THE

ANTE-NICENE FATHERS

TRANSLATIONS OF

The Writings of the Fathers down to A.D. 325

ORIGINAL SUPPLEMENT TO THE AMERICAN EDITION

ALLAN MENZIES, D.D.,

PROFESSOR OF BIBLICAL CRITICISM IN ST. MARY'S COLLEGE, ST. ANDREWS, SCOTLAND,

EDITOR

FIFTH EDITION

VOLUME X

THE GOSPEL OF PETER, THE DIATESSARON OF TATIAN, THE APOCALYPSE OF PETER, THE VISIO PAULI, THE APOCALYPSES OF THE VIRGIN AND SEDRACH, THE TESTAMENT OF ABRAHAM, THE ACTS OF XANTHIPPE AND POLYXENA, THE NARRATIVE OF ZOSIMUS, THE APOLOGY OF ARISTIDES, THE EPISTLES OF CLEMENT (COMPLETE TEXT), ORIGEN'S COMMENTARY ON JOHN, BOOKS I-X, AND COMMENTARY ON MATTHEW, BOOKS I, II, AND X-XIV.

WM. B. EERDMANS PUBLISHING COMPANY

GRAND RAPIDS MICHIGAN

NAMES OF TRANSLATORS

J. Armitage Robinson, B.D., Norrisian Professor of Divinity, Cambridge, Editor of *Texts and Studies* . .	*The Gospel of Peter.*
Do.	*The Passion of the Scillitan Martyrs.*
Andrew Rutherfurd, B.D. . . .	*The Gospel of Peter* (*Introduction and Synoptical Table*).
Do.	*The Apocalypse of Peter.*
Do.	*Visio Pauli.*
Do.	*Apocalypse of Maria Virgo.*
Do.	*Apocalypse of Sedrach.*
Do.	*The Passion of the Scillitan Martyrs* (*Introduction*).
Rev. Hope W. Hogg, B.D. . . .	*The Diatessaron of Tatian.*
W. A. Craigie, M.A., B.A. (Oxon.), Assistant in Humanity, St. Andrews University	*The Testament of Abraham.*
Do.	*The Acts of Xanthippe and Polyxena.*
Do.	*The Narrative of Zosimus.*
Rev. John Keith, B.D., Minister of Largs, Ayrshire	*The Epistles of Clement.*
Rev. D. M. Kay, B.Sc., B.D., Assistant in Semitic Languages, Edinburgh University	*The Apology of Aristides.*
Allan Menzies, D.D., Professor of Biblical Criticism, St. Andrews University	*Epistle to Gregory.*
Do.	*Origen's Commentary on John.*
Rev. John Patrick, D.D., Minister of Greenside, Edinburgh . . .	*Origen's Commentary on Matthew.*

Reprinted, *August 1980*

PHOTOLITHOPRINTED BY CUSHING - MALLOY, INC.
ANN ARBOR, MICHIGAN, UNITED STATES OF AMERICA

CONTENTS

PREFACE

The Ante-Nicene Fathers,[1] which seemed many years ago to have completed its task, now presents itself once more and ventures to solicit the renewal of the favour with which it was formerly received by the theological world. The publishers and the editor, who now stands, he well knows how unworthily, in the place of Principal Donaldson and Professor Roberts, believe that the volume now added to the series will be found most interesting in itself and not unworthy to stand beside its predecessors.

This volume consists of two distinct parts. The first is a collection of recently discovered additions to early Christian literature. The period which has elapsed since the last volumes of this series were published has been singularly rich in such discoveries. A portion of a gospel has been recovered which was read in the latter part of the second century in certain Christian churches and purports to be the work of the Apostle Peter. A harmony of the four canonical gospels has also been brought to our knowledge, which was made in the same century, and which, in a considerable district of Eastern Christendom, supplanted these gospels themselves. Another work bearing the name of the Apostle Peter, his Apocalypse, which once appeared to have some claim to a place in the canon, has also been found. The Epistles of Clement, which formerly broke off abruptly, have recovered their concluding portions, and the earliest public appeal to the head of the state on behalf of Christianity is also now in our possession. The circumstances of these various discoveries, and also of others of a similar nature, are stated in the introductions prefixed by the writers in this volume to the various pieces, and it will be seen that scholars of many lands have taken part in them. English scholarship, it is well known, has distinguished itself highly in this field. Many of the pieces now given first saw the light in the *Cambridge Texts and Studies*, a publication of singular interest and enduring value, without which the present volume would not have come into existence. The editor of the *Texts and Studies*, Professor Armitage Robinson, has taken a very kind interest in the present publication and has himself contributed translations of two pieces.

The history of the discussions awakened by these discoveries cannot yet be written, but it is not too early to place the English reader in possession of the documents thus restored to the Christian community. The reader of former volumes of *The Ante-Nicene Fathers* has already become acquainted with a number of uncanonical gospels, of apocalypses, and of early Christian apologies. In each of these classes of Christian literature he is now presented with pieces not less interesting than any known before. A glance at the table of contents will show the principle according to which the various works have been arranged. It may be stated that the *Diatessaron* of Tatian is here for the first time translated into English from the Arabic.

The second part of this volume contains portions of two of the most important commentaries of Origen. When *The Ante-Nicene Fathers* came to a close it was felt that more should have been done for a father who occupies a position of such singular importance in the history both of Scripture exegesis and of Christian thought. It is believed that the present translations will be welcomed by many who feel that growing interest in Origen which now appears in many quarters, and that they will be acceptable to all who care to know the varieties of treatment the Scriptures have met with in the church.

[1] All references to THE ANTE-NICENE FATHERS are to the American Edition, Christian Literature Co., New York, although sometimes referred to as "The Ante-Nicene Library."

PREFACE

THE GOSPEL OF PETER

BY

PROFESSOR J. ARMITAGE ROBINSON
Editor of the Cambridge *Texts and Studies*

INTRODUCTION AND SYNOPTICAL TABLE

By ANDREW RUTHERFURD, B.D.

THE GOSPEL OF PETER

INTRODUCTION

The important fragment of which Mr. J. Armitage Robinson's translation here follows was discovered by the French Archæological Mission, Cairo, in a grave (supposed to be a monk's) in an ancient cemetery at Akhmîm (Panopolis), in Upper Egypt, in 1886. It was published in 1892 under the care of M. Bouriant in vol. ix., fasc. i., of the *Memoirs of the French Archæological Mission at Cairo.* The same parchment which contained this fragment also contained a fragment of the Revelation of Peter and a fragment of the Book of Enoch in Greek. The parchment codex is assigned to a date between the eighth and the twelfth century.

Before this discovery the following is all that was known of the Gospel of Peter: 1. Serapion, Bishop of Antioch 190–203, writing to the church at Rhossus, says (Eusebius, *H. E.*, vi., 12, 2): "We, brethren, receive Peter and the other Apostles even as Christ; but the writings that go falsely by their names we, in our experience, reject, knowing that such things as these we never received. When I was with you I supposed you all to be attached to the right faith; and so without going through the gospel put forward under Peter's name, I said, 'If this is all that makes your petty quarrel,[1] why then let it be read.' But now that I have learned from information given me that their mind was lurking in some hole of heresy, I will make a point of coming to you again: so, brethren, expect me speedily. Knowing then, brethren, of what kind of heresy was Marcion— [*Here follows a sentence where the text is faulty.*] . . . From others who used this very gospel—I mean from the successors of those who started it, whom we call *Docetæ;* for most of its ideas are of their school—from them, I say, I borrowed it, and was able to go through it, and to find that most of it belonged to the right teaching of the Saviour, but some things were additions." From this we learn that a Gospel of Peter was in use in the church of Rhossus in the end of the second century, but that controversy had arisen as to its character, which, on a careful examination, Serapion condemned.

2. Origen († 253 A.D.), in commenting on Matthew x. 17, says: "But, proceeding on the tradition that is recorded in the Gospel according to Peter or in the Book of James, they say that there are certain brothers of Jesus, the sons of Joseph by a former wife, who lived with him before Mary."

3. Eusebius (*H. E.*, iii., 3, 2) says: "As to that work, however, which is ascribed to him, called 'The Acts,' and 'The Gospel according to Peter,' and that called 'The Preaching and the Revelations of Peter,' we know nothing of their being handed down as Catholic writings; since neither among the ancient nor the ecclesiastical writers of our own day has there been one that has appealed to testimony taken from them." And in *H. E.*, iii., 25, 6 sq., he includes the Gospel of Peter among the forged heretical gospels—"those that are adduced by the heretics under the name of the apostles, . . . of which no one of those writers in the ecclesiastical succession has condescended to make any mention in his works; and, indeed, the character of the style itself is very different from that of the apostles; and the sentiments, and the purport of those things that are advanced in them, deviating as far as possible from sound orthodoxy, evidently proves they are the fictions of heretical men; whence they are not only to be ranked

1 Παρέχειν μικροψυχίαν, perhaps "causes you ill-feeling." The translation ot Serapion's letter with this note is taken from Mr. Armitage Robinson's edition of the gospel.

among the spurious writings, but are to be rejected as altogether absurd and impious." It is, however, uncertain whether Eusebius himself was acquainted with the Gospel of Peter.

4. THEODORET († *c.* 455), in his *Religious History*, ii., 2, says that the Nazarenes used "the gospel called '*according to Peter*.'" Later references in Western literature, e.g., Jerome, *De vir. ill.*, i., and the *Decretum Gelasianum*, condemning the book, are based upon the judgement of Eusebius, and not upon direct knowledge (*cf.* Harnack, *Geschichte der altchristl. Lit.*, I. Th., p. 11).

This was all that was known of the Gospel of Peter till the publication of the Akhmîm fragment. The latter extends to about 174 stichi, counting 32 words to the stichus. It begins in the middle of the history of the Passion, just after Pilate has washed his hands of all responsibility, and ends in the middle of a sentence, with the departure of the disciples into Galilee at the end of the Feast of Unleavened Bread, exactly a week after the crucifixion, the ostensible author, Peter, and Andrew, his brother, taking their nets and going to the sea; "and there was with us Levi the son of Alphæus, whom the Lord . . ."

The accompanying Synoptical Table shows where the Petrine narrative agrees with and where it varies from those supplied by the canonical gospels. Of that part of the Passion history which it narrates, it gives an account which follows the main lines of the canonical tradition, but with important variations in detail. Of the events between the burial and the resurrection of our Lord, its account is much more ample and detailed than anything in the canonical tradition.

Harnack (*Texte und Untersuchungen*, ix., 2, 2d ed., p. 76) gives the following list of new traits contained in the Petrine account of the history of the Passion and burial:

1 Herod was the judge who condemned Jesus, and to him application had to be made for the body.
2 The Jews, Herod, and the judges would not wash their hands, and Pilate then raised the sitting.
3 Joseph was the friend of Pilate (sec. 2).
4 Joseph begged for the body before the crucifixion, and Pilate sent for permission from Herod.
5 The soldiers "pushed him as they ran," and their speech (sec. 3).
6 The mockery of the soldiers.
7 Mocking speech.
8 "As though having no pain" (sec. 4).
9 "Having placed his garments before him."
10 One of the malefactors blamed the multitude, and his speech.
11 The legs of either the malefactor or Jesus were not broken, *in order that he might die in torment.*
12 The gall and vinegar (sec. 5).
13 In the darkness many went about with lamps, and fell down.
14 The cry, "My power, my power."
15 The fact that when he had so cried Christ was taken up.
16 Mention of the nails in the hands at the taking down from the cross (sec. 6).
17 The earthquake when the body touched the ground.
18 The joy of the Jews when the sun shone again.
19 Joseph "had seen all the good things" that the Lord had done.
20 Joseph washed the body.
21 The cries of woe of the Jews and their leaders over their sins, and their expectation of the judgement on Jerusalem (sec. 7).
22 The disciples remained in concealment, full of grief, and fasted and wept till the Sabbath.
23 They were searched for as malefactors and as anxious to burn the temple.
24 The name of the centurion of the watch—Petronius (sec. 8).
25 The centurion, the soldiers, and the elders rolled up the stone.
26 The elders also watched at the grave.
27 Seven seals were placed on the stone.
28 A tent pitched for the watch.
29 The gathering of the multitude on the morning of the Sabbath to view the sealed grave (sec. 9).

The whole narrative of the resurrection is so different from that of the canonical gospels that it would be useless to go into details; but it is important to notice the prominence assigned to Mary Magdalene, and:

1 That the women fled from the grave and did not see the Lord (sec. 12).

2 That there is no account of any appearance of Christ for the first eight days after his death (sec. 13).

3 That the disciples, along with the rest of those who had taken part in the feast, returned home to Galilee on the seventh day of unleavened bread.

4 That they were then sad, and wept.

5 That the first appearance of Jesus must have taken place on the Lake of Gennesaret, either to Peter alone, or to Peter, Andrew, and Levi (Matthew), while fishing.

Moreover, according to section 13 (see sec. 5), the author puts the resurrection and ascension on the same day, or, rather, did not know of the latter as a separate event. He makes the angel say, "He is risen and gone away thither whence he was sent."

Whether the author used any other sources than the canonical gospels is a matter still in doubt. He is certainly influenced by views which are foreign to these gospels, and which are known from other quarters in early Christian literature. As between the Synpotists and the Fourth Gospel, the narrator is generally more closely akin both in matter and in manner to the Synoptists, but he agrees with the author of the Fourth Gospel in regard to the chronology of the crucifixion and several of the events at the cross, and in his general attitude towards the Jews and Pilate. With regard to the last two points, the Petrine Gospel seems to present a later and more exaggerated form of the tendency perceptible in the Johannine, and fully worked out in the Acts of Pilate, to blame the Jews and exculpate Pilate.

Of the new features in this fragment some are at least liable to a Docetic interpretation, e.g., the silence on the cross "as though he had no pain" (sec. 4), the cry, "My power, my power" (sec. 5), and "he was taken up" (sec. 5). This fact was recognised in subsequent times and condemned this gospel in the eye of the church. The date of the work is variously fixed by different scholars; Harnack assigns it to the first quarter of the second century, while Mr. Armitage Robinson and other scholars place it later.

THE GOSPEL ACCORDING TO PETER

1 But of the Jews none washed his hands, neither Herod nor any one of his judges. And when they had refused to wash them, Pilate rose up. And then Herod the king commandeth that the Lord be taken,[1] saying to them, What things soever I commanded you to do unto him, do.

2 And there was standing there Joseph the friend of Pilate and of the Lord; and, knowing that they were about to crucify [2] him, he came to Pilate and asked the body of the Lord for burial. And Pilate sent to Herod and asked his body. And Herod said, Brother Pilate, even if no one had asked for him, we purposed to bury him, especially as the sabbath draweth on:[3] for it is written in the law, that the sun set not upon one that hath been put to death.

3 And he delivered him to the people on the day before the unleavened bread, their feast. And they took the Lord and pushed him as they ran, and said, Let us drag away the Son of God, having obtained power over him. And they clothed him with purple, and set him on the seat of judgement, saying, Judge righteously, O king of Israel. And one of them brought a crown of thorns and put it on the head of the Lord. And others stood and spat in his eyes, and others smote his cheeks: others pricked him with a reed; and some scourged him, saying, With this honour let us honour the Son of God.

4 And they brought two malefactors, and they crucified the Lord between them. But he held his peace, as though having no pain. And when they had raised the cross, they wrote the title: This is the king of Israel. And having set his garments before him they parted them among them, and cast lots for them. And one of those malefactors reproached them, saying, We for the evils that we have done have suffered thus, but this man, who hath become the Saviour of men, what wrong hath he done to you? And they, being angered at him, commanded that his legs should not be broken, that he might die in torment.

5 And it was noon, and darkness came over all Judæa: and they were troubled and distressed, lest the sun had set, whilst he was yet alive: [for] it is written for them, that the sun set not on him that hath been put to death. And one of them said, Give him to drink gall with vinegar. And they mixed and gave him to drink, and fulfilled all things, and accomplished their sins against their own head. And many went about with lamps, supposing that it was night, and fell down.[4] And the Lord cried out, saying, My power, my power, thou hast forsaken me. And when he had said it he was taken up. And in that hour the vail of the temple of Jerusalem was rent in twain.[5]

6 And then they drew out the nails from the hands of the Lord, and laid him upon the earth, and the whole earth quaked, and great fear arose. Then the sun shone, and it was found the ninth hour: and the Jews rejoiced, and gave his body to Joseph that he might bury it, since he had seen what good things he had done. And he took the Lord, and washed him, and rolled him in a linen cloth, and brought him into his own tomb, which was called the Garden of Joseph.

7 Then the Jews and the elders and the priests, perceiving what evil they had done to themselves, began to lament and to say, Woe for our sins: the judgement hath drawn nigh, and the end of Jerusalem. And I with my companions was grieved; and being wounded in mind we hid ourselves: for we were being sought for by them as malefactors, and as wishing to set fire to the temple. And upon all these things we fasted and sat mourning and weeping night and day until the sabbath.

8 But the scribes and Pharisees and elders being gathered together one with another, when they heard that all the people murmured and beat their breasts saying, If by his death these most mighty signs have come to pass, see how righteous he is,—the elders were afraid and came

NOTE.—This translation is based on that which I published in *The Gospel and Apocalypse of Peter: Two Lectures*, etc. (Camb., 1892). It is now carefully revised in accordance with the photographic facsimile. A corrected Greek text will be found in Dr. Swete's edition (1893).

1 Παρ[αλημ]φθῆναι is perhaps supported by *παραλαβόντες*, Mt. xxiv. 27.

2 I know no other instance of *σταυρίσκειν*.

3 *cf.* Jo. xix. 31, where Syr. Pesch. reads: "They say, These bodies shall not remain on the cross, because the sabbath dawneth."

4 The text here is corrupt: for *ἐπέσαντο* I have provisionally read *ἔπεσάν τε*.

5 For *αὐτὸς ὥρας* we must read *αὐτῆς ὥρας* (*cf.* Clem., *Hom.*, xx., 16); *αὐτὴ* is the equivalent in later Greek literature of *ἐκείνη*, as in the modern tongue (*cf.* Lc. x. 7, 21, and xii. 12; || *ἐκείνῃ*, Mt., Mc.).

to Pilate, beseeching him and saying, Give us soldiers, that we may guard his sepulchre for three days, lest his disciples come and steal him away, and the people suppose that he is risen from the dead and do us evil. And Pilate gave them Petronius the centurion with soldiers to guard the tomb. And with them came elders and scribes to the sepulchre, and having rolled a great stone together with[1] the centurion and the soldiers, they all together who were there set it at the door of the sepulchre; and they affixed seven seals, and they pitched a tent there and guarded it. And early in the morning as the sabbath was drawing on, there came a multitude from Jerusalem and the region round about, that they might see the sepulchre that was sealed.

9 And in the night in which the Lord's day was drawing on, as the soldiers kept guard two by two in a watch, there was a great voice in the heaven; and they saw the heavens opened, and two men descend from thence with great light and approach the tomb. And that stone which was put at the door rolled of itself and made way in part; and the tomb was opened, and both the young men entered in.

10 When therefore those soldiers saw it, they awakened the centurion and the elders; for they too were hard by keeping guard. And, as they declared what things they had seen, again they see three men come forth from the tomb, and two of them supporting one, and a cross following them: and of the two the head reached unto the heaven, but the head of him that was led by them overpassed the heavens. And they heard a voice from the heavens, saying, Thou hast preached to them that sleep. And a response was heard from the cross, Yea.

11 They therefore considered one with another whether to go away and shew these things to Pilate. And while they yet thought thereon, the heavens again are seen to open, and a certain man to descend and enter into the sepulchre. When the centurion and they that were with him saw these things, they hastened in the night to Pilate, leaving the tomb which they were watching, and declared all things which they had seen, being greatly distressed and saying, Truly he was the Son of God. Pilate answered and said, I am pure from the blood of the Son of God: but it was ye who determined this. Then they all drew near and besought him and entreated him to command the centurion and the soldiers to say nothing of the things which they had seen: For it is better, say they, for us to be guilty of the greatest sin before God, and not to fall into the hands of the people of the Jews and to be stoned. Pilate therefore commanded the centurion and the soldiers to say nothing.

12 And at dawn upon the Lord's day Mary Magdalen, a disciple of the Lord, fearing because of the Jews, since they were burning with wrath, had not done at the Lord's sepulchre the things which women are wont to do for those that die and for those that are beloved by them —she took her friends with her and came to the sepulchre where he was laid. And they feared lest the Jews should see them, and they said, Although on that day on which he was crucified we could not weep and lament, yet now let us do these things at his sepulchre. But who shall roll away for us the stone that was laid at the door of the sepulchre, that we may enter in and sit by him and do the things that are due? For the stone was great, and we fear lest some one see us. And if we cannot, yet if we but set at the door the things which we bring for a memorial of him, we will weep and lament, until we come unto our home.

13 And they went and found the tomb opened, and coming near they looked in there; and they see there a certain young man sitting in the midst of the tomb, beautiful and clothed in a robe exceeding bright; who said to them, Wherefore are ye come? Whom seek ye? Him that was crucified?[2] He is risen and gone. But if ye believe not, look in and see the place where he lay, that he is not [here]; for he is risen and gone thither, whence he was sent. Then the women feared and fled.

14 Now it was the last day of the unleavened bread, and many were going forth, returning to their homes, as the feast was ended. But we, the twelve disciples of the Lord, wept and were grieved: and each one, being grieved for that which was come to pass, departed to his home. But I Simon Peter and Andrew my brother took our nets and went to the sea; and there was with us Levi the son of Alphæus, whom the Lord . . .

1 I have ventured to substitute μετὰ, "together with" (*cf.* Mt. xxvii 66), for κατὰ, "down upon." Dr. Swete, however, keeps κατὰ, and interprets it as "against," i.e., to guard the sepulchre against.

2 The form of the question in the Greek suggests a negative answer.

SYNOPTICAL TABLE

OF THE

FOUR CANONICAL GOSPELS

AND

THE GOSPEL ACCORDING TO PETER

MATTHEW XXVII.	MARK XV.	LUKE XXIII.	JOHN XIX.
24 ¶ When Pilate saw that he could prevail nothing, but *that* rather a tumult was made, he took water, and washed *his* hands before the multitude, saying, I am innocent of the blood of this just person: see ye *to it*. 25 Then answered all the people, and said, His blood *be* on us, and on our children.		[[2] *cf.* Lk. xxiii. 7.] [[3] *cf.* Lk. xxii. 66; Acts iv 27.]	[[1] *cf.* John *passim.*]
[*cf.* v. 57.]	[*cf.* v. 43.]	[*cf.* v. 50.]	[*cf.* v. 38.]
	[*cf.* v. 42.]	[[4] *cf.* Lk. xxiii. 12.]	[*cf.* xix. 31.]
26 ¶ Then released he Barabbas unto them: and when he had scourged Jesus, he delivered *him* to be crucified.	15 ¶ And *so* Pilate, willing to content the people, released Barabbas unto them, and delivered Jesus, when he had scourged *him*, to be crucified.	24 And Pilate gave sentence that it should be as they required. 25 And he released unto them him that for sedition and murder was cast into prison, whom they had desired; but he delivered Jesus to their will.	16 Then delivered he him therefore unto them to be crucified. And they took Jesus, and led *him* away.
27 Then the soldiers of the governor took Jesus into the common hall, and gathered unto him the whole band *of soldiers*. 28 And they stripped him, and put on him a scarlet robe. 29 ¶ And when they had platted a crown of thorns, they put *it* upon his head, and a reed in his right hand: and they bowed the knee before him, and mocked him, saying, Hail, King of the Jews! 30 And they spit upon	16 And the soldiers led him away into the hall, called Prætorium; and they call together the whole band. 17 And they clothed him with purple, and platted a crown of thorns, and put it about his *head*, 18 And began to salute him, Hail, King of the Jews! 19 And they smote him on the head with a reed, and did spit upon him, and bowing *their* knees worshipped him.		

PETER.

1 But of the Jews[1] none washed his hands, neither Herod[2] nor any one of his judges.[3] 2 And
when they had refused to wash them, Pilate rose up. And then Herod the king commandeth that
the Lord be taken, saying to them, What things soever I commanded you to do unto him, do.

3 And there was come there Joseph the friend of Pilate and of the Lord; and, knowing that
they were about to crucify him, he came to Pilate and asked the body of the Lord for burial.
4 And Pilate sent to Herod and asked his body. 5 And Herod said, Brother[4] Pilate, even if
no one had asked for him, we purposed to bury him, especially as the sabbath draweth on: for
it is written in the law, that the sun set not upon one that hath been put to death. And he
delivered him to the people on the day before the unleavened bread, their feast.

6 And they took the Lord and pushed him as they ran, and said, Let us drag away the Son
of God, having obtained power over him.

7 And they clothed him with purple, and set him on the seat of judgement, saying, Judge
righteously, O King of Israel. 8 And one of them brought a crown of thorns and put it on the
head of the Lord. 9 And others stood and spat in his eyes, and others smote his cheeks: others
pricked him with a reed; and some scourged him, saying, With this honour let us honour the
Son of God.

MATTHEW.	MARK.	LUKE.	JOHN.
him, and took the reed, and smote him on the head.			
31 And after that they had mocked him, they took the robe off from him, and put his own raiment on him, and led him away to crucify *him*.	20 And when they had mocked him, they took off the purple from him, and put his own clothes on him, and led him out to crucify him.		
32 And as they came out, they found a man of Cyrene, Simon by name: him they compelled to bear his cross.	21 And they compel one Simon a Cyrenian, who passed by, coming out of the country, the father of Alexander and Rufus, to bear his cross.	26 And as they led him away, they laid hold upon one Simon, a Cyrenian, coming out of the country, and on him they laid the cross, that he might bear *it* after Jesus.	
		27 ¶ And there followed him a great company of people, and of women, which also bewailed and lamented him.	
		28 But Jesus turning unto them said, Daughters of Jerusalem, weep not for me, but weep for yourselves, and for your children.	
		29 For, behold, the days are coming, in the which they shall say, Blessed *are* the barren, and the wombs that never bare, and the paps which never gave suck.	
		30 Then shall they begin to say to the mountains, Fall on us; and to the hills, Cover us.	
		31 For if they do these things in a green tree, what shall be done in the dry?	
		32 And there were also two other, malefactors, led with him to be put to death.	
33 And when they were come unto a place called Golgotha, that	22 And they bring him unto the place Golgotha, which is,	33 And when they were come to the place, which is called Calvary,	17 And he bearing his cross went forth into a place called *the place* of a skull, which is called in the Hebrew Golgotha:

PETER.

MATTHEW.	MARK.	LUKE.	JOHN.
is to say, a place of a skull, 34 ¶ They gave him vinegar to drink mingled with gall: and when he had tasted *thereof*, he would not drink. 35 And they crucified him;	being interpreted, The place of a skull. 23 And they gave him to drink wine mingled with myrrh: but he received *it* not.	there they crucified him, and the malefactors, one on the right hand, and the other on the left.	18 Where they crucified him, and two other with him, on either side one, and Jesus in the midst.
and parted his garments, casting lots: that it might be fulfilled which was spoken by the prophet, They parted my garments among them, and upon my vesture did they cast lots. 36 And sitting down they watched him there;	24 And when they had crucified him, they parted his garments, casting lots upon them, what every man should take. 25 And it was the third hour, and they crucified him.		[*cf.* vv. 23, 24.]
		34 ¶ Then said Jesus, Father, forgive them; for they know not what they do. And they parted his raiment, and cast lots. 35 And the people stood beholding. And the rulers also with them derided *him*, saying, He saved others; let him save himself, if he be Christ, the chosen of God. 36 And the soldiers also mocked him, coming to him, and offering him vinegar, 37 And saying, If thou be the King of the Jews, save thyself.	
37 And set up over his head his accusation written, THIS IS JESUS THE KING OF THE JEWS. 38 Then were there two thieves crucified with him, one on the right hand, and another on the left. 39 ¶ And they that	26 And the superscription of his accusation was written over, THE KING OF THE JEWS. 27 And with him they crucify two thieves; the one on his right hand, and the other on his left. 28 And the scripture	38 And a superscription also was written over him in letters of Greek, and Latin, and Hebrew, THIS IS THE KING OF THE JEWS.	19 ¶ And Pilate wrote a title, and put *it* on the cross. And the writing was, JESUS OF NAZARETH THE KING OF THE JEWS. 20 This title then read many of the Jews: for the place where Jesus was crucified was nigh to the city: and it was

PETER.

10 And they brought two malefactors, and they crucified the Lord between them.

But he held his peace, as though having no pain.

11 And when they had raised the cross, they wrote upon it, This is the King of Israel.
12 And having set his garments before him, they parted them among them, and cast lots for them.

[*cf.* v. 11.]

MATTHEW.	MARK.	LUKE.	JOHN.
passed by reviled him, wagging their heads, 40 And saying, Thou that destroyest the temple, and buildest *it* in three days, save thyself. If thou be the Son of God, come down from the cross. 41 Likewise also the chief priests mocking *him*, with the scribes and elders, said, 42 He saved others; himself he cannot save. If he be the King of Israel, let him now come down from the cross, and we will believe him. 43 He trusted in God; let him deliver him now, if he will have him: for he said, I am the Son of God.	was fulfilled, which saith, And he was numbered with the transgressors. 29 And they that passed by railed on him, wagging their heads, and saying, Ah, thou that destroyest the temple, and buildest *it* in three days, 30 Save thyself, and come down from the cross. 31 Likewise also the chief priests mocking said among themselves with the scribes, He saved others; himself he cannot save. 32 Let Christ the King of Israel descend now from the cross, that we may see and believe.		written in Hebrew, *and* Greek, *and* Latin. 21 Then said the chief priests of the Jews to Pilate, Write not, The King of the Jews; but that he said, I am King of the Jews. 22 Pilate answered, What I have written I have written.
[*cf.* v. 35.]	[*cf.* v. 24.]		23 ¶ Then the soldiers, when they had crucified Jesus, took his garments, and made four parts, to every soldier a part; and also *his* coat: now the coat was without seam, woven from the top throughout. 24 They said therefore among themselves, Let us not rend it, but cast lots for it, whose it shall be: that the scripture might be fulfilled, which saith, They parted my raiment among them, and for my vesture they did cast lots. These things therefore the soldiers did.
44 The thieves also, which were crucified with him, cast the same in his teeth.	And they that were crucified with him reviled him.	39 ¶ And one of the malefactors which were hanged railed on him, saying, If thou be Christ, save thyself and us. 40 But the other answering rebuked him, saying, Dost not thou fear God, seeing thou	

PETER.

[*cf.* v. 12.]

13 And one of those malefactors reproached them, saying, We for the evils that we have done have suffered thus, but this man, who hath become the Saviour of men, what wrong hath he done to you?

MATTHEW.	MARK.	LUKE.	JOHN.
		art in the same condemnation? 41 And we indeed justly; for we receive the due reward of our deeds: but this man hath done nothing amiss. 42 And he said unto Jesus, Lord, remember me when thou comest into thy kingdom. 43 And Jesus said unto him, Verily I say unto thee, To day shalt thou be with me in paradise.	
			25 ¶ Now there stood by the cross of Jesus his mother, and his mother's sister, Mary the *wife* of Cleophas, and Mary Magdalene. 26 When Jesus therefore saw his mother, and the disciple standing by, whom he loved, he saith unto his mother, Woman, behold thy son! 27 Then saith he to the disciple, Behold thy mother! And from that hour that disciple took her unto his own *home*.
45 Now from the sixth hour there was darkness over all the land unto the ninth hour.	33 And when the sixth hour was come, there was darkness over the whole land until the ninth hour.	44 And it was about the sixth hour, and there was a darkness over all the earth until the ninth hour. 45 And the sun was darkened, and the veil of the temple was rent in the midst.	
46 And about the ninth hour Jesus cried with a loud voice, saying, Eli, Eli, lama sabachthani? that is to say, My God, my God, why hast thou forsaken me?	34 And at the ninth hour Jesus cried with a loud voice, saying, Eloi, Eloi, lama sabachthani? which is, being interpreted, My God, my God, why hast thou forsaken me?		

PETER.

14 And they, being angered at him, commanded that his legs should not be broken, that he might die in torment.

15 And it was noon, and darkness came over all Judæa:

and they were troubled and distressed, lest the sun had set, whilst he was yet alive: [for] it is written for them, that the sun set not on him that hath been put to death.

MATTHEW.	MARK.	LUKE.	JOHN.
47 Some of them that stood there, when they heard *that*, said, This *man* calleth for Elias. 48 And straightway one of them ran, and took a spunge, and filled *it* with vinegar, and put *it* on a reed, and gave him to drink. 49 The rest said, Let be, let us see whether Elias will come to save him.	35 And some of them that stood by, when they heard *it*, said, Behold, he calleth Elias. 36 And one ran and filled a spunge full of vinegar, and put *it* on a reed, and gave him to drink, saying, Let alone; let us see whether Elias will come to take him down.		28 ¶ After this, Jesus knowing that all things were now accomplished, that the scripture might be fulfilled, saith, I thirst. 29 Now there was set a vessel full of vinegar: and they filled a spunge with vinegar, and put *it* upon hyssop, and put *it* to his mouth.
50 ¶ Jesus, when he had cried again with a loud voice, yielded up the ghost.	37 And Jesus cried with a loud voice, and gave up the ghost.	46 ¶ And when Jesus had cried with a loud voice, he said, Father, into thy hands I commend my spirit: and having said thus, he gave up the ghost.	30 When Jesus therefore had received the vinegar, he said, It is finished: and he bowed his head, and gave up the ghost.
51 And, behold, the veil of the temple was rent in twain from the top to the bottom;	38 And the veil of the temple was rent in twain from the top to the bottom.		
and the earth did quake, and the rocks rent; 52 And the graves were opened; and many bodies of the saints which slept arose, 53 And came out of the graves after his resurrection, and went into the holy city, and appeared unto many.			
			31 The Jews therefore, because it was the preparation, that the bodies should not remain upon the cross on the sabbath day, (for that sabbath day was an high day,) besought Pilate that their legs might be broken, and *that* they might be taken away. 32 Then came the soldiers, and brake the legs of the first, and of the other which was crucified with him. 33 But when they came to Jesus, and saw that he was dead already, they brake not his legs:

PETER.

16 And one of them said, Give him to drink gall with vinegar. And they mixed and gave
him to drink, 17 and fulfilled all things, and accomplished their sins against their own head.

18 And many went about with lamps, supposing that it was night, and fell down. 19 And
the Lord cried out, saying, My power, my power, thou hast forsaken me.

And when he had said it he was taken up.

20 And in that hour the vail of the temple of Jerusalem was rent in twain.

MATTHEW.	MARK.	LUKE.	JOHN.
			34 But one of the soldiers with a spear pierced his side, and forthwith came there out blood and water. 35 And he that saw *it* bare record, and his record is true: and he knoweth that he saith true, that ye might believe. 36 For these things were done, that the scripture should be fulfilled, A bone of him shall not be broken. 37 And again another scripture saith, They shall look on him whom they pierced.
54 Now when the centurion, and they that were with him, watching Jesus, saw the earthquake, and those things that were done, they feared greatly, saying, Truly this was the Son of God. 55 And many women were there beholding afar off, which followed Jesus from Galilee, ministering unto him: 56 Among which was Mary Magdalene, and Mary the mother of James and Joses, and the mother of Zebedee's children.	39 ¶ And when the centurion, which stood over against him, saw that he so cried out, and gave up the ghost, he said, Truly this man was the Son of God. 40 There were also women looking on afar off: among whom was Mary Magdalene, and Mary the mother of James the less and of Joses, and Salome; 41 (Who also, when he was in Galilee, followed him, and ministered unto him;) and many other women which came up with him unto Jerusalem.	47 Now when the centurion saw what was done, he glorified God, saying, Certainly this was a righteous man. 48 And all the people that came together to that sight, beholding the things which were done, smote their breasts, and returned. 49 And all his acquaintance, and the women that followed him from Galilee, stood afar off, beholding these things.	
	42 ¶ And now when the even was come, because it was the preparation, that is, the day before the sabbath,		
57 When the even was come, there came a rich man of Arimathæa, named Joseph, who also himself was Jesus' disciple:	43 Joseph of Arimathæa, an honourable counsellor, which also waited for the kingdom of God, came, and went in boldly unto Pilate,	50 ¶ And, behold, *there was* a man named Joseph, a counsellor; *and he was* a good man, and a just: 51 (The same had not	38 ¶ And after this Joseph of Arimathæa, being a disciple of Jesus, but secretly for fear of the Jews, besought Pilate that he might

PETER.

21 And then they drew out the nails from the hands of the Lord, and laid him upon the
earth, and the whole earth quaked, and great fear arose. 22 Then the sun shone, and it was found
the ninth hour: 23 and the Jews rejoiced, and

MATTHEW.	MARK.	LUKE.	JOHN.
58 He went to Pilate, and begged the body of Jesus. Then Pilate commanded the body to be delivered.	and craved the body of Jesus.	consented to the counsel and deed of them;) *he was* of Arimathæa, a city of the Jews: who also himself waited for the kingdom of God. 52 This *man* went unto Pilate, and begged the body of Jesus.	take away the body of Jesus: and Pilate gave *him* leave. He came therefore, and took the body of Jesus.
	44 And Pilate marvelled if he were already dead: and calling *unto him* the centurion, he asked him whether he had been any while dead. 45 And when he knew *it* of the centurion, he gave the body to Joseph.		
			39 And there came also Nicodemus, which at the first came to Jesus by night, and brought a mixture of myrrh and aloes, about an hundred pound *weight.*
59 And when Joseph had taken the body, he wrapped it in a clean linen cloth, 60 And laid it in his own new tomb, which he had hewn out in the rock: and he rolled a great stone to the door of the sepulchre, and departed. 61 And there was Mary Magdalene, and the other Mary, sitting over against the sepulchre.	46 And he bought fine linen, and took him down, and wrapped him in the linen, and laid him in a sepulchre which was hewn out of a rock, and rolled a stone unto the door of the sepulchre. 47 And Mary Magdalene and Mary *the mother* of Joses beheld where he was laid.	53 And he took it down, and wrapped it in linen, and laid it in a sepulchre that was hewn in stone, wherein never man before was laid. 54 And that day was the preparation, and the sabbath drew on. 55 And the women also, which came with him from Galilee, followed after, and beheld the sepulchre, and how his body was laid. 56 And they returned, and prepared spices and ointments; and rested the sabbath day according to the commandment.	40 Then took they the body of Jesus, and wound it in linen clothes with the spices, as the manner of the Jews is to bury. 41 Now in the place where he was crucified there was a garden; and in the garden a new sepulchre, wherein was never man yet laid. 42 There laid they Jesus therefore because of the Jews' preparation *day;* for the sepulchre was nigh at hand.

PETER.

gave his body to Joseph that he might bury it,

since he had seen what good things he had done.

24 And he took the Lord, and washed him, and wrapped him in a linen cloth, and brought him into his own tomb,

which was called the Garden of Joseph.

25 Then the Jews and the elders and the priests, perceiving what evil they had done to themselves, began to lament and to say, Woe for our sins: the judgement hath drawn nigh, and the end of Jerusalem.
26 And I with my companions was grieved; and being wounded in mind we hid ourselves: for we were being sought for by them as malefactors, and as wishing to set fire to the temple.

MATTHEW.	MARK.	LUKE.	JOHN.
[*cf.* Mt. xxvii. 24.]			
CHAPTER XXVIII.	CHAPTER XVI.	CHAPTER XXIV.	CHAPTER XX.
1 ¶ In the end of the sabbath, as it began to dawn toward the first *day* of the week, came Mary Magdalene and the other Mary to see the sepulchre.	1 ¶ And when the sabbath was past, Mary Magdalene, and Mary the *mother* of James, and Salome, had bought sweet spices, that they might come and anoint him. 2 And very early in the morning the first *day* of the week, they came unto the sepulchre at the rising of the sun.	1 Now upon the first *day* of the week, very early in the morning, they came unto the sepulchre, bringing the spices which they had prepared, and certain *others* with them.	1 ¶ The first *day* of the week cometh Mary Magdalene early, when it was yet dark, unto the sepulchre,
	3 And they said among themselves, Who shall roll us away the stone from the door of the sepulchre?		
2 And, behold, there was a great earthquake: for the angel of the Lord descended from heaven, and came and rolled back the stone from the door, and sat upon it.	4 And when they looked, they saw that the stone was rolled away: for it was very great.	2 And they found the stone rolled away from the sepulchre.	and seeth the stone taken away from the sepulchre.
	5 And entering into the sepulchre,	3 And they entered in, and found not the body of the Lord Jesus. 4 And it came to pass, as they were much perplexed thereabout, behold, two men stood by them in shining garments:	
3 His countenance was like lightning, and his raiment white as snow:	they saw a young man sitting on the right side, clothed in a long white garment; and they were affrighted.	5 And as they were afraid, and bowed down *their* faces to the earth,	

PETER.

watching, and declared all things which they had seen, being greatly distressed and saying, Truly
he was the Son of God. 46 Pilate answered and said, I am pure from the blood of the Son of
God: but ye determined this.
47 Then they all drew near and besought him and entreated him to command the centurion
and the soldiers to say nothing of the things which they had seen: 48 For it is better, say
they, for us to incur the greatest sin before God, and not to fall into the hands of the people
of the Jews and to be stoned. 49 Pilate therefore commanded the centurion and the soldiers
to say nothing.

50 And at dawn upon the Lord's day, Mary Magdalen, a disciple of the Lord, fearing because
of the Jews, since they were burning with wrath, had not done at the Lord's sepulchre the things
which the women are wont to do for those that die and for those that are beloved by them—
51 she took her friends with her and came to the sepulchre where he was laid.

52 And they feared lest the Jews should see them, and they said, Although on the day on
which he was crucified we could not weep and lament, yet now let us do these things at his
sepulchre.
53 But who shall roll away for us the stone that was laid at the door of the sepulchre, that we
may enter in and sit by him and do the things that are due? 54 For the stone was great, and
we fear lest some one see us. And if we cannot, yet if we but set at the door the things which
we bring for a memorial of him, we will weep and lament, until we come unto our home.

55 And they went away and found the tomb opened,

and coming near they looked in there;

and they see there a certain young man sitting in the midst of the tomb, beautiful and clothed in a robe exceeding bright;

MATTHEW.	MARK.	LUKE.	JOHN.
4 And for fear of him the keepers did shake, and became as dead *men*. 5 And the angel answered and said unto the women, Fear not ye: for I know that ye seek Jesus, which was crucified. 6 He is not here: for he is risen, as he said. Come, see the place where the Lord lay. 7 And go quickly, and tell his disciples that he is risen from the dead; and, behold, he goeth before you into Galilee; there shall ye see him: lo, I have told you. 8 And they departed quickly from the sepulchre with fear and great joy; and did run to bring his disciples word.	6 And he saith unto them, Be not affrighted: ye seek Jesus of Nazareth, which was crucified: he is risen; he is not here: behold the place where they laid him. 7 But go your way, tell his disciples and Peter that he goeth before you into Galilee: there shall ye see him, as he said unto you. 8 And they went out quickly, and fled from the sepulchre; for they trembled and were amazed: neither said they any thing to any *man;* for they were afraid. [Levi, etc.; *cf.* Mk. ii. 14.]	they said unto them, Why seek ye the living among the dead? 6 He is not here, but is risen: remember how he spake unto you when he was yet in Galilee, 7 Saying, The Son of man must be delivered into the hands of sinful men, and be crucified, and the third day rise again. 8 And they remembered his words, 9 And returned from the sepulchre, and told all these things unto the eleven, and to all the rest.	

PETER.

who said to them, 56 Wherefore are ye come? Whom seek ye? Him that was crucified? He is risen and gone. But if ye believe not, look in and see the place where he lay, that he is not [here]; for he is risen and gone away thither, whence he was sent.

57 Then the women feared and fled.

58 Now it was the last day of the unleavened bread, and many were going forth, returning to
their homes, as the feast was ended. 59 But we, the twelve disciples of the Lord, mourned and
were grieved: and each one, being grieved for that which was come to pass, departed to his home.
60 But I, Simon Peter and Andrew my brother, took our nets and went to the sea; and there was
with us Levi the son of Alphæus, whom the Lord . . .

THE DIATESSARON OF TATIAN

BY

REV. HOPE W. HOGG, B.D.

INTRODUCTION

THE aim of the following introductory paragraphs is neither to furnish a detailed restatement of facts already known, nor to offer an independent contribution to the discussion of the problems that arise, although in other circumstances such an attempt might be made with advantage. All that is needed and practicable here is to describe briefly, if possible, the nature of the connection between the English treatise forming the next part of this volume and the ancient work known as the *Diatessaron* of Tatian; and then to indicate in a few words some of the more important or interesting features of the work itself, and some of the historical and other problems that are in one way or another connected with it.

1 *The Text Translated.*—What is offered to the reader is a translation into English of an Arabic text, published at Rome in 1888, in a volume entitled in Arabic *Diatessaron, which Titianus Compiled from the Four Gospels*, with the alternative Latin title, *Tatiani Evangeliorum Harmoniæ, Arabice.* The Roman volume consists of two parts—the text, covering a little over 209 very clearly printed Arabic pages, and a Latin half, comprising a scholarly introduction (pp. v.–xv.), a Latin translation (pp. 1–99), and a table showing the order in which the passages taken from the gospels occur in the text. The editor is P. Agostino Ciasca, a well-known Orientalist, "scriptor" at the Vatican Library.

2 *Former Translations.*—In his Introduction (p. xiv. f.) Ciasca explains that in his translation he aimed at preserving *quantum, salva fidelitate, integrum fuit, indolem stylumque Clementinæ Vulgatæ.* This Latin version was in its turn translated into English by the Rev. J. Hamlyn Hill, B.D., and published in 1894 in a volume entitled *The Earliest Life of Christ*, with an interesting introduction and a number of valuable appendices. The MS. of Mr. Hill's translation of the Latin of Ciasca was compared with the Arabic original by Mr. G. Buchanan Gray, M.A., lecturer in Hebrew and the Old Testament in Mansfield College, Oxford.

3 *The Present Translation.*—The translation offered here is quite independent of either of these two. Ciasca's Latin was seldom consulted, except when it was thought the Arabic might perhaps be obscured by a misprint. After the translation was completed, Hill's English was compared with it to transfer Mr. Hill's valuable system of references to the margin of this work, and to lessen the risk of oversights passing the last revision unnoticed. In two or three cases this process led to the adoption of a different construction, and in a few of the more awkward passages a word was borrowed as being less harsh than that which had originally been written. Speaking generally, the present version appears to differ from Mr. Hill's in adhering more closely to the original.[1]

4 *The Arabic Text.*—Only two Arabic MSS. are known to exist. Ciasca tells us (p. xiv.) that he took as the basis of his text that MS. which is more careful in its orthography, the Cod. Vat. Arab. No. 14. He, however, printed at the foot of the page the variants of the other MS., and supplied from it two lacunæ in the Cod. Vat.,[2] substituted its readings for those of the Cod. Vat. where he thought them preferable, and followed its testimony in omitting two important passages.[3] Here and there Ciasca has emended the text, but he does not profess to have produced a critical edition.[4]

5 *The Arabic MSS.*—Unfortunately, the present writer has not had an opportunity of examining these two MSS.; but they have been described at some length by Ciasca; Codex XIV., in Pitra's *Analecta Sacra*, iv., 465 ff., and the other codex in the volume with which we are dealing, p. vi. ff. I. The former, which we shall call the Vatican MS. (in Ciasca's foot-notes it is called A), was brought to the Vatican from the East by Joseph S. Assemani[5] about A.D. 1719. It was described by Stephen E. Assemani,[6] Rosenmüller, and Akerblad,[7] and then at length by

1 For further explanation of the method followed see 20.
2 See notes to § 7, 47, and § 52, 36, of the present translation.
3 See below, 13, (2).
4 See also below, 6, and 20.
5 *Bibl. Or.*, i., 619.
6 Mai, *Vet. script. nova. collect.*, iv., 14.
7 *cf.* Zahn, *Forschungen*, i., 294 ff.

Ciasca, to whose account the reader must be referred for the details. It consists of 123 folios, of which the first seven are somewhat spoiled, and of which two are missing,[1] and is supposed by Ciasca, from the character of the writing, and from the presence of certain Coptic letters[2] by the first hand, to have been written in Egypt. S. Assemani assigned it to the twelfth century, and Ciasca accepts his verdict, while Akerblad says the thirteenth or fourteenth century. The text of the MS. is pretty fully vocalised, but there are few diacritical points. There are marginal notes, some of them by a later hand,[3] which Ciasca classifies as (1) emendations, (2) restorations, (3) explanations. II. The second MS., which we shall call the Borgian (in Ciasca's foot-notes it is called B), was brought to the Borgian Museum from Egypt in August, 1886. It has at the end the following inscription in Arabic: "A present from Halīm Dōs Ghālī, the Copt, the Catholic, to the Apostolic See, in the year of Christ 1886."[4] Antonius Morcos, Visitor Apostolic of the Catholic Copts, when, in the beginning of 1886, he was shown and informed about the Vatican MS., told of this other one and was the means of its being sent to Rome. The Borgian MS., which Ciasca refers to the fourteenth century, consists of 355 folios. Folios 1–85[5] contain an anonymous preface on the gospels, briefly described by Ciasca, who, however, does not say whether it appears to have been originally written in Arabic or to have been translated into that language. With folios 96*b*, 97*a*, which are reproduced in phototype in Ciasca's edition, begins the Introductory Note given in full at the beginning of the present translation. The text of the *Diatessaron* ends on folio 353*a*, but is followed by certain appendices, for which see below, §55, 17, note. This MS. is complete, and has, as we shall see,[6] in some respects a better text, though it is worse in its orthography than the Vatican MS.

6 *Condition of the Arabic Text.*—Ciasca's text does not profess to be critically determined, for which purpose a more careful study of each of the MSS. and an estimate of their respective texts would be indispensable. Although the Borgian MS. is supposed by Ciasca to be a century or two later than the Vatican MS. it is clearly not a copy of the latter, for not only does it sometimes offer more original readings, but, as we shall see, its text in some points coincides more exactly in scope with the original work. The list of various readings supplied by Ciasca,[7] which is equal to about a fifth or a quarter of the text itself, ought to yield, on being analysed, some canons of criticism. The foot-notes of the present edition are enough to show that a number of the peculiar features of Ciasca's text do not belong to the original Arabic MS.; and further study would dispose of still more. On the other hand, there are unfortunately some indications[8] that the common ancestor of both MSS., though perhaps less than two centuries removed from the original, was not the original itself, and therefore emendation may be necessary even where both MSS. agree. From first to last it has to be borne in mind that a great deal of work was done at Arabic versions of the gospels,[9] and the text of the copy from which our two MSS. are descended may already have suffered from contact with other versions; while the special activity of the thirteenth century may have left its mark in some places on the text of the Borgian MS., supposing it to be chronologically the later.

7 *Origin of the Arabic Text.*—If some of the uncouthness of the Arabic text is due to corruption in the course of transmission, much is also due to its being not an original work, but a translation. That it is, in the main, a translation from Syriac is too obvious to need proof.[10] The Introductory Notice and Subscription to the Borgian MS., moreover, expressly state that the work was translated by one Abu'l Fărăj 'Abdulla ibn-aṭ-Ṭayyib,[11] an "excellent and learned priest," and the inferiority of parts of the translation,[12] and entire absence of any confirmatory evidence,[13] hardly suffice to refute this assertion. Still, the Borgian MS. is a late witness, and although it most probably preserves a genuine tradition as to the author of our work, its statement need not therefore necessarily be correct in every point.

8 *The Arabic Editor and his Method.*—Ibn-aṭ-Ṭayyib (d. 1043) is a well-known man, a Nestorian monk and scholar, secretary to Elias I., Patriarch of Nisibis (for references to sources see, e.g., Ciasca's Introduction, p. xi. f. and Steinschneider's long note in his *Polemische und apologetische Lit. in Arabische Sprache*, pp. 52–55). As we are here concerned with him

1 See below, § 7, 47, note, and § 52, 36, note.
2 See below, § 28, 43, note.
3 See below, foot-notes, *passim*.
4 The first leaf bears a more pretentious Latin inscription, quoted by Ciasca, p. vi.
5 Can this be a misprint for 95?
6 See below, 13.
7 He does not state, in so many words, that the list is absolutely exhaustive.
8 See, e.g., below, § 13, 42, note, and § 14, 43, note.
9 See the valuable article of Guidi, "Le traduzioni degli Evangelii in arabo e in etiopico" (*Atti della R. Accademia dei Lincei; Classe di scienze morali, storiche e filologiche. Serie Quarta*, 1888, *Parte Prima—Memorie*, pp. 5–38). Some of his results are briefly stated in Scrivener, *A Plain Introd. to the Crit. of the N. T.*, 4th ed., ii., 162.
10 *cf.* the foot-notes *passim*, e.g., § 13, 14, § 14, 24.
11 See below, note to Subscription.
12 See a glaring case in § 52, 11.
13 The references to the readings of the *Diatessaron* in Ibn-aṭ-Ṭayyib's own commentary on the gospels (see next note) are remarkably impersonal for one who had made or was to make a translation of it.

simply as a link in the chain connecting our present work with its original source, the only point of interest for us is the method he followed in producing it. Did he prepare an independent translation or did he make use of existing Arabic versions, his own or others'? Until this question, which space forbids us to discuss here, has been more thoroughly investigated,[1] it must suffice to say that in view of the features in the present text that have not yet been shown to exist in any other Arabic version, it is still at least a tenable hypothesis that Ibn-aṭ-Ṭayyib's MS. constituted to a considerable extent a real translation rather than a sort of Arabic parallel to the Codex Fuldensis (see below, 12).

9 *The Syriac Text Translated*—The eleventh-century MS. of Ibn-aṭ-Ṭayyib, could we reach it, would bring us face to face with the more interesting question of the nature of his Syriac original. The Subscription to the Borgian MS. states, probably copying the statement from its exemplar, that this was a Syriac MS. in the handwriting of 'Isa ibn-'Ali al Motaṭabbib, pupil of Ḥonain ibn Isḥāḳ. This Ḥonain was a famous Arabic physician and medical writer of Bagdad (d. 873), whose school produced quite a number of translations and translators, among whom Ibn-'Ali, supposed to be identical with the Syriac lexicographer of the same name, is known to have had a high place. The Syriac MS., therefore, that Ibn-aṭ-Ṭayyib translated takes us back to about the year 900. But the Subscription to each of our MSS.[2] states that the work ended is the gospel called *Diatessaron*, compiled from the four gospels by Titianus; while the Introductory Note to the Borgian MS. adds that this Titianus was a Greek. The next step, therefore, is to inquire whether any traces exist of such a Syriac work, or any statements by which we can check the account just given of it.

10 *Other Traces of a Syriac Text.*—No copy of a Syriac *Diatessaron* has yet been shown to have survived.[3] A number of quotations[4] from such a work have, however, been found in a Syriac commentary on the New Testament by Isho'dad of Merv (*circ.* 852), a contemporary of Ḥonain, Ibn-'Ali's teacher.[5] The value of these extracts is apparent, for they take us back one generation earlier than Ibn-aṭ-Ṭayyib's Syriac exemplar. More important still, they do not entirely agree with the text of our Arabic version. To solve the problem thus raised, we must examine some of the statements about the *Diatessaron* to be found in ecclesiastical writers.

11 *Statements about the Diatessaron.*—One of the most widely known is that of Isho'dad himself, who, in his Preface to the Gospel of Mark, says: "Tatian, disciple of Justin, the philosopher and martyr, selected from the four gospels, and combined and composed a gospel, and called it *Diatessaron*, i.e., the Combined, . . . and upon this gospel Mar Ephraem commented."[6] Dionysius Bar Ṣalibi (twelfth century) repeats each of these phrases, adding, "Its commencement was, 'In the beginning was the Word.'"[7] These statements identify the author of the *Diatessaron* with a man otherwise known, and tell us that the great Syrian father Ephraem (d. 373) wrote a commentary on it. Unfortunately, no Syriac MS. of Ephraem's work is known to have survived;[8] but quotations from it, or allusions to it, are being found in other Syriac writers. One further reference will suffice for the present. Theodoret, Bishop of Cyrrhus, four hundred years before Isho'dad, wrote thus in his book on Heresies (written in 453): "Tatian the Syrian. . . . This [writer] also composed the gospel which is called *Diatessaron*, cutting out the genealogies and whatever other passages show that the Lord was born of the seed of David ac-

1 A specially important part of the general question is this, What are the mutual relations of the following: (1) a supposed version of at least Matthew and John made from the Syriac by Ibn-aṭ-Ṭayyib, mentioned by Ibn-al-'Assâl in the Preface to his scholarly recension of the gospels (MS. numbered Or. 3382 in Brit. Mus., folio 384*b*) and used by him in determining his text; (2) the gospel text interwoven with the commentary of Ibn-aṭ-Ṭayyib on the gospels, a commentary which De Slane says the author wrote in Syriac and then translated into Arabic; (3) our present work. Of MSS. testifying to No. 1 we have some dating from the time of Ibn-al-'Assâl himself; of No. 2 we have, in addition to others, an eleventh-century MS. in Paris, described by De Slane (catalogue No. 85) as being "un volume dépareillé du MS. original de l'ouvrage"; of No. 3 we have of course the Vatican and Borgian MSS. What is the mutual relation of these texts; were any two of them identical? The Brit. Mus. MS. of the second has many points of contact with the third, but is dated 1805 A.D. Does the older Paris MS. stand more or less closely related? Did Ibn-aṭ-Ṭayyib himself really translate any or all of these texts, or did he simply select or edit them? Space does not permit us to point out, far less to discuss, the various possibilities.

2 The text is given below in full at its proper place.

3 Prof. Gottheil, indeed, announced in 1892 in the *Journal of Biblical Literature* (vol. xi., pt. i., p. 71) that he had been privately informed of the existence of a complete copy of the Syriac *Diatessaron*. Unfortunately, however, as he has kindly informed me, he has reluctantly come to the conclusion that the MS. in question, which is not yet accessible, is "nothing more than the commentary of Isho'dad" mentioned in the text. A similar rumor lately circulated probably originated simply in the pamphlet of Goussen mentioned in the next note. S. Bäumer, on the other hand, in his article, "Tatians Diatessaron, seine bisher. Lit. u. die Reconstruction des Textes nach einer neuentdeckten Handschrift" (*Literarischer Handweiser*, 1890, 153-169) which the present writer has not been able to see, perhaps refers simply to the Borgian MS.

4 Attention was called to these by Profs. Isaac H. Hall and R. J. H. Gottheil (*Journ. of Bibl. Lit.*, x., 153 ff.; xi., 68 ff.); then by Prof. J. R. Harris (*Contemp. Rev.*, Aug., 1895, p. 271 ff., and, more fully, *Fragments of the Com. of Ephr. Syr. on the Diatess.*, London, 1895) and by Goussen (*Studia Theologica*, fasc. i., Lips., 1895).

5 Prof. Harris promises an edition of this commentary.

6 Harris, *Fragments*, p. 14, where the Syriac text is quoted.

7 *Bib. Or.*, ii., 159 f. Most of them are repeated again by Bar Hebræus (d. 1286), although some confusion is produced by his interweaving some phrases from Eusebius of Cæsarea. (*Bib. Or.*, i., 57 f., and a longer quotation in English in *Contemp. Rev.*, Aug., 1895, p. 274 f.)

8 Lagarde's statement (*Nachrichten von der Königl. Gesellsch. der Wiss., etc., zu Göttingen*, 1891, No. 4, p. 153) that a MS. had been discovered, appears to have been unfounded. Prof. Rahlfs of Göttingen kindly tells me that he believes this is so.

cording to the flesh." [1] Before examining the testimonials we have now adduced, we must notice certain more remote sources of information.

12 *Non-Syriac Texts of the Diatessaron.*—Although Ephraem's Syriac commentary on the *Diatessaron* is for the present lost, there is an Armenian version of it [2] extant in two MSS. dating from about the time of Bar Ṣalibi and our Vat. MS.[3] A Latin translation of this work, published in 1876 by Moesinger,[4] formed the main basis of Zahn's attempt [5] to reconstruct the *Diatessaron.* Appendix X in Hill's *Diatessaron* (pp. 334–377) contains an English translation of the texts commented on by Ephraem, made from Moesinger's Latin, but collated with the Armenian by Professor J. Armitage Robinson, of Cambridge. A comparison of this document with our Arabic text shows a remarkable agreement in the order and contents, but just as remarkable a lack of agreement in the kind of text presented. The same phenomenon is met with when we compare our Arabic text with a document that carries us back three hundred years before the time of Isho'dad, and therefore more than six hundred years before the Armenian MSS.—the Codex Fuldensis of the Vulgate.[6] This MS. contains an arrangement of the gospel matter that its discoverer and publisher, Bishop Victor of Capua (d. 554), rightly concluded must represent the *Diatessaron* of Tatian, but for the text of which was apparently substituted that of the Vulgate.[7] We are now ready to weigh the testimony we have gathered.[8]

13 *Accretions to the Diatessaron.*—The statements we are to consider are: (1) Bar Ṣalibi's, that Tatian's *Diatessaron* began with "In the beginning was the Word";[9] (2) Theodoret's, that Tatian cut out the genealogies; and (3) the same writer's, that Tatian also cut out "whatever other passages show that the Lord was born of the seed of David according to the flesh." Of these statements 1 conflicts with the Arabic text, which begins with Mark, and the Codex Fuldensis, which begins with Luke, but agrees with the Ephraem source; the same is true of 2; while 3 conflicts with all three texts. Our limits do not admit of our discussing these points in detail. It must suffice to say (1) that, although a more careful examination at first-hand of the introductory notices in the two Arabic MSS. seems needed before one can venture to propound a complete theory, a comparison of the two texts, and a consideration of the descriptions given by Ciasca and Lagarde,[10] make it almost certain that the genuine Arabic text of Ibn-aṭ-Ṭayyib began with John i. 1. Similarly the first four verses of Luke (on which see also below, § 1, 6, note) were probably not in the original text of the MS. that Victor found, for they are not mentioned in the (old) table of contents. We seem thus to detect a process of gradual accretion of material drawn from the ordinary gospel text. (2) The genealogies illustrate the same process. In the Vatican MS. they form part of the text.[11] But in the Borgian MS., although they precede the Subscription, and therefore *may* have been already in the ninth-century Syriac MS. used by Ibn-aṭ-Ṭayyib, they are still placed by themselves, after a blank space, at the end of the volume, with a title of their own.[12] Here, therefore, we actually see stages of the process of accretion. (3) It is therefore possible that the same account must also be given of 3, although in this case we have no direct proof.

14 *Passages Lost from the Diatessaron.*—If the *Diatessaron* has thus been growing so as to represent the ordinary text of the canonical gospels more completely, we have also evidence that suggests that it has been at some time or times purged of certain features that are lacking in these canonical gospels. For one case of this kind see below, § 4, 36, note.

15 *Preservation of the Text of the Diatessaron.*—We have observed already that the Latin, Armenian, and Arabic *Diatessarons* correspond pretty closely in subject-matter and arrangement, but differ markedly in text. The Codex Fuldensis is really a MS. of the Vulgate, although the text that Victor found was probably somewhat different. The Armenian text differs materially from the ordinary Syriac version of the New Testament (the Peshitta), showing a marked connection with another type of Syriac text represented now by the Curetonian and Sinaitic (Lewis) MSS. The Arabic text, on the other hand, almost systematically represents the Peshitta. The explanation of the condition of text in the Codex Fuldensis is obvious. On the other hand, the relationship of the Armenian and Arabic texts to the original *Diatessaron* must be determined by weighing

1 Migne, *Patrol. græc.*, tom. lxxxiii., col. 369, 372.

2 Published at Venice in 1836.

3 The two Armenian MSS. are dated A.D. 1195.

4 *Evangelii Concordantis Expositio, facta a S. Ephraemo* (Ven., 1876).

5 *Forschungen zur Geschichte des neutestamentlichen Kanons*, I. Theil.

6 Edited by Ernestus Ranke, Marb. and Lips., 1868.

7 For other forms of the *Diatessaron*, of no critical importance, see S. Hemphill, *The Diatessaron of Tatian* (London, 1888), Appendix D and the refs. there.

8 Further references, chiefly repetitions in one form or another of the statements we have quoted, may be found in a convenient form in Harnack, *Gesch. d. altchrist. Lit. bis Euseb.*, 493–496; *cf.* also the works mentioned by Hill (*op. cit.*) p. 378 f.

9 *cf.* the words of Aphraates, senior contemporary of Ephraem: "As it is written in the beginning of the Gospel of our Vivifier: In the beginning was the Word." (*Patrol. Syr.*, pars i., tom. i., 21, lines 17–19).

10 *Nachrichten von der Königl. Gesellsch. der Wiss.*, etc., March 17, 1886, No. 4, p. 151 ff.

11 See notes to § 2, 1, and § 4, 29.

12 See note to § 55, 17.

very multifarious evidence that cannot be even cited here (see above 6 ff.). The two texts depend, as we have seen, on late MSS.; but all the earlier references and quotations go to show that the Armenian text[1] stands much more closely related to the original than does the Arabic.

16 *Checkered History of the Diatessaron.*—What use the Arabic edition of Ibn-aṭ-Ṭayyib was put to when made we do not know. ʻAbd Ishoʻ (d. 1318) speaks in the highest terms of Tatian's work, saying, ". . . With all diligence he attended to the utmost degree to the right order of those things which were said and done by the Saviour; of his own he did not add a single saying."[2] But the leaders of the Syrian church had not always thought so. Theodoret (*loc. cit.*) some nine hundred years earlier had written thus: ". . . Even those that follow the apostolic doctrines, not perceiving the mischief of the composition," used "the book too simply as an abridgment." A few years earlier Rabbūlā, Bishop of Edessa (d. 435), had said:[3] "Let the presbyters and deacons give heed that in all the churches there be provided and read a copy of the Distinct Gospel," i.e., not the harmonized or mixed gospel. But obviously these men were trying to suppress traditional practice due to very different views. Theodoret (*loc. cit.*) found more than two hundred copies of the work "held in respect in the churches"; and the *Doctrine of Addai* (Edessa, third to fourth century) seems simply to identify the *Diatessaron* and the New Testament.[4] Outside of the Syriac-speaking churches we find no signs of any such use of the *Diatessaron*. It would seem, therefore, that at a quite early stage the *Diatessaron* was very widely if not universally read in the Syriac churches, and commented on by scholars as the gospel; that in time it fell under the condemnation of some at least of the church leaders, who made violent efforts to suppress it; that it could not be suppressed; that a commentary on it was (perhaps in the fifth century[5]) translated into Armenian; that it was still discussed by commentators, and new Syriac MSS. of it made in the ninth century, and thought worth the labor of reproduction in Arabic in the beginning of the eleventh century; that MSS. of the Armenian volume continued to be made down to the very end of the twelfth century, and of the Arabic edition down to the fourteenth century; but that this long life was secured at the expense of a more or less rapid assimilation of the text to that of the great Syriac Bible which from the fourth century onwards became more and more exclusively used—the Peshitta.

17 *The Author of the Diatessaron.*—The *Diatessaron* is such an impersonal work that we do not need to know very much about its compiler.[6] It will suffice here to say that he tells us himself that he was born "in the land of the Assyrians," and brought up a heathen. After travelling in search of knowledge, he settled at Rome, where he became a pupil of Justin Martyr, professed Christianity, and wrote in Greek his *Address to the Greeks*,[7] translated in vol. iii. of the *Ante-Nicene Christian Library*. He was too independent in his attitude to maintain a permanent popularity, and after Justin's death left Rome and returned to Mesopotamia. It was probably here that he issued in Syriac his most important work, the *Diatessaron*, which won such a warm place in the heart of the Syrian church. Among the Greek scholars, however, he became more and more regarded as a heretic, Encratite (ascetic), and Gnostic.

18 *The Diatessaron as a Harmony.*—Not very much need be said on this subject, as every reader can collect the facts for himself. In its present form the Harmony draws from all the four canonical gospels, and from very little else. Opinions differ as to whether it originally indicated the gospel from which any given piece was drawn, and some uncertainty must remain in special cases as to what gospel actually has been drawn upon. Professor G. F. Moore, in a very interesting article on the *Diatessaron*,[8] having counted the references in the Arabic MSS., states that the Arabic text contains 50 per cent. of Mark, 66 per cent. of Luke, 76.5 per cent. of Matthew, and 96 per cent. of John. The summation of his figures gives the following result: out of a total of 3780 verses in the four gospels, the *Diatessaron* quotes 2769 and omits 1011. As to the order in which the whole is arranged, Moore thinks that Matthew has chiefly been followed; while Zahn regards the Fourth Gospel as normative. For a specimen of the way in which words and phrases from the different gospels are woven together, we may refer to § 52, 35 ff., and the notes thereon. In the Arabic MSS., and probably in the Syriac exemplar, the work is divided into fifty-four almost equal chapters, followed by one short one—a feature that agrees well with what we have learned of the work as being of old the lectionary of the Syrian church.

1 The Armenian version of Ephraem is supposed to date from the fifth century.

2 Mai, *Script. vet. nov. Coll.*, x., 191.

3 Overbeck, *S. Ephraemi*, etc., *Opera Selecta*, p. 220, lines 3–5.

4 Phillips, *Doct. Add.*, p. 36, 15–17 [E. Tr. p. 34].

5 Moesinger, *Evang. Concord.*, etc., p. xi.

6 The latest discussion of the question whether this really was Tatian is Mr. Rendel Harris's article in the *Contemp. Rev.*, Aug., 1895.

7 Best ed. by Eduard Schwartz, in *Texte und Untersuchungen*, IV. Band, Heft 1.

8 "Tatian's *Diatessaron* and the Analysis of the Pentateuch," *Journ. of Bibl. Lit.*, vol. ix., 1890, pt. ii., 201–215.

19 *Problems Connected with the Diatessaron.*—The *Diatessaron* opens up a very wide field of study A few points may be here enumerated (see also above, 8, and note there). In what language was it written? On the view favoured by an increasing majority of scholars, that it was written in Syriac, was it a translation or simply a compilation? What precisely is its relation to the Syriac versions and the "Western" text generally? Then there is its bearing on the date and formation of the canonical gospels; the phenomenon of its so long supplying the place of those gospels; the analogy it presents to the Pentateuch, according to the critical view of the origin of the latter. These and other issues make the *Diatessaron* an important and interesting study.

20 *The Present Translation.*—The work of translation has been found much more tedious than was anticipated, notwithstanding the fact that considerably more than half of it is the work of my wife, which I have simply revised with special attention to the many obscurities dealt with in the foot-notes. We have, however, worked so much together that it is very doubtful whether any one could assign the various parts to their respective sources. My wife also verified the Arabic references to the gospels printed on the margin to the right of the text,[1] and prepared the Index to these references—an extremely laborious and perplexing piece of work. This Index is inserted merely for the practical purpose of enabling the reader to find any given gospel piece in the *Diatessaron*. When a verse is not found in the Index, an equivalent passage from some of the other gospels should be looked for. On the margin to the left of the text are indicated the pages of the Arabic text and the sections and verses in Hill's version.[2]

The aim has been to make a literal translation. As two freer translations already exist, it seemed best to incline to the side of being overliteral. If, however, features due simply to *Arabic* idiom have been preserved, this is an oversight. Uniformity could only have been secured by devoting a much longer time to the work than the editor was able to allow. The difficulties are due to the corrupt state of the Arabic text,[3] and to the awkward reproduction[4] or actual misunderstanding[5] of the Syriac original by the author or authors of the Arabic translation. It has been impossible to maintain consistency in dealing with these phenomena. If any rendering seem strange, it will be well to consult the Syriac versions before deciding that it is wrong. A good deal of attention, too, has to be paid to the usage of the Arabic text, which, though it has many points of contact with other Arabic versions of the gospels, e.g., the MS. described by Gildemeister (*De evangg. in arab. e simp. Syr.*, 1865), is as yet for us (see above, 8) a distinct version, possessed of an individuality of its own, one pronounced feature being its very close adherence to its Syriac original. Another revision of the present translation, in the light of a fuller study of these features, would doubtless lead to changes both in the text and in the foot-notes. The latter aim at preventing misunderstanding and giving some examples of the peculiarities of the text, and of the differences between the MSS. To have dealt systematically with the text and various readings would have required much more time and space than was available. The consequence of this incompleteness has been some uncertainty at times what text to translate. As already stated (paragraphs 4 and 6), Ciasca's printed text neither represents any one MS. nor professes to be based in its eclecticism on any systematic critical principles. On the whole Ciasca has here been followed somewhat mechanically in deciding what to exhibit in the text and what to relegate to the foot-notes. As a rule conjectural emendations have not been admitted into the *text* except where the MS. readings would hardly bear translation. Italics in the text denote words supplied for the sake of English idiom; in the foot-notes, quotations from the MSS. It is to be noted that many linguistic usages said, for shortness, in the foot-notes to be characteristic of the present work, i.e., as compared with ordinary Arabic, are common in Arabic versions. "Syriac versions" means the three (Pesh., Cur., Sin.), or as many of them as contain the passage in question; if the Peshitta alone is quoted, it may be assumed that Cur. and Sin. are missing or diverge.

In conclusion we may say that an effort has been made to preserve even the order of words; but it must be emphasized that it is very doubtful whether it is wise for any one to use the Arabic *Diatessaron* for critical purposes who is not acquainted with Arabic and Syriac. The tenses, e.g., are much vaguer in Arabic than in Greek and English, and are, moreover, in this work often accommodated to Syriac idiom. The Greek and the Revised Version have been

1 The refs., except where the foot-notes indicate otherwise, are to the verses of the English or Greek Bible. The numbers of the Arabic verse refs. (which follow the Vulgate and therefore in one or two passages differ from the English numbers by one) may, however, have been occasionally retained through oversight. It is only the name of the gospel that can possibly be ancient.

2 It may be mentioned that it has been found very convenient to mark these figures on the margin of the Arabic text. An English index (that given here, or that in Hill's volume) can then be used for the Arabic text also.

3 e.g., § 8, 10. For a list of suggested emendations see at end of Index. 4 e.g., § 52, 11. 5 e.g., § 45, 33.

used to determine in almost every case how the vague Arabic tenses and conjunctions should be rendered. It is therefore only where it *differs* from these that our translation can be quoted without investigation as giving positive evidence.

This is not a final translation. Few books have had a more remarkable literary history than the *Diatessaron*, and that history is by no means done. Much careful argument will yet be devoted to it, and perhaps discoveries as important as any hitherto made are yet to shed light on the problems that encircle it. If our work can help any one to take a step in advance, we shall not regret the toil.

OXFORD, 21st December, 1895.

THE DIATESSARON

INTRODUCTORY NOTES.

1. In the Borgian MS.

In the name of the one God, the Father, and the Son, and the Holy Spirit, to him be glory for ever. We shall begin, with the help of God most high, the writing of the pure gospel, the blooming garden, called *Diatessaron* (a word meaning "fourfold"), the work compiled by Titianus the Greek out of the four evangelists—Matthew the elect, whose symbol is M, Mark the chosen, whose symbol is R, Luke the approved, whose symbol is Ḳ, and John the beloved, whose symbol is Ḥ. The work was translated from Syriac into Arabic by the excellent and learned priest, Abu'l-Fārāj 'Abdulla ibn-aṭ-Ṭayyib,[1] may God grant him his favour. He began with the first of[2] And he said: The Beginning[3] of the Gospel of Jesus the Son of the living God. John:[4] In the beginning, etc.

2. In the Vatican MS.

In the name of the Father, and the Son, and the Holy Spirit, giver of life, the God that is one in substance in his essence, and three in persons in his attributes. The first of his Gospel is He began the first of his Gospel with Mark. And he said: The Beginning of the Gospel of Jesus the Messiah, the Son of God. John: In the beginning, etc.

[1] The MS. here has *Ṭabīb*, but the name is correctly given in the Subscription (*q.v.*).

[2] i.e., simply *He began with.*

[3] The vowel signs as printed by Ciasca imply some such construction as *And he said as a beginning: The Gospel*, etc. But the vocalisation is of course not authoritative, and a comparison with the preface in the Vatican MS. suggests the rendering given above. The word translated *Beginning* in the two Introductory Notes is the very word (whichever spelling be adopted) used by Ibn-aṭ-Ṭayyib himself in his comments on Mk. i. (at least according to the Brit. Mus. MS.), although not in the gospel text prefixed to the Comments *as it now stands*, or indeed in any MS. Arabic goṣpel in the Brit. Mus. This would seem to militate against our theory of the original form of this much-debated passage in the Introductory Notes, as indicated by the use of small type for the later inserted phrases; and the difficulty appears at first to be increased by the following words in Ibn-aṭ-Ṭayyib's comments on Mk. i. (Brit. Mus. MS., fol. 190*a*), "and some say that the Greek citation *and in the Diatessaron, which Tatianus the pupil of Justianus the philosopher wrote, the quotation is not written*, "Isaiah," but, "as it is written in the prophet." This is a remarkable statement about the *Diatessaron*. But the sentence is hardly grammatical. Perhaps the words printed in italics originally formed a complete sentence by themselves, possibly on the margin. If this conjecture be correct we might emend, e.g., by restoring them to the margin, and repeating the last three words or some equivalent phrase in the text. It would be interesting to know how the Paris MS. reads. See below, p. 138 (Suggested Emendations).

[4] Ciasca does not state whether the word *John* occurs here in the Borgian MS. or not.

THE TEXT OF THE DIATESSARON

[SECTION I.]

§1 1 In the beginning was the Word, and the Word was with God, and God is the Jo. 1, 1.
2, 3 Word. This *was* in the beginning with God. Everything was by his hand, and Jo. 1, 2. Jo. 1, 3.
4 without him not even one existing thing was *made*. In him was life, and the life Jo. 1, 4.
5 is the light of men. And the light shineth in the darkness, and the darkness appre- Jo. 1, 5.
hended it not.
6 There was in the days of Herod the king a priest whose name was Zacharias, of Lk. 1, 5.[1]
the family of Abijah; and his wife was of the daughters of Aaron, and her name
7 was Elizabeth. And they were both righteous before God, walking in all his com- Lk. 1, 6.
8 mands, and in the uprightness of God without reproach. And they had no son, for Lk. 1, 7.
9 Elizabeth was barren, and they had both advanced in age. And while he discharged Lk. 1, 8.
10 Arabic, the duties of priest in the order of his service before God, according to the Lk. 1, 9.
p. 2 custom of the priesthood it was his turn to burn incense; so he entered the
11 temple of the Lord. And the whole gathering of the people were praying without at the Lk. 1, 10.
12 time of the incense. And there appeared unto Zacharias the angel of the Lord, stand- Lk. 1, 11.
13 ing at the right of the altar of incense; and Zacharias was troubled when he saw him, Lk. 1, 12.
14 and fear fell upon him. But the angel said unto him, Be not agitated,[2] Zacharias, Lk. 1, 13.
for thy prayer is heard, and thy wife Elizabeth shall bear thee a son, and thou shalt
15 call his name John; and thou shalt have joy and gladness, and many shall rejoice Lk. 1, 14.
16 at his birth. And he shall be great before the Lord, and shall not drink wine nor Lk. 1, 15.
strong drink, and he shall be filled with the Holy Spirit[3] while he is in his mother's
17 womb. And he shall turn back many of the children of Israel to the Lord their Lk. 1, 16.
18 God. And he shall go before him in the spirit, and in the power of Elijah the Lk. 1, 17.
prophet, to turn back the heart of the fathers to the sons, and those that obey not to
the knowledge[4] of the righteous; and to prepare for the Lord a perfect people.
19 And Zacharias said unto the angel, How shall I know this, since I am an old man Lk. 1, 18.
20 and my wife is advanced in years? And the angel answered and said unto him, I Lk. 1, 19.
am Gabriel, that standeth before God; and I was sent to speak unto thee, and give
21 thee tidings of this. Henceforth thou shalt be speechless, and shalt not be able to Lk. 1, 20.
speak until the day in which this shall come to pass, because thou didst not trust
22 this my word, which shall be accomplished in its time. And the people were stand- Lk. 1, 21.
Arabic, ing awaiting Zacharias, and they were perplexed at his delaying in the temple.
23 p. 3 And when Zacharias went out, he was not able to speak unto them: so they Lk. 1, 22.
knew that he had seen in the temple a vision; and he made signs unto them, and
24 continued dumb. And when the days of his service were completed, he departed to Lk. 1, 23.
his dwelling.
25 And after those days Elizabeth his wife conceived; and she hid herself five Lk. 1, 24.
26 months, and said, This hath the Lord done unto me in the days when he looked Lk. 1, 25.
upon me, to remove my reproach from among men.
27 And[5] in the sixth month Gabriel the angel was sent from God to Galilee[6] to a Lk. 1, 26.
28 city called Nazareth, to a virgin given in marriage to a man named Joseph, of the Lk. 1, 27.
29 house of David; and the virgin's name was Mary. And the angel entered unto her Lk. 1, 28.
and said unto her, Peace be unto thee, thou who art filled with grace. Our Lord

1 On the margin of the Vatican MS., fol. 1*a*, are written by a later hand these words, *The first of his Gospel. The first of the Evangel (is) the Gospel of Luke;* followed by the text of the first four verses of Luke, and that in turn by the words, *Four complete Gospels, Matthew, and Mark, and Luke, and John.* See Ciasca's *Essay*, cited above (Introduction, 5), p. 468.

2 This word is constantly recurring in the sense of *fear*.

3 Everywhere, except in the introductory notes, the Arabic is *the Spirit of Holiness*, as in the Arabic versions.

4 See § 28, 17, note.

5 The Vat. MS. has over this verse, *The second section, from the Gospel of Luke*, i.e, as divided in the Syriac and Arabic versions.

6 The Borgian MS. omits *to Galilee*.

§1 30 is with thee, thou blessed amongst women. And she, when she beheld, was agitated Lk. 1, 29.
31 at his word, and pondered what this salutation could be. And the angel said unto Lk. 1, 30.
32 her, Fear not, Mary, for thou hast found favour with God. Thou shalt now con- Lk. 1, 31.
33 ceive, and bear a son, and call his name JESUS. This shall be great, and shall be Lk. 1, 32.
called the Son of the Most High; and the Lord God will give him the throne of
34 David his father: and he shall rule over the house of Jacob for ever; and to his Lk. 1, 33.
35 kingdom there shall be no end. Mary said unto the angel, How shall this be to Lk. 1, 34.
36 me when no man hath known me? The angel answered and said unto her, The Lk. 1, 35.
Arabic, Holy Spirit will come, and the power of the Most High shall rest upon thee,
p. 4 and therefore shall *he* that is born of thee be pure, and shall be called the Son
37 of God. And lo, Elizabeth thy kinswoman, she also hath conceived a son in her old Lk. 1, 36.
38 age; and this is the sixth month with her, her that is called barren. For nothing is Lk. 1, 37.
39 difficult for God. Mary said, Lo, I am the handmaid of the Lord; let it be unto me Lk. 1, 38.
according unto thy word. And the angel departed from her.
40 And then Mary arose in those days and went in haste into the hill country,[1] to a[2] Lk. 1, 39.
41 city of Judah; and entered into the house of Zacharias, and asked for the health of Lk. 1, 40.
42 Elizabeth. And when Elizabeth heard the salutation of Mary, the babe leaped in Lk. 1, 41.
43 her womb. And Elizabeth was filled with the Holy Spirit; and cried with a loud Lk. 1, 42.
voice and said unto Mary, Blessed art thou amongst women, and blessed is the
44 fruit that is in thy womb. Whence have I this *privilege*, that the mother of my Lk. 1, 43.
45 Lord should come unto me? When the sound of thy salutation reached my ears, Lk. 1, 44.
46 with great joy rejoiced[3] the babe in my womb. And blessed is she who believed Lk. 1, 45.
47 that what was spoken *to her* from the Lord would be fulfilled. And Mary said, Lk. 1, 46.
My soul doth magnify the Lord,
48 And my spirit hath rejoiced in God my Saviour, Lk. 1, 47.
49 Who hath looked upon the low estate of his handmaiden: Lk. 1, 48.
Lo, henceforth, all generations[4] shall pronounce blessing on me.
50 For[5] he hath done great things for me, who is mighty, Lk. 1, 49.
And holy is his name.
51 And his mercy embraceth them who fear him, Lk. 1, 50.
Throughout the ages and the times.
52 Arabic, He wrought the victory with his arm, Lk. 1, 51.
p. 5 And scattered them that prided themselves in their opinions.
53 He overthrew them that acted haughtily from their thrones, Lk. 1, 52.
And raised the lowly.
54 He satisfied with good things the hungry, Lk. 1, 53.
And left the rich without anything.
55 He helped Israel his servant, Lk. 1, 54.
And remembered his mercy
56 (According as he spake with our fathers) Lk. 1, 55.
Unto Abraham and unto his seed for ever.
57 And Mary abode with Elizabeth about three months, and returned unto her house. Lk. 1, 56.
58, 59 And Elizabeth's time of delivery was come; and she brought forth a son. And Lk. 1, 57. Lk. 1, 58.
her neighbours and kinsfolk heard that God had multiplied his mercy towards her;
60 and they rejoiced with her. And when[6] it was the eighth day, they came to cir- Lk. 1, 59.
cumcise the child, and called him Zacharias, *calling him* by the name of his father.
61 And his mother answered and said unto them, Not so; but he shall be called John. Lk. 1, 60.
62 And they said unto her, There is no man of thy kindred that is called by this name. Lk. 1, 61.
63, 64 And they made signs to his father, *saying*, How dost thou wish to name him? And Lk. 1, 62. Lk. 1, 63.
he asked for a tablet, and wrote and said, His name is John. And every one won-
65 dered. And immediately his mouth was opened, and his tongue, and he spake and Lk. 1, 64.
66 praised God. And fear fell on all their neighbours: and this was spoken of[7] in all Lk. 1, 65.

1 Vat. MS., like that described by Gildemeister (see Introduction, 20) has *into Galilee* (*cf.* § 8, 10, note).
2 Lit. *the*, a form due to Syriac influence (*cf.* § 2, 12, and *passim*).
3 The Syriac versions (like the Greek) have the same word here as in Lk. i. 41.
4 The Arabic word ordinarily means *tribe* or *nation*, but in this work it regularly represents the Syriac word used in the N. T. for *generation*.
5 The Arabic would naturally be rendered, *the blessing on me, That;* but a number of passages in this work seem to justify the rendering given in the text (*cf.*, e.g., § 46, 54, and especially § 15, 40).
6 The text is indistinct in the Vat. MS. The reading seems to be conflate, the doublets being *when it was*, which is the reading of Ibn-aṭ-Ṭayyib's Commentary, and *on*.
7 Lit. *described* (*cf.* § 2, 46).

§1 67 the mountains of Judah. And all who heard pondered in their hearts and said, Lk. 1, 66.
What shall this child be? And the hand of the Lord was with him.
68 And Zacharias his father was filled with the Holy Spirit, and prophesied and Lk. 1, 67.
said,
69 Blessed is the Lord, the God of Israel, Lk. 1, 68.
Who hath cared for his people, and wrought for it salvation;
70 And hath raised for us the horn of salvation Lk. 1, 69.
Arabic, In the house of David his servant
71 p. 6 (As he spake by the mouth of his holy prophets from eternity), Lk. 1, 70.
72 That he might save us from our enemies, Lk. 1, 71.
And from the hand of all them that hate us.
73 And he hath performed his mercy towards our fathers, Lk. 1, 72.
And remembered his holy covenants,
74 And the oath which he sware unto Abraham our father, Lk. 1, 73.
75 That he would give us deliverance from the hand of our enemies, Lk. 1, 74.
And without fear we shall[1] serve before him
76 All our days with equity and righteousness. Lk. 1, 75.
77 And as for thee, O child, prophet of the Most High shalt thou be called. Lk. 1, 76.
Thou shalt go forth before the face of the Lord to prepare his way,
78 To give the knowledge of salvation[2] unto his people, Lk. 1, 77.
For the forgiveness of their sins,
79 Through the mercy of[3] the compassion of our God, Lk. 1, 78.
With which he careth for[4] us, to appear[5] from on high
80 To give light to them that sit in darkness and under the shadow of death, Lk. 1, 79.
And to set straight our feet in the way of peace.
81 And the child grew and became strong in the spirit, and abode in the desert until Lk. 1, 80.
the time of his appearing unto the children of Israel.

SECTION II.

§2 1 Arabic, Now[6] the birth of Jesus the Messiah was on this wise: In the time when Mt. 1, 18.
p. 7 his mother was given in marriage to Joseph, before they came together,
2 she was found with child of the Holy Spirit. And Joseph her husband was a just Mt. 1, 19.
man and did not wish to expose her, and he purposed to put her away secretly.
3 But when he thought of this, the angel of the Lord appeared unto him in a dream, Mt. 1, 20.
and said unto him, Joseph, son of David, fear not to take Mary thy wife, for that
4 which is begotten[7] in her is of the Holy Spirit. She shall bear a son, and thou shalt Mt. 1, 21.
5 call his name Jesus, and he shall save[8] his people from their sins. And all this was Mt. 1, 22.
that the saying from the Lord by the prophet might be fulfilled:
6 Behold, the virgin shall conceive, and bear a son, Mt. 1, 23.
And they shall call his name Immanuel,
7 which is, being interpreted, With us is our God. And when Joseph arose from his Mt. 1, 24.
8 sleep, he did as the angel of the Lord commanded him, and took his wife; and knew Mt. 1, 25*a*.
her not until she brought forth her firstborn son.
9 And in those days there went forth a decree from Augustus Cæsar that all the Lk. 2, 1.

1 Or, *should*. 2 Here and elsewhere the Arabic translator uses *life* and *live* and *give life*, as in Syriac, for *salvation*, etc.
3 Borg. MS. has *and* for *of*.
4 The word used in the Peshitta means *visit*, either in the sense of *caring for* or in that of *frequenting*. See § 24, 29.
5 So Borg. MS. The Vat. MS. is very indistinct. Lagarde (see Introduction, 13, note), quoting Guidi, prints *Whereby there visiteth us the manifestation from on high*. The difference in Arabic is in a single stroke.
6 This is preceded in Vat. MS. by the genealogy, Mt. i., 1–17 (see Introduction, 13), with the marginal note *The Beginning of the Gospel of Matthew*. (Lagarde, *op. cit.*, 1886, p. 154.) The text presents nothing worthy of note in this place except that verse 16, construed on the same principle as the preceding verses, to which, except in the words printed in italics, it is strictly parallel in construction, reads thus: "Jacob begat Joseph, *the husband of Mary*, who *of her* begat Jesus, the Messiah" (*cf.* the remarkable reading of Sin. Syriac). As it stands, this is the only possible interpretation of the words, for *who* is masculine. But a mistake in the gender of a relative pronoun is very common in Arabic among illiterate people, while in Syriac there is, to begin with, no distinction. If then we correct the relative, *who of her* will become *of whom* (fem.), and *begat* will of course be construed as passive. We thus get the text followed in Ibn-aṭ-Ṭayyib's Commentary, the ordinary reading of the Peshitta, *of whom was born Jesus*.
7 The Arabic might even more naturally be rendered *born*, thus giving us the reading that Isho'dad tells us was that of the *Diatessaron* (Harris, *Fragments*, p. 16 f.); but throughout the whole genealogy (see § 1, 81, note) this word has been used by the Vat. MS. in the sense of *begat*. Here the Borg. MS. has *of her* for *in her*; but Ibn-aṭ-Ṭayyib in his Commentary discusses *why* Matthew wrote *in* and not *of*.
8 *cf.* § 1, 78.

§2 10 people of his dominion[1] should be enrolled. This first enrolment was[2] while Qui- Lk. 2, 2.
11, 12 rinius was governor of Syria. And every man went to be enrolled in his city. And Lk. 2, 3. Lk. 2, 4.
Joseph went up also from Nazareth, a city of Galilee, to Judæa, to the city of David
13 which is called Bethlehem (for he was of the house of David and of his tribe), with Lk. 2, 5.
14 Arabic, Mary his betrothed, she being with child, to be enrolled there. And while Lk. 2, 6.
15 p. 8 she was there the days for her being delivered were accomplished. And Lk. 2, 7.
she brought forth her firstborn son; and she wrapped him in swaddling cloths and laid
him in a manger, because there was no place for them where they were staying.
16 And there were in that region shepherds abiding, keeping their flock in the watch Lk. 2, 8.
17 of the night. And behold, the angel of God came unto them, and the glory of the Lk. 2, 9.
18 Lord shone upon them; and they were greatly terrified. And the angel said unto Lk. 2, 10.
them, Be not terrified; for I bring you tidings of great joy which shall be to the
19 whole world; there is born to you this day a Saviour, which is the Lord the Mes- Lk. 2, 11.
20 siah, in the city of David. And this is a sign for you: ye shall find a babe wrapped Lk. 2, 12.
21 in swaddling cloths and laid in a manger. And there appeared with the angels sud- Lk. 2, 13.
denly many heavenly forces praising[3] God and saying,
22 Praise be to God in the highest, Lk. 2, 14.
And on the earth peace, and good hope to men.
23 And when the angels departed from them to heaven, the shepherds spake to one Lk. 2, 15.
another and said, We will go to Bethlehem and see this word which hath been, as
24 the Lord made known unto us. And they came with haste, and found Mary and Lk. 2, 16.
25 Joseph, and the babe laid in a manger. And when they saw, they reported the word Lk. 2, 17.
26 which was spoken to them about the child. And all that heard wondered at the Lk. 2, 18.
27 description which the shepherds described[4] to them. But Mary kept these[5] sayings Lk. 2, 19.
28 and discriminated[6] them in her heart. And those shepherds returned, magnifying Lk. 2, 20.
and praising God for all that they had seen and heard, according as it was described
unto them.
29 Arabic, And when eight days were fulfilled that the child should be circumcised, Lk. 2, 21.
p. 9 his name was called Jesus, being that by which he was called by the angel
before his conception in the womb.
30 And when the days of their purification according to the law of Moses were Lk. 2, 22.
31 completed, they took him up to Jerusalem to present him before the Lord (as it Lk. 2, 23.
is written in the law of the Lord, Every male opening the womb shall be called the
32 holy *thing* of the Lord), and to give a sacrificial victim as it is said in the law of Lk. 2, 24.
33 the Lord, A pair of doves or two young pigeons. And there was in Jerusalem a Lk. 2, 25.
man whose name was Simeon; and this man was upright and pious, and expecting
34 the consolation of Israel; and the Holy Spirit was upon him. And it had been Lk. 2, 26.
said unto him by the Holy Spirit, that he should not see death till he had seen with
35 his eyes the Messiah[7] of the Lord. And this man came by the Spirit to the tem- Lk. 2, 27.
ple; and at the time when his parents brought in the child Jesus, that they might
36 present for him a sacrifice, as it is written in the law, he bare him in his arms and Lk. 2, 28.
praised God and said,
37 Now loosest thou the bonds of thy servant, O Lord, in peace,[8] Lk. 2, 29.
According to thy saying;
38 For mine eye hath witnessed thy mercy, Lk. 2, 30.
39 Which thou hast made ready because of the whole world; Lk. 2, 31.
40 A light for the unveiling[9] of the nations, Lk. 2, 32.
And a glory to thy people Israel.
41 And Joseph and his mother were marvelling at the things which were being said Lk. 2, 33.
42 concerning him. And Simeon blessed them and said to Mary his mother, Behold, Lk. 2, 34.
he is set for the overthrow and rising of many in Israel; and for a sign of conten-
43 tion; and a spear[10] shall pierce[11] through thine own soul; that the thoughts of the Lk. 2, 35.

1 The Arabic expression is clearly meant to represent that used in the Peshitta.
2 This is the most *natural* meaning of the Arabic sentence; which, however, is simply a word-for-word reproduction of the Peshitta.
3 The Arab. represents Syr. idiom.
4 *cf.* § 1, 66, note.
5 Borg. MS. inserts *all* above the line, after *these*. The meaning ought then to be, *these things, namely, all the sayings*.
6 The Arab. might mean *set them apart;* but the Syriac is against this.
7 Or, *anointed*.
8 For order *cf.* (in part) Sin. Syriac.
9 i.e., *becoming manifest*.
10 So also in Syriac versions and the quotation of Isho'dad from Ephraem (Harris, *Fragments*, p. 34), but not the Armenian version.
11 The Arabic sides with the Peshitta and Ibn-at-Tayyib's Commentary, against the remarkable reading of Sin. supported by Isho'dad, as in last note (*Syriac* text), and the Armenian in Hill, p. 336. See now also *The Guardian*, Dec. 18, 1895.

§2 44 Arabic, hearts of many may be revealed. And Anna the prophetess, the daughter Lk. 2, 36.
p. 10 of Phanuel, of the tribe of Asher, was also advanced in years (and she dwelt
45 with her husband seven years from her virginity, and she remained a widow about Lk. 2, 37.
eighty-four years); and she left not the temple, and served night and day with
46 fasting and prayer. And she also rose in that hour and thanked the Lord, and she Lk. 2, 38.
47 spake of him with every one who was expecting the deliverance of Jerusalem. And Lk. 2, 39.
when they had accomplished everything according to what is in the law of the
Lord, they returned to Galilee, to Nazareth their city.

SECTION III.

§3 1, 2 And after that,[1] the Magi came from the east to Jerusalem, and said, Where is Mt. 2, 1*b*.
the King of the Jews which was born? We have seen his star in the east, and have Mt. 2, 2.
3 come to worship him. And Herod the king heard, and he was troubled, and all Mt. 2, 3.
4 Jerusalem with him. And he gathered all the chief priests and the scribes of the Mt. 2, 4.
5 people, and asked them in what place[2] the Messiah should be born. They said, In Mt. 2, 5.
Bethlehem of Judæa: thus it is written in the prophet,

6 Thou also, Bethlehem of Judah, Mt. 2, 6.
Art not contemptible among the kings of Judah:
From thee shall go forth a king,
And he shall be a shepherd to my people Israel.

7 Then Herod called the Magi secretly, and inquired of them the time at which Mt. 2, 7.
8 the star appeared to them. And he sent them to Bethlehem, and said unto them, Mt. 2, 8.
Go and search about the child diligently; and when ye have found him, come and
9 make known to me, that I also may go and worship him. And they, when they Mt. 2, 9.
Arabic, heard the king, departed; and lo, the star which they had seen in the east
p. 11 went before them, until it came and stood above the place where the child
10, 11 was. And when they beheld the star, they rejoiced with very great joy. And they Mt. 2, 10. Mt. 2, 11.
entered the house and beheld the child with Mary his mother, and fell down wor-
shipping him, and opened their saddle-bags and offered to him offerings, gold and
12 myrrh and frankincense. And they saw in a dream[3] that they should not return to Mt. 2, 12.
Herod, and they travelled by another way in going to their country.
13 And when they had departed, the angel of the Lord appeared in a dream to Mt. 2, 13.
Joseph, and said unto him, Rise, take the child and his mother, and flee into Egypt,
and be thou there until I speak to thee; for Herod is determined to seek the child
14 to slay him. And Joseph arose and took the child and his mother in the night, and Mt. 2, 14.
15 fled into Egypt, and remained in it until the time of the death of Herod: that that Mt. 2, 15.
might be fulfilled which was said by the Lord in the prophet, which said, From
16 Egypt did I call my son. And Herod then, when he saw that he was mocked of Mt. 2, 16.
the Magi, was very angry, and sent and killed all the male children which were in
Bethlehem and all its borders, from two years old and under, according to the time
17 which he had inquired from the Magi. Then was fulfilled the saying in Jeremiah Mt. 2, 17.
the prophet, which said,

18 A voice was heard in Ramah, Mt. 2, 18.
Weeping and much lamentation;
Rachel weeping[4] for her children,
And not willing to be consoled for their loss.

19 But when Herod the king died, the angel of the Lord appeared in a dream to Mt. 2, 19.
20 Joseph in Egypt, and said unto him, Rise and take the child and his mother, and Mt. 2, 20.
Arabic, go into the land of Israel; for they have died who sought the child's life.
21 p. 12 And Joseph rose and took the child and his mother, and came to the land Mt. 2, 21.
22 of Israel. But when he heard that Archelaus had become king over Judæa instead Mt. 2, 22.
of Herod his father, he feared to go thither; and he saw in a dream that he should

1 On the substitution of this general phrase for Mt. 2, 1*a*, see the remarks of Harris in *Fragments*, etc., p. 37 ff.
2 This periphrasis for *where* is very characteristic of this work.
3 So in later Arabic and some Arabic versions. According to classical usage the word means *sleep*.
4 Or, *is weeping*, and so in next line *is not willing*.

§3 23 go into the land of Galilee, and that he should abide in a city called Nazareth: that Mt. 2, 23.
the saying in the prophet might be fulfilled, that he should be called a Nazarene.
24 And the child grew, and became strong in spirit, becoming filled with wisdom; Lk. 2, 40.
and the grace of God was upon him.
25 And his kinsfolk [1] used to go every year to Jerusalem at the feast of the pass- Lk. 2, 41.
26 over. And when he was twelve years old, they went up according to their custom, Lk. 2, 42.
27 to the feast. And when the days were accomplished, they returned; and the child Lk. 2, 43.
28 Jesus remained in Jerusalem, and Joseph and his mother knew not: and they sup- Lk. 2, 44.
posed that he was with the children of their company. And when they had gone
one day's journey, they sought him beside their people and those who knew them,
29 and they found him not; so they returned to Jerusalem and sought him again. Lk. 2, 45.
30 And after three days they found him in the temple, sitting in the midst of the teach- Lk. 2, 46.
31 ers, hearing them and asking them *questions;* and all who heard him wondered at Lk. 2, 47.
32 his wisdom and his words. And when they saw him they wondered, and his mother Lk. 2, 48.
said unto him, My son, why hast thou dealt with us thus? behold, I and thy father
33 have been seeking for thee with much anxiety. And he said unto them, Why were Lk. 2, 49.
34 ye seeking me? know [2] ye not that I must be in the house of my Father? And they Lk. 2, 50.
35 understood not the word which he spake unto them. And he went down with them, Lk. 2, 51.
and came to Nazareth; and he was obedient to them: and his mother used to keep
all these sayings in her heart.
36 Arabic, p. 13 And Jesus grew in his stature and wisdom, and in grace with God Lk. 2, 52.
and men.
37 And in the fifteenth year of the reign of Tiberius Cæsar, when Pontius Pilate Lk. 3, 1.
was governor in Judæa, and one of the four rulers, Herod, in Galilee; and Philip
his brother, one of the four rulers, in Ituræa and in the district of Trachonitis; and
38 Lysanias, one of the four rulers, in Abilene; in the chief-priesthood of Annas and Lk. 3, 2.
Caiaphas, the command [3] of God went forth to John the son of Zacharias in the
39 desert. And he came into all the region which is about Jordan, proclaiming the Lk. 3, 3.
40 baptism of repentance unto [4] the forgiveness of sins. And he was preaching in the Mt. 3, 1*b*.
41 wilderness of Judæa, and saying, Repent ye; the kingdom of heaven is come near. Mt. 3, 2.
42 This is he that was spoken *of* in Isaiah the prophet, Mt. 3, 3*a*.
The voice which crieth in the desert,
43 Prepare ye the way of the Lord, Lk. 3, 4*b*.
And make straight in the plain, paths for our God.
44 All the valleys shall become filled, Lk. 3, 5.
And all the mountains and hills shall become low;
And the rough shall become plain,
And the difficult place, easy;
45 And all flesh shall see the salvation [5] of God. Lk. 3, 6.
46 This *man* came to bear witness, that he might bear witness to the light, that Jo. 1, 7.
47 every man might believe through his mediation. He was not the light, but that he Jo. 1, 8.
48 might bear witness to the light, which was the light of truth, that giveth light to Jo. 1, 9.
49 every man coming into the world. He was in the world, and the world was made Jo. 1, 10.
50 by him, and the world knew him not. He came unto his own, and his own received Jo. 1, 11.
51 him not. And those who received him, to them gave he the power [6] that they might Jo. 1, 12.
52 be sons of God,—those which believe in his name: which were born, not of blood, Jo. 1, 13.
53 nor of the will of the flesh, nor of the will of a man, but of God. And the Word Jo. 1, 14.
became flesh, and took up his abode among us; and we saw his glory as the glory
54 of the only *Son* from the Father, which is full of grace and equity.[7] John bare wit- Jo. 1, 15.
Arabic, p. 14 ness of him, and cried, and said, This is he that I said cometh after me and
55 was before me, because he was before me.[8] And of his fulness received Jo. 1, 16.
56 we all grace for grace. For the law was given through the mediation of Moses, but Jo. 1, 17.
truth and grace were [9] through Jesus Christ.

1 A general word (*cf.* Syr. versions). 2 Or, *knew.*
3 There is a very rare use of this Arabic word in the Hebrew sense of *saying.*
4 So Vat. MS. The Borg. MS. has *with.* 5 See note on § 1, 78. 6 Or, *authority.*
7 In Syr. this word also means *truth.* 8 Or, *earlier than I.* 9 i.e., *came to be.*

SECTION IV.

§4 1 No man hath seen God at any time; the only *Son*, God,[1] which is in the bosom Jo. 1, 18.
of his Father, he hath told of *him*.
2 And this is the witness of John when the Jews sent to him from Jerusalem priests Jo. 1, 19.
3 and Levites to ask him, Who art thou? And he acknowledged, and denied not; Jo. 1, 20.
4 and he confessed that he was not the Messiah. And they asked him again, What Jo. 1, 21.
then? Art thou Elijah? And he said, I am not he. Art thou a prophet? He
5 said, No. They said unto him, Then who art thou? that we may answer them that Jo. 1, 22.
6 sent us. What sayest thou of thyself? And he said, I am the voice that crieth in Jo. 1, 23.
7 the desert, Repair ye the way of the Lord, as said Isaiah the prophet. And they Jo. 1, 24.
8 that were sent were from[2] the Pharisees. And they asked him and said unto him, Jo. 1, 25.
Why baptizest thou now, when thou art not the Messiah, nor Elijah, nor a prophet?
9 John answered and said unto them, I baptize with[3] water: among you is standing Jo. 1, 26.
10 one whom ye know not: this is he who I said cometh after me and was before Jo. 1, 27.
11 me, the latchets of whose shoes I am not worthy to unloose. And that was in Jo. 1, 28.
Bethany beyond Jordan, where John was baptizing.
12 Now John's raiment was camel's hair, and *he was* girded with skins, and his food Mt. 3, 4.
13 Arabic, was of locusts and honey of the wilderness.[4] Then went out unto him the Mt. 3, 5.
p. 15 people of Jerusalem, and all Judæa, and all the region which is about the
14, 15 Jordan; and they were baptized of him in the river Jordan, confessing their sins. But Mt. 3, 6. Mt. 3, 7.
when he saw many of the Pharisees[5] and Sadducees[6] coming to be baptized, he said
unto them, Ye children of vipers, who hath led you to flee from the wrath to come?
16, 17 Do now the fruits which are worthy of repentance; and think and say not within Mt. 3, 8. Mt. 3, 9.
yourselves, We have a father, *even* Abraham; for I say unto you, that God is able to
18 raise up of these stones children unto Abraham. Behold, the axe hath been laid at the Mt. 3, 10.
roots of the trees, and so every tree that beareth not good fruit shall be taken and
19 cast into the fire. And the multitudes were asking him and saying, What shall we do? Lk. 3, 10.
20 He answered and said unto them, He that hath two tunics shall[7] give to him that Lk. 3, 11.
21 hath not; and he that hath food shall[7] do likewise. And the publicans also came Lk. 3, 12.
22 to be baptized, and they said unto him, Teacher, what shall we do? He said unto Lk. 3, 13.
23 them, Seek not more than what ye are commanded to seek. And the servants[8] of Lk. 3, 14.
the guard asked him and said, And we also, what shall we do? He said unto them,
Do not violence to any man, nor wrong him; and let your allowances satisfy you.
24 And when the people were conjecturing about John, and all of them thinking Lk. 3, 15.
25 in their hearts whether he were haply[9] the Messiah, John answered and said unto Lk. 3, 16.
them, I baptize you with water; there cometh one after me who is stronger than I,
the latchets of whose shoes I am not worthy to loosen; he will baptize you with the
26 Holy Spirit and fire; who taketh the fan in his hand to cleanse his threshing-floors, Lk. 3, 17.
Arabic, and the wheat he gathereth into his garners, while the straw he shall burn
p. 16 in fire which can[10] not be put out.
27 And other things he taught and preached among the people. Lk. 3, 18.
28 Then came Jesus from Galilee to the Jordan to John, to be baptized of him. Mt. 3, 13.
29 And Jesus was about thirty years old, and it was supposed that he was the son of Lk. 3, 23*a*.
30 Joseph.[11] And John saw Jesus coming unto him, and said, This is the Lamb of Jo. 1, 29.
31 God, that taketh on itself the burden of the sins of the world! This is he concern- Jo. 1, 30.
ing whom I said, There cometh after me a man who was before me, because he was

1 *cf.* Peshitta, etc. (not Cur.): *cf.* also Gildemeister, *op. cit.*, p. 29, on Lk. 9, 20. 2 Lit. *from the side of.* 3 Or, *in.*

4 On the original *Diatessaron* reading, *honey and milk of the mountains*, or, *milk and honey of the mountains*, which latter Ibn-aṭ-Ṭayyib cites in his Commentary (folio 44b, 45a) as a reading, but without any allusion to the *Diatessaron*, see, e.g., now Harris, *Fragments of the Com. of Ephr. Syr. upon the Diat.* (London, 1895), p. 17 f.

5 The translator uses invariably an Arabic word (name of a sect) meaning *Separatists*.

6 Lit. *Zindiks*, a name given to Persian dualists and others.

7 Grammar requires this rendering, but solecisms in this kind of word are very common, and in this work (e.g., § 48, 21) the jussive particle is sometimes omitted. We should therefore probably render *let him give, let him do*, etc.

8 *cf.* Peshitta, where the word has its special meaning, *soldiers*.

9 Our translator constantly uses this Arabic word (which we render *haply*, or, *can it be?* or, *perhaps*, etc.) to represent the Syriac word used in this place. The latter is used in various ways, and need not be interrogative, as our translator renders it (*cf.* especially § 17, 6). 10 Or, *shall.*

11 The Vat. MS. here gives the genealogy (Lk. 3, 23–38), of which we shall quote only the last words: *the son of Adam; who (was) from God.* If this were not the reading of the Peshitta (against Sin.) and Ibn-aṭ-Ṭayyib's Commentary, one might explain *from* as a corruption of the Arabic *son of*, the words being very similar. On the Borg. MS. see § 55, 17, note.

§4 32 before me.[1] And I knew him not; but that he should be made manifest to Israel, Jo. 1, 31.
33 for this cause came I to baptize with water. And John was hindering him and Mt. 3, 14.
34 saying, I have need of being baptized by thee, and comest thou to me? Jesus Mt. 3, 15.
answered him and said, Suffer this now: thus it is our duty to fulfil all righteous-
35 ness. Then he suffered him. And when all the people were baptized, Jesus also Lk. 3, 21*b*.
36 was baptized. And immediately he went up out of the water, and heaven opened Mt. 3, 16*b*.
37 Arabic, to him,[2] and the Holy Spirit descended upon him in the similitude of the Lk. 3, 22*a*.
38 p. 17 body of a dove; and lo, a voice from heaven, saying, This is my beloved Mt. 3, 17.
39 Son, in whom I am well pleased. And John bare witness and said, I beheld the Jo. 1, 32.
40 Spirit descend from heaven like a dove; and it abode upon him. But I knew him Jo. 1, 33.
not; but he that sent me to baptize with water, he said unto me, Upon whomsoever
thou shalt behold the Spirit descending and lighting upon him, the same is he that
41 baptizeth with the Holy Spirit. And I have seen and borne witness that this is the Jo. 1, 34.
Son of God.
42, 43 And Jesus returned from the Jordan, filled with the Holy Spirit. And immedi- Lk. 4, 1*a*. Mk. 1, 12.
ately the Spirit took him out into the wilderness, to be tried of the devil;[3] and he Mk. 1, 13*b*.
44 was with the beasts. And he fasted forty days and forty nights. And he ate noth- Mt. 4, 2*a*. Lk. 4, 2*b*.
45 ing in those days, and at the end of them he hungered. And the tempter came and Mt. 4, 2*b*, 3.
said unto him, If thou art the Son of God, speak, and these stones shall become
46 bread. He answered and said, It is written, Not by bread alone shall man live, but Mt. 4, 4.
47 by every word that proceedeth out of the mouth of God. Then the devil[3] brought Mt. 4, 5.
48 him to the holy city, and set him on the pinnacle of the temple, and said unto him, Mt. 4, 6.
If thou art the Son of God, cast thyself down: for it is written,
He shall give his angels charge concerning thee:
And they shall take thee on their arms,
So that thy foot shall not stumble against a stone.
49 Jesus said unto him, And[4] it is written also, Thou shalt not tempt the Lord thy Mt. 4, 7.
50 God. And the devil[5] took him up to a high mountain, and shewed him all the king- Lk. 4, 5.
51 Arabic, doms of the earth, and their glory, in the least time; and the devil[5] said unto Lk. 4, 6.
p. 18 him, To thee will I give all this dominion, and its glory, which is delivered to
52 me that I may give it to whomsoever I will. If then thou wilt worship before me, all Lk. 4, 7.
of it shall be thine.

SECTION V.

§5 1 Jesus answered and said unto him, Get thee hence, Satan: for it is written, Thou Mt. 4, 10.
2 shalt worship the Lord thy God, and him alone shalt thou serve. And when the Lk. 4, 13.
3 devil[5] had completed all his temptations, he departed from him for a season. And Mt. 4, 11*b*.
behold, the angels drew near and ministered unto him.
4, 5 And next day John was standing, and two of his disciples; and he saw Jesus as Jo. 1, 35. Jo. 1, 36.
6 he was walking, and said, Behold, the Lamb of God! And his two disciples heard Jo. 1, 37.
7 him saying *this*,[6] and they followed Jesus. And Jesus turned and saw them coming Jo. 1, 38.
after him, and said unto them, What seek ye? They said unto him, Our master,
8 where art thou staying? And he said unto them, Come and see. And they came Jo. 1, 39.
and saw his place, and abode with him that day: and it was about the tenth hour.
9 One of the two which heard from[7] John, and followed Jesus, was Andrew the Jo. 1, 40.
10 brother of Simon. And he saw first Simon his brother, and said unto him, We have Jo. 1, 41*a*.
11 found the Messiah. And he brought him unto Jesus. And Jesus looked upon him Jo. 1, 42*a*.
and said, Thou art Simon, son of Jonah: thou shalt be called Cephas.[8]
12 And on the next day Jesus desired to go forth to Galilee, and he found Philip, Jo. 1, 43.
13 Arabic, and said unto him, Follow me. Now Philip was of Bethsaida, of the city Jo. 1, 44.
14 p. 19 of Andrew and Simon. And Philip found Nathanael, and said unto him, Jo. 1, 45.
He of whom Moses did write in the law and in the prophets, we have found that
15 he is Jesus the son of Joseph of Nazareth. Nathanael said unto him, Is it possible Jo. 1, 46.

1 *cf.* § 3, 54, note.
2 For the statement of Isho'dad (see above, Introduction, 10), "And straightway, as the *Diatessaron* testifieth, light shone forth," etc., see Harris, *Fragments*, etc., p. 43 f.
3 Lit. *calumniator*.
4 Borg. MS. omits *and*.
5 Lit. *backbiter*, a different word from that used above in § 4, 43, 47.
6 Or, *speaking*.
7 *cf.* Peshitta.
8 The Arabic word used throughout this work means *Stones*.

§ 5 that there can be any good thing from Nazareth? Philip said unto him, Come and
16 see. And Jesus saw Nathanael coming to him, and said of him, This is indeed a[1] Jo. 1, 47.
17 son of Israel in whom is no guile. And Nathanael said unto him, Whence knowest Jo. 1, 48.
thou me? Jesus said unto him, Before Philip called thee, while thou wast under the
18 fig tree, I saw thee. Nathanael answered and said unto him, My Master, thou art Jo. 1, 49.
19 the Son of God; thou art the King of Israel. Jesus said unto him, Because I said Jo. 1, 50.
unto thee, I saw thee under the fig tree, hast thou believed? thou shalt see what is
20 greater than this. And he said unto him, Verily, verily, I say unto you, Henceforth Jo. 1, 51.
ye shall see the heavens opened, and the angels of God ascending and descending
upon the Son of man.

21 And Jesus returned in the power of the Spirit to Galilee. Lk. 4, 14*a*.

22 And on the third day there was a feast in Cana,[2] a[1] city of Galilee; and the Jo. 2, 1.
23 mother of Jesus was there: and Jesus also and his disciples were invited to the Jo. 2, 2.
24 feast. And they lacked wine: and his mother said unto Jesus, They have no wine. Jo. 2, 3.
25 And Jesus said unto her, What have I to do with thee, woman? hath not mine Jo. 2, 4.
26 hour come?[3] And his mother said unto the servants, What he saith unto you, do. Jo. 2, 5.
27 And there were there six vessels of stone, placed for the Jews' purification, such as Jo. 2, 6.
28 Arabic, would contain two or three jars. And Jesus said unto them, Fill the vessels Jo. 2, 7.
29 p. 20 with water. And they filled them to the top. He said unto them, Draw Jo. 2, 8.
30 out now, and present to the ruler of the feast. And they did *so*. And when the ruler of Jo. 2, 9.
the company tasted that water which had become wine, and knew not whence it was
(but the servants knew, because they filled up the water), the ruler of the company called
31 the bridegroom, and said unto him, Every man presenteth first the good wine, and Jo. 2, 10.
on intoxication he bringeth what is poor; but thou hast kept the good wine until
32 now. And this is the first sign[4] which Jesus did in Cana of Galilee, and manifested Jo. 2, 11.
33 his glory; and his disciples believed on him. And his fame spread in all the coun- Lk. 4, 14*b*.
34 try which was around them. And he taught in their synagogues, and was glorified Lk. 4, 15.
35 by[5] every man. And he came to Nazareth, where he had been brought up, and Lk. 4, 16.
entered, according to his custom, into the synagogue on the sabbath day, and stood
36 up to read. And he was given the book of Isaiah the prophet. And Jesus opened Lk. 4, 17.
the book and found the place where it was written,
37 The Spirit of the Lord is upon me, Lk. 4, 18.
And for this anointed he me, to preach good tidings to the poor;
And he hath sent me to heal the broken-hearted,
And to proclaim forgiveness to the evil-doers,[6] and sight to the blind,
And to bring the broken into forgiveness,[7]
38 And to proclaim an acceptable year of the Lord. Lk. 4, 19.
39 And he rolled up the book and gave it to the servant, and went and sat down: Lk. 4, 20.
40 and the eyes of all that were in the synagogue were observing him. And he began Lk. 4, 21.
to say unto them, To-day hath this scripture been fulfilled which ye have heard with
41 your ears. And they all bare him witness, and wondered at the words of grace Lk. 4, 22*a*.
which were proceeding from his mouth.

42 Arabic, And from that time began Jesus to proclaim the gospel of the kingdom Mt. 4, 17*a*.
43 p. 21 of God, and to say, Repent ye, and believe in the gospel. The time is ful- Mk. 1, 15.
filled, and the kingdom of heaven hath come near.

44 And while he was walking on the shore of the sea of Galilee, he saw two breth- Mt. 4, 18.
ren, Simon who was called Cephas, and Andrew his brother, casting their nets into
45 the sea; for they were fishers. And Jesus said unto them, Follow me, and I will Mt. 4, 19.
46 make you fishers of men. And they immediately left their nets there and followed Mt. 4, 20.
47 him. And when he went on from thence, he saw other two brothers, James the son Mt. 4, 21.
of Zebedee, and John his brother, in the ship with Zebedee their father, mending
48 their nets; and Jesus called them. And they immediately forsook the ship and their Mt. 4, 22.
father Zebedee, and followed him.

1 Lit. *the* (*cf.* note to § 1, 40). 2 Arabic *Qaṭna;* at § 5, 32, *Qâṭîna*, following the Syriac form.
3 The reading of Cur. and Sin. is not known; but *cf.* Moesinger, p. 53, and Isho'dad quoted in Harris, *Fragments*, etc., p. 46. 4 Perhaps a comma should be inserted after *sign*.
5 If the text does not contain a misprint the word for *by* is wanting in both MSS. It should doubtless be restored as in § 7, 3.
6 *Evil-doers* could easily be an Arabic copyist's corruption of *captives;* but the word used here for *forgiveness* could hardly spring from an Arabic *release* (in Ibn-at-Ṭayyib's Commentary, where the thing seems to have happened, a different word is used). In Syriac, however, they are the same; while the first pair contain the same consonants.
7 See preceding note.

§5 49 And when the multitude gathered unto him to hear the word of God, while he Lk. 5, 1.
50 was standing on the shore of the sea of Gennesaret, he saw two boats standing be- Lk. 5, 2.
side the sea, while[1] the two fishers which were gone out of them were washing their
51 nets. And one of them belonged to Simon Cephas. And Jesus went up and sat Lk. 5, 3.
down in it, and commanded that they should move away a little from the land into
52 the water. And he sat down and taught the multitudes from the boat. And when Lk. 5, 4.
he had left off his speaking, he said unto Simon, Put out into the deep, and cast your
53 net for a draught. And Simon answered and said unto him, My Master, we toiled Lk. 5, 5.
54 all night and caught nothing; now[2] at thy word I will cast the net. And when Lk. 5, 6.
they did this, there were enclosed[3] a great many fishes; and their net was on the
55 point of breaking. And they beckoned to their comrades that were in the other Lk. 5, 7.
boat, to come and help them. And when they came, they filled both boats, so that
they were on the point of sinking.

SECTION VI.

§6 1 Arabic, p. 22 But when Simon Cephas saw *this* he fell before the feet of Jesus, and Lk. 5, 8.
said unto him, My Lord, I beseech of thee to depart from me, for I am
2 a sinful man. And amazement took possession of him, and of all who were with him, Lk. 5, 9.
3 because of the draught of the fishes which they had taken. And thus also were James Lk. 5, 10.
and John the sons of Zebedee overtaken,[4] who were Simon's partners. And Jesus said
4 unto Simon, Fear not; henceforth thou shalt be a fisher of men unto life. And they Lk. 5, 11.
brought the boats to the land; and they left everything, and followed him.
5 And after that came Jesus and his disciples into the land of Judæa; and he went Jo. 3, 22.
6 about there with them, and baptized. And John also was baptizing in Ænon, which Jo. 3, 23.
is beside Salim, because there was much water there: and they came, and were bap-
7, 8 tized. And John was not yet come into prison. And there was an inquiry between Jo. 3, 24. Jo. 3, 25.
9 one of John's disciples and one of the Jews about purifying. And they[5] came unto Jo. 3, 26.
John, and said unto him, Our master, he that was with thee beyond Jordan, to whom
10 thou hast borne witness, behold, he also baptizeth, and many come to him. John Jo. 3, 27.
answered and said unto them,[6] A man can receive nothing of himself, except it be
11 given him[7] from heaven. Ye are they that bear witness unto me that I said, I am Jo. 3, 28.
12 not the Messiah, but I am one sent[8] before him. And he that hath a bride is a Jo. 3, 29.
bridegroom: and the friend of the bridegroom is he that standeth and listeneth to
him, and rejoiceth greatly because of the bridegroom's voice. Lo now,[9] behold, my
13, 14 Arabic, p. 23 joy becometh complete.[10] And he must increase and I decrease. For[11] he Jo. 3, 30. Jo. 3, 31.
that is come from above is higher than everything; and he that is of the earth,
of the earth he is, and of the earth he speaketh; and he that came down from heaven is
15 higher than all. And he beareth witness of what he hath seen and heard; and no man Jo. 3, 32.
16 receiveth his witness. And he that hath received his witness hath asserted[12] that he is Jo. 3, 33.
17 truly God.[13] And he whom God hath sent speaketh the words[14] of God: God gave Jo. 3, 34.
18 not the Spirit by measure. The Father loveth the Son, and hath put everything in Jo. 3, 35.
19 his hands. Whosoever believeth in the Son hath eternal[15] life; but whosoever obey- Jo. 3, 36.
eth not the Son shall not see life, but the wrath of God cometh[16] upon him.
20 And Jesus learned[17] that the Pharisees had heard that he had received many dis- Jo. 4, 1.
21 ciples, and that he was baptizing more than John (not that Jesus was himself bap- Jo. 4, 2.
22 tizing, but his disciples); and *so* he left Judæa. Jo. 4, 3*a*.
23 And Herod the governor, because he used to be rebuked by John because of Lk. 3, 19.

1 Or, *but*. 2 Borg. MS. has *but*. The Arabic expressions are very similar.
3 Borg. MS. has *he did this, he enclosed,* on which see § 38, 43, note (end). Either reading could spring from the other, within the Arabic.
4 The verb may be active as well as passive, but does not agree in gender with *amazement*. Mistakes in gender are, however, very common transcriptional errors. 5 Dual.
6 Plural. In the Peshitta it is two individuals in verse 25. In Sin. the first is an individual and the second is ambiguous. In Cur. both are plural. 7 Or, *he be given it*. 8 The ordinary word for *apostle*. 9 See § 9, 21, note.
10 So Ciasca's printed text. The Vat. MS., however, probably represents a past tense.
11 *cf.* Peshitta. 12 *cf.* consonants of Syriac text.
13 Borg. MS., *that God is truly*, or, assuming a very common grammatical inaccuracy, *that God is true* or *truth*, the reading in Ibn-aṭ-Ṭayyib's Commentary. 14 Lit. *saying*.
15 Lit. *the life of eternity;* here and everywhere except § 21, 40.
16 i.e., alighteth-and-stayeth. 17 Or, *knew*.

§ 6 Herodias the wife of Philip his brother, and for all the sins which he was commit-
24 ting, added to all that also this, that he shut up John in prison. Lk. 3, 20.
25 And when Jesus heard that John was delivered up, he went away to Galilee. Mt. 4, 12.
26 And he entered again into Cana, where he had made the water wine. And there Jo. 4, 46.
27 was at Capernaum a king's servant, whose son was sick. And this *man* heard that Jo. 4, 47.
Jesus was come from Judæa to Galilee; and he went to him, and besought of him
that he would come down and heal his son; for he had come near unto death.
28, 29 Jesus said unto him, Except ye see signs and wonders, ye do[1] not believe. The Jo. 4, 48. Jo. 4, 49.
Arabic, king's servant said unto him, My Lord, come down, that the child die not.
30 p. 24 Jesus said unto him, Go; for thy son is alive. And that man believed the Jo. 4, 50.
31 word which Jesus spake, and went. And when he went down, his servants met him Jo. 4, 51.
32 and told him, and[2] said unto him, Thy son is alive. And he asked them at what Jo. 4, 52.
time he recovered. They said unto him, Yesterday at the seventh hour the fever left
33 him. And his father knew that that was at that hour in which Jesus said unto him, Jo. 4, 53.
34 Thy son is alive. And he believed, he and the whole people of his house. And this Jo. 4, 54.
35 is the second sign[3] which Jesus did when he returned from Judæa to Galilee. And Lk. 4, 44.
he was preaching in the synagogues of Galilee.
36 And he left Nazareth, and came and dwelt in Capernaum by the sea shore, in the Mt. 4, 13.
37 borders of Zebulun and Naphtali: that it might be fulfilled which was said in Isaiah Mt. 4, 14.
the prophet, who said,
38 The land of Zebulun, the land of Naphtali, Mt. 4, 15.
The way of the sea, the passage of the Jordan,
Galilee of the nations:
39 The people sitting in darkness Mt. 4, 16.
Saw a great light,
And those sitting in the region and in the shadow of death,
There appeared to them a light.
40 And he taught them on the sabbaths. And they wondered because of his doc- Lk. 4, 31*b*. Lk. 4, 32.
41 trine:[4] for his word was as if it were authoritative. And there was in the synagogue Lk. 4, 33.
42 a man with an unclean devil, and he cried out with a loud voice, and said, Let me Lk. 4, 34.
alone; what have I to do with thee, thou Jesus of Nazareth? art thou come for our
43 destruction? I know thee who thou art, thou Holy One of God. And Jesus rebuked Lk. 4, 35.
him, and said, Stop up thy mouth, and come out of him. And the demon threw him
44 in the midst and came out of him, having done him no harm. And great amaze- Lk. 4, 36.
Arabic, ment took hold upon every man. And they talked one with another, and
p. 25 said, What is this word that orders the unclean spirits with power and
45 authority, and they come out? And the news of him spread abroad in all the region Lk. 4, 37.
which was around them.
46 And when Jesus went out of the synagogue, he saw a man sitting among the Lk. 4, 38. Mt. 9, 9*b*.
publicans,[5] named Matthew: and he said unto him, Come after me. And he rose,
and followed him.
47, 48 And Jesus came to the house of Simon and Andrew with James and John. And Mk. 1, 29*b*. Lk. 4, 38*c*.
Simon's wife's mother was oppressed with a great fever, and they besought him for
49 her. And he stood over her and rebuked her fever, and it left her, and immediately Lk. 4, 39.
50 she rose and ministered to them. And at even they brought to him many that had Mt. 8, 16*a*.
51 demons: and he cast out their devils with the[6] word. And all that had sick, their Lk. 4, 40*b*.
diseases being divers *and* malignant, brought them unto him. And he laid his hand
52 on them one by one[7] and healed them: that that might be fulfilled which was said Mt. 8, 17.
53 in the prophet Isaiah, who said, He taketh our pains and beareth our diseases. And Mk. 1, 33.
54 all the city was gathered together unto the door of Jesus. And he cast out devils Lk. 4, 41.
also from many, as they were crying out and saying, Thou art the Messiah, the Son
of God; and he rebuked them. And he suffered not the demons to speak, because
they knew him that he was the Lord the Messiah.

1 Or, *will*. 2 Or, *good news, and*. 3 See § 5, 32, note.
4 Perhaps we might here render *learning;* but see § 28, 17, note.
5 So in the Arabic. It is, however, simply a misinterpretation of the expression in the Syriac versions for *at the place of toll* (*cf.* Ibn-aṭ-Ṭayyib's Commentary). 6 *cf.* § 1, 40, note 2. 7 Or, *each*.

SECTION VII.

§ 7 1 Arabic, And in the morning of that day he went out very early, and went to a Mk. 1, 35.
2 p. 26 desert place, and was there praying. And Simon and those that were with Mk. 1, 36.
3 him sought him. And when they found him, they said unto him, All the people seek for Mk. 1, 37.
4 thee. He said unto them, Let us go into the adjacent villages and towns, that I may Mk. 1, 38.
5 preach there also; for to this end did I come. And the multitudes were seeking Lk. 4, 42.
him, and came till they reached him; and they took hold of him, that he should not
6 go away from them. But Jesus said unto them, I must preach of the kingdom of Lk. 4, 43.
7 God in other cities also: for because of this gospel was I sent. And Jesus was going Mt. 9, 35.
about all the cities and the villages, and teaching in their synagogues, and preaching the gospel of the kingdom, and healing all the diseases and all the sicknesses, Mk. 1, 39.
8 and casting out the devils. And his fame became known that[1] he was teaching in Lk. 4, 14*b*.
9 every place and being glorified by every man. And when he passed by, he saw Levi Lk. 4, 15. Mk. 2, 14.
the son of Alphæus sitting among the tax-gatherers;[2] and he said unto him, Follow
10 me: and he rose and followed him. And the news of him was heard of in all the Mt. 4, 24.
land of Syria: and they brought unto him all those whom grievous ills had befallen
through divers diseases, and those that were enduring torment, and those that were
possessed, and lunatics,[3] and paralytics; and he healed them.
11, 12 And after some days Jesus entered into Capernaum again. And when they heard Mk. 2, 1. Mk. 2, 2.
that he was in the house,[4] many gathered, so that it could not hold them, even about
13 Arabic, the door; and he made known to them the word of God. And there were Lk. 5, 17*b*.
p. 27 there some of the Pharisees and the teachers of the law, sitting, come from
all the villages of Galilee, and Judæa, and Jerusalem; and the power of the Lord was
14 present to heal them. And some men brought a bed with a man on it who was para- Lk. 5, 18.
15 lytic. And they sought to bring him in and lay him before him. And when they Lk. 5, 19.
found no way to bring him in because of the multitude of people, they went up to
the roof, and let him down with his bed from the roofing,[5] into the midst before Jesus.
16 And when Jesus saw their faith, he said unto the paralytic, My son, thy sins are for- Lk. 5, 20.
17 given thee. And the scribes and Pharisees began to think within their hearts, Why Lk. 5, 21.
doth this man blaspheme?[6] Who is it that is able to forgive sins, but God alone?
18 And Jesus knew by the spirit that they were thinking this within themselves, and he Mk. 2, 8.
19 said unto them, Why do ye think this within your heart? Which is better,[7] that it Mk. 2, 9.
should be said to the paralytic, Thy sins are forgiven thee, or *that* it should be said
20 to him, Arise, and take thy bed, and walk? That ye may know that the Son of man Mk. 2, 10.
21 is empowered on earth to forgive sins (and he said to the paralytic), I say unto thee, Mk. 2, 11.
22 Arise, take thy bed, and go to thine house. And he rose forthwith, and took his Mk. 2, 12*a*.
bed, and went out in the presence of all. And he went to his house praising God. Lk. 5, 25*b*.
23 And when those multitudes saw, they feared; and amazement took possession of Mt. 9, 8*a*. Lk. 5, 26*a*.
24 them, and they praised God, who had given such power to men. And they said, Mt. 9, 8*b*. Lk. 5, 26*c*.
We have seen marvellous things to-day, of which we have never before seen the like. Mk. 2, 12*c*.
25 Arabic, And after that, Jesus went out, and saw a publican, named Levi, sitting Lk. 5, 27.
26 p. 28 among the publicans:[8] and he said unto him, Follow me. And he left Lk. 5, 28.
27 everything, and rose, and followed him. And Levi made him a great feast in his Lk. 5, 29.
house. And there was a great multitude of the publicans and others sitting with him.
28 And the scribes and Pharisees murmured, and said unto his disciples, Why do ye eat Lk. 5, 30.
29 and drink with the publicans and sinners? Jesus answered and said unto them, The Lk. 5, 31.
physician seeketh not those who are well, but those that are afflicted with grievous
30, 31 sickness.[9] I came not to call the righteous, but the sinners, to repentance. And Lk. 5, 32. Lk. 5, 33.
they said unto him, Why do the disciples of John fast always, and pray, and the
32 Pharisees also, but thy disciples eat and drink? He said unto them, Ye cannot make Lk. 5, 34.
33 the sons of the marriage feast[10] fast, while the bridegroom is with them. Days will Lk. 5, 35.

1 This may represent a Syriac *as*.
2 See above, note to § 6, 46, which applies, although the Arabic words are different.
3 Lit. *son-of-the-roofs*, a Syriac expression (*cf.* § 24, 31, note).
4 This is the end of verse 1 in the Greek.
5 This word may be either a singular or a plural.
6 This word ordinarily means *to forge lies against;* but our translator uses it regularly as here.
7 Peshitta has *easier*.
8 See above, note to § 6, 46.
9 A Syriacism.
10 The Arabic word, which occurs here in many of the Arabic versions, could also be read *bridegroom*. The Syriac word for *marriage chamber* is also used in the sense of *marriage feast*.

§ 7 come, when the bridegroom is taken away from them; then will they fast in those
34 days. And he spake unto them a parable: No man inserteth a new patch and Lk. 5, 36*a*. Mk. 2, 21.
seweth it in a worn garment, lest the newness of the new take from the worn, and
35 there occur a great rent. And no man putteth fresh wine into old skins, lest the Mk. 2, 22.
wine burst the skins, and the skins be destroyed, and the wine spilled; but they put
36 the fresh wine in the new skins, and both are preserved. And no man drinketh old Lk. 5, 38, 39.
wine and straightway desireth fresh; for he saith, The old is better.
37 And while Jesus was walking on the sabbath day among the sown fields, his dis- Mt. 12, 1.
Arabic, ciples hungered. And they were rubbing the ears with their hands, and
38 p. 29 eating. But some of the Pharisees, when they saw them, said unto him, See, Mt. 12, 2*a*. Mk. 2, 24.
39 why[1] do thy disciples on the sabbath day that which is not lawful? But Jesus said Mk. 2, 25.
unto them, Have ye not read in olden time what David did, when he had need and
40 hungered, he and those that were with him? how he entered the house of God, when Mk. 2, 26.
Abiathar was high priest, and ate the bread of the table of the Lord, which it was not
lawful that any should eat, save the priests, and gave to them that were with him also?
41 And he said unto them, The sabbath was created because of man, and man was not Mk. 2, 27.
42 created because of the sabbath. Or have ye not read in the law, that the priests in Mt. 12, 5.
43 the temple profane the sabbath, and *yet* they are blameless? I say unto you now, Mt. 12, 6.
44 that here is what[2] is greater than the temple. If ye had known *this*.[3] I love mercy, Mt. 12, 7.
45 not sacrifice, ye would not have condemned[4] those on whom is no blame. The Mt. 12, 8.
46 Lord of the sabbath is the Son of man. And his relatives heard, and went out to Mk. 3, 21.
take him, and said, He hath gone out of his mind.
47 And on the next[5] sabbath day he entered[6] into the synagogue and was teach- Lk. 6, 6.
48 ing. And there was there a man whose right hand was withered. And the scribes Lk. 6, 7.
and the Pharisees were watching him, whether he would heal on the sabbath day,
49 that they might find the means of accusing him. But he knew their thoughts, and Lk. 6, 8.
said unto the man whose hand was withered, Rise and come near into the midst of
50 the synagogue. And when he came and stood, Jesus said unto them, I ask you, Lk. 6, 9.
which is lawful to be done on the sabbath day, good or evil? shall lives be saved or
51 Arabic, destroyed? But they were silent. Regarding[7] them with anger, being Mk. 3, 4*b*. Mk. 3, 5.
p. 30 grieved because of the hardness of their hearts. And he said unto the
man, Stretch out thy hand. And he stretched it out: and his hand became straight.
52 Then he said unto them, What man of you shall have one sheep, and if it fall into a Mt. 12, 11.
53 well on the sabbath day, will not take it and lift it out? And how much is man Mt. 12, 12.
better than a sheep! Wherefore it is lawful on the sabbath to do good.

SECTION VIII.

§ 8 1 And the Pharisees went out, and consulted together concerning him, that they Mt. 12, 14.
2 might destroy him. And Jesus perceived, and removed thence: and great multitudes Mt. 12, 15.
3 followed him; and he healed all of them: and he forbade them that they should Mt. 12, 16.
4 not make him known:[8] that the saying in Isaiah the prophet might be fulfilled, Mt. 12, 17.
which said,

5 Behold, my servant[9] with whom I am pleased; Mt. 12, 18.
My beloved in whom my soul hath delighted:[10]
My spirit have I put upon him,
And he shall proclaim to the nations judgement.
6 He shall not dispute, nor cry out; Mt. 12, 19.
And no man shall hear his voice in the marketplace.
7 And a bruised reed shall he not break, Mt. 12, 20.
And a smoking lamp[11] shall he not extinguish,

1 Syr. In Arab. it means *what?*
2 This may be simply a misinterpretation of the ordinary Syriac reading, which in all probability agrees with the masculine reading found in the Text. Rec. of the Greek.
3 Is it possible that the Arabic word after *known* is not meant simply to introduce the quotation, but is to be taken in the adverbial sense, *how* representing the Syriac *what that is?*
4 See § 10, 13, note.
5 Lit. *other*. The definite article is a mistake of the translator.
6 Here, at the end of leaf 17 of Vat. MS., is a note by a later hand: "Here a leaf is missing." This first lacuna extends from § 7, 47, to § 8, 17.
7 An easy clerical error for *And so he regarded* (*cf.* Peshitta).
8 Lit. *lead to him.*
9 The Arabic word strictly means *young man.*
10 Or, *rested.*
11 Or, *wick.*

§ 8 Until he shall bring forth judgement unto victory.
8 And the nations shall rejoice in his name.[1] Mt. 12, 21.
9 And in those days Jesus went out to the mountain that he might pray, and he Lk. 6, 12.
10 spent the night[2] there in prayer to God. And when the morning was come, he called Lk. 6, 13a.
the disciples. And he went towards the sea: and there followed him much people Mk. 3, 7.
11 from Galilee that he might pray,[3] and from Judæa, and from Jerusalem, and from Mk. 3, 8.
Idumæa, and from beyond Jordan, and from Tyre, and from Sidon, and from De-
12 capolis; and great multitudes came unto him, which had heard what he did. And Mk. 3, 9.
he spake to his disciples to bring him the boat because of the multitudes, that they
13 might not throng him. And he healed many, so that they were almost falling on Mk. 3, 10.
Arabic, him[4] on account of their seeking to get near him. And[5] those that had
14 p. 31 plagues and unclean spirits, as soon as they beheld him, would fall, and Mk. 3, 11.
15 cry out, and say, Thou art the Son of God. And he rebuked them much, that they Mk. 3, 12.
16 should not make him known. And those that were under the constraint of[6] un- Lk. 6, 18.
17 clean spirits were healed. And all of the crowd were seeking to come near[7] him; Lk. 6, 19.
because power went out from him, and he healed them all.
18, 19 And when Jesus saw the multitudes, he went up to the mountain. And he Mt. 5, 1a. Lk. 6, 13b.
called his disciples, and chose from them twelve; and they are those whom he named
20 apostles: Simon, whom he named Cephas, and Andrew his brother, and James and Lk. 6, 14.
21 John, and Philip and Bartholomew, and Matthew and Thomas, and James the son Lk. 6, 15.
22 of Alphæus, and Simon which *was* called the Zealot, and Judas the son of James, Lk. 6, 16.
23 and Judas the Iscariot, being he that had betrayed him.[8] And Jesus went down Lk. 6, 17a.
with them and stood in the plain, and the company of his disciples, and the great
24 multitude of people. And these twelve he chose to be with him, and that he might Mk. 3, 14.
25 send them to preach, and to have power to heal the sick and to cast out devils.
26 Then he lifted up his eyes unto them, and opened his mouth, and taught them, Lk. 6, 20. Mt. 5, 2.
and said,
27 Blessed are the poor in spirit: for the kingdom of heaven is theirs. Mt. 5, 3.
28 Blessed are the sorrowful: for they shall be comforted. Mt. 5, 4.
29 Blessed are the humble: for they shall inherit the earth. Mt. 5, 5.
30 Blessed are they that hunger and thirst after righteousness: for they shall be Mt. 5, 6.
satisfied.
31 Blessed are the merciful: for on them shall be mercy. Mt. 5, 7.
32 Arabic, Blessed are the pure in their hearts: for they shall see God. Mt. 5, 8.
33 p. 32 Blessed are the peacemakers: for they shall be called the sons of God. Mt. 5, 9.
34 Blessed are they that were persecuted[9] for righteousness' sake: for the kingdom Mt. 5, 10.
of heaven is theirs.
35 Blessed are ye when men shall hate you, and separate you from them, and per- Lk. 6, 22a.
secute you, and reproach you, and shall speak against you with all evil talk, for my Mt. 5, 11b.
36 sake, falsely. Then rejoice and be glad, for your reward is great in heaven: for so Mt. 5, 12.
persecuted they the prophets before you.
37 But woe unto you rich! for ye have received your consolation. Lk. 6, 24.
38 Woe unto you that are satisfied! ye shall hunger. Lk. 6, 25.
Woe unto you that laugh now! ye shall weep and be sad.
39 Woe unto you when men praise you! for so did their fathers use to do to the Lk. 6, 26.
false prophets.
40 Unto you do I say, *ye* which hear, Ye are the salt of the earth: if then the salt Lk. 6, 27. Mt. 5, 13.
become tasteless, wherewith shall it be salted? For any purpose it is of no use, but
41 is thrown outside, and men tread upon it. Ye are the light of the world. It is Mt. 5, 14.
42 impossible that a city built on a mountain should be hid. Neither do they light a Mt. 5, 15.

1 The Arab. might also mean, *And he shall preach* (*the good tidings*) *to the peoples in his name* (*cf.* § 22, 47, note).
2 This phrase, in this case adopted from the Syriac, really means, in Arab., *morning found him.*
3 It must be remembered that we have here only one MS. The Arabic words for *Galilee* and for *mountain* are very similar. The words *that he might pray* have therefore probably made their way here by some error from § 8, 9, above.
4 So (with the Peshitta) by transposing two letters. The Arabic text as it stands can hardly be translated. *Almost* may be simply a corruption of the Arabic word *were.*
5 The syntax of the Arabic is ambiguous. The alternative followed above, which seems the most natural, is that which agrees most nearly with the Peshitta.
6 Or, *troubled with.*
7 This is the meaning of the Arabic word, as it is the primary meaning of the Syriac; but in this work a number of words meaning *approach* are used (and generally translated) in the sense of *touch.* The commonest word so used is that in § 12, 13 (*cf.* also § 12, 35).
8 So Vat. MS., followed by Ciasca (*cf.* Sin.). Borg. MS. has *he that was betraying* or *was a traitor* (*cf.* Peshitta).
9 This word, the ordinary meaning of which is *expel,* is freely used by our translator in the sense of *persecute.*

§8 lamp and place it under a bushel, but on the lamp-stand, and it giveth light to all
43 who are in the house. So shall[1] your light shine before men, that they may see Mt. 5, 16.
44 your good works, and glorify your Father which is in heaven. There is nothing Mk. 4, 22.
45 secret that shall not be revealed, or hidden that shall not be known. Whoever hath Mk. 4, 23.
ears that hear, let him hear.
46 Think not that I came to destroy the law or the prophets; I came not to destroy, Mt. 5, 17.
47 but to complete. Verily I say unto you, Until heaven and earth shall pass, there Mt. 5, 18.
Arabic, shall not pass one point or one letter of the law, until all of it shall be
48 p. 33 *accomplished*. Every one who shall violate now one of these small com- Mt. 5, 19.
mandments, and shall teach men so, shall be called lacking in the kingdom of
heaven: every one that shall do and teach shall[2] be called great in the kingdom
49 of heaven. I say unto you now, unless your righteousness abound more than that Mt. 5, 20.
of the scribes and Pharisees, ye shall not enter the kingdom of heaven.
50 Ye have heard that it was said to the ancients, Do not kill; and every one that Mt. 5, 21.
51 killeth is worthy of the judgement. But I say unto you that every one who is angry Mt. 5, 22.
with his brother without a cause is worthy of the judgement; and every one that
saith to his brother, Thou foul one, is condemned[3] by the synagogue; and whoso-
52 ever saith to him, Thou fool, is worthy of the fire of Gehenna. If thou art now Mt. 5, 23.
offering thy gift at the altar, and rememberest there that thy brother hath conceived
53 against thee any grudge, leave thy gift at the altar, and go first and satisfy thy Mt. 5, 24.
54 brother, and then return and offer thy gift. Join[4] thine adversary quickly, and Mt. 5, 25*a*. Lk. 12, 58*a*.
while thou art still with him in the way, give a ransom and free thyself from him;
55 lest thine adversary deliver thee to the judge, and the judge deliver thee to the tax- Mt. 5, 25*c*.
56 collector, and thou fall into prison. And verily I say unto thee, Thou shalt not go Mt. 5, 26.
out thence until thou payest the last farthing.
57, 58 Ye have heard that it was said, Do not commit adultery: but I now say unto Mt. 5, 27. Mt. 5, 28.
you, that every one that looketh at a woman lusting after her hath forthwith already
59 Arabic, committed adultery with her in his heart. If thy right eye injure thee, put Mt. 5, 29.
p. 34 it out and cast it from thee; for it is preferable for thee that one of thy
60 members should perish, and not thy whole body go into the fire *of hell*. And if thy Mt. 5, 30.
right hand injure thee, cut it off and cast it from thee; and it is better for thee that
61 one of thy members should perish, and not thy whole body fall into Gehenna. It Mt. 5, 31.
was said that he that putteth away his wife *should* give her a writing of divorcement:
62 but I say unto you, that every one that putteth away his wife, except for the cause Mt. 5, 32.
of adultery, hath made it lawful for[5] her to commit adultery: and whosoever taketh
one that is put away committeth adultery.

SECTION IX.

§9 1 Ye have heard also that it was said unto the ancients, Lie not, but perform unto Mt. 5, 33.
2 God in thy oaths: but I say unto you, Swear not at all; neither by heaven, for it Mt. 5, 34.
3 is God's throne; nor by the earth, for it is a footstool under his feet; nor yet by Mt. 5, 35.
4 Jerusalem, for it is the city of the great[6] King. Neither shalt thou swear by thy Mt. 5, 36.
5 head, for thou canst not make in it one lock of hair black or white. But your word Mt. 5, 37.
shall be either Yea or Nay, and what is in excess of this is of the evil one.
6, 7 Ye have heard that it was said, Eye for eye, and tooth for tooth: but I say unto Mt. 5, 38. Mt. 5, 39.
you, Stand not in opposition to the evil;[7] but whosoever smiteth thee on thy right
8 cheek,[8] turn to him also the other. And he that would sue thee, and take thy tunic, Mt. 5, 40.
9 leave to him also thy wrapper. And whosoever compelleth thee one mile, go with Mt. 5, 41.
10 Arabic, him twain. And he that asketh thee, give unto him: and he that would Mt. 5, 42.
p. 35 borrow of thee, prevent him not. And prosecute[9] not him that taketh thy Lk. 6, 30*b*.
11 substance. And as ye desire that men should do to you, so do ye also to them. Lk. 6, 31.
12, 13 Ye have heard that it was said, Love thy neighbour and hate thine enemy: but Mt. 5, 43. Mt. 5, 44.
I say unto you, Love your enemies, and pray for those that curse you, and deal well

1 Or, *let* (*cf.* § 4, 20, note). 2 Lit. *this* (*man*) *shall*. 3 See § 10, 13, note.
4 The text is rather uncertain.
5 The text is probably corrupt. Vat. MS. has on margin, *i.e.*, *caused her*. 6 The adj. is in the superlative.
7 A literal reproduction of the Greek, like that in Syr. versions. 8 Lit. *jaw*. 9 Or, *punish*.

§ **9** with those that hate you, and pray for those who take you with violence and per-
14 secute you; that ye may be sons of your heavenly Father, who maketh his sun to Mt. 5, 45.
rise on the good and the evil, and sendeth down his rain on the righteous and the
15 unrighteous. If ye love them that love you, what reward shall ye have? for the pub- Mt. 5, 46. Lk. 6, 32*b*.
16 licans and sinners also love those that love them. And if ye do a kindness to those Lk. 6, 33.
17 who treat you well, where is your superiority? for sinners also do likewise. And if Lk. 6, 34.
ye lend to him of whom ye hope for a reward,[1] where is your superiority? for the
18 sinners also lend to sinners, seeking recompense from [2] them. But love your enemies, Lk. 6, 35.
and do good to them, and lend, and cut not off the hope of any man; that your reward may be great, and ye may be the children of the Highest: for he is lenient
19 towards the wicked and the ungrateful. Be ye merciful, even as your Father also is Lk. 6, 36.
20 merciful. And if ye inquire for the good of your brethren only, what more have Mt. 5, 47.
21 ye done *than others?* is not this the conduct of the publicans also? Be ye now[3] Mt. 5, 48.
perfect, even as your Father which is in heaven is perfect.

22 Consider your alms; do them not before men to let them see you: and if it be not Mt. 6, 1.
23 so,[4] ye have no reward before your Father which is in the heavens. When then thou Mt. 6, 2.
givest an alms now, do not sound a trumpet before thee, as do the people of hypocrisy,
Arabic, in the synagogues and the marketplaces, that men may praise them. And
24 p. 36 verily say I unto you, They have received their reward. But thou, when Mt. 6, 3.
25 thou doest alms, let thy left hand not know what thy right hand doeth; that thine Mt. 6, 4.
alms may be concealed: and thy Father which seeth in secret shall reward thee openly.

26 And whenever thou prayest, be not as the hypocrites, who love to stand in the Mt. 6, 5.
synagogues and in the corners of the marketplaces for prayers, that men may be-
27 hold them. And verily say I unto you, They have received their reward. But Mt. 6, 6.
thou, when thou prayest, enter into thy closet, and fasten thy door, and pray to thy
Father in secret, and thy Father which seeth in secret shall reward thee openly.
28 And whenever ye pray, be not babblers, as the heathen; for they think that by the Mt. 6, 7.
29 abundance of their words they shall be heard. Then be not ye now like unto them; Mt. 6, 8.
30 for your Father knoweth your request before ye ask him. One of his disciples said Lk. 11, 1*b*.
31 unto him, Our Lord, teach us to pray, as John taught his disciples. Jesus said unto Lk. 11, 2*a*.
32 them, Thus now pray ye now:[5] Our Father which art in heaven, Hallowed be thy Mt. 6, 9.
33, 34 name. Thy kingdom come. Thy will be *done*,[6] as in heaven, so on earth. Give us the Mt. 6, 10. Mt. 6, 11.
35 food of to-day. And forgive us our trespasses, as we forgave those that trespass*ed* Mt. 6, 12.
36 against us. And bring us not into temptations, but deliver us from the evil one. For Mt. 6, 13.
37 thine is the kingdom, and the power, and the glory, for ever and ever.[7] If ye forgive Mt. 6, 14.
Arabic, men their wrong-doing,[8] your Father which is in heaven will forgive you.
38 p. 37 But if ye forgive not men, neither will your Father pardon your wrong-doing. Mt. 6, 15.
39 When ye fast, do not frown, as the hypocrites; for they make their faces austere, Mt. 6, 16.
that they may be seen of[9] men that they are fasting. Verily I say unto you, They
40 have received their reward. But when thou fastest, wash thy face and anoint thy Mt. 6, 17.
41 head; that thou make not an appearance to men of fasting, but to thy Father which Mt. 6, 18.
is in secret: and thy Father which seeth in secret shall reward thee.

42 Be not agitated, little flock; for your Father hath delighted to give you the king- Lk. 12, 32.
43 dom. Sell your possessions, and give in alms; take to yourselves purses that wax Lk. 12, 33*a*.
44 not old. Lay not up treasure on earth, where moth and worm corrupt, and where Mt. 6, 19.
45 thieves break through and steal: but lay up for yourselves treasure in heaven, where Mt. 6, 20.
46 moth and worm do not corrupt, nor thieves break through nor steal: for where your Mt. 6, 21.
47 treasure is, there also will your heart be. The lamp of the body is the eye: if then[10] Mt. 6, 22.
48 thine eye now be sound, thy whole body also shall be light. But if thine eye be Mt. 6, 23.
evil, all thy body shall be dark. And if the light which is in thee is darkness, how
49 great is[11] thy darkness! Be watchful that the light which is in thee be not darkness. Lk. 11, 35.
50 Because that, if thy whole body is light, and have no part dark, it shall all be light, Lk. 11, 36.
as the lamp giveth light to thee with its flame.

1 Or, *return*. 2 Or, *to be given back as much by*.
3 Our translator is continually using this word (*cf.* § 9, 23) where the context and the originals require *then* or *therefore*. We shall only occasionally reproduce the peculiarity. 4 A clumsy phrase.
5 The Arabic text makes Matthew begin here.
6 The text as printed reads, *That thy will may be* (*done*); but it is to be explained as a (very common grammatical) transcriptional error. The Cur., however, has *and*. 7 Lit. *unto the age of the ages*.
8 Or, *folly*; and so in following verse. 9 Or, *shew to*. 10 Or, *for if*. 11 Or, *will be*.

SECTION X.

§10 1 Arabic, No man can serve two masters; and that because it is necessary that he Mt. 6, 24.
p. 38 hate one of them and love the other, and honour one of them and despise the
2 other. Ye cannot serve God and possessions. And because of this I say unto you, Mt. 6, 25.
Be not anxious for yourselves,[1] what ye shall eat and what ye shall drink; neither for
your bodies, what ye shall put on. Is not the life better than the food, and the body
3 than the raiment? Consider the birds of the heaven, which sow not, nor reap, nor Mt. 6, 26.
store in barns; and *yet* your Father which is in heaven feedeth them. Are not ye
4 better than they? Who of you when he trieth is able to add to his stature one Mt. 6, 27.
5 cubit? If then ye are not able for a small *thing*, why are ye anxious about the Lk. 12, 26. Mt. 6, 28.
6, 7 rest? Consider the wild lily, how it grows, although it toils not, nor spins; and I Mt. 6, 29.
say unto you that Solomon in the greatness of his glory was not clothed like one of
8 them. And if God so clothe the grass of the field, which to-day is, and to-morrow Mt. 6, 30.
9 is cast[2] into the oven, how much more shall be unto you, O ye of little faith! Be Mt. 6, 31.
not anxious, so as to say, What shall we eat? or, What shall we drink? or, With
10 what shall we be clothed? Neither let your minds be perplexed in this: all these Lk. 12, 29*b*. Mt. 6, 32.
things the nations of the world seek; and your Father which is in heaven knoweth
11 your need of all these things. Seek ye first the kingdom of God, and his righteous- Mt. 6, 33.
12 Arabic, ness; and all these shall come to you as something additional for you. Be Mt. 6, 34.
p. 39 not anxious for the morrow; for the morrow shall be anxious for what
belongs to it. Sufficient unto the day is its evil.
13 Judge not, that ye be not judged: condemn[3] not, that ye be not condemned: Mt. 7, 1. Lk. 6, 37*b*.
14 forgive, *and* it shall be forgiven you: release, and ye shall be released: give, that ye Lk. 6, 38.
may be given *unto;* with good measure, abundant, full, they shall thrust[4] into your
15 bosoms. With what measure ye measure it shall be measured to you. See *to it* Mk. 4, 24*b*.
what ye hear: with what measure ye measure it shall be measured to you; and ye
16 shall be given more. I say unto those that hear, He that hath shall be given *unto;* Mk. 4, 25.
and he that hath not, that which he regards[5] as his shall be taken from him.
17 And he spake unto them a parable, Can a blind man haply guide a blind man? Lk. 6, 39.
18 shall[6] they not both fall into a hollow? A disciple is not better than his master; Lk. 6, 40.
19 every perfect man shall be as his master. Why lookest thou at the mote which is Lk. 6, 41.
in the eye of thy brother, but considerest not the column that is in thine *own* eye?
20 Or how canst thou say to thy brother, Brother, I will take out the mote from thine Lk. 6, 42.
eye; and the column which is in thine eye thou seest not? Thou hypocrite, take
out first the column from thine eye; and then shalt thou see to take out the mote
from the eye of thy brother.
21 Give not that which is holy unto the dogs, neither cast your pearls before the Mt. 7, 6.
swine, lest they trample them with their feet, and return and wound you.
22 And he said unto them, Who of you, that hath a friend, goeth to him at mid- Lk. 11, 5.
23 night, and saith unto him, My friend, lend me three loaves; for a friend hath come Lk. 11, 6.
24 to me from a journey, and I have nothing to offer to him: and that friend shall Lk. 11, 7.
Arabic, answer him from within, and say unto him, Trouble me not; for the door
p. 40 is shut, and my children are with me in bed, and I cannot rise and give thee?
25 And verily I say unto you, If he will not give him because of friendship, yet because Lk. 11, 8.
26 of *his* importunity he will rise and give him what he seeketh. And I also say unto Lk. 11, 9.
you, Ask, *and* ye shall be given *unto;* seek, *and* ye shall find; knock, *and* it shall be
27 opened unto you. Every one that asketh receiveth, and he that seeketh findeth, and Lk. 11, 10.
28 he that knocketh, it shall be opened to him. What father of you, shall his son ask for Lk. 11, 11.
bread—will he, think you, give him a stone?[7] and if he ask of him a fish, will he,
29 think you, instead of the fish give him a serpent? and if he ask him for an egg, will Lk. 11, 12.

1 Or, *your souls;* or, *your lives.* 2 Lit. *falleth* (*cf.* Syriac).
3 The word means *to contend successfully*, but is used throughout by our translator in the sense of *condemn*.
4 This is the reading adopted by Ciasca in his Latin version. The diacritical points in the Arabic text, as he has printed it (perhaps a misprint), give second person plural passive instead of third plural active.
5 *cf.* Lk. 8, 18*b*. Our translator uses the same word in § 50, 5=Lk. 23, 8*b;* and in both cases it represents the same word in the Syriac versions. 6 Or, *Do.*
7 The Arabic might also be rendered, ***What father of you, whom his son asketh for bread, will (think you) give him a stone?*** But as the Peshitta preserves the confused construction of the Greek, it is probably better to render as above.

§10 30 he, think you, extend to him a scorpion? If ye then, *although* being evil, know the Lk. 11, 13.
gifts *which are* good, and give them to your children, how much more shall your
31 Father which is in heaven give the Holy Spirit to them that ask him? Whatsoever Mt. 7, 12.
ye would that men should do to you, do ye even so to them: this is the law and the
prophets.
32 Enter[1] ye by the narrow gate; for the wide gate and the broad way lead to de- Mt. 7, 13.
33 struction, and many they be which go therein. How narrow is the gate and strait- Mt. 7, 14.
ened the way leading to life! and few be they that find it.
34 Beware of false prophets, which come to you in sheep's[2] clothing, while within Mt. 7, 15.
35 they are ravening wolves. But by their fruits ye shall know them. For every tree is Mt. 7, 16*a*.
known by its fruit. For figs are not gathered[3] of thorns, neither are grapes plucked of Lk. 6, 44.
36 briers. Even so every good tree bringeth forth good fruit, but the evil tree bringeth Mt. 7, 17.
37 Arabic, forth evil fruit. The good tree cannot bring forth evil fruit, neither *can* the Mt. 7, 18.
38 p. 41 evil tree bring forth good fruit. The good man from the good treasures that Lk. 6, 45.
are in his heart bringeth forth good *things;* and the evil man from the evil treasures
that are in his heart bringeth forth evil *things:* and from the overflowings of the
39 heart the lips speak. Every tree that beareth not good fruit is cut *down* and cast Mt. 7, 19.
40, 41 into the fire. Therefore by their fruits ye shall know them. Not all that say unto Mt. 7, 20.
me, My Lord, my Lord, shall enter the kingdom of the heavens; but he that doeth Mt. 7, 21.
42 the will of my Father which is in heaven. Many shall say unto me in that day, Mt. 7, 22.
My Lord, my Lord, did we not prophesy in thy name, and in thy name cast out
43 devils, and in thy name do many powers? Then shall I say unto them, I never Mt. 7, 23.
44 knew you: depart from me, ye servants of iniquity. Every man that cometh unto Lk. 6, 47.
45 me, and heareth my sayings, and doeth them, I will shew you to what he is like: he Lk. 6, 48.
is like the wise man which built a house, and digged and went deep, and laid the
46 foundations on a rock: and the rain came down, and the rivers overflowed, and the Mt. 7, 25.
winds blew, and shook that house, and it fell not: for its foundation was laid on
47 rocks. And every one that heareth these my words, and doeth them not, is like Mt. 7, 26.
48 the foolish man which built his house on sand, without foundation: and the rain de- Mt. 7, 27.
scended, and the rivers overflowed, and the winds blew, and smote upon that house,
and it fell: and the fall of it was great.

SECTION XI.

§11 1 Arabic, And when Jesus finished these sayings, the multitudes were astonished Mt. 7, 28.
2 p. 42 at his teaching; and that because he was teaching them as one having Mt. 7, 29.
authority, not as their scribes and the Pharisees.
3 And when he descended from the mountain, great multitudes followed him. Mt. 8, 1.
4 And when Jesus entered Capernaum, the servant of one of the chiefs was in an Mt. 8, 5*a*.
5 evil case, and he was precious to him, and he was at the point of death. And he Lk. 7, 2. Lk. 7, 3.
6 heard of Jesus, and came to him with the elders of the Jews; and he besought him, Mt. 8, 5*b*.
and said, My Lord, my boy is laid in the house paralysed,[4] and he is suffering griev- Mt. 8, 6.
7 ous torment. And the elders urgently requested of him, and said, He is worthy that Lk. 7, 4*b*.
8 this should be done unto him: for he loveth our people, and he also built the syna- Lk. 7, 5.
9, 10 gogue for us. Jesus said unto him, I will come and heal him. That chief answered Mt. 8, 7.
and said, My Lord, I am not worthy that my roof should shade thee; but it sufficeth Mt. 8, 8.
11 that thou speak a word, and my lad shall be healed. And I also am a man in obe- Lk. 7, 8.
dience to authority, having under my hand soldiers:[5] and I say to this *one*, Go, and
he goeth; and to another, Come, and he cometh; and to my servant that he do this,
12 and he doeth *it*. And when Jesus heard that, he marvelled at him,[6] and turned and Lk. 7, 9*a*.
said unto the multitude that were coming with him, Verily I say unto you, I have Mt. 8, 10*b*.
13 not found in Israel *the* like *of* this faith. I say unto you, that many shall come from Mt. 8, 11.
Arabic, the east and the west, and shall recline with Abraham and Isaac and Jacob
14 p. 43 in the kingdom of heaven: but the children of the kingdom shall be cast Mt. 8, 12.

1 There is nothing about *striving*. The verb is *walaga*, which means *enter* (*cf.* § 11, 48). 2 Or, *lambs'*.
3 The verbs might be *singular* active, but not *plural* as in Syriac versions (*cf.*, however, § 38, 43, note, end). In the Borg. MS. the nouns are in the accusative. 4 i.e., so as to be unable to walk.
5 Or, *bodies of soldiers*. 6 Or, *it*.

§11 15 forth into the outer darkness: and there shall be weeping and gnashing of teeth. And Mt. 8, 13.
Jesus said to that chief, Go thy way; as thou hast believed, *so* shall it be unto thee.
16 And his lad was healed in that hour. And that chief returned to the house and found Lk. 7, 10.
that sick servant healed.
17 And the day after, he was going to a city called Nain, and his disciples with him, Lk. 7, 11.
18 and a great multitude. And when he was come near the gate of the city, he saw a Lk. 7, 12.
crowd[1] accompanying one *that was* dead, the only son of his mother; and his
mother was a widow: and there was with her a great multitude of the people of the
19 city. And when Jesus saw her, he had compassion on her, and said unto her, Weep Lk. 7, 13.
20 not. And he went and advanced to the bier, and the bearers of it stood still; and Lk. 7, 14.
21 he said, Young man, I say unto thee, Arise. And that dead *man* sat up and began Lk. 7, 15.
22 to speak; and he gave him to his mother. And fear came on all the people: and Lk. 7, 16.
they praised God, and said, There hath risen among us a great prophet: and, God
23 hath had regard to his people. And this news concerning him spread in all Judæa, Lk. 7, 17.
and in all the region which was about them.
24 And when Jesus saw great multitudes surrounding him, he commanded them to Mt. 8, 18.
25 depart to the other side. And while they were going in the way, there came one Lk. 9, 57a. Mt. 8, 19.
of the scribes and said unto him, My Master, I will follow thee whithersoever thou
26 goest. Jesus said unto him, The foxes have holes, and the birds of the heaven have Mt. 8, 20.
27 nests; but the Son of man hath not a place in which to lay his head. And he said Lk. 9, 59.
unto another, Follow me. And he said unto him, My Lord, suffer me first to go and
28 bury my father. Jesus said unto him, Leave the dead to bury their dead; but thou, Lk. 9, 60.
29 follow me and preach the kingdom of God. And another said unto him, I will fol- Lk. 9, 61.
Arabic, low thee, my Lord; but first suffer me to go and salute my household and
30 p. 44 come. Jesus said unto him, There is no one who putteth his hand to the Lk. 9, 62.
plough[2] and looketh behind him, and *yet* is fit for the kingdom of God.
31 And he said to them on that day in the evening, Let us go over to the other side Mk. 4, 35. Lk. 8, 22d.
32 of the lake; and he left[3] the multitudes. And Jesus went up and sat in the ship, Mk. 4, 36a. Lk. 8, 22b.
33 he and his disciples, and there were with them other ships. And there occurred on Mk. 4, 36c. Mt. 8, 24a.
the sea a great tempest[4] of whirlwind and wind, and the ship was on the point of Lk. 8, 23c.
34 sinking from the greatness[5] of the waves. But Jesus was sleeping on a cushion in Mk. 4, 38a.
the stern of the ship; and his disciples came and awoke him, and said unto him, Our Mt. 8, 25.
35 Lord, save us; lo, we perish. And he rose, and rebuked the winds and the turbu- Lk. 8, 24b.
lence of the water, and said to the sea, Be still, for thou art rebuked; and the wind Mk. 4, 39b.
36 was still, and there was a great calm. And he said unto them, Why are ye thus Mk. 4, 40.
37 afraid? and why have ye no faith? And they feared greatly.[6] And they marvelled, Lk. 8, 25b.
and said one to another, Who, think you, is this, who commandeth also the wind
and the waves and the sea, and they obey him?
38 And they departed and came to the country of the Gadarenes, which is on the Lk. 8, 26.
39 other side, opposite the land of Galilee. And when he went out of the ship to the Lk. 8, 27a. Mk. 5, 2b.
land, there met him from among the tombs a man who had a devil for a long time, Lk. 8, 27c.
40 and wore no clothes, neither dwelt in a house, but among the tombs. And no man was Mk. 5, 3b.
Arabic, able to bind him with chains, because any time that he was bound with chains Mk. 5, 4a.
41 p. 45 and fetters he cut the chains and loosened the fetters; and he was snatched[7] Lk. 8, 29c.
42 away of the devil into the desert, and no man was able to quiet him; and at all times, Mk. 5, 4b, 5a.
in the night and in the day, he would be among the tombs and in the mountains;
and no man was able to pass by that way; and he would cry out and wound himself Mt. 8, 28b. Mk. 5, 5b.
43 with stones. And when he saw Jesus at a distance, he hastened and worshipped Mk. 5, 6.
44 him, and cried with a loud voice and said, What have we to do with thee, Jesus, Mk. 5, 7a. Lk. 8, 28b.
45 Son of the most high God? I adjure thee by God, torment me not. And Jesus Mk. 5, 7c. Lk. 8, 29a.
commanded the unclean spirit to come out of the man: and he had *suffered*[8] a long
46 time since the time when he came into captivity to it. And Jesus asked him, What Lk. 8, 30.
is thy name? He said unto him, Legion; for there had entered into him many
47 devils. And they besought him that he would not command them to depart into Lk. 8, 31.
48 the depths. And there was there a herd of many swine, feeding in the mountain, Lk. 8, 32.

1 Lit. *company*. 2 Lit. *plough of the yoke*.
3 *cf.*, e.g., at § 17, 19, § 23, 16, where the same Arabic and Syriac word is used; *cf.* also the ambiguity of the Greek (R. V. has *left*). 4 Lit. *commotion*. 5 Or, *abundance*.
6 The last clause belongs in the Greek to verse 41. 7 Imperfect tense. 8 Lit. *and it was for him*.

§11 and those devils besought him to give them leave to enter the swine; and he gave
49 them leave. And the devils went out of the man and entered into the swine. And Lk. 8, 33. Mk. 5, 13*b*.
that herd hastened to the summit and fell down into the midst of the sea, about two
50 thousand, and they were choked in the water. And when the keepers saw what Lk. 8, 34.
51 happened, they fled, and told those in the cities and villages. And the people went Lk. 8, 35.
out to see what had happened; and they came to Jesus, and found the man whose
Arabic, devils had gone out, clothed, modest,[1] seated at the feet of Jesus; and they
52 p. 46 feared. And they reported what they saw, and how the man was healed Lk. 8, 36.
who had a devil, and concerning those swine also. Mk. 5, 16*b*.

SECTION XII.

§12 1 And all the multitude of the Gadarenes entreated him to depart from them, be- Lk. 8, 37*a*.
cause that great fear took hold upon them.
2, 3 But Jesus went up into the ship, and crossed, and came to his city. And that Mt. 9, 1. Lk. 8, 38.
man from whom the devils went out entreated that he might stay with him; but
4 Jesus sent him away, and said unto him, Return to thy house, and make known what Lk. 8, 39*a*.
5 God hath done for thee. And he went, and began to publish in Decapolis[2] what Mk. 5, 20.
Jesus had done for him; and they all marvelled.
6 And when Jesus had crossed in the ship to that side, a great multitude received Mk. 5, 21*a*. Lk. 8, 40*b*.
7 him; and they were all looking for him. And a man named Jaïrus, the chief of the Lk. 8, 41*a*.
8 synagogue, fell before the feet of Jesus, and besought him much, and said unto him, Mk. 5, 23*a*.
I have an only daughter, and she is come nigh unto death; but come and lay thy Mt. 9, 18*b*.
9 hand upon her, and she shall live. And Jesus rose, and his disciples, and they fol- Mt. 9, 19.
10 lowed him. And there joined him a great multitude, and they pressed him. Mk. 5, 24*b*.
11, 12 And a woman, which had a flow of blood for twelve years, *had* suffered much Mk. 5, 25. Mk. 5, 26.
of many physicians, and spent all that she had, and was not benefited at all, but her
13 trouble increased further. And when she heard of Jesus, she came in the thronging of Mk. 5, 27.
14 Arabic, the crowd behind him, and touched[3] his garments; and she thought within Mk. 5, 28.
15 p. 47 herself, If I *could* reach to touch his garments, I should live. And immedi- Mk. 5, 29.
ately the fountain of her blood was dried; and she felt in her body that she was healed
16 of her plague. And Jesus straightway knew within himself that power had gone out Mk. 5, 30.
of him; and he turned to the crowd, and said, Who approached unto my garments?
17 And on their denying, all of them, Simon Cephas and those with him said unto him, Lk. 8, 45*b*.
Our Master, the multitudes throng thee and press thee, and sayest thou, Who ap-
18 proached unto me? And he said, Some one approached unto me; and I knew that Lk. 8, 46.
19 power went forth from me. And that woman, when she saw that she was not hid Lk. 8, 47*a*.
20 from him, came fearing and agitated (for she knew what had happened to her), and Mk. 5, 33*b*. Lk. 8, 47*c*.
fell down and worshipped him, and told, in the presence of all the people, for what
21 reason she touched *him*, and how she was healed immediately. And Jesus said unto Lk. 8, 48.
her, Be of good courage, daughter; thy faith hath made thee alive; depart in peace,
and be whole from thy plague. Mk. 5, 34*b*.
22 And while he was yet speaking, there came a man from the house of the chief Lk. 8, 49.
of the synagogue, and said unto him, Thy daughter hath died; so trouble not the
23 teacher. But Jesus heard, and said unto the father of the maid, Fear not: but be- Lk. 8, 50.
24 lieve only, and she shall live. And he suffered no man to go with him, except Mk. 5, 37.
25 Simon Cephas, and James, and John the brother of James. And they reached the Mk. 5, 38.
house of the chief of the synagogue; and he saw them agitated, weeping and wail-
26 ing. And he entered, and said unto them, Why are ye agitated *and* weeping? the Mk. 5, 39.
27 Arabic, maid hath not died, but she is sleeping. And they laughed at him, for Lk. 8, 53.
28 p. 48 they knew that she had died. And he put every man forth without, and Mk. 5, 40*b*.
took the father of the maid, and her mother, and Simon, and James, and John, and
29 entered into the place where the maid was laid. And he took hold of the hand of Mk. 5, 41.
the maid, and said unto her, Maid, arise. And her spirit returned, and straightway Lk. 8, 55*a*.
30 she arose and walked: and she was about twelve years *of age*. And he commanded Mk. 5, 42*b*. Lk. 8, 55*b*.
31 that there should be given to her something to eat. And her father wondered greatly: Lk. 8, 56.

1 *cf.* Syriac versions. 2 Lit. *the ten cities.* 3 See § 8, 17, note.

§12 32 and he warned them that they should tell no man what had happened. And this Mt. 9, 26.
report spread in all that land.
33 And when Jesus crossed over from there, there joined him two blind men, cry- Mt. 9, 27.
34 ing out, and saying, Have mercy on us, *thou* son of David. And when he came to Mt. 9, 28.
the house, those two blind men came to him: and Jesus said unto them, Believe ye
35 that I am able to do this? They said unto him, Yea, our Lord. Then he touched[1] Mt. 9, 29.
36 their eyes, and said, As ye have believed, it shall be unto you. And immediately Mt. 9, 30.
their eyes were opened. And Jesus forbade them, and said, See that no man know.
37 But they went out and published the news in all that land. Mt. 9, 31.
38 And when Jesus went out, they brought to him a dumb man having a devil. Mt. 9, 32.
39 And on the going out of the devil that dumb man spake. And the multitudes mar- Mt. 9, 33.
velled, and said, It was never so seen in Israel
40 And Jesus was going about in all the cities and *in* the villages, and teaching in their Mt. 9, 35.
synagogues, and proclaiming the good news of the kingdom, and healing every disease
41 Arabic, and sickness; and many followed him. And when Jesus saw the multitudes, Mt. 9, 36.
p. 49 he had compassion on them, for they were wearied and scattered,[2] as sheep
42 that have no shepherd. And he called his twelve disciples, and gave them power and Mt. 10, 1*a*. Lk. 9, 1*b*.
43 much authority over all devils and diseases; and sent them two and two, that they Lk. 9, 2.
44 might proclaim the kingdom of God, and *to* heal the sick. And he charged them, Mt. 10, 5.
and said, Walk not in the way of the heathen, nor enter into the cities of the Sa-
45, 46 maritans.[3] Go especially unto the sheep that are lost of the sons of Israel. And Mt. 10, 6. Mt. 10, 7.
47 when ye go, proclaim and say, The kingdom of heaven is come near. And heal the Mt. 10, 8.
sick, and cleanse the lepers, and cast out the devils: freely ye have received, freely
48, 49 give. Get you not gold, nor silver, nor brass in your purses; and take nothing for Mt. 10, 9 f.
the way, except a staff only; nor bag, nor bread; neither shall ye have two tunics, Mk. 6, 8*b*. Lk. 9, 3.
50 nor shoes, nor staff, but be shod with sandals; for the labourer is worthy of his food. Mt. 10, 10*c*.
51 And whatever city or village ye enter, inquire who is worthy in it, and there be until Mk. 6, 9*a*. Mt. 10, 10*d*.
52, 53 ye go out. And when ye enter into the house, ask for the peace of the house: and Mt. 10, 11. Mt. 10, 12.
if the house is worthy, your peace shall come upon it; but if it is not worthy, your Mt. 10, 13.
54 peace shall return unto you. And whosoever shall not receive you, nor hear your Mt. 10, 14*a*.
sayings, when ye go out from that house, or from that village, shake off the dust Mk. 6, 11*b*.
55 Arabic, that is under your feet against them for a testimony. And verily I say Mt. 10, 15.
p. 50 unto you, To the land of Sodom and Gomorrah there shall be rest in
the day of judgement, rather than to that city.

SECTION XIII.

§13 1 I am sending you as lambs among wolves: be ye now wise as serpents, and Mt. 10, 16.
2 harmless[4] as doves. Beware of men: they shall deliver you to the councils of the Mt. 10, 17.
3 magistrates, and scourge you in their synagogues; and shall bring you before gov- Mt. 10, 18.
ernors and kings for my sake, for a testimony against them and against the nations.
4 And when they deliver you up, be not[5] anxious, nor consider beforehand, what ye Mt. 10, 19.
5 shall say; but ye shall be given[6] in that hour what ye ought to speak. Ye do not Mt. 10, 20.
6 speak, but the Spirit of your Father speaketh in you. The brother shall deliver up Mt. 10, 21.
his brother to death, and the father his son; and the sons shall rise against their
7 parents, and put them to death. And ye shall be hated of every man because of Mt. 10, 22.
8 my name; but he that endureth unto the end of the matter shall be saved.[7] When Mt. 10, 23.
they expel you from this city, flee to another. Verily I say unto you, Ye shall not
finish all the cities of the people of Israel, until the Son of man come.
9, 10 A disciple is not superior to his lord, nor a servant to his master. For it is Mt. 10, 24. Mt. 10, 25.
enough then for the disciple that he be as his lord, and the servant as his master.
If they have called the master of the house Beelzebul, how much more the people

1 Lit. *went forward to* (*cf.* § 8, 17, note). 2 Lit. *cast away* (*cf.* meanings of Syriac word).
3 § 34, 40, shows that this Arabic form may be so translated.
4 The word is occasionally used in this sense, but ordinarily means *sound, unhurt.*
5 From this point down to Mt. 10, 27*a*, is assigned by Vat. MS. to Mark.
6 Borg. MS. reads, *but what ye are granted ye shall speak, and ye shall be given in*, etc., and there seems to be a trace of this reading in Ciasca's text. 7 See note to § 1, 78.

§ 13 11 of his house! Fear them not therefore:[1] for there is nothing covered, that shall Mt. 10, 26.
12 Arabic, not be revealed; nor hid, that shall not be disclosed and published. What Mt. 10, 27a.
p. 51 I say unto you in the darkness, speak ye in the light; and what ye have told Lk. 12, 3b.
13 secretly in the ears in closets, let it be proclaimed on the housetops. I say unto you Lk. 12, 4a.
now, my beloved, Be not agitated at[2] those who kill the body, but have no power to Mt. 10, 28b.
14 kill the soul. I will inform you whom ye shall fear: him[3] which is able to destroy
15 soul and body in hell. Yea, I say unto you, Be afraid of him especially. Are not two Lk. 12, 5. Mt. 10, 29.
sparrows sold for a farthing in a bond?[4] and one of them shall not fall on the
16 ground without your Father. But what concerns you: even the hair of your heads Mt. 10, 30.
17, 18 also is numbered. Fear not therefore; ye are better than many sparrows. Every Mt. 10, 31. Mt. 10, 32.
man who confesseth me now before men, I also will confess him before my Father
19 which is in heaven; but whosoever denieth me before men, I also will deny him be- Mt. 10, 33.
fore my Father which is in heaven.
20 Think ye that I am come to cast peace into the earth? I came not to cast peace, Lk. 12, 51.
21 but to cast dissension. Henceforth there shall be five in one house, three of them Lk. 12, 52.
22 disagreeing with two, and the two with the three. The father shall become hostile Lk. 12, 53.
to his son, and the son to his father; and the mother to her daughter, and the daughter to her mother; and the mother in law to her daughter in law, and the daughter
23 in law to her mother in law: and a man's enemies shall be the people of his house. Mt. 10, 36.
24 Whosoever loveth father or mother better than me is not worthy of me; and whoso- Mt. 10, 37.
Arabic, ever loveth son or daughter more than his love of me is not worthy of me.
25 p. 52 And every one that doth not take his cross and follow me is not worthy of Mt. 10, 38.
26 me. Whosoever findeth his life[5] shall lose it; and whosoever loseth his life[5] for my Mt. 10, 39.
sake shall find it.
27 And whosoever receiveth you receiveth me; and whosoever receiveth me re- Mt. 10, 40.
28 ceiveth him that sent me. And whosoever receiveth a prophet in the name of a Mt. 10, 41.
prophet shall take[6] a prophet's reward; and whosoever shall receive a righteous man
29 in the name of a righteous man shall take[6] a righteous man's reward. And every Mt. 10, 42a.
one that shall give to drink to one of these least ones a drink of water only, in the
name of a disciple, verily I say unto you, he shall not lose his reward. Mk. 9, 41b.
30 And when Jesus finished charging his twelve disciples, he removed thence to Mt. 11, 1.
31 teach and preach in their cities. And while they were going in the way they entered Lk. 10, 38.
into a certain village; and a woman named Martha entertained him in her house.
32 And she had a sister named Mary, and she came and sat at the feet of our Lord, Lk. 10, 39.
33 and heard his sayings. But Martha was disquieted by much serving; and she came Lk. 10, 40.
and said unto him, My Lord, givest thou no heed that my sister left me alone to
34 serve? speak to her that she help me. Jesus answered and said unto her, Martha, Lk. 10, 41.
35 Martha, thou art solicitous and impatient[7] on account of many things: but what is Lk. 10, 42.
sought is one *thing*. But Mary hath chosen for herself a good portion, and that
which shall not be taken from her.
36 And the apostles went forth, and preached to the people that they might repent. Mk. 6, 12.
37 And they cast out many devils, and anointed many sick with oil, and healed them. Mk. 6, 13.
38, 39 And the disciples of John told him[8] of all these things. And when John heard in Lk. 7, 18. Mt. 11, 2a.
Arabic, the prison of the doings of the Messiah, he called two of his disciples, and Lk. 7, 19.
p. 53 sent them to Jesus, and said, Art thou he that cometh, or look we for
40 another? And they came to Jesus, and said unto him, John the Baptist hath sent Lk. 7, 20.
41 us unto thee, and said, Art thou he that cometh, or look we for another? And in that Lk. 7, 21.
hour he cured many of diseases, and of plagues of an evil spirit; and he gave sight
42 to many blind. Jesus answered and said unto them, Go and tell John everything ye Lk. 7, 22.
have seen and heard: the blind see, and the lame walk, and the lepers are cleansed,
and the blind[9] hear, and the dead rise, and the poor have the gospel preached to
43 them. And blessed is he who doubteth not in me. Lk. 7, 23.

1 See note to § 9, 21.
2 Perhaps this Arabic word is a copyist's error for that used a few lines further down in Lk. 12, 5, the Arabic words being very similar; but see note on § 1, 14.
3 Syriac.
4 The Vat. MS., like the Brit. Mus. text of Ibn-aṭ-Ṭayyib's Commentary, omits *for a farthing*, retaining *in a bond*. The two phrases are simply different explanations of the same Syriac consonants. These are really the naturalised Greek word rendered *farthing* in Eng. version; but they also form a Syriac word meaning *bond*.
5 Or, *soul*.
6 Or, *receive*.
7 Or, *agitated*.
8 Lit. *And his disciples told John*, as in the Greek, etc.
9 A different word from that used in the preceding verse. It is either an Arabic copyist's error for the word for *deaf* used in Ibn-aṭ-Ṭayyib's Commentary, or a careless blunder.

§13 44 And when John's disciples departed, Jesus began to say to the multitudes con- Lk. 7, 24.
cerning John, What went ye out into the wilderness to see? a reed shaken with the
45 winds? And if not, then what went ye out to see ? a man clothed in soft raiment? Lk. 7, 25.
Behold, they that are in magnificent garments and in voluptuousness are in the abode
46 of kings. And if not, then what went ye out to see? a prophet? Yea, I say unto Lk. 7, 26.
47 you, and more than a prophet. This is he of whom it is written, Lk. 7, 27.
I am sending my messenger before thy face
To prepare the way before thee.

SECTION XIV.

§14 1 Verily I say unto you, There hath not arisen among those whom women have Mt. 11, 11.
borne a greater than John the Baptist; but he that is little now in the kingdom of
heaven is greater than he.
2 Arabic, And all the people which heard, and the publicans, justified[1] God, for Lk. 7, 29.
3 p. 54 they had been baptized with the baptism of John. But the Pharisees and the Lk. 7, 30.
scribes wronged[2] the purpose of God in themselves, in that they were not baptized of
4 him. And from the days of John the Baptist until now the kingdom of heaven is Mt. 11, 12*a*.
5 snatched away by violence. The law and the prophets *were* until John; and after that, Lk. 16, 16.
the kingdom of God is preached, and all press to enter it: and they that exert them- Mt. 11, 12*b*.
6, 7 selves snatch it away. All the prophets and the law until John prophesied. And if ye Mt. 11, 13. Mt. 11, 14.
8 will, then receive *it*, that he is Elijah, which is to come. Whosoever hath ears that hear Mt. 11, 15.
9 let him hear. Easier is the perishing of heaven and earth, than the passing away of Lk. 16, 17.
10 one point of the law. To whom then shall I liken the people of this generation,[3] and Lk. 7, 31*b*.
11 to whom are they like? They are like the children sitting in the market, which call Lk. 7, 32.
to their companions, and say, We sang to you, and ye danced not; we wailed to you,
12 and ye wept not. John the Baptist came neither eating bread nor drinking wine; Lk. 7, 33.
13 and ye said, He hath demons: and the Son of man came eating and drinking; and Lk. 7, 34.
ye said, Behold, a gluttonous man, and a drinker of wine, and an associate of pub-
14, 15 licans and sinners! And wisdom was justified of all her children. And when he Lk. 7, 35. Mk. 3, 20.[4]
said that, they came to the house. And there gathered unto him again multitudes,
16 so that they found not bread to eat. And while he was casting out a devil which Lk. 11, 14.
was dumb, when he cast out that devil, that dumb *man* spake. And the multitudes
17 Arabic, marvelled. And the Pharisees, when they heard, said, This *man* doth not cast Mt. 12, 24.
p. 55 out the devils, except by Beelzebul the chief of the demons, which is in him.
18, 19 And others requested of him a sign from heaven, to tempt him. And Jesus knew their Lk. 11, 16. Mt. 12, 25.
thoughts, and said unto them in parables, Every kingdom that withstandeth itself
shall become desolate; and every house or city that disagreeth with itself shall not
20 stand: and if a devil cast out a devil, he withstandeth himself; neither shall he be Mt. 12, 26*a*.
21 able to stand, but his end shall be. Then how now shall his kingdom stand? for ye Mk. 3, 26*b*. Mt. 12, 26*b*.
22 said that I cast out devils by Beelzebul. And if I by Beelzebul cast out the devils, Lk. 11, 18*b*. Mt. 12, 27.
then your children, by what do they cast them out? And for this cause they shall
23 be judges against you. But if I by the Spirit of God cast out devils, then the king- Mt. 12, 28.
24 dom of God is come near unto you. Or how can a man enter into the house of a Mt. 12, 29.
valiant *man*, and seize his garments,[5] if he do not beforehand secure himself[6] from
25 that valiant *man?* and then will he cut off[7] his house. But when the valiant man is Lk. 11, 21.
26 armed, guarding his house, his possessions are in peace. But if one come who is Lk. 11, 22.
more valiant than he, he overcometh him, and taketh his whole armour, on which
27 he relieth, and divideth his spoil. Whosoever is not with me is against me; and Lk. 11, 23.
28 whosoever gathereth not with me scattereth abroad. For this reason I say unto you, Mk. 3, 28.
Arabic, that all sins and blasphemies with which men blaspheme shall be forgiven
29 p. 56 them: but whosoever shall blaspheme against the Holy Spirit, there is no Mk. 3, 29.
30 forgiveness for him for ever, but he is deserving of eternal punishment: because they Mk. 3, 30.

1 Syriac. In Arabic the word ordinarily means *believed*.
2 See below, § 20, 28, note. 3 See § 1, 49, note. 4 And verse 19*b*.
5 The word used in the Syriac versions (Pesh. and Cur.) means *garments* as well as *utensils*, and the Arabic translator has chosen the wrong meaning (*cf.* § 42, 44).
6 Certain derivatives from the same root signify *bind*, but hardly this word.
7 The two Arab. MSS. differ in this word, but the meaning is about the same. Perhaps both are corrupt.

§ **14** 31 said that he had an unclean spirit. And he said also, Every one that speaketh a word Mt. 12, 32.
against the Son of man, it shall be forgiven him; but whosoever speaketh against
the Holy Spirit, it shall not be forgiven him, neither in this world, nor in the world to
32 come. Either ye must make a good tree[1] and its fruit good; or ye must make an evil Mt. 12, 33.
33 tree[2] and its fruit evil: for the tree is known by its fruit. Ye children of vipers, how Mt. 12, 34.
can ye, being evil, speak good things? from the overflowings of the heart the mouth
34 speaketh. The good man from the good treasures which are in his heart bringeth Lk. 6, 45*a*.
forth good things; and the wicked man from the evil treasures which are in his
35 heart bringeth forth evils. I say unto you, that every idle word which men shall Mt. 12, 36.
36 speak, they shall give an answer for in the day of judgement: for by thy sayings Mt. 12, 37.
thou shalt be justified, and by thy sayings thou shalt be judged.

37 And he said to the multitudes, When ye see the clouds appear from the west, Lk. 12, 54.
38 straightway ye say that there cometh rain; and so it cometh to pass. And when Lk. 12, 55.
39 the south wind bloweth, ye say that there will be heat; and it cometh to pass. And Mt. 16, 2*b*.
when the evening is come, ye say, It *will be* fair weather, for the heaven has become
40 red. And in the morning ye say, To-day there will be severe weather, for the redness Mt. 16, 3.
Arabic, of the heaven is paling. *Ye* hypocrites, ye know to examine the face of the Mt. 16, 4.[3]
p. 57 heaven and the earth; but the signs of this time ye know not to discern.
41 Then they brought to him one possessed of a demon, dumb *and* blind; and he Mt. 12, 22.
42 healed him, so that the dumb and blind began to speak and see. And all the mul- Mt. 12, 23.
titudes wondered, and said, Is this, think you, the son of David?

43 And the apostles returned unto Jesus, and told him everything that they had Mk. 6, 30.
44 done and wrought.[4] And he said unto them, Come, let us go into the desert alone, Mk. 6, 31.
and rest ye a little. And many were going and returning, and they had not leisure,
not even to eat bread.

45 And after that, there came to *him* one of the Pharisees, and besought him that Lk. 7, 36.
he would eat bread with him. And he entered into the house of that Pharisee, and
46 reclined. And there was in that city a woman *that was* a sinner; and when she Lk. 7, 37.
knew that he was sitting in the house of that Pharisee, she took a box of sweet oint-
47 ment, and stood behind him, towards his feet, weeping, and began to wet his feet Lk. 7, 38.
with her tears, and to wipe them with the hair of her head, and to kiss his feet, and
48 anoint them with the sweet ointment. And when that[5] Pharisee saw *it*, who invited Lk. 7, 39.
him, he thought within himself, and said, This *man*, if he were a prophet, would know
who she is and what is her history: for the woman which touched him was a sinner.

SECTION XV.

15 1 Jesus answered and said unto him, Simon, I have something to say unto thee. And Lk. 7, 40.
2 he said unto him, Say *on*, my Master. Jesus said unto him, There were two debtors Lk. 7, 41.
Arabic, to one creditor; and one of them owed five hundred pence, and the other
3 p. 58 owed fifty pence. And because they had not wherewith to pay, he forgave Lk. 7, 42.
4 them both. Which of them ought to love him more? Simon answered and said, I sup- Lk. 7, 43.
pose, he to whom he forgave most. Jesus said unto him, Thou hast judged rightly.
5 And he turned to that woman, and said to Simon, Dost thou see this woman? I Lk. 7, 44.
entered into thy dwelling, and thou gavest me not water to wash my feet: but this
6 *woman* hath bathed[6] my feet with her tears, and dried them with her hair. And Lk. 7, 45.
thou kissedst me not: but this *woman*, since she[7] entered, hath not ceased to kiss my
7 feet. And thou anointedst not my head with oil:[8] but this *woman* hath anointed Lk. 7, 46.
8 my feet with sweet ointment.[8] And for this, I say unto thee, Her many sins are for- Lk. 7, 47.
given her, because she loved much; for he to whom little is forgiven loveth little.
9, 10 And he said unto that woman, Thy sins are forgiven thee. And those that were in- Lk. 7, 48. Lk. 7, 49.
11 vited began to say within themselves, Who is this that forgiveth sins also? And Lk. 7, 50.
Jesus said to that woman, Thy faith hath saved thee; go in peace.

1 Or, *a tree good*. 2 Or, *a tree evil*. 3 This is reckoned to verse 3 in the Greek.
4 *Wrought* may have arisen from *taught* by a transcriptional error (transposition of *l* and *m*) *within* the Arabic text. As it appears to occur in both MSS., they would seem to have a common origin, which, however, can hardly have been the autograph of the translator. 5 A comparison with the Syriac text recommends this rendering.
6 Lit. *sunk*, a word the choice of which is explained by the Syriac. 7 Or, *I*. 8 Same word in Arabic.

§15 12 And many believed in him when they saw the signs which he was doing. Jo. 2, 23b.
13, 14 But Jesus did not trust[1] himself to them, for he knew every man, and he needed Jo. 2, 24. Jo. 2, 25.
not any man to testify to him concerning every man; for he knew what was in man.
15 And after that, Jesus set apart from his disciples other seventy, and sent them Lk. 10, 1.
two and two before his face to every region and city whither he was purposing to
16 go. And he said unto them, The harvest is abundant, and the labourers are few: Lk. 10, 2.
17 entreat now the Lord of the harvest, that he send forth labourers into his harvest. Go Lk. 10, 3.
18 Arabic, ye: and lo, I am sending you as lambs among wolves. Take not with you Lk. 10, 4.
19 p. 59 purses, nor a wallet, nor shoes; neither salute any man in the way. And Lk. 10, 5.
20 whatsoever house ye enter, first salute that house: and if there be there a son of peace, Lk. 10, 6.
21 let your peace rest upon him; but if there be not, your peace shall return to you. And Lk. 10, 7.
be ye in that house eating and drinking what they have:[2] for the labourer is worthy of
22 his hire. And remove not from house to house. And into whatsoever city ye enter, Lk. 10, 8.
23 and they receive you, eat what is presented to you: and heal the sick that are Lk. 10, 9.
24 therein, and say unto them, The kingdom of God is come near unto you. But Lk. 10, 10.
whatsoever city ye enter, and they receive you not, go out into the market, and say,
25 Even the dust that clave to our feet from your city, we shake off against you; but Lk. 10, 11.
26 know[3] this,[4] that the kingdom of God is come near unto you. I say unto you, that Lk. 10, 12.
for Sodom there shall be quiet in the day of judgement, but there shall not be for
27 that city. Then began Jesus to rebuke the cities in which there had been many Mt. 11, 20.
28 mighty works,[5] and they repented not. And he said, Woe unto thee, Chorazin! woe Mt. 11, 21.
unto thee, Bethsaida! if there had been in Tyre and Sidon the signs which were in
29 thee, it may be that they would have repented in sackcloth and ashes. Howbeit I Mt. 11, 22.
say unto you, that for Tyre and Sidon there shall be rest in the day of judgement,
30 more than for you. And thou, Capernaum, which art exalted unto heaven, shalt Mt. 11, 23.
sink down unto Hades; for if there had been in Sodom the wonders[6] which were
31 in thee, it would have remained until this day. And now I say unto thee, that for Mt. 11, 24.
the land of Sodom there shall be quiet in the day of judgement, more than for thee.
32 Arabic, And he said again unto his apostles, Whosoever heareth you heareth Lk. 10, 16.
p. 60 me; and whosoever heareth me heareth him that sent me: and whosoever
wrongeth[7] you wrongeth me; and whosoever wrongeth me wrongeth him that sent me.
33 And those seventy returned with great joy, and said unto him, Our Lord, even Lk. 10, 17.
34 the devils also are subject unto us in thy name. He said unto them, I beheld Lk. 10, 18.
35 Satan[8] fallen like lightning from heaven. Behold, I am giving you authority to tread Lk. 10, 19.
upon serpents and scorpions, and the whole race[9] of the enemy; and nothing shall
36 hurt you. Only ye must not rejoice that the devils are subject unto you; but be Lk. 10, 20.
glad that your names are written in heaven.
37 And in that hour Jesus rejoiced in the Holy Spirit, and said, I acknowledge thee, Lk. 10, 21.
my Father, Lord of heaven and earth, that thou didst hide these things from the
wise and understanding, and didst reveal them unto children: yea, my Father; so
38 was thy will. And he turned to his disciples,[10] and said unto them, Everything hath Lk. 10, 22.
been delivered to me of my Father: and no man knoweth who the Son is, save the
Father; and who the Father is, save the Son, and to whomsoever the Son willeth
39 to reveal *him*. Come unto me, all of you, ye *that are* wearied and bearers of bur- Mt. 11, 28.
40 dens, and I will give you rest. Bear my yoke upon you, and learn of me; for[11] I Mt. 11, 29.
41 am gentle and lowly in my heart: and ye shall find rest unto your souls. For my Mt. 11, 30.
yoke is pleasant, and my burden is light.
42 And while great multitudes were going with him, he turned, and said unto them, Lk. 14, 25.
43 Whosoever cometh unto me, and hateth not his father, and his mother, and his Lk. 14, 26.
brethren, and his sisters, and his wife, and his children, and himself[12] also, cannot
44 Arabic, be a disciple to me. And whosoever doth not take his cross, and follow Lk. 14, 27.
45 p. 61 me, cannot be a disciple to me. Which of you desireth to build a tower, Lk. 14, 28.

1 The meaning is not apparent. 2 *cf.* Syriac versions. 3 The first letter of the word has been lost.
4 Lit. *that*, as often in this work. 5 Lit. *powers*.
6 The word as printed by Ciasca perhaps means *gifts*, but by dropping a point from the second letter we get the post-classical word given in the text above. 7 See below, § 20, 28, note.
8 The word translated *devil* in preceding verse.
9 This is an Arabic clerical error for *forces*. The Syriac word for *power* means also *military forces*, which was apparently rendered in Arabic *army*, a word that differs from *race* only in diacritical points.
10 *cf.* Pesh. and A.V. margin. 11 Lit. *that* (*cf.* above, § 1, 50, note). 12 Or, *his life*; or, *his soul*.

§ 15 and doth not sit down first and reckon his expenses and whether he hath *enough* to
46 complete it?[1] lest, when he hath laid the foundations, and is not able to finish, all that Lk. 14, 29.
47 behold him[2] laugh at him, and say, This man began to build, and was not able to Lk. 14, 30.
48 finish. Or what king goeth to the battle to fight with another king,[3] and doth not Lk. 14, 31.
consider first whether he is able with ten thousand to meet him that cometh to him
49 with twenty thousand? And if he is not able, he sendeth unto him while he is afar Lk. 14, 32.
50 off, and seeketh peace. So shall[4] every man of you consider, that desireth to be a Lk. 14, 33.
disciple to me; for if he renounceth not all that he hath, he cannot be a disciple to me.

SECTION XVI.

§ 16 1 Then answered certain of the scribes and Pharisees, that they might tempt him, Mt. 12, 38.
2 and said, Teacher, we desire to see a sign from thee. He answered and said, This Mt. 12, 39.
evil and adulterous generation[5] seeketh a sign; and it shall not be given a sign,
3 except the sign of Jonah the prophet. And as Jonah was a sign to the inhabitants Lk. 11, 30.
4 of Nineveh, so shall the Son of man also be to this generation. And as Jonah was Mt. 12, 40.
in the belly of the great fish three days and three nights, so shall the Son of man
5 be in the heart of the earth three days and three nights. The queen of the south Lk. 11, 31.
shall rise in the judgement with the people of this generation, and condemn[6] them:
for she came from the ends of the earth that she might hear the wisdom of Solomon;
6 (Arabic, p. 62) and behold, here is a better than Solomon. The men of Nineveh shall stand Mt. 12, 41.
in the judgement with this generation, and condemn it: for they repented at
7 the preaching of Jonah; and behold, here is a greater than Jonah. The unclean spirit, Lk. 11, 24.
when he goeth out of the man, departeth, and goeth about through places wherein
are no waters, that he may find rest for himself; and when he findeth *it* not, he
8 saith, I will return to my house whence I came out. And if he come and find it Lk. 11, 25.
9 adorned *and* set in order, then he goeth, and associateth with himself seven other Lk. 11, 26.
spirits worse than himself; and they enter and dwell in it: and the end of that man
10 shall be worse than his beginning. Thus shall it be unto this evil generation. Mt. 12, 45*b*.
11 And while he was saying that, a woman from the multitude lifted up her voice, Lk. 11, 27.
and said unto him, Blessed is the womb that bare thee, and the breasts that nursed
12 thee. But he said unto her, Blessed is he that heareth the word of God, and keep- Lk. 11, 28.
eth it.
13 And while he was speaking unto the multitude, there came unto him his mother Mt. 12, 46*a*. Lk. 8, 19*a*.
14 and his brethren, and sought to speak with him; and they were not able, because of Mt. 12, 46*c*.
15 the multitude; and they stood without and sent, calling him unto them. A man said Lk. 8, 19*b*. Mk. 3, 31.
unto him, Behold, thy mother and thy brethren *are* standing without, and seek to Mt. 12, 47.
16 speak with thee. But he answered unto him that spake unto him, Who is my Mt. 12, 48.
17 mother? and who are my brethren? And he beckoned with his hand, stretching Mt. 12, 49.
it out towards his disciples, and said, Behold, my mother! and behold, my brethren!
18 And every man that shall do the will of my Father which is in heaven is my brother, Mt. 12, 50.
and my sister, and my mother.
19 And after that, Jesus was going about in the cities and in the villages, and pro- Lk. 8, 1.
(Arabic, p. 63) claiming and preaching the kingdom of God, and his[7] twelve with him,
20 and the women which had been healed of diseases and of evil spirits, Mary Lk. 8, 2.
21 that *was* called Magdalene, from whom he had cast out seven devils, and Joanna the Lk. 8, 3.
wife of Chuza Herod's steward, and Susanna, and many others, who were ministering
to them of their substance.
22 And after that, Jesus went out of the house, and sat on the sea shore. And there Mt. 13, 1.
23 gathered unto him great multitudes. And when the press of the people was great Mt. 13, 2.
upon him, he went up and sat in the boat; and all the multitude was standing on the
24 shore of the sea. And he spake to them much in parables, and said, The sower Mt. 13, 3.
25 went forth to sow: and when he sowed, some fell on the beaten highway; and it was Mt. 13, 4*a*. Lk. 8, 5*b*.
26 trodden upon, and the birds ate it. And other fell on the rocks: and some, where Mt. 13, 5.

1 This rendering assumes that *tower* is treated as feminine. 2 Or, *it*. 3 Or, *a king like him*.
4 Or, *let*. 5 See § 1, 49, note. 6 See note to § 10, 13.
7 The Arabic printed text gives no sense. A simple change in the diacritical points of one letter gives the reading of the Syriac versions, which is adopted here.

§16 there was not much earth; and straightway it sprang up, because it had no depth in
27 the earth: and when the sun rose, it withered; and because it had no root, it dried Mt. 13, 6.
28 up. And some fell among thorns; and the thorns sprang up with it, and choked it; Lk. 8, 7.
29 and it yielded no fruit. And other fell into excellent *and* good[1] ground; and it Mk. 4, 7b. Lk. 8, 8a.
came up, and grew, and brought forth fruit, some thirty, and some sixty, and some Mk. 4, 8b.
30 a hundred. And when he said that, he cried, He that hath ears that hear, let him Lk. 8, 8c.
31 hear. And when they were alone, his disciples came, and asked him, and said unto Mk. 4, 10.[2]
32 him, What is this parable? and why spakest thou unto them in parables? He Mk. 4, 11.[3]
Arabic, answered and said unto them, Unto you is given the knowledge of the
p. 64 secrets of the kingdom of God; but it is not given unto them that are
33 without. He that hath shall be given unto, and there shall be added; and he that Mt. 13, 12.
34 hath not, that which he hath shall be taken from him also. For this *cause* therefore Mt. 13, 13.
I speak unto them in parables; because they see, and see not; and hear, and hear
35 not, nor understand. And in them is being fulfilled the prophecy of Isaiah, who said, Mt. 13, 14.

Hearing they shall hear, and shall not understand;
And seeing they shall see, and shall not perceive:
36 The heart of this people is waxed gross, Mt. 13, 15.
And their hearing with their ears is become heavy,
And they have closed their eyes;
Lest they should see with their eyes,
And hear with their ears,
And understand with their hearts,
And should return,
And I should heal them.

37, 38 But ye, blessed are your eyes, which see; and your ears, which hear. Blessed Mt. 13, 16. Lk. 10, 23b.
39 are the eyes which see what ye see. Verily I say unto you, Many of the prophets Mt. 13, 17.
and the righteous longed to see what ye see, and saw not; and to hear what ye
40 hear, and heard not. When ye know not this parable, how shall ye know all para- Mk. 4, 13b.
41, 42 bles? Hear ye the parable of the sower. The sower which sowed, sowed the word Mt. 13, 18. Mk. 4, 14.
43 of God. Every one who heareth the word of the kingdom, and understandeth it Mt. 13, 19.
not, the evil one cometh and snatcheth away the word *that hath been* sown in his
44 heart: and this is that *which was* sown on the middle of the highway. But *that* Mt. 13, 20.
which was sown on the rocks is he that heareth the word, and straightway receiveth
45, 46 Arabic, it with joy; only, it hath no root in his soul, but his belief in it *is* for a Mt. 13, 21a. Lk. 8, 13b.
p. 65 time; and whenever there is distress or persecution because of a[4] word, he Mt. 13, 21c.
47 stumbleth[5] quickly. And *that which was* sown among the thorns is he that heareth Mt. 13, 22a.
the word; and the care of this world, and the error of riches, and the rest of the Mk. 4, 19b.
48 other lusts enter, and choke the word, and it becometh without fruit. And that Lk. 8, 15.
which was sown in good ground is he that heareth my word in a pure *and* good
heart, and understandeth it, and holdeth to it, and bringeth forth fruit with patience,
and produceth either a hundredfold or sixtyfold or thirty. Mt. 13, 23b.
49 And he said, So is the kingdom of God, like a man who casteth seed into the Mk. 4, 26.
50 earth, and sleepeth and riseth by night and day, and the seed groweth and cometh Mk. 4, 27.
51 up, whence[6] he knoweth not. And the earth bringeth it to the fruit; and first it Mk. 4, 28.
52 will be blade, and after it ear, and at last perfect wheat in the ear: and whenever Mk. 4, 29.
the fruit ripeneth,[7] he bringeth immediately the sickle, for the harvest hath come.

SECTION XVII.

§17 1 And he set forth to them another parable, and said, The kingdom of heaven is Mt. 13, 24.
2 like a man who sowed good seed in his field; but when men slept, his enemy came Mt. 13, 25.
3 and sowed tares among the wheat, and went away. And when the blade sprang up Mt. 13, 26.
4 and brought forth fruit, there were noticed the tares also. And the servants of the Mt. 13, 27.
master of the house came, and said unto him, Our lord, didst thou not sow good

1 *cf.* Peshitta (against Cur. and Sin.).
2 With additions from Mt. 13, 10, and Lk. 8, 9.
3 And Mt. 13, 11.
4 See above, § 1, 40, note 2.
5 Or, *is seduced* (*cf.* § 25, 17, note).
6 Or, *while.*
7 Lit. *fatteneth*, as in Peshitta.

§17 5 Arabic, seed in thy field? whence are there tares in it? He said unto them, An Mt. 13, 28.
p. 66 enemy hath done this. His servants said unto him, Wilt thou that we go
6 and separate it? He said unto them, Perhaps,[1] when ye separate the tares, ye would Mt. 13, 29.
7 root up with them wheat also. Leave them to grow both together until the harvest: Mt. 13, 30.
and in the time of the harvest I will say unto the reapers, Separate the tares first, and
bind them in bundles to be burned with fire; and gather the wheat into my barns.
8, 9 And he set forth to them another parable, and said, To what is the kingdom of Mt. 13, 31a. Lk. 13, 18b.
10 God like? and to what shall I liken it? and in what parable shall I set it forth? It Mk. 4, 30b. Lk. 13, 19a.
11 is like a grain of mustard seed, which a man took, and planted in his field: and of Mt. 13, 31c.
the number of the things that are sown in the earth it is smaller than all of the things Mk. 4, 31b.
12 which are sown, which are upon the earth; but when it is grown, it is greater than Mt. 13, 32b.
all the herbs, and produceth large branches, so that the birds of heaven make *their* Mk. 4, 32b.
nests in its branches.
13, 14 And he set forth to them another parable: To what shall I liken the kingdom of Mk. 4, 33.[2] Lk. 13, 20b.
15 God? It is like the leaven which a woman took, and kneaded into three measures Mt. 13, 33b.
of flour, until the whole of it was leavened.
16 And Jesus spake all that to the multitudes by way of parables, according as they Mt. 13, 34a. Mk. 4, 33b.
17 were able to hear. And without parables spake he not unto them; that the saying Mt. 13, 34b. Mt. 13, 35.
of the Lord through the prophet might be fulfilled:
I will open my mouth in parables;
And I will utter secrets which were before the foundations[3] of the world.
18 But he explained to his disciples privately everything. Mk. 4, 34b.
19 Then Jesus left[4] the multitudes, and came to the house. And his disciples came Mt. 13, 36.
Arabic, unto him, and said unto him, Explain unto us that parable about the tares
20 p. 67 and the field. He answered and said unto them, He that sowed good seed is Mt. 13, 37.
21 the Son of man; and the field is the world; and the good seed are the children of the Mt. 13, 38.
22 kingdom; and the tares are the children of the evil one; and the enemy that sowed them[5] Mt. 13, 39.
is Satan; and the harvest is the end of the world; and the reapers are the angels.
23 And as the tares are separated and burned in the fire, so shall it be in the end of Mt. 13, 40.
24 this world. The Son of man shall send his angels, and separate from his kingdom Mt. 13, 41.
25 all things that injure, and all the doers of iniquity, and they shall cast them into the Mt. 13, 42.
26 furnace of fire: and there shall be weeping and gnashing of teeth. Then the right- Mt. 13, 43.
eous shall shine as the sun in the kingdom of their Father. Whosoever hath ears that
hear, let him hear.
27 And again the kingdom of heaven is like treasure hid in a field: that which a Mt. 13, 44.
man found and hid; and, for his pleasure in it, went and sold all that he had, and
bought that field.
28 And again the kingdom of heaven is like a man *that is* a merchant seeking ex- Mt. 13, 45.
29 cellent pearls; and when he found one pearl of great price, he went and sold every- Mt. 13, 46.
thing that he had, and bought it.
30 And again the kingdom of heaven is like a net that was cast[6] into the sea, and Mt. 13, 47.
31 gathered of every kind: and when it was filled, they drew it up on to the shore of Mt. 13, 48.
the sea, and sat down to select; and the good of them they threw into the vessels,
32 and the bad they threw outside. Thus shall it be in the end of the world: the angels Mt. 13, 49.
33 shall go forth, and separate the wicked from among the good, and shall cast them Mt. 13, 50.
into the furnace of fire: there shall be weeping and gnashing of teeth.
34 Jesus said unto them, Have ye understood all these *things?* They said unto Mt. 13, 51.
35 Arabic, him, Yea, our Lord. He said unto them, Therefore every scribe that be- Mt. 13, 52.
p. 68 cometh a disciple of the kingdom of heaven is like a man that is a householder, who bringeth out of his treasures the new and the old.
36, 37 And when Jesus had finished all these parables, he removed thence, and came Mt. 13, 53. Mt. 13, 54.
to his city; and he taught them in their synagogues, so that they were perplexed.
38 And when the sabbath came, Jesus began to teach in the synagogue; and many of Mk. 6, 2.
39 those that heard marvelled, and said, Whence came these things to this *man?* And
many envied him and gave no heed to him, but said, What is this wisdom that is

1 See above, § 4, 24, note. 2 Or rather Mt. 13, 33a.
3 The word (if not a corruption of that used in the Brit. Mus. text of Ibn-aṭ-Ṭayyib's Commentary, and in § 43, 46, where, however, according to Ciasca's foot-note, it was not the word first written by the scribe) is Syriac. Perhaps it means *the ends of the earth* (see P. Smith, *Thes. Syr.*). Still a third word is used in § 47, 42.
4 *cf.* § 11, 32, note. 5 Singular. 6 *cf.* note to § 10, 8.

§17 given to this *man*, that there should happen at his hands such as these mighty works?[1]
40 Is not this a carpenter, son of a carpenter? and is not his mother called Mary? and Mt. 13, 55.
41 his brethren, James, and Joses, and Simon, and Judas? And his sisters, all of them, Mt. 13, 56.
42 lo, are they not all with us? Whence hath this *man* all these things? And they Mt. 13, 57.
were in doubt concerning him. And Jesus knew their opinion, and said unto them, Lk. 4, 23.
Will ye haply[2] say unto me this proverb, Physician, heal first thyself: and all that
43 we have heard that thou didst in Capernaum, do here also in thine own city? And Lk. 4, 24.
he said, Verily I say unto you, A prophet is not received in his own city, nor among
44 his brethren: for a prophet is not despised, save in his *own* city, and among his *own* Mk. 6, 4b.
45 kin, and in his *own* house. Verily I say unto you, In the days of Elijah the prophet, Lk. 4, 25.
there were many widows among the children of Israel, when the heaven held back
46 three years and six months, and there was a great famine in all the land; and Elijah Lk. 4, 26.
Arabic, was not sent to one of them, save to Zarephath of Sidon, to a woman that was
47 p. 69 a widow. And many lepers were among the children of Israel in the days of Lk. 4, 27.
Elisha the prophet; but not one of them was cleansed, save Naaman the Nabathæan.[3]
48 And he was not able to do there many mighty works,[4] because of their unbelief; Mk. 6, 5.
49 except that he laid his hand upon a few of the sick, and healed *them*. And he mar- Mk. 6, 6a.
50 velled at their lack of faith. And when those who were in the synagogue heard, Lk. 4, 28.
51 they were all filled with wrath; and they rose up, and brought him forth outside the Lk. 4, 29.
city, and brought him to the brow of the hill upon which their city was built, that
52 they might cast him from its summit: but he passed through among them and went Lk. 4, 30.
away.
53 And he went about in the villages which *were* around Nazareth, and taught in Mk. 6, 6b.
their synagogues.

SECTION XVIII.

§18 1 At that time Herod the tetrarch heard of the fame of Jesus, and all the things Mt. 14, 1. Lk. 9, 7b.
which came to pass at his hand; and he marvelled, for he had obtained excellent Mk. 6, 14b.
2 information concerning him.[5] And *some* men said that John the Baptist was risen Lk. 9, 7c.
3 from among the dead; and[6] others said that Elijah had appeared; and others, Jere- Lk. 9, 8a. Mt. 16, 14b.
4 miah; and others, that a prophet of the old prophets was risen; and others said that he Lk. 9, 8b. Mk. 6, 15b.
5 was a prophet like one of the prophets. Herod said to his servants, This is John the Mk. 6, 16.
Baptist, he whom I beheaded; he is risen from among the dead: therefore mighty Mt. 14, 2b.
6 Arabic, works result from him. For Herod him*self* had sent and taken John, and cast Mk. 6, 17.
p. 70 him into prison, for the sake of Herodias his brother Philip's wife, whom he
7 had taken. And John said to Herod, Thou hast no authority to take the wife of thy Mk. 6, 18.
8 brother. And Herodias avoided him and wished to kill him; and she could not. Mk. 6, 19.
9 But Herod feared John, for he knew that he was a righteous man *and* a holy; and Mk. 6, 20.
10 he guarded him, and heard him much, and did, and obeyed him with gladness. And Mt. 14, 5.
he wished to kill him; but he feared the people, for they adhered to him as the
11 prophet. And there was a celebrated day, and Herod had made a feast for his Mk. 6, 21.
great men on the day of his anniversary,[7] and for the officers and for the chief men
12 of Galilee. And the daughter of Herodias came in and danced in the midst of the Mk. 6, 22.
company, and pleased Herod and those that sat with him. And the king said to the
13 damsel, Ask of me what thou wilt, and I will give it thee. And he sware unto her, Mk. 6, 23.
14 Whatsoever thou shalt ask, I will give it thee, to the half of my kingdom. And she Mk. 6, 24.
went out, and said unto her mother, What shall I ask him?[8] She said unto her, The
15 head of John the Baptist. And immediately she came in hastily to the king, and Mk. 6, 25.
said unto him, I desire in this hour that thou give me on a dish the head of John
16 the Baptist. And the king was exceeding sorry; but because of the oath and the Mk. 6, 26.
17 guests he did not wish to refuse her. But immediately the king sent an executioner, Mk. 6, 27.
and commanded that he should bring the head of John: and he went and cut off

1 Lit. *powers*.
2 *cf.* above, § 4, 24, note.
3 Of the Syriac versions Cur. and Sin. are wanting. Pesh. has *Aramæan*.
4 Lit. *powers*.
5 There can be little doubt that this is the meaning of the Arabic. There is nothing like it in the Peshitta; the Curetonian is of course lacking; but the phrase in the Sinaitic is very similar.
6 Here begins verse 8a in Greek.
7 Perhaps *appointment* (*cf.* Moesinger, p. 165; but Isho'dad [Harris, *Fragments*, p. 65] and the Brit. Mus. text of Ibn-aṭ-Ṭayyib's Commentary have the ordinary reading).
8 Or simply *ask*.

§18 18 the head of John in the prison, and brought it on a dish, and delivered it to the Mk. 6, 28.
19 damsel; and the damsel gave it to her mother. And his disciples heard, and came Mk. 6, 29.
Arabic, and took his body, and buried it. And they came and told[1] Jesus what Mt. 14, 12b.
20 p. 71 had happened. And for this cause Herod said, I beheaded John: who Lk. 9, 9.
21 is this, of whom I hear these things. And he desired to see him. And Jesus, when Mt. 14, 13a.
he heard, removed thence in a boat to a waste place alone, to the other side of the Jo. 6, 1b.
sea of the Galilee of Tiberias.[2]

22 And many saw them going, and knew them, and hastened by land[3] from all the Mk. 6, 33a.
cities, and came thither beforehand; for they saw the signs which he was doing on the Jo. 6, 2b.
23, 24 sick. And Jesus went up into the mountain, and sat there with his disciples. And Jo. 6, 3. Jo. 6, 4.
25 the feast of the passover of the Jews was near. And Jesus lifted up his eyes, and saw Jo. 6, 5a.
great multitudes coming to him. And he was moved with compassion for them, for Mk. 6, 34b.
26 they were like sheep that *were* without a shepherd. And he received them, and spake Lk. 9, 11b.
to them concerning the kingdom of God, and healed those who had need of healing.

27 And when the evening approached,[4] his disciples came to him, and said unto Mt. 14, 15a.
28 him, The place is desert, and the time is past; send away the multitudes of the peo- Mk. 6, 36.
ple,[5] that they may go to the towns and villages which are around us, and buy for
29 themselves bread; for they have nothing to eat. But he said unto them, They have Mt. 14, 16.
30 no need to go away; give ye them what may be eaten. They said unto him, We have Mt. 14, 17a.
not here *enough*. He said unto Philip, Whence shall we buy bread that these may eat? Jo. 6, 5b.
31, 32 And he said that proving him; and he knew what he was resolved to do. Philip said Jo. 6, 6. Jo. 6, 7.
Arabic, unto him, Two hundred pennyworth of bread would not suffice them after[6]
33 p. 72 every one of them hath taken a small amount. One of his disciples said unto Jo. 6, 8.
34 him (namely, Andrew the brother of Simon Cephas), Here is a lad having five loaves Jo. 6, 9.
35 of barley and two fishes: but this amount, what is it for all these? But wilt thou Lk. 9, 13b.[7]
that we go and buy for all the people what may be eaten? for we have no more
36 than these five loaves and the two fishes. And the grass was plentiful in that place. Jo. 6, 10b.[8]
Jesus said unto them, Arrange all the people that they may sit down on the grass,
37 fifty people in a company. And the disciples did so. And all the people sat down Mk. 6, 40.
38 by companies, by hundreds and fifties. Then Jesus said unto them, Bring hither Mt. 14, 18.
39 those five loaves and the two fishes. And when they brought him that, Jesus took Mk. 6, 41a.
the bread and the fish, and looked to heaven, and blessed, and divided, and gave to
40 his disciples to set before them; and the disciples set for the multitudes the bread Mt. 14, 19b.
41 and the fish; and they ate, all of them, and were satisfied. And when they were Mt. 14, 20a. Jo. 6, 12.
satisfied, he said unto his disciples, Gather the fragments that remain over, that noth-
42 ing be lost. And they gathered, and filled twelve baskets with fragments, being Jo. 6, 13.
those that remained over from those which ate of the five barley loaves and the two
43 fishes. And those people who ate were five thousand, besides the women and children. Mt. 14, 21.
44 Arabic, And straightway he pressed his disciples to go up into the ship, and Mk. 6, 45.
p. 73 that they should go before him unto the other side to Bethsaida, while he
45 him*self* should send away the multitudes. And those people who saw the sign which Jo. 6, 14.
46 Jesus did, said, Of a truth this is a prophet who hath come into the world. And Jo. 6, 15.
Jesus knew their purpose to come and take him, and make him a king; and he left
them, and went up into the mountain alone for prayer.

47, 48 And when the nightfall was near, his disciples went down unto the sea, and sat[9] Jo. 6, 16. Jo. 6, 17.
in a boat, and came to the side of Capernaum. And the darkness came on, and Jesus
49 had not come to them. And the sea was stirred up against them by reason of a vio- Jo. 6, 18.
50 lent wind that blew. And the boat was distant from the land many furlongs, and Mt. 14, 24.
they were much damaged by the waves, and the wind was against them.

SECTION XIX.

§19 1 And in the fourth watch of the night Jesus came unto them, walking upon the Mt. 14, 25.
2 water, after they had rowed[10] with difficulty about twenty-five or thirty furlongs. Jo. 6, 19a, c.

1 Or, *to tell.*
2 A misunderstanding or slavish reproduction of the Syriac. The Brit. Mus. text of Ibn-aṭ-Ṭayyib's Commentary has *of Galilee, Tiberias.*
3 *cf.* Syriac versions and margin of R. V.
4 Or, *came.*
5 *cf.* the addition in the Sinaitic Syriac.
6 Probably a mistaken rendering of the ordinary Syriac reading.
7 Considerably changed.
8 And Lk. 9, 14b, 15a.
9 *cf.* Syriac versions.
10 Lit. *travelled.*

§19 3 And when he drew near unto their boat, his disciples saw him walking on the water; Mt. 14, 26.
and they were troubled, and supposed that it was a false appearance; and they cried
4 out from their fear. But Jesus straightway spake unto them, and said, Take courage, Mt. 14, 27.
5 for it is I; fear not. Then Cephas answered and said unto him, My Lord, if it be thou, Mt. 14, 28.
6 bid me to come unto thee on the water. And Jesus said unto him, Come. And Mt. 14, 29.
7 Cephas went down out of the boat, and walked on the water to come unto Jesus. But Mt. 14, 30.
Arabic, when he saw the wind strong, he feared, and was on the point of sink-
8 p. 74 ing; and he lifted up his voice, and said, My Lord, save me. And im- Mt. 14, 31.
mediately our Lord stretched out his hand and took *hold of* him, and said unto him,
9 Thou of little faith, why didst thou doubt? And when Jesus came near, he went up Mt. 14, 32.
10 unto them into the boat, he and Simon, and immediately the wind ceased. And Mt. 14, 33.
those that were in the ship came and worshipped him, and said, Truly thou art the
11 Son of God. And straightway that ship arrived at the land which they made for. Jo. 6, 21*b*.
12 And when they came out of the ship to the land, they marvelled greatly and were Mk. 6, 54*a*. Mk. 6, 51*b*.
13 perplexed in themselves: and they had not understood by means of [1] that bread, Mk. 6, 52.
because their heart was gross.

14 And when the people of that region knew of the arrival of Jesus, they made Mk. 6, 54. Mk. 6, 55.
haste in all that land, and began to bring those that were diseased,[2] borne in their
15 beds to the place where they heard that he was. And wheresoever the place *might* Mk. 6, 56.
be which he entered, of the villages or the cities, they laid the sick in the markets,
and sought of him that they might touch [3] were it only the edge of his garment:
and all that touched [4] him were healed and lived.[5]

16 And on the day after that, the multitude which was standing on the shore of the Jo. 6, 22*a*.
sea saw that there was there no other ship save that into which the disciples had
17 gone up, and that Jesus went not up into the ship with his disciples (but there were Jo. 6, 23.
other ships from Tiberias near [6] the place where they ate the bread when Jesus blessed
18 *it*): and when that multitude saw that Jesus was not there, nor yet his disciples, they Jo. 6, 24.
19 Arabic, went up into those ships, and came to Capernaum, and sought Jesus. And Jo. 6, 25.
p. 75 when they found him on the other side of the sea, they said unto him, Our
20 Master, when camest thou hither? Jesus answered and said unto them, Verily, verily, Jo. 6, 26.
I say unto you, Ye have not sought me because of [7] your seeing the signs, but because of
21 your eating the bread and being satisfied. Serve not the food which perisheth, but the Jo. 6, 27.
food which abideth in eternal life,[8] which the Son of man will give unto you: him [9]
22 hath God the Father sealed. They said unto him, What shall we do that we may Jo. 6, 28.
23 work the work of God? Jesus answered and said unto them, This is the work of Jo. 6, 29.
24 God, that ye believe in him whom he hath sent. They said unto him, What sign Jo. 6, 30.
hast thou done, that we may see, and believe in thee? what hast thou wrought?
25 Our fathers ate the manna in the wilderness; as it was written, Bread from heaven Jo. 6, 31.
26 gave he them to eat. Jesus said unto them, Verily, verily, I say unto you, Moses Jo. 6, 32.
gave you not bread from heaven; but my Father gave [10] you the bread of truth [11] from
27 heaven. The bread of God is that which came down from heaven and gave the Jo. 6, 33.
28, 29 world life. They said unto him, Our Lord, give us at all times this bread. Jesus Jo. 6, 34. Jo. 6, 35.
said unto them, I am the bread of life: whosoever cometh unto me shall not hun-
30 ger, and whosoever believeth in me shall not thirst for ever. But I said unto you, Jo. 6, 36.
31 Ye have seen me, and have not believed. And all that my Father hath given to me Jo. 6, 37.
cometh unto me; and whosoever cometh unto me I shall not cast him forth with-
32 out. I came down from heaven, not to do my *own* will, but to do the will of him Jo. 6, 38.
33 that sent me; and this is the will of him that sent me, that I should lose nothing of Jo. 6, 39.
34 Arabic, that which he gave me, but raise it up in the last day. This is the will of Jo. 6, 40.
p. 76 my Father, that every one that seeth the Son, and believeth in him, should
have eternal life; and I will raise him up in the last day.

35 The Jews therefore murmured against him because of his saying, I am the bread Jo. 6, 41.
36 which came down from heaven. And they said, Is not this Jesus, the son of Joseph, Jo. 6, 42.
whose father and mother we know? then how saith this *man*, I came down from
37, 38 heaven? Jesus answered and said unto them, Murmur not one with another. No Jo. 6, 43. Jo. 6, 44.

1 Lit. *from*. 2 Strictly used of severe chronic disease. 3 *cf.* § 12, 13, and note to § 8, 17.
4 The word used at § 12, 35. 5 Or, *revived*, i.e., *made to live*. 6 Lit. *on the border of*.
7 Or, *for the sake of*. 8 *Sic*. 9 Lit. *this*. 10 Represents a mistaken vocalisation of the Peshitta.
11 Lit. *equity;* see above, § 3, 53, note.

§ 19 man is able to come unto me, except the Father which sent me draw him; and I will
39 raise him up in the last day. It is written in the prophet, They shall all be the taught Jo. 6, 45.
of God. Every one who heareth from the Father now,[1] and learneth of him, cometh
40 unto me. No man now seeth the Father; but he that is from God, he it is that seeth Jo. 6, 46.
41 the Father. Verily, verily, I say unto you, Whosoever believeth in me hath eternal Jo. 6, 47.
42, 43 life. I am the bread of life. Your fathers ate the manna in the wilderness, and Jo. 6, 48. Jo. 6, 49.
44 they died. This is the bread which came down from heaven, that a man may eat Jo. 6, 50.
45 of it, and not die. I am the bread of life which came down from heaven: Jo. 6, 51.
and if a man eat of this bread he shall live for ever: and the bread which I shall give Jo. 6, 51*b*.[2]
is my body, which I give for the life of the world.
46 The Jews therefore quarrelled one with another, and said, How can he give us Jo. 6, 52.
47 Arabic, his body that we may eat it? Jesus said unto them, Verily, verily, I say unto Jo. 6, 53.
p. 77 you, If ye do not eat the body of the Son of man and drink his blood, ye shall
48 not have life in yourselves. Whosoever eateth of my body and drinketh of my blood Jo. 6, 54.
49 hath eternal life; and I will raise him up in the last day. My body truly is meat,[3] and Jo. 6, 55.
50 my blood truly is drink.[4] Whosoever eateth my body and drinketh my blood abideth Jo. 6, 56.
51 in me, and I in him—as the living Father sent me, and I am alive because of the Jo. 6, 57.
52 Father; and whosoever eateth me, he also shall live because of me. This is the Jo. 6, 58.
bread which came down from heaven: and not according as your fathers ate the
53 manna, and died: whosoever eateth of this bread shall live for ever. This he said in Jo. 6, 59.
54 the synagogue, when he was teaching in Capernaum. And many of his disciples, Jo. 6, 60.
when they heard, said, This word is hard; who is he that can hear it?

SECTION XX.

§ 20 1 And Jesus knew within himself that his disciples were murmuring because of Jo. 6, 61.
2 that, and he said unto them, Doth this trouble you? *What* if ye should see the Son Jo. 6, 62.
3 of man then ascend to the place where he was of old? It is the spirit that quick- Jo. 6, 63.
eneth, and the body profiteth nothing: the words[5] that I speak unto you are spirit
4 and life. But there are some of you that do not believe. And Jesus knew before- Jo. 6, 64.
hand who they were who should[6] not believe, and who it was that should betray
5 him. And he said unto them, Therefore I said unto you, No man can come unto Jo. 6, 65.
me, if that hath not been given him by the Father.
6 Arabic, And because of this word many of his disciples turned back and walked Jo. 6, 66.
7 p. 78 not with him. And Jesus said unto the twelve, Do ye haply also wish to Jo. 6, 67.
8 go away? Simon Cephas answered and said, My Lord, to whom shall we go? thou Jo. 6, 68.
9 hast the words of eternal life. And we have believed and known that thou art the Jo. 6, 69.
10 Messiah, the Son of the living God. Jesus said unto them, Did not I choose you, Jo. 6, 70.
11 ye company of the twelve, and of you one is a devil? He said that because of Judas Jo. 6, 71.
the son of Simon Iscariot; for he, being of the twelve, was purposed to[7] betray him.
12 And while he was speaking, one of the Pharisees came asking of him that he Lk. 11, 37.
13 would eat with him: and he went in, and reclined *to meat*. And that Pharisee, when Lk. 11, 38.
14 he saw it,[8] marvelled that he had not first cleansed himself before his eating. Jesus Lk. 11, 39.
said unto him, Now do ye Pharisees wash the outside of the cup and the dish, and
ye think that ye are cleansed; but your inside is full of injustice and wickedness.
15, 16 Ye of little mind, did not he that made the outside make the inside? Now give Lk. 11, 40. Lk. 11, 41.
what ye have[9] in alms, and everything *shall be* clean unto you.
17, 18 And there came to him Pharisees and scribes, come from Jerusalem. And when Mk. 7, 1. Mk. 7, 2.
they saw some of his disciples eating bread while they had not washed their hands,
19 they found fault. For all of the Jews and the Pharisees, if they wash not their Mk. 7, 3.
20 hands thoroughly, eat not; for they held[10] to the ordinance[11] of the elders. And they Mk. 7, 4.
ate not what was bought from the market, except they washed it; and many other
things did they keep of what they had received, such as the washing of cups, and
21 measures, and vessels of brass, and couches. And scribes[12] and Pharisees asked him, Mk. 7, 5.

1 i.e., *therefore* (see note, § 9, 21).
2 In Ciasca's text Jo. 6, 51*b*–71 are cited as 6, 52–72. (See Introduction, 20, note.) 3 Or, *eaten*.
4 Or, *drunk*. 5 Lit. *speech*. 6 Or, *did*. 7 Or, *was to*. 8 Or, *him*. 9 *cf.* Peshitta.
10 i.e., *were holding*. 11 Or, *custom, tradition;* and so wherever the word occurs. 12 *Sic*.

§ 20 Arabic, Why do thy disciples not walk according to the ordinances of the elders, but
22 p. 79 eat bread without washing their hands? Jesus answered and said unto Mt. 15, 3.
them, Why do ye also overstep the command of God by reason of your ordinance?
23 God said, Honour thy father and thy mother; and, Whosoever revileth his father and Mt. 15, 4*a*. Mk. 7, 10*b*.
24 his mother shall surely die. But ye say, If a man say to his father or to his mother, Mk. 7, 11.
25 What thou receivest [1] from me is an offering,—and ye [1] suffer him not to do any- Mk. 7, 12.
26 thing for his father or his mother; and ye [1] make void and reject the word of God Mk. 7, 13.
by reason of the ordinance that ye have ordained and commanded, such as the wash-
27 ing of cups and measures, and what resembles that ye do much. And ye forsook Mk. 7, 8.
28 the command of God, and held to the ordinance of men. Do [2] ye well to wrong [3] Mk. 7, 9.
29 the command of God in order that ye may establish your ordinance? Ye hypo- Mt. 15, 7.
crites, well did Isaiah the prophet prophesy concerning you, and say,
30 This people honoureth me with its [4] lips; Mt. 15, 8.
But their heart is very far from me.
31 But in vain do they fear me, Mt. 15, 9.
In that they teach the commands of men.
32 And Jesus called all the multitude, and said unto them, Hear me, all of you, and Mk. 7, 14.
33 understand: nothing without the man, which then enters him, is able to defile him; Mk. 7, 15.
34 but what goeth out of him, that it is which defileth the man. He that hath ears Mk. 7, 16.
35 that hear, let him hear. Then his disciples drew near, and said unto him, Knowest Mt. 15, 12.
36 thou that the Pharisees which heard this word were angry? He answered and said Mt. 15, 13.
unto them, Every plant which my Father which is in heaven planted not shall be
37 Arabic, uprooted. Let them alone; for they are blind leading blind. And if the Mt. 15, 14.
p. 80 blind lead [5] the blind, both of them shall fall into a hollow.
38 And when Jesus entered the house from the multitude, Simon Cephas asked him, Mk. 7, 17*a*. Mt. 15, 15.
39 and said unto him, My Lord, explain to us that parable. He said unto them, Do Mk. 7, 18*b*.
ye also thus not understand? Know ye not that everything that entereth into the
40 man from without cannot defile him; because it entereth not into his heart; it enter- Mk. 7, 19.
eth into his stomach only, and thence is cast forth in the cleansing which maketh
41 clean all the food? [6] The thing which goeth forth from the mouth of the man pro- Mt. 15, 18.
42 ceedeth from his heart, and it is that which defileth the man. From within [7] the Mk. 7, 21.
43 heart of men proceed evil thoughts, fornication, adultery, theft, false witness, mur- Mk. 7, 22.
der, injustice, wickedness, deceit, stupidity, evil eye, calumny, pride, foolishness:
44 these evils all of them from within proceed from the heart, and they are *the things* Mk. 7, 23.
45 which defile the man: but if a man eat while he washeth not his hands, he is not Mt. 15, 20*b*.
defiled.
46 And Jesus went out thence, and came to the borders of Tyre and Sidon. Mt. 15, 21*a*. Mk. 7, 24*b*.
And he entered into a certain house, and desired that no man should know it; [8] and
47 he could not be hid. But straightway a Canaanitish woman, whose daughter had an Mk. 7, 25*a*.
48, 49 unclean spirit, heard of him. And that woman was a Gentile of Emesa of Syria. And Mk. 7, 26*a*. Mt. 15, 22*b*.
she came out after him, crying out, and saying, Have mercy upon me, my Lord, *thou*
50 son of David; for my daughter is seized in an evil way by Satan. [9] And he answered Mt. 15, 23.
Arabic, her not a word. And his disciples came and besought him, and said, Send
51 p. 81 her away; for she crieth after us. He answered and said unto them, I was Mt. 15, 24.
52 not sent except to the sheep that are gone astray of the house of Israel. But she Mt. 15, 25.
came and worshipped him, and said, My Lord, help me, have mercy upon me.
53 Jesus said unto her, It is not seemly that the children's bread should be taken and Mt. 15, 26.
54 thrown to the dogs. But she said, Yea, my Lord: the dogs also eat of the crumbs Mt. 15, 27.
55 that fall from their masters' tables, and live. Then said Jesus unto her, O woman, Mt. 15, 28*a*.
56 great is thy faith: it shall be unto thee as thou hast desired. Go then *thy way;* and Mk. 7, 29*b*.
57 because of this word, the devil is gone out of thy daughter. And her daughter was Mt. 15, 28*b*.
58 healed in that hour. And that woman went away to her house, and found her Mk. 7, 30.
daughter laid upon the bed, and the devil gone out of her.

1 The printed Arabic text has *he receiveth* and *they*, resulting from a misplacement of diacritical points by an Arabic copyist. 2 Here begins verse 9 in Greek. 3 The Syriac word for *injure* also means *reject, deny*.
4 *Sic.* 5 The Arabic word is here used with a Syriac meaning.
6 This clause in the Peshitta is not very clear, and the Arabic version fails to get from it the meaning of the Greek.
7 Or, *From within, from.* 8 Or, *about him.* 9 Or, *the devil.*

SECTION XXI.

§ 21 1 And Jesus went out again from the borders of Tyre and Sidon, and came to the Mk. 7, 31.
2 sea of Galilee, towards the borders of Decapolis. And they brought unto him one Mk. 7, 32.
dumb and deaf, and entreated him that he would lay his hand upon him and heal
3 him. And he drew him away from the multitude, and went away alone, and spat Mk. 7, 33.
4 upon his fingers, and thrust *them* into his ears, and touched his tongue; and looked Mk. 7, 34.
5 to heaven, and sighed, and said unto him, Be opened. And in that hour his ears Mk. 7, 35.
6 were opened, and the bond of his tongue was loosed, and he spake with ease. And Mk. 7, 36.
Jesus charged them much that they should not tell this to any man: but the more
7 he charged them, *the more* they increased in publishing, and marvelled much, and Mk. 7, 37.
Arabic, said, This *man* doeth everything well: he made the deaf to hear, and those
p. 82 that lacked speech to speak.
8, 9 And while he was passing through the land of Samaria, he came to one of the Jo. 4, 4. Jo. 4, 5.
cities of the Samaritans, called Sychar, beside the field which Jacob gave to Joseph
10 his son. And there was there a spring of water of Jacob's. And Jesus was fatigued Jo. 4, 6.
from the exertion of the way, and sat at the spring. And the time was about the
11 sixth hour.[1] And a woman of Samaria came to draw water; and Jesus said unto Jo. 4, 7.
12 her, Give me water, that I may drink. And his disciples had entered into the city Jo. 4, 8.
13 to buy for themselves food. And that Samaritan woman said unto him, How dost Jo. 4, 9.
thou, being a Jew, ask me to give thee to drink, while I am a Samaritan woman?
14 (And the Jews mingle not with the Samaritans.[2]) Jesus answered and said unto Jo. 4, 10.
her, If thou knewest the gift of God, and who this is that said unto thee, Give me
15 to drink; thou wouldest ask him, and he would give thee the water of life. That Jo. 4, 11.
woman said unto him, My Lord, thou hast no bucket, and the well is deep: from
16 whence hast thou the water of life? Can it be that thou art greater than our father Jo. 4, 12.
Jacob, who gave us this well, and drank from it, and his children, and his sheep?
17 Jesus answered and said unto her, Every one that drinketh of this water shall thirst Jo. 4, 13.
18 again: but whosoever drinketh of the water which I shall give him shall not thirst for Jo. 4, 14.
ever; but the water which I shall give him shall be in him a spring of water springing
19 up unto eternal life. That woman said unto him, My Lord, give me of this water, that Jo. 4, 15.
20 I may not thirst again, neither come and draw water from here. Jesus said unto her, Jo. 4, 16.
21 Arabic, Go and call thy husband, and come hither. She said unto him, I have no Jo. 4, 17.
22 p. 83 husband. Jesus said unto her, Thou saidst well, I have no husband: five Jo. 4, 18.
husbands hast thou had, and this *man* whom thou hast now is not thy husband; and
23 in this thou saidst truly. That woman said unto him, My Lord, I perceive thee to Jo. 4, 19.
24 be a prophet. Our fathers worshipped in this mountain; and ye say that in Jeru- Jo. 4, 20.
25 salem is the place in which worship must be. Jesus said unto her, Woman, believe Jo. 4, 21.
me, an hour cometh, when neither in this mountain, nor yet in Jerusalem, shall ye wor-
26 ship the Father. Ye worship that which ye know not: but we worship that which Jo. 4, 22.
27 we know; for salvation is of the Jews. But an hour cometh, and now is, when the Jo. 4, 23.
true worshippers shall worship the Father in spirit and truth: and the Father also
28 seeketh such as these worshippers. For God is a Spirit: and they that worship him Jo. 4, 24.
29 must worship him in spirit and in truth. That woman said unto him, I know that Jo. 4, 25.
30 the Messiah cometh: and when he is come, he will teach us everything. Jesus said Jo. 4, 26.
unto her, I that speak unto thee am he.
31 And while he was speaking, his disciples came; and they wondered how he would Jo. 4, 27.
speak[3] with a woman; but not one of them said unto him, What seekest thou? or,
32 What[4] speakest thou with her? And the woman left her waterpot, and went to the Jo. 4, 28.
33 city, and said to the people, Come, and see a man who told me all that *ever* I did: Jo. 4, 29.
34 perhaps then he is the Messiah. And people went out from the city, and came to Jo. 4, 30.
35 him. And in the mean while his disciples besought him, and said unto him, Our Jo. 4, 31.
36, 37 master, eat. And he said unto them, I have food to eat that ye know not. And Jo. 4, 32. Jo. 4, 33.
the disciples said amongst themselves, Can any one have brought him aught to eat?[5]

1 Lit. *six hours* (*cf.* Syr.).
2 For the form *cf.* below, § 34, 40.
3 Or, *was speaking*.
4 But see note to § 7, 38.
5 The text is uncertain.

§21 38 Jesus said unto them, My food is to do the will of him that sent me, and to accom- Jo. 4, 34.
39 Arabic, plish his work. Said ye not that after four months cometh the harvest? Jo. 4, 35.
p. 84 behold, I therefore say unto you, Lift up your eyes, and behold the lands,
40 that they have become white, and the harvest is already come.[1] And he that reap- Jo. 4, 36.
eth receiveth his wages, and gathereth the fruit of eternal life;[2] and the sower and
41 the reaper rejoice together. For in this is found the word of truth, One soweth, and Jo. 4, 37.
42 another reapeth. And I sent you to reap that in which ye have not laboured: others Jo. 4, 38.
laboured, and ye have entered on their labour.
43 And from that city many of the Samaritans believed in him because of the words Jo. 4, 39.
44 of that woman, who testified and said, He told me all that *ever* I did. And when Jo. 4, 40.
those Samaritans came unto him, they besought him to abide with them; and he
45, 46 abode with them two days. And many believed in him because of his word; and Jo. 4, 41. Jo. 4, 42.
they said to that woman, Now not because of thy saying have we believed in him:
we have heard and known that this truly is the Messiah, the Saviour of the world.
47, 48 And after two days Jesus went out thence and departed to Galilee. And Jesus Jo. 4, 43. Jo. 4, 44.
49 testified that a prophet is not honoured in his own city. And when he came to Jo. 4, 45*a*.
Galilee, the Galilæans received him.

SECTION XXII.

§22 1 And when Jesus came to a certain village, there drew near to him a leper, and Lk. 5, 12.
fell at his feet, and besought him, and said unto him, If thou wilt, thou art able to
2 cleanse me. And Jesus had mercy upon him, and stretched forth his hand, and Mk. 1, 41.
3 touched him, and said, I will cleanse[3] thee. And immediately his leprosy departed Mk. 1, 42.
4 from him, and he was cleansed. And he sternly charged him, and sent him out, Mk. 1, 43.
5 Arabic, and said unto him, See that thou tell *not* any man: but go and shew thy- Mk. 1, 44.
p. 85 self to the priests, and offer an offering for thy cleansing as Moses com-
6 manded for their testimony. But he, when he went out, began to publish much, and Mk. 1, 45*a*.
spread abroad the news, so that Jesus could not enter into any of the cities openly,
for the extent to which the report of him spread, but he remained without in a des-
7 ert place. And much people came unto him from one place and another,[4] to hear Lk. 5, 15.
8 his word, and that they might be healed of their pains. And he used to withdraw Lk. 5, 16.
from them into the desert, and pray.
9 And after that, was the feast of the Jews; and Jesus went up to Jerusalem. Jo. 5, 1.
10 And there was in Jerusalem a place prepared for bathing,[5] which was called in Jo. 5, 2.
11 Hebrew the House of Mercy, having five porches. And there were laid in them Jo. 5, 3.
much people of the sick, and blind, and lame, and paralysed, waiting for the mov-
12 ing of the water. And the angel from time to time went down into the place of Jo. 5, 4.
bathing,[5] and moved the water; and the first that went down after the moving of
13 the water, every pain that he had was healed. And a man was there who had a Jo. 5, 5.
14 disease for thirty-eight years. And Jesus saw this *man* laid, and knew[6] that he had Jo. 5, 6.
15 been thus a long time; and he said unto him, Wouldest thou be made whole? That Jo. 5, 7.
diseased one answered and said, Yea, my Lord, I have no man, when the water mov-
eth, to put me into the bathing-place; but when I come, another goeth down before
16, 17 me. Jesus said unto him, Rise, take thy bed, and walk. And immediately that Jo. 5, 8. Jo. 5, 9.
man was healed; and he rose, and carried his bed, and walked.
18 And that day was a sabbath. And when the Jews saw that healed one, they[7] said Jo. 5, 10.
19 unto him, It is a sabbath; thou hast no authority to carry thy bed. And he answered Jo. 5, 11.
and said unto them, He that made me whole, the same said unto me, Take thy bed,
20 Arabic, and walk. They asked him therefore, Who is this man that said unto thee, Jo. 5, 12.
21 p. 86 Take thy bed, and walk? But he that was healed knew not who it was; for Jo. 5, 13.
Jesus had removed from that place to another, because of the press of the great mul-
22 titude which was in that place. And after two days Jesus happened upon him in the Jo. 5, 14.
temple, and said unto him, Behold, thou art whole: sin not again, lest there come upon

1 Or, *come beforehand*.
2 So in the Arabic, contrary to the usual practice of this writer (*cf.* § 6, 19).
3 Lit. *to cleanse*.
4 This phrase does not occur in the Syriac versions (Cur. wanting), but is obviously a Syriac construction.
5 Or, *baptism*. The phrase almost exactly reproduces the Syriac versions.
6 Or, *learned*.
7 Vat. MS. has *he*.

§22 23 thee what is worse than the first. And that man went, and said to the Jews that it Jo. 5, 15.
24 was Jesus that had healed him. And because of that the Jews persecuted Jesus and Jo. 5, 16.
25 sought to kill him, because he was doing this on the sabbath. And Jesus said unto Jo. 5, 17.
26 them, My Father worketh until now, and I also work. And because of this espe- Jo. 5, 18.
cially the Jews sought to kill him, not because he profaned the sabbath only; but
for his saying also that God was his Father, and his making himself equal with God.
27 Jesus answered and said unto them, Verily, verily, I say unto you, The Son cannot Jo. 5, 19.
do anything of himself, but what he seeth the Father do; what the Father doeth,
28 that the Son also doeth like him. The Father loveth his Son, and everything that Jo. 5, 20.
he doeth he sheweth him: and more than these works will he shew him, that ye
29 may marvel. And as the Father raiseth the dead and giveth them life, so the Son Jo. 5, 21.
30 also giveth life to whomsoever he will. And the Father judgeth no man, but hath Jo. 5, 22.
31 given all judgement unto the Son; that every man may honour the Son, as he honour- Jo. 5, 23.
eth the Father. And he that honoureth not the Son honoureth not the Father which
32 sent him. Verily, verily, I say unto you, Whosoever heareth my word, and believeth Jo. 5, 24.
in him that sent me, hath eternal life, and cometh not into judgement, but passeth from
33 Arabic, death unto life. Verily, verily, I say unto you, An hour shall come, and now Jo. 5, 25.
p. 87 is also, when the dead shall hear the voice of the Son of God; and those
34 which hear shall live. And as the Father hath life in himself,[1] likewise he gave to Jo. 5, 26.
35 the Son also that he might have life in himself,[1] and authority to do judgement also, Jo. 5, 27.
36 because[2] he is the Son of man. Marvel not then at that: I mean the coming of Jo. 5, 28.
the hour when all that are in the tombs shall hear his voice, and shall come forth; Jo. 5, 29.
37 those that have done good, to the resurrection of life; and those that have done evil
deeds, to the resurrection of judgement.

38 I am not able of myself to do anything; but as I hear, I judge: and my judge- Jo. 5, 30.
39 ment is just; I seek not my *own* will, but the will of him that sent me. I[3] bear wit- Jo. 5, 31.
40 ness of myself, and so[3] my witness is not true. It is another that beareth witness Jo. 5, 32.
41 of me; and I know that the witness which he beareth of me is true. Ye have sent Jo. 5, 33.
42 unto John, and he hath borne witness of the truth. But not from man do I seek Jo. 5, 34.
43 witness; but I say that ye may live.[4] That[5] was a lamp which shineth and Jo. 5, 35.
44 giveth light: and ye were pleased to glory now[6] in his light. But I have witness Jo. 5, 36.
greater than that of John: the works which my Father hath given me to accomplish,
45 those works which I do, bear witness of me, that the Father hath sent me. And Jo. 5, 37.
the Father which sent me, he hath borne witness of me. Ye have neither heard his
46 voice at any time, nor seen his appearance. And his word abideth not in you; because Jo. 5, 38.
47 in him whom he hath sent ye do not believe. Search the scriptures, in which ye rejoice[7] Jo. 5, 39.
48 that ye have eternal life; and they bear witness of me; and ye do not wish to come to Jo. 5, 40.
49, 50 Arabic, me, that ye may have eternal life. I seek not praise of men. But I know Jo. 5, 41. Jo. 5, 42.
51 p. 88 you, that the love of God is not in you. I am come in the name of my Jo. 5, 43.
Father, and ye received me not; but if another come in his own name, that *one* will
52 ye receive. And how can ye believe, while ye receive praise one from another, and Jo. 5, 44.
53 praise from God, the One, ye seek not? Can it be that ye think that I will accuse Jo. 5, 45.
you before the Father? Ye have one that accuseth you, Moses, in whom ye have
54 rejoiced.[7] If ye believed Moses, ye would believe me also; Moses wrote of me. Jo. 5, 46.
55 And if ye believed not his writings, how shall ye believe my words? Jo. 5, 47.

SECTION XXIII.

§23 1 And Jesus departed thence, and came to the side of the sea of Galilee, and went Mt. 15, 29.
2 up into the mountain, and sat there. And there came unto him great multitudes, Mt. 15, 30a.
having with them lame, and blind, and dumb, and maimed, and many others, and
3 they cast them at the feet of Jesus; for they had seen all the signs which he did in Jo. 4, 45b.
4 Jerusalem, when they were gathered at the feast. And he healed them all. And Mt. 15, 30b. Mt. 15, 31.

1 Borg. MS. reads *his person*. 2 Lit. *that*; or, *Verily*.
3 So Ciasca s Arabic text. Borg. MS. has *If I*, and instead *of and so, etc.*, simply *a witness which is not true, etc.*; but its text of the next sentence is quite corrupt. 4 Or, *be saved*. 5 Or, *that* (*man*).
6 Were it not also in Ibn-aṭ-Ṭayyib's Commentary (Brit. Mus. text) we should assume *now* to be a corruption of an original Arabic reading, *for a season* (*cf.* Syr.).
7 This word (often used by our translator) means in Syriac (transposed) *believe*, *think*, *hope* (*cf.* § 8, 8, note).

§23 those multitudes marvelled when they saw dumb *men* speak, and maimed *men* healed,
and lame *men* walk, and blind *men* see; and they praised the God of Israel.
5 And Jesus called his disciples, and said unto them, I have compassion on this mul- Mt. 15, 32.
titude, because of their continuing with me three days, having nothing to eat; and to
send them away fasting I am not willing, lest they faint in the way, some of them hav- Mk. 8, 3*b*.
6 Arabic, ing come from far. His disciples said unto him, Whence have we in the des- Mt. 15, 33.
7 p. 89 ert bread wherewith to satisfy all this multitude? Jesus said unto them, How Mt. 15, 34.
8 many loaves have ye? They said unto him, Seven, and a few small fishes. And he Mt. 15, 35.
9 commanded the multitudes to sit down upon the ground; and he took those seven Mt. 15, 36.
loaves and the fish, and blessed, and brake, and gave to his disciples to set before
10 them; and the disciples set before the multitudes. And they all ate, and were sat- Mt. 15, 37.
isfied: and they took that which remained over of the fragments, seven basketfuls.
11 And the people that ate were four thousand men, besides the women and children. Mt. 15, 38.
12 And when the multitudes departed, he went up into the boat, and came to the Mt. 15, 39.
borders of Magada.[1]
13 And the Pharisees and Sadducees came to him, and began to seek a discussion Mt. 16, 1*a*. Mk. 8, 11*b*.
with him. And they asked him to shew them a sign from heaven, tempting him.
14 And Jesus sighed within himself, and said, What sign seeketh this evil and adulter- Mk. 8, 12*a*. Mt. 16, 4.
ous generation? It seeketh a sign, and it shall not be given a sign, except the sign
15 of Jonah the prophet. Verily I say unto you, This generation shall not be given a Mk. 8, 12*b*.
16 sign. And he left[2] them, and went up into the boat, and went away to that side. Mk. 8, 13.
17 And his disciples forgot to take with them bread, and there was not with them Mk. 8, 14.
18 in the boat, not even[3] one loaf. And Jesus charged them, and said, Take heed, Mk. 8, 15.
and guard yourselves from the leaven of the Pharisees and Sadducees, and from the
19 leaven of Herod. And they reflected within themselves that they had taken with them Mt. 16, 7.
20 no bread. And Jesus knew, and said unto them, Why[4] think ye within yourselves, O Mt. 16, 8.
ye of little faith, and are anxious, because ye have no bread? until now do ye not per- Mk. 8, 17*b*.
21 ceive, neither understand? is your heart yet hard? And have ye eyes, and *yet* see not? Mk. 8, 18.
22 Arabic, and have ye ears, and *yet* hear not? and do ye not remember when I brake Mk. 8, 19.
p. 90 those five loaves for five thousand? and how many baskets full of broken
23 pieces took ye[5] up? They said, Twelve. He said unto them, And the seven also Mk. 8, 20.
for four thousand: how many baskets full of broken pieces took ye[5] up? They
24 said, Seven. He said unto them, How have ye not understood that I spake not to Mk. 8, 21*a*. Mt. 16, 11.
you because of[6] the bread, but that ye should beware of the leaven of the Pharisees
25 and Sadducees? Then they understood that he spake, not that they should beware Mt. 16, 12.
of the leaven of the bread, but of the doctrine of the Pharisees and Sadducees, which
he called leaven.
26 And after that, he came to Bethsaida. And they brought to him a certain[7] blind Mk. 8, 22.
27 *man*, and besought him that he would touch him. And he took the hand of that Mk. 8, 23.
blind man, and led him out without the village, and spat in his eyes, and laid his
28 hand on him,[8] and asked him, What seest thou? And that blind man looked in- Mk. 8, 24.
29 tently, and said unto him, I see men as trees walking. And he placed his hand Mk. 8, 25.
30 again on his eyes; and they were restored,[9] and he saw everything clearly. And Mk. 8, 26.
he sent him to his house, and said, Do not enter even into the village, nor tell any
man in the village.
31 And Jesus went forth, and his disciples, to the villages of Cæsarea Philippi. Mk. 8, 27*a*.
32 And while he was going in the way, and his disciples alone,[10] he asked his disciples, Mt. 16, 13*b*.
33 and said, What do men say of me that I am, the Son of man?[11] They said unto him, Mt. 16, 14.
Some say, John the Baptist; and others, Elijah; and others, Jeremiah, or one of the
34, 35 prophets. He said unto them, And ye, what say ye that I am? Simon Cephas an- Mt. 16, 15. Mt. 16, 16.
36 Arabic, swered and said, Thou art the Messiah, the Son of the living God. Jesus an- Mt. 16, 17.
p. 91 swered and said unto him, Blessed art thou, Simon son of Jonah: flesh and
37 blood hath not revealed *it* unto thee, but my Father which is in heaven. And I say unto Mt. 16, 18.

1 Arabic *Magadu*, as in Peshitta. 2 *cf.* § 11, 32, note.
3 The change of a single letter in the Arabic would turn *not even* into *except;* but Ibn-at-Tayyib's Commentary (Brit. Mus. text) also has *not even*. 4 Lit. *What*. See note to § 7, 38. 5 Or, *ye took*. 6 Or, *concerning*.
7 Lit. *one*, probably representing Syriac idiom (*cf.* Sinaitic?). 8 The Peshitta also omits *on him*.
9 An intransitive word. 10 Or, *his disciples being alone*. There is no such clause in the Syriac versions (Pesh., Sin.).
11 The Arabic, which reappears in Ibn-at-Ṭayyib's Commentary (Brit. Mus. text), and seems to represent the consonantal text of the Peshitta, is awkward. § 23, 34 (Arabic), shows, however, that the rendering given in the text is the meaning intended by the translator.

§ 23 thee also, that thou art Cephas,[1] and on this rock will I build my church; and the
38 gates of Hades shall not prevail against it. To thee will I give the keys of the kingdom Mt. 16, 19.
of heaven: and whatsoever thou shalt bind on earth shall be bound in heaven; and
39 whatsoever thou shalt loose on earth shall be loosed in heaven. And he sternly Mt. 16, 20.
charged his disciples, and warned them that they should not tell any man concern-
40 ing him, that he was the Messiah. And henceforth began Jesus to shew to his dis- Mt. 16, 21a.
41 ciples that he was determined[2] to go to Jerusalem, and suffer much, and be rejected Mk. 8, 31b.
of the elders, and of the chief priests, and of the scribes, and be killed, and on the
42 third day rise. And he was speaking[3] plainly. And Simon Cephas, as one grieved Mk. 8, 32a. Mt. 16, 22.
43 for him, said, Far be thou, my Lord, from that. And he turned, and looked upon Mk. 8, 33a
44 his disciples, and rebuked Simon, and said, Get thee behind me, Satan: for thou art Mt. 16, 23b.
a stumblingblock unto me: for thou thinkest not of what pertains to God, but of
what pertains to men.
45 And Jesus called the multitudes with his disciples, and said unto them, Whoso- Mk. 8, 34a.
ever would come after me, let him deny himself, and take his cross every day, and Lk. 9, 23b.
46 come after me. And whosoever would save his life shall lose it; and whosoever Mk. 8, 35.
47 loseth his life for my sake, and for the sake of my gospel, shall save it. What shall Lk. 9, 25.
48 a man profit, if he gain all the world, and destroy[4] his own life,[5] or lose it? or what Mk. 8, 37.
49 Arabic, will a man give *in* ransom for his life?[5] Whosoever shall deny me and my Mk. 8, 38.
p. 92 sayings in this sinful and adulterous generation, the Son of man also will
50 deny him, when he cometh in the glory of his Father with his holy angels. For the Mt. 16, 27.
Son of man is about to[6] come in the glory of his Father with his holy angels; and
then shall he reward each man according to his works.

SECTION XXIV.

§ 24 1 And he said unto them, Verily I say unto you, There be here now some standing Mk. 9, 1.
that shall not taste death, until they see the kingdom of God come[7] with strength,
and the Son of man who cometh in his kingdom. Mt. 16, 28b.
2 And after six days Jesus took Simon Cephas, and James, and John his brother, Mt. 17, 1.
3 and brought them up into a high mountain, the three of them only. And while they Lk. 9, 29a.
4 were praying, Jesus changed, and became after the fashion of another person; and Mt. 17, 2b.
his face shone like the sun, and his raiment was very white like the snow, and as Lk. 9, 29b.
5 the light of lightning, so that nothing on earth can whiten[8] like it. And there ap- Mk. 9, 3b. Mk. 9, 4.
6 peared unto him Moses and Elijah talking to Jesus. And they thought that the time Lk. 9, 31b.
7 of his decease which was to be accomplished at Jerusalem was come. And Simon and Lk. 9, 32.
those that were with him were heavy in the drowsiness of sleep; and with effort they
roused themselves, and saw his glory, and those two men that were standing with him.
8 Arabic, And when they began to depart from him, Simon said unto Jesus, My Lk. 9, 33a.
9 p. 93 Master, it is good for us to be here: and if thou wilt, we will make here Mt. 17, 4b.
three tabernacles; one for thee, and one for Moses, and one for Elijah; not know- Lk. 9, 33c.
10 ing what he said, because of the fear which took possession of them. And while he Mk. 9, 6b. Mt. 17, 5a.
11 was yet saying that, a bright cloud overshadowed them. And when they saw Moses Lk. 9, 34b.
12 and Elijah that they had entered into that cloud, they feared again. And a voice Mt. 17, 5b.
was heard out of the cloud, saying, This is my beloved Son, whom I have chosen;
13 hear ye therefore him. And when this voice was heard, Jesus was found alone. Lk. 9, 36a.
14 And the disciples, when they heard the voice, fell on their faces from the fear which Mt. 17, 6.
15 took hold of them. And Jesus came and touched them and said, Arise, be not Mt. 17, 7.
16 afraid. And they lifted up their eyes, and saw Jesus as he was. Mt. 17, 8.
17 And when they went down from the mountain, Jesus charged them, and said Mt. 17, 9.
unto them, Tell not what ye have seen to any man, until the Son of man rise from
18 among the dead. And they kept the word within themselves, and told no man in Mk. 9, 10a. Lk. 9, 36c.

1 Same Arabic word in both places. See note to § 5, 11.
2 The word is freely used in this work in the post-classical sense of *about to*.
3 The Arabic might perhaps be construed *and to speak*, depending on *began* in § 23, 40; but the clause agrees with the Sinaitic of Mark, as does the following. 4 Or, *lose*. 5 Or, *self*; or, *soul*.
6 See § 23, 40, note. 7 i.e., *already come*.
8 Or, *become white*. In the Pesh. the verb is transitive. In Sin. the clause is omitted.

§ 24 19 those days what they had seen. And they reflected among themselves, What is this Mk. 9, 10*b*.
20 word which he spake unto us, I, when I am risen from among the dead? And his Mk. 9, 11*a*.
disciples asked him, and said, What is that which the scribes say, then, that Elijah Mt. 17, 10*b*
21 must first come? He said unto them, Elijah cometh first to set in order everything, Mk. 9, 12.
Arabic, and as it was written of the Son of man, that he should suffer many things,
22 p. 94 and be rejected. But I say unto you, that Elijah is come, and they knew Mk. 9, 13.
him not, and have done unto him whatsoever they desired, as it was written of him.
23, 24 In like manner the Son of man is to suffer of them. Then understood the disciples Mt. 17, 12*b*. Mt. 17, 13.
that he spake unto them concerning John the Baptist.
25 And on that day whereon they came down from the mountain, there met him a Mk. 9, 14.
multitude of many people standing with his disciples, and the scribes were discuss-
26 ing with them. And the people, when they saw Jesus, were perplexed,[1] and in the Mk. 9, 15.
27 midst of their joy hastened[2] and saluted him. And on that day came certain of Lk. 13, 31.
the Pharisees, and said unto him, Get thee out, and go hence; for Herod seeketh
28 to kill thee. Jesus said unto them, Go ye and say to this fox, Behold, I am casting Lk. 13, 32.
out demons, and I heal to-day and to-morrow, and on the third day I am perfected.
29 Nevertheless I must be watchful[3] to-day and to-morrow, and on the last day I shall Lk. 13, 33.
depart; for it cannot be that a prophet perish outside of Jerusalem.
30 And after that, there came to him a man from that multitude, and fell upon his Lk. 9, 38*a*. Mt. 17, 14*b*.
knees, and said unto him, I beseech thee, my Lord, look upon my son; he is my Lk. 9, 38*b*.
31 only *child*: and the spirit cometh upon him suddenly. A lunacy[4] hath come upon Lk. 9, 39*a*. Mt. 17, 15*b*.
32 him, and he meeteth with evils. And when it cometh upon him, it beateth him about;[5] Mk. 9, 18*a*.
33 and he foameth, and gnasheth his teeth, and wasteth;[6] and many times it hath thrown Mt. 17, 15*c*.
him into the water and into the fire to destroy him, and it hardly leaveth him after Lk. 9, 39*c*.
34 Arabic, bruising him. And I brought him near to thy disciples, and they could Mt. 17, 16.
35 p. 95 not heal him. Jesus answered and said, O faithless and perverse genera- Mt. 17, 17.
tion, till when shall I be with you? and till when shall I bear with you? bring thy son
36 hither. And he brought him unto him: and when the spirit saw him, immediately Mk. 9, 20.
37 it beat him about; and he fell upon the ground, and was raging and foaming. And Mk. 9, 21.
Jesus asked his father, How long is the time during which he hath been thus? He
38 said unto him, From his youth until now. But, my Lord, help me wherein thou Mk. 9, 22*b*
39 canst, and have mercy upon me. Jesus said unto him, If thou canst believe! All Mk. 9, 23.
40 things are possible to him that believeth. And immediately the father of the child Mk. 9, 24.
41 cried out, weeping, and said, I believe, my Lord; help my lack of faith. And when Mk. 9, 25.
Jesus saw the hastening of the people, and their coming at the sound, he rebuked
that unclean spirit, and said to it, Thou dumb[7] spirit that speakest not, I command
42 thee,[8] come out of him, and enter not again into him. And that spirit, devil,[9] cried Mk. 9, 26.
out much, and bruised him, and came out; and that child fell as one dead, and
43 many thought that he had died. But Jesus took him by his hand, and raised him Mk. 9, 27*a*. Lk. 9, 42*b*.
44 up, and gave him to his father; and that child was healed from that hour. And Mt. 17, 18*b*.
the people all marvelled at the greatness of God. Lk. 9, 43*a*.
45 And when Jesus entered into the house, his disciples came, and asked him Mk. 9, 28.
46 privately,[10] and said unto him, Why were we not able to heal him? Jesus said unto Mt. 17, 20.
Arabic. them, Because of your unbelief. Verily I say unto you, If ye have faith
p. 96 as a grain of mustard seed, ye shall say to this mountain, Remove hence;
47 and it shall remove; and nothing shall overcome you. But it is impossible to cast Mk. 9, 29*b*.
out this kind by anything except by fasting and prayer.
48 And when he went forth thence, they passed through Galilee; and he would not Mk. 9, 30.
49 that any man should know it.[11] And he taught his disciples, and said unto them, Mk. 9, 31*a*.
50 Keep ye these sayings in your ears and your hearts: for the Son of man is to be Lk. 9, 44*a*. Mk. 9, 31*b*.

1 This rendering assumes that the diacritical point is due to a clerical error. The text as printed can hardly be translated without forcing.
2 This Arabic word repeatedly represents a Syriac *ran* (*cf.* § 53, 11). A different word is so used in § 26, 21.
3 The Syriac word used in the Peshitta is here translated just as it was translated in § 1, 79 (see note); but the Greek shows that in the present passage the Syriac word means *go about* (*cf.* Cur.).
4 Lit. *The son-of-the-roof*, a Syriac phrase meaning *a demon of lunacy*.
5 A word used in Arabic of the devil producing insanity; but here it reproduces the Peshitta.
6 Lit. *becometh light;* but a comparison with the Peshitta suggests that we should change one diacritical point and read *withereth*, as in Ibn-at-Ṭayyib's Commentary. An equally easy emendation would be *wasteth*.
7 In Syriac, but not in Arabic, the word means *deaf* or *dumb*, according to the context.
8 Ciasca's Arabic follows Vat. MS. in inserting a *that* (pronoun) after *thee*.
9 Doubtless alternative renderings of the same Syriac word (*demon*). 10 Lit. *between themselves and him.* 11 Or, *about him.*

§24 delivered into the hands of men, and they shall kill him; and when he is killed, he
51 shall rise on the third day. But they knew not the word which he spake unto them, Lk. 9, 45.
for it was concealed from them, that they should not perceive it; and they feared to
52 ask him about this word. And they were exceeding sorrowful. Mt. 17, 23*b*.

SECTION XXV.

§25 1 And in that day this thought presented itself to his disciples, and they said, which Lk. 9, 46.
2 haply should be the great*est* among them.[1] And when they came to Capernaum, Mk. 9, 33.
and entered into the house, Jesus said unto them, What were ye considering in the
3 way among yourselves? And they were silent because they had considered that Mk. 9, 34*a*.
matter.
4 And when Simon went forth without, those that received two dirhams for the Mt. 17. 24*b*.
tribute came to Cephas, and said unto him, Doth your master not give his two
5 dirhams? He said unto them, Yea. And when Cephas entered the house, Jesus Mt. 17, 25.
anticipated him, and said unto him, What thinkest thou, Simon? the kings of the
earth, from whom do they receive custom and tribute? from their sons, or from
6 Arabic, strangers? Simon said unto him, From strangers. Jesus said unto him, Mt. 17, 26.
p. 97 Children then are free. Simon said unto him, Yea. Jesus said unto him,
7 Give thou also unto them, like the stranger. But, lest it trouble them, go thou to Mt. 17, 27.
the sea, and cast *a* hook; and the first fish that cometh up, open its mouth, *and* thou
shalt find a stater: take therefore that, and give for me and thee.
8 And in that hour came the disciples to Jesus, and said unto him, Who, thinkest Mt. 18, 1.
9 thou, is greater in the kingdom of heaven? And Jesus knew the thought of their Lk. 9, 47*a*.
heart, and called a[2] child, and set him in the midst, and took him in his arms, and Mk. 9, 36.
10 said unto them, Verily I say unto you, If ye do not return, and become as children, Mt. 18, 3.
11 ye shall not enter the kingdom of heaven. Every one that shall receive in my Lk. 9, 48.
name such as this child hath received me: and whosoever receiveth me receiveth Mk. 9, 37*b*.
12 not me, but him that sent me. And he who is little in your company,[3] the same Lk. 9, 48*c*.
13 shall be great. But whosoever shall injure one of these little ones that believe in Mt. 18, 6.
me, it were better for him that a great millstone[4] should be hanged about his neck,
and *he should be* drowned in the depths of the sea.
14 John answered and said, Our Master, we saw one casting out devils in thy name; Lk. 9, 49.
15 and we prevented him, because he followed not thee with us. Jesus said unto them, Mk. 9, 39.
Prevent him not; for no man doeth powers in my name, and can hasten to speak evil
16, 17 of me. Every one who is not in opposition to you is with you. Woe unto the world Lk. 9, 50*b*. Mt. 18, 7*a*, *c*.
Arabic, because of trials![5] but woe unto that man by whose hand the trials come!
18 p. 98 If thy hand or thy foot injure thee, cut it off, and cast it from thee; for it Mt. 18, 8.
is better for thee to enter into life being halt or maimed, and not that thou shouldest
have two hands or two feet, and fall into the hell of fire that burneth[6] for ever;
19, 20 where their worm dieth not, and their fire is not quenched. And if thine eye seduce[7] Mk. 9, 44. Mt. 18, 9*a*.
21 thee, pluck it out, and cast it from thee; for it is better for thee to enter the king- Mk. 9, 47*b*.
dom of God with one eye, than that thou shouldest have two eyes, and fall into the
22, 23 fire of Gehenna; where their worm dieth not, and their fire is not quenched. Every Mk. 9, 48. Mk. 9, 49.
24 *one* shall be salted with fire, and every sacrifice shall be salted with salt. How good Mk. 9, 50*a*.
25 is salt! but if the salt also be tasteless, wherewith shall it be salted? It is fit neither Lk. 14, 34*b*. Lk. 14, 35.
for the land nor for dung, but they cast it out. He that hath ears to hear, let him
26 hear. Have ye salt in yourselves, and be in peace one with another. Mk. 9, 50*c*.
27 And he arose from thence, and came to the borders of Judæa beyond Jordan: Mk. 10, 1.
and there went unto him thither great multitudes, and he healed them; and he taught
28 them also, according to his custom. And the Pharisees came unto him, tempting Mk. 10, 2.
29 him, and asking him, Is it lawful for a man to put away his wife? He said, What Mk. 10, 3.
30 did Moses command you? They said, Moses made it allowable for us, *saying*, Who- Mk. 10, 4.
31 soever will, let him write a writing of divorcement, and put away his wife. Jesus Mk. 10, 5*a*.

1 Borg. MS. omits *among them*. 2 Lit. *one* (Syriac idiom).
3 In the present work this word frequently means *synagogue*. 4 Lit. *millstone of an ass*.
5 i.e., experiences that test one; or, *seductions*. The word is variously used. 6 Or, *is kindled*.
7 See note to § 25, 17.

§ answered and said unto them, Have ye not read, He that made *them* from the beginning Mt. 19, 4.
32 made them male and female, and said, For this reason shall the man leave his father Mt. 19, 5.
Arabic, and his mother, and cleave to his wife; and they both shall be one body?
33 p. 99 So then they are not twain, but one body; the thing, then, which God hath Mt. 19, 6.
34 joined together, let no man put asunder. And those Pharisees said unto him, Why did Mt. 19, 7.
Moses consent[1] that a *man* should give a writing of divorcement and put her away?
35 Jesus said unto them, Moses because of the hardness of your hearts gave you leave Mt. 19, 8.
36 to divorce your wives; but in the beginning it was not so. I say unto you, Whoso- Mt. 19, 9*a*.
ever putteth away[2] his wife without fornication, and marrieth another, hath exposed
37 her to adultery. And his disciples, when he entered the house, asked him again Mk. 10, 10.
38 about that. And he said unto them, Every one who putteth away his wife, and Mk. 10, 11.
39 marrieth another, hath exposed her to adultery. And any woman that leaveth her Mk. 10, 12.
husband, and becometh another's, hath committed adultery. And whosoever mar- Mt. 19, 9*b*.
40 rieth her that is divorced hath committed adultery. And his disciples said unto him, Mt. 19, 10.
If there be between the man and the woman such a case[3] as this, it is not good for
41 a man to marry. He said unto them, Not every man can endure this saying, except Mt. 19, 11.
42 him to whom it is given. There are eunuchs which from their mother's womb[4] Mt. 19, 12.
were born so; and there are eunuchs which through men became eunuchs; and
there are eunuchs which made themselves eunuchs for the sake of the kingdom of
heaven. He that is able to be content, let him be content.

43 Then they brought to him children, that he should lay his hand upon them, and Mt. 19, 13*a*.
44 pray: and his disciples were rebuking those that were bringing them. And Jesus Mk. 10, 13*b*. Mk. 10, 14.
saw, and it was distressing to him; and he said unto them, Suffer the children to
Arabic, come unto me, and prevent them not; for those that are like these have
45 p. 100 the kingdom of God. Verily I say unto you, Whosoever receiveth not the Mk. 10, 15.
46 kingdom of God as this child, shall not enter it. And he took them in his arms, and Mk. 10, 16.
laid his hand upon them, and blessed them.

SECTION XXVI.

§ 26 1, 2 And there came unto him publicans and sinners to hear his word. And the Lk. 15, 1. Lk. 15, 2.
scribes and the Pharisees murmured, and said, This man receiveth sinners, and
3 eateth with them. And Jesus, when he beheld their murmuring, spake unto them Lk. 15, 3.
4 this parable: What man of you, having an hundred sheep, if one of them were lost, Lk. 15, 4.
would not leave the ninety-nine in the wilderness, and go and seek the straying *one*
5 till he found it? Verily I say unto you, When he findeth it, he will rejoice over it Mt. 18, 13.
6 more than *over* the ninety-nine that went not astray; and bear it on his shoulders, Lk. 15, 5*b*.
and bring it to his house, and call his friends and neighbours, and say unto them, Lk. 15, 6.
7 Rejoice with me, since I have found my straying sheep. So your Father which is Mt. 18, 14.
in heaven willeth[5] not that one of these little ones that have strayed should perish,
8 and he seeketh for them repentance. I say unto you, Thus there shall be rejoicing Lk. 15, 7.
in heaven over one sinner that repenteth, more than *over* ninety-nine righteous
persons that do not need repentance.

9 And what woman having ten drachmas would lose one of them, and not light a Lk. 15, 8.
10 lamp, and sweep the house, and seek it with care till she found it; and when she Lk. 15, 9.
found it, call her friends and neighbours, and say unto them, Rejoice with me, as I
11 have found my drachma that was lost? I say unto you, Thus there shall be joy Lk. 15, 10.
Arabic, before the angels of God over the one sinner that repenteth, more than
p. 101 over the ninety-nine righteous *persons* that do not need repentance.

12, 13 And Jesus spake unto them also another parable: A man had two sons: and Lk. 15, 11. Lk. 15, 12.
the younger son said unto him, My father, give me my portion that belongeth to
14 me of thy goods. And he divided between them his property. And after a few Lk. 15, 13.
days the younger son gathered everything that belonged to him, and went into a
15 far country, and there squandered his property by living prodigally. And when he Lk. 15, 14.

1 So the Arabic; but the Syriac versions follow the Greek, and *consent* is doubtless a (very easy, and, in view of the succeeding context, natural) clerical error for an original Arabic *charge*. 2 Or, *leaveth*.
3 Lit. *blame*, a mistranslation (found also in the Brit. Mus. text of Ibn-aṭ-Tayyib's Commentary) of the Syriac word, which is ambiguous (*cf.* even the Greek). For a somewhat similar case see § 50, 11, note.
4 Lit. *wombs*. 5 Strictly, *preferreth*, but used also as in the text.

§ 26 had exhausted everything he had, there occurred a great dearth in that country.
16 And when he was in want, he went and joined himself to one of the people of a city Lk. 15, 15.
17 of that country; and that *man* sent him into the field[1] to feed the swine. And he Lk. 15, 16.
used to long to fill his belly with the carob that those swine were eating: and no man
18 gave him. And when he returned unto himself, he said, How many hired servants Lk. 15, 17.
now in my father's house have bread enough and to spare, while I here perish with
19 hunger! I will arise and go to my father's house, and say unto him, My father, I Lk. 15, 18.
20 have sinned in heaven and before thee, and am not worthy now to be called thy Lk. 15, 19.
21 son: make me as one of thy hired servants. And he arose, and came to his father. Lk. 15, 20.
But his father saw him while he was at a distance, and was moved with compassion
22 for him, and ran,[2] and fell on his breast,[3] and kissed him. And his son said unto Lk. 15, 21.
him, My father, I have sinned in heaven and before thee, and am not worthy to be
23 called thy son. His father said unto his servants, Bring forth a stately robe, and put Lk. 15, 22.
24 *it* on him; and put a ring on his hand, and put on him shoes on his feet: and bring and Lk. 15, 23.
25 slay a fatted ox, that we may eat and make merry: for this my son was dead, and is Lk. 15, 24.
26 Arabic, alive; and was lost, and is found. And they began to be merry.[4] Now his Lk. 15, 25.
p. 102 elder son was in the field; and when he came and drew near to the house,
27 he heard the sound of many singing.[5] And he called one of the lads, and asked him Lk. 15, 26.
28 what this was. He said unto him, Thy brother hath arrived; and thy father hath Lk. 15, 27.
29 slain a fatted ox, since he hath received him safe and sound.[6] And he was angry, Lk. 15, 28.
30 and would not enter; so his father went out, and besought him to enter. And he Lk. 15, 29.
said to his father, How many years do I serve thee in bondage, and I never transgressed a commandment of thine; and thou hast never given me a kid, that I might
31 make merry with my friends? but this thy son, when he had squandered thy Lk. 15, 30.
32 property with harlots, and come, thou hast slain for him a fatted ox. His father Lk. 15, 31.
said unto him, My son, thou art at all times with me, and everything I have is
33 thine. It behoveth thee to rejoice and make merry, since this thy brother was dead, Lk. 15, 32.
and is alive; and *was* lost, and is found.
34 And he spake a parable unto his disciples: There was a rich man, and he had Lk. 16, 1.
35 a steward; and he was accused to him that he had squandered his property. So Lk. 16, 2.
his lord called him, and said unto him, What is this that I hear regarding thee?
Give me the account of thy stewardship; for it is now impossible that thou shouldest
36 be a steward for me. The steward said within himself, What shall I do, seeing that Lk. 16, 3.
my lord taketh from me the stewardship? To dig I am not able; and to beg[7] I
37 am ashamed. I know what I will do, that, when I go out of the stewardship, they Lk. 16, 4.
38 may receive me into their houses. And he called one after another of his lord's Lk. 16, 5.
39 debtors, and said to the first, How much owest thou my lord? He said unto him, An Lk. 16, 6.
hundred portions[8] of oil. He said unto him, Take thy writing, and sit down, and write
40 quickly fifty portions.[8] And he said to the next, And thou, how much owest thou my Lk. 16, 7.
lord? He said unto him, An hundred cors of wheat. He said unto him, Take
41 Arabic, thy writing, and sit down, and write eighty cors. And our[9] lord com- Lk. 16, 8.
p. 103 mended the sinful steward[10] because he had done a wise deed; for the chil-
42 dren of this world are wiser than the children of the light in this their age. And I also Lk. 16, 9.
say unto you, Make unto yourselves friends with the wealth of this unrighteousness;[11]
43 so that, when it is exhausted, they may receive you into their tents for ever. He Lk. 16, 10.
who is faithful in[12] a little is faithful also in much: and he who is unrighteous in a
44 little is unrighteous also in much. If then in the wealth of unrighteousness ye were Lk. 16, 11.
45 not trustworthy, who will intrust you with the truth?[13] If ye are not found faithful Lk. 16, 12.
in what does not belong to you, who will give you what belongeth to you?

SECTION XXVII.

§ 27 1 Therefore the kingdom of heaven is like a certain king, who would make a Mt. 18, 23.
2 reckoning with his servants. And when he began to make *it*, they brought to him Mt. 18, 24.

1 This word is regularly used throughout this work in this sense. 2 See above, § 24, 26, note.
3 Did not Ibn-at-Ṭayyib's Commentary (Brit. Mus. text) also read *breast*, we might assume it to be a clerical error for a very similar (less common) word (same as the Syriac) for *neck*. 4 A different word. 5 *cf.* Peshitta. 6 One word.
7 Vat. MS. (followed by Ciasca's text) has *and if I beg*, by a common confusion of grammatical forms.
8 Or (otherwise vocalised), *farks*, a measure variously estimated. 9 *cf.* Peshitta. 10 Lit. *steward of sin*.
11 Lit. *injustice*. 12 Or, *intrusted with*. 13 Or, *true* (*wealth*); but *cf.* Syriac.

§ 27 3 one who owed him ten talents.[1] And because he had not wherewith to pay, his Mt. 18, 25.
lord ordered that he should be sold, he, and his wife, and children, and all that he
4 had, and payment be made. So that servant fell down and worshipped *him*, and Mt. 18, 26.
said unto him, My lord, have patience with me, and I shall pay thee everything.
5 And the lord of that servant had compassion, and released him, and forgave him his Mt. 18, 27.
6 debt. And that servant went out, and found one of his fellow-*servants*, who owed him Mt. 18, 28.
Arabic, a hundred pence;[2] and he took him, and dealt severely with him, and said
7 p. 104 unto him, Give me what thou owest. So the fellow-servant fell down at his Mt. 18, 29.
8 feet, and besought him, and said, Grant me respite, and I will pay thee. And he Mt. 18, 30.
would not; but took him, and cast him into prison, till he should give him his debt.
9 And when their fellow-*servants* saw what happened, it distressed them much; and Mt. 18, 31.
10 they came and told their lord of all that had taken place. Then his lord called Mt. 18, 32.
him, and said unto him, *Thou* wicked servant, all that debt I forgave thee, because
11 thou besoughtest me: was it not then incumbent on thee also to have mercy on thy Mt. 18, 33.
12 fellow-servant, as I had mercy on thee?[3] And his lord became wroth, and delivered Mt. 18, 34.
13 him to the scourgers, till he should pay all that he owed. So shall my Father which Mt. 18, 35.
is in heaven do unto you, if one forgive not his brother his wrong conduct[4] from
14 his heart. Take heed within[5] yourselves: if thy brother sin, rebuke him; and if he Lk. 17, 3.
15 repent, forgive him. And if he act wrongly towards thee seven times in a day, and Lk. 17, 4.
on that day return seven times unto thee, and say, I repent towards thee; forgive him.
16 And if thy brother act wrongly towards thee, go and reprove him between thee and Mt. 18. 15.
17 him alone: if he hear thee, thou hast gained thy brother. But if he hear thee not, Mt. 18. 16.
take with thee one or two, and so[6] at the mouth of two or three every saying shall
18 be established. And if he listen not to these also, tell the congregation;[7] and if he Mt. 18, 17.
listen not even to the congregation, let him be unto thee as a publican and a Gen-
19 tile.[8] Verily I say unto you, All that ye bind on earth shall be bound in heaven: Mt. 18, 18.
20 and what ye loose on earth shall be loosed in heaven. I say unto you also, If two Mt. 18, 19.
of you agree on earth to ask, everything shall[9] be granted them from my Father
21 Arabic, which is in heaven. For where two or three are gathered in my name, there Mt. 18, 20.
22 p. 105 am I amongst them. Then Cephas drew near to him, and said unto him, My Mt. 18, 21.
Lord, how many times, if my brother act wrongly towards me, should I forgive him?
23 until seven times? Jesus said unto him, I say not unto thee, Until seven; but, Until sev- Mt. 18, 22.
24 enty times seven, seven.[10] And the servant that knoweth his lord's will, and maketh not Lk. 12, 47.
25 ready for him according to his will, shall meet with much punishment; but he that Lk. 12, 48.
knoweth not, and doeth something for which he meriteth punishment, shall meet
with slight punishment. Every one to whom much hath been given, much shall
be asked of him; and he that hath had much committed to him, much shall be
26 required at his hand. I came to cast fire upon the earth; and I would that it had Lk. 12, 49.
27 been kindled already.[11] And I have a baptism to be baptized with, and greatly am Lk. 12, 50.
28 I straitened till it be accomplished. See *that ye* despise not[12] one of these little Mt. 18, 10.
ones that believe in me. Verily I say unto you, Their angels at all times see the
29 face of my Father which is in heaven. The Son of man came to save the thing Mt. 18, 11.
which was lost.

30 And after that, Jesus walked in Galilee; and he did not like to walk in Judæa, Jo. 7, 1.
31 because the Jews sought to kill him. And there came people who told him of Lk. 13, 1.
32 the Galilæans, those whose blood Pilate had mingled with their sacrifices. Jesus Lk. 13, 2.
answered and said unto them, Do ye imagine that those Galilæans were sinners
33 more than all the Galilæans, so that this thing has come upon them? Nay. Lk. 13, 3.
Verily I say unto you now,[13] that ye shall all also, if ye repent not, likewise perish.
34 Or perchance those eighteen on whom the palace fell in Siloam, and slew them, do Lk. 13, 4.
ye imagine that they were to be condemned[14] more than all the people that dwell
35 Arabic, in Jerusalem? Nay. Verily I say unto you, If ye do not all repent, ye Lk. 13, 5.
p. 106 shall perish like them.

36 And he spake unto them this parable: A man had a fig tree planted in his vine- Lk. 13, 6.

1 Lit. *badras*, an amount variously estimated. 2 Lit. *dinars*.
3 The interrogative particle is lacking in the Arabic. 4 Or, *folly*. 5 A very close reproduction of the Syriac.
6 Or, *for*. 7 This word usually means *synagogue* in this work. 8 Or, *heathen*.
9 Or, *to ask everything, it shall*. 10 So Vat. MS., following the Syriac versions; Borg. MS. has only one *seven*.
11 Lit. *beforehand*; and so often. 12 Or, repeating a letter, *See that ye despise not*. 13 Borg. MS. omits *now*.
14 See note, § 10, 13.

§27 37 yard; and he came and sought fruit thereon, and found none. So he said to the Lk. 13, 7.
husbandman, Lo, three years do I come and seek fruit on this fig tree, and find
38 none: cut it down; why doth it render the ground unoccupied? The husbandman Lk. 13, 8.
said unto him, My lord, leave it this year also, that I may dig about it, and dung
39 it; then if it bear fruit—! and if not, then cut it down in the coming year. Lk. 13, 9.
40 And when Jesus was teaching on the sabbath day in one of the synagogues, Lk. 13, 10.
41 there was there a woman that had a spirit of disease eighteen years; and she was Lk. 13, 11.
42 bowed down, and could not straighten herself at all. And Jesus saw her, and called Lk. 13, 12.
43 her, and said unto her, Woman, be loosed from thy disease. And he put his hand Lk. 13, 13.
44 upon her; and immediately she was straightened, and praised God. And the chief[1] Lk. 13, 14.
of the synagogue answered with anger, because Jesus had healed on a sabbath,
and said unto the multitudes, There are six days in which work ought to be done;
45 come in them and be healed, and not on the sabbath day. But Jesus answered Lk. 13, 15.
and said unto him, *Ye* hypocrites, doth not each of you on the sabbath day loose
46 his ox or his ass from the manger, and go and water it? Ought not this woman, Lk. 13, 16.
who is a daughter of Abraham, and whom the devil[2] hath bound eighteen years,
47 to be loosed from this bond on the sabbath day? And when he said this, they Lk. 13, 17.
were all put to shame, those standing, who were opposing him:[3] and all the people
were pleased with all the wonders that proceeded from his hand.

SECTION XXVIII.[4]

§28 1, 2 Arabic, p. 107 And at that time the feast of tabernacles of the Jews drew near. So the Jo. 7, 2. Jo. 7, 3.
brethren of Jesus said unto him, Remove now hence, and go to Judæa, that
3 thy disciples may see the deeds that thou doest. For no man doeth a thing secretly Jo. 7, 4.
4 and wisheth to be apparent. If thou doest this, shew thyself to the world. For Jo. 7, 5.
5 up to this time not even the brethren of Jesus believed on him. Jesus said unto Jo. 7, 6.
them, My time till now has not arrived; but as for you, your time is alway ready.
6 It is not possible for the world to hate you; but me it hateth, for I bear witness Jo. 7, 7.
7 against it, that its deeds are evil. As for you, go ye up unto this feast: but I go Jo. 7, 8.
8 not up now to this feast; for my time has not yet been completed. He said this, Jo. 7, 9.
and remained behind in Galilee.
9 But when his brethren went up unto the feast, he journeyed from Galilee, and Jo. 7, 10*a*. Mt. 19, 1*b*.
10 came to the borders of Judæa, to *the country* beyond Jordan; and there came after Mt. 19, 2.
11 him great multitudes, and he healed them all there. And he went out, and proceeded Jo. 7, 10*b*.
12 to the feast, not openly, but as one that conceals himself. And the Jews sought him Jo. 7, 11.
13 at the feast, and said, In what place is this *man?* And there occurred much mur- Jo. 7, 12.
muring there in the great multitude that came to the feast, on his account. For
14 some said, He is good; and others said, Nay, but he leadeth the people astray. But Jo. 7, 13.
no man spake of him openly for fear of the Jews.
15 Arabic, p. 108 But when the days of the feast of tabernacles were half over, Jesus went Jo. 7, 14.
16 up to the temple, and taught. And the Jews wondered, and said, How doth Jo. 7, 15.
17 this man know writing,[5] seeing he hath not learned? Jesus answered and said, My doc- Jo. 7, 16.
18 trine[6] is not mine, but his that sent me. Whoever wisheth to do his will understandeth Jo. 7, 17.
my doctrine,[6] whether it be from God, or whether I speak of mine own accord.
19 Whosoever speaketh of his own accord seeketh praise for himself; but whosoever Jo. 7, 18.
seeketh praise for him that sent him, he is true, and unrighteousness in his heart
20 there is none. Did not Moses give you the law, and no man of you keepeth the Jo. 7, 19.
21 law? Why seek ye to kill me? The multitude answered and said unto him, Thou Jo. 7, 20.
22 hast demons:[7] who seeketh to kill thee? Jesus answered and said unto them, I did Jo. 7, 21.
23 one deed, and ye all marvel because of this. Moses hath given you circumcision Jo. 7, 22.
(not because it is from Moses, but it is from the fathers); and ye on the sabbath

1 Lit. *great* (*man*). 2 Lit. *calumniator*. 3 *cf.* Syriac versions.
4 On margin of Vat. MS., in another hand: "This is the beginning of the second part of *Diatessaron*, which means *The Four*." See p. 467 of Ciasca's Essay, mentioned above (Introduction, 5). 5 Or, *the scripture*.
6 This word ordinarily means *knowledge*, but is used in this work in the sense of *doctrine*. The commoner form occurs perhaps only in § 50, 2. 7 *cf.* § 14, 12.

§28 24 circumcise a man. And if a man is circumcised on the sabbath day, that the law Jo. 7, 23.
of Moses may not be broken; are ye angry at me, because I healed on the sabbath
25 day the whole man? Judge not with hypocrisy, but judge righteous judgement. Jo. 7, 24.
26 And some people from Jerusalem said, Is not this he whom they seek to slay? Jo. 7, 25.
27 And lo, he discourseth with them openly, and they say nothing unto him. Think Jo. 7, 26.
28 you that our elders have learned that this is the Messiah indeed? But this man is[1] Jo. 7, 27.
known whence he is; and the Messiah, when he cometh, no man knoweth whence
29 he is. So Jesus lifted up his voice as he taught in the temple, and said, Ye both Jo. 7, 28.
know me, and know whence I am; and of my own accord am I not come, but he
30 Arabic, that sent me is true, he whom ye know not: but I know him; for I am Jo. 7, 29.
31 p. 109 from him, and he sent me. And they sought to seize him: and no man Jo. 7, 30.
32 laid a hand on him, because his hour had not yet come. But many of the multi- Jo. 7, 31.
tude believed on him; and they said, The Messiah, when he cometh, can it be that
he will do more than these signs that this *man* doeth?
33 And a man of that multitude said unto our Lord, Teacher, say to my brother Lk. 12, 13.
34 that he divide with me the inheritance. Jesus said unto him, Man, who is it that Lk. 12, 14.
35 appointed me over you as a judge and divider? And he said unto his disciples, Lk. 12, 15.
Take heed within yourselves of all inordinate desire; for it is not in abundance of
36 possessions that life shall be. And he gave them this parable: The ground of a Lk. 12, 16.
37 rich man brought forth abundant produce: and he pondered within himself, and Lk. 12, 17.
38 said, What shall I do, since I have no place to store my produce? And he said, I Lk. 12, 18.
will do this: I will pull down the buildings of my barns, and build them, and make
39 them greater; and store there all my wheat and my goods. And I will say to my Lk. 12, 19.
soul, Soul, thou hast much goods laid by for many years; take thine ease, eat,
40 drink, enjoy thyself. God said unto him, O *thou* of little intelligence, this night Lk. 12, 20.
shall thy soul be taken from thee; and this that thou hast prepared, whose shall it
41 be? So is he that layeth up treasures for himself, and is not rich in God. Lk. 12, 21.
42 And while Jesus was going in the way, there came near to him a young man[2] of Mk. 10, 17.
the rulers,[3] and fell on his knees, and asked him, and said, Good Teacher, what is
43 it that I *must* do that I may have eternal life? Jesus said unto him, Why callest thou Mk. 10, 18.
44 me good, while there is none good but the one, *even* God?[4] Thou knowest the com- Mk. 10, 19*a*.
45 mandments.[5] If thou wouldest enter into life, keep the commandments.[5] The young Mt. 19, 17*b*. Mt. 19, 18*a*.
Arabic, man said unto him, Which of the commandments?[6] Jesus said unto him,
46 p. 110 Thou shalt not commit adultery, Thou shalt not steal, Thou shalt not kill, Mk. 10, 19*b*.
Thou shalt not bear false witness, Thou shalt not do injury, Honour thy father
47 and thy mother: and, Love thy neighbour as thyself. That young man said unto Mt. 19, 19*b*. Mt. 19, 20.
48 him, All these have I kept from my youth: what then is it that I lack? And Jesus Mk. 10, 21*a*.
49 looked intently at him, and loved him, and said unto him, If thou wouldest be Mt. 19, 21*b*.
perfect, what thou lackest is one thing:[7] go away and sell everything that thou
hast, and give to the poor, and thou shalt have treasure in heaven: and take thy
50 cross, and follow me. And that young man frowned at this word, and went away Mt. 19, 22*a*. Lk. 18, 23*b*.
51 feeling sad; for he was very rich. And when Jesus saw his sadness, he looked Lk. 18, 24*a*. Mk. 10, 23.
towards his disciples, and said unto them, How hard it is for them that have possessions to enter the kingdom of God!

SECTION XXIX.

§29 1 Verily I say unto you, It is difficult for a rich man to enter the kingdom of Mt. 19, 23.
2 heaven. And I say unto you also, that it is easier for a camel to enter the eye of Mt. 19, 24.
3 a needle, than for a rich man to enter the kingdom of God. And the disciples Mk. 10, 24.
were wondering at these sayings. And Jesus answered and said unto them again,
My children, how hard it is for those that rely on their possessions to enter the
4 kingdom of God! And those that were listening wondered more, and said amongst Mk. 10, 26.
5 themselves, being agitated,[8] Who, thinkest thou, can be saved? And Jesus looked at Mk. 10, 27.

1 Or, *will be*. 2 From Matthew. 3 From Luke.
4 The scribe who wrote the Vat. MS. wrote first *God, the one*, and then reversed the order by writing the Coptic letters for B and A over the words. (See above, Introduction, 5.) 5 Different words. 6 The same word as in Mk. 10, 19*a*.
7 From Mark. 8 *cf.* note, § 1, 14. Borg. MS. omits *being agitated*.

§ 29 them intently, and said unto them, With men this is not possible, but with God *it is:*
6 Arabic, it is possible for God to do everything. Simon Cephas said unto him, Lo, we Lk. 18, 28.
p. 111 have left everything, and followed thee; what is it, thinkest thou, that we Mt. 19, 27*b*.
7 shall have? Jesus said unto them, Verily I say unto you, Ye that have followed me, Mt. 19, 28.
in the new world, when the Son of man shall sit on the throne of his glory, ye also
8 shall sit on twelve thrones, and shall judge the twelve tribes of Israel. Verily I say Mk. 10, 29*b*.
unto you, No man leaveth houses, or brothers, or sisters, or father, or mother, or
wife, or children, or kinsfolk, or lands, because of the kingdom of God, or for my
9 sake, and the sake of my gospel, who shall not obtain[1] many times as much in this Lk. 18, 30.
10 time, and in the world to come inherit eternal life: and now in this time, houses, Mk. 10, 30*b*.
and brothers, and sisters, and mothers, and children, and lands, with persecution;
11 and in the world to come *ever*lasting life. Many that are first shall be last,[2] and Mk. 10, 31.
that are last shall be first.
12 And when the Pharisees heard all this, because of their love for wealth they Lk. 16, 14.
13 scoffed at him. And Jesus knew what was in their hearts, and said unto them, Ye Lk. 16, 15.
are they that justify yourselves before men; while God knows your hearts: the
thing that is lofty with men is base before God.
14 And he began to say, A *certain* man was rich, and wore silk and purple, and en- Lk. 16, 19.
15 joyed himself every day in splendour: and there was a poor man named Lazarus, and Lk. 16, 20.
16 he was cast down at the door of the rich man, afflicted with sores, and he longed to fill Lk. 16, 21.
Arabic, his belly with the crumbs that fell from the table of that rich man; yea,
17 p. 112 even[3] the dogs used to come and lick his sores. And it happened that that Lk. 16, 22.
poor man died, and the angels conveyed him into the bosom of Abraham: and the
18 rich man also died, and was buried. And while he was being tormented in Hades, Lk. 16, 23.
19 he lifted up his eyes from afar, and saw Abraham with[4] Lazarus in his bosom. And Lk. 16, 24.
he called with a loud voice, and said, My father Abraham, have mercy upon me,
and send Lazarus to wet the tip of his finger with water, and moisten my tongue
20 for me; for, behold, I am burned in this flame. Abraham said unto him, My son, Lk. 16, 25.
remember that thou receivedst thy good things in thy life, and Lazarus his afflic-
21 tions: but now, behold, he is at rest here, and thou art tormented. And in addition Lk. 16, 26.
to all this, there is between us and you a great abyss placed, so that they that
would cross unto you from hence cannot, nor yet from thence do they cross unto
22 us. He said unto him, Then I beseech thee, my father, to send him to my father's Lk. 16, 27.
23 house; for I have five brethren; let him go, that they also sin not,[5] and come to Lk. 16, 28.
24 the abode of this torment.[6] Abraham said unto him, They have Moses and the Lk. 16, 29.
25 prophets; let them hear them. He said unto him, Nay,[7] my father Abraham: but Lk. 16, 30.
26 let a man from the dead go unto them, and they will repent. Abraham said unto Lk. 16, 31.
him, If they listen neither to Moses nor to the prophets, neither if a man from the
dead rose would they believe him.
27 The kingdom of heaven is like a man that is a householder, which went out early Mt. 20, 1.
28 in the morning to hire labourers for his vineyard. And he agreed with the labourers on Mt. 20, 2.
29 one penny a day for each labourer, and he sent them into his vineyard. And he went Mt. 20, 3.
30 Arabic, out in three hours, and saw others standing in the market idle. He said Mt. 20, 4.
p. 113 unto them, Go ye also into my vineyard, and what is right I will pay you.
31 And they went. And he went out also at the sixth and the ninth hour, and did like- Mt. 20, 5.
32 wise, and sent them. And about the eleventh hour he went out, and found others Mt. 20, 6.
standing idle. He said unto them, Why are ye standing the whole day idle?
33 They said unto him, Because no one hath hired us. He said unto them, Go ye Mt. 20, 7.
34 also into the vineyard, and what is right ye shall receive. So when evening came, Mt. 20, 8.
the lord of the vineyard said unto his steward, Call the labourers, and pay them
35 their wages; and begin with the later ones, and end with the former ones. And Mt. 20, 9.
36 those of eleven hours[8] came, and received each a penny. When therefore the first Mt. 20, 10.
came, they supposed that they should receive something more; and they also
37 received each a penny. And when they received *it*, they spake angrily against the Mt. 20, 11.

1 Lit. *meet with;* or, *be recompensed with.* 2 The Arabic words are not so strong. 3 Or, *so that.* 4 Or, *and.*
5 The Syriac and Arabic versions here agree with the Greek. For a plausible suggestion as to the origin of the strange reading in the text, see Harris, *The Diatessaron of Tatian*, p. 21, who cites a parallel from Aphraates.
6 This may be simply a corruption of the Peshitta. 7 Or, *Surely.* The word is omitted by Borg. MS.
8 i.e., probably *the eleventh hour* (*cf.* § 21, 10).

§29 38 householder, and said, These last worked one hour, and thou hast made them equal Mt. 20, 12.
39 with us, who have suffered the heat of the day, and its burden. He answered and Mt. 20, 13.
said unto one of them, My friend, I do thee no wrong: *was it* not for a penny *that*
40 thou didst bargain with me? Take what is thine, and go thy way; for I wish to Mt. 20, 14.
41 give this last as I have given thee. Or am I not entitled to do with what is mine[1] Mt. 20, 15.
42 what I choose? Or is thine eye perchance evil, because I am good? Thus shall Mt. 20, 16.
the last *ones* be first, and the first last. The called are many, and the chosen are
few.

43 And when Jesus entered into the house of one of the chiefs of the Pharisees to Lk. 14, 1.
eat bread on the sabbath day, and they were watching him to see what he would
44, 45 do, and there was before him a man which had the dropsy, Jesus answered and Lk. 14, 2. Lk. 14, 3.
46 said unto the scribes and the Pharisees, Is it lawful on the sabbath to heal? But Lk. 14, 4.
Arabic, they were silent. So he took him, and healed him, and sent him away.
47 p. 114 And he said unto them, Which of you shall *have* his son or his ox fall on Lk. 14, 5.
the sabbath day into a well, and not lift him up straightway, and draw water for
48 him? And they were not able to answer him a word to that. Lk. 14, 6.

SECTION XXX.

§30 1 And he spake a parable unto those which were bidden there, because he saw Lk. 14, 7.
2 them choose the places that were in the highest part of the sitting room: When a Lk. 14, 8.
man invites thee to a feast, do not go and sit at the head of the room; lest there
3 be there a man more honourable than thou, and he that invited you come and say Lk. 14, 9.
unto thee, Give the place to this man: and thou be ashamed when thou risest and
4 takest[2] another place. But when thou art invited, go and sit last; so that when Lk. 14, 10.
he that invited thee cometh, he may say unto thee, My friend, go up higher: and
5 thou shalt have praise before all that were invited with thee. For every one that Lk. 14, 11.
exalteth himself shall be abased; and every one that abaseth himself shall be
exalted.

6 And he said also to him that had invited him, When thou makest a feast[3] or a Lk. 14, 12.
banquet,[3] do not invite thy friends, nor even thy brethren, nor thy kinsmen, nor thy
7 rich neighbours; lest haply they also invite thee, and thou have this reward. But Lk. 14, 13.
when thou makest a feast, invite the poor, and those with withered hand, and the
8 lame, and the blind: and blessed art thou, since they have not the means to reward Lk. 14, 14.
9 thee; that thy reward may be at the rising of the righteous. And when one of Lk. 14, 15.
them that were invited heard that, he said unto him, Blessed is he that shall eat
bread in the kingdom of God.

10, 11 Jesus answered again in parables, and said, The kingdom of heaven hath been lik- Mt. 22, 1. Mt. 22, 2.
Arabic, ened to[4] a certain king, which made a feast[5] for his son, and prepared a Lk. 14, 16*b*.
12 p. 115 great banquet,[6] and invited many: and he sent his servants at the time of the Lk. 14, 17.
feast to inform them that were invited, Everything is made ready for you; come. And Mt. 22, 3*b*.
13 they would not come, but began all of them with one voice to make excuse. And Lk. 14, 18.
the first said unto them, Say to him, I have bought a field, and I must needs go out
14 to see it: I pray thee to release[7] me, for I ask to be excused. And another said, Lk. 14, 19.
I have bought five yoke of oxen, and I am going to examine them: I pray thee
15 to release me, for I ask to be excused. And another said, I have married a wife, Lk. 14, 20.
16 and therefore I cannot come. And the king sent also other servants, and said, Say Mt. 22, 4.
to those that were invited, that my feast is ready, and my oxen and my fatlings are
17 slain, and everything is ready: come to the feast. But they made light of it, and Mt. 22, 5.
18 went, one to his field, and another to his merchandise: and the rest took his Mt. 22, 6.
19 servants, and entreated them shamefully, and killed them. And one of the servants Lk. 14, 21*a*.
20 came, and informed his lord of what had happened. And when the king heard, he Mt. 22, 7.
became angry, and sent his armies; and they destroyed those murderers, and
21 burned their cities. Then he said to his servants, The feast is prepared, but those Mt. 22, 8.
22 that were invited were not worthy. Go out quickly into the markets and into the Lk. 14, 21*c*.

1 Lit. *my thing*. 2 Lit. *at thy rising and taking*. 3 Practically synonymous words.
4 Borg. MS., *is like*. 5 Used specially of a marriage feast.
6 Lit. *bread*, the Syriac word for which (*not* that in the versions) means also *feast*. 7 Or, *omit*.

§ 30 partings of the ways of the city, and bring in hither the poor, and those with pains,
and the lame, and the blind. And the servants did as the king commanded them.
23 And they came, and said unto him, Our lord, we have done all that thou com- Lk. 14, 22.
24 mandedst us, and there is here still room. So the lord said unto his servants, Go Lk. 14, 23*a*.
out into the roads, and the ways, and the paths, and every one that ye find, invite Mt. 22, 9*b*.
25 Arabic, to the feast, and constrain them to enter, till my house is[1] filled. I say unto Lk. 14, 23*b*. Lk. 14, 24.
p. 116 you, that no one of those people that were invited shall taste of my feast.
26 And those servants went out into the roads, and gathered all that they found, good and Mt. 22, 10.
27 bad: and the banquet-house was filled with guests. And the king entered to see those Mt. 22, 11.
28 who were seated, and he saw there a man not wearing a festive garment: and he Mt. 22, 12.
said unto him, My friend, how didst thou come in here not having on festive gar-
29 ments? And he was silent. Then the king said to the servants, Bind his hands Mt. 22, 13.
and his feet, and put him forth into the outer darkness; there shall be weeping and
30 gnashing of teeth. The called are many; and the chosen, few. Mt. 22, 14.
31 And after that, the time of the feast of unleavened bread of the Jews arrived, Jo. 5, 1*a*.
32 and Jesus went out to go to Jerusalem. And as he went in the way, there met him Lk. 17, 11. Lk. 17, 12.
33 ten persons who were lepers, and stood afar off: and they lifted up their voice, and Lk. 17, 13.
34 said, Our Master, Jesus, have mercy upon us. And when he saw them, he said Lk. 17, 14.
unto them, Go and shew yourselves unto the priests. And when they went, they
35 were cleansed. And one of them, when he saw himself cleansed, returned, and Lk. 17, 15.
36 was praising God with a loud voice; and he fell on his face before the feet of Lk. 17, 16.
37 Jesus, giving him thanks: and this *man* was a Samaritan. Jesus answered and said, Lk. 17, 17.
38 Were not those that were cleansed ten? where then are the nine? Not one of Lk. 17, 18.
them turned aside to come and praise God, but this *man* who is of a strange
39 people. He said unto him, Arise, and go thy way; for thy faith hath given thee Lk. 17, 19.
life.[2]
40 And while they were going up in the way to Jerusalem, Jesus went in front of them; Mk. 10, 32.
and they wondered, and followed him fearing. And he took his twelve disciples apart,
41 and began to tell them privately[3] what was about to befall him. And he said unto Lk. 18, 31*b*.
Arabic, them, We are going up to Jerusalem, and all the things shall be fulfilled
42 p. 117 that are written in the prophets concerning the Son of man. He shall be Mk. 10, 33*b*.
delivered to the chief priests and the scribes; and they shall condemn him to death,
43 and deliver him to the peoples;[4] and they shall treat him shamefully, and scourge Mk. 10, 34*a*.
44 him, and spit in his face, and humble him,[5] and crucify him, and slay him: and on Lk. 18, 33.
45 the third day he shall rise. But they understood not one thing of this; but this Lk. 18, 34.
word was hidden from them, and they did not perceive these things that were
addressed to them.
46 Then came near to him the mother of the (two) sons of Zebedee, she and her Mt. 20, 20.
(two) sons, and worshipped him, and asked of him a *certain* thing. And he said Mt. 20, 21*a*.
47 unto her, What wouldest thou? And James and John, her two sons, came Mk. 10, 35.
forward, and said unto him, Teacher, we would that all that we ask thou wouldest
48 do unto us. He said unto them,[6] What would ye that I should do unto you? Mk. 10, 36.
49 They said unto him, Grant us that we may sit, the one on thy right, and the other Mk. 10, 37.
50 on thy left, in thy kingdom and thy glory. And Jesus said unto them, Ye know Mk. 10, 38.
not what ye ask. Are ye able to drink the cup that I am to drink? and with the
51 baptism that I am to be baptized with, will ye be baptized? And they said unto Mk. 10, 39.
him, We are able. Jesus said unto them, The cup that I drink ye shall drink; and
52 with the baptism wherewith I am baptized ye shall be baptized: but that ye should Mk. 10, 40.
sit on my right and on my left is not mine to give; but *it is* for him for whom my
Father hath prepared *it*.

SECTION XXXI.

§ 31 1 And when the ten heard, they were moved with anger against James and John. Mk. 10, 41.
2 And Jesus called them, and said unto them, Ye know that the rulers of the nations Mk. 10, 42

1 Or, *that my house may be*. 2 Or, *saved thee*. 3 Lit. *between himself and them*.
4 i.e., Gentiles.
5 An obscure expression; perhaps it was originally a repetition of the preceding clause. It might be emended into *point at him* (*the finger of scorn*).
6 Lit. of course *the two of them*, and so all through the conversation.

§31 3 are their lords; and their great men are set in authority over them. Not thus shall it Mk. 10, 43.
Arabic, be amongst you: but he amongst you that would be great, let him be to you a
4 p. 118 servant; and whoever of you would be first,[1] let him be to every man a Mk. 10, 44.
5 bond-servant: *even* as the Son of man also came not to be served, but to serve, and Mt. 20, 28.
6 to give himself a ransom in place of the many. He said this, and was going about Lk. 13, 22.
7 the villages and the cities, and teaching; and he went to Jerusalem. And a man Lk. 13, 23.
asked him, Are those that shall be saved few? Jesus answered and said unto
8 them, Strive ye to enter at the narrow door: I say unto you now, that many shall Lk. 13, 24.
9 seek to enter, and shall not be able[2]—from the time when the master of the house Lk. 13, 25.
riseth, and closeth the door, and ye shall be standing without, and shall knock at
the door, and shall begin to say, Our lord, open unto us; and he shall answer and
10 say, I say unto you, I know you not whence ye are: and ye shall begin to say, Lk. 13, 26.
11 Before thee we did eat and drink, and in our markets didst thou teach; and he Lk. 13, 27.
shall say unto you, I know you not whence ye are; depart[3] from me, ye servants
12 of untruth. There shall be weeping and gnashing of teeth, when ye see Abraham, Lk. 13, 28.
and Isaac, and Jacob, and all the prophets, in the kingdom of God, while ye are
13 put forth without. And they shall come from the east and the west, and from the Lk. 13, 29.
14 north and the south, and shall sit down in the kingdom of God. And there shall Lk. 13, 30.
then be last that have become first, and first that have become last.

15, 16 And when Jesus entered and passed through Jericho, there was a man named Zac- Lk. 19, 1. Lk. 19, 2.
17 chæus, rich, and chief of the publicans. And he desired to see Jesus who he was; and Lk. 19, 3.
he was not able for the pressure of the crowd, because Zacchæus was little of stature.
18 Arabic, And he hastened, and went before Jesus, and went up into an unripe fig Lk. 19, 4.
19 p. 119 tree[4] to see Jesus: for he was to pass thus. And when Jesus came to Lk. 19, 5.
that place, he saw him, and said unto him, Make haste, and come down, Zacchæus:
20 to-day I must be in thy house. And he hastened, and came down, and received Lk. 19, 6.
21 him joyfully. And when they all saw, they murmured, and said, He hath gone in Lk. 19, 7.
22 and lodged with a man that is a sinner. So Zacchæus stood, and said unto Jesus, Lk. 19, 8.
My Lord, now half of my possessions I give to the poor, and what I have unjustly
23 taken[5] from every man I give him fourfold. Jesus said unto him, To-day is salva- Lk. 19, 9.
24 tion come to this house, because this *man* also is a[6] son of Abraham. For the Son Lk. 19, 10.
of man came to seek and save the thing that was lost.

25 And when Jesus went out of Jericho, he and his disciples, there came after him Lk. 18, 35a.[7] Mt. 20, 29b.
26 a great multitude. And there was a blind man sitting by the way side begging. Lk. 18, 35b.
27 And his name was Timæus, the son of Timæus. And he heard the sound of the Mk. 10, 46b. Lk. 18, 36.
28 multitude passing, and asked, Who is this? They said unto him, Jesus the Naza- Lk. 18, 37.
29 rene passeth by. And when he heard that it was Jesus, he called out with a loud Mk. 10, 47a. Lk. 18, 38.
30 voice, and said, Jesus, son of David, have mercy on me. And those that went Lk. 18, 39a.
before Jesus were rebuking him, that he should hold his peace: but he cried the Mk. 10, 48b
31 more, and said, Son of David, have mercy on me. And Jesus stood, and com- Mk. 10, 49.
manded that they should call him. And they called the blind man, and said unto
32 him, Be of good courage, and rise; for, behold, he calleth thee. And the blind Mk. 10, 50.
33 man threw away his garment, and rose, and came to Jesus. Jesus said unto him, Mk. 10, 51.
What dost thou wish that I should do unto thee? And that blind man said unto
him, My Lord and Master, that my eyes may be opened, so that I may see thee.[8]
34 Arabic, And Jesus had compassion on him, and touched his eyes, and said unto Mt. 20, 34a
35 p. 120 him, See; for thy faith hath saved thee. And immediately he received Lk. 18, 42b.
his sight,[9] and came after him, and praised God; and all the people that saw Lk. 18, 43.
praised God.

36 And he spake a parable because he was nearing[10] Jerusalem, and they supposed Lk. 19, 11b
37 that at that time the kingdom of God was about to appear. He said unto them, Lk. 19, 12.
A man, a son of a great race, went into a far country, to receive a kingdom, and
38 return. And he called his ten servants, and gave them ten shares, and said unto Lk. 19, 13.

1 Lit. *advanced.* 2 Lit. *find*, like the Syriac.
3 This rendering requires the omission of the diacritical point over the middle radical. The text as printed means *perish.*
4 *cf.* the extract from Isho'dad (Harris, *Fragments*, p. 19).
5 A diacritical point must be restored to the second letter of this word. As it stands it gives no sense.
6 Lit. *the.* 7 Rather, Mt. 20, 29a+Mk. 10, 46a. 8 *cf.* Mt. 20, 33, and Lk. 18, 41, both in Curetonian.
9 Lit. *saw.* 10 Or, *near.*

§31 39 them, Trade till the time of my coming. But the people of his city hated him, and Lk. 19, 14.
40 sent messengers after him, and said, We will not that this *man* reign over us. And Lk. 19, 15.
when he had received a[1] kingdom, and returned, he said that the servants to whom
he had given the money should be called unto him, that he might know what each
41 of them had traded. And the first came, and said, My lord, thy share hath gained Lk. 19, 16.
42 ten shares. The king said unto him, Thou good and faithful servant, who hast Lk. 19, 17.
43 been found faithful in a little, be thou set over ten districts. And the second came, Lk. 19, 18.
44 and said, My lord, thy portion hath gained five portions. And he said unto him Lk. 19, 19.
45 also, And thou shalt be set over five districts. And another came, and said, My Lk. 19, 20.
46 lord, here is thy portion, which was with me laid by in a napkin: I feared thee, Lk. 19, 21.
because thou art a hard man, and takest what thou didst not leave, and seekest
47 what thou didst not give, and reapest what thou didst not sow. His lord said unto Lk. 19, 22.
him, From thy mouth shall I judge thee, thou wicked and idle servant, who wast
untrustworthy. Thou knewest that I am a hard man, and take what I did not
48 leave, and reap what I did not sow: why didst thou not put my money at usury, Lk. 19, 23.
49 and so I might come and seek it, with its gains? And he said unto those that were Lk. 19, 24.
standing in front of him, Take from him the share, and give it to him that hath
50, 51 Arabic, ten shares. They said unto him, Our lord, he hath ten shares. He said Lk. 19, 25. Lk. 19, 26.
p. 121 unto them, I say unto you, Every one that hath shall be given unto; and
52 he that hath not, that which he hath also shall be taken from him. And those mine Lk. 19, 27.
enemies who would not that I should reign over them, bring them, and slay them
before me.

SECTION XXXII.

§32 1 And when Jesus entered Jerusalem, he went up to the temple of God, and found Mt. 21, 12*a*. Jo. 2, 14*a*.
2 there oxen and sheep and doves. And when he beheld those that sold and those Mt. 21, 12*b*.
that bought, and the money-changers sitting, he made for himself a scourge of rope, Jo. 2, 14*b*.
and drove them all out of the temple, and the sheep and the oxen, and the money-
changers; and he threw down their money, and upset their tables, and the seats of Mt. 21, 12*c*.
3 them that sold the doves; and he was teaching, and saying unto them, Is it not Mt. 21, 13.
written, My house is a house of prayer for all peoples? and ye have made it a den
4 for robbers. And he said unto those that sold the doves, Take this hence, and Jo. 2, 16.
5 make not my Father's house a house of merchandise. And he suffered not any Mk. 11, 16.
6 one to carry vessels inside the temple. And his disciples remembered the scripture, Jo. 2, 17.
7 The zeal of thy house hath eaten me up. The Jews answered and said unto him, Jo. 2, 18.
8 What sign hast thou shewn us, that thou doest this? Jesus answered and said unto Jo. 2, 19.
9 them, Destroy this temple, and I shall raise it in three days. The Jews said unto Jo. 2, 20.
him, This temple was built in forty-six years, and wilt thou raise it in three days?
10 But he spake unto them of the temple of his body, that when[2] they destroyed it, he Jo. 2, 21.
11 Arabic, would raise it in three days. When therefore he rose from among the Jo. 2, 22.
p. 122 dead, his disciples remembered that he said this; and they believed the
scriptures, and the word that Jesus spake.
12 And when Jesus sat down over against the treasury, he observed how the multi- Mk. 12, 41.
tudes were casting their offerings into the treasury: and many rich *men* were
13, 14 throwing in much. And there came a poor widow, and cast in two mites. And Mk. 12, 42*a*. Lk. 21, 3.
Jesus called his disciples, and said unto them, Verily I say unto you, This poor
15 widow cast into the treasury more than all the people: and all of these cast into Mk. 12, 44*a*.
the place of the offering of God[3] of the superfluity of their wealth; while this
woman of her want threw in all that she possessed.
16 And he spake unto them this parable, concerning people who trusted in them- Lk. 18, 9.
17 selves that they are righteous, and despised every man: Two men went up to the Lk. 18, 10.
18 temple to pray; one of them a Pharisee, and the other a publican. And the Lk. 18, 11.
Pharisee stood apart,[4] and prayed thus, O Lord, I thank thee, since I am not like
the rest of men, the unjust, the profligate, the extortioners, or even like this publican;

1 Doubtless a misinterpretation of the Syriac. 2 Or, *if*.
3 Lit. *house of the offering of God*, as in the MS. described by Gildemeister (at Lk. 21, 4); but it is simply a reproduction of the phrase used in the Peshitta at Lk. 21, 3. The parallel passages are a good deal fused together.
4 Lit. *between him and himself*.

§32 19 20 but I fast two days a week, and tithe all my possessions.[1] And the publican was Lk. 18, 12. Lk. 18, 13.
standing at a distance, and he would not even lift up his eyes to heaven, but was
21 beating upon his breast, and saying, O Lord, have mercy on me, me the sinner. I Lk. 18, 14.
say unto you, that this man went down justified to his house more than the Pharisee.
Every one that exalteth himself shall be abased; and every one that abaseth himself shall be exalted.
22 Arabic, And when eventide was come, he left all the people, and went outside the Mk. 11, 19a. Mt. 21, 17.
23 p. 123 city to Bethany, he and his twelve, and he remained there. And all the peo- Lk. 9, 11.
ple, because they knew the place, came to him, and he received them; and them that
24 had need of healing he healed. And on the morning of the next day, when he returned Mk. 11, 12.
25 to the city from Bethany, he hungered. And he saw a[2] fig tree at a distance on the Mk. 11, 13.
beaten highway, having on it leaves. And he came unto it, *expecting* to find something on it; and when he came, he found nothing on it but the leaves—it[3] was not
26 the season of figs—and he said unto it, Henceforward for ever let no man eat fruit Mk. 11, 14.
of thee. And his disciples heard.
27 And they came to Jerusalem. And there was there a man of the Pharisees, Mk. 11, 15a. Jo. 3, 1.
28 named Nicodemus, ruler of the Jews. This *man* came unto Jesus by night, and Jo. 3, 2.
said unto him, My Master, we know that thou hast been sent from God as a
teacher; and no man can do these signs that thou doest, except him whom God is
29 with. Jesus answered and said unto him, Verily, verily, I say unto thee, If a man Jo. 3, 3.
30 be not born a second *time*, he cannot see the kingdom of God. Nicodemus said Jo. 3, 4.
unto him, How can a man who is old be born? can he, think you, return again to
31 his mother's womb a second time, to enter and be born? Jesus answered and said Jo. 3, 5.
unto him, Verily, verily, I say unto thee, If a man be not born of water and the Spirit,
32 he cannot enter the kingdom of God. For he that is born of flesh is flesh; and he that Jo. 3, 6.
33 is born of Spirit is spirit. Wonder not that I said unto thee that ye must be born a Jo. 3, 7.
34 Arabic, second *time*. The wind bloweth where it listeth, and thou hearest its voice, Jo. 3, 8.
p. 124 but thou knowest not from what place it cometh, nor whither it goeth: so
35 is every man that is born of the Spirit. Nicodemus answered and said unto him, Jo. 3, 9.
36 How can that be? Jesus answered and said unto him, Art thou teaching[4] Israel, Jo. 3, 10.
37 and *yet* knowest not these things? Verily, verily, I say unto thee, What we know Jo. 3, 11.
38 we say, and what we have seen we witness; and ye receive not our witness. If I Jo. 3, 12.
said unto you what is on earth, and ye believed not, how then, if I say unto you
39 what is in heaven, will ye believe? And no man hath ascended up into heaven, Jo. 3, 13.
except him that descended from heaven, the Son of man, which is in heaven.
40 And as Moses lifted up the serpent in the wilderness, so is the Son of man to be Jo. 3, 14.
41 lifted up; so that every man who may believe in him may not perish, but have Jo. 3, 15.
42 eternal life. God so loved the world, that[5] he should give his only Son; and so Jo. 3, 16.
every one that believeth on him should not perish, but should have eternal life.
43 God sent not his Son into the world to judge the world; but that the world might Jo. 3, 17.
44 be saved by his hand. He that believeth in him shall not be judged: but he that Jo. 3, 18.
believeth not is condemned beforehand, because he hath not believed in the name
45 of the only *Son*, the Son of God.[6] This is the judgement, that the light came into Jo. 3, 19.
the world, and men loved the darkness more than the light; because their deeds
46 were evil. Whosoever doeth evil deeds hateth the light, and cometh not to the Jo. 3, 20.
47 light, lest his deeds be reproved. But he that doeth the truth cometh to the light, Jo. 3, 21.
that his deeds may be known, that they have been done in God.

SECTION XXXIII.

§33 1 Arabic, And when evening came, Jesus went forth outside of the city, he and his Mk. 11, 19.
2 p. 125 disciples. And as they passed in the morning, the disciples saw that fig tree Mk. 11, 20.
3 withered away from its root. And they passed by, and said, How did the fig tree dry Mt. 21, 20b.
4 up immediately? And Simon remembered, and said unto him, My Master, behold, Mk. 11, 21.

1 Or, *gains*. 2 Lit. *one* (Syriac). 3 Lit. *and it*. 4 Or *the teacher of*.
5 The Arabic particle means *in order that*. Perhaps it is a clerical error for *so that*; or it may be meant to represent the Syriac.
6 The translator has followed too closely the order of words in his Syriac original, which agrees with the Text. Rec.

§33 5 that fig tree which thou didst curse hath dried up. And Jesus answered and said Mk. 11, 22.
6 unto them, Let there be in you the faith of God. Verily I say unto you, if ye Mk. 11, 23.
believe, and doubt not in your hearts, and assure yourselves that that will be which
7 ye say, ye shall have what ye say. And if ye say to this mountain, Remove, and Mt. 21, 21*b*.
8 fall[1] into the sea, it shall be. And all that ye ask God in prayer, and believe, he Mt. 21, 22.
9, 10 will give you. And the apostles[2] said unto our Lord, Increase our[3] faith. He Lk. 17, 5. Lk. 17, 6.
said unto them, If there be in you faith like a grain of mustard, ye shall say to this
fig tree, Be thou torn up, and be thou planted in the sea; and it will obey you.
11 Who of you hath a servant driving a yoke of oxen or tending sheep, and if he Lk. 17, 7.
12 come from the field, will say unto him straightway, Go and sit down? Nay,[4] he Lk. 17, 8.
will say unto him, Make ready for me wherewith I may sup, and gird thy waist,
and serve me, till I eat and drink; and afterwards thou shalt eat and drink also.
13 Doth that servant haply, who did what he was bid, receive his praise? I think Lk. 17, 9.
14 not. So ye also, when ye have done all that ye were bid, say, We are idle servants; Lk. 17, 10.
what it was our duty to do, we have done.
15 For this reason I say unto you, Whatever ye pray and ask, believe that ye Mk. 11, 24.
16 Arabic, receive, and ye shall have. And when ye stand to pray, forgive what is Mk. 11, 25.
p. 126 in your heart against *any* man; and your Father which is in heaven will
17 forgive you also your wrong-doings. But if ye forgive not men their wrong-doings, Mk. 11, 26.
neither will your Father forgive you also your wrong-doings.
18 And he spake unto them a parable also, that they should pray at all times, and Lk. 18, 1.
19 not be slothful: There was a judge in a city, who feared not God, nor was ashamed Lk. 18, 2.
20 for men: and there was a widow in that city; and she came unto him, and said, Lk. 18, 3.
21 Avenge me of mine adversary. And he would not for a long time: but afterwards Lk. 18, 4.
he said within himself, If of God I have no fear, and before men I have no shame;
22 *yet* because this widow vexeth *me*, I will avenge her, that she come not at all times Lk. 18, 5.
23, 24 and annoy me. And our Lord said, Hear ye what the judge of injustice said. And Lk. 18, 6. Lk. 18, 7.
shall not God *still* more do vengeance for his elect, who call upon him in the night
25 and *in* the day, and grant them respite? I say unto you, He will do vengeance for Lk. 18, 8.
them speedily. Thinkest thou the Son of man will come and find faith on the
earth?
26, 27 And they came again to Jerusalem. And it came to pass, on one of the days, Mk. 11, 15*a*. Lk. 20, 1.
as Jesus was walking in the temple, and teaching the people, and preaching *the*
28 *gospel*, that the chief priests and the scribes with the elders came upon him, and Lk. 20, 2*a*.
said unto him, Tell us: By what power doest thou this? and who gave thee this Mk. 11, 28*b*.
29 power to do that? And Jesus said unto them, I also will ask you one word, and if Mk. 11, 29*a*. Mt. 21, 24*b*.
30 ye tell me, I also shall tell you by what power I do that. The baptism of John, from Mt. 21, 25*a*.
31 what place *is* it? from heaven or of men? Tell me. And they reflected within them- Mk. 11, 30*b*. Mt. 21, 25*b*.
Arabic, selves, and said, If we shall say unto him, From heaven; he will say unto
32 p. 127 us, For what reason did ye not believe him? But[5] if we shall say, Of men; Mt. 21, 26*a*.
33 we fear[6] that the people will stone us, all of them. And all of them were holding[7] Lk. 20, 6*b*. Mk. 11, 32*b*.
34 to John, that he was a true prophet. They answered and said unto him, We know Mk. 11, 33.
35 not. Jesus said unto them, Neither tell I you also by what power I work. What Mt. 21, 28.
think ye? A man had two sons; and he went to the first, and said unto him, My
36 son, go to-day, and till in the vineyard. And he answered and said, I do not wish Mt. 21, 29.
37 to: but finally he repented, and went. And he went to the other, and said unto Mt. 21, 30.
38 him likewise. And he answered and said, Yea, my lord: and went not. Which of Mt. 21, 31.
these two did the will of his father? They said unto him, The first. Jesus said
unto them, Verily I say unto you, The publicans and harlots go before you into
39 the kingdom of God. John came unto you in the way of righteousness, and ye Mt. 21, 32.
believed him not; but the publicans and harlots believed him; and ye, not even
when ye saw, did ye repent at last, that ye might believe in him.
40 Hear another parable: A man was a householder, and planted a vineyard, and Mt. 21, 33*a*.
surrounded it with a hedge, and digged in it a winepress, and built in it a tower,
41, 42 and gave it to husbandmen, and went to a distance for a long time. So when the Lk. 20, 9*b*. Mk. 21, 34.
time of the fruits came, he sent his servants[8] unto the husbandmen, that they might

1 Syr. 2 The Syriac word. 3 Lit. *Increase us in.* 4 Or, *But.* 5 Verse 26 begins here in the Greek.
6 From Mark. 7 *cf.* Syriac. 8 The difference between singular and plural is very slight in Arabic.

§33 43 send him of the produce[1] of his vineyard. And those husbandmen beat him, and Mk. 12, 3*b*.
44 sent him away empty. And he sent unto them another servant also; and they Mk. 12, 4.
45 stoned him, and wounded[2] him, and sent him away with shameful handling. And Mk. 12, 5*a*.
he sent again another; and they slew him. And he sent many other servants unto
46 them. And the husbandmen took his servants, and one they beat, and another they Mt. 21, 35.
47 stoned, and another they slew. So he sent again other servants more than the first; and Mt. 21, 36.
48 Arabic, they did likewise with them. So the owner of the vineyard said, What shall Lk. 20, 13.
p. 128 I do? I will send my beloved son: it may be they will see him and be
49, 50 ashamed. So at last he sent unto them his beloved son that he had. But the Mk. 12, 6*a*. Mt. 21, 38*a*.
husbandmen, when they saw the son, said amongst themselves, This is the heir.
51, 52 And they said, We will slay him, and so the inheritance will be ours. So they took Lk. 20, 14*b*. Mt. 21, 39.
53 him, and put him forth without the vineyard, and slew him. When then the lord Mt. 21, 40.
54 of the vineyard shall come, what will he do with those husbandmen? They said Mt. 21, 41.
unto him, He will destroy them in the worst of ways,[3] and give the vineyard to
55 other husbandmen, who will give him fruit in its season. Jesus said unto them, Mt. 21, 42*a*.
Have ye never read in the scripture,

The stone which the builders declared to be base,
The same came to be at the head of the corner: Lk. 20, 17*b*.
56 From God was this, Mt. 21, 42*c*.
And it is wonderful in our eyes?

57 Therefore I say unto you, The kingdom of God shall be taken from you, and Mt. 21, 43.
58 given to a people that will produce fruit. And whosoever falleth on this stone Mt. 21, 44.
shall be broken in pieces: but on whomsoever it falleth, it will grind him to
59 powder. And when the chief priests and the Pharisees heard his parables, they Mt. 21, 45.
60 perceived that it was concerning them he spake. And they sought to seize him; Mt. 21, 46.
and they feared the multitude, because they were holding to him as the prophet.

SECTION XXXIV.

§34 1 Then went the Pharisees and considered how they might ensnare him in a word, Mt. 22, 15.
2 and deliver him into the power of the judge,[4] and into the power of the ruler. And Lk. 20, 20*b*. Mt. 22, 16.
they sent unto him their disciples, with the kinsfolk of Herod; and they said unto him,
Arabic, Teacher, we know that thou speakest the truth, and teachest the way of God
p. 129 with equity,[5] and art not lifted up[6] by any man: for thou actest not so as to
3 be seen of any man. Tell us now, What is thy opinion? Is it lawful that we should Mt. 22, 17.
4 pay the tribute to Cæsar, or not? shall we give, or shall we not give? But Jesus knew Mk. 12, 15*a*.
5 their deceit, and said unto them, Why tempt ye me, ye hypocrites? Shew me the Mt. 22, 18*b*. Mt. 22, 19.
6 penny of the tribute. So they brought unto him a penny. Jesus said unto them, Mt. 22, 20.
To whom belongeth this image and inscription? They said unto him, To Cæsar.
7, 8 He said unto them, Give what is Cæsar's to Cæsar, and what is God's to God. And Mt. 22, 21. Lk. 20, 26.
they could not make him slip in a *single* word before the people; and they marvelled
at his word, and refrained.
9 And on that day came the Sadducees, and said unto him,[7] There is no life for Mt. 22, 23.
10 the dead. And they asked him, and said unto him, Teacher, Moses said unto us, Mt. 22, 24.
If a man die, not having children, let his brother take his wife, and raise up seed
11 for his brother. Now there *were* with us seven brethren: and the first took a wife, Mt. 22, 25. Lk. 20, 29*b*.
12 and died without children; and the second took his wife, and died without children; Lk. 20, 30.
13 and the third also took her; and in like manner the seven of them also, and they Lk. 20, 31.
14, 15 died without leaving children. And last of them all the woman died also. At the Mt. 22, 27. Mt. 22, 28.
resurrection, then, which of these seven shall have this woman? for all of them took
16 her. Jesus answered and said unto them, Is it not for this that ye have erred, Mt. 22, 29*a*. Mk. 12, 24*b*.
17 because ye know not the scriptures, nor the power of God? And the sons of this Lk. 20, 34*b*.
18 world take wives, and the women become the men's;[8] but those that have become Lk. 20, 35.
worthy of that world, and the resurrection from among the dead, do[9] not take

1 Lit. *property*. 2 A word used specially of wounding the head. 3 *cf.* Syriac versions.
4 Vat. MS. omits *the power*. We should then translate (with Pesh. and Sin.) *unto judgement*. 5 See note, § 3, 53.
6 Possibly this is the meaning of the Arabic phrase, which occurs also in Ibn-aṭ-Ṭayyib's Commentary (Brit. Mus. text).
7 *cf.* the Syriac versions. 8 *cf.* the Syriac versions. 9 Or, *shall*.

§34 19 Arabic, wives, and the women also do[1] not become the men's. Nor is it possible Lk. 20, 36.
p. 130 that they should die; but they[2] are like the angels, and are the children of
20 God, because they have become the children of the resurrection. For in[3] the resur- Mt. 22, 30*a*.
rection of the dead, have ye not read in the book of Moses, how from the bush God Mk. 12, 26*b*.
said unto him, I am the God of Abraham, and the God of Isaac, and the God of Jacob?
21 And God is not *the God* of the dead, but of the living: for all of them are alive Lk. 20, 38.
with him. And ye have erred greatly. Mk. 12, 27*b*.
22, 23 And when the multitudes heard, they were wondering at his teaching. And Mt. 22, 33. Lk. 20, 39.
24 some of the scribes answered and said unto him, Teacher, thou hast well said. But Mt. 22, 34.
the rest of the Pharisees, when they saw his silencing the Sadducees on this point,
gathered against him to contend with him.
25 And one of the scribes, of those that knew the law, when he saw the excellence Mt. 22, 35*a*. Mk. 12, 28*b*.
26 of his answer to them, desired to try him, and said unto him, What shall I do to Lk. 10, 25*b*.
inherit eternal life? and, Which of the commandments is greater, and has precedence Mk. 12, 28*b*.
27 in the law? Jesus said unto him, The first of all the commandments is, Hear, O Mk. 12, 29.
28 Israel; The Lord our God, the Lord is one: and thou shalt love the Lord thy Mk. 12, 30*a*.
God with all thy heart, and with all thy soul, and with all thy thought, and with all thy Mt. 22, 37*b*.[4]
29, 30 strength. This is the great and preëminent[5] commandment. And the second, which Mt. 22, 38. Mk. 12, 31.
is like it, is, Thou shalt love thy neighbour as thyself. And another commandment
31 greater than these two there is not. On these two commandments, then, are hung the Mt. 22, 40.
32 Arabic, law and the prophets. That scribe said unto him, Excellent! my Master;[6] Mk. 12, 32.
p. 131 thou hast said truly that he is one, and there is no other outside of him:
33 and that a man should love him with all his heart, and with all his thought, and Mk. 12, 33.
with all his soul, and with all his strength, and that he should love his neighbour as
34 himself, is better than all savours and sacrifices. And Jesus saw him that he had Mk. 12, 34*a*.
answered wisely; and he answered and said unto him, Thou art not far from the
35, 36 kingdom of God. Thou hast spoken rightly: do this, and thou shalt live. And Lk. 10, 28*b*. Lk. 10, 29.
he, as his desire was to justify himself, said unto him, And who is my neighbour?
37 Jesus said unto him, A man went down from Jerusalem to Jericho; and the robbers Lk. 10, 30.
fell upon him, and stripped[7] him, and beat him, his life remaining in him *but* little,[8]
38 and went away. And it happened that there came down a certain priest that way; Lk. 10, 31.
39 and he saw him, and passed by. And likewise a Levite also came and reached Lk. 10, 32.
40 that place, and saw him, and passed by. And a certain Samaritan, as he journeyed, Lk. 10, 33.
41 came to[9] the place where he was, and saw him, and had compassion on him, and Lk. 10, 34.
came near, and bound up his strokes,[10] and poured on them wine and oil; and he
set[11] him on the ass, and brought him to the inn, and expended his care upon him.
42 And on the morrow of that day he took out two pence, and gave them to the inn- Lk. 10, 35.
keeper, and said unto him, Care for him; and if thou spendest upon him more,
43 when I return, I shall give thee. Who of these three now, thinkest thou, is nearest Lk. 10, 36.
44 to him that fell among the robbers? And he said unto him, He that had compas- Lk. 10, 37.
45 Arabic, sion on him. Jesus said unto him, Go, and do thou also likewise. And Mk. 12, 34*b*.
p. 132 no man dared afterwards to ask him anything.
46 And he was teaching every day in the temple. But the chief priests and scribes Lk. 19, 47.
and the elders of the people sought to destroy him: and they could[12] not *find* what Lk. 19, 48.
47 they should do with him; and all the people were hanging upon him to hear him.
48 And many of the multitude believed on him, and said, The Messiah, when he Jo. 7, 31.
49 cometh, can it be that he will do more than these signs that this *man* doeth? And Jo. 7, 32.
the Pharisees heard the multitudes say that of him; and the chief priests sent
50 officers[13] to seize him. And Jesus said unto them, I am with you *but* a short time Jo. 7, 33.

1 Or, *shall*. 2 Borg. MS., *all of them* instead of *but they*. 3 Or, *Moreover, regarding*.
4 Rather, Mk. 12, 30*b*. 5 This simply represents *first* in Syriac.
6 Vat. MS. has a corruption of *Excellent! Rabbi*, better preserved by Borg. MS., which, however, adds our translator's ordinary rendering of *Rabbi—my Master*. This explanation is confirmed by Ibn-aṭ-Ṭayyib's Commentary. Ciasca's emended text cannot be right. 7 The diacritical point over the third radical must be removed. 8 *cf.* Peshitta.
9 Ciasca's Arabic text (apparently following Borg. MS.) has *till he* before *came*. This is unsupported by any of the three Syriac texts, although they differ from one another. Perhaps *till* and *came* should be transposed. The translation would then be as given in the text above; but this rendering may also be obtained according to § 54, 1, note.
10 The Syriac word used means both *wounds* and *strokes*.
11 The Arabic word is a favourite of the translator's, and may therefore be original. One cannot help thinking, however, that it is a clerical error for *mounted* (*cf.* Cur. and Sin.).
12 In Syriac *could* and *found* are represented by the same word. The Arabic translator has chosen the wrong one.
13 See note, § 11, 11.

§ 34 51 yet, and I go to him that sent me. And ye shall seek me, and shall not find me: Jo. 7, 34.
52 and where I shall be, ye shall not be able to come. The Jews said within them- Jo. 7, 35.
selves, Whither hath this *man* determined to go that we shall not be able [1] *to find*
him? can it be that he is determined to go to the regions of the nations,[2] and teach
53 the heathen? What is this word that he said, Ye shall seek me, and shall not find Jo. 7, 36.
me: and where I am, ye cannot come?

SECTION XXXV.

§ 35 1 And on the great day, which is the last of the feast, Jesus stood, crying out and Jo. 7, 37.
2 saying, If *any* man is thirsty, let him come unto me, and drink. Every one that Jo. 7, 38.
believeth in me, as the scriptures said, there shall flow from his belly rivers of pure
3 water. He said that referring to the Spirit, which those who believed in him were Jo. 7, 39.
to receive: for the Spirit was not yet granted; and because Jesus had not yet been
4 Arabic, glorified. And many of the multitude that heard his words said, This is Jo. 7, 40.
5 p. 133 in truth the prophet. And others said, This is the Messiah. But others Jo. 7, 41.
6 said, Can it be that the Messiah will come from Galilee? Hath not the scripture Jo. 7, 42.
said that from the seed of David, and from Bethlehem, the village of David, the
7 Messiah cometh? And there occurred a dissension in the multitude because of him. Jo. 7, 43.
8 And some of them were wishing to seize him; but no man laid a hand upon him. Jo. 7, 44.
9 And those officers came to the chief priests and Pharisees; and the priests said Jo. 7, 45.
10 unto them, Why did ye not bring him? The officers said, Never spake man thus Jo. 7, 46.
11 as speaketh this man. The Pharisees said unto them, Perhaps ye also have gone Jo. 7, 47.
12, 13 astray? Hath any of the rulers or the Pharisees haply believed in him? except Jo. 7, 48. Jo. 7, 49.
14 this people which knows not the law; they are accursed. Nicodemus, one of them, Jo. 7, 50.
15 he that had come to Jesus by night, said unto them, Doth our law haply condemn Jo. 7, 51.
16 a man, except it hear him first and know what he hath done? They answered and Jo. 7, 52.
said unto him, Art thou also haply from Galilee? Search, and see that a prophet
riseth not from Galilee.
17, 18 And when the Pharisees assembled, Jesus asked them, and said, What say ye of Mt. 22, 41. Mt. 22, 42.
19 the Messiah? whose son is he? They said unto him, The son of David. He said Mt. 22, 43.
unto them, And how doth David in the Holy Spirit call him Lord? for he said,
20 The Lord said unto my Lord, Mt. 22, 44.
Sit on my right hand,
That I may put thine enemies under thy feet.
21, 22 If then David calleth him Lord, how is he his son? And no one was able to Mt. 22, 45. Mt. 22, 46.
answer him; and no man dared from that day again to ask him of anything.
23 And Jesus addressed them again, and said, I am the light of the world; and he that Jo. 8, 12.
24 followeth me shall not walk in darkness, but shall find the light of life. The Pharisees Jo. 8, 13.
Arabic, said unto him, Thou bearest witness to thyself; thy witness is not true. Jesus Jo. 8, 14.
25 p. 134 answered and said unto them, If I bear witness to myself, my witness is true;
for I know whence I came, and whither I go; but ye know not whence I came, or
26, 27 whither I go. And ye judge after the flesh; and I judge no man. And even if I Jo. 8, 15. Jo. 8, 16.
judge, my judgement is true; because I am not alone, but I and my Father which
28, 29 sent me. And in your law it is written, that the witness of two men is true. I am Jo. 8, 17. Jo. 8, 18.
he that beareth witness to myself, and my Father which sent me beareth witness to
30 me. They said unto him, Where is thy Father? Jesus answered and said unto Jo. 8, 19.
them, Ye know not me, nor my Father: for did ye know me, ye would know my
31 Father. He said these sayings in the treasury, where he was teaching in the Jo. 8, 20.
32 temple: and no man seized him; because his hour had not yet come. Jesus said Jo. 8, 21.
unto them again, I go truly, and ye shall seek me and not find me, and ye shall die
33 in your sins: and where I go, ye cannot come. The Jews said, Will he haply kill Jo. 8, 22.
34 himself, that he saith, Where I go, ye cannot come? He said unto them, Ye are Jo. 8, 23.
from below; and I am from above: ye are of this world; and I am not of this
35 world. I said unto you, that ye shall die in your sins: if ye believe not that I am Jo. 8, 24.
36 *he*, ye shall die in your sins. The Jews said, And thou, who art thou? Jesus said Jo. 8, 25.

1 See note above, on § 34, 46.   2 i.e., Gentiles.

§35 37 unto them, If I should begin to speak unto you, I have concerning you many words Jo. 8, 26.
and judgement: but he that sent me is true; and I, what I heard from him is what
38, 39 I say in the world. And they knew not that he meant by that the Father. Jesus Jo. 8, 27. Jo. 8, 28.
Arabic, said unto them again, When ye have lifted up the Son of man, then ye
p. 135 shall know that I am he: and I do nothing of myself, but as my Father
40 taught me, so I speak. And he that sent me is with me; and my Father hath not Jo. 8, 29.
41 left me alone; because I do what is pleasing to him at all times. And while he was Jo. 8, 30.
saying that, many believed in him.
42 And Jesus said to those Jews that believed in him, If ye abide in my words, truly Jo. 8, 31.
43 ye are my disciples; and ye shall know the truth, and the truth shall make you free. Jo. 8, 32.
44 They said unto him, We are the seed of Abraham, and have never served any man Jo. 8, 33.
45 in the way of slavery: how then sayest thou, Ye shall be free children? Jesus said Jo. 8, 34.
unto them, Verily, verily, I say unto you, Every one that doeth a sin is a slave of
46 sin. And the slave doth not remain for ever in the house; but the son remaineth Jo. 8, 35.
47, 48 for ever. And if the Son set you free, truly ye shall be free children. I know that Jo. 8, 37.
ye are the seed of Abraham; but ye seek to slay me, because ye are unable for my
49 word. And what I saw with my Father, I say: and what ye saw with your father, Jo. 8, 38.
50 ye do. They answered and said unto him, Our father is Abraham. Jesus said Jo. 8, 39.
unto them, If ye were the children of Abraham, ye would do the deeds of Abraham.
51 Now, behold, ye seek to kill me, a man that speak[1] with you[2] the truth, that I Jo. 8, 40.
52 heard from God: this did Abraham not do. And ye do the deeds of your father. Jo. 8, 41.
They said unto him, We were not *born* of fornication;[3] we have one Father, who is
53 God. Jesus said unto them, If God were your Father, ye would love me: I pro- Jo. 8, 42.
ceeded and came[4] from God; and it was not of my own self that I came,[4] but he sent
54 Arabic, me. Why then do ye not know my word? Because ye cannot hear my word. Jo. 8, 43.
55 p. 136 Ye are from the father, the devil,[5] and the lust of your father do ye desire Jo. 8, 44.
to do, who from the beginning is a slayer of men, and in the truth standeth not,
because the truth is not in him. And when he speaketh untruth, he speaketh from
56 himself: for he is a liar, and the father of untruth. And I who speak the truth, ye Jo. 8, 45.
57 believe me not. Who of you rebuketh me for a sin? And if I speak the truth, ye Jo. 8, 46.
58 do not believe me.[6] Whosoever is of God heareth the words of God: therefore do Jo. 8, 47.
59 ye not hear, because ye are not of God. The Jews answered and said unto him, Jo. 8, 48.
60 Did we not say well that thou art a Samaritan, and hast demons? Jesus said unto Jo. 8, 49.
them, As for me, I have not a devil; but my Father do I honour, and ye dishonour
61 me. I seek not my glory: here is one who seeketh and judgeth. Jo. 8, 50.

SECTION XXXVI.

§36 1 Verily, verily, I say unto you, Whosoever keepeth my word shall not see death Jo. 8, 51.
2 for ever. The Jews said unto him, Now we know that thou hast demons. Abraham Jo. 8, 52.
is dead, and the prophets; and thou sayest, Whosoever keepeth my word shall not
3 taste death for ever. Art thou haply greater than our father Abraham, who is Jo. 8, 53.
4 dead, and than the prophets, which are dead? whom makest thou thyself? Jesus Jo. 8, 54.
said unto them, If I glorify myself, my glory is nothing: my Father is he that
5 glorifieth me; *of* whom ye say, that he is our[7] God; and *yet* ye have not known Jo. 8, 55.
him: but I know him; and if I should say that I know him not, I should become
6 Arabic, a liar like you: but I know him, and keep his word. Abraham your father Jo. 8, 56.
7 p. 137 longed to see my day; and he saw, and rejoiced. The Jews said unto him, Jo. 8, 57.
8 Thou art now not fifty years old, and hast thou seen Abraham? Jesus said unto Jo. 8, 58.
9 them, Verily, verily, I say unto you, Before Abraham was, I am. And they take[8] Jo. 8, 59.
stones to stone him: but Jesus concealed himself, and went out of the temple. And Jo. 8, 60.[9]
he passed through them, and went *his way*.

1 Lit. *speaketh*, according to Arabic idiom. 2 Borg. MS. omits *with you*.
3 Borg. MS. has *an adulteress*, mistaking the less common Arabic word for a clerical error.
4 Different words are used in the Arabic; so in the Greek, but not in the Peshitta. Sin. and Cur. are wanting.
5 Lit. *backbiter*.
6 This is probably simply a clerical error for the ordinary reading, *why have ye not believed me?* The Arabic words *why* and *not* having the same consonants, one of them was purposely or accidentally omitted by a copyist.
7 *cf.* Peshitta. The Sinaitic omits *our*.
8 The Vat. MS. has *took him*, probably omitting *stones*, though Ciasca does not say so. *Take* is probably a copyist's error (change in diacritical points) for *took*. 9 Reckoned to verse 59 in the Greek.

§36 10 And as he passed, he saw a man blind from his mother's womb. And his Jo. 9, 1.
11 disciples asked him, and said, Our Master, who sinned, this *man*, or his parents, so Jo. 9, 2.
12 that he was born blind?[1] Jesus said unto them, Neither did he sin, nor his parents: Jo. 9, 3.
13 but that the works of God may be seen in him.[2] It is incumbent on me to do the Jo. 9, 4.
deeds of him that sent me, while it is day: a night will come, and no man will be
14 able to busy himself. As long as I am in the world, I am the light of the world. Jo. 9, 5.
15 And when he said that, he spat upon the ground, and made clay of his spittle, and Jo. 9, 6.
16 smeared *it* on the eyes of the blind man, and said unto him, Go and wash thyself in Jo. 9, 7.
17 the pool[3] of Siloam.[4] And he went and washed, and came seeing. And his neigh- Jo. 9, 8.
bours, which saw him of old begging, said, Is not this he that was sitting begging?
18 And some said, It is he; and others said, Nay, but he resembles him much. He Jo. 9, 9.
19, 20 said, I am he. They said unto him, How then were thine eyes opened? He Jo. 9, 10. Jo. 9, 11.
answered and said unto them, A man named Jesus made clay, and smeared *it* on
my eyes, and said unto me, Go and wash in the water of Siloam: and I went and
21 washed, and received sight.[5] They said unto him, Where is he? He said, I know not. Jo. 9, 12.
22, 23 Arabic, And they brought him that was previously blind to the Pharisees. And Jo. 9, 13. Jo. 9, 14.
p. 138 the day in which Jesus made clay and opened with it his eyes was a sabbath
24 day. And again the Pharisees asked him, How didst thou receive sight? And he said Jo. 9, 15.
25 unto them, He put clay on mine eyes, and I washed, and received sight. The people[6] Jo. 9, 16.
of the Pharisees said, This man is not from God, for he keepeth not the sabbath.
And others said, How can a man *that is* a sinner do these signs? And there came
26 to be a division amongst them. And again they said to that blind man, Thou, Jo. 9, 17.
then, what sayest thou of him that opened for thee thine eyes? He said unto them,
27 I say that he is a prophet. And the Jews did not believe concerning him, that he Jo. 9, 18.
was blind, and received sight, until they summoned the parents of him who received
28 sight, and asked them, Is this[7] your son, *of* whom ye said that he was born blind? Jo. 9, 19.
29 how then, behold, doth he now see? His parents answered and said, We know Jo. 9, 20.
30 that this is our son, and that he was born blind: but how he has come to see now, Jo. 9, 21.
or who it is that opened his eyes, we know not: and he also has reached his prime;
31 ask him, and he will speak for himself. This said his parents, because they were Jo. 9, 22.
fearing the Jews: and the Jews decided, that if any man should confess of him that
32 he was the Messiah, they would put him out of the synagogue. For this reason Jo. 9, 23.
33 said his parents, He hath reached his prime; ask him. And they called the man a Jo. 9, 24.
second time, him that was blind, and said unto him, Praise God: we know that this
34 man is a sinner. He answered and said unto them, Whether he be a sinner, I know Jo. 9, 25.
35 not: I know one thing, that I was blind, and I now see. They said unto him again, Jo. 9, 26.
36 Arabic, What did he unto thee? how opened he for thee thine eyes? He said unto Jo. 9, 27.
p. 139 them, I said unto you, and ye did not hear: what[8] wish ye further to hear?
37 ye also, do ye wish to become disciples to him? And they reviled him, and said unto Jo. 9, 28.
him, Thou art the disciple[9] of that *man;* but as for us, we are the disciples of
38 Moses. And we know that God spake unto Moses: but this man, we know not Jo. 9, 29.
39 whence he is. The man answered and said unto them, From this is the wonder, Jo. 9, 30.
40 because ye know not whence he is, and mine eyes hath he opened. And we know Jo. 9, 31.
that God heareth not the voice of sinners: but whosoever feareth him, and doeth
41 his will, him he heareth. From eternity hath it not been heard of, that a man Jo. 9, 32.
42 opened the eyes of a blind *man*, who had been born in blindness. If then this *man* Jo. 9, 33.
43 were not from God, he could not do that. They answered and said unto him, Thou Jo. 9, 34.
wast all of thee born in sins, and dost thou teach us? And they put him forth without.
44 And Jesus heard of his being put forth without, and found him, and said unto Jo. 9, 35.
45 him, Dost thou believe in the Son of God? He that was made whole answered Jo. 9, 36.
46 and said, Who is he, my Lord, that I may believe in him? Jesus said unto him, Jo. 9, 37.
47 Thou hast seen him, and he that speaketh to thee is he. And he said, I believe, Jo. 9, 38.
my Lord. And he fell down worshipping him.

1 A different word in Arabic from that used in verses 1 and 6.
2 The Vat. MS. has *that we may see the works of God in him.* By the addition of a diacritical point this would give the same sense as in the text above, and more grammatically.
3 The Arabic word properly means *baptism.* The Syriac has both meanings.
4 Lit. *Shīlōḥa*, as in Syriac. 5 Lit. *saw.* 6 An easy clerical error for *Some.*
7 Lit. *them, whether this be.* 8 Or, *why* (*cf.* note, § 7, 38).
9 *Disciples* is probably simply a misprint in Ciasca's text.

SECTION XXXVII.

§ 37 1 And Jesus said, To judge the world am I come, so that they that see not may Jo. 9, 39.
2 see, and they that see may become blind. And some of the Pharisees which were Jo. 9, 40.
3 with him heard that, and they said unto him, Can it be that we are blind? Jesus Jo. 9, 41.
said unto them, If ye were blind, ye should not have sin: but now ye say, We see:
and because of this your sin remaineth.[1]

4 Arabic, p. 140 Verily, verily, I say unto you, Whosoever entereth not into the fold of the Jo. 10, 1.
sheep by the door, but goeth up from another place, that *man* is a thief and a
5, 6 stealer. But he that entereth by the door is the shepherd of the sheep. And therefore[2] Jo. 10, 2. Jo. 10, 3.
the keeper of the door openeth for him the door; and the sheep hear his voice: and
7 he calleth his sheep[3] by their names, and they go forth unto him. And when he Jo. 10, 4.
putteth forth his sheep, he goeth before them, and his sheep[3] follow him: because
8 they know his voice. And after a stranger will the sheep not go, but they flee from Jo. 10, 5.
9 him: because they hear not the voice of a stranger. This parable spake Jesus unto Jo. 10, 6.
them: but they knew not what he was saying unto them.

10 Jesus said unto them again, Verily, verily, I say unto you, I am the door of the Jo. 10, 7.
11 sheep. And all that came are thieves and stealers: but the sheep heard them not. Jo. 10, 8.
12 I am the door: and if a man enter by me, he shall live, and shall go in and go out, Jo. 10, 9.
13 and shall find pasture. And the stealer cometh not, save that he may steal, and Jo. 10, 10.
kill, and destroy: but I came that they might have life, and that they might have
14 the thing *that is* better.[4] I am the good shepherd; and the good shepherd giveth Jo. 10, 11.
15 himself[5] for his sheep. But the hireling, who is not a shepherd, and whose the Jo. 10, 12.
sheep[6] are not, when he seeth the wolf as it cometh, leaveth the sheep, and fleeth,
16 and the wolf cometh, and snatcheth away the sheep, and scattereth[7] them: and the Jo. 10, 13.
17 hireling fleeth because he is an hireling, and hath no care for the sheep. I am the Jo. 10, 14.
18 good shepherd; and I know what is mine, and what is mine knoweth me, as my Jo. 10, 15.
Father knoweth me, and I know my Father; and I give myself[8] for the sheep.
19 And I have other sheep also, that are not of this flock: them also I must invite, Jo. 10, 16.
and they shall hear my voice; and all the sheep shall be one, and the shepherd one.
20 Arabic, p. 141 And therefore doth my Father love me, because I give my life, that I may Jo. 10, 17.
21 take it again. No man taketh it from me, but I leave it of my own choice. Jo. 10, 18.
And I have the right to leave it, and have the right also to take it. And this commandment did I receive of my Father.

22 And there occurred a disagreement among the Jews because of these sayings. Jo. 10, 19.
23 And many of them said, He hath a devil, and is afflicted with madness;[9] why listen Jo. 10, 20.
24 ye to him? And others said, These sayings are not those of *men* possessed with Jo. 10, 21.
demons. Can a demon haply open the eyes of a blind *man?*

25, 26 And the feast of the dedication came on at Jerusalem: and it was winter. And Jo. 10, 22. Jo. 10, 23.
27 Jesus was walking in the temple in the porch of Solomon. The Jews therefore Jo. 10, 24.
surrounded him, and said unto him, Until when dost thou make our hearts anxious?
28 If thou art the Messiah, tell us plainly. He answered and said unto them, I told Jo. 10, 25.
you, and ye believe not: and the deeds that I do in my Father's name bear witness
29, 30 to me. But ye believe not, because ye are not of my sheep,[10] as I said unto you. Jo. 10, 26.
31 And my sheep[10] hear my voice, and I know them, and they come after me: and I Jo. 10, 27. Jo. 10, 28.
give them eternal life; and they shall not perish for ever, nor shall any man snatch
32 them out of my hands.[11] For the Father, who hath given *them* unto me, is greater Jo. 10, 29.
33 than all; and no man is able to take *them* from the hand of my[12] Father. I and Jo. 10, 30.
34, 35 my Father are one. And the Jews took stones to stone him. Jesus said unto them, Jo. 10, 31. Jo. 10, 32.
Many good deeds from my Father have I shewed you; because of which[13] of them,
36 then, do ye stone me? The Jews said unto him, Not for the good deeds do we Jo. 10, 33.
stone thee, but because thou blasphemest; and, whilst thou art a man, makest thy-

1 Or, *is permanent.* 2 Or, *to him.*
3 A different word (lit. *rams*) from that used in the other verses; so in Peshitta (*cf.* Sin., which, however, differs somewhat); *cf.* also § 54, 40 f., note. 4 Or, *best thing.* Vat. MS. omits from *but I came.* 5 Or, *his life.*
6 *cf.* note to § 37, 6. 7 Or, *to snatch . . . and scatter.* 8 Or, *my life.* 9 Lit. *epilepsy.*
10 *cf.* § 37, 6. 11 Or, *hand;* but probably dual (*cf.* Syr.).
12 So Peshitta; but Sin. *the.* Borg. MS. omits *the hand of.* 13 Lit. *which deed.*

§ **37** 37 self God. Jesus said unto them, Is it not thus written in your law, I said, Ye are gods? Jo. 10, 34.
38 Arabic, And if he called those gods—for [1] to them came the word of God (and it is Jo. 10, 35.
39 p. 142 not possible in [2] the scripture that *anything* should be undone)—he then, Jo. 10, 36.
whom the Father hath sanctified and sent into the world, do ye say that he blasphemeth;
40 because I said unto you, I am the Son of God? If then I do not the deeds of my Jo. 10, 37.
41 Father, ye believe me not.[3] But if I do, *even* if ye believe not me, believe the Jo. 10, 38.
deeds: that ye may know and believe that my Father is in me, and I in my Father.
42 And they sought again to take him: and he went forth out of their hands. Jo. 10, 39.
43 And he went beyond Jordan to the place where John was baptizing formerly; Jo. 10, 40.
44 and abode there. And many people came unto him; and they said, John did not Jo. 10, 41.
45 work even one sign: but all that John said of this man is truth. And many believed Jo. 10, 42.
in him.
46 And there was a sick *man*, named Lazarus, of the village of Bethany, the brother Jo. 11, 1.
47 of Mary and Martha. And Mary was she that anointed with sweet ointment the Jo. 11, 2.
feet of Jesus, and wiped *them* with her hair; and Lazarus, who was sick, was the
48 brother of this *woman*.[4] And his sisters sent unto Jesus, and said unto him, Our Jo. 11, 3.
49 Lord, behold, he whom thou lovest is sick. But Jesus said, This sickness is not Jo. 11, 4.
unto death, but for the glorifying of God, that the Son of God may be glorified
50, 51 because of it. And Jesus loved Martha, and Mary, and Lazarus. And when he Jo. 11, 5. Jo. 11, 6.
52 heard that he was sick, he abode in the place where he was two days. And after that, Jo. 11, 7.
53 he said unto his disciples, Come, let us go into Judæa. His disciples said unto him, Our Jo. 11, 8.
Arabic, Master, now the Jews desire to stone thee; and goest thou again thither?
54, 55 p. 143 Jesus said unto them, Is not the day of twelve hours? If then a man Jo. 11, 9.
walk in the day, he stumbleth not, because he seeth the light of the world. But if Jo. 11, 10.
56 a man walk in the night, he stumbleth, because there is no lamp in him. This said Jo. 11, 11.
Jesus: and after that, he said unto them, Lazarus our friend hath fallen asleep; but
57 I am going to awaken him. His disciples said unto him, Our Lord, if he hath Jo. 11, 12.
58 fallen asleep, he will recover. But Jesus said that concerning his death: while they Jo. 11, 13.
59 supposed that he spake of lying down to sleep. Then Jesus said unto them plainly, Jo. 11, 14.
60 Lazarus is dead. And I am glad that I was not there for your sakes, that ye may Jo. 11, 15.
61 believe; but let us go thither. Thomas, who is called Thama,[5] said to the disciples, Jo. 11, 16.
his companions, Let us also go, and die with him.

SECTION XXXVIII.

§ **38** 1, 2 And Jesus came to Bethany, and found him *already* four days in the grave. And Jo. 11, 17. Jo. 11, 18.
Bethany was beside Jerusalem, and its distance from it *was* a sum of fifteen fur-
3 longs;[6] and many of the Jews came unto Mary and Martha, to comfort their heart Jo. 11, 19.
4 because of their brother. And Martha, when she heard that Jesus had come, went Jo. 11, 20.
5 out to meet him: but Mary was sitting in the house. Martha then said unto Jesus, Jo. 11, 21.
6 My Lord, if thou hadst been here, my brother had not died. But I know now that, Jo. 11, 22.
7 whatever thou shalt ask of God, he will give thee. Jesus said unto her, Thy brother shall Jo. 11, 23.
8 rise. Martha said unto him, I know that he shall rise in the resurrection at the last day. Jo. 11, 24.
9 Jesus said unto her, I am the resurrection, and the life: whosoever believeth in Jo. 11, 25.
10 Arabic, me, even though he die, he shall live: and every living one that believeth Jo. 11, 26.
11 p. 144 in me shall never die. Believest thou this? She said unto him, Yea, my Jo. 11, 27.
Lord: I believe that thou art the Messiah, the Son of God, that cometh into the
12 world. And when she had said that, she went and called Mary her sister secretly, Jo. 11, 28.
13 and said unto her, Our Master hath come, and summoneth thee. And Mary, when Jo. 11, 29.
14 she heard, rose in haste, and came unto him. (And Jesus then had not come into Jo. 11, 30.
15 the village, but was in the place where Martha met him.) And the Jews also that Jo. 11, 31.
were with her in the house, to comfort her, when they saw that Mary rose up and
went out in haste, went after her, because they supposed that she was going to the
16 tomb to weep. And Mary, when she came to where Jesus was, and saw him, fell Jo. 11, 32.
at his feet, and said unto him, If thou hadst been here, my Lord, my brother had

1 *cf.* Peshitta. 2 This *in* could more easily arise as a clerical error (repetition) in the Syriac text.
3 So Ciasca's text, following Vat. MS. But this is probably a clerical error for the reading of Borg. MS., which omits *ye*.
4 *cf.* Peshitta. 5 The Syriac word for *Twin*. 6 Arabic *mil*, a somewhat indefinite distance.

§38 17 not died. And Jesus came; and when he saw her weeping, and the Jews that were Jo. 11, 33.
18 with her weeping, he was troubled[1] in himself, and sighed; and he said, In what Jo. 11, 34.
19 place have ye laid him? And they said unto him, Our Lord, come and see. And Jo. 11, 35.
20 the tears of Jesus came.[2] The Jews therefore said, See the greatness of his love for Jo. 11, 36.
21 him! But some of them said, Could not this *man*, who opened the eyes of that Jo. 11, 37.
22 blind *man*, have caused that this *man* also should not die? And Jesus came to the Jo. 11, 38.
place of burial, being troubled within himself. And the place of burial was a cave,
23 and a stone was placed at its door. Jesus therefore said, Take these stones *away*. Jo. 11, 39.
Martha, the sister of him *that was* dead, said unto him, My Lord, he hath come to
24 stink for some time: he hath been[3] four days *dead*. Jesus said unto her, Did not I say Jo. 11, 40.
25 Arabic, unto thee, If thou believest, thou shalt see the glory of God? And they re- Jo. 11, 41.
p. 145 moved those stones. And Jesus lifted his eyes on high, and said, My Father,
26 I thank thee since thou didst hear me. And I know that thou at all times hearest Jo. 11, 42.
me: but I say this unto thee because of this multitude that is standing, that they
27 may believe that thou didst send me. And when he had said that, he cried with a Jo. 11, 43.
28 loud voice, Lazarus, come forth. And that dead *man* came out, having his hands Jo. 11, 44.
and feet bound with bandages, and his face wrapped in a scarf. Jesus said unto
them, Loose him, and let him go.
29 And many of the Jews which came unto Mary, when they saw the deed of Jesus, Jo. 11, 45.
30 believed in him. But some of them went to the Pharisees, and informed them of Jo. 11, 46.
all that Jesus did.
31 And the chief priests and the Pharisees gathered, and said, What shall we do? Jo. 11, 47.
32 for lo, this man doeth many signs. And if we leave him thus, all men will believe Jo. 11, 48.
33 in him: and the Romans will come and take our country and people. And one of Jo. 11, 49.
them, who was called Caiaphas, the chief priest he was in that year, said unto them,
34 Ye know not anything, nor consider that it is more advantageous for us that one Jo. 11, 50.
35 man should die instead of the people, and not that the whole people perish. And Jo. 11, 51.
this he said not of himself: but because he was the chief priest of[4] that year, he
36 prophesied that Jesus was to die instead of the people; and not instead of the Jo. 11, 52.
people alone, but that he might gather the scattered children of God together.
37 And from that day they considered *how* to kill him. Jo. 11, 53.
38 Arabic, And Jesus did not walk openly amongst the Jews, but departed thence to a Jo. 11, 54.
p. 146 place near the wilderness, to a town[5] called Ephraim; and he was there, going
39 about with his disciples. And the passover of the Jews was near: and many went Jo. 11, 55.
40 up from the villages unto Jerusalem before the feast, to purify themselves. And Jo. 11, 56.
they sought for Jesus, and said one to another in the temple, What think ye of his
41 holding back from the feast? And the chief priests and the Pharisees had given Jo. 11, 57.
commandment, that, if any man knew in what place he was, he should reveal *it* to
them, that they might take him.
42 And when the days of his going up were accomplished, he prepared himself that Lk. 9, 51.
43 he might go[6] to Jerusalem. And he sent messengers before him, and departed,[7] and Lk. 9, 52.
44 entered into a village[8] of Samaria, that they might make ready for him. And they Lk. 9, 53.
45 received him not, because he[9] was prepared for going to Jerusalem. And when Lk. 9, 54.
James and John his disciples saw *it*, they said unto him, Our Lord, wilt thou that
we speak, and fire come down from heaven, to extirpate them, as did Elijah also?
46 And Jesus turned, and rebuked them, and said, Ye know not of what spirit ye are. Lk. 9, 55.
47 Verily the Son of man did not come to destroy lives, but to give life. And they Lk. 9, 56.
went to another village.

1 This is the Syriac word (*cf.* the versions, and below, § 44, 44; see also Ibn-at-Ṭayyib's Commentary, *ad loc*).
2 So in Syriac versions. 3 Borg. MS. omits *some time: he hath been.*
4 So both MSS.; but the Vat. MS. had originally a reading equivalent to the text above with *of* omitted.
5 The Arabic word as printed (following Vat. MS.) means *a place for monks to live in*, but we should certainly restore a diacritical point *over* the last letter, and thus obtain another Syriac loan-word (that used here in the Peshitta), meaning *town*. See also Ibn-at-Ṭayyib's Commentary, *ad loc.*
6 The present Arabic reading *in going* could pretty easily arise from that assumed in the translation above.
7 This and the following verb are singular in the printed Arabic (against the versions), although Ciasca renders them plural. A copyist using a carelessly written Arabic exemplar might conceivably overlook the plural terminations. Besides, they are often omitted in Syriac MSS. 8 *cf.* note, § 1, 40. 9 Lit. *his body.*

SECTION XXXIX.

§39 1 And Jesus six days before the passover[1] came to Bethany, where was Lazarus, Jo. 12, 1.
2 whom Jesus raised from among the dead. And they made[2] a feast for him there: Jo. 12, 2.
3 and Martha was serving; while Lazarus was one of them that sat with him. And Mk. 14, 3a.
4 at the time of Jesus' being at Bethany in the house of Simon the leper, great multitudes Jo. 12, 9.
of the Jews heard that Jesus was there: and they came, not because of Jesus alone, but
Arabic, that they might look also on Lazarus, whom he raised from among the dead.
5, 6 p. 147 And the chief priests considered *how* they might kill Lazarus also; because Jo. 12, 10. Jo. 12, 11.
7 many of the Jews were going on his account, and believing in Jesus. And Mary Jo. 12, 3a.
took a case of the ointment of fine nard, of great price, and opened it, and poured Mk. 14, 3b.
8 it out on the head of Jesus as he was reclining; and she anointed his feet, and Jo. 12, 3b.
wiped them with her hair: and the house was filled with the odour of the ointment.
9, 10 But Judas Iscariot, one of the disciples, he that was to betray him, said, Why was Jo. 12, 4. Jo. 12, 5.
11 not this ointment sold for three hundred pence, and given unto the poor? This he Jo. 12, 6.
said, not because of his care for the poor, but because he was a thief, and the chest
12 was with him, and what was put[3] into it he used to bear. And that displeased the Mk. 14, 4.
rest of the disciples also within themselves, and they said, Why went this ointment
13 to waste? It was possible that it should be sold for much, and the poor be given Mt. 26, 9. Mk. 14, 5b.
14 it. And they were angry with[4] Mary. And Jesus perceived *it*, and said unto them, Mt. 26, 10a.
Leave her; why molest ye her? a good work hath she accomplished on me: for the Mk. 14, 6b. Jo. 12, 7b.
15 day of my burial kept she it. At all times the poor are with you, and when ye Jo. 12, 8a.
16 wish ye can do them a kindness: but I am not at all times with you. And for this Mk. 14, 7b. Mt. 26, 12.
cause, when she poured[5] this ointment on my body, it is as if she did it for my bur-
17 ial, and anointed my body beforehand. And verily I say unto you, In every place Mk. 14, 8b. Mk. 14, 9.
where this my gospel shall be proclaimed in all the world, what she did shall be told
for a memorial of her.
18, 19 Arabic, And when Jesus said that, he went out leisurely to go to Jerusalem. And Lk. 19, 28. Lk. 19, 29a.
p. 148 when he arrived at Bethphage and at Bethany, beside the mount which is Mt. 21, 1b.
20 called the mount of Olives, Jesus sent two of his disciples, and he said unto them, Go Mt. 21, 2a. Mk. 11, 2b.
21 into this village that is opposite you: and when ye enter it, ye shall find an ass tied, and Mt. 21, 2b. Lk. 19, 30b.
22 a colt with him,[6] which no man ever yet mounted: loose him, and bring them[7] unto Mt. 21, 2c.
me. And if any man say unto you, Why loose ye them? say unto him thus, We Lk. 19, 31a. Mt. 21, 3b.
23 seek them for our Lord; and straightway send them hither. All this was, that what Mt. 21, 4.
was said in the prophet might be fulfilled, which said,

24 Say ye unto the daughter of Zion, Mt. 21, 5.
Behold, thy King cometh unto thee,
Meek, and riding upon an ass,
And upon a colt the foal of an ass.

25 And the disciples did not know this at that time: but after that Jesus was glori- Jo. 12, 16.
fied, his disciples remembered that these *things* were written of him, and *that* this
26 they had done unto him. And when the two disciples went, they found as he had Mt. 21, 6a. Lk. 19, 32b.
27 said unto them, and they did as Jesus charged them. And when they loosed them, Mt. 21, 6b. Lk. 19, 33.
28 their owners said unto them, Why loose ye them? They said unto them, We seek Lk. 19, 34.
29 them for our Lord. And they let them *go*. And they brought the ass and the colt, Mk. 11, 6b. Mt. 21, 7.
30 and they placed on the colt their garments; and Jesus mounted it. And most of the Mt. 21, 8.
multitudes spread their garments on the ground before him; and others cut branches
31 from the trees, and threw *them* in the way. And when he neared his[8] descent from Lk. 19, 37.
Arabic, the mount of Olives, all the disciples began to rejoice and to praise God with
32 p. 149 a loud voice for all the powers which they had seen; and they said, Praise Mt. 21, 9b.[9]
in the highest; Praise to the Son of David: Blessed is he that cometh in the name
33 of the Lord; and blessed[10] is the kingdom that cometh, *that* of[11] our father David: Mk. 11, 10a.
Peace in heaven, and praise in the highest. Lk. 19, 38c.

1 *cf.* the Greek phrase. 2 Lit. *he made* (*cf.* first note to § 38, 43, last sentence). 3 Lit. *fell* (*cf.* § 25, 18).
4 Or, *spake angrily to.* 5 Lit. *cast*, as in Greek. 6 *Sic.* 7 Dual in Arabic.
8 The Syriac versions have *the.* 9 Or better Lk. 19, 38a. 10 Or, *and, Blessed.*
11 The Arabic has *to*, but it probably represents the Syriac text with the meaning given above.

§39 34 And a great multitude, that which came to the feast, when they heard that Jesus Jo. 12, 12*b*.
35 was coming to Jerusalem, took young palm branches,[1] and went forth to meet him, Jo. 12, 13.
and cried and said, Praise: Blessed is he that cometh in the name of the Lord, the
36 King of Israel. Certain therefore of the Pharisees from among the multitudes Lk. 19, 39.
37 said unto him, Our Master, rebuke thy disciples. He said unto them, Verily I say Lk. 19, 40.
unto you, If these were silent, the stones would cry out.
38, 39 And when he drew near, and saw the city, he wept over it, and said, Would that Lk. 19, 41. Lk. 19, 42.
thou hadst known the things that are[2] for thy peace, in this thy day! now that is
40 hidden from thine eyes. There shall come unto thee days when thine enemies Lk. 19, 43.
41 shall encompass thee, and straiten thee from every quarter, and shall get possession Lk. 19, 44.
of[3] thee, and thy children within thee; and they shall not leave in thee a stone upon
another; because thou knewest not the time of thy visitation.
42 And when he entered into Jerusalem, the whole city was agitated, and they said, Mt. 21, 10.
43 Who is this? And the multitudes said, This is Jesus, the prophet that is from Naza- Mt. 21, 11.
44 reth of Galilee. And the multitude which was with him bare witness that he called Jo. 12, 17.
45 Lazarus from the grave, and raised him from among the dead. And for this *cause* Jo. 12, 18.
great multitudes went out to meet him, because they heard the sign which he did.

SECTION XL.

§40 1 Arabic, And when Jesus entered the temple, they brought unto him blind and Mt. 21, 14.
2 p. 150 lame: and he healed them. But when the chief priests and the Pharisees Mt. 21, 15.
saw the wonders that he did, and the children that were crying in the temple and
3 saying, Praise be to the Son of David; it distressed them, and they said, Hearest Mt. 21, 16.
thou not what these say? Jesus said unto them, Yea: did ye not read long ago, From
4 the mouths of children and infants thou hast chosen my praise? And the Pharisees Jo. 12, 19.
said one to another, Behold, do ye not see that nothing availeth us? for lo, the whole
world hath followed him.
5 And there were among them certain Gentiles also, which had come up to wor- Jo. 12, 20.
6 ship at the feast: these therefore came to Philip, who was of Bethsaida of Galilee, Jo. 12, 21.
7 and asked him, and said unto him, My lord, we wish to see Jesus. And Philip Jo. 12, 22.
8 came and told Andrew: and Andrew and Philip told Jesus. And Jesus answered Jo. 12, 23.
and said unto them, The hour is come nigh, in which the Son of man is to be glori-
9 fied. Verily, verily, I say unto you, A grain of wheat, if it fall not and die in the Jo. 12, 24.
10 earth, remaineth alone; but if it die, it beareth much fruit. He that loveth his life[4] Jo. 12, 25.
destroyeth it; and he that hateth his life[4] in this world shall keep it unto the life eter-
11 nal. If a man serve me, he will follow me; and where I am, there shall my servant be Jo. 12, 26.
12 also: and whosoever serveth me, the Father will honour him. Now is my soul trou- Jo. 12, 27.
Arabic, bled; and what shall I say? My Father, deliver me from this hour. But
13 p. 151 for this cause came I unto this hour. My Father, glorify thy name. And a Jo. 12, 28.
14 voice was heard from heaven, I have glorified *it*, and shall glorify *it*. And the Jo. 12, 29.
multitude that were standing heard, and said, This is thunder: and others said, An
15 angel speaketh to him. Jesus answered and said unto them, Not because of me Jo. 12, 30.
16 was this voice, but because of you. Now is the judgement of this world; and the Jo. 12, 31.
17 prince of this world shall now be cast forth. And I, when I am lifted up from the Jo. 12, 32.
18 earth, shall draw every man unto me. This he said, that he might shew by what Jo. 12, 33.
19 manner of death he should die. The multitudes said unto him, We have heard out Jo. 12, 34.
of the law that the Messiah abideth for ever: how then sayest thou, that the Son of
20 man is to be lifted up? who is this, the Son of man? Jesus said unto them, Another Jo. 12, 35.
little while is the light with you. Walk so long as ye have light, lest the darkness
overtake you; for he that walketh in the darkness knoweth not whither he goeth.
21 So long as ye have light, believe the light, that ye may be the children of the light. Jo. 12, 36.
22 And when certain of the Pharisees asked of Jesus, when the kingdom of God Lk. 17, 20.
should come, he answered and said unto them, The kingdom of God cometh not

1 Lit. *the heart* (or, *pith*) *of the palm*. The word *pith*, which occurs also in the Æthiopic version (Ezek. 27, 25; Jubilees, ch. 16) and in Ibn-aṭ-Ṭayyib's exposition, though not in the Brit. Mus. gospel text, is perhaps used here of the inner branches from its resemblance to the post-biblical Hebrew word employed in accounts of the Feast of Tabernacles.
2 Lit. *are found*, a rendering due to the Syriac.
3 So Ciasca's text, following Vat. MS. The other MS. has *drag*, which by restoring a diacritical point to the third radical would give *destroy*, the reading of the Syriac versions. Ibn-aṭ-Ṭayyib's Commentary has *hide*. 4 Or, *soul*; or, *self*.

§40 23 with expectation: neither shall they say, Lo, it is here! nor, Lo, it is there! for the Lk. 17, 21.
kingdom of God is within you.
24 And in the day*time* he was teaching in the temple; and at night he used to go Lk. 21, 37.
25 out, and pass the night in the mount called the mount of Olives. And all the Lk. 21, 38.
people came [1] to him in the morning in the temple, to hear his word.
26, 27 Then spake Jesus unto the multitudes and his disciples, and said unto them, On Mt. 23, 1. Mt. 23, 2.
28 Arabic, the seat of Moses are seated the scribes and Pharisees: everything that Mt. 23, 3.
p. 152 they say unto you now to keep, keep and do: but according to their deeds
29 do ye not; for they say, and do not. And they bind heavy burdens, and lay them Mt. 23, 4.
on the shoulders of the people; while they with one of their fingers will not come
30, 31 near [2] them. But all their deeds they do to make a shew before men. And all the Mt. 23, 5*a*. Mk. 12, 37*b*.
multitude were hearing that with pleasure.
32 And in the course of his teaching he said unto them, Guard yourselves from the Mk. 12, 38.
33 scribes, who desire to walk in robes, and love salutation in the marketplaces, and Mk. 12, 39.
sitting in the highest places of the synagogues, and at feasts in the highest parts of
34 the rooms: and they broaden their amulets, and lengthen the cords of their cloaks, Mt. 23, 5*b*.
35 and *love* that they should be called by men, My master, and devour widows' houses, Mt. 23, 7*b*. Mk. 12, 40.
because [3] of their prolonging their prayers; these then shall receive greater judge-
36 ment. But ye, be ye not called masters: [4] for your master is one; all ye are brethren. Mt. 23, 8.
37 Call not then to yourselves *any one* [5] father on earth: for your Father is one, who is Mt. 23, 9.
38 in heaven. And be not called directors: for your director is one, *even* the Messiah. Mt. 23, 10.
39, 40 He that is great among you shall be unto you a minister. Whosoever shall exalt Mt. 23, 11. Mt. 23, 12.
himself shall be abased; and whosoever shall abase himself shall be exalted.
41 Woe unto you, Pharisees! because ye love the highest places in the synagogues, Lk. 11, 43.
and salutation in the marketplaces.
42 Woe unto you, scribes and Pharisees, hypocrites! because ye devour widows' Mt. 23, 14.
houses, because [6] of your prolonging your prayers: for this *reason* then ye shall
receive greater judgement.
43 Woe unto you, scribes and Pharisees, hypocrites! because ye have shut the Mt. 23, 13*a*.
kingdom of God before men.
44 Arabic, Woe unto you that know the law! for ye concealed the keys of know- Lk. 11, 52*a*.
p. 153 ledge: ye enter not, and those that are entering ye suffer not to enter. Mt. 23, 13*b*.
45 Woe unto you, scribes and Pharisees, hypocrites! because [7] ye compass land and Mt. 23, 15.
sea to draw [8] one proselyte; and when he is *become so*, ye make him a son of hell
twice as much [9] as yourselves.
46 Woe unto you, ye blind guides! because ye say, Whosoever sweareth by the Mt. 23, 16.
temple, it is nothing; but whosoever sweareth by the gold that is in the temple,
47 shall be condemned.[10] Ye blind foolish *ones:* which is greater, the gold, or the Mt. 23, 17.
48 temple which sanctifieth the gold? And, Whosoever sweareth by the altar, it is Mt. 23, 18.
nothing; but whosoever sweareth by the offering that is upon it, shall be condemned.[10]
49 Ye blind foolish *ones:* which is greater, the offering, or the altar which sanctifieth Mt. 23, 19.
50 the offering? Whosoever then sweareth by the altar, hath sworn by it, and by all Mt. 23, 20.
51 that is upon it. And whosoever sweareth by the temple, hath sworn by it, and by Mt. 23, 21.
52 him that is dwelling in it. And whosoever sweareth by heaven, hath sworn by the Mt. 23, 22.
throne of God, and by him that sitteth upon it.
53 Woe unto you, scribes and Pharisees, hypocrites! because ye tithe mint and rue Mt. 23, 23.
and dill and cummin and all herbs, and ye leave the important *matters* of the law,
judgement, and mercy, and faith, and the love of God: this ought ye to do, and
54 not to leave that *undone*. Ye blind guides, which strain out a gnat, and swallow [11] Mt. 23, 24.
camels.
55 Woe unto you, scribes and Pharisees, hypocrites! because ye cleanse the outside Mt. 23, 25.

1 i.e., *used to come*. 2 Or, *touch*.
3 The Syriac word means *on the pretext of* as well as *because of* (*cf.* § 50, 11, note).
4 This word is not spelled in the ordinary way. Doubtless we should supply two diacritical points and read, with the Syriac versions, *My master*. 5 *cf.* Peshitta. 6 Syriac, same as in § 40, 35; Arabic different.
7 Adopting the reading of Borg. MS. (*cf.* next verse).
8 Perhaps this reading is due to the easy confusion of *d* and *r* in Syriac; but it might also conceivably be a corruption of the Arabic word in the next clause. It occurs also in the text of Ibn-at-Tayyib's Commentary.
9 Doubtless the Arabic word should be read as a monosyllable, as in Ibn-at-Tayyib's Commentary. 10 See § 10, 13.
11 The Arabic word as printed gives no suitable sense. Either the last radical has been omitted, or the last two radicals have exchanged places.

§40 of the cup and of the platter, while the inside of them is full of injustice and wrong.
56 Ye blind Pharisees, cleanse first the inside of the cup and of the platter, then shall Mt. 23, 26.
the outside of them be cleansed.
57 Arabic, p. 154 Woe unto you, scribes and Pharisees, hypocrites! because ye resem- Mt. 23, 27.
ble whited sepulchres, which appear[1] from the outside beautiful, but within
58 full of the bones of the dead, and all uncleanness. So ye also from without appear Mt. 23, 28.
unto men like the righteous, but within ye are full of wrong and hypocrisy.
59 One of the scribes answered and said unto him, Teacher, in this saying of thine Lk. 11, 45.
60 thou art casting a slur on us. He said, And to you also, ye scribes, woe! for ye Lk. 11, 46.
lade men with heavy burdens, and ye with one of your fingers come not near[2] those
burdens.
61 Woe unto you, scribes and Pharisees, hypocrites! for ye build the tombs of the Mt. 23, 29*a*.
prophets, which your fathers killed, and adorn the burying-places of the righteous, Lk. 11, 47*b*. Mt. 23, 29*b*.
62 and say, If we had been in the days of our fathers, we should not have been partakers Mt. 23, 30.
63 with them in the blood of the prophets. Wherefore, behold, ye witness against Mt. 23, 31.
64 yourselves, that ye are the children of those that slew the prophets. And ye also, Mt. 23, 32.
65 ye fill up the measure[3] of your fathers. Ye serpents, ye children of vipers, where Mt. 23, 33.
shall ye flee from the judgement of Gehenna?

SECTION XLI.

§41 1 Therefore, behold, I, the wisdom of God, am sending unto you prophets, and Mt. 23, 34.
apostles, and wise men, and scribes: and some of them ye shall slay and crucify;
and some of them ye shall beat in your synagogues, and persecute[4] from city to
2 city: that there may come on you all the blood of the righteous that hath been Mt. 23, 35.
poured upon the ground,[5] from the blood of Abel the pure to the blood of Zacha-
riah the son of Barachiah, whom ye slew between the temple[6] and the altar.
3 Verily I say unto you, All these *things* shall come upon this generation.[7] Mt. 23, 36.
4 Arabic, p. 155 O Jerusalem, Jerusalem, slayer of the prophets, and stoner of them that Mt. 23, 37.
are sent unto her! how many times did I wish to gather thy children, as
5 a hen gathereth her chickens under her wings, and ye would not! Your house shall Mt. 23, 38.
6 be left over you desolate. Verily I say unto you, Ye shall not see me henceforth, Mt. 23, 39.
till ye shall say, Blessed is he that cometh in the name of the Lord.
7 And many of the rulers also believed on him; but because of the Pharisees they Jo. 12, 42.
8 were not confessing *him*, lest they be put[8] out of the synagogue: and they loved Jo. 12, 43.
9 the praise of men more than the praising of God. And Jesus cried and said, Jo. 12, 44.
10 Whosoever believeth in me, believeth not in me, but in him that sent me. And Jo. 12, 45.
11 whosoever seeth me hath seen him that sent me. I am come a light[9] into the Jo. 12, 46.
12 world, and so every one that believeth in me abideth not in the darkness. And Jo. 12, 47.
whosoever heareth my sayings, and keepeth them not, I judge him not: for I came
13 not to judge the world, but to give the world life.[10] Whosoever wrongeth[11] me, and Jo. 12, 48.
receiveth not my sayings, there is one that judgeth him: the word that I spake, it
14 shall judge him at the last day. I from myself did not speak; but the Father Jo. 12, 49.
which sent me, he hath given me commandment,[12] what I should say, and what I
15 should speak; and I know that his commandment[12] is eternal life. The things that Jo. 12, 50.
I say now, as my Father hath said unto me, *even* so I say.
16 And when he said that unto them, the scribes and Pharisees began their evil- Lk. 11, 53.
doing, being angry with *him*, and finding fault with his sayings, and harassing[13] him
17 in many things; seeking to catch something from his mouth, that they might be Lk. 11, 54.
able to calumniate him.
18 And when there gathered together myriads of great multitudes, which almost trode Lk. 12, 1.

1 Lit. *are seen*. 2 Or, *touch*. 3 Lit. *boundary* or *limit*. 4 *cf.* § 8, 34.
5 Or, *earth*. 6 Or, *sanctuary*. 7 See § 1, 49, note. 8 Lit. *become*.
9 The text as it stands ought to mean *I am a light. I am come;* but it is a word-for-word reproduction of the Peshitta, and should therefore doubtless be rendered as above. 10 Or, *to save the world* (*cf.* § 1, 78, note).
11 See § 20, 28, note. 12 Not the same word.
13 So Ciasca, following Vat. MS. The true reading, however, is probably that underlying the Borg. MS. If we restore diacritical points to the radical letters we get *deceiving* (*cf.* § 41, 31), an alternative meaning for the word *laying wait for*, used in the Peshitta. The Arabic follows the Peshitta very closely in this and the following verse.

§41 Arabic, one upon another, Jesus began to say unto his disciples, Preserve yourselves
19 p. 156 from the leaven of the Pharisees, which is hypocrisy. For there is nothing Lk. 12, 2.
20 concealed, that shall not be revealed: nor hid, that shall not be known. Everything Lk. 12, 3.
that ye have said in the darkness shall be heard in the light; and what ye have
spoken secretly in the ears in the inner chambers shall be proclaimed on the roofs.
21, 22 This said Jesus, and he went and hid himself from them. But notwithstanding Jo. 12, 36*b*. Jo. 12, 37.
23 his having done all these signs before them, they believed not in him: that the word Jo. 12, 38.
of Isaiah the prophet might be fulfilled, who said,

My Lord, who is he that hath believed to hear us?
And the arm of the Lord, to whom hath it appeared?

24 And for this reason it is not possible for them to believe, because Isaiah also said, Jo. 12, 39
25 They have blinded their eyes, and made dark their heart; Jo. 12, 40.
That they may not see with their eyes, and understand with their heart,
And turn,
So that I should heal them.

26 This said Isaiah when he saw his glory, and spake of him. Jo. 12, 41.
27 And when Jesus went out of the temple, certain of his disciples came forward Mt. 24, 1.
28 to shew[1] him the buildings of the temple, and its beauty and greatness, and the Mk. 13, 1*b*.
strength of the stones that were laid in it, and the elegance of its building, and that Lk. 21, 5*b*.
29 it was adorned with noble stones and beautiful colours. Jesus answered and said Mt. 24, 2*a*.
30 unto them, See ye these great buildings? verily I say unto you, Days will come, Lk. 19, 43*a*.
when there shall not be left here a stone upon another, that shall not be cast down. Lk. 19, 44*b*.[2]
31 And two days before[3] the passover of unleavened bread, the chief priests and Mk. 14, 1.
32 the scribes sought how they might take him by deceit,[4] and kill him: and they said, Mk. 14, 2.
It shall not be at the feast, lest the people be agitated.
33 And when Jesus sat on the mount of Olives opposite the temple, his disciples, Simon Mk. 13, 3.
Cephas and James and John and Andrew, came forward unto him, and said unto him
34 between themselves and him, Teacher, tell us when that shall be, and what is the sign Lk. 21, 7*b*. Mt. 24, 3*b*.
35 Arabic, of thy coming and the end of the world. Jesus answered and said unto them, Mt. 24, 4*a*. Lk. 17, 22*b*.
p. 157 Days will come, when ye shall long to see one of the days of the Son of Mt. 24, 4*b*.
36, 37 man, and shall not behold. Take heed lest any man lead you astray. Many shall Mt. 24, 5*a*. Lk. 21, 8*b*.
38 come in my name, and say, I am the Messiah; and they shall say, The time is come Mk. 13, 6*b*.
39 near, and shall lead many astray: go not therefore after them. And when ye hear Lk. 21, 8*c*. Mk. 13, 7*a*.
of wars and tidings of insurrections, see *to it*, be[5] not agitated: for these *things* must Mt. 24, 6*b*. Lk. 21, 9*b*.
40 first be; only the end is not yet come. Nation shall rise against nation, and king- Mt. 24, 7*a*.
41 dom against kingdom: and great earthquakes shall be in one place and another, Lk. 21, 11.
and there shall be famines and deaths and agitations; and there shall be fear and
terror and great signs that[6] shall appear from heaven, and there shall be great
42, 43 storms. All these *things* are the beginning of travail. But before all of that, they Mt. 24, 8. Lk. 21, 12.
shall lay hands upon you, and persecute you, and deliver you unto the synagogues
44 and into prisons, and bring you before kings and judges for my name's sake. And Lk. 21, 13.
45 that shall be unto you for a witness. But first must my gospel be preached unto all Mk. 13, 10.
46 nations. And when they bring you into the synagogues before the rulers and the Lk. 12, 11.
authorities, be not anxious beforehand how ye shall answer for yourselves, or what ye
47, 48 shall say: because it is not ye that speak, but the Holy Spirit. Lay it to your heart, not Mk. 13, 11*b*. Lk. 21, 14.
49 Arabic, to be anxious before the time what ye shall say: and I shall[7] give you under- Lk. 21, 15.
p. 158 standing and wisdom,[8] which all your adversaries shall not be able to gainsay.
50 And then shall they deliver you unto constraint, and shall kill you: and ye shall be Mt. 24, 9.
51 hated of all nations because of my name. And then shall many go astray,[9] and they Mt. 24, 10.
52 shall hate one another, and deliver one another unto death. And your parents, and Lk. 21, 16.
your brethren, and your kinsfolk, and your friends shall deliver you up, and shall
53, 54 slay some of you. But a lock of hair from your heads shall not perish. And by Lk. 21, 18. Lk. 21, 19.
55 your patience ye shall gain[10] your souls. And many *men*,[11] false prophets, shall arise, Mt. 24, 11.
56 and lead many astray. And because of the abounding of iniquity, the love of many Mt. 24, 12.

1 Or, *and shewed*. 2 Or rather Mt. 24, 2*b*, or Mk. 13, 2*b*.
3 Lit. *before two days would be* (*cf.* Sin. and above, § 39, 1, note). 4 *cf.* § 41, 16, note.
5 Or, *that ye be*, if we suppose the present text to have resulted from the loss of the second of two *alifs*.
6 Or, omit *that*. 7 The Arabic text lacks a letter.
8 Borg. MS. reads *you the fruits of wisdom*. 9 See § 25, 17, note. 10 Or, *possess*.
11 So the Arabic text; but it doubtless simply represents the Syriac, which here agrees with the Greek.

§41 57 shall wax cold. But he that endureth to the end, the same shall be saved. And Mt. 24, 13. Mt. 24, 14.
58 this, the[1] gospel of the kingdom, shall be preached in all the world for a testimony
to all nations; and then shall come the end of all.

SECTION XLII.

§42 1 But when ye see Jerusalem with the army compassing it about, then know that Lk. 21, 20.
2 its desolation is come near. Those then that are in Judæa at that time shall flee Lk. 21, 21.
to the mountain; and those that are within her shall flee; and those that are in the
3 villages shall not enter her. For these days are the days of vengeance, that all that Lk. 21, 22.
4 is written may be fulfilled. And when ye see the unclean sign of desolation,[2] spoken Mt. 24, 15.
of in Daniel the prophet, standing in the pure place, he that readeth shall understand,
5, 6 and then he that is in Judæa shall flee in to the mountain: and let him that is on the Mt. 24, 16. Mk. 13, 15.
7 roof not go down, nor enter in to take anything from his house: and let him that is in Mk. 13, 16.
8 Arabic, the field not turn behind him to take his garment. Woe to them that are Lk. 21, 23.
p. 159 with child and to them that give suck in those days! there shall be great
9 distress in the land, and wrath against this nation. And they shall fall on the edge Lk. 21, 24.
of the sword,[3] and shall be taken captive to every land: and Jerusalem shall be
trodden down of the nations, until the times of the nations be ended.
10 Then if any man say unto you, The Messiah is here; or, Lo, he is there; believe Mk. 13, 21.
11 him not: there shall rise then false Messiahs and prophets of lying, and shall do Mt. 24, 24.
signs and wonders, in order that they may lead astray even the elect also, if they
12 be able. But as for you, beware: for I have acquainted you with everything Mk. 13, 23.
13 beforehand. If then they say unto you, Lo, he is in the desert; go not out, lest ye Mt. 24, 26.
14 be taken: and if they say unto you, Lo, he is in the chamber; believe not. And Mt. 24, 27.
as the lightning appeareth from the east, and is seen unto the west; so shall be the
15 coming of the Son of man. But first he must suffer much and be rejected by this Lk. 17, 25.
16 generation.[4] Pray therefore that your flight be not in winter, nor on a sabbath: Mt. 24, 20.
17 there shall be then great tribulation,[5] the like of which there hath not been from the Mt. 24, 21.
18 beginning of the world till now, nor shall be. And except the Lord had shortened Mk. 13, 20.
those days, no flesh would have lived: but because of the elect, whom he elected,
19 he shortened those days. And there shall be signs in the sun and the moon and the Lk. 21, 25.
stars; and upon the earth affliction[5] of the nations, and rubbing of hands for the con-
20 Arabic, fusion[6] of the noise of the sea, and an earthquake: the souls of men shall Lk. 21, 26*a*.
21 p. 160 go forth from fear of that which is to come upon the earth. And in those Mk. 13, 24*a*.
days, straightway after the distress of those days, the sun shall become dark, and the Mt. 24, 29.
moon shall not shew its light, and the stars shall fall from heaven, and the powers
22 of heaven shall be convulsed: and then shall appear the sign of the Son of man in Mt. 24, 30.
heaven: and at that time all the tribes of the earth shall wail, and look unto the Son
23 of man coming on the clouds of heaven with power and much glory. And he shall Mt. 24, 31.
send his angels with the great trumpet, and they shall gather his elect from the four
24 winds, from one end of heaven to the other.[7] But when these things begin to be, Lk. 21, 28.
be of good cheer, and lift up your heads; for your salvation[8] is come near.
25 Learn the example of the fig tree: when it letteth down its branches,[9] and put- Mt. 24, 32.
26 teth forth its leaves, ye know that the summer is come; so ye also, when ye see Mt. 24, 33.
these things begun to be, know ye that the kingdom of God hath arrived at the
27 door. Verily I say unto you, This generation shall not pass away, until all these Mt. 24, 34.
28 *things* shall be. Heaven and earth shall pass away, but my sayings shall not pass Mt. 24, 35.
away.
29 Take heed to yourselves, that your hearts become not heavy with inordinate Lk. 21, 34.
desire,[10] and drunkenness, and the care of the world at any time, and that day come

1 So the Arabic text; but it doubtless simply represents the Syriac, which here agrees with the Greek.
2 So Vat. MS., following the Peshitta. Ciasca follows Borg. MS., which by a change of diacritical points has the hardly grammatical reading, *see that it is the desolation, the unclean thing spoken of.* Ibn-aṭ-Ṭayyib's Commentary supports Vat. MS.
3 This word has a Syriac meaning given to it. In Arabic it means *war.*
4 *cf.* § 16, 2.
5 Same Arabic (and Syriac) word as in § 41, 50.
6 So the Borg. MS. The Vat. MS., followed by Ciasca, has *grief.*
7 Lit. *the end of heaven unto its end.*
8 Or, *deliverance.*
9 *cf.* Peshitta, which text the translator seems to have misread.
10 *cf.* Peshitta.

§ **42** 30 upon you suddenly: for it is as a shock that shocks all the inhabitants that are on the Lk. 21, 35.
31 face of the whole earth. Watch at all times, and pray, that ye may be worthy to escape Lk. 21, 36.
Arabic, from all the things that are to be, and that ye may stand before the Son of
32 p. 161 man. Of that day and of that hour hath no man learned, not even the angels Mk. 13, 32.
33 of heaven, neither the Son, but the Father. See ye, and watch and pray: for ye know Mk. 13, 33.
34 not when that time *will be*. *It is* as a man, who journeyed, and left his house, and Mk. 13, 34.
gave his authority to his servants, and appointed every man to his work, and
35 charged the porter to be wakeful. Be wakeful then:[1] since ye know not when the Mk. 13, 35.
lord of the house cometh, in the evening, or in the middle of the night, or when the
36 cock croweth, or in the morning; lest he come unexpectedly, and find you sleeping. Mk. 13, 36.
37 The thing that I say unto you, unto all of you do I say it, Be ye watchful. Mk. 13, 37.
38 For as it was in the days of Noah, so shall the coming of the Son of man be. Mt. 24, 37.
39 As they were before the flood eating and drinking, and taking wives, and giving Mt. 24, 38.
40 *wives* to men, until the day in which Noah entered into the ark, and they perceived Mt. 24, 39.
not till the flood came, and took them all; so shall the coming of the Son of man
41 be. And as it was in the days of Lot; they were eating and drinking, and selling Lk. 17, 28.
42 and buying, and planting and building, on the day in which Lot went out from Lk. 17, 29.
Sodom, and the Lord rained fire and brimstone from heaven, and destroyed them
43, 44 all: so shall it be in the day in which the Son of man is revealed.[2] And in that day, Lk. 17, 30. Lk. 17, 31.
whosoever is on the roof, and his garments[3] in the house, let him not go down to
45 take them: and he that is in the field shall not turn behind him. Remember Lot's Lk. 17, 32.
46 wife. Whosoever shall desire to save his life shall destroy it: but whosoever shall Lk. 17, 33.
47 destroy his life shall save it. Verily I say unto you, In that night there shall be two on Lk. 17, 34.
48 Arabic, one bed; one shall be taken, and another left. And two *women* shall be grind- Lk. 17, 35.
49 p. 162 ing at one mill; one shall be taken, and another left. And two shall be in the Lk. 17, 36.
50 field; one shall be taken, and another left. They answered and said unto him, To what Lk. 17, 37.
place, our Lord? He said unto them, Where the body is, there will the eagles
51, 52 gather. Be attentive now: for ye know not at what hour your Lord cometh. Know Mt. 24, 42. Mt. 24, 43.
this: if the master of the house had known in what watch the thief would come, he
would have been attentive, and would not make it possible that his house should be
53 broken through. Therefore be ye also ready: for in the hour that ye think not the Mt. 24, 44.
Son of man cometh.

SECTION XLIII.

§ **43** 1 Simon Cephas said unto him, Our Lord, *is it* to us *that* thou hast spoken this Lk. 12, 41.
2 parable, or also to every man? Jesus said unto him, Who, thinkest thou, is the Lk. 12, 42*a*.[4] Mt. 24, 45.
servant, the master of the house,[5] trusted with control,[6] whom his lord set over his
3 household, to give them their food in its season? Blessed is that servant, whom his Mt. 24, 46.
4 lord shall come and find having done so. Verily I say unto you, He will set him Lk. 12, 44*a*. Mt. 24, 47*b*.
5 over all that he hath. But if that evil servant say in his heart, My lord delayeth his Mt. 24, 48.
6 coming; and shall begin to beat his servants and the maidservants of his lord, and Lk. 12, 45*b*. Mt. 24, 49*b*.
7 shall begin to eat and to drink with the drunken; the lord of that servant shall come Mt. 24, 50.
8 in the day that he thinketh not, and in the hour that he knoweth not, and shall Mt. 24, 51*a*.
Arabic, judge him, and appoint his portion with the hypocrites, and with those that Lk. 12, 46*b*.
p. 163 are not faithful: there shall be weeping and gnashing of teeth. Mt. 24, 51*b*.
9 Then shall the kingdom of heaven be like unto ten virgins, those that took their Mt. 25, 1.
10 lamps, and went forth to meet the bridegroom and the bride. Five of them were Mt. 25, 2.
11 wise, and five foolish. And those foolish *ones* took their lamps, and took not with Mt. 25, 3.
12, 13 them oil: but those wise *ones* took oil in vessels along with their lamps. When then Mt. 25, 4. Mt. 25, 5.
14 the bridegroom delayed, they all slumbered and slept. But in the middle of the Mt. 25, 6.
night there occurred a cry, Behold, the bridegroom cometh! Go forth therefore to
15, 16 meet him. Then all those virgins arose, and made ready their lamps. The foolish Mt. 25, 7. Mt. 25, 8.
17 said unto the wise, Give us of your oil; for our lamps are gone out. But those wise Mt. 25, 9.
answered and said, Perhaps[7] there will not be enough for us and you: but go ye to

1 *cf.* § 9, 21. 2 Or, *appeareth*. 3 *cf.* § 14, 24, note. 4 Borg. MS. omits Lk. 12, 42*a*. 5 i.e., *the steward*.
6 Borg. MS. has *trusted and faithful*. Doubtless we should supply diacritical points to the reading of Vat. MS., and translate *trusted and wise*. Ibn-aṭ-Ṭayyib's Commentary, however, has both *and wise* and the word translated *with control*, used in a different sense. 7 See § 10, 17, and § 4, 24, note.

§43 18 the sellers, and buy for yourselves. And when they went away to buy, the bride- Mt. 25, 10.
groom came; and those that were ready went in with him to the marriage feast: and
19 the door was shut. And at last those other virgins also came and said, Our Lord, Mt. 25, 11.
20 our Lord, open unto us. He answered and said unto them, Verily I say unto you, Mt. 25, 12.
21 I know you not. Watch then, for ye know not that day nor that hour. Mt. 25, 13.
22 *It is* as a man, who went on a journey, and called his servants, and delivered unto Mt. 25, 14.
23 them his possessions. And unto one he gave five talents,[1] and another two, and another Mt. 25, 15.
24 one; every one according to his strength; and went on *his* journey forthwith. He Mt. 25, 16.
Arabic, then that received the five talents went and traded with them, and gained
25, 26 p. 164 other five. And so also he of the two gained other two. But he that re- Mt. 25, 17. Mt. 25, 18.
27 ceived the one went and digged in the earth, and hid the money of his lord. And Mt. 25, 19.
after a long time the lord of those servants came, and took from them the account.
28 And he that received five talents came near and brought other five, and said, My Mt. 25, 20.
lord, thou gavest me five talents: lo, I have gained other five in addition to them.
29 His lord said unto him, Well done, thou good and faithful servant: over a little hast Mt. 25, 21.
30 thou been faithful, over much will I set thee: enter into the joy of thy lord. And Mt. 25, 22.
he that had the two came near and said, My lord, thou gavest me two talents: lo,
31 other two have I gained in addition to them. His lord said unto him, Good,[2] thou Mt. 25, 23.
faithful servant: over a little hast thou been faithful, over much will I set thee: enter
32 into the joy of thy lord. And he also that received the one talent came forward Mt. 25, 24.
and said, My lord, I knew thee that thou art a severe man, who reapest where thou
33 sowest not, and gatherest where thou didst not scatter: and so I was afraid, and Mt. 25, 25.
34 went away and hid thy talent in the earth: lo, thou hast what is thine. His lord Mt. 25, 26.
answered and said unto him, Thou wicked and slothful servant, thou knewest me
35 that I reap where I sowed not, and gather where I did not scatter; it was incumbent Mt. 25, 27.
on thee to put my money to the bank,[3] and *then* I should come and seek it with its
36 gains. Take now from him the talent, and give it to him that hath ten talents. Mt. 25, 28.
37 Whosoever hath shall be given, and he shall have more: but he that hath not, even Mt. 25, 29.
38 Arabic, what he hath shall be taken from him. And the unprofitable servant, put Mt. 25, 30.
p. 165 him forth into the outer darkness: there shall be the weeping and gnashing of teeth.
39, 40 Your loins shall be girded, and your lamps lit; and ye shall be like the people Lk. 12, 35. Lk. 12, 36.
that are looking for their lord, when he shall return from the feast; so that, when
41 he cometh and knocketh, they may at once open unto him. Blessed are those ser- Lk. 12, 37.
vants, whom their lord shall come and find attentive: verily I say unto you, that
he will gird his waist, and make them sit down, and pass through[4] *them* and serve
42 them. And if he come in the second watch, or the third, and find thus, blessed are Lk. 12, 38.
those servants.
43 But when the Son of man cometh in his glory, and all his pure angels with him, Mt. 25, 31.
44 then shall he sit on the throne of his glory: and he will gather before him all the Mt. 25, 32.
nations, and separate them the one from the other, like the shepherd who separateth
45 the sheep from the goats; and will set[5] the sheep on his right, and the goats on his Mt. 25, 33.
46 left. Then shall the King say to those that are at his right, Come, ye blessed of my Mt. 25, 34.
Father, inherit the kingdom prepared for you from the foundations[6] of the world:
47 I hungered, and ye gave me to eat; and I thirsted, and ye gave me to drink; and I Mt. 25, 35.
48 was a stranger, and ye took me in; and I was naked, and ye clothed me; and I Mt. 25, 36.
49 was sick, and ye visited me; and I was in prison, and ye cared for me. Then shall Mt. 25, 37.
those righteous say unto him, Our Lord, when saw we thee hungry, and fed thee?
50 or thirsty, and gave thee to drink? And when saw we thee a stranger, and took Mt. 25, 38.
51 thee in? or naked, and clothed thee? And when saw we thee sick, or imprisoned, and Mt. 25, 39.
52 cared for thee? The King shall answer and say[7] unto them, Verily I say unto you, What Mt. 25, 40.
53 Arabic, ye did to one of these my brethren, the little ones, ye did unto me. Then Mt. 25, 41.
p. 166 shall he say unto those that are on his left also, Depart from me, ye cursed,
54 into the eternal fire prepared for the devil and his hosts: I hungered, and ye fed me Mt. 25, 42.
55 not; and I thirsted, and ye did not give me to drink; and I was a stranger, and ye Mt. 25, 43.

1 *cf.* § 27, 2, note. 2 A Persian word. The Vat. MS. omits it. 3 Lit. *table* (*cf.* Peshitta).
4 *cf.* Peshitta (and Greek). 5 Or, *and setteth;* but the Peshitta confirms the rendering given above.
6 *cf.* § 17, 17, note. 7 Perfect tenses, as in Peshitta.

§43 took me not in; and I was naked, and ye clothed me not; and I was sick, and im-
56 prisoned, and ye visited me not. Then shall those also answer and say, Our Lord, Mt. 25, 44.
when saw we thee an hungred, or athirst, or naked, or a stranger, or sick, or im-
57 prisoned, and did not minister unto thee? Then shall he answer and say unto them, Mt. 25, 45.
Verily I say unto you, When ye did *it* not unto one of these little *ones*, ye did *it* not
58 unto me also. And these shall go away into eternal punishment: but the righteous Mt. 25, 46.
into eternal life.

SECTION XLIV.

§44 1,2 And when Jesus[1] finished all these sayings, he said unto his disciples, Ye know Mt. 26, 1. Mt. 26, 2.
that after two days will be the passover, and the Son of man is delivered up to be
3 crucified. Then gathered together the chief priests, and the scribes, and the elders Mt. 26, 3.
4 of the people, unto the court of the chief priest, who was called Caiaphas; and they Mt. 26, 4.
took counsel together concerning Jesus, that they might seize him by subtilty, and
5 kill him. But they said, Not during the feast, lest there take place a disturbance Mt. 26, 5.
among the people; for they feared the people. Lk. 22, 2*b*.
6 And Satan entered into Judas who was called Iscariot, who was of the number Lk. 22, 3.
7 of the twelve. And he went away, and communed with the chief priests, and the Lk. 22, 4*a*.
scribes, and those that held command in the temple, and said unto them, What Mt. 26, 15*a*.
8 Arabic, would ye pay me, and I will deliver him unto you? And they, when they Mk. 14, 11*a*.
p. 167 heard *it*, were pleased, and made ready[2] for him thirty *pieces* of money.[3] Mt. 26, 15*b*.
9 And he promised[4] them, and from that time he sought an opportunity[5] that he might Lk. 22, 6.
deliver unto them Jesus without the multitude.
10 And on the first day of unleavened bread the disciples came to Jesus, and said Mk. 14, 12.
unto him, Where wilt thou that we go and make ready for thee that thou mayest
eat the passover?
11 And before the feast of the passover, Jesus knew that the hour was arrived for Jo. 13, 1.
his departure from this world unto his Father; and he loved his own in this world,
12 and to the last he loved them. And at the time of the feast, Satan put into the Jo. 13, 2.
13 heart of Judas, the son of Simon Iscariot, to deliver him up. And Jesus, because Jo. 13, 3.
he knew that the Father had delivered into his hands everything, and that he came
14 forth from the Father, and goeth unto God, rose from supper, and laid *aside* his Jo. 13, 4.
15 garments; and took a towel, *and* girded his waist, and poured water into a bason, Jo. 13, 5.
and began to wash the feet of his disciples, and to wipe them with the towel where-
16 with his waist was girded. And when he came to Simon Cephas, Simon said unto Jo. 13, 6.
17 him, Dost thou, my Lord, wash for me my feet? Jesus answered and said unto Jo. 13, 7.
18 him, What I do, now thou knowest not; but afterwards thou shalt learn. Simon Jo. 13, 8.
said unto him, Thou shalt never wash for me my feet. Jesus said unto him, If I
19 wash thee not, thou hast no part with me. Simon Cephas said unto him, Then, my Jo. 13, 9.
20 Lord, wash not for me my feet alone, but my hands also and my head. Jesus said Jo. 13, 10.
unto him, He that batheth[6] needeth not to wash save his feet, whereas his whole
21 *body* is clean: and ye also are clean, but not all of you. For Jesus knew him that Jo. 13, 11.
should betray him; therefore said he, Ye are not all clean.
22 Arabic, So when he had washed their feet, he took his garments, and sat down, and Jo. 13, 12.
23 p. 168 said unto them, Know ye what I have done unto you? Ye call me, Master, Jo. 13, 13.
24 and, Lord: and ye say well; so I am. If then I, now, who am your Lord and Master, Jo. 13, 14.
have washed for you your feet, how needful is it that ye should wash one another's feet!
25 This have I given you as an example, that as I have done to you so ye should do Jo. 13, 15.
26 also. Verily, verily, I say unto you, No servant is greater than his lord; nor an Jo. 13, 16.
27 apostle greater than he that sent him. If ye know that, ye are happy if ye do it. Jo. 13, 17.
28 My saying this[7] is not for all of you: for I know whom I have chosen: but that Jo. 13, 18.
the scripture might be fulfilled, He that eateth with me bread lifted against me his

1 Borg. MS., *the Lord Jesus*.
2 Probably the letter that stands for *and* should be repeated, and the phrase rendered *and appointed*.
3 So Vat. MS. (following Peshitta) and Ibn-aṭ-Ṭayyib's Commentary. Borg. MS., followed by Ciasca, has *dirhams of money*. 4 Lit. *became responsible unto*. Syriac versions as in text above (*cf.* § 44, 33).
5 The Arabic (lit. *a stumbling* or *a cause of stumbling*) doubtless represents the Syriac.
6 The Arabic word means *swimmeth*. The Syriac versions have *is bathed*, which Borg. MS. misreads *bathed*, and Vat. MS. (followed by Ciasca) corrupts into *batheth*, rendering it *swimmeth*. 7 Or, *This my saying*.

§ **44** 29 heel. Henceforth I say unto you before it come to pass, that, when it cometh to Jo. 13, 19.
30 pass, ye may believe that I am *he*. Verily, verily, I say unto you, Whosoever Jo. 13, 20.
receiveth whomsoever I send receiveth me; and whosoever receiveth me receiveth
him that sent me.
31 Who is the great *one*, he that sitteth, or he that serveth? is it not he that sitteth? Lk. 22, 27.
32 I am among you as he that serveth. But ye are they that have continued with me Lk. 22, 28.
33 in my temptations; I promise[1] you, as my Father promised[1] me, the kingdom, that Lk. 22, 29. Lk. 22, 30.
ye may eat and drink at the table of my kingdom.
34 And the first day[2] came, the feast of unleavened bread, on which the Jews were Lk. 22, 7.
35 wont[3] to sacrifice[4] the passover. And Jesus sent two of his disciples, Cephas and Lk. 22, 8.
John, and said unto them, Go and make ready for us the passover, that we may eat.
36, 37 And they said unto him, Where wilt thou that we make ready for thee? He said Lk. 22, 9. Lk. 22, 10*a*.
unto them, Go, enter the city; and at the time of your entering, there shall meet you Mk. 14, 13*b*. Lk. 22, 10*b*.
a man bearing a pitcher of water; follow him, and the place where he entereth, say Lk. 22, 11*a*.
38 to such an one, the master of the house, Our Master saith, My time is come, and Mt. 26, 18*b*.
Arabic, at thy *house* I keep the passover. Where then is the lodging-place where Lk. 22, 11*b*.
39 p. 169 I shall eat with my disciples? And he will shew you a large upper room Lk. 22, 12.
40 spread and made ready: there then make ready for us. And his two disciples went Mk. 14, 15. Mk. 14, 16.
out, and came to the city, and found as he had said unto them: and they made
ready the passover as he had said unto them.
41 And when the evening was come, and the time arrived, Jesus came and reclined, Lk. 22, 14.
42 and the twelve apostles with him. And he said unto them, With desire I have Lk. 22, 15.
43 desired to eat this passover with you before I suffer: I say unto you, that hence- Lk. 22, 16.
forth I shall not eat it, until it is fulfilled in the kingdom of God.
44 Jesus said that, and was agitated[5] in his spirit, and testified, and said, Verily, Jo. 13, 21*a*.
45 verily, I say unto you, One of you, *he* that eateth with me, shall betray me. And Mk. 14, 18*b*. Mk. 14, 19.
they were very sorrowful; and they began to say unto him, one after another of
46 them, Can it be I, Lord? He answered and said unto them, One of the twelve, Mk. 14, 20.
47 *he* that dippeth his hand with me in the dish, will betray me. And lo, the hand of Lk. 22, 21.
48 him that betrayeth me is on the table. And the Son of man goeth, as it is written Mk. 14, 21.
of him: woe then to that man by whose hand the Son of man is betrayed! for it
49 would have been better for that man had he not been born. And the disciples Jo. 13, 22.
50 looked one on another, for they knew not to whom he referred; and they began Lk. 22, 23.
to search among themselves, who that might be who was to do *this*.

SECTION XLV.

§ **45** 1, 2 Arabic, And one of his disciples was sitting[6] in his bosom, *he* whom Jesus loved. Jo. 13, 23.
p. 170 To him Simon Cephas beckoned, that he should ask him who this *was*, con- Jo. 13, 24.
3 cerning whom he spake. And that disciple leaned[7] on Jesus' breast, and said unto him, Jo. 13, 25.
4 My Lord, who is this? Jesus answered and said, He to whom I shall dip bread, Jo. 13, 26.
and give it. And Jesus dipped bread, and gave to Judas, the son of Simon Iscariot.
5 And after the bread, Satan entered him. And Jesus said unto him, What thou Jo. 13, 27.
6 desirest to do, hasten the doing of it. And no man of them that sat knew why he Jo. 13, 28.
7 said this unto him. And some of them thought, because Judas had the box, that Jo. 13, 29.
he was bidding him buy what would be needed for the feast; or, that he might pay
8 something to the poor. Judas the betrayer answered and said, Can it be I, my Mt. 26, 25.
9 Master? Jesus said unto him, Thou hast said. And Judas took the bread straight- Jo. 13, 30.
way, and went forth without: and it was still night.
10 And Jesus said, Now is the Son of man being glorified,[8] and God is being glorified[8] Jo. 13, 31.
11 in him; and if God is glorified in him, God also will glorify him in him, and straight- Jo. 13, 32.
way will glorify him.
12 And while they were eating, Jesus took bread, and blessed, and divided; and he Mk. 14, 22*a*. Mt. 26, 26*b*.

1 *cf.* § 44, 9, note. 2 Vat. MS. has the word *day* on the margin, added by a late hand.
3 The misprint in the Arabic text has been overlooked in the list of *Corrigenda*. 4 Or, *kill*.
5 The Syriac word is retained. In Arabic it properly means *become strong* or *proud* (*cf.* § 38, 17).
6 The Syriac versions have *reclining*. 7 Lit. *fell*.
8 A simple change of diacritical points would give the reading of the Greek and of the Syriac versions.

§45 13 gave to his disciples, and said unto them, Take and eat; this is my body. And he Mk. 14, 23a.
Arabic, took a cup, and gave thanks, and blessed, and gave them, and said, Take Mt. 26, 27b.
14, 15 p. 171 and drink of it, all of you. And they drank of it, all of them. And he Mk. 14, 23b. Mk. 14, 24a.
said unto them, This is my blood, the new covenant, that is shed for many for the Mt. 26, 28.
16 forgiveness of sins. I say unto you, I shall not drink henceforth of this, the juice Mt. 26, 29.
of the vine, until the day in which I drink[1] with you new *wine* in the kingdom of
17 God. And thus do ye in remembrance of me. And Jesus said unto Simon, Simon, Lk. 22, 19b. Lk. 22, 31.
18 behold, Satan asketh that he may sift you like wheat: but I entreat[2] for thee, that Lk. 22, 32.
thou lose not thy faith:[3] and do thou, at some time, turn[4] and strengthen thy brethren.
19 My children, another little *while* am I with you. And ye shall seek me: and as Jo. 13, 33.
20 I said unto the Jews, Whither I go, ye cannot come; I say unto you now also. A Jo. 13, 34.
new commandment I give you, that ye may love one another; and as I have loved
21 you, so shall ye also love one another. By this shall every man know that ye are Jo. 13, 35.
22 my disciples, if ye have love one to another. Simon Cephas said unto him, Our Jo. 13, 36.
Lord, whither goest thou? Jesus answered and said unto him, Whither I go, thou
canst not now follow me; but later thou shalt come.
23 Then said Jesus unto them, Ye all shall desert[5] me this night:[6] it is written, I Mt. 26, 31.
24 will smite the shepherd, and the sheep of the flock shall be scattered. But after my Mt. 26, 32.
25 rising, I shall go before you into Galilee. Simon Cephas answered and said unto Mt. 26, 33.
26 him, My Lord, if every man desert thee, I shall at no time desert thee. I am with Lk. 22, 33b.
thee ready for imprisonment and for death. And my life will I give up for thee. Jo. 13, 37b.
27 Arabic, Jesus said unto him, Wilt thou give up thy life for me? Verily, verily, Jo. 13, 38a. Mk. 14, 30b.
p. 172 I say unto thee, Thou shalt to-day, during this night, before the cock crow
28 twice, three times deny me, that thou knowest me not. But Cephas said the more,[7] Lk. 22, 34b. Mk. 14, 31.
Even if it lead to[8] death with thee, I shall not deny thee, my Lord. And in like
manner said all the disciples also.
29 Then Jesus said unto them, Let not your hearts be troubled:[9] believe in God, Jo. 14, 1.
30 and believe in me. The stations[10] in my Father's house are many, else I should Jo. 14, 2.
31 have told[11] you. I[12] go to prepare for you a place. And if I go *to* prepare for you Jo. 14, 3.
a place, I shall return again, and take you unto me; and so where I am, there ye
32, 33 shall be also. And the place that I go ye know,[13] and the way ye know.[13] Thomas Jo. 14, 4. Jo. 14, 5.
said unto him, Our Lord, we know not whither thou goest; and how is the way for
34 us to the knowledge of that?[14] Jesus said unto him, I am the way, and the truth, Jo. 14, 6.
35 and the life: and no man cometh unto my Father, but through me. And if ye had Jo. 14, 7.
known me, ye should have known my Father: and from henceforth ye know[15] him,
36 and have seen him. Philip[16] said unto him, Our Lord, shew us the Father, and it suf- Jo. 14, 8.
37 ficeth us. Jesus said unto him, Have I been all this time with you, and dost thou not Jo. 14, 9.
know[17] me, Philip?[16] whosoever hath seen me hath seen the Father; how then sayest
38 thou, Shew us the Father? Believest thou not that I am in my Father, and my Father Jo. 14, 10.
in me? and the saying that I say, I say not of myself: but my Father who dwelleth in
39 me, he doeth these deeds. Believe that I am in my Father, and my Father in me: Jo. 14, 11.
40 Arabic, or else believe for the sake of the deeds. Verily, verily, I say unto you, Jo. 14, 12.
p. 173 Whosoever believeth in me, the deeds that I do shall he do also; and
41 more than that shall he do; I go unto the Father. And what ye shall ask in my Jo. 14, 13.
42 name, I shall do unto you, that the Father may be glorified in his Son. And if ye Jo. 14, 14.
43, 44 ask me[18] in my name, I will do *it*. If ye love me, keep my commandments. And Jo. 14, 15. Jo. 14, 16.
I will entreat of my Father, and he will send unto you another Paraclete, that he
45 may be with you for ever, *even* the Spirit of truth: whom the world cannot receive; Jo. 14, 17.
for it hath not seen him, nor known him: but ye know him; for he hath dwelt[19]

1 Peshitta adds *it*. The reading of the Sinaitic is doubtful. 2 Past tense in Syriac versions.
3 We may translate, with the Syriac versions, *that thy faith fail not*, only if we assign a somewhat Syriac meaning to the verb, and assume either an error in diacritical points (*t* for *y*) or an unusual (Syriac) gender for *faith*.
4 *cf.* Syriac versions. 5 The Arabic word is not unlike the word for *stumble*, and Borg. MS. omits *me*.
6 Vat. MS. omits *this night*. 7 Or, *went on saying*. 8 Lit. *end in*. Or, *if I come to* (*the point of*).
9 The diacritical points in both Vat. (followed by Ciasca) and Borg. MSS. appear to demand a rendering *inquire* for *be troubled*. In Ibn-at-Ṭayyib's comments (not the *text*), however (with other points), we have the meaning *wail* (root *nhb*). Every Syriac version uses a different word. 10 Or, *ranks*. 11 Or, *should tell*.
12 Probably the Arabic represents a Syriac *For I*. 13 Different words.
14 *cf.* Ibn-at-Ṭayyib's Commentary (f. 352a) and order of words in Peshitta (not Sin.). 15 Lit. *have known*.
16 Different forms, as in Peshitta. 17 More exactly, *hast thou not come to know*.
18 The Borg. MS. has *me* clearly (*cf.* Peshitta). The Vat. MS. is ambiguous.
19 Probably a misreading of the Peshitta (not Sin. or Cur.), since the next clause also agrees with it.

§45 46 with you, and is in you. I will not leave you orphans: I will come unto you. Jo. 14, 18.
47 Another little *while*, and the world seeth me not; but ye see me that I live, and ye Jo. 14, 19.
48 shall live also. And in that day ye shall know that I am in my Father, and ye in Jo. 14, 20.
me, and I in you.

SECTION XLVI.

§46 1 Whosoever hath my commandments, and keepeth them, he it is that loveth me: Jo. 14, 21.
and he that loveth me shall be loved of my Father, and I will love him, and will
2 shew myself unto him. Judas (not Iscariot) said unto him, My Lord, what is the Jo. 14, 22.
3 purpose of thy intention to shew thyself to us, and not to the world? Jesus Jo. 14, 23.
answered and said unto him, Whosoever loveth me will keep my word: and my
Father will love him, and to him will we come, and make our[1] abode with him.
4 But he that loveth me not keepeth not my word: and this word that ye hear is not Jo. 14, 24.
my word, but the Father's which sent me.
5, 6 This have I spoken unto you, while I was yet with you. But the Paraclete, the Jo. 14, 25. Jo. 14, 26.
Holy Spirit, whom my Father will send in my name, he will teach you everything, and
7 Arabic, he will bring to your remembrance all that I say unto you. Peace I leave you; Jo. 14, 27.
p. 174 my peace I give unto you: and not as this world giveth, give I unto you.
8 Let your heart not be troubled,[2] nor fearful. Ye heard that I said unto you, that I go Jo. 14, 28.
away, and come unto you. If[3] ye loved me, ye would rejoice, that I go away to my
9 Father: for my Father is greater than I. And now I say unto you before it come Jo. 14, 29.
10 to pass, that, when it cometh to pass, ye may believe me. Now I will not speak Jo. 14, 30.
with you much: the Archon of the world will come, and he will have nothing in
11 me: but that the world may know that I love my Father, and as my Father charged Jo. 14, 31*a*.
me, so I do.
12 And he said unto them, When I sent you without purses, or wallets, and shoes,[4] Lk. 22, 35.
13 lacked ye perchance anything? They said unto him, Nothing. He said unto Lk. 22, 36.
them, Henceforth, whosoever hath a purse, let him take it, and likewise the wallet
also: and whosoever hath not a sword, shall sell his garment, and buy for himself a
14 sword. I say unto you, that this scripture also must be fulfilled in me, that I Lk. 22, 37.
should be reckoned[5] with the transgressors: for all that is said of me is fulfilled in
15 me. His disciples said unto him, Our Lord, lo, here are two swords. He said Lk. 22, 38.
16 unto them, They are sufficient. Arise, let us go hence. And they arose, and Jo. 14, 31*b*. Lk. 22, 39.
praised, and went forth, and went, according to their custom, to the mount of Olives,
he and his disciples.
17 And he said unto them, I am the true vine, and my Father is the husbandman. Jo. 15, 1.
18 Every branch that produceth not fruit in me, he taketh it: and that which giveth fruit, Jo. 15, 2.
19 he cleanseth it, that it may give much fruit. Ye are already clean because of the word Jo. 15, 3.
20 that I have spoken unto you. Abide in me, and I in you. And as the branch of the Jo. 15, 4.
Arabic, vine cannot produce fruit of itself, if it be not abiding in the vine; so too ye
21 p. 175 also, if ye abide not in me. I am the vine, and ye are the branches: He Jo. 15, 5.
then that abideth in me, and I in him, he giveth much fruit: for without me ye can-
22 not do anything. And if a man abide not in me, he is cast without, like a withered Jo. 15, 6.
23 branch; and it is gathered, and cast[6] into the fire, that it may be burned. If ye Jo. 15, 7.
abide in me, and my word abide in you, everything that ye desire to ask shall be
24 *done* unto you. And herein is the Father glorified, that ye may give much fruit; Jo. 15, 8.
25 and ye *shall* be my disciples. And as my Father loved me, I loved you also: Jo. 15, 9.
26 abide in my love. If ye keep my commands, ye shall abide in my love; as I have Jo. 15, 10.
27 kept my Father's commands, and abode in his love. I have spoken that unto you, Jo. 15, 11.
28 that my joy[7] may be in you, and your joy[7] be fulfilled. This is my commandment, Jo. 15, 12.
29 that ye love one another, as I loved you. And no love is greater than this, namely, Jo. 15, 13.
30 that a man should give his life for his friends. Ye are my friends, if ye do all that Jo. 15, 14.
31 I command you. I call you not now servants; for the servant knoweth not what Jo. 15, 15.

1 Lit. *the* (*cf.* Syriac versions). 2 This word is quite unlike that used in § 45, 29.
3 The Syriac form of the introductory particle is wrongly used, for in Arabic it has interrogative force.
4 The first letter of the Arabic word has lost its diacritical point.
5 A possible rendering of the Syriac *he was reckoned*.
6 The verbs may be active or passive, but are singular (*cf.* § 38, 43, note). 7 Two words from the same root.

§ 46 his lord doeth: my friends have I now called you; for everything that I heard from
32 my Father I have made known unto you. Ye did not choose [1] me, but I chose [1] you, Jo. 15, 16.
and appointed you, that ye also should go and bear fruit, and *that* your fruit should [2]
33 abide; and *that* all that ye shall ask my Father in my name, he may [2] give you. This Jo. 15, 17.
34 I command [3] you, that ye love one another. And if the world hate you, know that Jo. 15, 18.
35 before you it hated me. If then ye were of the world, the world would love its own: Jo. 15, 19.
but ye are not of the world: I chose you out of the world: therefore the world
36 Arabic, p. 176 hateth you. Remember the word that I said unto you, that no servant is Jo. 15, 20.
greater than his lord. And if they persecuted [4] me, you also will they
37 persecute; [4] and if they kept my word, your word also will they keep. But all these Jo. 15, 21.
things will they do unto you for my name's sake, for they have not known [5] him
38 that sent me. And if I had not come and spoken unto them, they had not had sin: Jo. 15, 22.
39 but now they have no excuse for their sins. Whosoever hateth me, also hateth my Jo. 15, 23.
40 Father. And if I had not done the deeds before them that no other man did, they Jo. 15, 24.
would not have had sin: but now they have seen and hated me and my Father
41 also: that the word may be fulfilled that is written in their law, They hated me for Jo. 15, 25.
42 nothing. But when the Paraclete is come, whom I will send unto you from my Father, Jo. 15, 26.
even the Spirit of truth, which goeth forth from my Father, he shall bear witness of
43 me: and ye also bear witness, because from the beginning ye *have been* with me. Jo. 15, 27.
44, 45 I have said that unto you, that ye may not stumble.[6] And they shall put you Jo. 16, 1. Jo. 16, 2.
out of their synagogues: and there cometh an [7] hour when every one that killeth
46 you shall think that he hath offered unto God an offering. And they will do that, Jo. 16, 3.
47 because they do not know me, nor my Father. I have said that unto you, so that Jo. 16, 4.
48 when its time is come, ye may remember it, that I told you. And this hitherto I said Jo. 16, 5.[8]
not unto you, because I was with you. But [8] now I go unto him that sent me; and no
49 man of you asketh me whither I go. I have said that unto you now, and grief hath Jo. 16, 6.
50 come and taken possession of your hearts. But I say the truth unto you; It is better [9] Jo. 16, 7.
for you that I go away: for if I go not away, the Paraclete will not come unto you;
51 Arabic, p. 177 but if I go away, I will send him unto you. And when he cometh, he Jo. 16, 8.
will reprove the world for sin, and for righteousness, and for judgement:
52, 53 for sin, because they have not believed in me; and for righteousness, because I go Jo. 16, 9. Jo. 16, 10.
54 to my Father; and for judgement, because [10] the Archon of this world hath been Jo. 16, 11.
55 judged. And further have I many things to speak unto you, but ye cannot tarry [11] Jo. 16, 12.
56 now. Howbeit [12] when the Spirit of truth is come, he will remind [13] you of all the Jo. 16, 13.
truth: he will say nothing from himself; but everything that he heareth, that shall
57 he say: and he shall make known unto you the things that are to be. And he shall Jo. 16, 14.
58 glorify me; for from me shall he take and shew you. All that my Father hath is Jo. 16, 15.
mine: therefore said I unto you, that he taketh [14] of mine, and shall shew [14] you.

SECTION XLVII.

§ 47 1 A little *while*, and ye shall not behold me; and a little *while* again, and ye shall Jo. 16, 16.
2 behold me; because I go to the Father. His disciples therefore said one to Jo. 16, 17.
another, What is this that he hath said unto us, A little *while*, and ye shall not
behold me; and a little *while* again, and ye shall behold me: and, I go to my
3 Father? And they said, What is this little *while* that he hath said? We know not Jo. 16, 18.
4 what he speaketh. And Jesus perceived that they were seeking to ask him, and Jo. 16, 19.
said unto them, Do ye inquire among yourselves concerning this, that I said unto
you, A little *while*, and ye behold me not, and a little while again, and ye shall
5 behold me? Verily, verily,[15] I say unto you, that ye shall weep and grieve, but the Jo. 16, 20.
world shall rejoice: and ye shall be sorrowful, but your grief shall turn [16] to joy.

1 Different words. 2 Or, *shall* and *will*, respectively. 3 Or, *have commanded*. 4 *cf.* § 8, 34, note.
5 The Arabic text (Vat.) is grammatically inaccurate, and the Borg. MS. has *know not*.
6 Lit. *sway* (*as one does in dozing*). 7 Or, *the*, as in Borg. MS.
8 In the Greek and English verse 5 begins at *But*. 9 Or, *best*. 10 Lit. *that* (*cf.* Peshitta).
11 Or perhaps *receive* (*them*). Possibly a Syriac *d* has been read *r*. But Ibn-aṭ-Ṭayyib in the text of his Commentary (f. 357*a*) has a word which perhaps might be rendered *accommodate yourselves* (*to them*) (same letters, but last two transposed), while his comment (f. 357*b*) gives *ye cannot bear it*. 12 Or, *And*.
13 The Syriac words for *remind* and *lead* differ only in the length of a single stroke. Ibn-aṭ-Ṭayyib (*ibid.* f. 357*b*) almost seems to have read *illumine you with*, although he calls attention to the "Greek" reading. 14 Same tense.
15 Not quite the usual formula, there being here no article.
16 The Arabic might also be rendered *be turned*, but the Syriac is intransitive.

§47 6 For, a woman when the time is come for her that she should bring forth, the arrival Jo. 16, 21.
of the day of her bringing forth distresseth her: but whenever she hath brought
forth a son, she remembereth not her distress, for joy at the birth of a man into the
7 world. And ye now also grieve: but I shall see you, and your hearts shall rejoice, Jo. 16, 22.
8 Arabic, and your joy no man taketh from you. And in that day ye shall ask me Jo. 16, 23.
p. 178 nothing. And verily, verily,[1] I say unto you, All that ye ask my Father
9 in my name, he will give you. Hitherto ye have asked nothing in my name: ask, Jo. 16, 24.
and ye shall receive, that your joy may be complete.
10 I have spoken unto you now in ænigmas:[2] but there will come an hour when[3] Jo. 16, 25.
I shall not speak to you in ænigmas,[2] but shall reveal unto you the Father plainly,
11 in that day when[4] ye shall ask in my name: and I say not unto you, that I shall Jo. 16, 26.
12 entreat the Father for you; for the Father loveth you, because ye have loved me, Jo. 16, 27.
13 and have believed that I came forth from my Father. I came forth from my Jo. 16, 28.
Father, and came into the world: and I leave the world, and go unto my Father.
14 His disciples said unto him, Lo, thy speech is now plain, and thou hast not said one Jo. 16, 29.
15 thing in an ænigma. Now, lo, we know that thou knowest everything, and needest Jo. 16, 30.
not that any man should ask thee: and by this we believe that thou camest forth
16, 17 from God. Jesus said unto them, Believe that an hour cometh, and lo, it hath Jo. 16, 31. Jo. 16, 32.
come, and ye shall be scattered, every one of you to his place, and shall leave me
18 alone: and *yet* I am not alone, because the Father is with me. This have I said Jo. 16, 33.
unto you, that in me ye may have peace. And in the world trouble shall overtake
you: but be of good courage; for I have overcome the world.
19 This said Jesus, and lifted up his eyes unto heaven, and said, My Father, the hour Jo. 17, 1.
20 is come; glorify thy Son, that thy Son may glorify thee: as thou gavest him authority Jo. 17, 2.
21 over all flesh, that all that thou hast given him, he might give them[5] eternal life. And Jo. 17, 3.
this is eternal life, that they should[6] know that thou alone art true God, and *that he*
22 Arabic, whom thou didst send is Jesus the Messiah.[7] I glorified thee in the earth, Jo. 17, 4.
23 p. 179 and the work which thou gavest me to do I have accomplished. And Jo. 17, 5.
now glorify thou me, O Father, beside thee, with that glory which I had with thee
24 before the world was. I made known thy name to the men whom thou gavest me Jo. 17, 6.
out of the world: thine they were, and thou gavest them to me; and they have kept
25, 26 thy word. Now they[8] know that all that thou hast given me is from thee: and the Jo. 17, 7. Jo. 17, 8.
sayings which thou gavest me I have given unto them; and they received *them*, and
knew of a truth that I came forth from thee, and believed that thou didst send me.
27 And I ask for their sake: and my asking is not for the world, but for those whom Jo. 17, 9.
28 thou hast given me; for they are thine: and all that is mine is thine, and all that is Jo. 17, 10.
29 thine is mine: and I am glorified in them. And now I am not in the world, and Jo. 17, 11.
they are in the world, and I come to thee. My[9] holy Father, keep them in thy
30 name which[10] thou hast given unto me, that they may be one, as we are. When I Jo. 17, 12.
was with them in the world, I kept them in thy name: and I kept those whom thou
gavest unto me: and no man of them hath perished, but the son of perdition; that
31 the scripture might be fulfilled. Now I come to thee; and this I say in the world, Jo. 17, 13.
32 that my joy may be complete in them. I have given them thy word; and the world Jo. 17, 14.
33 hated them, because they were not of the world, as I was not of the world. And I Jo. 17, 15.
ask not this, that thou take them from the world, but that thou keep them from the
34, 35 evil one. They were not of the world, as I was not of the world. O Father, sanctify Jo. 17, 16. Jo. 17, 17.
36 them in thy truth: for thy word is truth. And as thou didst send me into the world, I Jo. 17, 18.
37 Arabic, also send them into the world. And for their sake I sanctify myself, that they Jo. 17, 19.
38 p. 180 also may be sanctified in the truth. Neither for these alone do I ask, but for Jo. 17, 20.
39 the sake of them that believe in me through their word; that they may be all one; Jo. 17, 21.

1 Not quite the usual formula, there being here no article (*cf.* also § 47, 5).
2 Not the usual word for *proverb* or *parable* (*cf.* Syriac versions).
3 So Vat. MS. and Peshitta. The Borg. MS., followed by Ciasca, has *and a time when.*
4 *cf.* Peshitta. 5 Lit. *it* or *him.*
6 In the Borg. MS. the sentence begins with *that they might*, the preceding clause being omitted.
7 The above is perhaps the most natural rendering of the Arabic; but the latter is really only an awkward word-for-word reproduction of the Peshitta, which means *know thee, who alone art the God of truth, and him whom thou didst send, (even) Jesus the Messiah.*
8 So Ciasca's text. The Vat. MS. has *I*, with the Peshitta and probably Sinaitic.
9 So in Sinaitic. The Peshitta omits *My.*
10 Singular in both Arabic MSS., as in the Peshitta. Ciasca prints the plural form. The Sin. passes directly from *name* to *When.*

§47 as thou art in me, and I in thee, and so they also shall be one in us: that the world
40 may believe that thou didst send me. And the glory which thou hast given unto Jo. 17, 22.
41 me I have given unto them; that they may be one, as we are one; I in them, and Jo. 17, 23.
thou in me, that they may be perfect into[1] one; and *that* the world may know that
42 thou didst send me, and that I[2] loved them, as thou lovedst me. Father, and those Jo. 17, 24.
whom thou hast given me, I wish that, where I am, they may be with me also; that
they may behold my glory, which thou hast given me: for thou lovedst me before
43 the foundation[3] of the world. My righteous Father,[4] and the world knew thee not, Jo. 17, 25.
44 but I know thee; and they knew that thou didst send me; and I made known unto Jo. 17, 26.
them thy name, and will make *it* known to them; that the love *wherewith* thou
lovedst me may be in them, and I shall[5] be in them.

SECTION XLVIII.

§48 1 This said Jesus, and went forth with his disciples to a place which was called Jo. 18, 1.
Gethsemane,[6] on[7] the side that is in the plain[8] of Kidron, the mountain,[9] the place
2 in which was a garden; and he entered thither, he and his disciples. And Judas the Jo. 18, 2.
3 betrayer knew that place: for Jesus oft-times met with his disciples there. And when Lk. 22, 40*a*.
Jesus came to the place, he said to his disciples, Sit ye here, so that I may go and pray; Mt. 26, 36*b*.
4, 5 (Arabic, p. 181) and pray ye, that ye enter not into temptations. And he took with him Lk. 22, 40*b*. Mt. 26, 37.
Cephas and the sons of Zebedee together, James and John; and he began to
6 look sorrowful, and to be anxious. And he said unto them, My soul is distressed unto Mt. 26, 38.
7 death: abide ye here, and watch with me. And he withdrew from them a little, Lk. 22, 41*a*.
8 the space of a stone's throw; and he kneeled,[10] and fell on his face, and prayed, so Mk. 14, 35*b*.
9 that, if it *were* possible, this hour *might* pass[11] him. And he said, Father, thou art Mk. 14, 36*a*.
able for all things; if thou wilt, let this cup pass me: but let not my will be *done*, Lk. 22, 42*b*.
10 but let thy will be *done*. And he came to his disciples, and found them sleeping; Mt. 26, 40*a*.
11 and he said unto Cephas, Simon, didst thou sleep? Could ye thus not for one hour Mk. 14, 37*b*. Mt. 26, 40*b*.
12 watch with me? Watch and pray, that ye enter not into temptations: the spirit is Mt. 26, 41*a*. Mk. 14, 38*b*.
13 willing and ready, but the body is weak.[12] And he went again a second time, and Mt. 26, 42.
prayed, and said, My Father, if it is not possible with regard to[13] this cup that it pass,
14 except I drink it, thy will be *done*. And he returned again, and found his disciples Mk. 14, 40.
sleeping, for their eyes were heavy from their grief and anxiety; and they knew not
15 what to say to him. And he left them, and went away again, and prayed a third Mt. 26, 44.
16 time, and said the very same word. And there appeared unto him an angel from Lk. 22, 43.
17 heaven, encouraging him. And being afraid[14] he prayed continuously:[15] and his sweat Lk. 22, 44.
18 (Arabic, p. 182) became like a stream of blood, and fell on the ground. Then he rose from Lk. 22, 45*a*.
19 his prayer, and came to his disciples, and found them sleeping. And he Lk. 22, 46.
20 said unto them, Sleep now, and rest: the end hath arrived,[16] and the hour hath come; Mt. 26, 45*b*. Mk. 14, 41*b*.
21 and behold, the Son of man is betrayed into the hands of sinners. Arise, let us go:[17] for Mk. 14, 42*a*. Mt. 26, 46*b*.
he hath come that betrayeth me.

22 And while he was still speaking, came Judas the betrayer, one of the twelve, and Mt. 26, 47.
with him a great multitude carrying lanterns and torches[18] and swords and staves,
from the chief priests and scribes and elders of the people, and with him the foot-
23 soldiers of the Romans.[19] And Judas the betrayer gave them a sign, and said, He Mt. 26, 48.
whom I shall kiss, he is he: take him with care,[20] and lead him *away*.[21] Mk. 14, 44*b*.

1 Vat. MS. has *as*. 2 *cf.* Peshitta, as pointed in the editions. 3 *cf.* § 17, 17, note.
4 The Arabic as it stands should mean *My Father is righteous;* but it is simply the ordinary Syriac reading, and is so rendered above. 5 Or perhaps *may*. 6 Mt. 26, 36. 7 Vat. MS. has *and on*.
8 The word rendered *plain* (*cf.* Dozy, *Supplément, sub voc.*), which occurs also in the text of Ibn-aṭ-Ṭayyib (*loc. cit.*, f. 362*b*), properly means *lake*. The word in the *Jerusalem Lectionary* means *valley* as well as *stream*. For the whole clause *cf.* the text of Jo. 18, in *Die vier Evangelien, arabisch, aus der Wiener Handschrift*, edited by P. de Lagarde, 1864. 9 *cf.* Sinaitic Syriac and Lk. 22, 39.
10 Lit. *fell on his knees*. 11 Lit. *let this hour pass*. The Borg. MS. omits *him*.
12 Lit. *diseased*. The Arabic word is rare in the sense required by the context (*cf.* Pesh.).
13 This reading would perhaps more easily arise out of the Sinaitic than out of the Peshitta.
14 *cf.* Peshitta. Or, *And although he was afraid*. 15 The Peshitta (hardly Cur.) is capable of this interpretation.
16 *cf.* Syr., especially Peshitta. 17 *cf.* § 4, 20, note. 18 Jo. 18, 3.
19 *cf.* Jo. 18, 3 (*Jerusalem Lectionary*). In Syriac *Romans* means *soldiers*. The Arabic *footsoldiers* might be *man* (singular).
20 *cf.* Syriac versions. Obviously we must supply a diacritical point over the last radical, or read the middle one as *dhal*.
21 Lit. *him to—*. Borg. MS. probably means *bear him away*.

§ **48** 24 And Jesus, because he knew everything that should come upon him, went forth Jo. 18, 4*a*.
25 unto them. And immediately Judas the betrayer came to Jesus, and said, Peace, Mt. 26, 49.
26 my Master; and kissed him. And Jesus said unto him, Judas, with a kiss betrayest Mt. 26, 50*a*. Lk. 22, 48*b*.
27 thou the Son of man? *Was it* for that thou camest, my friend? And Jesus said Mt. 26, 50*b*. Lk. 22, 52*a*,*c*.
28 to those that came unto him, Whom seek ye? They said unto him, Jesus the Naz- Jo. 18, 4*b*.
arene. Jesus said unto them, I am he. And Judas the betrayer also was standing Jo. 18, 5.
29 with them. And when Jesus said unto them, I am he, they retreated backward, and Jo. 18, 6.
30 fell to the ground. And Jesus asked them again, Whom seek ye? They answered, Jo. 18, 7.
31 Jesus the Nazarene. Jesus said unto them, I told you that I am he: and if ye seek Jo. 18, 8.
32 me, let these go away: that the word might be fulfilled which he spake, Of those Jo. 18, 9.
33 Arabic, whom thou hast given me I lost not even one. Then came those that were Mt. 26, 50*c*.
p. 183 with Judas, and seized Jesus, and took him.
34 And when his disciples saw what happened, they said, Our Lord, shall we smite Lk. 22, 49.
35 them with swords? And Simon Cephas had a sword, and he drew it, and struck Jo. 18, 10.
the servant of the chief priest, and cut off his right ear. And the name of that ser-
36 vant was Malchus. Jesus said unto Cephas, The cup which my Father hath given Jo. 18, 11*a*.
37 me, shall I not drink it? Put the sword into its sheath: for all that take with[1] the Jo. 18, 11*c*. Mt. 26, 52*b*.
38 sword shall die by the sword. Thinkest[2] thou that I am not able to ask of my Mt. 26, 53.
39 Father, and he shall now raise up for me more than[3] twelve tribes of angels? Then Mt. 26, 54.
40 how should the scriptures which were spoken be fulfilled, that thus it must be? Your Lk. 22, 51*b*.
41 leave in this.[4] And he touched the ear of him that was struck, and healed it. And Mt. 26, 55.
in that hour Jesus said to the multitudes, As they come out against a thief are ye
come out against me with swords and staves to take me? Daily was I with you in
42 the temple sitting teaching, and ye took me not: but this is your hour, and the power Lk. 22, 53*b*.
43 of darkness. And that was, that the scriptures of the prophets might be fulfilled. Mt. 26, 56.
44 Then the disciples all left him, and fled. And the footsoldiers and the officers Jo. 18, 12*a*.
45 and the soldiers[5] of the Jews seized Jesus, and came. And a certain[6] young man Mk. 14, 51.
46 followed him, and he was wrapped in a towel, naked: and they seized him; so he Mk. 14, 52.
47 Arabic, left the towel, and fled naked. Then they took Jesus, and bound him, and Jo. 18, 12*b*. Jo. 18, 13.
p. 184 brought him to Annas first; because he was the father in law of Caiaphas,
48 who was chief priest that year. And Caiaphas was he that counselled the Jews, that Jo. 18, 14.
it was necessary that one man should die instead of the people.
49 And Simon Cephas and one of the other disciples followed Jesus. And the chief Jo. 18, 15.
50 priest knew that disciple, and he entered with Jesus into the court; but Simon was Jo. 18, 16.
standing without at the door. And that other disciple, whom the chief priest knew,
51 went out and spake unto her that kept the door, and she brought Simon in. And Jo. 18, 17*a*.
when the maid that kept the door saw Simon, she looked stedfastly at him, and said
unto him, Art not thou also one of the disciples of this man, I mean Jesus the
52 Nazarene? But he denied, and said, Woman, I know him not, neither know I even Lk. 22, 57. Mk. 14, 68*b*.
53 what thou sayest. And the servants and the soldiers rose, and made a fire in the Jo. 18, 18*a*.
54 middle of the court, that they might warm themselves; for it was cold. And when Lk. 22, 55*a*.
55 the fire burned up, they sat down around it. And Simon also came, and sat down Jo. 18, 18*c*.
with them to warm himself, that he might see the end of what should happen. Mt. 26, 58*b*.

SECTION XLIX.

§ **49** 1,2 And the chief priest asked Jesus about his disciples, and about his doctrine.[7] And Jo. 18, 19. Jo. 18, 20.
Jesus said unto him, I was speaking[8] openly to the people; and I ever taught in the
synagogue, and in the temple, where all the Jews gather; and I have spoken nothing in
3 Arabic, secret. Why askest thou me? ask those that have heard, what I spake unto Jo. 18, 21.
4 p. 185 them: for they know all that I said. And when he had said that, one of Jo. 18, 22.
the soldiers which were standing *there* struck the cheek[9] of Jesus, and said unto him,

1 *With* is doubtless an accidental repetition of *by* (the same Arabic particle) in the next clause.
2 The introductory interrogative particle may represent an original *Or*.
3 Vat. MS. omits *than*, and has *more* only in the margin by another hand.
4 The phrase is awkward. The rendering is different in the text (f. 292*a*; *cf.* Lagarde, *Die vier Evv.*), and yet again in the comment (f. 293*a*) of Ibn-at-Ṭayyib's Commentary. 5 *cf.* § 11, 11. 6 Lit. *one*. 7 *cf.* § 6, 40, note.
8 Peshitta, *spake;* Sin. omits the verse; Cur. lacking. 9 See § 9, 7, note.

§ 49 5 Dost thou thus answer the chief priest? Jesus answered and said unto him, If I Jo. 18, 23.
6 have spoken evil, bear witness of evil:[1] but if well, why didst thou smite me? And Jo. 18, 24.
Annas sent Jesus bound unto Caiaphas the chief priest.

7 And when Jesus went out, Simon Cephas was standing in the outer court warm- Jo. 18, 25a.
8 ing himself. And that maid saw him again, and began to say to those that stood Mk. 14, 69a.
9 *by*, This *man* also was there with Jesus the Nazarene. And those that stood *by* Mt. 26, 71b. Mt. 26, 73b.
10 came forward and said to Cephas, Truly thou art one of his disciples. And he Mt. 26, 72.
11 denied again with an oath, I know not the man. And after a little one of the ser- Lk. 22, 58a. Jo. 18, 26a.
vants of the chief priest, the kinsman of him whose ear Simon cut off, saw him; and
12 he disputed[2] and said, Truly this *man* was with him: and he also is a Galilæan; Lk. 22, 59b.
13 and his speech resembles.[3] And he said unto Simon, Did not I see thee with him Mt. 26, 73c. Jo. 18, 26b.
14 in the garden? Then began Simon to curse,[4] and to swear, I know not this man Mk. 14, 71.
15 whom ye have mentioned. And immediately, while he was speaking, the cock crew Lk. 22, 60b.
16 twice. And in that hour Jesus turned, he being without, and looked stedfastly at Lk. 22, 61a.
Cephas. And Simon remembered the word of our Lord, which he said unto him,
17, 18 Before the cock crow twice, thou shalt deny me thrice. And Simon went forth Mk. 14, 30b, c. Lk. 22, 62.
without, and wept bitterly.

19 Arabic, p. 186 And when the morning approached, the servants of all the chief priests Lk. 22, 66a.
and the scribes and the elders of the people and all the multitude assembled,
20, 21 and made a plot; and they took counsel against Jesus to put him to death. And they Mt. 27, 1b. Mt. 26, 59b.
sought false witnesses who should witness against him, that they might put him to
22, 23 death, and they found not; but many false witnesses came, but their witness did not Mt. 26, 60a. Mk. 14, 59.
24, 25 agree. But at last there came two lying witnesses, and said, We heard him say, I will Mt. 26, 60b. Mk. 14, 57b.
destroy this[5] temple of God that is made with hands, and will build another not Mk. 14, 58.
26, 27 made with hands after three days. And not even so did their witness agree. But Mk. 14, 59. Mt. 26, 63a.
Jesus was silent. And the chief priest rose in the midst, and asked Jesus, and said, Mk. 14, 60a.
28 Answerest thou not a word concerning anything? what do these[6] witness against Mt. 26, 62b.
29, 30 thee? But Jesus was silent, and answered him nothing. And they took him up Mk. 14, 61a. Lk. 22, 66b.
31 into their assembly,[7] and said unto him, If thou art the Messiah, tell us. He said Lk. 22, 67.
32 unto them, If I tell you, ye will not believe me: and if I ask you, ye will not answer Lk. 22, 68.
33 me a word, nor let me go. And the chief priest answered and said unto him, I Mt. 26, 63b.
adjure thee by the living God, that thou tell us whether thou art the Messiah, the
34, 35 Son of the living God. Jesus said unto him, Thou hast said that I am he. They Mt. 26, 64a. Lk. 22, 70.
all said unto him, Then thou art now the Son of God? Jesus said, Ye have said
36 that I am he. I say unto you, that henceforth ye shall see the Son of man sitting Mt. 26, 64b.
37 Arabic, at the right hand of power, and coming on the clouds of heaven. Then the Mk. 14, 63a.
38 p. 187 chief priest rent his tunic,[8] and said, He hath blasphemed. And they all said, Mt. 26, 65b. Lk. 22, 71.
Why should we seek now witnesses? we have heard now the blasphemy from his mouth.
39, 40 What then think ye? They all answered and said, He is worthy of death. Then Mk. 14, 64b. Mt. 26, 66.
some of them drew near, and spat in his face, and struck him, and scoffed at him. Mk. 14, 65a. Lk. 22, 63b.
41 And the soldiers struck him on his cheeks,[9] and said, Prophesy unto us, *thou* Mes- Mk. 14, 65c. Mt. 26, 68.
42 siah: who is he that struck thee? And many other things spake they falsely,[10] and Lk. 22, 65.
said against him.

43 And all of their assembly arose,[11] and took Jesus, and brought him bound[12] to Jo. 18, 28. Mk. 15, 1b.
44 the prætorium,[13] and delivered him up to Pilate the judge; but they entered not into Jo. 18, 28c.
the prætorium, that they might not be defiled when they should eat the passover.
45 And Jesus stood before the judge. And Pilate went forth unto them without, and Mt. 27, 11a. Jo. 18, 29.
46 said unto them, What accusation[14] have ye against this man? They answered and Jo. 18, 30.
said unto him, If he had not been doing evils, neither should we have delivered
47 him up unto thee. We found this *man* leading our people astray, and restraining Lk. 23, 2b.
from giving tribute to Cæsar, and saying of himself that he is the King, the Messiah.
48 Pilate said unto them, Then take ye him, and judge him according to your law. Jo. 18, 31.

1 Borg. MS. has *the evil.*
2 This is an alternative meaning of the Syriac word *affirmed*, used in the Peshitta.
3 *cf.* Sinaitic (Curetonian wanting). Vat. MS., which Ciasca follows, adds *him* or *it*.
4 Borg. MS., by adding diacritical points, gets *asserted*.
5 Syriac order, but not in agreement with the versions.
6 Vat. MS. has *anything, when these*.
7 The word usually means *synagogue* in this work.
8 The foreign word used in the Peshitta is preserved. The Sinaitic uses a Syriac word meaning *garment*.
9 See § 9, 7, note.
10 See § 7, 17, note.
11 *cf.* Lk. 23, 1a.
12 *cf.* Mt. 27, 2; Mk. 15, 1.
13 Arabic, *dîwân*.
14 Lit. *plea*.

§ 49 Arabic, The Jews said unto him, We have no authority to put a man to death:
49 p. 188 that the word might be fulfilled, which Jesus spake, when he made known Jo. 18, 32.
by what manner of death he was to die.
50 And Pilate entered into the prætorium, and called Jesus, and said unto him, Art Jo. 18, 33.
51 thou the King of the Jews? Jesus said unto him, Of thyself saidst thou this, or Jo. 18, 34.
52 did others tell it thee concerning me? Pilate said unto him, Am I, forsooth,[1] a Jo. 18, 35.
Jew? The sons of thy nation[2] and the chief priests delivered thee unto me: what
53 hast thou done? Jesus said unto him, My kingdom is not of this world: if my Jo. 18, 36.
kingdom were of this world, then would my servants fight, that I should not be
54 delivered to the Jews: now my kingdom is not from hence. Pilate said unto him, Jo. 18, 37.
Then *thou art* a king? Jesus said unto him, Thou hast said that I am a king. And
for this was I born, and for this came I into the world, that I should bear witness
55 of the truth. And every one that is of the truth heareth my voice. Pilate said Jo. 18, 38*a*.
unto him, And what is the truth? And when he said that, he went out again unto
the Jews.

SECTION L.

§ 50 1 And Pilate said unto the chief priests and the multitude, I have not found Lk. 23, 4.
2 against this man anything. But they cried out and said, He hath disquieted[3] our Lk. 23, 5.
people with his teaching in all Judæa, and he began[4] from Galilee and unto this
3 place. And Pilate, when he heard the name of Galilee, asked, Is this man a Gali- Lk. 23, 6.
4 læan? And when he learned that he was under the jurisdiction of Herod, he sent Lk. 23, 7.
him to Herod: for he was in Jerusalem in those days.
5 And Herod, when he saw Jesus, rejoiced exceedingly: for he had desired to see him Lk. 23, 8.
for a long time, because he had heard regarding him many things; and he counted on[5]
6 Arabic, seeing some sign from him. And he questioned him with many words; but Lk. 23, 9.
7 p. 189 Jesus answered him not a word. And the scribes and chief priests were Lk. 23, 10.
8 standing *by*, and they accused him vehemently. And Herod scoffed at him, he and Lk. 23, 11.
his servants; and when he had scoffed at him, he clothed him in robes of scarlet,
9 and sent him to Pilate. And on that day Pilate and Herod became friends, there Lk. 23, 12.
having been[6] enmity between them before that.
10, 11 And Pilate called the chief priests and the rulers of the people, and said unto Lk. 23, 13. Lk. 23, 14.
them, Ye brought unto me this man, as the perverter of your people: and I have
tried him before you, and have not found in this man any cause[7] of all that ye
12 seek[8] against him: nor yet Herod: for I sent him unto him; and he hath done Lk. 23, 15.
13 nothing for which he should deserve death. So now I will chastise him, and let Lk. 23, 16.
14, 15 him go. The multitude all cried out and said, Take him from us, take him. And Lk. 23, 18*a*. Mk. 15, 3*a*.
16 the chief priests and the elders accused him of many things. And during their Mt. 27, 12.
17 accusation he answered not a word. Then Pilate said unto him, Hearest thou not Mt. 27, 13.
18 how many *things* they witness against thee? And he answered him not, not even Mt. 27, 14.
one word: and Pilate marvelled at that.
19 And when the judge sat on his tribune, his wife sent unto him, and said unto Mt. 27, 19.
him, See that thou have nothing to do with that righteous *man:* for I have suffered
much in my dream[9] to-day because of him.
20 And at every feast the custom of the judge was to release to the people one Mt. 27, 15.
21 prisoner, him whom they would. And there was in their prison a well-known pris- Mt. 27, 16.
22, 23 oner, called Barabbas. And when they assembled, Pilate said unto them, Ye have Mt. 27, 17*a*. Jo. 18, 39.
a custom, that I should release unto you a prisoner at the passover: will ye that I
24 release unto you the King of the Jews? And they all cried out and said, Release not Jo. 18, 40.
Arabic, unto us this *man*, but release unto us Barabbas. And this Barabbas was a
25 p. 190 robber, who for sedition[10] and murder, which was in the city, was cast into the Lk. 23, 19.

1 See § 4, 24, note. 2 The Syriac word. 3 Or, *led astray* (*cf.* § 25, 17, note). 4 *cf.* Syriac versions.
5 Same word as in § 10, 16 (see note there). 6 Lit. *and there was*.
7 The Arabic word may also, like the Syriac, mean *thing*, but hardly, as that does here, *fault* or *crime*. The Vat. MS., pointing differently, reads *thing*. The same confusion occurs at § 40, 35 (*cf.* a converse case in § 25, 40).
8 So Ciasca's text, following the Borg. MS. The Vat. MS. has *plotted*, which is nearer the Syriac *accuse*.
9 See § 3, 12, note.
10 Ciasca's text, following the Vat. MS., has *disorder*. Borg. MS. has *division* (*cf. heresies*, Curetonian of § 50, 37), which by addition of a diacritical point gives *sedition; cf.* § 50, 37 (Ciasca, following Vat. MS.), and Peshitta (both places).

§ 50 26 prison. And all the people cried out and began to ask *him to do* as the custom was Mk. 15, 8.
27 that he should do with them. And Pilate answered and said unto them, Whom Mk. 15, 9a. Mt. 27, 17b.
will ye that I release unto you? Barabbas, or Jesus which is called the Messiah, the
28 King of the Jews? For Pilate knew that envy had moved them to deliver him up. Mt. 27, 18.
29 And the chief priests and the elders asked the multitudes to deliver Barabbas, and Mt. 27, 20.
30 to destroy Jesus. The judge answered and said unto them, Whom of the two will Mt. 27, 21.
31 ye that I release unto you? They said, Barabbas. Pilate said unto them, And Mt. 27, 22a.
32 Jesus which is called the Messiah, what shall I do with him? They all cried out Mk. 15, 13.
33 and said, Crucify him. And Pilate spake to them again, for he desired to release Lk. 23, 20.
34 Jesus; but they cried out and said, Crucify him, crucify him, and release unto us Lk. 23, 21.
35 Barabbas. And Pilate said unto them a third time, What evil hath this *man* done? Lk. 23, 22.
I have not found in him any cause[1] to necessitate death: I will chastise him and
36 let him go. But they increased in importunity[2] with a loud voice, and asked him Lk. 23, 23.
to crucify him. And their voice, and the voice of the chief priests, prevailed.
37 Then Pilate released unto them that one who was cast into prison for sedition and Mk. 15, 15a. Lk. 23, 25a.
murder, Barabbas, whom they asked for: and he scourged Jesus with whips.[3] Mt. 27, 26b.
38 Then the footsoldiers of the judge took Jesus, and went into the prætorium, and Mt. 27, 27.
39 Arabic, gathered unto him all of the footsoldiers. And they stripped him, and put on Mt. 27, 28.
40 p. 191 him a scarlet cloak. And they clothed him in garments of purple, and plaited Jo. 19, 2.
41 a crown of thorns, and placed it on his head, and a reed in his right hand; and while Mt. 27, 29b.
they mocked at him and laughed, they fell down on their knees before him, and bowed
42 down to[4] him, and said, Hail,[5] King of the Jews! And they spat in his face, and Mt. 27, 30.
took the reed from his hand, and struck him on his head, and smote his cheeks. Jo. 19, 3b.
43 And Pilate went forth without again, and said unto the Jews, I bring him forth to Jo. 19, 4.
44 you, that ye may know that I do not find, in examining[6] him, even one crime.[7] And Jo. 19, 5.
Jesus went forth without, wearing the crown of thorns and the purple garments.
45 Pilate said unto them, Behold, the man! And when the chief priests and the Jo. 19, 6.
soldiers[8] saw him, they cried out and said, Crucify him, crucify him. Pilate said
unto them, Take him yourselves, and crucify him: for I find not a cause[9] against
46 him. The Jews said unto him, We have a law, and according to our law he deserves Jo. 19, 7.
47 death, because he made himself the Son of God. And when Pilate heard this word, Jo. 19, 8.
48 his fear increased; and he entered again into the porch, and said to Jesus, Whence Jo. 19, 9.
49 art thou? But Jesus answered him not a word. Pilate said unto him, Speakest[10] Jo. 19, 10.
thou not unto me? knowest thou not that I have authority to release thee, and have
50 authority to crucify thee? Jesus said unto him, Thou hast not any[11] authority over Jo. 19, 11.
me, if thou wert not given *it* from above: therefore the sin of him that delivered
51 me up unto thee is greater than thy sin. And for this word Pilate wished to release Jo. 19, 12.
him: but the Jews cried out, If thou let him go, thou art not a friend of Cæsar: for
every one that maketh himself a king is against Cæsar.

SECTION LI.

§ 51 1 Arabic, And when Pilate heard this saying, he took Jesus out, and sat on the Jo. 19, 13.
p. 192 tribune in the place which was called the pavement of stones, but in the He-
2 brew called Gabbatha. And that day was the Friday of the passover: and it had reached Jo. 19, 14.
3 about the sixth hour.[12] And he said to the Jews, Behold, your King! And they cried Jo. 19, 15.
out, Take him, take him, crucify him, crucify him. Pilate said unto them, Shall I
crucify your King? The chief priests said unto him, We have no king except
4 Cæsar. And Pilate, when he saw *it*, and[13] he was gaining nothing, but the tumult Mt. 27, 24.

1 Our translator has retained the Syriac word, which in this context means *fault* (see § 50, 11, note).
2 The word used in Vat MS. means a repeated *charge* or *attack*. That in Borg. MS. is probably used in the post-classical sense of *importuning him*. Either word might be written by a copyist for the other. The same double reading probably occurs again at § 53, 55.
3 *cf.* Syriac versions.
4 This may be a mere clerical error (very natural in Arabic) for *scoffed at*, the reading of the Syriac versions. This being so, it is worthy of remark that the reading is apparently common to the two MSS. The Syriac words are, however, also somewhat similar. The *Jerusalem Lectionary* has a word agreeing with the text above.
5 Lit. *Peace*.
6 This reading may be a corruption of a very literal rendering of the Peshitta.
7 *cf.* § 50, 11.
8 *cf.* § 11, 11, note.
9 See § 50, 35, note.
10 Borg. MS., *Why speakest;* a reading that might be a corruption of the Peshitta.
11 Lit. *even one* (Pesh.).
12 Lit. *six hours.*
13 Or, *that.*

§ 51 was increasing, took water, and washed his hands before the multitude, and said, I
5 am innocent of the blood of this innocent *man:* ye shall know.[1] And all the people Mt. 27, 25.
6 answered and said, His blood be on us, and on our children. Then Pilate com- Jo. 19, 16*a*.
manded to grant them their request; and delivered up Jesus to be crucified,
according to their wish.
7 Then Judas the betrayer, when he saw Jesus wronged, went and returned the Mt. 27, 3.
8 thirty *pieces* of money to the chief priests and the elders, and said, I have sinned in Mt. 27, 4.
my betraying innocent blood. And they said unto him, And we, what must we *do?*
9 know thou. And he threw down the money in the temple, and departed; and *he* Mt. 27, 5.
10 went away[2] and hanged[3] himself. And the chief priests took the money, and said, Mt. 27, 6.
We have not authority to cast it into the place of the offering,[4] for it is the price
11 of blood. And they took counsel, and bought with it the plain of the potter, for Mt. 27, 7.
12 the burial of strangers. Therefore that plain was called, The field of blood, unto Mt. 27, 8.
13 Arabic, p. 193 this day. Therein[5] was fulfilled the saying in the prophet which said, I Mt. 27, 9.
took thirty *pieces* of money, the price of the precious *one, which was* fixed
14 by the children of Israel; and I paid them for the plain of the potter, as the Lord Mt. 27, 10.
commanded me.
15 And the Jews took Jesus, and went away to crucify him. And when he bare his Jo. 19, 16*b*. Mk. 15, 20*b*. Jo. 19, 17*a*.
16 cross and went out, they stripped him of those purple and scarlet garments which he Mt. 27, 31*b*.
17 had on, and put on him his *own* garments. And while they were going with him, Mt. 27, 32*a*.
they found a man, a Cyrenian, coming from the country, named Simon, the father Mk. 15, 21*b*.
of Alexander and Rufus: and they compelled this *man* to bear the cross of Jesus. Mt. 27, 32*b*.
18 And they took the cross and laid it upon him, that he might bear it, and come after Lk. 23, 26*b*.
Jesus; and Jesus went, and his cross behind him.
19 And there followed him much people, and women which were lamenting and Lk. 23, 27.
20 raving.[6] But Jesus turned unto them and said, Daughters of Jerusalem, weep not Lk. 23, 28.
21 for me: weep for yourselves, and for your children. Days are coming, when they Lk. 23, 29.
shall say, Blessed are the barren, and the wombs that bare not, and the breasts
22 that gave not suck. Then shall they begin to say to the mountains, Fall on us; and Lk. 23, 30.
23 to the hills, Cover us. For if they do so in the green tree,[7] what shall be in the dry? Lk. 23, 31.
24 And they brought with Jesus two others of the malefactors,[8] to be put to death. Lk. 23, 32.
25 And when they came unto a certain place called The skull, and called in the Lk. 23, 33*a*. Jo. 19, 17*c*.
Hebrew Golgotha, they crucified him there: they crucified with him these two Lk. 23, 33*b*.
26 malefactors, one on his right, and the other on his left. And the scripture was Mk. 15, 28.
27 Arabic, p. 194 fulfilled, which saith, He was numbered with the transgressors. And they Mk. 15, 23*a*.
gave him to drink wine and myrrh, and vinegar which had been mixed
with the myrrh; and he tasted, and would not drink; and he received it not. Mt. 27, 34*b*. Mk. 15, 23*b*.
28 And the soldiers, when they had crucified Jesus, took his garments, and cast lots Jo. 19, 23.
for them in four parts, to every party of the soldiers a part; and his tunic was
29 without sewing, from the top woven throughout. And they said one to another, Jo. 19, 24.
Let us not rend it, but cast lots for it, whose it shall be: and the scripture was
fulfilled, which saith,

They divided my garments among them,
And cast the lot for my vesture.

30, 31 This the soldiers did. And they sat and guarded him there. And Pilate wrote on Mt. 27, 36. Jo. 19, 19.
a tablet the cause of his death, and put it on the wood of the cross above his head.[9]
And there was written upon it thus: THIS IS JESUS THE NAZARENE, THE KING OF THE
32 JEWS. And this tablet[10] read many of the Jews: for the place where Jesus was Jo. 19, 20.
crucified was near the city: and it was written in Hebrew and Greek and Latin.
33 And the chief priests said unto Pilate, Write not, The King of the Jews; but, He it is Jo. 19, 21.
34 that[11] said, I am the King of the Jews. Pilate said unto them, What hath been Jo. 19, 22.
35 written hath been written.[12] And the people were standing beholding; and they Lk. 23, 35*a*. Mt. 27, 39.

1 *cf.* Peshitta. Or, *Ye know* (*cf.* Sinaitic).
2 Borg. MS. omits *and he went away*.
3 Lit. *strangled*.
4 *cf.* § 32, 15, note.
5 Or, *at that* (*time*).
6 Lit. *being burned*. The text is probably corrupt.
7 Lit. *wood* (*cf.* Syr. and Greek).
8 Or, *others, malefactors*.
9 Mt. 27, 37.
10 A different word from that in the preceding verse; in each case, the word used in the Peshitta (Cur. and Sin. lacking).
11 The Syriac words, retained in Ibn-aṭ-Ṭayyib's Commentary (f. 366*a*), seem to have been transposed. Vat. MS. omits *he*, probably meaning *but that he said*.
12 In a carelessly written Arabic MS. there is almost no difference between *hath been written* and *I have written*, as it is in Ibn-aṭ-Ṭayyib (*loc. cit.*, f. 366*a*).

§ 51 36 that passed by were reviling[1] him, and shaking[2] their heads, and saying, Thou that Mt. 27, 40a. Mk. 15, 29.
destroyest the temple, and buildest it in three days, save thyself if thou art the Son Mt. 27, 40c.
37 of God, and come down from the cross. And in like manner the chief priests and the Mt. 27, 41.
Arabic, scribes and the elders and the Pharisees derided him, and laughed one with
38, 39 p. 195 another, and said, The saviour of others cannot save himself. If he is the Mt. 27, 42a. Lk. 23, 35c.
Messiah, the chosen of God, and the King of Israel,[3] let him come down now from the Mt. 27, 42c.
40 cross, that we may see, and believe in him. He that relieth on God—let him deliver him Mt. 27, 43.
41 now, if he is pleased with him: for he said, I am the Son of God. And the soldiers Lk. 23, 36.
42 also scoffed at him, in that they came near unto him, and brought him vinegar, and Lk. 23, 37.
43 said unto him, If thou art the King of the Jews, save thyself. And likewise the Mt. 27, 44.
two robbers[4] also that were crucified with him reproached him.
44 And one of those two malefactors who were crucified with him reviled him, and Lk. 23, 39.
45 said, If thou art the Messiah, save thyself, and save us also. But his comrade Lk. 23, 40.
rebuked him, and said, Dost thou not even fear God, being thyself also in this
46 condemnation? And we with justice, and as we deserved, and according to our Lk. 23, 41.
deed,[5] have we been rewarded: but this *man* hath not done anything unlawful.
47 And he said unto Jesus, Remember me, my Lord, when thou comest in thy kingdom. Lk. 23, 42.
48 Jesus said unto him, Verily[6] I say unto thee, To-day shalt thou be with me in Paradise. Lk. 23, 43.
49 And there stood by the cross of Jesus his mother, and his mother's sister,[7] Jo. 19, 25.
50 Mary[8] that was related to Clopas, and Mary Magdalene. And Jesus saw his Jo. 19, 26.
mother, and that disciple whom he loved standing *by;* and he said to his mother,
51 Woman, behold, thy son! And he said to that disciple, Behold, thy mother! And Jo. 19, 27.
from that hour that disciple took her unto him*self*.
52 Arabic, And from the sixth hour[9] darkness was on all the land unto the ninth Mt. 27, 45a. Lk. 23, 44b.
53 p. 196 hour,[9] and the sun became dark. And at the ninth hour Jesus cried out Lk. 23, 45a. Mk. 15, 34.
with a loud voice, and said, Yāil, Yāili,[10] why hast thou forsaken me? which[11] is, My
54 God, my God, why hast thou forsaken me? And some of those that stood there, Mt. 27, 47.
when they heard, said,[12] This *man* called Elijah.

SECTION LII.

§ 52 1 And after that, Jesus knew that all things were finished; and that the scripture Jo. 19, 28.
2 might be accomplished, he said, I thirst. And there was set a vessel full of vinegar: Jo. 19, 29a.
and in that hour one of them hasted, and took a sponge, and filled it with that Mt. 27, 48.
3 vinegar, and fastened it on a reed, and brought it near[13] his mouth to give him a Mk. 15, 36b.
4 drink. And when Jesus had taken that vinegar, he said, Everything is finished. Jo. 19, 30a.
5 But the rest said, Let be, that we may[14] see whether Elijah cometh to save him. Mt. 27, 49. Lk. 23, 34.
6, 7 And Jesus said, My Father, forgive them; for they know not what they do. And Lk. 23, 46a.
Jesus cried again with a loud voice, and said, My Father, into thy hands I commend[15] my spirit. He said that, and bowed his head, and gave up his spirit. Jo. 19, 30b.
8 And immediately the face of[16] the door of the temple was rent into two parts from Mt. 27, 51.
9 top to bottom; and the earth was shaken; and the stones were split to pieces; and the Mt. 27, 52.
Arabic, tombs were opened; and the bodies of many saints which slept, arose and
10 p. 197 came forth; and after his resurrection they entered into the holy city and Mt. 27, 53.
11 appeared unto many. And the officer of the footsoldiers, and they that were with him Mt. 27, 54.
who were guarding Jesus,[17] when they saw the earthquake, and the things which came
12 to pass, feared greatly, and praised God, and said, This man *was* righteous; and, Lk. 23, 47b. Mt. 27, 54b.
13 Truly he was the Son of God. And all the multitudes that were come together to Lk. 23, 48.
the sight, when they saw what came to pass, returned and smote upon their breasts.

1 *cf.* § 7, 17, note. Borg. MS. has *jesting at.*
2 The Arabic text has *deriding* (*cf.* § 51, 37). Either *with* is accidentally omitted, or, more probably, we should correct the spelling to *shaking* (*cf.* Syriac versions). 3 Verse 37 or Mt. 4 Borg. MS. has *boys* (an easy clerical error).
5 *Our deed* might be read *we have done*, and perhaps our translator's style would justify our writing *as* for *to*.
6 Borg. MS. has *Verily, verily.* 7 A single word in Arabic. 8 Vat. MS. has *and Mary.*
9 Lit. *six hours* and *nine hours* respectively.
10 In Vat. MS. the second word is like the first. The syllable *Ya* doubtless is the Arabic interjection *O!*
11 The Borg. MS. omits from *which* to *me.* 12 Borg. MS. omits *when they*, and has *and said.*
13 *cf.* § 12, 13, note. 14 Or, *Let us.* 15 Lit. *lay down.*
16 *cf.* Syriac versions and Ibn-aṭ-Ṭayyib's Commentary. Vat. MS. omits *the face of.*
17 This sentence is a good example of word-for-word translation of the Peshitta.

§ 52 14 And the Jews, because of the Friday, said, Let these bodies not remain on their Jo. 19, 31.
crosses,[1] because it is the morning of the sabbath (for that sabbath was a great
day); and they asked of Pilate that they might break the legs of those that were
15 crucified, and take them down. And the soldiers came, and brake the legs of the Jo. 19, 32.
16 first, and that other which was crucified with him: but when they came to Jesus, Jo. 19, 33.
17 they saw that he had died before, so they brake not his legs: but one of the soldiers Jo. 19, 34.
pierced[2] him in his side with a spear, and immediately there came forth blood and
18 water. And he that hath seen hath borne witness, and his witness is true: and he Jo. 19, 35.
19 knoweth that he hath said the truth, that ye also may believe. This he did, that Jo. 19, 36.
20 the scripture might be fulfilled, which saith, A bone shall not be broken in him; and Jo. 19, 37.
the scripture also which saith, Let them look upon him whom they pierced.[2]
21 And there were in the distance all the acquaintance of Jesus standing, and the Lk. 23, 49*a*.
women that came with him from Galilee, those that followed him and ministered. Mk. 15, 41*b*.
22 One of them *was* Mary Magdalene; and Mary the mother of James the little and Mt. 27, 56*a*. Mk. 15, 40*b*.
23 Arabic, Joses, and the mother of the sons of Zebedee, and Salome, and many others Mt. 27, 56*c*. Mk. 15, 40*c*, 41*c*
p. 198 which came up with him unto Jerusalem; and they saw that. Lk. 23, 49*b*.
24 And when the evening of the Friday was come, because of the entering of the Mk. 15, 42.
25 sabbath, there came a rich man,[3] a noble[4] of Ramah,[5] a city of Judah,[6] named Lk. 23, 50.
Joseph, and he was a good man and upright; and he was a[7] disciple of Jesus, but Jo. 19, 38*b*.
26 was concealing himself for fear of the Jews. And he did not agree with the accusers Lk. 23, 51*a*.
27 in their desire and their deeds: and he was looking for the kingdom of God. And Lk. 23, 51*c*. Mk. 15, 43*b*.
this *man* went boldly, and entered in unto Pilate, and asked of him the body of
28 Jesus. And Pilate wondered how he had died already: and he called the officer of Mk. 15, 44.
29 the footsoldiers, and asked him concerning his death before the time. And when Mk. 15, 45*a*.
30 he knew, he commanded him to deliver up his body unto Joseph. And Joseph Mt. 27, 58*b*. Mk. 15, 46*a*.
bought for him a winding cloth of pure linen, and took down the body of Jesus,
31 and wound it in it; and they came and took it. And there came unto him Nicode- Jo. 19, 38*d*. Jo. 19, 39.
mus also, who of old came unto Jesus by night; and he brought with him perfume[8]
32 of myrrh and aloes, about a hundred pounds. And they took the body of Jesus, Jo. 19, 40.
and wound it in the linen and the perfume, as was the custom of the Jews to bury.
33 And there was in the place where Jesus was crucified a garden; and in that garden Jo. 19, 41.
34 a new tomb cut out in a rock,[9] wherein was never man yet laid. And they left Jo. 19, 42.
35 Jesus there because the sabbath had come in, and because the tomb was near. And Mt. 27, 60*b*.
they pushed[10] a great stone, and thrust[11] it against the door of the sepulchre, and
36 went away. And Mary Magdalene and Mary that was related to Joses came to Mk. 15, 47*a*.
37 Arabic, the sepulchre after them,[12] and sat opposite the sepulchre,[13] and saw the Lk. 23, 55*b*.
38 p. 199 body, how they took it in and laid it there. And they returned, and bought Lk. 23, 56*a*. Mk. 16, 1*b*.
ointment[14] and perfume,[15] and prepared[16] *it*, that they might come and anoint him.
39 And on the day which was the sabbath day they desisted according to the command. Lk. 23, 56*c*.
40, 41 And the chief priests and the Pharisees gathered unto Pilate, and said unto him, Mt. 27, 62. Mt. 27, 63.
Our lord, we remember that that misleader said, while he was alive, After three days
42 I rise. And now send beforehand and guard the tomb[17] until the third day,[18] lest Mt. 27, 64.
his disciples come and steal him by night, and they will say unto the people that he
43 is risen from the dead: and the last error shall be worse than the first. He said Mt. 27, 65.
unto them, And have ye not guards?[19] go, and take precautions as ye know *how*.
44 And they went, and set *guards* at the tomb, and sealed that stone, with the guards. Mt. 27, 66.
45 And in the evening of the sabbath, which is the morning of the first *day*, and in Mt. 28, 1*a*. Lk. 24, 1*b*.
46 the dawning[20] while the darkness yet remained, came Mary Magdalene and the Mt. 28, 1*b*.
other Mary and other women to see the tomb. They brought with them the Lk. 24, 1*d*.
47 perfume which they had prepared, and said among themselves, Who is it that will Mk. 16, 3.

1 The word is probably plural. 2 Lit. *ripped*. 3 Mt. 27, 57. 4 Borg. MS. omits.
5 Lk. 23, 51*b*. 6 Syriac versions. 7 Lit. *the*. 8 The preparation used in embalming.
9 Mk. 15, 46. Lit. *a stone*.
10 On the plural, which is to be found also in Ibn-aṭ-Tayyib's Commentary, see § 38, 43, note (end). The word chosen might be simply a clerical error for an original Arabic *rolled*. 11 Lit. *cast* (*cf.* Sinaitic).
12 Dual. The clause (from *came*) is found verbatim in Sin. and Cur. at Lk. 23, 55. Here, after the word *Luke* of the reference, at the end of leaf 117 of Vat. MS., is a note by a later hand: "Here a leaf is wanting." This second and last lacuna extends from § 52, 37, to § 53, 4. 13 Mt. 27, 61*b*. 14 *cf.* Sinaitic.
15 The two *Arabic* words are practically synonymous (*cf.* Lk. 23, 56, Pesh.). 16 Lk. 23, 56.
17 The MS. omits *the tomb*. 18 Lit. *three days*.
19 The word might be taken as a collective noun, singular. But *cf.* Peshitta and § 52, 51.
20 *cf.* Peshitta. The Arabic word is variously explained.

§ 52 48 remove for us the stone from the door of the tomb? for it was very great. And Mk. 16, 4b. Mt. 28, 2a.
when they said thus, there occurred a great earthquake; and an angel came down
49 from heaven, and came and removed the stone from the door. And they came Lk. 24, 2.
and found the stone removed from the sepulchre, and the angel sitting upon the Mt. 28, 2b.
50 stone. And his appearance was as the lightning, and his raiment white as the Mt. 28, 3.
51 snow: and for fear of him the guards were troubled, and became as dead *men*. Mt. 28, 4.
52 And when he went away, the women entered into the sepulchre; and they found Lk. 24, 3.
53 Arabic, not the body of Jesus. And they saw there a young man sitting on the Mk. 16, 5b.
54 p. 200 right, arrayed in a white garment; and they were amazed.[1] And the angel Mt. 28, 5.
answered and said unto the women, Fear ye not: for I know that ye seek Jesus the
55 Nazarene, who hath been crucified. He is not here; but he is risen, as he said. Come Mt. 28, 6.
and see the place where our Lord lay.

SECTION LIII.[2]

§ 53 1 And while they marvelled at that, behold, two men standing above them, their Lk. 24, 4.
2 raiment shining: and they were seized with fright, and bowed down their face to Lk. 24, 5.
3 the earth: and they said unto them, Why seek ye the living *one* with the dead? He Lk. 24, 6.
is not here; he is risen: remember what he was speaking unto you while he was in
4 Galilee, and saying, The Son of man is to be delivered up into the hands of sinners, Lk. 24, 7.
5 and to be crucified, and on the third day to rise. But go in haste, and say to his Mt. 28, 7a.
disciples and to Cephas, He is risen from among the dead; and lo, he goeth before
6 you into Galilee; and there ye shall see him, where[3] he said unto you: lo, I have Mk. 16, 7b. Mt. 28, 7c.
7 told you. And they remembered his sayings; and they departed in haste from the Lk. 24, 8. Mt. 28, 8a.
8 tomb with joy and great fear, and hastened and went; and perplexity and fear Mk. 16, 8b.
9 encompassed them; and they told no man anything, for they were afraid. And Jo. 20, 2.
Mary hastened, and came to Simon Cephas, and to that other disciple whom Jesus
loved, and said unto them, They have taken our Lord from the sepulchre, and I
10 know not where they have laid him. And Simon went out, and that other disciple, Jo. 20, 3.
11 and came to the sepulchre. And they hastened both together: and that disciple Jo. 20, 4.
12 outran[4] Simon, and came first to the sepulchre; and he looked down, and saw the Jo. 20, 5.
13 linen laid; but he went not in. And Simon came after him, and entered into the Jo. 20, 6.
14 Arabic, sepulchre, and saw the linen laid; and the scarf with which his head was Jo. 20, 7.
p. 201 bound was not with the linen, but wrapped and laid aside in a certain place.
15 Then entered that disciple which came first to the sepulchre, and saw, and believed. Jo. 20, 8.
16 And they knew not yet from the scriptures that the Messiah was to rise from among Jo. 20, 9.
17 the dead. And those two disciples went to their place. Jo. 20, 10.
18 But Mary remained[5] at the tomb weeping: and while she wept, she looked Jo. 20, 11.
19 down into the tomb; and she saw two angels sitting in white raiment, one of them Jo. 20, 12.
toward his pillow, and the other toward his feet, where the body of Jesus had been
20 laid. And they said unto her, Woman, why weepest thou? She said unto them, Jo. 20, 13.
21 They have taken my Lord, and I know not where they have left him. She said Jo. 20, 14.
that, and turned behind her, and saw Jesus standing, and knew not that it was
22 Jesus. Jesus said unto her, Woman, why weepest thou? whom seekest thou? And Jo. 20, 15.
she supposed[6] him *to be* the gardener, and said, My lord, if thou hast taken him,
23 tell me where thou hast laid him, that I may go and take him Jesus said unto Jo. 20, 16.
her, Mary. She turned, and said unto him in Hebrew, Rabboni; which is, being
24 interpreted, Teacher. Jesus said unto her, Touch me not;[7] for I have not ascended Jo. 20, 17.
yet unto my Father: go to my brethren, and say unto them, I ascend unto my
Father and your Father, and my God and your God.
25 And on the First-day on which he rose, he appeared first unto Mary Magdalene, Mk. 16, 9.
from whom he had cast out seven demons.

1 The diacritical points of the first letter must be corrected.
2 The Borg. MS. indicates the beginning of the sections, not by titles, but by "*vittas amplinsculas auroque oblinitas*" (Ciasca, Introduction). Ciasca indicates in the *Corrigenda*, opposite p. 210 of the Arabic text, where this section should begin.
3 Possibly the translator's style would warrant the translation *as*.
4 Lit. *hastened and preceded*.
5 Probably an Arabic copyist's emendation (addition of *alif*) for *stood*.
6 *cf.* § 10, 16.
7 *cf.* § 12, 13.

§ 53 26 And some of those guards[1] came to the city, and informed the chief priests of Mt. 28, 11b.
27 Arabic, all that had happened. And they assembled with the elders, and took Mt. 28, 12.
28 p. 202 counsel; and they gave money, not a little, to the guards, and said unto Mt. 28, 13.
them, Say ye, His disciples came and stole him by night, while we were sleeping.
29 And if the judge hear that, we will make a plea with him, and free you of blame. Mt. 28, 14.
30 And they, when they took the money, did according to what they taught them. And Mt. 28, 15.
this word spread among the Jews unto this day.
31 And then came Mary Magdalene, and announced to the disciples that she had Jo. 20, 18.
seen our Lord, and that he had said that unto her.
32 And while the first[2] women[3] were going in the way to inform[4] his disciples,[3] Mt. 28, 8b.
33 Jesus met them, and said unto them, Peace unto you. And they came and took Mt. 28, 9.
34 hold of his feet, and worshipped him. Then said Jesus unto them, Fear not: but Mt. 28, 10.
go and say to my brethren that they depart into Galilee, and there they shall see
35 me. And those women returned, and told all that to the eleven, and to the rest of Lk. 24, 9.
the disciples; and to those that had been with him, for they were saddened and Mk. 16, 10b.
36 weeping. And those were Mary Magdalene, and Joanna, and Mary the mother of Lk. 24, 10.
James, and the rest who were with them: and they were those that told the apostles.
37 And they, when they heard them say that he was alive and had appeared unto them, Mk. 16, 11.
38 did not believe them: and these sayings were before their eyes as the sayings of madness. Lk. 24, 11a.
39 Arabic, And after that, he appeared to two of them, on that day, and while they Mk. 16, 12a. Lk. 24, 13b.
p. 203 were going to the village which was named Emmaus, and whose distance
40 from Jerusalem was sixty furlongs.[5] And they were talking the one of them with the Lk. 24, 14.
41 other of all the things which had happened. And during the time of their talking and Lk. 24, 15.
42 inquiring with one another, Jesus came and reached them, and walked with them. But Lk. 24, 16.
43 their eyes were veiled that they should not know him. And he said unto them, What Lk. 24, 17.
are these sayings which ye address the one of you to the other, as ye walk and are
44 sad? One of them, whose name was Cleopas, answered and said unto him, Art Lk. 24, 18.
thou perchance alone a stranger to Jerusalem, since thou knowest not what was in
45 it in these days? He said unto them, What was? They said unto him, Concerning Lk. 24, 19.
Jesus, he who was from Nazareth, a man who was a prophet, and powerful in
46 speech and deeds before God and before all the people: and the chief priests and Lk. 24, 20.
47 the elders delivered him up to the sentence of[6] death, and crucified him. But we Lk. 24, 21.
supposed that he was the one who was to deliver Israel. And since all[7] these
48 things happened there have passed three days. But *certain* women of us also Lk. 24, 22.
49 informed us that they had come to the sepulchre; and when they found not his Lk. 24, 23.
body, they came and told us that they had seen there the angels, and they[8] said
50 concerning him that he was alive. And some of us also went to the sepulchre, and Lk. 24, 24.
51 found the matter as the women had said: only they saw him not. Then said Jesus Lk. 24, 25.
52 unto them, Ye lacking in discernment, and heavy in heart to believe! Was it not Lk. 24, 26.
in all the sayings of the prophets that the Messiah was to suffer these things, and to
53 Arabic, enter into his glory? And he began from Moses and from all the prophets, Lk. 24, 27.
54 p. 204 and interpreted to them concerning himself from all the scriptures. And Lk. 24, 28.
they drew near unto the village, whither they were going: and he was leading them to
55 imagine that he was as if going to a distant region. And they pressed[9] him, and said Lk. 24, 29.
unto him, Abide with us: for the day hath declined now to the darkness. And he went
56 in to abide with them. And when he sat with them, he took bread, and blessed, Lk. 24, 30.
57 and brake, and gave to them. And straightway their eyes were opened, and they Lk. 24, 31.
58 knew him; and he was taken away from them.[10] And they said the one to the Lk. 24, 32.
other, Was not our heart heavy within us, while he was speaking to us in the way,
and interpreting to us the scriptures?
59 And they rose in that hour, and returned to Jerusalem, and found the eleven Lk. 24, 33.
60 gathered, and those that were with them, saying, Truly our Lord is risen, and hath Lk. 24, 34.
61 appeared to Simon. And they related what happened in the way, and how they Lk. 24, 35.
knew him when he brake the bread. Neither believed they that also. Mk. 16, 13b.

1 The Vat. MS. has a form that is distinctively plural. The Borg. MS. uses, with a plural adjective, the form found in § 52, 43. In the next verse the relation of the MSS. is reversed.
2 The word *first* is less correctly spelled in Borg. MS.
3 The Vat. MS. omits *women* and *to inform his disciples*.
4 *Inform* is dual and masc. in the MS., while the other verbs and pronouns are plural and feminine.
5 Lit. *mils*.
6 Borg. MS., *to judgement and*.
7 Borg. MS. omits *all*.
8 Masc. plural.
9 *cf.* § 50, 36, note.
10 Vat. MS. omits this clause.

SECTION LIV.

§ 54 1 And while they talked together,[1] the evening of that day arrived which was the Lk. 24, 36a. Jo. 20, 19.
First-day; and the doors were shut where the disciples were, because of the fear of the
2 Jews; and Jesus came and stood among them, and said unto them, Peace *be* with you: Lk. 24, 36c.
I am he; fear not. But they were agitated, and became afraid, and supposed that they Lk. 24, 37.
3 saw a spirit. Jesus said unto them, Why are ye agitated? and why do thoughts rise Lk. 24, 38.
4 Arabic, p. 205 in[2] your hearts? See my hands and my feet, that I am he: feel me, and Lk. 24, 39.
know that a spirit hath not flesh and bones, as ye see me having that.
5 And when he had said this, he shewed them his hands and his feet and his side.[3] Lk. 24, 40.
6 And they were until this time unbelieving, from their joy and their wonder. He Lk. 24, 41.
7 said unto them, Have ye anything here to eat? And they gave him a portion of Lk. 24, 42.
broiled fish and of honey.[4] And he took *it*, and ate before them. Lk. 24, 43.
8 And he said unto them, These are the sayings which I spake unto you, while I Lk. 24, 44.
was with you, that[5] everything must be fulfilled, which is written in the law of
9 Moses, and the prophets, and the psalms, concerning me. Then opened he their Lk. 24, 45.
10 heart, that they might understand the scriptures; and he said unto them, Thus it is Lk. 24, 46.
written, and thus it is necessary[6] that the Messiah suffer, and rise from among the
11 dead on the third day; and *that* repentance unto the forgiveness of sins be preached Lk. 24, 47.
12 in his name among all the peoples; and the beginning shall be from Jerusalem. And Lk. 24, 48.
13 ye shall be witnesses of that. And I send unto you the promise of my Father. And Lk. 24, 49a. Jo. 20, 20b.
14 when the disciples heard that, they were glad. And Jesus said unto them again, Jo. 20, 21.
15 Peace *be* with you: as my Father hath sent me, I also send you. And when he had Jo. 20, 22.
said this, he breathed on them, and said unto them, Receive ye the Holy Spirit:
16 and if ye forgive sins to *any* man, they shall be forgiven him; and if ye retain them Jo. 20, 23.
against *any* man, they shall be retained.
17 But Thomas, one of the twelve, called Thama, was not there with the disciples Jo 20, 24.
18 when Jesus came. The disciples therefore said unto him, We have seen our Lord. Jo. 20, 25.
But he said unto them, If I do not see in his hands the places of the nails, and put
on them my fingers, and pass my hand over his side, I will not believe.
19 And after eight days, on the next First-day, the disciples were assembled again Jo. 20, 26.
within, and Thomas with them. And Jesus came, the doors being shut, and stood
20 Arabic, p. 206 in the midst, and said unto them, Peace *be* with you. And he said to Jo. 20, 27.
Thomas, Bring hither thy finger, and behold my hands; and bring *hither*
21 thy hand, and spread it on my side: and be not unbelieving, but believing. Thomas Jo. 20, 28.
22 answered and said unto him, My Lord and my God. Jesus said unto him, Now since Jo. 20, 29.
thou hast seen me, thou hast believed: blessed are they that have not seen me, and
have believed.
23 And many other signs did Jesus before his disciples, and they are they which Jo. 20, 30.
24 are not written in this book: but these that[7] are written also *are* that ye may believe Jo. 20, 31.
in Jesus the Messiah, the Son of God; and *that* when ye have believed, ye may
have in his name eternal life.
25 And after that, Jesus shewed himself again to his disciples at the sea of Tiberias; Jo. 21, 1.
26 and he shewed *himself* unto them thus. And there were together Simon Cephas, Jo. 21, 2.
and Thomas which was called Twin,[8] and Nathanael who was of Cana of Galilee,
27 and the sons of Zebedee, and two other of the disciples. Simon Cephas said unto Jo. 21, 3.
them, I go to catch fish. They said unto him, And we also come with thee. And
they went forth, and went up into the boat; and in that night they caught nothing.
28 And when the morning arrived, Jesus stood on the shore of the sea: but the disciples Jo. 21, 4.
29 knew not that it was Jesus. And Jesus said unto them, Children, have ye anything Jo. 21, 5.
30 to eat? They said unto him, No. He said unto them, Cast your net from the Jo. 21, 6.
right side of the boat, and ye shall find.[9] And they threw, and they were not able
31 to draw the net for the abundance of the fish that were come[10] into it. And that Jo. 21, 7.

1 The Arabic word after *together* looks as if it might be due to a misreading of the Syriac, but it is probably a usage cited by Dozy, *Supplément*, etc., i., 247.
2 Lit. *on* (*cf.* Pesh.).
3 Borg. MS. has *sides*.
4 Borg. MS. omits *and of honey*.
5 Vat. MS., *for*.
6 Borg. MS. omits *it is necessary*.
7 *cf.* Peshitta.
8 Apparently the Vat. MS. means to translate the word. The Borg. MS. retains *Tāmī*, as both MSS. did in § 37, 61.
9 So Peshitta. Vat. MS. has a form that might possibly be a corruption of *take*.
10 Or, *were taken*.

§ 54 disciple whom Jesus loved said to Cephas, This is our Lord. And Simon, when he
heard that it was our Lord, took his tunic, and girded it on his waist (for he was
32 naked), and cast himself into the sea to come to Jesus. But some others of the Jo. 21, 8.
disciples came in the boat[1] (and they were not far from the land, but about two
33 Arabic, hundred cubits), and drew that net of fish. And when they went up on the Jo. 21, 9.
34 p. 207 land, they saw live coals laid, and fish laid thereon, and bread. And Jesus Jo. 21, 10.
35 said unto them, Bring of this fish which ye have now caught. Simon Cephas therefore Jo. 21, 11.
went up, and dragged the net to the land, full of great fish, a hundred and fifty-three
36 fishes: and with all this weight that net was not rent. And Jesus said unto them, Jo. 21, 12.
Come and sit down. And no man of the disciples dared to ask him who he was,
for they knew that it was our Lord. But he did not appear to them in his *own*
37, 38 form. And Jesus came, and took bread and fish, and gave unto them. This is Jo. 21, 13. Jo. 21, 14.
the third time that Jesus appeared to his disciples, when he had risen from among
the dead.

39 And when they had breakfasted, Jesus said to Simon Cephas, Simon, son of Jo. 21, 15.
Jonah, lovest thou me more than these? He said unto him, Yea, my Lord; thou
40 knowest that I love thee. Jesus said unto him, Feed for me my lambs. He said Jo. 21, 16.
unto him again a second time, Simon, son of Jonah, lovest thou me? He said unto
him, Yea, my Lord; thou knowest that I love thee. He said unto him, Feed for
41 me my sheep.[2] He said unto him again the third time, Simon, son of Jonah, lovest Jo. 21, 17.
thou me? And it grieved Cephas that he said unto him three times, Lovest thou
me? He said unto him, My Lord, thou knowest everything; thou knowest that I
42 love thee. Jesus said unto him, Feed for me my sheep.[3] Verily, verily, I say unto Jo. 21, 18.
thee, When thou wast a child, thou didst gird thy waist for thyself, and go whither
Arabic, thou wouldest: but when thou shalt be old, thou shalt stretch out thy hands,
p. 208 and another shall gird thy waist, and take thee whither thou wouldest not.
43 He said that to him to explain by what death he was to glorify God. And when he Jo. 21, 19.
44 had said that, he said unto him, Come after me. And Simon Cephas turned, and saw Jo. 21, 20.
that disciple whom Jesus loved following him; he which at the supper leaned[4] on
45 Jesus' breast, and said, My Lord, who is it that betrayeth thee? When therefore Jo. 21, 21.
Cephas saw him, he said to Jesus, My Lord, and this *man*, what shall be in his
46 case?[5] Jesus said unto him, If I will that this *man* remain until I come, what is Jo. 21, 22.
47 that to thee? follow thou me. And this word spread among the brethren, that that Jo. 21, 23.
disciple should not die: but Jesus said not that he should not die; but, If I will that
this *man* remain until I come, what is that to thee?

48 This is the disciple which bare witness of that, and wrote it: and we know that Jo. 21, 24.
his witness is true.

SECTION LV.

§ 55 1 But the eleven disciples went into Galilee, to the mountain[6] where Jesus had Mt. 28, 16.
2 appointed them. And when they saw him, they worshipped him: but there were of Mt. 28, 17.
3 them who doubted. And while they sat there he appeared to them again, and Mk. 16, 14.
upbraided *them* for their lack of faith and the hardness of their hearts, those that
saw him when he was risen, and believed not.[7]

4 Arabic, Then said Jesus unto them, I have been given all authority in heaven Mt. 28, 18*b*.
5 p. 209 and earth; and as my Father hath sent me, so I also send you. Go now into Jo. 20, 21*b*. Mk. 16, 15*b*.
6 all the world, and preach my gospel in all the creation; and teach[8] all the peoples, and Mt. 28, 19*b*.
7 baptize them in the name of the Father and the Son and the Holy Spirit; and teach Mt. 28, 20.
them to keep all whatsoever I commanded you: and lo, I am with you all the days, unto
8 the end of the world. For whosoever believeth and is baptized shall be saved; but Mk. 16, 16.
9 whosoever believeth not shall be rejected. And the signs[9] which shall attend those Mk. 16, 17.
that believe in me are these: that they shall cast out devils in my name; and they
10 shall speak with new tongues; and they shall take *up* serpents, and if they drink Mk. 16, 18.

1 Vat. MS. adds *unto Jesus*. 2 Lit. *rams*. 3 Lit. *ewes*. For the three words *cf.* Peshitta and Sinaitic.
4 *cf.* § 45, 3, note. 5 Lit. *of him*. 6 Vat. MS. omits *to the mountain*.
7 This seems to be the meaning of the text of the MSS. Ciasca conjecturally emends it by printing in his Arabic text *because they* after *hearts*; but this is of no use unless one also ignores the *and* before *believed*.
8 Or, *make disciples of*. 9 Not the usual word, although that is used in the Peshitta.

§ 55 deadly poison,[1] it shall not injure them; and they shall lay their hands on the dis-
11 eased, and they shall be healed. But ye, abide in the city of Jerusalem, until ye be Lk. 24, 49*b*.
clothed with power from on high.
12 And our Lord Jesus, after speaking to them, took them out to Bethany: and he Mk. 16, 19*a*. Lk. 24, 50.
13 lifted up his hands, and blessed them. And while he blessed them, he was sepa- Lk. 24, 51.
rated from them, and ascended into heaven, and sat down at the right hand of God. Mk. 16, 19*c*.
14, 15 And they worshipped him, and returned to Jerusalem with great joy: and at all Lk. 24, 52. Lk. 24, 53.
times they were in the temple, praising and blessing God. Amen.
16 And from thence they went forth, and preached in every place; and our Lord Mk. 16, 20.
helped them, and confirmed their sayings by the signs which they did.[2]
17 And here are also many other things which Jesus did, which if they were written Jo. 21, 25.
every one of them, not even the world, according to my opinion, would contain the
books which should be written.[3]

1 The Arabic translator renders it *the poison of death*. 2 *cf.* Peshitta.

3 In the Borg. MS. the text ends on folio 353*a*. On folios 354*a*–355*a* are found the genealogies, with the title, *Book of the Generation of Jesus*, that of Luke following that of Matthew without any break. Ciasca has told us nothing of the nature of the text. The Subscription follows on folio 355*b*.

SUBSCRIPTIONS

1. IN BORGIAN MS

Here endeth the Gospel which Tatianus compiled and named *Diatessaron*, i.e., The Fourfold, a compilation from the four Gospels of the holy Apostles, the excellent Evangelists (peace be upon them). It was translated by the excellent and learned priest, Abu'l Fărăj 'Abdulla ibn-aṭ-Ṭayyib [1] (may God grant him favour), from Syriac into Arabic, from an exemplar written by 'Isa [2] ibn-'Ali al-Motaṭabbib,[3] pupil of Ḥonain ibn-Isḥāḳ (God have mercy on them both). Amen.

2. IN VATICAN MS.[4]

Here endeth, by the help of God, the holy Gospel that Titianus compiled from the four Gospels, which is known as *Diatessaron*. And praise be to God, as he is entitled to it and lord of it! And to him be the glory for ever.

1 See note 1 to Introductory Note in Borg. MS. (above, p. 42).
2 MS., by misplacing the diacritical signs, has *Ghobasi*.
3 The MS. has *Moṭṭayyib;* but Ciasca, in an additional note inserted after the volume was printed, gives the correct form.
4 The Arabic text of this Subscription is given by Ciasca in his essay, *De Tatiani Diatessaron arabica Versione*, in I. B. Pitra's *Analecta Sacra*, tom. iv., p. 466.

INDEX

SHOWING DIATESSARON SELECTIONS FROM THE GOSPELS IN BIBLICAL ORDER IN THE LEFT-HAND COLUMN, AND OPPOSITE EACH ITS PLACE IN THE SECTIONS OF THE DIATESSARON.

SUGGESTED EMENDATIONS.

We collect here a number of references to places where emendations of the Arabic text of varying degrees of importance and plausibility have been suggested in the notes:

§8, 10, 13; §10, 14; §13, 15, 42; §14, 43; §15, 25, 30, 35; §16, 19; §20, 25 f.; §22, 43; §24, 26, 32; §25, 34; §26, 21; §31, 11, 22; §34, 32, 37, 41; §35, 57; §36, 9, 25; §38, 38 (42); §39, 2, 41; §40, 36, 45, 54; §41, 11, 16, 49; §43, 2; §44, 8, 34; §45, 10 f., 23, (29); §46, 12; §48, 23, 37; §51, 35; §52, 53; §53, 18.

[On the last part of note 3, p. 42, see now Zahn's review of Harris's *Fragments*, in *Theologisches Literaturblatt*, Leipzig, 3 Jan. 1896, col. 3.]

THE APOCALYPSE OF PETER

VISIO PAULI

APOCALYPSE OF MARIA VIRGO

APOCALYPSE SEDRACH

BY

ANDREW RUTHERFURD, B.D.

THE REVELATION OF PETER

INTRODUCTION.

THE fragment here translated was discovered in 1886 by the French Archæological Mission in an ancient burying-place at Akhmîm in Upper Egypt. It was published at Paris in 1892 (BOURIANT, *Mémoires publiés par les membres de la Mission Archéologique Française au Caire,* T. ix., fasc. 1, 1892). The MS. is now in the Gizeh Museum and has been held to be of a date between the eighth and twelfth centuries.

Until the discovery of the fragment, the following was all that was known about the Revelation of Peter.

1. The so-called *Muratorian Fragment,* a list of sacred writings, first published by Muratori in 1740, and found by him in a seventh or eighth century MS. belonging to the Ambrosian Library in Milan, but which had previously belonged to the Columban Monastery of Bobbio, is assigned on internal evidence to the third quarter of the second century. (*Vide* WESTCOTT, *Canon of the N. T.*, p. 514.) At line 69 it says: "the Apocalypses also of John and Peter only do we receive, which (latter) some among us would not have read in church."

2. CLEMENT of Alexandria (fl. c. 200 A.D.) in his *Hypotoposes,* according to the testimony of EUSEBIUS, *H. E.*, vi., 14, gave "abridged accounts of all the canonical Scriptures, not even omitting those that are disputed, I mean the book of Jude and the other general epistles. Also the Epistle of Barnabas and that called the Revelation of Peter." Also in his *Eclogæ Propheticæ,* chapters 41, 48 and 49, he gives three, or as some think, four quotations from the Revelation of Peter, mentioning it twice by name.

3. The *Catalogus Claromontanus,* an Eastern list of Holy Scriptures, belonging to the third century, gives at the end the Revelation of Peter (v. WESTCOTT, *Canon,* p. 555). This catalogue gives the length of the various books it enumerates measured in stichoi. Our book is said to have two hundred and seventy, which makes it rather longer than the Epistle to the Colossians which has two hundred and fifty-one.

4. METHODIUS, bishop of Olympus in Lycia in the beginning of the fourth century, in his *Symposium,* ii., 6, says, "wherefore we have also learned from divinely inspired Scriptures that untimely births even if they are the offspring of adultery are delivered to care-taking angels." Though Peter is not here mentioned, the purport of the passage is the same as that of one of the quotations given by Clement of Alexandria.

5. EUSEBIUS († c. 339 A.D.), in his *Ecclesiastical History,* iii., 25, expressly mentions the *Revelation of Peter* along with the *Acts of Paul* and the *Pastor* as spurious books, while at iii., 3, he says: "as to that which is called the *Preaching* and that called the *Apocalypse of Peter,* we know nothing of their being handed down as Catholic writings. Since neither among the ancients nor among the ecclesiastical writers of our own day, has there been anyone that has appealed to testimony taken from them."

6. MACARIUS MAGNES (beginning of fifth century) in his *Apocritica,* iv., 6, quotes as from a heathen opponent of Christianity the following: "Let us by way of superfluity cite also that saying in the Apocalypse of Peter. It thus introduces the heaven as being about to undergo judgment along with the earth. 'The earth,' it says, 'shall present all men before God at the day of judgment, being itself also to be judged along with the heaven also which encompasses it.'" And at iv., 16, he examines this passage again, naming the Revelation of Peter, and supporting the doctrine of the passage by the authority of prophecy (Isaiah xxxiv., 4) and the Gospel (Matt. xxiv., 35).

7. SOZOMEN (middle of fifth century), *H. E.*, vii., 19, says: "For instance, the so-called Apocalypse of Peter which was esteemed as entirely spurious by the ancients, we have discovered to be read in certain churches of Palestine up to the present day, once a year, on the day of preparation, during which the people most religiously fast in commemoration of the Saviour's Passion" (*i.e.*, on Good Friday). It is to be noted that Sozomen himself belonged to Palestine.

8. In the list of *the Sixty Books* which is assigned to the fifth or sixth century the Revelation of Peter is mentioned among the Apocrypha (*v.* WESTCOTT, *Canon*, p. 551).

9. The so-called *Stichometry of Nicephorus*, a list of scriptures with notes of their extent, ascribed to NICEPHORUS, Patriarch of Constantinople, 806–814 A.D., includes the Revelation of Peter among the *antilegomena* or disputed writings of the New Testament, and gives it three hundred stichoi or thirty more than the above-mentioned Catalogus Claromontanus.

10. The Armenian annalist Mkhitan (thirteenth century) in a list of the New Testament antilegomena mentions the Revelation of Peter, after the *Gospel of Thomas* and before the *Periodoi Pauli*, and remarks that he has himself copied these books. (Cf. Harnack, *Geschichte der altchristlichen Literatur.*)

Up till lately these facts represented all that was positively known of the Revelation of Peter. From them we gather that it must have been written before the middle of the second century (so as to be known at Rome and included in the Muratorian Canon), that it had a wide circulation, that it was for some time very popular, so that it would appear to have run a considerable chance of achieving a place in the canon, but that it was ultimately rejected and in the long run dropped out of knowledge altogether.

But even previously to the discovery at Akhmîm, the general character of the book had been inferred from the scanty fragments preserved in ancient writers and from the common elements contained in other and later apocalyptic writings which seemed to require some such book as the Revelation of Peter as their ultimate source. Such writings are the (Christian) Apocalypse of Esdras, the Vision of Paul, the Passion of S. Perpetua and the visions contained in the History of Barlaam and Josaphat. (Cf. Robinson, *Texts and Studies*, i., 2, p. 37–43, and Robinson and James, *The Gospel according to Peter and the Revelation of Peter*, 1892.)

The Revelation of Peter affords the earliest embodiment in Christian literature of those pictorial presentations of heaven and hell which have exercised so widespread and enduring an influence. It has, in its imagery, little or no kinship with the Book of Daniel, the Book of Enoch, or the Revelation of S. John. Its only parallels in canonical scripture, with the notable exception of the Second Epistle of Peter, are to be found in Isaiah lxvi., 24, Mark ix., 44, 48, and the parable of Dives and Lazarus in Luke xvi., 19. It is indeed Judaic in the severity of its morality and even in its phraseology (*cf.* the frequent use of the word *righteous*, and the idea that God and not Christ will come to judge sinners). But the true parallels for, if not the sources of, its imagery of the rewards and punishments which await men after death are to be found in Greek beliefs which have left their traces in such passages as the Vision of Er at the end of Plato's *Republic*.

The heaven of the Petrine Apocalypse is akin to the Elysian Fields and the Islands of the Blest. In it the saints are crowned as with flowers and beautiful of countenance, singing songs of praise in the fragrant air, in a land all lighted up with the light of the sun.[1] We are reminded of "the Elysian Fields and the world's end where is Rhadamanthus of the fair hair, where life is easiest for men. No snow is there, nor yet great storm, nor any rain; but alway Ocean sendeth forth the breeze of the shrill West to blow cool on men" (*Odyssey*, iv., 563), and of the garden of the gods on Olympus, which "is not shaken by winds, or ever wet with rain, nor doth the snow come nigh thereto, but most clear air is spread about it cloudless, and the white light floats over it" (*Odyssey*, vi., 43, Butcher and Lang's transl.). Perhaps the most striking parallel of all is afforded by the fragment of a dirge of Pindar: "For them shineth below the strength of the sun, while in our world it is night, and the space of crimson-flowered meadow before their city is full of the shade of frankincense trees, and of fruits of gold. And some in horses, and in bodily

[1] *Cf.*

". . . the island valley of Avilion;
Where falls not rain or hail or any snow,
Nor ever wind blows loudly; but it lies
Deep-meadowed, happy, fair with orchard lawns
And bowery hollows crowned with summer seas."

TENNYSON, *Passing of Arthur.*

feats, and some in dice, and some in harp-playing have delight; and among them thriveth all fair-flowering bliss; and fragrance streameth ever through the lovely land, as they mingle incense of every kind upon the altars of the gods" (Pindar, E. Myer's transl., p. 176). Beside this heaven the New Jerusalem of the canonical Apocalypse is austere. But it is the spiritual city. "For the city had no need of the sun, neither of the moon to shine on it, for the Lord God Almighty and the Lamb were in the midst of it and the Lamb was the light thereof."

So likewise in the case of the torments of the wicked as presented in the Revelation of Peter. We are not here in the Jewish Sheol, or among the fires of the valley of Hinnom, so much as among the tortures of Tartarus and the boiling mud of the Acherusian Lake (*cf.* Plato, *Phædo*, p. 113; Aristophanes, *Frogs*, line 145), or where "wild men of fiery aspect . . . seized and carried off several of them, and Ardiæus and others, they bound head and foot and hand, and threw them down and flayed them with scourges, and dragged them along the road at the side, carding them on thorns like wool, and declaring to the passers-by what were their crimes, and that they were being taken away to be cast into hell" (*Republic*, x., p. 616, Jowett's transl.). It is not surprising that in later visions of the same kind the very names of the Greek under-world are ascribed to localities of hell. It is across the river Oceanus. It is called Tartarus. In it is the Acherusian Lake. Notice in this connection that the souls of innocent victims are present along with their murderers to accuse them.

The Revelation of Peter shows remarkable kinship in ideas with the Second Epistle of Peter. The parallels will be noted in the margin of the translation. It also presents notable parallels to the Sibylline Oracles (*cf. Orac. Sib.*, ii., 255 sqq.), while its influence has been conjectured, almost with certainty, in the Acts of Perpetua and the visions narrated in the Acts of Thomas and the History of Barlaam and Josaphat. It certainly was one of the sources from which the writer of the Vision of Paul drew. And directly or indirectly it may be regarded as the parent of all the mediæval visions of the other world.

The fragment begins in the middle of an eschatological discourse of Jesus, probably represented as delivered after the resurrection, for verse 5 implies that the disciples had begun to preach the Gospel. It ends abruptly in the course of a catalogue of sinners in hell and their punishments. The fragments preserved in the writings of Clement of Alexandria and Methodius probably belonged to the lost end of the book; that preserved by Macarius Magnes may have belonged to the eschatological discourse at the beginning. Taking the length of the whole at from two hundred and seventy to three hundred stichoi, the Akhmîm fragment contains about the half.

The present translation is made from Harnack's edition of the text, 2d ed., Leipzig, 1893.

There is another and later Apocalypse of Peter in Arabic, of which MSS. exist in Rome and Oxford. It is called the *Apocalypse of Peter, or the narrative of things revealed to him by Jesus Christ which had taken place from the beginning of the world and which shall take place till the end of the world or the second coming of Christ*. The book is said to have been written by Clement, to whom Peter had communicated the secrets revealed to him. The writer himself calls the book *Librum Perfectionis* or *Librum Completum*. Judging from the analysis of its contents quoted by Tischendorf (*Apocalypses Apocr.*) it has no connection with the present work.

THE APOCALYPSE OF PETER

1. . . . many of them will be false prophets,[1] and will teach divers ways and doctrines of perdition: but these will become sons of perdition.[2] 3. And then God will come unto my faithful ones who hunger and thirst and are afflicted and purify their souls in this life; and he will judge the sons of lawlessness.[3]

4. And furthermore the Lord said: Let us go into the mountain:[4] Let us pray. 5. And going with him, we, the twelve disciples, begged that he would show us one of our brethren, the righteous who are gone forth out of the world, in order that we might see of what manner of form they are, and having taken courage, might also encourage[5] the men who hear us.

6. And as we prayed, suddenly there appeared two men standing before the Lord towards the East, on whom we were not able to look;[6] 7, for there came forth from their countenance a ray as of the sun, and their raiment was shining, such as eye of man[7] never saw; for no mouth is able to express or heart to conceive the glory with which they were endued, and the beauty of their appearance. 8. And as we looked upon them, we were astounded; for their bodies were whiter than any snow and ruddier than any rose;[8] 9, and the red thereof was mingled with the white, and I am utterly unable to express their beauty; 10, for their hair was curly and bright and seemly both on their face and shoulders, as it were a wreath[9] woven of spikenard and divers-coloured flowers, or like a rainbow in the sky, such was their seemliness.

11. Seeing therefore their beauty we became astounded at them, since they appeared suddenly. 12. And I approached the Lord and said: Who are these? 13. He saith to me: These are your brethren the righteous, whose forms ye desired to see. 14. And I said to him: And where are all the righteous ones and what is the æon in which they are and have this glory?

15. And the Lord showed me[10] a very great country outside of this world, exceeding bright with light, and the air there lighted with the rays of the sun, and the earth itself blooming with unfading flowers and full of spices and plants, fair-flowering and incorruptible and bearing blessed fruit. 16. And so great was the perfume that it[11] was borne thence even unto us. 17. And the dwellers in that place were clad in the raiment of shining angels and their raiment was like unto their country; and angels hovered about them there. 18. And the glory of the dwellers there was equal, and with one voice they sang praises alternately to the Lord God, rejoicing in that place. 19. The Lord saith to us: This is the place of your high-priests,[12] the righteous men.

20. And over against that place I saw another, squalid, and it was the place of punishment; and those who were punished there and the punishing angels had their raiment dark[13] like the air of the place.

21. And there were certain there hanging by the tongue: and these were the blasphemers of the way of righteousness; and under them lay fire,[14] burning and punishing them.

22. And there was a great lake, full of

[1] False prophets. Cf. Matt. vii. 15; xxiv. 5, 11. Cf. Pastor of Hermas, *Mand.* xi.

[2] Sons of perdition. Cf. 2 Peter ii. 1–3; iii. 7, 16; 2 Thess. ii. 3, and Ep. of Lyons and Vienne, Euseb. *H. E.* v. 1.

[3] Purify their souls. Cf. 2 Peter i. 18. Sons of lawlessness. Cf. Pastor Herm. *Vis.* iii. 6.

[4] Mountain. Cf. 2 Peter i. 18.

[5] The righteous. Cf. 2 Peter i. 1; iii. 19. What manner of. Cf. 2 Peter iii. 11. Encourage. Cf. Pastor Herm. *Vis.* iii. 3.

[6] Not able to look. Cf. 2 Cor. iii. 7 ff.

[7] Eye of man, etc. Cf. 1 Cor. ii. 9.

[8] Snow and rose. Cf. Bk. of Enoch cvi. 2.

[9] Wreath. Cf. Ep. of Lyons and Vienne, ap. Euseb. *H. E.* v 1, 36.

[10] Apparently all the disciples are supposed to have had the vision of heaven, but Peter alone that of hell. Unfading. Cf. 1 Peter i. 4.

[11] Odour. Cf. Ep. of Lyons and Vienne, l. c., and Passion of S. Perpetua, ch. xiii.

[12] High-priests. Cf. Didache 13, 3.

[13] Squalid. Cf. 2 Peter i. 19. Punishment. Cf. 2 Peter ii. 9. Punishing angels. Cf. Pastor Herm. *Sim.* vi. 3. Dark. Cf. Jude, vv. 6 and 13.

[14] Blasphemers. Cf. 2 Peter ii. 12; Pastor Herm. *Sim.* viii. 6; ix. 18. Fire. Cf. 2 Peter iii. 7.

flaming mire, in which were certain men that pervert righteousness,[1] and tormenting angels afflicted them.

23. And there were also others, women, hanged by their hair over that mire that bubbled up: and these were they who adorned themselves for adultery; and the men who mingled with them in the defilement[2] of adultery, were hanging by the feet and their heads in that mire. *And* I said: I did not believe that I should come into this place.

24. And I saw the murderers and those who conspired with them, cast into a certain strait place, full of evil snakes, and smitten by those beasts, and thus turning to and fro in that punishment; and worms,[3] as it were clouds of darkness, afflicted them. And the souls of the murdered stood and looked upon the punishment of those murderers and said: O God, thy judgment is just.

25. And near that place I saw another strait place into which the gore and the filth of those who were being punished ran down and became there as it were a lake: and there sat women having the gore up to their necks, and over against them sat many children who were born to them out of due time, crying; and there came forth from them sparks of fire and smote the women in the eyes: and these were the accursed who conceived and caused abortion.

26. And other men and women were burning up to the middle and were cast into a dark place and were beaten by evil spirits, and their inwards were eaten by restless worms:[4] and these were they who persecuted the righteous and delivered them up.

27. And near those there were again women and men gnawing their own lips, and being punished and receiving a red-hot iron in their eyes: and these were they who blasphemed and slandered[5] the way of righteousness.

28. And over against these again other men and women gnawing their tongues and having flaming fire in their mouths: and these were the false witnesses.[6]

29. And in a certain other place there were pebbles sharper than swords or any spit, red-hot, and women and men in tattered and filthy raiment rolled about on them in punishment: and these were the rich who trusted in their riches and had no pity for orphans and widows, and despised the commandment[7] of God.

30. And in another great lake, full of pitch and blood and mire bubbling up, there stood men and women up to their knees: and these were the usurers and those who take interest on interest.

31. And other men and women were being hurled down from a great cliff and reached the bottom, and again were driven by those who were set over them to climb up upon the cliff, and thence were hurled down again, and had no rest from this punishment: and these were they who defiled[8] their bodies acting as women; and the women who were with them were those who lay with one another as a man with a woman.

32. And alongside of that cliff there was a place full of much fire, and there stood men who with their own hands had made for themselves carven images instead of God. And alongside of these were other men and women, having rods and striking each other and never ceasing from such punishment.

33. And others again near them, women and men, burning and turning themselves and roasting: and these were they that leaving the way of God[9] . . .

FRAGMENTS OF THE APOCALYPSE OF PETER.

1. Clemens Alexandrinus, *Eclog.* 48. For instance, Peter in the Apocalypse says that the children who are born out of due time shall be of the better part: and that these are delivered over to a care-taking angel that they may attain a share of knowledge and gain the better abode [after suffering what they would have suffered if they had been in the body: but the others shall merely obtain salvation as injured beings to whom mercy is shown, and remain without punishment, receiving this as a reward].*

2. Clem. Alex. *Eclog.* 49. But the milk of the women running down from their breasts and congealing shall engender small flesh-

[1] Mire. Cf. 2 Peter ii. 22. Pervert righteousness. Cf. Pastor Herm. *Sim.* viii. 6. Cf. Titus i. 14.

[2] Cf. Jude 7. Defilement. Cf. 2 Peter ii. 10, 14, 17, 20, and Jude 8. Cf. Pastor Herm. *Sim.* vi. 5.

[3] Darkness. Cf. 2 Peter ii. 17. Worms. Cf. Isaiah lxvi. 24 and Mark ix. 48.

[4] Restless worms. Cf. Isaiah lxvi. 24 and Mark ix. 48. Cf. Esdras, Ante-Nicene Lib., vol. viii., p. 572; Pastor Herm. *Sim.* ix. 19; viii. 6.

[5] Slandered. Cf. 2 Peter ii. 2 and Jude, vv. 8, 10.

[6] False witnesses. Cf. Hermas. *Mand.* viii. 5.

[7] The rich. etc. Cf. 2 Peter ii. 14. Cf. Pastor Herm. *Vis.* iii. 9; *Sim.* ix. 20; *Sim.* i. 8, and *Mand.* viii. 5. Commandment. Cf. 2 Peter ii. 21; iii. 2.

[8] Defiled. 2 Peter ii. 10. Cf. Rom. i. 26 ff.; Jude 8.

[9] Way of God. 2 Peter ii. 2. Pastor Herm. *Vis.* iii. 7; viii. 6; ix. 19, 22.

* The part of the quotation between square brackets is assigned by Harnack to Clement himself and not to the Apocalypse.

eating beasts: and these run up upon them and devour them.[1]

3. MACARIUS MAGNES, *Apocritica* iv., 6 cf. 16. The earth, it (sc. the Apoc. of Peter) says, "shall present all men before God at the day of judgment, being itself also to be judged, with the heaven also which encompasses it."

[1] Cf. Esdras, Ante-Nicene Lib., vol. viii., p. 573.

4. CLEM. ALEX. *Eclog.* 41. The scripture says that infants that have been exposed are delivered to a care-taking angel, by whom they are educated and so grow up, and they will be, it says, as the faithful of a hundred years old are here.

5. METHODIUS, *Conviv.* ii., 6. Whence also we have received in divinely-inspired scriptures that untimely births are delivered to care-taking angels, even if they are the offspring of adultery.

THE VISION OF PAUL

INTRODUCTION

THE present translation of the Vision of Paul is made from the text of a Latin version, edited by Mr. M. R. James in the *Cambridge Texts and Studies,* ii., 3, p. 11 ff.—from a MS. of the eighth century now in the Bibliothèque Nationale at Paris.

Tischendorf's Greek text was based on two MSS., the earliest of which is at Munich and is of the thirteenth century. This version has already been translated in the Ante-Nicene Library, vol. xvi.

A translation into English from a Syriac version (date unknown) was published by the Rev. J. Perkins, D.D., in the *Journal of Sacred Literature,* N. S., vol. vi., 1865, and re-published by Tischendorf alongside of the Greek version in his *Apocalypses Apocryphæ.*

The Revelation of Paul was known to S. Augustine, who thus refers to it in his *Tractate* 98 on the Gospel of John, § 8: ". . . There have been some vain individuals, who, with a presumption that betrays the grossest folly, have forged a Revelation of Paul, crammed with all manner of fables, which has been rejected by the Orthodox Church; affirming it to be that whereof he had said that he was caught up into the third heavens, and there heard unspeakable words 'which it is not lawful for a man to utter.' Nevertheless, the audacity of such might be tolerable, had he said that he heard words which it is not as yet lawful for a man to utter; but when he said 'which it is not lawful for a man to utter,' who are they that dare to utter them with such impudence and non-success?"

Sozomen, *H. E.*, vii., 19, after speaking of the Apocalypse of Peter, continues: "So the work entitled 'The Apocalypse of the Apostle Paul,' though rejected by the ancients, is still esteemed by most of the monks. Some persons affirm that the book was found during this reign (*i.e.*, of Theodosius) by divine revelation, in a marble box, buried beneath the soil, in the house of Paul, at Tarsus, in Cilicia. I have been informed that this report is false, by a presbyter of Tarsus, a man of very advanced age, as is indicated by his grey hairs."

The book was probably composed, or rather compiled, for it is largely indebted to previous Apocalyptic writings, about the time when it purports to have been discovered at Tarsus, *i.e.*, 388 A.D., the year of the consulship of Theodosius the Less and Cynegius. The alleged sending of a copy of the original to Jerusalem probably indicates the place where it was composed, or, at least, first found currency.

The *Vision of Paul* seems to have enjoyed great popularity during the Middle Ages. Brandes (Halle, 1885), in his edition of two shorter Latin versions, enumerates twenty-two different MSS. of the Latin and "gives particulars of French, English, Danish, and Slavonic forms of the legend."

Of the three main versions, the Latin and Syriac are longer and fuller than the Greek, which in its present form has been abbreviated. Taking advantage of the excellent comparative table presented by Mr. M. R. James in his edition of the text, the translator has endeavoured to point out to the reader, by notes in the margin, the passages where the Latin varies from the Greek, and, to a less extent, from the Syriac.

Parallel passages in other and earlier Apocalyptic writings are also indicated in the notes.

THE VISION OF PAUL

HERE BEGINS THE VISION OF SAINT PAUL THE APOSTLE.

"But I will come to visions and revelations of the Lord: I know a man in Christ fourteen years ago (whether in the body, I know not; or out of the body, I know not, God knoweth) snatched up in this manner to the third heaven: and I know such a man, whether in the body or out of the body I know not, God knoweth; how that he was snatched up into Paradise and heard secret words which it is not lawful for men to speak; on behalf of such a one will I glory; but on mine own behalf I will not glory, save in my infirmities." —2 Cor. xii. 1-5.

1. At what time was this revelation made? In the consulship of Theodosius Augustus the Younger and Cynegius,[1] a certain nobleman then living in Tharsus, in the house which was that of Saint Paul, an angel appearing in the night revealed to him, saying that he should open the foundations of the house and should publish what he found, but he thought that these things were dreams.

2. But the angel coming for the third time beat him and forced him to open the foundation. And digging he found a marble box, inscribed on the sides; there was the revelation of Saint Paul, and his shoes in which he walked teaching the word of God. But he feared to open that box and brought it to the judge; when he had received it, the judge, because it was sealed with lead, sent it to the Emperor Theodosius, fearing lest it might be something else; which when he had received the emperor opened it, and found the revelation of Saint Paul; a copy of it he sent to Jerusalem, and retained the original himself.

3. While I was in the body in which I was snatched up to the third heaven, the word of the Lord came to me saying: speak to the people: until when will ye transgress, and heap sin upon sin, and tempt the Lord who made you? Ye are the sons of God, doing the works of the devil in the faith of Christ, on account of the impediments of the world. Remember therefore and know that while every creature serves God, the human race alone sins. But it reigns over every creature and sins more than all nature.

4. For indeed the sun, the great light, often addressed the Lord saying: Lord God Almighty, I look out upon the impieties and injustices of men; permit me and I shall do unto them what are my powers, that they may know that thou art God alone. And there came a voice saying to him: I know all these things, for mine eye sees and ear hears, but my patience bears them until they shall be converted and repent. But if they do not return to me I will judge them all.

5. For sometimes the moon and stars addressed the Lord saying: Lord God Almighty, to us thou hast given the power of the night; till when shall we look down upon the impieties and fornications and homicides done by the sons of men? Permit us to do unto them according to our powers, that they may know that thou art God alone. And there came a voice unto them saying: I know all these things, and mine eye looks forth and ear hears, but my patience bears with them until they shall be converted and repent. But if they do not return unto me I will judge them.

6. And frequently also the sea exclaimed saying: Lord God Almighty, men have defiled thy holy name in me; permit me to arise and cover every wood and orchard and the whole world, until I blot out all the sons of men from before thy face, that they may know that thou art God alone. And the voice came again and said: I know all things; mine eye seeth everything, and mine ear heareth, but my patience bears with them until they be converted and repent. But if they do not return, I will judge them. Sometimes the waters[2] also spoke against the sins of men saying: Lord God Almighty,

[1] Theodosius the Younger and Cynegius, Consuls, 388 A.D.

[2] The waters (not in Greek version); rivers in Syriac.

all the sons of men have defiled thy holy name. And there came a voice saying: I know all things before they come to pass, for mine eye seeth and mine ear heareth all things, but my patience bears with them until they be converted. But if not I will judge them. Frequently also the earth[1] too exclaimed to the Lord against the sons of men saying: Lord God Almighty, I above every other creature of thine am harmed, supporting the fornications, adulteries, homicides, thefts, perjuries and magic and ill-doings of men and all the evil they do, so that the father rises up against the son, and the son upon the father, the alien against the alien, so that each one defiles his neighbour's wife. The father ascends upon the bed of his own son, and the son likewise ascends the couch of his own father; and in all these evils, they who offer the sacrifice to thy name have defiled thy holy place. Therefore I am injured above every creature, desiring not to shew my power to myself, and my fruits to the sons of men. Permit me and I will destroy the virtue of my fruits. And there came a voice and said: I know all things, and there is none who can hide himself from his sin. Moreover I know their impieties, but my holiness suffers them until they be converted and repent. But if they do not return unto me I will judge them.

7. Behold, ye sons of men, the creature is subject to God, but the human race alone sins. For this cause, therefore, ye sons of men, bless the Lord God unceasingly, every hour and every day: but more especially when the sun has set:[2] for at that hour all the angels proceed to the Lord to worship him and to present the works of men, which every man has wrought from the morning till the evening, whether good or evil. And there is a certain angel who proceeds rejoicing concerning the man in whom he dwells. When therefore the sun[3] has set in the first hour of night, in the same hour the angel of every people and every man and woman, who protect and preserve them, because man is the image of God: similarly also in the matin hour which is the twelfth of the night, all the angels of men and women, go up to God to worship God, and present every work which each man has wrought, whether good or evil. Moreover every day and night the angels show to God an account[4] of all the acts of the human race. To you, therefore, I say, ye sons of men, bless the Lord God without fail all the days of your life.

8. Therefore at the appointed hour all the angels whatever, rejoicing at once together, proceed before God that they may meet to worship at the hour determined. And behold suddenly it became the hour of meeting, and the angels came to worship in the presence of God, and the spirit proceeded to meet them: and there came a voice and said: Whence come ye, our angels, bearing the burdens of tidings?

9. They answered and said: We come from those who have renounced this world for the sake of thy holy name, wandering as pilgrims, and in caves of the rocks, and weeping every hour in which they inhabited the earth, and hungering and thirsting because of thy name, with their loins girded, having in their hands the incense of their hearts, and praying and blessing every hour, and restraining and overcoming themselves, weeping and wailing above the rest that inhabit the earth. And we indeed, their angels, mourn along with them: whither therefore it shall please thee, command us to go and minister, lest others also do it, but the destitute above the rest who are on earth. And there came the voice of God to them saying: Know ye that now henceforward my grace is appointed unto you, and my help, who is my well-beloved Son, shall be present with them, guiding them every hour; ministering also to them, never deserting them, since their place is his habitation.

10. When therefore these angels had retired, behold other angels came to adore in the presence of honour, in the assembly, who wept; and the spirit of God proceeded to meet them, and there came the voice of God and said: Whence come ye, our angels, bearing the burdens of the ministry of the tidings of the world? They answered and said in the presence of God: We have arrived from those who called upon thy name, and the impediments of the world made them wretched, devising many occasions every hour, not even making one pure prayer, nor out of their whole heart, in all the time of their life; what need, therefore, is there to be present with men who are sinners? And there came the voice of God to them: It is necessary that ye should minister to them, until they be converted and repent: but if they do not return to me I will judge them. Know therefore, sons of men, that whatever things are wrought by you, these angels relate to God, whether good or evil.

[1] The earth (not in Greek version, but in Syriac).
[2] Cf. Test. of Abraham, Rec. B, iv.
[3] Cf. Test. of Abraham, Rec. B, § 4.
[4] Cf. Test. of Abraham, Rec. A, § 12.

11. And the angel answered and said unto me: Follow me, and I will show you the place of the just where they are led when they are deceased, and after these things taking thee into the abyss, I will show thee the souls of sinners and what sort of place they are led into when they have deceased. And I proceeded back after the angel, and he led me into heaven, and I looked back upon the firmament, and I saw in the same place power, and there was there oblivion which deceives and draws down to itself the hearts of men, and the spirit of detraction, and the spirit of fornication, and the spirit of madness, and the spirit of insolence, and there were there the princes of vices: these I saw under the firmament of heaven: and again I looked back, and I saw angels without mercy, having no pity, whose countenance was full of madness, and their teeth sticking out beyond the mouth: their eyes shone like the morning star of the east, and from the hairs of their head sparks of fire went out, or from their mouth. And I asked the angel saying: Sir, who are those? And the angel answered and said unto me: These are those who are destined to the souls of the impious in the hour of need, who did not believe that they had the Lord for their helper, nor hoped in him.

12. And I looked on high and I saw other angels whose countenance shone as the sun, their loins girded with golden girdles, having palms in their hands, and the sign of God, clothed with garments in which was written the name of the Son of God, filled moreover with all meekness and pity; and I asked the angels saying: Who are these, Lord, in so great beauty and pity? And the angel answered and said unto me: These are the angels of justice who are sent to lead up the souls of the just, in the hour of need, who believed that they had the Lord for their helper. And I said to him: Do the just and sinners necessarily meet witnesses when they have died? And the angel answered and said to me: There is one way by which all pass over to God, but the just having their helper with them are not confounded when they go to appear in the sight of God.

13. And I said to the angel: I wished to see the souls of the just and of sinners going out of the world. And the angel answered and said unto me: Look down upon the earth. And I looked down from heaven upon the earth, and saw the whole world, and it was nothing in my sight and I saw the sons of men as though they were naught, and a-wanting, and I wondered and said to the angel: Is this the greatness of men? And the angel answered and said unto me: It is, and these are they who do evil from morning till evening. And I looked and saw a great cloud of fire spread over the whole world, and I said to the angel: What is this, my Lord? and he said to me: This is injustice stirred up by the princes of sinners.

14. I indeed when I had heard this sighed and wept, and said to the angel: I wished to see the souls of the just and of sinners, and to see in what manner they go out of the body. And the angel answered and said unto me: Look again upon the earth. And I looked and saw all the world, and men were as naught and a-wanting: and I looked carefully and saw a certain man about to die, and the angel said to me: This one whom thou seest is a just man. And I looked again and saw all his works, whatever he had done for the sake of God's name, and all his desires, both what he remembered, and what he did not remember; they all stood in his sight in the hour of need; and I saw the just man advance and find refreshment and confidence, and before he went out of the world the holy and the impious angels both attended: and I saw them all, but the impious found no place of habitation in him, but the holy took possession of his soul, guiding it till it went out of the body: and they roused the soul saying: Soul, know thy body whence thou goest out, for it is necessary that thou shouldst return to the same body on the day of the resurrection, that thou mayest receive the things promised to all the just. Receiving therefore the soul from the body, they immediately kissed it as familiarly known to them, saying to it: Do manfully, for thou hast done the will of God while placed in the earth. And there came to meet him the angel who watched him every day, and said to him: Do manfully, soul; for I rejoice in thee, because thou hast done the will of God on earth: for I related to God all thy works, such as they were. Similarly also the spirit proceeded to meet him and said: Soul, fear not, nor be disturbed, until thou comest into a place which thou hast never known, but I will be a helper unto thee: for I found in thee a place of refreshment in the time when I dwelt in thee, while I was on earth. And his spirit strengthened him, and his angel received him, and led him into heaven: and an angel said: Whither runnest thou, O soul, and dost thou dare to enter into heaven? Wait and let us see if there is anything of ours in thee: and behold

we find nothing in thee. I see also thy divine helper and angel, and the spirit is rejoicing along with thee, because thou hast done the will of God on earth. And they led him along till he should worship in the sight of God. And when they had ceased, immediately Michael and all the army of angels, with one voice, adored the footstool of his feet, and his doors, saying at the same time to the soul: This is your God of all things, who made you in his own image and likeness. Moreover the angel returns and points him out saying: God, remember his labours: for this is the soul, whose works I related to thee, doing according to thy judgment. And the spirit said likewise: I am the spirit of vivification inspiring him: for I had refreshment in him, in the time when I dwelt in him, doing according to thy judgment. And there came the voice of God and said: In as much as this man did not vex me, neither will I vex him; for according as he had pity, I also will have pity. Let him therefore be handed over to Michael, the angel of the Covenant, and let him lead him into the Paradise of joy, that he himself may become co-heir with all the saints. And after these things I heard the voices of a thousand thousand angels, and archangels, and cherubim, and twenty-four elders saying hymns, and glorifying the Lord and crying: thou art just, O Lord, and just are thy judgments, and there is no acceptance of persons with thee, but thou rewardest unto every man according to thy judgment. And the angel answered and said unto me: Hast thou believed and known, that whatever each man of you has done, he sees in the hour of need? And I said: Yes, sir.

15. And he saith to me: Look again down on the earth, and watch the soul of an impious man going out of the body, which vexed the Lord day and night, saying: I know nothing else in this world, I eat and drink, and enjoy what is in the world; for who is there who has descended into hell, and ascending has declared to us that there is judgment there! And again I looked carefully, and saw all the scorn of the sinner, and all that he did, and they stood together before him in the hour of need: and it was done to him in that hour, in which he was threatened about his body at the judgment, and I said: It were better for him if he had not been born. And after these things, there came at the same time, the holy angels, and the malign, and the soul of the sinner and the holy angels did not find a place in it. Moreover the malign angels cursed it; and when they had drawn it out of the body, the angels admonished it a third time, saying: O wretched soul, look upon thy flesh, whence thou camest out: for it is necessary that thou shouldst return to thy flesh in the day of resurrection, that thou mayest receive the due for thy sins and thy impieties.

16. And when they had led it forth, the customary angel preceded it, and said to it: O wretched soul, I am the angel belonging to thee, relating daily to the Lord thy malign works, whatever thou didst by night or day: and if it were in my power, not for one day would I minister to thee, but none of these things was I able to do: the judge is pitiful and just, and he himself commanded us that we should not cease to minister to the soul, till you should repent, but thou hast lost the time of repentance. I indeed was strange to thee and thou to me. Let us go on then to the just judge: I will not dismiss thee, before I know from to-day why I was strange to thee. And the spirit confounded him, and the angel troubled him. When, therefore, they had arrived at the power, when he started to enter heaven, a labour was imposed upon him, above all other labour: error and oblivion and murmuring met him, and the spirit of fornication, and the rest of the powers, and said to him: Whither goest thou, wretched soul, and darest thou to rush into heaven? hold, that we may see if we have our qualities in thee, since we do not see that thou hast a holy helper. And after that I heard voices in the height of heaven saying: Present that wretched soul to God, that it may know that it is God that it despised. When, therefore, it had entered heaven, all the angels saw it, a thousand thousand exclaimed with one voice, all saying: Woe to thee, wretched soul, for the sake of thy works which thou didst on earth; what answer art thou about to give to God when thou shalt have approached to adore him? The angel who was with it answered and said: Weep with me, my beloved, for I have not found rest in this soul. And the angels answered him and said: Let such a soul be taken away from the midst of ours, for from the time he entered, the stink of him crosses to us angels. And after these things it was presented, that it might worship in the sight of God, and an angel of God showed him God who made him after his own image and likeness. Moreover his angel ran before him saying: Lord God Almighty, I am the angel of this soul, whose works I presented to thee day and night, not doing according to thy judg-

ment. And the spirit likewise said: I am the spirit who dwelt in it from the time it was made, in itself moreover I know it, and it has not followed my will: judge it, Lord, according to thy judgment. And there came the voice of God to it and said: Where is thy fruit which thou has made worthy of the goods which thou hast received? Have I put a distance of one day between thee and the just man? Did I not make the sun to arise upon thee as upon the just? But the soul was silent, having nothing to answer: and again there came a voice saying: Just is the judgment of God, and there is no acceptance of persons with God, for whoever shall have done mercy, on them shall he have mercy, and whoever shall not have pitied neither shall God pity him. Let him therefore be handed over to the angel Tartaruch, who is set over the punishments, and let him place him in outer darkness, where there is weeping and gnashing of teeth, and let him be there till the great day of judgment. And after these things I heard the voice of angels and archangels saying: Thou art just, Lord, and thy judgment is just.

17. And again I saw, and behold a soul which was led forward by two angels, weeping and saying: Have pity on me, just God, God the judge, for to-day is seven days since I went out of my body, and I was handed over to these two angels, and they led me through to those places, which I had never seen. And God, the just judge, saith to him: What hast thou done? for thou never didst mercy, wherefore thou wast handed over to such angels as have no mercy, and because thou didst not do uprightly, so neither did they act piously with thee in the hour of thy need. Confess therefore thy sins which thou didst commit when placed in the world. And he answered and said: Lord, I did not sin. And the Lord, the just Lord, was angered in fury when it said: I did not sin, because it lied; and God said: Dost thou think thou art still in the world? if any one of you, sinning there, conceal and hide his sin from his neighbour, here indeed nothing whatever shall be hid: for when the souls come to adore in sight of the throne, both the good works and the sins of each one are made manifest. And hearing these things the soul was silent, having no answer. And I heard the Lord God, the just judge, again saying: Come, angel of this soul, and stand in the midst. And the angel of the sinful soul came, having in his hands a manuscript, and said: These, Lord, in my hands, are all the sins of this soul from his youth till to-day, from the tenth year of his birth: and if thou command, Lord, I will also relate his acts from the beginning of his fifteenth year. And the Lord God, the just judge, said: I say unto thee, angel, I do not expect of thee an account of him since he began to be fifteen years old, but state his sins for five years before he died and before he came hither. And again God, the just judge, said: For by myself I swear, and by my holy angels, and by my virtue, that if he had repented five years before he died, on account of one year's life, oblivion would now be thrown over all the evils which he sinned before, and he would have indulgence and remission of sins: now indeed he shall perish. And the angel of the sinful soul answered and said: Lord, command that angel to exhibit those souls.

18. And in that same hour the souls were exhibited in the midst, and the soul of the sinner knew them; and the Lord said to the soul of the sinner: I say unto thee, soul, confess thy work which thou wroughtest in these souls, whom thou seest, when they were in the world. And he answered and said: Lord, it is not yet a full year since I slew this one and poured his blood upon the ground, and with another (a woman) I committed fornication: not this alone, but I also greatly harmed her in taking away her goods. And the Lord God, the just judge, said: Either thou didst not know that he who does violence to another, if he dies first who sustains the violence, is kept in this place until the doer of hurt dies, and then both stand in the presence of the judge, and now each receives according to his deed. And I heard a voice of one saying: Let that soul be delivered into the hands of Tartarus, and led down into hell: he shall lead him into the lower prison and he shall be put in torments, and left there till the great day of judgment. And again I heard a thousand thousand angels saying hymns to the Lord, and crying: Thou art just, O Lord, and just are thy judgments.

19. The angel answered and said unto me: Hast thou perceived all these things? and I said, Yes, sir. And he said to me: Follow me again, and I will take thee, and show thee the places of the just. And I followed the angel, and he raised me to the third heaven, and placed me at the entry of the door: and looking carefully I saw, and the door was of gold, and two columns of gold, full above of golden letters, and the angel turned again to me and said: Blessed wert thou, if thou hadst entered into these doors, for it is not allowed to any to enter except only to those who have

goodness and innocence of body in all things. And I asked the angel about everything and said: Sir, tell me on what account these letters are put upon those tables? The angel answered and said unto me: These are the names of the just, serving God with their whole heart, who dwell on the earth. And again I said: Sir, therefore their names and countenance and the likeness of these who serve God are in heaven, and are known to the angels: for they know who are the servants of God with all their heart, before they go out of the world.

20. And when I had entered the interior of the gate of Paradise,[1] there came out to meet me an old man whose countenance shone as the sun; and when he had embraced me he said: Hail, Paul, beloved of God. And he kissed me with a cheerful countenance. He wept, and I said to him: Brother, why dost thou weep? And again sighing and lamenting he said: We are hurt by men, and they vex us greatly; for many are the good things which the Lord has prepared, and great is his promise, but many do not perceive them. And I asked the angel, and said: Sir, who is this? And he said to me: This is Enoch, the scribe of righteousness. And I entered into the interior of that place, and immediately I saw the sun,[2] and coming it saluted me laughing and rejoicing. And when it had seen (me), it turned away and wept, and said to me: Paul, would that thou shouldst receive thy labours which thou hast done in the human race. For me, indeed, I have seen the great and many good things, which God has prepared for the just, and the promises of God are great, but many do not perceive them; but even by many labours scarcely one or two enters into these places.

21. And the angel answered and said to me,[3] Whatever I now show thee here, and whatever thou shalt hear, tell it not to any one in the earth. And he led me and shewed me: and there I heard words which it is not lawful for a man to speak. And again he said, For now follow me, and I will shew thee what thou oughtest to narrate in public and relate.

And he took me down from the third heaven, and led me into the second heaven, and again he led me on to the firmament and from the firmament he led me over the doors of heaven: the beginning of its foundation was on the river which waters all the earth. And I asked the angel and said, Lord, what is this river of water? and he said to me, This is Oceanus! And suddenly I went out of heaven, and I understood that it is the light of heaven which lightens all the earth. For the land there is seven times brighter[4] than silver. And I said, Lord, what is this place? And he said to me, This is the land of promise. Hast thou never heard what is written: Blessed are the meek: for they shall inherit the earth? The souls therefore of the just, when they have gone out of the body, are meanwhile dismissed to this place. And I said to the angel, Then this land will be manifested before the time? The angel answered and said to me, When Christ, whom thou preachest, shall come to reign, then, by the sentence of God,[5] the first earth will be dissolved and this land of promise will then be revealed, and it will be like dew or cloud, and then the Lord Jesus Christ, the King Eternal, will be manifested and will come with all his saints to dwell in it, and he will reign over them a thousand years, and they will eat of the good things which I shall now show unto thee.

22. And I looked around upon that land and I saw a river flowing of milk and honey, and there were trees planted by the bank of that river, full of fruit: moreover each single tree bore twelve fruits in the year, having various and diverse fruits: and I saw the created things which are in that place and all the work of God, and I saw there palms of twenty cubits, but others of ten cubits: and that land was seven times brighter than silver. And there were trees full of fruits from the roots to the highest branches, of ten thousand fruits of palms upon ten thousand fruits. The grape-vines moreover had ten thousand plants.[6] Moreover in the single vines there were ten thousand thousand bunches and in each of these a thousand single grapes: moreover these single trees bore a thousand fruits. And I said to the angel, Why does each tree bear a thousand fruits? The angel answered and said unto me, Because the Lord God gives an abounding flood of gifts to the worthy, because they also of their own will afflicted themselves when they were placed in the world doing all things on account of his holy name. And again I said to the angel, Sir, are these the only promises which the Most Holy God makes? And he answered and said to me: No! there are seven times greater than these. But I say unto

[1] Cf. Ascension of Isaiah ix. 9.
[2] And the sun. Not in Greek: *Elias* in Syriac.
[3] (Not in Syriac.)
[4] Cf. Rev. of Peter. 15.
[5] Cf. Enoch.
[6] Cf. Papias. ap. Iren. *Haer.* v. 33. 3, 4.

thee that when the just go out of the body they shall see the promises and the good things which God has prepared for them. Till then, they shall sigh, and lament saying: Have we emitted any word from our mouth to vex our neighbour even on one day? I asked and said again: Are these alone the promises of God? And the angel answered and said unto me: These whom you now see are the souls of the married[1] and those who kept the chastity of their nuptials, containing themselves. But to the virgins and those who hunger and thirst after righteousness and those who afflicted themselves for the sake of the name of God, God will give seven times greater than these, which I shall now show thee.

And then he took me up from that place where I saw these things and behold, a river, and its waters were greatly whiter than milk, and I said to the angel, What is this? And he said to me: This is the Acherousian Lake where is the City of Christ, but not every man is permitted to enter that city; for this is the journey which leads to God, and if anyone is a fornicator and impious, and is converted and shall repent and do fruits worthy of repentance, at first indeed when he shall have gone out of the body, he is led and adores God, and thence by command of the Lord he is delivered to the angel Michael and he baptizes him in the Acherousian Lake—thus he leads them into the City of Christ alongside of those who have never sinned. But I wondered and blessed the Lord God for all the things which I saw.

23. And the angel answered and said unto me: Follow me and I will lead thee into the City of Christ. And he was standing on the Acherousian Lake and he put me into a golden ship[2] and angels as it were three thousand were saying hymns before me till I arrived at the City of Christ. Moreover those who inhabited the City of Christ greatly rejoiced over me as I went to them, and I entered and saw the City of Christ, and it was all of gold, and twelve walls encircled it, and twelve interior towers, and each wall had between them single stadia in the circuit: And I said to the angel, Sir, how much is a stadium? The angel answered and said to me: As much as there is between the Lord God and the men who are on the earth, for the City of Christ is alone great. And there were twelve gates in the circuit of the city, of great beauty, and four rivers which encircled it. There was, moreover, a river of honey and a river of milk, and a river of wine and a river of oil. And I said to the angel: What are these rivers surrounding that city? And he saith to me: These are the four rivers which flow sufficiently for those who are in this land of promise, of which the names[3] are: the river of honey is called Fison, and the river of milk Euphrates, and the river of oil Gion, and the river of wine Tigris, such therefore they are for those who when placed in the world did not use the power of these things, but they hungered for these things and afflicted themselves for the sake of the Lord God: so that when these enter into this city, the Lord will assign them these things on high above all measure.

24. I indeed entering the gates saw trees great and very high before the doors of the city, having no fruit but leaves only, and I saw a few men scattered in the midst of the trees, and they lamented greatly when they saw anyone enter the city. And those trees were sorry for them and humbled themselves and bowed down and again erected themselves. And I saw and wept with them and I asked the angel and said: Sir, who are these who are not admitted to enter into the City of Christ? And he said to me: These are they who zealously abstained day and night in fasts, but they had a proud heart above other men, glorifying and praising themselves and doing nothing for their neighbours. For they gave some friendly greeting, but to others they did not even say hail! and indeed they shewed hospitality to those only whom they wished, and if they did anything whatever for their neighbour they were immoderately puffed up. And I said: What then, Sir? Did their pride prevent them from entering into the City of Christ? And the angel answered and said unto me: Pride is the root of all evils. Are they better than the Son of God who came to the Jews with much humility? And I asked him and said: Why is it that the trees humble themselves and erect themselves again? And the angel answered and said to me: The whole time which these men passed on earth zealously serving God, on account of the confusion and reproaches of men at the time, they blushed and humiliated themselves, but they were not saddened, nor did they repent that they should recede from their pride which was in them. This is why the trees humble themselves, and again

[1] (In Syriac, but not in Greek version.)

[2] The Greek has not the golden ship, the angels or the walls. They are given in the Syriac.

[3] Not in the Greek, but given in the Syriac. Cf. Genesis ii. 11 ff.

are raised up. And I asked and said: For what cause were they admitted to the doors of the city? The angel answered and said unto me: Because of the great goodness of God, and because there is the entry of his holy men entering into this city: for this cause they are left in this place, but when Christ the King Eternal enters with his saints, as he enters just men may pray for these, and then they may enter into the city along with them: but yet none of them is able to have assurance such as they have who humbled themselves, serving the Lord God all their lives.

25. But I went on while the angel instructed me, and he carried me to the river of honey, and I saw there Isaiah and Jeremiah[1] and Ezekiel and Amos, and Micah and Zechariah, the minor and major prophets, and they saluted me in the city. I said to the angel: What way is this? And he said to me: This is the way of the prophets, every one who shall have afflicted his soul and not done his own will because of God, when he shall have gone out of the world and have been led to the Lord God and adored him, then by the command of God he is handed over to Michael, and he leads him into the city to this place of the prophets, and they salute him as their friend and neighbour because he did the will of God.

26. Again he led me where there is a river of milk, and I saw in that place all the infants whom Herod slew because of the name of Christ, and they saluted me, and the angel said to me: All who keep their chastity with purity, when they shall have come out of the body, after they adore the Lord God are delivered to Michael and are led to the infants and they salute them, saying that they are our brothers and friends and members; in themselves they shall inherit the promises of God.

27. Again he took me up and carried me to the north of the city and led me where there was a river of wine, and there I saw Abraham and Isaac and Jacob, Lot and Job and other saints,[2] and they saluted me: and I asked and said: What is this place, my Lord? The angel answered and said to me: All who are receivers of pilgrims, when they go out of the world, first adore the Lord God, and are delivered to Michael and by this way are led into the city, and all the just salute him as son and brother, and say unto him: Because thou hast observed humanity and the receiving of pilgrims, come, have an inheritance in the city of the Lord our God: every just man shall receive good things of God in the city, according to his own action.

28. And again he carried me near the river of oil on the east of the city. And I saw there men rejoicing and singing psalms, and I said: Who are those, my Lord? And the angel saith to me: Those are they who devoted themselves to God with their whole heart and had no pride in themselves. For all those who rejoice in the Lord God and sing psalms to the Lord with their whole heart are here led into this city.

29. And he carried me into the midst of the city near the twelve walls.[3] But there was in this place a higher wall, and I asked and said: Is there in the City of Christ a wall which in honour exceeds this place? And the angel answering said to me: There is a second better than the first, and similarly a third than the second, as each exceeds the other, unto the twelfth wall. And I said: Tell me, Sir, why one exceeds another in glory? And the angel answered and said unto me: All who have in themselves even a little detraction or zeal or pride, something of his glory would be made void even if he were in the city of Christ: look backward!

And turning round I saw golden thrones placed in each gate, and on them men having golden diadems and gems:[4] and I looked carefully and I saw inside between the twelve men thrones placed in another rank which appeared of much glory, so that no one is able to recount their praise. And I asked the angel and said: My lord, who is on the throne? And the angel answered and said unto me: Those thrones belong to those who had goodness and understanding of heart and made themselves fools for the sake of the Lord God, nor knew new Scriptures nor psalms, but, mindful of one chapter of the commands of God, and hearing what it contained they wrought thereby in much diligence and had a right zeal before the Lord God, and the admiration of them will seize all the saints in presence of the Lord God, for talking with one another they say, Wait and see the unlearned who know nothing more: by which means they merited so great and such a garment and so great glory on account of their innocence.

And I saw in the midst of this city a great

[1] Names not in the Greek. Isaiah, Jeremiah, Ezekiel, Moses and all the Prophets in the Syriac.
[2] Names not in the Greek or Syriac.
[3] Not in Greek, which here has the altar in the city and David. The Syriac is the same as the Latin.
[4] Not in the Greek. Cf. Ascension of Isaiah viii. 36.

altar, very high, and there was one standing near the altar whose countenance shone as the sun, and he held in his hands a psaltery and harp, and he sang psalms, saying Halleluia! And his voice filled the whole city: at the same time when all they who were on the towers and gates heard him they responded Halleluia! so that the foundations of the city were shaken: and I asked the angel and said, Sir, who is this of so great power? And the angel said to me: This is David: this is the city of Jerusalem, for when Christ the King of Eternity shall come with the assurance of His kingdom, he again shall go before him that he may sing psalms, and all the just at the same time shall sing psalms responding Halleluia! And I said, Sir, how did David alone above the other saints make a beginning of psalm-singing? And the angel answered and said unto me: Because Christ the Son of God sits at the right hand of His Father, and this David sings psalms before him in the seventh heaven, and as is done in the heavens so also below, because the host may not be offered to God without David, but it is necessary that David should sing psalms in the hour of the oblation of the body and blood of Christ: as it is performed in heaven so also on earth.

30. And I said to the angel: Sir, what is Alleluia? And the angel answered and said to me: You ask questions about everything. And he said to me, Alleluia is said in the Hebrew language of God and angels, for the meaning of Alleluia is this : *tecel cat. marith macha.*[1] And I said, Sir, what is *tecel cat. marith macha?* And the angel answered and said unto me : *Tecel cat. marith macha* is : Let us all bless him together. I asked the angel and said, Sir, do all who say Alleluia bless the Lord? And the angel answered and said to me: It is so, and again, therefore, if any one sing Alleluia and those who are present do not sing at the same time, they commit sin because they do not sing along with him. And I said: My lord, does he also sin if he be hesitating or very old? The angel answered and said unto me: Not so, but he who is able and does not join in the singing, know such as a despiser of the Word, and it would be proud and unworthy that he should not bless the Lord God his maker.

31. Moreover when he had ceased speaking to me, he led me outside the city through the midst of the trees and far from the places of the land of the good, and put me across the river of milk and honey: and after that he led me over the ocean which supports the foundations of heaven.

The angel answered and said unto me: Dost thou understand why thou goest hence? And I said: Yes, sir. And he said to me Come and follow me, and I will show thee the souls of the impious and sinners, that thou mayest know what manner of place it is. And I proceeded with the angel and he carried me by the setting of the sun, and I saw the beginning of heaven founded on a great river of water, and I asked: What is this river of water? And he said to me: This is Ocean which surrounds all the Earth. And when I was at the outer limit of Ocean I looked, and there was no light in that place, but darkness and sorrow and sadness: and I sighed.

And I saw there a fervent river of fire, and in it a multitude of men and women immersed up to the knees, and other men up to the navel, others even up to the lips, others moreover up to the hair. And I asked the angel and said: Sir, who are those in the fiery river? And the angel answered and said to me: They are neither hot nor cold, because they were found neither in the number of the just nor in the number of the impious.[2] For those spent the time of their life on earth passing some days in prayer, but others in sins and fornications, until their death. And I asked him and said: Who are these, Sir, immersed up to their knees in fire? He answered and said to me: These are they who when they have gone out of church throw themselves into strange conversations to dispute. Those indeed who are immersed up to the navel are those who, when they have taken the body and blood of Christ go and fornicate and did not cease from their sins till they died. Those who are immersed up to the lips are the detractors of each other when they assemble in the church of God: those up to the eyebrows are those who nod approval of themselves and plot spite against their neighbour.[3]

32. And I saw on the north a place of various and diverse punishments full of men and women,[4] and a river of fire ran down into it. Moreover I observed and I saw pits great in depth, and in them several souls together, and the depth of that place was as it were three thousand cubits, and I saw them groaning

[1] These letters are unintelligible. In the Greek version, the interpretation of Alleluia is given as *thebel marematha,* which is also unintelligible. In the Syriac the interpretation of Alleluia is correctly given.

[2] Not in Greek or Syriac.

[3] Not in the Greek or Syriac.

[4] The Greek has here *thieves* and *slanderers.*

and weeping and saying: Have pity on us, O Lord! and none had pity on them. And I asked the angel and said: Who are these, Sir? And the angel answered and said unto me: These are they who did not hope in the Lord, that they would be able to have him as their helper. And I asked and said: Sir, if these souls remain for thirty or forty generations thus one upon another, if they were sent deeper, the pits I believe would not hold them. And he said to me: The Abyss has no measure, for beyond[1] this it stretches down below him who is down in it: and so it is, that if perchance anyone should take a stone and throw it into a very deep well and after many hours it should reach the bottom, such is the abyss. For when the souls are thrown in there, they hardly reach the bottom in fifty years.

33. I, indeed, when I heard this, wept and groaned over the human race. The angel answered and said unto me: Why dost thou weep? Art thou more pitiful than God? For though God is good, He knows also that there are punishments, and He patiently bears with the human race, dismissing each one to work his own will in the time in which he dwells on the earth.

34. I further observed the fiery river and saw there a man being tortured by Tartaruchian angels having in their hands an iron with three hooks with which they pierced the bowels of that old man: and I asked the angel, and said: Sir, who is that old man on whom such torments are imposed? And the angel answered and said to me: He whom you see was a presbyter who did not perform well his ministry: when he had been eating and drinking and committing fornication he offered the host to the Lord at his holy altar.

35. And I saw not far away another old man led on by malign angels running with speed, and they pushed him into the fire up to his knees, and they struck him with stones and wounded his face like a storm, and did not allow him to say: Have pity on me! And I asked the angel and he said to me: He whom you see was a bishop, and did not perform well his episcopate, who indeed accepted the great name but did not enter into the witness of him who gave him the name in all his life, seeing that he did not do just judgment, and did not pity widows and orphans, but now he receives retribution according to his iniquity and his works.

36. And I saw another man in the fiery river up to his knees. Moreover his hands were stretched out and bloody, and worms proceeded from his mouth and nostrils and he was groaning and weeping, and crying he said: Have pity on me! for I am hurt above the rest who are in this punishment. And I asked, Sir, who is this? And he said to me: This man whom thou seest, was a deacon who devoured the oblations and committed fornications and did not right in the sight of God, for this cause he unceasingly pays this penalty.

And I looked closely and saw alongside of him another[2] man whom they delivered up with haste and cast into the fiery river, and he was (in it) up to the knees: and there came the angel who was set over the punishments having a great fiery razor, and with it he cut the lips of that man and the tongue likewise. And sighing, I lamented and asked: Who is that, sir. And he said to me, He whom thou seest was a reader and read to the people, but he himself did not keep the precepts of God: now he also pays the proper penalty.

37. And I saw another multitude of pits in the same place, and in the midst of it a river full of a multitude of men and women,[3] and worms[4] consumed them. But I lamented and sighing asked the angel and said: Sir, who are these? And he said to me: These are those who exacted interest[5] on interest and trusted in their riches and did not hope in God that He was their helper.

And after that I looked and saw another place, very narrow, and it was like a wall, and fire round about it. And I saw inside men and women gnawing[6] their tongues, and I asked: Sir, who are these. And he said to me: These are they who in church disparage the Word of God, not attending to it, but as it were make naught of God and His angels: for that cause they now likewise pay the proper penalty.

38. And I observed and saw another old man down in a pit and his countenance was like blood, and I asked and said, Sir, what is this place? And he said to me: Into that pit stream all the punishments. And I saw men and women immersed up to the lips and I asked, Sir, who are these? And he said to me: These are the magicians who prepared for men and women evil magic arts and did not find how to stop them till they died.

And again I saw men and women with very

[1] Passage probably corrupt.

[2] Not in the Greek but in the Syriac.

[3] Not in the Greek. The Syriac has simply those who trusted in their riches

[4] Cf. Rev. of Peter, 27.

[5] Cf. Rev. of Peter, 31.

[6] Cf. Rev. of Peter, 29.

black faces in a pit of fire,[1] and I sighed and lamented and asked, Sir, who are these? And he said to me: These are fornicators and adulterers who committed adultery having wives of their own: likewise also the women committed adultery having husbands of their own: therefore they unceasingly suffer penalties.

39. And I saw there girls having black[2] raiment, and four terrible angels having in their hands burning chains, and they put them on the necks of the girls and led them into darkness: and I, again weeping, asked the angel: Who are these, Sir? And he said to me: These are they who, when they were virgins, defiled their virginity unknown to their parents; for which cause they unceasingly pay the proper penalties.

And again I observed there men and women with hands cut and their feet placed naked in a place of ice and snow, and worms devoured them. But seeing them I lamented and asked: Sir, who are these? And he said to me: These are they who harmed orphans and widows and the poor,[3] and did not hope in the Lord, for which cause they unceasingly pay the proper penalties.

And I observed and saw others hanging over a channel of water, and their tongues were very dry, and many fruits were placed in their sight, and they were not permitted to take of them, and I asked: Sir, who are these? And he said to me: These are they who break their fast[4] before the appointed hour, for this cause they unceasingly pay these penalties.

And I saw other men and women hanging by their eyebrows and their hair,[5] and a fiery river drew them, and I said: Who are these, my Lord? And he said to me:[6] These are they who join themselves not to their own husbands and wives but to whores, and therefore they unceasingly pay the proper penalties.

And I saw other men and women covered with dust, and their countenance was like blood, and they were in a pit of pitch and sulphur and running down into a fiery river, and I asked: Sir, who are these?[7] And he said to me: These are they who committed the iniquity of Sodom and Gomorrah, the male with the male, for which reason they unceasingly pay the penalties.

40. And[8] I observed and saw men and women clothed in bright garments, having their eyes blind, placed in a pit, and I asked: Sir, who are these? And he said to me: These are of the people who did alms, and knew not the Lord God, for which reason they unceasingly pay the proper penalties. And I observed and saw other men and women on an obelisk of fire, and beasts tearing them in pieces, and they were not allowed to say, Lord have pity on us! And I saw the angel[9] of penalties putting heavy punishments on them and saying: Acknowledge the Son of God; for this was predicted to you, when the divine Scriptures were read to you, and you did not attend; for which cause God's judgment is just, for your actions have apprehended you and brought you into these penalties. But I sighed and wept, and I asked and said: Who are these men and women who are strangled in fire and pay their penalties? And he answered me: These are women who defiled the image of God when bringing forth infants out of the womb, and these are the men who lay with them. And their infants addressed the Lord God and the angels who were set over the punishments, saying:[10] Cursed be the hour to our parents, for they defiled the image of God, having the name of God but not observing His precepts: they gave us for food to dogs and to be trodden down of swine: others they threw into the river. But their infants[11] were handed over to the angels of Tartarus who were set over the punishments, that they might lead them to a wide place of mercy: but their fathers and mothers were tortured in a perpetual punishment.

And after that I saw men and women clothed with rags full of pitch and fiery sulphur, and dragons were coiled about their necks and shoulders and feet, and angels having fiery horns restrained them and smote them, and closed their nostrils, saying to them: Why did ye not know the time in which it was right to repent and serve God, and did not do it? And I asked: Sir, who are these? And he said to me: These are they who seem to give up the world for God,[12] putting on our garb, but the impediments of the world made them wretched, not main-

[1] Cf. Rev. of Peter, 24. Not in the Greek. The Syriac has darkness the torment of patriarchs, bishops, etc.
[2] Cf. Rev. of Peter xxi. 30. Not in Syriac.
[3] Cf. Rev. of Peter, 30. Not in the Greek.
[4] Not in the Greek.
[5] Not in the Greek.
[6] Cf. Rev. of Peter, 24.
[7] Cf. Rev. of Peter, 32. Not in the Greek.
[8] Not in the Greek. Whole section omitted in the Syriac.
[9] Cf. Rev. of Peter xxi. 23.
[10] Cf. Rev. of Peter, 26.
[11] Cf. Rev. of Peter. Fragments 4, 5.
[12] Not in the Greek.

taining *agapæ*, and they did not pity widows and orphans: they did not receive the stranger and the pilgrim, nor did they offer the oblations, and they did not pity their neighbour. Moreover their prayer did not even on one day ascend pure to the Lord God, but many impediments of the world detained them, and they were not able to do right in the sight of God, and the angels enclosed them in the place of punishments. Moreover they saw those who were in punishments and said to them: We indeed when we lived in the world neglected God, and ye also did likewise: as we also truly when we were in the world knew that ye were sinners. But ye said: These are just and servants of God, now we know why ye were called by the name of the Lord: for which cause they also pay their own penalties.

And sighing I wept and said: Woe unto men, woe unto sinners! why were they born? And the angel answered and said unto me: Why dost thou lament?[1] Art thou more pitiful than the Lord God who is blessed forever, who established judgment and sent forth every man to choose good and evil in his own will and do what pleases him? Then I lamented again very greatly, and he said to me: Dost thou lament when as yet thou hast not seen greater punishments? Follow me and thou shalt see seven times greater than these.

41. And he carried me south and placed me above a well, and I found it sealed with seven seals: and answering, the angel who was with me said to the angel of that place: Open the mouth of the well that Paul, the well-beloved of God, may see, for authority is given him that he may see all the pains of hell. And the angel said to me: Stand afar off that thou mayest be able to bear the stench of this place. When therefore the well was opened, immediately there arose from it a certain hard and malign stench, which surpasses all punishments: and I looked into the well and I saw fiery masses glowing in every part, and narrow places, and the mouth of the well was narrow so as to admit one man only. And the angel answered and said unto me: If any man shall have been put into this well of the abyss and it shall have been sealed over him, no remembrance of him shall ever be made in the sight of the Father and His Son and the holy angels. And I said: Who are these, Sir, who are put into this well? And he said to me: They are whoever shall not confess that Christ has come in the flesh and that the Virgin Mary brought him forth, and whoever says that the bread and cup of the Eucharist of blessing are not this body and blood of Christ.

42. And I looked to the south in the west and I saw there a[2] restless worm and in that place there was gnashing of teeth: moreover the worms were one cubit long, and had two heads, and there I saw men and women in cold and gnashing of teeth. And I asked and said, Sir, who are these in this place? And he said to me: These are they who say that Christ did not rise from the dead and that this flesh will not rise again. And I asked and said: Sir, is there no fire nor heat in this place? And he said to me: In this place there is nothing else but cold and snow:[3] and again he said to me: Even if the sun should rise upon them, they do not become warm on account of the superabundant cold of that place and the snow.

But hearing these things I stretched out my hands and wept, and sighing again, I said: It were better for us if we had not been born,[4] all of us who are sinners.

43. But when those who were in the same place saw me weeping with the angel, they themselves cried out and wept saying, Lord God have mercy upon us! And after these things I saw the heavens open, and Michael[5] the archangel descending from heaven, and with him was the whole army of angels, and they came to those who were placed in punishment and seeing him, again weeping, they cried out and said, Have pity on us! Michael the archangel, have pity on us and on the human race, for on account of thy prayers the earth standeth. We now see the judgment and acknowledge the Son of God! It was impossible for us before these things to pray for this, before we entered into this place: for we heard that there was a judgment before we went out of the world, but impediments and the life of the world did not allow us to repent. And Michael answered and said: Hear Michael speaking! I am he who stands in the sight of God every hour: As the Lord liveth, in whose sight I stand, I do not intermit one day or one night praying incessantly for the human race, and I indeed pray for those who are on the earth: but they do not cease doing iniquity and fornications, and they do not bring to me any good while they are placed on earth: and ye have con-

[1] Not in the Greek.

[2] Cf. Rev. of Peter, 27.

[3] Not in the Greek.

[4] Cf. Esdras, Ante-Nicene Lib., vol. viii., p. 571.

[5] *Gabriel* in the Greek version.

sumed in vanity the time in which ye ought to have repented. But I have always prayed thus and I now beseech that God may send dew and send forth rains upon the earth, and now I desire until the earth produce its fruits and verily I say, that if any have done but a little good, I will agonise for him, protecting him till he have escaped the judgment of penalties. Where therefore are your prayers? Where are your penances? Ye have lost your time contemptuously. But now weep and I will weep with you and the angels who are with me with the well-beloved Paul, if perchance the merciful God will have pity and give you refreshment. But hearing these words they cried out and wept greatly, and all said with one voice: Have pity on us, Son of God! And I, Paul, sighed and said: O Lord God! have pity on thy creature, have pity on the sons of men, have pity on thine image.

44. And I looked and saw the heaven move like a tree shaken by the wind. Suddenly, moreover, they threw themselves on their faces in the sight of the throne. And I saw twenty-four elders and twenty-four thousand adoring God, and I saw an altar and veil and throne, and all were rejoicing; and the smoke of a good odour was raised near the altar of the throne of God, and I heard the voice of one saying: For the sake of what do ye our angels and ministers intercede? And they cried out saying: We intercede seeing thy many kindnesses to the human race. And after these things I saw the Son of God descending from heaven, and a diadem was on his head. And seeing him those who were placed in punishment exclaimed all with one voice saying: Have pity, Son of the High God! Thou art He who shewest refreshment for all in the heavens and on earth, and on us likewise have pity, for since we have seen Thee, we have refreshment. And a voice went out from the Son of God through all the punishments saying: And what work have ye done that ye demand refreshment from me? My blood was poured out for your sakes, and not even so did ye repent: for your sakes I wore the crown of thorns on my head: for you I received buffets on my cheeks, and not even so did ye repent. I asked water when hanging on the cross and they gave me vinegar mixed with gall, with a spear they opened my right side, for my name's sake they slew my prophets and just men, and in all these things I gave you a place of repentance and ye would not. Now, however, for the sake of Michael the archangel of my covenant and the angels who are with him, and because of Paul the well-beloved, whom I would not vex, for the sake of your brethren who are in the world and offer oblations, and for the sake of your sons, because my precepts are in them, and more for the sake of mine own kindness, on the day on which I rose from the dead, I give to you all who are in punishment a night and a day of refreshment forever. And they all cried out and said, We bless thee, Son of God, that Thou hast given us a night and a day of respite. For better to us is a refreshment of one day above all the time of our life which we were on earth, and if we had plainly known that this was intended for those who sin, we would have worked no other work, we would have done no business, and we would have done no iniquity: what need had we for pride in the world? For here our pride is crushed which ascended from our mouth against our neighbour: our plagues and excessive straitness and the tears and the worms which are under us, these are much worse to us than the pains which we have left behind us. When they said thus, the malign angels of the penalties were angered with them, saying: How long do ye lament and sigh? for ye had no pity. For this is the judgment of God who had no pity. But ye received this great grace of a day and a night's refreshment on the Lord's Day for the sake of Paul the well-beloved of God who descended to you.

45. And after that the angel said to me: Hast thou seen all these things? And I said: Yes, Sir. And he said to me: Follow me and I will lead thee into Paradise, that the just who are there may see thee, for lo! they hope to see thee, and they are ready to come to meet thee in joy and gladness. And I followed the angel by the impulse of the Holy Spirit, and he placed me in Paradise and said to me: This is Paradise in which Adam and his wife erred. Moreover I entered Paradise and saw the beginning of waters, and there was an angel making a sign to me and he said to me: Observe, said he, the waters, for this is the river of Physon which surrounds all the land of Evilla, and the second is Geon which surrounds all the land of Egypt and Ethiopia, and the third is Thigris which is over against the Assyrians, and another is Eufrates which waters all the land of Mesopotamia. And when I had gone inside I saw a tree planted from whose roots water flowed out, and from this beginning there were four rivers. And the spirit of God rested on that tree, and when the Spirit blew, the waters flowed forth,

and I said: My Lord, is it this tree itself which makes the waters flow? And he said to me: That from the beginning, before the heavens and earth were manifested, and all things here invisible, the Spirit of God was borne upon the waters, but from the time when the command of God made the heavens and earth to appear, the Spirit rested upon this tree: wherefore whenever the Spirit blows, the waters flow forth from the tree. And he held me by the hand and led me near the tree of knowledge of good and evil, and he said: This is the tree by which death entered into the world, and receiving of it through his wife Adam ate and death entered into the world. And he shewed me another tree in the midst of Paradise, and saith to me: This is the tree of life.

46. While I was yet looking upon the tree, I saw a virgin coming from afar and two hundred angels before her saying hymns, and I asked and said: Sir, who is she who comes in so great glory? And he said to me: This is Mary the Virgin, the Mother of the Lord. And coming near she saluted me and said: Hail, Paul! well-beloved of God and angels and men. For all the saints prayed my Son Jesus who is my Lord that thou mightest come hither in the body that they might see thee before thou goest out of the world. And the Lord said to them: Bear and be patient: yet a little and ye shall see him and he shall be with you for ever: and again they all said to him together: Do not vex us, for we desire to see him in the flesh, for by him Thy name was greatly glorified in the world, and we have seen that he endured all the labours whether of the greater or of the less. This we learn from those who come hither. For when we say: Who is he who directed you in the world? they reply to us: There is one in the world whose name is Paul, he preaches and announces Christ, and we believe that many have entered into the kingdom through the virtue and sweetness of his speeches. Behold all the just men are behind me coming to meet thee, Paul, and I first come for this cause to meet them who did the will of my Son and my Lord Jesus Christ, I first advance to meet them and do not send them away to be as wanderers until they meet in peace.

47. When she had thus spoken, I saw three coming from afar, very beautiful in the likeness of Christ, and their forms were shining, and their angels, and I asked: Sir, who are these? And he said to me: Dost thou not know those? And I said: No, Sir. And he answered: These are the fathers of the people, Abraham, Isaac, and Jacob. And coming near they saluted me, and said: Hail, Paul, well-beloved of God and men; blessed is he who suffers violence for the Lord's sake. And Abraham answered me and said: This is my son Isaac, and Jacob my well-beloved, and we have known the Lord and followed him; blessed are all they who believed in thy word, that they may be able to inherit the Kingdom of God by labour, by renunciation, and sanctification, and humility, and charity, and meekness, and right faith in the Lord; and we also have had devotion to the Lord whom thou preachest in the testament, that we might assist those who believed in him with their whole soul, and might minister unto them as fathers minister to their children.

When they had thus spoken, I saw other twelve coming from afar in honour, and I asked: Sir, who are these? And he said: These are the patriarchs. And coming near they saluted me and said: Hail, Paul, well-beloved of God and men: the Lord did not vex us, that we might see thee yet in the body, before thou goest out of the world. And each one of them reminded me of his name in order, from Ruben to Benjamin: and Joseph said to me: I am he who was sold; but I say to thee, Paul, that all the things, whatever my brothers did to me, in nothing did I act maliciously with them, nor in all the labour which they imposed on me, nor in any point was I hurt by them on that account from morning till evening: blessed is he who receives some hurt on account of the Lord, and bears it, for the Lord will repay it to him manifold, when he shall have gone out of the world.

48. When he had spoken thus far, I saw another beautiful one coming from afar, and his angels saying hymns, and I asked: Sir, who is this that is beautiful of countenance? And he saith to me: Dost thou not know him? And I said: No, Sir. And he said to me: This is Moses the law-giver, to whom God gave the law. And when he had come near me, he immediately wept, and after that he saluted me: and I said to him: What dost thou lament? for I have heard that thou excellest every man in meekness. And he answered saying: I weep for those whom I planted with toil, because they did not bear fruit, nor did any profit by them; and I saw all the sheep whom I fed, that they were scattered and become as if they had no shepherd, and because all the toils which I

endured for the sake of the sons of Israel were accounted as naught, and how greatsoever virtues I did in the midst of them these they did not understand, and I wonder that strangers and uncircumcised and idol-worshippers have been converted and have entered into the promises of God, but Israel has not entered; and now I say unto thee, brother Paul, that in that hour when the people hanged Jesus whom thou preachest, that the Father, the God of all, who gave me the law, and Michael and all the angels and archangels, and Abraham and Isaac, and Jacob, and all the just wept over the Son of God hanging on the cross. In that hour all the saints attended on me looking (upon me) and they said to me: See, Moses, what men of thy people have done to the Son of God. Wherefore thou art blessed, Paul, and blessed the generation and race which believed in thy word.

49. When he had spoken thus far, there came other twelve, and seeing me said: Art thou Paul the glorified in heaven and on earth? And I answered and said: What are ye? The first answered and said: I am Esaias whom Manasses cut asunder with a wooden saw. And the second said likewise: I am Jeremias who was stoned by the children of Israel and slain. And the third said: I am Ezekiel whom the children of Israel dragged by the feet over a rock in a mountain till they knocked out my brains, and we endured all these toils, wishing to save the children of Israel: and I say unto thee that after the toils which they laid upon me, I cast myself on my face in the sight of the Lord praying for them, bending my knees until the second hour of the Lord's day, till Michael came and lifted me up from the earth. Blessed art thou, Paul, and blessed the nation which believed through thee.

And as these passed by, I saw another, beautiful of countenance, and I asked: Sir, Who is this? Who when he had seen me, rejoiced and said to me: This is Lot[1] who was found just in Sodom. And approaching[2] he saluted me and said: Blessed art thou, Paul, and blessed the generation to which thou didst minister. And I answered and said to him: Art thou Lot who wast found just in Sodom? And he said: I entertained angels, as travellers, and when they of the city wished to violate them, I offered them my two virgin daughters who had not yet known men, and gave them to them saying: use them as ye will, but only to these men ye shall do no evil; for this cause they entered under the roof of my house. For this cause, therefore, we ought to be confident and know that if anyone shall have done anything, God shall repay him manifold when they shall come to him. Blessed art thou, Paul, and blessed the nation which believed in thy word.

When, therefore, he had ceased talking to me, I saw another coming from a distance, very beautiful of countenance, and smiling, and his angels saying hymns: and I said to the angel who was with me: Has then each of the just an angel for companion? And he said to me: Each one of the saints has his own (angel) assisting him, and saying a hymn, and the one does not depart from the other. And I said: Who is this, Sir? And he said: This is Job. And approaching, he saluted me and said: Brother Paul, thou hast great praise with God and men. And I am Job, who laboured much for a period of thirty years from a plague in the blood; and verily in the beginning, the wounds which went forth from my body were like grains of wheat. But on the third day, they became as the foot of an ass; worms moreover which fell four digits in length: and on the third (day) the devil appeared and said to me: Say something against God and die. I said to him: If such be the will of God that I should remain under a plague all the time of my life till I die, I shall not cease from blessing the Lord, and I shall receive more reward. For I know that the labours of that world are nothing to the refreshment which is afterwards: for which cause blessed art thou, Paul, and blessed the nation which believed through thee.

50. When he had spoken thus far, another came calling from afar and saying: Blessed art thou, Paul, and blessed am I because I saw thee, the beloved of the Lord. And I asked the angel: Sir, who is this? And he answered and said unto me: This is Noe in the time of the deluge. And immediately we saluted each other: and greatly rejoicing he said to me: Thou art Paul the most beloved of God. And I asked him: Who art thou? And he said: I am Noe, who was in the time of the deluge. And I say to thee, Paul, that working for a hundred years, I made the ark, not putting off the tunic with which I was clad, nor did I cut the hair of my head. Till then also I cherished continence, not approaching my own wife: in those hundred years not a hair of my head grew in length, nor did my garments

[1] Lot and Job, in the Syriac but not in the Greek.
[2] For *adproprians* read *adpropinquans*.

become soiled: and I besought men at all times saying: Repent, for a deluge of waters will come upon you. But they laughed at me, and mocked my words; and again they said to me: But this is the time of those who are able to play and sin freely, desiring her with whom it is possible to commit fornication frequently: for God does not regard this, and does not know what things are done by us men, and there is no flood of waters straightway coming upon this world. And they did not cease from their sins, till God destroyed all flesh which had the breath of life in it. Know then that God loveth one just man more than all the world of the impious. Wherefore, blessed art thou, Paul, and blessed is the nation which believes through thee.

51. And turning round, I saw other just ones coming from afar, and I asked the angel: Sir, who are those? And he answered me: These are Elias and Eliseus.[1] And they saluted me: and I said to them: Who are ye? And one of them answered and said: I am Elias, the prophet of God; I am Elias who prayed, and because of my word, the heaven did not rain for three years and six months, on account of the unrighteousness of men. God is just and true, who doeth the will of his servants: for the angels often besought the Lord for rain, and he said: Be patient till my servant Elias shall pray and petition for this and I will send rain on the earth.[2]

[1] Elias and Eliseus. Latin and Syriac. The Greek has Enoch and Elijah.

[2] The Latin version here breaks off abruptly, as does also the Greek. In the Syriac as translated by the Rev. J. Perkins, D.D. (cf. Journal of Sacred Literature, N. S., vi., 1865, p. 399), the narrative runs as follows: "And often the angels asked that he would give them rain, and he gave not, until I called upon him again; then he gave unto them. But blessed art thou, O Paul, that thy generation, and those thou teachest, are the sons of the kingdom. And know thou, O Paul, that every man who believes through thee hath a great blessing, and a blessing is reserved for him." Then he departed from me.

And the angel who was with me led me forth, and said unto me: "Lo, unto thee is given this mystery and revelation; as thou pleasest, make it known unto the sons of men." And I, Paul, returned unto myself, and I knew all that I had seen; and in life I had not rest that I might reveal this mystery, but I wrote it and deposited it under the ground and the foundation of a certain faithful man with whom I used to be, in Tarsus, a city of Cilicia. And when I was released from this life of time and stood before my Lord, thus said He unto me: "Paul, have we shown all these things unto thee, that thou shouldst deposit them under the foundation of a house? Then send, and disclose, concerning this Revelation that men may read it, and turn to the way of truth, that they also may not come to these bitter torments."

Then follows the story of the discovery of the Revelation at Tarsus in the reign of Theodosius as given at the beginning of the Greek and Latin versions.

THE END OF THE VISION OF SAINT PAUL.

THE APOCALYPSE OF THE VIRGIN

The present translation of this Apocalypse[1] is made from the text as published by Mr. M. R. James in *Texts and Studies*, ii., 3, from a MS. in the Bodleian Library, which he assigns to the eleventh century. The original he conjecturally assigns to the ninth century, and regards it as a late and clumsy compilation based on (1) the Assumption Legends and (2) the Apocalypse of Paul. Its main feature, intercession for the lost, it has in common with the Testament of Abraham, the Apocalypse of Paul, 4 Esdras, the Apocalypse of Baruch, the Apocalypse of Esdras and the Apocalypse of Sedrach. Parallels are pointed out in the notes.

[1] In this Apocalypse and that of Sedrach which follows, the text is in many places so obviously corrupt that the translator cannot be confident that he has given the correct meaning of the original in all cases.—A. R.

THE APOCALYPSE OF THE HOLY MOTHER OF GOD CONCERNING THE CHASTISEMENTS

I. The all-holy mother of God was about to proceed to the Mount of Olives to pray; and praying to the Lord our God she said: In the name of the Father and the Son and the Holy Spirit; let the archangel Gabriel descend, that he may tell me concerning the chastisements and concerning things in heaven and on the earth and under the earth. And as she said the word the archangel Michael descended with the angels of the East and the West and angels of the South and the North, and they saluted the highly favoured one and said to her: Hail, reflection of the Father, hail dwelling of the Son, hail command of the Holy Spirit, hail firmament of the seven heavens, hail firmament of the eleven strongholds, hail worship of the angels, hail loftier than the prophets unto the throne of God. And the holy mother of God said to the angel: Hail Michael, commander-in-chief, the minister of the invisible Father, hail· Michael, commander-in-chief, associate of my Son, hail Michael, commander-in-chief, most dread of the six-winged, hail Michael, commander-in-chief, who rules through all things and art worthy to stand beside the throne of the Lord, hail Michael, commander-in-chief, who art about to sound the trumpet and awaken those who have been asleep for ages: hail Michael, commander-in-chief, first of all unto the throne of God.

II. And having greeted all the angels in like manner, the highly favoured one prayed the commander-in-chief regarding the chastisements, saying: Tell to me all things on the earth. And the commander-in-chief said to her: If thou askest me, highly favoured one, I will tell thee. And the highly favoured one said to him: How many are the chastisements with which the race of man is chastised? And the archangel said to her: The chastisements are innumerable. And the highly favoured one said to him: Tell me the things in heaven and on the earth.

III. Then the commander-in-chief, Michael, commanded the Western angels that revelation should be made, and Hades opened, and she saw those who were chastised[1] in Hades: and there lay there a multitude of men and women, and there was a great lamentation. And the highly favoured one asked the commander-in-chief: Who are these and what is their sin? And the commander-in-chief said: These, all holy, are those who did not worship the Father and the Son and the Holy Spirit and for this cause they are thus chastised here.

IV. And she saw in another place[2] a great darkness: and the all holy said: What is this darkness and who are they who are being chastised? And the commander-in-chief said: Many souls are lying in this darkness. And the all holy one said: Let this darkness be taken away in order that I may see this chastisement also. And the commander-in-chief said to the highly favoured one: It is not possible, all holy, that thou shouldst see this chastisement also. And the angels guarding them answered and said: We have a command from the invisible Father that they shall not see the light till thy blessed Son shall shine forth. And plunged in grief the all holy lifted up her eyes to the angels touching the undefiled word of the Father, and said: In the name of the Father and the Son and the Holy Spirit let the darkness be taken away, that I may see this chastisement also. And straightway that darkness was lifted up and covered the seven heavens: and there lay a great multitude of both men and women, and there arose

---

[1] Cf. Vision of Paul, 31.
[2] Rev. of Peter, 21. Paul, 37.

a great lamentation and a great cry began. And seeing them the all holy wept and said to them: What are ye doing, wretched ones? Who are ye? And how are ye found there? and there was no voice or hearkening. And the angels guarding them said: Why do ye not speak to the highly favoured one? And those who were under chastisement said to her: O highly favoured one, from eternity we see not the light, and we are not able to keep off that up there. And splashing pitch flowed down upon them: and seeing them the all holy wept. And again those who were being chastised said to her: How dost thou ask concerning us, holy lady, Mother of God? Thy blessed Son came to the earth and did not make enquiry concerning us, neither Abraham the patriarch, nor John the Baptist, nor Moses the great prophet, nor the Apostle Paul, and unto us their light shone not: and now, all holy Mother of God, the armour of the Christians, the bringer of great comfort on account of the Christians, how dost thou ask concerning us? Then the all holy Mother of God said to Michael, the commander-in-chief: What is their sin? And Michael, the commander-in-chief, said: These are they who did not believe in the Father and the Son and the Holy Spirit, and did not confess thee[1] to be the Mother of God, and that the Lord Jesus Christ was born of thee and took flesh, and for this cause they are chastised there. And again weeping, the all holy Mother of God said to them: Why did ye so greatly err, wretched ones? Did ye not hear that the whole creation names my name? And having said these words the darkness fell over them as it was from the beginning.

V. And the commander-in-chief said: Whither wouldst thou go, highly favoured one? to the West or to the South? And the highly favoured answered: Let us go to the South. And immediately there appeared the cherubim and the seraphim and four hundred angels, and led out the highly favoured one to the South, where came out the river of fire,[2] and there there lay a multitude of men and women, some up to the girdle, others up to the neck, and others up to the crown of the head: and seeing them the all holy Mother of God cried out with a loud voice to the commander-in-chief and said: Who are these, and what is their sin who stand in the fire up to the girdle? And the commander-in-chief said: These, all holy one, are they who inherited the curse of father and mother, and for this cause they are thus chastised here as accursed.

VI. And the all holy one said: And who are these standing in the fire up to the breasts? And the commander-in-chief said: These are whosoever cast off their wives and defiled them in adultery, and for this cause they are thus chastised here.

VII. And the all holy one said to the commander-in-chief: Who are these standing up to the neck in the flame of the fire? And the commander-in-chief said: These, all holy one, are whosoever ate of the flesh of men. And the all holy one said: And how is it possible for one man to eat of the flesh of another? And the commander-in-chief said: Listen, all holy one, and I will tell thee: These are they whosoever brought down their own children out of their own wombs and cast them out[3] as food for dogs, and whosoever gave up their brothers in the presence of kings and governors, these ate the flesh of man, and for this cause they are thus chastised.

VIII. And the all holy one said: Who are these set in the fire up to the crown? And the commander-in-chief said: These, all holy one, are whosoever lay hold of the precious cross and swear to a lie: by the power of the cross of the Lord. The angels tremble and worship with fear, and men lay hold of it and swear to a lie and do not know what they testify: and for this cause they are thus chastised here.

IX. And in another place the all holy one saw a man hung by the feet,[4] and worms devoured him. And she asked the commander-in-chief: Who is this and what is his sin? And the commander-in-chief said: This is he who took usury[5] for his gold, and for this cause he is thus chastised here.

X. And she saw a woman hanging by her two ears, and all the beasts[6] came out of her mouth and gnawed her in pieces: and the highly favoured one asked the commander-in-chief: Who is she, and what is her sin? And the commander-in-chief said: She is she who turned aside into strange houses and those of her neighbours and spoke evil words to make strife, and for that cause she is thus chastised here.

XI. And seeing these things the all holy Mother of God wept and said to the commander-in-chief: It were well for man that he

[1] Cf. Paul, 41.
[2] Cf. Paul, 31.
[3] Cf. Peter, Frag.; Paul, 40; Peter, 27.
[4] Cf. Peter, 24.
[5] Cf. Peter, 31; Paul, 37.
[6] Cf. Peter, Frag. 2.

had not been born. And the commander-in-chief said: Verily, all holy one, thou hast not seen the great chastisements. And the all holy one said to the commander-in-chief: Come, Michael, great commander-in-chief, and lead me that I may see all the chastisements. And the commander-in-chief said: Where dost thou wish, all holy one, that we should go? And the highly favoured one answered: To the West: and straightway the cherubim appeared and led the highly favoured to the West.

XII. And she saw a cloud full of fire and in it there was a[1] multitude of men and women. And the all holy one said: What was their sin? And the commander-in-chief said: These, all holy one, are they who on the morning of the Lord's day sleep like the dead, and for that reason they are thus chastised here. And the all holy one said: If anyone cannot rise, what shall he do? And the commander-in-chief said: Listen, all holy one: if anyone's house is fastened on the four (sides?) and surrounds him and he cannot come out, he has forgiveness.

XIII. And she saw in another place burning benches of fire and on them sat a multitude of men and women and burned on them. And the all holy one asked: Who are these and what is their sin? And the commander-in-chief said: These, all holy one, are they who do not rise up to the presbyter when they enter into the church of God, and for this cause they are thus chastised here.

XIV. And the all holy one saw in another place an iron tree and it had branches of iron, and on it there hung a multitude of men and women by their tongues.[2] And seeing them the all holy one wept, and asked the commander-in-chief saying: Who are these and what was their sin? And the commander-in-chief said: These are perjurers, blasphemers, slanderers, whosoever divided brothers from brothers. And the all holy one said: How is it possible to divide brothers from brothers? And the commander-in-chief said: Listen, all holy one, and I will tell thee about this: When some from among the nations desired to be baptised, he would say to them one word: Thou foul-feeding, unbelieving Gentile; because he thus blasphemed, he shall receive ceaseless retribution.

XV. And in another place the all holy one saw a man hanging from his four extremities, and from his nails blood gushed vehemently, and his tongue[3] was tied in a flame of fire, and he was unable to groan and say the *Kyrie eleïson me*. And when she had seen him the all holy one wept and herself said the *Kyrie eleïson* thrice : and after the saying of the prayer, came the angel who had authority over the scourge and loosed the man's tongue: and the all holy one asked the commander-in-chief: Who is this wretched one who has this chastisement? And the commander-in-chief said: This, all holy one, is the steward who did not the will of God, but ate the things of the church and said: "He who ministers to the altar shall be nourished from the altar":[4] and for this cause he is thus chastised here. And the all holy one said: Let it be unto him according to his faith. And again he tied his tongue.

XVI. And Michael, the commander-in-chief said: Come hither, all holy one, and I will show unto thee where the priests are chastised. And the all holy one came out and saw presbyters hanging by their twenty nails, and fire came out of their heads. And seeing them the all holy one asked the commander-in-chief: Who are these and what is their sin? And the commander-in-chief said: These, all holy one, are they who stand beside the throne of God, and when they sang of the body of our Lord Jesus Christ, the pearls fell out, and the awful throne of heaven shook and the footstool of our Lord Jesus Christ trembled, and they did not perceive it: and for this cause they are thus chastised here.

XVII. And the all holy one saw a man and a winged beast having three heads like flames of fire: the two heads were towards his eyes and the third head towards his mouth. And seeing him the all holy one asked the commander-in-chief: Who is this, that he cannot save himself from the mouth of the dragon? And the commander-in-chief said to her: This, all holy one, is the reader who does not practise in his own habits according to what is worthy of the holy Gospel: and for this cause he is thus chastised here.

XVIII. And the commander-in-chief said: Come hither, all holy one, and I will show thee where the angelic and archangelic form is chastised. She proceeded and saw[5] them lying in the fire and the sleepless worm gnawed them: and the all holy one said: Who are these, and what is their sin? And the commander-in-chief said: These, all holy one,

[1] Cf. Peter, 25.
[2] Cf. Peter, 22.
[3] Cf. Peter, 29.
[4] Cf. Lev. x. 12ff; Num. xviii. 7ff.
[5] Cf. Peter, 27.

are they who possessed the archangelic and apostolic form: hearken, all holy one, concerning this: on earth they were called patriarchs and bishops, and they were not worthy of their name: on earth they heard 'Bless (the Lord) ye saints,' and in heaven they were not called saints, because they did not act as bearers of the archangelic form: and for this cause they are thus chastised here.

XIX. And she saw women hanging by their nails, and a flame of fire came out of their mouth and burned them: and all the beasts[1] coming out of the fire gnawed them to pieces, and groaning they cried out: Have pity on us, have pity, for we are chastised worse than all those who are under chastisement. And seeing them the all holy one wept, and asked the commander-in-chief, Michael: Who are these and what is their sin? And the commander-in-chief said: These are the wives of presbyters who did not honour the presbyters, but after the death of the presbyter took husbands, and for this cause they are thus chastised here.

XX. And the all holy one saw after the same manner also a deaconess hanging from a crag and a beast with two heads devoured her breasts. And the all holy one asked: What is her sin? And the commander-in-chief said: She, all holy one, is an archdeaconess who defiled her body in fornication, and for this cause she is thus chastised here.

XXI. And she saw other women hanging over the fire, and all the beasts devoured them. And the all holy one asked the commander-in-chief: Who are these and what is their sin? And he said: These are they who did not do the will of God, lovers of money and those who took interest[2] on accounts, and the immodest.

XXII. And when she had heard these things the all holy one wept and said: Woe unto sinners. And the commander-in-chief said: Why dost thou lament, all holy one? Now verily thou hast not seen the great chastisemnts. And the highly favoured one said: Come, Michael, the great commander-in-chief of the powers above, tell me how I may see all the chastisements. And the commander-in-chief said: Where dost thou wish that we should go, all holy one? to the East or towards the left parts of Paradise? And the all holy one said: To the left parts of Paradise.

XXIII. And immediately when she had spoken, the cherubim and seraphim stood beside her and led the highly favoured one out to the left parts of Paradise. And behold, there was a great river, and the appearance of the river was blacker than pitch, and in it there were a multitude[3] of men and women: it boiled like a furnace of forges, and its waves were like a wild sea over the sinners: and when the waves rose, they sank the sinners ten thousand cubits and they were unable to keep it off and say: Have mercy on us, thou just judge: for the sleepless worm devoured them, and there was no reckoning of the number of those who devoured them. And seeing the all holy Mother of God the angels[4] who chastised them cried out with one voice: Holy is God who has compassion on account of the Mother of God: we give thee thanks, O Son of God, that from eternity we did not see the light, and to-day through the Mother of God we have seen the light: and again they shouted with one voice, saying: Hail, highly favoured Mother of God: Hail, lamp of the inaccessible light: Hail to thee also, Michael, the commander-in-chief, thou that art ambassador from the whole creation: for we, seeing the chastisement of sinners are greatly grieved. And the all holy one, when she saw the angels humbled on account of the sinners, lamented and said: Woe to sinners and their neighbours. And the all holy one said: Let us see the sinners. And the highly favoured one, coming with the archangel Michael and all the armies of the angels lifted up one voice saying: Lord have mercy. And after the making of the prayer earnestly, the wave of the river rested and the fiery waves grew calm, and the sinners appeared as a grain of mustard-seed: and seeing them the all holy one lamented and said: What is this river, and what are its waves? And the commander-in-chief said: This river is the outer fire, and those who are being tortured are the Jews who crucified our Lord Jesus Christ the Son of God, and who refused holy baptism, and those who commit fornication and sin against the sweet and passionless perfume of marriage, and he who debauches mother and daughter, and the poisoners and those who slay with the sword, and the women who strangle their offspring. And the all holy one said: According to their faith so be it unto them. And straightway the waves rose over the sinners and the darkness

[1] Cf. Peter fr. ap. Clem. Alex.
[2] Cf. Peter, 31.
[3] Cf. Paul, 31.
[4] Cf. Peter, 23.

covered them. And the commander-in-chief said: Hearken, thou highly favoured one: if anyone shall be cast into this darkness,[1] his remembrance shall never be in the sight of God. And the all holy Mother of God said: Woe to sinners, because the flame of the fire is everlasting.

XXIV. And the commander-in-chief said: Come hither, all holy one, and I will show unto thee the lake of fire: and see thou where the race of the Christians is chastised.[2] And the all holy one proceeded and saw: and some she heard, but others she did not see: and she asked the commander-in-chief: Who are these, and what is their sin? And the commander-in-chief said: These, all holy one, are those who were baptised and arrayed under the oracle of Christ, but worked the works of the devil and wasted the time of their repentance: and for this cause they are thus chastised here.

XXV. And she said: I pray, one request will I make of thee, let me also be chastised with the Christians, because they are the children of my son. And the commander-in-chief said: Rest thou in Paradise, holy lady, Mother of God. And the all holy one said: I pray thee, move the fourteen firmaments and the seven heavens, and let us pray for the Christians that the Lord our God may hearken unto us and have mercy on them.[3] And the commander-in-chief said: As the Lord God liveth, the great name, seven times a day and seven times a night, when we lead up the hymn of the Lord, we make remembrance for the sake of sinners, and the Lord accounts us as naught.

XXVI. And the all holy one said: I pray thee, commander-in-chief, command the armies of the angels and let them place me on the height of heaven and let me into the presence of the invisible Father. And immediately the commander-in-chief commanded, and the chariot of the cherubim and seraphim appeared, and they exalted the highly favoured one to the height of heaven and placed her in the presence of the invisible Father: And she stretched forth her hands to the undefiled throne of the Father and said: Have mercy, O Lord, on the Christian sinners, for I saw them being chastised and I cannot bear their complaint. Let me go forth and be chastised myself for the Christians. I do not pray, O Lord, for the unbelieving Jews, but for the Christians I entreat thy compassion. And there came a second voice from the invisible Father saying: How can I have mercy on them, when they did not have mercy on their own brothers?[4] And the all holy one said: Lord, have mercy on the sinners: behold the chastisements, for every creature on the earth calls upon my name: and when the soul comes forth out of the body, it cries saying, "Holy Lady, Mother of God." Then the Lord said to her: Hearken, all holy Mother of God, if anyone names and calls upon thy name, I will not forsake him, either in heaven or on earth.

XXVII. And the all holy one said: Where is Moses? Where are all the prophets and fathers who never sinned? Where art thou, holy Paul of God? where is the holy Lord's Day, the boast of the Christians? where is the power of the precious and life-giving cross, which delivered Adam and Eve from the ancient curse? Then Michael and all the angels raised one voice saying: Lord, have mercy on the sinners. Then Moses also cried: Have mercy, Lord, on those to whom I gave thy law. Then John also called: Have mercy, Lord, on those to whom I gave thy Gospel. Then Paul cried: Have mercy, Lord, on those to whom I brought thy epistles in the Church. And the Lord God said: Hearken, all ye righteous: if according to the law which Moses gave, and according to the Gospel which John gave, and according to the epistles which Paul carried, they thus be judged. And they had nothing to say except, Have mercy, O just judge.

XXVIII. And the all holy Mother of God said: Have mercy, Lord, on the Christians, because they kept thy law and gave heed to thy gospel, but they were simple ones. Then the Lord said to her: Hearken, all holy one: if anyone did evil to them and they did not requite him the evil, thou sayest well that they attended to both my law and my gospel, but if he did not do them wrong and they requited him evil, how may I say that these are holy men? now they shall be rewarded according to their wrongdoing. Then all hearing the voice of the Lord had nothing to answer; and the all holy one, when she saw that the saints were at a loss, and their Lord did not hear, and his mercy was hidden from them, then the all holy one said: Where is Gabriel, who announced unto me the "Hail, thou that from eternity shalt conceive him who is without beginning like the Father," and now does not look upon sinners? Where

[1] Cf. Paul, 41.
[2] Cf. Esdras. Ante-Nicene Lib., vol. viii., p. 573.
[3] Cf. Paul, 43.
[4] Cf. Esdras, l. c., pp. 469, 470.

is the great commander-in-chief? come hither, all ye saints whom God justified, and let us fall down in the presence of the invisible Father, in order that the Lord God may hear us, and have mercy on sinners. Then Michael, the commander-in-chief, and all the saints fell on their faces in the presence of the invisible Father, saying: Have mercy, Lord, on the Christian sinners.

XXIX. Then the Lord, seeing the prayer of the saints, had compassion and said: Go down, my beloved son, and because of the prayer of the saints let thy face shine on earth to sinners. Then the Lord came down from his undefiled throne: and when they saw Him, those who were under chastisement raised one voice saying: Have mercy on us, King of ages. Then the Lord of all things said: Hearken, all ye sinners and righteous men: I made paradise and made man after my image: but he transgressed, and for his own sins was delivered to death: but I did not suffer the works of my hands to be tyrannized over by the serpent: wherefore I bowed the heavens and came down and was born of Mary, the holy undefiled Mother of God, that I might set you free: I was baptised in Jordan in order that I might save the creature (nature) which had grown old under sin: I was nailed to the cross[1] to free you from the ancient curse: I asked for water and ye gave me vinegar mingled with gall: I was laid in the grave: I trampled on the enemy: I raised up mine elect, and even thus ye would not hear me. But now, because[2] of the prayer of my mother Mary, because she has wept much for your sake, and because of Michael my archangel, and because of the multitude of my saints, I grant you to have rest on the day of Pentecost to glorify the Father and the Son and the Holy Spirit.

XXX. Then all the angels and archangels, thrones, lordships, authorities, governments, powers, and the many-eyed cherubim and the six-winged seraphim and all the apostles and prophets and martyrs and all the saints raised one voice, saying: Glory to thee, O Lord: glory to thee, lover of men: glory to thee, King of ages: glory be to thy compassion: glory be to thy long suffering: glory be to thy unspeakable justice of judgment, because thou hast been long-suffering with sinners and impious men: Thine is it to pity and to save. To him be the glory and the power to the Father and to the Son and to the Holy Spirit for ever and ever. Amen.

[1] Cf. Paul, 44; Esdras, l. c., p. 470.
[2] Cf. Paul, 44.

THE APOCALYPSE OF SEDRACH

THE translation is from Mr. M. R. James's text in *Texts and Studies*, ii. 3, p. 130ff., published from a fifteenth century MS. in the Bodleian Library. The original, Mr. James conjecturally assigns to the tenth or eleventh century. It is notable for its close resemblance in several passages to 4 Esdras, to the Greek original of which the author seems to have had direct access.

Like the Apocalypse of Esdras it deals with the subject of intercession for sinners and the reluctance of the seer to die. The parallel passages in 4 Esdras and the Apocalypse of Esdras are pointed out in the margin of the translation.

Chapter I. consists of a few lines from the beginning and end of a homily on love which appears in the MS. at the beginning of the Apocalypse, but which Mr. James regards as "quite unimportant and quite irrelevant."

THE APOCALYPSE OF SEDRACH

THE APOCALYPSE OF SEDRACH

THE Word of the holy and blessed Sedrach concerning love and concerning repentance and Orthodox Christians, and concerning the Second Coming of our Lord Jesus Christ. Lord give thy blessing.

I. Beloved, let us prefer nothing in honour except sincere love: for in many things we stumble every day and night and hour. And for this cause let us gain love, for it covereth a multitude of sins: for what is the profit, my children, if we have all things, and have not saving love . . .

O blessed love, supplier of all good things. Blessed is the man who has gained the true faith and sincere love, according as the Master said, there is no greater love than this that a man should lay down his life for his friend. Cf. John xv. 13.

II. And invisibly he received a voice in his ears: Come hither, Sedrach, since thou wishest and desirest to converse with God and ask of him that he may reveal unto thee whatever thou wishest to ask. And Sedrach said: What, Sir? And the voice said to him: I was sent to thee to raise thee here into heaven. And he said: I desired to speak mouth to mouth with God: I am not fit, Sir, to come into heaven. And stretching out his wings he took him up and he came into heaven to the very flame, and he set him as high as the third heaven, and in it stood the flame of the divinity.

III. And the Lord saith to him: Welcome, my beloved Sedrach: What suit hast thou against God who created thee, that thou saidst, I desired to speak face to face with God? Sedrach saith to him:[1] Yea, verily, the son hath a suit with the Father: my Lord, why didst thou make the earth? The Lord saith to him: For man's sake. Sedrach saith: And why didst Thou make the sea? Why didst Thou scatter every good thing on the earth? The Lord saith to him: For man's sake. Sedrach saith to him:[2] If thou didst these things,[3] why wilt Thou destroy him? And the Lord said: Man is my work and the creature of my hands, and I discipline him as I find good.

IV. Sedrach saith to him: Chastisement and fire are thy discipline: they are bitter, my Lord:[4] it were well for man if he had not been born: why then didst thou make him, my Lord? Why didst thou weary thine undefiled hands[5] and create man, since thou didst not intend to have mercy on him? God saith to him: I made Adam the first creature and placed him in Paradise in the midst of the tree of life and said to him: Eat of all the fruits, but beware of the tree of life: for if thou eat of it, thou shalt die the death. But he transgressed my commandment, and being beguiled by the devil ate of the tree.

V. Sedrach saith to him: Of thy will Adam was beguiled, my Lord: Thou commandest thine[6] angels to make approach to Adam, and the first of the angels himself transgressed thy commandment and did not make approach to him, and Thou didst banish him, because he transgressed thy commandment and did not make any approach to the work of thine hands: if thou lovedst man, why didst Thou not slay the devil, the worker of unrighteousness? Who is able to fight an invisible spirit? And he as a smoke enters into the hearts of men and teaches them every sin: he fights against thee, the immortal God, and what can wretched man then do to him? But have mercy, O Lord, and stop the chastisements: but if not, count me also with the sinners: if thou wilt have no mercy on the sinners, where are thy mercies, where is thy[7] compassion, O Lord?

VI. God saith to him: Be it known unto thee that I ordered all things to be placable

[1] Cf. Esdras. Ante-Nicene Lib., viii., 571.

[2] Cf. 4 Esdras viii. 15ff.

[3] Cf. Esdras, Ante-Nicene Lib., viii., p. 572.

[4] Cf. Esdras, Ante-Nicene Lib., vol. viii., p. 571.

[5] Undefiled hands. Cf. Esdras, p. 571.

[6] Angels. Cf. Esdras, p. 571.

[7] Compassion. Cf. Esdras, p. 571.

to him: I gave him understanding and made him the heir of heaven and earth, and I subjected all things to him, and every living thing flees from him and from before his face: but he, having received of mine, became alien, adulterous, and sinful: tell me, what father, having given his son his portion, when he takes his substance and leaves his father and goes away and becomes an alien and serves an alien, when the father sees that the son has deserted him, does not darken his heart, and does not the father go and take his substance and banish him from his glory because he deserted his father? And how have I, the wonderful and jealous God, given him everything, and he having received these things has become an adulterer and a sinner?

VII. Sedrach saith to him: Thou, O Lord, didst create man. Thou knewest of what sort of mind he was and of what sort of knowledge we are, and thou makest it a cause for chastisement: but cast him forth; for shall not I alone fill up the heavenly places? But if that is not to be so save man too, O Lord. He failed by thy will, wretched man. Why dost thou waste words on me, Sedrach? I created Adam and his wife and the sun and said: Behold each other how bright he is, and the wife of Adam is brighter in the beauty of the moon and he was the giver of her life.[1] Sedrach saith: but of what profit are beauties if they die away into the earth? How didst thou say, O Lord, Thou shalt not return evil for evil? How is it, O Lord? the word of Thy divinity never lies, and why dost Thou retaliate on man? or dost thou not in so doing render evil for evil? I know that among the quadrupeds there is no other so wily and unreasonable as the mule. But we strike it with the bridle when we wish: and thou hast angels: send them forth to guard them, and when man inclines towards sin, to take hold of his foot and not let him go whither he would.

VIII. God saith to him: If I catch him by the foot, he will say, Thou hast given me no joy in the world. But I have left him to his own will because I loved him. Wherefore I sent forth my righteous angels to guard him night and day. Sedrach saith:[2] I know, O Lord, that of all thy creatures Thou chiefly lovedst man, of the quadrupeds the sheep, of woods the olive, of fruits the vine, of flying things the bee, of rivers the Jordan, of cities Jerusalem. And all these man also loves, my Lord. God saith to Sedrach: I will ask thee one thing, Sedrach: if thou answerest me, then I may fitly help thee, even though thou hast tempted thy creator. Sedrach saith: Speak.[3] The Lord God saith: Since I made all things, how many men were born and how many died, and how many are to die and how many hairs have they? Tell me, Sedrach,[4] since the heaven was created and the earth, how many trees grew in the world, and how many fell, and how many are to fall, and how many are to arise, and how many leaves have they? Tell me, Sedrach, since I made the sea, how many waves arose and how many fell, and how many are to arise, and how many winds blow along the margin of the sea? Tell me, Sedrach, from the creation of the world of the æons, when the air rained, how many drops fell upon the world, and how many are to fall? And Sedrach said: Thou alone knowest all these things, O Lord; thou only understandest all these things: only, I pray thee, deliver man from chastisement, and I shall not be separated from our race.

IX. And God said to his only begotten Son: Go,[5] take the soul of Sedrach my beloved, and place it in Paradise. The only begotten Son saith to Sedrach: Give me the trust which our Father deposited in the womb of thy mother in the holy tabernacle of thy body from a child. Sedrach saith: I will not give thee my soul. God saith to him: And wherefore was I sent to come hither, and thou pleadest against me? For I was commanded by my Father not to take thy soul with violence; but if not, (then) give me thy most greatly desired soul.

X. And Sedrach saith to God : And whence dost Thou intend to take my soul, and from which limb? And God saith to him: Dost thou not know that it is placed in the midst of thy lungs and thy heart and is dispersed into all thy limbs? It is brought up through the throat and gullet and the mouth and at whatever hour it is predestined to come forth, it is scattered, and brought together from the points of the nails and from all the limbs, and there is a great necessity that it should be separated from the body and parted from the heart. When Sedrach had heard all these things and had considered the memory of death he was greatly astounded, and Sedrach said to God: O Lord,

[1] Passage corrupt; the above appears to be the best sense it admits of as it stands.
[2] Cf. iv. Esdras v. 23ff.
[3] Cf. iv. Esdras iv. 4–11, v. 36.
[4] Cf. Esdras, p. 574.
[5] Cf. *Apoc. of Esdras,* in Ante-Nicene Lib., vol. viii., p. 574, and *Testament of Abraham,* Rec. A., Chaps. vii. and xvi.

give me a little respite that I may weep, for I have heard that tears are able to do much and much remedy comes to the lowly body of thy creature.

XI. And weeping and bewailing he began to say: O marvellous head of heavenly adornment: O radiant as the sun which shines on heaven and earth: thy hairs are known from Teman, thine eyes from Bosor, thine ears from thunder, thy tongue from a trumpet, and thy brain is a small creation, thy head the energy of the whole body: O friendly and most fair beloved by all, and now falling into the earth it must become forgotten. O hands, mild, fair-fingered, worn with toil by which the body is nourished: O hands, deftest of all, heaping up from all quarters ye made ready houses. O fingers adorned and decked with gold and silver (rings): and great worlds are led by the fingers: the three joints enfold the palms, and heap up beautiful things: and now ye must become aliens to the world. O feet, skilfully walking about, self-running, most swift, unconquerable: O knees, fitted together, because without you the body does not move: the feet run along with the sun and the moon in the night and in the day, heaping up all things, foods and drinks, and nourishing the body: O feet, most swift and fair runners, moving on the face of the earth, getting ready the house with every good thing: O feet which bear up the whole body, that run up to the temples, making repentance and calling on the saints, and now ye are to remain motionless. O head and hands and feet, until now I have kept you. O soul, what sent thee into the humble and wretched body? and now being separated from it, thou art going up where the Lord calleth thee, and the wretched body goes away to judgment. O body well-adorned, hair clothed with stars, head of heavenly adornment and dress: O face well-anointed, light-bringing eyes, voice trumpet-like, tongue placable, chin fairly adorned, hairs like the stars, head high as heaven, body decked out, light-bringing eyes that know all things—and now you shall fall into the earth and under the earth your beauty shall disappear.

XII. Christ saith to him: Stay, Sedrach; how long dost thou weep and groan? Paradise is opened to thee, and, dying, thou shalt live. Sedrach saith to him: Once more I will speak unto thee, O Lord: How long shall I live before I die? and do not disregard my prayer. The Lord saith to him: Speak, O Sedrach. Sedrach saith: If a man shall live eighty or ninety or an hundred years, and live these years in sin, and again shall turn, and the man live in repentance, in how many days dost thou forgive him his sins? God saith to him: If he shall live an hundred or eighty years and shall turn and repent for three years and do the fruit of righteousness, and death shall overtake him, I will not remember all his sins.

XIII. Sedrach saith to him: The three years are a long time, my Lord, lest death overtake him and he fulfil not his repentance: have mercy, Lord, on thine image and have compassion, for the three years are many. God saith to him: If a man live an hundred years and remember his death and confess before men and I find him, after a time I will forgive all his sins. Sedrach saith again: I will again beseech thy compassion for thy creature. The time is long lest death overtake him and snatch him suddenly. The Saviour saith to him: I will ask thee one word, Sedrach, my beloved, then thou shalt ask me in turn: if the man shall repent for forty days I will not remember all his sins which he did.

XIV. And Sedrach saith[1] to the archangel Michael: Hearken to me, O powerful chief, and help thou me and be my envoy that God may have mercy on the world. And falling on their faces, they besought the Lord and said: O Lord, teach us how and by what sort of repentance and by what labour man shall be saved. God saith: By repentances, by intercessions, by liturgies, by tears in streams, in hot groanings. Dost thou not know that my prophet David was saved by tears, and the rest were saved in one moment? Thou knowest, Sedrach, that there are nations which have not the law and which do the works of the law: for if they are unbaptized and my divine spirit come unto them and they turn to my baptism, I also receive them with my righteous ones into Abraham's bosom. And there are some who have been baptized with my baptism and who have shared in my divine part and become reprobate in complete reprobation and will not repent: and I suffer them with much compassion and much pity and wealth[2] in order that they may repent, but they do the things which my divinity hates, and did not hearken to the wise man asking (them), saying, we by no means justify a sinner. Dost thou not most certainly know that it is written: And those who repent never see chastisement? And they did not hearken to the Apostles or to my word in the Gospels, and they

[1] Cf. Test. of Abraham, Rec. A. §§ xiv., xviii.
[2] Rom. ii. 4.

grieve my angels, and verily they do not attend to my messenger in the assemblies (for communion) and in my services, and they do not stand in my holy churches, but they stand and do not fall down and worship in fear and trembling, but boast things which I do not accept, or my holy angels.

XV. Sedrach saith to God: O Lord, Thou alone art sinless and very compassionate, having compassion and pity for sinners, but thy divinity said: I am not come to call the righteous but sinners to repentance. And the Lord said to Sedrach: Dost thou not know, Sedrach, that the thief was saved in one moment to repent? Dost thou not know that my apostle and evangelist was saved in one moment? "*Peccatores enim non salvantur,*" for their hearts are like rotten stone: these are they who walk in impious ways and who shall be destroyed with Antichrist. Sedrach saith: O my Lord, Thou also saidst: My divine spirit entered into the nations which, not having the law, do the things of the law. So also the thief and the apostle and evangelist and the rest of those who have already got into thy Kingdom. O my Lord; so likewise do Thou pardon those who have sinned to the last: for life is very toilsome and there is no time for repentance.

XVI. The Lord saith to Sedrach: I made man in three stages: when he is young, I overlooked his stumblings as he was young: and again when he was a man I considered his purpose: and again when he grows old, I watch him till he repent. Sedrach saith: O Lord, Thou knowest and understandest all these things: but have sympathy for sinners. The Lord saith to him: Sedrach, my beloved, I promise to have sympathy and bring down the forty days to twenty: and whosoever shall remember thy name shall not see the place of chastisement, but shall be with the just in a place of refreshment and rest: and if anyone shall record this wonderful word his sins shall not be reckoned against him for ever and ever.[1] And Sedrach saith: O Lord, and if anyone shall bring enlightenment to thy servant, save him, O Lord, from all evil. And Sedrach, the servant of the Lord, saith: Now take my soul, O Lord. And God took him and placed him in Paradise with all the saints. To whom be the glory and the power for ever and ever. Amen.

[1] Cf. Esdras, p. 574.

THE TESTAMENT OF ABRAHAM,
THE ACTS OF XANTHIPPE AND POLYXENA,
THE NARRATIVE OF ZOSIMUS

TRANSLATED BY

W. A. CRAIGIE, M.A., B.A. (Oxon.)

THE TESTAMENT OF ABRAHAM

INTRODUCTION

THE Greek text of both the recensions of this work is published for the first time in "Texts and Studies," Vol. II., No. 2 (Cambridge, 1892), by Montague Rhodes James, M.A. None of the manuscripts are older than the thirteenth century; of the six which contain the longer version the best is a Paris MS. written 1315, and the principal MS. of the shorter recension (also in Paris) belongs to the fifteenth century. There are also versions in Roumanian, Slavonic, Ethiopic, and Arabic.

The work itself has hitherto been little noticed, and it is doubtful how far it was well known in ancient times. It is perhaps that cited as "Abraham" in early lists of Apocryphal works, and some passages in early Christian writers may indicate their knowledge of such a work. The evidence for this is given in full by the editor of the Greek text in his introduction (pp. 7–29). The conclusions drawn by him from these notices, and from the work itself, are "that it was written in the second century, that it embodies legends earlier than that century, that it received its present form perhaps in the ninth or tenth century." Certain features in it also "seem to point to Egypt as its birthplace," such as the conception of Death in the longer recension, which has parallels in the Coptic Apocryphal books, the weighing of souls, and the presence of recording angels at the judgment scene.

Neither of the two versions can be supposed to be true copies of the original work. They differ from each other not only in length, but in arrangement. The shorter recension may preserve more of the original language, but it transposes certain sections, thereby confusing the order of the narrative, and in this the Arabic version generally agrees with it. The most essential discrepancy begins with Chap. X. of the longer recension, where Abraham, after being taken up on the cloud, is first shown the iniquities that take place on earth. The shorter text places this at the end of his journey, quite destroying the original moral of the writer, who wishes to emphasize the mercy of God, and to show how Abraham's righteous indignation is replaced by feelings of compassion for the sinner. The vision of judgment is then altered in the shorter version, the doubtful soul being there condemned, instead of being saved by the intercession of Abraham. In this point the editor thinks that the shorter recension may have been influenced by the Apocalypse of Paul, as would also seem to be the case with Michael's reason for leaving Abraham in Chap. IV, which is quite different from the pretext given in the longer text. It is also remarkable that in the shorter form there is no word of Abraham's unwillingness to die, which is so prominent a feature of the other, and is no doubt original, as the idea is not otherwise unknown in Apocryphal literature. The conclusion of the shorter version is very much curtailed, compared with the longer one.

On account of these many differences between the recensions of this remarkable work, it has been judged best to give both of them entire, and so arranged that the reader can readily discover in what respects the one differs from the other.

The tone of the work is perhaps rather Jewish than Christian, but as phrases and conceptions of a New Testament character appear in it, especially in the judgment scene, it is most probably to be assigned to a Jewish Christian, who for the substance of it drew partly on older legends, and partly on his own imagination. Some of its features are very striking, and a few of them do not seem to occur elsewhere in literature of this class; it is possible that some of these do not go further back than the medieval editors of the text. Among the most remarkable points may be noticed the age of Abraham, variously given in different MSS., his hospitality, and the sending of Michael to announce his death (Chap. I.) : Michael's refusal to mount a horse (Chap. II.): the tree speaking with a human voice (Chap. III.); the tears of Michael turning into precious stones (ibid.) ; and the devouring spirit sent to consume the food for him (Chap. IV.). In Chap. VI. the narrative of Genesis is recalled by Sarah's recognizing Michael as one of the three who came to Abraham at the oak of Mamre, with the added circumstance of the calf rising up whole after being eaten. The dream of Isaac in Chap. VII. is perhaps remotely suggested by that of Joseph. The whole vision of judgment, with the presence of Adam and Abel, is very noteworthy, as also the conception of Death, and the explanation of his various forms.

THE TESTAMENT OF ABRAHAM

I. Abraham lived the measure of his life, nine hundred and ninety-five years, and having lived all the years of his life in quietness, gentleness, and righteousness, the righteous one was exceeding hospitable; for, pitching his tent in the cross-ways at the oak of Mamre, he received every one, both rich and poor, kings and rulers, the maimed and the helpless, friends and strangers, neighbours and travellers, all alike did the devout, all-holy, righteous, and hospitable Abraham entertain. Even upon him, however, there came the common, inexorable, bitter lot of death, and the uncertain end of life. Therefore the Lord God, summoning his archangel Michael, said to him: Go down, chief-captain[1] Michael, to Abraham and speak to him concerning his death, that he may set his affairs in order, for I have blessed him as the stars of heaven, and as the sand by the sea-shore, and he is in abundance of long life and many possessions, and is becoming exceeding rich. Beyond all men, moreover, he is righteous in every goodness, hospitable and loving to the end of his life; but do thou, archangel Michael, go to Abraham, my beloved friend, and announce to him his death and assure him thus: Thou shalt at this time depart from this vain world, and shalt quit the body, and go to thine own Lord among the good.

II. And the chief-captain departed from before the face of God, and went down to Abraham to the oak of Mamre, and found the righteous Abraham in the field close by, sitting beside yokes of oxen for ploughing, together with the sons of Masek and other servants, to the number of twelve. And behold the chief-captain came to him, and Abraham, seeing the chief-captain Michael coming from afar, like to a very comely warrior, arose and met him as was his custom, meeting and entertaining all strangers. And the chief-captain saluted him and said: Hail, most honoured father, righteous soul chosen

[1] Literally Commander-in-chief, or Chief-General.

I. It came to pass, when the days of the death of Abraham drew near, that the Lord said to Michael: Arise and go to Abraham, my servant, and say to him, Thou shall depart from life, for lo! the days of thy temporal life are fulfilled: so that he may set his house in order before he die.

II. And Michael went and came to Abraham, and found him sitting before his oxen for ploughing, and he was exceeding old in appearance, and had his son in his arms. Abraham, therefore, seeing the archangel Michael, rose from the ground and saluted him, not knowing who he was, and said to him: The Lord preserve thee. May thy journey be prosperous with thee. And Michael answered him: Thou art kind, good father. Abraham answered and said to him: Come, draw near to me, brother, and sit down a little while, that I may order a beast to be brought that we may go to my house, and thou mayest rest with me, for it is toward evening, and in the morning arise and go

of God, true son of the heavenly one. Abraham said to the chief-captain: Hail, most honoured warrior, bright as the sun and most beautiful above all the sons of men; thou art welcome; therefore I beseech thy presence, tell me whence the youth of thy age has come; teach me, thy suppliant, whence and from what army and from what journey thy beauty has come hither. The chief-captain said: I, O righteous Abraham, come from the great city. I have been sent by the great king to take the place of a good friend of his, for the king has summoned him. And Abraham said, Come, my lord, go with me as far as my field. The chief-captain said: I come; and going into the field of the ploughing, they sat down beside the company. And Abraham said to his servants, the sons of Masek: Go ye to the herd of horses, and bring two horses, quiet, and gentle and tame, so that I and this stranger may sit thereon. But the chief-captain said, Nay, my lord, Abraham, let them not bring horses, for I abstain from ever sitting upon any four-footed beast. Is not my king rich in much merchandise, having power both over men and all kinds of cattle? but I abstain from ever sitting upon any four-footed beast. Let us go, then, O righteous soul, walking lightly until we reach thy house. And Abraham said, Amen, be it so.

III. And as they went on from the field toward his house, beside that way there stood a cypress tree, and by the command of the Lord the tree cried out with a human voice, saying, Holy, holy, holy is the Lord God that calls himself to those that love him; but Abraham hid the mystery, thinking that the chief-captain had not heard the voice of the tree. And coming nigh to the house they sat down in the court, and Isaac seeing the face of the angel said to Sarah his mother, My lady mother, behold, the man sitting with my father Abraham is not a son of the race of those that dwell on the earth. And Isaac ran, and saluted him, and fell at the feet of the Incorporeal, and the Incorporeal blessed him and said, The Lord God will grant thee his promise that he made to thy father Abraham and to his seed, and will also grant thee the precious prayer of thy father and thy mother. Abraham said to Isaac his son, My son Isaac, draw water from the well, and bring it me in the vessel, that we may wash the feet of this stranger, for he is tired, having come to us from off a long journey. And Isaac ran to the well and drew water in the vessel and brought it to them, and Abraham went up and washed

whithersoever thou wilt, lest some evil beast meet thee and do thee hurt. And Michael enquired of Abraham, saying: Tell me thy name, before I enter thy house, lest I be burdensome to thee. Abraham answered and said, My parents called me Abram, and the Lord named me Abraham, saying: Arise and depart from thy house, and from thy kindred, and go into the land which I shall show unto thee. And when I went away into the land which the Lord showed me, he said to me: Thy name shall no more be called Abram, but thy name shall be Abraham. Michael answered and said to him: Pardon me, my father, experienced man of God, for I am a stranger, and I have heard of thee that thou didst go forty furlongs and didst bring a goat and slay it, entertaining angels in thy house, that they might rest there. Thus speaking together, they arose and went towards the house. And Abraham called one of his servants, and said to him: Go, bring me a beast that the stranger may sit upon it, for he is wearied with his journey. And Michael said: Trouble not the youth, but let us go lightly until we reach the house, for I love thy company.

III. And arising they went on, and as they drew nigh to the city, about three furlongs from it, they found a great tree having three hundred branches, like to a tamarisk tree. And they heard a voice from its branches singing, "Holy art thou, because thou hast kept the purpose for which thou wast sent." And Abraham heard the voice, and hid the mystery in his heart, saying within himself, What is the mystery that I have heard? As he came into the house, Abraham said to his servants, Arise, go out to the flocks, and bring three sheep, and slay them quickly, and make them ready that we may eat and drink, for this day is a feast for us. And the servants brought the sheep, and Abraham called his son Isaac, and said to him, My son Isaac, arise and put water in the vessel that we may wash the feet of this stranger. And he brought it as he was commanded, and Abraham said, I perceive, and so it shall be, that in this basin I shall never again wash the feet of any man coming to us as a guest. And Isaac hearing his father say this wept, and said to him, My father what is this that thou sayest, This is my last time to wash the feet of a stranger? And Abraham seeing his son weeping, also wept ex-the feet of the chief captain Michael, and the heart of Abraham was moved, and he wept over the stranger. And Isaac, seeing his father weeping, wept also, and the chief captain, seeing them weeping, also wept with them, and the tears of the chief captain fell upon the vessel into the water of the basin and became precious stones. And Abraham seeing the marvel, and being astonished, took the stones secretly, and hid the mystery, keeping it by himself in his heart.

IV. And Abraham said to Isaac his son: Go, my beloved son, into the inner chamber of the house and beautify it. Spread for us there two couches, one for me and one for this man that is guest with us this day. Prepare for us there a seat and a candlestick and a table with abundance of every good thing. Beautify the chamber, my son, and spread under us linen and purple and fine linen. Burn there every precious and excellent incense, and bring sweet-smelling plants from the garden and fill our house with them. Kindle seven lamps full of oil, so that we may rejoice, for this man that is our guest this day is more glorious than kings or rulers, and his appearance surpasses all the sons of men. And Isaac prepared all things well, and Abraham taking the archangel Michael went into the chamber, and they both sat down upon the couches, and between them he placed a table with abundance of every good thing. Then the chief captain arose and went out, as if by constraint of his belly to make issue of water, and ascended to heaven in the twinkling of an eye, and stood before the Lord, and said to him: Lord and Master, let thy power know that I am unable to remind that righteous man of his death, for I have not seen upon the earth a man like him, pitiful, hospitable, righteous, truthful, devout, refraining from every evil deed. And now know, Lord, that I cannot remind him of his death. And the Lord said: Go down, chief-captain Michael, to my friend Abraham, and whatever he say to thee, that do thou also, and whatever he eat, eat thou also with him. And I will send my holy spirit upon his son Isaac, and will put the remembrance of his death into the heart of Isaac, so that even he in a dream may see the death of his father, and Isaac will relate the dream, and thou shalt interpret it, and he himself will know his end. And the chief-captain said, Lord, all the heavenly spirits are incorporeal, and neither eat nor drink, and this man has set before me a table with abundance of all good things earthly and corruptible. Now, Lord, what shall I do? How shall I escape him,

ceedingly, and Michael seeing them weeping, wept also, and the tears of Michael fell upon the vessel and became a precious stone.

IV. When Sarah, being inside in her house, heard their weeping, she came out and said to Abraham, Lord, why is it that ye thus weep? Abraham answered, and said to her, It is no evil. Go into thy house, and do thy own work, lest we be troublesome to the man. And Sarah went away, being about to prepare the supper. And the sun came near to setting, and Michael went out of the house, and was taken up into the heavens to worship before God, for at sunset all the angels worship God and Michael himself is the first of the angels. And they all worshipped him, and went each to his own place, but Michael spoke before the Lord and said, Lord, command me to be questioned before thy holy glory! And the Lord said to Michael, Announce whatsoever thou wilt! And the Archangel answered and said, Lord, thou didst send me to Abraham to say to him, Depart from thy body, and leave this world; the Lord calls thee; and I dare not, Lord, reveal myself to him, for he is thy friend, and a righteous man, and one that receives strangers. But I beseech thee, Lord, command the remembrance of the death of Abraham to enter into his own heart, and bid not me tell it him, for it is great abruptness to say, Leave the world, and especially to leave one's own body, for thou didst create him from the beginning to have pity on the souls of all men. Then the Lord said to Michael, Arise and go to Abraham, and lodge with him, and whatever thou seest him eat, eat thou also, and where-ever he shall sleep, sleep thou there also. For I will cast the thought of the death of Abraham into the heart of Isaac his son in a dream.

sitting at one table with him? The Lord said: Go down to him, and take no thought for this, for when thou sittest down with him, I will send upon thee a devouring spirit, and it will consume out of thy hands and through thy mouth all that is on the table. Rejoice together with him in everything, only thou shalt interpret well the things of the vision, that Abraham may know the sickle of death and the uncertain end of life, and may make disposal of all his possessions, for I have blessed him above the sand of the sea and as the stars of heaven.

V. Then the chief captain went down to the house of Abraham, and sat down with him at the table, and Isaac served them. And when the supper was ended, Abraham prayed after his custom, and the chief-captain prayed together with him, and each lay down to sleep upon his couch. And Isaac said to his father, Father, I too would fain sleep with you in this chamber, that I also may hear your discourse, for I love to hear the excellence of the conversation of this virtuous man. Abraham said, Nay, my son, but go to thy own chamber and sleep on thy own couch, lest we be troublesome to this man. Then Isaac, having received the prayer from them, and having blessed them, went to his own chamber and lay down upon his couch. But the Lord cast the thought of death into the heart of Isaac as in a dream, and about the third hour of the night Isaac awoke and rose up from his couch, and came running to the chamber where his father was sleeping together with the archangel. Isaac, therefore, on reaching the door cried out, saying, My father Abraham, arise and open to me quickly, that I may enter and hang upon thy neck, and embrace thee before they take thee away from me. Abraham therefore arose and opened to him, and Isaac entered and hung upon his neck, and began to weep with a loud voice. Abraham therefore being moved at heart, also wept with a loud voice, and the chief-captain, seeing them weeping, wept also. Sarah being in her room, heard their weeping, and came running to them, and found them embracing and weeping. And Sarah said with weeping, My lord Abraham, what is this that ye weep? Tell me, my lord, has this brother that has been entertained by us this day brought thee tidings of Lot, thy brother's son, that he is dead? is it for this that ye grieve thus? The chief-captain answered and said to her, Nay, my sister Sarah, it is not as thou sayest, but thy son Isaac, methinks, beheld a dream, and came to us weeping, and we seeing him were moved in our hearts and wept.

V. Then Michael went into the house of Abraham on that evening, and found them preparing the supper, and they ate and drank and were merry. And Abraham said to his son Isaac, Arise, my son, and spread the man's couch that he may sleep, and set the lamp upon the stand. And Isaac did as his father commanded him, and Isaac said to his father, I too am coming to sleep beside you. Abraham answered him, Nay, my son, lest we be troublesome to this man, but go to thy own chamber and sleep. And Isaac not wishing to disobey his father's command, went away and slept in his own chamber.

VI. And it happened about the seventh hour of the night Isaac awoke, and came to the door of his father's chamber, crying out and saying, Open, father, that I may touch thee before they take thee away from me. Abraham arose and opened to him, and Isaac entered and hung upon his father's neck weeping, and kissed him with lamentations. And Abraham wept together with his son, and Michael saw them weeping and wept likewise. And Sarah hearing them weeping called from her bed-chamber, saying, My lord Abraham, why is this weeping? Has the stranger told thee of thy brother's son Lot that he is dead? or has aught else befallen us? Michael answered and said to Sarah, Nay, Sarah, I have brought no tidings of Lot, but I knew of all your kindness of heart, that therein ye excel all men upon earth, and the Lord has remembered you.

VI. Then Sarah, hearing the excellence of the conversation of the chief-captain, straightway knew that it was an angel of the Lord that spoke. Sarah therefore signified to Abraham to come out towards the door, and said to him, My lord Abraham, knowest thou who this man is? Abraham said, I know not. Sarah said, Thou knowest, my lord, the three men from heaven that were entertained by us in our tent beside the oak of Mamre, when thou didst kill the kid without blemish, and set a table before them. After the flesh had been eaten, the kid rose again, and sucked its mother with great joy. Knowest thou not, my lord Abraham, that by promise they gave to us Isaac as the fruit of the womb? Of these three holy men this is one. Abraham said, O Sarah, in this thou speakest the truth. Glory and praise from our God and the Father. For late in the evening when I washed his feet in the basin I said in my heart, These are the feet of one of the three men that I washed then; and his tears that fell into the basin then became precious stones. And shaking them out from his lap he gave them to Sarah, saying, If thou believest me not, look now at these. And Sarah receiving them bowed down and saluted and said, Glory be to God that showeth us wonderful things. And now know, my lord Abraham, that there is among us the revelation of some thing, whether it be evil or good!

Then Sarah said to Abraham, How durst thou weep when the man of God has come in to thee, and why have thy eyes [1] shed tears for to-day there is great rejoicing? Abraham said to her, How knowest thou that this is a man of God? Sarah answered and said, Because I say and declare that this is one of the three men who were entertained by us at the oak of Mamre, when one of the servants went and brought a kid and thou didst kill it, and didst say to me, Arise, make ready that we may eat with these men in our house. Abraham answered and said, Thou has perceived well, O woman, for I too, when I washed his feet knew in my heart that these were the feet which I had washed at the oak of Mamre, and when I began to enquire concerning his journey, he said to me, I go to preserve Lot thy brother from the men of Sodom, and then I knew the mystery.

VII. And Abraham left Sarah, and went into the chamber, and said to Isaac, Come hither, my beloved son, tell me the truth, what it was thou sawest and what befell thee that thou camest so hastily to us. And Isaac answering began to say, I saw, my lord, in this night the sun and the moon above my head, surrounding me with its rays and giving me light. As I gazed at this and rejoiced, I saw the heaven opened, and a man bearing light descend from it, shining more than seven suns. And this man like the sun came and took away the sun from my head, and went up into the heavens from whence he came, but I was greatly grieved that he took away the sun from me. After a little, as I was still sorrowing and sore troubled, I saw this man come forth from heaven a second time, and he took away from me the moon also from off my head, and I wept greatly and called upon that man of light, and said, Do not, my lord, take away my glory from me; pity me and hear me, and if thou takest away the sun from me, then leave the moon to me. He said, Suffer them to be taken up to the king above, for he wishes them there. And he took them away from me, but he left the

VII. And Abraham said to Michael, Tell me, man of God, and show to me why thou hast come hither. And Michael said. Thy son Isaac will show thee. And Abraham said to his son, My beloved son, tell me what thou hast seen in thy dream to-day, and wast frightened. Relate it to me. Isaac answered his father, I saw in my dream the sun and the moon, and there was a crown upon my head, and there came from heaven a man of great size, and shining as the light that is called the father of light. He took the sun from my head, and yet left the rays behind with me. And I wept and said, I beseech thee, my lord, take not away the glory of my head, and the light of my house, and all my glory. And the sun and the moon and the stars lamented, saying, Take not away the glory of our power. And that shining man answered and said to me, Weep not that I take the light of thy house, for it is taken up from troubles into rest, from a low estate to a high one; they lift him up from a narrow to a wide place; they raise him from darkness to light. And I said to him, I beseech thee, Lord, take also the

[1] "Eyes of the fountain of light" is apparently what the text has.

rays upon me. The chief-captain said, Hear, O righteous Abraham; the sun which thy son saw is thou his father, and the moon likewise is Sarah his mother. The man bearing light who descended from heaven, this is the one sent from God who is to take thy righteous soul from thee. And now know, O most honored Abraham, that at this time thou shalt leave this worldly life, and remove to God. Abraham said to the chief captain, O strangest of marvels! and now art thou he that shall take my soul from me? The chief-captain said to him, I am the chief-captain Michael, that stands before the lord, and I was sent to thee to remind thee of thy death, and then I shall depart to him as I was commanded. Abraham said, Now I know that thou art an angel of the Lord, and wast sent to take my soul, but I will not go with thee; but do thou whatever thou art commanded.

VIII. The chief-captain hearing these words immediately vanished, and ascending into heaven stood before God, and told all that he had seen in the house of Abraham; and the chief-captain said this also to his Lord, Thus says thy friend Abraham, I will not go with thee, but do thou whatever thou art commanded; and now, O Lord Almighty, doth thy glory and immortal kingdom order aught? God said to the chief-captain Michael, Go to my friend Abraham yet once again, and speak to him thus, Thus saith the Lord thy God, he that brought thee into the land of promise, that blessed thee above the sand of the sea and above the stars of heaven, that opened the womb of barrenness of Sarah, and granted thee Isaac as the fruit of the womb in old age, Verily I say unto thee that blessing I will bless thee, and multiplying I will multiply thy seed, and I will give thee all that thou shalt ask from me, for I am the Lord thy God, and besides me there is no other. Tell me why thou hast rebelled against me, and why there is grief in thee, and why thou rebelled against my archangel Michael? Knowest thou not that all who have come from Adam and Eve have died, and that none of the prophets has escaped death? None of those that rule as kings is immortal; none of thy forefathers has escaped the mystery of death. They have all died, they have all departed into Hades, they are all gathered by the sickle of death. But upon thee I have not sent death, I have not suffered any deadly disease to come upon thee, I have not permitted the sickle of death to meet thee, I have not allowed the nets of Hades to enfold thee, I have never wished thee to meet with any evil. But for good comfort I have sent my rays with it. He said to me, There are twelve hours of the day, and then I shall take all the rays. As the shining man said this, I saw the sun of my house ascending into heaven, but that crown I saw no more, and that sun was like thee my father. And Michael said to Abraham, Thy son Isaac has spoken truth, for thou shalt go, and be taken up into the heavens, but thy body shall remain on earth, until seven thousand ages are fulfilled, for then all flesh shall arise. Now therefore, Abraham, set thy house in order, and thy children, for thou hast heard fully what is decreed concerning thee.

chief-captain Michael to thee, that thou mayst know thy departure from the world, and set thy house in order, and all that belongs to thee, and bless Isaac thy beloved son. And now know that I have done this not wishing to grieve thee. Wherefore then hast thou said to my chief-captain, I will not go with thee? Wherefore hast thou spoken thus? Knowest thou not that if I give leave to death and he comes upon thee, then I should see whether thou wouldst come or not?

IX. And the chief-captain receiving the exhortations of the Lord went down to Abraham, and seeing him the righteous one fell upon his face to the ground as one dead, and the chief-captain told him all that he had heard from the Most High. Then the holy and just Abraham rising with many tears fell at the feet of the Incorporeal, and besought him, saying, I beseech thee, chief-captain of the hosts above, since thou hast wholly deigned to come thyself to me a sinner and in all things thy unworthy servant, I beseech thee even now, O chief-captain, to carry my word yet again to the Most High, and thou shalt say to him, Thus saith Abraham thy servant, Lord, Lord, in every work and word which I have asked of thee thou hast heard me, and hast fulfilled all my counsel. Now, Lord, I resist not thy power, for I too know that I am not immortal but mortal. Since therefore to thy command all things yield, and fear and tremble at the face of thy power, I also fear, but I ask one request of thee, and now, Lord and Master, hear my prayer, for while still in this body I desire to see all the inhabited earth, and all the creations which thou didst establish by one word, and when I see these, then if I shall depart from life I shall be without sorrow. So the chief-captain went back again, and stood before God, and told him all, saying, Thus saith thy friend Abraham, I desired to behold all the earth in my lifetime before I died. And the Most High hearing this, again commanded the chief-captain Michael, and said to him, Take a cloud of light, and the angels that have power over the chariots, and go down, take the righteous Abraham upon a chariot of the cherubim, and exalt him into the air of heaven that he may behold all the earth.

X. And the archangel Michael went down and took Abraham upon a chariot of the cherubim, and exalted him into the air of heaven, and led him upon the cloud together with sixty angels, and Abraham ascended upon the chariot over all the earth. And Abraham saw the world as it was in that day, some ploughing, others driving wains, in one place men herding flocks, and in another

Abraham answered and said to Michael, I beseech thee, lord, if I shall depart from my body, I have desired to be taken up in my body that I may see the creatures that the Lord my God has created in heaven and on earth. Michael answered and said, This is not for me to do, but I shall go and tell the Lord of this, and if I am commanded I shall show thee all these things.

VIII. And Michael went up into heaven, and spoke before the Lord concerning Abraham, and the Lord answered Michael, Go and take up Abraham in the body, and show him all things, and whatsoever he shall say to thee do to him as to my friend. So Michael went forth and took up Abraham in the body on a cloud, and brought him to the river of Ocean.

watching them by night, and dancing and playing and harping, in another place men striving and contending at law, elsewhere men weeping and having the dead in remembrance. He saw also the newly-wedded received with honour, and in a word he saw all things that are done in the world, both good and bad. Abraham therefore passing over them saw men bearing swords, wielding in their hands sharpened swords, and Abraham asked the chief-captain, Who are these? The chief-captain said, These are thieves, who intend to commit murder, and to steal and burn and destroy. Abraham said, Lord, Lord, hear my voice, and command that wild beasts may come out of the wood and devour them. And even as he spoke there came wild beasts out of the wood and devoured them. And he saw in another place a man with a woman committing fornication with each other, and said, Lord, Lord, command that the earth may open and swallow them, and straightway the earth was cleft and swallowed them. And he saw in another place men digging through a house, and carrying away other men's possessions, and he said, Lord, Lord, command that fire may come down from heaven and consume them. And even as he spoke, fire came down from heaven and consumed them. And straightway there came a voice from heaven to the chief-captain, saying thus, O chief-captain Michael, command the chariot to stop, and turn Abraham away that he may not see all the earth, for if he behold all that live in wickedness, he will destroy all creation. For behold, Abraham has not sinned, and has no pity on sinners, but I have made the world, and desire not to destroy any one of them, but wait for the death of the sinner, till he be converted and live. But take Abraham up to the first gate of heaven, that he may see there the judgments and recompenses, and repent of the souls of the sinners that he has destroyed.

XI. So Michael turned the chariot and brought Abraham to the east, to the first gate of heaven; and Abraham saw two ways, the one narrow and contracted, the other broad and spacious, and there he saw two gates, the one broad on the broad way, and the other narrow on the narrow way. And outside the two gates there he saw a man sitting upon a gilded throne, and the appearance of that man was terrible, as of the Lord.[1] And they saw many souls driven by angels and led in through the broad gate, and other souls, few in number, that were taken by the angels through the narrow gate. And when the

[1] Two MSS. read, "Of our Lord Jesus Christ."

XII. And after Abraham had seen the place of judgment, the cloud took him down upon the firmament below, and Abraham, looking down upon the earth, saw a man committing adultery with a wedded woman. And Abraham turning said to Michael, Seest thou this wickedness? but, Lord, send fire from heaven to consume them. And straightway there came down fire and consumed them, for the Lord had said to Michael, Whatsoever Abraham shall ask thee to do for him, do thou. Abraham looked again, and saw other men railing at their companions, and said, Let the earth open and swallow them, and as he spoke the earth swallowed them alive. Again the cloud led him to another place, and Abraham saw some going into a desert place to commit murder, and he said to Michael, Seest thou this wickedness? but let wild beasts come out of the desert, and tear them in pieces, and that same hour wild beasts came out of the desert, and devoured them. Then the Lord God spoke to Michael saying, Turn away Abraham to his own house, and let him not go round all the creation that I have made, because he has no compassion on sinners, but I have compassion on sinners that they may turn and live, and repent of their sins and be saved.

(VIII.) And Abraham looked and saw two gates, the one small and the other large, and between the two gates sat a man upon a throne of great glory, and a multitude of angels round about him, and he was weeping, and again laughing, but his weeping exceeded his laughter seven-fold. And Abraham said to Michael, Who is this that sits between the two gates in great glory; sometimes he laughs, and sometimes he weeps, and his weeping exceeds his laughter seven-fold? And Michael said to Abraham, Knowest thou not who it is? And he said, No, lord. And Michael said to Abraham, Seest thou these two gates, the small and the great? These are they which

wonderful one who sat upon the golden throne saw few entering through the narrow gate, and many entering through the broad one, straightway that wonderful one tore the hairs of his head and the sides of his beard, and threw himself on the ground from his throne, weeping and lamenting. But when he saw many souls entering through the narrow gate, then he arose from the ground and sat upon his throne in great joy, rejoicing and exulting. And Abraham asked the chief-captain, My lord chief-captain, who is this most marvelous man, adorned with such glory, and sometimes he weeps and laments, and sometimes he rejoices and exults? The incorporeal one said: This is the first-created Adam who is in such glory, and he looks upon the world because all are born from him, and when he sees many souls going through the narrow gate, then he arises and sits upon his throne rejoicing and exulting in joy, because this narrow gate is that of the just, that leads to life, and they that enter through it go into Paradise. For this, then, the first-created Adam rejoices, because he sees the souls being saved. But when he sees many souls entering through the broad gate, then he pulls out the hairs of his head, and casts himself on the ground weeping and lamenting bitterly, for the broad gate is that of sinners, which leads to destruction and eternal punishment. And for this the first-formed Adam falls from his throne weeping and lamenting for the destruction of sinners, for they are many that are lost, and they are few that are saved, for in seven thousand there is scarcely found one soul saved, being righteous and undefiled.

XII. While he was yet saying these things to me, behold two angels, fiery in aspect, and pitiless in mind, and severe in look, and they drove on thousands of souls, pitilessly lashing them with fiery thongs. The angel laid hold of one soul, and they drove all the souls in at the broad gate to destruction. So we also went along with the angels, and came within that broad gate, and between the two gates stood a throne terrible of aspect, of terrible crystal, gleaming as fire, and upon it sat a wondrous man bright as the sun, like to the Son of God. Before him stood a table like crystal, all of gold and fine linen, and upon the table there was lying a book, the thickness of it six cubits, and the breadth of it ten cubits, and on the right and left of it stood two angels holding paper and ink and pen. Before the table sat an angel of light, holding in his hand a balance, and on his left sat an angel all fiery, pitiless, and severe, holding in his hand a trumpet, having within it

lead to life and to destruction. This man that sits between them is Adam, the first man whom the Lord created, and set him in this place to see every soul that departs from the body, seeing that all are from him. When, therefore, thou seest him weeping, know that he has seen many souls being led to destruction, but when thou seest him laughing, he has seen many souls being led into life. Seest thou how his weeping exceeds his laughter? Since he sees the greater part of the world being led away through the broad gate to destruction, therefore his weeping exceeds his laughter seven-fold.

IX. And Abraham said, And he that cannot enter through the narrow gate, can he not enter into life? Then Abraham wept, saying, Woe is me, what shall I do? for I am a man broad of body, and how shall I be able to enter by the narrow gate, by which a boy of fifteen years cannot enter? Michael answered and said to Abraham, Fear not, father, nor grieve, for thou shalt enter by it unhindered, and all those who are like thee.

And as Abraham stood and marveled. behold an angel of the Lord driving sixty thousand souls of sinners to destruction, And Abraham said to Michael, Do all these go into destruction? And Michael said to him, Yea, but let us go and search among these souls, if there is among them even one righteous. And when they went, they found an angel holding in his hand one soul of a woman from among these sixty thousand, because he had found her sins weighing equally with all her works, and they were neither in motion nor at rest, but in a state between; but the other souls he led away to destruction. Abraham said to Michael, Lord, is this the angel that removes the souls from the body or not? Michael answered and said, This is death, and he leads them into the place of judgment, that the judge may try them.

X. And Abraham said, My lord, I beseech thee to lead me to the place of judgment so

all-consuming fire with which to try the sinners. The wondrous man who sat upon the throne himself judged and sentenced the souls, and the two angels on the right and on the left wrote down, the one on the right the righteousness and the one on the left the wickedness. The one before the table, who held the balance, weighed the souls, and the fiery angel, who held the fire, tried the souls. And Abraham asked the chief-captain Michael, What is this that we behold? And the chief-captain said, These things that thou seest, holy Abraham, are the judgment and recompense. And behold the angel holding the soul in his hand, and he brought it before the judge, and the judge said to one of the angels that served him, Open me this book, and find me the sins of this soul. And opening the book he found its sins and its righteousness equally balanced, and he neither gave it to the tormentors, nor to those that were saved, but set it in the midst.

XIII. And Abraham said, My lord chief-captain, who is this most wondrous judge? and who are the angels that write down? and who is the angel like the sun, holding the balance? and who is the fiery angel holding the fire? The chief-captain said, "Seest thou, most holy Abraham, the terrible man sitting upon the throne? This is the son of the first created Adam, who is called Abel, whom the wicked Cain killed, and he sits thus to judge all creation, and examines righteous men and sinners. For God has said, I shall not judge you, but every man born of man shall be judged. Therefore he has given to him judgment, to judge the world until his great and glorious coming, and then, O righteous Abraham, is the perfect judgment and recompense, eternal and unchangeable, which no one can alter. For every man has come from the first-created, and therefore they are first judged here by his son, and at the second coming they shall be judged by the twelve tribes of Israel,

that I too may see how they are judged. Then Michael took Abraham upon a cloud, and led him into Paradise, and when he came to the place where the judge was, the angel came and gave that soul to the judge. And the soul said, Lord have mercy on me. And the judge said, How shall I have mercy upon thee, when thou hadst no mercy upon thy daughter which thou hadst, the fruit of thy womb? Wherefore didst thou slay her? It answered, Nay, Lord, slaughter has not been done by me, but my daughter has lied upon me. But the judge commanded him to come that wrote down the records, and behold cherubim carrying two books. And there was with them a man of exceeding great stature, having on his head three crowns, and the one crown was higher than the other two. These are called the crowns of witness. And the man had in his hand a golden pen, and the judge said to him, Exhibit the sin of this soul. And that man. opening one of the books of the cherubim, sought out the sin of the woman's soul and found it. And the judge said, O wretched soul, why sayest thou that thou hast not done murder? Didst thou not, after the death of thy husband, go and commit adultery with thy daughter's husband, and kill her? And he convicted her also of her other sins, whatsoever she had done from her youth. Hearing these things the woman cried out, saying, Woe is me, all the sins that I did in the world I forgot, but here they were not forgotten. Then they took her away also and gave her over to the tormentors.

XI. And Abraham said to Michael, Lord, who is this judge, and who is the other, who convicts the sins? And Michael said to Abraham, Seest thou the judge? This is Abel, who first testified, and God brought him hither to judge, and he that bears witness here is the teacher of heaven and earth, and the scribe of righteousness, Enoch, for the Lord sent them hither to write down the sins and righteousnesses of each one. Abraham said, And how can Enoch bear the weight of the souls, not having seen death? or how can he give sentence to all the souls? Michael said, If he gives sentence concerning the souls, it is not permitted; but Enoch himself does not give sentence, but it is the Lord who does so, and he has no more to do than only to write. For Enoch prayed to the Lord saying, I desire not, Lord, to give sentence on the souls, lest I be grievous to anyone; and the Lord said to Enoch, I shall command thee to write down the sins of the soul that makes atonement and it shall enter every breath and every creature. But the third time they shall be judged by the Lord God of all, and then, indeed, the end of that judgment is near, and the sentence terrible, and there is none to deliver. And now by three tribunals the judgment of the world and the recompense is made, and for this reason a matter is not finally confirmed by one or two witnesses, but by three witnesses shall everything be established. The two angels on the right hand and on the left, these are they that write down the sins and the righteousness, the one on the right hand writes down the righteousness, and the one on the left the sins. The angel like the sun, holding the balance in his hand, is the archangel, Dokiel the just weigher, and he weighs the righteousnesses and sins with the righteousness of God. The fiery and pitiless angel, holding the fire in his hand, is the archangel Puruel, who has power over fire, and tries the works of men through fire, and if the fire consume the work of any man, the angel of judgment immediately seizes him, and carries him away to the place of sinners, a most bitter place of punishment. But if the fire approves the work of anyone, and does not seize upon it, that man is justified, and the angel of righteousness takes him and carries him up to be saved in the lot of the just. And thus, most righteous Abraham, all things in all men are tried by fire and the balance."

XIV. And Abraham said to the chief-captain, My lord the chief-captain, the soul which the angel held in his hand, why was it adjudged to be set in the midst? The chief-captain said, Listen, righteous Abraham. Because the judge found its sins and its righteousnesses equal, he neither committed it to judgment nor to be saved, until the judge of all shall come. Abraham said to the chief-captain, And what yet is wanting for the soul to be saved? The chief-captain said, If it obtains one righteousness above its sins, it enters into salvation. Abraham said to the chief-captain, Come hither, chief-captain Michael, let us make prayer for this soul, and see whether God will hear us. The chief-captain said, Amen, be it so; and they made prayer and entreaty for the soul, and God heard them, and when they rose up from their prayer they did not see the soul standing there. And Abraham said to the angel, Where is the soul that thou didst hold in the midst? And the angel answered, It has been saved by thy righteous prayer, and behold an angel of light has taken it and carried it up into Paradise. Abraham said, I glorify the name of God, the Most High, and his immeasurable mercy. And Abraham said to the chief-captain, I beseech thee, archangel, hearken to my prayer, and let us yet call upon the Lord, and supplicate his compassion, and entreat his mercy for the souls of the sinners whom I formerly, in my anger, cursed and destroyed, whom the earth devoured, and the wild beasts tore in pieces, and the fire consumed through my words. Now I know that I have sinned before the Lord our God. Come then, O Michael, chief-captain of the hosts above, come, let us call upon God with tears that he may forgive me my sin, and grant them to me. And the chief-captain heard him, and they made entreaty before the Lord, and when they had called upon him for a long space, there came a voice from heaven saying, Abraham, Abraham, I have hearkened to thy voice and thy prayer, and forgive thee thy sin, and those whom thou thinkest that I destroyed I have called up and brought them into life by my exceeding kindness, because for a season I have requited them in judgment, and those whom I destroy living upon earth I will not requite in death.

XV. And the voice of the Lord said also to the chief-captain Michael, Michael, my servant, turn back Abraham to his house, for behold his end has come nigh, and the measure of his life is fulfilled, that he may make disposition of all things, and then take him and bring him to me. And the chief-captain turned the chariot and the cloud, and brought Abraham to his house, and he went into his chamber and sat upon his couch. And Sarah his wife came and embraced the feet of the Incorporeal, and spoke humbly, saying, I give thee thanks, my lord, that thou hast brought my lord Abraham, for behold we thought he had been taken up from us. And his son Isaac also came and fell upon his neck, and in like manner all his men-servants and maid-servants surrounded Abraham, and embraced him, glorifying God. And the Incorporeal one said to them, Hearken, righteous Abraham. Behold thy wife Sarah, behold also thy beloved son Isaac, behold also all thy men-servants and maid-servants round about thee. Make disposition of all that thou hast, for the day has drawn nigh in which thou shalt depart from the body and go to the Lord once for all. Abraham said, Has the Lord said it, or sayest thou this of thyself? The chief-captain answered and said, Hearken, righteous Abraham. The Lord has commanded, and I tell it thee. Abraham said, I will not go with thee. The chief-captain, when he heard these words, straightway went forth from the presence of Abraham, and went up into the heavens, and stood before God the Most High, and said, Lord Almighty, behold I have hearkened to thy friend Abraham in all he has said to thee, and have fulfilled his request. I have shown to him thy power, and all the earth and sea that is under heaven. I have shown to him judgment and recompense by means of cloud and chariots, and again he says, I will not go with thee. And the Most High said to the angel, Does my friend Abraham say thus again, I will not go with thee? The archangel said, Lord Almighty, he says thus, and I refrain from laying hands on him, because from the beginning he is thy friend, and has done all things pleasing in thy sight. And there is no man like him on earth, not even Job the wonderful man, and for this reason I refrain from laying hands on him. Command, therefore, immortal King, what shall be done.

XVI. Then the Most High said, Call me hither Death that is called the shameless countenance and the pitiless look. And Michael the Incorporeal went and said to Death, Come hither; the Lord of creation, the immortal King, calls thee. And Death, hearing this, shivered and trembled, being possessed with great terror, and came with great fear and stood before the invisible Father, shivering, groaning and trembling, awaiting the command of the Lord. Then the invisible God said to Death, Come hither, thou bitter and fierce name of the world, hide thy fierceness, cover thy corruption, and cast away thy bitterness from thee, and put on thy beauty and all thy glory, and go down to Abraham my friend, and take him and bring him to me. But now also I tell thee not to terrify him, but bring him with fair speech, for he is my own friend. Having heard this, Death went out from the presence of the Most High, and put on a robe of great brightness, and made his appearance like the sun, and became fair and beautiful above the sons of men, assuming the form of an archangel, having his cheeks flaming with fire, and he departed to Abraham. Now righteous Abraham went out of his chamber, and sat under the trees of Mamre, holding his chin in his hand, and awaiting the coming of the archangel Michael. And behold, a smell of sweet odor came to him, and a flashing of light, and Abraham turned and saw Death coming towards him in great glory and beauty. And Abraham arose and went to meet him, thinking that it was the chief-captain of God, and Death beholding him saluted him, saying, Rejoice, precious Abraham, righteous soul, true friend of the Most High God, and companion of the holy angels. Abraham said to Death, Hail thou of appearance and form like the sun, most glorious helper, bringer of light, wondrous man, from whence does thy glory come to us, and who art thou, and whence comest thou? Then Death said, Most righteous Abraham, behold I tell thee the truth. I am the bitter lot of death. Abraham said to him, Nay, but thou art the comeliness of the world, thou art the glory and beauty of angels and men, thou art fairer in form than every other, and sayest thou, I am the bitter lot of death, and not rather, I am fairer than every good thing? Death said, I tell thee the truth. What the Lord has named me, that also I tell thee. Abraham said, For what art thou come hither? Death said, For thy holy soul am I come. Then Abraham said, I know what thou meanest, but I will not go with thee; and Death was silent and answered him not a word.

XVII. Abraham arose, and went into his house, and Death also accompanied him thither. And Abraham went up into his chamber, and Death went up with him. And Abraham lay down upon his couch, and Death came and sat by his feet. Then Abraham said, Depart, depart from me, for I desire to rest upon my couch. Death said, I will not depart until I take thy spirit from thee. Abraham said to him, By the immortal God I charge thee to tell me the truth. Art thou death? Death said to him, I am Death. I am the destroyer of the world. Abraham said, I pray thee, since thou art Death, tell me if thou comest thus to all in such fairness and glory and beauty? Death said, Nay, my lord Abraham, for thy righteousnesses, and the boundless sea of thy hospitality, and the greatness of thy love towards God has become a crown upon my head, and in beauty and great peace and gentleness I approach the righteous, but to sinners I come in great corruption and fierceness and the greatest bitterness and with fierce and pitiless look. Abraham said, I pray thee, hearken to me, and show me thy fierceness and all thy corruption and bitterness. And Death said, Thou canst not behold my fierceness, most righteous Abraham. Abraham said, Yea, I shall be able to behold all thy fierceness by means of the name of the living God, for the might of my God that is in heaven is with me. Then Death put off all his comeliness and beauty, and all his glory and the form like the sun with which he was clothed, and put upon himself a tyrant's robe, and made his appearance gloomy and fiercer than all kinds of beasts, and more unclean than all uncleanness. And he showed to Abraham seven fiery heads of dragons and fourteen faces, (one) of the most flaming fire and of great fierceness, and a face of darkness, and a most gloomy face of a viper, and a face of a most horrible precipice, and a face fiercer than an asp, and a face of a terrible lion, and a face of a cerastes and basilisk. He showed him also a face of a fiery scimitar, and a swordlike face, and another face of lightning flashing terribly, and a noise of dreadful thunder. He showed him also another face of a fierce stormy sea, and a fierce rushing river, and a terrible three-headed dragon, and a mingled cup of poisons, and in short he showed to him great fierceness and unendurable bitterness, and every mortal disease as of the odor of death. And from the great bitterness and fierceness there died servants and maid-servants in number about seven thousand, and the righteous Abraham came into indifference of death so that his spirit failed him.

into life, and if the soul make not atonement and repent, thou shalt find its sins written down and it shall be cast into punishment.

ham said to the chief-captain, I beseech thee, archangel, hearken to my prayer, and let us yet call upon the Lord, and supplicate his compassion, and entreat his mercy for the souls of the sinners whom I formerly, in my anger, cursed and destroyed, whom the earth devoured, and the wild beasts tore in pieces, and the fire consumed through my words. Now I know that I have sinned before the Lord our God. Come then, O Michael, chief-captain of the hosts above, come, let us call upon God with tears that he may forgive me my sin, and grant them to me. And the chief-captain heard him, and they made entreaty before the Lord, and when they had called upon him for a long space, there came a voice from heaven saying, Abraham, Abraham, I have hearkened to thy voice and thy prayer, and forgive thee thy sin, and those whom thou thinkest that I destroyed I have called up and brought them into life by my exceeding kindness, because for a season I have requited them in judgment, and those whom I destroy living upon earth, I will not requite in death.

XV. And the voice of the Lord said also to the chief-captain Michael, Michael, my servant, turn back Abraham to his house, for behold his end has come nigh, and the measure of his life is fulfilled, that he may set all things in order, and then take him and bring him to me. So the chief-captain, turning the chariot and the cloud, brought Abraham to his house, and going into his chamber he sat upon his couch. And Sarah his wife came and embraced the feet of the Incorporeal, and spoke humbly, saying, I give thee thanks, my lord, that thou hast brought my lord Abraham, for behold we thought he had been taken up from us. And his son Isaac also came and fell upon his neck, and in the same way all his men-slaves and women-slaves surrounded Abraham and embraced him, glorifying God. And the Incorporeal one said to them, Hearken, righteous Abraham. Behold thy wife Sarah, behold also thy beloved son Isaac, behold also all thy men-servants and maid-servants round about thee. Make disposition of all that thou hast, for the day has come nigh in which thou shalt depart from the body and go to the Lord once for all. Abraham said, Has the Lord said it, or sayest thou this of thyself? The chief-captain answered, Hearken, righteous Abraham. The Lord has commanded, and I tell it thee. Abraham said, I will not go with thee. The chief-captain, hearing these words, straightway went forth from the presence of Abraham, and went up into the heavens, and

And about the ninth hour Michael brought Abraham back to his house. But Sarah his wife, not seeing what had become of Abraham, was consumed with grief, and gave up the ghost, and after the return of Abraham he found her dead, and buried her.

stood before God the Most High, and said, Lord Almighty, behold I have hearkened to Thy friend Abraham in all he has said to Thee, and have fulfilled his requests. I have shown to him Thy power, and all the earth and sea that is under heaven. I have shown to him judgment and recompense by means of cloud and chariots, and again he says, I will not go with thee. And the Most High said to the angel, Does my friend Abraham say thus again, I will not go with thee? The archangel said, Lord Almighty, he says thus, and I refrain from laying hands on him, because from the beginning he is Thy friend, and has done all things pleasing in Thy sight. There is no man like him on earth, not even Job the wondrous man, and therefore I refrain from laying hands on him. Command, therefore, Immortal King, what shall be done.

XVI. Then the Most High said, Call me hither Death that is called the shameless countenance and the pitiless look. And Michael the Incorporeal went and said to Death, Come hither; the lord of creation, the immortal king, calls thee. And Death, hearing this, shivered and trembled, being possessed with great terror, and coming with great fear it stood before the invisible father, shivering, groaning and trembling, awaiting the command of the Lord. Therefore the invisible God said to Death, Come hither, thou bitter and fierce name of the world, hide thy fierceness, cover thy corruption, and cast away thy bitterness from thee, and put on thy beauty and all thy glory, and go down to Abraham my friend, and take him and bring him to me. But now also I tell thee not to terrify him, but bring him with fair speech, for he is my own friend. Having heard this, Death went out from the presence of the Most High, and put on a robe of great brightness, and made his appearance like the sun, and became fair and beautiful above the sons of men, assuming the form of an archangel, having his cheeks flaming with fire, and he departed to Abraham. Now the righteous Abraham went out of his chamber, and sat under the trees of Mamre, holding his chin in his hand, and awaiting the coming of the archangel Michael. And behold, a smell of sweet odor came to him, and a flashing of light, and Abraham turned and saw Death coming towards him in great glory and beauty, And Abraham arose and went to meet him, thinking that it was the chief-captain of God, and Death beholding him saluted him, saying, Rejoice, precious Abraham, righteous soul, true friend of the Most High God, and companion of the holy angels.

XIII. But when the day of the death of Abraham drew nigh, the Lord God said to Michael, Death will not dare to go near to take away the soul of my servant, because he is my friend, but go thou and adorn Death with great beauty, and send him thus to Abraham, that he may see him with his eyes. And Michael straightway, as he was commanded, adorned Death with great beauty, and sent him thus to Abraham that he might see him. And he sat down near to Abraham, and Abraham seeing Death sitting near to him was afraid with a great fear. And Death said to Abraham, Hail, holy soul! hail, friend of the Lord God! hail, consolation and entertainment of travelers! And Abraham said, Thou art welcome, servant of the Most High God. I beseech thee, tell me who thou art; and entering into my house partake of food and drink, and depart from me, for since I have seen thee sitting near to me my soul has been troubled. For I am not at all worthy to come near thee, for thou art an exalted spirit and I am flesh and blood, and therefore I cannot bear thy glory, for I see that thy beauty is not of this world. And Death said to Abraham, I tell thee, in all the creation that God has made, there has not been found one like thee, for even the Lord himself by searching has not found such an one upon the whole earth. And Abraham said to Death, How durst thou lie? for I see that thy

Abraham said to Death, Hail thou of appearance and form like the sun, most glorious helper, bringer of light, wondrous man, from whence does thy glory come to us, and who art thou, and whence comest thou? Then Death said, Most righteous Abraham, behold I tell thee the truth. I am the bitter lot of death. Abraham said to him, Nay, but thou art the comeliness of the world, thou art the glory and beauty of angels and men, thou art fairer in form than every other, and sayest thou, I am the bitter lot of death, and not rather, I am fairer than every good thing. Death said, I tell thee the truth. What the Lord has named me, that also I tell thee. Abraham said, For what art thou come hither? Death said, For thy holy soul am I come. Then Abraham said, I know what thou meanest, but I will not go with thee; and Death was silent and answered him not a word.

XVII. Then Abraham arose, and went into his house, and Death also accompanied him thither. And Abraham went up into his chamber, and Death went up with him. And Abraham lay down upon his couch, and Death came and sat by his feet. Then Abraham said, Depart, depart from me, for I desire to rest upon my couch. Death said, I will not depart until I take thy spirit from thee. Abraham said to him, By the immortal God I charge thee to tell me the truth. Art thou death? Death said to him, I am Death. I am the destroyer of the world. Abraham said, I beseech thee, since thou art Death, tell me if thou comest thus to all in such fairness and glory and beauty? Death said, Nay, my lord Abraham, for thy righteousnesses, and the boundless sea of thy hospitality, and the greatness of thy love towards God has become a crown upon my head, and in beauty and great peace and gentleness I approach the righteous, but to sinners I come in great corruption and fierceness and the greatest bitterness and with fierce and pitiless look. Abraham said, I beseech thee, hearken to me, and show me thy fierceness and all thy corruption and bitterness. And Death said, Thou canst not behold my fierceness, most righteous Abraham. Abraham said, Yes, I shall be able to behold all thy fierceness by means of the name of the living God, for the might of my God that is in heaven is with me. Then Death put off all his comeliness and beauty, and all his glory and the form like the sun with which he was clothed, and put upon himself a tyrant's robe, and made his appearance gloomy and fiercer than all kind of wild beasts, and more unclean than all uncleanness. And he showed to Abraham seven

beauty is not of this world. And Death said to Abraham, Think not, Abraham, that this beauty is mine, or that I come thus to every man. Nay, but if any one is righteous like thee, I thus take crowns and come to him, but if it is a sinner I come in great corruption, and out of their sin I make a crown for my head, and I shake them with great fear, so that they are dismayed. Abraham therefore said to him, And whence comes thy beauty? And Death said, There is none other more full of corruption than I am. Abraham said to him, And art thou indeed he that is called Death? He answered him and said, I am the bitter name. I am weeping. . . .

XIV. And Abraham said to Death, Show us thy corruption. And Death made manifest his corruption; and he had two heads, the one had the face of a serpent and by it some die at once by asps, and the other head was like a sword; by it some die by the sword as by bows.

fiery heads of serpents and fourteen faces, (one) of flaming fire and of great fierceness, and a face of darkness, and a most gloomy face of a viper, and a face of a most terrible precipice, and a face fiercer than an asp, and a face of a terrible lion, and a face of a cerastes and basilisk. He showed him also a face of a fiery scimitar, and a sword-bearing face, and a face of lightning, lightening terribly, and a noise of dreadful thunder. He showed him also another face of a fierce stormy sea, and a fierce rushing river, and a terrible three-headed serpent, and a cup mingled with poisons, and in short he showed to him great fierceness and unendurable bitterness, and every mortal disease as of the odour of Death. And from the great bitterness and fierceness there died servants and maid-servants in number about seven thousand, and the righteous Abraham came into indifference of death so that his spirit failed him.

XVIII. And the all-holy Abraham, seeing these things thus, said to Death, I beseech thee, all-destroying Death, hide thy fierceness, and put on thy beauty and the shape which thou hadst before. And straightway Death hid his fierceness, and put on his beauty which he had before. And Abraham said to Death, Why hast thou done this, that thou hast slain all my servants and maid-servants? Has God sent thee hither for this end this day? Death said, Nay, my lord Abraham, it is not as thou sayest, but on thy account was I sent hither. Abraham said to Death, How then have these died? Has the Lord not spoken it? Death said, Believe thou, most righteous Abraham, that this also is wonderful, that thou also wast not taken away with them. Nevertheless I tell thee the truth, for if the right hand of God had not been with thee at that time, thou also wouldst have had to depart from this life. The righteous Abraham said, Now I know that I have come into indifference of death, so that my spirit fails, but I beseech thee, all-destroying Death, since my servants have died before their time, come let us pray to the Lord our God that he may hear us and raise up those who died by thy fierceness before their time. And death said, Amen, be it so. Therefore Abraham arose and fell upon the face of the ground in prayer, and Death together with him, and the Lord sent a spirit of life upon those that were dead and they were made alive again. Then the righteous Abraham gave glory to God.

XIX. And going up into his chamber he lay down, and Death came and stood before him. And Abraham said to him, Depart from me, for I desire to rest, because my

In that day the servants of Abraham died through fear of Death, and Abraham seeing them prayed to the Lord, and he raised them up.

spirit is in indifference. Death said, I will not depart from thee until I take thy soul. And Abraham with an austere countenance and angry look said to Death, Who has ordered thee to say this? Thou sayest these words of thyself boastfully, and I will not go with thee until the chief-captain Michael come to me, and I shall go with him. But this also I tell thee, if thou desirest that I shall accompany thee, explain to me all thy changes, the seven fiery heads of serpents and what the face of the precipice is, and what the sharp sword, and what the loud-roaring river, and what the tempestuous sea that rages so fiercely. Teach me also the unendurable thunder, and the terrible lightning, and the evil-smelling cup mingled with poisons. Teach me concerning all these. And Death answered, Listen, righteous Abraham. For seven ages I destroy the world and lead all down to Hades, kings and rulers, rich and poor, slaves and free men, I convoy to the bottom of Hades, and for this I showed thee the seven heads of serpents. The face of fire I showed thee because many die consumed by fire, and behold death through a face of fire. The face of the precipice I showed thee, because many men die descending from the tops of trees or terrible precipices and losing their life, and see death in the shape of a terrible precipice. The face of the sword I showed thee because many are slain in wars by the sword, and see death as a sword. The face of the great rushing river I showed thee because many are drowned and perish snatched away by the crossing of many waters and carried off by great rivers, and see death before their time. The face of the angry raging sea I showed thee because many in the sea falling into great surges and becoming shipwrecked are swallowed up and behold death as the sea. The unendurable thunder and the terrible lightning I showed thee because many men in the moment of anger meet with unendurable thunder and terrible lightning coming to seize upon men, and see death thus. I showed thee also the poisonous wild beasts, asps and basilisks, leopards and lions and lions' whelps, bears and vipers, and in short the face of every wild beast I showed thee, most righteous one, because many men are destroyed by wild beasts, and others by poisonous snakes, serpents and asps and cerastes and basilisks and vipers, breathe out their life and die. I showed thee also the destroying cups mingled with poison, because many men being given poison to drink by other men straightway depart unexpectedly.

XX. Abraham said, I beseech thee, is there also an unexpected death? Tell me. Death said, Verily, verily, I tell thee in the truth of God that there are seventy-two deaths. One is the just death, having its fixed time, and many men in one hour enter into death being given over to the grave. Behold, I have told thee all that thou hast asked, now I tell thee, most righteous Abraham, to dismiss all counsel, and cease from asking anything once for all, and come, go with me, as the God and judge of all has commanded me. Abraham said to Death, Depart from me yet a little, that I may rest on my couch, for I am very faint at heart, for since I have seen thee with my eyes my strength has failed me, all the limbs of my flesh seem to me a weight as of lead, and my spirit is distressed exceedingly. Depart for a little; for I have said I cannot bear to see thy shape. Then Isaac his son came and fell upon his breast weeping, and his wife Sarah came and embraced his feet, lamenting bitterly. There came also his men slaves and women slaves and surrounded his couch, lamenting greatly. And Abraham came into indifference of death, and Death said to Abraham, Come, take my right hand, and may cheerfulness and life and strength come to thee. For Death deceived Abraham, and he took his right hand, and straightway his soul adhered to the hand of Death. And immediately the archangel Michael came with a multitude of angels and took up his precious soul in his hands in a divinely woven linen cloth, and they tended the body of the just Abraham with divine ointments and perfumes until the third day after his death, and buried him in the land of promise, at the oak of Mamre, but the angels received his precious soul, and ascended into heaven, singing the hymn of "thrice holy" to the Lord the God of all, and they set it there to worship the God and Father. And after great praise and glory had been given to the Lord, and Abraham bowed down to worship, there came the undefiled voice of the God and Father saying thus, Take therefore my friend Abraham into Paradise, where are the tabernacles of my righteous ones, and the abodes of my saints Isaac and Jacob in his bosom, where there is no trouble, nor grief, nor sighing, but peace and rejoicing and life unending. (And let us, too, my beloved brethren, imitate the hospitality of the patriarch Abraham, and attain to his virtuous way of life, that we may be thought worthy of the life eternal, glorifying the Father, Son and Holy Ghost; to whom be glory and power forever. Amen.)

But God returned and removed the soul of Abraham as in a dream, and the archangel Michael took it up into the heavens. And Isaac buried his father beside his mother Sarah, glorifying and praising God, for to him is due glory, honour and worship, of the Father, Son and Holy Ghost, now and always and to all eternity. Amen.

THE ACTS OF XANTHIPPE AND POLYXENA

INTRODUCTION

THE original Greek text of this work is edited for the first time in Text and Studies, Vol. II., No. 3 (1893), by Montague Rhodes James, M.A., from the only MS. known to him, a Paris one of the eleventh century. References to these Acts are not common in works dealing with the saints of the early church, and few writers seem to have known the work itself.

In substance the Acts are a religious novel, similar in form, and to some extent in matter, to the Greek romances by Achilles Tatius, Heliodorus, and others, and based upon the belief that St. Paul actually did visit Spain, according to the intention expressed by him in Romans xv. 24. The editor of the Greek text is inclined to assign its composition to about the middle of the third century, reasoning from its relations to the Acts of Paul, and those of other apostles, which its author apparently knew and made use of. Thus a knowledge of the Acts of Paul and Thecla may be inferred from c. xxvi., of the Acts of Peter from c. xxiv., and of those of Andrew from cc. xxviii.–xxxi.

The first and longest part of the story (from c. i. to xxi.) gives an account of the conversion of Xanthippe, wife of Probus, a man of rank in Spain. In this part the narrative is less prominent than the speeches and prayers, which are numerous, and of considerable length. With c. xxii. a new section of the story begins, of which no previous warning has been given except in the title, containing the adventures of Polyxena, the sister of Xanthippe, who is carried off in the latter's absence. The rest of the story is much more diversified than the early part, being full of incident and introducing a great variety of persons—the apostles Peter, Philip, and Andrew, an ass-driver, the Jewess Rebecca, a wicked prefect and his kind-hearted son, and finally Onesimus, who brings Polyxena back to Spain.

This difference in the character of the narrative in the two parts causes also some difference in the language, which in the earlier section is more diffuse and more difficult of exact translation than in the later one. The meaning of some words is also doubtful: those translated "lamp-stand" and "destroyer," towards the end of c. xxi., are so rendered in accordance with suggestions by his Exc. M. Gennadius, who also characterises the language of the text as full of errors.

LIFE AND CONDUCT OF THE HOLY WOMEN XANTHIPPE, POLYXENA, AND REBECCA

I. When the blessed Paul was at Rome through the word of the Lord, it happened that a certain servant of a ruler of Spain came to Rome with letters of his master's, and heard the word of God from Paul, the truly golden and beautiful nightingale. This servant being greatly touched, and being unable to remain and be filled with the divine word because he was hastened by the letters, returned into Spain in great grief, and being unable to show his desire to any one, because his master was an idolater, he was always pained at heart and sighing greatly. Now this servant was honoured and faithful to his masters, and as time went past, the servant fell sick and grew lean of flesh, which his master perceiving said to him, What has happened to thee that thou art thus fallen together in countenance? The servant said, There is a great pain in my heart, and I can in no way find rest. His master said to him, And what is the pain that cannot receive healing from my chief physician? The servant said, While I was still in Rome, this pain and its recurring mishap made itself known to me. His master said, And knowest thou not of any who have fallen into this disease and been healed? The servant said, Yes, but where that physician is I know not, for I left him in Rome. So many as have been attended by that physician and have gone through the water in his hands, have received healing immediately. His master said, I ought not to grudge to send thee yet again to Rome, if perchance thou mightest obtain healing.

II. And while they spoke thus, behold his mistress, by name Xanthippe, overhearing these words, and learning of the teaching of Paul, said, What is the name of that physician, and what is the healing to ward off such a disease? The servant said to her, The calling upon a new name, and anointing with oil and washing with water. By this treatment I have seen many that had incurable pains receive healings. As he said this, the images of the idols that stood in the house began to be shaken and fall down. And his mistress beckoned to him, saying, Seest thou, brother, the images of the idols being shaken, how they cannot endure the power of the word? And his master, by name Probus, arose from his mid-day sleep with a very gloomy countenance, for the Devil had greatly disturbed him, because the knowledge of God had come into his house. And he questioned the servant of everything in order, and the servant having been seized by sickness by the foreknowledge of God, disclosed to him the life of man, and Xanthippe was incurable in her soul concerning this teaching. So Probus too was grieved for Xanthippe, because from that time she was wasting herself away with waking and abstinence and other austerities.

III. And Xanthippe going away to her couch and groaning, said, Woe is me, wretched one, lying in darkness, that I have not learned the name of the new teacher, that I might summon his prayer to help me, and what to say I know not. Shall I call upon him by the name of his God? but I cannot say, The God that is preached by such a one. Nevertheless I shall say thus by conjecture, O God, giving light in Hades, and guiding those in darkness, Lord of free men and kings, and preached by worthy servants in all the world, called upon as a brother by sinful men and quick to hear, to whom not even archangels can send up worthy songs of praise, who hast shown to me, humble and unworthy, the ever-living and abiding seed (though my ignorance permits me not to receive it), hasten also the things that concern me, Lord, since by thy will thou hast made thyself heard by me, and in thy compassion show me the proclamation of thy herald, that I may learn of him what is pleasing to thee. Yea, I beseech thee look upon my ignorance, O God, and enlighten me with the light of thy countenance, thou that never overlookest any of those that call upon thee in truth. Probus, her husband said to her, Why troublest thou thyself so much, lady, and dost not at all turn to sleep? Xanthippe said, I cannot sleep, for there is in me an incurable pain. Probus said to her, And what is thy pain or grief, O lady, that I am not sufficient to comfort thee? All that thou hast wished unto this day I have served thee in, and now what is it that thou hast, and dost not tell me? Xanthippe says to him, I beseech thee this thing only, my lord, permit me for a little and for this day only to sleep apart from thee. And Probus said to her, Be it as thou wilt, lady; only leave off thy groaning.

IV. Then entering into her bed-chamber alone, she spoke thus with tears, In what way, my God, I shall act, or what counsel I shall take, I know not. Shall I declare the thought that has come upon me? I fear the madness and disorder of the city. Shall I fly from this impious city? I fear the contrivance of the devil for seizing the sheep. Shall I await the mercy and swiftness of the Lord? Again I fear the untimely snatching away of life, for the death of sinners has no warning. Shall I depart and flee away to Rome? I fear the length of the journey, being unable to go on foot. But while I say these things by conjecture, constrained by my desire (for I cannot speak with surety), may I find pardon with thee, my God, and do thou fulfil my desire with excess of right words, and think me but worthy to hear thy preacher, for if I say, to see his face, I ask a great thing. Blessed is he that is found in the company of thy preachers, and is satisfied with their precious countenances. Blessed are they that are yoked under the preaching of thy commandments. Blessed are they that keep thy commandments; but where now, Lord, are thy mercies to our fathers, that we also may be their successors in love toward thee and heirs of faith. But behold now, Lord, I cannot find any one that has love for thee, that communing with him I might even a little refresh my soul. Speed therefore, Lord, to yoke me in desire for thee, and keep me under the shadow of thy wings, for thou alone art God, glorified to all eternity. Amen.

V. Therefore Xanthippe saying these words and others like them, groaned continually all the night, and Probus heard her and was greatly distressed, and arising from his couch when the morning came he went in to her, and seeing her eyes inflamed with tears, he said, Wherefore, lady, dost thou thus vex me, and wilt not tell me thy pain? Tell it me, that I may do whatever is pleasing to thee, and distress me not with thy trouble. Xanthippe says to him, Be of good cheer rather, my lord, and be not vexed, for my trouble shall not harm thee, but if I have found favour before thee, go forth now to the salutation, and allow me to indulge myself in it as I will, for it is not possible for man to take from me the insatiable pain. And listening to her he went out immediately to receive the salutations of the men of the city, for he was the great man among them, and was also known to Nero, the Emperor. And sitting down, great grief appeared in his countenance, and being asked the reason of his grief by the chief men of the city, he said to them that he had fallen into many and unfounded charges.

VI. And Xanthippe went out into the garden, that she might await there looking closely for certainty of her husband, and she saw the delight of the trees, and the various warbling of the birds, and said, groaning, O beauty of the world! for that which we hitherto thought to come of itself, we know now that all things are beautifully fashioned by the beautiful One. O power and invention of wisdom! for not only has he placed in men a thousand tongues, but also in birds he has distinguished various voices, as if from anthems and responses to receive sweet-voiced and heart-stirring hymns from his own works. O delightfulness of the air, declaring the inimitable creator! Who shall turn my sorrow into rejoicing? And again she said, God to whom praise is sung by all, give me peace and comfort. As she said these things, Probus also came up from the street to break his fast, and when he saw her countenance altered by tears, he began to pull out the hairs of his head, but he dared not speak to her then so as not to mingle other trouble with her trouble. So he went and fell upon his couch, and said, groaning, Alas, that I had not even the consolation of a child from her, but only acquire grief upon grief. Two years are not yet full since I was wedded to her, and already she meditates divorce.

VII. But Xanthippe was always keeping watch through the doors into the streets of the city, and the blessed Paul, the preacher and teacher and illuminator of the world, left Rome and came even into Spain by the fore-knowledge of God. And coming up to the gates of the city he stood and prayed, and crossing himself entered the city. When Xanthippe saw the blessed Paul walking quietly and equally, and adorned with all virtue and understanding, she was greatly delighted in him and her heart leaped continually, and as possessed with an unexpected joy she said with herself, Why does my heart beat vehemently at the sight of this man? Why is his walk quiet and equable, as of one who expects to take in his arms one that is pursued? Why is his countenance kindly, as of one that tends the sick? Why does he look so lovingly hither and thither, as one who desires to assist those who are seeking to flee from the mouths of dragons? Who shall tell me that this is one from the flock of preachers? If it were possible for me, I should wish to touch the hem of his garments, that I may behold his kindness and readiness to receive and sweet odour; for the servant had told her this also, that the hems of his garments had the odour of precious perfumes.

VIII. Now Probus heard her words, and straightway ran out by himself into the street, and laying hold of Paul's hand said to him, Man, who thou art I know not, but deign to enter into my house; perchance thou mayest be to me a cause of salvation. Paul said to him, It will be well with thee, son, after thy request! And they went in together to Xanthippe. When Xanthippe therefore saw the great Paul, the intellectual eyes of her heart were uncovered, and she read upon his forehead, having as it were golden seals, these words, PAUL THE PREACHER OF GOD. Then exulting and rejoicing she threw herself at his feet, and twisting her hair together she wiped his feet, saying, Welcome, O man of God, to us humble ones, that live as shadows among shadows. For thou hast looked upon those who were running into Hades as into something beautiful, who addressed the crooked serpent and destroyer as provider and protector, who were running into the dark Hades as to their father, those that were fashioned with a rational nature but have become like irrational creatures. Thou hast sought me, lowly one, having the sun of righteousness in my heart. Now the poison is stayed, when I have seen thy precious face. Now he that troubled me is flown away, when thy most beautiful counsel has appeared to me. Now I shall be considered worthy of repentance, when I have received the seal of the preacher of the Lord. Before now I have deemed many happy who met with you, but I say boldly that from this time forth I myself shall be called happy by others, because I have touched thy hem, because I have received thy prayers, because I have enjoyed thy sweet and honeyed teaching. Thou hast not hesitated to come to us, thou that fishest the dry land in thy course, and gatherest the fish that fall in thy way into the net of the kingdom of heaven.

IX. The great Paul said to her, Arise, daughter, and look not upon me as having been sought out of thy ignorance by my foresight. For Christ, the provider of the world, the searcher out of sinners and the lost, who has not only called to mind those upon earth, but also by his own presence has redeemed those in Hades, he himself has pitied thee, and sent me hither that he might visit and pity many others together with thee. For this mercy and visitation are not of us, but are his injunction and command, even as we also have received mercy and been saved by him. Probus hearing this was astonished at their words, for he was altogether ignorant of these things. But Paul by force raised up Xanthippe from his feet, and she running set a new gilded chair for Paul to sit down upon. The great Paul said to her, My daughter Xanthippe, do not thus, for ye have not yet accorded to the faith of Christ, but wait a little, till the Lord shall set in order what is necessary! Xanthippe said to Paul, Sayest thou this to try me, O preacher of God, or hast thou any foreknowledge? Paul said, No, daughter, but the devil, who hates the servants of God, sows wickedness in the hearts of his own servants, to oppose those that labour for Christ in preaching, for his wickedness has extended to the apostles and even to the Lord himself. Therefore it is fitting to approach the unbelievers gently and kindly! Xanthippe said to Paul, I beseech thee, if thou lovest thy servants, make prayer for Probus, and let me see if he that is hated by thee can work in him; let me see if he can even stand against thy prayer. And Paul rejoiced exceedingly at the words of her faith, and said to her, Believe me, daughter, that by his suggestion and working I have not passed a single hour without chains and blows. Xanthippe said to him, But thou sufferest these things by thy own free will, since thou hast not neglected thy preaching even to scourging, but this again I tell thee, that thy bonds shall be the defeat of the prompter, and thy humiliation their overthrow.

X. Now the report of his presence ran through the whole city and the country round about, for some of that city having been at Rome had seen the signs and wonders that were done by the blessed Paul, and came to see if this was he. Many therefore came into the house of Probus, and he began to be annoyed and to say, I will not suffer my house to be made an inn. Xanthippe knowing that the face of Probus had begun to be estranged, and that he spoke thus, was greatly distressed, saying, Alas, wretched me, that we are not thought fully worthy to keep this man in our house; for if Paul goes hence, the church also will be held elsewhere. Then Xanthippe, considering these matters, put her hand on the foot of Paul, and taking dust she called Probus to her, and placing her hand on his breast said, O Lord, my God, who hast sought out me, lowly one and ignorant of thee, send what is fitting into this heart. And Paul perceived her prayer, and made the sign of the cross, and for several days the people entered unhindered, and as many as had sick and vexed by unclean spirits brought them, and all were healed.

XI. And Xanthippe said to Paul, Teacher, my heart is greatly consumed because I have not as yet received baptism. And after this Probus being again moved by the devil, cast Paul out of the house and shut up Xanthippe in her chamber. Then one of the chief men, Philotheus by name, besought the great Paul to come into his house, but the great Paul was unwilling to do so, saying, Lest Probus trouble thy house on my account. Philotheus said to him, Nay, father, I am not at all subject to him, for in no other thing is he greater than me, except in rank, and that because the parents of Xanthippe are above me. But if Probus come to me, I am above him in riches and in war. Then Paul, the great apostle of the Lord, was persuaded, and went into the house of Philotheus the ex-prefect. All this was done by the Evil one that Xanthippe might receive holy baptism with tribulation, and be faint-hearted concerning the commandments of Christ.

XII. Xanthippe therefore, with tears, said to her servants, Have ye learned where Paul is gone to? They said, Yea, in the house of Philotheus the ex-prefect, and Xanthippe rejoiced greatly that Philotheus also believed, being able, as she said, to persuade Probus also. Then Probus called Xanthippe to supper, and when she consented not, Probus said, Think not that in bed also thou wilt keep away from me. But when he lay down to supper, Xanthippe bending her knees, prayed to the Lord, saying, Eternal and immortal God, that didst take dust from the ground, and didst not value it according to the nature of its creation, but didst call it the son of immortality, thou who didst come from the heart of the father to the heart of the earth for our sake, on whom the cherubim dare not fix their gaze, and for us wast hidden in the womb that by taking up thy abode in a mother thou mightest make good the offence of Eve. Thou that didst drink gall and vinegar, and wast pierced in the side by a spear, that thou mightest heal the wound given by the rib to Adam. For Eve being his rib wrought a blow for Adam, and through him for all the world. Thou that gavest a sleep without perception to the serpent, so that he might not know thy Incarnation, remember also my groaning and tears, and grant fulfilment to my sleep,[1] and bring sleep upon Probus until I shall be deemed worthy of the gift of holy baptism, for I vehemently desire to obtain this, to the glory and praise of thy holy name.

XIII. But Probus, while still at supper, commanded the doors of their house to be secured by cruel and wicked soldiers, and having given these orders, he straightway fell asleep upon the couch. Then the servants came and announced this to Xanthippe that he might be awakened, but she said, Put out the lights, my children, and leave him thus. And in the first sleep, taking three hundred pieces of gold, she went to the doors, saying with herself, Perchance the porter will be persuaded by the amount of money. But he, being evil and froward, would not be persuaded to do this, and she, loosing also her girdle, which was set with precious stones and worth two hundred pieces of gold, gave it to him and went out saying, Lord, I win over my own slaves with money, that thy preacher Paul may not be oppressed by Probus. And Xanthippe went on to the house of Philotheus the ex-prefect, as to a great and incredible work, running and praising God. As she therefore passed through a certain place, the demons pursued her with fiery torches and lightnings, and she, turning, saw behind her this terrible sight, and being possessed with great fear said, What has happened to thee now, wretched soul? Thou hast been deprived of thy desire. Thou wast running to salvation, thou wast running to baptism, and thou hast fallen into the serpent and his ministers, and these things thy sins have prepared for thee. Speaking thus she was even fainting at heart from great despair, but the great Paul being forewarned by God of the assault of the demons, immediately stood beside her, being also preceded by a beautiful youth. And straightway the vision of the demons disappeared, and Paul said to her, Arise, daughter Xanthippe, and behold the Lord desired by thee, by whose flame the heavens are

[1] So the text; perhaps "prayer" ought to be read.

shaken and the deep is dried up, coming to thee and pitying and saving thee. Behold him that accepts thy prayers and straightway gives ear. See him coming in the shape of a man, and take courage against the demons. Then she rising from the ground said to him, Master, why hast thou left me solitary? Even now make haste to seal me, so that if death come upon me I may depart to him who is full of compassion and has no arrogance.

XIV. Therefore the great Paul straightway taking her hand, went into the house of Philotheus, and baptised her in the name of the Father and of the Son and the Holy Ghost. Then taking bread also he gave her the eucharist saying, Let this be to thee for a remission of sins and for a renewing of thy soul. Then the blessed Xanthippe, receiving the divine grace of holy baptism, returned to her own house, rejoicing and praising the Lord. The porter seeing her complained loudly in violent words, that her going out might be deemed to have been without his will if Probus should notice it; but he that gave her light along with Paul kept the whole house, together with Probus, in a deep sleep, and they did not hear his words at all. Then she went running into her bed-chamber, saying, What shall I say of thee, searcher out of sinners, who art most present with us in tribulations. Thy goodness does these things, since for the sake of man whom thou didst make thou didst go down even to death, for, however much man stir thee to anger many times, yet thou, Lord, pourest out thy mercies upon him. O depth of compassion and wealth of mercy; O immeasurable goodness and incomparable kindness; O treasure of good things, and giver of mercy, and enricher of all that believe in thee! If, therefore, one who loves thee say, Be near me, Lord, thou hast already anticipated him. If he say, I give thee thanks; hear my words, before they are spoken, thou understandest. And as for those that ask of thee, thou givest to each after his asking. Thy goodness seeks out those that know thee not, and thou runnest to sinners. O cheerful look, filling the ways of sinners with mercy; O excellent watching and exhortation of the ignorant! Who shall tell my lord Paul of the salvation that has now befallen me, that he might come and give words of thanksgiving for me to this protector of sinners? Come many and behold and know the Lord, who hates sin, but has mercy on sinners. Come, now, O Paul, preacher of God, for with thee even now I sit under instruction, and give words of thanksgiving for me, for I desire to keep silence, since human reason makes me afraid, lest I have not the grace of eloquence. I desire to keep silence, and am compelled to speak, for some one inflames and sweetens me within. If I say, I will shut my mouth, there is some one that murmurs in me. Shall I say a great thing? Is it not that teacher that is in Paul, without arrogance, filling the heavens, speaking within and waiting without, sitting on the throne with the father and stretched upon the cross by man. What, therefore, I shall do I know not. My worthless mind delights me, and is not unfolded to the end. Thou that hadst thy hands fixed with nails and thy side pierced with the spear, thou star out of Jacob and lion's whelp out of Judah, thou rod out of Jesse, and man and God out of Mary, thou invisible God in the bosom of the Father, and that canst not be looked upon by cherubim, and art mocked in Israel, glory be to thee, who didst appear on the earth and wast taken by the people, hung upon the tree and by the report of the wicked falsely said to be stolen, and that hast bought us all together.

XV. While she was still speaking thus, there appeared a cross on the eastern wall, and straightway there entered through it a beautiful youth, having round about him trembling rays, and under him an extended light, on which also he walked. And as he entered within, all the foundations of that house shook and sounded with a great trembling. Xanthippe seeing him cried out and fell to the ground as if dead; but he being pitiful and kind, changing immediately into the shape of Paul, raised her up, saying, Arise, Xanthippe, and fear not, for the servants of God are thus glorified. Then Xanthippe arising, gazed upon him, and thinking it to be Paul, said, How art thou come in hither, preacher of God, seeing that I have given five hundred pieces of gold to the porter, and that although he is my slave, while thou hast no money? The Lord said to her, My servant Paul is richer than all wealth, for whatsoever treasure he acquires here he sends it before him into the kingdom of heaven, that departing thither he may rest in the unending and eternal rest. This is the treasure of Paul, thou and thy like. Then Xanthippe gazing upon him, desirous to say something, saw his face shining as the light; and being greatly amazed, and putting both her hands over her face she threw herself to the ground, and said, Hide thyself, Lord, from my bodily eyes and enlighten my understanding, for I know now who thou art. Thou art he whose precursor was the cross, the only begotten son of the Father alone above, and only son of the Virgin alone below. Thou art he who was pierced in the hands and who rent the rocks. Thou art he whom none other can carry except the bosom of the Father.

XVI. And as she spoke thus the Lord was again hidden from her, and Xanthippe, coming to herself, said, Woe is me wretched one, that no one has told me what is the gratitude of slaves towards their master. If Paul the preacher of the Lord were here, how could he give praise ? But perchance in the face of such favors and gifts they are silent, possessed only with tears, for it is not possible worthily to praise any one according to his favour. Saying this she was seized with great faintness from lack of food, for having been strongly possessed with desire for Christ she had forgotten to take nourishment. Therefore, being greatly exhausted by abstinence and the vision and want of sleep and other austerities, she was unable to rise from the ground.

XVII. And Probus arose from his couch with a very gloomy countenance, for in his sleep he had seen a dream, and was greatly troubled concerning it. But the porter seeing him about to issue to the market-place, having his countenance thus troubled, was greatly afraid, Lest, said he, he know what has happened, and will miserably destroy me. Probus, however, having gone forth and signified to those in the market what was fitting for the day and season, speedily returned into the house, and said to his servants, Call me quickly the wise men Barandus and Gnosteas. When they were summoned he said to them, I have seen a very terrible vision, and what appeared in it is difficult for our power to interpret. This, however, do ye disclose to me, as being the most excellent of all the world. Expound it to me when I tell it you. Barandus says to him, If the vision can be interpreted by our wisdom, we shall explain it to thee, but if it be of the faith that is now spoken of we cannot expound it to thee, for it is of another wisdom and understanding. However, let our lord and master tell the dream, and let us see if there is any explanation for it. Probus says to Gnosteas, Wherefore answerest thou nothing ? Gnosteas said, I have not heard the dream, and what can I say but whatever it may be, if it is by reason of Paul ? Tell me now, and thou wilt find it so. Probus said, I thought I was standing in a certain unknown and strange country, and that there sat there an Ethiop king, who ruled over all the earth and seemed never to have any successor. There stood beside him multitudes of servants, and all hastened to destruction and had mastery far and wide. And when that Ethiop seemed to have gained his purpose, there arose a raven and standing above him croaked with a pitiful voice. And straightway there arose from the eastern parts an eagle, and seized his kingdom, and his power was made vain, and those standing by him fled to the eagle. Then that king strove against those that fled to the eagle, but the eagle carried it up into heaven, and, behold, there came a helper to those that fled to the eagle and left his staff to them. Then they laying hold of it were not overcome by the violence of that king. So many as ran to those who had the staff, he washed them in pure water, and they that were washed had power over his kingdom. And by that staff the enemies of the king were put to flight, therefore capable men laying hold of the staff turned to themselves great multitudes. And that king strove against them, and had no might at all, but he hindered many from believing in him that sent out the men into the world to bear witness, and for that reason many were grieved. Nevertheless, this one did not constrain any like the other, for he himself was ruler of all light. This then was the end.

XVIII. Then the wise Barandus said, By the grace of God I shall tell the things sent into the world by the Lord. The king whom thou sawest is the Devil, and the multitudes of his servants are the demons, and the throngs about him are they that worship the gods. Whereas he thought to have no successor, he looked not for the coming of Christ. The raven betokened the weakness of his kingdom, for the raven kept not obedience to the righteous Noah, but loved pitiful things. The eagle that arose and took away his kingdom and carried it up into heaven, and that there came a protector of those that fled to the eagle, having a staff, that is the Lord Jesus Christ, who left to them his staff, that is, his precious cross; and that he washed those that fled to him signifies the invulnerable breast-plate of baptism, and therefore they were not overcome. The capable men sent into the world with the cross are the preachers of God like Paul who is now with us, against whom that king has no power. This was made known to thee because even on those who are hard of belief God has compassion in some way. See therefore whether even thou wilt be able to injure Paul though thou desirest, for the mighty power that shields him has been shown thee by the Lord. Therefore, understand what has been said to thee by me, and serve not that king of darkness, for as thou sawest his kingdom vanish away, so shall all his servants perish with him. Come now, therefore, my Lord, let us go to Paul and receive baptism from him, lest Satan have mastery over us also. Probus said, Let us first go to Xanthippe and see whether she still lives, for behold there are twenty-nine days since she has tasted anything; for I saw her face in the evening, and it was as of one prepared to depart.

XIX. And as they went into the chamber, they heard her singing.

Praise the Lord ye sinners also, because he accepts your prayers also. Alleluia.

Praise the Lord ye that have despaired like me, for many are his mercies. Alleluia.

Praise him ye ungodly, because for you he was crucified. Alleluia.

Praise him ye that strive for the salvation of sinners, because God loves you. Alleluia.

Praise him, ye that rejoice at the calling of sinners, because ye are fellow-citizens with the saints. Alleluia.

As she said these words and more than these with tears, the wise men Barandus and Gnosteas opening the door entered and fell at her feet, saying, Pray for us lowly ones, O servant of Christ, that he may bring us also into thy number. But she said to them, Brethren, I am not Paul who remits sins, but neither is he far from you. Therefore fall not before my knees, but go to him, who is also more able to benefit you. Then they came running to the house of Philotheus to Paul, and found him teaching a great multitude. And Probus also came to hear Paul, and Xanthippe entered along with him to salute him, and coming near to Paul and bending her knees she did him reverence. Probus seeing this marvelled that her so proud spirit had changed to so great humility, for she sat beside the feet of Paul on the ground humbly and as one of the worthless. And Probus was greatly grieved, not yet attending to the hearing of the word, but was ever gazing and fixing his attention on Xanthippe.

XX. The great Paul was teaching thus, Let those that burn in the flesh observe lawful marriage, avoiding fornication, especially that with another's wife, and let those that are united keep to one another. Probus heard this teaching with delight, and said, O Paul, how excellently and wisely thou employest this teaching. Why then has Xanthippe withdrawn from me? And Paul said, My son Probus, they that foresee that the works of men shall be tried with fire, and that have always in their mind the inexorableness of death, cast out all desire that cleaves to the flesh. But woe when the desire shall judge him that desired, then he shall gnash his teeth to no effect and in vain, for the amendment of repentance is past. Hearing this Probus went up into his house marvelling, and tasted nothing that day, but went and lay down upon his bed. And about the third hour of the night he arose and said, Alas, how wretched was the day in which I was wedded to Xanthippe. Would that I had died and not seen her. Saying this he arose and said, I shall pray to the God of Paul. Perchance he will do to me also what is fitting, that I may not become a reproach in the world, being rejected by her. And straightway falling upon the ground he said, O God of Paul, if, as I have heard from Xanthippe, thou dost seek after the ignorant and turn back those that are astray, do to me also what is fitting; for thou art the king of life and death, as I have heard, and hast dominion over things in heaven and on earth and under the earth, and over all the thoughts and desires of men, and to thee alone belongs glory to all eternity. Amen.

XXI. Then Probus arising from the ground fell again upon the couch, and arising early he came to Paul, and finding him baptising many in the name of the life-giving Trinity, he said, My lord Paul, if only I were worthy to receive baptism, behold the hour. Paul said to him, Son, behold the water is ready for the cleansing of those that come to Christ. Therefore immediately taking off his garments, and Paul laying hold of him, he leapt into the water, saying, Jesus Christ, son of God, and everlasting God, let all my sins be taken away by this water. And Paul said, We baptise thee in the name of the Father and Son and Holy Ghost. After this he made him to receive the eucharist of Christ. Then Xanthippe, being greatly rejoiced, began in the house toward evening together with her husband to give good cheer to all those in the house, and to prepare a feast, and when they came, after giving orders for the supper to be magnificent she herself went up to the chamber. And behold on the stairs a demon coming in the likeness of one of the actors, and standing in a dark corner, was desirous to frighten and terrify Xanthippe. But she thinking it to be the actor that she ordinarily had, said in anger, Many a time have I said to him that I no longer care for toys, and he despises me as being a woman; and straightway seizing an iron lamp-stand, she hurled it at his face, and crushed all his features. Then the demon cried out, saying, O violence, from this destroyer even women have received power to strike us. But Xanthippe was greatly afraid.

XXII. After supper then Probus went forth to hear the word, but Xanthippe sitting in her bed-chamber was reading the prophets, her sister Polyxena lying upon the couch. Xanthippe loved Polyxena exceedingly, because she was younger than herself, and beautiful in appearance, and Probus also loved her greatly. And as Polyxena lay upon the couch she saw this dream, that a dragon, hideous in appearance, came and signified to her to come to him, and when she did not obey him to go to him, he came running and swallowed her. From fear of this the girl leapt up trembling, and Xanthippe running to her said, What has happened to thee, dearest, that thou hast leapt up thus suddenly? She for a long time was unable to speak; then coming to herself she said, Alas, my sister Xanthippe, what danger or tribulation awaits me, I know not; for I saw in my dream that a hideous dragon came and signed to me to go to him, and, when I would not go, he came running and swallowed me, beginning at my feet. While I was terrified at this, there suddenly spoke out of the air, in the light of the sun, a beautiful youth, whom I thought to be the brother of Paul, saying, Verily, thou hast no power. Who also took me by the hand and straightway drew me out of him, and straightway the dragon disappeared. And behold his hand was full of sweet odour as of balsam or aught else for fragrance. Xanthippe said to her, Truly thou must be greatly troubled, my sister Polyxena, but God has thee dear, seeing that he has shown thee strange and marvellous things. Therefore arise quickly in the morning and receive the holy baptism, and ask in the baptism to be delivered from the snares of the dragon.

XXIII. Xanthippe, having said this to Polyxena, and having made a cross of wood, went to Paul, but Polyxena remained alone in the bed-chamber, her nurse having gone together with Xanthippe. And about the middle of the night, a certain man, powerful in wealth and assistance, finding the doors open and using magical arts, entered within, desiring to carry away Polyxena. She discovering this fled into the mill, but the magicians led by the demons found her. And she, not finding any door to escape by, said, Alas that I am given over to this destroyer; for she had heard that he was at enmity with her suitor, and he did this to assail and vex him, being a man who was a robber and exceeding cruel. Therefore seizing her they went out of the city, dragging her to the sea. She looked round this way and that, but there was none to deliver her, and groaning she said, Alas, my sister Xanthippe, thou didst send seven hundred pieces of gold to Rome and buy books, that through them thou mightest prophesy by me; for this evening thou didst read, I looked to my right hand and beheld, but there was no one that knew me; flight perished from me and there is no one that seeketh out my soul.[1]

XXIV. While she said these words, those that were dragging her away walked in haste, and coming to the shore they hired a ship and sailed for Babylonia, for he that carried her off had a brother there, a ruler of a district. But the wind blew against them, so that they could not proceed by reason of it, and as they were rowing on the sea, behold the great apostle of the Lord, Peter, was sailing past in a ship, being urged by a dream to go to Rome, because when Paul departed for Spain there had entered into Rome a certain deceiver and magician, Simon by name, and had broken up the church which Paul had established. And, behold, as he journeyed he heard a voice from heaven saying to him, Peter, to-morrow there will meet thee a ship coming from Spain; arise, therefore, and pray for the soul that is troubled in it. As soon therefore as Peter saw the ship, remembering the dream, he said, O Jesus, that hast care for the troubled, whom the tribulation of those in a strange land moves to compassion, whom the weeping of those in captivity made to come upon the earth, who givest us at all time whatsoever we desire, and never turnest away from our request, show now also pity and assistance to the soul that is tossed about in that ship, because thou, O Lord, pitiest at all time those in pain. The demons then, perceiving his prayer, said to the magicians, Avoid ye the course of that ship, for if we meet with it, we cannot move.

XXV. But the loving God taking care for Polyxena, the vessel arrived in Greece, the blessed Philip being there, and having come down to the shore by a vision, and there accompanied him also great multitudes of those who were being taught by him. And behold the vessel wherein was Polyxena appeared, terribly tossed about. And the blessed Philip said, Behold the vessel on account of which we came down here, in which there is a soul in trouble. When the vessel arrived and all had disembarked upon the dry land, they lay as half dead, because they had been greatly

[1] Psalm 142. 4.

tossed about in the sea. But the apostle Philip ordered Polyxena to be lifted and taken to the place where he was lodging, and the rest to be looked to. But he that had carried off Polyxena, recovering from the disorder of the sea, was desirous to take her again, for Philip, having entrusted Polyxena to one of those that were taught by him, went on his way rejoicing. But he that had her said, She was committed to me by a holy man, and I cannot give her up to thee. He, however, giving no heed to him and finding there a kinsman of his, a nobleman, prepared for war, gathering eight thousand men. Polyxena, knowing this, went forth by night and departed, but he that had charge of Polyxena said, Taking the tunic of Philip, I shall go forth alone to meet them; but as he said this it was announced to him that the maid was not there. Then he, leaving all thought of the war, ran into the bed-chamber, and not finding the maid threw himself on the ground, saying, Woe is me, wretched one, that have become an enemy of Philip. What shall I answer him, when he asks the maiden from me? His servants came and said to him, Arise, our lord, from the ground, for the forces have surrounded thy house, and the maid cannot be found. He said, Leave me thus to die on her account. Perhaps, even by this, Philip the servant of Christ may be fully satisfied, since I shall be found despising his command. Then the servants, seeing that he heeded them not, took counsel to flee from the enemies, but again after a little, being moved by the fore-knowledge of God, they said, It is not right for our master to die. Come, let us go forth to meet them, raising the sign of the cross. Then raising the precious cross they went forth, about thirty men, upon the enemy, and slew five thousand, and the rest fled. And they returned with victory to their master, praising God and saying, What God is so great as our God, who has not suffered his servant to be slain by the wicked? And coming upon their lord, still weeping, they said to him, Arise, lord, and weep not, for it befits it to be not as we will, but as the Lord wills.

XXVI. Polyxena, however, going out of the city, and not knowing by what way she should walk, found herself in desert places of the hills, and sitting down said thus with tears, Woe is me, outcast and captive, that I cannot find even a wild beast's den to rest in. Woe is me, left desolate, that not even Hades, that no one escapes, has devoured me. Woe is me, who at one time showed myself not even to my servants, and now display myself to demons. Woe is me, that I am now made manifest to all those by whom I disdained to be seen. Alas for me that was formerly devoted to idols; for this now even the mercy of God has passed me in silence. Whom, then, shall I call upon to help me? The God of Paul whom I have constantly offended? But who shall help me now? No one sees or heeds or hears my groaning. Verily I shall beseech Him that sees the hidden things, for who is more pitiful and compassionate than He who always keeps watch over the oppressed? But because my mouth is unclean and defiled, I dare not ask help from Him. Would that I were as one of the wild beasts that I might not know what captivity is. Would that I had been drowned in the sea; perhaps having received the divine baptism I should have gone where no one is made captive. What then shall I do, for death delays, and night has come on, and there is no help anywhere. Having said thus, she arose and began to walk onwards, and passing through a small defile she fell into a wood very thick and large, and finding there a hollow in a tree, which was the den of a lioness, she sat down there, for the lioness had gone forth for her food. And sitting down she said, O wretched begetting, O grievous hour in which I, unhappy one, came into this world; O mother that bore me, why, foreseeing my troubles and wanderings, didst thou name me Polyxena? Has any other ever fallen into such tribulations and misfortunes? Truly, my sister Xanthippe, didst thou read concerning me, unhappy one, saying, I have suffered affliction and been utterly bowed down (—Psalm xxxviii. 6). These words thou didst utter with grief, while I lay upon the couch, thinking not at all of my sorrows. On this account I have now come into the depths of evils, and pass the night in deserts like a wild beast. But the beasts live with others of their kind, while I am left solitary, as not being of one race with mankind.

XXVII. And as she was saying these words, and more than these, the morning dawned, and the lioness came from her hunting. Polyxena, seeing the wild beast, trembled and said, By the God of Paul, O wild beast, have compassion on me and tear me not until I receive baptism. And the wild beast, fearing the adjuration, immediately went away, and standing afar off gazed at her. And she said, Behold, the beast has obeyed me; I will also retire from its dwelling. And immediately she began to journey towards the east, and the beast went before her until she was come out of the wood. Then Polyxena said, What shall I give to thee in return,

O beast? The God of Paul will repay thee this kindness; and the wild beast, hearing her prayer, immediately returned to its place. Then she, descending, found a public road, and standing on it wept, not knowing whither she should go, and though many went past, she turned to none of them, but said, Perchance the God of Paul will remember me, and whoever shall have pity upon me, to him will I go.

XXVIII. As she said this, Andrew, the apostle of the Lord, also came journeying to that place, and as he drew near to Polyxena he felt in his heart some commotion arising in himself. Standing, therefore, to pray, and folding his arms in the shape of the cross, he said, Lord Jesus Christ, partaker of light and knower of things hidden, from whom nothing on earth is hid, do unto me kindness and mercy, and make clear to me this commotion of heart, and calm my reason, thou that makest peace always with those that love peace. Then Polyxena ran to him, and Andrew, the apostle of the Lord, said to her, Approach me not, daughter, but tell me who and whence thou art. Polyxena said, My lord, I am a stranger here, but I see thy face is gracious, and thy words as the words of Paul, and I suppose thee to be of the same God. Andrew understood that she spoke of the apostle Paul, and said to her, And whence dost thou know of Paul? She said, From my own country, for I left him in Spain. Andrew said to her, And how happenest thou to be here, the country being far distant? She said, Because it was thus appointed for me, and came to pass; but I beseech thee and fall at thy feet, seal me, as Paul seals, by the baptism of regeneration, so that even I, lowly one, may be known by our God, for the kind God, seeing my tribulation and distress, sent thee to pity me. Andrew, the great apostle of the Lord, said to her, Let us go, daughter, where there is water.

XXIX. And when they had gone no long way, they came to a well most transparent and pure. And as the blessed Andrew stood to pray beside the well, behold a certain maiden named Rebecca, of the tribe of Israel, brought as a captive to that country, came to draw water at the well, and seeing the blessed Andrew, knew him by his appearance. For Rebecca said, This is the appearance of a Prophet, and this is one of the apostles. And bowing down to him she said, Have mercy on me, servant of the true God, who am captive and sold for the third time, who was once honored by prophets, and am now insulted by idolaters, and recall me, lowly one, thou that wast sent to call back many sinners. Andrew, the apostle of Christ, said, God will care for thee also, daughter, as well as for this stranger. Therefore, receive ye now baptism, and be ye as of one people, glorifying God always.

XXX. Therefore the apostle standing prayed, and, behold, the lioness came running, and stood gazing upon him. And Andrew the apostle of the Lord said, What then does this beast wish? The lioness opening her mouth spoke with a human voice, Andrew, apostle of Christ, the prayer of her, that stands on thy right hand, has overtaken me. Therefore confirm thou and instruct and admonish them in the right and true faith of Christ, for they greatly desire the name of the Lord. And, behold, the wonderful condescension of God, that even on irrational and untamable beasts he has poured out his mercy. The blessed Andrew weeping said, What shall I say or what shall I speak concerning thy mercy, O God, that thus thou at all times cleavest to the lowly, and takest care for those in ignorance, being without arrogance and full of mercy? And having completed the prayer he baptised the maidens in the name of the Father, Son and Holy Ghost. Then the lioness immediately set off to the mountain, and the Apostle Andrew said to the maidens, Be zealous, daughters, to be of good repute before God by living well in a strange land, and separate not from each other, and God, that is always present to those that call upon him, keep you in holiness, driving away from you the Evil One. And pray ye also for me. Polyxena said, We will follow thee whithersoever thou goest. The Apostle Andrew said, This was not made known to me by the Lord, daughters; therefore remain with peace, hoping in the Lord, and he will preserve you to the end.

XXXI. And Andrew went his way rejoicing and glorifying God. Then said Polyxena, Whither shall we go, sister? Rebecca said, Let us depart whither thou wilt, lest my mistress send and separate us. Polyxena said, Come, let us depart into the mountain to the lioness. Rebecca said, It is indeed better for us to live with wild beasts and perish of hunger than to be compelled by Greeks and idolaters to fall into the filth of marriage. So they began to journey, and, behold, by the providence of God, they met a man driving asses, who seeing them said, Ye are not of this country, and, as I see, ye wear not its dress. Command therefore of your servant to eat bread and receive one piece of silver that ye may remember your servant when ye buy bread. And he made haste and took the sacks off his asses and spread them on the ground, and made the maidens to sit upon them and said to them, Seeing that the wine which your servant carries is gathered by Greeks, tell me of what faith ye are, that thus we may taste of it. Polyxena said, We, brother, taste no wine, and are of the God of Paul. The ass-driver said, Is this God upon earth? Polyxena said to him, God is everywhere, both in heaven and on earth. The ass-driver, being desirous to learn clearly, said, Does this Paul then have the same God that is preached by Philip? Polyxena, learning that he was a Christian, said, Yea, brother, this is the God of all, whom Paul and Philip preach.

XXXII. The ass-driver hearing this wept unceasingly, and Polyxena said, Has then the providence of God overtaken thee, that thou weepest thus? The ass-driver said, If thou art desirous to learn wherefore I weep, hear the truth, for one ought not to grudge to tell the things of Christ. I was a disciple of Philip, the apostle of Christ, and seeing how all his thought was towards the poor, I took all that I had and sold it. And taking the price, I bought bread and wine, and divided them throughout the cities to those that had need, when therefore I had done this for some time in the neighbouring city, a certain maimed person cried out, saying (though it was not himself that spoke, but Satan through his mouth), I desire nothing, I take nothing from thee, because thou art a Christian. Then the whole city arose against me and sought to take me, but some ran one way and some another, while I go through their midst and no one sees me. And issuing from the city I gave praise and glory to God that thus I had been rewarded, and I prayed to my God that I should meet some one who knew his all-holy name, so that relating these things I might obtain relief. For the men of this country will not hear at all concerning Christ, being full of impiety and filled with wickedness. I exhort you therefore, take ye also one coin from me, and if it seem good, take ye rest also upon the asses. Polyxena said, Mayest thou obtain mercy from God, brother. But if thou wilt receive a full reward, save us as far as the sea, so that, if God wills, we may sail for Spain.

XXXIII. The ass-driver, as if commanded by the voice of God, eagerly receiving the maidens, went on his way rejoicing in the Lord. And he said to Polyxena, Alter thy appearance to that of a man, lest for thy beauty's sake some one snatch thee away from me. And coming to an inn, they stayed there, and on the morrow they went forward taking heed to the way. And behold there came past a certain prefect journeying to Greece, who seeing the maidens ordered Polyxena to be carried off on his chariot. Then the ass-driver followed, crying and saying, A prefect does violence to none. Why do ye this? Then they beat him and drove him away.

XXXIV. And he going on his way lamented, saying, Woe is me, wretched and abominable one. Woe is me that thought to do good, but now I have wrought mischief. Woe is me that my trouble and my running were unacceptable. Would that I had died before yesterday, that I might not have met with these maidens at all. But why troublest thou me, O wretched soul? Let us go to Philip the apostle of God. If there is not forgiveness for me, it is better for me to choose death in whatsoever fashion than to live with such evil and bitter conscience. So he went and found Philip the apostle of Christ, and said to him, O disciple and preacher of Christ, thus and thus it has happened to me and befallen me. Has my soul salvation? Philip the apostle of Christ said, Be not distressed concerning this, my son, it is impossible for them to be dishonoured, seeing that no one ever overcomes God; for this same Polyxena, when she first came from the sea, I entrusted to a certain brother, who also was greatly distressed because of her running away secretly from his house. Him also I persuaded not to grieve, for through her tribulation and wanderings many shall know God.

XXXV. The prefect therefore carried Polyxena to the city where he stayed, and ordered her to be shut up in a chamber. And one of the soldiers seized Rebecca, but the maid secretly escaping fled into the house of an old woman, who received the maiden kindly and entreated her well. And sitting down she wept, saying, Alas, my sister Polyxena, I wretched one did not think that anyone was oppressed like myself, but now I am persuaded and know that all my misfortunes and tribulations do not compare with one day of thine. And most grievous of all, behold I have been separated from thee and am again a captive, but do thou search for me even into the next world, my sister Polyxena. The old woman said to her, What ails thee, daughter, that thou weepest thus bitterly? Rebecca said, Suffer me, mother, to be distressed and to lament the great and incurable pain of my heart. The old woman greatly compassionating her wept exceedingly, for the maid had told her all that had happened to her, and how through Polyxena she had believed in Christ. So too Polyxena, shut up in the chamber, said, Woe is me, wretched one ; alas for me miserable one ; now I know clearly how the devil hates virginity, but O Lord Jesus Christ, God of all, since I dare not beseech thee of myself, I bring to thee the prayers of thy holy preacher Paul, that thou mayst not suffer my virginity to be destroyed by any one.

XXXVI. And as she was yet praying, the attendants came to lead her to the couch of the prefect. But Polyxena said to them, Brethren, make not haste to any one's destruction, for this time shall quickly pass away, and they that work together with the destroyers shall perish with them. Rather assist strangers, that ye be not found strangers to the angels of God. The men, being shamed by these words, went to the prefect and said, The maid from fear is seized with a violent fever. And the prefect said, Let her alone. And, behold, the son of the prefect came to Polyxena by night, and she seeing him was afraid, but the youth said to her, Fear not, girl. I seek not to be wedded with thee as the bridegroom of destruction, for I know from thy prayer that thou art the bride of the God of heaven. I know this God who is never overcome by any one, for a certain man of glorious countenance lately in Antioch preached this God, and a certain maid, whose name was Thecla, believing him followed him, and encountered dangers on account of her beauty, of whom I have heard that she was condemned to the wild beasts. I therefore continually gazed upon the man, and he having observed me said to me, God give heed to thee, my son. From that time therefore by the grace of Christ I have not gone into the sacrifices of idols, but sometimes feigning illness and sometimes involving myself in some business, my father said to me, Because thou hast no zeal for the sacrifices of the gods, therefore neither art thou in health, not being worthy of the gods. But I rejoiced, hearing that I was not worthy of the sacrifices to idols ; and, by the grace of God, art thou come hither as a providence to me. Polyxena said, And what is the name of that man ? The youth said, Paul is his name. Polyxena said, He is in my city. The youth said, Come then, girl, put on my appearance, and go down to the shore and wait me there ; I having taken money will come quickly.

XXXVII. And one of the servants overhearing them told all this to the prefect, who being filled with great anger condemned them to be cast to the wild beasts. And when they were cast into the arena, a fierce lioness was let loose upon them, which ran and embraced the feet of Polyxena, and licked the soles of her feet. Then the prefect and all the city, seeing this fearful and wonderful sight, gave praise and glory to the merciful God, saying, Of a truth thou art, and he, that is named by Polyxena, alone is God, for the gods of the heathen are the works of men's hands, unable to save or assist any one. Let them perish now, both themselves and their makers. And the prefect straightway taking his son and Polyxena into the palace, heard from them in order the faith and religion in Christ without omission, and he and all in the city believed, and there was great joy and giving of glory to God. And Polyxena said to the prefect, Be of good cheer, my lord, for the man of God will quickly come, who will perfectly teach, exhort, instruct, and enlighten you in the knowledge of Christ. She however prepared in all haste to depart into Spain.

XXXVIII. And as I, Onesimus, was sailing into Spain to Paul, I received from the Lord a revelation saying to me, Onesimus, the vessel in which thou now art will land in the parts of Greece, and thou wilt find on the shore of the harbour two maids and one youth. Assist them and take them to Paul. When we reached this place according to the command of the Lord, we found the maids together with the youth seeking a vessel. When the maids saw us therefore, they knew that we were of the hope of Christ, and Polyxena running to us said, Verily the man of God cannot be concealed, for the grace and kindliness of his countenance makes him manifest. And when we sought to sail away, the sea was troubled by the providence of God. And there was with us a disciple of Paul, by name Lucius, capable in word to teach the city. Therefore we remained seven days, and God opened to that place a great door of faith, and twenty thousand believed, and there was great joy and rejoicing in all the city. And when the season was favourable for us to sail the prefect again constrained us, and we stayed another seven days, until all believed and rejoiced in the Lord.

XXXIX. Thus now by the fore-knowledge of Christ, the prefect sent us away with supplies for the voyage, sending also his son with us. And when we had sailed twenty days, Polyxena was greatly exhausted, and we touched at a certain island for the sake of rest. And behold, certain fierce and hardened men, coming down to us and seeing

Polyxena, prepared for battle; but by the grace of Christ our men defended Polyxena and vanquished them, although the strangers were more numerous and more powerful. Polyxena therefore fearing again to become a captive threw herself into the sea; but the pilot dragged her out, having suffered no harm. Then we embarked in the vessel and fled, for the places were rough and wooded, and we were afraid to remain, and in twelve days we arrived in Spain, by the grace of God.

XL. And Paul seeing us rejoiced greatly, and said, Welcome ye that have been troubled. And Polyxena, laying hold of his feet, said, It may be that this trouble came upon me because I would have blasphemed thee, but now I beseech and entreat that I may not again be delivered into such troubles and misfortunes. And Paul said, weeping, Thus must we be troubled, my daughter, that we may know our defender, Jesus Christ.

XLI. And while we were giving the letters of the brethren to Paul, one ran and told Xanthippe of the arrival of Polyxena. And she made haste and came to us, and seeing Polyxena, was overcome by an unspeakable joy and fell to the ground; but Polyxena embracing her and caressing her for a long time brought her back to life. Then Xanthippe said to her, I, my true sister Polyxena, went not forth at all for forty days, praying much for thee to the loving God, that thy virginity might not be taken away. And Paul, the preacher of God, said to me, Her virginity will not be taken away, and she will come quickly. And Probus said to me, It was assigned to her by God to be thus afflicted. Seest thou how by many devices God saves many? But now, my beloved sister, having unexpectedly seen thy face, now I shall willingly die.

XLII. Then he who had carried her away came up again and sought for Polyxena, but the great Paul persuaded him to refrain from her, and he also believed and was baptised by Paul, as also the suitor of Polyxena believed, and there was great joy in all that city of Spain for the recovery of Polyxena. From that time forward she left not at all the blessed Paul in her fear of temptations. These things then being thus, all rejoiced in the Lord, glorifying Father, Son and Holy Ghost, one God, to whom is glory and power, now and ever and to all eternity. Amen.

THE NARRATIVE OF ZOSIMUS

INTRODUCTION

THE Greek text of this work is printed for the first time in the same part of "Texts and Studies" as the Acts of Xanthippe and Polyxena. The sources for it are two manuscripts—one in Paris, belonging to the twelfth century, and the other in Oxford, dating from the fifteenth or sixteenth. The latter, however, only extends to the close of c. viii., the copy used by the scribe having been imperfect. There are versions of the work in Slavonic, Syriac, Ethiopic, and Arabic; in the former of these the Blessed Ones are called the Brachmani.

From two passages in the poems of Commodian (c. 250 A.D.) it would seem that the work was known in his day, and the canon of Nicephorus (c. 850 A.D.) places it among certain apocryphal books which are to be rejected. At the same time, it is doubtful whether, in its present form, it can be put as far back as the earlier of these dates.

It professes to be the account of a visit to the Makares, or Blessed Ones, given by a hermit, Zosimus, who was privileged to visit them. For forty years he had abstained from bread and wine and from seeing the face of man, always praying to be permitted to see the life of the Blessed. With the second chapter the narrative begins in the first person, and is continued in this up to c. xxi., just where the angels come to receive the soul of Zosimus, and the work is then finished off by one of the hermits who were present at his last moments.

While the style is inelegant and sometimes obscure, the matter of the book is very interesting, and shows considerable powers of imagination. The land of the Blessed is reached by means of a camel, which comes from the desert, and then by a storm of wind, which carries Zosimus along with it. He is addressed by the river to which he comes, as well as by the wall of cloud which rises above it, and is finally lifted across it by two trees. The origin of the Blessed Ones is noteworthy, as connecting the story with early literature on the Lost Tribes. They are the descendants of Rechab in the days of Jeremiah the prophet, who, for refusing to give up their observances, are cast into prison by the king. From this they are delivered by an angel, and brought to the place they now inhabit,—a level land covered with flowers,—a view of Paradise which continues all through the Middle Ages. The chapters (x.-xv.) in which the Blessed describe their life and death are of special merit, and form the best part of the whole. In striking contrast to its lofty tone is the appearance of Satan with his 1360 demons, whom Zosimus finally overcomes and drives away.

To the various accounts of the Earthly Paradise, the story of Zosimus forms an important addition; on these it may, either directly or indirectly, have had considerable influence, although the difficulty of assigning a definite date to it makes this very uncertain.

THE NARRATIVE OF ZOSIMUS CONCERNING THE LIFE OF THE BLESSED

I. About that time there was in the desert a certain man named Zosimus, who for forty years ate no bread, and drank no wine, and saw not the face of man. This man was entreating God that he might see the way of life of the blessed, and behold an angel of the Lord was sent saying to him, Zosimus, man of God, behold I am sent by the Most High, the God of all, to tell thee that thou shalt journey to the blessed, but shalt not dwell with them. But exalt not thy heart, saying, For forty years I have not eaten bread, for the word of God is more than bread, and the spirit of God is more than wine. And as for thy saying, I have not seen the face of man, behold the face of the great king is nigh thee. Zosimus said, I know that the Lord can do whatsoever he will. The angel said to him, Know this also, that thou art not worthy of one of their delights, but arise and set out.

II. And I, Zosimus, issuing from my cave with God leading me, set out not knowing which way I went, and after I had travelled forty days my spirit grew faint and my body failed, and being exhausted I sat down, and continued praying in that place for three days. And, behold, there came a beast from the desert, whose name is the camel, and placing its knees on the ground, it received me upon its neck and went into the desert and set me down. There there was much howling of wild beasts, and gnashing of teeth, and deadly poison. And becoming afraid, I prayed to the Lord, and there came in that place a great earthquake with noise, and a storm of wind blew and lifted me from the earth, and exalted me on its wing, and I was praying and journeying till it set me upon a place beside a river, and the name of the river is Eumĕles. And behold when I desired to cross the river, some one cried as if from the water, saying, Zosimus, man of God, thou canst not pass through me, for no man can divide my waters: but look up from the waters to the heaven. And looking up I saw a wall of cloud stretching from the waters to the heaven, and the cloud said, Zosimus, man of God, through me no bird passes out of this world, nor breath of wind, nor the sun itself, nor can the tempter in this world pass through me.

III. And I was astonished at these words, and at the voice that spake these things to me. And as I prayed, behold two trees sprang up out of the earth, fair and beautiful, laden with fragrant fruits. And the tree on this side bent down and received me on its top, and was lifted up exceedingly above the middle of the river, and the other tree met me and received me in its branches and bending down set me on the ground; and both trees were lifted up and set me away from the river on the other side. In that place I rested three days, and arising again I went forward, whither I knew not, and that place was filled with much fragrance, and there was no mountain on either hand, but the place was level and flowery, all crowned with garlands, and all the land beautiful.

IV. And I saw there a naked man sitting, and said in myself, Surely this is not the tempter. And I remembered the voice of the cloud that it said to me, Not even the tempter in this world passes through me. And thus taking courage I said to him, Hail, brother. And he answering said to me, The grace of my God be with thee. Again I said to him, Tell me, man of God, who thou art? He answered and said to me, Who art thou rather? And I answered and told him all concerning myself, and that I had prayed to God and he had brought me into that place. He answered and said to me, I also know that thou art a man of God, for if not, thou couldst not have passed through the cloud and the river and the air. For the breadth of the river is about thirty thousand paces, and the cloud reaches to heaven, and the depth of the river to the abyss.

V. And having ended this discourse the man spoke again, Hast thou come hither out of the vanity of the world? I said to him, Wherefore art thou naked? He said, How knowest thou that I am naked? Thou wearest skins of the cattle of the earth, that decay together with thy body, but look up to the height of heaven and behold of what nature my clothing is. And looking up into heaven I saw his face as the face of an angel, and his clothing as lightning, which passes from the east to the west, and I was greatly afraid, thinking that it was the son of God, and trembled, falling upon the ground. And giving me his hand he raised me up, saying, Arise, I also am one of the blessed. Come with me, that I may lead thee to the elders. And laying hold of my hand he walked about with me and led me toward a certain crowd, and there were in that crowd elders like sons of God, and young men were standing beside the elders. And as I came near to them, they said, This man has come hither out of the vanity of the world; come, let us beseech the Lord and he will reveal to us this mystery. Surely the end is not at hand, that the man of vanity is come hither? Then they arose and besought the Lord with one accord, and behold two angels came down from heaven and said, Fear not the man, for God has sent him, that he may remain seven days and learn your ways of life, and then he shall go forth and depart to his own place. The angels of God having said this ascended into heaven before our eyes.

VI. Then the elders of the blessed gave me over to one of the attendants, saying, Keep him for seven days. So the attendant receiving me led me to his cave, and we sat under a tree partaking of food. For from the sixth hour even to the sixth, then we ate, and the water came out from the root of the tree sweeter than honey, and we drank our fill, and again the water sank down into its place. And all the country of those there heard of me, that there had come thither a man out of the vanity of the world, and all the country was stirred up, and they came to see me because it seemed strange to them. Therefore they were asking me all things and I was answering them, and I became faint in spirit and in body, and besought the man of God that served me, and said, I beseech thee, brother, if any come to see me, tell them He is not here, so that I may rest a little. And the man of God cried out saying, Woe is me, that the story of Adam is summed up in me, for Satan deceived him through Eve, and this man by his flattery desires to make me a liar while he is here. Take me away from hence, for I shall flee from the place. For behold he wishes to sow in me seeds of the world of vanity. And all the multitude and the elders rose up against me, and said, Depart from us, man; we know not whence thou art come to us. But I lamented with great lamentation, and my senses left me, and I cried out to the elders, saying, Forgive me, my lords, and the elders stilled them and made quietness. Then I related to them all from the beginning till that time, and said, I besought the Lord to come to you, and he deemed me worthy. And the elders said, And now what wilt thou we should do to thee? I said to them, I desire to learn of you your way of life.

VII. And they rejoiced with great joy, and taking up tables of stone they wrote on them with their nails, thus, Hear, ye sons of men, hear ye us who are become blessed, that we also are of you; for when the prophet Jeremiah proclaimed that the city of Jerusalem should be delivered into the hands of the destroyers, he rent his garments, and put sackcloth upon his loins, and sprinkled dust upon his head, and took earth upon his bed, and told all the people to turn from their wicked way. And our father Rechab, the son of Aminadab, heard him and said to us, Ye sons and daughters of Rechab, hearken to your father, and put off your garments from your body, and drink no vessel of wine, and eat no bread from the fire, and drink not strong drink and honey until the Lord hear your entreaty. And we said, All that he has commanded us we shall do and hearken. So we cast away our clothing from our bodies, and we ate no bread from the fire, and drank no vessel of wine nor honey nor strong drink, and we lamented with a great lamentation and besought the Lord, and he heard our prayer and turned away his anger from the city of Jerusalem, and there came to the city of Jerusalem mercy from the Lord, and he pitied its people, and turned away his deadly anger.

VIII. And after these things the king of the city of Jerusalem died, and there arose another king. And all the people gathered to him and informed him concerning us, and said, There are certain of thy people, who have changed their way from us. Therefore the king summoned them, and asked them wherefore they had done this; and he sent for us and asked, Who are ye and of what worship and of what country? And we said to him, We are the sons of thy servant, and our father is Rechab the son of Jonadab, and when Jeremiah the prophet preached in the days of thy father the king, he proclaimed death to the city of Jerusalem, saying, Yet three days and all the city shall be put to death. And the king thy father hearing this repented of his sins, and issued a command to all to turn aside from their wicked way. And our father thy servant hearing it charged us, saying, Drink no vessel of wine, and eat no bread from the fire, until the Lord shall hear your entreaty. And we hearkened to the commandment of our father, and made naked our bodies, we drank no wine and ate no bread, and we prayed to the Lord for the city of Jerusalem, and the Lord pitied his people and turned away his anger, and we saw it and our soul was rejoiced, and we said, It is good for us to be so.

IX. And the king said to us, Ye have done well. Now therefore mingle with my people, and eat bread and drink wine, and glorify your Lord, and ye shall be serving God and the king. But we said, We will not disobey God. Then the king was enraged and set us in prison, and we passed that night there. And behold a light shone in the building, and an angel uncovered the prison and laid hold of the crowns of our heads, and took us out of the prison, and set us beside the water of the river, and said to us, Whithersoever the water goes, go ye also. And we travelled with the water and with the angel. When therefore he had brought us to this place, the river was dried up and the water was swallowed up by the abyss, and he made a wall round this country, and there came a wall of cloud, and shadowed above the water; and he did not scatter us over all the earth, but gave to us this country.

X. Hear, ye sons of men, hear the way of life of the blessed. For God placed us in this land, for we are holy but not immortal. For the earth produces most fragrant fruit, and out of the trunks of the trees comes water sweeter than honey, and these are our food and drink. We are also praying night and day, and this is all our occupation. Hear, ye sons of men; with us there is no vine, nor ploughed field, nor works of wood or iron, nor have we any house or building, nor fire nor sword, nor iron wrought or unwrought, nor silver nor gold, nor air too heavy or too keen. Neither do any of us take to themselves wives, except for so long as to beget two children, and after they have produced two children they withdraw from each other and continue in chastity, not knowing that they were ever in the intercourse of marriage, but being in virginity as from the beginning. And the one child remains for marriage, and the other for virginity.

XI. And there is no count of time, neither weeks nor months nor years, for all our day is one day. In our caves lie the leaves of trees, and this is our couch under the trees. But we are not naked of body, as ye wrongly imagine, for we have the garment of immortality and are not ashamed of each other. At the sixth hour of every day we eat, for the fruit of the tree falls of itself at the sixth hour, and we eat and drink our fill, and again the water sinks into its place. We also know you who are there in the world, and who are in sins, and your works, for every day the angels of the Lord come and tell them to us, and the number of your years. But we pray for you to the Lord, because we also are of you and of your race, except that God has chosen us, and has set us in this place without sin. And the angels of God dwell with us every day, and tell us all things concerning you, and we rejoice with the angels over the works of the just, but over the works of sinners we mourn and lament, praying to the Lord that he may cease from his anger and spare your offences.

XII. But when the time of the forty days comes, all the trees cease from their fruits, and the manna that he gave to our fathers rains down from heaven, and the manna is sweeter than honey. Thus we know that the season of the year is changed. But when the time of the holy passover comes, then again the trees put forth fragrant fruit, and thus we know that it is the beginning of the year. But the feast of the resurrection of the Lord is performed with much watching, for we continue watching for three days and three nights.

XIII. We know also the time of our end, for we have no torment nor disease nor pain in our bodies, nor exhaustion nor weakness, but peace and great patience and love. For our soul is not troubled by the angels to go forth, for the angels rejoice when they receive our souls, and the souls also rejoice with the angels when they behold them; as a bride receives the bridegroom, so our soul receives the announcement of the holy angels, saying nothing more than only this, The Lord calls thee. Then the soul quits the body and goes to the angels, and the angels seeing the soul coming forth spotless rejoice, and spreading out their robes receive it. Then the angels call it blessed, saying, Blessed art thou, O soul, because the will of the Lord is fulfilled in thee.

XIV. The time of our life is this. If one quits the body in his youth, the days of his life here are three hundred and sixty years, and he that quits the body in old age, the days of his life here are six hundred and eighty-eight years. And the day of our completion is made known to us by the angels, and when the angels of God come to take us, we go with them, and the elders, seeing the angels, gather together all the people and we depart together with the angels, singing psalms, until the angels arrive at the place of our abode. And because we have no tools, the angels of God themselves make the grave for our body, and thus he that is called by God goes down, and all salute him from small to great, sending him on his way and bidding him farewell. Then the soul quits the body and the angels receive it, but we see the shape of the soul as a shape of light, perfect in all the body apart from the distinction of male and female.

XV. Then the angels taking it up sing a song and hymn, making melody to God, and again other troops of angels come in haste to meet them, saluting the soul that is coming and entering into the firmaments. And when it has come to the place where it is to worship God, the son of God himself, together with the angels, receives the soul of the blessed one and bears it to the undefiled father of the ages, and again, when the angels sing above, we being below listen to them, and again we sing and they listen in heaven above, and thus between us and the angels there arises a giving of praise in hymns. But when the soul of the blessed one, falling upon its face, worships the Lord, then we also falling down worship the Lord in that same hour, and when the Lord raises it up then we also arise; and when it goes to its appointed place, we also go into the church, fulfilling the eucharist of the Lord.

Having written these things, and all the life of the blessed, we gave them to our brother Zosimus, and escorted him as far as the place of trees beside the river Euměles.

XVI. And I, Zosimus, besought again the blessed ones to make entreaty for me to the Lord that the trees might receive me to take me across. And they all cried to the Lord and said, O God that hast shown us thy marvels and hast made thy servant Zosimus to come to us out of the world of vanity, set him again in his own place with peace, and command these trees to bow down and take up thy servant and set him on the further side. And as they finished their prayer, the trees straightway bent down before them, and received me as on the second day before; and being set on the other side of the river I cried with a loud voice and said, Men of righteousness, who are brothers of the holy angels, grant me your prayer in peace, for behold I depart from you. And making prayer they all cried out, saying, Peace, peace be with you, brother.

XVII. Then I prayed to the Lord, and there came to me a storm of wind, and received me upon its wings, and carried me to the place where it found me sitting, and left me there in peace. And raising its voice the wind said to me, Blessed art thou, Zosimus, that thou hast been numbered with the blessed. And the beast from the desert, whose name is the camel, came and received me upon its neck and carried me eighty and five stations, and set me in the place where it found me praying, and left me in peace, crying and saying, Blessed art thou, Zosimus, that thou hast been numbered with the blessed.

XVIII. But seeing me thus praised, Satan desired to tempt me and throw his dart at me from his station, but an angel of God came and said to me, Zosimus, behold Satan is coming to tempt thee, but the Lord will fight for thee, for the glory of thy faith must bind[1] Satan. And an angel of God appeared, crying and saying, Welcome, blessed one of Christ. Come and I shall lead thee to the cave that is the dwelling-place of thy body, for thy cave shall be a testimony of the desert, a healing of the sick that come to it, a place of trial and touch-stone of demons. And laying hold of my hand he strengthened me, and led me for forty days to the cave where I had dwelt. And there was there a table of righteousness, and I spent the night with the angels of God. And I placed the tablets that were given me by the holy blessed ones on the step of the altar in my cave.

XIX. And, behold, when the angels of God ascended, the Devil came, having a fierce shape, and possessed with anger and gall, and said to me, I knew that God would do with thee as with the blessed ones, and that they shall be free from sin and be above the angels, and therefore I brought in an evil design, and entered into the vessel of the serpent, an evil-doer added to evil-doer. And by this I made the first man Adam to transgress and taste of the tree of life, since God had commanded him not to eat of it, that he might remain equal in glory to God and the holy angels; and thou again hast gone and brought this commandment, but now that they may not be without sin, I shall show thee how I shall destroy thee and all those that receive this commandment, so that they may not be without sin, and the book that thou hast brought.

[1] Text corrupt; "bind" is conjectural.

XX. Saying these things the Devil departed from me, and after eight days he brought with him one thousand three hundred and sixty demons, and dragged me from the cave as I prayed, and they beat me, tossing me about between them, for forty days. And after the forty days the devil lamented before me and said, Woe is me that through one man I have lost the world, for he has vanquished me by his prayer. And he began to run from me, but I laying hold of him stayed him and said, Thou shalt not run away and flee from me until thou swearest to me never again to tempt man. And lamenting with great and violent lamentation he swore to me by the firmament of heaven, So long as thy dwelling is here, and after thee, I will not come upon this place. Then I let him go, sending him and the demons with him into eternal fire. Then the angel came, who had companied with me at the table, and led me into my cave with great glory.

XXI. After this I lived thirty-six years, and communicated the way of life of the blessed to the fathers in the desert. But the Devil wept because of the tables of the life of the blessed, saying, If this get abroad in the world, I shall be mocked, and these will remain without sin and I alone in folly. And after the completion of the thirty-six years, the angels of God came to me as to the blessed.

And all the monks were gathered together and all who heard it, and this testament was read to all of them, and in such life he gave up his soul to God.

XXII. And I, Cryseos,[1] being one of those in the desert, spread it abroad and gave it to all that were willing to learn it and profit by it. Therefore the angels of God helped to bury the body of Zosimus as a precious gift, and we saw the soul of the blessed one shining seven times brighter than the sun. And straightway upon that place there came up seven palm-trees and overshadowed the cave. There came up also a fountain of water in that place, holy water, and unto this day a healing and salvation to all the sick that come to it. Peace be to all that have heard the memorial of the holy Zosimus; the Lord is the advocate and helper of all to the endless ages of ages. Amen.

---

1 The name is corrupt.

THE EPISTLES OF CLEMENT

Reprinted from the translation given in the 1st vol. of the Ante-Nicene Fathers. Completed and revised from a manuscript discovered after the publication of that volume.

BY

REV. JOHN KEITH, B.D.

INTRODUCTORY NOTICE TO 1ST CLEMENT

[*From Vol. I. of the Ante-Nicene Fathers.*]

THE first Epistle, bearing the name of Clement, has been preserved to us in a single manuscript only. Though very frequently referred to by ancient Christian writers, it remained unknown to the scholars of Western Europe until happily discovered in the Alexandrian manuscript. This MS. of the sacred Scriptures (known and generally referred to as Codex A) was presented in 1628 by Cyril, Patriarch of Constantinople, to Charles I., and is now preserved in the British Museum. Subjoined to the books of the New Testament contained in it, there are two writings described as the Epistles of one Clement. Of these, that now before us is the first. It is tolerably perfect, but there are many slight *lacunæ,* or gaps, in the MS., and one whole leaf is supposed to have been lost towards the close. These *lacunæ,* however, so numerous in some chapters, do not generally extend beyond a word or syllable, and can for the most part be easily supplied.

Who the Clement was to whom these writings are ascribed, cannot with absolute certainty be determined. The general opinion is, that he is the same as the person of that name referred to by St. Paul (Phil. iv. 3). The writings themselves contain no statement as to their author. The first, and by far the longer of them, simply purports to have been written in the name of the church at Rome to the church at Corinth. But in the catalogue of contents prefixed to the MS. they are both plainly attributed to one Clement; and the judgment of most scholars is, that, in regard to the first epistle at least, this statement is correct, and that it is to be regarded as an authentic production of the friend and fellow-worker of St. Paul. This belief may be traced to an early period in the history of the church. It is found in the writings of Eusebius (*Hist. Eccl.*, iii. 15), of Origen (*Comm. in Joan.*, i. 29), and others. The internal evidence also tends to support this opinion. The doctrine, style, and manner of thought are all in accordance with it; so that, although, as has been said, positive certainty cannot be reached on the subject, we may with great probability conclude that we have in this epistle a composition of that Clement who is known to us from Scripture as having been an associate of the great apostle.

The date of this epistle has been the subject of considerable controversy. It is clear from the writing itself that it was composed soon after some persecution (chap. i.) which the Roman church had endured; and the only question is, whether we are to fix upon the persecution under Nero or Domitian. If the former, the date will be about the year 68; if the latter, we must place it towards the close of the first century or the beginning of the second. We possess no external aid to the settlement of this question. The lists of early Roman bishops are in hopeless confusion, some making Clement the immediate successor of St. Peter, others placing Linus, and others still Linus and Anacletus, between him and the apostle. The internal evidence, again, leaves the matter doubtful, though it has been strongly pressed on both sides. The probability seems, on the whole, to be in favour of the Domitian period, so that the epistle may be dated about A.D. 97.

This epistle was held in very great esteem by the early church. The account given of it by Eusebius (*Hist. Eccl.*, iii. 16) is as follows: "There is one acknowledged epistle of this Clement (whom he has just identified with the friend of St. Paul), great and admirable, which he wrote in the name of the church of Rome to the church at Corinth, sedition having then arisen in the latter church. We are aware that this epistle has been publicly read in very many churches, both in old times and also in our own day." The epistle before us thus appears to have been read in numerous churches, as being almost on a level with the canonical writings. And its place in the Alexandrian MS., immediately after the inspired books, is in harmony with the position thus assigned it in the primitive church. There does indeed appear a great difference between it and the inspired writings in many respects, such as the fanciful use sometimes made of Old Testament statements, the fabulous stories which are accepted by its author, and the general diffuseness and feebleness of style by which it is distinguished. But the high tone of evangelical truth which pervades it, the simple and earnest appeals which it makes to the heart and conscience, and the anxiety which its writer so constantly shows to promote the best interests of the church of Christ, still impart an undying charm to this precious relic of later apostolic times.

ADDITIONAL INTRODUCTION.

Towards the close of 1875, at Constantinople, Philotheus Bryennius, Metropolitan of Serræ, published the first complete edition of the epistles ascribed to Clement. This he was enabled to do by the discovery of a MS. in the library of the Holy Sepulchre at Fanari in Constantinople. This MS., of vellum, consists of one hundred and twenty leaves in small octavo, nearly seven and a half inches in length and six in breadth. The MS. bears the date 1056, and was written by one Leo. Its contents are:

1. Chrysostom's Synopsis of the Old Testament (the New also being included in the title).
2. Epistle of Barnabas.
3. Clement to the Corinthians I.
4. Clement to the Corinthians II.
5. Teaching of the Twelve Apostles.
6. Ignatian Epistles.

The MS. is written with comparative accuracy and clearness. Internal evidence seems to establish its independent value; *e.g.*, words carelessly omitted in the Codex Alexandrinus are found in this MS. It also supplies the *lacunæ*, notably chapters 57 (concluding sentence)—63 inclusive of the first Epistle and chapters 12 (concluding sentences)—20, being the close of the second Epistle. Harnack seems to prove that the new MS. is as complete as the original Alexandrian.

The *lacuna* of the first Epistle consists mainly of a prayer, the writer somewhat abruptly passing from the *oratio obliqua* to the *oratio recta*. The prayer is indicative of intense earnestness and emotion rather than official authority. It is marked by wealth of quotation, especially from the Septuagint. Perhaps, too, the nature of the sufferings referred to in the opening chapters may be inferred from the petitions of this prayer.

In the Notes the old MS. is indicated by A, the recently discovered MS. by I.

THE FIRST EPISTLE OF CLEMENT TO THE CORINTHIANS[1]

CHAP. I.—THE SALUTATION. PRAISE OF THE CORINTHIANS BEFORE THE BREAKING FORTH OF SCHISM AMONG THEM.

THE church of God which sojourns at Rome, to the church of God sojourning at Corinth, to them that are called and sanctified by the will of God, through our Lord Jesus Christ: Grace unto you, and peace, from Almighty God through Jesus Christ, be multiplied.

Owing, dear brethren, to the sudden and successive calamitous events[2] which have happened to ourselves, we feel that we have been somewhat tardy in turning our attention to the points respecting which you consulted us; and especially to that shameful and detestable sedition, utterly abhorrent to the elect of God, which a few rash and self-confident persons have kindled to such a pitch of frenzy, that your venerable and illustrious name, worthy to be universally loved, has suffered grievous injury.[3] For who ever dwelt even for a short time among you, and did not find your faith to be as fruitful of virtue as it was firmly established?[4] Who did not admire the sobriety and moderation of your godliness in Christ? Who did not proclaim the magnificence of your habitual hospitality? And who did not rejoice over your perfect and well-grounded knowledge? For ye did all things without respect of persons, and walked in the commandments of God, being obedient to those who had the rule over you, and giving all fitting honour to the presbyters among you. Ye enjoined young men to be of a sober and serious mind, ye instructed your wives to do all things with a blameless, becoming, and pure conscience, loving their husbands as in duty bound; and ye taught them that, living in the rule of obedience, they should manage their household affairs becomingly, and be in every respect marked by discretion.

CHAP. II.—PRAISE OF THE CORINTHIANS CONTINUED.

Moreover, ye were all distinguished by humility, and were in no respect puffed up with pride, but yielded obedience rather than extorted it,[5] and were more willing to give than to receive.[6] Content with the provision which God[7] had made for you, and carefully attending to His words, ye were inwardly filled[8] with His doctrine, and His sufferings were before your eyes. Thus a profound and abundant peace was given to you all, and ye had an insatiable desire for doing good, while a full outpouring of the Holy Spirit was upon you all. Full of holy designs, ye did, with true earnestness of mind and a godly confidence, stretch forth your hands to God Almighty, beseeching Him to be merciful unto you, if ye had been guilty of any involuntary transgression. Day and night ye were anxious for the whole brotherhood,[9] that the number of God's elect might be saved with mercy[10] and a good conscience.[11] Ye were sincere and uncorrupted, and forgetful of injuries between

---

[1] According to I, the title is "Clement's (Epistle) to the Corinthians." A includes in a Table of Contents of the New Testament after the Apocalypse:
"Clement's Epistle I."
"Clement's Epistle II."
The space for the title for the 1st Epistle is mutilated, and we find only ". . . . Corinthians I.;" the 2d Epistle has no title.
On the authority of Eusebius, Jerome, Georgius Syncellus, the earlier editions give the titles, "First Epistle of Saint Clement, Bishop of Rome, to the Corinthians, written in name of the Church of Rome," "Second Epistle of Saint Clement, Bishop of Rome, to the Corinthians."

[2] I. περιστάσεις (critical experiences).

[3] Literally "is greatly blasphemed."

[4] Literally, "did not prove your all-virtuous and firm faith."

[5] Eph. v. 21; 1 Pet. v. 5.

[6] Acts xx. 35.

[7] I. Χριστοῦ (Christ). In the monophysite controversy, the theologians of Alexandria preferred to call the Lord "God" rather than "Christ."

[8] Literally, "ye embraced it in your bowels."

[9] 1 Pet. ii. 17.

[10] I. δέους (fear).

[11] So in the MS., but many have suspected that the text is here corrupt. Perhaps the best emendation is that which substitutes συναισθήσεως "compassion," for συνειδήσεως "conscience."

one another. Every kind of faction and schism was abominable in your sight. Ye mourned over the transgressions of your neighbours: their deficiencies you deemed your own. Ye never grudged any act of kindness, being "ready to every good work."[1] Adorned by a thoroughly virtuous and religious life, ye did all things in the fear of God. The commandments and ordinances of the Lord were written upon the tablets of your hearts.[2]

CHAP. III.—THE SAD STATE OF THE CORINTHIAN CHURCH AFTER SEDITION AROSE IN IT FROM ENVY AND EMULATION.

Every kind of honour and happiness[3] was bestowed upon you, and then was fulfilled that which is written, "My beloved did eat and drink, and was enlarged and became fat, and kicked."[4] Hence flowed emulation and envy, strife and sedition, persecution and disorder, war and captivity. So the worthless rose up against the honoured, those of no reputation against such as were renowned, the foolish against the wise, the young against those advanced in years. For this reason righteousness and peace are now far departed from you, inasmuch as every one abandons the fear of God, and is become blind in His faith,[5] neither walks in the ordinances of His appointment, nor acts a part becoming a Christian,[6] but walks after his own wicked lusts, resuming the practice of an unrighteous and ungodly envy, by which death itself entered into the world.[7]

CHAP. IV.—MANY EVILS HAVE ALREADY FLOWED FROM THIS SOURCE IN ANCIENT TIMES.

For thus it is written: "And it came to pass after certain days, that Cain brought of the fruits of the earth a sacrifice unto God; and Abel also brought of the firstlings of his sheep, and of the fat thereof. And God had respect to Abel and to his offerings, but Cain and his sacrifices He did not regard. And Cain was deeply grieved, and his countenance fell. And God said to Cain, Why art thou grieved, and why is thy countenance fallen? If thou offerest rightly, but dost not divide rightly, hast thou not sinned? Be at peace: thine offering returns to thyself, and thou shalt again possess it. And Cain said to Abel his brother, Let us go into the field. And it came to pass, while they were in the field, that Cain rose up against Abel his brother, and slew him."[8] Ye see, brethren, how envy and jealousy led to the murder of a brother. Through envy, also, our father Jacob fled from the face of Esau his brother.[9] Envy made Joseph be persecuted unto death, and to come into bondage.[10] Envy compelled Moses to flee from the face of Pharaoh king of Egypt, when he heard these words from his fellow-countryman, "Who made thee a judge or a ruler over us? Wilt thou kill me, as thou didst kill the Egyptian yesterday?"[11] On account of envy, Aaron and Miriam had to make their abode without the camp.[12] Envy brought down Dathan and Abiram alive to Hades, through the sedition which they excited against God's servant Moses.[13] Through envy, David not only underwent the hatred of foreigners, but was also persecuted by Saul king of Israel.[14]

CHAP. V.—NO LESS EVILS HAVE ARISEN FROM THE SAME SOURCE IN THE MOST RECENT TIMES. THE MARTYRDOM OF PETER AND PAUL.

But not to dwell upon ancient examples, let us come to the most recent spiritual heroes.[15] Let us take the noble examples furnished in our own generation. Through envy[16] and jealousy, the greatest and most righteous pillars [of the church] have been persecuted and put to death.[17] Let us set before our eyes the illustrious[18] apostles. Peter, through unrighteous envy, endured not one or two, but numerous labours; and when he had at length suffered martyrdom, departed to the place of glory due to him. Owing to envy, Paul also obtained[19] the reward of patient endurance, after being seven times thrown into captivity,[20] compelled[21] to flee, and

[1] Tit. iii. 1.
[2] Prov. vii. 3.
[3] Literally, "enlargement."
[4] Deut. xxxii. 15.
[5] It seems necessary to refer αὐτοῦ to *God*, in opposition to the translation given by Abp. Wake and others.
[6] Literally, "Christ;" comp. 2 Cor. i. 21; Eph. iv. 20.
[7] Wisd. ii. 24.

[8] Gen. iv. 3–8. The writer here, as always, follows the reading of the Septuagint, which in this passage both alters and adds to the Hebrew text. We have given the rendering approved by the best critics; but some prefer to translate, as in our English version, "unto thee shall be his desire, and thou shalt rule over him." See, for an ancient explanation of the passage, Irenæus, *Adv. Hær.*, iv. 18, 3.
[9] Gen. xxvii. 41, etc.
[10] Gen. xxxvii.
[11] Ex. ii. 14.
[12] Num. xii. 14, 15.
[13] Num. xvi. 33.
[14] 1 Kings xviii. 8, etc.
[15] Literally, "those who have been athletes."
[16] I. ἔριν (strife).
[17] I. ἕως θανάτου ἤθλησαν (contended unto death).
[18] Literally "good."
[19] I. ἔδειξεν (displayed).
[20] *Seven* imprisonments of St. Paul are not referred to in Scripture.
[21] I. φυγαδευθείς (having become a fugitive). Archbishop Wake here reads "scourged." We have followed the most recent critics in filling up the numerous *lacunæ* in this chapter.

stoned. After preaching both in the east and west, he gained the illustrious reputation due to his faith, having taught righteousness[1] to the whole world, and come to the extreme limit of the west,[2] and suffered martyrdom under the prefects.[3] Thus was he removed from the world, and went into the holy place, having proved himself a striking example of patience.

CHAP. VI. — CONTINUATION. SEVERAL OTHER MARTYRS.

To these men who spent their lives in the practice of holiness, there is to be added a great multitude of the elect, who, having through envy endured many indignities and tortures, furnished us with a most excellent example. Through envy, those women, the Danaids[4] and Dircæ, being persecuted, after they had suffered terrible and unspeakable torments, finished the course of their faith with stedfastness,[5] and though weak in body, received a noble reward. Envy has alienated wives from their husbands, and changed that saying of our father Adam, "This is now bone of my bones, and flesh of my flesh."[6] Envy and strife have overthrown[7] great cities, and rooted up mighty nations.

CHAP. VII.—AN EXHORTATION TO REPENTANCE.

These things, beloved, we write unto you, not merely to admonish you of your duty, but also to remind ourselves. For we are struggling on the same arena, and the same conflict is assigned to both of us. Wherefore let us give up vain and fruitless cares, and approach to the glorious and venerable rule of our holy calling.[8] Let us attend to what is good, pleasing, and acceptable in the sight of Him who formed us. Let us look stedfastly to the blood of Christ, and see how precious that blood is to God[9] which, having been shed for our salvation, has set the grace of repentance before the whole world.[10] Let us turn to[11] every age that has passed, and learn that, from generation to generation, the Lord has granted a place of repentance to all such as would be converted unto Him. Noah preached repentance, and as many as listened to him were saved.[12] Jonah proclaimed destruction to the Ninevites;[13] but they, repenting of their sins, propitiated God by prayer, and obtained salvation, although they were aliens [to the covenant] of God.

CHAP. VIII.—CONTINUATION RESPECTING REPENTANCE.

The ministers of the grace of God have, by the Holy Spirit, spoken of repentance; and the Lord of all things has himself declared with an oath regarding it, "As I live, saith the Lord, I desire not the death of the sinner, but rather his repentance;"[14] adding, moreover, this gracious declaration, "Repent, O house of Israel, of your iniquity."[15] Say to the children of my people, Though your sins reach from earth to heaven, and though they be redder[16] than scarlet, and blacker than sack-cloth, yet if ye turn to me with your whole heart, and say, Father! I will listen to you, as to a holy[17] people. And in another place He speaks thus: "Wash you and become clean; put away the wickedness of your souls from before mine eyes; cease from your evil ways, and learn to do well; seek out judgment, deliver the oppressed, judge the fatherless, and see that justice is done to the widow; and come, and let us reason together. He declares, Though your sins be like crimson, I will make them white as snow; though they be like scarlet, I will whiten them like wool. And if ye be willing and obey me, ye shall eat the good of the land; but if ye refuse, and will not hearken unto me, the sword shall devour you, for the mouth of the Lord hath spoken these things."[18] Desiring, therefore, that all His beloved should be partakers of repentance, He has, by His almighty will, established [these declarations].

CHAP. IX.—EXAMPLES OF THE SAINTS.

Wherefore, let us yield obedience to His excellent and glorious will; and imploring His mercy and loving-kindness, while we forsake all fruitless labours,[19] and strife, and envy, which leads to death, let us turn and have recourse to His compassions. Let us

[1] I. punctuates ἔλαβε δικαιοσύνην, διδάξας (received righteousness, having taught).
[2] Some think *Rome*, others *Spain*, and others even *Britain*, to be here referred to.
[3] That is, under Tigellinus and Sabinus, in the last year of the Emperor Nero; but some think Helius and Polycletus referred to; and others, both here and in the preceding sentence, regard the words as denoting simply the *witness* borne by Peter and Paul to the truth of the gospel before the rulers of the earth.
[4] Some suppose these to have been the names of two eminent female martyrs under Nero; others regard the clause as an interpolation.
[5] Literally, "have reached to the stedfast course of faith."
[6] Gen. ii. 23.
[7] I. κατέσκαψεν (razed to the ground).
[8] I. τῆς παραδόσεως ἡμῶν (of our tradition).
[9] I. τῷ πατρὶ αὐτοῦ τῷ θεῷ (to His Father God).
[10] I. ἐπήνεγκεν (conferred).
[11] I. διέλθωμεν (traverse, trace).
[12] Gen. vii.; 1 Pet. iii. 20; 2 Pet. ii. 5.
[13] Jonah iii.
[14] Ezek. xxxiii. 11.
[15] Ezek. xviii. 30.
[16] Comp. Isa. i. 18.
[17] These words are not found in Scripture, though they are quoted again by Clem. Alex. (*Pædag.* i. 10) as from Ezekiel.
[18] Isa. i. 16-20.
[19] Some read *ματαιολογίαν*, *vain talk*.

stedfastly contemplate those who have perfectly ministered to his excellent glory. Let us take (for instance) Enoch, who, being found righteous in obedience, was translated, and death was never known to happen to him.[1] Noah, being found faithful, preached regeneration to the world through his ministry; and the Lord saved by him the animals which, with one accord, entered into the ark.

CHAP. X.—CONTINUATION OF THE ABOVE.

Abraham, styled "the friend,"[2] was found faithful, inasmuch as he rendered obedience to the words of God. He, in the exercise of obedience, went out from his own country, and from his kindred, and from his father's house, in order that, by forsaking a small territory, and a weak family, and an insignificant house, he might inherit the promises of God. For God said to him, "Get thee out from thy country, and from thy kindred, and from thy father's house, into the land which I shall show thee. And I will make thee a great nation, and will bless thee, and make thy name great, and thou shalt be blessed. And I will bless them that bless thee, and curse them that curse thee; and in thee shall all the families of the earth be blessed."[3] And again, on his departing from Lot, God said to him, "Lift up thine eyes, and look from the place where thou now art, northward, and southward, and eastward, and westward; for all the land which thou seest, to thee will I give it, and to thy seed for ever. And I will make thy seed as the dust of the earth, [so that] if a man can number the dust of the earth, then shall thy seed also be numbered."[4] And again [the Scripture] saith, "God brought forth Abram, and spake unto him, Look up now to heaven, and count the stars if thou be able to number them; so shall thy seed be. And Abram believed God, and it was counted to him for righteousness."[5] On account of his faith and hospitality, a son was given him in his old age; and in the exercise of obedience, he offered him as a sacrifice to God on one of the mountains which He showed him.[6]

CHAP. XI.—CONTINUATION. LOT.

On account of his hospitality and godliness, Lot was saved out of Sodom when all the country round was punished by means of fire and brimstone, the Lord thus making it manifest that He does not forsake those that hope in Him, but gives up such as depart from Him to punishment and torture.[7] For Lot's wife, who went forth with him, being of a different mind from himself, and not continuing in agreement with him [as to the command which had been given them], was made an example of, so as to be a pillar of salt unto this day.[8] This was done that all might know that those who are of a double mind, and who distrust the power of God, bring down judgment on themselves,[9] and become a sign to all succeeding generations.

CHAP. XII.—THE REWARDS OF FAITH AND HOSPITALITY. RAHAB.

On account of her faith and hospitality, Rahab the harlot was saved. For when spies were sent by Joshua, the son of Nun, to Jericho, the king of the country ascertained that they were come to spy out their land, and sent men to seize them, in order that, when taken, they might be put to death. But the hospitable Rahab receiving them, concealed them on the roof of her house under some stalks of flax. And when the men sent by the king arrived and said, "There came men unto thee who are to spy out our land; bring them forth, for so the king commands," she answered them, "The two men whom ye seek came unto me, but quickly departed again and are gone," thus not discovering the spies to them. Then she said to the men, "I know assuredly that the Lord your God hath given you this city, for the fear and dread of you have fallen on its inhabitants. When therefore ye shall have taken it, keep ye me and the house of my father in safety." And they said to her, "It shall be as thou hast spoken to us. As soon, therefore, as thou knowest that we are at hand, thou shalt gather all thy family under thy roof, and they shall be preserved, but all that are found outside of thy dwelling shall perish."[10] Moreover, they gave her a sign to this effect, that she should hang forth from her house a scarlet thread. And thus they made it manifest that redemption should flow through the blood of the Lord to all them that believe and hope in God.[11] Ye see, beloved, that there was not only faith, but prophecy, in this woman.

1 Gen. v. 24; Heb. xi. 5. Literally, "and his death was not found."
2 Isa. xli. 8; 2 Chron. xx. 7; Judith viii. 19; James ii. 23.
3 Gen. xii. 1–3.
4 Gen. xiii. 14–16.
5 Gen. xv. 5, 6; Rom. iv. 3.
6 Gen. xii. 22; Heb. xi. 17.
7 Gen. xix.; comp. 2 Pet. ii. 6–9.
8 So Joseph., *Antiq.*, i. 11, 4; Irenæus, *Adv. Hær.*, iv. 31.
9 Literally, "become a judgment and sign."
10 Josh. ii.; Heb xi. 31.
11 Others of the fathers adopt the same allegorical interpretation, *e. g.*, Justin Mar., *Dial. c. Tryph.*, n. 111; Irenæus, *Adv. Hær.*, iv. 20.

CHAP. XIII.—AN EXHORTATION TO HUMILITY.

Let us therefore, brethren, be of humble mind, laying aside all haughtiness, and pride, and foolishness, and angry feelings; and let us act according to that which is written (for the Holy Spirit saith, "Let not the wise man glory in his wisdom, neither let the mighty man glory in his might, neither let the rich man glory in his riches; but let him that glorieth glory in the Lord, in diligently seeking Him, and doing judgment and righteousness"[1]), being especially mindful of the words of the Lord Jesus which He spake, teaching us meekness and long-suffering. For thus He spoke: "Be ye merciful, that ye may obtain mercy; forgive, that it may be forgiven to you; as ye do, so shall it be done unto you; as ye judge, so shall ye be judged; as ye are kind, so shall kindness be shown to you; with what measure ye mete, with the same it shall be measured to you."[2] By this precept and by these rules let us stablish ourselves, that we walk with all humility in obedience to His holy words. For the holy word saith, "On whom shall I look, but on him that is meek and peaceable, and that trembleth at my words?"[3]

CHAP. XIV.—WE SHOULD OBEY GOD RATHER THAN THE AUTHORS OF SEDITION.

It is right and holy therefore, men and brethren, rather to obey God than to follow those who, through pride and sedition, have become the leaders of a detestable emulation. For we shall incur no slight injury, but rather great danger, if we rashly yield ourselves to the inclinations of men who aim at exciting strife and tumults,[4] so as to draw us away from what is good. Let us be kind one to another after the pattern of the tender mercy and benignity of our Creator. For it is written, "The kind-hearted shall inhabit the land, and the guiltless shall be left upon it, but transgressors shall be destroyed from off the face of it."[5] And again [the Scripture] saith, "I saw the ungodly highly exalted, and lifted up like the cedars of Lebanon: I passed by, and, behold, he was not; and I diligently sought his place, and could not find it. Preserve innocence, and look on equity: for there shall be a remnant to the peaceable man.[6]

CHAP. XV.—WE MUST ADHERE TO THOSE WHO CULTIVATE PEACE, NOT TO THOSE WHO MERELY PRETEND TO DO SO.

Let us cleave, therefore, to those who cultivate peace with godliness, and not to those who hypocritically profess to desire it. For [the Scripture] saith in a certain place, "This people honoureth me with their lips, but their heart is far from me."[7] And again: "They bless with their mouth, but curse with their heart."[8] And again it saith, "They loved Him with their mouth, and lied[9] to Him with their tongue; but their heart was not right with Him, neither were they faithful in His covenant."[10] "Let the deceitful lips become silent,[11] [and "let the Lord destroy all the lying lips,[12]] and the boastful tongue of those who have said, Let us magnify our tongue: our lips are our own; who is lord over us? For the oppression of the poor, and for the sighing of the needy, will I now arise, saith the Lord: I will place him in safety; I will deal confidently with him."[13]

CHAP. XVI.—CHRIST AS AN EXAMPLE OF HUMILITY.

For Christ is of those who are humble-minded, and not of those who exalt themselves over His flock. Our Lord Jesus Christ, the Sceptre of the majesty of God, did not come in the pomp of pride or arrogance, although He might have done so, but in a lowly condition, as the Holy Spirit had declared regarding Him. For He says, "Lord, who hath believed our report, and to whom is the arm of the Lord revealed? We have declared [our message] in His presence: He is, as it were, a child, and like a root in thirsty ground; He has no form nor glory, yea, we saw Him, and He had no form nor comeliness; but His form was without eminence, yea, deficient in comparison with the [ordinary] form of men. He is a man exposed to stripes and suffering, and acquainted with the endurance of grief: for His countenance was turned away; He was despised, and not esteemed. He bears our iniquities, and is in sorrow for our sakes; yet we supposed that [on His own account] He was exposed to labour, and stripes, and affliction. But He was wounded for our transgressions, and bruised for our iniquities.

1 Jer. ix. 23, 24; 1 Cor. i. 31; 2 Cor. x. 17.
2 Comp. Matt. vi. 12-15, vii. 2; Luke vi. 36-38.
3 Isa. lxvi. 2.
4 I. εἰς αἱρέσεις (sects).
5 Prov. ii. 21, 22.
6 Ps. xxxvii. 35-37. "Remnant" probably refers either to the *memory* or *posterity* of the righteous.

7 Isa. xxix. 13; Matt. xv. 8; Mark vii. 6.
8 Ps. lxii. 4.
9 I. ἔψεξαν (blamed).
10 Ps. lxxviii. 36, 37.
11 Ps. xxxi. 18.
12 These words within brackets are not found in the MS., but have been inserted from the Septuagint by most editors.
13 Ps. xii. 3-5.

The chastisement of our peace was upon Him, and by His stripes we were healed. All we, like sheep, have gone astray ; [every] man has wandered in his own way ; and the Lord has delivered Him up for our sins, while He in the midst of His sufferings openeth not His mouth. He was brought as a sheep to the slaughter, and as a lamb before her shearer is dumb, so He openeth not His mouth. In His humiliation His judgment was taken away ; who shall declare His generation ? for His life is taken from the earth. For the transgressions of my people was He brought down to death. And I will give the wicked for His sepulchre, and the rich for His death,[1] because He did no iniquity, neither was guile found in His mouth. And the Lord is pleased to purify him by stripes.[2] If ye make[3] an offering for sin, your soul shall see a long-lived seed. And the Lord is pleased to relieve Him of the affliction of His soul, to show Him light, and to form Him with understanding,[4] to justify the Just One who ministereth well to many ; and He Himself shall carry their sins. On this account He shall inherit many, and shall divide the spoil of the strong ; because His soul was delivered to death, and He was reckoned among the transgressors, and He bare the sins of many, and for their sins was He delivered."[5] And again He saith, "I am a worm, and no man ; a reproach of men, and despised of the people. All that see me have derided me ; they have spoken with their lips ; they have wagged their head, [saying] He hoped in God, let Him deliver Him, let Him save Him, since He delighteth in Him."[6] Ye see, beloved, what is the example which has been given us ; for if the Lord thus humbled Himself, what shall we do who have through Him come under the yoke of His grace ?

CHAP. XVII.—THE SAINTS AS EXAMPLES OF HUMILITY.

Let us be imitators also of those who in goat-skins and sheep-skins[7] went about proclaiming the coming of Christ ; I mean Elijah, Elisha, and Ezekiel among the prophets, with those others to whom a like testimony is borne [in Scripture]. Abraham was specially honoured, and was called the friend of God ; yet he, earnestly regarding the glory of God, humbly declared, "I am but dust and ashes."[8] Moreover, it is thus written of Job, "Job was a righteous man, and blameless, truthful, God-fearing, and one that kept himself from all evil."[9] But bringing an accusation against himself, he said, "No man is free from defilement, even if his life be but of one day.[10] Moses was called faithful in all God's house ;[11] and through his instrumentality,[12] God punished Egypt with plagues and tortures. Yet he, though thus greatly honoured, did not adopt lofty language, but said, when the divine oracle came to him out of the bush, "Who am I, that Thou sendest me ? I am a man of a feeble voice and a slow tongue."[13] And again he said, "I am but as the smoke of a pot."[14]

CHAP. XVIII.—DAVID AS AN EXAMPLE OF HUMILITY.

But what shall we say concerning David, to whom such testimony was borne, and of whom[15] God said, "I have found a man after mine own heart, David the son of Jesse ; and in everlasting mercy have I anointed him ?"[16] Yet this very man saith to God, "Have mercy on me, O Lord, according to Thy great mercy ; and according to the multitude of Thy compassions, blot out my transgression.[17] Wash me still more from mine iniquity, and cleanse me from my sin. For I acknowledge mine iniquity, and my sin is ever before me. Against Thee only have I sinned, and done that which is evil in Thy sight ; that Thou mayest be justified in Thy sayings, and mayest overcome when Thou[18] art judged. For, behold, I was conceived in transgressions, and in sins did my mother conceive me. For, behold, Thou hast loved truth ; the secret and hidden things of wisdom hast Thou shown me. Thou shalt sprinkle me with hyssop, and I shall be cleansed ; Thou shalt wash me, and I shall be whiter than snow. Thou shalt make me to hear joy and gladness ; my bones, which have been humbled, shall exult. Turn away Thy face from my sins, and blot out all mine iniquities. Create in me a clean heart, O God, and

[1] The Latin of Cotelerius, adopted by Hefele and Dressel, translates this clause as follows : "I will set free the wicked on account of His sepulchre, and the rich on account of His death."

[2] The reading of the MS., is τῆς πληγῆς, "purify, or free Him, from stripes." We have adopted the emendation of Junius.

[3] Wotton reads, "If He make."

[4] Or, "*fill* Him with understanding," if πλῆσαι should be read instead of πλάσαι, as Grabe suggests.

[5] Isa. liii. The reader will observe how often the text of the Septuagint, here quoted, differs from the Hebrew as represented by our authorized English version.

[6] Ps. xxii. 6–8.

[7] Heb. xi. 37.

[8] Gen. xviii. 27.

[9] Job i. 1.

[10] Job xiv. 4, 5.

[11] Num. xii. 7; Heb. iii. 2.

[12] I. ὑπηρεσίας (service).

[13] Ex. iii. 11, iv. 10.

[14] This is not found in Scripture.

[15] Or, as some render "to whom."

[16] Ps . lxxxix. 21.

[17] "Wash me . . . ." and following verses omitted in I.

[18] Or, "when Thou judgest."

renew a right spirit within me.[1] Cast me not away from Thy presence, and take not Thy Holy Spirit from me. Restore to me the joy of Thy salvation, and establish me by Thy governing Spirit. I will teach transgressors Thy ways, and the ungodly shall be converted unto Thee. Deliver me from bloodguiltiness,[2] O God, the God of my salvation: my tongue shall exult in Thy righteousness. O Lord, Thou shalt open my mouth, and my lips shall show forth Thy praise. For if Thou hadst desired sacrifice, I would have given it; Thou wilt not delight in burnt-offerings. The sacrifice [acceptable] to God is a bruised spirit; a broken and a contrite heart God will not despise."[3]

CHAP. XIX.—IMITATING THESE EXAMPLES, LET US SEEK AFTER PEACE.

Thus the humility and godly submission of so great and illustrious men have rendered not only us, but also all the generations before us, better; even as many as have received His oracles in fear and truth. Wherefore, having so many great and glorious examples set before us, let us turn again to the practice of that peace which from the beginning was the mark set before us;[4] and let us look stedfastly to the Father and Creator of the universe, and cleave to His mighty and surpassingly great gifts and benefactions of peace. Let us contemplate Him with our understanding, and look with the eyes of our soul to His long-suffering will. Let us reflect how free from the wrath He is towards all His creation.

CHAP. XX.—THE PEACE AND HARMONY OF THE UNIVERSE.

The heavens, revolving under His government, are subject to Him in peace. Day and night run the course appointed by Him, in no wise hindering each other. The sun and moon, with the companies of the stars, roll on in harmony according to His command, within their prescribed limits, and without any deviation. The fruitful earth, according to His will, brings forth food in abundance, at the proper seasons, for man and beast and all the living beings upon it, never hesitating, nor changing any of the ordinances which He has fixed. The unsearchable places of abysses, and the indescribable arrangements of the lower world, are restrained by the same laws. The vast unmeasurable sea, gathered together by His working into various basins,[5] never passes beyond the bounds placed around it, but does as He has commanded. For He said, "Thus far shalt thou come, and thy waves shall be broken within thee."[6] The ocean, impassable to man and the worlds beyond it, are regulated by the same enactments of the Lord. The seasons of spring, summer, autumn, and winter, peacefully give place[7] to one another. The winds in their several quarters[8] fulfil, at the proper time, their service without hindrance. The ever-flowing fountains, formed both for enjoyment and health, furnish without fail their breasts for the life of men. The very smallest of living beings meet together in peace and concord. All these the great Creator and Lord of all has appointed to exist in peace and harmony; while He does good to all, but most abundantly to us who have fled for refuge to His compassions through Jesus Christ our Lord, to whom be glory and majesty for ever and ever. Amen.

CHAP. XXI.—LET US OBEY GOD, AND NOT THE AUTHORS OF SEDITION.

Take heed, beloved, lest His many kindnesses lead to the condemnation of us all. [For thus it must be] unless we walk worthy of Him, and with one mind do those things which are good and well-pleasing in His sight. For [the Scripture] saith in a certain place, "The Spirit of the Lord is a candle searching the secret parts of the belly."[9] Let us reflect how near He is, and that none of the thoughts or reasonings in which we engage are hid from Him. It is right, therefore, that we should not leave the post which His will has assigned us. Let us rather offend those men who are foolish, and inconsiderate, and lifted up, and who glory in the pride of their speech, than [offend] God. Let us reverence the Lord Jesus Christ,[10] whose blood was given for us; let us esteem those who have the rule over us;[11] let us honour the aged[12] among us; let us train up the young men in the fear of God; let us direct our wives to that which is good. Let them exhibit the lovely habit of purity [in all their conduct]; let them show forth the sincere disposition of meekness; let them make

1 Literally, "in my inwards."
2 Literally, "bloods."
3 Ps. li. 1–17.
4 Literally, "Becoming partakers of many great and glorious deeds, let us return to the aim of peace delivered to us from the beginning." Comp. Heb. xii. 1.

5 Or, "collections."
6 Job xxxviii. 11.
7 I. μεταδιδόασι (transfer from one to another).
8 Or "stations."
9 Prov. xx. 27.
10 I. omits "Christ."
11 Comp. Heb. xiii. 17; 1 Thess. v. 12, 13.
12 Or, "the presbyters."

manifest the command which they have of their tongue, by their manner[1] of speaking; let them display their love, not by preferring[2] one to another, but by showing equal affection to all that piously fear God. Let your children be partakers of true Christian training; let them learn of how great avail humility is with God—how much the spirit of pure affection can prevail with Him—how excellent and great His fear is, and how it saves all those who walk in[3] it with a pure mind. For He is a Searcher of the thoughts and desires [of the heart]: His breath is in us; and when He pleases, He will take it away.

CHAP. XXII. —THESE EXHORTATIONS ARE CONFIRMED BY THE CHRISTIAN FAITH, WHICH PROCLAIMS THE MISERY OF SINFUL CONDUCT.

Now the faith which is in Christ confirms all these [admonitions]. For He Himself by the Holy Ghost thus addresses us: "Come, ye children, hearken unto me; I will teach you the fear of the Lord.[4] What man is he that desireth life, and loveth to see good days? Keep thy tongue from evil, and thy lips from speaking guile. Depart from evil, and do good; seek peace, and pursue it. The eyes of the Lord are upon the righteous, and His ears are [open] unto their prayers. The face of the Lord is against them that do evil, to cut off the remembrance of them from the earth. The righteous cried, and the Lord heard him, and delivered him out of all his troubles."[5] "Many are the stripes [appointed for] the wicked; but mercy shall compass those about who hope in the Lord."[6]

CHAP. XXIII.—BE HUMBLE, AND BELIEVE THAT CHRIST WILL COME AGAIN.

The all-merciful and beneficent Father has bowels [of compassion] towards those that fear Him, and kindly and lovingly bestows His favours upon those who come to Him with a simple mind. Wherefore let us not be double-minded; neither let our soul be lifted[7] up on account of His exceedingly great and glorious gifts. Far from us be that which is written, "Wretched are they who are of a double mind, and of a doubting heart; who say, These things we have heard even in the times of our fathers; but, behold, we have grown old, and none of them has happened unto us;"[8] Ye foolish ones! compare yourselves to a tree; take [for instance] the vine. First of all, it sheds its leaves,[9] then it buds, next it puts forth leaves, and then it flowers; after that comes the sour grape, and then follows the ripened fruit. Ye perceive how in a little time the fruit of a tree comes to maturity. Of a truth, soon and suddenly shall His will be accomplished, as the Scripture also bears witness, saying, "Speedily will He come, and will not tarry;[10] and, "The Lord shall suddenly come to His temple, even the Holy One, for whom ye look."[11]

CHAP. XXIV.—GOD CONTINUALLY SHOWS US IN NATURE THAT THERE WILL BE A RESURRECTION.

Let us consider, beloved, how the Lord continually proves to us that there shall be a future resurrection, of which He has rendered the Lord Jesus Christ[12] the first-fruits[13] by raising Him from the dead. Let us contemplate, beloved, the resurrection which is at all times[14] taking place. Day and night declare to us a resurrection. The night sinks to sleep, and the day arises; the day [again] departs, and the night comes on. Let us behold[15] the fruits [of the earth], how the sowing of grain takes place. The sower[16] goes forth, and casts it into the ground,[17] and the seed being thus scattered, though dry and naked when it fell upon the earth, is gradually dissolved. Then out of its dissolution the mighty power of the providence of the Lord raises it up again, and from one seed many arise and bring forth fruit.

CHAP. XXV.—THE PHŒNIX AN EMBLEM OF OUR RESURRECTION.

Let us consider that wonderful sign [of the resurrection] which takes place in eastern lands, that is, in Arabia and the countries round about. There is a certain bird which is called a phœnix. This is the only one of its kind, and lives five hundred years. And when the time of its dissolution draws near that it must die, it builds itself a nest of

---

1 I. σιγῆς (silence).
2 I. προσκλήσεις (summonses). Comp. 1 Tim. v. 21.
3 Some translate, "who turn to Him."
4 I. omits rest of quotation as far as "Many," etc.
5 Ps. xxxiv. 11-17.
6 Ps. xxxii. 10.
7 Or, as some render, "neither let us have any doubt of."

8 Some regard these words as taken from an apocryphal book, others as derived from a fusion of James i. 8 and 2 Pet. iii. 3, 4.
9 I. omits.
10 Hab. ii. 3; Heb. x. 37.
11 Mal. iii. 1.
12 I. omits "Christ."
13 Comp. 1 Cor. xv. 20; Col. i. 18.
14 I. κατὰ καιρόν (in due season).
15 I. λάβωμεν (let us take).
16 Comp. Luke viii. 5.
17 I. adds ἕκαστον τῶν σπερμάτων (the seeds severally.)

frankincense, and myrrh, and other spices, into which, when the time is fulfilled, it enters and dies. But as the flesh decays a certain kind of worm is produced, which, being nourished by the juices of the dead bird, brings forth feathers. Then, when it has acquired strength, it takes up that nest in which are the bones of its parent, and bearing these it passes[1] from the land of Arabia into Egypt, to the city called Heliopolis. And, in open day, flying[2] in the sight of all men, it places them on the altar of the sun, and having done this, hastens back to its former abode. The priests then inspect the registers of the dates, and find that it has returned exactly as the five hundredth year was completed.[3]

CHAP. XXVI.—WE SHALL RISE AGAIN, THEN, AS THE SCRIPTURE ALSO TESTIFIES.

Do we then deem it any great and wonderful thing for the Maker of all things to raise up again those that have piously served Him in the assurance of a good faith, when even by a bird He shows us the mightiness of His power to fulfil His promise?[4] For [the Scripture] saith in a certain place, "Thou shalt raise me up, and I shall confess unto Thee";[5] and again, "I laid me down, and slept"; "I awaked, because Thou art with me;"[6] and again, Job says, "Thou shalt raise up this flesh of mine, which has suffered all these things."[7]

CHAP. XXVII.—IN THE HOPE OF THE RESURRECTION, LET US CLEAVE TO THE OMNIPOTENT AND OMNISCIENT GOD.

Having then this hope, let our souls be bound to Him who is faithful in His promises, and just in His judgments. He who has commanded us not to lie, shall much more Himself not lie; for nothing is impossible with God, except to lie.[8] Let His faith therefore be stirred up again within us, and let us consider that all things are nigh unto Him. By the word of His might[9] He established all things, and by His word He can overthrow them. "Who shall say unto Him, What hast thou done? or, Who shall resist the power of His strength?"[10] When, and as He pleases, He will do all things, and none of the things determined by Him shall pass away.[11] All things are open before Him, and nothing can be hidden from His counsel. "The heavens[12] declare the glory of God, and the firmament showeth His handy-work.[13] Day unto day uttereth speech, and night unto night showeth knowledge. And there are no words or speeches of which the voices are not heard."[14]

CHAP. XXVIII.—GOD SEES ALL THINGS: THEREFORE LET US AVOID TRANSGRESSION.

Since then all things are seen and heard [by God], let us fear Him, and forsake those wicked works which proceed from evil[15] desires;[16] so that, through His mercy, we may be protected from the judgments to come. For whither can any of us flee from His mighty hand? Or what world will receive any of those who run away from Him? For the Scripture saith in a certain place, "Whither shall I go, and where shall I be hid from Thy presence? If I ascend into heaven, Thou art there; if I go away even to the uttermost parts of the earth, there is Thy right hand;[17] if I make my bed in the abyss, there is Thy Spirit."[18] Whither, then, shall any one go, or where shall he escape from Him who comprehends all things?

CHAP. XXIX.—LET US ALSO DRAW NEAR TO GOD IN PURITY OF HEART.

Let us then draw near to Him with holiness of spirit, lifting up pure and undefiled hands unto Him, loving our gracious and merciful Father, who has made us partakers in the blessings of His elect.[19] For thus it is written, "When the Most High divided the nations, when He scattered[20] the sons of Adam, He fixed the bounds of the nations according to the number of the angels of God. His people Jacob became the portion of the Lord, and Israel the lot of His inheritance.[21] And in another place [the Scripture] saith,

[1] I. διανύει (accomplishes its journey).
[2] I. omits ἐπιπτὰς (on the wing, flying).
[3] This fable respecting the phœnix is mentioned by Herodotus (ii. 73), and by Pliny (*Nat. Hist.*, x. 2), and is used as above by Tertullian (*De Resurr.*, § 13), and by others of the fathers.
[4] Literally, "the mightiness of His promise."
[5] Ps. xxviii. 7, or from some apocryphal book.
[6] Comp. Ps. iii. 6.
[7] Job xix. 25, 26.
[8] Comp. Tit. i. 2; Heb. vi. 18.
[9] Or "majesty."
[10] Wisd. xii. 12, xi. 21.
[11] Comp. Matt. xxiv. 35.
[12] Literally, "if the heavens," etc.
[13] I. omits.
[14] Ps. xix. 1–3. I. omits Ps. xix, 2–4, with the exception of the concluding words, ἀκούονται αἱ φωναὶ αὐτῶν (their voices are heard), which are connected with the opening words of the following chapter.
[15] I. βλαβεράς (hurtful).
[16] Literally, "abominable lusts of evil deeds."
[17] I. σὺ ἐκεῖ εἶ (Thou art there).
[18] Ps. cxxxix. 7–10.
[19] Literally, "has made us to Himself a part of election."
[20] Literally, "sowed abroad."
[21] Deut. xxxii. 8, 9.

"Behold, the Lord taketh unto Himself a nation out of the midst of the nations, as a man takes the first-fruits of his threshing-floor; and from that nation shall come forth the Most Holy."[1]

CHAP. XXX.—LET US DO THOSE THINGS THAT PLEASE GOD, AND FLEE FROM THOSE HE HATES, THAT WE MAY BE BLESSED.

Seeing, therefore, that we are the portion of the Holy One,[2] let us do all those things which pertain to holiness, avoiding all evil-speaking, all abominable and impure embraces, together with all drunkenness, seeking after change,[3] all abominable lusts, detestable adultery, and execrable pride. "For God," [saith the Scripture], "resisteth the proud, but giveth grace to the humble."[4] Let us cleave, then, to those to whom grace has been given by God. Let us clothe ourselves with concord and humility, ever exercising self-control, standing far off from all whispering and evil-speaking, being justified by our works, and not our words. For [the Scripture] saith, "He that speaketh much, shall also hear much in answer. And does he that is ready in speech deem himself righteous? Blessed[5] is he that is born of woman, who liveth but a short time: be not given to much speaking."[6] Let our praise be in God, and not of ourselves; for God hateth those that commend themselves. Let testimony to our good[7] deeds be borne by others, as it was in the case of our righteous forefathers. Boldness, and arrogance, and audacity belong to[8] those that are accursed of God; but moderation, humility, and meekness to such as are blessed by Him.

CHAP. XXXI.—LET US SEE BY WHAT MEANS WE MAY OBTAIN THE DIVINE BLESSING.

Let us cleave then to His blessing, and consider what are the means[9] of possessing it. Let us think[10] over the things which have taken place from the beginning. For what reason was our father Abraham blessed? Was it not because he wrought righteousness and truth through faith? Isaac,[11] with perfect confidence, as if knowing what was to happen,[12] cheerfully yielded himself as a sacrifice.[13] Jacob, through reason[14] of his brother, went forth with humility from his own land, and came to Laban and served him; and there was given to him the sceptre of the twelve tribes of Israel.

CHAP. XXXII.—WE ARE JUSTIFIED NOT BY OUR OWN WORKS, BUT BY FAITH.

Whosoever will candidly consider each particular, will recognise the greatness of the gifts which were given by him.[15] For from him[16] have sprung the priests and all the Levites who minister at the altar of God. From him also [was descended] our Lord Jesus Christ according to the flesh.[17] From him [arose] kings, princes, and rulers of the race of Judah. Nor are his other tribes in small glory,[18] inasmuch as God had promised, "Thy seed shall be as the stars of heaven."[19] All these, therefore, were highly honoured, and made great, not for their own sake, or for their own works, or for the righteousness which they wrought, but through the operation of His will. And we, too, being called by His will[20] in Christ Jesus, are not justified by ourselves, nor by our own wisdom, or understanding, or godliness, or works which we have wrought in holiness of heart; but by that faith through which, from the beginning, Almighty God has justified all men; to whom be glory for ever and ever. Amen.

CHAP. XXXIII.—BUT LET US NOT GIVE UP THE PRACTICE OF GOOD WORKS AND LOVE. GOD HIMSELF IS AN EXAMPLE TO US OF GOOD WORKS.

What shall we do,[21] then, brethren? Shall we become slothful in well-doing, and cease from the practice of love? God forbid that any such course should be followed by us! But rather let us hasten with all energy and readiness of mind to perform every good work. For the Creator and Lord of all Himself rejoices in His works. For by His infinitely great power He established the heavens, and by His incomprehensible wisdom He adorned them. He also divided the earth from the water which surrounds it, and fixed it upon

---

1 Formed apparently from Num. xviii. 27 and 2 Chron. xxxi. 14. Literally, the closing words are, "the holy of holies."
2 I. ἅγια μέρη (holy parts.)
3 Some translate, "youthful lusts."
4 Prov. iii. 34; James iv. 6; 1 Pet. v. 5.
5 I. omits.
6 Job xi. 2, 3. The translation is doubtful.
7 I. omits.
8 I. ἐδόθη (was given).
9 Literally, "what are the ways of His blessing."
10 Literally, "unroll."
11 Comp. James ii. 21.
12 Some translate, "knowing what was to come."
13 Gen. xxii., 6–10.
14 So Jacobson: Wotton reads, "fleeing from his brother."
15 The meaning here is very doubtful. Some translate, "the gifts which were given to Jacob by Him," *i.e.* God.
16 MS. αὐτῶν, referring to the gifts: we have followed the emendation αὐτοῦ, adopted by most editors. Some refer the word to *God*, and not *Jacob*.
17 Comp. Rom. ix. 5.
18 I. τάξει (rank).
19 Gen. xxii. 17, xxviii. 4.
20 I. omits.
21 I. ἐροῦμεν (shall we say).

the immovable foundation of His own will. The animals also which are upon it He commanded by His own word[1] into existence. So likewise, when He had formed[2] the sea, and the living creatures which are in it, He enclosed them [within their proper bounds] by His own power. Above all,[3] with His holy and undefiled hands He formed man, the most excellent [of His creatures], and truly great through the understanding given him—the express likeness of His own image. For thus says God: "Let us make man in our image, and after our likeness. So God made man; male and female He created them."[4] Having thus finished all these things, He approved them, and blessed them, and said, "Increase and multiply."[5] We see,[6] then, how all righteous men have been adorned with good works, and how the Lord Himself, adorning Himself with His works, rejoiced. Having therefore such an example, let us without delay accede to His will, and let us work the work of righteousness with our whole strength.

CHAP. XXXIV.—GREAT IS THE REWARD OF GOOD WORKS WITH GOD. JOINED TOGETHER IN HARMONY, LET US IMPLORE THAT REWARD FROM HIM.

The good servant[7] receives the bread of his labour with confidence; the lazy and slothful cannot look his employer in the face. It is requisite, therefore, that we be prompt in the practice of well-doing; for of Him are all things. And thus He forewarns us: "Behold, the Lord [cometh], and His reward is before His face, to render to every man according to his work."[8] He exhorts us, therefore,[9] with our whole heart to attend to this,[10] that we be not lazy or slothful in any good work. Let our boasting and our confidence be in Him. Let us submit ourselves to His will. Let us consider the whole multitude of His angels, how they stand ever ready to minister to His will. For the Scripture saith, "Ten thousand times ten thousand stood around Him, and thousands of thousands ministered unto Him,[11] and cried, Holy, holy, holy, [is] the Lord of Sabaoth; the whole creation[12] is full of His glory."[13] And let us therefore, conscientiously gathering together in harmony, cry to Him earnestly, as with one mouth, that we may be made partakers of His great and glorious promises. For [the Scripture] saith, "Eye hath not seen, nor ear heard, neither have entered into the heart of man, the things which He hath prepared for them that wait for[14] Him."[15]

CHAP. XXXV.—IMMENSE IS THIS REWARD. HOW SHALL WE OBTAIN IT?

How blessed and wonderful, beloved, are the gifts of God! Life in immortality, splendour in righteousness, truth in perfect confidence,[16] faith in assurance, self-control in holiness! And all these fall under the cognizance of our understandings [now]; what then shall those things be which are prepared for such as wait for Him? The Creator and Father of all worlds,[17] the Most Holy,[18] alone knows their amount and their beauty. Let us therefore earnestly strive to be found in the number of those that wait for Him, in order that we may share in His promised gifts. But how, beloved, shall this be done? If our understanding be fixed by faith towards God; if we earnestly seek the things[19] which are pleasing and acceptable to Him; if we do the things which are in harmony with His blameless will; and if we follow the way of truth, casting away from us all unrighteousness and inquity,[20] along with all covetousness,[21] strife, evil practices, deceit, whispering, and evil-speaking, all hatred of God, pride and haughtiness, vainglory and ambition.[22] For they that do such things are hateful to God; and not only they that do them, but also those that take pleasure in them that do them.[23] For the Scripture saith, "But to the sinner God said, Wherefore dost thou declare my statutes, and take my covenant into thy mouth, seeing thou hatest instruction, and castest my words behind thee? When thou sawest a thief, thou consentedst with[24] him, and didst make thy portion with adulterers. Thy mouth has abounded with wickedness, and

[1] Or, "commandment."
[2] I. προετοιμάσας (having previously prepared).
[3] Or, "in addition to all."
[4] Gen. i. 26, 27.
[5] Gen. i. 28.
[6] Or, "let us consider."
[7] Or, "labourer."
[8] Isa. xl. 10, lxii. 11; Rev. xxii. 12.
[9] I. πιστεύοντας (believing).
[10] The text here seems to be corrupt. Some translate, "He warns us with all His heart to this end, that," etc.
[11] Dan. vii. 10.
[12] I. γῆ (earth).
[13] Isa. vi. 3.
[14] I. ἀγαπῶσιν (love).
[15] 1 Cor. ii. 9.
[16] Some translate, "in liberty."
[17] Or, "of the ages."
[18] I. ὁ δημιοῦργος τῶν αἰώνων καὶ ποτὴρ πανάγιος (the Creator Eternal and Father All-Holy.)
[19] I. τὰ ἀγαθά (good things) added.
[20] I. πονηρίαν (wickedness).
[21] I. omits πλεονεξία (covetousness).
[22] The reading is doubtful: some have ἀφιλοξενίαν, "want of a hospitable spirit."
[23] Rom. i. 32.
[24] Literally, "didst run with."

thy tongue contrived[1] deceit. Thou sittest, and speakest against thy brother; thou slanderest[2] thine own mother's son. These things thou hast done, and I kept silence; thou thoughtest, wicked one, that I should be like to thyself. But I will reprove thee, and set thyself before thee. Consider now these things, ye that forget God, lest He tear you in pieces, like a lion, and there be none to deliver.[3] The sacrifice of praise will glorify me, and a way is there by which I will show him the salvation of God."[4]

CHAP. XXXVI.—ALL BLESSINGS ARE GIVEN TO US THROUGH CHRIST.

This is the way, beloved, in which we find our Saviour,[5] even Jesus Christ, the High Priest of all our offerings, the defender and helper of our infirmity. By Him we look up to the heights of heaven. By Him we behold, as in a glass, His immaculate and most excellent visage. By Him are the eyes of our hearts opened. By Him our foolish and darkened understanding blossoms[6] up anew towards His marvellous light. By Him the Lord has willed that we should taste of immortal knowledge,[7] "who, being the brightness of His majesty, is by so much greater than the angels, as He hath by inheritance obtained a more excellent name than they."[8] For it is thus written, "Who maketh His angels spirits, and His ministers a flame of fire."[9] But concerning His Son[10] the Lord spoke thus: "Thou art my Son, to-day have I begotten Thee. Ask of me, and I will give Thee the heathen for Thine inheritance, and the uttermost parts of the earth for Thy possession."[11] And again He saith to Him, "Sit Thou at my right hand, until I make Thine enemies Thy footstool."[12] But who are His enemies? All the wicked, and those who set themselves to oppose the will of God.[13]

CHAP. XXXVII. —CHRIST IS OUR LEADER, AND WE HIS SOLDIERS.

Let us then, men and brethren, with all energy act the part of soldiers, in accordance with His holy commandments. Let us consider those who serve under our generals, with what order, obedience,[14] and submissiveness they perform the things which are commanded them. All are not prefects, nor commanders of a thousand, nor of a hundred, nor of fifty, nor the like, but each one in his own rank performs the things commanded by the king and the generals. The great cannot subsist without the small, nor the small without the great. There is a kind of mixture in all things, and thence arises mutual advantage.[15] Let us take our body for an example.[16] The head is nothing without the feet, and the feet are nothing without the head; yea, the very smallest members of our body are necessary and useful to the whole body. But all work[17] harmoniously together, and are under one common rule[18] for the preservation of the whole body.

CHAP. XXXVIII.—LET THE MEMBERS OF THE CHURCH SUBMIT THEMSELVES, AND NO ONE EXALT HIMSELF ABOVE ANOTHER.

Let our whole body, then, be preserved in Christ Jesus;[19] and let every one be subject to his neighbour, according to the special gift[20] bestowed upon him. Let the strong not despise[21] the weak, and let the weak show respect unto the strong. Let the rich man provide for the wants of the poor; and let the poor man bless God, because He hath given him one by whom his need may be supplied. Let the wise man display his wisdom, not by [mere] words, but through good deeds. Let the humble not bear testimony to himself, but leave witness to be borne to him by another.[22] Let him that is pure in the flesh not grow proud[23] of it, and boast, knowing that it was another who bestowed on him the gift of continence. Let us consider, then, brethren, of what matter we were made,—who and what manner of beings we came into the world, as it were out of a sepulchre, and from utter darkness.[24] He who made us and fashioned us, having prepared His bountiful gifts for us before we were born, introduced us into His world. Since, therefore, we receive all these things from Him, we ought for everything to give Him thanks; to whom be glory for ever and ever. Amen.

---

1 Literally, "did weave."

2 Or, "layest a snare for."

3 I. omit "σὺ δὲ ἐμίσησας . . . ὁ ῥυόμενος Ps. l., 17–22, and connects by ἐν τῷ τέλει (in the end).

4 Ps. l. 16–23. The reader will observe how the Septuagint followed by Clement differs from the Hebrew.

5 Literally, "that which saves us."

6 Or, "rejoices to behold."

7 Or, "knowledge of immortality."

8 Heb. i. 3, 4.

9 Ps. civ. 4; Heb. i. 7.

10 Some render, "to the Son."

11 Ps. ii. 7, 8; Heb. i. 5.

12 Ps. cx. 1; Heb. i. 13.

13 Some read, "who oppose their own will to that of God."

14 I. ἑκτικῶς (habitually).

15 Literally, "in these there is use."

16 1 Cor., xii. 12, etc.

17 Literally, "all breathe together."

18 Literally, "use one subjection."

19 I. omits "Jesus."

20 Literally, "according as he has been placed in his charism."

21 I. τημελείτω (attend to).

22 Comp. Prov. xxvii. 2.

23 The MS. is here slightly torn, and we are left to conjecture.

24 Comp. Ps. cxxxix. 15.

CHAP. XXXIX.—THERE IS NO REASON FOR SELF-CONCEIT.

Foolish and inconsiderate[1] men, who have neither wisdom[2] nor instruction, mock and deride us, being eager to exalt themselves in their own conceits. For what can a mortal man do, or what strength is there in one made out of the dust? For it is written, "There was no shape before mine eyes, only I heard a sound,[3] and a voice [saying], What then? Shall a man be pure before the Lord? Or shall such an one be [counted] blameless in his deeds, seeing He does not confide in His servants, and has charged[4] even His angels with perversity? The heaven is not clean in His sight: how much less they that dwell in houses of clay, of which also we ourselves were made! He smote them as a moth; and from morning even until evening they endure not. Because they could furnish no assistance to themselves, they perished. He breathed upon them, and they died, because they had no wisdom. But call now, if any one will answer thee, or if thou wilt look to any of the holy angels; for wrath destroys the foolish man, and envy killeth him that is in error. I have seen the foolish taking root, but their habitation was presently consumed. Let their sons be far from safety; let them be despised[5] before the gates of those less than themselves, and there shall be none to deliver. For what was prepared for them, the righteous shall eat; and they shall not be delivered from evil."[6]

CHAP. XL.—LET US PRESERVE IN THE CHURCH THE ORDER APPOINTED BY GOD.

These things therefore being manifest to us, and since we look into the depths of the divine knowledge, it behoves us to do all things in [their proper] order, which the Lord has commanded us to perform at stated times.[7] He has enjoined offerings [to be presented] and service to be performed [to Him], and that not thoughtlessly or irregularly, but at the appointed times and hours. Where and by whom He desires these things to be done, He Himself has fixed by His own supreme will, in order that all things, being piously done according to His good pleasure, may be acceptable unto Him.[8] Those, therefore, who present their offerings at the appointed times, are accepted and blessed; for inasmuch as they follow the laws of the Lord, they sin not. For his own peculiar services are assigned to the high priest, and their own proper place is prescribed to the priests, and their own special ministrations devolve on the Levites. The layman is bound by the laws that pertain to laymen.

CHAP. XLI.—CONTINUATION OF THE SAME SUBJECT.

Let every one of you, brethren, give thanks[9] to God in his own order, living in all good conscience, with becoming gravity, and not going beyond the rule of the ministry prescribed to him. Not in every place, brethren, are the daily sacrifices offered, or the peace-offerings, or the sin-offerings and the trespass-offerings, but in Jerusalem only. And even there they are not offered in any place, but only at the altar before the temple, that which is offered being first carefully examined by the high priest and the ministers already mentioned. Those, therefore, who do anything beyond that which is agreeable to His will, are punished with death. Ye see,[10] brethren, that the greater the knowledge that has been vouchsafed to us, the greater also is the danger to which we are exposed.

CHAP. XLII.—THE ORDER OF MINISTERS IN THE CHURCH.

The apostles have preached the gospel to us from[11] the Lord Jesus Christ; Jesus[12] Christ [has done so] from God. Christ therefore was sent forth by God,[13] and the apostles by Christ. Both these appointments,[14] then, were made in an orderly way, according to the will of God. Having therefore received their orders, and being fully assured by the resurrection of our Lord Jesus Christ, and established[15] in the word of God, with full assurance of the Holy Ghost, they went forth proclaiming that the kingdom of God was at hand. And thus preaching through countries and cities, they appointed the first fruits [of their labours], having first proved them by the Spirit,[16] to be bishops and deacons of those who should afterwards believe. Nor was this any new thing, since indeed many ages before it was written con-

[1] I omits καὶ ἀσύνετοι (and without understanding).
[2] Literally, "and silly and uninstructed."
[3] Literally, "a breath."
[4] Or, "has perceived."
[5] Some render, "they perished at the gates."
[6] Job iv. 16–18, 19–21, v. 1–5, xv. 15.
[7] Some join κατὰ καιροὺς τεταγμένους, "at stated times," to the next sentence.
[8] Literally, "to His will."

[9] I. εὐαρεστείτω (be well-pleasing).
[10] Or, "consider."
[11] Or, "by the command of."
[12] A. "the Christ," I. "Christ."
[13] I. omits.
[14] Literally, "both things were done."
[15] Or, "confirmed by."
[16] Or, "having tested them in spirit."

cerning bishops and deacons. For thus saith the Scripture in a certain place, "I will appoint their bishops[1] in righteousness, and their deacons[2] in faith."[3]

CHAP. XLIII.—MOSES OF OLD STILLED THE CONTENTION WHICH AROSE CONCERNING THE PRIESTLY DIGNITY.

And what wonder is it if those in Christ who were entrusted with such a duty by God, appointed those [ministers] before mentioned, when the blessed Moses also, "a faithful servant in all his house,"[4] noted down in the sacred books all the injunctions which were given him, and when the other prophets also followed him, bearing witness with one consent to the ordinances which he had appointed? For, when rivalry arose concerning the priesthood, and the tribes were contending among themselves as to which of them should be adorned with that glorious title, he commanded the twelve princes of the tribes to bring him their rods, each one being inscribed with the name[5] of the tribe. And he took them and bound them [together], and sealed them with the rings of the princes of the tribes, and laid them up in the tabernacle of witness on the table of God. And having shut the doors of the tabernacle, he sealed the keys, as he had done the rods, and said to them, Men and brethren, the tribe whose rod shall blossom has God chosen to fulfil the office of the priesthood, and to minister unto Him. And when the morning was come, he assembled all Israel, six hundred thousand men, and showed the seals to the princes of the tribes, and opened the tabernacle of witness, and brought forth the rods. And the rod of Aaron was found not only to have blossomed, but to bear fruit upon it.[6] What think ye, beloved? Did not Moses know beforehand that this would happen? Undoubtedly he knew; but he acted thus, that there might be no sedition in Israel, and that the name of the true and only God might be glorified; to whom be glory for ever and ever. Amen.

CHAP. XLIV. — THE ORDINANCES OF THE APOSTLES, THAT THERE MIGHT BE NO CONTENTION RESPECTING THE PRIESTLY OFFICE.

Our apostles also knew, through our Lord Jesus Christ, that there would be strife on account of the office[7] of the episcopate. For this reason, therefore, inasmuch as they had obtained a perfect fore-knowledge of this, they appointed those [ministers] already mentioned, and afterwards gave instructions,[8] that when these should fall asleep, other approved men should succeed them in their ministry. We are of opinion, therefore, that those appointed by them,[9] or afterwards by other eminent men, with the consent of the whole church, and who have blamelessly served the flock of Christ, in a humble, peaceable, and disinterested spirit, and have for a long time possessed the good opinion of all, cannot be justly dismissed from the ministry. For our sin will not be small, if we eject from the episcopate[10] those who have blamelessly and holily fulfilled its duties.[11] Blessed are those presbyters who, having finished their course before now, have obtained a fruitful and perfect departure [from this world]; for they have no fear lest any one deprive them of the place now appointed them. But we see that ye have removed some men of excellent behaviour from the ministry, which they fulfilled blamelessly and with honour.

CHAP. XLV. — IT IS THE PART OF THE WICKED TO VEX THE RIGHTEOUS.

Ye are fond of contention, brethren, and full of zeal about things which do not pertain to salvation. Look carefully into the Scriptures, which are the true utterances of the Holy Spirit. Observe[12] that nothing of an unjust or counterfeit character is written in them. There[13] you will not find that the righteous were cast off by men who themselves were holy. The righteous were indeed persecuted, but only by the wicked. They were cast into prison, but only by the unholy; they were stoned, but only by transgressors; they were slain, but only by the accursed, and such as had conceived an unrighteous envy against them. Exposed to such sufferings, they endured them gloriously. For what shall we say, brethren? Was Daniel[14] cast into the den of lions by such as

---

[1] Or, "overseers."
[2] Or, "servants."
[3] Isa. lx. 17, Sept.; but the text is here altered by Clement. The LXX. have, "I will give thy rulers in peace, and thy overseers in righteousness."
[4] Num. xii. 10; Heb. iii. 5.
[5] Literally, "every tribe being written according to its name."
[6] See Num. xvii.

[7] Literally, "on account of the title of the oversight." Some understand this to mean, "in regard to the dignity of the episcopate;" and others simply, "on account of the oversight." I. for ἐπινομή gives ἐπιδομή. Bryennius conjectures ἐπιδοχή, which, perhaps, may be rendered "Succession" (διαδοχή).
[8] The meaning of this passage is much controverted. Some render, "left a list of other approved persons;" while others translate the unusual word ἐπινομὴ, which causes the difficulty, by "testamentary direction," and many others deem the text corrupt. We have given what seems the simplest version of the text as it stands.
[9] *i.e.* the apostles.
[10] Or, "oversight."
[11] Literally, "presented the offerings."
[12] Or, "Ye perceive."
[13] Or, "For."
[14] Dan. vi. 16.

feared God? Were Ananias, and Azarias, and Mishael shut up in a furnace[1] of fire by those who observed[2] the great and glorious worship of the Most High? Far from us be such a thought! Who, then, were they that did such things? The hateful, and those full of all wickedness, were roused to such a pitch of fury, that they inflicted torture on those who served God with a holy and blameless purpose [of heart], not knowing that the Most High is the Defender and Protector of all such as with a pure conscience venerate[3] His all-excellent name; to whom be glory for ever and ever. Amen. But they who with confidence endured [these things] are now heirs of glory and honour, and have been exalted and made illustrious[4] by God in their memorial for ever and ever. Amen.

CHAP. XLVI. — LET US CLEAVE TO THE RIGHTEOUS: YOUR STRIFE IS PERNICIOUS.

Such examples, therefore, brethren, it is right that we should follow;[5] since it is written, "Cleave to the holy, for those that cleave to them shall [themselves] be made holy."[6] And again, in another place, [the Scripture] saith, "With a harmless man thou shalt prove[7] thyself harmless, and with an elect man thou shalt be elect, and with a perverse man thou shalt show[8] thyself perverse."[9] Let us cleave, therefore, to the innocent and righteous, since these are the elect of God. Why are there strifes, and tumults, and divisions, and schisms, and wars[10] among you? Have we not [all] one God and one Christ? Is there not one Spirit of grace poured out upon us? And have we not one calling in Christ?[11] Why do we divide and tear in pieces the members of Christ, and raise up strife against our own body, and have reached such a height of madness as to forget that "we are members one of another?"[12] Remember the words of our Lord Jesus Christ, how[13] He said, "Woe to that man [by whom[13] offences come]! It were better for him that he had never been born, than that he should cast a stumbling-block before one of my elect. Yea, it were better for him that a millstone should be hung about [his neck], and he should be sunk in the depths of the sea, than that he should cast a stumbling-block before one of my little ones."[14] Your schism has subverted [the faith of] many, has discouraged many, has given rise to doubt in many, and has caused grief to us all. And still your sedition continueth.

CHAP. XLVII.—YOUR RECENT DISCORD IS WORSE THAN THE FORMER WHICH TOOK PLACE IN THE TIMES OF PAUL.

Take up the epistle of the blessed Apostle Paul. What did he write to you at the time when the gospel first began to be preached?[15] Truly, under the inspiration[16] of the Spirit, he wrote to you concerning himself, and Cephas, and Apollos,[17] because even then parties[18] had been formed among you. But that inclination for one above another entailed less guilt upon you, inasmuch as your partialities were then shown towards apostles, already of high reputation, and towards a man whom they had approved. But now reflect who those are that have perverted you, and lessened the renown of your far-famed brotherly love. It is disgraceful, beloved, yea, highly disgraceful, and unworthy of your Christian profession,[19] that such a thing should be heard of as that the most stedfast and ancient church of the Corinthians should, on account of one or two persons, engage in sedition against its presbyters. And this rumour has reached not only us, but those also who are unconnected[20] with us; so that, through your infatuation, the name of the Lord is blasphemed, while danger is also brought upon yourselves.

CHAP. XLVIII.—LET US RETURN TO THE PRACTICE OF BROTHERLY LOVE.

Let us therefore, with all haste, put an end[21] to this [state of things]; and let us fall down before the Lord, and beseech Him with tears, that He would mercifully[22] be reconciled to us, and restore us to our former seemly and holy practice of brotherly love. For [such conduct] is the gate of righteousness, which is set open for the attainment of life, as it is written, "Open to me the gates of righteousness; I will go in by them, and will praise the Lord: this is the gate of the

---

1 Dan. iii. 20.
2 Literally, "worshipped."
3 Literally, "serve."
4 Or, "lifted up." I. ἔγγραφοι (inscribed).
5 Literally, "to such examples it is right that we should cleave."
6 Not found in Scripture.
7 Literally, "be."
8 Or, "thou wilt overthrow."
9 Ps. xviii. 25, 26.
10 Or. "war." Comp. James iv. 1.
11 Comp. Eph. iv. 4–6.
12 Rom. xii. 5.
13 This clause is wanting in the text.

14 Comp. Matt. xviii 6, xxvi. 24; Mark ix. 42; Luke xvii. 2.
15 Literally, "in the beginning of the gospel."
16 Or, "spiritually."
17 1 Cor. iii. 13, etc.
18 Or, "inclinations for one above another." I. προσκλήσεις (summonses) throughout for προσκλίσεις.
19 Literally, "of conduct in Christ." I. ἀγάπη (love).
20 Or, "aliens from us," *i.e.* the Gentiles.
21 Literally, "remove."
22 Literally, "becoming merciful."

Lord: the righteous shall enter in by it."[1] Although, therefore, many gates have been set open, yet this gate of righteousness is that gate in Christ by which blessed are all they that have entered in and have directed their way in holiness and righteousness, doing all things without disorder. Let a man be faithful: let him be powerful in the utterance of knowledge; let him be wise in judging of words; let him be pure in all his deeds; yet the more he seems to be superior to others [in these respects], the more humble-minded ought he to be, and to seek the common good of all, and not merely his own advantage.

CHAP. XLIX.—THE PRAISE OF LOVE.

Let him who has love in Christ keep the commandments of Christ. Who can describe the [blessed] bond of the love of God? What man is able to tell the excellence of its beauty, as it ought to be told? The height to which love exalts is unspeakable. Love unites us to God. Love covers a multitude of sins.[2] Love beareth all things, is long-suffering in all things.[3] There is nothing base, nothing arrogant in love. Love admits of no schisms: love gives rise to no seditions: love does all things in harmony. By love have all the elect of God been made perfect; without love nothing is well-pleasing to God. In love has the Lord taken us to Himself. On account of the love He bore us, Jesus Christ our Lord gave His blood for us by the will of God; His flesh for our flesh, and His soul for our souls.

CHAP. L.—LET US PRAY TO BE THOUGHT WORTHY OF LOVE.

Ye see, beloved, how great and wonderful a thing is love, and that there is no declaring its perfection. Who is fit to be found in it, except such as God has vouchsafed to render so? Let us pray,[4] therefore, and implore of His mercy, that we may live[5] blameless in love, free from all human partialities for one above another. All the generations from Adam even unto this day have passed away; but those who, through the grace of God, have been made perfect in love, now possess a place among the godly, and shall be made manifest at the revelation[6] of the kingdom of Christ.[7] For it is written, "Enter into thy secret chambers for a little time, until my wrath and fury pass away; and I will remember a propitious[8] day, and will raise you up out of your graves."[9] Blessed are we, beloved, if we keep the commandments of God in the harmony of love; that so through love our sins may be forgiven us. For it is written, "Blessed are they whose transgressions are forgiven, and whose sins are covered. Blessed is the man whose sin the Lord will not impute to him, and in whose mouth there is no guile.[10] This blessedness cometh upon those who have been chosen by God through Jesus Christ our Lord; to whom be glory for ever and ever. Amen.

CHAP. LI.—LET THE PARTAKERS IN STRIFE ACKNOWLEDGE THEIR SINS.

Let us therefore implore forgiveness for all those transgressions which through any [suggestion] of the adversary we have committed. And those who have been the leaders of sedition and disagreement ought to have respect[11] to the common hope. For such as live in fear and love would rather that they themselves than their neighbours should be involved in suffering. And they prefer to bear blame themselves, rather than that the concord which has been well and piously[12] handed down to us should suffer. For it is better that a man should acknowledge his transgressions than that he should harden his heart, as the hearts of those were hardened who stirred up sedition against Moses the servant[13] of God, and whose condemnation was made manifest [unto all]. For they went down alive into Hades, and death swallowed them up.[14] Pharaoh with his army and all the princes of Egypt, and the chariots with their riders, were sunk in the depths of the Red Sea, and perished,[15] for no other reason than that their foolish hearts were hardened, after so many signs and wonders had been wrought in the land of Egypt by Moses the servant of God.

CHAP. LII.—SUCH A CONFESSION IS PLEASING TO GOD.

The Lord, brethren, stands in need of nothing; and He desires nothing of any one, except that confession be made to Him.

1 Ps. cxviii. 19, 20.
2 James v. 20; 1 Pet. iv. 8.
3 Comp. 1 Cor. xiii. 4, etc.
4 I. gives indicative mood.
5 I. εὑρεθῶμεν (may be found).
6 Literally, "visitation."
7 I. θεοῦ (God).
8 Or, "good."
9 Isa. xxvi. 20.
10 Ps. xxxii. 1, 2.
11 Or, "look to."
12 Or, "righteously."
13 I. ἄνθρωπον (man).
14 Num. xvi. I. θάνατος ποιμανεῖ αὐτούς—"Death shall feed on them," Ps. xlix., 14 A. V.—should be, "Death shall tend them."
15 Ex. xiv.

For, says the elect David, "I will confess unto the Lord; and that will please Him more than a young bullock[1] that hath horns and hoofs. Let the poor see it, and be glad."[2] And again he saith, "Offer[3] unto God the sacrifice of praise, and pay thy vows unto the Most High. And call upon me in the day of thy trouble: I will deliver thee, and thou shalt glorify me."[4] For "the sacrifice of God is a broken spirit."[5]

CHAP. LIII.—THE LOVE OF MOSES TOWARDS HIS PEOPLE.

Ye understand, beloved, ye understand well the sacred Scriptures, and ye have looked very earnestly into the oracles of God. Call then these things to your remembrance. When Moses went up into the mount, and abode there, with fasting and humiliation, forty days and forty nights, the Lord said unto him, "Moses, Moses, get thee down quickly from hence; for thy people whom thou didst bring out of the land of Egypt have committed iniquity. They have speedily departed from the way in which I commanded them to walk, and have made to themselves molten images."[6] And the Lord said unto him, "I have spoken to thee once and again, saying, I have seen this people, and, behold, it is a stiff-necked people: let me destroy them, and blot out their name from under heaven; and I will make thee a great and wonderful nation, and one much more numerous than this."[7] But Moses said, "Far be it from Thee, Lord: pardon the sin of this people; else blot me also out of the book of the living."[8] O marvellous[9] love! O insuperable perfection! The servant[10] speaks freely to his Lord, and asks forgiveness for the people, or begs that he himself might perish[11] along with them.

CHAP. LIV.—HE WHO IS FULL OF LOVE WILL INCUR EVERY LOSS, THAT PEACE MAY BE RESTORED TO THE CHURCH.

Who then among you is noble-minded? who compassionate? who full of love? Let him declare, "If on my account sedition and disagreement and schisms have arisen, I will depart, I will go away whithersoever ye desire, and I will do whatever the majority[12] commands; only let the flock of Christ live on terms of peace with the presbyters set over it." He that acts thus shall procure to himself great glory in the Lord;[13] and every place will welcome[14] him. For "the earth is the Lord's, and the fulness thereof.[15] These things they who live a godly life that is never to be repented of, both have done and always will do.

CHAP. LV.—EXAMPLES OF SUCH LOVE.

To bring forward some examples[16] from among the heathen: Many kings and princes, in times of pestilence, when they had been instructed by an oracle, have given themselves up to death, in order that by their own blood they might deliver their fellow-citizens [from destruction]. Many have gone forth from their own cities, that so sedition might be brought to an end within them. We know many among ourselves who have given themselves up to bonds, in order that they might ransom others. Many, too, have surrendered themselves to slavery, that with the price[17] which they received for themselves, they might provide food for others. Many women also, being strengthened by the grace of God, have performed numerous manly exploits. The blessed Judith, when her city was besieged, asked of the elders permission to go forth into the camp of the strangers; and, exposing herself to danger, she went out for the love which she bare to her country and people then besieged; and the Lord delivered Holofernes into the hands of a woman.[18] Esther also, being perfect in faith, exposed herself to no less danger, in order to deliver the twelve tribes of Israel from impending destruction. For with fasting and humiliation she entreated the everlasting[19] God, who seeth all things; and He, perceiving the humility of her spirit, delivered the people for whose sake she had encountered peril.[20]

CHAP. LVI.—LET US ADMONISH AND CORRECT ONE ANOTHER.

Let us then also pray for those who have fallen into any sin, that meekness and humil-

1 I. omits from Ps. lxix., 31, 32 the words following "bullock."
2 Ps. lxix. 31, 32.
3 Or, "sacrifice."
4 Ps. l. 14, 15. I. omits Ps. l., 15.
5 Ps. li. 17.
6 Ex. xxxii. 7, etc.; Deut. ix. 12, etc.
7 Ex. xxxii. 9, etc.
8 Ex. xxxii. 32.
9 Or, "mighty."
10 I. δεσπότης (master).
11 Literally, "be wiped out."
12 Literally, "the multitude."
13 I. ἐν Χριστῷ (in Christ).
14 Or, "receive."
15 Ps. xxiv. 1; 1 Cor. x. 26, 28.
16 I. ὑπομνήματα (memorials).
17 Literally, "and having received their prices, fed others."
18 Judith viii. 30.
19 I. omits δεσπότην (Lord).
20 Esther vii. viii.

ity may be given to them, so that they may submit, not unto us, but to the will of God. For in this way they shall secure a fruitful and perfect remembrance from us, with sympathy for them, both in our prayers to God, and our mention of them to the saints.[1] Let us receive correction, beloved, on account of which no one should feel displeased. Those exhortations by which we admonish one another are both good [in themselves], and highly profitable, for they tend to unite[2] us to the will of God. For thus saith the holy Word: "The Lord hath severely chastened me, yet hath not given me over to death."[3] "For whom the Lord loveth He chasteneth, and scourgeth every son whom He receiveth."[4] "The righteous,"[5] saith it, "shall chasten me in mercy, and reprove me;" but let not the oil of sinners make fat my head.[6] And again he saith, "Blessed is the man whom the Lord reproveth, and reject not thou the warning of the Almighty. For He causes sorrow, and again restores [to gladness]; He woundeth, and His hands make whole. He shall deliver thee in six troubles, yea, in the seventh no evil shall touch thee. In famine He shall rescue thee from death, and in war He shall free thee from the power[7] of the sword. From the scourge of the tongue will He hide thee, and thou shalt not fear when evil cometh. Thou shalt laugh at the unrighteous and the wicked, and shalt not be afraid of the beasts of the field. For the wild beasts shall be at peace with thee: then shalt thou know that thy house shall be in peace, and the habitation of thy tabernacle shall not fail.[8] Thou shalt know also that thy seed shall be great, and thy children like the grass of the field. And thou shalt come to the grave like ripened corn which is reaped in its season, or like a heap of the threshing-floor which is gathered together at the proper time."[9] Ye see, beloved, that[10] "protection is afforded to those that are chastened of the Lord; for since God is good,[11] He corrects us, that we may be admonished"[12] by His holy chastisement.

CHAP. LVII.—LET THE AUTHORS OF SEDITION SUBMIT THEMSELVES.

Ye therefore, who laid the foundation of this sedition, submit yourselves to the presbyters, and receive correction so as to repent, bending the knees of your hearts. Learn to be subject, laying aside the proud and arrogant self-confidence of your tongue. For it is better for you that ye should occupy[13] a humble but honourable place in the flock of Christ, than that, being highly exalted, ye should be cast out from the hope of His people.[14] For thus speaketh all-virtuous Wisdom: "Behold, I will bring forth to you the words of my Spirit, and I will teach you my speech. Since I called, and ye did not hear; I held forth my words, and ye regarded not, but set at naught my counsels, and yielded not at my reproofs; therefore I too will laugh at your destruction; yea, I will rejoice when ruin cometh upon you, and when sudden confusion overtakes you, when overturning presents itself like a tempest, or when tribulation and oppression[15] fall upon you. For it shall come to pass, that when ye call upon me, I will not hear you; the wicked shall seek me, and they shall not find me. For they hated wisdom, and did not choose the fear of the Lord; nor would they listen to my counsels, but despised my reproofs. Wherefore they shall eat the fruits of their own way, and they shall be filled[16] with their own ungodliness.[17] . . . For, in punishment for the wrongs which they practised upon babes, shall they be slain, and inquiry will be death to the ungodly; but he that heareth me shall rest in hope and be undisturbed by the fear of any evil."

CHAP. LVIII.—SUBMISSION THE PRECURSOR OF SALVATION.

Let us, therefore, flee from the warning threats pronounced by Wisdom on the disobedient, and yield submission to His all-holy and glorious name, that we may stay our trust upon the most hallowed name of His majesty. Receive our counsel, and ye shall be without repentance. For, as God liveth, and as the Lord Jesus Christ and the Holy Ghost live,—both the faith and hope of the elect, he who in lowliness of mind, with instant gentleness, and without repentance hath observed the ordinances and appointments given by God—the same shall obtain a place and name in the number of those who are being saved through Jesus Christ, through whom is glory to Him for ever and ever. Amen.

---

1 Literally, "there shall be to them a fruitful and perfect remembrance, with compassions both towards God and the saints."

2 Or, "they unite."

3 Ps. cxviii. 18.

4 Prov. iii. 12; Heb. xii. 6.

5 I. κύριος (Lord).

6 Ps. cxli. 5.

7 Literally, "hand."

8 Literally, "err" or "sin."

9 Job v. 17–26.

10 I. βλέπετε πόσος (ye see how great).

11 I. (δεσπότου) πατὴρ γὰρ ἀγαθὸς ὢν (being a good father).

12 I. ἐλεηθῆναι (be pitied).

13 Literally, "to be found small and esteemed."

14 Literally, "His hope."

15 I. adds στενοχωρία (straits).

16 Here begins the *lacuna* in the old text referred to in the Introduction. The newly discovered portion of the Epistle extends from this point to the end of Chap. lxiii.

17 Prov. i. 22–33.

CHAP. LIX. — WARNING AGAINST DISOBEDIENCE. PRAYER.

If, however, any shall disobey the words spoken by Him through us, let them know that they will involve themselves in transgression and serious danger; but we shall be innocent of this sin, and, instant in prayer and supplication, shall desire that the Creator of all preserve unbroken the computed number of His elect in the whole world through His beloved Son Jesus Christ, through whom He called us from darkness to light, from ignorance to knowledge of the glory of His name, our hope resting on Thy name which is primal cause of every creature,—having opened the eyes of our heart to the knowledge of Thee, who alone "dost rest highest among the highest, holy among the holy,"[1] who "layest low the insolence of the haughty,"[2] who "destroyest the calculations of the heathen,"[3] who "settest the low on high and bringest low the exalted;"[4] who "makest rich and makest poor,"[5] who "killest and makest to live,"[6] only Benefactor of spirits and God of all flesh,[7] who beholdest the depths, the eye-witness of human works, the help of those in danger, the Saviour of those in despair, the Creator and Guardian of every spirit, who multipliest nations upon earth, and from all madest choice of those who love Thee through Jesus Christ, Thy beloved Son, through whom Thou didst instruct, sanctify, honour us. We would have Thee, Lord, to prove our help and succour. Those of us in affliction save, on the lowly take pity; the fallen raise; upon those in need arise; the sick[8] heal; the wandering ones of Thy people turn; fill the hungry; redeem those of us in bonds; raise up those that are weak; comfort the faint-hearted; let all the nations know that Thou art God alone and Jesus Christ Thy Son, and we are Thy people and the sheep of Thy pasture.

CHAP. LX.— PRAYER CONTINUED.

Thou didst make to appear the enduring fabric of the world by the works of Thy hand; Thou, Lord, didst create the earth on which we dwell,—Thou, who art faithful in all generations, just in judgments, wonderful in strength and majesty, with wisdom creating and with understanding fixing the things which were made, who art good among them that are being saved[9] and faithful among them whose trust is in Thee; O merciful and Compassionate One, forgive us our iniquities and offences and transgressions and trespasses. Reckon not every sin of Thy servants and handmaids, but Thou wilt purify us with the purification of Thy truth; and direct our steps that we may walk in holiness of heart and do what is good and well-pleasing in Thy sight and in the sight of our rulers. Yea, Lord, make Thy face to shine upon us for good in peace, that we may be shielded by Thy mighty hand and delivered from every sin by Thine uplifted arm, and deliver us from those who hate us wrongfully. Give concord and peace to us and all who dwell upon the earth, even as Thou gavest to our fathers, when they called upon Thee in faith and truth, submissive as we are to Thine almighty and all-excellent Name.

CHAP. LXI. — PRAYER CONTINUED — FOR RULERS AND GOVERNORS. CONCLUSION.

To our rulers and governors on the earth —to them Thou, Lord, gavest the power of the kingdom by Thy glorious and ineffable might, to the end that we may know the glory and honour given to them by Thee and be subject to them, in nought resisting Thy will; to them, Lord, give health, peace, concord, stability, that they may exercise the authority given to them without offence. For Thou, O heavenly Lord and King eternal, givest to the sons of men glory and honour and power over the things that are on the earth; do Thou, Lord, direct their counsel according to that which is good and well-pleasing in Thy sight, that, devoutly in peace and meekness exercising the power given them by Thee, they may find Thee propitious. O Thou, who only hast power to do these things and more abundant good with us, we praise Thee through the High Priest and Guardian of our souls Jesus Christ, through whom be glory and majesty to Thee both now and from generation to generation and for evermore. Amen.

CHAP. LXII.—SUMMARY AND CONCLUSORY—CONCERNING GODLINESS.

Concerning the things pertaining to our religious observance which are most profitable for a life of goodness to those who would pursue a godly and righteous course, we have

[1] Is. lvii. 15.
[2] Is. xiii. 11.
[3] Ps. xxxiii. 10.
[4] Job v. 11; Ezek. xvii. 24.
[5] 1 Sam. ii. 7.
[6] Deut. xxxii. 39.
[7] Numb. xvi. 22, xxvii. 16; Jer. xxxii. 27.
[8] I. gives ἀσεβεῖς (ungodly) where ἀσθενεῖς (sick) is substituted.

[9] σωζομένοις is the emendation of Harnack for ὁρωμένοις (seen).

written to you, men and brethren, at sufficient length. For concerning faith and repentance and true love and continence and soberness and patience, we have touched upon every passage, putting you in mind that you ought in righteousness and truth and long-suffering to be well-pleasing[1] to Almighty God with holiness, being of one mind—not remembering evil—in love and peace with instant gentleness, even as also our fathers fore-mentioned found favour by the humility of their thoughts towards the Father and God and Creator and all mankind. And of these things we put you in mind with the greater pleasure, since we were well assured that we were writing to men who were faithful and of highest repute and had peered into the oracles of the instruction of God.

CHAP. LXIII.—HORTATORY, LETTER SENT BY SPECIAL MESSENGERS.

Right is it, therefore, to approach examples so good and so many, and submit the neck and fulfil the part of obedience, in order that, undisturbed by vain sedition, we may attain unto the goal set before us in truth wholly free from blame. Joy and gladness will ye afford us, if ye become obedient to the words written by us and through the Holy Spirit root out the lawless wrath of your jealousy according to the intercession which we have made for peace and unity in this letter. We have sent men faithful and discreet, whose conversation from youth to old age has been blameless amongst us,—the same shall be witnesses between you and us. This we have done, that ye may know that our whole concern has been and is that ye may be speedily at peace.

CHAP. LXIV.—BLESSINGS SOUGHT FOR ALL THAT CALL UPON GOD.

May God, who seeth all things, and who is the Ruler of all spirits and the Lord of all flesh—who chose our Lord Jesus Christ and us through Him to be a peculiar[2] people—grant to every soul that calleth upon His glorious and holy name, faith, fear, peace, patience, long-suffering, self-control, purity, and sobriety, to the well-pleasing of His name, through our High Priest and Protector, Jesus Christ, by whom be to Him glory, and majesty, and power, and honour, both now and for evermore. Amen.

CHAP. LXV.—THE CORINTHIANS ARE EXHORTED SPEEDILY TO SEND BACK WORD THAT PEACE HAS BEEN RESTORED. THE BENEDICTION.

Send back speedily to us in peace and with joy these our messengers to you: Claudius Ephebus and Valerius Bito, with Fortunatus; that they may the sooner announce to us the peace and harmony we so earnestly desire and long for [among you], and that we may the more quickly rejoice over the good order re-established among you. The grace of our Lord Jesus Christ be with you, and with all everywhere that are the called of God through Him, by whom be to Him glory, honour, power, majesty, and eternal dominion,[3] from everlasting to everlasting.[4] Amen.

---

[1] εὐαριστεῖν is emendation for εὐχαριστεῖν (give thanks).

[2] Comp. Tit. ii. 14.

[3] Literally, "an eternal throne."

[4] Literally, "from the ages to the ages of ages."

INTRODUCTORY NOTICE

[*From Vol. VII., p. 515 of the Ante-Nicene Fathers.*]

THE first certain reference which is made by any early writer to this so-called Epistle of Clement is found in these words of Eusebius (*Hist. Eccl.*, iii. 38): "We must know that there is also a second Epistle of Clement. But we do not regard it as being equally notable with the former, since we know of none of the ancients that have made use of it." Several critics in modern times have endeavoured to vindicate the authenticity of this epistle. But it is now generally regarded as one of the many writings which have been falsely ascribed to Clement. Besides the want of external evidence, indicated even by Eusebius in the above extract, the diversity of style clearly points to a different writer from that of the first epistle. A commonly accepted opinion among critics at the present day is, that this is not an epistle at all, but a fragment of one of the many homilies falsely ascribed to Clement. There can be no doubt, however, that in the catalogue of writings contained in the Alexandrian MS. it is both styled an epistle, and, as well as the other which accompanies it, is attributed to Clement. As the MS. is certainly not later than the fifth century, the opinion referred to must by that time have taken firm root in the Church; but in the face of internal evidence, and in want of all earlier testimony, such a fact goes but a small way to establish its authenticity.

THE second epistle differs from the first in several respects. The range of Scriptural quotation is wider, the quotations of the first epistle being taken mainly from the Septuagint version of the Old Testament. The attitude of the writer is in accordance with this fact; it is distinctively Gentile. For example, Chapter XII. contains a report of words purporting to have been spoken by the Lord; these, Clemens Alexandrinus states, are taken from the Apocryphal Gospel according to the Egyptians, not now extant. The reference in Chapter XIV. to the spiritual church, recalling Eph. i. 3–5, is parallel to the Pastor of Hermas, Vision II. 4. These passages help to determine the date; for the quotation from the Apocryphal Gospel would not have been made after the four gospels of the New Testament obtained exclusive authority—toward the close of the second century; while similarity of idea and exposition would seem to make the second epistle and the Pastor of Hermas somewhat contemporaneous.

The conclusion of the second epistle, as in the recently discovered MS., goes to establish the speculation made before this MS. was discovered, that it is a homily to be read in churches.

THE SECOND EPISTLE OF CLEMENT[1]

CHAP. I.—WE OUGHT TO THINK HIGHLY OF CHRIST.

BRETHREN, it is fitting that you should think of Jesus Christ as of God,—as the Judge of the living and the dead. And it does not become us to think lightly of our salvation; for if we think little of Him, we shall also hope but to obtain little [from Him]. And those of us who hear carelessly of these things, as if they were of small importance, commit sin, not knowing whence we have been called, and by whom, and to what place, and how much Jesus Christ submitted to suffer for our sakes. What return, then, shall we make to Him, or what fruit that shall be worthy of that which He has given to us? For, indeed, how great are the benefits[2] which we owe to Him! He has graciously given us light; as a Father, He has called us sons; He has saved us when we were ready to perish. What praise, then, shall we give to Him, or what return shall we make for the things which we have received?[3] We were deficient[4] in understanding, worshipping stones and wood, and gold, and silver, and brass, the works of men's hands;[5] and our whole life was nothing else than death. Involved in blindness, and with such darkness[6] before our eyes, we have received sight, and through His will have laid aside that cloud by which we were enveloped. For He had compassion on us, and mercifully saved us, observing the many errors in which we were entangled, as well as the destruction to which we were exposed,[7] and that we had no hope of salvation except it came to us from Him. For He called us when we were not,[8] and willed that out of nothing we should attain a real existence.[9]

CHAP. II.—THE CHURCH, FORMERLY BARREN, IS NOW FRUITFUL.

"Rejoice, thou barren that bearest not; break forth and cry, thou that travailest not; for she that is desolate hath many more children than she that hath an husband."[10] In that He said, "Rejoice, thou barren that bearest not," He referred to us, for our church was barren before that children were given to her. But when He said, "Cry out, thou that travailest not," He means this, that we should sincerely offer up our prayers to God, and should not, like women in travail, show signs of weakness.[11] And in that He said, "For she that is desolate hath many more children than she that hath an husband," [He means] that our people seemed to be outcast from God, but now, through believing, have become more numerous than those who are reckoned to possess God.[12] And another Scripture saith, "I came not to call the righteous, but sinners."[13] This means that those who are perishing must be saved. For it is indeed a great and admirable thing to establish not the things which are standing, but those that are falling. Thus also did Christ[14] desire to save the things which were perishing,[15] and has saved many by coming and calling us when hastening to destruction.[16]

CHAP. III. — THE DUTY OF CONFESSING CHRIST.

Since, then, He has displayed so great mercy towards us, and especially in this respect, that we who are living should not offer sacrifices to gods that are dead, or pay them worship,[17] but should attain through Him to

[1] No title, not even a letter, is preserved in A. I. inserts "Clement's (Epistle) to the Corinthians II."
[2] Literally, "holy things."
[3] Comp. Ps. cxvi. 12.
[4] Literally, "lame." I. πονηροί (wicked).
[5] Literally, "of men."
[6] Literally, "being full of such darkness in our sight."
[7] Literally, "having beheld in us much error and destruction."
[8] Comp. Hos ii. 23; Rom. iv. 17, ix. 25.
[9] Literally, "willed us from not being to be."

[10] Isa. liv. 1; Gal. iv. 27.
[11] Some render, "should not cry out, like women in travail." The text is doubtful. I. ἐκκακῶμεν (faint).
[12] It has been remarked that the writer here implies he was a Gentile.
[13] Matt. ix. 13; Luke v. 32.
[14] I. Κύριος (Lord).
[15] Comp. Matt. xviii. 11.
[16] Literally, "already perishing."
[17] I. omits.

the knowledge of the true Father,[1] whereby shall we show that we do indeed know Him,[2] but by not denying Him through whom this knowledge has been attained? For He himself declares, "Whosoever shall confess me before men, him will I confess before my Father."[3] This, then, is our reward if we shall confess Him by whom we have been saved. But in what way shall we confess Him? By doing what He says, and not transgressing His commandments, and by honouring Him not with our lips only, but with all our heart and all our mind.[4] For He says in Isaiah, "This people honoureth me with their lips, but their heart is far from me."[5]

CHAP. IV.—TRUE CONFESSION OF CHRIST.

Let us, then, not only call Him Lord, for that will not save us. For He saith, "Not every one that saith to me, Lord, Lord, shall be saved, but he that worketh righteousness."[6] Wherefore, brethren, let us confess Him by our works, by loving one another, by not committing adultery, or speaking evil of one another, or cherishing envy; but by being continent, compassionate, and good. We ought also to sympathize with one another, and not be avaricious. By such works let us confess Him,[7] and not by those that are of an opposite kind. And it is not fitting that we should fear men, but rather God. For this reason, if we should do such [wicked] things, the Lord hath said, "Even though ye were gathered together to[8] me in my very bosom, yet if ye were not to keep my commandments, I would cast you off, and say unto you, Depart from me; I know you not whence ye are, ye workers of iniquity."[9]

CHAP. V.—THIS WORLD SHOULD BE DESPISED.

Wherefore, brethren, leaving [willingly] our sojourn in this present world, let us do the will of Him that called us, and not fear to depart out of this world. For the Lord saith, "Ye shall be as lambs in the midst of wolves."[10] And Peter answered and said unto Him,[11] "What, then, if the wolves shall tear in pieces the lambs?" Jesus said unto Peter, "The lambs have no cause after they are dead to fear[12] the wolves; and in like manner, fear not ye them that kill you, and can do nothing more unto you; but fear Him who, after you are dead, has power over both soul and body to cast them into hell-fire."[13] And consider,[14] brethren, that the sojourning in the flesh in this world is but brief and transient, but the promise of Christ is great and wonderful, even the rest of the kingdom to come, and of life everlasting.[15] By what course of conduct, then, shall we attain these things, but by leading a holy and righteous life, and by deeming these worldly things as not belonging to us, and not fixing our desires upon them? For if we desire to possess them, we fall away from the path of righteousness.

CHAP. VI.—THE PRESENT AND FUTURE WORLDS ARE ENEMIES TO EACH OTHER.

Now the Lord declares, "No servant can serve two masters."[16] If we desire, then, to serve both God and mammon, it will be unprofitable for us. "For what will it profit if a man gain the whole world, and lose his own soul?"[17] This world and the next are two enemies. The one urges[18] to adultery and corruption, avarice and deceit; the other bids farewell to these things. We cannot, therefore, be the friends of both; and it behoves us, by renouncing the one, to make sure[19] of the other. Let us reckon[20] that it is better to hate the things present, since they are trifling, and transient, and corruptible; and to love those [which are to come,] as being good and incorruptible. For if we do the will of Christ, we shall find rest; otherwise, nothing shall deliver us from eternal punishment, if we disobey His commandments. For thus also saith the Scripture in Ezekiel, "If Noah, Job, and Daniel should rise up, they should not deliver their children in captivity."[21] Now, if men so eminently righteous are not able by their righteousness to deliver their children, how[22] can we hope to enter into the royal residence[23] of God unless we keep our baptism holy and undefiled? Or who shall be our advocate,

---

[1] I. τῆς ἀληθείας (of truth).
[2] Literally, "what is the knowledge which is towards Him."
[3] Matt. x. 32.
[4] Comp. Matt. xxii. 37.
[5] Isa. xxix. 13.
[6] Matt. vii. 21, loosely quoted.
[7] Some read, "God."
[8] Or, "with me."
[9] The first part of this sentence is not found in Scripture; for the second comp., Matt. vii. 23; Luke xiii. 27.
[10] Matt. x. 16.
[11] No such conversation is recorded in Scripture.
[12] Or, "Let not the lambs fear."
[13] Matt. x. 28; Luke xii. 4, 5.
[14] Or, "know."
[15] The text and translation are here doubtful.
[16] Matt. vi. 24; Luke xvi. 13.
[17] Matt. xvi. 26. I. omits ὅλον (whole).
[18] Literally, "speaks of."
[19] Or, "enjoy."
[20] The MS. has, "we reckon."
[21] Ezek. xiv. 14, 20.
[22] Literally, "with what confidence shall we."
[23] Wake translates "kingdom," as if the reading had been βασιλείαν; but the MS. has βασίλειον, "palace."

unless we be found possessed of works of holiness and righteousness?

CHAP. VII.—WE MUST STRIVE IN ORDER TO BE CROWNED.

Wherefore, then, my brethren, let us struggle with all earnestness, knowing that the contest is [in our case] close at hand, and that many undertake long voyages to strive for a corruptible reward;[1] yet all are not crowned, but those only that have laboured hard and striven gloriously. Let us therefore so strive, that we may all be crowned. Let us run the straight[2] course, even the race that is incorruptible; and let us in great numbers set out[3] for it, and strive that we may be crowned. And should we not all be able to obtain the crown, let us at least come near to it. We must remember[4] that he who strives in the corruptible contest, if he be found acting unfairly,[5] is taken away and scourged, and cast forth from the lists. What then think ye? If one does anything unseemly in the incorruptible contest, what shall *he* have to bear? For of those who do not preserve the seal[6] [unbroken], [the Scripture] saith, "Their worm shall not die, and their fire shall not be quenched, and they shall be a spectacle to all flesh."[7]

CHAP. VIII.—THE NECESSITY OF REPENTANCE WHILE WE ARE ON EARTH.

As long, therefore, as we are upon earth, let us practise repentance, for we are as clay in the hand of the artificer. For as the potter, if he make a vessel, and it be distorted or broken in his hands, fashions it over again; but if he have before this cast it into the furnace of fire, can no longer find any help for it: so let us also, while we are in this world, repent with our whole heart of the evil deeds we have done in the flesh, that we may be saved by the Lord, while we have yet an opportunity of repentance. For after we have gone out of the world, no further power of confessing or repenting will there belong to us. Wherefore, brethren, by doing the will of the Father, and keeping the flesh holy, and observing the commandments of the Lord, we shall obtain eternal life. For the Lord saith in the Gospel, "If ye have not kept that which was small, who will commit to you the great? For I say unto you, that he that is faithful in that which is least, is faithful also in much."[8] This, then, is what He means: "Keep the flesh holy and the seal undefiled, that[9] ye may receive eternal life."[10]

CHAP. IX.—WE SHALL BE JUDGED IN THE FLESH.

And let no one of you say that this very flesh shall not be judged, nor rise again. Consider ye in what [state] ye were saved, in what ye received sight,[11] if not while ye were in this flesh. We must therefore preserve the flesh as the temple of God. For as ye were called in the flesh, ye shall also come [to be judged] in the flesh. As Christ[12] the Lord who saved us, though He was first a Spirit[13] became flesh, and thus called us, so shall we also receive the reward in this flesh. Let us therefore love one another, that we may all attain to the kingdom of God. While we have an opportunity of being healed, let us yield ourselves to God that healeth us, and give to Him a recompense. Of what sort? Repentance out of a sincere heart; for He knows all things beforehand, and is acquainted with what is in our hearts. Let us therefore give Him praise, not with the mouth only, but also with the heart, that He may accept us as sons. For the Lord has said, "Those are my brethren who do the will of my Father."[14]

CHAP. X.—VICE IS TO BE FORSAKEN, AND VIRTUE FOLLOWED.

Wherefore, my brethren, let us do the will of the Father who called us, that we may live; and let us earnestly[15] follow after virtue, but forsake every wicked tendency[16] which would lead us into transgression; and flee from ungodliness, lest evils overtake us. For if we are diligent in doing good, peace will follow us. On this account, such men cannot find it [*i.e.* peace] as are[17] influenced by

---

1 Literally, "that many set sail for corruptible contests," referring probably to the concourse at the Isthmian games.
2 Or, "Let us place before us."
3 Or, "set sail."
4 Literally, "know."
5 Literally, "if he be found corrupting."
6 Baptism is probably meant.
7 Isa. lxvi. 24.

8 Comp. Luke xvi. 10–12.
9 MS. has "we," which is corrected by all editors as above. I. ἀπολάβητε.
10 Some have thought this a quotation from an unknown apocryphal book, but it seems rather an explanation of the preceding words.
11 Literally, "looked up."
12 The MS. has εἷς, "one," which Wake follows, but it seems clearly a mistake for ὡς.
13 I. λόγος (word).
14 Matt. xii. 50.
15 Literally, "rather."
16 Literally, "malice, as it were, the precursor of our sins." Some deem the text corrupt.
17 Literally, according to the MS., "it is not possible that a man should find it who *are*"—the passage being evidently corrupt.

human terrors, and prefer rather present enjoyment[1] to the promise which shall afterwards be fulfilled. For they know not what torment present enjoyment incurs, or what felicity is involved in the future promise. And if, indeed, they themselves only did such things, it would be [the more] tolerable; but now they persist in imbuing innocent souls with their pernicious doctrines, not knowing that they shall receive a double condemnation, both they and those that hear them.

CHAP. XI.—WE OUGHT TO SERVE GOD, TRUSTING IN HIS PROMISES.

Let us therefore serve God with a pure heart, and we shall be righteous; but if we do not serve Him, because we believe not the promise of God, we shall be miserable. For the prophetic word also declares, "Wretched are those of a double mind, and who doubt in their heart, who say, All these things[2] have we heard even in the times of our fathers; but though we have waited day by day, we have seen none of them [accomplished]. Ye fools! compare yourselves to a tree; take, for instance, the vine. First of all it sheds its leaves, then the bud appears; after that the sour grape, and then the fully-ripened fruit. So, likewise, my people have borne disturbances and afflictions, but afterwards shall they receive their good things."[3] Wherefore, my brethren, let us not be of a double mind, but let us hope and endure, that we also may obtain the reward. For He is faithful who has promised that He will bestow on every one a reward according to his works. If, therefore, we shall do righteousness in the sight of God, we shall enter into His kingdom, and shall receive the promises, which "ear hath not heard, nor eye seen, neither have entered into the heart of man."[4]

CHAP. XII.—WE ARE CONSTANTLY TO LOOK FOR THE KINGDOM OF GOD.

Let us expect, therefore, hour by hour, the kingdom of God in love and righteousness, since we know not the day of the appearing of God. For the Lord Himself, being asked by one when His kingdom would come, replied, "When two shall be one, that which is without as that which is within, and the male with the female, neither male nor female."[5] Now, two are one when we speak the truth one to another, and there is unfeignedly one soul in two bodies. And "that which is without as" that which is within meaneth this: He calls the soul "that which is within," and the body "that which is without." As, then, thy body is visible to sight, so also let thy soul be manifest by good works. And "the male with the female, neither male nor female," this[6] He saith, that brother seeing sister may have no thought concerning her as female, and that she may have no thought concerning him as male. "If ye do these things," saith He, "the kingdom of my Father shall come."[7]

CHAP. XIII.—GOD'S NAME NOT TO BE BLASPHEMED.

Brethren, then, let us now at length repent, let us soberly turn to that which is good; for we are full of abundant folly and wickedness. Let us wipe out from us our former sins, and repenting from the heart be saved; and let us not be men-pleasers, nor be willing to please one another only, but also the men without, for righteousness' sake, that the name may not be, because of us, blasphemed. For the Lord saith, "Continually my name is blasphemed among all nations," and "Wherefore my name is blasphemed; blasphemed in what? In your not doing the things which I wish."[8] For the nations, hearing from our mouth the oracles of God, marvel at their excellence and worth; thereafter learning that our deeds are not worthy of the words which we speak,—receiving this occasion they turn to blasphemy, saying that they are a fable and a delusion. For, whenever they hear from us that God saith, "No thank have ye, if ye love them which love you, but ye have thank, if ye love your enemies and them which hate you"[9]—whenever they hear these words, they marvel at the surpassing measure of their goodness; but when they see, that not only do we not love those who hate, but that we love not even those who love, they laugh us to scorn, and the name is blasphemed.

CHAP. XIV.—THE CHURCH SPIRITUAL.

So, then, brethren, if we do the will of our Father God, we shall be members of the first church, the spiritual,—that which was created before sun and moon; but if we shall not do the will of the Lord, we shall come under the Scripture which saith, "My house became a den of robbers."[10] So, then, let us

---

1 I. ἀνάπαυσιν (rest),
2 I. πάλαι (long ago).
3 The same words occur in Clement's first epistle, chap. xxiii.
4 1 Cor. ii. 9.
5 These words are quoted (Clem. Alex., *Strom.*, iii. 9, 1.) from the Gospel according to the Egyptians, no longer extant.

6 Here the piece formerly broke off. From this point to the end the text of Gebhardt, Harnack, Zahn has been followed.
7 Comp. 1 Cor. vii. 29.
8 Is. lii. 5.
9 Luke vi. 32 *sqq.*
10 Jer. vii. 11.

elect to belong to the church of life,[1] that we may be saved. I think not that ye are ignorant that the living church is the body of Christ (for the Scripture saith, "God created man, male and female;"[2] the male is Christ, the female the church,) and that the Books[3] and the Apostles teach that the church is not of the present, but from the beginning. For it was spiritual, as was also our Jesus, and was made manifest at the end of the days in order to save us.[4] The church being spiritual, was made manifest in the flesh of Christ, signifying to us that if any one of us shall preserve it in the flesh and corrupt it not, he shall receive it in the Holy Spirit. For this flesh is the type of the spirit; no one, therefore, having corrupted the type, will receive afterwards the antitype. Therefore is it, then, that He saith, brethren, "Preserve ye the flesh, that ye may become partakers of the spirit." If we say that the flesh is the church and the spirit Christ, then it follows that he who shall offer outrage to the flesh is guilty of outrage on the church. Such an one, therefore, will not partake of the spirit, which is Christ. Such is the life and immortality, which this flesh may afterwards receive, the Holy Spirit cleaving to it; and no one can either express or utter what things the Lord hath prepared for His elect.[5]

CHAP. XV.—HE WHO SAVES AND HE WHO IS SAVED.

I think not that I counted trivial counsel concerning continence; following it, a man will not repent thereof, but will save both himself and me who counselled.[6] For it is no small reward to turn back a wandering and perishing soul for its salvation.[7] For this recompense we are able to render to the God who created us, if he who speaks and hears both speak and hear with faith and love. Let us, therefore, continue in that course in which we, righteous and holy, believed, that with confidence we may ask God who saith, "Whilst thou art still speaking, I will say, Here I am."[8] For these words are a token of a great promise, for the Lord saith that He is more ready to give than he who asks. So great, then, being the goodness of which we are partakers, let us not grudge one another the attainment of so great blessings. For in proportion to the pleasure with which these words are fraught to those who shall follow them, in that proportion is the condemnation with which they are fraught to those who shall refuse to hear.

CHAP. XVI.—PREPARATION FOR THE DAY OF JUDGMENT.

So, then, brethren, having received no small occasion to repent, while we have opportunity, let us turn to God who called us, while yet we have One to receive us. For if we renounce these indulgences and conquer the soul by not fulfilling its wicked desires, we shall be partakers of the mercy of Jesus. Know ye that the day[9] of judgment draweth nigh like a burning oven, and certain of the heavens and all the earth will melt, like lead melting in fire; and then will appear the hidden and manifest deeds of men. Good, then, is alms as repentance from sin; better is fasting than prayer, and alms than both; "charity covereth a multitude of sins,"[10] and prayer out of a good conscience delivereth from death. Blessed is every one that shall be found complete in these; for alms lightens the burden of sin.

CHAP. XVII.—SAME SUBJECT CONTINUED.

Let us, then, repent with our whole heart, that no one of us may perish amiss. For if we have commands and engage in withdrawing from idols and instructing others, how much more ought a soul already knowing God not to perish. Rendering, therefore, mutual help, let us raise the weak also in that which is good, that all of us may be saved and convert one another and admonish. And not only now let us seem to believe and give heed, when we are admonished by the elders;[11] but also when we take our departure home, let us remember the commandments of the Lord, and not be allured back by worldly lusts, but let us often and often draw near and try to make progress in the Lord's commands, that we all having the same mind may be gathered together for life. For the Lord said, "I come to gather all nations [kindreds] and tongues."[12] This means the day of His appearing, when He will come and redeem us—each one according to his works. And the unbelievers will see His glory and might, and, when they see the empire of the world in Jesus, they will be surprised, saying, "Woe to us, because Thou wast, and we knew not and believed not and obeyed not the elders[13] who show us

---

1 Comp. 1 Pet. ii. iv. *sqq.*
2 Gen. i. 27; comp. Eph. v. 22–23.
3 i. e., The Old Testament.
4 1 Pet. i. 20.
5 1 Cor. ii. 9.
6 1 Tim. iv. 16.
7 Jas. v. 19–25.
8 Is. lviii. 9.

9 2 Pet. ii. 9, iii. 5–10.
10 1 Pet. iv. 8.
11 i. e., Presbyters.
12 This passage proves this so-called Epistle to be a homily.
13 Is. lxvi. 18.

plainly of our salvation." And "their worm shall not die, neither shall their fire be quenched; and they shall be a spectacle unto all flesh."[1] It is of the great day of judgment He speaks, when they shall see those among us who were guilty of ungodliness and erred in their estimate of the commands of Jesus Christ. The righteous, having succeeded both in enduring the trials and hating the indulgences of the soul, whenever they witness how those who have swerved and denied Jesus by words or deeds are punished with grievous torments in fire unquenchable, will give glory to their God and say, "There will be hope for him who has served God with his whole heart."

CHAP. XVIII. — THE AUTHOR SINFUL, YET PURSUING.

And let us, then, be of the number of those who give thanks, who have served God, and not of the ungodly who are judged. For I myself, though a sinner every whit and not yet fleeing temptation but continuing in the midst of the tools of the devil, study to follow after righteousness, that I may make, be it only some, approach to it, fearing the judgment to come.

CHAP. XIX. — REWARD OF THE RIGHTEOUS, ALTHOUGH THEY MAY SUFFER.

So then, brothers and sisters,[2] after the God of truth[3] I address to you an appeal that ye may give heed to the words written,[4] that ye may save both yourselves and him who reads an address in your midst. For as a reward I ask of you repentance with the whole heart, while ye bestow upon yourselves salvation and life. For by so doing we shall set a mark for all the young who wish to be diligent in godliness and the goodness of God. And let not us, in our folly, feel displeasure and indignation, whenever any one admonishes us and turns us from unrighteousness to righteousness. For there are some wicked deeds which we commit, and know it not, because of the double-mindedness and unbelief present in our breasts, and our understanding is darkened by vain desires. Let us, therefore, work righteousness, that we may be saved to the end. Blessed are they who obey these commandments, even if for a brief space they suffer in this world, and they will gather the imperishable fruit of the resurrection. Let not the godly man, therefore, grieve; if for the present he suffer affliction, blessed is the time that awaits him there; rising up to life again with the fathers he will rejoice for ever without a grief.

CHAP. XX. — GODLINESS, NOT GAIN, THE TRUE RICHES.

But let it not even trouble your mind, that we see the unrighteous possessed of riches and the servants of God straitened. Let us, therefore, brothers and sisters, believe; in a trial of the living God we strive and are exercised in the present life, that we may obtain the crown in that which is to come. No one of the righteous received fruit speedily, but waiteth for it. For if God tendered the reward of the righteous in a trice, straightway were it commerce that we practised, and not godliness. For it were as if we were righteous by following after not godliness but gain; and for this reason the divine judgment baffled[5] the spirit that is unrighteous and heavily weighed the fetter.

To the only God, invisible, Father of truth, who sent forth to us the Saviour and Author of immortality, through whom He also manifested to us the truth and the heavenly life, to Him be glory for ever and ever. Amen.

[1] Is. lxvi. 24.
[2] Indicative of the approaching close.
[3] Bryennius interprets this to refer to the Scripture-lesson.
[4] Either the Scripture-lesson or the homily.

[5] Some take the aorist here used to be the iterative aorist of proverbs and, therefore, translated by the present tense.

THE APOLOGY

OF

ARISTIDES THE PHILOSOPHER

TRANSLATED FROM THE GREEK AND FROM THE SYRIAC VERSION

IN

PARALLEL COLUMNS.

BY

D. M. KAY, B.Sc., B.D.,

ASSISTANT TO THE PROFESSOR OF SEMITIC LANGUAGES IN THE UNIVERSITY OF EDINBURGH.

THE APOLOGY OF ARISTIDES

INTRODUCTION.

The Church Histories, hitherto in dealing with early Christian literature, have given Aristides along with Quadratus the first place in the list of lost apologists. It was known that there had been such early defenders of the faith, and that Quadratus had seen persons who had been miraculously healed by Christ; but beyond this little more could be said. To Justin Martyr, who flourished about A.D. 150, belonged the honour of heading the series of apologists whose works are extant, viz., Tatian, Melito, Athenagoras, Theophilus, the author of the Epistle to Diognetus, who all belonged to the second century and wrote in Greek; and Tertullian, Minucius Felix, Arnobius, and Lactantius, who wrote in Latin, and Clement and Origen who wrote in Greek, during the third century. While Christianity was winning its way to recognition in the Roman empire, these writers tried to disprove the gross calumnies current about Christians, to enlighten rulers and magistrates as to the real character and conduct of the adherents of the new religion, and to remove the prejudice which led to the violent persecutions of the populace. They also endeavoured to commend Christianity to "the cultured among its despisers," by showing that it is philosophy as well as revelation, that it can supply the answers sought by philosophy, and is unlike human wisdom in being certain because divinely revealed. At the same time they demonstrated the folly of polytheism and pointed out its disastrous effects on morality. This faithful company of the defenders of the faith has now regained Aristides as their leader in place of Justin Martyr. It will be well to recount briefly what was previously known about Aristides, and to tell how the lost Apology has been found.

Eusebius, in his History of the Church, written during the reign of Constantine, A.D. 306–337, has a chapter (bk. iv., c. 3) headed "The authors that wrote in defence of the faith in the reign of Hadrian, A.D. 117–138." After describing and quoting the Apology of Quadratus, he adds:

"Aristides also, a man faithfully devoted to the religion we profess, like Quadratus, has left to posterity a defence of the faith, addressed to Hadrian. This work is also preserved by a great number, even to the present day."

The same Eusebius in his *Chronicon* states that the Emperor Hadrian visited Athens in the eighth year of his reign (i.e., A.D. 125) and took part in the Eleusinian mysteries. In the same connection the historian mentions the presentation of Apologies to the Emperor by Quadratus and Aristides, "an Athenian philosopher;" and implies that Hadrian was induced by these appeals, coupled with a letter from Serenius Granianus, proconsul of Asia, to issue an Imperial rescript forbidding the punishment of Christians without careful investigation and trial.

About a century later Jerome (died A.D. 420) tells us that Aristides was a philosopher of Athens, that he retained his philosopher's garb after his conversion to Christianity, and that he presented a defence of the faith to Hadrian at the same time as Quadratus. This Apology, he says, was extant in his day, and was largely composed of the opinions of philosophers ("contextum philosophorum sententiis"), and was afterwards imitated by Justin Martyr.

After this date Aristides passes out of view. In the mediæval martyrologies there is a faint reflection of the earlier testimony, as, e.g., the 31st of August is given as the saint's day "of the blessed Aristides, most renowned for faith and wisdom, who presented books on the Christian religion to the prince Hadrian, and most brilliantly proclaimed in the presence of the Emperor himself how that Christ Jesus is the only God."

In the seventeenth century there were rumours that the missing Apology of Aristides was to be found in various monastic libraries in Greece; and Spon, a French traveller, made a fruitless search for it. The book had apparently disappeared for ever.

But in recent times Aristides has again "swum into our ken." Armenian literature, which has done service to Christendom by preserving so many of its early documents, supplied also the first news of the recovery of Aristides. In the Mechitarite convent of S. Lazarus at Venice there is a body of Armenian monks who study Armenian and other literature. In 1878 these Armenians surprised the learned world by publishing a Latin translation of an Armenian fragment (the first two chapters) of the lost Apology of Aristides. Renan at once set it down as spurious because it contained theological terms of a later age, e.g., "bearer of God" applied to the Virgin Mary. These terms were afterwards seen to be due to the translator. At what time the translation from Greek into Armenian was made is not apparent; but it may reasonably be connected with the work begun by the famous Armenian patriarch Mesrobes. This noble Christian invented an alphabet for his country, established schools, and sent a band of young Armenians to Edessa, Athens, and elsewhere with instructions to translate into Armenian the best sacred and classical books. And in spite of Mohammedans and Turks Armenia has remained Christian, and now restores to the world the treasures committed to its keeping in the early centuries.

Opinions as to the Armenian fragment of Aristides remained undecided till 1889. In the spring of that year Professor J. Rendel Harris, of Cambridge, had the honour of discovering a Syriac version of the whole Apology in the library of the Convent of St. Catharine, on Mount Sinai. He found the Apology of Aristides among a collection of Syriac treatises of an ethical character; and he refers the MS. to the seventh century. Professor Harris has translated the Syriac into English, and has carefully edited the Syriac text with minute discussions of every point of interest.[1]

The recovery of the Syriac version by Professor Harris placed the genuineness of the Armenian fragment beyond question. It also led to the strange reappearance of the greater part of the original Greek. Professor J. A. Robinson, the general editor of the Cambridge *Texts and Studies*, having read the translation of the Syriac version, discovered that the Apology of Aristides is incorporated in the early Christian Romance entitled, *The Life of Barlaam and Josaphat.*

Some account must be given of this remarkable book in order to show its connection with the Apology of Aristides. Its author is said to be John of Damascus, who died about A.D. 760. Whoever wrote it, the book soon became very popular. In the East it was translated into Arabic, Ethiopic, Armenian, and Hebrew; in the West there are versions of it in nearly a dozen languages, including an English metrical rendering. As early as 1204 a king of Norway had it translated into Icelandic. It is now known to be the story of Buddha in a Christian setting, furnished with fables and parables which have migrated from the far East and can be traced back to an extreme antiquity.

The outline of the story is as follows: A king in India, Abenner by name, who is an enemy of the Christians, has an only son Josaphat (or Joasaph). At his birth the astrologers predict that he will become great, but will embrace the new doctrine. To prevent this, his father surrounds the prince with young and beautiful attendants, and takes care that Josaphat shall see nothing of illness, old age, or death. At length Josaphat desires his freedom, and then follow the excursions as in the case of Buddha. Josaphat seeing so much misery possible in life is sunk in despair. In this state he is visited by a Christian hermit—Barlaam by name. Josaphat is converted to Christianity, and Barlaam withdraws again to the desert.

To undo his son's conversion the king arranges that a public disputation shall be held; one of the king's sages, Nachor by name, is to personate Barlaam and to make a very weak statement of the Christian case, and so be easily refuted by the court orators. When the day comes, the prince Josaphat charges Nachor, the fictitious monk, to do his best on pain of torture. Thus stimulated, Nachor begins, and "like Balaam's ass he spake that which

[1] *Texts and Studies.* Contributions to Biblical and Patristic Literature. Edited by J. A. Robinson, B.D. Vol. i., No. 1, the *Apology* of Aristides, edited and translated by J. Rendel Harris, M.A., with an Appendix by J. A. Robinson, B.D. (Cambridge University Press.)

he had not purposed to speak; and he said, 'I, O king, in the providence of God,' etc." He then recites the Apology of Aristides to such purpose that he converts himself, the king, and all his people. Josaphat finally relinquishes his kingdom, and retires into the desert with the genuine Barlaam for prayer and meditation. Not only so, but the churches of the Middle Ages, forgetting the fabulous character of the story, raised Barlaam and Josaphat to the rank of saints, with a holy day in the Christian calendar. Thus the author of *Barlaam and Josaphat* caused Christianity unwittingly to do honour to the founder of Buddhism under the name of St. Josaphat; and also to read the Apology of Aristides in nearly twenty languages without suspecting what it was.

The speech of Nachor in Greek, that is to say, the greater part of the original Greek of the Apology of Aristides, has been extracted from this source by Professor Robinson and is published in *Texts and Studies,* Vol. I., so that there is now abundant material for making an estimate of Aristides.

It may be asked whether we have in any of our three sources the actual words of Aristides. The circumstances under which the Apology was incorporated in *The Life of Barlaam and Josaphat* are such as to render it unlikely that the author of the Romance should copy with the faithfulness of a scribe; but examination proves that very few modifications have been made. The Greek divides men into three races (the Syriac and Armenian into four); the introductory accounts of these races are in the Greek blended with the general discussion; and at the close the description of early Christian customs is shortened. These few differences from the Syriac are all explained by the fact that the Apology had to be adapted to the circumstances of an Indian court in a later age. On the other hand, when the Syriac is compared with the Greek and Armenian in passages where these two agree, it is found that explanatory clauses are added; and there is throughout a cumbrous redundancy of pronouns in the Syriac. In short, the actual words of Aristides may be restored with tolerable certainty—a task which has been already accomplished by a German scholar, Lic. Edgar Hennecke.[1] In any case we have the substance of the Apology of Aristides with almost verbal precision.

In regard to the date of Aristides, Eusebius says expressly that the Apology was presented to Hadrian while he was in Athens about the year A.D. 125. The only ground for questioning this statement is the second superscription given in the Syriac version, which implies that the Apology was presented to Antoninus Pius, A.D. 138–161. This heading is accepted by Professor Harris as the true one; and he assigns the Apology to "the early years of the reign of Antoninus Pius; and it is at least conceivable," he adds, "that it may have been presented to the Emperor along with other Christian writings during an unrecorded visit of his to his ancient seat of government at Smyrna." But this requires us to suppose that Eusebius was wrong; that Jerome copied his error; that the Armenian version curiously fell into the same mistake; and that the Syriac translator is at this point exceptionally faithful. So perhaps it is better with Billius, "not to trust more in one's own suspicions, than in Christian charity which believeth all things," and to rest in the comfortable hypothesis that Eusebius spoke the truth.

Writing in A.D. 125, or even twenty years later, Aristides becomes an important witness as to the nature of early Christianity. His Apology contains no express quotation from Scripture; but the Emperor is referred for information to a gospel which is written. Various echoes of New Testament expressions will at once be recognized; and "the language-moulding power of Christianity" is discernible in the new meaning given to various classical words. Some topics are conspicuous by their absence. Aristides has no trace of ill-feeling to the Jews; no reference to the Logos doctrine, nor to the distinctive ideas of the Apostle Paul; he has no gnosticism or heresy to denounce, and he makes no appeal to miracle and prophecy. Christianity, in his view, is worthy of a philosophic emperor because it is eminently reasonable, and gives an impulse and power to live a good life. On the whole, Aristides represents that type of Christian practice which is found in the *Teaching of the Twelve Apostles;* and to this he adds a simple Christian philosophy which may be compared with that of St. Paul at Athens. Although the details about the elements and the heathen gods are discussed with tedious minuteness, still his closing section describing the lives of the early Christians should always be good reading.

The translation of the Syriac given here is independently made from the Syriac text, edited by Professor Harris.[2] Full advantage has been taken of his notes and *apparatus criti-*

[1] *Die Apologie des Aristides.* Recension und Rekonstruktion des Textes, von Lic. Edgar Hennecke. (*Die Griechischen Apologeten*: Heft 3.)

[2] The Cambridge *Texts and Studies,* vol i., No. 1.

cus, but no use has been made of his translation. In obscure passages the German translation of Dr. Richard Raabe[1] has been compared; and the *Text-Rekonstruktion* of Hennecke has been consulted on textual points in both translations. The Greek translation is made from the text edited by Professor Robinson.[2] The translations from the Greek and from the Syriac are arranged side by side, so that their relation to one another is apparent at a glance. No attempt has been made to force the same English words from passages which are evidently meant to be identical in the two languages; but the literal tenour of each has been allowed to assert itself.

[1] *Texte und Untersuchungen zur Geschichte der Altchristlichen Litteratur,* Gebhardt und Harnack, IX. Band, Heft 1.
[2] The Cambridge *Texts and Studies,* vol. i., No. 1.

THE APOLOGY OF ARISTIDES

AS IT IS PRESERVED IN THE HISTORY OF

BARLAAM AND JOSAPHAT.

Translated from the Greek.

I. I, O King in the providence of God came into the world; and when I had considered the heaven and the earth, the sun and the moon and the rest, I marvelled at their orderly arrangement.

And when I saw that the universe and all that is therein is moved by necessity, I perceived that the mover and controller is God.

For everything which causes motion is stronger than that which is moved, and that which controls is stronger than that which is controlled.

The self-same being, then, who first established and now controls the universe—him do I affirm to be God

who is without beginning and without end,

THE APOLOGY OF ARISTIDES THE PHILOSOPHER.

Translated from the Syriac.

ARISTIDES.

Here follows the defence which Aristides the philosopher made before Hadrian the King on behalf of reverence for God.

. . . All-powerful Cæsar Titus Hadrianus Antoninus, venerable and merciful, from Marcianus Aristides, an Athenian philosopher.[1]

I. I, O King, by the grace of God came into this world; and when I had considered the heaven and the earth and the seas, and had surveyed the sun and the rest of creation, I marvelled at the beauty of the world. And I perceived that the world and all that is therein are moved by the power of another; and I understood that he who moves them is God, who is hidden in them, and veiled by them. And it is manifest that that which causes motion is more powerful than that which is moved. But that I should make search concerning this same mover of all, as to what is his nature (for it seems to me, he is indeed unsearchable in his nature), and that I should argue as to the constancy of his government, so as to grasp it fully,—this is a vain effort for me; for it is not possible that a man should fully comprehend it. I say, however, concerning this mover of the world, that he is God of all, who made all things for the sake of mankind. And it seems to me that this is reasonable, that one should fear God and should not oppress man.

I say, then, that God is not born, not made, an ever-abiding nature without beginning and without

---

1 The superscription seems to be duplicate in the Syriac. It is absent from the Greek as we have it; the Armenian has "To the Emperor Cæsar Hadrian from Aristides." Various explanations are offered. (*a*) Both emperors, as colleagues, may be meant. In support of this the Syriac adjectives for "venerable and merciful" are marked plural; the phrase "Your majesty" occurring later has a plural suffix; and two Imperatives, "Take and read," are plural. On the other hand "O King" occurs constantly in the singular; and the emperors were colleagues only for a few months in the year A.D. 138.

(*b*) The longer heading is the true one—the shorter being due perhaps to a scribe who had a collection of works to copy. In that case the word "Hadrian" has been selected from the full title of Antonine, and the two adjectives "venerable and merciful" are proper names, Augustus Pius. (Harris.)

(*c*) The shorter heading has the support of Eusebius and the Armenian version; and the translator into Syriac may have amplified.

(ܟܠ ܐܚܝܕ) Almighty is separated from the word for "God" by a pause, and is not an attribute which a Christian would care to apply to a Roman emperor. παντοκράτωρ may have been confounded with αὐτοκράτωρ. Raabe supplies [Syriac] giving the sense "qui imperium (postatem) habet," as an epithet of Cæsar. If . . . ܡܚܕܬ ܠ = "Renewed, or dedicated again to. . . Antoninus Pius," could be read, both headings might be retained.

GREEK.

immortal and self-sufficing, above all passions and infirmities, above

anger and forgetfulness

and ignorance and the rest.

Through Him too all things consist. He requires not sacrifice and libation nor any one of the things that appear to sense; but all men stand in need of Him.

II. Having thus spoken concerning God, so far as it was possible for me to speak of Him,[1] let us next proceed to the human race, that we may see which of them participate in the truth and which of them in error.

For it is clear to us, O King,[2] that there are three[3] classes of men in this world; these being the worshippers of the gods acknowledged among you, and Jews, and Christians. Further they who pay homage to many gods are themselves divided into three classes, Chaldæans namely, and Greeks, and Egyptians; for these have been guides and preceptors to the rest of the nations in the service and worship of these many-titled deities.

SYRIAC.

end, immortal, perfect, and incomprehensible. Now when I say that he is "perfect," this means that there is not in him any defect, and he is not in need of anything but all things are in need of him. And when I say that he is "without beginning," this means that everything which has beginning has also an end, and that which has an end may be brought to an end. He has no name, for everything which has a name is kindred to things created. Form he has none, nor yet any union of members; for whatsoever possesses these is kindred to things fashioned. He is neither male nor female.[4] The heavens do not limit him, but the heavens and all things, visible and invisible, receive their bounds from him. Adversary he has none, for there exists not any stronger than he. Wrath and indignation he possesses not, for there is nothing which is able to stand against him. Ignorance and forgetfulness are not in his nature, for he is altogether wisdom and understanding; and in Him stands fast all that exists. He requires not sacrifice and libation, nor even one of things visible; He requires not aught from any, but all living creatures stand in need of him.

II. Since, then, we have addressed you concerning God, so far as our discourse can bear upon him, let us now come to the race of men, that we may know which of them participate in the truth of which we have spoken, and which of them go astray from it.

This is clear to you, O King, that there are four classes of men in this world:—Barbarians and Greeks, Jews and Christians. The Barbarians, indeed, trace the origin of their kind of religion from Kronos and from Rhea and their other gods; the Greeks, however, from Helenos, who is said to be sprung from Zeus. And by Helenos there were born Aiolos and Xuthos; and there were others descended from Inachos and Phoroneus, and lastly from the Egyptian Danaos and from Kadmos and from Dionysos.

The Jews, again, trace the origin of their race from Abraham, who begat Isaac, of whom was born Jacob. And he begat twelve sons who migrated from Syria to Egypt; and there they were called the nation of the Hebrews, by him who made their laws; and at length they were named Jews.

---

[1] The Greek might be rendered, "so far as there was room for me to speak of Him," i.e., the attributes of the Deity are not further relevant to the discussion—as the translator into Syriac takes it. The Armenian adopts the other meaning, viz., the theme is beyond man's power to discuss. As translated by F. C. Conybeare, the Armenian is in these words: "Now by the grace of God it was given me to speak wisely concerning Him. So far as I have received the faculty I will speak, yet not according to the measure of the inscrutability of His greatness shall I be able to do so, but by faith alone do I glorify and adore Him."

[2] The "King" in the Greek is Abenner, the father of Josaphat; in the Syriac, as in the Greek originally, he is the Roman Emperor, Hadrian.

[3] The Armenian and Syriac agree in giving four races, which was probably the original division. To a Greek, men were either Greeks or Barbarians: to a Greek Christian it would seem necessary to add two new peoples, Jews and Christians. The Greek calls the Barbarians "Chaldæans." This change of classification is probably the cause of the omission in the Greek of the preliminary accounts of the four classes. The Greek blends the summaries with the fuller accounts.

[4] The Armenian adds, "For that which is subject to this distinction is moved by passions."

GREEK.

III. Let us see then which of them participate in truth and which of them in error.

The Chaldæans, then, not knowing God went astray after the elements and began to worship the creation more than their Creator. And of these they formed certain shapes and styled them a representation of the heaven and the earth and the sea, of the sun too and the moon and the other primal bodies or luminaries. And they shut them up together in shrines, and worship them, calling them gods, even though they have to guard them securely for fear they should be stolen by robbers. And they did not perceive that anything which acts as guard is greater than that which is guarded, and that he who makes is greater than that which is made. For if their gods are unfit to look after their own safety, how shall they bestow protection upon others? Great

SYRIAC.

The Christians, then, trace the beginning of their religion from Jesus the Messiah; and he is named the Son of God Most High. And it is said that God came down from heaven, and from a Hebrew virgin assumed and clothed himself with flesh; and the Son of God lived in a daughter of man. This is taught in the gospel, as it is called, which a short time ago was preached among them; and you also if you will read therein, may perceive the power which belongs to it. This Jesus, then, was born of the race of the Hebrews; and he had twelve disciples in order that the purpose of his incarnation [1] might in time be accomplished. But he himself was pierced by the Jews, and he died and was buried; and they say that after three days he rose and ascended to heaven. Thereupon these twelve disciples went forth throughout the known parts of the world, and kept showing his greatness with all modesty and uprightness. And hence also those of the present day who believe that preaching are called Christians, and they are become famous.

So then there are, as I said above, four classes of men:—Barbarians and Greeks, Jews and Christians.

Moreover the wind is obedient to God, and fire to the angels; the waters also to the demons and the earth to the sons of men.[2]

III. Let us begin, then, with the Barbarians, and go on to the rest of the nations one after another, that we may see which of them hold the truth as to God and which of them hold error.

The Barbarians, then, as they did not apprehend God, went astray among the elements, and began to worship things created instead of their Creator; [3] and for this end they made images and shut them up in shrines, and lo! they worship them, guarding them the while with much care, lest their gods be stolen by robbers. And the Barbarians did not observe that that which acts as guard is greater than that which is guarded, and that every one who creates is greater than that which is created. If it be, then, that their gods are too feeble to see to their own safety, how will they take thought for the safety of men? Great then is the error into which the Barbarians wandered in worshipping lifeless images which can do nothing to help them. And I am led to wonder, O King, at their philosophers, how that even they went astray, and gave the name of gods to images which were made in honour of the elements; and that their sages did not perceive that the elements also are dissoluble and perishable. For if a small part of an element is dissolved or destroyed, the whole of it may be dissolved and destroyed. If then the elements themselves are dis-

[1] Literally: "a certain dispensation of his." The Greek term οἰκονομία, "dispensation," suggests to the translator into Syriac the idea of the Incarnation, familiar, as it seems, by his time. Professor Sachau reads the equivalent of θαυμαστή instead of מדעם (τις). In the translation given מדעם is taken adverbially=aliquamdiu.

[2] This irrelevant sentence is found in the Armenian version also, and therefore was probably in the original Greek. It seems to be an *obiter dictum.* Men fall into four groups, and, by the way, so do the elements, air, fire, earth, and water; and the powers that govern them. One quaternion suggests others.

[3] Cf. Rom. i. 25 and Col. ii. 8.

GREEK.

then is the error into which the Chaldæans wandered in adoring lifeless and good-for-nothing images.

And it occurs to me as surprising, O King, how it is that their so-called philosophers have quite failed to observe that the elements themselves are perishable. And if the elements are perishable and subject to necessity, how are they gods? And if the elements are not gods, how do the images made in their honour come to be gods?

IV. Let us proceed then, O King, to the elements themselves that we may show in regard to them that they are not gods, but perishable and mutable, produced out of that which did not exist at the command of the true God, who is indestructible and immutable and invisible; yet He sees all things and as He wills, modifies and changes things. What then shall I say concerning the elements?

They err who believe that the sky is a god. For we see that it revolves and moves by necessity and is compacted of many parts, being thence called the ordered universe (Kosmos). Now the universe is the construction of some designer; and that which has been constructed has a beginning and an end. And the sky with its luminaries moves by necessity. For the stars are carried along in array at fixed intervals from sign to sign, and, some setting, others rising, they traverse their courses in due season so as to mark off summers and winters, as it has been appointed for them by God; and obeying the inevitable necessity of their nature they transgress not their proper limits, keeping company with the heavenly order. Whence it is plain that the sky is not a god but rather a work of God.

They erred also who believed the earth to be a goddess. For we see that it is despitefully used and tyrannized over by men, and is furrowed and kneaded and becomes of no account. For if it be burned with fire, it becomes devoid of life; for nothing will grow from the ashes. Besides if there fall upon it an excess of rain it dissolves away,

SYRIAC.

solved and destroyed and forced to be subject to another that is more stubborn than they, and if they are not in their nature gods, why, forsooth, do they call the images which are made in their honour, God? Great, then, is the error which the philosophers among them have brought upon their followers.

IV. Let us turn now, O King, to the elements in themselves, that we may make clear in regard to them, that they are not gods, but a created thing, liable to ruin and change, which is of the same nature as man; whereas God is imperishable and unvarying, and invisible, while yet He sees, and overrules, and transforms all things.

Those then who believe concerning the earth that it is a god have hitherto deceived themselves, since it is furrowed and set with plants and trenched; and it takes in the filthy refuse of men and beasts and cattle. And at times it becomes unfruitful, for if it be burnt to ashes it becomes devoid of life, for nothing germinates from an earthen jar. And besides if water be collected upon it, it is dissolved together with its products. And lo! it is trodden under foot of men and beast, and receives the blood-

GREEK.

both it and its fruits. Moreover it is trodden under foot of men and the other creatures; it is dyed with the blood of the murdered; it is dug open and filled with dead bodies and becomes a tomb for corpses. In face of all this, it is inadmissible that the earth is a goddess but rather it is a work of God for the use of men.

V. They also erred who believed the water to be a god. For it, too, has been made for the use of men, and is controlled by them; it is defiled and destroyed and suffers change on being boiled and dyed with colours; and it is congealed by the frost, and polluted with blood, and is introduced for the washing of all unclean things. Wherefore it is impossible that water should be a god, but it is a work of God.

They also err who believe that fire is a god. For fire was made for the use of men, and it is controlled by them, being carried about from place to place for boiling and roasting all kinds of meat, and even for (the burning of) dead bodies. Moreover it is extinguished in many ways, being quenched through man's agency. So it cannot be allowed that fire is a god, but it is a work of God.

They also err who think the blowing of the winds is a goddess. For it is clear that it is under the dominion of another; and for the sake of man it has been designed by God for the transport of ships and the conveyance of grain and for man's other wants. It rises too and falls at the bidding of God, whence it is concluded that the blowing of the winds is not a goddess but only a work of God.

VI. They also err who believe the

SYRIAC.

stains of the slain; and it is dug open, and filled with the dead, and becomes a tomb for corpses. But it is impossible that a nature, which is holy and worthy and blessed and immortal, should allow of any one of these things. And hence it appears to us that the earth is not a god but a creation of God.

V. In the same way, again, those erred who believed the waters to be gods. For the waters were created for the use of man, and are put under his rule in many ways. For they suffer change and admit impurity, and are destroyed and lose their nature while they are boiled into many substances. And they take colours which do not belong to them; they are also congealed by frost and are mingled and permeated with the filth of men and beasts, and with the blood of the slain. And being checked by skilled workmen through the restraint of aqueducts, they flow and are diverted against their inclination, and come into gardens and other places in order that they may be collected and issue forth as a means of fertility for man, and that they may cleanse away every impurity and fulfil the service man requires from them. Wherefore it is impossible that the waters should be a god, but they are a work of God and a part of the world.

In like manner also they who believed that fire is a god erred to no slight extent. For it, too, was created for the service of men, and is subject to them in many ways:—in the preparation of meats, and as a means of casting metals, and for other ends whereof your Majesty is aware. At the same time it is quenched and extinguished in many ways.

Again they also erred who believed the motion of the winds to be a god. For it is well known to us that those winds are under the dominion of another, at times their motion increases, and at times it fails and ceases at the command of him who controls them. For they were created by God for the sake of men, in order to supply the necessity of trees and fruits and seeds; and to bring over the sea ships which convey for men necessaries and goods from places where they are found to places where they are not found; and to govern the quarters of the world. And as for itself, at times it increases and again abates; and in one place brings help and in another causes disaster at the bidding of him who rules it. And mankind too are able by known means to confine and keep it in check in order that it may fulfil for them the service they require from it. And of itself it has not any authority at all. And hence it is impossible that the winds should be called gods, but rather a thing made by God.

VI. So also they erred who believed that the sun

GREEK.

sun to be a god. For we see that it moves by necessity and revolves and passes from sign to sign, setting and rising so as to give warmth to plants and tender shoots for the use of man.

Besides it has its part in common with the rest of the stars, and is much smaller than the sky; it suffers eclipse of its light and is not the subject of its own laws. Wherefore it is concluded that the sun is not a god, but only a work of God. They also err who believe that the moon is a goddess. For we see that it moves by necessity and revolves and passes from sign to sign, setting and rising for the benefit of men; and it is less than the sun and waxes and wanes and has eclipses. Wherefore it is concluded that the moon is not a goddess but a work of God.

VII. They also err who believe that man[1] is a god. For we see that he is moved by necessity, and is made to grow up, and becomes old even though he would not. And at one time he is joyous, at another he is grieved when he lacks food and drink and clothing. And we see that he is subject to anger and jealousy and desire and change of purpose and has many infirmities. He is destroyed too in many ways by means of the elements and animals, and by ever-assailing death. It cannot be admitted, then, that man is a god, but only a work of God.

Great therefore is the error into which the Chaldæans wandered, following after their own desires.

For they reverence the perishable elements and lifeless images, and do not perceive that they themselves make these things to be gods.

VIII. Let us proceed then to the Greeks, that we may see whether they have any discernment concerning God. The Greeks, indeed, though they call themselves wise proved more deluded than the Chaldæans in alleging that many gods have come into being, some of them

SYRIAC.

is a god. For we see that it is moved by the compulsion of another, and revolves and makes its journey, and proceeds from sign to sign, rising and setting every day, so as to give warmth for the growth of plants and trees, and to bring forth into the air wherewith it (sunlight) is mingled every growing thing which is upon the earth. And to it there belongs by comparison a part in common with the rest of the stars in its course; and though it is one in its nature it is associated with many parts for the supply of the needs of men; and that not according to its own will but rather according to the will of him who rules it. And hence it is impossible that the sun should be a god, but the work of God; and in like manner also the moon and the stars.

VII. And those who believed of the men of the past, that some of them were gods, they too were much mistaken. For as you yourself allow, O King, man is constituted of the four elements and of a soul and a spirit (and hence he is called a microcosm),[2] and without any one of these parts he could not consist. He has a beginning and an end, and he is born and dies. But God, as I said, has none of these things in his nature, but is uncreated and imperishable. And hence it is not possible that we should set up man to be of the nature of God:—man, to whom at times when he looks for joy, there comes trouble, and when he looks for laughter there comes to him weeping,—who is wrathful and covetous and envious, with other defects as well. And he is destroyed in many ways by the elements and also by the animals.

And hence, O King, we are bound to recognize the error of the Barbarians, that thereby, since they did not find traces of the true God, they fell aside from the truth, and went after the desire of their imagination, serving the perishable elements and lifeless images, and through their error not apprehending what the true God is.

VIII. Let us turn further to the Greeks also, that we may know what opinion they hold as to the true God. The Greeks, then, because they are more subtle than the Barbarians, have gone further astray than the Barbarians; inasmuch as they have introduced many fictitious gods, and have set up some of them as males and some as females; and in that some of their gods were found who were adulterers, and did murder, and were deluded, and envious, and wrathful and passionate, and parricides, and thieves, and

[1] "I do not think it out of place here to mention Antinous of our day [a slave of the Emperor Hadrian], whom all, notwithstanding they knew who and whence he was, yet affected to worship as a god."—Justin Martyr quoted in Eusebius Hist. Bk. IV., c. 8.

[2] Or "and hence the world also gets its name κόσμος." The Syriac is the equivalent of the Greek "διὸ καὶ κόσμος καλεῖται,', which occurs (Chap. IV.) in discussing the supposed divinity of the sky or heaven.

GREEK.

male, some female, practised masters in every passion and every variety of folly. [And the Greeks themselves represented them to be adulterers and murderers, wrathful and envious and passionate, slayers of fathers and brothers, thieves and robbers, crippled and limping, workers in magic, and victims of frenzy. Some of them died (as their account goes), and some were struck by thunderbolts, and became slaves to men, and were fugitives, and they mourned and lamented, and changed themselves into animals for wicked and shameful ends.] [1]

Wherefore, O King, they are ridiculous and absurd and impious tales that the Greeks have introduced, giving the name of gods to those who are not gods, to suit their unholy desires, in order that, having them as patrons of vice, they might commit adultery and robbery and do murder and other shocking deeds. For if their gods did such deeds why should not they also do them?

So that from these misguided practices it has been the lot of mankind to have frequent wars and slaughters and bitter captivities.

IX. But, further, if we be minded to discuss their gods individually, you will see how great is the absurdity; for instance, how Kronos is brought forward by them as a god above all, and they sacrifice their own children to him. And he had many sons by Rhea, and in his madness devoured his own offspring. And they say that Zeus cut off his members and cast them into the sea, whence Aphrodite is said in fable to be engendered. Zeus, then, having bound his own father, cast him

SYRIAC.

robbers. And some of them, they say, were crippled and limped, and some were sorcerers, and some actually went mad, and some played on lyres, and some were given to roaming on the hills, and some even died, and some were struck dead by lightning, and some were made servants even to men, and some escaped by flight, and some were kidnapped by men, and some, indeed, were lamented and deplored by men. And some, they say, went down to Sheol, and some were grievously wounded, and some transformed themselves into the likeness of animals to seduce the race of mortal women, and some polluted themselves [2] by lying with males. And some, they say, were wedded to their mothers and their sisters and their daughters. And they say of their gods that they committed adultery with the daughters of men; and of these there was born a certain race which also was mortal. And they say that some of the females disputed about beauty, and appeared before men for judgment. Thus, O King, have the Greeks put forward foulness, and absurdity, and folly about their gods and about themselves, in that they have called those that are of such a nature gods, who are no gods. And hence mankind have received incitements to commit adultery and fornication, and to steal and to practise all that is offensive and hated and abhorred. For if they who are called their gods practised all these things which are written above, how much more should men practise them—men, who believe that their gods themselves practised them. And owing to the foulness of this error there have happened to mankind harassing wars, and great famines, and bitter captivity, and complete desolation. And lo! it was by reason of this alone that they suffered and that all these things came upon them; and while they endured those things they did not perceive in their mind that for their error those things came upon them.

IX. Let us proceed further to their account of their gods that we may carefully demonstrate all that is said above. First of all, the Greeks bring forward as a god Kronos, that is to say Chiun [3] (Saturn). And his worshippers sacrifice their children to him, and they burn some of them alive in his honour. And they say that he took to him among his wives Rhea, and begat many children by her. By her too he begat Dios, who is called Zeus. And at length he (Kronos) went mad, and through fear of an oracle that had been made known to him, he began to devour his sons. And from him Zeus was stolen away without his knowledge; and at length Zeus bound him, and mutilated the signs of his manhood, and flung them into the sea. And hence, as they say in fable, there was engendered Aphrodite, who is called Astarte. And he (Zeus) cast out Kronos fettered

[1] The passage in brackets occurs earlier in "Barlaam and Josaphat," and is restored to its place by J. A. Robinson.

[2] Professor Nöldeke's emendation, [illegible] in place of [illegible] = "they were reviled," is adopted in the translation given.

[3] Cf. Amos v. 26, "Chiun, your star god," and Acts vii. 43.

GREEK.

into Tartaros. You see the error and brutality which they advance against their god? Is it possible, then, that a god should be manacled and mutilated? What absurdity! Who with any wit would ever say so?

Next Zeus is introduced, and they say that he was king of their gods, and that he changed himself into animals that he might debauch mortal women.

For they allege that he transformed himself into a bull for Europe, and into gold for Danae, and into a swan for Leda, and into a satyr for Antiope, and into a thunderbolt for Semele. Then by these there were many children, Dionysos and Zethus and Amphion and Herakles and Apollo and Artemis and Perseus, Kastor and Helenes and Polydeukes and Minos and Rhadamanthys and Sarpedon, and the nine daughters whom they called the Muses. Then too they bring forward statements about the matter of Ganymedes.

Hence it happened, O King, to mankind to imitate all these things and to become adulterous men and lascivious women, and to be workers of other terrible iniquities, through the imitation of their god. Now how is it possible that a god should be an adulterer or an obscene person or a parricide?

X. Along with him, too, they bring forward one Hephaistos as a god, and they say that he is lame and wields a hammer and tongs, working as a smith for his living.

Is he then badly off? But it cannot be admitted that a god should be a cripple, and besides be dependent on mankind.

Then they bring forward Hermes as a god, representing him to be lust-

SYRIAC.

into darkness. Great then is the error and ignominy which the Greeks have brought forward about the first of their gods, in that they have said all this about him, O King. It is impossible that a god should be bound or mutilated; and if it be otherwise, he is indeed miserable.

And after Kronos they bring forward another god Zeus. And they say of him that he assumed the sovereignty, and was king over all the gods. And they say that he changed himself into a beast and other shapes in order to seduce mortal women, and to raise up by them children for himself. Once, they say, he changed himself into a bull through love of Europe and Pasiphae.[1] And again he changed himself into the likeness of gold through love of Danae, and to a swan through love of Leda, and to a man through love of Antiope, and to lightning through love of Luna,[2] and so by these he begat many children. For by Antiope, they say, that he begat Zethus and Amphion, and by Luna Dionysos, by Alcmena Hercules, and by Leto, Apollo and Artemis, and by Danae Perseus, and by Leda, Castor and Polydeuces, and Helene and Paludus,[3] and by Mnemosyne he begat nine daughters whom they styled the Muses, and by Europe, Minos and Rhadamanthos and Sarpedon. And lastly he changed himself into the likeness of an eagle through his passion for Ganydemos (Ganymede) the shepherd.

By reason of these tales, O King, much evil has arisen among men, who to this day are imitators of their gods, and practise adultery and defile themselves with their mothers and their sisters, and by lying with males, and some make bold to slay even their parents. For if he who is said to be the chief and king of their gods do these things how much more should his worshippers imitate him? And great is the folly which the Greeks have brought forward in their narrative concerning him. For it is impossible that a god should practise adultery or fornication or come near to lie with males, or kill his parents; and if it be otherwise, he is much worse than a destructive demon.

X. Again they bring forward as another god Hephaistos. And they say of him, that he is lame, and a cap is set on his head, and he holds in his hands firetongs and a hammer; and he follows the craft of iron working, that thereby he may procure the necessaries of his livelihood. Is then this god so very needy? But it cannot be that a god should be needy or lame, else he is very worthless.

And further they bring in another god and call him Hermes. And they say that he is a thief,[4] a lover of avarice, and greedy for gain, and a magician

[1] Pasiphae's unnatural passion for Taurus is not in the Greek mythology charged to Zeus.

[2] The visit of Zeus to Semele (not Selene) is evidently referred to. Σελήνη Luna would give the Syriac ܣܠܝܢܐ

[3] Professor Rendel Harris pronounces "Paludus" a *vox nihili*, and explains its presence as due to a corrupt repetition of the preceding Polydeuces. The Syriac word in the text suggests Pollux—the Latin equivalent of Polydeuces. Clytemnestra is the name required.

[4] Adopting Professor Harris's emendation ܓܢܒܐ = κλέπτης instead of ܓܒܪܐ = vir.

GREEK.

ful, and a thief, and covetous, and a magician (and maimed) and an interpreter of language. But it cannot be admitted that such an one is a god.

They also bring forward Asklepios as a god who is a doctor and prepares drugs and compounds plasters for the sake of a living. For he was badly off. And afterwards he was struck, they say, with a thunderbolt by Zeus on account of Tyndareos, son of Lacedaimon; and so was killed. Now if Asklepios in spite of his divinity could not help himself when struck by lightning, how will he come to the rescue of others?

Again Ares is represented as a god, fond of strife and given to jealousy, and a lover of animals and other such things. And at last while corrupting Aphrodite, he was bound by the youthful Eros and by Hephaistos. How then was he a god who was subject to desire, and a warrior, and a prisoner and an adulterer?

They allege that Dionysos also is a god who holds nightly revels and teaches drunkenness, and carries off the neighbours' wives, and goes mad and takes to flight. And at last he was put to death by the Titans. If then Dionysos could not save himself when he was being killed, and besides used to be mad, and drunk with wine, and a fugitive, how should he be a god?

They allege also that Herakles got drunk and went mad and cut the throats of his own children, then he was consumed by fire and so died. Now how should he be a god, who was drunk and a slayer of children and burned to death? or how will he come to the help of others, when he was unable to help himself?

XI. They represent Apollo also as a jealous god, and besides as the master of the bow and quiver, and sometimes of the lyre and flute, and as divining to men for pay? Can he then be very badly off? But it cannot be admitted that a god should be in want, and jealous, and a harping minstrel.

SYRIAC.

and mutilated and an athlete, and an interpreter of language. But it is impossible that a god should be a magician or avaricious, or maimed, or craving for what is not his, or an athlete. And if it be otherwise, he is found to be useless.

And after him they bring forward as another god Asklepios. And they say that he is a physician and prepares drugs and plaster that he may supply the necessaries of his livelihood. Is then this god in want? And at length he was struck with lightning by Dios on account of Tyndareos of Lacedæmon, and so he died. If then Asklepios were a god, and, when he was struck with lightning, was unable to help himself, how should he be able to give help to others? But that a divine nature should be in want or be destroyed by lightning is impossible.

And again they bring forward another as a god, and they call him Ares. And they say that he is a warrior, and jealous, and covets sheep and things which are not his. And he makes gain by his arms. And they say that at length he committed adultery with Aphrodite, and was caught by the little boy Eros and by Hephaistos the husband of Aphrodite. But it is impossible that a god should be a warrior or bound or an adulterer.

And again they say of Dionysos that he forsooth! is a god, who arranges carousals by night, and teaches drunkenness, and carries off women who do not belong to him. And at length, they say, he went mad and dismissed his handmaidens and fled into the desert; and during his madness he ate serpents. And at last he was killed by Titanos. If then Dionysos were a god, and when he was being killed was unable to help himself, how is it possible that he should help others?

Herakles next they bring forward and say that he is a god, who hates detestable things, a tyrant,[1] and warrior and a destroyer of plagues. And of him also they say that at length he became mad and killed his own children, and cast himself into a fire and died. If then Herakles is a god, and in all these calamities was unable to rescue himself, how should others ask help from him? But it is impossible that a god should be mad, or drunken or a slayer of his children, or consumed by fire.

XI. And after him they bring forward another god and call him Apollon. And they say that he is jealous and inconstant, and at times he holds the bow and quiver, and again the lyre and plectron. And he utters oracles for men that he may receive rewards from them. Is then this god in need of rewards? But it is an insult that all these things should be found with a god.

[1] "Tyrant," ܛܪܘܢܐ, seems out of place when connected with Herakles. Perhaps ܪܘܝܐ =ebrius, which occurs at the close of the paragraph, should be read here. Cf. also the Greek.

GREEK.

They represent Artemis also as his sister, who is a huntress and has a bow with a quiver; and she roams alone upon the hills with the dogs to hunt the stag or the wild boar. How then should such a woman, who hunts and roams with her dogs, be a divine being?

Even Aphrodite herself they affirm to be a goddess who is adulterous. For at one time she had Ares as a paramour, and at another time Anchises and again Adonis, whose death she also laments, feeling the want of her lover. And they say that she even went down to Hades to purchase back Adonis from Persephone. Did you ever see, O King, greater folly than this, to bring forward as a goddess one who is adulterous and given to weeping and wailing?

And they represent that Adonis is a hunter god, who came to a violent end, being wounded by a wild boar and having no power to help himself in his distress. How then will one who is adulterous and a hunter and mortal give himself any concern for mankind?

All this and much more of a like nature, and even far more disgraceful and offensive details, have the Greeks narrated, O King, concerning their gods;—details which it is not proper either to state or for a moment to remember. And hence mankind, taking an impulse from their gods, practised all lawlessness and brutality and impiety, polluting both earth and air by their awful deeds.

XII. The Egyptians, again, being

SYRIAC.

And after him they bring forward as a goddess Artemis, the sister of Apollo; and they say that she was a huntress and that she herself used to carry a bow and bolts, and to roam about upon the mountains, leading the hounds to hunt stags or wild boars of the field. But it is disgraceful that a virgin maid should roam alone upon the hills or hunt in the chase for animals. Wherefore it is impossible that Artemis should be a goddess.

Again they say of Aphrodite that she indeed is a goddess. And at times she dwells with their gods, but at other times she is a neighbour to men. And once she had Ares as a lover, and again Adonis who is Tammuz. Once also, Aphrodite was wailing and weeping for the death of Tammuz, and they say that she went down to Sheol that she might redeem Adonis from Persephone, who is the daughter of Sheol (Hades). If then Aphrodite is a goddess and was unable to help her lover at his death, how will she find it possible to help others? And this cannot be listened to, that a divine nature should come to weeping and wailing and adultery.

And again they say of Tammuz that he is a god. And he is, forsooth! a hunter and an adulterer. And they say that he was killed by a wound from a wild boar, without being able to help himself. And if he could not help himself, how can he take thought for the human race? But that a god should be an adulterer or a hunter or should die by violence is impossible.

Again they say of Rhea that she is the mother of their gods. And they say that she had once a lover Atys, and that she used to delight in depraved men. And at last she raised a lamentation and mourned for Atys her lover. If then the mother of their gods was unable to help her lover and deliver him from death, how can she help others? So it is disgraceful that a goddess should lament and weep and take delight in depraved men.

Again they introduce Kore and say that she is a goddess, and she was stolen away by Pluto, and could not help herself. If then she is a goddess and was unable to help herself how will she find means to help others? For a god who is stolen away is very powerless.

All this, then, O King, have the Greeks brought forward concerning their gods, and they have invented and declared it concerning them. And hence all men received an impulse to work all profanity and all defilements; and hereby the whole earth was corrupted.

XII. The Egyptians, moreover, because they are

GREEK.

more stupid and witless than these have gone further astray than all the nations. For they were not content with the objects of worship of the Chaldæans and the Greeks, but in addition to these brought forward also brute creatures as gods, both land and water animals, and plants and herbs; and they were defiled with all madness and brutality more deeply than all the nations on the earth.

For originally they worshipped Isis, who had Osiris as brother and husband. He was slain by his own brother Typhon; and therefore Isis with Horos her son fled for refuge to Byblus in Syria, mourning for Osiris with bitter lamentation, until Horos grew up and slew Typhon. So that neither had Isis power to help her own brother and husband; nor could Osiris defend himself when he was being slain by Typhon; nor did Typhon, the slayer of his brother, when he was perishing at the hands of Horos and Isis, find means to rescue himself from death. And though they were revealed in their true character by such mishaps, they were believed to be very gods by the simple Egyptians, who were not satisfied even with these or the other deities of the nations, but brought forward also brute creatures as gods. For some of them worshipped the sheep, and some the goat; another tribe (worshipped) the bull and the pig; others again, the raven and the hawk, and the vulture and the eagle; and others the crocodile; and some the cat and the dog, and the wolf and the ape, and the dragon and the asp; and others the onion and the garlic and thorns and other created things. And the poor creatures do not perceive about all these that they are utterly helpless. For though they see their gods eaten by men of other tribes, and burnt as offerings and

SYRIAC.

more base and stupid than every people that is on the earth, have themselves erred more than all. For the deities (or religion) of the Barbarians and the Greeks did not suffice for them, but they introduced some also of the nature of the animals, and said thereof that they were gods, and likewise of creeping things which are found on the dry land and in the waters. And of plants and herbs they said that some of them were gods. And they were corrupted by every kind of delusion and defilement more than every people that is on the earth. For from ancient times they worshipped Isis, and they say that she is a goddess whose husband was Osiris her brother. And when Osiris was killed by Typhon his brother, Isis fled with Horos her son to Byblus in Syria, and was there for a certain time till her son was grown. And he contended with Typhon his uncle, and killed him. And then Isis returned and went about with Horos her son and sought for the dead body of Osiris her lord, bitterly lamenting his death. If then Isis be a goddess, and could not help Osiris her brother and lord, how can she help another? But it is impossible that a divine nature should be afraid, and flee for safety, or should weep and wail; or else it is very miserable.

And of Osiris also they say that he is a serviceable god. And he was killed by Typhon and was unable to help himself. But it is well known that this cannot be asserted of divinity. And further, they say of his brother Typhon that he is a god, who killed his brother and was killed by his brother's son and by his bride, being unable to help himself. And how, pray, is he a god who does not save himself?

As the Egyptians, then, were more stupid than the rest of the nations, these and such like gods did not suffice for them. Nay, but they even apply the name of gods to animals in which there is no soul at all. For some of them worship the sheep and others the calf; and some the pig and others the shad fish; and some the crocodile and the hawk and the fish and the ibis and the vulture and the eagle and the raven. Some of them worship the cat, and others the turbot-fish, some the dog, some the adder, and some the asp, and others the lion; and others the garlic and onions and thorns, and others the tiger and other such things. And the poor creatures do not see that all these things are nothing, although they daily witness their gods being eaten and consumed by men and also by their fellows; while some of them are cremated,

GREEK.

slain as victims and mouldering in decay, they have not perceived that they are not gods.

XIII. So the Egyptians and the Chaldæans and the Greeks made a great error in bringing forward such beings as gods, and in making images of them, and in deifying dumb and senseless idols.

And I wonder how they saw their gods sawn out and hacked and docked by the workmen, and besides aging with time and falling to pieces, and being cast from metal, and yet did not discern concerning them that they were not gods.

For when they have no power to see to their own safety, how will they take forethought for men?

But further, the poets and philosophers, alike of the Chaldæans and the Greeks and the Egyptians, while they desired by their poems and writings to magnify the gods of their countries, rather revealed their shame, and laid it bare before all men. For if the body of man while consisting of many parts does not cast off any of its own members, but preserving an unbroken unity in all its members, is harmonious with itself, how shall variance and discord be so great in the nature of God?

For if there had been a unity of nature among the gods, then one god ought not to have pursued or slain or injured another. And if the gods were pursued by gods, and slain, and kidnapped and struck with lightning by them, then there is no longer any unity of nature, but

SYRIAC.

and some die and decay and become dust, without their observing that they perish in many ways. So the Egyptians have not observed that such things which are not equal to their own deliverance, are not gods. And if, forsooth, they are weak in the case of their own deliverance, whence have they power to help in the case of deliverance of their worshippers? Great then is the error into which the Egyptians wandered;—greater, indeed, than that of any people which is upon the face of the earth.

XIII, But it is a marvel, O King, with regard to the Greeks, who surpass all other peoples in their manner of life and reasoning, how they have gone astray after dead idols and lifeless images. And yet they see their gods in the hands of their artificers being sawn out, and planed and docked, and hacked short, and charred, and ornamented, and being altered by them in every kind of way. And when they grow old, and are worn away through lapse of time, and when they are molten and crushed to powder, how, I wonder, did they not perceive concerning them, that they are not gods? And as for those who did not find deliverance for themselves, how can they serve the distress of men?

But even the writers and philosophers among them have wrongly alleged that the gods are such as are made in honour of God Almighty. And they err in seeking to liken (them) to God whom man has not at any time seen nor can see unto what He is like. Herein, too (they err) in asserting of deity that any such thing as deficiency can be present to it; as when they say that He receives sacrifice and requires burnt-offering and libation and immolations of men, and temples. But God is not in need, and none of these things is necessary to Him; and it is clear that men err in these things they imagine.

Further their writers and their philosophers represent and declare that the nature of all their gods is one. And they have not apprehended God our Lord who while He is one, is in all. They err therefore. For if the body of a man while it is many in its parts is not in dread, one member of another, but, since it is a united body, wholly agrees with itself; even so also God is one in His nature. A single essence is proper to Him, since He is uniform in His nature and His essence; and He is not afraid of Himself. If then the nature of the gods is one, it is not proper that a god should either pursue or slay or harm a god. If then gods be pursued and wounded by gods, and some be kidnapped and some struck dead by lightning, it is obvious that the nature of their gods is not one. And hence it is known, O King, that it is a mistake when they reckon and bring the natures of their gods under a single

GREEK.

divided counsels, all mischievous. So that not one of them is a god. It is clear then, O King, that all their discourse on the nature of the gods is an error.

But how did the wise and erudite men of the Greeks not observe that inasmuch as they make laws for themselves they are judged by their own laws? For if the laws are righteous, their gods are altogether unrighteous, as they have committed transgressions of laws, in slaying one another, and practising sorceries, and adultery and thefts and intercourse with males. If they were right in doing these things, then the laws are unrighteous, being framed contrary to the gods. Whereas in fact, the laws are good and just, commending what is good and forbidding what is bad. But the deeds of their gods are contrary to law. Their gods, therefore, are lawbreakers, and all liable to the punishment of death; and they are impious men who introduce such gods. For if the stories about them be mythical, the gods are nothing more than mere names; and if the stories be founded on nature, still they who did and suffered these things are no longer gods; and if the stories be allegorical, they are myths and nothing more.

It has been shown then, O King, that all these polytheistic objects of worship are the works of error and perdition. For it is not right to give the name of gods to beings which may be seen but cannot see; but one ought to reverence the invisible and all-seeing and all-creating God.

XIV. Let us proceed then, O King, to the Jews also, that we may see what truth there is in their view of God. For they were descendants of Abraham and Isaac and Jacob, and migrated to Egypt. And thence God brought them forth with a mighty hand and an uplifted arm through Moses, their lawgiver; and by many wonders and signs He made known His power to them. But even they

SYRIAC.

nature. If then it becomes us to admire a god which is seen and does not see, how much more praiseworthy is it that one should believe in a nature which is invisible and all-seeing? And if further it is fitting that one should approve the handiworks of a craftsman, how much more is it fitting that one should glorify the Creator of the craftsman?

For behold! when the Greeks made laws they did not perceive that by their laws they condemn their gods. For if their laws are righteous, their gods are unrighteous, since they transgressed the law in killing one another, and practising sorcery, and committing adultery, and in robbing and stealing, and in lying with males, and by their other practises as well. For if their gods were right in doing all these things as they are described, then the laws of the Greeks are unrighteous in not being made according to the will of their gods. And in that case the whole world is gone astray.

For the narratives about their gods are some of them myths, and some of them nature-poems (lit: natural—*φυσικαί*), and some of them hymns and elegies. The hymns indeed and elegies are empty words and noise. But these nature-poems, even if they be made as they say, still those are not gods who do such things and suffer and endure such things. And those myths are shallow tales with no depth whatever in them.

XIV. Let us come now, O King, to the history of the Jews also, and see what opinion they have as to God. The Jews then say that God is one, the Creator of all, and omnipotent; and that it is not right that any other should be worshipped except this God alone. And herein they appear to approach the truth more than all the nations, especially in that they worship God and not His works. And they imitate God by the philanthropy which prevails among them; for they have compassion on the poor, and they release the captives, and bury the dead, and do such things as these, which are acceptable before God and well-pleasing also to men,—which (customs) they have received from their forefathers.

GREEK.

proved stubborn and ungrateful, and often served the idols of the nations, and put to death the prophets and just men who were sent to them. Then when the Son of God was pleased to come upon the earth, they received him with wanton violence and betrayed him into the hands of Pilate the Roman governor; and paying no respect to his good deeds and the countless miracles he wrought among them, they demanded a sentence of death by the cross. And they perished by their own transgression; for to this day they worship the one God Almighty, but not according to knowledge. For they deny that Christ is the Son of God; and they are much like to the heathen, even although they may seem to make some approach to the truth from which they have removed themselves. So much for the Jews.

XV. Now the Christians[1] trace their origin from the Lord Jesus Christ. And He is acknowledged by the Holy Spirit to be the son of the most high God, who came down from heaven for the salvation of men. And being born of a pure virgin, unbegotten and immaculate, He assumed flesh and revealed himself among men that He might recall them to Himself from their wandering after many gods. And having accomplished His wonderful dispensation, by a voluntary choice He tasted death on the cross, fulfilling an august dispensation. And after three days He came to life again and ascended into heaven. And if you would read, O King, you may judge the glory of His presence from the holy gospel writing, as it is called among themselves. He had twelve disciples, who after His ascension to heaven went forth into the provinces of the whole world, and declared His greatness. As for instance, one of them traversed the countries about us, proclaiming the doctrine of the truth. From this it is, that they who still observe the righteousness enjoined by their preaching are called Christians.

And these are they who more than

SYRIAC.

Nevertheless they too erred from true knowledge. And in their imagination they conceive that it is God they serve; whereas by their mode of observance it is to the angels and not to God that their service is rendered:—as when they celebrate sabbaths and the beginning of the months, and feasts of unleavened bread, and a great fast; and fasting and circumcision and the purification of meats, which things, however, they do not observe perfectly.

XV. But the Christians, O King, while they went about and made search,[2] have found the truth; and as we learned from their writings, they have come nearer to truth and genuine knowledge than the rest of the nations. For they know and trust in God, the Creator of heaven and of earth, in whom and from whom are all things, to whom there is no other god as companion, from whom they received commandments which they engraved upon their minds and observe in hope and expectation of the world which is to come. Wherefore they do not commit adultery nor fornication, nor bear false witness, nor embezzle what is held in pledge, nor covet what is not theirs. They honour father and mother, and show kindness to those near to them; and whenever they are judges, they judge uprightly. They do not worship idols (made) in the image of man; and whatsoever they would not that others should do unto them, they do not to others; and of the food which is consecrated to idols they do not eat, for they are pure. And their oppressors they appease (lit: comfort) and make them their friends; they do good to their enemies; and their women, O King, are pure as virgins, and their daughters are modest; and their men keep themselves from every unlawful union and from all uncleanness, in the hope of a recompense to come in the other world. Further, if one or other of them have bondmen and bondwomen or children, through love towards them they persuade them to become Christians, and when they have done so, they call them brethren without distinction. They do not worship strange gods, and they go their way in all modesty and cheerfulness. Falsehood is not found

[1] This, the "Christological" passage, occurs earlier in the Syriac. Chap. II.
[2] The same two words are used of Isis. The Christians are unlike her in finding what they sought.

GREEK.

all the nations on the earth have found the truth. For they know God, the Creator and Fashioner of all things through the only-begotten Son and the Holy Spirit[1]; and beside Him they worship no other God. They have the commands of the Lord Jesus Christ Himself graven upon their hearts; and they observe them, looking forward to the resurrection of the dead and life in the world to come. They do not commit adultery nor fornication, nor bear false witness, nor covet the things of others; they honour father and mother, and love their neighbours; they judge justly, and they never do to others what they would not wish to happen to themselves; they appeal to those who injure them, and try to win them as friends; they are eager to do good to their enemies; they are gentle and easy to be entreated; they abstain from all unlawful conversation and from all impurity; they despise not the widow, nor oppress the orphan; and he that has, gives ungrudgingly for the maintenance of him who has not.

If they see a stranger, they take him under their roof, and rejoice over him as over a very brother; for they call themselves brethren not after the flesh but after the spirit.

And they are ready to sacrifice their lives for the sake of Christ; for they observe His commands without swerving, and live holy and just lives, as the Lord God enjoined upon them.

And they give thanks unto Him every hour, for all meat and drink and other blessings.

SYRIAC.

among them; and they love one another, and from widows they do not turn away their esteem; and they deliver the orphan from him who treats him harshly. And he, who has, gives to him who has not, without boasting. And when they see a stranger, they take him in to their homes and rejoice over him as a very brother; for they do not call them brethren after the flesh, but brethren after the spirit and in God. And whenever one of their poor passes from the world, each one of them according to his ability gives heed to him and carefully sees to his burial. And if they hear that one of their number is imprisoned or afflicted on account of the name of their Messiah, all of them anxiously minister to his necessity, and if it is possible to redeem him they set him free. And if there is among them any that is poor and needy, and if they have no spare food, they fast two or three days in order to supply to the needy their lack of food. They observe the precepts of their Messiah with much care, living justly and soberly as the Lord their God commanded them. Every morning[2] and every hour they give thanks and praise to God for His loving-kindnesses toward them; and for their food and their drink they offer thanksgiving to Him. And if any righteous man among them passes from the world, they rejoice and offer thanks to God; and they escort his body as if he were setting out from one place to another near. And when a child has been born to one of them, they give thanks to God;

[1] The Armenian agrees with the Greek against the Syriac. "Uná cum Spiritu Sancto" Arm.

[2] Cf. Pliny's letter to the Emperor Trajan, A.D. 112, "The Christians are wont to meet at dawn on an appointed day, and to sing a hymn to Christ as God."

GREEK.

SYRIAC.

and if moreover it happen to die in childhood, they give thanks to God the more, as for one who has passed through the world without sins. And further if they see that any one of them dies in his ungodliness or in his sins, for him they grieve bitterly, and sorrow as for one who goes to meet his doom.

XVI. Such, O King, is the commandment of the law of the Christians, and such is their manner of life. As men who know God, they ask from Him petitions which are fitting for Him to grant and for them to receive. And thus they employ their whole lifetime. And since they know the loving-kindnesses of God toward them, behold! for their sake the glorious things which are in the world flow forth to view. And verily, they are those who found the truth when they went about and made search for it; and from what we considered, we learned that they alone come near to a knowledge of the truth. And they do not proclaim in the ears of the multitude the kind deeds they do, but are careful that no one should notice them; and they conceal their giving just as he who finds a treasure and conceals it. And they strive to be righteous as those who expect to behold their Messiah, and to receive from Him with great glory the promises made concerning them. And as for their words and their precepts, O King, and their glorying in their worship, and the hope of earning according to the work of each one of them their recompense which they look for in another world,—you may learn about these from their writings. It is enough for us to have shortly informed your Majesty concerning the conduct and the truth of the Christians. For great indeed, and wonderful is their doctrine to him who will search into it and reflect upon it. And verily, this is a new people, and there is something divine (lit: a divine admixture) in the midst of them.

XVI. Verily then, this is the way of the truth which leads those who travel therein to the everlasting kingdom promised through Christ in the life to come. And that you may know, O King, that in saying these things I do not speak at my own instance, if you deign to look into the writings of the Christians, you will find that I state nothing beyond the truth. Rightly then, did thy son[1] apprehend, and justly was he taught to serve the living God and to be saved for the age that is destined to come upon us. For great and wonderful are the sayings and deeds of the Christians; for they speak not the words of men but those of God. But the rest of the nations go astray and

Take, then, their writings, and read therein, and lo! you will find that I have not put forth these things on my own authority, nor spoken thus as their advocate; but since I read in their writings I was fully assured of these things as also of things which are to come. And for this reason I was constrained to declare the truth to such as care for it and seek the world to come. And to me there is no doubt but that the earth abides through the supplication of the Christians. But the rest of the nations err and cause error in wallowing before the elements of the world, since beyond these their mental vision will not pass. And they search about as if in darkness because they will not recognize the truth; and like drunken men they reel and jostle one another and fall.

[1] The reference is to Josaphat, son of Abenner, who was taught to be a Christian by the monk Barlaam.

GREEK.

deceive themselves; for they walk in darkness and bruise themselves like drunken men.

XVII. Thus far, O King, extends my discourse to you, which has been dictated in my mind by the Truth.[2] Wherefore let thy foolish sages cease their idle talk against the Lord; for it is profitable for you to worship God the Creator, and to give ear to His incorruptible words, that ye may escape from condemnation and punishment, and be found to be heirs of life everlasting.

SYRIAC.

XVII. Thus far, O King, I have spoken; for concerning that which remains, as is said above,[1] there are found in their other writings things which are hard to utter and difficult for one to narrate,—which are not only spoken in words but also wrought out in deeds.

Now the Greeks, O King, as they follow base practises in intercourse with males, and a mother and a sister and a daughter, impute their monstrous impurity in turn to the Christians. But the Christians are just and good, and the truth is set before their eyes, and their spirit is long-suffering; and, therefore, though they know the error of these (the Greeks), and are persecuted by them, they bear and endure it; and for the most part they have compassion on them, as men who are destitute of knowledge. And on their side, they offer prayer that these may repent of their error; and when it happens that one of them has repented, he is ashamed before the Christians of the works which were done by him; and he makes confession to God, saying, I did these things in ignorance. And he purifies his heart, and his sins are forgiven him, because he committed them in ignorance in the former time, when he used to blaspheme and speak evil of the true knowledge of the Christians. And assuredly the race of the Christians is more blessed than all the men who are upon the face of the earth.

Henceforth let the tongues of those who utter vanity and harass the Christians be silent; and hereafter let them speak the truth. For it is of serious consequence to them that they should worship the true God rather than worship a senseless sound. And verily whatever is spoken in the mouth of the Christians is of God; and their doctrine is the gateway of light. Wherefore let all who are without the knowledge of God draw near thereto; and they will receive incorruptible words, which are from all time and from eternity. So shall they appear before the awful judgment which through Jesus the Messiah is destined to come upon the whole human race.

The Apology of Aristides the Philosopher is finished.

---

[1] The Christian Scriptures are previously referred to as a source of information, not as containing difficulties. cf. 2 Peter iii. 16.

[2] Nachor, the fictitious monk who represented Barlaam, intended to make a weak defence of Christianity, but, according to the story, he was constrained to speak what he had not intended. It is evidently the author's intention to make it an instance of "suggestio verborum" or plenary inspiration, in the case of the fictitious monk.

THE PASSION OF THE SCILLITAN MARTYRS

BY

ANDREW RUTHERFURD, B.D.

TRANSLATION BY PROF. J. A. ROBINSON. INTRODUCTION BY A. R.

INTRODUCTION

THE Scillitan Martyrs were condemned and executed at Carthage on the 17th July, A.D. 180. The martyrs belonged to Scili, a place in that part of Numidia which belonged to proconsular Africa. The proconsul at the time, who is said by Tertullian to have been the first to draw the sword against the Christians there, was P. Vigellius Saturninus. The consuls for the year were Præsens II. and Condianus. Marcus Aurelius had died only a few months before.

The exact date of the martyrdom was long under dispute, and the question has recently arisen whether the Acts were originally written in Latin or Greek. Baronius placed the date as late as 202. The text had become corrupt in passing through various Latin and Greek versions and transcriptions, and it was long impossible to recognize the names of the consuls for the year in the first line of the piece. But M. Leon Renier conjectured that the word *bis* pointed to a consul's name underlying the word preceding it, and suggested the year 180, when Præsens and Condianus were consuls. This conjecture was confirmed by Usener's publication in 1881 of a Greek version from a ninth century MS. in the Bibliothèque Nationale at Paris, though even here the names, though recognizable, were in a corrupt form. Usener believed this version to be a translation from a Latin original, and his theory has been confirmed by Mr. Armitage Robinson's discovery of a Latin MS. of the ninth century in the British Museum, containing the Acts of the Scillitan Martyrs in a form briefer than any of the other versions and believed to be the original. Mr. A. Robinson's translation which follows, is from the Latin which he discovered, and which is printed in *Texts and Studies*, vol. i., No. 2.

THE PASSION OF THE SCILLITAN MARTYRS

WHEN Præsens, for the second time, and Claudianus were the consuls, on the seventeenth day of July, at Carthage, there were set in the judgment-hall Speratus, Nartzalus, Cittinus, Donata, Secunda and Vestia.

Saturninus the proconsul said: Ye can win the indulgence of our lord the Emperor, if ye return to a sound mind.

Speratus said: We have never done ill, we have not lent ourselves to wrong, we have never spoken ill, but when ill-treated we have given thanks; because we pay heed to OUR EMPEROR.

Saturninus the proconsul said: We too are religious, and our religion is simple, and we swear by the genius of our lord the Emperor, and pray for his welfare, as ye also ought to do.

Speratus said: If thou wilt peaceably lend me thine ears, I can tell thee the mystery of simplicity.

Saturninus said: I will not lend mine ears to thee, when thou beginnest to speak evil things of our sacred rites; but rather swear thou by the genius of our lord the Emperor.

Speratus said: The empire of this world I know not; but rather I serve that God, *whom no man hath seen, nor* with these eyes *can see.*[1] I have committed no theft; but if I have bought anything I pay the tax; because I know my Lord, the King of kings and Emperor of all nations.

Saturninus the proconsul said to the rest: Cease to be of this persuasion.

Speratus said: It is an ill persuasion to do murder, to speak false witness.

Saturninus the proconsul said: Be not partakers of this folly.

Cittinus said: We have none other to fear, save only our Lord God, who is in heaven.

Donata said: Honour to Cæsar as Cæsar: but fear to God.[2]

Vestia said: I am a Christian.

Secunda said: What I am, that I wish to be.

Saturninus the proconsul said to Speratus: Dost thou persist in being a Christian?

Speratus said: I am a Christian. And with him they all agreed.

Saturninus the proconsul said: Will ye have a space to consider?

Speratus said: In a matter so straightforward there is no considering.

Saturninus the proconsul said: What are the things in your chest?

Speratus said: Books and epistles of Paul, a just man.

Saturninus the proconsul said: Have a delay of thirty days and bethink yourselves.

Speratus said a second time: I am a Christian. And with him they all agreed.

Saturninus the proconsul read out the decree from the tablet: Speratus, Nartzalus, Cittinus, Donata, Vestia, Secunda and the rest having confessed that they live according to the Christian rite, since after opportunity offered them of returning to the custom of the Romans they have obstinately persisted, it is determined that they be put to the sword.

Speratus said: We give thanks to God.

Nartzalus said: To-day we are martyrs in heaven; thanks be to God.

Saturninus the proconsul ordered it to be declared by the herald: Speratus, Nartzalus, Cittinus, Veturius, Felix, Aquilinus, Laetantius, Januaria, Generosa, Vestia, Donata and Secunda, I have ordered to be executed.

They all said: Thanks be to God.

And so they all together were crowned with martyrdom; and they reign with the Father and the Son and the Holy Ghost, for ever and ever. Amen.

[1] 1 Tim. vi. 16.

[2] Cf. Rom. xiii. 7.

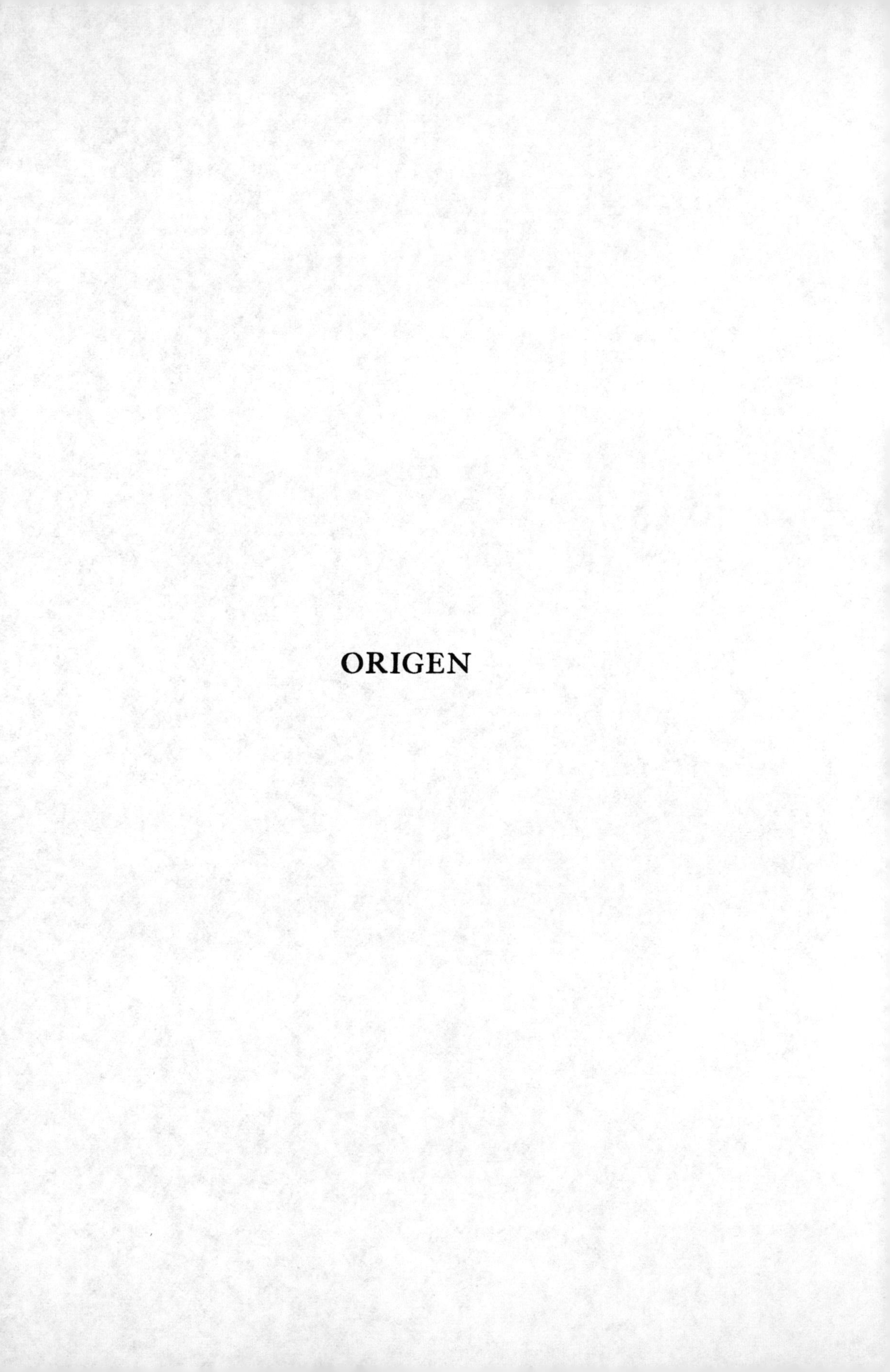

ORIGEN

EPISTLE TO GREGORY

AND

ORIGEN'S COMMENTARY

ON THE

GOSPEL OF JOHN

BY

ALLAN MENZIES, D.D.

COMMENTARIES OF ORIGEN

INTRODUCTION

For a general account of Origen and of his works we may refer to Dr. Crombie's *Life of Origen,* in vol. iv. of this series (xxiii. in Clark's issue). The principal facts of his career are as follows : He was born of Christian parents at Alexandria about the year 185 A.D., and from his earliest youth devoted himself to the study of Scripture in such a way as to suggest that he was destined for a great career. His father suffered martyrdom in the year 202, and Origen very soon afterwards succeeded the great Clement as head of the school at Alexandria. Thirteen years after, the persecution of Caracalla drove him from his own country to Cæsarea, where though still a layman he preached at church meetings. Recalled to Alexandria, he laboured there for fifteen years further as teacher and author, till in the year 231 his ordination at Cæsarea to the office of presbyter drew upon him the condemnation of the bishop of Alexandria and became the occasion of his permanent withdrawal from the place of his birth. At Cæsarea he now formed a new school of Christian training similar to that from which he had been driven. At this time, as well as in the earlier period of his life, he made various journeys to different parts of the world. His death was brought about by sufferings inflicted on him in the persecution of Decius, and took place at Tyre, probably in the year 254.

Part of the Commentary on John, the first great work of Christian interpretation, and part of that on Matthew, written by the father at a later period of his life, are here presented to the reader ; and a few words of introduction may be added on Origen's work as an expositor and on these two works in particular.

Though Origen was the first great interpreter of Scripture in the Church, commentaries had been written before his. He speaks of those who had preceded him in this activity ; and though but little survives of the labours of these earlier expositors, we know that the work of commenting on Scripture was zealously carried on in the Gnostic churches in the latter part of the second century, and several of the older exegetes in the Church are also known to us by name and reputation. Heracleon the Gnostic commentator on John, who is often cited and often rather unfairly dealt with by Origen, as he follows him over the same ground, belonged to the Valentinian school. Many of his comments the reader will find to be very just and shrewd ; but the tenets of his school led him into many extravagances. Of Pantænus, head of the catechetical school at Alexandria in the end of the second and early years of the third century, we hear that he interpreted many of the books of Scripture. We also learn that he preceded Clement and Origen, his successors in office, in the application of Gentile learning to Christian studies ; the broad and liberal tone of Alexandrian theology may be due in part to his influence. Much of his exegetical work was still extant in the days of Jerome, who, however, reports that he did more for the Church as a teacher than as a writer. Only fragments of his Commentaries now remain. In Clement's works, on the contrary, we find, if not any set commentaries, various extended discussions of particular texts. We also find in him a theory of Scripture, its inspiration and its nature, which is followed also by Origen, and which determines the whole character of Alexandrian exegesis. In accordance with the general tendency of that age, which witnessed a reaction from the independence of philosophy and an appeal in many quarters to the authority of ancient oracles and writings, the Alexandrian school treats Scripture as an inspired and infallible storehouse of truth,—of truth, however, not patent to the simple reader, but requiring the spiritual man to discern its mystic import. Clement discusses the question why divine things are wrapped up in mysteries, and holds that all who have spoken of such things have dealt with them in this way. Everything in Scripture, therefore, has a mystical in addition to its obvious meaning. Every minute particular about the tabernacle and its furniture is charged with an unseen truth. The effect of such a view of Scripture on exegesis is necessarily that the interpreter finds in the inspired words not what they plainly convey, but what most interests his own mind. In assigning to each verse its spiritual meaning, he is neither guided nor restrained by any rule or system, but enjoys complete liberty. The natural good sense of these great scholars curbed to some extent the licence of their theory; but with such a view of Scripture they could not but run into many an extravagance; and the allegorical method of interpretation, which so long prevailed in Christendom and is still practised in some quarters, dates from Alexandria. The roots of it lie further back, in Jewish rabbinical treatment of the Old Testament, and in the Greek philosophy of Alexandria. In Philo, the great contemporary of Christ at Alexandria, rabbinical and Greek learning met, and Scripture being a divine authority and having to furnish evidence of Greek philosophical doctrines, the allegorical method of interpretation was called to perform large services. To Philo's eyes all wisdom was contained in the Pentateuch, and many an idea of which Moses never dreamed had to be extracted from that ancient record. The method was older than Clement and Origen, but it was through them that it became so firmly established in the Church.

In Origen we first find a great teacher who deliberately sets himself to the task of explaining Scripture. He became, at the early age of eighteen, the head of the catechetical school at Alexandria, an institution which not only trained catechumens but provided open lectures, on every part of Christian learning, and from that time to his death, at the age of sixty-nine, he was constantly engaged in the work of public exposition. At Alexandria his expositions took place in the school, but at Cæsarea they formed part of the church services, so that the reports of those belonging to the Cæsarean period provide us with the earliest examples we possess of the discourse at Christian meetings. In an activity which he practised so much Origen acquired extraordinary skill and facility, and gained the highest reputation, even beyond the limits of the Church. It is no wonder, therefore, if he succeeded in treating nearly the whole Bible in this way, a thing which might no doubt be said of many a Christian teacher since his day; for he was not one who was apt to repeat himself, but was constantly pressing on to break new ground.

But the reported homilies form only a part—and that not the most important part—of his exegetical works. What he gave in his homilies was necessarily designed for edification; it had to be plain enough to be understood by a mixed audience, and serviceable to their needs. Origen believed, however, that there was very much in Scripture that lay beyond the capacity of the ordinary mind, and that the highest way of treating Scripture was not that of practical application, but that of searching after its hidden sense. In the fourth book of his *De Principiis* (vol. iv., American Ed.) he sets forth his views about the Scriptures. "As man," he there says, "consists of body, soul, and spirit, so in the same way does Scripture, which has been arranged to be given by God for the salvation of man." Scripture, therefore, has three senses, the bodily (somatic) or the obvious matter-of-fact sense, the psychical or moral sense, which serves for edification of the pious, and, highest of all, the spiritual sense. For this latter sense of Scripture Origen has many names,—as many as forty have been counted,—he calls it the heavenly sense, the intellectual, the anagogical, the mystic, the hidden. This is what chiefly engages his interest in the work of expounding. Scripture is to him full of mysteries, every jot and tittle has its secret, and to read these heavenly mysteries is the highest object of the interpreter. In addition, therefore, to his oral expositions (*ὁμιλίαι*) and the short notes (*σημειώσεις*) which are generally reckoned as a third class of his exegetical works, we have the written commentaries, books, or *τόμοι* of Origen, in which he discusses Scripture without being hampered by the requirements of edification, according to the method which alone he recognizes as adequate. He was enabled to devote himself to this labour by the generosity of a rich friend, Ambrosius, who urged him to undertake it, and provided funds for the payment of shorthand writers and copyists. We are told that seven of the former were at one time placed at his disposal. The work which he was thus led to undertake Origen felt to be very responsible and burdensome; it was not to be approached without fervent prayer, and he sometimes complains that it is too much for him, and that it is only the urgent commands of Ambrosius that make him go on with it. (See the opening chapters of the various books on John.)

What has been said will to some extent explain the nature of these commentaries, parts of which are now for the first time presented to the English reader. There is a side of them, however, of which we have not yet spoken. Origen was a great scholar as well as a great theologian; and he thought it right, as the reader may see from the letter to Gregory also here given, that scholarship should contribute all it could to the study of Scripture. Of his multifarious knowledge and of his easy command of all the science and philosophy of his day, the reader may judge for himself even from what is now presented to him. His work on the words of Scripture has a value quite independently of his theological views. Some of the most important qualifications of the worthy interpreter of Scripture he possesses in a supreme degree. His knowledge of Scripture is extraordinary both for its range and its minute accuracy. He had no concordance to help him; but he was himself a concordance. Whatever word occurs he is able to bring from every part of Scripture the passages in which it is used. He quotes passages, it is true, which are only verbally connected with the text before him and have no affinity of idea; the wealth of illustration he has at his command does not always assist, but sometimes, as the reader will see, impedes his progress: yet the wonder is not diminished of such a knowledge of all parts of the Bible as is probably without parallel. It has to be added that he is strong in grammar, and has a true eye for the real meaning of his text; the discussions in which he does this often leave nothing to be desired. In defining his terms he often goes far astray; he has to define them according to the science of his day; but he is not guilty of loose construction of sentences. Another matter in which he is distinguished is that of textual criticism. He is the first great textual critic of the Church. That his name occurs more frequently than that of any other father in the digests of early readings of the text of the New Testament, is due no doubt to the fact that he is the earliest writer of commentaries which have been preserved; his commentaries contain complete texts of the portions of Scripture commented on, as well as copious quotations from other parts of Scripture. But he was keenly interested in the text of the New Testament for its own sake. He tells us that many variations already existed in his day in different copies. And he preserves many readings which afterwards disappeared from the Bible. It has also to be said that he often quotes the same text differently in different passages, so that it appears probable that he used several copies of the N. T. books, and that these copies differed from each other. If, therefore, as Tischendorf suggests, Origen made a collation of the various texts of the N. T. with which he was acquainted, as he did with his texts of the O. T. in his Hexapla, he had no strong views as to which text was to be followed. He sometimes expresses an opinion as to which is the true reading (pp. 368 sq.), but he does so on grounds which the textual critics of the present day could not approve.

It may be stated here that the translators of Origen in this volume have sought to represent their author's critical position with regard to Scripture by translating his Scripture quotations from his text. As he used the Septuagint version of the Old Testament, many of his quotations from that part of Scripture appear in a form unfamiliar to the English reader. In the New Testament, also, his text is also very different from that which afterwards prevailed in the Church.

The weakness of Origen as an interpreter is his want of historical feeling or of any conception of such a thing as growth or development in revelation. His mind slips incessantly away from the real scenes and events recorded in Scripture, to the ideal region where he conceives that the truths reside which these prefigure. Scripture is to him not a record of actual occurrences which took place as they are narrated, but a storehouse of types of heavenly things, which alone are real. He scoffs at the notion that historical facts should be regarded as the chief outcome of a Scripture narrative (John, book x. 15–17, pp. 389–394). When he does treat the facts as facts he has many a shrewd observation and many a beautiful application. But the facts are to a large extent in his way; they have to give place to something more important. He sees very well how the synoptic narratives clash with that of John; no better demonstration of this need be looked for than he gives in the tenth book of his John; from this, however, he infers not that the books must have had different sources of information, but that the literal meaning of the passages must be altogether disregarded, and their true purport looked for, not in the things of history, but in the things of the Spirit. The water-pots at the feast in Cana (*De Principiis*), the shoe latchet of the Saviour (John, book vi. 17), the ass and foal (John, book x. 18), each must receive a transcendent application.

It follows from this that the commentaries are deficient in order and sequence. The method which calls the writer to look at every step for spiritual meanings, combined with his own extraordinary fertility of imagination and wealth of matter, makes these books very disconnected. At each point a number of questions suggests itself as to possible meanings; a host of texts is brought at once from every part of Scripture to afford illustration, and these again have to be considered. Very modestly are the questions and themes introduced. The tone is as far as possible from being *ex cathedra;* it is rather that of a student groping his way, and asking at each step for assistance. And the great mass of the questions thus raised is left, apparently, unanswered. So that the work as a whole is rather a great collection of materials for future consideration than a finished treatise.

Such being the characteristics of Origen's commentaries, they have by many been regarded as unsuitable for the general reader, and unfavourably compared with those of later writers, to whom the interpretation of Scripture was not weighted with such difficulties as Origen had to contend with. Our author does not carry us along in his commentaries with a stream of golden eloquence; his interests are intellectual more than literary or practical, his work is scientific rather than popular. Perhaps the historical student has more to gain from them than the preacher. But among the pages which witness chiefly to restless intellectual energy and unwearied diligence, there are also many passages of rare and touching beauty, when the writer realizes the greatness of the Christian salvation, or when the heavenly things to the search for which all his labour is devoted shine by their own brightness on his sight.

The Commentaries on John are the earliest work of Christian exegesis which has come down to us, and are therefore placed in this volume before those on Matthew. The first five books on John were written at Alexandria before Origen's compulsory withdrawal from that city to Cæsarea in 231. In chaps. 4 and 8 of the first book he speaks of this work as being the first fruits of his activity as a writer on Holy Scripture. The sixth book, as he tells us in vi. 1, had been begun at Alexandria, but the manuscript had been left behind, so that a new beginning had to be made at Cæsarea. The work was again interrupted by the persecution of Maximian in 238; the volumes from the twenty-second to the last were written after that date. At the end of the thirty-second volume, which is the last we now possess, the writer has only reached John xiii. 33, but he tells us in his Commentary on Matthew that he has spoken of the two thieves in his work on John. In the time of Eusebius only twenty-two books survived out of the whole number, which seems to have been thirty-nine. We now possess books i., ii., vi., x., xiii., xix., xx., xxviii., xxxii., some of which, however, are not complete, and a few fragments. The thirteenth book begins in the middle of the story of the Samaritan woman. Ambrosius had wished that story to be completed in the twelfth book, but Origen did not like to make his books too long, and on this point disregarded the authority of his mentor. The nineteenth and twentieth books are both occupied with the eighth chapter of John, which, if it was all treated on the same scale, must have occupied two more books in addition to these. The thirty-second book scarcely completes the thirteenth chapter of the Gospel; and if the remaining chapters only occupied seven books, the treatment of these must have been much more condensed.

Two Latin translations of Origen's John were made in the sixteenth century, one by Ambrosius Ferrarius of Milan from the Venice Codex, the other by Joachim Perionius.

The Commentaries on John and on Matthew are both embraced in several manuscripts. Of those on John, Mr. A. E. Brooke (*Texts and Studies*, vol. i. No. 4; *The Fragments of Heracleon*, pp. 1–30; "the MSS. of Origen's Commentaries on S. John") enumerates eight or nine. The Munich MS. of the thirteenth century is the source of all the rest. Huet, the first editor (1668), used the Codex Regius (Paris) of the sixteenth century, which is in many passages mutilated and disfigured. The brothers Delarue (1733–1759) used the MSS. Barberinus aud Bodleianus, which are more complete, and Lommatzsch (1831) follows his predecessors. The present translations are from the text of Lommatzsch, which is in many places very defective.[1]

[1] Mr. Brooke's revised text of the Commentary of Origen on St. John's Gospel (2 vols., Cambridge University Warehouse) appeared unfortunately too late to be used in the preparation of this volume.

LETTER OF ORIGEN TO GREGORY.

When and to whom the Learning derived from Philosophy may be of Service for the Exposition of the Holy Scriptures; with a lively Personal Appeal.

This letter to Gregory, afterwards bishop of Cæsarea, and called Thaumaturgus, was preserved in the Philocalia, or collection of extracts from Origen's works drawn up by Gregory of Nyssa and Basil of Cæsarea. It is printed by Delarue and Lommatzsch in the forefront of their editions of the works. It forms a good preface to the commentaries, as it shows how Origen considered the study of Scripture to be the highest of all studies, and how he regarded scientific learning, in which he was himself a master, as merely preparatory for this supreme learning. Dräseke [1] has shown that it was written about 235, when Origen, after having had Gregory as his pupil at Cæsarea for some years, had fled before the persecution under Maximinus Thrax to Cappadocia; while Gregory, to judge from the tenor of this Epistle, had gone to Egypt. The Panegyric on Origen,[2] pronounced by Gregory at Cæsarea about 239, when the school had reassembled there after the persecution, shows that the master's solicitude for his pupil's true advancement was not disappointed.

1. GREGORY IS URGED TO APPLY HIS GENTILE LEARNING TO THE STUDY OF SCRIPTURE.

All hail to thee in God, most excellent and reverend Sir, son Gregory, from Origen. A natural quickness of understanding is fitted, as you are well aware, if it be diligently exercised, to produce a work which may bring its owner so far as is possible, if I may so express myself, to the consummation of the art the which he desires to practise, and your natural aptitude is sufficient to make you a consummate Roman lawyer and a Greek philosopher too of the most famous schools. But my desire for you has been that you should direct the whole force of your intelligence to Christianity as your end, and that in the way of production. And I would wish that you should take with you on the one hand those parts of the philosophy of the Greeks which are fit, as it were, to serve as general or preparatory studies for Christianity, and on the other hand so much of Geometry and Astronomy as may be helpful for the interpretation of the Holy Scriptures. The children of the philosophers speak of geometry and music and grammar and rhetoric and astronomy as being ancillary to philosophy; and in the same way we might speak of philosophy itself as being ancillary to Christianity.

2. THIS PROCEDURE IS TYPIFIED BY THE STORY OF THE SPOILING OF THE EGYPTIANS.

It is something of this sort perhaps that is enigmatically indicated in the directions God is represented in the Book of Exodus [3] as giving to the children of Israel. They are directed to beg from their neighbours and from those dwelling in their tents vessels of silver and of gold, and raiment; thus they are to spoil the Egyptians, and to obtain materials for making the things they are told to provide in connection with the worship of God. For out of the things of which the children of Israel spoiled the Egyptians the furniture of the Holy of Holies was made, the ark with its cover, and the cherubim and the mercy-seat and the gold jar in which the manna, that bread of angels, was stored. These probably were made from the finest of the gold of the Egyptians, and from a second quality, perhaps, the solid golden candlestick which stood near the inner veil, and the lamps on it, and the golden table on which stood the shewbread, and between these two the golden altar of incense. And if there was gold of a third and of a fourth quality, the sacred vessels were made of it. And of the Egyptian silver, too, other things were made; for it was from their sojourn in Egypt that the children of Israel derived the great advantage of being supplied with such a quantity of precious materials for the use of the service of God. Out of the Egyptian raiment probably were made all those requisites named in Scripture in embroidered work; the embroiderers working [1] with the wisdom of God,[2] such garments for such purposes, to produce the hangings and the inner and outer courts. This is not a suitable opportunity to enlarge on such a theme or to show in how many ways the children of Israel found those things useful which they got from the Egyptians. The Egyptians had not made a proper use of them; but the Hebrews used them, for the wisdom of God was with them, for religious purposes. Holy Scripture knows, however, that it was an evil thing to descend from the land of the children of Israel into Egypt; and in this a great truth is wrapped up. For some it is of evil that they should dwell

[1] *Jahrbucher fur Prot. Theol.* 1881, 1.
[2] See *Ante-Nicene Fathers*, vol. vi.
[3] ix. 2.

[1] Reading with Dräseke, *ραφιδευόντων*, *συρραπτόντων τῶν ραφιδευτῶν*.
[2] Exod. xxxi. 3, 6; xxxvi. 1, 2, 8.

with the Egyptians, that is to say, with the learning of the world, after they have been enrolled in the law of God and in the Israelite worship of Him. Ader the Edomite,[1] as long as he was in the land of Israel and did not taste the bread of the Egyptians, made no idols; but when he fled from the wise Solomon and went down into Egypt, as one who had fled from the wisdom of God he became connected with Pharaoh, marrying the sister of his wife, and begetting a son who was brought up among the sons of Pharaoh. Therefore, though he did go back to the land of Israel, he came back to it to bring division into the people of God, and to cause them to say to the golden calf, "These are thy gods, O Israel, which brought thee up out of the land of Egypt." I have learned by experience and can tell you that there are few who have taken of the useful things of Egypt and come out of it, and have then prepared what is required for the service of God; but Ader the Edomite on the other hand has many a brother. I mean those who, founding on some piece of Greek learning, have brought forth heretical ideas, and have as it were made golden calves in Bethel, which is, being interpreted, the house of God. This appears to me to be intended to convey that such persons set up their own images in the Scriptures in which the Word of God dwells, and which therefore are tropically called Bethel. The other image is said in the word to have been set up in Dan. Now the borders of Dan are at the extremities and are contiguous to the country of the heathens, as is plainly recorded in the Book of Jesus, son of Nave. Some of these images, then, are close to the borders of the heathen, which the brothers, as we showed, of Ader have devised.

[3] 1 Kings xi. 14 (Hadad). Origen confuses him with Jeroboam.

3. PERSONAL APPEAL.

Do you then, sir, my son, study first of all the divine Scriptures. Study them I say. For we require to study the divine writings deeply, lest we should speak of them faster than we think; and while you study these divine works with a believing and God-pleasing intention, knock at that which is closed in them, and it shall be opened to thee by the porter, of whom Jesus says,[1] "To him the porter openeth." While you attend to this divine reading seek aright and with unwavering faith in God the hidden sense which is present in most passages of the divine Scriptures. And do not be content with knocking and seeking, for what is most necessary for understanding divine things is prayer, and in urging us to this the Saviour says not only,[2] "Knock, and it shall be opened to you," and "Seek, and ye shall find," but also "Ask, and it shall be given you." So much I have ventured on account of my fatherly love to you. Whether I have ventured well or not, God knows, and His Christ, and he who has part of the Spirit of God and the Spirit of Christ. May you partake in these; may you have an always increasing share of them, so that you may be able to say not only, "We are partakers of Christ,"[3] but also "We are partakers of God."

[1] John x. 3. [2] Matt. vii. 7. [3] Heb. iii. 14.

ORIGEN'S COMMENTARY ON THE GOSPEL OF JOHN

BOOK I

1. HOW CHRISTIANS ARE THE SPIRITUAL ISRAEL.

That people which was called of old the people of God was divided into twelve tribes, and over and above the other tribes it had the levitical order, which itself again carried on the service of God in various priestly and levitical sub-orders. In the same manner, it appears to me that the whole people of Christ, when we regard it in the aspect of the hidden man of the heart,[1] that people which is called "Jew inwardly," and is circumcised in the spirit, has in a more mystic way the characteristics of the tribes. This may be more plainly gathered from John in his Apocalypse, though the other prophets also do not by any means conceal the state of matters from those who have the faculty of hearing them. John speaks as follows:[2] "And I saw another angel ascending from the sunrising, having the seal of the living God, and he cried with a loud voice to the four angels to whom it was given to hurt the earth and the sea, saying, Hurt not either the earth, or the sea, or the trees, till we have sealed the servants of our God on their foreheads. And I heard the number of them that were sealed, a hundred and forty-four thousand who were sealed, out of every tribe of the children of Israel; of the tribe of Juda were sealed twelve thousand, of the tribe of Roubem twelve thousand." And he mentioned each of the tribes singly, with the exception of Dan. Then, some way further on,[3] he continues: "And I saw, and behold the Lamb standing on Mount Zion, and with Him a hundred and forty-four thousand, having His name and the name of His Father written on their foreheads. And I heard a voice from heaven as the voice of many waters, and as the voice of a great thunder. And the voice which I heard was as the voice of harpers harping with their harps; and they sing a new song before the throne and before the four beasts and the elders, and no one could learn the song but the hundred and forty-four thousand who had been purchased from the earth. These are they which were not defiled with women, for they are virgins. These are they who follow the Lamb whithersover He goeth. These were purchased from among men, a first fruits to God and to the Lamb; and in their mouth was found no lie, for they are without blemish." Now this is said in John with reference to those who have believed in Christ, for they also, even if their bodily descent cannot be traced to the seed of the Patriarchs, are yet gathered out of the tribes. That this is so we may conclude from what is further said about them: "Hurt not," he says, "the earth, nor the sea, nor the trees, till we have sealed the servants of our God on their foreheads. And I heard the number of them that were sealed, a hundred and forty-four thousand, sealed from every tribe of the children of Israel."

[1] Rom. ii. 29. [2] Apoc. vii. 2–5. [3] Apoc. xiv. 1–5.

2. THE 144,000 SEALED IN THE APOCALYPSE ARE CONVERTS TO CHRIST FROM THE GENTILE WORLD.

These, then, who are sealed on their foreheads[1] from every tribe of the children of Israel, are a hundred and forty-four thousand in number; and these hundred and forty-four thousand are afterwards said in John to have the name of the Lamb and of His Father written on their foreheads, and to be virgins, not having defiled themselves with women. What else could the seal be which is on their foreheads but the name of the Lamb and the name of His Father? In both passages their foreheads are said to have the seal; in one the seal is spoken of, in the other it appears to contain the letters forming the

[1] Apoc. vii. 3, 4.

name of the Lamb, and the name of His Father. Now these taken from the tribes are, as we showed before, the same persons as the virgins. But the number of believers is small who belong to Israel according to the flesh ; one might venture to assert that they would not nearly make up the number of a hundred and forty-four thousand. It is clear, therefore, that the hundred and forty-four thousand who have not defiled themselves with women must be made up of those who have come to the divine word out of the Gentile world. In this way the truth of the statement may be upheld that the first fruits of each tribe are its virgins. For the passage goes on : "These were brought from among men to be a first fruits to God and to the Lamb ; and in their mouth was found no guile, for they are without blemish." The statement about the hundred and forty-four thousand no doubt admits of mystical interpretation ; but it is unnecessary at this point, and would divert us from our purpose, to compare with it those passages of the prophets in which the same lesson is taught regarding those who are called from among the Gentiles.

3. IN THE SPIRITUAL ISRAEL THE HIGH-PRIESTS ARE THOSE WHO DEVOTE THEMSELVES TO THE STUDY OF SCRIPTURE.

But what is the bearing of all this for us? So you will ask when you read these words, Ambrosius, thou who art truly a man of God, a man in Christ, and who seekest to be not a man only, but a spiritual man.[1] The bearing is this. Those of the tribes offer to God, through the levites and priests, tithes and first fruits ; not everything which they possess do they regard as tithe or first fruit. The levites and priests, on the other hand, have no possessions but tithes and first fruits ; yet they also in turn offer tithes to God through the high-priests, and, I believe, first fruits too. The same is the case with those who approach Christian studies. Most of us devote most of our time to the things of this life, and dedicate to God only a few special acts, thus resembling those members of the tribes who had but few transactions with the priest, and discharged their religious duties with no great expense of time. But those who devote themselves to the divine word and have no other employment but the service of God may not unnaturally, allowing for the difference

[1] 1 Cor. ii. 14.

of occupation in the two cases, be called our levites and priests. And those who fulfil a more distinguished office than their kinsmen[1] will perhaps be high-priests, according to the order of Aaron, not that of Melchisedek. Here some one may object that it is somewhat too bold to apply the name of high-priests to men, when Jesus Himself is spoken of in many a prophetic passage as the one great priest, as[2] "We have a great high-priest who has passed through the heavens, Jesus, the Son of God." But to this we reply that the Apostle clearly defined his meaning, and declared the prophet to have said about the Christ, "Thou[3] art a priest for ever, according to the order of Melchisedek," and not according to the order of Aaron. We say accordingly that men can be high-priests according to the order of Aaron, but according to the order of Melchisedek only the Christ of God.

4. THE STUDY OF THE GOSPELS IS THE FIRST FRUITS OFFERED BY THESE PRIESTS OF CHRISTIANITY.

Now our whole activity is devoted to God, and our whole life, since we are bent on progress in divine things. If, then, it be our desire to have the whole of those first fruits spoken of above which are made up of the many first fruits, if we are not mistaken in this view, in what must our first fruits consist, after the bodily separation we have undergone from each other, but in the study of the Gospel? For we may venture to say that the Gospel is the first fruits of all the Scriptures. Where, then, could be the first fruits of our activity, since the time when we came to Alexandria, but in the first fruits of the Scriptures? It must not be forgotten, however, that the first fruits are not the same as the first growth. For the first fruits[4] are offered after all the fruits (are ripe), but the first growth[5] before them all. Now of the Scriptures which are current and are believed to be divine in all the churches, one would not be wrong in saying that the first growth is the law of Moses, but the first fruits the Gospel. For it was after all the fruits of the prophets who prophesied till the Lord Jesus, that the perfect word shot forth.

[1] Reading with Neander and Lommatzsch (note), διαφέρον τι for διαφέροντες.
[2] Heb. iv. 14.
[3] Ps. cx. 4; Heb. v. 6. Cf. vii. 11.
[4] ἀπαρχή, Exod. xxii. 29.
[5] πρωτογέννημα, Exod. xxiii. 16.

5. ALL SCRIPTURE IS GOSPEL; BUT THE GOSPELS ARE DISTINGUISHED ABOVE OTHER SCRIPTURES.

Here, however, some one may object, appealing to the notion just put forward of the unfolding of the first fruits last, and may say that the Acts and the letters of the Apostles came after the Gospels, and that this destroys our argument to the effect that the Gospel is the first fruits of all Scripture. To this we must reply that it is the conviction of men who are wise in Christ, who have profited by those epistles which are current, and who see them to be vouched for by the testimonies deposited in the law and the prophets,[1] that the apostolic writings are to be pronounced wise and worthy of belief, and that they have great authority, but that they are not on the same level with that "Thus sayeth the Lord Almighty."[2] Consider on this point the language of St. Paul. When he declares that[3] "Every Scripture is inspired of God and profitable," does he include his own writings? Or does he not include his dictum,[4] "I say, and not the Lord," and[5] "So I ordain in all the churches," and[6] "What things I suffered at Antioch, at Iconium, at Lystra," and similar things which he writes in virtue of his own authority, and which do not quite possess the character of words flowing from divine inspiration. Must we also show that the old Scripture is not Gospel, since it does not point out the Coming One, but only foretells Him and heralds His coming at a future time; but that all the new Scripture is the Gospel. It not only says as in the beginning of the Gospel,[7] "Behold the Lamb of God, which taketh away the sin of the world;" it also contains many praises of Him, and many of His teachings, on whose account the Gospel is a Gospel. Again, if God set in the Church[8] apostles and prophets and evangelists (gospellers), pastors and teachers, we must first enquire what was the office of the evangelist, and mark that it is not only to narrate how the Saviour cured a man who was blind from his birth,[9] or raised up a dead man who was already stinking,[10] or to state what extraordinary works he wrought; and the office of the evangelist being thus defined, we shall not hesitate to find Gospel in such discourse also as is not narrative but hortatory and intended to strengthen belief in the mission of Jesus; and thus we shall arrive at the position that whatever was written by the Apostles is Gospel. As to this second definition, it might be objected that the Epistles are not entitled "Gospel," and that we are wrong in applying the name of Gospel to the whole of the New Testament. But to this we answer that it happens not unfrequently in Scripture when two or more persons or things are named by the same name, the name attaches itself most significantly to one of those things or persons. Thus the Saviour says,[1] "Call no man Master upon the earth;" while the Apostle says that Masters[2] have been appointed in the Church. These latter accordingly will not be Masters in the strict sense of the dictum of the Gospel. In the same way the Gospel in the Epistles will not extend to every word of them, when it is compared with the narrative of Jesus' actions and sufferings and discourses. No: the Gospel is the first fruits of all Scripture, and to these first fruits of the Scriptures we devote the first fruits of all those actions of ours which we trust to see turn out as we desire.

[1] This passage is difficult and disputed.
[2] 2 Cor. vi. 18.
[3] 2 Tim. iii. 16.
[4] 1 Cor. vii. 12.
[5] 1 Cor. vii. 17.
[6] 2 Tim. iii. 11.
[7] John i. 29.
[8] Ephes. iv. 11.
[9] John ix. 1.
[10] John xi. 39.

6. THE FOURFOLD GOSPEL. JOHN'S THE FIRST FRUITS OF THE FOUR. QUALIFICATIONS NECESSARY FOR INTERPRETING IT.

Now the Gospels are four. These four are, as it were, the elements of the faith of the Church, out of which elements the whole world which is reconciled to God in Christ is put together; as Paul says,[3] "God was in Christ, reconciling the world to Himself;" of which world Jesus bore the sin; for it is of the world of the Church that the word is written,[4] "Behold the Lamb of God which taketh away the sin of the world." The Gospels then being four, I deem the first fruits of the Gospels to be that which you[5] have enjoined me to search into according to my powers, the Gospel of John, that which speaks of him whose genealogy had already been set forth, but which begins to speak of him at a point before he had any genealogy. For Matthew, writing for the Hebrews who looked for Him who was to come of the line of Abraham and of David, says:[6] "The book of the generation of Jesus Christ, the son of David, the son of Abraham." And Mark, knowing what he writes, narrates the beginning of the Gospel; we may perhaps find what he aims at in John; in the beginning the Word, God the Word. But Luke, though he says at the beginning of Acts, "The former treatise did I make about all that Jesus began to do and to teach," yet

[1] Matt. xxiii. 8, 9.
[2] διδάσκαλοι, Ephes. iv. 11.
[3] 2 Cor. v. 19.
[4] John i. 29.
[5] Ambrosius.
[6] Matt. i. 1.

leaves to him who lay on Jesus' breast the greatest and completest discourses about Jesus. For none of these plainly declared His Godhead, as John does when he makes Him say, "I am the light of the world," "I am the way and the truth and the life," "I am the resurrection," "I am the door," "I am the good shepherd;" and in the Apocalypse, "I am the Alpha and the Omega, the beginning and the end, the first and the last." We may therefore make bold to say that the Gospels are the first fruits of all the Scriptures, but that of the Gospels that of John is the first fruits. No one can apprehend the meaning of it except he have lain on Jesus' breast and received from Jesus Mary to be his mother also. Such an one must he become who is to be another John, and to have shown to him, like John, by Jesus Himself Jesus as He is. For if Mary, as those declare who with sound mind extol her, had no other son but Jesus, and yet Jesus says to His mother, "Woman, behold thy son,"[1] and not "Behold you have this son also," then He virtually said to her, "Lo, this is Jesus, whom thou didst bear." Is it not the case that every one who is perfect lives himself no longer,[2] but Christ lives in him; and if Christ lives in him, then it is said of him to Mary, "Behold thy son Christ." What a mind, then, must we have to enable us to interpret in a worthy manner this work, though it be committed to the earthly treasure-house of common speech, of writing which any passer-by can read, and which can be heard when read aloud by any one who lends to it his bodily ears? What shall we say of this work? He who is accurately to apprehend what it contains should be able to say with truth,[3] "We have the mind of Christ, that we may know those things which are bestowed on us by God." It is possible to quote one of Paul's sayings in support of the contention that the whole of the New Testament is Gospel. He writes in a certain place:[4] "According to my Gospel." Now we have no written work of Paul which is commonly called a Gospel. But all that he preached and said was the Gospel; and what he preached and said he was also in the habit of writing, and what he wrote was therefore Gospel. But if what Paul wrote was Gospel, it follows that what Peter wrote was also Gospel, and in a word all that was said or written to perpetuate the knowledge of Christ's sojourn on earth, and to prepare for His second coming, or to bring it about as a present reality in those souls which were willing to receive the Word of God as He stood at the door and knocked and sought to come into them.

[1] John xix. 26. [2] Gal ii. 20. [3] 1 Cor. ii. 12, 16. [4] Rom. ii. 16.

7. WHAT GOOD THINGS ARE ANNOUNCED IN THE GOSPELS.

But it is time we should inquire what is the meaning of the designation "Gospel," and why these books have this title. Now the Gospel is a discourse containing a promise of things which naturally, and on account of the benefits they bring, rejoice the hearer as soon as the promise is heard and believed. Nor is such a discourse any the less a Gospel that we define it with reference to the position of the hearer. A Gospel is either a word which implies the actual presence to the believer of something that is good, or a word promising the arrival of a good which is expected. Now all these definitions apply to those books which are named Gospels. For each of the Gospels is a collection of announcements which are useful to him who believes them and does not misinterpret them; it brings him a benefit and naturally makes him glad because it tells of the sojourn with men, on account of men, and for their salvation, of the first-born of all creation,[1] Christ Jesus. And again each Gospel tells of the sojourn of the good Father in the Son with those minded to receive Him, as is plain to every believer; and moreover by these books a good is announced which had been formerly expected, as is by no means hard to see. For John the Baptist spoke in the name almost of the whole people when he sent to Jesus and asked,[2] "Art thou He that should come or do we look for another?" For to the people the Messiah was an expected good, which the prophets had foretold, and they all alike, though under the law and the prophets, fixed their hopes on Him, as the Samaritan woman bears witness when she says:[3] "I know that the Messiah comes, who is called Christ; when He comes He will tell us all things." Simon and Cleopas too, when talking to each other about all that had happened to Jesus Christ Himself, then risen, though they did not know that He had risen, from the dead, speak thus,[4] "Dost thou sojourn alone in Jerusalem, and knowest not the things which have taken place there in these days? And when he said what things? they answered, The things concerning Jesus of Nazareth,[5] which was a prophet, mighty in

[1] Col. i. 15. [2] Matt. xi. 3. [3] John iv. 25. [4] Luke xxiv. 18–21. [5] Ναζαρηνοῦ.

deed and in word before God and all the people, and how the chief priests and our rulers delivered Him up to be sentenced to death and crucified Him. But we hoped that it was He which should redeem Israel." Again, Andrew the brother of Simon Peter found his own brother Simon and said to him,[1] "We have found the Messiah, which is, being interpreted, Christ." And a little further on Philip finds Nathanael and says to him,[2] "We have found Him of whom Moses in the law, and the prophets, wrote, Jesus the son of Joseph, from Nazareth."

8. HOW THE GOSPELS CAUSE THE OTHER BOOKS OF SCRIPTURE ALSO TO BE GOSPEL.

Now an objection might be raised to our first definition, because it would embrace books which are not entitled Gospels. For the law and the prophets also are to our eyes books containing the promise of things which, from the benefit they will confer on him, naturally rejoice the hearer as soon as he takes in the message. To this it may be said that before the sojourn of Christ, the law and the prophets, since He had not come who interpreted the mysteries they contained, did not convey such a promise as belongs to our definition of the Gospel; but the Saviour, when He sojourned with men and caused the Gospel to appear in bodily form, by the Gospel caused all things to appear as Gospel. Here I would not think it beside the purpose to quote the example of Him who . . . a few things . . . and yet all.[3] For when he had taken away the veil which was present in the law and the prophets, and by His divinity had proved the sons of men that the Godhead was at work, He opened the way for all those who desired it to be disciples of His wisdom, and to understand what things were true and real in the law of Moses, of which things those of old worshipped the type and the shadow, and what things were real of the things narrated in the histories which "happened to them in the way of type,"[4] but these things "were written for our sakes, upon whom the ends of the ages have come." With whomsoever, then, Christ has sojourned, he worships God neither at Jerusalem nor on the mountain of the Samaritans; he knows that God is a spirit, and worships Him spiritually, in spirit and in truth; no longer by type does he worship the Father and Maker of all. Before that Gospel, therefore, which came into being by the sojourning of Christ, none of the older works was a Gospel. But the Gospel, which is the new covenant, having delivered us from the oldness of the letter, lights up for us, by the light of knowledge,[1] the newness of the spirit, a thing which never grows old, which has its home in the New Testament, but is also present in all the Scriptures. It was fitting, therefore, that that Gospel, which enables us to find the Gospel present, even in the Old Testament, should itself receive, in a special sense, the name of Gospel.

[1] John i. 42. [2] John i. 46.
[3] Text defective here. The words as they stand would yield the sense, "the formula, little and yet all." [4] 1 Cor. x. 11.

9. THE SOMATIC AND THE SPIRITUAL GOSPEL.

We must not, however, forget that the sojourning of Christ with men took place before His bodily sojourn, in an intellectual fashion, to those who were more perfect and not children, and were not under pedagogues and governors. In their minds they saw the fulness of the time to be at hand—the patriarchs, and Moses the servant, and the prophets who beheld the glory of Christ. And as before His manifest and bodily coming He came to those who were perfect, so also, after His coming has been announced to all, to those who are still children, since they are under pedagogues and governors and have not yet arrived at the fulness of the time, forerunners of Christ have come to sojourn, discourses (*logoi*) suited for minds still in their childhood, and rightly, therefore, termed pedagogues. But the Son Himself, the glorified God, the Word, has not yet come; He waits for the preparation which must take place on the part of men of God who are to admit His deity. And this, too, we must bear in mind, that as the law contains a shadow of good things to come, which are indicated by that law which is announced according to truth, so the Gospel also teaches a shadow of the mysteries of Christ, the Gospel which is thought to be capable of being understood by any one. What John calls the eternal Gospel, and what may properly be called the spiritual Gospel, presents clearly to those who have the will to understand, all matters concerning the very Son of God, both the mysteries presented by His discourses and those matters of which His acts were the enigmas. In accordance with this we may conclude that, as it is with Him who is a Jew outwardly and circumcised in the flesh, so it is with the Christian and with baptism. Paul and Peter were, at an earlier period, Jews outwardly and circumcised, but later they received from Christ that they should be so

[1] γνῶσις.

in secret, too; so that outwardly they were Jews for the sake of the salvation of many, and by an economy they not only confessed in words that they were Jews, but showed it by their actions. And the same is to be said about their Christianity. As Paul could not benefit those who were Jews according to the flesh, without, when reason shows it to be necessary, circumcising Timothy, and when it appears the natural course getting himself shaved and making a vow, and, in a word, being to the Jews a Jew that he might gain the Jews—so also it is not possible for one who is responsible for the good of many to operate as he should by means of that Christianity only which is in secret. That will never enable him to improve those who are following the external Christianity, or to lead them on to better and higher things. We must, therefore, be Christians both somatically and spiritually, and where there is a call for the somatic (bodily) Gospel, in which a man says to those who are carnal that he knows nothing but Jesus Christ and Him crucified, so we must do. But should we find those who are perfected in the spirit, and bear fruit in it, and are enamoured of the heavenly wisdom, these must be made to partake of that Word which, after it was made flesh, rose again to what it was in the beginning, with God.

10. HOW JESUS HIMSELF IS THE GOSPEL.

The foregoing inquiry into the nature of the Gospel cannot be regarded as useless; it has enabled us to see what distinction there is between a sensible Gospel and an intellectual and spiritual one. What we have now to do is to transform the sensible Gospel into a spiritual one. For what would the narrative of the sensible Gospel amount to if it were not developed to a spiritual one? It would be of little account or none; any one can read it and assure himself of the facts it tells—no more. But our whole energy is now to be directed to the effort to penetrate to the deep things of the meaning of the Gospel and to search out the truth that is in it when divested of types. Now what the Gospels say is to be regarded in the light of promises of good things; and we must say that the good things the Apostles announce in this Gospel are simply Jesus. One good thing which they are said to announce is the resurrection; but the resurrection is in a manner Jesus, for Jesus says:[1] "I am the resurrection." Jesus preaches to the poor those things which are laid up for the

[1] John xi. 25.

saints, calling them to the divine promises. And the holy Scriptures bear witness to the Gospel announcements made by the Apostles and to that made by our Saviour. David says of the Apostles, perhaps also of the evangelists:[1] "The Lord shall give the word to those that preach with great power; the King of the powers of the beloved;" teaching at the same time that it is not skilfully composed discourse, nor the mode of delivery, nor well practised eloquence that produces conviction, but the communication of divine power. Hence also Paul says:[2] "I will know not the word that is puffed up, but the power; for the kingdom of God is not in word but in power." And in another passage:[3] "And my word and my preaching were not in persuasive words of wisdom, but in demonstration of the spirit and of power." To this power Simon and Cleophas bear witness when they say:[4] "Was not our heart burning within us by the way, as he opened to us the Scriptures?" And the Apostles, since the quantity of the power is great which God supplies to the speakers, had great power, according to the word of David: "The Lord will give the word to the preachers with great power." Isaiah too says:[5] "How beautiful are the feet of them that proclaim good tidings;" he sees how beautiful and how opportune was the announcement of the Apostles who walked in Him who said, "I am the way," and praises the feet of those who walk in the intellectual way of Christ Jesus, and through that door go in to God. They announce good tidings, those whose feet are beautiful, namely, Jesus.

11. JESUS IS ALL GOOD THINGS; HENCE THE GOSPEL IS MANIFOLD.

Let no one wonder if we have understood Jesus to be announced in the Gospel under a plurality of names of good things. If we look at the things by the names of which the Son of God is called, we shall understand how many good things Jesus is, whom those preach whose feet are beautiful. One good thing is life; but Jesus is the life. Another good thing is the light of the world, when it is true light, and the light of men; and all these things the Son of God is said to be. And another good thing which one may conceive to be in addition to life or light is the truth. And a fourth in addition to these is the way which leads to the truth. And all these things our Saviour teaches that He is,

[1] Ps. lxviii. 11, 12.
[2] 1 Cor. iv. 19, 20 (with a peculiar reading).
[3] 1 Cor. ii. 4. [4] Luke xxiv. 32. [5] Isa. lii. 7; Rom. x. 15.

when He says :[1] "I am the way and the truth and the life." Ah, is not that good, to shake off earth and mortality, and to rise again, obtaining this boon from the Lord, since He is the resurrection, as He says :[2] "I am the resurrection." But the door also is a good, through which one enters into the highest blessedness. Now Christ says :[3] "I am the door." And what need is there to speak of wisdom, which "the Lord created[4] the first principle of His ways, for His works," in whom the father of her rejoiced, delighting in her manifold intellectual beauty, seen by the eyes of the mind alone, and provoking him to love who discerns her divine and heavenly charm ? A good indeed is the wisdom of God, proclaimed along with the other good foresaid by those whose feet are beautiful. And the power of God is the eighth good we enumerate, which is Christ. Nor must we omit to mention the Word, who is God after the Father of all. For this also is a good, less than no other. Happy, then, are those who accept these goods and receive them from those who announce the good tidings of them, those whose feet are beautiful. Indeed even one of the Corinthians to whom Paul declared that he knew nothing but Jesus Christ and Him crucified, should he learn Him who for our sakes became man, and so receive Him, he would become identified with the beginning of the good things we have spoken of ; by the man Jesus he would be made a man of God, and by His death he would die to sin. For "Christ,[5] in that He died, died unto sin once." But from His life, since "in that He liveth, He liveth unto God," every one who is conformed to His resurrection receives that living to God. But who will deny that righteousness, essential righteousness, is a good, and essential sanctification, and essential redemption ? And these things those preach who preach Jesus, saying[6] that He is made to be of God righteousness and sanctification and redemption. Hence we shall have writings about Him without number, showing that Jesus is a multitude of goods ; for from the things which can scarcely be numbered and which have been written we may make some conjecture of those things which actually exist in Him in whom[7] "it pleased God that the whole fulness of the Godhead should dwell bodily," and which are not contained in writings. Why should I say, "are not contained in writings"? For John speaks of the whole world in this connection, and says :[1] "I suppose that not even the world itself would contain the books which would be written." Now to say that the Apostles preach the Saviour is to say that they preach these good things. For this is He who received from the good Father that He Himself should be these good things, so that each man receiving from Jesus the thing or things he is capable of receiving may enjoy good things. But the Apostles, whose feet were beautiful, and those imitators of them who sought to preach the good tidings, could not have done so had not Jesus Himself first preached the good tidings to them, as Isaiah says:[2] "I myself that speak am here, as the opportunity on the mountains, as the feet of one preaching tidings of peace, as one preaching good things ; for I will make My salvation to be heard, saying, God shall reign over thee, O Zion ! " For what are the mountains on which the speaker declares that He Himself is present, but those who are less than none of the highest and the greatest of the earth ? And these must be sought by the able ministers of the New Covenant, in order that they may observe the injunction which says :[3] Go up into a high mountain, thou that preachest good tidings to Zion ; thou that preachest good tidings to Jerusalem, lift up thy voice with strength ! " Now it is not wonderful if to those who are to preach good tidings Jesus Himself preaches good tidings of good things, which are no other than Himself ; for the Son of God preaches the good tidings of Himself to those who cannot come to know Him through others. And He who goes up into the mountains and preaches good things to them, being Himself instructed by His good Father,[4] who "makes His sun to rise on the evil and on the good, and sends rain on the just and on the unjust," He does not despise those who are poor in soul. To them He preaches good tidings, as He Himself bears witness to us when He takes Isaiah[5] and reads : "The spirit of the Lord is upon me, for the Lord hath anointed me to preach good tidings to the poor, He hath sent me to proclaim liberty to the captives, and sight to the blind. For closing the book He handed it to the minister and sat down. And when the eyes of all were fastened upon Him, He said, This day is this Scripture fulfilled in your ears."

12. THE GOSPEL CONTAINS THE ILL DEEDS ALSO WHICH WERE DONE TO JESUS.

It ought not to be forgotten that in such a

[1] John xiv. 6. [2] John xi. 25. [3] John x. 9.
[4] Prov. viii 22. [5] Rom. vi. 10. [6] Cor. i. 30.
[7] Coloss. i. 19 ; ii. 9.

[1] John xxi. 25. [2] Isa. lii. 6. [3] Isa. xl. 9.
[4] Matt. v. 45. [5] Luke iv. 18 sq.

Gospel as this there is embraced every good deed which was done to Jesus; as, for example, the story of the woman[1] who had been a sinner and had repented, and who, having experienced a genuine recovery from her evil state, had grace to pour her ointment over Jesus so that every one in the house smelt the sweet savour. Hence, too, the words, "Wherever this Gospel shall be preached among all the nations, there also this that she has done shall be spoken of, for a memorial of her." And it is clear that whatever is done to the disciples of Jesus is done to Him. Pointing to those of them who met with kind treatment, He says to those who were kind to them,[2] "What ye did to these, ye did to Me." So that every good deed we do to our neighbours is entered in the Gospel, that Gospel which is written on the heavenly tablets and read by all who are worthy of the knowledge of the whole of things. But on the other side, too, there is a part of the Gospel which is for the condemnation of the doers of the ill deeds which have been done to Jesus. The treachery of Judas and the shouts of the wicked crowd when it said,[3] "Away with such a one from the earth," and "Crucify Him, crucify Him," the mockings of those who crowned Him with thorns, and everything of that kind, is included in the Gospels. And as a consequence of this we see that every one who betrays the disciples of Jesus is reckoned as betraying Jesus Himself. To Saul,[4] when still a persecutor, it is said, "Saul, Saul, why persecutest thou Me?" and, "I am Jesus whom thou persecutest." There are those who still have thorns with which they crown and dishonour Jesus, those, namely, who are choked by the cares, and riches, and pleasures of life, and though they have received the word of God, do not bring it to perfection.[5] We must beware, therefore, lest we also, as crowning Jesus with thorns of our own, should be entered in the Gospel and read of in this character by those who learn the Jesus, who is in all and is present in all rational and holy lives, learn how He is anointed with ointment, is entertained, is glorified, or how, on the other side, He is dishonoured, and mocked, and beaten. All this had to be said; it is part of our demonstration that our good actions, and also the sins of those who stumble, are embodied in the Gospel, either to everlasting life or to reproach and everlasting shame.

[1] Matt. xxvi. 6–13, combined with Luke vii. 36–50.
[2] Matt. xxv. 40.
[3] John xix. 6, 15.
[4] Acts ix. 4, 5.
[5] Luke viii. 14.

13. THE ANGELS ALSO ARE EVANGELISTS.

Now if there are those among men who are honoured with the ministry of evangelists, and if Jesus Himself brings tidings of good things, and preaches the Gospel to the poor, surely those messengers who were made spirits by God,[1] those who are a flame of fire, ministers of the Father of all, cannot have been excluded from being evangelists also. Hence an angel standing over the shepherds made a bright light to shine round about them, and said:[2] "Fear not; behold I bring you good tidings of great joy, which shall be to all the people; for there is born to you, this day, a Saviour, who is Christ the Lord, in the city of David." And at a time when there was no knowledge among men of the mystery of the Gospel, those who were greater than men and inhabitants of heaven, the army of God, praised God, saying, "Glory to God in the highest, and on earth peace, good will among men."[3] And having said this, the angels go away from the shepherds into heaven, leaving us to gather how the joy preached to us through the birth of Jesus Christ is glory in the highest to God; they humbled themselves even to the ground, and then returned to their place of rest, to glorify God in the highest through Jesus Christ. But the angels also wonder at the peace which is to be brought about on account of Jesus on the earth, that seat of war, on which Lucifer, star of the morning, fell from heaven, to be warred against and destroyed by Jesus.

14. THE OLD TESTAMENT, TYPIFIED BY JOHN, IS THE BEGINNING OF THE GOSPEL.

In addition to what we have said, there is also this to be considered about the Gospel, that in the first instance it is that of Christ Jesus, the head of the whole body of the saved; as Mark says,[4] "The beginning of the Gospel of Jesus Christ." Then also it is the Gospel of the Apostles; whence Paul[5] says, "According to my Gospel." But the beginning of the Gospel—for in respect of its extent it has a beginning, a continuation, a middle, and an end—is nothing but the whole Old Testament. John is, in this respect, a type of the Old Testament, or, if we regard the connection of the New Testament with the Old, John represents the termination of the Old. For the same Mark says:[6] "The beginning of the Gospel of Jesus Christ, as it is written in Isaiah the prophet, Behold I send my messenger be-

[1] Ps. civ. 4.
[2] Luke ii. 10, 11.
[3] Origen, however, appears also to have read εὐδοκιας: "among men of good will."
[4] Mark i. 1.
[5] Rom. ii. 16.
[6] i. 2, 3.

fore thy face, who shall prepare thy way. The voice of one crying in the wilderness, Prepare ye the way of the Lord, make His paths straight." And here I must wonder how the dissentients[1] can connect the two Testaments with two different Gods. These words, were there no others, are enough to convict them of their error. For how can John be the beginning of the Gospel if they suppose he belongs to a different God, if he belongs to the demiurge, and, as they hold, is not acquainted with the new deity? And the angels are not entrusted with but one evangelical ministry, and that a short one, not only with that addressed to the shepherds. For at the end an exalted and flying angel, having the Gospel, will preach it to every nation, for the good Father has not entirely deserted those who have fallen away from Him. John, son of Zebedee, says in his Apocalypse:[2] "And I saw an angel flying in the midst of heaven, having the Eternal Gospel, to preach it to those who dwell upon the earth, and to every nation, and tribe, and tongue, and people, saying, with a loud voice, Fear God and give Him glory, for the hour of His judgment hath come, and worship Him that made the heaven, and the earth, and the sea, and the fountains of waters."

15. THE GOSPEL IS IN THE OLD TESTAMENT, AND INDEED IN THE WHOLE UNIVERSE. PRAYER FOR AID TO UNDERSTAND THE MYSTICAL SENSE OF THE WORK IN HAND.

As, then, we have shown that the beginning of the Gospel, according to one interpretation, is the whole Old Testament, and is signified by the person of John, we shall add, lest this should be called a mere unsupported assertion, what is said in the Acts about the eunuch of the queen of the Ethiopians and Philip. Philip, it is said, began at the passage of Isaiah: "He was led as a lamb to the slaughter, and as a lamb before his shearer is dumb," and so preached to him the Lord Jesus. How can he begin with the prophet and preach Jesus, if Isaiah was not a part of the beginning of the Gospel? From this we may derive a proof of the assertion made at the outset, that every divine Scripture is Gospel. If he who preaches the Gospel preaches good things, and all those who spoke before the sojourn of Jesus in the flesh preach Christ, who is as we saw good things, then the words spoken by all of them alike are in a sense a part of the Gospel. And when the Gospel is said to be declared throughout the whole world, we infer that it is actually preached in the whole world, not, that is to say, in this earthly district only, but in the whole system of heaven and earth, or from heaven and earth. And why should we discuss any further what the Gospel is? What we have said is enough. Besides the passages we have adduced,—passages by no means inept or unsuited for our purpose,—much to the same effect might be collected from the Scriptures, so that it is clearly seen what is the glory of the good things in Jesus Christ shed forth by the Gospel, the Gospel ministered by men and angels, and, I believe, also by authorities and powers,[1] and thrones and dominions, and every name that is named, not only in this world, but also in the world to come, and indeed even by Christ Himself. Here, then, let us bring to a close what has to be said before proceeding to read the work itself. And now let us ask God to assist us through Jesus Christ by the Holy Spirit, so that we may be able to unfold the mystical sense which is treasured up in the words before us.

16. MEANING OF "BEGINNING." (1) IN SPACE.

"*In the beginning was the Word.*"[2] It is not only the Greeks who consider the word "beginning" to have many meanings. Let any one collect the Scripture passages in which the word occurs, and with a view to an accurate interpretation of it note what it stands for in each passage, and he will find that the word has many meanings in sacred discourse also. We speak of a beginning in reference to a transition. Here it has to do with a road and with length. This appears in the saying:[3] "The beginning of a good way is to do justice." For since the good way is long, there have first to be considered in reference to it the question connected with action, and this side is presented in the words "to do justice;" the contemplative side comes up for consideration afterwards. In the latter the end of it comes to rest at last in the so-called restoration of all things, since no enemy is left them to fight against, if that be true which is said:[4] "For He must reign until He have placed His enemies under His feet. But the last enemy to be destroyed is death." For then but one activity will be left for those who have come to God on account of His word which is with Him, that, namely, of

[1] ἑτερόδοξοι. [2] Apoc. xiv. 6, 7. [3] Acts viii. 26, sqq.

[1] Ephes. i. 21. [2] John i. 1. [3] Prov. xvi. 5. [4] 1 Cor. xv. 25, 26.

knowing God, so that, being found by the knowledge of the Father, they may all be His Son, as now no one but the Son knows the Father. For should any one enquire carefully at what time those are to know the Father to whom He who knows the Father reveals Him, and should he consider how a man now sees only through a glass and in a riddle, never having learned to know as he ought to know, he would be justified in saying that no one, no apostle even, and no prophet had known the Father, but when he became one with Him as a son and a father are one. And if any one says that it is a digression which has led us to this point, our consideration of that one meaning of the word beginning, we must show that the digression is necessary and useful for the end we have in view. For if we speak of a beginning in the case of a transition, and of a way and its length, and if we are told that the beginning of a good way is to do justice, then it concerns us to know in what manner every good way has for its beginning to do justice, and how after such beginning it arrives at contemplation, and in what manner it thus arrives at contemplation.

17. (2) IN TIME. THE BEGINNING OF CREATION.

Again, there is a beginning in a matter of origin, as might appear in the saying:[1] "In the beginning God made the heaven and the earth." This meaning, however, appears more plainly in the Book of Job in the passage:[2] "This is the beginning of God's creation, made for His angels to mock at." One would suppose that the heavens and the earth were made first, of all that was made at the creation of the world. But the second passage suggests a better view, namely, that as many beings were framed with a body, the first made of these was the creature called dragon, but called in another passage[3] the great whale (leviathan) which the Lord tamed. We must ask about this; whether, when the saints were living a blessed life apart from matter and from any body, the dragon, falling from the pure life, became fit to be bound in matter and in a body, so that the Lord could say, speaking through storm and clouds, "This is the beginning of the creation of God, made for His angels to mock at." It is possible, however, that the dragon is not positively the beginning of the creation of the Lord, but that there were many creatures made with a body for the angels to mock at, and that the dragon was the first of these, while others could subsist in a body without such reproach. But it is not so. For the soul of the sun is placed in a body, and the whole creation, of which the Apostle says:[1] "The whole creation groaneth and travaileth in pain together until now," and perhaps the following is about the same: "The creation was made subject to vanity, not willingly, but on account of Him who subjected it for hope;" so that bodies might be in vanity, and doing the things of the body, as he who is in the body must.[2] . . . One who is in the body does the things of the body, though unwillingly. Wherefore the creation was made subject to vanity, not willingly, but he who does unwillingly the things of the body does what he does for the sake of hope, as if we should say that Paul desired to remain in the flesh, not willingly, but on account of hope. For though he thought it better[3] to be dissolved and to be with Christ, it was not unreasonable that he should wish to remain in the flesh for the sake of the benefit to others and of advancement in the things hoped for, not only by him, but also by those benefited by him. This meaning of the term "beginning," as of origin, will serve us also in the passage in which Wisdom speaks in the Proverbs.[4] "God," we read, "created me the beginning of His ways, for His works." Here the term could be interpreted as in the first application we spoke of, that of a way: "The Lord," it says, "created me the beginning of His ways." One might assert, and with reason, that God Himself is the beginning of all things, and might go on to say, as is plain, that the Father is the beginning of the Son; and the demiurge the beginning of the works of the demiurge, and that God in a word is the beginning of all that exists. This view is supported by our: "In the beginning was the Word." In the Word one may see the Son, and because He is in the Father He may be said to be in the beginning.

18. (3) OF SUBSTANCE.

In the third place a beginning may be that out of which a thing comes, the underlying matter from which things are formed. This, however, is the view of those who hold matter itself to be uncreated, a view which we believers cannot share, since we believe God to have made the things that are out of the things which are not, as the

[1] Gen. i. 1. [2] Job xl. 19. [3] Job iii. 8.

[1] Rom. viii. 22, 20. [2] The text is defective here. [3] Phil. i. 23. [4] viii. 22.

mother of the seven martyrs in the Maccabees teaches,[1] and as the angel of repentance in the Shepherd inculcated.[2]

19. (4) OF TYPE AND COPY.

In addition to these meanings there is that in which we speak of an arche,[3] according to form; thus if the first-born of every creature[4] is the image of the invisible God, then the Father is his arche. In the same way Christ is the arche of those who are made according to the image of God. For if men are according to the image, but the image according to the Father; in the first case the Father is the arche of Christ, and in the other Christ is the arche of men, and men are made, not according to that of which he is the image, but according to the image. With this example our passage will agree: "In the arche was the Word."

20. (5) OF ELEMENTS AND WHAT IS FORMED FROM THEM.

There is also an arche in a matter of learning, as when we say that the letters are the arche of grammar. The Apostle accordingly says:[5] "When by reason of the time you ought to be teachers, you have need again that some one teach you what are the elements of the arche of the oracles of God." Now the arche spoken of in connection with learning is twofold; first in respect of its nature, secondly in its relation to us; as we might say of Christ, that by nature His arche is deity, but that in relation to us who cannot, for its very greatness, command the whole truth about Him, His arche is His manhood, as He is preached to babes, "Jesus Christ and Him crucified." In this view, then, Christ is the arche of learning in His own nature, because He is the wisdom and power of God; but for us, the Word was made flesh, that He might tabernacle among us who could only thus at first receive Him. And perhaps this is the reason why He is not only the firstborn of all creation, but is also designated the man, Adam. For Paul says He is Adam:[6] "The last Adam was made a life-giving spirit."

21. (6) OF DESIGN AND EXECUTION.

Again we speak of the arche of an action, in which there is a design which appears after the beginning. It may be considered whether wisdom is to be regarded as the arche of the works of God because it is in this way the principle of them.

[1] 2 Macc. vii. 28. [2] Herm. Sim. viii.
[3] We must here reproduce the Greek word, as Origen passes to meanings of it which the English "beginning" does not cover.
[4] Coloss. i. 15. [5] Heb. v. 12. [6] 1 Cor. xv. 45.

22. THE WORD WAS IN THE BEGINNING, I.E., IN WISDOM, WHICH CONTAINED ALL THINGS IN IDEA, BEFORE THEY EXISTED. CHRIST'S CHARACTER AS WISDOM IS PRIOR TO HIS OTHER CHARACTERS.

So many meanings occur to us at once of the word arche. We have now to ask which of them we should adopt for our text, "In the beginning was the Word." It is plain that we may at once dismiss the meaning which connects it with transition or with a road and its length. Nor, it is pretty plain, will the meaning connected with an origin serve our purpose. One might, however, think of the sense in which it points to the author, to that which brings about the effect, if, as we read,[1] "God commanded and they were created." For Christ is, in a manner, the demiurge, to whom the Father says, "Let there be light," and "Let there be a firmament." But Christ is demiurge as a beginning (arche), inasmuch as He is wisdom. It is in virtue of His being wisdom that He is called arche. For Wisdom says in Solomon:[2] "God created me the beginning of His ways, for His works," so that the Word might be in an arche, namely, in wisdom. Considered in relation to the structure of contemplation and thoughts about the whole of things, it is regarded as wisdom; but in relation to that side of the objects of thought, in which reasonable beings apprehend them, it is considered as the Word. And there is no wonder, since, as we have said before, the Saviour is many good things, if He comprises in Himself thoughts of the first order, and of the second, and of the third. This is what John suggested when he said about the Word:[3] "That which was made was life in Him." Life then came in the Word. And on the one side the Word is no other than the Christ, the Word, He who was with the Father, by whom all things were made; while, on the other side, the Life is no other than the Son of God, who says:[4] "I am the way and the truth and the life." As, then, life came into being in the Word, so the Word in the arche. Consider, however, if we are at liberty to take this meaning of arche for our text: "In the beginning was the Word," so as to obtain the meaning that all things came into being according to wisdom and according to the models of the system which are present in his thoughts. For I consider that as a house or a ship is built and fashioned in accordance with the sketches of the builder or designer,

[1] Ps. cxlviii. 5. [2] Prov. viii. 22.
[3] John i. 3, 4. [4] John xiv. 6.

the house or the ship having their beginning (arche) in the sketches and reckonings in his mind, so all things came into being in accordance with the designs of what was to be, clearly laid down by God in wisdom. And we should add that having created, so to speak, ensouled[1] wisdom, He left her to hand over, from the types which were in her, to things existing and to matter, the actual emergence of them, their moulding and their forms.[2] But I consider, if it be permitted to say this, that the beginning (arche) of real existence was the Son of God, saying:[3] "I am the beginning and the end, the *A* and the *Ω*, the first and the last." We must, however, remember that He is not the arche in respect of every name which is applied to Him. For how can He be the beginning in respect of His being life, when life came in the Word, and the Word is manifestly the arche of life? It is also tolerably evident that He cannot be the arche in respect of His being the first-born from the dead. And if we go through all His titles carefully we find that He is the arche only in respect of His being wisdom. Not even as the Word is He the arche, for the Word was in the arche. And so one might venture to say that wisdom is anterior to all the thoughts that are expressed in the titles of the first-born of every creature. Now God is altogether one and simple; but our Saviour, for many reasons, since God[4] set Him forth a propitiation and a first fruits of the whole creation, is made many things, or perhaps all these things; the whole creation, so far as capable of redemption, stands in need of Him.[5] And, hence, He is made the light of men, because men, being darkened by wickedness, need the light that shines in darkness, and is not overtaken by the darkness; had not men been in darkness, He would not have become the light of men. The same thing may be observed in respect of His being the first-born of the dead. For supposing the woman had not been deceived, and Adam had not fallen, and man created for incorruption had obtained it, then He would not have descended into the grave, nor would He have died, there being no sin, nor would His love of men have required that He should die, and if He had not died, He could not have been the first-born of the dead. We may also ask whether He would ever have become a shepherd, had man not been thrown together with the beasts which are devoid of reason, and made like to them. For if God saves man and beasts, He saves those beasts which He does save, by giving them a shepherd, since they cannot have a king. Thus if we collect the titles of Jesus, the question arises which of them were conferred on Him later, and would never have assumed such importance if the saints had begun and had also persevered in blessedness. Perhaps Wisdom would be the only remaining one, or perhaps the Word would remain too, or perhaps the Life, or perhaps the Truth, not the others, which He took for our sake. And happy indeed are those who in their need for the Son of God have yet become such persons as not to need Him in His character as a physician healing the sick, nor in that of a shepherd, nor in that of redemption, but only in His characters as wisdom, as the word and righteousness, or if there be any other title suitable for those who are so perfect as to receive Him in His fairest characters. So much for the phrase "In the beginning."

23. THE TITLE "WORD" IS TO BE INTERPRETED BY THE SAME METHOD AS THE OTHER TITLES OF CHRIST. THE WORD OF GOD IS NOT A MERE ATTRIBUTE OF GOD, BUT A SEPARATE PERSON. WHAT IS MEANT WHEN HE IS CALLED THE WORD.

Let us consider, however, a little more carefully what is the Word which is in the beginning. I am often led to wonder when I consider the things that are said about Christ, even by those who are in earnest in their belief in Him. Though there is a countless number of names which can be applied to our Saviour, they omit the most of them, and if they should remember them, they declare that these titles are not to be understood in their proper sense, but tropically. But when they come to the title Logos (Word), and repeat that Christ alone is the Word of God, they are not consistent, and do not, as in the case of the other titles, search out what is behind the meaning of the term "Word." I wonder at the stupidity of the general run of Christians in this matter. I do not mince matters; it is nothing but stupidity. The Son of God says in one passage, "I am the light of the world," and in another, "I am the resurrection," and again, "I am the way and the truth and the life." It is also written, "I am the door," and we have the saying, "I am the good shepherd," and when the woman of Samaria says, "We know the

[1] Opp. to embodied.
[2] Mr. Brooke, *T. & S.* I. iv. p. 15, discusses this corrupt passage and suggests an improved text which would yield the sense, that wisdom was to give to things and matter, "it might be rash to say bluntly their essences, but their moulding and their forms."
[3] Apoc. xxii. 13.
[4] Rom. iii. 25.
[5] Passage obscure and probably corrupt.

Messiah is coming, who is called Christ; when He comes, He will tell us all things," Jesus answers, "I that speak unto thee am He." Again, when He washed the disciples' feet, He declared Himself in these words [1] to be their Master and Lord: "You call Me Master and Lord, and you say well, for so I am." He also distinctly announces Himself as the Son of God, when He says,[2] "He whom the Father sanctified and sent unto the world, to Him do you say, Thou blasphemest, because I said, I am the Son of God?" and [3] "Father, the hour is come; glorify Thy Son, that the Son also may glorify Thee." We also find Him declaring Himself to be a king, as when He answers Pilate's question,[4] "Art Thou the King of the Jews?" by saying, "My kingdom is not of this world; if My kingdom were of this world, then would My servants fight, that I should not be delivered to the Jews, but now is My kingdom not from hence." We have also read the words,[5] "I am the true vine and My Father is the husbandman," and again, "I am the vine, ye are the branches." Add to these testimonies also the saying,[6] "I am the bread of life, that came down from heaven and giveth life to the world." These texts will suffice for the present, which we have picked up out of the storehouse of the Gospels, and in all of which He claims to be the Son of God. But in the Apocalypse of John, too, He says,[7] "I am the first and the last, and the living One, and I was dead. Behold, I am alive for evermore." And again,[8] "I am the *A* and the *Ω*, and the first and the last, the beginning and the end." The careful student of the sacred books, moreover, may gather not a few similar passages from the prophets, as where He calls Himself[9] a chosen shaft, and a servant of God,[10] and a light of the Gentiles.[11] Isaiah also says,[12] "From my mother's womb hath He called me by my name, and He made my mouth as a sharp sword, and under the shadow of His hand did He hide me, and He said to me, Thou art My servant, O Israel, and in thee will I be glorified." And a little farther on: "And my God shall be my strength, and He said to me, This is a great thing for thee to be called My servant, to set up the tribes of Jacob and to turn again the diaspora of Israel. Behold I have set thee for a light of the Gentiles, that thou shouldest be for salvation to the end of the earth." And in

1 John xiii. 13.
2 John x. 36.
3 John xvii. 1.
4 John xviii. 33, 36.
5 John xv. 1, 5.
6 John vi. 35, 41, 33.
7 Apoc. i. 18.
8 Apoc. xxii. 13.
9 Isa. xlix. 2.
10 Isa. xlii. 1, etc.
11 Isa. xlix. 6.
12 Isa. xlix. 1, 2, 3.

Jeremiah too [1] He likens Himself to a lamb, as thus: "I was as a gentle lamb that is led to the slaughter." These and other similar sayings He applies to Himself. In addition to these one might collect in the Gospels and the Apostles and in the prophets a countless number of titles which are applied to the Son of God, as the writers of the Gospels set forth their own views of what He is, or the Apostles extol Him out of what they had learned, or the prophets proclaim in advance His coming advent and announce the things concerning Him under various names. Thus John calls Him the Lamb of God, saying,[2] "Behold the Lamb of God which taketh away the sins of the world," and in these words he declares Him as a man,[3] "This is He about whom I said, that there cometh after me a man who is there before me; for He was before me." And in his Catholic Epistle John says that He is a Paraclete for our souls with the Father, as thus:[4] "And if any one sin, we have a Paraclete with the Father, Jesus Christ the righteous," and he adds that He is a propitiation for our sins, and similarly Paul says He is a propitiation:[5] "Whom God set forth as a propitiation through faith in His blood, on account of forgiveness of the forepast sins, in the forbearance of God." According to Paul, too, He is declared to be the wisdom and the power of God, as in the Epistle to the Corinthians:[6] "Christ the power of God and the wisdom of God." It is added that He is also sanctification and redemption: "He was made to us of God," he says, "wisdom and righteousness and sanctification and redemption." But he also teaches us, writing to the Hebrews, that Christ is a High-Priest:[7] "Having, therefore, a great High-Priest, who has passed through the heavens, Jesus the Son of God, let us hold fast our profession." And the prophets have other names for Him besides these. Jacob in his blessing of his sons [8] says, "Judah, thy brethren shall extol thee; thy hands are on the necks of thine enemies. A lion's whelp is Judah, from a shoot, my son, art thou sprung up; thou hast lain down and slept as a lion; who shall awaken him?" We cannot now linger over these phrases, to show that what is said of Judah applies to Christ. What may be quoted against this view, viz., "A ruler shall not part from Judah nor a leader from his loins, until He come for whom it is reserved;" this can better be cleared up on another occa-

1 Jerem. xi. 19.
2 John i. 29.
3 John i. 30, 31.
4 1 John ii. 1, ἱλασμός.
5 Rom. iii. 25, 26, ἱλαστήριον.
6 1 Cor. i. 24, 30.
7 Heb. iv. 14.
8 Gen. xlix. 10.

sion. But Isaiah knows Christ to be spoken of under the names of Jacob and Israel, when he says,[1] "Jacob is my servant, I will help Him; Israel is my elect, my soul hath accepted Him. He shall declare judgment to the Gentiles. He shall not strive nor cry, neither shall any one hear His voice on the streets. A bruised rod shall He not break, and smoking flax shall He not quench, till He bring forth judgment from victory, and in His name shall the nations hope." That it is Christ about whom such prophecies are made, Matthew shows in his Gospel, where he quotes from memory and says:[2] "That the saying might be fulfilled, He shall not strive nor cry," etc. David also is called Christ, as where Ezekiel in his prophecy to the shepherds adds as from the mouth of God:[3] "I will raise up David my servant, who shall be their shepherd." For it is not the patriarch David who is to rise and be the shepherd of the saints, but Christ. Isaiah also called Christ the rod and the flower:[4] "There shall come forth a rod out of the root of Jesse, and a flower shall spring out of his root, and the spirit of God shall rest upon Him, the spirit of wisdom and understanding, the spirit of counsel and of might, the spirit of knowledge and of godliness, and He shall be full of the spirit of the fear of the Lord." And in the Psalms our Lord is called the stone, as follows:[5] "The stone which the builders rejected is made the head of the corner. It is from the Lord, and it is wonderful in our eyes." And the Gospel shows, as also does Luke in the Acts, that the stone is no other than Christ; the Gospel as follows:[6] "Have ye never read, the stone which the builders rejected is made the head of the corner. Whosoever falls on this stone shall be broken, but on whomsoever it shall fall, it will scatter him as dust." And Luke writes in Acts:[7] "This is the stone, which was set at naught of you the builders, which has become the head of the corner." And one of the names applied to the Saviour is that which He Himself does not utter, but which John records;—the Word who was in the beginning with God, God the Word. And it is worth our while to fix our attention for a moment on those scholars who omit consideration of most of the great names we have mentioned and regard this as the most important one. As to the former titles, they look for any account of them that any one may offer, but in the case of this one they proceed differently and ask, What is the Son of God when called the Word? The passage they employ most is that in the Psalms,[1] "My heart hath produced a good Word;" and they imagine the Son of God to be the utterance of the Father deposited, as it were, in syllables, and accordingly they do not allow Him, if we examine them farther, any independent hypostasis, nor are they clear about His essence. I do not mean that they confuse its qualities, but the fact of His having an essence of His own. For no one can understand how that which is said to be "Word" can be a Son. And such an animated Word, not being a separate entity from the Father, and accordingly as it, having no subsistence, is not a Son, or if he is a Son, let them say that God the Word is a separate being and has an essence of His own. We insist, therefore, that as in the case of each of the titles spoken of above we turn from the title to the concept it suggests and apply it and demonstrate how the Son of God is suitably described by it, the same course must be followed when we find Him called the Word. What caprice it is, in all these cases, not to stand upon the term employed, but to enquire in what sense Christ is to be understood to be the door, and in what way the vine, and why He is the way; but in the one case of His being called the Word, to follow a different course. To add to the authority, therefore, of what we have to say on the question, how the Son of God is the Word, we must begin with those names of which we spoke first as being applied to Him. This, we cannot deny, will seem to some to be superfluous and a digression, but the thoughtful reader will not think it useless to ask as to the concepts for which the titles are used; to observe these matters will clear the way for what is coming. And once we have entered upon the theology concerning the Saviour, as we seek with what diligence we can and find the various things that are taught about Him, we shall necessarily understand more about Him not only in His character as the Word, but in His other characters also.

24. CHRIST AS LIGHT; HOW HE, AND HOW HIS DISCIPLES ARE THE LIGHT OF THE WORLD.

He said, then, that He was the light of the world; and we have to examine, along with this title, those which are parallel to it; and, indeed, are thought by some to be not merely parallel, but identical with

[1] Isa. xlii. 1-4. [2] Matt. xii. 17, 19. [3] Ezek. xxxiv. 23. [4] Isa. xi. 1-3. [5] Ps. cxviii. 22, 23. [6] Matt. xxi. 42, 44. [7] Acts iv. 11.

[1] Ps. xlv. 1.

it. He is the true light, and the light of the Gentiles. In the opening of the Gospel now before us He is the light of men: "That which was made,"[1] it says, "was life in Him, and the life was the light of men; and the light shines in darkness, and the darkness did not overtake it." A little further on, in the same passage, He is called the true light:[2] "The true light, which lightens every man, was coming into the world." In Isaiah, He is the light of the Gentiles, as we said before. "Behold,[3] I have set Thee for a light of the Gentiles, that Thou shouldest be for salvation to the end of the earth." Now the sensible light of the world is the sun, and after it comes very worthily the moon, and the same title may be applied to the stars; but those lights of the world are said in Moses to have come into existence on the fourth day, and as they shed light on the things on the earth, they are not the true light. But the Saviour shines on creatures which have intellect and sovereign reason, that their minds may behold their proper objects of vision, and so he is the light of the intellectual world, that is to say, of the reasonable souls which are in the sensible world, and if there be any beings beyond these in the world from which He declares Himself to be our Saviour. He is, indeed, the most determining and distinguished part of that world, and, as we may say, the sun who makes the great day of the Lord. In view of this day He says to those who partake of His light, "Work[4] while it is day; the night cometh when no man can work. As long as I am in the world, I am the light of the world." Then He says to His disciples,[5] "Ye are the light of the world," and "Let your light shine before men." Thus we see the Church, the bride, to present an analogy to the moon and stars, and the disciples have a light, which is their own or borrowed from the true sun, so that they are able to illuminate those who have no command of any spring of light in themselves. We may say that Paul and Peter are the light of the world, and that those of their disciples who are enlightened themselves, but are not able to enlighten others, are the world of which the Apostles were the light. But the Saviour, being the light of the world, illuminates not bodies, but by His incorporeal power the incorporeal intellect, to the end that each of us, enlightened as by the sun, may be able to discern the rest of the things of the mind. And as when the sun is shining the moon

[1] John i. 3-5. [2] John i. 9. [3] Isa. xlix. 6.
[4] John ix. 4, 5. [5] Matt. v. 14, 16.

and the stars lose their power of giving light, so those who are irradiated by Christ and receive His beams have no need of the ministering apostles and prophets—we must have courage to declare this truth—nor of the angels; I will add that they have no need even of the greater powers when they are disciples of that first-born light. To those who do not receive the solar beams of Christ, the ministering saints do afford an illumination much less than the former; this illumination is as much as those persons can receive, and it completely fills them. Christ, again, the light of the world, is the true light as distinguished from the light of sense; nothing that is sensible is true. Yet though the sensible is other than the true, it does not follow that the sensible is false, for the sensible may have an analogy with the intellectual, and not everything that is not true can correctly be called false. Now I ask whether the light of the world is the same thing with the light of men, and I conceive that a higher power of light is intended by the former phrase than by the latter, for the world in one sense is not only men. Paul shows that the world is something more than men when he writes to the Corinthians in his first Epistle:[1] "We are made a spectacle unto the world, and to angels, and to men." In one sense, too, it may be considered,[2] the world is the creation which is being delivered from the bondage of corruption into the liberty of the glory of the children of God, whose earnest expectation is waiting for the manifestation of the sons of God. We also draw attention to the comparison which may be drawn between the statement, "I am the light of the world," and the words addressed to the disciples, "Ye are the light of the world." Some suppose that the genuine disciples of Jesus are greater than other creatures, some seeking the reason of this in the natural growth of these disciples, others inferring it from their harder struggle. For those beings which are in flesh and blood have greater labours and a life more full of dangers than those which are in an ethereal body, and the lights of heaven might not, if they had put on bodies of earth, have accomplished this life of ours free from danger and from error. Those who incline to this argument may appeal to those texts of Scripture which say the most exalted things about men, and to the fact that the Gospel is addressed directly to men; not so much is said about the creation, or, as we understand it, about the

[1] 1 Cor. iv. 9. [2] Rom. viii. 24, 19.

world. We read, [1] "As I and Thou are one, that they also may be one in Us," and [2] "Where I am, there will also My servant be." These sayings, plainly, are about men; while about the creation it is said that it is delivered from the bondage of corruption into the liberty of the glory of the children of God. It might be added that not even when it is delivered will it take part in the glory of the sons of God. Nor will those who hold this view forget that the first-born of every creature, honouring man above all else, became man, and that it was not any of the constellations existing in the sky, but one of another order, appointed for this purpose and in the service of the knowledge of Jesus, that was made to be the Star of the East, whether it was like the other stars or perchance better than they, to be the sign of Him who is the most excellent of all. And if the boasting of the saints is in their tribulations, since [3] "tribulation worketh patience, and patience probation, and probation hope, and hope maketh not ashamed," then the afflicted creation cannot have the like patience with man, nor the like probation, nor the like hope, but another degree of these, since [4] "the creation was made subject to vanity, not willingly, but on account of Him who subjected it, for hope." Now he who shrinks from conferring such great attributes on man will turn to another direction and say that the creature being subjected to vanity groans and suffers greater affliction than those who groan in this tabernacle, for has she not suffered for the utmost extent of time in her service of vanity—nay, many times as long as man? For why does she do this not willingly, but that it is against her nature to be subject to vanity, and not to have the best arrangement of her life, that which she shall receive when she is set free, when the world is destroyed and released even from the vanity of bodies. Here, however, we may appear to be stretching too far, and aiming at more than the question now before us requires. We may return, therefore, to the point from which we set out, and ask for what reason the Saviour is called the light of the world, the true light, and the light of men. Now we saw that He is called the true light with reference to the sensible light of the world, and that the light of the world is the same thing as the light of men, or that we may at least enquire whether they are the same. This discussion is not superfluous. Some students do not take anything at all out of the statement that the Saviour is the Word; and it is important for us to assure ourselves that we are not chargeable with caprice in fixing our attention on that notion. If it admits of being taken in a metaphorical sense we ought not to take it literally.[1] When we apply the mystical and allegorical method to the expression "light of the world" and the many analogous terms mentioned above, we should surely do so with this expression also.

25. CHRIST AS THE RESURRECTION.

Now He is called the light of men and the true light and the light of the word, because He brightens and irradiates the higher parts of men, or, in a word, of all reasonable beings. And similarly it is from and because of the energy with which He causes the old deadness to be put aside and that which is *par excellence* life to be put on, so that those who have truly received Him rise again from the dead, that He is called the resurrection. And this He does not only at the moment at which a man says,[2] "We are buried with Christ through baptism and have risen again with Him," but much rather when a man, having laid off all about him that belongs to death, walks in the newness of life which belongs to Him, the Son, while here. We always [3] "carry about in our body the dying of the Lord Jesus," and thus we reap the vast advantage, "that the life of the Lord Jesus might be made manifest in our bodies."

26. CHRIST AS THE WAY.

But that progress too, which is in wisdom and which is found by those who seek their salvation in it to do for them what they require both in respect of exposition of truth in the divine word and in respect of conduct according to true righteousness, it lets us understand how Christ is the way. In this way we have to take nothing with us,[4] neither wallet nor coat; we must travel without even a stick, nor must we have shoes on our feet. For this road is itself sufficient for all the supplies of our journey; and every one who walks on it wants nothing. He is clad with a garment which is fit for one who is setting out in response to an invitation to a wedding; and on this road he cannot meet anything that can annoy him. "No one," Solomon says,[5] "can find out the way of a serpent upon a

[1] John xvii. 21. [2] John xii. 26. [3] Rom. v. 3-5.
[4] Rom. viii. 20.

[1] Text corrupt. The above seems to be the meaning. Cf. chap. 23 init. p. 306.
[2] Rom. vi. 4. [3] 2 Cor. iv. 10.
[4] Matt. x. 10. [5] Prov. xxx. 19.

rock." I would add, or that of any other beast. Hence there is no need of a staff on this road, on which there is no trace of any hostile creature, and the hardness of which, whence also it is called rock (*petra*), makes it incapable of harbouring anything hurtful.

27. CHRIST AS THE TRUTH.

Further, the Only-begotten is the truth, because He embraces in Himself according to the Father's will the whole reason of all things, and that with perfect clearness, and being the truth communicates to each creature in proportion to its worthiness. And should any one enquire whether all that the Father knows, according to the depth of His riches and His wisdom and His knowledge, is known to our Saviour also, and should he, imagining that he will thereby glorify the Father, show that some things known to the Father are unknown to the Son, although He might have had an equal share of the apprehensions of the unbegotten God, we must remind him that it is from His being the truth that He is Saviour, and add that if He is the truth complete, then there is nothing true which He does not know; truth must not limp for the want of the things which, according to those persons, are known to the Father only. Or else let it be shown that some things are known to which the name of truth does not apply, but which are above the truth.

28. CHRIST AS LIFE.

It is clear also that the principle of that life which is pure and unmixed with any other element, resides in Him who is the first-born of all creation, taking from which those who have a share in Christ live the life which is true life, while all those who are thought to live apart from this, as they have not the true light, have not the true life either.

29. CHRIST AS THE DOOR AND AS THE SHEPHERD.

But as one cannot be in the Father or with the Father except by ascending from below upwards and coming first to the divinity of the Son, through which one may be led by the hand and brought to the blessedness of the Father Himself, so the Saviour has the inscription "The Door." And as He is a lover of men, and approves the impulse of human souls to better things, even of those who do not hasten to reason (the Logos), but like sheep have a weakness and gentleness apart from all accuracy and reason, so He is the Shepherd. For the Lord saves men and beasts,[1] and Israel and Juda are sowed with the seed not of men only but also of beasts.[2]

30. CHRIST AS ANOINTED (CHRIST) AND AS KING.

In addition to these titles we must consider at the outset of our work that of Christ, and we must also consider that of King, and compare these two so as to find out the difference between them. Now it is said in the forty-fourth Psalm,[3] "Thou hast loved righteousness and hated iniquity, whence Thou art anointed (Christ) above Thy fellows." His loving righteousness and hating iniquity were thus added claims in Him; His anointing was not contemporary with His being nor inherited by Him from the first. Anointing is a symbol of entering on the kingship, and sometimes also on the priesthood; and must we therefore conclude that the kingship of the Son of God is not inherited nor congenital to Him? But how is it conceivable that the First-born of all creation was not a king and became a king afterwards because He loved righteousness, when, moreover, He Himself was righteousness? We cannot fail to see that it is as a man that He is Christ, in respect of His soul, which was human and liable to be troubled and sore vexed, but that He is conceived as king in respect of the divine in Him. I find support for this in the seventy-first Psalm,[4] which says, "Give the king Thy judgment, O God, and Thy righteousness to the king's Son, to judge Thy people in righteousness and Thy poor in judgment." This Psalm, though addressed to Solomon, is evidently a prophecy of Christ, and it is worth while to ask to what king the prophecy desires judgment to be given by God, and to what king's Son, and what king's righteousness is spoken of. I conceive, then, that what is called the King is the leading nature of the First-born of all creation, to which judgment is given on account of its eminence; and that the man whom He assumed, formed and moulded by that nature, according to righteousness, is the King's Son. I am the more led to think that this is so, because the two beings are here brought together in one sentence, and are spoken of as if they were not two but one. For the Saviour made both one,[5] that is, He made them according to the prototype of the two which had been made one in Himself before all things. The two I refer to human nature, since each man's soul is

[1] Ps. xxxvi. 6. [2] Jer. xxxi. 27. [3] Ps. xlv. 8.
[4] Ps. lxxii. 1, 2. [5] Ephes. ii 14.

mixed with the Holy Spirit, and each of those who are saved is thus made spiritual. Now as there are some to whom Christ is a shepherd, as we said before, because of their meek and composed nature, though they are less guided by reason; so there are those to whom He is a king, those, namely, who are led in their approach to religion rather by the reasonable part of their nature. And among those who are under a king there are differences; some experience his rule in a more mystic and hidden and more divine way, others in a less perfect fashion. I should say that those who, led by reason, apart from all agencies of sense, have beheld incorporeal things, the things which Paul speaks of as "invisible," or "not seen," that they are ruled by the leading nature of the Only-begotten, but that those who have only advanced as far as the reason which is conversant with sensible things, and on account of these glorify their Maker, that these also are governed by the Word, by Christ. No offence need be taken at our distinguishing these notions in the Saviour; we draw the same distinctions in His substance.

31. CHRIST AS TEACHER AND MASTER.

It is plain to all how our Lord is a teacher and an interpreter for those who are striving towards godliness, and on the other hand a master of those servants who have the spirit of bondage to fear,[1] who make progress and hasten towards wisdom, and are found worthy to possess it. For[2] "the servant knoweth not what the master wills," since he is no longer his master, but has become his friend. The Lord Himself teaches this, for He says to hearers who were still servants:[3] "You call Me Master and Lord, and you say well, for so I am," but in another passage,[4] "I call you no longer servants, for the servant knoweth not what is the will of his master, but I call you friends," because[5] "you have continued with Me in all My temptations." They, then, who live according to fear, which God exacts from those who are not good servants, as we read in Malachi,[6] "If I am a Master, where is My fear?" are servants of a master who is called their Saviour.

32. CHRIST AS SON.

None of these testimonies, however, sets forth distinctly the Saviour's exalted birth; but when the words are addressed to Him, "Thou art My Son, this day have I begotten Thee,"[1] this is spoken to Him by God, with whom all time is to-day, for there is no evening with God, as I consider, and there is no morning, nothing but time that stretches out, along with His unbeginning and unseen life. The day is to-day with Him in which the Son was begotten, and thus the beginning of His birth is not found, as neither is the day of it.

33. CHRIST THE TRUE VINE, AND AS BREAD.

To what we have said must be added how the Son is the true vine. Those will have no difficulty in apprehending this who understand, in a manner worthy of the prophetic grace, the saying:[2] "Wine maketh glad the heart of man." For if the heart be the intellectual part, and what rejoices it is the Word most pleasant of all to drink which takes us off human things, makes us feel ourselves inspired, and intoxicates us with an intoxication which is not irrational but divine, that, I conceive, with which Joseph made his brethren merry,[3] then it is very clear how He who brings wine thus to rejoice the heart of man is the true vine. He is the *true* vine, because the grapes He bears are the truth, the disciples are His branches, and they, also, bring forth the truth as their fruit. It is somewhat difficult to show the difference between the vine and bread, for He says, not only that He is the vine, but that He is the bread of life. May it be that as bread nourishes and makes strong, and is said to strengthen the heart of man, but wine, on the contrary, pleases and rejoices and melts him, so ethical studies, bringing life to him who learns them and reduces them to practice, are the bread of life, but cannot properly be called the fruit of the vine, while secret and mystical speculations, rejoicing the heart and causing those to feel inspired who take them in, delighting in the Lord, and who desire not only to be nourished but to be made happy, are called the juice of the true vine, because they flow from it.

34. CHRIST AS THE FIRST AND THE LAST; HE IS ALSO WHAT LIES BETWEEN THESE.

Further, we have to ask in what sense He is called in the Apocalypse the First and the Last, and how, in His character as the First, He is not the same as the Alpha and the beginning, while in His character as the Last He is not the same as the Omega and the end. It appears to me, then, that the reason-

[1] Rom. viii. 15.
[2] John xv. 15; θέλει for ποιεῖ.
[3] John xiii. 13.
[4] John xv. 15.
[5] Luke xxii. 28.
[6] i. 6.

[1] Mark i. 11; Ps. ii. 7; Heb. i. 5.
[2] Ps. civ. 15.
[3] Gen. xliii. 34.

able beings which exist are characterized by many forms, and that some of them are the first, some the second, some the third, and so on to the last. To pronounce exactly, however, which is the first, what kind of a being the second is, which may truly be designated third, and to carry this out to the end of the series, this is not a task for man, but transcends our nature. We shall yet venture, such as we are, to stand still a little at this point, and to make some observations on the matter. There are some gods of whom God is god, as we hear in prophecy,[1] "Thank ye the God of gods," and[2] "The God of gods hath spoken, and called the earth." Now God, according to the Gospel,[3] "is not the God of the dead but of the living." Those gods, then, are living of whom God is god. The Apostle, too, writing to the Corinthians, says:[4] "As there are gods many and lords many," and so we have spoken of these gods as really existing. Now there are, besides the gods of whom God is god, certain others, who are called thrones, and others called dominions, lordships, also, and powers in addition to these. The phrase,[5] "above every name that is named, not only in this world, but also in that which is to come," leads us to believe that there are yet others besides these which are less familiar to us; one kind of these the Hebrews called Sabai, from which Sabaoth was formed, who is their ruler, and is none other than God. Add to all these the reasonable being who is mortal, man. Now the God of all things made first in honour some race of reasonable beings; this I consider to be those who are called gods, and the second order, let us say, for the present, are the thrones, and the third, undoubtedly, the dominions. And thus we come down in order to the last reasonable race, which, perhaps, cannot be any other than man. The Saviour accordingly became, in a diviner way than Paul, all things to all, that He might either gain all or perfect them; it is clear that to men He became a man, and to the angels an angel. As for His becoming man no believer has any doubt, but as to His becoming an angel, we shall find reason for believing it was so, if we observe carefully the appearances and the words of the angels, in some of which the powers of the angels seem to belong to Him. In several passages angels speak in such a way as to suggest this, as when[6] "the angel of the Lord appeared in a flame of fire. And he said, I am the God of Abraham and of Isaac and of Jacob." But Isaiah also says:[1] "His name is called Angel of Great Counsel." The Saviour, then, is the first and the last, not that He is not what lies between, but the extremities are named to show that He became all things. Consider, however, whether the last is man, or the things said to be under the earth, of which are the demons, all of them or some. We must ask, too, about those things which the Saviour became which He speaks of through the prophet David,[2] "And I became as a man without any to help him, free among the dead." His birth from the Virgin and His life so admirably lived showed Him to be more than man, and it was the same among the dead. He was the only free person there, and His soul was not left in hell. Thus, then, He is the first and the last. Again, if there be letters of God, as such there are, by reading which the saints may say they have read what is written on the tablets of heaven, these letters, by which heavenly things are to be read, are the notions, divided into small parts, into *A* and so on to Ω, the Son of God. Again, He is the beginning and the end, but He is this not in all His aspects equally. For He is the beginning, as the Proverbs teach us, inasmuch as He is wisdom; it is written: "The Lord founded Me in the beginning of His ways, for His works." In the respect of His being the Logos He is not the beginning. "The Word was *in* the beginning." Thus in His aspects one comes first and is the beginning, and there is a second after the beginning, and a third, and so on to the end, as if He had said, I am the beginning, inasmuch as I am wisdom, and the second, perhaps, inasmuch as I am invisible, and the third in that I am life, for "what was made was life in Him." One who was qualified to examine and to discern the sense of Scripture might, no doubt, find many members of the series; I cannot say if he could find them all. "The beginning and the end" is a phrase we usually apply to a thing that is a completed unity; the beginning of a house is its foundation and the end the parapet. We cannot but think of this figure, since Christ is the stone which is the head of the corner, to the great unity of the body of the saved. For Christ the only-begotten Son is all and in all, He is as the beginning in the man He assumed, He is present as the end in the last of the saints, and He is also in those between, or else He is present

[1] Ps. cxxxvi. 2. [2] Ps. l. 1. [3] Matt. xx. 2, [4] 1 Cor. viii. 5. [5] Ephes. i. 21. [6] Exod. iii. 2, 6.

[1] Isa. ix. 6. [2] Ps. lxxxviii. 4,5.

as the beginning in Adam, as the end in His life on earth, according to the saying: "The last Adam was made a quickening spirit." This saying harmonizes well with the interpretation we have given of the first and the last.

35. CHRIST AS THE LIVING AND THE DEAD.

In what has been said about the first and the last, and about the beginning and the end, we have referred these words at one point to the different forms of reasonable beings, at another to the different conceptions of the Son of God. Thus we have gained a distinction between the first and the beginning, and between the last and the end, and also the distinctive meaning of *A* and *Ω*. It is not hard to see why he is called[1] "the Living and the Dead," and after being dead He that is alive for evermore. For since we were not helped by His original life, sunk as we were in sin, He came down into our deadness in order that, He having died to sin, we,[2] bearing about in our body the dying of Jesus, might then receive that life of His which is for evermore. For those who always carry about in their body the dying of Jesus shall obtain the life of Jesus also, manifested in their bodies.

36. CHRIST AS A SWORD.

The texts of the New Testament, which we have discussed, are things said by Himself about Himself. In Isaiah, however, He said[3] that His mouth had been set by His Father as a sharp sword, and that He was hidden under the shadow of His hand, made like to a chosen shaft and kept close in the Father's quiver, called His servant by the God of all things, and Israel, and Light of the Gentiles. The mouth of the Son of God is a sharp sword, for[4] "The word of God is living, and active, and sharper than any two-edged sword, and piercing to the dividing of soul and spirit, of both joints and marrow, and quick to discern the thoughts and intents of the heart." And indeed He came not to bring peace on the earth, that is, to corporeal and sensible things, but a sword, and to cut through, if I may say so, the disastrous friendship of soul and body, so that the soul, committing herself to the spirit which was against the flesh, may enter into friendship with God. Hence, according to the prophetic word, He made His mouth as a sword, as a sharp sword. Can any one behold so many wounded by the divine love, like her in the Song of Songs, who complained that she was wounded:[1] "I am wounded with love," and find the dart that wounded so many souls for the love of God, in any but Him who said, "He hath made Me as a chosen shaft."

37. CHRIST AS A SERVANT, AS THE LAMB OF GOD, AND AS THE MAN WHOM JOHN DID NOT KNOW.

Again, let any one consider how Jesus was to His disciples, not as He who sits at meat, but as He who serves, and how though the Son of God He took on Him the form of a servant for the sake of the freedom of those who were enslaved in sin, and he will be at no loss to account for the Father's saying to Him:[2] "Thou art My servant," and a little further on: "It is a great thing that thou shouldst be called My servant." For we do not hesitate to say that the goodness of Christ appears in a greater and more divine light, and more according to the image of the Father, because[3] "He humbled Himself, becoming obedient unto death, even the death of the cross," than if He had judged it a thing to be grasped to be equal with God, and had shrunk from becoming a servant for the salvation of the world. Hence He says,[4] desiring to teach us that in accepting this state of servitude He had received a great gift from His Father: "And My God shall be My strength. And He said to Me, It is a great thing for Thee to be called My servant." For if He had not become a servant, He would not have raised up the tribes of Jacob, nor have turned the heart of the diaspora of Israel, and neither would He have become a light of the Gentiles to be for salvation to the ends of the earth. And it is no great thing for Him to become a servant, even if it is called a great thing by His Father, for this is in comparison with His being called with an innocent sheep and with a lamb. For the Lamb of God became like an innocent sheep being led to the slaughter, that He may take away the sin of the world. He who supplies reason (λογος) to all is made like a lamb which is dumb before her shearer, that we might be purified by His death, which is given as a sort of medicine against the opposing power, and also against the sin of those who open their minds to the truth. For the death of Christ reduced to impotence those powers which war against the human race, and it set free

[1] Apoc. i. 17, 18.
[2] 2 Cor. iv. 10.
[3] Isa. xlix. , 3.
[4] Heb. iv. 12.

[1] Song ii. 5.
[2] Isa. xlix. 3, 6.
[3] Philipp. ii. 6, 8.
[4] Isa. xlix. 5, 6.

from sin by a power beyond our words the life of each believer. Since, then, He takes away sin until every enemy shall be destroyed and death last of all, in order that the whole world may be free from sin, therefore John points to Him and says:[1] "Behold the Lamb of God which taketh away the sin of the world." It is not said that He will take it away in the future, nor that He is at present taking it, nor that He has taken it, but is not taking it away now. His taking away sin is still going on, He is taking it away from every individual in the world, till sin be taken away from the whole world, and the Saviour deliver the kingdom prepared and completed to the Father, a kingdom in which no sin is left at all, and which, therefore, is ready to accept the Father as its king, and which on the other hand is waiting to receive all God has to bestow, fully, and in every part, at that time when the saying[2] is fulfilled, "That God may be all in all." Further, we hear of a man who is said to be coming after John, who was made before him and was before him. This is to teach us that the man also of the Son of God, the man who was mixed with His divinity, was older than His birth from Mary. John says he does not know this man, but must he not have known Him when he leapt for joy when yet a babe unborn in Elisabeth's womb, as soon as the voice of Mary's salutation sounded in the ears of the wife of Zacharias? Consider, therefore, if the words "I know Him not" may have reference to the period before the bodily existence. Though he did not know Him before He assumed His body, yet he knew Him when yet in his mother's womb, and perhaps he is here learning something new about Him beyond what was known to him before, namely, that on whomsoever the Holy Spirit shall descend and abide on him, that is he who is to baptize with the Holy Spirit and with fire. He knew him from his mother's womb, but not all about Him. He did not know perhaps that this is He who baptizes with the Holy Spirit and with fire, when he saw the Spirit descending and abiding on Him. Yet that He was indeed a man, and the first man, John did not know.

38. CHRIST AS PARACLETE, AS PROPITIATION, AND AS THE POWER OF GOD.

But none of the names we have mentioned expresses His representation of us with the Father, as He pleads for human nature, and makes atonement for it; the Paraclete, and

[1] John i. 29. [2] 1 Cor. xv. 28.

the propitiation, and the atonement. He has the name Paraclete in the Epistle of John:[1] "If any man sin, we have a Paraclete with the Father, Jesus Christ the righteous." And He is said in the same epistle to be the atonement[2] for our sins. Similarly, in the Epistle to the Romans, He is called a propitiation:[3] "Whom God set forth to be a propitiation through faith." Of this proportion there was a type in the inmost part of the temple, the Holy of Holies, namely, the golden mercy-seat placed upon the two cherubim. But how could He ever be the Paraclete, and the atonement, and the propitiation without the power of God, which makes an end of our weakness, flows over the souls of believers, and is administered by Jesus, who indeed is prior to it and Himself the power of God, who enables a man to say:[4] "I can do all things through Jesus Christ who strengtheneth me." Whence we know that Simon Magus, who gave himself the title of "The power of God, which is called great," was consigned to perdition and destruction, he and his money with him. We, on the contrary, who confess Christ as the true power of God, believe that we share with Him, inasmuch as He is that power, all things in which any energy resides.

39. CHRIST AS WISDOM AND SANCTIFICATION AND REDEMPTION.

We must not, however, pass over in silence that He is of right the wisdom of God, and hence is called by that name. For the wisdom of the God and Father of all things does not apprehend His substance in mere visions, like the phantasms of human thoughts. Whoever is able to conceive a bodiless existence of manifold speculations which extend to the rationale of all existing things, living and, as it were, ensouled, he will see how well the Wisdom of God which is above every creature speaks of herself, when she says:[5] "God created me the beginning of His ways, for His works." By this creating act the whole creation was enabled to exist, not being unreceptive of that divine wisdom according to which it was brought into being; for God, according to the prophet David,[6] made all things in wisdom. But many things came into being by the help of wisdom, which do not lay hold of that by which they were created; and few things indeed there are which lay hold not only of that wisdom which con-

[1] 1 John ii. 1, 2. [2] *ἱλασμὸς.* [3] *ἱλαστήριον*, Rom. iii. 25.
[4] Philipp. iv. 13. [5] Prov. viii. 22. [6] Ps. civ. 24.

cerns themselves, but of that which has to do with many things besides, namely, of Christ who is the whole of wisdom. But each of the sages, in proportion as he embraces wisdom, partakes to that extent of Christ, in that He is wisdom; just as every one who is greatly gifted with power, in proportion as he has power, in that proportion also has a share in Christ, inasmuch as He is power. The same is to be thought about sanctification and redemption; for Jesus Himself is made sanctification to us and redemption. Each of us is sanctified with that sanctification, and redeemed with that redemption. Consider, moreover, if the words "to us," added by the Apostle, have any special force. Christ, he says, "was made to us of God, wisdom, and righteousness, and sanctification, and redemption." In other passages, he speaks about Christ as being wisdom, without any such qualification, and of His being power, saying that Christ is the power of God and the wisdom of God, though we might have conceived that He was not the wisdom of God or the power of God, absolutely, but only for us. Now, in respect of wisdom and power, we have both forms of the statement, the relative and the absolute; but in respect of sanctification and redemption, this is not the case. Consider, therefore, since[1] "He that sanctifies and they that are sanctified are all of one," whether the Father is the sanctification of Him who is our sanctification, as, Christ being our head, God is His head. But Christ is our redemption because we had become prisoners and needed ransoming. I do not enquire as to His own redemption, for though He was tempted in all things as we are, He was without sin, and His enemies never reduced Him to captivity.

40. CHRIST AS RIGHTEOUSNESS; AS THE DEMIURGE, THE AGENT OF THE GOOD GOD, AND AS HIGH-PRIEST.

Having expiscated the "to us" and the "absolutely"—santification and redemption being "to us" and not absolute, wisdom and redemption both to us and absolute—we must not omit to enquire into the position of righteousness in the same passage. That Christ is righteousness relatively to us appears clearly from the words: "Who was made to us of God wisdom and righteousness and sanctification and redemption." And if we do not find Him to be righteousness absolutely as He is the wisdom and the power of God absolutely, then we must enquire whether to Christ Himself, as the Father is santification, so the Father is also righteousness. There is, we know, no unrighteousness with God;[1] He is a righteous and holy Lord,[2] and His judgments are in righteousness, and being righteous, He orders all things righteously.

The heretics drew a distinction for purposes of their own between the just and the good. They did not make the matter very clear, but they considered that the demiurge was just, while the Father of Christ was good. That distinction may, I think, if carefully examined, be applied to the Father and the Son; the Son being righteousness, and having received power[3] to execute judgment, because He is the Son of Man and will judge the world in righteousness, but the Father doing good to those who have been disciplined by the righteousness of the Son. This is after the kingdom of the Son; then the Father will manifest in His works His name the Good, when God becomes all in all. And perhaps by His righteousness the Saviour prepares everything at the fit times, and by His word, by His ordering, by His chastisements, and, if I may use such an expression, by His spiritual healing aids, disposes all things to receive at the end the goodness of the Father. It was from His sense of that goodness that He answered him who addressed the Only-begotten with the words "Good Master,"[4] and said, "Why callest thou Me good? None is good but one, God, the Father." This we have treated of elsewhere, especially in dealing with the question of the greater than the demiurge; Christ we have taken to be the demiurge, and the Father the greater than He. Such great things, then, He is, the Paraclete, the atonement, the propitiation, the sympathizer with our weaknesses, who was tempted in all human things, as we are, without sin; and in consequence He is a great High-Priest, having offered Himself as the sacrifice which is offered once for all, and not for men only but for every rational creature. For without[5] God He tasted death for every one. In some copies of the Epistle to the Hebrews the words are "by the grace of God." Now, whether He tasted death for every one without God, He died not for men only but for all other intellectual beings too, or whether He tasted death for every one by the grace of God, He died for all without

[1] Heb. ii. 11.

[1] John vii. 18.
[2] Apoc. xvi. 5, 7.
[3] John v. 27.
[4] Heb. ii. 9.
[5] χωρις for χαριτι, a widely diffused early variant.

God, for by the grace of God He tasted death for every one. It would surely be absurd to say that He tasted death for human sins and not for any other being besides man which had fallen into sin, as for example for the stars. For not even the stars are clean in the eyes of God, as we read in Job,[1] "The stars are not clean in His sight," unless this is to be regarded as a hyperbole. Hence he is a great High-Priest, since He restores all things to His Father's kingdom, and arranges that whatever defects exist in each part of creation shall be filled up so as to be full of the glory of the Father. This High-Priest is called, from some other notion of him than those we have noticed, Judas, that those who are Jews secretly[2] may take the name of Jew not from Judah, son of Jacob, but from Him, since they are His brethren, and praise Him for the freedom they have attained. For it is He who sets them free, saving them from their enemies on whose backs He lays His hand to subdue them. When He has put under His feet the opposing power, and is alone in presence of His Father, then He is Jacob and Israel; and thus as we are made light by Him, since He is the light of the world, so we are made Jacob since He is called Jacob, and Israel since He is called Israel.

41. CHRIST AS THE ROD, THE FLOWER, THE STONE.

Now He receives the kingdom from the king whom the children of Israel appointed, beginning the monarchy not at the divine command and without even consulting God. He therefore fights the battles of the Lord and so prepares peace for His Son, His people, and this perhaps is the reason why He is called David. Then He is called a rod;[3] such He is to those who need a harder and severer discipline, and have not submitted to the love and gentleness of God. On this account, if He is a rod, He has to "go forth;" He does not remain in Himself, but appears to go beyond His earlier state. Going forth, then, and becoming a rod, He does not remain a rod, but after the rod He becomes a flower that rises up, and after being a rod He is made known as a flower to those who, by His being a rod, have met with visitation. For "God will visit their iniquities with a rod,"[4] that is, Christ. But "His mercy He will not take from him," for He will have mercy on him, for on whom the Son has mercy the Father has mercy also. An interpretation may be given which makes Him a rod and a flower in respect of different persons, a rod to those who have need of chastisement, a flower to those who are being saved; but I prefer the account of the matter given above. We must add here, however, that, perhaps, looking to the end, if Christ is a rod to any man He is also a flower to him, while it is not the case that he who receives Him as a flower must also know Him as a rod. And yet as one flower is more perfect than another and plants are said to flower, even though they bring forth no perfect fruit, so the perfect receive that of Christ which transcends the flower. Those, on the other hand, who have known Him as a rod will partake along with it, not in His perfection, but in the flower which comes before the fruit. Last of all, before we come to the word Logos, Christ was a stone,[1] set at naught by the builders but placed on the head of the corner, for the living stones are built up as on a foundation on the other stones of the Apostles and prophets, Christ Jesus Himself our Lord being the chief corner-stone, because He is a part of the building made of living stones in the land of the living; therefore He is called a stone. All this we have said to show how capricious and baseless is the procedure of those who, when so many names are given to Christ, take the mere appellation "the Word," without enquiring, as in the case of His other titles, in what sense it is used; surely they ought to ask what is meant when it is said of the Son of God that He was the Word, and God, and that He was in the beginning with the Father, and that all things were made by Him.

42. OF THE VARIOUS WAYS IN WHICH CHRIST IS THE LOGOS.

As, then, from His activity in enlightening the world whose light He is, Christ is named the Light of the World, and as from His making those who sincerely attach themselves to Him put away their deadness and rise again and put on newness of life, He is called the Resurrection, so from an activity of another kind He is called Shepherd and Teacher, King and Chosen Shaft, and Servant, and in addition to these Paraclete and Atonement and Propitiation. And after the same fashion He is also called the Logos,[2] because He takes away from us all that is

[1] Job xxv. 5.
[2] Rom. ii. 29.
[3] Isa. xi. 1.
[4] Ps. lxxxix. 32, 33.

[1] Ps. cxviii. 22.
[2] It is impossible to render by any one English word the Greek λόγος as used by Origen in the following discussion. We shall therefore in many passages leave it untranslated.

irrational, and makes us truly reasonable, so that we do all things, even to eating and drinking, to the glory of God, and discharge by the Logos to the glory of God both the commoner functions of life and those which belong to a more advanced stage. For if, by having part in Him, we are raised up and enlightened, herded also it may be and ruled over, then it is clear that we become in a divine manner reasonable, when He drives away from us what in us is irrational and dead, since He is the Logos (reason) and the Resurrection. Consider, however, whether all men have in some way part in Him in His character as Logos. On this point the Apostle teaches us that He is to be sought not outside the seeker, and that those find Him in themselves who set their heart on doing so; "Say not[1] in thy heart, Who shall ascend into heaven? That is to bring Christ down; or, Who shall descend into the abyss? That is to bring Christ up from the dead. But what saith the Scripture? The Word is very nigh thee, in thy mouth and in thy heart," as if Christ Himself were the same thing as the Word said to be sought after. But when the Lord Himself says[2] "If I had not come and spoken unto them, they had not had sin; but now they have no cloak for their sin," the only sense we can find in His words is that the Logos Himself says that those are not chargeable with sin to whom He (reason) has not fully come, but that those, if they sin, are guilty who, having had part in Him, act contrary to the ideas by which He declares His full presence in us. Only when thus read is the saying true: "If I had not come and spoken to them, they had not had sin." Should the words be applied, as many are of opinion that they should, to the visible Christ, then how is it true that those had no sin to whom He did not come? In that case all who lived before the advent of the Saviour will be free from sin, since Jesus, as seen in flesh, had not yet come. And more—all those to whom He has never been preached will have no sin, and if they have no sin, then it is clear they are not liable to judgment. But the Logos in man, in which we have said that our whole race had part, is spoken of in two senses; first, in that of the filling up of ideas which takes place, prodigies excepted, in every one who passes beyond the age of boyhood, but secondly, in that of the consummation, which takes place only in the perfect. The words, therefore, "If I had not come and spoken to them, they would not have had sin, but now they have no cloak for their sin," are to be understood in the former sense; but the words,[1] "All that ever came before me are thieves and robbers, and the sheep did not hear them," in the latter. For before the consummation of reason comes, there is nothing in man but what is blameworthy; all is imperfect and defective, and can by no means command the obedience of those irrational elements in us which are tropically spoken of as sheep. And perhaps the former meaning is to be recognized in the words "The Logos was made flesh," but the second in "The Logos was God." We must accordingly look at what there is to be seen in human affairs between the saying, "The Word (reason) was made flesh" and "The Word was God." When the Word was made flesh can we say that it was to some extent broken up and thinned out, and can we say that it recovered from that point onward till it became again what it was at first, God the Word, the Word with the Father; the Word whose glory John saw, the verily only-begotten, as from the Father. But the Son may also be the Logos (Word), because He reports the secret things of His Father who is intellect in the same way as the Son who is called the Word. For as with us the word is a messenger of those things which the mind perceives, so the Word of God, knowing the Father, since no created being can approach Him without a guide, reveals the Father whom He knows. For no one knows the Father save the Son,[2] and he to whomsoever the Son reveals Him, and inasmuch as He is the Word He is the Messenger of Great Counsel,[3] who has the government upon His shoulders; for He entered on His kingdom by enduring the cross. In the Apocalypse,[4] moreover, the Faithful and True (the Word), is said to sit on a white horse, the epithets indicating, I consider, the clearness of the voice with which the Word of truth speaks to us when He sojourns among us. This is scarcely the place to show how the word "horse" is often used in passages spoken for our encouragement in sacred learning. I only cite two of these: "A horse is deceitful for safety,"[5] and "Some trust in chariots and some in horses, but we will rejoice in the name of the Lord our God."[6] Nor must we leave unnoticed a passage in the forty-fourth Psalm,[7] frequently quoted by many writers as if they understood it: "My heart

[1] Rom. x. 6 8.
[2] John xv. 22.

[1] John x. 8.
[2] Matt. xi. 27.
[3] Isa. ix. 5, 6.
[4] xix. 11.
[5] Ps. xxxiii. 17.
[6] Ps. xx. 7.
[7] Ps. xlv. 1.

hath belched forth a good word, I speak my works to the King." Suppose it is God the Father who speaks thus; what is His heart, that the good word should appear in accordance with His heart? If, as these writers suppose, the Word (Logos) needs no interpretation, then the heart is to be taken in the natural sense too. But it is quite absurd to suppose God's heart to be a part of Him as ours is of our body. We must remind such writers that as when the hand of God is spoken of, and His arm and His finger, we do not read the words literally but enquire in what sound sense we may take them so as to be worthy of God, so His heart is to be understood of His rational power, by which He disposes all things, and His word of that which announces what is in this heart of His. But who is it that announces the counsel of the Father to those of His creatures who are worthy and who have risen above themselves, who but the Saviour? That "belched forth" is not, perhaps, without significance; a hundred other terms might have been employed; "My heart has produced a good word," it might have been said, or "My heart has spoken a good word." But in belching, some wind that was hidden makes its way out to the world, and so it may be that the Father gives out views of truth not continuously, but as it were after the fashion of belching, and the word has the character of the things thus produced, and is called, therefore, the image of the invisible God. We may enter our agreement, therefore, with the ordinary acceptation of these words, and take them to be spoken by the Father. It is not, however, a matter of course, that it is God Himself who announces these things. Why should it not be a prophet? Filled with the Spirit and unable to contain himself, he brings forth a word about his prophecy concerning Christ: "My heart hath belched forth a good word, I speak my works to the King, my pen is the tongue of a ready writer. Excellent in beauty is He beyond the sons of men." Then to the Christ Himself: "Grace is poured out on Thy lips." If the Father were the speaker, how could He go on after the words, "Grace is poured out on thy lips," to say, "Therefore God hath blessed thee for ever," and a little further on, "Therefore God, thy God, hath anointed thee with the oil of gladness above thy fellows." Some of those who wish to make the Father the speaker may appeal to the words, "Hear, O daughter, and behold and incline thine ear, and forget thy people and thy father." The prophet, it may be said, could not address the Church in the words, "Hear, O daughter." It is not difficult, however, to show that changes of person occur frequently in the Psalms, so that these words, "Hear, O daughter," might be from the Father, in this passage, though the Psalm as a whole is not. To our discussion of the Word we may here add the passage,[1] "By the word of the Lord were the heavens founded, and all the power of them by the breath of His mouth." Some refer this to the Saviour and the Holy Spirit. The passage, however, does not necessarily imply any more than that the heavens were founded by the reason (logos) of God, as when we say that a house is built by the plan (logos) of the architect, or a ship by the plan (logos) of the shipbuilder. In the same way the heavens were founded (made solid) by the Word of God, for they are[2] of a more divine substance, which on this account is called solid;[3] it has little fluidity for the most part, nor is it easily melted like other parts of the world, and specially the lower parts. On account of this difference the heavens are said in a special manner to be constituted by the Word of God.

The saying then stands, first, "In the beginning was the Logos;" we are to place that full in our view; but the testimonies we cited from the Proverbs led us to place wisdom first, and to think of wisdom as preceding the Word which announces her. We must observe, then, that the Logos is in the beginning, that is, in wisdom, always. Its being in wisdom, which is called the beginning, does not prevent it from being with God and from being God, and it is not simply with God, but is in the beginning, in wisdom, with God. For he goes on: "He was in the beginning with God." He might have said, "He was with God;" but as He was in the beginning, so He was with God in the beginning, and "All things were made by Him," being in the beginning, for God made all things, as David tells us, in wisdom. And to let us understand that the Word has His own definite place and sphere as one who has life in Himself (and is a distinct person), we must also speak about powers, not about power. "Thus saith the Lord of powers, (A.V. hosts)" we frequently read; there are certain creatures, rational and divine, which are called powers; and of these Christ was the highest and best, and is called not only the wisdom of God but

[1] Ps. xxxiii. 6.

[2] Reading τυγχάνομτας.

[3] στερεός, of which the στερέωμα, firmament, is made.

also His power. As, then, there are several powers of God, each of them in its own form, and the Saviour is different from these, so also Christ, even if that which is Logos in us is not in respect of form outside of us, will be understood from our discussion up to this point to be the Logos, who has His being in the beginning, in wisdom. This for the present may suffice, on the word: "In the beginning was the Logos."

BOOK II.

1. "*And the Word was with God, and the Word was God.*" In the preceding section, my revered brother Ambrosius, brother formed according to the Gospel, we have discussed, as far as is at present in our power, what the Gospel is, and what is the beginning in which the Word was, and what the Word is which was in the beginning. We now come to consider the next point in the work before us, How the Word was with God. To this end it will be of service to remember that what is called the Word came to certain persons; as "The Word of the Lord[1] which came to Hosea, the son of Beeri," and "The Word[2] which came to Isaiah, the son of Amos, concerning Judah and concerning Jerusalem," and "The Word which came to Jeremiah[3] concerning the drought." We must enquire how this Word came to Hosea, and how it came also to Isaiah the son of Amos, and again to Jeremiah concerning the drought; the comparison may enable us to find out how the Word was with God. The generality will simply look at what the prophets said, as if that were the Word of the Lord or the Word, that came to them. May it not be, however, that as we say that this person comes to that, so the Son, the Word, of whom we are now theologizing, came to Hosea, sent to him by the Father; historically, that is to say, to the son of Beeri, the prophet Hosea, but mystically to him who is saved, for Hosea means, etymologically, *Saved;* and to the son of Beeri, which etymologically means wells, since every one who is saved becomes a son of that spring which gushes forth out of the depths, the wisdom of God. And it is nowise marvellous that the saint should be a son of wells. From his brave deeds he is often called a son, whether, from his works shining before men, of light, or from his possessing the peace of God which passes all understanding, of peace, or, once more, from the help which wisdom brings him, a child of wisdom; for wisdom,[1] it says, is justified of her children. Thus he who by the divine spirit searches all things, and even the deep things of God, so that he can exclaim,[2] "O the depth of the riches both of the wisdom and the knowledge of God!" he can be a son of wells, to whom the Word of the Lord comes. Similarly the Word comes also to Isaiah, teaching the things which are coming upon Judæa and Jerusalem in the last days; and so also it comes to Jeremiah lifted up by a divine elation. For Iᴀᴏ means etymologically lifting up, elation. Now the Word comes to men who formerly could not receive the advent of the Son of God who is the Word; but to God it does not come, as if it had not been with Him before. The Word was always with the Father; and so it is said, "And the Word was with God." He did not come to God, and this same word "was" is used of the Word because He was in the beginning at the same time when He was with God, neither being separated from the beginning nor being bereft of His Father. And again, neither did He come to be in the beginning after He had not been in it, nor did He come to be with God after not having been with Him. For before all time and the remotest age[3] the Word was in the beginning, and the Word was with God. Thus to find out what is meant by the phrase, "The Word was with God," we have adduced the words used about the prophets, how He came to Hosea, to Isaiah, to Jeremiah, and we have noticed the difference, by no means accidental, between "became" and "was." We have to add that in His coming to the prophets He illuminates the prophets with the light of knowledge, causing them to see things which had been before them, but which they had not understood till then. With God, however, He is God, just because

[1] Hos. i. 1. [2] Isa. ii. 1. [3] Jer. xiv. 1.

[1] Matt. xi. 19. [2] Rom. xi. 33.
[3] Omitting τὸ, with Jacobi.

He is with Him. And perhaps it was because he saw some such order in the Logos, that John did not place the clause "The Word was God" before the clause "The Word was with God." The series in which he places his different sentences does not prevent the force of each axiom from being separately and fully seen. One axiom is, "In the beginning was the Word," a second, "The Word was with God," and then comes, "And the Word was God." The arrangement of the sentences might be thought to indicate an order; we have first "In the beginning was the Word," then, "And the Word was with God," and thirdly, "And the Word was God," so that it might be seen that the Word being with God makes Him God.

2. IN WHAT WAY THE LOGOS IS GOD. ERRORS TO BE AVOIDED ON THIS QUESTION.

We next notice John's use of the article in these sentences. He does not write without care in this respect, nor is he unfamiliar with the niceties of the Greek tongue. In some cases he uses the article, and in some he omits it. He adds the article to the Logos, but to the name of God he adds it sometimes only. He uses the article, when the name of God refers to the uncreated cause of all things, and omits it when the Logos is named God. Does the same difference which we observe between God with the article and God without it prevail also between the Logos with it and without it? We must enquire into this. As the God who is over all is God with the article, not without it, so "the Logos" is the source of that reason (Logos) which dwells in every reasonable creature; the reason which is in each creature is not, like the former, called *par excellence* The Logos. Now there are many who are sincerely concerned about religion, and who fall here into great perplexity. They are afraid that they may be proclaiming two Gods, and their fear drives them into doctrines which are false and wicked. Either they deny that the Son has a distinct nature of His own besides that of the Father, and make Him whom they call the Son to be God all but the name, or they deny the divinity of the Son, giving Him a separate existence of His own, and making His sphere of essence fall outside that of the Father, so that they are separable from each other. To such persons we have to say that God on the one hand is Very God (Autotheos, God of Himself); and so the Saviour says in His prayer to the Father,[1] "That they may know Thee the only true God;" but that all beyond the Very God is made God by participation in His divinity, and is not to be called simply God (with the article), but rather God (without article). And thus the first-born of all creation, who is the first to be with God, and to attract to Himself divinity, is a being of more exalted rank than the other gods beside Him, of whom God is the God, as it is written,[2] "The God of gods, the Lord, hath spoken and called the earth." It was by the offices of the first-born that they became gods, for He drew from God in generous measure that they should be made gods, and He communicated it to them according to His own bounty. The true God, then, is "The God," and those who are formed after Him are gods, images, as it were, of Him the prototype. But the archetypal image, again, of all these images is the Word of God, who was in the beginning, and who by being with God is at all times God, not possessing that of Himself, but by His being with the Father, and not continuing to be God, if we should think of this, except by remaining always in uninterrupted contemplation of the depths of the Father.

3. VARIOUS RELATIONS OF THE LOGOS TO MEN.

Now it is possible that some may dislike what we have said representing the Father as the one true God, but admitting other beings besides the true God, who have become gods by having a share of God. They may fear that the glory of Him who surpasses all creation may be lowered to the level of those other beings called gods. We drew this distinction between Him and them that we showed God the Word to be to all the other gods the minister of their divinity. To this we must add, in order to obviate objections, that the reason which is in every reasonable creature occupied the same relation to the reason who was in the beginning with God, and is God the Word, as God the Word occupies to God. As the Father who is Very God and the True God is to His image and to the images of His image—men are said to be according to the image, not to be images of God—so He, the Word, is to the reason (word) in every man. Each fills the place of a fountain—the Father is the fountain of divinity, the Son of reason. As, then, there are many gods, but to us there is but one God the Father, and many Lords, but to us there is one Lord, Jesus Christ, so there are many λόγοι, but we, for our

[1] John xvii. 3.

[2] Ps. l. 1.

part, pray that that one Λόγος may be with us who was in the beginning and was with God, God the Logos. For whoever does not receive this Logos who was in the beginning with God, or attach himself to Him as He appeared in flesh, or take part in some of those who had part in this Logos, or whoever having had part in Him falls away from Him again, he will have his portion in what is called most opposite to reason. What we have drawn out from the truths with which we started will now be clear enough. First, we spoke about God and the Word of God, and of Gods, either, that is, beings who partake in deity or beings who are called Gods and are not. And again of the Logos of God and of the Logos of God made flesh, and of logoi, or beings which partake in some way of the Logos, of second logoi or of third, thought to be logoi, in addition to that Logos that was before them all, but not really so. Irrational Reasons these may be styled; beings are spoken of who are said to be Gods but are not, and one might place beside these Gods who are no Gods, Reasons which are no Reasons. Now the God of the universe is the God of the elect, and in a much greater degree of the Saviours of the elect; then He is the God of these beings who are truly Gods, and then He is the God, in a word, of the living and not of the dead. But God the Logos is the God, perhaps, of those who attribute everything to Him and who consider Him to be their Father. Now the sun and the moon and the stars were connected, according to the accounts of men of old times, with beings who were not worthy to have the God of gods counted their God. To this opinion they were led by a passage in Deuteronomy which is somewhat on this wise:[1] "Lest when thou liftest up thine eyes to heaven, and seest the sun and the moon and the whole host of heaven, thou wander away and worship them and serve them which the Lord thy God hath appointed to all the peoples. But to you the Lord thy God hath not so given them." But how did God appoint the sun and the moon and all the host of heaven to all the nations, if He did not give them in the same way to Israel also, to the end that those who could not rise to the realm of intellect, might be inclined by gods of sense to consider about the Godhead, and might of their own free will connect themselves with these and so be kept from falling away to idols and demons? Is it not the case that some have for their God the God of the universe, while a second class, after these, attach themselves to the Son of God, His Christ, and a third class worship the sun and the moon and all the host of heaven, wandering, it is true, from God, but with a far different and a better wandering than that of those who invoke as gods the works of men's hands, silver and gold,—works of human skill. Last of all are those who devote themselves to the beings which are called gods but are no gods. In the same way, now, some have faith in that Reason which was in the beginning and was with God and was God; so did Hosea and Isaiah and Jeremiah and others who declared that the Word of the Lord, or the Logos, had come to them. A second class are those who know nothing but Jesus Christ and Him crucified, considering that the Word made flesh is the whole Word, and knowing only Christ after the flesh. Such is the great multitude of those who are counted believers. A third class give themselves to logoi (discourses) having some part in the Logos which they consider superior to all other reason: these are they who follow the honourable and distinguished philosophical schools among the Greeks. A fourth class besides these are they who put their trust in corrupt and godless discourses, doing away with Providence, which is so manifest and almost visible, and who recognize another end for man to follow than the good. It may appear to some that we have wandered from our theme, but to my thinking the view we have reached of four things connected with the name of God and four things connected with the Logos comes in very well at this point. There was God with the article and God without the article, then there were gods in two orders, at the summit of the higher order of whom is God the Word, transcended Himself by the God of the universe. And, again, there was the Logos with the article and the Logos without the article, corresponding to God absolutely and a god; and the Logoi in two ranks. And some men are connected with the Father, being part of Him, and next to these, those whom our argument now brings into clearer light, those who have come to the Saviour and take their stand entirely in Him. And third are those of whom we spoke before, who reckon the sun and the moon and the stars to be gods, and take their stand by them. And in the fourth and last place those who submit to soulless and dead idols. To all this we find analogies in what concerns the Logos. Some are adorned with the Word Himself; some with what is next to Him and appears to be

[1] Deut. iv. 19, quoted apparently from memory.

the very original Logos Himself, those, namely, who know nothing but Jesus Christ and Him crucified, and who behold the Word as flesh. And the third class, as we described them a little before. Why should I speak of those who are thought to be in the Logos, but have fallen away, not only from the good itself, but from the very traces of it and from those who have a part in it?

4. THAT THE LOGOS IS ONE, NOT MANY. OF THE WORD, FAITHFUL AND TRUE, AND OF HIS WHITE HORSE.

"*He was in the beginning with God.*" By his three foregoing propositions the Evangelist has made us acquainted with three orders, and he now sums up the three in one, saying, "This (Logos) was in the beginning with God." In the first premiss we learned where the Logos was; He was in the beginning; then we learned with whom He was, with God; and then who He was, that He was God. He now points out by this word "He," the Word who is God, and gathers up into a fourth proposition the three which went before, "In the beginning was the Word," "The Word was with God," and "The Word was God." Now he says, He, this (Word) was in the beginning with God. The term beginning may be taken of the beginning of the world, so that we may learn from what is said that the Word was older than the things which were made from the beginning. For if "in the beginning God created heaven and earth," but "He" was in the beginning, then the Logos is manifestly older than those things which were made at the beginning, older not only than the firmament and the dry land, but than the heavens and earth. Now some one might ask, and not unreasonably, why it is not said, "In the beginning was the Word of God, and the Word of God was with God, and the Word of God was God." But he who asked such a question could be shown to be taking for granted that there are a plurality of logoi, differing perhaps from each other in kind, one being the word of God, another perhaps the word of angels, a third of men, and so on with the other logoi. Now, if this were so with the Logos, the case would be the same with wisdom and with righteousness. But it would be absurd that there should be a number of things equally to be called "The Word;" and the same would apply to wisdom and to righteousness. We shall be driven to confess that we ought not to look for a plurality of logoi, or of wisdom, or of righteousness, if we look at the case of truth. Any one will confess that there is only one truth; it could never be said in this case that there is one truth of God, and another of the angels, and another of man,—it lies in the nature of things that the truth about anything is one. Now, if truth be one, it is clear that the preparation of it and its demonstration, which is wisdom, must in reason be conceived as one, since what is regarded as wisdom cannot justly claim that title where truth, which is one, is absent from its grasp. But if truth is one and wisdom one, then Reason (Logos) also, which announces truth and makes truth simple and manifest to those who are fitted to receive it, will be one. This we say, by no means denying that truth and wisdom and reason are of God, but we wish to indicate the purpose of the omission in this passage of the words "of God," and of the form of the statement, "In the beginning the Logos was with God." The same John in the Apocalypse gives Him His name with the addition "of God," where he says:[1] "And I saw heaven opened, and behold a white horse, and He that sat thereon called Faithful and True; and in righteousness doth He judge and make war. And His eyes are as a flame of fire, and on His head are many diadems, and He hath a name written which no one knoweth but He Himself. And He is arrayed in a garment sprinkled with blood, and His name is called[2] Word of God. And His armies in heaven followed Him on white horses, clothed in pure fine linen. And out of His mouth proceedeth a sharp sword, that with it He should smite the nations, and He shall rule them with a rod of iron, and He treadeth the winepress of the fierceness of the wrath of Almighty God. And He hath on His garment and on His thigh a name written: King of kings, and Lord of lords." In this passage Logos is necessarily spoken of absolutely without the article, and also with the addition Logos of God; had the first not been the case (*i.e.*, had the article been given) we might have been led to take up the meaning wrongly,[3] and so to depart from the truth about the Logos. For if it had been called simply Logos, and had not been said to be the Logos of God, then we would not be clearly informed that the Logos is the Logos of God. And, again, had it been called Logos of God but not said to be Logos absolutely, then we might imagine many logoi, according to the constitution

[1] Apoc. xix. 11-16. [2] In the Greek the article is here omitted.
[3] Reading παρεκδέξασθαι, with Huet.

of each of the rational beings which exist; then we might assume a number of logoi properly so called. Again, in his description in the Apocalypse of the Logos of God, the Apostle and Evangelist (and the Apocalypse entitles him to be styled a prophet, too) says he saw the Word of God in the opened heaven, and that He was riding on a white horse. Now we must consider what he means to convey when he speaks of heaven being opened and of the white horse, and of the Word of God riding on the white horse, and also what is meant by saying that the Word of God is Faithful and True, and that in righteousness He judges and makes war. All this will greatly advance our study on the subject of the Word of God. Now I conceive heaven to have been shut against the ungodly, and those who bear the image of the earthly, and to have been opened to the righteous and those adorned with the image of the heavenly. For to the former, being below and still dwelling in the flesh, the better things are closed, since they cannot understand them and have neither power nor will to see their beauty, looking down as they do and not striving to look up. But to the excellent, or those who have their commonwealth in heaven,[1] he opens, with the key of David, the things in heavenly places and discloses them to their view, and makes all clear to them by riding on his horse. These words also have their meaning; the horse is white because it is the nature of higher knowledge (γνῶσις) to be clear and white and full of light. And on the white horse sits He who is called Faithful, seated more firmly, and so to speak more royally, on words which cannot be set aside, words which run sharply and more swiftly than any horse, and overbear in their rushing course every so-called word that simulates the Word, and every so-called truth that simulates the Truth. He who sits on the white horse is called Faithful, not because of the faith He cherishes, but of that which He inspires, because He is worthy of faith. Now the Lord Jehovah, according to Moses,[2] is Faithful and True. He is true also in respect of His relation to shadow, type, and image; for such is the Word who is in the opened heaven, for He is not on earth as He is in heaven; on earth He is made flesh and speaks through shadow, type, and image. The multitude, therefore, of those who are reputed to believe are disciples of the shadow of the Word, not of the true Word of God which is in the opened heaven. Hence Jeremiah says,[1] "The Spirit of our face is Christ the Lord, of whom we said, In His shadow shall we live among the nations." Thus the Word of God who is called Faithful is also called True, and in righteousness He judges and makes war; since He has received from God the faculty of judging in very righteousness and very judgment, and of apportioning its due to every existing creature. For none of those who have some portion of righteousness and of the faculty of judgment can receive on his soul such copies and impressions of righteousness and judgment as to come short in no point of absolute righteousness and absolute justice, just as no painter of a picture can communicate to the representation all the qualities of the original. This, I conceive, is the reason why David says,[2] "Before Thee shall no living being be justified." He does not say, no man, or no angel, but no living being, since even if any being partakes of life and has altogether put off mortality, not even then can it be justified in comparison of Thee, who art, as it were, Life itself. Nor is it possible that one who partakes of life and is therefore called living, should become life itself, or that one who partakes of righteousness and, therefore, is called righteous should become equal to righteousness itself. Now it is the function of the Word of God, not only to judge in righteousness, but also to make war in righteousness, that by making war on His enemies by reason and righteousness, so that what is irrational and wicked is destroyed,[3] He may dwell in the soul of him who, for his salvation, so to speak, has become captive to Christ, and may justify that soul and cast out from her all adversaries. We shall, however, obtain a better view of this war which the Word carries on if we remember that He is an ambassador for the truth, while there is another who pretends to be the Word and is not, and one who calls herself the truth and is not, but a lie. Then the Word, arming Himself against the lie, slays it with the breath of His mouth and brings it to naught by the manifestation of His coming.[4] And consider whether these words of the Apostle to the Thessalonians may be understood in an intellectual sense. For what is that which is destroyed by the breath of the mouth of Christ, Christ being the Word and Truth and Wisdom, but the lie? And what is that which is brought

[1] Philipp. iii. 20.

[2] Deut. xxxii. 4.

[1] Lam. iv. 20.

[2] Ps. cxliii. 2.

[3] Omitting λεγεσθαι, with Jacobi.

[4] 2 Thess. ii. 8.

to naught by the manifestation of Christ's coming, Christ being conceived as wisdom and reason, what but that which announces itself as wisdom, when in reality it is one of those things with which God deals as the Apostle describes,[1] "He taketh the wise, those who are not wise with the true wisdom, in their own craftiness"? To what he says of the rider on the white horse, John adds the wonderful statement: "His eyes are like a flame of fire." For as the flame of fire is bright and illuminating, but at the same time fiery and destructive of material things, so, if I may so say, are the eyes of the Logos with which He sees, and every one who has part in Him; they have not only the inherent quality of laying hold of the things of the mind, but also that of consuming and putting away those conceptions which are more material and gross, since whatever is in any way false flees from the directness and lightness of truth. It is in a very natural order that after speaking of Him who judges in righteousness and makes war in accordance with His righteous judgments, and then after His warring of His giving light, the writer goes on to say, "On His head are many diadems." For had the lie been one, and of one form only, against which the True and Faithful Word contended, and for conquering which He was crowned, then one crown alone would naturally have been given Him for the victory. As it is, however, as the lies are many which profess the truth and for warring against which the Word is crowned, the diadems are many which surround the head of the conqueror of them all. As He has overcome every revolting power many diadems mark His victory. Then after the diadems He is said to have a name written which no one knows but He Himself. For there are some things which are known to the Word alone; for the beings which come into existence after Him have a poorer nature than His, and none of them is able to behold all that He apprehends. And perhaps it is the case that only those who have part in that Word know the things which are kept from the knowledge of those who do not partake of Him. Now, in John's vision, the Word of God as He rides on the white horse is not naked: He is clothed with a garment sprinkled with blood, for the Word who was made flesh and therefore died is surrounded with marks of the fact that His blood was poured out upon the earth, when the soldier pierced His side. For of that passion, even should it be our lot some day to come to that highest and supreme contemplation of the Logos, we shall not lose all memory, nor shall we forget the truth that our admission was brought about by His sojourning in our body. This Word of God is followed by the heavenly armies one and all; they follow the Word as their leader, and imitate Him in all things, and chiefly in having mounted, they also, white horses. To him that understands, this secret is open. And as sorrow and grief and wailing fled away at the end of things, so also, I suppose, did obscurity and doubt, all the mysteries of God's wisdom being precisely and clearly opened. Look also at the white horses of the followers of the Word and at the white and pure linen with which they were clothed. As linen comes out of the earth, may not those linen garments stand for the dialects on the earth in which those voices are clothed which make clear announcements of things? We have dealt at some length with the statements found in the Apocalypse about the Word of God; it is important for us to know clearly about Him.

5. HE (THIS ONE) WAS IN THE BEGINNING WITH GOD.

To those who fail to distinguish with care the different propositions of the context the Evangelist may appear to be repeating himself. "He was in the beginning with God" may seem to add nothing to "And the Word was with God." We must observe more carefully. In the statement "The Word was with God" we are not told anything of the when or the where; that is added in the fourth axiom. There are four axioms, or, as some call them, propositions, the fourth being "He was in the beginning with God." Now "The Word was with God" is not the same thing as "He was," etc; for here we are told, not only that He was with God, but when and where He was so: "He was in the beginning with God." The "He," too, used as it is for a demonstration, will be considered to refer to the Word, or by a less careful enquirer, to God. What was noted before is now summed up in this designation "He," the notion of the Logos and that of God; and as the argument proceeds the different notions are collected in one; for the notion God is not included in the notion Logos, nor the notion Logos in that of God. And perhaps the proposition before us is a summing up in one of the three which have preceded. Taking the statement that the

[1] 1 Cor. iii. 19.

Word was in the beginning, we have not yet learned that He was with God, and taking the statement that the Word was with God it is not yet clear to us that He was with God in the beginning; and taking the statement that the Word was God, it has neither been shown that He was in the beginning, nor that He was with God.

Now when the Evangelist says, "He was in the beginning with God," if we apply the pronoun "He" to the Word and to God (as He is God) and consider that "in the beginning" is conjoined with it, and "with God" added to it, then there is nothing left of the three propositions that is not summed up and brought together in this one. And as "in the beginning" has been said twice, we may consider if there are not two lessons we may learn. First, that the Word was in the beginning, as if He was by Himself and not with any one, and secondly, that He was in the beginning with God. And I consider that there is nothing untrue in saying of Him both that He was in the beginning, and in the beginning with God, for neither was He with God alone, since He was also in the beginning, nor was He in the beginning alone and not with God, since "He was in the beginning with God."

6. HOW THE WORD IS THE MAKER OF ALL THINGS, AND EVEN THE HOLY SPIRIT WAS MADE THROUGH HIM.

"*All things were made through Him.*" The "through[1] whom" is never found in the first place but always in the second, as in the Epistle to the Romans,[2] "Paul a servant of Christ Jesus, a called Apostle, separated to the Gospel of God which He promised before by His prophets in Holy Scriptures, concerning His Son, who was born of the seed of David according to the flesh, determined the Son of God in power according to the Spirit of holiness, by the resurrection of the dead, Jesus Christ our Lord, through whom we received grace and apostleship, for obedience of the faith among all the nations, for His name's sake." For God promised aforehand by the prophets His own Gospel, the prophets being His ministers, and having their word to speak about Him "through whom." And again God gave grace and apostleship to Paul and to the others for the obedience of the faith among all the nations, and this He gave them through Jesus Christ the Saviour, for the "through whom" belonged to Him. And the Apostle Paul says in the Epistle to the Hebrews:[1] "At the end of the days He spoke to us in His Son, whom He made the heir of all things, 'through whom' also He made the ages," showing us that God made the ages through His Son, the "through whom" belonging, when the ages were being made, to the Only-begotten. Thus, if all things were made, as in this passage also, *through* the Logos, then they were not made *by* the Logos, but by a stronger and greater than He. And who else could this be but the Father? Now if, as we have seen, all things were made through Him, we have to enquire if the Holy Spirit also was made through Him. It appears to me that those who hold the Holy Spirit to be created, and who also admit that "all things were made through Him," must necessarily assume that the Holy Spirit was made through the Logos, the Logos accordingly being older than He. And he who shrinks from allowing the Holy Spirit to have been made through Christ must, if he admits the truth of the statements of this Gospel, assume the Spirit to be uncreated. There is a third resource besides these two (that of allowing the Spirit to have been made by the Word, and that of regarding it as uncreated), namely, to assert that the Holy Spirit has no essence of His own beyond the Father and the Son. But on further thought one may perhaps see reason to consider that the Son is second beside the Father, He being the same as the Father, while manifestly a distinction is drawn between the Spirit and the Son in the passage,[2] "Whosoever shall speak a word against the Son of Man, it shall be forgiven him, but whosoever shall blaspheme against the Holy Spirit, he shall not have forgiveness, either in this world or in the world to come." We consider, therefore, that there are three hypostases, the Father and the Son and the Holy Spirit; and at the same time we believe nothing to be uncreated but the Father. We therefore, as the more pious and the truer course, admit that all things were made by the Logos, and that the Holy Spirit is the most excellent and the first in order[3] of all that was made by the Father through Christ. And this, perhaps, is the reason why the Spirit is not said to be God's own Son. The Only-begotten only is by nature and from the beginning a Son, and the Holy Spirit seems to have need of the Son, to minister to Him His essence, so as to enable Him not only to exist, but to be wise and reasonable and just, and all that we must think of Him as being. All this He has by participation of

[1] See R. V. margin, John i. 3. [2] Rom. i. 1–5.

[1] i. 1, 2. [2] Matt. xii. 32. [3] Reading πρὸ πάντων, with Jacobi.

the character of Christ, of which we have spoken above. And I consider that the Holy Spirit supplies to those who, through Him and through participation in Him, are called saints, the material of the gifts, which come from God; so that the said material of the gifts is made powerful by God, is ministered by Christ, and owes its actual existence in men to the Holy Spirit. I am led to this view of the charisms by the words of Paul which he writes somewhere,[1] "There are diversities of gifts but the same Spirit, and diversities of ministrations, and the same Lord. And there are diversities of workings, but it is the same God that worketh all in all." The statement that all things were made by Him, and its seeming corollary, that the Spirit must have been called into being by the Word, may certainly raise some difficulty. There are some passages in which the Spirit is placed above Christ; in Isaiah, for example, Christ declares that He is sent, not by the Father only, but also by the Holy Spirit. "Now the Lord hath sent Me," He says,[2] "and His Spirit." And in the Gospel He declares that there is forgiveness for the sin committed against Himself, but that for blasphemy against the Holy Spirit there is no forgiveness, either in this age or in the age to come. What is the reason of this? Is it because the Holy Spirit is of more value than Christ that the sin against Him cannot be forgiven? May it not rather be that all rational beings have part in Christ, and that forgiveness is extended to them when they repent of their sins, while only those have part in the Holy Spirit who have been found worthy of it, and that there cannot well be any forgiveness for those who fall away to evil in spite of such great and powerful co-operation, and who defeat the counsels of the Spirit who is in them. When we find the Lord saying, as He does in Isaiah, that He is sent by the Father and by His Spirit, we have to point out here also that the Spirit is not originally superior to the Saviour, but that the Saviour takes a lower place than He in order to carry out the plan which has been made that the Son of God should become man. Should any one stumble at our saying that the Saviour in becoming man was made lower than the Holy Spirit, we ask him to consider the words used in the Epistle to the Hebrews,[3] where Jesus is shown by Paul to have been made less than the angels on account of the suffering of death. "We behold Him," he says, "who hath been made a little lower than the angels, Jesus, because of the suffering of death, crowned with glory and honour." And this, too, has doubtless to be added, that the creation, in order to be delivered from the bondage of corruption, and not least of all the human race, required the introduction into human nature of a happy and divine power, which should set right what was wrong upon the earth, and that this action fell to the share, as it were, of the Holy Spirit; but the Spirit, unable to support such a task, puts forward the Saviour as the only one able to endure such a conflict. The Father therefore, the principal, sends the Son, but the Holy Spirit also sends Him and directs Him to go before, promising to descend, when the time comes, to the Son of God, and to work with Him for the salvation of men. This He did, when, in a bodily shape like a dove, He flew to Him after the baptism. He remained on Him, and did not pass Him by, as He might have done with men not able continuously to bear His glory. Thus John, when explaining how he knew who Christ was, spoke not only of the descent of the Spirit on Jesus, but also of its remaining upon him. For it is written that John said:[1] "He who sent me to baptize said, On whomsoever thou shalt see the Spirit descending and abiding upon Him, the same is He that baptizeth with the Holy Spirit and with fire." It is not said only, "On whomsoever thou shalt see the Spirit descending," for the Spirit no doubt descended on others too, but "descending and abiding on Him." Our examination of this point has been somewhat extended, since we were anxious to make it clear that if all things were made by Him, then the Spirit also was made through the Word, and is seen to be one of the "all things" which are inferior to their Maker. This view is too firmly settled to be disturbed by a few words which may be adduced to the opposite effect. If any one should lend credence to the Gospel according to the Hebrews, where the Saviour Himself says, "My mother, the Holy Spirit took me just now by one of my hairs and carried me off to the great mount Tabor," he will have to face the difficulty of explaining how the Holy Spirit can be the mother of Christ when it was itself brought into existence through the Word. But neither the passage nor this difficulty is hard to explain. For if he who does the will of the Father in heaven[2] is Christ's brother and sister and mother, and if the name of brother of Christ may be applied, not only to the race of men, but to beings of diviner rank than they,

[1] 1 Cor. xii. 4–6. [2] Isa. xlviii. 16. [3] ii. 9.

[1] John i. 32. [2] Matt. xii. 50.

then there is nothing absurd in the Holy Spirit's being His mother, every one being His mother who does the will of the Father in heaven.

On the words, "All things were made by Him," there is still one point to be examined. The "word" is, as a notion, from "life," and yet we read, "What was made in the Word was life, and the life was the light of men." Now as all things were made through Him, was the life made through Him, which is the light of men, and the other notions under which the Saviour is presented to us? Or must we take the "all things were made by Him" subject to the exception of the things which are in Himself? The latter course appears to be the preferable one. For supposing we should concede that the life which is the light of men was made through Him, since it said that the life "was made" the light of men, what are we to say about wisdom, which is conceived as being prior to the Word? That, therefore, which is about the Word (His relations or conditions) was not made by the Word, and the result is that, with the exception of the notions under which Christ is presented, all things were made through the Word of God, the Father making them in wisdom. "In wisdom hast Thou made them all," it says,[1] not *through*, but *in* wisdom.

7. OF THINGS NOT MADE THROUGH THE LOGOS.

Let us see, however, why the words are added, "And without Him was not anything (Gr. even one thing) made." Some might think it superfluous to add to the words "All things were made through Him," the phrase "Without Him was not anything made." For if everything whatsoever was made through the Logos, then nothing was made without Him. Yet it does not follow from the proposition that without the Logos nothing was made, that all things were made through the Logos. It is possible that though nothing was made without the Logos, all things were made, not through the Logos only, but some things by Him. We must, therefore, make ourselves sure in what sense the "all things" is to be understood, and in what sense the "nothing." For, without a clear preliminary definition of these terms, it might be maintained that, if all things were made through the Logos, and evil is a part of all things, then the whole matter of sin, and everything that is wicked, that these also were made through the Logos. But this we must regard as false. There is nothing absurd in thinking that creatures were made through the Logos, and also that men's brave deeds have been done through Him, and all the useful acts of those who are now in bliss; but with the sins and misfortunes of men it is otherwise. Now some have held that since evil is not based in the constitution of things—for it did not exist at the beginning and at the end it will have ceased—that, therefore, the evils of which we spoke are the Nothing; and as some of the Greeks say that genera and forms, such as the (general) animal and the man, belong to the category of No-things, so it has been supposed that all that is not of God is Nothing, and has not even obtained through the Word the subsistence it appears to have. We ask whether it is possible to show from Scripture in any convincing way that this is so. As for the meanings of the word "Nothing" and "Not-being," they would appear to be synonymous, for Nothing can be spoken of as Not-being, and the Not-being can be described as Nothing. The Apostle, however, appears to count the things which are not, not among those which have no existence whatever, but rather among things which are evil. To him the Not-being is evil; "God," he says,[1] "called the things that are not as things that are." And Mardochæus, too, in the Esther of the Septuagint, calls the enemies of Israel "those that are not," saying,[2] "Deliver not Thy sceptre, O Lord, to those that are not." We may also notice how evil men, on account of their wickedness, are said not to be, from the name ascribed to God in Exodus:[3] "For the Lord said to Moses, I am, that is My name." The good God says this with respect of us also who pray that we may be part of His congregation. The Saviour praises him, saying,[4] "None is good but one, God the Father." The good, then, is the same as He who is. Over against good is evil or wickedness, and over against Him who is that which is not, whence it follows that evil and wickedness are that which is not. This, perhaps, is what has led some to affirm that the devil is not created by God. In respect that he is the devil he is not the work of God, but he who is the devil is a created being, and as there is no other creator but our God, he is a work of God. It is as if we should say that a murderer is not a work of God, while we may say that in respect he is a man, God made him. His being as a man he received from God;

[1] Ps. civ. 24.

[1] Rom. iv. 17.
[2] Esth. iv. 22.
[3] Exod. iii.14, 15.
[4] Mark x. 18.

we do not assert that he received from God his being as a murderer. All, then, who have part in Him who is, and the saints have part in Him, may properly be called Beings; but those who have given up their part in the Being, by depriving themselves of Being, have become Not-beings. But we said when entering on this discussion, that Not-being and Nothing are synonymous, and hence those who are not beings are Nothing, and all evil is nothing, since it is Not-being, and thus since they are called Not-being came into existence without the Logos, not being numbered among the all things which were made through Him. Thus we have shown, so far as our powers admit, what are the "all things" which were made through the Logos, and what came into existence without Him, since at no time is it Being, and it is, therefore, called "Nothing."

HERACLEON'S VIEW THAT THE LOGOS IS NOT THE AGENT OF CREATION.

It was, I consider, a violent and unwarranted procedure which was adopted by Heracleon,[1] the friend, as it is said, of Valentinus, in discussing this sentence: "All things were made through Him." He excepted the whole world and all that it contains, excluding, as far as his hypothesis goes, from the "all things" what is best in the world and its contents. For he says that the æon (age), and the things in it, were not made by the Logos; he considers them to have come into existence before the Logos. He deals with the statement, "Without Him was nothing made," with some degree of audacity, nor is he afraid of the warning:[2] "Add not to His words, lest He find thee out and thou prove a liar," for to the "Nothing" he adds: "Of what is in the world and the creation." And as his statements on the passage are obviously very much forced and in the face of the evidence, for what he considers divine is excluded from the all, and what he regards as purely evil is, that and nothing else, the all things, we need not waste our time in rebutting what is, on the face of it, absurd, when, without any warrant from Scripture, he adds to the words, "Without Him was nothing made," the further words, "Of what is in the earth and the creation." In this proposal, which has no inner probability to recommend it, he is asking us, in fact, to trust him as we do the prophets, or the Apostles, who had authority and were not responsible to men for the writings belonging to man's salvation, which they handed to those about them and to those who should come after. He had, also, a private interpretation of his own of the words: "All things were made through Him," when he said that it was the Logos who caused the demiurge to make the world, not, however, the Logos from whom or by whom, but Him through whom, taking the written words in a different sense from that of common parlance.[1] For, if the truth of the matter was as he considers, then the writer ought to have said that all things were made through the demiurge by the Word, and not through the Word by the demiurge. We accept the "through whom," as it is usually understood, and have brought evidence in support of our interpretation, while he not only puts forward a new rendering of his own, unsupported by the divine Scripture, but appears even to scorn the truth and shamelessly and openly oppose it. For he says: "It was not the Logos who made all things, as under another who was the operating agent," taking the "through whom" in this sense, "but another made them, the Logos Himself being the operating agent." This is not a suitable occasion for the proof that it was not the demiurge who became the servant of the Logos and made the world; but that the Logos became the servant of the demiurge and formed the world. For, according to the prophet David,[2] "God spake and they came into being, He commanded and they were created." For the unbegotten God commanded the first-born of all creation,[3] and they were created, not only the world and what is therein, but also all other things, whether thrones or dominions or principalities or powers, for all things were made through Him and unto Him, and He is before all things."

9. THAT THE LOGOS PRESENT IN US IS NOT RESPONSIBLE FOR OUR SINS.

One point more on the words: "Without Him was not anything made." The question about evil must receive adequate discussion; what was said of it has not, it is true, a very likely appearance, and yet it appears to me that it ought not to be simply overlooked. The question is whether evil, also, was made through the Logos, taking the Logos, now be it well noted, in the sense of that reason which is in every one, as thus brought into being by the reason

[1] On the fragments of Heracleon in this work of Origen, see *Texts and Studies*, vol. i. part iv. by A. E. Brooke, M.A.
[2] Prov. xxx. 6.

[1] Accepting Jacobi's and Brook's correction παρα τὴν.
[2] Ps. cxlviii. 5.
[3] Coloss. i. 15, 16.

which was from the beginning. The Apostle says:[1] "Without the law sin was dead," and adds, "But when the commandment came sin revived," and so teaches generally about sin that it has no power before the law and the commandment (but the Logos is, in a sense, law and commandment), and there would be no sin were there no law, for,[2] "sin is not imputed where there is no law." And, again, there would be no sin but for the Logos, for "if I had not come and spoken unto them," Christ says,[3] "they had not had sin." For every excuse is taken away from one who wants to make excuse for his sin, if, though the Word is in him and shows him what he ought to do, he does not obey it. It seems, then, that all things, the worse things not excepted, were made by the Logos, and without Him, taking the nothing here in its simpler sense, was nothing made. Nor must we blame the Logos if all things were made by Him, and without Him nothing was made, any more than we blame the master who has showed the pupil his duty, when the instruction has been such as to leave the pupil, should he sin, no excuse or room to say that he erred through ignorance. This appears the more plainly when we consider that master and pupil are inseparable. For as master and pupil are correlatives, and belong together, so the Logos is present in the nature of reasonable beings as such, always suggesting what they ought to do, even should we pay no heed to his commands, but devote ourselves to pleasure and allow his best counsels to pass by us unregarded. As the eye is a servant given us for the best purposes, and yet we use it to see things on which it is wrong for us to look, and as we make a wrong use of our hearing when we spend our time in listening to singing competitions and to other forbidden sounds, so we outrage the Logos who is in us, and use Him otherwise than as we ought, when we make Him assist in our transgressions. For He is present with those who sin, for their condemnation, and He condemns the man who does not prefer Him to everything else. Hence we find it written:[4] "The word which I have spoken unto you, the same shall judge you." That is as if He should say: "I, the Word, who am always lifting up my voice in you, I, myself, will judge you, and no refuge or excuse will then be left you." This interpretation, however, may appear somewhat strained, as we have taken the Word in one sense to be the Word in the beginning, who was with God, God the Word, and have now taken it in another sense, speaking of it, not only in reference to the principal works of creation, as in the words, "All things were made through Him," but as related to all the acts of reasonable beings, this last being the Logos (reason), without whose presence none of our sins are committed. The question arises whether the Logos in us is to be pronounced the same being as that which was in the beginning and was with God, God the Word. The Apostle, certainly, does not appear to make the Logos in us a different being from the Logos who was in the beginning with God. "Say not in thine heart," he says,[1] "who shall go up into heaven; that is to bring Christ down, or who shall go down into the abyss; that is to bring Christ up from the dead. But what saith the Scripture? The Logos is very nigh thee, in thy mouth and in thy heart."

10. "THAT WHICH WAS MADE WAS LIFE IN HIM, AND THE LIFE WAS THE LIGHT OF MEN." THIS INVOLVES THE PARADOX THAT WHAT DOES NOT DERIVE LIFE FROM THE LOGOS DOES NOT LIVE AT ALL.

The Greeks have certain apothegms, called paradoxes, in which the wisdom of their sages is presented at its highest, and some proof, or what appears to be proof, is given. Thus it is said that the wise man alone, and that every wise man, is a priest, because the wise man alone and every wise man possesses knowledge as to the service of God. Again, that the wise man alone and that every wise man is free and has received from the divine law authority to do what he himself is minded to do, and this authority they call lawful power of decision. Why should we say more about these so-called paradoxes? Much discussion is devoted to them, and they call for a comparison of the sense of Scripture with the doctrine thus conveyed, so that we may be in a position to determine where religious doctrine agrees with them and where it differs from them. This has been suggested to us by our study of the words, "That which was made was life in Him;" for it appears possible to follow the words of Scripture here and to make out a number of things which partake of the character of the paradoxes and are even more paradoxical than these sentences of the Greeks. If we consider the Logos in the beginning, who was with God, God the

[1] Rom. vii. 8, 9.
[2] Rom. v. 13.
[3] John xv. 22.
[4] John xii. 48.

[1] Rom. x. 6–8.

Word, we shall perhaps be able to declare that only he who partakes of this being, considered in this character, is to be pronounced reasonable ("logical"), and thus we should demonstrate that the saint alone is reasonable. Again, if we apprehend that life has come in the Logos, he, namely, who said, "I am the life," then we shall say that no one is alive who is outside the faith of Christ, that all are dead who are not living to God, that their life is life to sin, and therefore, if I may so express myself, a life of death. Consider however, whether the divine Scriptures do not in many places teach this; as where the Saviour says,[1] "Or have ye not read that which was spoken at the bush, I am the God of Abraham and the God of Isaac and the God of Jacob. He is not God of the dead but of the living." And[2] "Before Thee shall no living being be justified." But why need we speak about God Himself or the Saviour? For it is disputed to which of them the voice belongs which says in the prophets,[3] "As I live, saith the Lord."

11. HOW NO ONE IS RIGHTEOUS OR CAN TRULY BE SAID TO LIVE IN COMPARISON WITH GOD.

First let us look at the words, "He is not the God of the dead but of the living." That is equivalent to saying that He is not the God of sinners but of saints. For it was a great gift to the Patriarchs that God in place of His own name should add their name to His own designation as God, as Paul says,[4] "Therefore God is not ashamed to be called their God." He is the God, therefore, of the fathers and of all the saints; it might be hard to find a passage to the effect that God is the God of any of the wicked. If, then, He is the God of the saints, and is said to be the God of the living, then the saints are the living and the living are saints; neither is there any saint outside the living, nor when any one is called living is the further implication absent that in addition to his having life he is a holy one. Near akin to this is the lesson to be drawn from the saying,[5] "I shall be well pleasing to the Lord in the land of the living." The good pleasure of the Lord, he appears to say, is in the ranks of the saints, or in the place of the saints, and it is there that he hopes to be. No one pleases God well who has not entered the rank of the saints, or the place of the saints; and to that place every one must come who has assumed beforehand, as it were in this life, the shadow and image of true God-pleasing. The passage which declares that before God no living being shall be justified shows that in comparison with God and the righteousness that is in Him none, even of the most finished saints, will be justified. We might take a parable from another quarter and say that no candle can give light before the sun, not that the candle will not give light, only it will not when the sun outshines it. In the same way every "living" will be justified, only not before God, when it is compared with those who are below and who are in the power of darkness. To them the light of the saints will shine. Here, perhaps, we have the key to the meaning of that verse:[1] "Let your light shine before men." He does not say, Let your light shine before God; had he said so he would have given a commandment impossible of fulfilment, as if he had bidden those lights which have souls to let their light shine before the sun. It is not only, therefore, the ordinary mass of the living who will not be justified before God, but even those among the living who are distinguished above the rest, or, to put it more truly, the whole righteousness of the living will not be justified before God, as compared with the righteousness of God, as if I were to call together all the lights which shine on the earth by night, and to say that they could not give light in comparison with the rays of the sun. We rise from these considerations to a higher level when we take the words before our minds, "I live, saith the Lord." Life, in the full sense of the word, especially after what we have been saying on the subject, belongs perhaps to God and none but Him. Is this the reason why the Apostle, after speaking of the supreme excellency of the life of God and being led to the highest expression about it, says about God (showing in this a true understanding of that saying, "I live, saith the Lord"); "who only hath immortality."[2] No living being besides God has life free from change and variation. Why should we be in further doubt? Even Christ did not share the Father's immortality; for He "tasted death for every man."

12. IS THE SAVIOUR ALL THAT HE IS, TO ALL?

We have thus enquired as to the life of God, and the life which is Christ, and the living who are in a place by themselves, and have seen how the living are not justified before God, and we have noticed the cognate statement, "Who alone hath im-

[1] Mark xii. 26. [2] Ps. cxliii. 2. [3] Numb xiv. 28.
[4] Heb. xi. 16. [5] Ps. cxvi. 9.

[1] Matt. v. 16. [2] 1 Tim. iv. 16.

mortality." We may now take up the assumption which may appear to be involved in this, namely, that whatever being is gifted with reason does not possess blessedness as a part of its essence, or as an inseparable part of its nature. For if blessedness and the highest life were an inseparable characteristic of reasonable being, how could it be truly said of God that He only has immortality? We should therefore remark, that the Saviour is some things, not to Himself but to others, and some things both to Himself and others, and we must enquire if there are some things which He is to Himself and to no other. Clearly it is to others that He is a Shepherd, not a shepherd like those among men who make gain out of their occupation; unless the benefit conferred on the sheep might be regarded, on account of His love to men, as a benefit to Himself also. Similarly it is to others that He is the Way and the Door, and, as all will admit, the Rod. To Himself and to others He is Wisdom and perhaps also Reason (Logos). It may be asked whether, as He has in Himself a system of speculations, inasmuch as He is wisdom, there are some of those speculations which cannot be received by any nature that is begotten, but His own, and which He knows for Himself only. Nor should the reverence we owe to the Holy Spirit keep us from seeking to answer this question. For the Holy Spirit Himself receives instruction, as is clear from what is said about the Paraclete and the Holy Spirit,[1] "He shall take of mine and shall declare it to you." Does He, then, from these instructions, take in everything that the Son, gazing at the Father from the first, Himself knows? That would require further consideration. And if the Saviour is some things to others, and some things it may be to Himself, and to no other, or to one only, or to few, then we ask, in so far as He is the life which came in the Logos, whether he is life to Himself and to others, or to others, and if to others, to what others. And are life and the light of men the same thing, for the text says, "That which was made was life in Him and the life was the light of men." But the light of men is the light only of some, not of all, rational creatures; the word "men" which is added shows this. But He is the light of men, and so He is the life of those whose light he is also. And inasmuch as He is life He may be called the Saviour, not for Himself but to be life to others, whose light also He is. And this life comes to the Logos and is inseparable from Him, once it has come to Him. But the Logos, who cleanses the soul, must have been in the soul first; it is after Him and the cleansing that proceeds from Him, when all that is dead or weak in her has been taken away, that pure life comes to every one who has made himself a fit dwelling for the Logos, considered as God.

[1] John xvi. 14, 15.

13. HOW THE LIFE IN THE LOGOS COMES AFTER THE BEGINNING.

Here, we must carefully observe, we have two things which are one, and we have to define the difference between them. First, what is before us in *The Word in the beginning*, then what is implied in *The Life in the Word*. The Word was not *made* in the beginning; there was no time when the beginning was devoid of the Word, and hence it is said, "In the beginning was the Word." Of life, on the other hand, we read, not that it was as the Word, but that it was made; if at least it be the case that the life is the light of men. For when man was not yet, there was no light of men; for the light of men is conceived only in relation to men. And let no one annoy us with the objection that we have put this under the category of time, though it be the order of the things themselves, that make them first and second and so on, and even though there should have been no time when the things placed by the Logos third and fourth were not in existence. As, then, all things *were made* by Him, not all things *were* by Him, and as without Him *was* nothing *made*, not, without Him nothing *was*, so what *was made* in Him, not what *was* in Him, was life. And, again, not what *was made* in the beginning was the Word, but what *was* in the beginning was the Word. Some of the copies, it is true, have a reading which is not devoid of probability, "What was made is life in Him." But if life is the same thing as the light of men, then no one who is in darkness is living, and none of the living is in darkness; but every one who is alive is also in light, and every one who is in light is living, so that not he only who is living, but every one who is living, is a son of light; and he who is a son of light is he whose work shines before men.

14. HOW THE NATURES OF MEN ARE NOT SO FIXED FROM THE FIRST, BUT THAT THEY MAY PASS FROM DARNKESS TO LIGHT.

We have been discussing certain things which are opposite, and what has been said of them may serve to suggest what has been omitted. We are speaking of life and the light of men, and the opposite to life is death; the opposite to the light of men, the darkness of men. It is therefore plain that he who is in the darkness of men is in death, and that he who works the works of death is nowhere but in darkness. But he who is mindful of God, if we consider what it is to be mindful of Him, is not in death, according to the saying,[1] "In death there is no one who remembers Thee." Are the darkness of men, and death, such as they are by nature? On this point we have another passage,[2] "We were once darkness, but now light in the Lord," even if we be now in the fullest sense saints and spiritual persons. Thus he who was once darkness has become, like Paul, capable of being light in the Lord. Some consider that some natures are spiritual from the first, such as those of Paul and the holy Apostles; but I scarcely see how to reconcile with such a view, what the above text tells us, that the spiritual person was once darkness and afterwards became light. For if the spiritual was once darkness what can the earthy have been? But if it is true that darkness became light, as in the text, how is it unreasonable to suppose that all darkness is capable of becoming light? Had not Paul said, "We were once in darkness, but now are we light in the Lord," and thus implied of those whom they consider to be naturally lost, that they were darkness, or are darkness still, the hypothesis about the different natures might have been admissible. But Paul distinctly says that he had once been darkness but was now light in the Lord, which implies the possibility that darkness should turn into light. But he who perceives the possibility of a change on each side for the better or for the worse, will not find it hard to gain an insight into every darkness of men, or into that death which consists in the darkness of men.

15. HERACLEON'S VIEW THAT THE LORD BROUGHT LIFE ONLY TO THE SPIRITUAL. REFUTATION OF THIS.

Heracleon adopts a somewhat violent course when he arrives at this passage, "What was made in Him was life." Instead of the "In Him" of the text he understands "to those men who are spiritual," as if he considered the Logos and the spiritual to be identical, though this he does not plainly say; and then he proceeds to give, as it were, an account of the origin of the matter and says, "He (the Logos) provided them with their first form at their birth, carrying further and making manifest what had been sown by another,[1] into form and into illumination and into an outline of its own." He did not observe how Paul speaks of the spiritual,[2] and how he refrains from saying that they are men. "A natural man receiveth not the things of the spirit of God, for they are foolishness to him; but the spiritual judgeth all things." We maintain that it was not without a meaning that he did not add the word *men* to the word *spiritual.* Spiritual is something better than man, for man receives his form either in soul, or in body, or in both together, not in what is more divine than these, namely, in spirit; and it is after he has come to have a prevailing share of this that he is called "spiritual." Moreover, in bringing forward such a hypothesis as this, he furnishes not even the pretence of a proof, and shows himself unable to reach even a moderate degree of plausibility for his argument on the subject. So much, then, for him.

16. THE LIFE MAY BE THE LIGHT OF OTHERS BESIDES MEN.

Let us suggest another question, namely, whether the life was the light of men only, and not of every being as well that is in blessedness. For if the life were the same thing as the light of men, and if the light of Christ were for men alone, then the life also would be only for men. But such a view is both foolish and impious, since the other Scriptures testify against this interpretation and declare that, when we are somewhat more advanced, we shall be equal to the angels.[3] The question is to be solved on the principle that when a predicate is applied to certain persons, it is not to be at once taken to apply to them alone. Thus, when the light of men is spoken of, it is not the light of men only; had that been the meaning, a word would have been added to express it; the life, it would have read, was the light of men only. For it is possible for the light of men to be the light of others besides men, just as it is possible that certain animals and certain plants may form the food of men, and that the same animals and plants should be the food of other creatures too. That is an example from common life; it is fitting that another analogy should be adduced from the inspired books. Now the question here

[1] Ps. vi. 6. [2] Ephes. v. 8.

[1] The demiurge. [2] 1 Cor. ii. 14, 15.
[3] Matt. xxii. 30.

before us, is why the light of men should not be the light of other creatures also, and we have seen that to speak of the light of men by no means excludes the possibility that the light may be that of other beings besides man, whether inferior to him or like him. Now a name is given to God; He is said to be the God of Abraham and of Isaac and of Jacob. He, then, who infers from the saying, "The life was the light of men," that the light is for no other than for men, ought also to conclude that the God of Abraham and the God of Isaac and the God of Jacob is the God of no one else but these three patriarchs. But He is also the God of Elijah,[1] and, as Judith says,[2] of her father Simeon, and the God of the Hebrews. By analogy of reasoning, then, if nothing prevents Him from being the God of others, nothing prevents the light of men from being the light of others besides men.

17. THE HIGHER POWERS ARE MEN; AND CHRIST IS THEIR LIGHT ALSO.

Another, again, appeals to the text, "Let us make man according to our image and likeness," and maintains that whatever is made according to God's image and likeness is man. To support this, numberless instances are adduced to show that in Scripture "man" and "angel" are used indifferently, and that the same subject is entitled both angel and man. This is true of the three who were entertained by Abraham, and of the two who came to Sodom; in the whole course of Scripture, persons are styled sometimes men, sometimes angels. Those who hold this view will say that since persons are styled angels who are manifestly men, as when Zechariah says,[4] "The messenger of the Lord, I am with you, saith the Lord Almighty," and as it is written of John the Baptist,[5] "Behold I send My messenger before thy face," the angels (messengers) of God are so called on account of their office, and are not here called men on account of their nature. It confirms this view that the names applied to the higher powers are not those of species of living beings, but those of the orders, assigned by God to this and to that reasonable being. "Throne" is not a species of living being, nor "dominion," nor "principality," nor "power"; these are names of the businesses to which those clothed with the names have been appointed; the subjects themselves are nothing but men, but the subject has come to be a throne, or a dominion, or a principality, or a power. In Joshua, the son of Nun, we read[1] that in Jericho there appeared to Joshua a man who said, "I am captain of the Lord's host, now am I come." The outcome of this is that the light of men must be held to be the same as the light of every being endowed with reason; for every reasonable being is man, since it is according to the image and likeness of God. It is spoken of in three different ways, "the light of men," and simply "the light," and "the true light." It is the light of men either, as we showed before, because there is nothing to prevent us from regarding it as the light of other beings besides men, or because all beings endowed with reason are called men because they are made in the image of God.

18. HOW GOD ALSO IS LIGHT, BUT IN A DIFFERENT WAY; AND HOW LIFE CAME BEFORE LIGHT.

The Saviour is here called simply light. But in the Catholic Epistle of this same John[2] we read that God is light. This, it has been maintained, furnishes a proof that the Son is not in substance different from the Father. Another student, however, looking into the matter more closely and with a sounder judgment, will say that the light which shines in darkness and is not overtaken by it, is not the same as the light in which there is no darkness at all. The light which shines in darkness comes upon this darkness, as it were, and is pursued by it, and, in spite of attempts made upon it, is not overtaken. But the light in which there is no darkness at all neither shines on darkness, nor is at first pursued by it, so as to prove victor and to have it recorded that it was not overtaken by its pursuer. The third designation was "the true light." But in proportion as God, since He is the Father of truth, is more and greater than truth, and since He is the Father of wisdom is greater and more excellent than wisdom, in the same proportion He is more than the true light. We may learn, perhaps, in a more suggestive manner, how the Father and the Son are two lights, from David, who says in the thirty-fifth Psalm,[3] "In Thy light we shall see light." This same light of men which shines in darkness, the true light, is called, further on in the Gospel, the light of the world; Jesus says,[4] "I am the light of the world." Nor must we omit to notice that whereas the passage might very well have

[1] 2 Kings ii. 14. [2] Judith ix. 2. [3] Gen. i. 26.
[4] Zechar. i.; Hagg. i. 13. [5] Mal. iii. 1; Mark i. 2.

[1] v. 13, 14. [2] i. 5.
[3] Ps. xxxvi. 10. [4] viii. 12.

run, "That which was made was in Him the light of men, and the light of men was life," he chose the opposite order. He puts life before the light of men, even if life and the light of men are the same thing; in thinking of those who have part in life, though that life is also the light of men, we are to come first to the fact that they are living the divine life spoken of before; then we come to their enlightenment. For life must come first if the living person is to be enlightened; it would not be a good arrangement to speak of the illumination of one not yet conceived as living, and to make life come after the illumination. For though "life" and "the light" of men are the same thing, the notions are taken separately. This light of men is also called, by Isaiah, "the light of the Gentiles," where he says,[1] "Behold I have set Thee for a covenant of the generation, for a light of the Gentiles;" and David, placing his confidence in this light, says in the twenty-sixth Psalm,[2] "The Lord is my illumination and my Saviour; whom shall I fear?"

19. THE LIFE HERE SPOKEN OF IS THE HIGHER LIFE, THAT OF REASON.

As for those who make up a mythology about the æons and arrange them in syzygies (yokes or pairs), and who consider the Logos and Life to have been emitted by Intellect and Truth, it may not be beside the point to state the following difficulties. How can life, in their system, the yokefellow of the Word, derive his origin from his yokefellow? For "what was made in Him," he says, evidently referring to the Word, mentioned immediately before, "was life." Will they tell us how life, the yokefellow, as they say, of the Word, came into being in the Word, and how life rather than the Word is the light of men. It would be quite natural if men of reasonable minds, who are perplexed with such questions and find the point we have raised hard to dispose of, should turn round upon us and invite us to discuss the reason why it is not the Word that is said to be the light of men, but life which originated in the Word. To such an enquiry we shall reply that the life here spoken of is not that which is common to rational beings and to beings without reason, but that life which is added to us upon the completion of reason in us, our share in that life, being derived from the first reason (Logos). It is when we turn away from the life which is life in appearance only, not in truth, and when we yearn to be filled with the true life, that we are made partakers of it, and when it has arisen in us it becomes the foundation of the light of the higher knowledge (gnosis). With some it may be that this life is only potentially and not actually light, with those who do not strive to search out the things of the higher knowledge, while with others it is actually light. With these it clearly is so who act on Paul's injunction, "Seek earnestly the best gifts;" and among the greatest gifts is that which all are enjoined to seek, namely, the word of wisdom, and it is followed by the word of knowledge. This wisdom and this knowledge lie side by side; into the difference between them this is not a fitting occasion to enquire.

20. DIFFERENT KINDS OF LIGHT; AND OF DARKNESS.

"And[1] the light shineth in darkness and the darkness hath not overtaken it." We are still enquiring about the light of men, since it is what was spoken of in the preceding verse, and also, I consider, about darkness, which is named as its adversary, the darkness also being, if the definition of it is correct, that of men. The light of men is a generic notion covering two special things; and with the darkness of men it is the same. He who has gained the light of men and shares its beams will do the work of light and know in the higher sense, being illuminated by the light of the higher knowledge. And we must recognize the analogous case of those on the other side, and of their evil actions, and of that which is thought to be but is not really knowledge, since those who exercise it have the reason (Logos) not of light but of darkness. And because the sacred word knows the things which produce light, Isaiah says:[2] "Because Thy commandments are a light upon the earth," and David says in the Psalm,[3] "The precept of the Lord is clear, enlightening the eyes." But since in addition to the commandments and the precepts there is a light of higher knowledge, we read in one of the twelve (prophets),[4] "Sow to yourselves for righteousness, reap to yourselves for the fruit of life, make light for yourselves the light of knowledge." There is a further light of knowledge in addition to the commandments, and so we read, "Make light for yourselves," not simply light, but what light?—the light of knowledge. For if any light that a man kindles for himself were a

[1] Isa. xlii. 6. [2] Ps. xxvii. 1.

[1] i. 5. [2] xxvi. 9.
[3] xix. 9. [4] Hosea x. 12.

light of knowledge, then the added words, "Make light for yourselves, the light of knowledge," would have no meaning. And again that darkness is brought upon men by their evil deeds, we learn from John himself, when he says in his epistle,[1] "If we say that we have fellowship with Him and walk in darkness, we lie and do not the truth," and again, "He that saith he is in the light, and hateth his brother, is in darkness even until now," and again, "He that hateth his brother is in darkness, and walketh in darkness, and knoweth not whither he goeth, because darkness hath blinded his eyes." Walking in darkness signifies evil conduct, and to hate one's brother, is not that to fall away from that which is properly called knowledge? But he also who is ignorant of divine things walks in darkness, just because of that ignorance; as David says,[2] "They knew not, they understood not, they walk in darkness." Consider, however, this passage,[3] "God is light and in Him is no[4] darkness," and see if the reason for this saying is not that darkness is not one, being either two, because there are two kinds of it, or many, because it is taken distributively, individually with reference to the many evil actions and the many false doctrines; so that there are many darknesses, not one of which is in God. The saying of the Saviour could not be spoken of the Holy One, "Ye are the light of the world;" for the Holy One is light of the world (absolute, not particular), and there is not in Him any darkness.

21. CHRIST IS NOT, LIKE GOD, QUITE FREE FROM DARKNESS: SINCE HE BORE OUR SINS.

Now some one will ask how this statement that there is no darkness in Him can be regarded as a thing peculiar to Him, when we consider that the Saviour also was quite without sin. Could it not be said of Him also that "He is light, and that there is no darkness in Him"? The difference between the two cases has been partly set forth above. We will now, however, go a step further than we did before, and add, that if God made Christ who knew no sin to be sin for us,[5] then it could not be said of Him that there was no darkness in Him. For if Jesus was in the likeness[6] of the flesh of sin and for sin, and condemned sin by taking upon Him the likeness of the flesh of sin, then it cannot be said of Him, absolutely and directly, that there was no darkness in Him. We may add that "He[1] took our infirmities and bare our sicknesses," both infirmities of the soul and sicknesses of the hidden man of our heart. On account of these infirmities and sicknesses which He bore away from us, He declares His soul to be sorrowful and sore troubled,[2] and He is said in Zechariah to have put on filthy garments,[3] which, when He was about to take them off, are said to be sins. "Behold, it is said, I have taken away thy sins." Because He had taken on Himself the sins of the people of those who believed in Him, he uses many such expressions as these: "Far from my salvation are the words of my transgressions,"[4] and "Thou knowest my foolishness, and my sins were not hid from Thee."[5] And let no one suppose that we say this from any lack of piety towards the Christ of God; for as the Father alone has immortality and our Lord took upon Himself, for His love to men, the death He died for us, so to the Father alone the words apply, "In Him is no darkness," since Christ took upon Himself, for His goodwill towards men, our darknesses. This He did, that by His power He might destroy our death and remove the darkness which is in our soul, so that the saying in Isaiah might be fulfilled,[6] "The people that sat in darkness saw a great light." This light, which came into being in the Logos, and is also life, shines in the darkness of our souls, and it has come where the rulers of this darkness carry on their struggle with the race of men and strive to subdue to darkness those who do not stand firm with all their power; that they might be enlightened the light has come so far, and that they might be called sons of light. And shining in darkness this light is pursued by the darkness, but not overtaken.

22. HOW THE DARKNESS FAILED TO OVERTAKE THE LIGHT.

Should any one consider that we are adding something that is not written, namely, the pursuit of the light by the darkness, let him reflect that unless the darkness had pursued the light the words, "The darkness did not overtake it," would have no meaning. John writes for those who have wit to see what is omitted and to supply it as the context requires, and so he wrote, "The darkness did not overtake it." If it did not overtake it, it must first have pursued it,

[1] 1 John i. 6; ii. 9, 11. [2] Ps. lxxxii. 5. [3] 1 John i. 5. [4] οὐδεμία, not one. [5] 2 Cor. v. 21. [6] Rom. viii. 3.

[1] Matt. viii. 17. [2] Matt. xxvi. 38. [3] Zech. iii. 4. [4] Ps. xxii. 1. [5] Ps. lxix. 5. [6] ix. 2.

and that the darkness did pursue the light is clear from what the Saviour suffered, and those also who received His teachings, His own children, when darkness was doing what it could against the sons of light and was minded to drive light away from men. But since, if God be for us,[1] no one, however that way minded, can be against us, the more they humbled themselves the more they grew, and they prevailed exceedingly. In two ways the darkness did not overtake the light. Either it was left far behind and was itself so slow, while the light was in its course so sharp and swift, that it was not even able to keep following it, or if the light sought to lay a snare for the darkness, and waited for it in pursuance of the plan it had formed, then darkness, coming near the light, was brought to an end. In either case the darkness did not overtake the light.

23. THERE IS A DIVINE DARKNESS WHICH IS NOT EVIL, AND WHICH ULTIMATELY BECOMES LIGHT.

In connection with this subject it is necessary for us to point out that darkness is not to be understood, every time it is mentioned, in a bad sense; Scripture speaks of it sometimes in a good sense. The heterodox have failed to observe this distinction, and have accordingly adopted most shameful doctrines about the Maker of the world, and have indeed revolted from Him, and addicted themselves to fictions and myths. We must, therefore, show how and when the name of darkness is taken in a good sense. Darkness and clouds and tempest are said in Exodus[2] to be round about God, and in the seventeenth Psalm,[3] "He made darkness His secret place, His tent round about Him, dark water in clouds of the air." Indeed, if one considers the multitude of speculation and knowledge about God, beyond the power of human nature to take in, beyond the power, perhaps, of all originated beings except Christ and the Holy Spirit, then one may know how God is surrounded with darkness, because the discourse is hid in ignorance which would be required to tell in what darkness He has made His hiding-place when He arranged that the things concerning Him should be unknown and beyond the grasp of knowledge. Should any one be staggered by these expositions, he may be reconciled to them both by the "dark sayings" and by the "treasures of darkness," hidden, invisible, which are given

[1] Rom. viii. 31. [2] xix. 9, 16. [3] Ps. xviii. 11.

to Christ by God. In nowise different, I consider, are the treasures of darkness which are hid in Christ, from what is spoken of in the text, "God made darkness His secret place," and (the saint) "shall understand parable and dark saying."[1] And consider if we have here the reason of the Saviour's saying to His disciples, "What ye have heard in darkness, speak ye in the light." The mysteries committed to them in secret and where few could hear, hard to be known and obscure, He bids them, when enlightened and therefore said to be in the light, to make known to every one who is made light. I might add a still stranger feature of this darkness which is praised, namely, that it hastens to the light and overtakes it, and so at last, after having been unknown as darkness, undergoes for him who does not see its power such a change that he comes to know it and to declare that what was formerly known to him as darkness has now become light.

24. JOHN THE BAPTIST WAS SENT. FROM WHERE? HIS SOUL WAS SENT FROM A HIGHER REGION.

"There was a man sent from God, whose name was John."[2] He who is sent is sent from somewhere to somewhere; and the careful student will, therefore, enquire from what quarter John was sent, and whither. The "whither" is quite plain on the face of the story; he was sent to Israel, and to those who were willing to hear him when he was staying in the wilderness of Judæa and baptizing by the banks of the Jordan. According to the deeper sense, however, he was sent into the world, the world being understood as this earthly place where men are; and the careful student will have this in view in enquiring from where John was sent. Examining the words more closely, he will perhaps declare that as it is written of Adam,[3] "And the Lord sent him forth out of the Paradise of pleasure to till the earth, out of which he was taken," so also John was sent, either from heaven or from Paradise, or from some other quarter to this place on the earth. He was sent that he might bear witness of the light. There is, however, an objection to this interpretation, which is not to be lightly dismissed. It is written in Isaiah:[4] "Whom shall I send, and who will go to the people?" The prophet answers: "Here am I,—send me." He, then, who objects to that rendering of

[1] Prov. i. 6. [2] John i. 6.
[3] Gen. iii. 23. [4] vi. 1, 9.

our passage which appears to be the deeper may say that Isaiah was sent not to this world from another place, but after having seen "the Lord sitting on a throne high and lifted up," was sent to the people, to say, "Hearing, ye shall hear and shall not understand," and so on; and that in the same manner John, the beginning of his mission not being narrated, is sent after the analogy of the mission of Isaiah, to baptize,[1] and to make ready for the Lord a people prepared for Him, and to bear witness of the light. So much we have said of the first sense; and now we adduce certain solutions which help to confirm the deeper meaning about John. In the same passage it is added, "He came for witness, to bear witness of the light." Now, if he came, where did he come from? To those who find it difficult to follow us, we point to what John says afterwards of having seen the Holy Spirit as a dove descending on the Saviour. "He that sent me," he says,[2] "to baptize with water, He said unto me, Upon whomsoever thou shalt see the Holy Spirit descending and abiding upon Him, the same is He that baptizeth with the Holy Spirit and with fire." When did He send him and give him this injunction? The answer to this question will probably be that when He sent him to begin to baptize, then He who was dealing with him uttered this word. But a more convincing argument for the view that John was sent from another region when he entered into the body, the one object of his entry into this life being that he should bear witness of the truth, may be drawn from the narrative of his birth. Gabriel, when announcing to Zacharias the birth of John, and to Mary the advent of our Saviour among men, says:[3] That John is to be "filled with the Holy Spirit even from his mother's womb." And we have also the saying, "For behold, when the voice of thy salutation came into mine ears, the babe leaped in my womb for joy." He who sedulously guards himself in his dealings with Scripture against forced, or casual, or capricious procedure, must necessarily assume that John's soul was older than his body, and subsisted by itself before it was sent on the ministry of the witness of the light. Nor must we overlook the text, "This is Elijah which is to come."[4] For if that general doctrine of the soul is to be received, namely, that it is not sown at

[1] Luke i. 17. [2] John i. 33.
[3] Luke i. 13, 15. [4] Matt. xi. 14.

the same time with the body, but is before it, and is then, for various causes, clothed with flesh and blood; then the words "sent from God" will not appear to be applicable to John alone. The most evil of all, the man of sin, the son of perdition, is said by Paul to be sent by God:[1] "God sendeth them a working of error that they should believe a lie; that they all might be judged who believed not the truth, but had pleasure in unrighteousness." But our present question may, perhaps, be solved in this way, that as every man is a man of God, simply because God created him, but not every man is called a man of God, but only he who has devoted himself to God, such as Elijah and those who are called men of God in the Scriptures, thus every man might be said in ordinary language to be sent from God, but in the absolute sense no one is to be spoken of in this way who has not entered this life for a divine ministry and in the service of the salvation of mankind. We do not find it said of any one but the saints that he is sent by God. It is said of Isaiah as we showed before; it is also said of Jeremiah, "To whomsoever I shall send thee thou shalt go";[2] and it is said of Ezekiel,[3] "I send thee to nations that are rebellious and have not believed in Me." The examples, however, do not expressly speak of a mission from the region outside life into life, and as it is a mission into life that we are enquiring about, they may seem to have little bearing on our subject. But there is nothing absurd in our transferring the argument derived from them to our question. They tell us that it is only the saints, and we were speaking of them, whom God is said to send, and in this sense they may be applied to the case of those who are sent into this life.

25. ARGUMENT FROM THE PRAYER OF JOSEPH, TO SHOW THAT THE BAPTIST MAY HAVE BEEN AN ANGEL WHO BECAME A MAN.

As we are now engaged with what is said of John, and are asking about his mission, I may take the opportunity to state the view which I entertain about him. We have read this prophecy about him, "Behold, I send My messenger (angel) before Thy face, who shall prepare Thy way before Thee;" and at this we ask if it can be one of the holy angels who is sent down on this ministry as forerunner of our Saviour. No wonder if, when the first-born of all creation was assuming a human body, some of them should

[1] 2 Thess. ii. 11, 12. [2] Jer. i. 7. [3] Ezek. ii. 3.

have been filled with love to man and become admirers and followers of Christ, and thought it good to minister to his kindness towards man by having a body like that of men. And who would not be moved at the thought of his leaping for joy when yet in the belly, surpassing as he did the common nature of man? Should the piece entitled "The prayer of Joseph," one of the apocryphal works current among the Hebrews, be thought worthy of credence, this dogma will be found in it clearly expressed. Those at the beginning, it is represented, having some marked distinction beyond men, and being much greater than other souls, because they were angels, they have come down to human nature. Thus Jacob says: "I, Jacob, who speak to you, and Israel, I am an angel of God, a ruling spirit, and Abraham and Isaac were created before every work of God; and I am Jacob, called Jacob by men, but my name is Israel, called Israel by God, a man seeing God, because I am the first-born of every creature which God caused to live." And he adds: "When I was coming from Mesopotamia of Syria, Uriel, the angel of God, came forth, and said, I have come down to the earth and made my dwelling among men, and I am called Jacob by name. He was wroth with me and fought with me and wrestled against me, saying that his name and the name of Him who is before every angel should be before my name. And I told him his name and how great he was among the sons of God; Art not thou Uriel my eighth, and I am Israel and archangel of the power of the Lord and a chief captain among the sons of God? Am not I Israel, the first minister in the sight of God, and I invoked my God by the inextinguishable name?" It is likely that this was really said by Jacob, and was therefore written down, and that there is also a deeper meaning in what we are told, "He supplanted his brother in the womb." Consider whether the celebrated question about Jacob and Esau has a solution. We read,[1] "The children being not yet born, neither having done anything good or bad, that the purpose of God according to election might stand, not of works but of him that calleth, it was said, "The elder shall serve the younger." Even as it is written: "Jacob I loved, but Esau I hated." What shall we say, then? Is there unrighteousness with God? God forbid." If, then, when they were not yet born, and had not done anything either good or evil, in order that God's purpose according to election might stand, not of works, but of him that calleth, if at such a period this was said, how if we do not go back to the works done before this life, can it be said that there is no unrighteousness with God when the elder serves the younger and is hated (by God) before he has done anything worthy of slavery or of hatred? We have made something of a digression in introducing this story about Jacob and appealing to a writing which we cannot well treat with contempt; but it certainly adds weight to our argument about John, to the effect that as Isaiah's voice declares[1] he is an angel who assumed a body for the sake of bearing witness to the light. So much about John considered as a man.

[1] Rom. ix. 11–14.

26. JOHN IS VOICE, JESUS IS SPEECH. RELATION OF THESE TWO TO EACH OTHER.

Now we know voice and speech to be different things. The voice can be produced without any meaning and with no speech in it, and similarly speech can be reported to the mind without voice, as when we make mental excursions, within ourselves. And thus the Saviour is, in one view of Him, speech, and John differs from Him; for as the Saviour is speech, John is voice. John himself invites me to take this view of him, for to those who asked who he was, he answered, "I am the voice of one crying in the wilderness, Prepare the way of the Lord! make His paths straight!" This explains, perhaps, how it was that Zacharias lost his voice at the birth of the voice which points out the Word of God, and only recovered it when the voice, forerunner of the Word, was born. A voice must be perceived with the ears if the mind is afterwards to receive the speech which the voice indicates. Hence, John is, in point of his birth, a little older than Christ, for our voice comes to us before our speech. But John also points to Christ; for speech is brought forward by the voice. And Christ is baptized by John, though John declares himself to have need to be baptized by Christ; for with men speech is purified by voice, though the natural way is that speech should purify the voice which indicates it. In a word, when John points out Christ, it is man pointing out God, the Saviour incorporeal, the voice pointing out the Word.

27. SIGNIFICANCE OF THE NAMES OF JOHN AND OF HIS PARENTS.

The force that is in names may be applied

[1] Isa. xl. 3.

in many matters, and it may be worth our while to ask at this point what is the significance of the names John and Zacharias. The relatives wish, as the giving of a name is a thing not to be lightly disposed of, to call the child Zacharias, and are surprised that Elisabeth should want him to be called John. Zacharias then writes, "His name is John," and is at once freed from his troublesome silence. On examining the names, then, we find "Joannes" to be "Joa" without the "nes." The New Testament gives Hebrew names a Greek form and treats them as Greek words; Jacob is changed into Jacobus, Symeon into Simon, and Joannes is the same as Joa. Zacharias is said to be memory, and Elisabeth "oath of my God," or "strength of my God." John then came into the world from grace of God (=Joa=Joannes), and his parents were Memory (about God) and the Oath of our God, about the fathers. Thus was he born to make ready for the Lord a people fit for Him, at the end of the Covenant now grown old, which is the end of the Sabbatic period. Hence it is not possible that the rest after the Sabbath should have come into existence from the seventh of our God; on the contrary, it is our Saviour who, after the pattern of His own rest, caused us to be made in the likeness of His death, and hence also of His resurrection.[1]

28. THE PROPHETS BORE WITNESS TO CHRIST AND FORETOLD MANY THINGS CONCERNING HIM.

"He came for a witness that He might bear witness of the light, that all through Him might believe."[2] Some of the dissenters from the Church's doctrine, men who profess to believe in Christ, have desired another being, as indeed their system requires, besides the Creator, and hence cannot allow His coming to the world to have been foretold by the prophets.[3] They therefore endeavour to get rid of the testimonies of the prophets about Christ, and say that the Son of God has no need of witnesses, but that He brings with Him His own evidence, partly in the sound words full of power which He proclaimed and partly in the wonderful works He did, which were sufficient at once to convince any one whatever. Then they say: If Moses is believed on account of his word and his works, and has no need of any witnesses to announce him beforehand, and if the prophets were received, every one of them, by these people, as messengers from God, how should not one who is much greater than Moses and the prophets accomplish His mission and benefit the human race, without prophets to bear witness about Him? They regard it as superfluous that He should have been foretold by the prophets, since the prophets were concerned, as these opponents would say, that those who believed in Christ should not receive Him as a new God, and therefore did what they could to bring them to that same God whom Moses and the prophets taught before Jesus. To this we must say that as there are many causes which may lead men to believe, since men who are not moved by one argument may be by another, so God is able to provide for men a number of occasions, any of which may cause their minds to open to the truth that God, who is over all, has taken on Himself human nature. It is manifest to all, how some are brought by the prophetic writings to the admiration of Christ. They are astounded at the voices of so many prophets before Him, which establish the place of His birth, the country of His upbringing, the power of His teaching, His working of wonderful works, and His human passion brought to a close by His resurrection. We must notice, too, that Christ's stupendous acts of power were able to bring to the faith those of Christ's own time, but that they lost their demonstrative force with the lapse of years and began to be regarded as mythical. Greater evidential value than that of the miracles then performed attaches to the comparison which we now make between these miracles and the prophecy of them; this makes it impossible for the student to cast any doubt on the former. The prophetic testimonies do not declare merely the advent of the Messiah; it is by no means the case that they teach this and nothing else. They teach a great deal of theology. The relation of the Father to the Son and of the Son to the Father may be learned not less from what the prophets announce about Christ, than from the Apostles narrating the splendours of the Son of God. A parallel case, which we may venture to adduce, is that of the martyrs, who were honoured by the witness they bore Him, and by no means conferred any favour on Him by their witnessing for the Son of God. And how is it if, as many of Christ's true disciples were honoured by having thus to witness for Him, so the

[1] Origen appears to be pointing to the fact that the Christian rest which is connected in its origin with the resurrection of Christ is not held as the Jewish Sabbath rest on the seventh but on the first day of the week. John marking the end of the old period is the son of Elisabeth the oath, or seventh, of God, and is thus connected with the seventh day; but not so Jesus.

[2] John i. 7.

[3] The Old Testament belongs to the Creator, the Demiurge.

prophets received from God as their special gift that of understanding about Christ and announcing Him before, and that they taught not only those living after Christ's advent how they should regard the Son of God, but those also who lived in the generations before Him? As he who in these times does not know the Son has not the Father either,[1] so also we are to understand it was in these earlier times. Hence "Abraham rejoiced to see the day of Christ, and he saw it and was glad."[2] He, therefore, who declares that they are not to testify about Christ is seeking to deprive the chorus of the prophets of the greatest gift they have; for what office of equal importance would be left to prophecy, inspired as it is by the Holy Spirit, if all connection with the economy of our Lord and Master were taken away from it? For as these have their faith well ordered who approach the God of the universe through Mediator and High-Priest and Paraclete, and as his religion is a halting one who does not go in through the door to the Father, so also in the case of men of old time. Their religion was sanctified and made acceptable to God by their knowledge and faith and expectation of Christ. For we have observed that God declares Himself to be a witness and exhorts them all to declare the same about Christ, and to be imitators of Him, bearing witness of Him to all who require it. For he says,[3] "Be witnesses for Me, and I am witness, saith the Lord God, and My servant whom I have chosen." Now every one who bears witness to the truth, whether he support it by words or deeds, or in whatever way, may properly be called a witness (martyr); but it has come to be the custom of the brotherhood, since they are struck with admiration of those who have contended to the death for truth and valour, to keep the name of martyr more properly for those who have borne witness to the mystery of godliness by shedding their blood for it. The Saviour gives the name of martyr to every one who bears witness to the truth He declares; thus at the Ascension He says to His disciples:[4] "You shall be my witnesses in Jerusalem and in Judæa and in Samaria and unto the uttermost parts of the earth." The leper who was cleansed[5] had still to bring the gift which Moses commanded for a testimony to those who did not believe in the Christ. In the same way the martyrs bear witness for a testimony to the unbelieving, and so do all the saints whose deeds shine before men. They spend their life rejoicing in the cross of Christ and bearing witness to the true light.

29. THE SIX TESTIMONIES OF THE BAPTIST ENUMERATED. JESUS' "COME AND SEE." SIGNIFICANCE OF THE TENTH HOUR.

Accordingly John came to bear witness of the light, and in his witness-bearing he cried, saying,[1] "He that cometh after me exists before me; for He was before me; for of His fulness we have all received and grace for grace, for the law was given by Moses, but grace and truth came through Jesus Christ. No one hath seen God at any time; the only-begotten God, who is in the bosom of the Father, He hath declared Him." This whole speech is from the mouth of the Baptist bearing witness to the Christ. Some take it otherwise, and consider that the words from "for of His fulness" to "He hath declared Him" are from the writer, John the Apostle. The true state of the case is that John's first testimony begins, as we said before, "He that cometh after me," and ends, "He hath declared Him," and his second testimony is that spoken to the priests and levites sent from Jerusalem, whom the Jews had sent. To them he confesses and does not deny the truth, namely, that he is not the Christ, nor Elijah, nor the prophet, but "the voice of one crying in the wilderness, Make straight the way of the Lord, as saith Isaiah the prophet."[2] After this there is another testimony of the same Baptist to Christ, still teaching His superior nature, which goes forth into the whole world and enters into reasonable souls. He says,[3] "There standeth One among you whom you know not, even He that cometh after me, the latchet of whose shoe I am not worthy to unloose." Consider if, since the heart is in the middle of the whole body, and the ruling principle in the heart, the saying, "There standeth One among you whom you know not," can be understood of[4] the reason which is in every man. John's fourth testimony of Christ after these points to His human sufferings. He says,[5] "Behold the Lamb of God, which taketh away the sin of the world. This is He of whom I said, After me cometh a man who exists before me, for He was before me. And I knew Him not, but that He should be made

[1] 1 John ii. 23. [2] John viii. 56. [3] Isa. xliii. 10. [4] Acts i. 8. [5] Matt. viii. 4.

[1] i. 7, 15–18. [2] i. 23. [3] i. 26. [4] Reading κατὰ for καί. [5] i. 29–31.

manifest to Israel, therefore am I come baptizing with water." And the fifth testimony is recorded in the words,[1] "I beheld the Spirit descending as a dove out of heaven, and it abode upon Him, and I knew Him not, but He that sent me to baptize with water, He said unto me, Upon whomsoever thou shalt see the Spirit descending and abiding upon Him, the same is He that baptizeth with the Holy Spirit. And I have seen and borne witness that this is the Son of God." In the sixth place John witnesses of Christ to the two disciples:[2] "He looked on Jesus as He walked and saith, Behold the Lamb of God." After this testimony the two disciples who heard it followed Jesus; and Jesus turned and beheld them following, and saith unto them, "What seek ye?" Perhaps it is not without significance that after six testimonies John ceases from his witness-bearing and Jesus brings forward in the seventh place His "What seek ye?" Very becoming in those who have been helped by John's testimony is the speech in which they address Christ as their Master, and declare their wish to see the dwelling of the Son of God; for they say to Him, "Rabbi," which answers to "Master," in our language, "where dwellest Thou?" And since every one that seeketh findeth, when John's disciples seek Jesus' dwelling, Jesus shows it to them, saying, "Come and see." By the word "Come" He exhorts them perhaps to the practical part of life, while the "see" is to suggest to them that that speculation which comes in the train of right conduct will be vouchsafed to those who desire it; in Jesus' dwelling they will have it. After they had asked where Jesus dwells, and had followed the Master and had seen, they desired to stay with Him and to spend that day with the Son of God. Now the number ten is a sacred one, not a few mysteries being indicated by it; and so we are to understand that the mention of the tenth hour as that at which these disciples turned in with Jesus, is not without significance. Of these disciples, Andrew, the brother of Simon Peter, is one; and he having profited by this day with Jesus and having found his own brother Simon (perhaps he had not found him before), told him that he had found the Messiah, which is, being interpreted, Christ. It is written that "he that seeketh findeth." Now he had sought where Jesus dwelt, and had followed Him and looked upon His dwelling; he stays with the Lord "at the tenth hour," and finds the Son of God, the Word, and Wisdom, and is ruled by Him as King. That is why he says, "We have found the Messiah," and this a thing which every one can say who has found this Word of God and is ruled as by a king, by His Divinity. As a fruit he at once brings his brother to Christ, and Christ deigned to look upon Simon, that is to say, by looking at him to visit and enlighten his ruling principle; and Simon by Jesus' looking at him was enabled to grow strong, so as to earn a new name from that work of firmness and strength, and to be called Peter.

30. HOW JOHN WAS A WITNESS OF CHRIST, AND SPECIALLY OF "THE LIGHT."

It may be asked why we should have gone through all this when the verse before us is, "He came for witness, that he might bear witness of the light." But it was necessary to give John's testimonies to the light, and to show the order in which they took place, and also, in order to show how effective John's testimony proved, to set forth the help it afforded afterwards to those to whom he bore it. But before all these testimonies there was an earlier one when the Baptist leaped in the womb of Elisabeth at the greeting of Mary. That was a testimony to Christ and attested His divine conception and birth. And what more need I say? John is everywhere a witness and forerunner of Christ. He anticipates His birth and dies a little before the death of the Son of God, and thus witnesses not only for those at the time of the birth, but to those who were expecting the freedom which was to come for man through the death of Christ. Thus, in all his life, he is a little before Christ, and everywhere makes ready for the Lord a people prepared for Him. And John's testimony precedes also the second and diviner coming of Christ, for we read,[1] "If ye will receive it, this is Elijah which is to come. He that hath ears to hear let him hear." Now, there was a beginning, in which the Word was,—and we saw from Proverbs that that beginning was wisdom,—and the Word was in existence, and in the Word life was made, and the life was the light of men; and all this being so, I ask why the man who came, sent from God, whose name was John, why he came for witness to bear witness especially of the light? Why did he not come to bear witness of the life, or of the Word, or about the

[1] i. 32-34.

[2] i. 35-38.

[1] Matt. xi. 14, 15.

beginning, or about any other of the many aspects in which Christ appears? Consider here the texts, "The people which sat in darkness saw a great light," and "The light shineth in darkness, and the darkness overtook it not," and consider how those who are in darkness, that is, men, have need of light. For if the light of men shines in darkness, and there is no active power in darkness to attain to it, then we must partake of other aspects of Christ; at present we have no real share of Him at all. For what share have we of life, we who are still in the body of death, and whose life is hid with Christ in God?[1] "For when Christ who is our life shall appear, then shall we also appear with Him in glory." It was not possible, therefore, that he who came should bear witness about a life which is still hid with Christ in God. Nor did he come for witness to bear witness of the Word, for we know the Word who was in the beginning with God and who is God the Word; for the Word was made flesh on the earth. And though the witness had been, at least apparently, about the Word, it would in fact have been about the Word made flesh and not about the word of God. He did not come, therefore, to bear witness of the Word. And how could there be any witness-bearing about wisdom, to those who, even if they appear to know something, cannot understand pure truth, but behold it through a glass and in an enigma? It is likely, however, that before the second and diviner advent of Christ, John or Elias will come to bear witness about life a little before Christ our life is made manifest, and that then they will bear witness about the Word, and offer also their testimony about wisdom. Some inquiry is necessary whether a testimony such as that of John is to precede each of the aspects of Christ. So much for the words, "He came for witness, to bear witness of the light." What we are to understand by the further words, "That all might believe through Him," may be considered later.

[1] Coloss. iii. 3, 4.

FRAGMENTS OF THE FOURTH BOOK[1]

(*Three Leaves from the Beginning.*)

1. He who distinguishes in himself voice and meaning and things for which the meaning stands, will not be offended at rudeness of language if, on enquiry, he finds the things spoken of to be sound. The more may this be so when we remember how the holy men acknowledge their speech and their preaching to be not in persuasion of the wisdom of words, but in demonstration of the Spirit and of power. . . .

[*Then, after speaking of the rudeness of style of the Gospel, he proceeds:*]

2. The Apostles are not unaware that in some things they give offence, and that in some respects their culture is defective, and they confess themselves[2] accordingly to be rude in speech but not in knowledge; for we must consider that the other Apostles would have said this, too, as well as Paul. As for the text,[3] "But we have this treasure in earthen vessels, that the excellency of the power may be of God and not of us," we interpret it in this way. By "treasures" we understand here, as in other passages, the treasure of knowledge (gnosis) and of hidden wisdom. By "earthen vessels" we understand the humble diction of the Scriptures, which the Greek might so readily be led to despise, and in which the excellency of God's power appears so clearly. The mystery of the truth and the power of the things said were not hindered by the humble diction from travelling to the ends of the earth, nor from subduing to the word of Christ, not only the foolish things of the world, but sometimes its wise things, too. For we see our calling,[1] not that no wise man according to the flesh, but that not many wise according to the flesh. But Paul, in his preaching of the Gospel, is a debtor[2] to deliver the word not to Barbarians only, but also to Greeks, and not only to the unwise, who would easily agree with him, but also to the wise. For he was made sufficient[3] by God to be a minister of the New Covenant, wielding the demonstration of the spirit and of power, so that when the believers agreed with him their belief should

[1] From the *Philocalia*. [2] 2 Cor. xi. 6. [3] 2 Cor. iv. 7.

[1] 1 Cor. i. 26, 27. [2] Rom. i. 14. [3] 2 Cor. iii. 6.

not be in the wisdom of men, but in the power of God. For, perhaps, if the Scripture possessed, like the works the Greeks admire, elegance and command of diction, then it would be open to suppose that not the truth of them had laid hold of men, but that the apparent sequence and splendour of language had carried off the hearers, and had carried them off by guile.

FROM THE FIFTH BOOK.

(*From the Preface.*)[1]

You are not content to fulfil the office, when I am present with you, of a taskmaster to drive me to labour at theology; even when I am absent you demand that I should spend most of my time on you and on the task I have to do for you.[2] I, for my part, am inclined to shrink from toil, and to avoid that danger which threatens from God those who give themselves to writing on divinity; thus I would take shelter in Scripture in refraining from making many books. For Solomon says in Ecclesiastes,[3] "My son, beware of making many books; there is no end of it, and much study is a weariness of the flesh." For we, except that text have some hidden meaning which we do not yet perceive, have directly transgressed the injunction, we have not guarded ourselves against making many books.

[*Then, after saying that this discussion of but a few sentences of the Gospel have run to four volumes, he goes on :*]

2. HOW SCRIPTURE WARNS US AGAINST MAKING MANY BOOKS.

For, to judge by the words of the phrase, "My son, beware of making many books," two things appear to be indicated by it: first, that we ought not to possess many books, and then that we ought not to compose many books. If the first is not the meaning the second must be, and if the second is the meaning the first does not necessarily follow. In either case we appear to be told that we ought not to make many books. I might take my stand on this dictum which now confronts us, and send you the text as an excuse, and I might appeal in support of this position to the fact that not even the saints found leisure to compose many books; and thus I might cry off from the bargain we made with each other, and give up writing what I was to send to you. You, on your side, would no doubt feel the force of the text I have cited, and might, for the future, excuse me. But we must treat Scripture conscientiously, and must not congratulate ourselves because we see the primary meaning of a text, that we understand it altogether. I do not, therefore, shrink from bringing forward what excuse I think I am able to offer for myself, and to point out the arguments, which you would certainly use against me, if I acted contrary to our agreement. And in the first place, the Sacred History seems to agree with the text in question, inasmuch as none of the saints composed several works, or set forth his views in a number of books. I will take up this point: when I proceed to write a number of books, the critic will remind me that even such a one as Moses left behind him only five books.

[1] From the Philocalia.
[2] This is addressed to Ambrose, who was at the time absent from Alexandria. Cf. book i. chap. 6, p. 299.
[3] xii. 12.

3. THE APOSTLES WROTE LITTLE.[1]

But he who was made fit to be a minister of the New Covenant, not of the letter, but of the spirit, Paul, who fulfilled the Gospel from Jerusalem round about to Illyricum,[2] did not write epistles to all the churches he taught, and to those to whom he did write he sent no more than a few lines. And Peter, on whom the Church of Christ is built, against which the gates of hell shall not prevail,[3] left only one epistle of acknowledged genuineness. Suppose we allow that he left a second; for this is doubtful. What are we to say of him who leaned on Jesus' breast, namely, John, who left one Gospel, though confessing[4] that he could make so many that the world would not contain them? But he wrote also the Apocalypse, being commanded to be silent and not to write the voices of the seven thunders.[5] But he also left an epistle of very few lines.

[1] From Eusebius, *Hist. Eccl.* vi. 25.
[2] Rom. xv. 19.
[3] Matt. xvi. 18.
[4] John i. 20, 25.
[5] Apoc. x. 4.

Suppose also a second and a third, since not all pronounce these to be genuine; but the two together do not amount to a hundred lines.

[*Then, after enumerating the prophets and Apostles, and showing how each wrote only a little, or not even a little, he goes on:*][1]

4. I feel myself growing dizzy with all this, and wonder whether, in obeying you, I have not been obeying God, nor walking in the footsteps of the saints, unless it be that my too great love to you, and my unwillingness to cause you any pain, has led me astray and caused me to think of all these excuses. We started from the words of the preacher, where he says: "My son, beware of making many books." With this I compare a saying from the Proverbs of the same Solomon,[2] "In the multitude of words thou shalt not escape sin; but in sparing thy lips thou shalt be wise." Here I ask whether speaking many words of whatever kind is a multitude of words (in the sense of the preacher), even if the many words a man speaks are sacred and connected with salvation. If this be the case, and if he who makes use of many salutary words is guilty of "multitude of words," then Solomon himself did not escape this sin, for "he spoke[3] three thousand proverbs, and five thousand songs, and he spoke of trees from the cedar that is in Lebanon even unto the hyssop that springeth out of the wall, he spoke also of beasts and of fowl, and of creeping things and of fishes." How, I may ask, can any one give any course of instruction, without a multitude of words, using the phrase in its simplest sense? Does not Wisdom herself say to those who are perishing,[4] "I stretched out my words, and ye heeded not"? Do we not find Paul, too, extending his discourse from morning to midnight,[5] when Eutychus was borne down with sleep and fell down, to the dismay of the hearers, who thought he was killed? If, then, the words are true, "In much speaking thou wilt not escape sin," and if Solomon was yet not guilty of great sin when he discoursed on the subjects above mentioned, nor Paul when he prolonged his discourse till midnight, then the question arises, What is that much speaking which is referred to? and then we may pass on to consider what are the many books. Now the entire Word of God, who was in the beginning with God, is not much speaking, is not *words;* for the Word is one, being composed of the many speculations (theoremata), each of which is a part of the Word in its entirety. Whatever words there be outside of this one, which promise to give any description and exposition, even though they be words about truth, none of these, to put it in a somewhat paradoxical way, is Word or Reason, they are all words or reasons. They are not the monad, far from it; they are not that which agrees and is one in itself, by their inner divisions and conflicts unity has departed from them, they have become numbers, perhaps infinite numbers. We are obliged, therefore, to say that whoever speaks that which is foreign to religion is using many words, while he who speaks the words of truth, even should he go over the whole field and omit nothing, is always speaking the one word. Nor are the saints guilty of much speaking, since they always have the aim in view which is connected with the one word. It appears, then, that the much speaking which is condemned is judged to be so rather from the nature of the views propounded, than from the number of the words pronounced. Let us see if we cannot conclude in the same way that all the sacred books are one book, but that those outside are the "many books" of the preacher. The proof of this must be drawn from Holy Scripture, and it will be most satisfactorily established if I am able to show that it is not only one book, taking the word now in its commoner meaning, that we find to be written about Christ. Christ is written about even in the Pentateuch; He is spoken of in each of the Prophets, and in the Psalms, and, in a word, as the Saviour Himself says, in all the Scriptures. He refers us to them all, when He says:[1] "Search the Scriptures, for in them ye think ye have eternal life, and these are they which testify of Me." And if He refers us to the Scriptures as testifying of Him, it is not to one that He sends us, to the exclusion of another, but to all that speak of Him, those which, in the Psalms, He calls the chapter of the book, saying,[2] "In the chapter of the book it is written of Me." If any one proposes to take these words, "In the chapter of the book it is written of Me," literally, and to apply them to this or that special passage where Christ is spoken of, let him tell us on what principle he warrants his preference for one

[1] The following fragments is found in *Philocalia*, pp. 27–30.
[2] x. 19.
[3] 1 Kings iv. 32.
[4] Prov. i. 24.
[5] Acts xx. 7–9.

[1] John v. 39.
[2] xl. 7.

book over another. If any one supposes that we are doing something of this kind ourselves, and applying the words in question to the book of Psalms, we deny that we do so, and we would urge that in that case the words should have been, "In this book it is written of Me." But He speaks of all the books as one chapter, thus summing up in one all that is spoken of Christ for our instruction. In fact the book was seen by John,[1] "written within and without, and sealed; and no one could open it to read it, and to loose the seals thereof, but the Lion of the tribe of Judah, the root of David, who has the key of David,[2] he that openeth and none shall shut, and that shutteth and none shall open." For the book here spoken of means the whole of Scripture; and it is written within (lit. in front), on account of the meaning which is obvious, and on the back, on account of its remoter and spiritual sense. Observe, in addition to this, if a proof that the sacred writings are one book, and those of an opposite character many, may not be found in the fact that there is one book of the living from which those who have proved unworthy to be in it are blotted out, as it is written:[3] "Let them be blotted out of the book of the living," while of those who are to undergo the judgment, there are books in the plural, as Daniel says:[4] "The judgment was set, and the books were opened." But Moses also bears witness to the unity of the sacred book, when he says:[5] "If Thou forgive the people their sins, forgive, but if not, then wipe me out of the book which Thou hast written." The passage in Isaiah,[6] too, I read in the same way. It is not peculiar to his prophecy that the words of the book should be sealed, and should neither be read by him who does not know letters, because he is ignorant of letters, nor by him who is learned, because the book is sealed. This is true of every writing, for every written work needs the reason (Logos) which closed it to open it. "He shall shut, and none shall open,"[7] and when He opens no one can cast doubt on the interpretation He brings. Hence it is said that He shall open and no man shall shut. I infer a similar lesson from the book spoken of in Ezekiel,[8] in which was written lamentation, and a song, and woe. For the whole book is full of the woe of the lost, and the song of the saved, and the lamentation of those between these two. And John, too,

[1] Apoc. v. 1-5. [2] Apoc. iii. 7. [3] Ps. lxix. 28. [4] Dan. vii. 10. [5] Exod. xxxii. 32. [6] xxix. 11, 12. [7] Isa. xxii. 22. [8] ii. 10.

when he speaks of his eating the one roll,[1] in which both front and back were written on, means the whole of Scripture, one book which is, at first, most sweet when one begins, as it were, to chew it, but bitter in the revelation of himself which it makes to the conscience of each one who knows it. I will add to the proof of this an apostolic saying which has been quite misunderstood by the disciples of Marcion, who, therefore, set the Gospels at naught. The Apostle says:[2] "According to my Gospel in Christ Jesus;" he does not speak of Gospels in the plural, and, hence, they argue that as the Apostle only speaks of one Gospel in the singular, there was only one in existence. But they fail to see that, as He is one of whom all the evangelists write, so the Gospel, though written by several hands, is, in effect, one. And, in fact, the Gospel, though written by four, is one. From these considerations, then, we learn what the one book is, and what the many books, and what I am now concerned about is, not the quantity I may write, but the effect of what I say, lest, if I fail in this point, and set forth anything against the truth itself, even in one of my writings, I should prove to have transgressed the commandment, and to be a writer of "many books." Yet I see the heterodox assailing the holy Church of God in these days, under the pretence of higher wisdom, and bringing forward works in many volumes in which they offer expositions of the evangelical and apostolic writings, and I fear that if I should be silent and should not put before our members the saving and true doctrines, these teachers might get a hold of curious souls, which, in the absence of wholesome nourishment, might go after food that is forbidden, and, in fact, unclean and horrible. It appears to me, therefore, to be necessary that one who is able to represent in a genuine manner the doctrine of the Church, and to refute those dealers in knowledge, falsely so-called, should take his stand against historical fictions, and oppose to them the true and lofty evangelical message in which the agreement of the doctrines, found both in the so-called Old Testament and in the so-called New, appears so plainly and fully. You yourself felt at one time the lack of good representatives of the better cause, and were impatient of a faith which was at issue with reason and absurd, and you then, for the love you bore to the Lord, gave yourself to composition from which, however, in

[1] Apoc. x. 9, 10. [2] Rom. ii 16.

the exercise of the judgment with which you are endowed, you afterwards desisted. This is the defence which I think admits of being made for those who have the faculty of speaking and writing. But I am also pleading my own cause, as I now devote myself with what boldness I may to the work of exposition; for it may be that I am not endowed with that habit and disposition which he ought to have who is fitted by God to be a minister of the New Covenant, not of the letter but of the spirit.

SIXTH BOOK

1. THE WORK IS TAKEN UP AFTER A VIOLENT INTERRUPTION, WHICH HAS DRIVEN THE WRITER FROM ALEXANDRIA. HE ADDRESSES HIMSELF TO IT AGAIN, WITH THANKS FOR HIS DELIVERANCE, AND PRAYER FOR GUIDANCE.

When a house is being built which is to be made as strong as possible, the building takes place in fine weather and in calm, so that nothing may hinder the structure from acquiring the needed solidity. And thus it turns out so strong and stable that it is able to withstand the rush of the flood, and the dashing of the river, and all the agencies accompanying a storm which are apt to find out what is rotten in a building and to show what parts of it have been properly put together. And more particularly should that house which is capable of sheltering the speculations of truth, the house of reason, as it were, in promise or in letters, be built at a time when God can add His free co-operation to the projector of so noble a work, when the soul is quiet and in the enjoyment of that peace which passes all understanding, when she is turned away from all disturbance and not buffeted by any billows. This, it appears to me, was well understood by the servants of the prophetic spirit and the ministers of the Gospel message; they made themselves worthy to receive that peace which is in secret from Him who ever gives it to them that are worthy and who said,[1] "Peace I leave with you, My peace I give unto you; not as the world giveth give I unto you." And look if some similar lesson is not taught under the surface with regard to David and Solomon in the narrative about the temple. David, who fought the wars of the Lord and stood firm against many enemies, his own and those of Israel, desired to build a temple for God. But God, through Nathan, prevents him from doing so, and Nathan says to him,[2] "Thou shalt not build me an house, because thou art a man of blood." But Solomon, on the other hand, saw God in a dream, and in a dream received wisdom, for the reality of the vision was kept for him who said, "Behold a greater than Solomon is here." The time was one of the profoundest peace, so that it was possible for every man to rest under his own vine and his own fig-tree, and Solomon's very name was significant of the peace which was in his days, for Solomon means peaceful; and so he was at liberty to build the famous temple of God. About the time of Ezra, also, when "truth conquers wine and the hostile king and women,"[1] the temple of God is restored again. All this is said by way of apology to you, reverend Ambrosius. It is at your sacred encouragement that I have made up my mind to build up in writing the tower of the Gospel; and I have therefore sate down to count the cost,[2] if I have sufficient to finish it, lest I should be mocked by the beholders, because I laid the foundation but was not able to finish the work. The result of my counting, it is true, has been that I do not possess what is required to finish it; yet I have put my trust in God, who enriches us[3] with all wisdom and all knowledge. If we strive to keep His spiritual laws we believe that He does enrich us; He will supply what is necessary so that we shall get on with our building, and shall even come to the parapet of the structure. That parapet it is which keeps from falling those who go up on the house of the Word; for people only fall off those houses which have no parapet, so that the buildings themselves are to blame for their fall and for their death. We proceeded as far as the fifth volume in spite of the obstacles presented by the storm in Alexandria, and spoke what was given us to speak, for Jesus rebuked the winds and the waves of the sea. We emerged from the storm, we were brought out of Egypt, that God delivering

[1] John xiv. 27.

[2] 1 Chron. xxii. 8, 9.

[1] 3 Esdras iv. 37, 41, 47.

[2] Luke xiv. 28.

[3] 1 Cor. i. 5.

us who led His people forth from there. Then, when the enemy assailed us with all bitterness by his new writings, so directly hostile to the Gospel, and stirred up against us all the winds of wickedness in Egypt, I felt that reason called me rather to stand fast for the conflict, and to save the higher part in me, lest evil counsels should succeed in directing the storm so as to overwhelm my soul, rather to do this than to finish my work at an unsuitable season, before my mind had recovered its calm. Indeed, the ready writers who usually attended me brought my work to a stand by failing to appear to take down my words. But now that the many fiery darts directed against me have lost their edge, for God extinguished them, and my soul has grown accustomed to the dispensation sent me for the sake of the heavenly word, and has learned from necessity to disregard the snares of my enemies, it is as if a great calm had settled on me, and I defer no longer the continuation of this work. I pray that God will be with me, and will speak as a teacher in the porch of my soul, so that the building I have begun of the exposition of the Gospel of John may arrive at completion. May God hear my prayer and grant that the body of the whole work may now be brought together, and that no interruption may intervene which might prevent me from following the sequence of Scripture. And be assured that it is with great readiness that I now make this second beginning and enter on my sixth volume, because what I wrote before at Alexandria has not, I know not by what chance, been brought with me. I feared I might neglect this work, if I were not engaged on it at once, and therefore thought it better to make use of this present time and begin without delay the part which remains. I am not certain if the part formerly written will come to light, and would be very unwilling to waste time in waiting to see if it does. Enough of preamble, let us now attend to our text.

2. HOW THE PROPHETS AND HOLY MEN OF THE OLD TESTAMENT KNEW THE THINGS OF CHRIST.

"And this is the witness of John."[1] This is the second recorded testimony of John the Baptist to Christ. The first begins with "This was He of whom I said, He that cometh after me," and goes down to "The only-begotten Son of God who is in the bosom of the Father, He hath declared him." Heracleon supposes the words, "No one has seen God at any time," etc., to have been spoken, not by the Baptist, but by the disciple. But in this he is not sound. He himself allows the words, "Of his fulness we all received, and grace for grace; for the law was given by Moses, but grace and truth came by Jesus Christ," to have been spoken by the Baptist. And does it not follow that the person who received of the fulness of Christ, and a second grace in addition to that he had before, and who declared the law to have been given by Moses, but grace and truth to have come through Jesus Christ, is it not clear that this is the person who understood, from what he received from the fulness of Christ, how "no one hath seen God at any time," and how "the only-begotten who is in the bosom of the Father" had delivered the declaration about God to him and to all those who had received of His fulness? He was not declaring here for the first time Him that is in the bosom of the Father, as if there had never before been any one fit to receive what he told His Apostles. Does he not teach us that he was before Abraham, and that Abraham rejoiced and was glad to see his day? The words "Of his fulness all we received," and "Grace for grace," show, as we have already made clear, that the prophets also received their gift from the fulness of Christ and received a second grace in place of that they had before; for they also, led by the Spirit, advanced from the introduction they had in types to the vision of truth. Hence not all the prophets, but many of them,[1] desired to see the things, which the Apostles saw. For if there was a difference among the prophets, those who were perfect and more distinguished of them did not desire to see what the Apostles saw, but actually beheld them, while those who rose less fully than these to the height of the Word were filled with longing for the things which the Apostles knew through Christ. The word "saw" we have not taken in a physical sense, and the word "heard" we have taken to refer to a spiritual communication; only he who has ears is prepared to hear the words of Jesus—a thing which does not happen too frequently. There is the further point, that the saints before the bodily advent of Jesus had an advantage over most believers in their insight into the mysteries of divinity, since the Word of God was their teacher before He became flesh, for He was always work-

[1] John i. 19.

[1] Matt. xiii. 17.

ing, in imitation of His Father, of whom He says, "My father worketh hitherto." On this point we may adduce the words He addresses to the Sadducees, who do not believe the doctrine of the resurrection. "Have you not read," He says,[1] "what is said by God at the Bush, I am the God of Abraham, and the God of Isaac, and the God of Jacob; He is not the God of the dead but of the living." If, then, God is not ashamed to be called the God of these men, and if they are counted by Christ among the living, and if all believers are sons of Abraham,[2] since all the Gentiles are blessed with faithful Abraham, who is appointed by God to be a father of the Gentiles, can we hesitate to admit that those living persons made acquaintance with the learning of living men, and were taught by Christ who was born before the daystar,[3] before He became flesh? And for this cause they lived, because they had part in Him who said, "I am the life," and as the heirs of so great promises received the vision, not only of angels, but of God in Christ. For they saw, it may be, the image of the invisible God,[4] since he who hath seen the Son hath seen the Father, and so they are recorded to have known God, and to have heard God's words worthily, and, therefore, to have seen God and heard Him. Now, I consider that those who are fully and really sons of Abraham are sons of his actions, spiritually understood, and of the knowledge which was made manifest to him. What he knew and what he did appears again in those who are his sons, as the Scripture teaches those who have ears to hear,[5] "If ye were the children of Abraham, ye would do the works of Abraham." And if it is a true proverb[6] which says, "A wise man will understand that which proceeds from his own mouth, and on his lips he will bear prudence," then we must at once repudiate some things which have been said about the prophets, as if they were not wise men, and did not understand what proceeded from their own mouths. We must believe what is good and true about the prophets, that they were sages, that they did understand what proceeded from their mouths, and that they bore prudence on their lips. It is clear indeed that Moses understood in his mind the truth (real meaning) of the law, and the higher interpretations of the stories recorded in his books. Joshua, too, understood the meaning of the allotment of the land after the destruction of the nine and twenty kings, and could see better than we can the realities of which his achievements were the shadows. It is clear, too, that Isaiah saw the mystery of Him who sat upon the throne, and of the two seraphim, and of the veiling of their faces and their feet, and of their wings, and of the altar and of the tongs. Ezekiel, too, understood the true significance of the cherubim and of their goings, and of the firmament that was above them, and of Him that sat on the throne, than all which what could be loftier or more splendid? I need not enter into more particulars; the point I aim at establishing is clear enough already, namely, that those who were made perfect in earlier generations knew not less than the Apostles did of what Christ revealed to them, since the same teacher was with them as He who revealed to the Apostles the unspeakable mysteries of godliness. I will add but a few points, and then leave it to the reader to judge and to form what views he pleases on this subject. Paul says in his Epistle to the Romans,[1] "Now, to him who is able to establish you according to my Gospel, according to the revelation of the mystery which hath been kept in silence through times eternal, but is now made manifest by the prophetic Scriptures and the appearance of our Lord Jesus Christ." For if the mystery concealed of old is made manifest to the Apostles through the prophetic writings, and if the prophets, being wise men, understood what proceeded from their own mouths, then the prophets knew what was made manifest to the Apostles. But to many it was not revealed, as Paul says,[2] "In other generations it was not made known to the sons of men as it hath now been revealed unto His holy Apostles and prophets by the Spirit, that the Gentiles are fellow-heirs and members of the same body." Here an objection may be raised by those who do not share the view we have propounded; and it becomes of importance to define what is meant by the word "*revealed.*" It is capable of two meanings: firstly, that the thing in question is understood, but secondly, if a prophecy is spoken of, that it is accomplished. Now, the fact that the Gentiles were to be fellow-heirs and members of the same body, and partakers of the promise, was known to the prophets to this extent, that they knew the Gentiles were to be fellow-heirs and members of the same

[1] Mark xii. 20. [2] Rom. iv. 11. [3] Ps. cv. 3. [4] Coloss. i. 15; John xiv. 19. [5] John viii. 39. [6] Prov. xvi. 23.

[1] xvi. 25. [2] Ephes. iii. 5.

body, and partakers of the promise in Christ. When this should be, and why, and what Gentiles were spoken of, and how, though strangers from the covenants, and aliens to the promises, they were yet to be members of one body and sharers of the blessings; all this was known to the prophets, being revealed to them. But the things prophesied belong to the future, and are not revealed to those who know them, but do not witness their fulfilment, as they are to those who have the event before their eyes. And this was the position of the Apostles. Thus, I conceive, they knew the events no more than the fathers and the prophets did; and yet it is truly said of them that "what to other generations was not revealed was now revealed to the Apostles and prophets, that the Gentiles were fellow-heirs and members of the same body, and partakers in the promise of Christ." For, in addition to knowing these mysteries, they saw the power at work in the accomplished fact. The passage, "Many prophets and righteous men desired to see the things ye see and did not see them; and to hear the things ye hear and did not hear them," may be interpreted in the same way. They also desired to see the mystery of the incarnation of the Son of God, and of His coming down to carry out the design of His suffering for the salvation of many, actually put in operation. This may be illustrated from another quarter. Suppose one of the Apostles to have understood the "unspeakable words which it is not lawful for a man to utter,"[1] but not to witness the glorious bodily appearing of Jesus to the faithful, which is promised, although He desired to see it and suppose another had not only not[2] marked and seen what that Apostle marked and saw, but had a much feebler grasp of the divine hope, and yet is present at the second coming of our Saviour, which the Apostle, as in the parallel above, had desired, but had not seen. We shall not err from the truth if we say that both of these have seen what the Apostle, or indeed the Apostles, desired to see, and yet that they are not on that account to be deemed wiser or more blessed than the Apostles. In the same way, also, the Apostles are not to be deemed wiser than the fathers, or than Moses and the prophets, than those in fact who, for their virtue, were found worthy of epiphanies and of divine manifestations and of revelations of mysteries.

3. "GRACE AND TRUTH CAME THROUGH JESUS CHRIST." THESE WORDS BELONG TO THE BAPTIST, NOT THE EVANGELIST. WHAT THE BAPTIST TESTIFIES BY THEM.

We have lingered rather long over these discussions, but there is a reason for it. There are many who, under the pretence of glorifying the advent of Christ, declare the Apostles to be wiser than the fathers or the prophets; and of these teachers some have invented a greater God for the later period, while some, not venturing so far, but moved, according to their own account of the matter, by the difficulty connected with doctrine, cancel the whole of the gift conferred by God on the fathers and the prophets, through Christ, through whom all things were made. If all things were made through Him, clearly so must the splendid revelations have been which were made to the fathers and prophets, and became to them the symbols of the sacred mysteries of religion. Now the true soldiers of Christ must always be prepared to do battle for the truth, and must never, so far as lies with them, allow false convictions to creep in. We must not, therefore, neglect this matter. It may be said that John's earlier testimony to Christ is to be found in the words, "He who cometh after me exists before me, for He was before me," and that the words, "For of His fulness we all received, and grace for grace," are in the mouth of John the disciple. Now, we must show this exposition to be a forced one, and one which does violence to the context; it is rather a strong proceeding to suppose the speech of the Baptist to be so suddenly and, as it were, inopportunely interrupted by that of the disciple, and it is quite apparent to any one who can judge, in whatever small degree, of a context, that the speech goes on continuously after the words, "This is He of whom I spoke, He that cometh after me exists before me, for He was before me." The Baptist brings a proof that Jesus existed before him because He was before him, since He is the first-born of all creation; he says, "For of His fulness all we received." That is the reason why he says, "He exists before me, for He was before me." That is how I know that He is first and in higher honour with the Father, since of His fulness both I and the prophets before me received the more divine prophetic grace instead of the grace we received at His hands before in

[1] 2 Cor. xii. 4.
[2] Lommatzsch omits οὐ before ἠκριβωκότα, but it is necessary to the sense.

respect of our election. That is why I say, "He exists before me, for He was before me," because we know what we have received from His fulness; namely, that the law was given through Moses, not by Moses, while grace and truth not only were given but came into existence[1] through Jesus Christ. For His God and Father both gave the law through Moses, and made grace and truth through Jesus Christ, that grace and truth which came to man. If we give a reasonable interpretation to the words, "Grace and truth came through Jesus Christ," we shall not be alarmed at the possible discrepancy with them of that other saying, "I am the way and the truth and the life." If it is Jesus who says, "I am the truth," then how does the truth come through Jesus Christ, since no one comes into existence through himself? We must recognize that this very truth, the essential truth, which is prototypal, so to speak, of that truth which exists in souls endowed with reason, that truth from which, as it were, images are impressed on those who care for truth, was not made through Jesus Christ, nor indeed through any one, but by God;—just as the Word was not made through any one which was in the beginning with the Father;—and as wisdom which God created the beginning of His ways was not made through any one, so the truth also was not made through any one. That truth, however, which is with men came through Jesus Christ, as the truth in Paul and the Apostles came through Jesus Christ. And it is no wonder, since truth is one, that many truths should flow from that one. The prophet David certainly knew many truths, as he says,[2] "The Lord searcheth out truths," for the Father of truth searches out not the one truth but the many through which those are saved who possess them. And as with the one truth and many truths, so also with righteousness and righteousnesses. For the very essential righteousness is Christ, "Who was made to us of God wisdom and righteousness and sanctification and redemption." But from that righteousness is formed the righteousness which is in each individual, so that there are in the saved many righteousnesses, whence also it is written,[3] "For the Lord is righteous, and He loved righteousnesses." This is the reading in the exact copies, and in the other versions besides the Septuagint, and in the Hebrew. Consider if the other things which Christ is said to be in a unity admit of

[1] ἐγένετο. [2] Ps. xxxi. 24. [3] Ps. xi. 7.

being multiplied in the same way and spoken of in the plural. For example, Christ is our life as the Saviour Himself says,[1] "I am the way and the truth and the life." The Apostle, too, says,[2] "When Christ our life shall appear, then shall ye also appear with Him in glory." And in the Psalms again we find,[3] "Thy mercy is better than life;" for it is on account of Christ who is life in every one that there are many lives. This, perhaps, is also the key to the passage,[4] "If ye seek a proof of the Christ that speaketh in me." For Christ is found in every saint, and so from the one Christ there come to be many Christs, imitators of Him and formed after Him who is the image of God; whence God says through the prophet,[5] "Touch not my Christs." Thus we have explained in passing the passage which we appeared to have omitted from our exposition, viz.: "Grace and truth came through Jesus Christ;" and we have also shown that the words belong to John the Baptist and form part of his testimony to the Son of God.

4. JOHN DENIES THAT HE IS ELIJAH OR "THE" PROPHET. YET HE WAS "A" PROPHET.

Now let us consider John's second testimony. Jews from Jerusalem,[6] kindred to John the Baptist, since he also belonged to a priestly race, send priests and levites to ask John who he is. In saying, "I am not the Christ," he made a confession of the truth. The words are not, as one might suppose, a negation; for it is no negation to say, in the honour of Christ, that one is not Christ. The priests and levites sent from Jerusalem, having there heard in the first place that he is not the expected Messiah, put a question about the second great personage whom they expected, namely, Elijah, whether John were he, and he says he is not Elijah, and by his "I am not" makes a second confession of the truth. And, as many prophets had appeared in Israel, and one in particular was looked for according to the prophecy of Moses, who said,[7] "A prophet shall the Lord your God raise up to you of your brethren, like unto me, him shall ye hear; and it shall come to pass that every soul that shall not hear that prophet shall be destroyed from among the people," they, therefore, ask a third question, not whether he is a prophet, but whether he is the prophet. Now, they did not apply this

[1] John xiv. 6. [2] Coloss. iii. 4. [3] Ps. lxiii. 3.
[4] 2 Cor. xiii. 3. [5] Ps. cv. 15. [6] John i. 19–21.
[7] Deut. xviii. 15.

name to the Christ, but supposed the prophet to be a second figure beside the Christ. But John, on the contrary, who knew that He whose forerunner he was was both the Christ and the prophet thus foretold, answered "No;" whereas, if they had asked if he was a prophet, he would have answered "Yes;"[1] for he was not unconscious that he was a prophet. In all these answers John's second testimony to Christ was not yet completed; he had still to give his questioners the answer they were to take back to those who sent them, and to declare himself in the terms of the prophecy of Isaiah, which says, "The voice of one crying in the wilderness, Prepare ye the way of the Lord."

5. THERE WERE TWO EMBASSIES TO JOHN THE BAPTIST; THE DIFFERENT CHARACTERS OF THESE.

Here the enquiry suggests itself whether the second testimony is concluded, and whether there is a third, addressed to those who were sent from the Pharisees. They wished to know why he baptized, if he was neither the Christ, nor Elijah, nor the prophet; and he said:[2] "I baptize with water; but there standeth one among you whom you know not, He that cometh after me, the latchet of whose shoe I am not worthy to unloose." Is this a third testimony, or is this which they were to report to the Pharisees a part of the second? As far as the words allow me to conjecture I should say that the word to the emissaries of the Pharisees was a third testimony. It is to be observed, however, that the first testimony asserts the divinity of the Saviour, while the second disposes of the suspicion of those who were in doubt whether John could be the Christ, and the third declares one who was already present with men, although they saw Him not, and whose coming was no longer in the future. Before going on to the subsequent testimonies in which he points out Christ and witnesses to Him, let us look at the second and third, word for word, and let us, in the first place, observe that there are two embassies to the Baptist, one "from Jerusalem" from the Jews, who send priests and levites, to ask him, "Who art thou?" the second sent by the Pharisees,[3] who were in doubt about the answer which had been made to the priests and levites. Observe how what is said by the first envoys is in keeping with the character of priests and levites, and shows gentleness and a willingness to learn. "Who art thou?" they say, and "What then? art thou Elijah?" and "Art thou that prophet?" and then, "Who art thou, that we may give an answer to them that sent us? What sayest thou of thyself?" There is nothing harsh or arrogant in the enquiries of these men; everything agrees well with the character of true and careful servants of God; and they raise no difficulties about the replies made to them. Those, on the contrary, who are sent from the Pharisees assail the Baptist, as it were, with arrogant and unsympathetic words: "Why then baptizest thou if thou be not the Christ nor Elijah nor the prophet?" This mission is sent scarcely for the sake of information, as in the former case of the priests and levites, but rather to debar the Baptist from baptizing, as if it were thought that no one was entitled to baptize but Christ and Elijah and the prophet. The student who desires to understand the Scripture must always proceed in this careful way; he must ask with regard to each speech, who is the speaker and on what occasion it was spoken. Thus only can we discern how speech harmonizes with the character of the speaker, as it does all through the sacred books.

6. MESSIANIC DISCUSSION WITH JOHN THE BAPTIST.

Then the Jews sent priests and levites from Jerusalem to ask him, Who art thou? And he confessed and denied not; and he confessed, I am not the Christ.[1] What legates should have been sent from the Jews to John, and where should they have been sent from? Should they not have been men held to stand by the election of God above their fellows, and should they not have come from that place which was chosen out of the whole of the earth, though it is all called good, from Jerusalem where was the temple of God? With such honour, then, do they enquire of John. In the case of Christ nothing of this sort is reported to have been done by the Jews; but what the Jews do to John, John does to Christ, sending his own disciples to ask him,[2] "Art thou He that should come, or do we look for another?" John confesses to those sent to him, and denies not, and he afterwards declares, "I am the voice of one crying in the wilderness;" but Christ, as having a greater testimony than John the Baptist, makes His answer by words and deeds, saying, "Go and tell John those things which ye do

[1] John i. 25. [2] John i. 25 sqq. [3] Ver. 24.

[1] John i. 19, 20. [2] Matt. xi. 3.

hear and see; the blind receive their sight, and the lame walk, the lepers are cleansed and the deaf hear, and the poor have the Gospel preached to them." On this passage I shall, if God permit, enlarge in its proper place. Here, however, it might be asked reasonably enough why John gives such an answer to the question put to him. The priests and levites do not ask him, "Art thou the Christ?" but "Who art thou?" and the Baptist's reply to this question should have been, "I am the voice of one crying in the wilderness." The proper reply to the question, "Art thou the Christ?" is, "I am not the Christ;" and to the question, "Who art thou?"—"The voice of one crying in the wilderness." To this we may say that he probably discerned in the question of the priests and levites a cautious reverence, which led them to hint the idea in their minds that he who was baptizing might be the Christ, but withheld them from openly saying so, which might have been presumptuous. He quite naturally, therefore, proceeds in the first place to remove any false impressions they might have taken up about him, and declares publicly the true state of the matter, "I am not the Christ." Their second question, and also their third, show that they had conceived some such surmise about him. They supposed that he might be that second in honour to whom their hopes pointed, namely, Elijah, who held with them the next position after Christ; and so when John had answered, "I am not the Christ," they asked, "What then? Art thou Elijah?" And he said, "I am not." They wish to know, in the third place, if he is the prophet, and on his answer, "No," they have no longer any name to give the personage whose advent they expected, and they say, "Who art thou, then, that we may give an answer to them that sent us. What sayest thou of thyself?" Their meaning is: "You are not, you say, any of those personages whose advent Israel hopes and expects, and who you are, to baptize as you do, we do not know; tell us, therefore, so that we may report to those who sent us to get light upon this point." We add, as it has some bearing on the context, that the people were moved by the thought that the period of Christ's advent was near. It was in a manner imminent in the years from the birth of Jesus and a little before, down to the publication of the preaching. Hence it was, in all likelihood, that as the scribes and lawyers had deduced the time from Holy Scripture and were expecting the Coming One, the idea was taken up by Theudas, who came forward as the Messiah and brought together a considerable multitude, and after him by the famous Judas of Galilee in the days of the taxing.[1] Thus the coming of the Messiah was more warmly expected and discussed, and it was natural enough for the Jews to send priests and levites from Jerusalem to John, to ask him, "Who art thou?" and learn if he professed to be the Christ.

7. OF THE BIRTH OF JOHN, AND OF HIS ALLEGED IDENTITY WITH ELIJAH. OF THE DOCTRINE OF TRANSCORPORATION.

"And[2] they asked him, What then? Art thou Elijah? and he said, I am not." No one can fail to remember in this connection what Jesus says of John,[3] "If ye will receive it, this is Elijah which is to come." How, then, does John come to say to those who ask him, "Art thou Elijah?"—"I am not." And how can it be true at the same time that John is Elijah who is to come, according to the words of Malachi,[4] "And behold I send unto you Elijah the Tishbite, before the great and notable day of the Lord come, who shall restore the heart of the father to the son, and the heart of a man to his neighbour, lest I come, and utterly smite the earth." The words of the angel of the Lord, too, who appeared to Zacharias, as he stood at the right hand of the altar of incense, are somewhat to the same effect as the prophecy of Malachi: "And[5] thy wife Elisabeth shall bear thee a son, and thou shalt call his name John." And a little further on:[6] "And he shall go before His face in the spirit and power of Elijah to turn the hearts of the fathers to the children, and the disobedient to the wisdom of the just, to make ready for the Lord a people prepared for Him." As for the first point, one might say that John did not know that he was Elijah. This will be the explanation of those who find in our passage a support for their doctrine of transcorporation, as if the soul clothed itself in a fresh body and did not quite remember its former lives. These thinkers will also point out that some of the Jews assented to this doctrine when they spoke about the Saviour as if He was one of the old prophets, and had risen not from the tomb but from His birth. His mother Mary was well known, and Joseph the carpenter was supposed to be His father, and it could readily be supposed that He was one of the old prophets risen from the dead.

---

[1] Acts v. 36, 37.
[2] John i. 21.
[3] Matt. xi. 14.
[4] Mal. iv. 5, 6.
[5] Luke i. 13.
[6] Luke i. 17.

The same person will adduce the text in Genesis,[1] "I will destroy the whole resurrection," and will thereby reduce those who give themselves to finding in Scripture solutions of false probabilities to a great difficulty in respect of this doctrine. Another, however, a churchman, who repudiates the doctrine of transcorporation as a false one, and does not admit that the soul of John ever was Elijah, may appeal to the above-quoted words of the angel, and point out that it is not the soul of Elijah that is spoken of at John's birth, but the spirit and power of Elijah. "He shall go before him," it is said, "in the spirit and power of Elijah, to turn the hearts of the fathers to the children." Now it can be shown from thousands of texts that the spirit is a different thing from the soul, and that what is called the power is a different thing from both the soul and the spirit. On these points I cannot now enlarge; this work must not be unduly expanded. To establish the fact that power is different from spirit, it will be enough to cite the text,[2] "The Holy Spirit shall come upon thee, and the power of the Highest shall overshadow thee." As for the spirits of the prophets, these are given to them by God, and are spoken of as being in a manner their property (slaves), as "The spirits of the prophets are subject to the prophets,"[3] and "The spirit of Elijah rested upon Elisha."[4] Thus, it is said, there is nothing absurd in supposing that John, "in the spirit and power of Elijah," turned the hearts of the fathers to the children, and that it was on account of this spirit that he was called "Elijah who was to come." And to reinforce this view it may be argued that if the God of the universe identified Himself with His saints to such an extent as to be called the God of Abraham and the God of Isaac and the God of Jacob, much more might the Holy Spirit so identify Himself with the prophets as to be called their spirit, so that when the spirit is spoken of it might be the spirit of Elijah or the spirit of Isaiah. Our churchman, to go on with his views, may further say that those who supposed Jesus to be one of the prophets risen from the dead were probably misled, partly by the doctrine above mentioned, and partly by supposing Him to be one of the prophets, and that as for this misconception that He was one of the prophets, these persons probably fell into their error from not knowing about Jesus' supposed father and actual mother, and considering that He had risen

[1] vii. 4. [2] Luke i. 35.
[3] 1 Cor. xiv. 32. [4] 2 Kings ii. 15.

from the tombs. As for the text in Genesis about the resurrection, the churchman will rejoin with a text to an opposite effect, "God hath raised up for me another seed in place of Abel whom Cain slew;"[1] showing that the resurrection occurs in Genesis. As for the first difficulty which was raised, our churchman will meet the view of the believers in transcorporation by saying that John is no doubt, in a certain sense, as he has already shown, Elijah who is to come; and that the reason why he met the enquiry of the priests and levites with "I am not," was that he divined the object they had in view in making it. For the enquiry laid before John by the priests and levites was not intended to bring out whether the same spirit was in both, but whether John was that very Elijah who was taken up, and who now appeared according to the expectation of the Jews without being born (for the emissaries, perhaps, did not know about John's birth); and to such an enquiry he naturally answered, "I am not;" for he who was called John was not Elijah who was taken up, and had not changed his body for his present appearance. Our first scholar, whose view of transcorporation we have seen based upon our passage, may go on with a close examination of the text, and urge against his antagonist, that if John was the son of such a man as the priest Zacharias, and if he was born when his parents were both aged, contrary to all human expectation, then it is not likely that so many Jews at Jerusalem would be so ignorant about him, or that the priests and levites whom they sent would not be acquainted with the facts of his birth. Does not Luke declare[2] that "fear came upon all those who lived round about,"—clearly round about Zacharias and Elisabeth—and that "all these things were noised abroad throughout the whole hill country of Judæa"? And if John's birth from Zacharias was a matter of common knowledge, and the Jews of Jerusalem yet sent priests and levites to ask, "Art thou Elijah?" then it is clear that in saying this they assumed the doctrine of transcorporation to be true, and that it was a current doctrine of their country, and not foreign to their secret teaching. John therefore says, I am not Elijah, because he does not know about his own former life. These thinkers, accordingly, entertain an opinion which is by no means to be despised. Our churchman, however, may return to the charge, and ask if it is worthy of a prophet,

[1] Gen. iv. 25. [2] Luke i. 65.

who is enlightened by the Holy Spirit, who is predicted by Isaiah, and whose birth was foretold before it took place by so great an angel, one who has received of the fulness of Christ, who shares in such a grace, who knows truth to have come through Jesus Christ, and has taught such deep things about God and about the only-begotten, who is in the bosom of the Father, is it worthy of such a one to lie, or even to hesitate, out of ignorance of what he was. For with respect to what was obscure, he ought to have refrained from confessing, and to have neither affirmed nor denied the proposition put before him. If the doctrine in question really was widely current, ought not John to have hesitated to pronounce upon it, lest his soul had actually been in Elijah? And here our churchman will appeal to history, and will bid his antagonists ask experts of the secret doctrines of the Hebrews, if they do really entertain such a belief. For if it should appear that they do not, then the argument based on that supposition is shown to be quite baseless. Our churchman, however, is still free to have recourse to the solution given before, and to insist that attention be paid to the meaning with which the question was put. For if, as I showed, the senders knew John to be the child of Zacharias and Elisabeth, and if the messengers still more, being men of priestly race, could not possibly be ignorant of the remarkable manner in which their kinsman Zacharias had received his son, then what could be the meaning of their question, "Art thou Elijah?" Had they not read that Elijah had been taken up into heaven, and did they not expect him to appear? Then, as they expect Elijah to come at the consummation before Christ, and Christ to follow him, perhaps their question was meant less in a literal than in a tropical sense: Are you he who announces beforehand the word which is to come before Christ, at the consummation? To this he very properly answers, "I am not." The adversary, however, tries to show that the priests could not be ignorant that the birth of John had taken place in so remarkable a manner, because "all these things had been much spoken of in the hill country of Judæa;" and the churchman has to meet this. He does so by showing that a similar mistake was widely current about the Saviour Himself; for "some said that He was John the Baptist, others Elijah, others Jeremiah or one of the prophets."[1]

[1] Matt. xvi. 13, 14.

So the disciples told the Lord when He was in the parts of Cæsarea Philippi, and questioned them on that subject. And Herod, too, said,[1] "John whom I beheaded, he is risen from the dead;" so that he appears not to have known what was said about Christ, as reported in the Gospel,[2] "Is not this the son of the carpenter, is not His mother called Mary, and His brothers James, and Joseph, and Simon, and Judas? And His sisters, are they not all with us?" Thus in the case of the Saviour, while many knew of His birth from Mary, others were under a mistake about Him; and so in the case of John, there is no wonder if, while some knew of his birth from Zacharias, others were in doubt whether the expected Elijah had appeared in him or not. There was not more room for doubt about John, whether he was Elijah, than about the Saviour, whether He was John. Of the two, the question of the outward form of Elijah could be disposed of from the words of Scripture, though not from actual observation, for we read,[3] "He was a hairy man, and girt with a leather girdle about his loins." John's outward appearance, on the contrary, was well known, and was not like that of Jesus; and yet there were those who surmised that John had risen from the dead, and taken the name of Jesus. As for the change of name, a thing which reminds us of mysteries, I do not know how the Hebrews came to tell about Phinehas, son of Eleazar, who admittedly prolonged his life to the time of many of the judges, as we read in the Book of Judges,[4] to tell about him what I now mention. They say that he was Elijah, because he had been promised immortality (in Numbers[5]), on account of the covenant of peace granted to him because he was jealous with a divine jealousy, and in a passion of anger pierced the Midianitish woman and the Israelite, and stayed the wrath of God as it is called, as it is written, "Phinehas, the son of Eleazar, the son of Aaron, hath turned my wrath away from the children of Israel, in that he was jealous with my jealousy among them." No wonder, then, if those who conceived Phinehas and Elijah to be the same person, whether they judged soundly in this or not, for that is not now the question, considered John and Jesus also to be the same. This, then, they doubted, and desired to know if John and Elijah were the same. At another time than this, the point would certainly

[1] Mark vi. 16. [2] Matt. xiii. 55. [3] 2 Kings i. 8.
[4] Jud. xx. 28. [5] Numb. xxv. 12.

call for a careful enquiry, and the argument would have to be well weighed as to the essence of the soul, as to the principle of her composition, and as to her entering into this body of earth. We should also have to enquire into the distributions of the life of each soul, and as to her departure from this life, and whether it is possible for her to enter into a second life in a body or not, and whether that takes place at the same period, and after the same arrangement in each case, or not; and whether she enters the same body, or a different one, and if the same, whether the subject remains the same while the qualities are changed, or if both subject and qualities remain the same, and if the soul will always make use of the same body or will change it. Along with these questions, it would also be necessary to ask what transcorporation is, and how it differs from incorporation, and if he who holds transcorporation must necessarily hold the world to be eternal. The views of these scholars must also be taken into account, who consider that, according to the Scriptures, the soul is sown along with the body, and the consequences of such a view must also be looked at. In fact the subject of the soul is a wide one, and hard to be unravelled, and it has to be picked out of scattered expressions of Scripture. It requires, therefore, separate treatment. The brief consideration we have been led to give to the problem in connection with Elijah and John may now suffice; we go on to what follows in the Gospel.

8. JOHN IS A PROPHET, BUT NOT THE PROPHET.

"Art thou that prophet? And he answered No."[1] If the law and the prophets were until John,[2] what can we say that John was but a prophet? His father Zacharias, indeed, says, filled with the Holy Ghost and prophesying,[3] "And thou, child, shalt be called the prophet of the Highest, for thou shalt go before the Lord to prepare His ways." (One might indeed get past this passage by laying stress on the word called: he is to be called, he is not said to be, a prophet.) And still more weighty is it that the Saviour said to those who considered John to be a prophet,[4] "But what went ye out to see? A prophet? Yea, I say unto you, and more than a prophet." The words, Yea, I say unto you, manifestly affirm that John is a prophet, and that is nowhere denied afterwards. If, then, he is

[1] John i. 21. [2] Luke xvi. 16.
[3] Luke i. 76. [4] Matt. xi. 9.

said by the Saviour to be not only a prophet but "more than a prophet," how is it that when the priests and levites come and ask him, "Art thou the Prophet?" he answers No! On this we must remark that it is not the same thing to say, "Art thou the Prophet?" and "Art thou a prophet?" The distinction between the two expressions has already been observed, when we asked what was the difference between the God and God, and between the Logos and Logos.[1] Now it is written in Deuteronomy,[2] "A prophet shall the Lord your God raise up unto you, like me; Him shall ye hear, and it shall be that every soul that will not hear that prophet shall be cut off from among His people." There was, therefore, an expectation of one particular prophet having a resemblance to Moses in mediating between God and the people and receiving a new covenant from God to give to those who accepted his teaching; and in the case of each of the prophets, the people of Israel recognized that he was not the person of whom Moses spoke. As, then, they doubted about John, whether he were not the Christ,[3] so they doubted whether he could not be the prophet. And there is no wonder that those who doubted about John whether he were the Christ, did not understand that the Christ and the prophet are the same person; their doubt as to John necessarily implied that they were not clear on this point. Now the difference between "the prophet" and "a prophet" has escaped the observation of most students; this is the case with Heracleon, who says, in these very words: "As, then, John confessed that he was not the Christ, and not even a prophet, nor Elijah." If he interpreted the words before us in such a way, he ought to have examined the various passages to see whether in saying that he is not a prophet nor Elijah he is or is not saying what is true. He devotes no attention, however, to these passages, and in his remaining commentaries he passes over such points without any enquiry. In the sequel, too, his remarks, of which we shall have to speak directly, are very scanty, and do not testify to careful study.

9. JOHN I. 22.

"They said therefore unto him, Who art thou? that we may give an answer to them that sent us. What sayest thou of thyself?" This speech of the emissaries amounts to the following: We had a surmise what you were and came to learn if it was

[1] P. 321. [2] xviii. 15 sq. [3] Luke iii. 15.

so, but now we know that you are not that. It remains for us, therefore, to hear your account of yourself, so that we may report your answer to those who sent us.

10. OF THE VOICE JOHN THE BAPTIST IS.

"He said, I am the voice of one crying in the wilderness: Make straight the way of the Lord, as said Isaiah the prophet." As He who is peculiarly the Son of God, being no other than the Logos, yet makes use of Logos (reason)—for He was the Logos in the beginning, and was with God, the Logos of God—so John, the servant of that Logos, being, if we take the Scripture to mean what it says, no other than a voice, yet uses his voice to point to the Logos. He, then, understanding in this way the prophecy about himself spoken by Isaiah the prophet, says he is a voice, not crying in the wilderness, but "of one crying in the wilderness," of Him, namely, who stood and cried,[1] "If any man thirst, let him come unto Me and drink." He it was, too, who said,[2] "Prepare ye the way of the Lord, make His paths straight. Every valley shall be filled and every mountain and hill shall be brought low; and all the crooked shall be made straight." For as we read in Exodus that God said to Moses,[3] "Behold I have given thee for a God to Pharaoh, and Aaron thy brother shall be thy prophet;" so we are to understand—the cases are at least analogous if not altogether similar—it is with the Word in the beginning, who is God, and with John. For John's voice points to that word and demonstrates it. It is therefore a very appropriate punishment that falls on Zacharias on his saying to the angel,[4] "Whereby shall I know this? For I am an old man and my wife well stricken in years." For his want of faith with regard to the birth of the voice, he is himself deprived of his voice, as the angel Gabriel says to him, "Behold, thou shalt be silent and not able to speak until the day that these things shall come to pass, because thou hast not believed my words, which shall be fulfilled in their season." And afterwards when he had "asked for a writing tablet and written, His name is John; and they all marvelled," he recovered his voice; for "his mouth was opened immediately and his tongue, and he spake, blessing God." We discussed above how it is to be understood that the Logos is the Son of God, and went over the ideas connected with that; and a similar sequence of ideas is to be observed at this point. John came for a witness; he was a man sent from God to bear witness of the light, that all men through him might believe; he was that voice, then, we are to understand, which alone was fitted worthily to announce the Logos. We shall understand this aright if we call to mind what was adduced in our exposition of the texts: "That all might believe through Him," and "This is he of whom it is written, Behold I send My messenger before thy face, who shall prepare thy way before thee."[1] There is fitness, too, in his being said to be the voice, not of one saying in the wilderness, but of one crying in the wilderness. He who cries, "Prepare ye the way of the Lord," also says it; but he might say it without crying it. But he cries and shouts it, that even those may hear who are at a distance from the speaker, and that even the deaf may understand the greatness of the tidings, since it is announced in a great voice; and he thus brings help, both to those who have departed from God and to those who have lost the acuteness of their hearing. This, too, was the reason why "Jesus stood and cried, saying, If any man thirst, let him come unto Me and drink." Hence, too,[2] "John beareth witness of Him, and cried, saying," "Hence also God commands Isaiah to cry, with the voice of one saying, Cry. And I said, What shall I cry?" The physical voice we use in prayer need not be great nor startling; even should we not lift up any great cry or shout, God will yet hear us. He says to Moses,[3] "Why criest thou unto Me?" when Moses had not cried audibly at all. It is not recorded in Exodus that he did so; but Moses had cried mightily to God in prayer with that voice which is heard by God alone. Hence David also says,[4] "With my voice I cried unto the Lord, and He heard me." And one who cries in the desert has need of a voice, that the soul which is deprived of God and deserted of truth—and what more dreadful desert is there than a soul deserted of God and of all virtue, since it still goes crookedly and needs instruction—may be exhorted to make straight the way of the Lord. And that way is made straight by the man who, far from copying the serpent's crooked journey; while he who is of the contrary disposition perverts his way. Hence the rebuke directed to a man of this kind and to all who resemble him, "Why pervert ye the right ways of the Lord?"[5]

[1] John vii. 37. [2] Luke iii. 4. [3] vii. 1. [4] Luke i. 18.

[1] Matt. xi. 10. [2] John i. 15. [3] Exod. xiv. 15. [4] Ps. lxxvii. 7. [5] Acts xiii. 10.

11. OF THE WAY OF THE LORD, HOW IT IS NARROW, AND HOW JESUS IS THE WAY.

Now the way of the Lord is made straight in two fashions. First, in the way of contemplation, when thought is made clear in truth without any mixture of falsehood; and then in the way of conduct, after the sound contemplation of what ought to be done, when action is produced which harmonizes with sound theory of conduct. And that we may the more clearly understand the text, "Make straight the way of the Lord," it will be well to compare with it what is said in the Proverbs,[1] "Depart not, either to the right hand or to the left." For he who deviates in either direction has given up keeping his path straight, and is no longer worthy of regard, since he has gone apart from the straightness of the journey, for "the Lord[2] is righteous, and loves righteousness, and His face beholds straightness." Hence he who is the object of regard, and receives the benefit that comes from this oversight, says,[3] "The light of Thy countenance was shown upon us, O Lord." Let us stand, then, as Jeremiah[4] exhorts, upon the ways, and let us see and ask after the ancient ways of the Lord, and let us see which is the good way, and walk in it. Thus did the Apostles stand and ask for the ancient ways of the Lord; they asked the Patriarchs and the Prophets, enquiring into their writings, and when they came to understand these writings they saw the good way, namely, Jesus Christ, who said, "I am the way," and they walked in it. For it is a good way that leads the good man to the good father, the man who, from the good treasure of his heart, brings forth good things, and who is a good and faithful servant. This way is narrow, indeed, for the many cannot bear to walk in it and are lovers of their flesh; but it is also hard-pressed[5] by those who use violence[6] to walk in it, for it is not called afflicting, but afflicted.[5] For that way which is a living way, and feels the qualities of those who tread it, is pressed and afflicted, when he travels on it who has not taken off his shoes from off his feet,[7] nor truly realized that the place on which he stands, or indeed treads, is holy ground. And it will lead to Him who is the life, and who says, "I am the life." For the Saviour, in whom all virtues are combined, has many aspects. To him who, though by no means near the end, is yet advancing, He is the way; to him who has put off all that is dead He is the life. He who travels on this way is told to take nothing with him on it, since it provides bread and all that is necessary for life, enemies are powerless on it, and he needs no staff, and since it is holy, he needs no shoes.

[1] iv. 27.
[2] Ps. xi. 7.
[3] Ps. iv. 7.
[4] Jer. iv. 16.
[5] τεθλιμμένη, the word translated "narrow" in Matt. vii. 14.
[6] Matt. xi. 12.
[7] Exod. iii. 5.

12. HERACLEON'S VIEW OF THE VOICE, AND OF JOHN THE BAPTIST.

The words, however, "I am the voice of one crying in the wilderness," etc., may be taken as equivalent to "I am He of whom the 'voice in the wilderness' is written." Then John would be the person crying, and his voice would be that crying in the wilderness, "Make straight the way of the Lord." Heracleon, discussing John and the prophets, says, somewhat slanderously, that "the Word is the Saviour; the voice, that in the wilderness which John interpreted; the sound is the whole prophetic order." To this we may reply by reminding him of the text,[1] "If the trumpet give an uncertain sound, who shall prepare himself for the battle," and that which says that though a man have knowledge of mysteries, or have prophecy but wants love, he is a sounding or a tinkling cymbal.[2] If the prophetic voice be nothing but sound, how does our Lord come to refer us to it as where He says,[3] "Search the Scriptures, for in them you think you have eternal life, and these are they which bear witness," and[4] "If ye believed Moses, ye would believe Me," and[5] "Well did Isaiah prophesy concerning you, saying, This people honours me with their lips"? I do not know if any one can reasonably admit that the Saviour thus spoke in praise of an uncertain sound, or that there is any preparation to be had from the Scriptures to which we are referred as from the voice of a trumpet, for our war against opposing powers, should their sound give an uncertain voice. If the prophets had not love, and if that is why they were sounding brass or a tinkling cymbal, then how does the Lord send us to their sound, as these writers will have it, as if we could get help from that? He asserts, indeed, that a voice, when well fitted to speech, becomes speech, as if one should say that a woman is turned into a man; and the assertion is not supported by argument. And, as if he were in a position to put forth a dogma on the subject and to get on in this way, he declares that sound can be changed in a similar way

[1] 1 Cor. xiv. 8.
[2] 1 Cor. xiii. 1.
[3] John v. 39.
[4] John v. 46.
[5] Matt. xv. 7; Isa. xxix. 13.

into voice, and the voice, which is changed into speech, he says, is in the position of a disciple, while sound passing into voice is in that of a slave. If he had taken any kind of trouble to establish these points we should have had to devote some attention to refuting them ; but as it is, the bare denial is sufficient refutation. There was a point some way back which we deferred taking up, that, namely, of the motive of John's speeches. We may now take it up. The Saviour, according to Heracleon, calls him both a prophet and Elijah, but he himself denies that he is either of these. When the Saviour, Heracleon says, calls him a prophet and Elijah, He is speaking not of John himself, but of his surroundings ; but when He calls him greater than the prophets and than those who are born of women, then He is describing the character of John himself. When John, on the other hand, is asked about himself, his answers relate to himself, not to his surroundings. This we have examined as carefully as possible, comparing each of the terms in question with the statements of Heracleon, lest he should not have expressed himself quite accurately. For how it comes that the statements that he is Elijah and that he is a prophet apply to those about him, but the statement that he is the voice of one crying in the wilderness, to himself, no attempt whatever is made to show Heracleon only gives an illustration, namely, this : His surroundings were, so to speak, his clothes, and other than himself, and when he was asked about his clothes, if he were his clothes, he could not answer "Yes." Now that his being Elijah, who was to come, was his clothes, is scarcely consistent, so far as I can see, with Heracleon's views ; it might consist, perhaps, with the exposition we ourselves gave of the words, "In the spirit and power of Elijah ;" it might, in a sense, be said that this spirit of Elijah is equivalent to the soul of John. He then goes on to try to determine why those who were sent by the Jews to question John were priests and levites, and he answers by no means badly, that it was incumbent on such persons, being devoted to the service of God, to busy themselves and to make enquiries about such matters. When he goes on, however, to say that it was "because John was of the levitical tribe, this is less well considered. We raised the question ourselves above, and saw that if the Jews who were sent knew John's birth, it was not open to them to ask if he was Elijah. Then, again, in dealing with the question, "Art thou the prophet?" Heracleon does not regard the addition of the article as having any special force, and says, "They asked him if he were a prophet, wishing to know this more general fact." Again, not Heracleon alone, but, so far as I am informed, all those who diverge from our views, as if they had not been able to deal with a trifling ambiguity and to draw the proper distinction, suppose John to be greater than Elijah and than all the prophets. The words are, "Of those born of women there is none greater than John ;" but this admits of two meanings, that John is greater than they all, or again, that some of them are equal to him. For though many of the prophets were equal to him, still it might be true in respect of the grace bestowed on him, that none of them was greater than he. He regards it as confirming the view that John was greater, that "he is predicted by Isaiah ;" for no other of all those who uttered prophecies was held worthy by God of this distinction. This, however, is a venturesome statement and implies some disrespect of what is called the Old Testament, and total disregard of the fact that Elijah himself was the subject of prophecy. For Elijah is prophesied by Malachi, who says,[1] "Behold, I send unto you Elijah, the Tishbite, who shall restore the heart of the father to the son." Josiah, too, as we read in third Kings,[2] was predicted by name by the prophet who came out of Judah ; for he said, Jeroboam also being present at the altar, "Thus saith the Lord, Behold a son is born to David, his name is Josiah." There are some also who say that Samson was predicted by Jacob, when he said,[3] "Dan shall judge his own people, he is as one tribe in Israel," for Samson who judged Israel was of the tribe of Dan. So much by way of evidence of the rashness of the statement that John alone was the subject of prophecy, made by Heracleon in his attempted explanation of the words, "I am the voice of one crying in the wilderness."

13. JOHN I. 24, 25. OF THE BAPTISM OF JOHN, THAT OF ELIJAH, AND THAT OF CHRIST.

And they that were sent were of the Pharisees. And they asked him, and said unto him,[4] "Why baptizest thou then, if thou art not the Christ, nor Elijah, nor the prophet?" Those who sent from Jerusalem the priests and levites who asked John these questions, having learned who John was not, and who he was, preserve a decent silence, as if tacitly assenting and indicating that they ac-

---

[1] iv. 5, 6.
[2] 1 Kings xiii. 2.
[3] Gen. xlix. 16.
[4] John i. 24, 25.

cepted what was said, and saw that baptism was suited to a voice crying in the wilderness for the preparing of the way of the Lord. But the Pharisees being, as their name indicates, a divided and seditious set of people, show that they do not agree with the Jews of the metropolis and with the ministers of the service of God, the priests and levites. They send envoys who deal in rebukes, and so far as their power extends debar him from baptizing; their envoys ask, Why baptizest thou, then, if thou art not the Christ, nor Elijah, nor the prophet? And if we were to stitch together into one statement what is written in the various Gospels, we should say that at this time they spoke as is here reported, but that at a later time, when they wished.to received baptism, they heard the address of John:[1] "Generations of vipers, who hath warned you to flee from the wrath to come? Bring forth therefore fruits worthy of repentance." This is what the Baptist says in Matthew, when he sees many of the Pharisees and Sadducees coming to his baptism, without, it is clear, having the fruits of repentance, and pharisaically boasting in themselves that they had Abraham for their father. For this they are rebuked by John, who has the zeal of Elijah according to the communication of the Holy Spirit. For that is a rebuking word, "Think not to say within yourselves, We have Abraham for our father," and that is the word of a teacher, when he speaks of those who for their stony hearts are called unbelieving stones, and says that by the power of God these stones may be changed into children of Abraham; for they were present to the eyes of the prophet and did not shrink from his divine glance. Hence his words: "I say unto you that God is able of these stones to raise up children to Abraham." And since they came to his baptism without having done fruits meet for repentance, he says to them most appropriately, "Already is the axe laid to the root of the tree; every tree that bringeth not forth good fruit is hewn down and cast into the fire." This is as much as to say to them: Since you have come to baptism without having done fruits meet for repentance, you are a tree that does not bring forth good fruit and which has to be cut down by the most sharp and piercing axe of the Word which is living and powerful and sharper than every two-edged sword. The estimation in which the Pharisees held themselves is also set forth by Luke in the passage:[2] "Two men went up to the temple to pray, the one a Pharisee and the other a publican. And the Pharisee stood and prayed thus with himself: God, I thank Thee that I am not as other men are, extortioners, unjust, adulterers, or even as this publican." The result of this speech is that the publican goes down to his house justified rather than the Pharisee, and the lesson is drawn, that every one who exalts himself is abased. They came, then, in the character in which the Saviour's reproving words described them, as hypocrites to John's baptism, nor does it escape the Baptist's observation that they have the poison of vipers under their tongue and the poison of asps, for "the poison of asps is under their tongue."[1] The figure of serpents rightly indicates their temper, and it is plainly revealed in their bitter question: "Why baptizest thou then, if thou art not the Christ, nor Elijah, nor the prophet?" To these I would fain reply, if it be the case that the Christ and Elijah and the prophet baptize, but that the voice crying in the wilderness has no authority to do so, "Most harshly, my friends, do you question the messenger sent before the face of Christ to prepare His way before Him. The mysteries which belong to this point are all hidden to you; for Jesus being, whether you will or not, the Christ, did not Himself baptize but His disciples, He who was Himself the prophet. And how have you come to believe that Elijah who is to come will baptize?" He did not baptize the logs upon the altar in the times of Ahab,[2] though they needed such a bath to be burned up, what time the Lord appeared in fire. No, he commands the priests to do this for him, and that not only once; for he says, "Do it a second time," upon which they did it a second time, and "Do it a third time," and they did it a third time. If, then, he did not at that time himself baptize but left the work to others, how was he to baptize at the time spoken of by Malachi? Christ, then, does not baptize with water, but His disciples. He reserves for Himself to baptize with the Holy Spirit and with fire. Now Heracleon accepts the speech of the Pharisees as distinctly implying that the office of baptizing belonged to the Christ and Elijah and to every prophet, for he uses these words, "Whose office alone it is to baptize." He is refuted by what we have just said, and especially by the consideration that he takes the word "prophet" in a general sense;[3] for he can-

[1] Matt. iii. 7, 8.

[2] Luke xviii. 10, 11.

[1] Ps. xiv. 3.

[2] 1 Kings xviii. 33 sq.

[3] By not noticing the difference between "a prophet" and "the prophet." *Vide supra*, p. 355.

not show that any of the prophets baptized. He adds, not incorrectly, that the Pharisees put the question from malice, and not from a desire to learn.

14 COMPARISON OF THE STATEMENTS OF THE FOUR EVANGELISTS RESPECTING JOHN THE BAPTIST, THE PROPHECIES REGARDING HIM, HIS ADDRESSES TO THE MULTITUDE AND TO THE PHARISEES, ETC.

We deem it necessary to compare with the expression of the passage we are considering the similar expressions found elsewhere in the Gospels. This we shall continue to do point by point to the end of this work, so that terms which appear to disagree may be shown to be in harmony, and that the peculiar meanings present in each may be explained. This we shall do in the present passage. The words, "The voice of one crying in the wilderness, Make straight the way of the Lord," are placed by John, who was a disciple, in the mouth of the Baptist. In Mark, on the other hand, the same words are recorded at the beginning of the Gospel of Jesus Christ, in accordance with the Scripture of Isaiah, as thus: "The beginning of the Gospel of Jesus Christ, as it is written in Isaiah the prophet, Behold, I send My messenger before thy face, who shall prepare thy way before thee. The voice of one crying in the wilderness, Prepare ye the way of the Lord, make His paths straight." Now the words, "Make straight the way of the Lord," added by John, are not found in the prophet. Perhaps John was seeking to compress the "Prepare ye the way of the Lord, make straight the paths of our God," and so wrote, "Make straight the way of the Lord;" while Mark combined two prophecies spoken by two different prophets in different places, and made one prophecy out of them, "As it is written in Isaiah the prophet, Behold I send My messenger before thy face, who shall prepare thy way. The voice of one crying in the wilderness, Prepare ye the way of the Lord, make His paths straight." The words, "The voice of one crying in the wilderness," are written immediately after the narrative of Hezekiah's recovery from his sickness,[1] while the words, "Behold I send My messenger before thy face," are written by Malachi.[2] What John does here, abbreviating the text he quotes, we find done by Mark also at another point. For while the words of the prophet are, "Prepare ye the way of the Lord, make straight the paths of our God," Mark writes, "Prepare ye the way of the Lord, make His paths straight." And John practises a similar abbreviation in the text, "Behold I send My messenger before thy face, who shall prepare thy way before thee," when he does not add the words "before thee," as in the original. Coming now to the statement, "They were sent from the Pharisees and they asked Him,"[1] we have been led by our examination of the passage to prefix the enquiry of the Pharisees—which Matthew does not mention—to the occurrence recorded in Matthew, when John saw many of the Pharisees and Sadducees coming to his baptism, and said to them, "Ye generations of vipers," etc. For the natural sequence is that they should first enquire and then come. And we have to observe how, when Matthew reports that there went out to John Jerusalem and all Judæa, and all the region round about Jordan, to be baptized by him in Jordan, confessing their sins, it was not these people who heard from the Baptist any word of rebuke or refutation, but only those many Pharisees and Sadducees whom he saw coming. They it was who were greeted with the address, "Ye offspring of vipers," etc.[2] Mark, again, does not record any words of reproof as having been used by John to those who came to him, being all the country of Judæa and all of them of Jerusalem, who were baptized by him in the Jordan and confessed their sins. This is because Mark does not mention the Pharisees and Sadducees as having come to John. A further circumstance which we must mention is that both Matthew and Mark state that, in the one case, all Jerusalem and all Judæa, and the whole region round about Jordan, in the other, the whole land of Judæa and all they of Jerusalem, were baptized, confessing their sins; but when Matthew introduces the Pharisees and Sadducees as coming to the baptism, he does not say that they confessed their sins, and this might very likely and very naturally be the reason why they were addressed as "offspring of vipers." Do not suppose, reader, that there is anything improper in our adducing in our discussion of the question of those who were sent from the Pharisees and put questions to John, the parallel passages from the other Gospels too. For if we have indicated the proper connection between the enquiry of the Pharisees, re-

[1] Isa. xl. 3. [2] iii. 1.

[1] John i. 24. [2] Matt. iii. 7.

corded by the disciple John, and their baptism which is found in Matthew, we could scarcely avoid inquiring into the passages in question, nor recording the observations made on them. Luke, like Mark, remembers the passage, "The voice of one crying in the wilderness," but he for his part treats it as follows :[1] "The word of God came unto John, the son of Zacharias, in the wilderness. And he came into all the region round about Jordan preaching the baptism of repentance unto remission of sins ; as it is written in the book of the words of Isaiah the prophet, The voice of one crying in the wilderness, Prepare ye the way of the Lord, make His paths straight." Luke, however, added the continuation of the prophecy : "Every valley shall be filled, and every mountain and hill shall be brought low, and the crooked shall become straight, and the rough ways smooth, and all flesh shall see the salvation of God." He writes, like Mark, "Make His ways straight ;" curtailing, as we saw before, the text, "Make straight the ways of our God." In the phrase, "And all the crooked shall become straight," he leaves out the "all," and the word "straight" he converts from a plural into a singular. Instead of the phrase, moreover, "The rough land into a plain," he gives, "The rough ways into smooth ways," and he leaves out "And the glory of the Lord shall be revealed," and gives what follows, "And all flesh shall see the salvation of God." These observations are of use as showing how the evangelists are accustomed to abbreviate the sayings of the prophets. It has also to be observed that the speech, "Offspring of vipers," etc., is said by Matthew to have been spoken to the Pharisees and Sadducees when coming to baptism, they being a different set of people from those who confessed their sins, and to whom no words of this kind were spoken. With Luke, on the contrary, these words were addressed to the multitudes who came out to be baptized by John, and there were not two divisions of those who were baptized, as we found in Matthew. But Matthew, as the careful observer will see, does not speak of the multitudes in the way of praise, and he probably means the Baptist's address, Offspring of vipers, etc., to be understood as addressed to them also. Another point is, that to the Pharisees and Sadducees he says, "Bring forth a fruit," in the singular, "worthy of repentance," but to the multitudes he uses the plural, "Bring forth fruits worthy of repentance." Perhaps the Pharisees are required to yield the special fruit of repentance, which is no other than the Son and faith in Him, while the multitudes, who have not even a beginning of good things, are asked for all the fruits of repentance, and so the plural is used to them. Further, it is said to the Pharisees, "Think not to say within yourselves, We have Abraham for our father." For the multitudes now have a beginning, appearing as they do to be introduced into the divine Word, and to approach the truth ; and thus they begin to say within themselves, "We have Abraham for our father." The Pharisees, on the contrary, are not beginning to this, but have long held it to be so. But both classes see John point to the stones aforesaid and declare that even from these children can be raised up to Abraham, rising up out of unconsciousness and deadness. And observe how it is said to the Pharisees,[1] according to the word of the prophet,[2] "Ye have eaten false fruit," and they have false fruit,—"Every tree which bringeth not forth good fruit is hewn down and cast into the fire," while to the multitudes which do not bear fruit at all,[3] "Every tree which bringeth not forth fruit is hewn down." For that which has no fruit at all has not good fruit, and, therefore, it is worthy to be hewn down. But that which bears fruit has by no means good fruit, whence it also calls for the axe to lay it low. But, if we look more closely into this about the fruit, we shall find that it is impossible that that which has just begun to be cultivated, even should it not prove fruitless, should bear the first good fruits. The husbandman is content that the tree just coming into cultivation should bear him at first such fruits as it may ; afterwards, when he has pruned and trained it according to his art, he will receive, not the fruits it chanced to bear at first, but good fruits. The law itself favours this interpretation, for it says[4] that the planter is to wait for three years, having the trees pruned and not eating the fruit of them. "Three years," it says, "the fruit shall be unpurified to you, and shall not be eaten, but in the fourth year all the fruit shall be holy, for giving praise unto the Lord." This explains how the word "good" is omitted from the address to the multitudes, "Every tree, therefore, which bears not fruit is hewn down and cast into the fire." The tree

[1] Luke iii. 2.

[1] Matt. iii. 10.
[2] Hos. x. 13.
[3] Luke iii. 9.
[4] Deut. xix. 23.

which goes on bearing such fruit as it did at first, is a tree which does not bear good fruit, and is, therefore, cut down, and cast into the fire, since, when the three years have passed and the fourth comes round, it does not bear good fruit, for praise unto the Lord. In thus adducing the passages from the other Gospels I may appear to be digressing, but I cannot think it useless, or without bearing on our present subject. For the Pharisees send to John, after the priests and levites who came from Jerusalem, men who came to ask him who he was, and enquire, Why baptizest thou then, if thou be not the Christ, nor Elijah, nor the prophet? After making this enquiry they straightway come for baptism, as Matthew records, and then they hear words suited to their quackery and hypocrisy. But the words addressed to them were very similar to those spoken to the multitudes, and hence the necessity to look carefully at both speeches, and to compare them together. It was while we were so engaged that various points arose in the sequence of the matter, which we had to consider. To what has been said we must add the following. We find mention made in John of two orders of persons sending: the one, that of the Jews from Jerusalem sending priests and levites; the other, that of the Pharisees who want to know why he baptizes. And we found that, after the enquiry, the Pharisees present themselves for baptism. May it not be that the Jews, who had sent the earlier mission from Jerusalem, received John's words before those who sent the second mission, namely, the Pharisees, and hence arrived before them? For Jerusalem and all Judæa, and, in consequence, the whole region round about Jordan, were being baptized by him in the river Jordan, confessing their sins; or, as Mark says, "There went out to him the whole land of Judæa, and all they of Jerusalem, and were baptized of him in the river Jordan, confessing their sins." Now, neither does Matthew introduce the Pharisees and Sadducees, to whom the words, "Offspring of vipers," etc., are addressed; nor does Luke introduce the multitudes who meet with the same rebuke, as confessing their sins. And the question may be raised how, if the whole city of Jerusalem, and the whole of Judæa, and the whole region round about Jordan, were baptized of John in Jordan, the Saviour could say,[1] "John the Baptist came neither eating nor drinking, and ye say he hath a devil;" and how could He say to those who asked Him,[1] "By what authority doest thou these things? I also will ask you one word, which if ye tell me, I also will tell you by what authority I do these things. The baptism of John, whence was it? from heaven or of men? And they reason, and say, If we shall say, From heaven, He will say, Why did ye not believe him?" The solution of the difficulty is this. The Pharisees, addressed by John, as we saw before, with his "Offspring of vipers," etc., came to the baptism, without believing in him, probably because they feared the multitudes, and, with their accustomed hypocrisy towards them, deemed it right to undergo the washing, so as not to appear hostile to those who did so. Their belief was, then, that he derived his baptism from men, and not from heaven, but, on account of the multitude, lest they should be stoned, they are afraid to say what they think. Thus there is no contradiction between the Saviour's speech to the Pharisees and the narratives in the Gospels about the multitudes who frequented John's baptism. It was part of the effrontery of the Pharisees that they declared John to have a devil, as, also, that they declared Jesus to have performed His wonderful works by Beelzebub, the prince of the devils.

15. HOW THE BAPTIST ANSWERS THE QUESTION OF THE PHARISEES AND EXALTS THE NATURE OF CHRIST. OF THE SHOE-LATCHET WHICH HE IS UNABLE TO UNTIE.

John[2] answered them, saying, "I baptize with water, but in the midst of you standeth one whom ye know not, even He who cometh after me, the latchet of whose shoe I am not worthy to unloose." Heracleon considers that John's answers to those sent by the Pharisees refer not to what they asked, but to what he wished, not observing that he accuses the prophet of a want of manners, by making him, when asked about one thing, answer about another; for this is a fault to be guarded against in conversation. We assert, on the contrary, that the reply accurately takes up the question. It is asked, "Why baptizest thou then, if thou art not the Christ?" And what other answer could be given to this than to show that his baptism was in its nature a bodily thing? I, he says, "baptize with water;" this is his answer to, "Why baptizest thou." And to the second part of their question, "If thou art not the Christ," he answers by exalting the

[1] Matt. xi. 13.

[1] Matt. xxi. 23.

[2] John i. 26.

superior nature of Christ, that He has such virtue as to be invisible in His deity, though present to every man and extending over the whole universe. This is what is indicated in the words, "There standeth one among you." The Pharisees, moreover, though expecting the advent of Christ, saw nothing in Him of such a nature as John speaks of; they believed Him to be simply a perfect and holy man. John, therefore, rebukes their ignorance of His superiority, and adds to the words, "There standeth one among you," the clause, "whom ye know not." And, lest any one should suppose the invisible One who extends to every man, or, indeed, to the whole world, to be a different person from Him who became man, and appeared upon the earth and conversed with men, he adds to the words, "There standeth one among you whom you know not," the further words, "Who cometh after me," that is, He who is to be manifested after me. By whose surpassing excellence he well understood that his own nature was far surpassed, though some doubted whether he might be the Christ; and, therefore, desiring to show how far he is from attaining to the greatness of the Christ, that no one should think of him beyond what he sees or hears of him, he goes on: "The latchet of whose shoe I am not worthy to unloose." By which he conveys, as in a riddle, that he is not fit to solve and to explain the argument about Christ's assuming a human body, an argument tied up and hidden (like a shoe-tie) to those who do not understand it,—so as to say anything worthy of such an advent, compressed, as it was, into so short a space.

16. COMPARISON OF JOHN'S TESTIMONY TO JESUS IN THE DIFFERENT GOSPELS.

It may not be out of place, as we are examining the text, "I baptize with water," to compare the parallel utterances of the evangelists with this of John. Matthew reports that the Baptist, when he saw many of the Pharisees and Sadducees coming to his baptism, after the words of rebuke which we have already studied, went on:[1] "I indeed baptize you with water unto repentance; but He that cometh after me is mightier than I, whose shoes I am not worthy to bear; He shall baptize you with the Holy Ghost, and with fire." This agrees with the words in John, in which the Baptist declares himself to those sent by the Pharisees, on the subject of his baptizing with water. Mark, again, says,[1] "John preached, saying, There cometh after me He that is mightier than I, the latchet of whose shoes I am not worthy to stoop down and unloose. I baptized you with water, but He shall baptize you with the Holy Ghost." And Luke says[2] that, as the people were in expectation, and all were reasoning in their hearts concerning John, whether haply he were the Christ, John answered them all, saying, "I indeed baptize you with water; but there cometh one mightier than I, whose shoe-latchet I am not worthy to unloose; He shall baptize you with the Holy Ghost, and with fire."

17. OF THE TESTIMONY OF JOHN TO JESUS IN MATTHEW'S GOSPEL.

These, then, are the parallel passages of the four; let us try to see as clearly as we can what is the purport of each and wherein they differ from each other. And we will begin with Matthew, who is reported by tradition to have published his Gospel before the others, to the Hebrews, those, namely, of the circumcision who believed. I, he says, baptize you with water unto repentance, purifying you, as it were, and turning you away from evil courses and calling you to repentance; for I am come to make ready for the Lord a people prepared for Him, and by my baptism of repentance to prepare the ground for Him who is to come after me, and who will thus benefit you much more effectively and powerfully than my strength could. For His baptism is not that of the body only; He fills the penitent with the Holy Ghost, and His diviner fire does away with everything material and consumes everything that is earthy, not only from him who admits it to his life, but even from him who hears of it from those who have it. So much stronger than I is He who is coming after me, that I am not able to bear even the outskirts of the powers round Him which are furthest from Him (they are not open and exposed, so that any one could see them), nor even to bear those who support them. I know not of which I should speak. Should I speak of my own great weakness, which is not able to bear even these things about Christ which in comparison with the greater things in Him are least, or should I speak of His transcendent Deity, greater than all the world? If I who have received such grace, as to be thought worthy of prophecy predicting my arrival in this human life, in the words, "The

[1] Matt. iii. 11.

[1] Mark i. 6. 7.

[2] Luke iii. 16.

voice of one crying in the wilderness," and "Behold I send my messenger before thy face;" if I whose birth Gabriel who stands before God announced to my father so advanced in years, so much against his expectation, I at whose name Zacharias recovered his voice and was enabled to use it to prophesy, I to whom my Lord bears witness that among them that are born of women there is none greater than I, I am not able so much as to bear His shoes! And if not His shoes, what can be said about His garments? Who is so great as to be able to guard His coat? Who can suppose that He can understand the meaning contained in His tunic which is without seam from the top because it is woven throughout? It is to be observed that while the four represent John as declaring himself to have come to baptize with water, Matthew alone adds the words "to repentance," teaching that the benefit of baptism is connected with the intention of the baptized person; to him who repents it is salutary, but to him who comes to it without repentance it will turn to greater condemnation. And here we must note that as the wonderful works done by the Saviour in the cures He wrought, which are symbolical of those who at any time are set free by the word of God from any sickness or disease, though they were done to the body and brought a bodily relief, yet also called those who were benefited by them to an exercise of faith, so the washing with water which is symbolic of the soul cleansing herself from every stain of wickedness, is no less in itself to him who yields himself to the divine power of the invocation of the Adorable Trinity, the beginning and source of divine gifts; for "there are diversities of gifts." This view receives confirmation from the narrative recorded in the Acts of the Apostles, which shows the Spirit to have descended so manifestly on those who receive baptism, after the water had prepared the way for him in those who properly approached the rite. Simon Magus, astonished at what he saw, desired to receive from Peter this gift, but though it was a good thing he desired, he thought to attain it by the mammon of unrighteousness. We next remark in passing that the baptism of John was inferior to the baptism of Jesus which was given through His disciples. Those persons in the Acts[1] who were baptized to John's baptism and who had not heard if there was any Holy Ghost are baptized over again by the Apostle. Regeneration did not take place with John, but with Jesus through His disciples it does so, and what is called the laver of regeneration takes place with renewal of the Spirit; for the Spirit now comes in addition since it comes from God and is over and above the water and does not come to all after the water. So far, then, our examination of the statements in the Gospel according to Matthew.

[1] Acts xix. 2.

18. OF THE TESTIMONY IN MARK. WHAT IS MEANT BY THE SAVIOUR'S SHOES AND BY UNTYING HIS SHOE-LATCHETS.

Now let us consider what is stated by Mark. Mark's account of John's preaching agrees with the other. The words are, "Ther ecometh after me He that is mightier than I," which amounts to the same thing as "He that cometh after me is mightier than I." There is a difference, however, in what follows, "The latchets of His shoes I am not worthy to stoop down and untie." For it is one thing to bear a person's shoes,—they must, it is evident, have been untied already from the feet of the wearer,—and it is another thing to stoop down and untie the latchet of his shoes. And it follows, since believers cannot think that either of the Evangelists made any mistake or misrepresentation, that the Baptist must have made these two utterances at different times and have meant them to express different things. It is not the case, as some suppose, that the reports refer to the same incident and turned out differently because of a looseness of memory as to some of the facts or words. Now it is a great thing to bear the shoes of Jesus, a great thing to stoop down to the bodily features of His mission, to that which took place in some lower region, so as to contemplate His image in the lower sphere, and to untie each difficulty connected with the mystery of His incarnation, such being as it were His shoe-latchets. For the fetter of obscurity is one as the key of knowledge also is one; not even He who is greatest among those born of women is sufficient of Himself to loose such things or to open them, for He who tied and locked at first, He also grants to whom He will to loose His shoe-latchet and to unlock what He has shut. If the passage about the shoes has a mystic meaning we ought not to scorn to consider it. Now I consider that the inhumanisation when the Son of God assumes flesh and bones is one of His shoes, and that the other is the descent to Hades, whatever that Hades be, and the journey with the Spirit to the prison. As to the descent into Hades, we read in the sixteenth Psalm, "Thou wilt not leave my soul in Hades," and as for the journey in prison with the Spirit we read in Peter in his Catholic Epistle,[1] "Put to death," he says, "in the flesh, but quickened in the Spirit; in which also He went and preached unto the spirits in prison, which at one time were disobedient, when the long-suffering of God once waited in the days of Noah while the ark was a preparing." He, then, who is able worthily to set forth the meaning of these two journeys is able to untie the latchet of the shoes of Jesus; he, bending down in his mind and going with Jesus as He goes down into Hades, and descending from heaven and the mysteries of Christ's deity to the advent He of necessity made with us when He took on man (as His shoes). Now He who put on man also put on the dead, for[2] "for this end Jesus both died and revived, that He might be Lord both of dead and living." This is why He put on both living and dead, that is, the inhabitants of the earth and those of Hades, that He might be the Lord of both dead and living. Who, then, is able to stoop down and untie the latchet of such shoes, and having untied them not to let them drop, but by the second faculty he has received to take them up and bear them, by bearing the meaning of them in his memory?

19. LUKE AND JOHN SUGGEST THAT ONE MAY LOOSE THE SHOE-LATCHETS OF THE LOGOS WITHOUT STOOPING DOWN.

We must not, however, omit to ask how it comes that Luke and John give the speech without the phrase "to stoop down." He, perhaps, who stoops down may be held to unloose in the sense which we have stated. On the other hand, it may be that one who fixes his eyes on the height of the exaltation of the Logos, may find the loosing of those shoes which when one is seeking them seem to be bound, so that He also looses those shoes which are separable from the Logos, and beholds the Logos divested of inferior things, as He is, the Son of God.

20. THE DIFFERENCE BETWEEN NOT BEING "SUFFICIENT" AND NOT BEING "WORTHY."

John records that the Baptist said he was not worthy, Mark that he was not sufficient, and these two are not the same. One who was not worthy might yet be sufficient, and one who was worthy might not be sufficient. For even if it be the case that gifts are bestowed to profit withal and not merely according to the proportion of faith, yet it would seem to be the part of a God who loves men and who sees before what harm must come from the rise of self-opinion or conceit, not to bestow sufficiency even on the worthy. But it belongs to the goodness of God by conferring bounties to conquer the object of His bounty, taking in advance him who is destined to be worthy, and adorning him even before he becomes worthy with sufficiency, so that after his sufficiency he may come to be worthy; he is not first to be worthy and then to anticipate the giver and take His gifts before the time and so arrive at being sufficient. Now with the three the Baptist says he is not sufficient, while in John he says he is not worthy. But it may be that he who formerly declared that he was not sufficient became sufficient afterwards, even though perhaps he was not worthy, or again that while he was saying he was not worthy, and was in fact not worthy, he arrived at being worthy, unless one should say that human nature can never come to perform worthily this loosing or this bearing, and that John, therefore, says truly that he never became sufficient to loose the latchets of the Saviour's shoes, nor worthy of it either. However much we take into our minds there are still left things not yet understood; for, as we read in the wisdom of Jesus, son of Sirach,[1] "When a man hath done, then he beginneth, and when he leaveth off, then he shall be doubtful."

21. THE FOURTH GOSPEL SPEAKS OF ONLY ONE SHOE, THE OTHERS OF BOTH. THE SIGNIFICANCE OF THIS.

As to the shoes, too, which are spoken of in the three Gospels, we have a question to consider; we must compare them with the single shoe named by the disciple John. "I am not worthy," we read there, "to untie the latchet of His shoe." Perhaps he was conquered by the grace of God, and received the gift of doing that which of himself he would not have been worthy to do, of untying, namely, the latchet of one of the shoes, namely, after he had seen the Saviour's sojourn among men, of which he bears witness. But he did not know the things which were to follow, namely, whether Jesus was to come to that place also, to which he was to go after being beheaded in prison, or whether he was to look for another; and hence he alludes enigmatically to that doubt which was afterwards cleared

[1] 1 Pet. iii. 18-20. [2] Rom. xiv. 9.

[1] xviii. 7.

up to us, and says, "I am not worthy to untie His shoe-latchet." If any one considers this to be a superfluous speculation, he can combine in one the speech about the shoes and that about the shoe, as if John said, I am by no means worthy to loose His shoestring, not even at the beginning, the string of one of His shoes. Or the following may be a way to combine what is said in the Four. If John understands about Jesus sojourn here, but is in doubt about the future, then he says with perfect truth that he is not worthy to loose the latchet of His shoes; for though he loosed that of one shoe, he did not loose both. And on the other hand, what he says about the latchet of the shoe is quite true also; since as we saw he is still in doubt whether Jesus is He that was to come, or whether another is to be looked for, in that other region.

22. HOW THE WORD STANDS IN THE MIDST OF MEN WITHOUT BEING KNOWN OF THEM.

As for the saying, "There standeth one among you whom you know not," we are led by it to consider the Son of God, the Word, by whom all things were made, since He exists in substance throughout the underlying nature of things, being the same as wisdom. For He permeated, from the beginning, all creation, so that what is made at any time should be made through Him, and that it might be always true of anything soever, that "All things were made by Him, and without Him was not anything made that was made;" and this saying also, "By wisdom didst thou make them all." Now, if He permeates all creation, then He is also in those questioners who ask, "Why baptizest thou, if thou art not the Christ, nor Elijah, nor the prophet?" In the midst of them stands the Word, who is the same and steadfast, being everywhere established by the Father. Or the words, "There standeth among you," may be understood to say, In the midst of you men, because you are reasonable beings, stands He who is proved by Scripture to be the sovereign principle in the midst of every body, and so to be present in your heart. Those, therefore, who have the Word in the midst of them, but who do not consider His nature, nor from what spring and principle He came, nor how He gave them the nature they have,[1] these, while having Him in the midst of them, know Him not. But John knew Him: for the words, "Whom you know not," used in reproach to the Pharisees, show that he well knew the Word whom they did not know. And the Baptist, therefore, knowing Him, saw Him coming after himself, who was now in the midst of them, that is to say, dwelling after him and the teaching he gave in his baptism, in those who, according to reason (or the Word), submitted to that purifying rite. The word "after," however, has not the same meaning here as it has when Jesus commands us to come "after" Him; for in this case we are bidden to go after Him, so that, treading in His steps, we may come to the Father; but in the other case, the meaning is that after the teachings of John (since "He came in order that all men through Him might believe"), the Word dwells with those who have prepared themselves, purified as they are by the lesser words for the perfect Word. Firstly, then, stands the Father, being without any turning or change; and then stands also His Word, always carrying on His work of salvation, and even when He is in the midst of men, not comprehended, and not even seen. He stands, also, teaching, and inviting all to drink from His abundant spring, for [1] "Jesus stood and cried, saying, If any man thirst, let him come unto Me and drink."

23. HERACLEON'S VIEW OF THIS UTTERANCE OF JOHN THE BAPTIST, AND INTERPRETATION OF THE SHOE OF JESUS.

But Heracleon declares the words, "There standeth one among you," to be equivalent to "He is already here, and He is in the world and in men, and He is already manifest to you all." By this He does away with the meaning which is also present in the words, that the Word had permeated the whole world. For we must say to him, When is He not present, and when is He not in the world? Does not this Gospel say, "He was in the world, and the world was made by Him, and the world knew Him not." And this is why those to whom the Logos is He "whom you know not," do not know Him: they have never gone out of the world, but the world does not know Him. But at what time did He cease to be among men? Was He not in Isaiah, when He said,[2] "The Spirit of the Lord is upon me, because He hath anointed me," and [3] "I became manifest to those who sought me not." Let them say, too, if He was not in David when he said, not from himself,[4] "But I was established by Him a

[1] Reading αὐτούς.

[1] John vii. 37.
[2] Isa. lxi. 1.
[3] Isa. lxv. 1.
[4] Ps. ii. 6.

king in Zion His holy hill," and the other words spoken in the Psalms in the person of Christ. And why should I go over the details of this proof, truly they are hard to be numbered, when I can show quite clearly that He was always in men? And that is enough to show Heracleon's interpretation of "There standeth in the midst of you," to be unsound, when he says it is equivalent to "He is already here, and He is in the world and in men." We are disposed to agree with him when he says that the words, "Who cometh after me," show John to be the forerunner of Christ, for he is in fact a kind of servant running before his master. The words, however, "Whose shoe-latchet I am not worthy to unloose," receive much too simple an interpretation when it is said that "in these words the Baptist confesses that he is not worthy even of the least honourable ministration to Christ." After this interpretation he adds, not without sense, "I am not worthy that for my sake He should come down from His greatness and should take flesh as His footgear, concerning which I am not able to give any explanation or description, nor to unloose the arrangement of it." In understanding the world by his shoe, Heracleon shows some largeness of mind, but immediately after he verges on impiety in declaring that all this is to be understood of that person whom John here has in his mind. For he considers that it is the demiurge of the world who confesses by these words that he is a lesser person than the Christ; and this is the height of impiety. For the Father who sent Him, He who is the God of the living as Jesus Himself testifies, of Abraham and of Isaac and of Jacob, and He who is greater than heaven and earth for the reason that He is the Maker of them, He also alone is good and is greater than He who was sent by Him. And even if, as we said, Heracleon's idea was a lofty one, that the whole world was the shoe of Jesus, yet I think we ought not to agree with him. For how can it be harmonized with such a view, that "Heaven is My throne and the earth My footstool," a testimony which Jesus accepts as said of the Father?[1] "Swear not by heaven," He says, "for it is God's throne, nor by the earth, for it is the footstool of His feet." How, if he takes the whole world to be the shoe of Jesus, can he also accept the text,[2] "Do not I fill heaven and earth?" saith the Lord. It is also worth while to enquire, whether as the Word and wisdom permeated the whole world, and as the Father was in the Son, the words are to be understood as above or in this way, that He who first of all was girded about with the whole creation, in addition to the Son's being in Him, granted to the Saviour, as being second after Him and being God the Word, to pervade the whole creation. To those who have it in them to take note of the uninterrupted movement of the great heaven, how it carries with it from East to West so great a multitude of stars, to them most of all it will seem needful to enquire what that force is, how great and of what nature, which is present in the whole world. For to pronounce that force to be other than the Father and the Son, that perhaps might be inconsistent with piety.

[1] Matt. v. 34, 35.

[2] Jer. xxiii. 24.

24. THE NAME OF THE PLACE WHERE JOHN BAPTIZED IS NOT BETHANY, AS IN MOST COPIES, BUT BETHABARA. PROOF OF THIS. SIMILARLY "GERGESA" SHOULD BE READ FOR "GERASA," IN THE STORY OF THE SWINE. ATTENTION IS TO BE PAID TO THE PROPER NAMES IN SCRIPTURE, WHICH ARE OFTEN WRITTEN INACCURATELY, AND ARE OF IMPORTANCE FOR INTERPRETATION.

"These things were done in Bethabara, beyond Jordan, where John was baptizing."[1] We are aware of the reading which is found in almost all the copies, "These things were done in Bethany." This appears, moreover, to have been the reading at an earlier time; and in Heracleon we read "Bethany." We are convinced, however, that we should not read "Bethany," but "Bethabara." We have visited the places to enquire as to the footsteps of Jesus and His disciples, and of the prophets. Now, Bethany, as the same evangelist tells us,[2] was the town of Lazarus, and of Martha and Mary; it is fifteen stadia from Jerusalem, and the river Jordan is about a hundred and eighty stadia distant from it. Nor is there any other place of the same name in the neighbourhood of the Jordan, but they say that Bethabara is pointed out on the banks of the Jordan, and that John is said to have baptized there. The etymology of the name, too, corresponds with the baptism of him who made ready for the Lord a people prepared for Him; for it yields the meaning "House of preparation," while Bethany means "House of obedience." Where else was it fitting that he should baptize, who was sent as a messenger before the face of the Christ, to pre-

[1] John i. 28.

[2] John xi. 1, 18.

pare His way before Him, but at the House of preparation? And what more fitting home for Mary, who chose the good part,[1] which was not taken away from her, and for Martha, who was cumbered for the reception of Jesus, and for their brother, who is called the friend of the Saviour, than Bethany, the House of obedience? Thus we see that he who aims at a complete understanding of the Holy Scriptures must not neglect the careful examination of the proper names in it. In the matter of proper names the Greek copies are often incorrect, and in the Gospels one might be misled by their authority. The transaction about the swine, which were driven down a steep place by the demons and drowned in the sea, is said to have taken place in the country of the Gerasenes.[2] Now, Gerasa is a town of Arabia, and has near it neither sea nor lake. And the Evangelists would not have made a statement so obviously and demonstrably false; for they were men who informed themselves carefully of all matters connected with Judæa. But in a few copies we have found, "into the country of the Gadarenes;" and, on this reading, it is to be stated that Gadara is a town of Judæa, in the neighbourhood of which are the well-known hot springs, and that there is no lake there with overhanging banks, nor any sea. But Gergesa, from which the name Gergesenes is taken, is an old town in the neighbourhood of the lake now called Tiberias, and on the edge of it there is a steep place abutting on the lake, from which it is pointed out that the swine were cast down by the demons. Now, the meaning of Gergesa is "dwelling of the casters-out," and it contains a prophetic reference to the conduct towards the Saviour of the citizens of those places, who "besought Him to depart out of their coasts." The same inaccuracy with regard to proper names is also to be observed in many passages of the law and the prophets, as we have been at pains to learn from the Hebrews, comparing our own copies with theirs which have the confirmation of the versions, never subjected to corruption, of Aquila and Theodotion and Symmachus. We add a few instances to encourage students to pay more attention to such points. One of the sons of Levi,[3] the first, is called Geson in most copies, instead of Gerson. His name is the same as that of the first-born of Moses;[4] it was given appropriately in each case, both children being born, because of the sojourn in Egypt, in a strange land. The second son of Juda,[1] again, has with us the name Annan, but with the Hebrews Onan, "their labour." Once more, in the departures of the children of Israel in Numbers,[2] we find, "They departed from Sochoth and pitched in Buthan;" but the Hebrew, instead of Buthan, reads Aiman. And why should I add more points like these, when any one who desires it can examine into the proper names and find out for himself how they stand? The place-names of Scripture are specially to be suspected where many of them occur in a catalogue, as in the account of the partition of the country in Joshua, and in the first Book of Chronicles from the beginning down to, say, the passage about Dan,[3] and similarly in Ezra. Names are not to be neglected, since indications may be gathered from them which help in the interpretation of the passages where they occur. We cannot, however, leave our proper subject to examine in this place into the philosophy of names.

25. JORDAN MEANS "THEIR GOING DOWN." SPIRITUAL MEANINGS AND APPLICATION OF THIS.

Let us look at the words of the Gospel now before us. "Jordan" means "their going down." The name "Jared" is etymologically akin to it, if I may say so; it also yields the meaning "going down;" for Jared was born to Maleleel, as it is written in the Book of Enoch—if any one cares to accept that book as sacred—in the days when the sons of God came down to the daughters of men. Under this descent some have supposed that there is an enigmatical reference to the descent of souls into bodies, taking the phrase "daughters of men" as a tropical expression for this earthly tabernacle. Should this be so, what river will "their going down" be, to which one must come to be purified, a river going down, not with its own descent, but "theirs," that, namely, of men, what but our Saviour who separates those who received their lots from Moses from those who obtained their own portions through Jesus (Joshua)? His current, flowing in the descending stream, makes glad, as we find in the Psalms,[4] the city of God, not the visible Jerusalem—for it has no river beside it—but the blameless Church of God, built

[1] Luke x. 41, 43.
[2] Matt. viii. 28, 32; Mark v. 1, 13; Luke viii. 26–37.
[3] Gen. xlvi. 11; Ex. vi. 16.
[4] Ex. ii. 22.

[1] Gen. xxxviii. 4.
[2] xxxiii. 6.
[3] The name "Saul" or "David" should probably stand here. 1 Chron. x., where the genealogies give place to narrative.
[4] xlvi. 4.

on the foundation of the Apostles and Prophets, Christ Jesus our Lord being the chief corner-stone. Under the Jordan, accordingly, we have to understand the Word of God who became flesh and tabernacled among us, Jesus who gives us as our inheritance the humanity which He assumed, for that is the head corner-stone, which being taken up into the deity of the Son of God, is washed by being so assumed, and then receives into itself the pure and guileless dove of the Spirit, bound to it and no longer able to fly away from it. For "Upon whomsoever," we read, "thou shalt see the Spirit descending and abiding upon Him, the same is He that baptizeth with the Holy Spirit." Hence, he who receives the Spirit abiding on Jesus Himself is able to baptize those who come to him in that abiding Spirit. But John baptizes beyond Jordan, in the regions verging on the outside of Judæa, in Bethabara, being the forerunner of Him who came to call not the righteous but sinners, and who taught that the whole have no need of a physician, but they that are sick. For it is for forgiveness of sins that this washing is given.

26. THE STORY OF ISRAEL CROSSING JORDAN UNDER JOSHUA IS TYPICAL OF CHRISTIAN THINGS, AND IS WRITTEN FOR OUR INSTRUCTION.

Now, it may very well be that some one not versed in the various aspects of the Saviour may stumble at the interpretation given above of the Jordan; because John says, "I baptize with water, but He that cometh after me is stronger than I; He shall baptize you with the Holy Spirit." To this we reply that, as the Word of God in His character as something to be drunk is to one set of men water, and to another wine, making glad the heart of man, and to others blood, since it is said,[1] "Except ye drink My blood, ye have no life in you," and as in His character as food He is variously conceived as living bread or as flesh, so also He, the same person, is baptism of water, and baptism of Holy Spirit and of fire, and to some, also, of blood. It is of His last baptism, as some hold, that He speaks in the words,[2] "I have a baptism to be baptized with, and how am I straitened till it be accomplished?" And it agrees with this that the disciple John speaks in his Epistle[3] of the Spirit, and the water, and the blood, as being one. And again He declares Himself to be the way and the door, but clearly He is not the door to those to whom He is the way, and He is no longer the way to those to whom He is the door. All those, then, who are being initiated in the beginning of the oracles of God, and come to the voice of him who cries in the wilderness, "Make straight the way of the Lord," the voice which sounds beyond Jordan at the house of preparation, let them prepare themselves so that they may be in a state to receive the spiritual word, brought home to them by the enlightenment of the Spirit. As we are now, as our subject requires, bringing together all that relates to the Jordan, let us look at the "river." God, by Moses, carried the people through the Red Sea, making the water a wall for them on the right hand and on the left, and by Joshua He carried them through Jordan. Now, Paul deals with this Scripture, and his warfare is not according to the flesh of it, for he knew that the law is spiritual in a spiritual sense. And he shows us that he understood what is said about the passage of the Red Sea; for he says in his first Epistle to the Corinthians,[1] "I would not, brethren, have you ignorant, how that our fathers were all under the cloud, and all passed through the sea, and were all baptized into Moses in the cloud and in the sea, and did all eat the same spiritual meat, and drink the same spiritual drink; for they drank of the spiritual rock which followed them, and the rock was Christ." In the spirit of this passage let us also pray that we may receive from God to understand the spiritual meaning of Joshua's passage through Jordan. Of it, also, Paul would have said, "I would not, brethren, have you ignorant, that all our fathers went through Jordan, and were all baptized into Jesus in the spirit and in the river." And Joshua, who succeeded Moses, was a type of Jesus Christ, who succeeds the dispensation through the law, and replaces it by the preaching of the Gospel. And even if those Paul speaks of were baptized in the cloud and in the sea, there is something harsh and salt in their baptism. They are still in fear of their enemies, and crying to the Lord and to Moses, saying,[2] "Because there were no graves in Egypt, hast thou brought us forth to slay us in the wilderness? Why hast thou dealt thus with us, to bring us forth out of Egypt?" But the baptism to Joshua, which takes place in quite sweet and drinkable water, is in many ways superior to that earlier one, religion having by this time grown clearer and assuming a becoming

[1] John vi. 53. [2] Luke xii. 50. [3] 1 John v. 8.

[1] x. 1–4. [2] Exod. xiv. 11.

order. For the ark of the covenant of the Lord our God is carried in procession by the priests and levites, the people following the ministers of God, it, also, accepting the law of holiness. For Joshua says to the people,[1] "Sanctify yourselves against to-morrow; the Lord will do wonders among you." And he commands the priests to go before the people with the ark of the covenant, wherein is plainly showed forth the mystery of the Father's economy about the Son, which is highly exalted by Him who gave the Son this office; "That at the name of Jesus[2] every knee should bow, of things in heaven and things on earth and things under the earth, and that every tongue should confess that Jesus Christ is Lord, to the glory of God the Father." This is pointed out by what we find in the book called Joshua,[3] "In that day I will begin to exalt thee before the children of Israel." And we hear our Lord Jesus saying to the children of Israel,[4] "Come hither and hear the words of the Lord your God. Hereby ye shall know that the living God is in (among) you;" for when we are baptized to Jesus, we know that the living God is in us. And, in the former case, they kept the passover in Egypt, and then began their journey, but with Joshua, after crossing Jordan on the tenth day of the first month they pitched their camp in Galgala; for a sheep had to be procured before invitations could be issued to the banquet after Joshua's baptism. Then the children of Israel, since the children of those who came out of Egypt had not received circumcision, were circumcised by Joshua with a very sharp stone; the Lord declares that He takes away the reproach of Egypt on the day of Joshua's baptism, when Joshua purified the children of Israel. For it is written:[5] "And the Lord said to Joshua, the son of Nun, This day have I taken away the reproach of Egypt from off you." Then the children of Israel kept the passover on the fourteenth day of the month, with much greater gladness than in Egypt, for they ate unleavened bread of the corn of the holy land, and fresh food better than manna. For when they received the land of promise God did not entertain them with scantier food, nor when such a one as Joshua was their leader do they get inferior bread. This will be plain to him who thinks of the true holy land and of the Jerusalem above. Hence it is written in this same Gospel:[1] Your fathers did eat bread in the wilderness, and are dead; he that eateth of this bread shall live for ever. For the manna, though it was given by God, yet was bread of travel, bread supplied to those still under discipline, well fitted for those who were under tutors and governors. And the new bread Joshua managed to get from corn they cut in the country, in the land of promise, others having laboured and his disciples reaping,—that was bread more full of life, distributed as it was to those who, for their perfection, were able to receive the inheritance of their fathers. Hence, he who is still under discipline to that bread may receive death as far as it is concerned, but he who has attained to the bread that follows that, eating it, shall live for ever. All this has been added, not, I conceive, without appropriateness, to our study of the baptism at the Jordan, administered by John at Bethabara.

27. OF ELIJAH AND ELISHA CROSSING THE JORDAN.

Another point which we must not fail to notice is that when Elijah was about to be taken up in a whirlwind, as if to heaven,[2] he took his mantle and wrapped it together and smote the water, which was divided hither and thither, and they went over both of them, that is, he and Elisha. His baptism in the Jordan made him fitter to be taken up, for, as we showed before, Paul gives the name of baptism to such a remarkable passage through the water. And through this same Jordan Elisha receives, through Elijah, the gift he desired, saying, "Let a double portion of thy spirit be upon me." What enabled him to receive this gift of the spirit of Elijah was, perhaps, that he had passed through Jordan twice, once with Elijah, and the second time, when, after receiving the mantle of Elijah, he smote the water and said, "Where is the God of Elijah, even He? And he smote the waters, and they were divided hither and thither."

28. NAAMAN THE SYRIAN AND THE JORDAN. NO OTHER STREAM HAS THE SAME HEALING POWER.

Should any one object to the expression "He smote the water," on account of the conclusion we arrived at above with respect to the Jordan, that it is a type of the Word who descended for us our descending, we rejoin that with the Apostle the rock is plainly said to be Christ, and that it is

[1] Josh. iii. 5. [2] Philipp. ii. 9–11. [3] iii. 7.
[4] Josh. iii. 9, 10. [5] Josh. v. 9.

[1] vi. 49. [2] 2 Kings ii. 8, 11.

smitten twice with the rod, so that the people may drink of the spiritual rock which follows them. The "smiting" in this new difficulty is that of those who are fond of suggesting something that contradicts the conclusion even before they have learned what the question is which is in hand. From such God sets us free, since, on the one hand, He gives us to drink when we are thirsty, and on the other He prepares for us, in the immense and trackless deep, a road to pass over, namely, by the dividing of His Word, since it is by the reason which distinguishes (divides) that most things are made plain to us. But that we may receive the right interpretation about this Jordan, so good to drink, so full of grace, it may be of use to compare the cleansing of Naaman the Syrian from his leprosy, and what is said of the rivers of religion of the enemies of Israel. It is recorded of Naaman [1] that he came with horse and chariot, and stood at the door of the house of Elisha. And Elisha sent a messenger to him, saying, "Go, wash seven times in the Jordan, and thy flesh shall come again unto thee, and thou shalt be cleansed." Then Naaman is angry; he does not see that our Jordan is the cleanser of those who are impure from leprosy, from that impurity, and their restorer to health; it is the Jordan that does this, and not the prophet; the office of the prophet is to direct to the healing agency. Naaman then says, not understanding the great mystery of the Jordan, "Behold, I said that he will certainly come out to me, and will call upon the name of the Lord his God, and lay his hand upon the place, and restore the leper." For to put his hand on the leprosy [2] and cleanse it is a work belonging to our Lord Jesus only; for when the leper appealed to Him with faith, saying, "If Thou wilt Thou canst make me clean," He not only said, "I will, be thou clean," but in addition to the word He touched him, and he was cleansed from his leprosy. Naaman, then, is still in error, and does not see how far inferior other rivers are to the Jordan for the cure of the suffering; he extols the rivers of Damascus, Arbana, and Pharpha, saying, "Are not Arbana and Pharpha, rivers of Damascus, better than all the waters of Israel? Shall I not wash in them and be clean?" For as none is good [3] but one, God the Father, so among rivers none is good but the Jordan, nor able to cleanse from his leprosy him who with faith washes his soul in Jesus. And this, I suppose, is the reason why the Israelites are recorded to have wept when they sat by the rivers of Babylon and remembered Zion; those who are carried captive, on account of their wickedness, when they taste other waters after sacred Jordan, are led to remember with longing their own river of salvation. Therefore it is said of the rivers of Babylon, "There we sat down," clearly because they were unable to stand, "and wept." And Jeremiah rebukes those who wish to drink the waters of Egypt, and desert the water which comes down from heaven, and is named from its so coming down—namely, the Jordan. He says,[1] "What hast thou to do with the way of Egypt, to drink the water of Geon, and to drink the water of the river," or, as it is in the Hebrew, "to drink the water of Sion." Of which water we have now to speak.

[1] 2 Kings v. 9, 10. [2] Matt. viii. 2, 3.
[3] Matt. xix. 17; Mark x. 18; Luke xviii. 19.

29. THE RIVER OF EGYPT AND ITS DRAGON, CONTRASTED WITH THE JORDAN.

But that the Spirit in the inspired Scriptures is not speaking mainly of rivers to be seen with the eyes, may be gathered from Ezekiel's prophecies against Pharaoh, king of Egypt:[2] "Behold I am against thee, Pharaoh, king of Egypt, the great dragon, seated in the midst of rivers, who sayest, Mine are the rivers, and I made them. And I will put traps in thy jaws, and I will make the fishes of the river to stick to thy fins, and I will bring thee up from the midst of thy river, and all the fish of the river, and I will cast thee down quickly and all the fish of the river; thou shalt fall upon the face of thy land, and thou shalt not be gathered together, and thou shalt not be adorned." For what real bodily dragon has ever been reported as having been seen in the material river of Egypt? But consider if the river of Egypt be not the dwelling of the dragon who is our enemy, who was not even able to kill the child Moses. But as the dragon is in the river of Egypt, so is God in the river which makes glad the city of God; for the Father is in the Son. Hence those who come to wash themselves in Him put away the reproach of Egypt, and become more fit to be restored. They are cleansed from that foulest leprosy, receive a double portion of spiritual gifts, and are made ready to receive the Holy Spirit, since the spiritual dove does not light on any other stream. Thus we have considered in a way more worthy of the sacred

[1] ii. 18. [2] xxix. 3-5.

subject the Jordan and the purification that is in it, and Jesus being washed in it, and the house of preparation. Let us, then, draw from the river as much help as we require.

30. OF WHAT JOHN LEARNED FROM JESUS WHEN MARY VISITED ELISABETH IN THE HILL COUNTRY.

"The next day John seeth Jesus coming unto him."[1] The mother of Jesus had formerly, as soon as she conceived, stayed with the mother of John, also at that time with child, and the Former then communicated to the Formed with some exactness His own image, and caused him to be conformed to His glory. And from this outward similarity it came that with those who did not distinguish between the image itself and that which was according to the image, John was thought to be Christ[2] and Jesus was supposed[3] to be John risen from the dead. So now Jesus, after the testimonies of John to Him which we have examined, is Himself seen by the Baptist coming to him. It is to be noticed that on the former occasion, when the voice of Mary's salutation came to the ears of Elisabeth, the babe John leaped in the womb of his mother, who then received the Holy Spirit, as it were, from the ground. For it came to pass, we read,[4] "when Elisabeth heard the salutation of Mary, the babe leaped in her womb; and Elisabeth was filled with the Holy Spirit, and she lifted up her voice with a loud cry and said," etc. On this occasion, similarly, John sees Jesus coming to him and says, "Behold the Lamb of God which taketh away the sin of the world." For with regard to matters of great moment one is first instructed by hearing and afterwards one sees them with one's own eyes. That John was helped to the shape he was to wear by the Lord who, still in the process of formation and in His mother's womb, approached Elisabeth, will be clear to any one who has grasped our proof that John is a voice but that Jesus is the Word, for when Elisabeth was filled with the Holy Spirit at the salutation of Mary there was a great voice in her, as the words themselves bear; for they say, "And she spake out with a loud voice." Elisabeth, it is plain, did this, "and she spake." For the voice of Mary's salutation coming to the ears of Elisabeth filled John with itself; hence John leaps, and his mother becomes, as it were, the mouth of her son and a prophetess, crying out with a loud voice and saying, "Blessed art thou among women, and blessed is the fruit of thy womb." Now we see clearly how it was with Mary's hasty journey to the hill country, and her entrance into the house of Zacharias, and the greeting with which she salutes Elisabeth; it was that she might communicate some of the power she derived from Him she had conceived, to John, yet in his mother's womb, and that John too might communicate to his mother some of the prophetic grace which had come to him, that all these things were done. And most rightly was it in the hill country that these transactions took place, since no great thing can be entertained by those who are low and may be thence called valleys. Here, then, after the testimonies of John,—the first, when he cried and spoke about His deity; the second, addressed to the priests and levites who were sent by the Jews from Jerusalem; and the third, in answer to the sharper questions of those from the Pharisees,—Jesus is seen by the witness-bearer coming to him while he is still advancing and growing better. This advance and improvement is symbolically indicated in the phrase, "On the morrow." For Jesus came in the consequent illumination, as it were, and on the day after what had preceded, not only known as standing in the midst even of those who knew Him not, but now plainly seen advancing to him who had formerly made such declarations about Him. On the first day the testimonies take place, and on the second Jesus comes to John. On the third John, standing with two of his disciples and looking upon Jesus as He walked, said, "Behold the Lamb of God," thus urging those who were there to follow the Son of God. On the fourth day, too, He was minded to go forth into Galilee, and He who came forth to seek that which was lost finds Philip and says to him, "Follow Me." And on that day, after the fourth, which is the sixth from the beginning of those we have enumerated, the marriage takes place in Cana of Galilee, which we shall have to consider when we get to the passage. Note this, too, that Mary being the greater comes to Elisabeth, who is the less, and the Son of God comes to the Baptist; which should encourage us to render help without delay to those who are in a lower position, and to cultivate for ourselves a moderate station.

[1] John. i. 29.
[2] Luke iii. 14.
[3] Matt. xiv. 2.
[4] Luke i. 41, 42.

31. OF THE CONVERSATION BETWEEN JOHN AND JESUS AT THE BAPTISM, RECORDED BY MATTHEW ONLY.

John the disciple does not tell us where the Saviour comes from to John the Baptist, but we learn this from Matthew, who writes:[1] "Then cometh Jesus from Galilee to Jordan to John, to be baptized of him." And Mark adds the place in Galilee; he says,[2] "And it came to pass in those days, that Jesus came from Nazareth in Galilee and was baptized by John in Jordan." Luke does not mention the place Jesus came from, but on the other hand he tells us what we do not learn from the others, that immediately after the baptism, as He was coming up, heaven was opened to Him, and the Holy Spirit descended on Him in bodily form like a dove. Again, it is Matthew alone who tells us of John's preventing the Lord, saying to the Saviour, "I have need to be baptized of Thee, and comest Thou to me?" None of the others added this after Matthew, so that they might not be saying just the same as he. And what the Lord rejoined, "Suffer it now, for thus it becometh us to fulfil all righteousness," this also Matthew alone recorded.

32. JOHN CALLS JESUS A "LAMB." WHY DOES HE NAME THIS ANIMAL SPECIALLY? OF THE TYPOLOGY OF THE SACRIFICES, GENERALLY.

"And he sayeth, Behold the Lamb of God, which taketh away the sin of the world."[3] There were five animals which were brought to the altar, three that walk and two that fly; and it seems to be worth asking why John calls the Saviour a lamb and not any of these other creatures, and why, when each of the animals that walk is offered of three kinds he used for the sheep-kind the term "lamb." The five animals are as follows: the bullock, the sheep, the goat, the turtle-dove, the pigeon. And of the walking animals these are the three kinds —bullock, ox, calf; ram, sheep, lamb; he-goat, goat, kid. Of the flying animals, of pigeons we only hear of two young ones; of turtle doves only of a pair. He, then, who would accurately understand the spiritual rationale of the sacrifices must enquire of what heavenly things these were the pattern and the shadow, and also for what end the sacrifice of each victim is prescribed, and he must specially collect the points connected with the lamb. Now that the principle of the sacrifice must be apprehended with reference to certain heavenly mysteries, appears from the words of the Apostle, who somewhere[1] says, "Who serve a pattern and shadow of heavenly things," and again, "It was necessary that the patterns of the things in the heavens should be purified with these, but the heavenly things themselves with better sacrifices than these." Now to find out all the particulars of these and to state in its relation to them that sacrifice of the spiritual law which took place in Jesus Christ (a truth greater than human nature can comprehend)—to do this belongs to no other than the perfect man,[2] who, by reason of use, has his senses exercised to discern good and evil, and who is able to say, from a truth-loving disposition,[3] "We speak wisdom among them that are perfect." Of these things truly and things like these, we can say,[4] "Which none of the rulers of this world knew."

33. A LAMB WAS OFFERED AT THE MORNING AND EVENING SACRIFICE. SIGNIFICANCE OF THIS.

Now we find the lamb offered in the continual (daily) sacrifice. Thus it is written,[4] "This is that which thou shalt offer upon the altar; two lambs of the first year day by day continually, for a continual sacrifice. The one lamb thou shalt offer in the morning, and the other lamb thou shalt offer at even, and a tenth part of fine flour mingled with beaten oil, the fourth part of a hin; and for a drink-offering the fourth part of a hin of wine to the first lamb. And the other lamb thou shalt offer in the evening, according to the first sacrifice and according to its drink-offering. Thou shalt offer a sweet savour, an offering to the Lord, a continual burnt offering throughout your generations at the door of tent of witness before the Lord, where I will make myself known to thee, to speak unto thee. And I will appoint thee for the children of Israel, and I will be sanctified in my glory, and with sanctification I will sanctify the tent of witness." But what other continual sacrifice can there be to the man of reason in the world of mind, but the Word growing to maturity, the Word who is symbolically called a lamb and who is offered as soon as the soul receives illumination. This would be the continual sacrifice of the morning, and it is offered again when the sojourn of the mind with divine things comes to an end. For it cannot maintain for ever its inter-

[1] iii. 13. [2] i. 9. [3] John i. 29.

[1] Heb. viii. 5; ix. 23. [2] Heb. v. 14. [3] 1 Cor. ii. 6. [4] Exod. xxix. 38–44.

course with higher things, seeing that the soul is appointed to be yoked together with the body which is of earth and heavy.

34. THE MORNING AND EVENING SACRIFICES OF THE SAINT IN HIS LIFE OF THOUGHT.

But if any one asks what the saint is to do in the time between morning and evening, let him follow what takes place in the cultus and infer from it the principle he asks for. In that case the priests begin their offerings with the continual sacrifice, and before they come to the continuous one of the evening they offer the other sacrifices which the law prescribes, as, for example, that for transgression, or that for involuntary offences, or that connected with a prayer for salvation, or that of jealousy, or that of the Sabbath, or of the new moon, and so on, which it would take too long to mention. So we, beginning our oblation with the discourse of that type which is Christ, can go on to discourse about many other most useful things. And drawing to a close still in the things of Christ, we come, as it were, to evening and night, when we arrive at the bodily features of His manifestation.

35. JESUS IS A LAMB IN RESPECT OF HIS HUMAN NATURE.

If we enquire further into the significance of Jesus being pointed out by John, when he says, "This is the Lamb of God which taketh away the sin of the world," we may take our stand at the dispensation of the bodily advent of the Son of God in human life, and in that case we shall conceive the lamb to be no other than the man. For the man "was led like a sheep to the slaughter, and as a lamb, dumb before his shearers,"[1] saying, "I was as like a gentle lamb led to the slaughter."[2] Hence, too, in the Apocalypse[3] a lamb is seen, standing as if slain. This slain lamb has been made, according to certain hidden reasons, a purification of the whole world, for which, according to the Father's love to man, He submitted to death, purchasing us back by His own blood from him who had got us into his power, sold under sin. And He who led this lamb to the slaughter was God in man, the great High-Priest, as he shows by the words:[4] "No one taketh My life away from Me, but I lay it down of Myself. I have power to lay it down, and I have power to take it again."

[1] Isa. liii. 7.
[2] Jer. xi. 19.
[3] v. 6.
[4] John x. 18.

36. OF THE DEATH OF THE MARTYRS CONSIDERED AS A SACRIFICE, AND IN WHAT WAY IT OPERATES TO THE BENEFIT OF OTHERS.

Akin to this sacrifice are the others of which the sacrifices of the law are symbols, and another kind of sacrifice also appears to me to be of the same nature; namely, the shedding of the blood of the noble martyrs, whom the disciple John saw, for this is not without significance, standing beside the heavenly altar. "Who is wise,[1] and he shall understand these things, prudent, and he shall know them?" It is a matter of higher speculation to consider even slightly the rationale of those sacrifices which cleanse those for whom they are offered. Jephthah's sacrifice of his daughter should receive attention; it was by vowing it that he conquered the children of Ammon, and the victim approved his vow, for when her father said,[2] "I have opened my mouth unto the Lord against thee," she answered, "If thou hast opened thy mouth unto the Lord against me, do that which thou hast vowed." The story suggests that the being must be a very cruel one to whom such sacrifices are offered for the salvation of men; and we require some breadth of mind and some ability to solve the difficulties raised against Providence, to be able to account for such things and to see that they are mysteries and exceed our human nature. Then we shall say,[3] "Great are the judgments of God, and hard to be described; for this cause untutored souls have gone astray." Among the Gentiles, too, it is recorded that many a one, when pestilential disease broke out in his country, offered himself a victim for the public good. That this was the case the faithful Clement assumes,[4] on the faith of the narratives, to whom Paul bears witness when he says,[5] "With Clement also, and the others, my fellow-labourers, whose names are in the book of life." If there is anything in these narratives that appears incongruous to one who is minded to carp at mysteries revealed to few, the same difficulty attaches to the office that was laid on the martyrs, for it was God's will that we should rather endure all the dreadful reproaches connected with confessing Him as God, than escape for a short time from such sufferings (which men count evil) by allowing ourselves by our words to conform to the will of the enemies of the truth. We are, therefore, led to believe that the powers of evil do suffer

[1] Hosea xiv. 10.
[2] Judges xi. 35.
[3] Wisdom xvii. 1.
[4] 1 Clement, 55.
[5] Philipp. iv. 3.

defeat by the death of the holy martyrs; as if their patience, their confession, even unto death, and their zeal for piety blunted the edge of the onset of evil powers against the sufferer, and their might being thus dulled and exhausted, many others of those whom they had conquered raised their heads and were set free from the weight with which the evil powers formerly oppressed and injured them. And even the martyrs themselves are no longer involved in suffering, even though those agents which formerly wrought ill to others are not exhausted; for he who has offered such a sacrifice overcomes the power which opposed him, as I may show by an illustration which is suited to this subject. He who destroys a poisonous animal, or lulls it to sleep with charms, or by any means deprives it of its venom, he does good to many who would otherwise have suffered from that animal had it not been destroyed, or charmed, or emptied of its venom. Moreover, if one of those who were formerly bitten should come to know of this, and should be cured of his malady and look upon the death of that which injured him, or tread on it, or touch it when dead, or taste a part of it, then he, who was formerly a sufferer, would owe cure and benefit to the destroyer of the poisonous animal. In some such way must we suppose the death of the most holy martyrs to operate, many receiving benefit from it by an influence we cannot describe.

37. OF THE EFFECTS OF THE DEATH OF CHRIST, OF HIS TRIUMPH AFTER IT, AND OF THE REMOVAL BY HIS DEATH OF THE SINS OF MEN.

We have lingered over this subject of the martyrs and over the record of those who died on account of pestilence, because this lets us see the excellence of Him who was led as a sheep to the slaughter and was dumb as a lamb before the shearer. For if there is any point in these stories of the Greeks, and if what we have said of the martyrs is well founded,—the Apostles, too, were for the same reason the filth of the world and the offscouring of all things,[1]—what and how great things must be said of the Lamb of God, who was sacrificed for this very reason, that He might take away the sin not of a few but of the whole world, for the sake of which also He suffered? If any one sin, we read,[2] "We have an advocate with the Father, Jesus Christ the righteous; and He is the propitiation for our sins, and not for ours only, but for those of the whole world," since He is the Saviour of all men,[1] especially of them that believe, who [2] blotted out the written bond that was against us by His own blood, and took it out of the way, so that not even a trace, not even of our blotted-out sins, might still be found, and nailed it to His cross; who having put off from Himself the principalities and powers, made a show of them openly, triumphing over them by His cross. And we are taught to rejoice when we suffer afflictions in the world, knowing the ground of our rejoicing to be this, that the world has been conquered and has manifestly been subjected to its conqueror. Hence all the nations, released from their former rulers, serve Him, because He [3] saved the poor from his tyrant by His own passion, and the needy who had no helper. This Saviour, then, having humbled the calumniator by humbling Himself, abides with the visible sun before His illustrious church, tropically called the moon, from generation to generation. And having by His passion destroyed His enemies, He who is strong in battle and a mighty Lord [4] required after His mighty deeds a purification which could only be given Him by His Father alone; and this is why He forbids Mary to touch Him, saying,[5] "Touch Me not, for I am not yet ascended to My Father; but go and tell My disciples, I go to My Father and your Father, to My God and your God." And when He comes, loaded with victory and with trophies, with His body which has risen from the dead,—for what other meaning can we see in the words, "I am not yet ascended to My Father," and "I go unto My Father,"—then there are certain powers which say, Who is this that cometh from Edom, red garments from Bosor; this that is beautiful?[6] Then those who escort Him say to those that are upon the heavenly gates,[7] "Lift up your gates, ye rulers, and be ye lifted up, ye everlasting doors, and the king of glory shall come in." But they ask again, seeing as it were His right hand red with blood and His whole person covered with the marks of His valour, "Why are Thy garments red, and Thy clothes like the treading of the full winefat when it is trodden?" And to this He answers, "I have crushed them." For this cause He had need to wash "His robe in wine, and His garment in the blood of the grape."[8] For when He had taken up our

[1] 1 Cor. iv. 13.
[2] 1 John ii. 1, 2.

[1] 1 Tim. iv. 10.
[2] Coloss. ii. 14, 15.
[3] Ps. lxxii. 12.
[4] Ps. xxiv. 8.
[5] John xx. 17.
[6] Isa. lxiii. 1.
[7] Ps. xxiv. 7 9.
[8] Gen. xlix. 2.

infirmities and carried our diseases, and had borne the sin of the whole world, and had conferred blessings on so many, then, perhaps, He received that baptism which is greater than any that could ever be conceived among men, and of which I think He speaks when He says,[1] "I have a baptism to be baptized with, and how am I straitened till it be accomplished?" I enquire here with boldness and I challenge the ideas put forward by most writers. They say that the greatest baptism, beyond which no greater can be conceived, is His passion. But if this be so, why should He say to Mary after it, "Touch Me not"? He should rather have offered Himself to her touch, when by His passion He had received His perfect baptism. But if it was the case, as we said before, that after all His deeds of valour done against His enemies, He had need to wash "His robe in wine, His garment in the blood of the grape," then He was on His way up to the husbandman of the true vine, the Father, so that having washed there and after having gone up on high, He might lead captivity captive and come down bearing manifold gifts—the tongues, as of fire, which were divided to the Apostles, and the holy angels which are to be present with them in each action and to deliver them. For before these economies, they were not yet cleansed and angels could not dwell with them, for they too perhaps do not desire to be with those who have not prepared themselves nor been cleansed by Jesus. For it was of Jesus' benignity alone that He ate and drank with publicans and sinners, and suffered the penitent woman who was a sinner to wash His feet with her tears, and went down even to death for the ungodly, counting it not robbery to be equal with God, and emptied Himself, assuming the form of a servant. And in accomplishing all this He fulfils rather the will of the Father who gave Him up for sinners than His own. For the Father is good, but the Saviour is the image of His goodness; and doing good to the world in all things, since God was in Christ reconciling the world to Himself, which formerly for its wickedness was an enemy to Him, He accomplishes His good deeds in order and succession, and does not all at once take all His enemies for His footstool. For the Father says to Him, to the Lord of us all,[2] "Sit Thou on My right hand, until I make Thy enemies the footstool of Thy feet." And this goes on till the last enemy, Death, is overcome by Him.

[1] Luke xii. 50. [2] Ps. cx. 1.

And if we consider what is meant by this subjection to Christ and find an explanation of this mainly from the saying,[1] "When all things shall have been put under Him, then shall the Son Himself be subjected to Him who put all things under Him," then we shall see how the conception agrees with the goodness of the God of all, since it is that of the Lamb of God, taking away the sin of the world. Not all men's sin, however, is taken away by the Lamb of God, not the sin of those who do not grieve and suffer affliction till it be taken away. For thorns are not only fixed but deeply rooted in the hand of every one who is intoxicated by wickedness and has parted with sobriety, as it is said in the Proverbs,[2] "Thorns grow in the hand of the drunkard," and what pain they must cause him who has admitted such growth in the substance of his soul, it is hard even to tell. Who has allowed wickedness to establish itself so deeply in his soul as to be a ground full of thorns, he must be cut down by the quick and powerful word of God, which is sharper than a two-edged sword, and which is more caustic than any fire. To such a soul that fire must be sent which finds out thorns, and by its divine virtue stands where they are and does not also burn up the threshing-floors or standing corn. But of the Lamb which takes away the sin of the world and begins to do so by His own death there are several ways, some of which are capable of being clearly understood by most, but others are concealed from most, and are known to those only who are worthy of divine wisdom. Why should we count up all the ways by which we come to believe among men? That is a thing which every one living in the body is able to see for himself. And in the ways in which we believe in these also, sin is taken away; by afflictions and evil spirits and dangerous diseases and grievous sicknesses. And who knows what follows after this? So much as we have said was not unnecessary—we could not neglect the thought which is so clearly connected with that of the words, "Behold the Lamb of God that taketh away the sin of the world," and had therefore to attend somewhat closely to this part of our subject. This has brought us to see that God convicts some by His wrath and chastens them by His anger, since His love to men is so great that He will not leave any without conviction and chastening; so that we should do what in us lies to be spared such

[1] 1 Cor. xv. 26. [2] xxvi. 9.

conviction and such chastening by the sorest trials.

38. THE WORLD, OF WHICH THE SIN IS TAKEN AWAY, IS SAID TO BE THE CHURCH. REASONS FOR NOT AGREEING WITH THIS OPINION.

The reader will do well to consider what was said above and illustrated from various quarters on the question what is meant in Scripture by the word "world"; and I think it proper to repeat this. I am aware that a certain scholar understands by the world the Church alone, since the Church is the adornment of the world,[1] and is said to be the light of the world. "You," he says,[2] "are the light of the world." Now, the adornment of the world is the Church, Christ being her adornment, who is the first light of the world. We must consider if Christ is said to be the light of the same world as His disciples. When Christ is the light of the world, perhaps it is meant that He is the light of the Church, but when His disciples are the light of the world, perhaps they are the light of others who call on the Lord, others in addition to the Church, as Paul says on this point in the beginning of his first Epistle to the Corinthians, where he writes, "To the Church of God, with all who call on the name of the Lord Jesus Christ." Should any one consider that the Church is called the light of the world, meaning thereby of the rest of the race of men, including unbelievers, this may be true if the assertion is taken prophetically and theologically; but if it is to be taken of the present, we remind him that the light of a thing illuminates that thing, and would ask him to show how the remainder of the race is illuminated by the Church's presence in the world. If those who hold the view in question cannot show this, then let them consider if our interpretation is not a sound one, that the light is the Church, and the world those others who call on the Name. The words which follow the above in Matthew will point out to the careful enquirer the proper interpretation. "You," it is said, "are the salt of the earth," the rest of mankind being conceived as the earth, and believers are their salt; it is because they believe that the earth is preserved. For the end will come if the salt loses its savour, and ceases to salt and preserve the earth, since it is clear that if iniquity is multiplied and love waxes cold upon the earth,[1] as the Saviour Himself uttered an expression of doubt as to those who would witness His coming, saying,[2] "When the Son of man cometh, shall He find faith upon the earth?" then the end of the age will come. Supposing, then, the Church to be called the world, since the Saviour's light shines on it—we have to ask in connection with the text, "Behold the Lamb of God, which taketh away the sin of the world," whether the world here is to be taken intellectually of the Church, and the taking away of sin is limited to the Church. In that case what are we to make of the saying of the same disciple with regard to the Saviour, as the propitiation for sin? "If any man sin," we read, "we have an advocate with the Father, Jesus Christ the righteous; and He is the propitiation for our sins, and not for our sins only, but for the sins of the whole world?" Paul's dictum appears to me to be to the same effect, when he says,[3] "Who is the Saviour of all men, especially of the faithful." Again, Heracleon, dealing with our passage, declares, without any proof or any citation of witnesses to that effect, that the words, "Lamb of God," are spoken by John as a prophet, but the words, "who taketh away the sin of the world," by John as more than a prophet. The former expression he considers to be used of His body, but the latter of Him who was in that body, because the lamb is an imperfect member of the genus sheep; the same being true of the body as compared with the dweller in it. Had he meant to attribute perfection to the body he would have spoken of a ram as about to be sacrificed. After the careful discussions given above, I do not think it necessary to enter into repetitions on this passage, or to controvert Heracleon's careless utterances. One point only may be noted, that as the world was scarcely able to contain Him who had emptied Himself, it required a lamb and not a ram, that its sin might be taken away.

[1] κοσμος means both "ornament" and "world."
[2] Matt. v. 14.

[1] Matt. xxiv. 12. [2] Luke xviii. 8. [3] 1 Tim. iv. 10.

TENTH BOOK

1. JESUS COMES TO CAPERNAUM. STATEMENTS OF THE FOUR EVANGELISTS REGARDING THIS.

"After this[1] He went down to Capernaum, He and His mother and His brothers and His disciples; and there they abode not many days. And the passover of the Jews was at hand, and Jesus went up to Jerusalem, and He found in the temple those that sold oxen and sheep and doves, and the changers of money sitting, and He made a sort of scourge of cords, and cast them all out of the temple, and the sheep and the oxen, and He poured out the small money of the changers and overthrew their tables, and to those that sold the doves He said, Take these things hence; make not My Father's house a house of merchandize. Then His disciples remembered that it was written, that the zeal of thy house shall eat me up. The Jews therefore answered and said unto Him, What sign showest Thou unto us, that Thou doest such things? Jesus answered and said unto them, Destroy this temple, and in three days I will raise it up. The Jews therefore answered, Forty-six years was this temple in building, and wilt thou raise it up in three days? But He spoke of the temple of His body. When therefore He rose from the dead, His disciples remembered that He said this, and they believed the Scripture and the word which Jesus said. Now when He was at Jerusalem at the passover at the feast, many believed in His name, beholding His signs which He did. But Jesus Himself did not trust Himself to them, for that He knew all men, and because He had no need that any should bear witness concerning man. For He Himself knew what was in man."

The numbers which are recorded in the book of that name[2] obtained a place in Scripture in accordance with some principle which determines their proportion to each thing. We ought therefore to enquire whether the book of Moses which is called Numbers teaches us, should we be able to trace it out, in some special way, the principle with regard to this matter. This remark I make to you at the outset of my tenth book, for in many passages of Scripture I have observed the number ten to have a peculiar privilege, and you may consider carefully whether the hope is justified that this volume will bring you from God some special benefit. That this may prove to be the case, we will seek to yield ourselves as fully as we can to God, who loves to bestow His choicest gifts. The book begins at the words: "After this He went down to Capernaum, He and His mother and His brothers and His disciples, and there they abode not many days." The other three Evangelists say that the Lord, after His conflict with the devil, departed into Galilee. Matthew and Luke represent that he was first at Nazara,[1] and then left them and came and dwelt in Capernaum. Matthew and Mark also state a certain reason why He departed thither, namely, that He had heard that John was cast into prison. The words are as follows: Matthew says,[2] "Then the devil leaveth Him, and behold, angels came and ministered unto Him. But when He heard that John was delivered up, He departed into Galilee, and leaving Nazareth He came and dwelt at Capernaum on the seashore in the borders of Zebulun and Naphtali, that it might be fulfilled which was spoken by Isaiah the prophet, saying, The land of Zebulun and the land of Naphtali;" and after the quotation from Isaiah: "From that time Jesus began to preach and to say, Repent ye; for the kingdom of heaven is at hand." Mark has the following:[3] "And He was in the desert forty days and forty nights tempted by Satan, and He was with the wild beasts; and the angels ministered unto Him. But after John was delivered up Jesus came into Galilee, preaching the Gospel of God, that the time is fulfilled and the kingdom of God is at hand; repent ye, and believe in the Gospel." Then after the narrative about Andrew and Peter and James and John, Mark writes: "And He entered into Capernaum, and straightway on the Sabbath He was teaching in the synagogue." Luke has,[4] "And having finished the temptation the devil departed from Him for a season. And Jesus returned in the power of the Spirit into Galilee, and a fame went out

[1] John ii. 12–25.
[2] The text is doubtful here, but the above seems to be the meaning.

[1] Nazara is with Origen a neuter plural.
[2] iv. 11–15, 17. [3] i. 13, 14, 21. [4] iv. 13–16.

concerning Him into all the region round about, and He taught in their synagogues being glorified of all. And He came to Nazara, where He had been brought up, and He entered as His custom was into the synagogue on the Sabbath day." Then Luke[1] gives what He said at Nazara, and how those in the synagogue were enraged at Him and cast Him out of the city and brought Him to the brow of the hill on which their cities were built, to cast Him down headlong, and how going through the midst of them the Lord went His way; and with this he connects the statement, "And He came down to Capernaum, a city of Galilee, and He was teaching them on the Sabbath day."

2. THE DISCREPANCY BETWEEN JOHN AND THE FIRST THREE GOSPELS AT THIS PART OF THE NARRATIVE. LITERALLY READ, THE NARRATIVES CANNOT BE HARMONIZED: THEY MUST BE INTERPRETED SPIRITUALLY.

The truth of these matters must lie in that which is seen by the mind. If the discrepancy between the Gospels is not solved, we must give up our trust in the Gospels, as being true and written by a divine spirit, or as records worthy of credence, for both these characters are held to belong to these works. Those who accept the four Gospels, and who do not consider that their apparent discrepancy is to be solved anagogically (by mystical interpretation), will have to clear up the difficulty, raised above, about the forty days of the temptation, a period for which no room can be found in any way in John's narrative; and they will also have to tell us when it was that the Lord came to Capernaum. If it was after the six days of the period of His baptism, the sixth being that of the marriage at Cana of Galilee, then it is clear that the temptation never took place, and that He never was at Nazara, and that John was not yet delivered up. Now, after Capernaum, where He abode not many days, the passover of the Jews was at hand, and He went up to Jerusalem, where He cast the sheep and oxen out of the temple, and poured out the small change of the bankers. In Jerusalem, too, it appears that Nicodemus, the ruler and Pharisee, first came to Him by night, and heard what we may read in the Gospel. "After these things,[2] Jesus came, and His disciples, into the land of Judæa, and there He tarried with them and baptized, at the same time at which John also was baptizing in Ænon near Salim, because there were many waters there, and they came and were baptized; for John was not yet cast into prison." On this occasion, too, there was a questioning on the part of John's disciples with the Jews about purification, and they came to John, saying of the Saviour, "Behold, He baptizeth, and all come to Him." They had heard words from the Baptist, the exact tenor of which it is better to take from Scripture itself. Now, if we ask when Christ was first in Capernaum, our respondents, if they follow the words of Matthew, and of the other two, will say, After the temptation, when, "leaving Nazareth, He came and dwelt in Capernaum by the sea." But how can they show both the statements to be true, that of Matthew and Mark, that it was because He heard that John was delivered up that He departed into Galilee, and that of John,[1] found there, after a number of other transactions, subsequent to His stay at Capernaum, after His going to Jerusalem, and His journey from there to Judæa, that John was not yet cast into prison, but was baptizing in Ænon near Salim? There are many other points on which the careful student of the Gospels will find that their narratives do not agree; and these we shall place before the reader, according to our power, as they occur. The student, staggered at the consideration of these things, will either renounce the attempt to find all the Gospels true, and not venturing to conclude that all our information about our Lord is untrustworthy, will choose at random one of them to be his guide; or he will accept the four, and will consider that their truth is not to be sought for in the outward and material letter.

3. WHAT WE ARE TO THINK OF THE DISCREPANCIES BETWEEN THE DIFFERENT GOSPELS.

We must, however, try to obtain some notion of the intention of the Evangelists in such matters, and we direct ourselves to this. Suppose there are several men who, by the spirit, see God, and know His words addressed to His saints, and His presence which He vouchsafes to them, appearing to them at chosen times for their advancement. There are several such men, and they are in different places, and the benefits they receive from above vary in shape and character. And let these men report, each of them separately, what he sees in spirit about God and His words, and His appearances to His saints, so that one of them speaks of

[1] iv. 21 sqq.

[2] John iii. 23–26.

[1] iii. 24.

God's appearances and words and acts to one righteous man in such a place, and another about other oracles and great works of the Lord, and a third of something else than what the former two have dealt with. And let there be a fourth, doing with regard to some particular matter something of the same kind as these three. And let the four agree with each other about something the Spirit has suggested to them all, and let them also make brief reports of other matters besides that one; then their narratives will fall out something on this wise: God appeared to such a one at such a time and in such a place, and did to him thus and thus; as if He had appeared to him in such a form, and had led him by the hand to such a place, and then done to him thus and thus. The second will report that God appeared at the very time of the foresaid occurrences, in a certain town, to a person who is named, a second person, and in a place far removed from that of the former account, and he will report a different set of words spoken at the same time to this second person. And let the same be supposed to be the case with the third and with the fourth. And let them, as we said, agree, these witnesses who report true things about God, and about His benefits conferred on certain men, let them agree with each other in some of the narratives they report. He, then, who takes the writings of these men for history, or for a representation of real things by a historical image, and who supposes God to be within certain limits in space, and to be unable to present to several persons in different places several visions of Himself at the same time, or to be making several speeches at the same moment, he will deem it impossible that our four writers are all speaking truth. To him it is impossible that God, who is in certain limits in space, could at the same set time be saying one thing to one man and another to another, and that He should be doing a thing and the opposite thing as well, and, to put it bluntly, that He should be both sitting and standing, should one of the writers represent Him as standing at the time, and making a certain speech in such a place to such a man, while a second writer speaks of Him as sitting.

4. SCRIPTURE CONTAINS MANY CONTRADICTIONS, AND MANY STATEMENTS WHICH ARE NOT LITERALLY TRUE, BUT MUST BE READ SPIRITUALLY AND MYSTICALLY.

In the case I have supposed where the historians desire to teach us by an image what they have seen in their mind, their meaning would be found, if the four were wise, to exhibit no disagreement; and we must understand that with the four Evangelists it is not otherwise. They made full use for their purpose of things done by Jesus in the exercise of His wonderful and extraordinary power; they use in the same way His sayings, and in some places they tack on to their writing, with language apparently implying things of sense, things made manifest to them in a purely intellectual way. I do not condemn them if they even sometimes dealt freely with things which to the eye of history happened differently, and changed them so as to subserve the mystical aims they had in view; so as to speak of a thing which happened in a certain place, as if it had happened in another, or of what took place at a certain time, as if it had taken place at another time, and to introduce into what was spoken in a certain way some changes of their own. They proposed to speak the truth where it was possible both materially and spiritually, and where this was not possible it was their intention to prefer the spiritual to the material. The spiritual truth was often preserved, as one might say, in the material falsehood. As, for example, we might judge of the story of Jacob and Esau.[1] Jacob says to Isaac, "I am Esau thy firstborn son," and spiritually he spoke the truth, for he already partook of the rights of the first-born, which were perishing in his brother, and clothing himself with the goatskins he assumed the outward semblance of Esau, and was Esau all but the voice praising God, so that Esau might afterward find a place to receive a blessing. For if Jacob had not been blessed as Esau, neither would Esau perhaps have been able to receive a blessing of his own. And Jesus too is many things, according to the conceptions of Him, of which it is quite likely that the Evangelists took up different notions; while yet they were in agreement with each other in the different things they wrote. Statements which are verbally contrary to each other, are made about our Lord, namely, that He was descended from David and that He was not descended from David. The statement is true, "He was descended from David," as the Apostle says,[2] "born of the seed of David according to the flesh," if we apply this to the bodily part of Him; but the self-same statement is untrue if we understand His being born of

[1] Gen. xxvii.

[2] Rom. i. 3.

the seed of David of His diviner power; for He was declared to be the Son of God with power. And for this reason too, perhaps, the sacred prophecies speak of Him now as a servant, and now as a Son. They call Him a servant on account of the form of a servant which he wore, and because He was of the seed of David, but they call Him the Son of God according to His character as first-born. Thus it is true to call Him man and to call Him not man; man, because He was capable of death; not man, on account of His being diviner than man. Marcion, I suppose, took sound words in a wrong sense, when he rejected His birth from Mary, and declared that as to His divine nature He was not born of Mary, and hence made bold to delete from the Gospel the passages which have this effect. And a like fate seems to have overtaken those who make away with His humanity and receive His deity alone; and also those opposites of these who cancel His deity and confess Him as a man to be a holy man, and the most righteous of all men. And those who hold the doctrine of Dokesis, not remembering that He humbled Himself even unto death [1] and became obedient even to the cross, but only imagining in Him the absence of suffering, the superiority to all such accidents, they do what they can to deprive us of the man who is more just than all men, and are left with a figure which cannot save them, for as by one man came death, so also by one man is the justification of life. We could not have received such benefit as we have from the Logos had He not assumed the man, had He remained such as He was from the beginning with God the Father, and had He not taken up man, the first man of all, the man more precious than all others, purer than all others and capable of receiving Him. But after that man we also shall be able to receive Him, to receive Him so great and of such nature as He was, if we prepare a place in proportion to Him in our soul. So much I have said of the apparent discrepancies in the Gospels, and of my desire to have them treated in the way of spiritual interpretation.

5. PAUL ALSO MAKES CONTRADICTORY STATEMENTS ABOUT HIMSELF, AND ACTS IN OPPOSITE WAYS AT DIFFERENT TIMES.

On the same passage one may also make use of such an example as that of Paul, who at one place [2] says that he is carnal, sold under sin, and thus was not able to judge anything, while in another place he is the spiritual man who is able to judge all things and himself to be judged by no man. Of the carnal one are the words, "Not what I would that do I practise, but what I hate that do I." And he too who was caught up to the third heaven and heard unspeakable words [1] is a different Paul from him who says, Of such an one I will glory, but of myself I will not glory. If he becomes [2] to the Jews as a Jew that he may gain the Jews, and to those under the law as under the law that he may gain those under the law, and to them that are without law as without law, not being without law to God, but under law to Christ, that he may gain those without law, and if to the weak he becomes weak that he may gain the weak, it is clear that these statements must be examined each by itself, that he becomes a Jew, and that sometimes he is under the law and at another time without law, and that sometimes he is weak. Where, for example, he says something by way of permission [3] and not by commandment, there we may recognize that he is weak; for who, he says, [4] is weak, and I am not weak? When he shaves his head and makes an offering, [5] or when he circumcises Timothy, [6] he is a Jew; but when he says to the Athenians, [7] "I found an altar with the inscription, To the unknown God. That, then, which ye worship not knowing it, that declare I unto you," and, "As also some of your own poets have said, For we also are His offspring," then he becomes to those without the law as without the law, adjuring the least religious of men to espouse religion, and turning to his own purpose the saying of the poet, "From Love do we begin; his race are we." [8] And instances might perhaps be found where, to men not Jews and yet under the law, he is under the law.

6. DIFFERENT ACCOUNTS OF THE CALL OF PETER, AND OF THE IMPRISONMENT OF THE BAPTIST. THE MEANING OF "CAPERNAUM."

These examples may be serviceable to illustrate statements not only about the Saviour, but about the disciples too, for here also there is some discrepancy of statement. For there is a difference in thought perhaps between Simon who is found by his own brother Andrew, and who is addressed "Thou shalt be called Cephas," [9] and him who is seen by Jesus when walking by the sea of Galilee, [10] along with his brother, and

[1] Philipp. ii. 8.
[2] Rom. vii. 14.

[1] 2 Cor. xii. 3, 4, 5.
[2] 1 Cor. ix. 20–22.
[3] 1 Cor. vii. 6.
[4] 2 Cor. xi. 29.
[5] Acts xxi. 24, 26.
[6] Acts xvi. 3.
[7] Acts xvii. 23.
[8] Aratus phenom. 5.
[9] John i. 41.
[10] Matt. iv. 18. Cf. Mark i. 16.

addressed conjointly with that brother, "Come after Me, and I will make you fishers of men." There was some fitness in the fact that the writer who goes more to the root of the matter and tells of the Word becoming flesh, and hence does not record the human generation of the Word who was in the beginning with God, should not tell us of Simon's being found at the seashore and called away from there, but of his being found by his brother who had been staying with Jesus at the tenth hour, and of his receiving the name Cephas in connection with his being thus found out. If he was seen by Jesus when walking by the sea of Galilee, it would scarcely be on a later occasion that he was addressed, "Thou art Peter and upon this rock I will build My church." With John again the Pharisees know Jesus to be baptizing with His disciples,[1] adding this to His other great activities; but the Jesus of the three does not baptize at all. John the Baptist, too, with the Evangelist of the same name, goes on a long time without being cast into prison. With Matthew, on the contrary, he is put in prison almost at the time of the temptation of Jesus, and this is the occasion of Jesus retiring to Galilee, to avoid being put in prison. But in John there is nothing at all about John's being put in prison. Who is so wise and so able as to learn all the things that are recorded about Jesus in the four Evangelists, and both to understand each incident by itself, and have a connected view of all His sojournings and words and acts at each place? As for the passage presently before us, it gives in the order of events that on the sixth day the Saviour, after the business of the marriage at Cana of Galilee, went down with His mother and His brothers and His disciples to Capernaum, which means "field of consolation." For after the feasting and the wine it was fitting that the Saviour should come to the field of consolation with His mother and His disciples, to console those whom He was training for disciples and the soul which had conceived Him by the Holy Ghost, with the fruits which were to stand in that full field.

7. WHY HIS BROTHERS ARE NOT CALLED TO THE WEDDING; AND WHY HE ABIDES AT CAPERNAUM NOT MANY DAYS.

But we must ask why His brothers are not called to the wedding: they were not there, for it is not said they were; but they go down to Capernaum with Him and His mother and His disciples. We must also

[1] iv. 1, 2.

examine why on this occasion they do not "*go in to*" Capernaum, nor "*go up to*," but "go down to" it. Consider if we must not understand by His brothers here the powers which went down along with Him, not called to the wedding according to the explanations given above, since it is in lower and humbler places than those who are called disciples of Christ, and in another way, that these brothers receive assistance. For if His mother is called, then there are some bearing fruit, and even to these the Lord goes down with the servants and disciples of the Word, to help such persons, His mother also being with Him. Those indeed who are called Capernaum appear not to be able to allow Jesus and those who went down with Him to make a longer stay with them: hence they remain with them not many days. For the lower field of consolation does not admit the illumination of many doctrines, but is only capable of a few. To get a clear view of the difference between those who receive Jesus for longer and for shorter time, we may compare with this, "They abode there not many days," the words recorded in Matthew as spoken by Christ when risen from the dead to His disciples who were being sent out to teach all nations,[1] "Behold, I am with you always, even to the end of the world." To those who are to know all that human nature can know while it still is here, is said with emphasis, "I am with you;" and as the rise of each new day upon the field of contemplation brings more days before the eyes of the blessed, therefore He says, "All the days till the end of the world." As for those in Capernaum, on the contrary, to whom they go down as to the more needy, not only Jesus, but also His mother and His brothers and His disciples "abode there not many days."

8. HOW CHRIST ABIDES WITH BELIEVERS TO THE END OF THE AGE, AND WHETHER HE ABIDES WITH THEM AFTER THAT CONSUMMATION.

Some may very likely and not unreasonably ask, whether, when all the days of this age are over, there will no longer be any one to say, "Lo, I am with you," with those, namely, who received Him till the fulfilment of the age, for the "until" seems to indicate a certain limit of time. To this we must say that the phrase, "I am with you," is not the same as "I am in you." We might say more properly that the Saviour was not in His disciples but with them, so

[1] xxviii. 20.

long as they had not arrived in their minds at the consummation of the age. But when they see to be at hand, as far as their effort is concerned, the consummation of the world which is crucified to them, then Jesus will be no longer with them, but in them, and they will say, "It is no longer I that live but Christ that lives in me,"[1] and "If ye seek a proof of Christ that speaketh in me."[2] In saying this we are keeping for our part also to the ordinary interpretation which makes the "always" the time down to the consummation of the age, and are not asking more than is attainable to human nature as it is here. That interpretation may be adhered to and justice yet be done to the "I." He who is with His disciples who are sent out to teach all the nations, until the consummation, may be He who emptied Himself and took the form of a servant, and yet afterwards may be another in point of state; afterwards He may be such as He was before He emptied Himself, until all His enemies are made by His Father the footstool of His feet; and after this, when the Son has delivered up the kingdom to God and the Father, it may be the Father who says to them, "Behold, I am with you." But whether it is "all the days" up to that time, or simply "all the days," or not "all days" but "every day," any one may consider that likes. Our plan does not allow us at present to digress so far.

9. HERACLEON SAYS THAT JESUS IS NOT STATED TO HAVE DONE ANYTHING AT CAPERNAUM. BUT IN THE OTHER GOSPELS HE DOES MANY THINGS THERE.

But Heracleon, dealing with the words, "After this He went down to Capernaum," declares that they indicate the introduction of another transaction, and that the word "went down" is not without significance. "Capernaum," he says, "means these farthest-out parts of the world, these districts of matter, into which He descended, and because the place was not suitable, he says, He is not reported either to have done anything or said anything in it." Now if the Lord had not been reported in the other Gospels either as having done or said anything at Capernaum, we might perhaps have hesitated whether this view ought or ought not to be received. But that is far from being the case. Matthew says our Lord left Nazareth and came and dwelt at Capernaum on the seaside, and that from that time He began to preach, saying, "Repent ye, for the kingdom of heaven is at hand." And Mark, starting in his narrative[1] from the temptation by the devil, relates that after John was cast into prison, Jesus came into Galilee, proclaiming the Gospel of God, and after the call of the four fishermen to the Apostleship, "they enter into Capernaum; and straightway on the Sabbath day He taught in the synagogue, and they were astonished at His doctrine." And Mark records an action of Jesus also which took place at Capernaum, for he goes on to say, "In their synagogue there was a man with an unclean spirit, and he cried out, saying, Ah! what have we to do with Thee, Thou Jesus of Nazareth? Art Thou come to destroy us? We know Thee who Thou art, the Son of God. And Jesus rebuked him, saying, Hold thy peace and come out of him; and the unclean spirit, tearing him and crying with a loud voice, came out of him. And they were all amazed." And at Capernaum Simon's mother-in-law is cured of her fever. And Mark adds that when evening was come all those were cured who were sick and who were possessed with demons. Luke's report is very like Mark's about Capernaum.[2] He says, "And He came to Capernaum, a city of Galilee, and He was teaching them on the Sabbath day, and they were astonished at His teachings, for His word was with power. And in the synagogue there was a man having a spirit of an unclean demon, and he cried out with a loud voice, Ah! what have we to do with Thee, Thou Jesus of Nazareth? Hast Thou come to destroy us? I know Thee who Thou art, the holy one of God. And Jesus rebuked him, saying, Hold thy peace and come out of him. Then the demon having thrown him down in the midst, went out of him, doing him no harm." And then Luke reports how the Lord rose up from the synagogue and went into the house of Simon, and rebuked the fever in his mother-in-law, and cured her of her disease; and after this cure, "when the sun was setting," he says, "all, as many as had persons sick with divers diseases, brought them to Him, and He laid his hands on each one of them and cured them. And demons also went out from many, crying and saying, Thou art the Son of God, and He rebuked them and suffered them not to speak because they knew that He was the Christ." We have presented all these statements as to the Saviour's sayings and doings at Capernaum in order to refute Heracleon's interpretation of our

[1] Gal. ii. 20.
[2] 2 Cor. xiii. 3.

[1] i. 14–27.
[2] iv. 31–41.

passage, "Hence He is not said to have done or to have spoken anything there." He must either give two meanings to Capernaum, and show us his reasons for them, or if he cannot do this he must give up saying that the Saviour visited any place to no purpose. We, for our part, should we come to passages where even a comparison of the other Gospels fails to show that Jesus' visit to this place or that was not accompanied by any results, will seek with the divine assistance to make it clear that His coming was not in vain.

10. SIGNIFICANCE OF CAPERNAUM.

Matthew for his part adds,[1] that when the Lord had entered into Capernaum the centurion came to him, saying, "My boy is lying in my house sick of the palsy, grievously tormented," and after telling the Lord some more about him, received the reply, "Go, and as thou hast believed, so be it unto thee." And Matthew then gives us the story of Peter's mother-in-law, in close agreement with the other two. I conceive it to be a creditable piece of work and becoming to one who is anxious to hear about Christ, to collect from the four Gospels all that is related about Capernaum, and the discourses spoken, and the works done there, and how many visits the Lord paid to the place, and how, at one time, He is said to have gone down to it, and at another to have entered into it, and where He came from when He did so. If we compare all these points together, we shall not go astray in the meaning we ascribe to Capernaum. On the one hand, the sick are healed, and other works of power are done there, and on the other, the preaching, Repent ye, for the kingdom of heaven is at hand, begins there, and this appears to be a sign, as we showed when entering on this subject, of some more needy place of consolation, made so perhaps by Jesus, who comforted men by what He taught and by what He did there, in that place of consolation. For we know that the names of places agree in their meaning with the things connected with Jesus; as Gergesa, where the citizens of these parts besought Him to depart out of their coasts, means, "The dwelling of the casters-out." And this, also, we have noticed about Capernaum, that not only did the preaching, "Repent ye, for the kingdom of heaven is at hand," begin there, but that according to the three Evangelists Jesus performed there His first miracles. None of the three, however, added to the first wonders which he records as done in Capernaum, that note attached by John the disciple to the first work of Jesus, "This beginning of His signs did Jesus in Cana of Galilee." For that which was done in Capernaum was not the beginning of the signs, since the leading sign of the Son of God was good cheer, and in the light of human experience it is also the most representative of Him. For the Word of God does not show forth His own beauty so much in healing the sick, as in His tendering the temperate draught to make glad those who are in good health and are able to join in the banquet.

11. WHY THE PASSOVER IS SAID TO BE THAT OF THE "JEWS." ITS INSTITUTION, AND THE DISTINCTION BETWEEN "FEASTS OF THE LORD" AND FEASTS NOT SO SPOKEN OF.

"And the passover of the Jews was at hand."[1] Inquiring into the accuracy of the most wise John (on this passage), I put myself the question, What is indicated by the addition "of the Jews"? Of what other nation was the passover a festival? Would it not have been enough to say, "And the passover was at hand"? It may, however, be the case that the human passover is one thing when kept by men not as Scripture intended, and that the divine passover is another thing, the true passover, observed in spirit and truth by those who worship God in spirit and in truth; and then the distinction indicated in the text may be that between the divine passover and that said to be of the Jews. We should attend to the passover law and observe what the Lord says of it when it is first mentioned in Scripture.[2] "And the Lord spake unto Moses and Aaron in the land of Egypt, saying, This month is to you the beginning of months, it is the first for you among the months of the year. Speak thou to all the congregation of the children of Israel, saying, On the tenth of this month shall every man take a sheep, according to the houses of your families;" then after some directions in which the word passover does not occur again, he adds,[3] "Thus shall ye eat it, your loins girt and your shoes on your feet, and your staves in your hands, and ye shall eat it with haste. It is the passover of the Lord." He does not say, "It is your passover." And a little further on He names the festival again in the same way,[4] "And it shall come to pass, when your sons say to

[1] viii. 5 sqq.

[1] John ii. 13.
[2] Exod. xii. 1–3.
[3] Ver. 11.
[4] Ver. 26.

you, What is this service? And ye shall say to them, It is the sacrifice, the passover of the Lord, how He guarded the houses of the children of Israel." And again, a little further on,[1] "And the Lord spake to Moses and Aaron, saying, This is the law of the passover. No alien shall eat of it." And again in a little,[2] "But if a proselyte come to you, and keep the passover of the Lord, every male of him shall be circumcised." Observe that in the law we never find it said, "Your passover;" but in all the passages quoted the phrase occurs once without any adjunct, while we have three times "The passover of the Lord." To make sure that there is such a distinction between the passover of the Lord and the passover of the Jews, we may consider the way in which Isaiah speaks of the matter:[3] "Your new moons and your Sabbaths and your great day I cannot bear; your fast and your holiday and your new moons and your feasts my soul hateth." The Lord does not call them His own, these observances of sinners (they are hated of His soul, if such there be); neither the new moons, nor the Sabbaths, nor the great day, nor the fast, nor the festivals. And in the legislation about the Sabbath in Exodus, we read,[4] "And Moses said unto them, This is the word which the Lord spake, The Sabbath is a holy rest unto the Lord." And a little further on, "And Moses said, Eat ye; for to-day is a Sabbath unto the Lord." And in Numbers,[5] before the sacrifices which are offered at each festival, as if all the festivals came under the law of the continuous and daily sacrifice, we find it written, "And the Lord spake unto Moses, Announce to the children of Israel, and thus shalt thou say unto them, My gifts, My offerings, My fruits for a smell of sweet savour, ye shall observe to offer unto Me at My festivals. And thou shalt say unto them, These are the offerings which ye shall offer unto the Lord." The festival set forth in Scripture He calls His own, not those of the people receiving the law, He speaks of *His* gifts, *His* offerings. A similar way of speaking is that in Exodus with regard to the people; it is said by God to be His own people, when it does not sin; but in the section about the calf He abjures it and calls it the people of Moses.[6] On the one hand, "Thou shalt say to Pharaoh, Thus saith the Lord, Let My people go, that they may serve Me in the wilderness. But if thou wilt not let My people go, behold, I will send against thee and against thy servants, and against thy people and against thy houses, the dog-fly; and the houses of the Egyptians shall be full of the dog-fly, and on the land on which they are, against it will I send them. And I will glorify on that day the land of Gesem, on which My people are; on it there shall be no dog-fly, that thou mayest know that I am the Lord, the Lord of all the earth. And I will make a distinction between My people and thy people." To Moses, on the other hand, He says,[1] "Go, descend quickly, for thy people hath transgressed, which thou leddest out of the land of Egypt." As, then, the people when it does not sin is the people of God, but when it sins is no longer spoken of as His, thus, also, the feasts when they are hated by the Lord's soul are said to be feasts of sinners, but when the law is given regarding them, they are called feasts of the Lord. Now of these feasts passover is one, which in the passage before us is said to be that not of the Lord, but of the Jews. In another passage, too,[2] we find it said, "These are the feasts of the Lord, which ye shall call chosen, holy." From the mouth of the Lord Himself, then, we see that there is no gainsaying our statement on this point. Some one, no doubt, will ask about the words of the Apostle, where he writes to the Corinthians:[3] "For our Passover also was sacrificed for us, namely, Christ;" he does not say, "The Passover of the Lord was sacrificed, even Christ." To this we must say, either that the Apostle simply calls the passover our passover because it was sacrificed for us, or that every sacrifice which is really the Lord's, and the passover is one of these, awaits its consummation not in this age nor upon earth, but in the coming age and in heaven when the kingdom of heaven appears. As for those feasts, one of the twelve prophets says,[4] "What will ye do in the days of assembly, and in the days of the feast of the Lord?" But Paul says in the Epistle to the Hebrews:[5] "But ye are come unto Mount Zion, and to the city of the living God, the heavenly Jerusalem, and to ten thousands of angels, the assembly and church of the firstborn, who are written in heaven." And in the Epistle to the Colossians:[6] "Let no one judge you in meat and in drink, or in respect of a feast-day or a new moon, or a sabbath-day; which are a shadow of the things to come."

---

[1] Ver. 43–48. [2] Ver. 48. [3] Isa. i. 13. [4] xvi. 23. [5] xxviii. 1. [6] Exod. viii. 21–23.

[1] Exod. xxxii. 7. [2] Levit. xxiii. 2. [3] 1 Cor. v. 7. [4] Hosea ix. 5. [5] xii. 22, 23. [6] ii. 16.

12. OF THE HEAVENLY FESTIVALS, OF WHICH THOSE ON EARTH ARE TYPICAL.

Now in what manner, in those heavenly things of which the shadow was present to the Jews on earth, those will celebrate festivals who have first been trained by tutors and governors under the true law, until the fulness of the time should come, namely, above, when we shall be able to receive into ourselves the perfect measure of the Son of God, this it is the work of that wisdom to make plain which has been hidden in a mystery; and it also may show to our thought how the laws about meats are symbols of those things which will there nourish and strengthen our soul. But it is vain to think that one desiring to work out in his fancy the great sea of such ideas, even if he wished to show how local worship is still a pattern and shadow of heavenly things, and that the sacrifices and the sheep are full of meaning, that he should advance further than the Apostle, who seeks indeed to lift our minds above earthly views of the law, but who does not show us to any extent how these things are to be. Even if we look at the festivals, of which passover is one, from the point of view of the age to come, we have still to ask how it is that our passover is now sacrificed, namely, Christ, and not only so, but is to be sacrificed hereafter.

13. SPIRITUAL MEANING OF THE PASSOVER.

A few points may be added in connection with the doctrines now under consideration, though it would require a special discussion in many volumes to treat of all the mystical statements about the law, and specially of those connected with the festivals, and more particularly still with the passover. The passover of the Jews consists of a sheep which is sacrificed, each taking a sheep according to his father's house; and the passover is accompanied by the slaughter of thousands of rams and goats, in proportion to the number of the houses of the people. But our Passover is sacrificed for us, namely, Christ. Another feature of the Jewish festival is unleavened bread; all leaven is made to disappear out of their houses; but "we keep the feast[1] not with the old leaven, nor with the leaven of malice and wickedness, but with the unleavened bread of sincerity and truth." Whether there be any passover and any feast of leaven beyond the two we have mentioned, is a point we must examine more carefully, since these serve for a pattern and a shadow of the heavenly ones we spoke of, and not only such things as food and drink and new moons and sabbaths, but the festivals also, are a shadow of the things to come. In the first place, when the Apostle says, "Our passover is sacrificed, Christ," one may feel with regard to this such doubts as these. If the sheep with the Jews is a type of the sacrifice of Christ, then one should have been offered and not a multitude, as Christ is one; or if many sheep were offered it is to follow out the type, as if many Christs were sacrificed. But not to dwell on this, we may ask how the sheep, which was the victim, contains an image of Christ, when the sheep was sacrificed by men who were observing the law, but Christ was put to death by transgressors of the law, and what application can be found in Christ of the direction,[1] "They shall eat the flesh this night, roast with fire, and unleavened bread on bitter herbs shall they eat," and "Eat not of it raw, nor sodden with water, but roast with fire; the head with the feet and the entrails; ye shall not set any of it apart till the morning, and a bone thereof ye shall not break. But that which is left thereof till the morning ye shall burn." The sentence, "A bone of it ye shall not break," John appears to have made use of in his Gospel, as applying to the transactions connected with Christ, and connecting with them the occasion spoken of in the law when those eating the sheep are bidden not to break a bone of it. He writes as follows:[2] "The soldiers therefore came and brake the legs of the first, and of the other who was crucified with him; but when they came to Jesus and saw that He was already dead, they brake not His legs, but one of the soldiers with a spear pierced His side, and straightway there came out blood and water. And he that hath seen hath borne witness and his witness is true, and he knoweth that he sayeth truth that ye also may believe. And these things took place that the Scripture might be fulfilled, "A bone of Him ye shall not break." There are a myriad other points besides this in the Apostle's language which would call for inquiry, both about the passover and the unleavened bread, but they would have to be dealt with, as we said above, in a special work of great length. At present we can only give an epitome of them as they bear on the text presently before us, and aim at a short solution of the principal problem. We call to mind the words, "This is the Lamb of God that taketh away the sin of the

[1] 1 Cor. v. 8.

[1] Exod. xii. 8.

[2] xix. 32.

world," for it is said of the passover,[1] "Ye shall take it of the lambs or of the goats." The Evangelist here agrees with Paul, and both are involved in the difficulties we spoke of above. But on the other hand we have to say that if the Word became flesh, and the Lord says,[2] "Unless ye eat the flesh of the Son of Man, and drink His blood, ye have no life in you. He that eateth My flesh and drinketh My blood, hath eternal life, and I will raise him up at the last day. For My flesh is meat indeed and My blood is drink indeed. He that eateth My flesh and drinketh My blood abideth in Me, and I in him,"—then the flesh thus spoken of is that of the Lamb that takes away the sin of the world; and this is the blood, some of which was to be put on the two side posts of the door, and on the lintels in the houses, in which we eat the passover. Of the flesh of this Lamb it is necessary that we should eat in the time of the world, which is night, and the flesh is to be roast with fire, and eaten with unleavened bread; for the Word of God is not flesh and flesh only. He says, in fact, Himself,[3] "I am the bread of life," and "This is the bread of life which came down from heaven, that a man should eat of it, and not die. I am the bread of life that came down from heaven; if a man eat of this bread, he shall live for ever." We must not overlook, however, that by a loose use of words, any food is called bread, as we read in Moses in Deuteronomy,[4] "Forty days He ate no bread and drank no water," instead of, He took no food, either wet or dry. I am led to this observation by John's saying, "And the bread which I will give is My flesh, for the life of the world." Again, we eat the flesh of the Lamb, with bitter herbs, and unleavened bread, when we repent of our sins and grieve with the sorrow which is according to God, a repentance which operates for our salvation, and is not to be repented of; or when, on account of our trials, we turn to the speculations which are found to be those of truth, and are nourished by them. We are not, however, to eat the flesh of the Lamb raw, as those do who are slaves of the letter, like irrational animals, and those who are enraged at men truly reasonable, because they desire to understand spiritual things; truly, they share the nature of savage beasts. But we must strive to convert the rawness of Scripture into well-cooked food, not letting what is written grow

[1] Exod. xii. 5. [2] John vi. 53. [3] John vi. 48–50. [4] ix. 9.

flabby and wet and thin, as those do who have itching ears,[1] and turn away their ears from the truth; their methods tend to a loose and flabby conduct of life. But let us be of a fervent spirit and keep hold of the fiery words given to us of God, such as Jeremiah received from Him who spoke to him,[2] "Behold, I have made My words in thy mouth like fire," and let us see that the flesh of the Lamb be well cooked, so that those who partake of it may say, as Christ speaks in us, "Our heart burned by the way, as He opened to us the Scriptures."[3] Further, if it is our duty to enquire into such a point as the roasting of the flesh of the Lamb with fire, we must not forget the parallel of what Jeremiah suffered on account of the words of God, as he says:[4] "And it was as a glowing fire, burning in my bones, and I am without any strength, and I cannot bear it." But, in this eating, we must begin at the head, that is to say, at the principal and the most essential doctrines about heavenly things, and we must end at the feet, the last branches of learning which enquire as to the final nature in things, or about more material things, or about things under the earth, or about wicked spirits and unclean demons. For it may be that the account of these things is not obvious, like themselves, but is laid away among the mysteries of Scripture, so that it may be called, tropically, the feet of the Lamb. Nor must we fail to deal with the entrails, which are within and hidden from us; we must approach the whole of Scripture as one body, we must not lacerate nor break through the strong and well-knit connections which exist in the harmony of its whole composition, as those do who lacerate, so far as they can, the unity of the Spirit that is in all the Scriptures. But this aforesaid prophecy of the Lamb is to be our nourishment only during the night of this dark life of ours; what comes after this life is, as it were, the dawn of day, and why should we leave over till then the food which can only be useful to us now? But when the night is passed, and the day which succeeds it is at hand, then we shall have bread to eat which has nothing to do with the leavened bread of the older and lower state of things, but is unleavened, and that will serve our turn until that which comes after the unleavened bread is given us, the manna, which is food for angels rather than men. Every one of us, then, may sacrifice his lamb in every house of our fathers; and

[1] 2 Tim. iv. 3, 4. [2] Jer. v. 14. [3] Luke xxiv. 32. [4] xx. 9.

while one breaks the law, not sacrificing the lamb at all, another may keep the commandment entirely, offering his sacrifice, and cooking it aright, and not breaking a bone of it. This, then, in brief, is the interpretation of the Passover sacrificed for us, which is Christ, in accordance with the view taken of it by the Apostles, and with the Lamb in the Gospel. For we ought not to suppose that historical things are types of historical things, and material things of material, but that material things are typical of spiritual things, and historical things of intellectual. It is not necessary that our discourse should now ascend to that third passover which is to be celebrated with myriads of angels in the most perfect and most blessed exodus; we have already spoken of these things to a greater extent than the passage demands.

14. IN THE FIRST THREE GOSPELS THE PASSOVER IS SPOKEN OF ONLY AT THE CLOSE OF THE MINISTRY; IN JOHN AT THE BEGINNING. REMARKS ON THIS. HERACLEON ON THE PASSOVER.

We must not, however, fail to enquire into the statement that the passover of the Jews was at hand, when the Lord was at Capernaum with His mother and His brothers and His disciples. In the Gospel according to Matthew,[1] after being left by the devil, and after the angels came and ministered to Him, when He heard that John was delivered up He withdrew into Galilee, and leaving Nazara He came and dwelt in Capernaum. Then He began to preach, and chose the four fishermen for His Apostles, and taught in the synagogues of the whole of Galilee and healed those who were brought to Him. Then He goes up into the mountain and speaks the beatitudes and what follows them; and after finishing that instruction He comes down from the mountain and enters Capernaum a second time.[2] Then He embarked in a ship and crossed over to the other side to the country of the Gergesenes. On their beseeching Him to depart out of their coasts He embarked[3] in a ship and crossed over and came to His own city. Then He wrought certain cures and went about all the cities and the villages, teaching in their synagogues; after this most of the events of the Gospels take place, before Matthew indicates the approach of the time of passover.[4] With the other Evangelists also, after the stay at Capernaum it is long till we come to any mention of the passover; which may confirm in their opinion those who take the view about Capernaum which was set forth above. That stay, in the neighbourhood of the passover of the Jews, is set in a brighter light by that nearness, both because it was better in itself, and still more because at the passover of the Jews there are found in the temple those who sell oxen and sheep and doves. This adds emphasis to the statement that the passover was not that of the Lord but that of the Jews; the Father's house was made, in the eyes of those who did not hallow it, a house of merchandise, and the passover of the Lord became for those who took a low and material view of it a Jewish passover. A fitter occasion than the present will occur for enquiring as to the time of the passover, which took place about the spring equinox, and for any other enquiry which may arise in connection with it. As for Heracleon, he says, "This is the great festival; for it was a type of the passion of the Saviour; not only was the lamb put to death, the eating of it afforded relaxation, the killing it pointed to what of the passion of the Saviour was in this world, and the eating it to the rest at the marriage." We have given his words, that it may be seen with what a want of caution and how loosely he proceeds, and with what an absence of constructive skill even on such a theme as this; and how little regard in consequence is to be paid to him.

15. DISCREPANCY OF THE GOSPEL NARRATIVES CONNECTED WITH THE CLEANSING OF THE TEMPLE.

"And Jesus went up to Jerusalem.[1] And He found in the temple those that sold oxen and sheep and doves and the changers of money sitting; and He made a scourge of cords, and cast out of the temple the sheep and the oxen, and poured out the small coin of the changers, and overturned their tables, and to those who sold the doves He said, Take these things hence; make not My Father's house a house of merchandise. Then His disciples remembered that it was written, The zeal of thy house shall eat me up." It is to be noted that John makes this transaction of Jesus with those He found selling oxen and sheep and doves in the temple His second work; while the other Evangelists narrate a similar incident almost at the end and in connection with the story of the passion. Matthew has it thus:[2] "At Jesus' entry into Jerusalem the whole city was stirred, saying, Who is this? And the multitudes said, This is Jesus the prophet, from Nazareth of Galilee. And Jesus went into the temple

[1] iv. 11 sqq. [2] Matt. viii. [3] viii. 23. [4] xxvi. 2.

[1] John ii. 13-17. [2] Matt. xxi. 10-13.

and cast out all them that sold and bought in the temple, and He overturned the tables of the money-changers and the seats of them that sold doves. And He says to them, It is written, My house shall be called a house of prayer, but you make it a den of robbers." Mark has the following: "And they came to Jerusalem. And having entered into the temple He began to cast out those that sold and bought in the temple, and the tables of the money-changers He overthrew and the seats of them that sold doves. And He suffered not that any should carry a vessel through the temple; and He taught and said unto them, Is it not written that My house shall be called a house of prayer for all the nations? But you have made it a den of robbers." And Luke:[1] "And when he came near, He beheld the city and wept over it, saying that, if thou hadst known in this day, even thou, the things that belong to peace; but now they are hid from thine eyes. For the days shall come upon thee, when they shall surround thee and shut thee in on every side, and shall dash thee to the ground and thy children, and they shall not leave in thee one stone upon another, because thou knewest not the time of thy visitation. And He entered into the temple and began to cast out those that sold, saying to them, It is written, My house shall be a house of prayer, but ye have made it a den of robbers." It is further to be observed that what is recorded by the three as having taken place in connection with the Lord's going up to Jerusalem, when He did these things in the temple, is narrated in a very similar manner by John as taking place long after this, after another visit to Jerusalem different from this one. We must consider the statements, and in the first place that of Matthew, where we read:[2] "When He drew nigh to Jerusalem and came to Bethphage over against the Mount of Olives, then Jesus sent two disciples, saying unto them, Go ye into the village over against you, and straightway ye shall find an ass tied and a colt with her; loose them and bring them to Me. And if any man say unto you, What are you doing? you shall say, The Lord hath need of them, and straightway he will send them. But this was done that it might be fulfilled which was spoken by the prophet, saying, Say ye to the daughter of Zion, Behold, thy king cometh, meek and seated upon an ass and upon the colt of an ass. And the disciples went and did as Jesus commanded them; they brought the ass and the foal, and they placed on them their garments, and He sat thereon. And the most part of the multitude spread their garments on the road, but the multitudes that went before Him, and they that followed, cried, Hosanna to the Son of David, blessed is He that cometh in the name of the Lord. Hosanna in the highest." After this comes, "And when He had entered into Jerusalem the whole city was stirred," which we cited above. Then we have Mark's account:[1] "And when they drew nigh unto Jerusalem, to Bethphage and Bethany, to the Mount of Olives, He sends two of His disciples and says to them, Go ye into the village over against you. And straightway as ye enter into it ye shall find a colt tied, on which no man hath ever sat, loose it and bring it. And if any one say to you, Why do ye this? say, Because the Lord hath need of him, and straightway he will send him back hither. And they went and found the colt tied at the door outside on the road, and they loose him. And some of them that stood there said to them, What do ye, loosing the colt? And they said to them as Jesus told them, and they let them go. And they brought the colt to Jesus, and cast on it their garments. But others cut down branches from the field and spread them in the way. And they that went before and they that followed cried, Hosanna, blessed is He that cometh in the name of the Lord; blessed be the kingdom that cometh, of our father David! Hosanna in the highest! And He went into Jerusalem to the temple, and looked round about on all things, and as it was already evening, He went out to Bethany with the twelve. And on the morrow when they were come forth from Bethany He was hungry." Then, after the affair of the withered fig tree, "They came to Jerusalem. And He went into the temple and began to cast out them that sold." Luke narrates as follows:[2] "And it came to pass, when He drew near to Bethphage and Bethany at the mount that is called the Mount of Olives, He sent two of his disciples, saying, Go ye into the village over against you, in which when ye enter, ye shall find a colt tied, on which no man ever hath sate; loose him and bring him. And if any man asks you, Why do ye loose him? Ye shall say thus, The Lord hath need of him. And the disciples went and found as He said to them. And when they were loosing the colt its owners said to them, Why loose ye the colt?

[1] Luke xix. 41, 42.

[2] Matt. xxi. 1.

[1] Mark xi. 1–12.

[2] Luke xix. 29.

and they said, Because the Lord hath need of him. And they brought him to Jesus, and they threw their garments on the colt, and set Jesus thereon. And as He went, they strewed their garments in the way. And when He was drawing near, being now at the descent of the Mount of Olives, the whole multitude of the disciples began to rejoice and praise God with a loud voice for all the mighty works which they had seen, saying, Blessed is the King in the name of the Lord ; peace in heaven and glory in the highest. And some of the Pharisees from the multitude said unto Him, Master, rebuke Thy disciples. And He answered and said, I say unto you, If these shall hold their peace, the stones will cry out. And when He drew near He beheld the city and wept over it," and so on, as we cited above. John, on the contrary, after giving an account nearly identical with this, as far as, "And Jesus went up to Jerusalem, and He found in the temple those who were selling oxen and sheep," gives a second account of an ascent of the Lord to Jerusalem, and then goes on to tell of the supper in Bethany six days before the passover, at which Martha served and Lazarus was at table. "On the morrow,[1] a great multitude that had come to the feast, having heard that Jesus was coming to Jerusalem, took branches of palm trees and went forth to meet Him ; and they cried, Hosanna, blessed be the King of Israel in the name of the Lord. And Jesus, having found a young ass, sat thereon, as it is written, Fear not, daughter of Zion ; behold thy King cometh, sitting on the foal of an ass." I have written out long sections from the Gospels, but I have thought it necessary to do so, in order to exhibit the discrepancy at this part of our Gospel. Three of the Gospels place these incidents, which we supposed to be the same as those narrated by John, in connection with one visit of the Lord to Jerusalem. While John, on the other hand, places them in connection with two visits which are widely separated from each other and between which were various journeys of the Lord to other places. I conceive it to be impossible for those who admit nothing more than the history in their interpretation to show that these discrepant statements are in harmony with each other. If any one considers that we have not given a sound exposition, let him write a reasoned rejoinder to this declaration of ours.

[1] John xii. 12–15.

16. THE STORY OF THE PURGING OF THE TEMPLE SPIRITUALIZED. TAKEN LITERALLY, IT PRESENTS SOME VERY DIFFICULT AND UNLIKELY FEATURES.

We shall, however, expound according to the strength that is given to us the reasons which move us to recognize here a harmony ; and in doing so we entreat Him who gives to every one that asks and strives acutely to enquire, and we knock that by the keys of higher knowledge the hidden things of Scripture may be opened to us. And first, let us fix our attention on the words of John, beginning, "And Jesus went up to Jerusalem."[1] Now Jerusalem, as the Lord Himself teaches in the Gospel according to Matthew,[2] "is the city of the great King." It does not lie in a depression, or in a low situation, but is built on a high mountain, and there are mountains round about it,[3] and the participation of it is to the same place,[4] and thither the tribes of the Lord went up, a testimony for Israel. But that city also is called Jerusalem, to which none of those upon the earth ascends, nor goes in ; but every soul that possesses by nature some elevation and some acuteness to perceive the things of the mind is a citizen of that city. And it is possible even for a dweller in Jerusalem to be in sin (for it is possible for even the acutest minds to sin), should they not turn round quickly after their sin, when they have lost their power of mind and are on the point not only of dwelling in one of those strange cities of Judæa, but even of being inscribed as its citizens. Jesus goes up to Jerusalem, after bringing help to those in Cana of Galilee, and then going down to Capernaum, that He may do in Jerusalem the things which are written. He found in the temple, certainly, which is said to be the house of the Father of the Saviour, that is, in the church or in the preaching of the ecclesiastical and sound word, some who were making His Father's house a house of merchandise. And at all times Jesus finds some of this sort in the temple. For in that which is called the church, which is the house of the living God, the pillar and ground of the truth,[5] when are there not some money-changers sitting who need the strokes of the scourge Jesus made of small cords, and dealers in small coin who require to have their money poured out and their tables overturned ? When are there not those who are inclined to merchandise, but

[1] John ii. 13. [2] Matt. v. 35. [3] Ps. cxxv. 2.
[4] Ps. cxxii. 2, 3, 4. [5] Tim. iii. 15.

need to be held to the plough and the oxen, that having put their hand to it and not turning round to the things behind them, they may be fit for the kingdom of God? When are there not those who prefer the mammon of unrighteousness to the sheep which give them the material for their true adornment? And there are always many who look down on what is sincere and pure and unmixed with any bitterness or gall, and who, for the sake of miserable gain, betray the care of those tropically called doves. When, therefore, the Saviour finds in the temple, the house of His Father, those who are selling oxen and sheep and doves, and the changers of money sitting, He drives them out, using the scourge of small cords which He has made, along with the sheep and oxen of their trade, and pours out their stock of coin, as not deserving to be kept together, so little is it worth. He also overturns the tables in the souls of such as love money, saying even to those who sell doves, "Take these things hence," that they may no longer traffic in the house of God. But I believe that in these words He indicated also a deeper truth, and that we may regard these occurrences as a symbol of the fact that the service of that temple was not any longer to be carried on by the priests in the way of material sacrifices, and that the time was coming when the law could no longer be observed, however much the Jews according to the flesh desired it. For when Jesus casts out the oxen and sheep, and orders the doves to be taken away, it was because oxen and sheep and doves were not much longer to be sacrificed there in accordance with Jewish practices. And possibly the coins which bore the stamp of material things and not of God were poured out by way of type; because the law which appears so venerable, with its letter that kills, was, now that Jesus had come and had used His scourge to the people, to be dissolved and poured out, the sacred office (episcopate) being transferred to those from the Gentiles who believed, and the kingdom of God being taken away from the Jews[1] and given to a nation bringing forth the fruits of it. But it may also be the case that the natural temple is the soul skilled in reason, which, because of its inborn reason, is higher than the body; to which Jesus ascends from Capernaum, the lower-lying place of less dignity, and in which, before Jesus' discipline is applied to it, are found tendencies which are earthly and senseless and dangerous, and things which have the name but not the reality of beauty, and which are driven away by Jesus with His word plaited out of doctrines of demonstration and of rebuke, to the end that His Father's house may no longer be a house of merchandize but may receive, for its own salvation and that of others, that service of God which is performed in accordance with heavenly and spiritual laws. The ox is symbolic of earthly things, for he is a husbandman. The sheep, of senseless and brutal things, because it is more servile than most of the creatures without reason. Of empty and unstable thoughts, the dove. Of things that are thought good but are not, the small change. If any one objects to this interpretation of the passage and says that it is only pure animals that are mentioned in it, we must say that the passage would otherwise have an unlikely air. The occurence is necessarily related according to the possibilities of the story. It could not have been narrated that a herd of any other animals than pure ones had found access to the temple, nor could any have been sold there but those used for sacrifice. The Evangelist makes use of the known practice of the merchants at the times of the Jewish feasts; they did bring in such animals to the outer court; this practice, with a real occurrence He knew of, were His materials. Any one, however, who cares to do so may enquire whether it is in agreement with the position held by Jesus in this world, since He was reputed to be the Son of a carpenter, to venture upon such an act as to drive out a crowd of merchants from the temple? They had come up to the feast to sell to a great number of the people, the sheep, several myriads in number, which they were to sacrifice according to their fathers' houses. To the richer Jews they had oxen to sell, and there were doves for those who had vowed such animals, and many no doubt bought these with a view to their good cheer at the festival. And did not Jesus do an unwarrantable thing when He poured out the money of the money-changers, which was their own, and overthrew their tables? And who that received a blow from the scourge of small cords at the hands of One held in but slight esteem, was driven out of the temple, would not have attacked Him and raised a cry and avenged himself with his own hand, especially when there was such a multitude present who might all feel themselves insulted by Jesus in the same way? To think, moreover, of the Son of God taking the small cords in His hands

[1] Matt. xxi. 43.

and plaiting a scourge out of them for this driving out from the temple, does it not bespeak audacity and temerity and even some measure of lawlessness? One refuge remains for the writer who wishes to defend these things and is minded to treat the occurrence as real history, namely, to appeal to the divine nature of Jesus, who was able to quench, when He desired to do so, the rising anger of His foes, by divine grace to get the better of myriads, and to scatter the devices of tumultuous men; for "the Lord scatters the counsels of the nations[1] and brings to naught devices of the peoples, but the counsel of the Lord abideth for ever." Thus the occurrence in our passage, if it really took place, was not second in point of the power it exhibits to any even of the most marvellous works Christ wrought, and claimed no less by its divine character the faith of the beholders. One may show it to be a greater work than that done at Cana of Galilee in the turning of water into wine; for in that case it was only soulless matter that was changed, but here it was the soul and will of thousands of men. It is, however, to be observed that at the marriage the mother of Jesus is said to be there, and Jesus to have been invited and His disciples, but that no one but Jesus is said to have descended to Capernaum. His disciples, however, appear afterwards as present with Him; they remembered that "the zeal of thine house shall devour me." And perhaps Jesus was in each of the disciples as He ascended to Jerusalem, whence it is not said, Jesus went up to "Jerusalem and His disciples," but He went down to Capernaum, "He and His mother and His brothers and His disciples."

17. MATTHEW'S STORY OF THE ENTRY INTO JERUSALEM. DIFFICULTIES INVOLVED IN IT FOR THOSE WHO TAKE IT LITERALLY.

We have now to take into consideration the statements of the other Gospels on the expulsion from the temple of those who made it a house of merchandise. Take in the first place what we find in Matthew. On the Lord's entering Jerusalem, he says,[2] "All the city was stirred, saying, Who is this?" But before this he has the story of the ass and the foal which were taken by command of the Lord and found by the two disciples whom he sent from Bethphage into the village over against them. These two disciples loose the ass which was tied, and they have orders, if any one says anything to them, to answer that "the Lord has need of them; and immediately he will send them." By these incidents Matthew declares that the prophecy was fulfilled which says, "Behold, the King cometh, meek and sitting on an ass and a colt the foal of an ass," which we find in Zechariah.[1] When, then, the disciples went and did as Jesus commanded them, they brought the ass and the colt, and placed on them, he says, their own garments, and the Lord sat upon them, clearly on the ass and the colt. Then "the most part of the multitude spread their garments in the way, and others cut down branches from the trees and strewed them in the way, and the multitudes that went before and that followed cried, Hosanna to the Son of David, blessed is He that cometh in the name of the Lord. Hosanna in the highest." Hence it was that when He entered Jerusalem, the whole city was moved, saying, Who is this? "and the multitudes said," those obviously who went before Him and who followed Him, to those who were asking who He was, "This is the prophet Jesus of Nazareth of Galilee. And Jesus entered into the temple and cast out all those that sold and bought in the temple, and overthrew the tables of the money-changers and the seats of them that sold doves: and He saith unto them, It is written, My house shall be called a house of prayer; but ye make it a den of robbers." Let us ask those who consider that Matthew had nothing but the history in his mind when he wrote his Gospel, what necessity there was for two of the disciples to be sent to the village over against Bethphage, to find an ass tied and its colt with it and to loose them and bring them? And how did it deserve to be recorded that He sat upon the ass and the foal and entered into the city? And how does Zechariah prophesy about Christ when he says,[2] "Rejoice greatly, thou daughter of Zion, proclaim it, thou daughter of Jerusalem. Behold thy king cometh unto thee, just is He and bringing salvation, meek and sitting on an ass and a young foal"? If it be the case that this prophecy predicts simply the material incident described by the Evangelists, how can those who stand on the letter maintain that this is so with regard to the following part also of the prophecy, which runs: "And He shall destroy chariots from Ephraim and horse from Jerusalem, and the bow of the warrior shall be destroyed, and a multitude and peace from the

[1] Ps. xxxiii. 10.

[2] xxi. 10.

[1] Zech. ix. 9.

[2] Zech. ix. 9.

Gentiles, and He shall rule over the waters as far as the sea, and the rivers to the ends of the earth," etc. It is to be noted, too, that Matthew does not give the words as they are found in the prophet, for instead of "Rejoice greatly, thou daughter of Zion, proclaim it, thou daughter of Jerusalem," he makes it, "Tell ye the daughter of Zion." He curtails the prophetic utterance by omitting the words, "Just is He and bringing salvation," then he gives, "meek and sitting," as in the original, but instead of "on an ass and a young colt," he gives, "on an ass and a colt the foal of an ass." The Jews, examining into the application of the prophecy to what is recorded about Jesus, press us in a way we cannot overlook with the enquiry how Jesus destroyed chariots out of Ephraim and horse from Jerusalem, and how He destroyed the bow of the enemy and did the other deeds mentioned in the passage. So much with regard to the prophecy. Our literal interpreters, however, if there is nothing worthy of the appearance of the Son of God in the ass and the foal, may perhaps point to the length of the road for an explanation. But, in the first place, fifteen stades are not a great distance and afford no reasonable explanation of the matter, and, in the second place, they would have to tell us how two beasts of burden were needed for so short a journey; "He sat," it is said, "on them." And then the words: "If any man say aught unto you, say ye that the Lord hath need of them, and straightway he will send them." It does not appear to me to be worthy of the greatness of the Son's divinity to say that such a nature as His confessed that it had need of an ass to be loosed from its bonds and of a foal to come with it; for everything the Son of God has need of should be great and worthy of His goodness. And then the very great multitude strewing their garments in the way, while Jesus allows them to do so and does not rebuke them, as is clear from the words used in another passage,[1] "If these should hold their peace, the stones will cry out." I do not know if it does not indicate a certain degree of stupidity on the part of the writer to take delight in such things, if nothing more is meant by them than what lies on the surface. And the branches being cut down from the trees and strewn on the road where the asses go by, surely they are rather a hindrance to Him who is the centre of the throng than a well-devised reception of Him. The difficulties which met us on the part of those who were cast out of the temple by Jesus meet us here in a still greater degree. In the Gospel of John He casts out those who bought, but Matthew says that He cast out those who sold and those who bought in the temple. And the buyers would naturally be more numerous than the sellers. We have to consider if the casting out of buyers and sellers in the temple was not out of keeping with the reputation of one who was thought to be the Son of a carpenter, unless, as we said before, it was by a divine power that He subjected them. The words addressed to them, too, are harsher in the other Evangelists than in John. For John says that Jesus said to them, "Make not My Father's house a house of merchandise," while in the others they are rebuked for making the house of prayer a den of robbers. Now the house of His Father did not admit of being turned into a den of robbers, though by the acts of sinful men it was brought to be a house of merchandise. It was not only the house of prayer, but in fact the house of God, and by force of human neglect it harboured robbers, and was turned not only into their house but their den—a thing which no skill, either of architecture or of reason, could make it.

18. THE ASS AND THE COLT ARE THE OLD AND THE NEW TESTAMENT. SPIRITUAL MEANING OF THE VARIOUS FEATURES OF THE STORY. DIFFERENCES BETWEEN JOHN'S NARRATIVE AND THAT OF THE OTHER EVANGELISTS.

Now to see into the real truth of these matters is the part of that true intelligence which is given to those who can say,[1] "But we have the mind of Christ that we may see those things which are freely given to us of God;" and doubtless it is beyond our powers. For neither is the ruling principle in our soul free from agitation, nor are our eyes such as those of the fair bride of Christ should be, of which the bridegroom says,[2] "Thy eyes are doves," signifying, perhaps, in a riddle, the observant power which dwells in the spiritual, because the Holy Spirit came like a dove to our Lord and to the lord in every one. Such as we are, however, we will not delay, but will feel about the words of life which have been spoken to us and strive to lay hold of that power in them which flows to him who touches them in faith. Now Jesus is the word of God which goes into the soul that is called Jerusalem, riding on the ass freed by the disciples from its bonds. That is to

[1] Luke xix. 40.

[1] 1 Cor. ii. 16.

[2] Song of Sol. i. 15.

say, on the simple language of the Old Testament, interpreted by the two disciples who loose it: in the first place him who applies what is written to the service of the soul and shows the allegorical sense of it with reference to her, and in the second place him who brings to light by the things which lie in shadow the good and true things of the future. But He also rides on the young colt, the New Testament; for in both alike we find the word of truth which purifies us and drives away all those thoughts in us which incline to selling and buying. But He does not come alone to Jerusalem, the soul, nor only with a few companions; for many things have to enter into us before the word of God which makes us perfect, and as many things have to come after Him, all, however, hymning and glorifying Him and placing under Him their ornaments and vestures, so that the beasts He rides on may not touch the ground, when He who descended out of heaven is seated on them. But that His bearers, the old and the new words of Scripture, may be raised yet higher above the ground, branches have to be cut down from the trees that they may tread on reasonable expositions. But the multitudes which go before and follow Him may also signify the angelic ministrations, some of which prepare the way for Him in our souls, and help in their adorning, while some come after His presence in us, of which we have often spoken, so that we need not now adduce testimonies about it. And perhaps it is not without reason that I have likened to an ass the surrounding voices which conduct the Word Himself to the soul; for it is a beast of burden, and many are the burdens, heavy the loads, which are brought into view from the text, especially of the Old Testament, as he can clearly see who observes what is done in this connection on the part of the Jews. But the foal is not a beast of burden in the same way as the ass. For though every load of the latter be heavy to those who have not in themselves the upbearing and most lightening power of the Spirit, yet the new word is less heavy than the old. I know some who interpret the tied-up ass as being believers from the circumcision, who are freed from many bonds by those who are truly and spiritually instructed in the word; and the foal they take to be those from the Gentiles, who before they receive the word of Jesus are free from any control and subject to no yoke in their unbridled and pleasure-loving existence. The writers I am speaking of do not say who those are that go before and who those follow after; but there would be no absurdity in saying that those who went before were like Moses and the prophets, and those who followed after the holy Apostles. To what Jerusalem all these go in it is now our business to enquire, and what is the house which has many sellers and buyers to be driven out by the Son of God. And perhaps the Jerusalem above to which the Lord is to ascend driving like a charioteer those of the circumcision and the believers of the Gentiles, while prophets and Apostles go before Him and follow after Him (or is it the angels who minister to Him, for they too may be meant by those who go before and those who follow), perhaps it is that city which before He ascended to it contained the so-called[1] "spiritual hosts of wickedness in heavenly places," or the Canaanites and Hittites and Amorites and the other enemies of the people of god, and in a word, the foreigners. For in that region, too, it was possible for the prophecy to be fulfilled which says,[2] "Your country is desolate, your cities are burned with fire, your land, strangers devour it in your presence." For these are they who defile and turn into a den of robbers, that is, of themselves the heavenly house of the Father, the holy Jerusalem, the house of prayer; having spurious money, and giving pence and small change, cheap worthless coinage, to all who come to them. These are they who, contending with the souls, take from them what is most precious, robbing them of their better part to return to them what is worth nothing. But the disciples go and find the ass tied and loose it, for it cannot have Jesus on account of the covering that is laid upon it by the law.[3] And the colt is found with it, both having been lost till Jesus came; I mean, namely, those of the circumcision and those of the Gentiles who afterwards believed. But how these are sent back again after Jesus has ascended to Jerusalem seated upon them, it is somewhat dangerous to say; for there is something mystical about it, in connection with the change of saints into angels. After that change they will be sent back, in the age succeeding this one, like the ministering spirits,[4] who are sent to do service for the sake of them who will thereby inherit salvation. But if the ass and the foal are the old and the new Scriptures, on which the Word of God rides, it is easy to see how, after the Word has appeared in them, they are

[1] Ephes. vi. 12.
[2] Isa. i. 7.
[3] 2 Cor. iii. 14.
[4] Heb. i. 11.

sent back and do not wait after the Word has entered Jerusalem among those who have cast out all the thoughts of selling and buying. I consider, too, that it is not without significance that the place where the ass was found tied, and the foal, was a village, and a village without a name. For in comparison with the great world in heaven, the whole earth is a village where the ass is found tied and the colt, and it is simply called "the village" without any other designation being added to it. From Bethphage Matthew says the disciples are sent out who are to fetch the ass and the colt; and Bethphage is a priestly place, the name of which means "House of Jaw-bones." So much we have said, as our power allowed, on the text of Matthew, reserving for a further opportunity, when we may be permitted to take up the Gospel of Matthew by itself, a more complete and accurate discussion of his statements. Mark and Luke say that the two disciples, acting on their Master's instructions, found a foal tied, on which no one had ever sat, and that they loosed it and brought it to the Lord. Mark adds that they found the foal tied at the door, outside on the road. But who is outside? Those of the Gentiles who were strangers[1] from the covenants, and aliens to the promise of God; they are on the road, not resting under a roof or a house, bound by their own sins, and to be loosed by the twofold knowledge spoken of above, of the friends of Jesus. And the bonds with which the foal was tied, and the sins committed against the wholesome law and reproved by it,—for it is the gate of life,—in respect of it, I say, they were not inside but outside the door, for perhaps inside the door there cannot be any such bond of wickedness. But there were some persons standing beside the tied-up foal, as Mark says; those, I suppose, who had tied it; as Luke records, it was the masters of the foal who said to the disciples, Why loose ye the foal? For those lords who subjected and bound the sinner are illegal masters and cannot look the true master in the face when he frees the foal from its bonds. Thus when the disciples say, "The Lord hath need of him," these wicked masters have nothing to say in reply. The disciples then bring the foal to Jesus naked, and put their own dress on it, so that the Lord may sit on the disciples' garments which are on it, at His ease. What is said further will not, in the light of Matthew's statements, present any difficulty; how [1] "They come to Jerusalem, and entering into the temple He began to cast out them that sold and bought in the temple," or how [2] "When He drew nigh and beheld the city He wept over it; and entering into the temple He began to cast out them that sold." For in some of those who have the temple in themselves He casts out all that sell and buy in the temple; but in others who do not quite obey the word of God, He only makes a beginning of casting out the sellers and buyers. There is a third class also besides these, in which He began to cast out the sellers only, and not also the buyers. With John, on the contrary, they are all cast out by the scourge woven of small cords, along with the sheep and the oxen. It should be carefully considered whether it is possible that the changes of the things described and the discrepancies found in them can be satisfactorily solved by the anagogic method. Each of the Evangelists ascribes to the Word different modes of action, which produce in souls of different tempers not the same effects but yet similar ones. The discrepancy we noticed in respect of Jesus' journeys to Jerusalem, which the Gospel now in hand reports quite differently from the other three, as we have expounded their words, cannot be made good in any other way. John gives statements which are similar to those of the other three but not the same; instead of branches cut from the trees or stubble brought from the fields and strewed on the road he says they took branches of palm trees. He says that much people had come to the feast, and that these went out to meet Him, crying, "Blessed is He that cometh in the name of the Lord," and "Blessed is the King of Israel." He also says that it was Jesus Himself who found the young ass on which Christ sat, and the phrase, young ass, doubtless conveys some additional meaning, as the small animal afforded a benefit not of men, nor through men, but through Jesus Christ. John moreover does not, any more than the others, reproduce the prophetic words exactly; instead of them he gives us "Fear not, O daughter of Zion; behold thy King cometh sitting" (instead of "mounted") "on the foal of an ass" (for "on an ass and a young foal"). The words "Fear not, daughter of Zion," are not in the prophet at all. But as the prophetic utterance has been applied by all in this way, let us see if there was not a necessity that the daughter of Zion should rejoice greatly and that the

[1] Ephes. ii. 12.

[1] Mark xi. 15. [2] Luke xix. 41.

greater than she, the daughter of Jerusalem, should not only rejoice greatly but should also proclaim it when her king was coming to her, just and bringing salvation, and meek, having mounted an ass and a young colt. Whoever, then, receives Him will no longer be afraid of those who are armed with the specious discourses of the heterodox, those chariots of Ephraim said to be destroyed by the Lord,[1] nor the horse, the vain thing for safety,[2] that is the mad desire which has accustomed itself to the things of sense and which is injurious to many of those who desire to dwell in Jerusalem and to attend to the sound word. It is also fitting to rejoice at the destruction by Him who rides on the ass and the young foal of every hostile dart, since the fiery darts of the enemy are no longer to prevail over him who has received Jesus to his own temple. And there will also be a multitude from the Gentiles with peace[3] at the Saviour's coming to Jerusalem, when He rules over the waters that He may bruise the head of the dragon on the water,[4] and we shall tread upon the waves of the sea and to the mouths of all the rivers on the earth. Mark, however, writing about the foal,[5] reports the Lord to have said, "On which never man sat;" and he seems to me to hint at the circumstance that those who afterwards believed had never submitted to the Word before Jesus' coming to them. For of men, perhaps, no one had ever sate on the foal, but of hearts or of powers alien to the Word some had sate on it, since in the prophet Isaiah the wealth of opposing powers is said to be borne on asses and camels.[6] "In the distress and the affliction," he writes, "the lion and the lion's whelp, whence also the offspring of flying asps, who carried their riches on asses and camels." The question occurs again, for those who have no mind but for the bare words, if according to their view the words, "on which never man sat," are not quite meaningless. For who but a man ever sits on a foal? So much of our views.

19. VARIOUS VIEWS OF HERACLEON ON THE PURGING OF THE TEMPLE.

Let us see what Heracleon makes of this. He says that the ascent to Jerusalem signifies the Lord's going up from material things to the spiritual place, which is a likeness of Jerusalem. And he considers that the words are, "He found in the temple," and not "in the sanctuary,"[1] because the Lord is not to be understood as instrumental in that call only, which takes place where the spirit is not. He considers the temple to be the Holy of Holies, into which none but the High-Priest enters, and there I believe he says that the spiritual go; while the court of the temple, where the levites also enter, is a symbol of these psychical ones who are saved, but outside the Pleroma. Then those who are found in the temple selling oxen and sheep and doves, and the money-changers sitting, he took to represent those who attribute nothing to grace, but regard the entrance of strangers to the temple as a matter of merchandise and gain, and who minister the sacrifices for the worship of God, with a view to their own gain and love of money. And the scourge which Jesus made of small cords and did not receive from another, he expounds in a way of his own, saying that the scourge is an image of the power and energy of the Holy Spirit, driving out by His breath those who are bad. And he declares that the scourge and the linen and the napkin and other things of such a kind are symbolic of the power and energy of the Holy Spirit. Then he assumes what is not written, as that the scourge was tied to a piece of wood, and this wood he takes to be a type of the cross; on this wood the gamblers, merchants, and all evil was nailed up and done away. In searching into the act of Jesus, and discussing the composition of the scourge out of two substances, he romances in an extraordinary way; He did not make it, he says, of dead leather. He wished to make the Church no longer a den of robbers, but the house of His Father. We must here say what is most necessary on the divinity, as referred to in Heracleon's text. If Jesus calls the temple at Jerusalem the house of His Father, and that temple was made in honour of Him who made heaven and earth, why are we not at once told that He is the Son of no one else than the Maker of heaven and earth, that He is the Son of God? To this house of the Father of Jesus, as being the house of prayer, the Apostles of Christ also, as we find in their "Acts," are told[2] by the angel to go and to stand there and preach all the words of this life. But they came to the house of prayer, through the Beautiful Gate, to pray there, a thing they

[1] Zech. ix. 10. [2] Ps. xxxiii. 17. [3] Zech. ix. 9, 10. [4] Ps. lxxiv. 13. [5] xi. 2. [6] Isa. xxx. 6.

[1] ἐν τῶ ἱερῷ, not τῷ ναῷ. The latter is Neander's correction for τῶν ἄνω, "the things above." Heracleon's point is that the ἱερόν, the Holy of Holies, represents the spiritual realm; and that Jesus entered it as being, as well as the ναος, in need of His saving work.
[2] Acts v. 20.

would not have done had they not known Him to be the same with the God worshipped by those who had dedicated that temple. Hence, too, they say, those who obeyed God rather than men, Peter and the Apostles, "The God[1] of our Fathers raised up Jesus, whom ye slew, hanging Him on a tree;" for they know that by no other God was Jesus raised from the dead but the God of the fathers, whom Jesus also extols as the God of Abraham and Isaac and Jacob, who are not dead but living. How, too, could the disciples, if the house was not that of the same God with the God of Christ, have remembered the saying in the sixty-ninth Psalm, "The zeal of thy house shall devour Me;" for thus it is found in the prophet, and not "hath devoured Me." Now Christ is zealous principally for that house of God which is in each of us; He does not wish that it should be a house of merchandise, nor that the house of prayer should be a den of robbers; for He is the Son of a jealous God. We ought to give a liberal intepretation to such utterances of Scripture; they speak of human things, but in the way of metaphor, to show that God desires that nothing foreign should be mixed up with His will in the soul of all men, indeed, but principally of those who are minded to accept the message of our most divine faith. But we must remember that the sixty-ninth Psalm, which contains the words, "The zeal of thy house shall devour me," and a little further on, "They gave Me gall for My drink and for My thirst they gave Me vinegar," both texts being recorded in the Gospels, that that Psalm is spoken in the person of the Christ, and nowhere shows any change of person. It shows a great want of observation on Heracleon's part that he considers the words, "The zeal of thy house shall devour Me," to be spoken in the person of those powers which were cast out and destroyed by the Saviour; he fails to see the connection of the prophecy in the Psalm. For if these words are understood as spoken by the expelled and destroyed powers, it follows that he must take the words, "They gave Me vinegar to drink," which are a part of the same psalm, to be also spoken by those powers. What misled him was probably that he could not understand how the "shall devour Me" could be spoken by Christ, since He did not appreciate the way in which anthropopathic statements are applied to God and to Christ.

[1] Acts v. 29, 30.

20. THE TEMPLE WHICH CHRIST SAYS HE WILL RAISE UP IS THE CHURCH. HOW THE DRY BONES WILL BE MADE TO LIVE AGAIN.

"The Jews then answered and said unto Him, What sign showest Thou unto us, seeing that Thou doest these things?[1] Jesus answered and said unto them, Destroy this temple, and in three days I will raise it up." Those of the body, and those who incline to material things, seem to me to be meant by the Jews, who, after Jesus has driven out those who make God's house a house of merchandise, are angry at Him for treating these matters in such a way, and demand a sign, a sign which will show that the Word, whom they do not receive, has a right to do such things. The Saviour joins on to His statement about the temple a statement which is really one with the former, about His own body, and to the question, What sign doest Thou, seeing that Thou doest such things? answers, "Destroy this temple, and in three days I will raise it up." He could have exhibited a thousand other signs, but to the question, "Seeing that Thou doest such things," He could not answer anything else; He fittingly gave the answer about the sign connected with the temple, and not about signs unconnected with the temple. Now, both of these two things, the temple and the body of Jesus, appear to me, in one interpretation at least, to be types of the Church, and to signify that it is built of living stones,[2] a spiritual house for a holy priesthood, built[3] on the foundation of the Apostles and prophets, Christ Jesus being the head corner-stone; and it is, therefore, called a temple. Now, from the text,[4] "Ye are the body of Christ, and members each in his part," we see that even though the harmonious fitting of the stones of the temple appear to be dissolved and scattered, as it is written in the twenty-second Psalm[5] that all the bones of Christ are, by the plots made against it in persecutions and afflictions, on the part of those who war against the unity of the temple in persecutions, yet the temple will be raised again, and the body will rise again on the third day after the day of evil which threatens it,[6] and the day of consummation which follows. For the third day will rise on the new heaven and the new earth, when these bones, the whole house of Israel,[7] will rise in the great Lord's day, death having been overcome. And thus the resurrection of

[1] John ii. 18, 19. [2] 1 Pet. ii. 5. [3] Ephes. ii. 20. [4] 1 Cor. xii. 27. [5] Ver. 14. [6] 2 Peter iii. 3, 10, 13. [7] Ezek. xxxvii. 11.

the Saviour from the passion of the cross contains the mystery of the resurrection of the whole body of Christ. But as that material body of Jesus was sacrificed for Christ, and was buried, and was afterwards raised, so the whole body of Christ's saints is crucified along with Him, and now lives no longer; for each of them, like Paul, glories[1] in nothing but the cross of our Lord Jesus Christ, through which He is crucified to the world, and the world to Him. Not only, therefore, is it crucified with Christ, and crucified to the world; it is also buried with Christ, for we were buried with Christ, Paul says.[2] And then he says, as if enjoying some earnest of the resurrection, "We rose with Him,"[3] because He walks in a certain newness of life, though not yet risen in that blessed and perfect resurrection which is hoped for. Either, then, he is now crucified, and afterwards is buried, or he is now buried and taken down from the cross, and, being now buried, is to rise at some future time. But to most of us the mystery of the resurrection is a great one, and difficult of contemplation; it is spoken of in many other passages of Scripture, and is specially announced in the following passage of Ezekiel:[4] "And the hand of the Lord was upon me, and He led me out in the Spirit of the Lord, and set me in the midst of the plain, and it was full of human bones. And He led me round about them in a circle, and behold there were very many on the face of the plain, and behold they were very dry. And He said to me, Son of man, shall these bones live? And I said, Lord, Lord, Thou knowest. And He said to me, Prophesy to these bones, and thou shalt say to them, Hear the word of the Lord, ye dry bones;" and a little further on, "And the Lord spake to me, saying, Son of man, these bones are the house of Israel. And they say, Our bones are become dry, our hope is lost, we have breathed our last." For what bones are these which are addressed, "Hear ye the word of the Lord," as if they heard the word of the Lord? They belong to the house of Israel, or to the body of Christ, of which the Lord says,[5] "All My bones are scattered," although the bones of His body were not scattered, and not even one of them was broken. But when the resurrection itself takes place of the true and more perfect body of Christ, then those who are now the members of Christ, for they will then be dry bones, will be brought together, bone to bone, and fitting to fitting (for none of those who are destitute of fitting ἁρμονία) will come to the perfect man), to the measure[1] of the stature of the fulness of the body of Christ. And then the many members[2] will be the one body, all of them, though many, becoming members of one body. But it belongs to God alone to make the distinction of foot and hand and eye and hearing and smelling, which in one sense fill up the head, but in another the feet and the rest of the members, and the weaker and humbler ones, the more and the less honourable. God will temper the body together, and then, rather than now, He will give to that which lacks the more abundant honour, that there may be, by no means, any schism in the body, but that the members may have the same care for one another, and, if any member be well off, all the members may share in its good things, or if any member be glorified, all the members may rejoice with it.

[1] Gal. vi. 14. [2] Rom. vi. 4.
[3] These words do not occur in Rom. vi. 4.
[4] xxxvii. 1-4. [5] Ps. xxii. 13.

21. THAT THE SON WAS RAISED UP BY THE FATHER. THE CHARGE BROUGHT AGAINST JESUS AT HIS TRIAL WAS BASED ON THE INCIDENT NOW BEFORE US.

What I have said is not alien to the passage now engaging us, dealing as it does with the temple and those cast out from it, of which the Saviour says, "The zeal of thy house shall devour Me;" and with the Jews who asked that a sign should be showed them, and the Saviour's answer to them, in which He combines the discourse on the temple with that on His own body, and says, "Destroy this temple and in three days I will raise it up." For from this temple, which is the body of Christ, everything that is irrational and savours of merchandise must be driven away, that it may no longer be a house of merchandise. And this temple must be destroyed by those who plot against the Word of God, and after its destruction be raised again on that third day which we discussed above; when the disciples also will remember what He, the Word, said before the temple of God was destroyed, and will believe, not only their knowledge but their faith also being then made perfect, and that by the word which Jesus spoke. And every one who is of this nature, Jesus purifying him,[3] puts away things that are irrational and things that savour of selling, to be destroyed on account of the zeal of the

[1] Ephes. iv. 13. [2] 1 Cor. xii. 12 sq. [3] John xv. 3.

Logos that is in Him. But they are destroyed to be raised again by Jesus, not on the third day, if we attend to the exact words before us, but "in three days." For the rising again of the temple takes place on the first day after it has been destroyed and on the second day, and its resurrection is accomplished in all the three days. Hence a resurrection both has been and is to be, if indeed we were buried with Christ, and rose with Him. And since the word, "We rose with Him," does not cover the whole of the resurrection, "in Christ shall all be made alive,[1] but every one in his own order, Christ the first fruits, then they that are Christ's at His coming, and then the end." It belongs to the resurrection that one should be on the first day in the paradise of God,[2] and it belongs to the resurrection when Jesus appears and says, "Touch Me not; for I am not yet ascended to My Father,"[3] but the perfection of the resurrection was when He came to the Father. Now there are some who fall into confusion on this head of the Father and the Son, and we must devote a few words to them. They quote the text,[4] "Yea, and we are found false witnesses for God, because we testified against God that He raised up Christ, whom He raised not up," and other similar texts which show the raiser-up to be another person than He who was raised up; and the text, "Destroy this temple and in three days I will raise it up," as if it resulted from these that the Son did not differ in number from the Father, but that both were one, not only in point of substance but in point of subject, and that the Father and the Son were said to be different in some of their aspects but not in their hypostases. Against such views we must in the first place adduce the leading texts which prove the Son to be another than the Father, and that the Son must of necessity be the son of a Father, and the Father, the father of a Son. Then we may very properly refer to Christ's declaration that He cannot do anything but what He sees the Father doing and saying,[5] because whatever the Father does that the Son also does in like manner, and that He had raised the dead, *i.e.*, the body, the Father granting Him this, who must be said to have been the principal agent in raising up Christ from the dead. But Heracleon says, "In three days," instead of "On the third day," not having examined the point (and yet having noted the words "in three"), that the resurrection is brought about in three days. But he also calls the third the spiritual day, in which they consider the resurrection of the Church to be indicated. It follows from this that the first day is to be called the "earthly" day, and the second the psychical, the resurrection of the Church not having taken place on them. Now the statements of the false witnesses, recorded in the Gospel according to Matthew and Mark[1] towards the end of the Gospel, and the accusation they brought against our Lord Jesus Christ, appear to have reference to this utterance of His, "Destroy this temple, and I will build it up in three days." For He was speaking of the temple of His body, but they supposed His words to refer to the temple of stone, and so they said when accusing Him, "This man said, I am able to destroy the temple of God and to build it up in three days," or, as Mark has it, "We heard Him say, that I will destroy this temple made with hands, and in three days I will build up another temple not made with hands." Here the high-priest stood up and said to Him, "Answerest Thou nothing? What do these witness against Thee? But Jesus held His peace." Or, as Mark says, "And the high-priest stood up in the midst, and asked Jesus saying, Answerest Thou nothing? What do these witness against Thee? But He held His peace and answered nothing." These words must, I think, necessarily have reference to the text now before us.

22. THE TEMPLE OF SOLOMON DID NOT TAKE FORTY-SIX YEARS TO BUILD. WITH REGARD TO THAT OF EZRA WE CANNOT TELL HOW LONG IT TOOK. SIGNIFICANCE OF THE NUMBER FORTY-SIX.

The Jews therefore said, "Forty and six years was this temple in building,[2] and wilt thou raise it up in three days?" How the Jews said that the temple had been forty-six years building, we cannot tell, if we adhere to the history. For it is written in the third Book of Kings,[3] that they prepared the stones and the wood three years, and in the fourth year, in the second month,[4] when Solomon was king over Israel, the king commanded, and they brought great precious stones for the foundation of the house, and unhewn stones. And the sons of Solomon and the sons of Hiram hewed the stones and laid them in the fourth year, and they founded the house of the Lord in the month Nisan and the second month: in the tenth

[1] 1 Cor. xv. 22–24. [2] Luke xxiii. 43. [3] John xx. 17. [4] 1 Cor. xv. 15. [5] John v. 19.

[1] Matt. xxvi. 61; Mark xiv. 58. [2] John ii. 20. [3] 1 Kings v. 18. [4] 1 Kings vi. 1.

year in the month Baal, which was the eighth month, the house was finished according to the whole count and the whole plan of it. Thus comparing the time of its completion with the period of building, the building of it occupies less than eleven years. How, then, do the Jews come to say that the temple was forty-six years in building? One might, indeed, do violence to the words and make out the period of forty-six years at all costs, by counting from the time when David, after planning about the building of the temple, said to Nathan the prophet,[1] "Behold I dwell in a house of cedar, and the ark of God dwelleth in the midst of the tent," for though it is true that he was prevented, as being a man of blood,[2] from carrying out the building, he seems to have busied himself in collecting materials for it. In the first Book of Chronicles,[3] certainly, David the king says to all the congregation, "Solomon my son, whom the Lord hath chosen, is young and tender, and the work is great, because he is not to build for man but for the Lord God. According to my whole power I have prepared for the house of my God, gold, silver, brass, and iron, wood, stones of Soom, and stones for filling up, and precious stones of many kinds, and all sorts of precious wood, and a large quantity of Parian marble. And besides this, for the pleasure I have taken in the house of my God, the gold and the silver I possess, lo, I have given it for the house of my Lord, to the full; from such supplies[4] I prepared for the house of the saints, three thousand talents of gold from Suphir, and seven thousand talents of stamped silver, that the houses of God may be overlaid with them by the hands of artificers." For David reigned seven years in Hebron and thirty-three years in Jerusalem;[5] so that if it could be shown that the beginning of the preparations for the temple and of David's collecting the necessary material, was in the fifth year of his reign, then, with some forcing, the statement about forty-six years might stand. But some one else will say that the temple spoken of was not that built by Solomon, for that it was destroyed at the period of the captivity, but the temple built at the time of Ezra,[6] with regard to which the forty-six years can be shown to be quite accurate. But in this Maccabean period things were very unsettled with regard to the people and the temple, and I do not know if the temple was really built in that number of years. Heracleon pays no attention to the history, but says that in that he was forty-six years preparing the temple, Solomon was an image of the Saviour. The number six he connects with matter, that is, the image, and the number forty, which he says is the tetrad, not admitting of combination, he connects with the inspiration and the seed in the inspiration. Consider if the forty cannot be taken as due to the four elements of the world arranged in the building of the temple at the points at issue,[1] and the six to the fact that man was created on the sixth day.

[1] 2 Sam. vii. 2.
[2] 1 Chron. xxii. 8; xxvii. 3.
[3] 1 Chron. xxix. 1–5.
[4] LXX. reads "besides what;" neither reading yields a good sense.
[5] 1 Kings ii. 11.
[6] Ezra vi. 1.

23. THE TEMPLE SPOKEN OF BY CHRIST IS THE CHURCH. APPLICATION TO THE CHURCH OF THE STATEMENTS REGARDING THE BUILDING OF SOLOMON'S TEMPLE, AND THE NUMBERS STATED IN THAT NARRATIVE.

"But He spake of the temple of His body.[2] When, therefore, He was raised from the dead, His disciples remembered that He said this, and they believed the Scripture and the word which Jesus had said." This refers to the statement that the body of the Son is His temple. It may be asked whether this is to be taken in its plain sense, or whether we should try to connect each statement that is recorded about the temple, with the view we take about the body of Jesus, whether the body which He received from the Virgin, or that body of Christ which the Church is said to be, as we are said by the Apostle[3] to be all members of His body. One may, on the one hand, suppose it to be hopeless to get everything that is said about the temple properly connected with the body, in whatever sense the body be taken, and one may have recourse to a simpler explanation, and say that the body (in either of these senses) is called the temple, because as the temple had the glory of God dwelling in it, so He who was the image and glory of God, the first-born of every creature, could rightly be called, in respect of His body or the Church, the temple containing the image. We, for our part, see it to be a hard task to expound every particular of what is said about the temple in the third Book of Kings, and far beyond our powers of language, and we defer it in the meantime, as a thing beyond the scale of the present work. We also

[1] Reading ἠγωνισμένοις. Another suggested reading is γεγωνιωμένοις, which might give the sense "at the corners." Neither is satisfactory.
[2] John ii. 21.
[3] 1 Cor. xii. 27.

have a strong conviction that in such matters, which transcend human nature, it must be the work of divine wisdom to make plain the meaning of inspired Scripture, of that wisdom which is hidden in a mystery, which none of the rulers of this world knew. We are well aware, too, that we need the assistance of that excellent Spirit of wisdom, in order to understand such matters, as they should be understood by ministers of sacred things; and in this connection we will attempt to describe, as shortly as we may, our view of what belongs to this subject. The body is the Church, and we learn from Peter[1] that it is a house of God, built of living stones, a spiritual house for a holy priesthood. Thus the son of David, who builds this house, is a type of Christ. He builds it when his wars are at an end,[2] and a period of profound peace has arrived; he builds the temple for the glory of God in the Jerusalem on earth, so that worship may no longer be celebrated in a moveable erection like the tabernacle. Let us seek to find in the Church the truth of each statement made about the temple. If all Christ's enemies are made the footstool of His feet,[3] and Death, the last enemy, is destroyed, then there will be the most perfect peace. Christ will be Solomon, which means "Peaceful,"[4] and the prophecy will find its fulfilment in Him, which says,[5] "With those who hated peace I was peaceful." And then each of the living stones will be, according to the work of his life here, a stone of that temple, one, at the foundation, an apostle or a prophet, bearing those placed upon him, and another, after those in the foundation, and supported by the Apostles, will himself, with the Apostles, help to bear those in more need. One will be a stone of the inmost parts, where the ark is, and the cherubim, and the mercy-seat; another will be on the outer wall, and another even outside the outer wall of the levites and priests, a stone of the altar of whole burnt offerings. And the management and service of these things will be entrusted to holy powers, angels of God, being, respectively, lordships, thrones, dominions, or powers; and there will be others subject to these, typified by three thousand six hundred[6] chief officers, who were appointed over the works of Solomon, and the seventy thousand of those who bore burdens, and the eighty thousand stone-cutters in the mountain, who wrought in the work, and prepared the stones and the wood. It is to be remarked that those reported as bearing burdens are related to the Hebdomad. The quarrymen and stone-cutters, who make the stones fitted for the temple, have some kinship to the ogdoad. And the officers, who are six hundred in number, are connected with the perfect number six multiplied into itself. The preparation of the stones, as they are taken out and fitted for the building, extends over three years; this appears to me to point solely to the time of the eternal interval which is akin to the triad. This will come to pass when peace is consummated after the number of years of the transaction of the matters connected with the exodus from Egypt, namely, three hundred and forty, and of what took place in Egypt four hundred and thirty years after the covenant made by God with Abraham. Thus, from Abraham to the beginning of the building of the temple, there are two sabbatic numbers, the 700 and the 70; and at that time, too, our King Christ will command the seventy thousand burden-bearers not to take any chance stones for the foundation of the temple, but great stones, precious, unhewn, that they may be hewn, not by any chance workmen, but by the sons of Solomon; for so we find it written in the third Book of Kings. Then, too, on account of the profound peace, Hiram, king of Tyre, co-operates in the building of the temple, and gives his own sons to the sons of Solomon, to hew, in company with them, the great and precious stones for the holy place, which, in the fourth year, are placed in the foundation of the house of the Lord. But in an ogdoad of years the house is finished in the eighth month of the eighth year after its foundation.

24. THE ACCOUNT OF THE BUILDING OF SOLOMON'S TEMPLE CONTAINS SERIOUS DIFFICULTIES AND IS TO BE INTERPRETED SPIRITUALLY.

For the sake of those, however, who consider that nothing further than the narrative itself is meant to be indicated in these words, it may not be unfitting to introduce at this point some considerations which they can scarcely withstand, to show that the words ought to be regarded as those of the Spirit, and that the mind of the Spirit should be sought for in them. Did the sons of the kings really spend their time in hewing the great and precious stones, and practise a craft so little in keeping with royal birth? And the number of the burden-bearers and of the stone-cutters and of the officers, the duration, too, of the period of preparing the stones and marking them, is all this recorded

[1] 1 Pet. ii. 5. [2] 1 Kings v. 3-5. [3] 1 Cor. xv. 25.
[4] 1 Chron. xxii. 9. [5] Ps. cxx. 7. [6] 1 Kings v. 15-18.

as it really was? The holy house, too, was got ready in peace and was to be built for God without hammer or axe or any iron tool, that there might be no disturbance in the house of God. And again I would ask those who are in bondage to the letter how it is possible that there should be eighty thouand stone-cutters and that the house of God should be built out of hard white stones without the noise of hammer or axe or any iron tool being heard in His house while the building was going on? Is it not living stones that are hewn without any noise or tumult somewhere outside the temple, so that they are brought ready prepared to the place which awaits them in the building? And there is some sort of an ascent about the temple of God, not with angles, but with bends of straight lines. For it is written,[1] "And there was a winding staircase to the middle, and from the middle to the third floor;" for the staircase in the house of God had to be spiral, thus imitating in its ascent the circle, which is the most perfect figure. But that this house might be secure, five ties are built in it,[2] as fair as possible, a cubit high, that on looking up one might see it to be suggested how we rise from sensible things to the so-called divine perceptions, and so be brought to perceive those things which are seen only by the mind. But the place of the happier stones appears to be that called Dabir,[3] where the ark of the covenant of the Lord was, and, as I may say, the handwriting of God, the tables written with His own finger. And the whole house is overlaid with gold; "the whole house," we read,[4] "he overlaid with gold until all the house was finished." But there were two cherubim in Dabir, a word which the translators of the Hebrew Bible into Greek failed to render satisfactorily. Some, failing to do justice to the language, render it the temple; but it is more sacred than the temple. Now everything about the house was made golden, for a sign that the mind which is quite made perfect estimates accurately the things perceived by the intellect. But it is not given to all to approach and know them; and hence the veil of the court is erected, since to most of the priests and levites the things in the inmost part of the temple are not revealed.

25. FURTHER SPIRITUALIZING OF SOLOMON'S TEMPLE-BUILDING.

It is worth while to enquire how, on the one hand, Solomon the king is said to have built the temple, and on the other the master-builder whom Solomon sent and fetched,[1] "Hiram of Tyre, the son of a woman who was a widow; and he was of the tribe of Naphtali, and his father was a man of Tyre, a worker in brass, and filled with wisdom and understanding, to work all works in brass; and he was brought in to King Solomon and wrought all his works." Here I ask whether Solomon can be taken for the first-born of all creation,[2] and Hiram for the man whom he assumed, from the constraint of men—for the word Tyrians means "constrainers"—the man who derived his birth from nature, and being filled with all manner of art and wisdom and understanding, was brought in to co-operate with the first-born of all creation, and to build the temple. In this temple there are also windows,[3] placed obliquely and out of sight, so that the illumination of the divine light may enter for salvation, and —why should I go into particulars?—that the body of Christ, the Church, may be found having the plan of the spiritual house and temple of God. As I said before, we require that wisdom which is hidden in a mystery, and which he alone can apprehend who is able to say, "But we have the mind of Christ,"—we require that wisdom to interpret spiritually each detail of what is said in accordance with the will of Him who caused it to be written. To enter into these details is not in accordance with our present subject. What has been said may suffice to let us understand how "He spake about the temple of His body."

26. THE PROMISES ADDRESSED TO JERUSALEM IN THE PROPHETS REFER TO THE CHURCH, AND ARE STILL TO BE FULFILLED.

After all this it is proper to ask whether what is narrated as having taken place about the temple has ever taken place or ever will take place about the spiritual house. The argument may seem to pinch in whichever way we take it. If we say that it is possible that something like what is told about the temple may take place with regard to the spiritual house, or has already taken place in it, then those who hear us will, with difficulty, be brought to admit that a change can take place in such good things as these, firstly, because they do not wish it, and secondly, because of the incongruity of thinking that such things admit of change. If, on the other hand, we seek to maintain the unchangeableness of the good things once

[1] 1 Kings vi. 8.
[2] 1 Kings vi. 10.
[3] 1 Kings vi. 16, 19, the "oracle."
[4] 1 Kings vi. 21.

[1] 1 Kings vii. 13.
[2] Coloss. i. 15.
[3] 1 Kings vi. 4.

given to the saints, then we cannot apply to them what we find in the history, and we shall seem to be doing what those of the heresies do, who fail to maintain the unity of the narrative of Scripture from beginning to end. If we are not to take the view proper to old wives or Jews, of the promises recorded in the prophets, and especially in Isaiah, if, that is to say, we are to look for their fulfilment in connection with the Jerusalem on earth, then, as certain remarkable things connected with the building of the temple and the restoration of the people from the captivity are spoken of as happening after the captivity and the destruction of the temple, we must say that we are now the temple and the people which was carried captive, but is to come up again to Judæa and Jerusalem, and to be built with the precious stones of Jerusalem. But I cannot tell if it be possible that, at the revolution of long periods of time, things of the same nature should take place again, but in a worse way. The prophecies of Isaiah which we mentioned are the following:[1] "Behold I prepare for thy stone carbuncle and for thy foundation sapphire; and I will make thy battlements jasper, and thy gates stones of crystal, and thy outer wall choice stones; and all thy sons shall be taught of the Lord, and in great peace shall thy children be, and in righteousness shalt thou be built." And a little further on, to the same Jerusalem:[2] "And the glory of Lebanon shall come to thee with cypress, and pine, and cedar, along with those who will glorify My holy place. And the sons of them that humbled thee and insulted thee shall come to thee in fear; and thou shalt be called the city of the Lord, Sion of holy Israel, because thou wert desolate and hated, and there was none to help thee. And I will make thee an eternal delight, a joy of generations of generations. And thou shalt suck the milk of the Gentiles and shalt eat the riches of kings, and thou shalt know that I am the Lord that saveth thee and the God of Israel that chooseth thee. And instead of brass I will bring thee gold, and instead of iron I will bring thee silver, and for wood I will bring thee brass, and for stones iron. And I will establish thy rulers in peace and thy overseers in righteousness. And wickedness shall no more be heard in thy land, nor affliction and distress in thy borders, but thy walls shall be called salvation and thy gates sculpture. And the sun shall no longer be to thee for light by day, nor shall the rising of the moon give light to thee by night, but Christ shall be to thee an everlasting light and thy God thy glory. For thy sun shall no more go down, and thy moon shall not fail, for thy Lord shall be to thee an everlasting light, and the days of thy mourning shall be fulfilled." These prophecies clearly refer to the age still to come, and they are addressed to the children of Israel in their captivity, to whom He was sent and came, who said, "I am not sent but to the lost sheep of the house of Israel."[1] Such things, though they are captives, they are to receive in their own land; and proselytes also are to come to them at that time through Christ, and are to fly to them, according to the saying,[2] "Behold, proselytes shall come to thee through Me, and shall flee to thee for refuge." And if all this is to take place with the captives, then it is plain that they must be about their temple, and that they must go up there again to be built up, having become the most precious of stones. For we find with John in his Apocalyse,[3] the promise made to him that overcomes, that he will be a pillar in the temple of God, and will go no more out. All this I have said with a view to our obtaining a cursory view at least of the matters pertaining to the temple, and the house of God, and the Church and Jerusalem, which we cannot now take up systematically. Those, however, who, in their reading of the prophets, do not shrink from the labour of seeking after their spiritual meaning, must enquire into these matters with the greatest particularity, and must take account of every possibility. So far of "the temple of His body."

27. OF THE BELIEF THE DISCIPLES AFTERWARDS ATTAINED IN THE WORDS OF JESUS.

"When He was raised from the dead,[4] His disciples remembered that He spake this, and they believed the Scripture and the word which Jesus had said." This tells us that after Jesus' resurrection from the dead His disciples saw that what He had said about the temple had a higher application to His passion and His resurrection; they remembered that the words, "In three days I will raise it up," pointed to the resurrection; "And they believed the Scripture and the word which Jesus had said." We are not told that they believed the Scripture or the word which Jesus said, before. For faith in its full sense is the act of him who accepts with his whole soul what is pro-

[1] Isa. liv. 11–14.

[2] Isa. lx. 13–20.

[1] Matt. xv. 24.

[2] Isa. liv. 15.

[3] Apoc. iii. 12.

[4] John ii. 22.

fessed at baptism. As for the higher sense, as we have already spoken of the resurrection from the dead of the whole body of the Lord, we have now to note that the disciples were put in mind by the fulfilment of the Scripture which when they were in life they had not fully understood; its meaning was now brought under their eyes and made quite clear to them, and they knew of what heavenly things it was the pattern and shadow. Then they believed the Scripture who formerly did not believe it, and believed the word of Jesus which, as the speaker means to convey, they had not believed before the resurrection. For how can any one be said in the full sense to believe the Scripture when he does not see in it the mind of the Holy Spirit, which God would have us to believe rather than the literal meaning? From this point of view we must say that none of those who walk according to the flesh believe the spiritual things of the law, of the very beginnings of which they have no conception. But, they say, those are more blessed who have not seen and yet believe, than those who have seen and have believed, and for this they quote the saying to Thomas at the end of the Gospel of John,[1] "Blessed are they that have not seen and yet have believed." But it is not said here that those who have not seen and yet have believed are more blessed than those who have seen and believed. According to their view those after the Apostles are more blessed than the Apostles; than which nothing can be more foolish. He who is to be blessed must see in his mind the things which he believes, and must be able with the Apostles to hear the words spoken to him, "Blessed are your eyes, for they see, and your ears, for they hear,"[2] and "Many prophets and righteous men have desired to see the things which ye see, and have not seen them, and to hear the things which ye hear, and have not heard them." Yet he may be content who only receives the inferior beatitude, which says:[3] "Blessed are they who have not seen and yet have believed." But how much more blessed are those eyes which Jesus calls blessed for the things which they have seen, than those which have not attained to such a vision; Simeon is content to take into his arms the salvation of God, and after seeing it, he says,[4] "Now, O Lord, lettest Thou Thy servant depart in peace, according to Thy word; for mine eyes have seen Thy salvation." We must strive, therefore, as Solomon says, to open our eyes that we may be satisfied with bread; "Open thine eyes," he says, "and be satisfied with bread." What I have said on the text, "They believe the Scripture and the word which Jesus had said unto them," may lead us to understand, after discussing the subject of faith, that the perfection of our faith will be given us at the great resurrection from the dead of the whole body of Jesus which is His Holy Church. For what is said about knowledge, "Now I know in part,"[1] that, I think, may be said in the same way of every other good; and one of these others is faith. "Now I believe in part," we may say, "but when that which is perfect is come, then the faith which is in part will be done away." As with knowledge, so with faith, that which is through sight is far better, if I may say so, than that which is through a glass and in an enigma.

28. THE DIFFERENCE BETWEEN BELIEVING IN THE NAME OF JESUS AND BELIEVING IN JESUS HIMSELF.

"Now, when He was in Jerusalem at the passover, during the feast, many believed in His name, beholding His signs which He did. But He, Jesus, did not trust Himself to them, because He knew all (men) and because He needed not that any should testify of man, for he Himself knew what was in man."[2] One might ask how Jesus did not Himself believe in those of whom we are told that they believed. To this we must say it was not those who believed in Him that Jesus did not trust, but those who believed in His name; for believing in His name is a different thing from believing in Him. He who will not be judged because of his faith is exempted from the judgment, not for believing in His name, but for believing in Him; for the Lord says,[3] "He that believeth in Me is not judged," not, "He who believes in My name is not judged;" the latter believes, and hence he is not worthy to be condemned already, but he is inferior to the other who believes in Him. Hence it is that Jesus does not trust Himself to him who believes in His name. We must, therefore, cleave to Him rather than to His name, lest after we have done wonders in His name, we should hear these words addressed to us which He will speak to those who boast of His name alone.[4] With the Apostle Paul[5] let us seek

[1] xx. 29. [2] Matt. xiii. 16. [3] John xx. 29. [4] Luke ii. 29, 30.

[1] 1 Cor. xiii. 12. [2] ii. 23–25. [3] John iii. 18. [4] Matt. vii. 21–23. [5] Philipp. iv. 13.

joyfully to say, "I can do all things in Christ Jesus strengthening me." We have also to notice that in a former passage[1] the Evangelist calls the passover that of the Jews, while here he does not say that Jesus was at the passover of the Jews, but at the passover at Jerusalem; and in the former case when the passover is called that of the Jews, it is not said to be a feast; but here Jesus is recorded to have been at the feast; when at Jerusalem He was at the passover during the feast, and many believed, even though only in His name. We ought to notice certainly that "many" are said to believe, not in Him, but in His name. Now, those who believe in Him are those who walk in the straight and narrow way,[2] which leads to life, and which is found by few. It may well be, however, that many of those who believe in His name will sit down with Abraham and Isaac and Jacob in the kingdom of heaven, the Father's house, in which are many mansions. And it is to be noted that the many who believe in His name do not believe in the same way as Andrew does, and Peter, and Nathanael, and Philip. These believe the testimony of John when he says, "Behold the Lamb of God," or they believe in Christ as found by Andrew, or Jesus saying to Philip, "Follow Me," or Philip saying, "We have found Him of whom Moses and the prophets did write, Jesus the Son of Joseph from Nazareth." Those, on the other hand, of whom we now speak, "believed in His name, beholding His signs which He did." And as they believe the signs and not in Him but in His name, Jesus "did not trust Himself to them, because He knew all men, and needed not that any should testify of man, because He knew what is in every man."

29. ABOUT WHAT BEINGS JESUS NEEDED TESTIMONY.

The words, "He needed not that any should testify of man," may fitly be used to show that the Son of God is able of Himself to see the truth about each man and is in no need of such testimony as any other could supply. The words, however, "He had no need that any should testify of man," are not equivalent to "He had no need of testimony about any being." If we take the word "man" to include every being who is according to the image of God, or every reasonable creature, then He will have no need that any should testify to Him of any reasonable being whatever, since He Himself, by the power given Him by the Father, knows them all. But if the term "man" be restricted to mortal animated reasonable beings, then it might be said, on the one hand, that He had need of testimony respecting the beings above man, and while His knowledge was adequate with regard to man it did not extend to those other beings. On the other hand, however, it might be said that He who humbled Himself had no need that any should testify to Him concerning man, but that He had such need in respect of beings higher than men.

30. HOW JESUS KNEW THE POWERS, BETTER OR WORSE, WHICH RESIDE IN MAN.

It may also be asked what signs those many saw Him do who believed on Him, for it is not recorded that He did any signs at Jerusalem, though some may have been done which are not recorded. One may, however, consider if what He did may be called signs, when He made a scourge of small cords, and cast them all out of the temple, and the sheep, and the oxen, and poured out the changers' money, and overthrew the tables. As for those who suppose that it was only about men that He had no need of witnesses, it has to be said that the Evangelist attributes to Him two things, that He knew all beings, and that He had no need that any one should testify of man. If He knew all beings, then He knew not only men but the beings above men, all beings who are without such bodies as ours; and He knew what was in man, since He was greater than those who reproved and judged by prophesying, and who brought to the light the secret things of the hearts of those whom the Spirit suggested to them to be thus dealt with. The words, "He knew what was in man," could also be taken as referring to the powers, better or worse, which work in men. For if any one gives place to the devil, Satan enters into him; thus did Judas give place, and thus did the devil put it in his heart to betray Jesus, and "after the sop," therefore, "the devil entered into him."[1] But if any one gives place to God, he becomes blessed; for blessed is the man whose help is from God, and the ascent is in his heart from God.[2] Thou knowest what is in man, Thou who knowest all things, O Son of God. And now that our tenth book has come to be large enough we will here pause in our theme.

[1] John ii. 13.

[2] Matt. vii. 14.

[1] John xiii. 2–27.

[2] Ps. lxxxiv. 5.

ORIGEN'S COMMENTARY

ON THE

GOSPEL OF MATTHEW

BY

JOHN PATRICK, D.D.

COMMENTARY ON MATTHEW

INTRODUCTION

According to Eusebius (*H. E.* vi. 36) the Commentaries on the Gospel of Matthew were written about the same time as the *Contra Celsum*, when Origen was over sixty years of age, and may therefore be probably assigned to the period 246–248. This statement is confirmed by internal evidence. In the portion here translated, books x.–xiv., he passes by the verses Matt. xviii. 12, 13, and refers for the exposition of them to his Homilies on Luke (book xiii. 29). Elsewhere, he refers his readers for a fuller discussion on certain points to his Commentaries on John (book xvi. 20), and on Romans (book xvii. 32). Of the twenty-five books into which the work was divided, the first nine, with the exception of two fragments, are lost; books x.–xvii., covering the portion from Matt. xiii. 36 to xxii. 33, are extant in the Greek, and the greater part of the remaining books survives in a Latin version, which is co-extensive with the Greek from book xii. 9 to book xvii. 36, and contains further the exposition from Matt. xxii. 34 to xxvii. 66. The passages in Cramer's *Catena* do not seem to be taken from the Commentaries. Of the numerous quotations from Matthew only one (Matt. xxi. 35) can be definitely traced to this section of the writings of Origen; and as this differs greatly from our present text, and is moreover purely narrative, it is probably taken like the others either from the Scholia (*commaticum interpretationis genus*), or from the Homilies to which reference is made by Jerome (*Prol. in Matt.* I. iv). The majority of them may be ascribed to the Scholia.

In addition to the MSS. already referred to (p. 294) the old Latin version is often useful for determining the text, though it contains some interpolations and has many omissions. The omissions (cf. book xiii. 28, book xiv. 1, 3, book xiv. 19–22) are not due to any dogmatic bias, but have been made by the translator or some subsequent transcriber on the ground that the passages were uninteresting or unimportant. The version is otherwise for the most part literal, and has in some cases preserved the correct reading, though it often fails just when it would have been of most service. For an estimate of the work and method of Origen as an exegete, see pp. 291–294; and for a fuller statement on some of the points here touched upon, see Westcott's article on Origen in Smith's *Dictionary of Christian Biography* (vol. iv.).

FROM THE FIRST BOOK OF THE COMMENTARY ON MATTHEW [1]

CONCERNING the four Gospels which alone are uncontroverted in the Church of God under heaven, I have learned by tradition that the Gospel according to Matthew, who was at one time a publican and afterwards an Apostle of Jesus Christ, was written first; and that he composed it in the Hebrew tongue and published it for the converts from Judaism. The second written was that according to Mark, who wrote it according to the instruction of Peter, who, in his General Epistle, acknowledged him as a son, saying, "The church that is in Babylon, elect together with you, saluteth you; and so doth Mark my son." [2] And third, was that according to Luke, the Gospel commended by [3] Paul, which he composed for the converts from the Gentiles. Last of all, that according to John.

[1] This fragment is found in Eusebius, *H. E.* vi. 25.

[2] 1 Pet. v. 13.

[3] *Or*, who is commended by Paul.

FROM THE SECOND BOOK OF THE COMMENTARY ON THE GOSPEL ACCORDING TO MATTHEW

BOOK II.[1]

THE UNITY AND HARMONY OF SCRIPTURE.

"*Blessed are the peacemakers. . . .*"[2] To the man who is a peacemaker in either sense there is in the Divine oracles nothing crooked or perverse, for they are all plain to those who understand.[3] And because to such an one there is nothing crooked or perverse, he sees therefore abundance of peace[4] in all the Scriptures, even in those which seem to be at conflict, and in contradiction with one another. And likewise he becomes a third peacemaker as he demonstrates that that which appears to others to be a conflict in the Scriptures is no conflict, and exhibits their concord and peace, whether of the Old Scriptures with the New, or of the Law with the Prophets, or of the Gospels with the Apostolic Scriptures, or of the Apostolic Scriptures with each other. For, also, according to the Preacher, all the Scriptures are "words of the wise like goads, and as nails firmly fixed which were given by agreement from one shepherd;"[5] and there is nothing superfluous in them. But the Word is the one Shepherd of things rational which may have an appearance of discord to those who have not ears to hear, but are truly at perfect concord. For as the different chords of the psalter or the lyre, each of which gives forth a certain sound of its own which seems unlike the sound of another chord, are thought by a man who is not musical and ignorant of the principle of musical harmony, to be inharmonious, because of the dissimilarity of the sounds, so those who are not skilled in hearing the harmony of God in the sacred Scriptures think that the Old is not in harmony with the New, or the Prophets with the Law, or the Gospels with one another, or the Apostle with the Gospel, or with himself, or with the other Apostles. But he who comes instructed in the music of God, being a man wise in word and deed, and, on this account, like another David—which is, by interpretation, skilful with the hand—will bring out the sound of the music of God, having learned from this at the right time to strike the chords, now the chords of the Law, now the Gospel chords in harmony with them, and again the Prophetic chords, and, when reason demands it, the Apostolic chords which are in harmony with the Prophetic, and likewise the Apostolic with those of the Gospels. For he knows that all the Scripture is the one perfect and harmonised[1] instrument of God, which from different sounds gives forth one saving voice to those willing to learn, which stops and restrains every working of an evil spirit, just as the music of David laid to rest the evil spirit in Saul, which also was choking him.[2] You see, then, that he is in the third place a peacemaker, who sees in accordance with the Scripture the peace of it all, and implants this peace in those who rightly seek and make nice distinctions in a genuine spirit.

---

[1] This fragment, which is preserved in the *Philocalia*, c. vi., is all that is extant of Book II.
[2] Matt. v. 9.
[3] Prov. viii. 8, 9.
[4] Ps. lxxii. 7
[5] Ecc. xii. 11.

[1] *Or*, fitted,
[2] 1 Sam. xvi. 14.

BOOK X.

1. THE PARABLE OF THE TARES: THE HOUSE OF JESUS.

"*Then He left the multitudes and went into His house, and His disciples came unto Him saying, Declare to us the parable of the tares of the field.*"[1] When Jesus then is with the multitudes, He is not in His house, for the multitudes are outside of the house, and it is an act which springs from His love of men to leave the house and to go away to those who are not able to come to Him. Now, having discoursed sufficiently to the multitudes in parables, He sends them away and goes to His own house, where His disciples, who did not abide with those whom He had sent away, come to Him. And as many as are more genuine hearers of Jesus first follow Him, then having inquired about His abode, are permitted to see it, and, having come, see and abide with Him, all for that day, and perhaps some of them even longer. And, in my opinion, such things are indicated in the Gospel according to John in these words, "On the morrow again John was standing and two of his disciples."[2] And in order to explain the fact that of those who were permitted to go with Jesus and see His abode, the one who was more eminent becomes also an Apostle, these words are added: "One of the two that heard John speak and followed him was Andrew, Simon Peter's brother."[3] And if then, unlike the multitudes whom He sends away, we wish to hear Jesus and go to the house and receive something better than the multitudes, let us become friends of Jesus, so that as His disciples we may come to Him when He goes into the house, and having come may inquire about the explanation of the parable, whether of the tares of the field, or of any other. And in order that it may be more accurately understood what is represented by the house of Jesus, let some one collect from the Gospels whatsoever things are spoken about the house of Jesus, and what things were spoken or done by Him in it; for all the passages collected together will convince any one who applies himself to this reading that the letters of the Gospel are not absolutely simple as some suppose, but have become simple to the simple by a divine concession;[1] but for those who have the will and the power to hear them more acutely there are concealed things wise and worthy of the Word of God.

[1] Matt. xiii. 36. [2] John i. 35. [3] John i. 40.

2. EXPOSITION OF THE PARABLE.

"*After these things He answered and said to them, He that soweth the good seed is the Son of man.*"[2] Though we have already, in previous sections, according to our ability discussed these matters, none the less shall we now say what is in harmony with them, even if there is reasonable ground for another explanation. And consider now, if in addition to what we have already recounted, you can otherwise take the good seed to be the children of the kingdom, because whatsoever good things are sown in the human soul, these are the offspring of the kingdom of God and have been sown by God the Word who was in the beginning with God,[3] so that wholesome words about anything are children of the kingdom. But while men are asleep who do not act according to the command of Jesus, "Watch and pray that ye enter not into temptation,"[4] the devil on the watch sows what are called tares—that is, evil opinions—over and among what are called by some natural conceptions, even the good seeds which are from the Word. And according to this the whole world might be called a field, and not the Church of God only, for in the whole world the Son of man sowed the good seed, but the wicked one tares,—that is, evil words,—which, springing from wickedness, are children of the evil one. And at the end of things, which is called "the consummation of the age,"[5] there will of necessity be a harvest, in order that the angels of God who have been appointed for this work may gather up the bad opinions that have grown upon the soul, and overturning them may give them over to fire which is said to burn, that they may be consumed. And so the angels and servants of the Word will gather from all the kingdom of Christ all things that cause a

[1] *Or*, by a dispensation.
[2] Matt. xiii. 37.
[3] John i. 2.
[4] Matt. xxvi. 41.
[5] Matt. xiii. 39. *Or*, reading ὅς καλεῖται for ὃ, and at the end of things, there will of necessity be a harvest, which is called the consummation of the age.

stumbling-block to souls and reasonings that create iniquity, which they will scatter and cast into the burning furnace of fire. Then those who become conscious that they have received the seeds of the evil one in themselves, because of their having been asleep, shall wail and, as it were, be angry against themselves; for this is the "gnashing of teeth."[1] Wherefore, also, in the Psalms it is said, "They gnashed upon me with their teeth."[2] Then above all "shall the righteous shine," no longer differently as at the first, but all "as one sun in the kingdom of their Father."[3] Then, as if to indicate that there was indeed a hidden meaning, perhaps, in all that is concerned with the explanation of the parable, perhaps most of all in the saying, "Then shall the righteous shine as the sun in the kingdom of their Father," the Saviour adds, "He that hath ears to hear, let him hear,"[4] thereby teaching those who think that in the exposition, the parable has been set forth with such perfect clearness that it can be understood by the vulgar,[5] that even the things connected with the interpretation of the parable stand in need of explanation.

3. THE SHINING OF THE RIGHTEOUS. ITS INTERPRETATION.

But as we said above in reference to the words, "Then shall the righteous shine as the sun," that the righteous will shine not differently as formerly, but as one sun, we will, of necessity, set forth what appears to us on the point. Daniel, knowing that the intelligent are the light of the world, and that the multitudes of the righteous differ in glory, seems to have said this, "And the intelligent shall shine as the brightness of the firmament, and from among the multitudes of the righteous as the stars for ever and ever."[6] And in the passage, "There is one glory of the sun, and another glory of the moon, and another glory of the stars: for one star differeth from another star in glory: so also is the resurrection of the dead,"[7] the Apostle says the same thing as Daniel, taking this thought from his prophecy. Some one may inquire how some speak about the difference of light among the righteous, while the Saviour on the contrary says, "They shall shine as one sun." I think, then, that at the beginning of the blessedness enjoyed by those who are being saved (because those who are not such are not yet purified), the difference connected with the light of the saved takes place: but when, as we have indicated, he gathers from the whole kingdom of Christ all things that make men stumble, and the reasonings that work iniquity are cast into the furnace of fire, and the worse elements utterly consumed, and, when this takes place, those who received the words which are the children of the evil one come to self-consciousness, then shall the righteous having become one light of the sun shine in the kingdom of their Father. For whom will they shine? For those below them who will enjoy their light, after the analogy of the sun which now shines for those upon the earth? For, of course, they will not shine for themselves. But perhaps the saying, "Let your light shine before men,"[1] can be written "upon the table of the heart,"[2] according to what is said by Solomon, in a threefold way; so that even now the light of the disciples of Jesus shines before the rest of men, and after death before the resurrection, and after the resurrection "until all shall attain unto a full-grown man,"[3] and all become one sun. Then shall they shine as the sun in the kingdom of their Father.

4. CONCERNING THE PARABLE OF THE TREASURE HIDDEN IN THE FIELD. THE PARABLE DISTINGUISHED FROM THE SIMILITUDE.

"*Again the kingdom of heaven is like unto a treasure hidden in the field, which a man found and hid.*"[4] The former parables He spoke to the multitudes; but this and the two which follow it, which are not parables but similitudes in relation to the kingdom of heaven, He seems to have spoken to the disciples when in the house. In regard to this and the next two, let him who "gives heed to reading"[5] inquire whether they are parables at all. In the case of the latter the Scripture does not hesitate to attach in each case the name of parable; but in the present case it has not done so; and that naturally. For if He spoke to the multitudes in parables, and "spake all these things in parables, and without a parable spake nothing to them,"[6] but on going to the house He discourses not to the multitudes but to the disciples who came to Him there, manifestly the things spoken in the house were not parables: for, to them that are without, even to those to whom "it is not given to know the mysteries of the kingdom of heaven,"[7] He speaks in parables. Some one will then say, If they are not really parables,

[1] Matt. xiii. 42. [2] Ps. xxxv. 16. [3] Matt. xiii. 43. [4] Matt. xiii. 43. [5] *Or*, in little details. [6] Dan. xii. 3. [7] 1 Cor. xv. 41, 42.

[1] Matt. v. 16. [2] Prov. vii. 3. *Or*, on the breadth of the heart. [3] Eph. iv. 13. [4] Matt. xiii. 44. [5] 1 Tim. iv. 13. [6] Matt. xiii. 34. [7] Matt. xiii. 11.

what are they? Shall we then say in keeping with the diction of the Scripture that they are similitudes (comparisons)? Now a similitude differs from a parable; for it is written in Mark, "To what shall we compare the kingdom of God, or in what parable shall we set it forth?"[1] From this it is plain that there is a difference between a similitude and a parable. The similitude seems to be generic, and the parable specific. And perhaps also as the similitude, which is the highest genus of the parable, contains the parable as one of its species, so it contains that particular form of similitude which has the same name as the genus. This is the case with other words as those skilled in the giving of many names have observed; who say that "impulse"[2] is the highest genus of many species, as, for example, of "disinclination"[3] and "inclination," and say that, in the case of the species which has the same name as the genus, "inclination" is taken in opposition to and in distinction from "disinclination."

5. THE FIELD AND THE TREASURE INTERPRETED.

And here we must inquire separately as to the field, and separately as to the treasure hidden in it, and in what way the man who has found this hidden treasure goes away with joy and sells all that he has in order to buy that field; and we must also inquire—what are the things which he sells. The field, indeed, seems to me according to these things to be the Scripture, which was planted with what is manifest in the words of the history, and the law, and the prophets, and the rest of the thoughts; for great and varied is the planting of the words in the whole Scripture; but the treasure hidden in the field is the thoughts concealed and lying under that which is manifest, "of wisdom hidden in a mystery," "even Christ, in whom are all the treasures of wisdom and knowledge hidden."[4] But another might say that the field is that which is verily full, which the Lord blessed, the Christ of God; but the treasure hidden in it is the things said to have been "hidden in Christ" by Paul, who says about Christ, "in whom are the treasures of wisdom and knowledge hidden." The heavenly things, therefore, even the kingdom of heaven, as in a figure it is written in the Scriptures,—which are the kingdom of heaven, or Christ—Himself the king of the ages, are the kingdom of heaven which is likened to a treasure hidden in the field.

[1] Mark iv. 30.
[2] ὁρμή; *also*, inclination.
[3] ἀφορμή.
[4] Col. ii. 3.

6. THE EXPOSITION CONTINUED.

And at this point you will inquire, whether the kingdom of heaven is likened only to the treasure hidden in the field, so that we are to think of the field as different from the kingdom, or is likened to the whole of this treasure hidden in the field, so that the kingdom of heaven contains according to the similitude both the field and the treasure hidden in the field. Now a man who comes to the field, whether to the Scriptures or to the Christ who is constituted both from things manifest and from things hidden, finds the hidden treasure of wisdom whether in Christ or in the Scriptures. For, going round to visit the field and searching the Scriptures and seeking to understand the Christ, he finds the treasure in it; and, having found it, he hides it, thinking that it is not without danger to reveal to everybody the secret meanings of the Scriptures, or the treasures of wisdom and knowledge in Christ. And, having hidden it, he goes away, working and devising how he shall buy the field, or the Scriptures, that he may make them his own possession, receiving from the people of God the oracles of God with which the Jews were first entrusted.[1] And when the man taught by Christ has bought the field, the kingdom of God which, according to another parable, is a vineyard, "is taken from them and is given to a nation bringing forth the fruits thereof,"[2]—to him who in faith has bought the field, as the fruit of his having sold all that he had, and no longer keeping by him anything that was formerly his; for they were a source of evil to him. And you will give the same application, if the field containing the hidden treasure be Christ, for those who give up all things and follow Him, have, as it were in another way, sold their possessions, in order that, by having sold and surrendered them, and having received in their place from God—their helper—a noble resolution, they may purchase, at great cost worthy of the field, the field containing the treasure hidden in itself.

7. THE PARABLE OF THE PEARL OF GREAT PRICE. THE FORMATION AND DIFFERENCE OF PEARLS.

"*Again the kingdom of heaven is like unto a man that is a merchant seeking goodly pearls.*"[3] There are many merchants engaged in many forms of merchandise, but not to any one of these is the kingdom of heaven like, but only to him who is seeking

[1] Rom. iii. 2.
[2] Matt. xxi. 43.
[3] Matt. xiii. 45

goodly pearls, and has found one equal in value to many, a very costly pearl which he has bought in place of many. I consider it reasonable, then, to make some inquiry into the nature of the pearl.[1] Be careful however to note, that Christ did not say, "He sold all the pearls that he had," for he sold not only those which one seeking goodly pearls had bought, but also everything which he had, in order to buy that goodly pearl. We find then in those who write on the subject of stones, with regard to the nature of the pearl, that some pearls are found by land, and some in the sea. The land pearls are produced among the Indians only, being fitted for signet-rings and collets and necklaces; and the sea pearls, which are superior, are found among the same Indians, the best being produced in the Red Sea. The next best pearls are those taken from the sea at Britain; and those of the third quality, which are inferior not only to the first but to the second, are those found at Bosporus off Scythia. Concerning the Indian pearl these things further are said. They are found in mussels, like in nature to very large spiral snail-shells; and these are described as in troops making the sea their pasture-ground, as if under the guidance of some leader, conspicuous in colour and size, and different from those under him, so that he has an analogous position to what is called the queen of the bees. And likewise, in regard to the fishing for the best—that is, those in India—the following is told. The natives surround with nets a large circle of the shore, and dive down, exerting themselves to seize that one of them all which is the leader; for they say that, when this one is captured, the catching of the troop subject to it costs no trouble, as not one of those in the troop remains stationary, but as if bound by a thong follows the leader of the troop. It is said also that the formation of the pearls in India requires periods of time, the creature undergoing many changes and alterations until it is perfected. And it is further reported that the shell—I mean, the shell of the animal which bears the pearl—opens and gapes, as it were, and being opened receives into itself the dew of heaven; when it is filled with dew pure and untroubled, it becomes illumined and brings forth a large and well-formed pearl; but if at any time it receives dew darkened, or uneven, or in winter, it conceives a pearl cloudy and disfigured with spots. And this we also find that if it be intercepted by lightning when it is on the way towards the completion of the stone with which it is pregnant, it closes, and, as it were in terror, scatters and pours forth its offspring, so as to form what are called "physemata." And sometimes, as if premature, they are born small, and are somewhat cloudy though well-formed. As compared with the others the Indian pearl has these features. It is white in colour, like to silver in transparency, and shines through as with a radiance somewhat greenish yellow, and as a rule is round in form; it is also of tender skin, and more delicate than it is the nature of a stone to be; so it is delightful to behold, worthy to be celebrated among the more notable, as he who wrote on the subject of stones used to say. And this is also a mark of the best pearl, to be rounded off on the outer surface, very white in colour, very translucent, and very large in size. So much about the Indian pearl. But that found in Britain, they say, is of a golden tinge, but somewhat cloudy, and duller in sparkle. And that which is found in the strait of Bosporus is darker than that of Britain, and livid, and perfectly dim, soft and small. And that which is produced in the strait of Bosporus is not found in the "pinna" which is the pearl-bearing species of shells, but in what are called mussels; and their habitat—I mean those at Bosporus—is in the marshes. There is also said to be a fourth class of pearls in Acarnania in the "pinnæ" of oysters. These are not greatly sought after, but are irregular in form, and perfectly dark and foul in colour; and there are others also different from these in the same Acarnania which are cast away on every ground.

8. THE PARABLE INTERPRETED IN THE LIGHT OF THESE VIEWS.

Now, having collected these things out of dissertations about stones, I say that the Saviour with a knowledge of the difference of pearls, of which some are in kind goodly and others worthless, said, "The kingdom of heaven is like unto a man that is a merchant seeking goodly pearls;"[1] for, if some of the pearls had not been worthless, it would not have been said, "to a man seeking goodly pearls." Now among the words of all kinds which profess to announce truth, and among those who report them, he seeks pearls. And let the prophets be, so to speak, the mussels which conceive the dew of heaven, and become pregnant with the word of truth from heaven, the

[1] Cf. Pliny, *Nat. Hist.* ix. 54, etc.

[1] Matt. xiii. 45.

goodly pearls which, according to the phrase here set forth, the merchantman seeks. And the leader of the pearls, on the finding of which the rest are found with it, is the very costly pearl, the Christ of God, the Word which is superior to the precious letters and thoughts in the law and the prophets, on the finding of which also all the rest are easily taken. And the Saviour holds converse with all the disciples, as merchantmen who are not only seeking the goodly pearls but who have found them and possess them, when He says, "Cast not your pearls before swine."[1] Now it is manifest that these things were said to the disciples from that which is prefixed to His words, "And seeing the multitudes He went up into the mountain, and when He had sat down His disciples came unto Him;"[2] for, in the course of those words, He said, "Give not that which is holy unto the dogs, neither cast your pearls before the swine."[3] Perhaps, then, he is not a disciple of Christ, who does not possess pearls or the very costly pearl, the pearls, I mean, which are goodly; not the cloudy, nor the darkened, such as the words of the heterodox, which are brought forth not at the sunrise, but at the sunset or in the north, if it is necessary to take also into the comparison those things on account of which we found a difference in the pearls which are produced in different places. And perhaps the muddy words and the heresies which are bound up with works of the flesh, are the darkened pearls, and those which are produced in the marshes, not goodly pearls.

9. CHRIST THE PEARL OF GREAT PRICE.

Now you will connect with the man seeking goodly pearls the saying, "Seek and ye shall find,"[4] and this—"Every one that seeketh findeth."[5] For what seek ye? Or what does every one that seeketh find? I venture to answer, pearls and the pearl which he possesses, who has given up all things, and counted them as loss; "for which," says Paul, "I have counted all things but loss that I may win Christ;"[6] by "all things" meaning the goodly pearls, "that I may win Christ," the one very precious pearl. Precious, then, is a lamp to men in darkness, and there is need of a lamp until the sun rise; and precious also is the glory in the face of Moses, and of the prophets also, I think, and a beautiful sight,

1 Matt. vii. 6.
2 Matt. v. 1.
3 Matt. vii. 6.
4 Matt. vii. 7.
5 Matt. vii. 8
6 Phil. iii. 8.

by which we are introduced so as to be able to see the glory of Christ, to which the Father bears witness, saying, "This is My beloved Son in whom I am well-pleased."[1] But "that which hath been made glorious hath not been made glorious in this respect by reason of the glory that surpasseth;"[2] and there is need to us first of the glory which admits of being done away, for the sake of the glory which surpasseth; as there is need of the knowledge which is in part, which will be done away when that which is perfect comes.[3] Every soul, therefore, which comes to childhood, and is on the way to full growth, until the fulness of time is at hand, needs a tutor and stewards and guardians, in order that, after all these things, he who formerly differed nothing from a bond-servant, though he is lord of all,[4] may receive, when freed from a tutor and stewards and guardians, the patrimony corresponding to the very costly pearl, and to that which is perfect, which on its coming does away with that which is in part, when one is able to receive "the excellency of the knowledge of Christ,"[5] having been previously exercised, so to speak, in those forms of knowledge which are surpassed by the knowledge of Christ. But the multitude, not perceiving the beauty of the many pearls of the law, and all the knowledge, "in part," though it be, of the prophets, suppose that they can, without a clear exposition and apprehension of these, find in whole[6] the one precious pearl, and behold "the excellency of the knowledge of Christ," in comparison with which all things that came before such and so great knowledge, although they were not refuse in their own nature, appear to be refuse. This refuse is perhaps the "dung" thrown down beside the fig tree by the keeper of the vineyard, which is the cause of its bearing fruit.[7]

10. THE PEARL OF THE GOSPEL IN RELATION TO THE OLD TESTAMENT.

"To everything then is its season, and a time for everything under heaven,"[8] a time to gather the goodly pearls, and a time after their gathering to find the one precious pearl, when it is fitting for a man to go away and sell all that he has in order that he may buy that pearl. For as every man who is going to be wise in the words of truth must first be taught the rudiments, and further pass through the elementary instruction, and

1 Matt. iii. 17.
2 2 Cor. iii. 10.
3 1 Cor. xiii. 9, 10.
4 Cf. Gal. iv. 1, 2.
5 Phil. iii. 8.
6 *Or*, absolutely.
7 Luke xiii. 8.
8 Eccles. iii. 1.

appreciate it highly but not abide in it, as one who, having honoured it at the beginning but passed over towards perfection, is grateful for the introduction because it was useful at the first; so the perfect apprehension of the law and the prophets is an elementary discipline for the perfect apprehension of the Gospel, and all the meaning in the words and deeds of Christ.

11. THE PARABLE OF THE DRAG-NET.

"*Again the kingdom of heaven is like unto a net that was cast into the sea.*"[1] As in the case of images and statues, the likenesses are not likenesses in every respect of those things in relation to which they are made; but, for example, the image painted with wax on the plane surface of wood has the likeness of the surface along with the colour, but does not further preserve the hollows and prominences, but only their outward appearance; and in the moulding of statues an endeavour is made to preserve the likeness in respect of the hollows and the prominences, but not in respect of the colour; and, if the cast be formed of wax, it endeavours to preserve both, I mean both the colour and also the hollows and the prominences, but is not indeed an image of the things in the respect of depth; so conceive with me also that, in the case of the similitudes in the Gospel, when the kingdom of heaven is likened unto anything, the comparison does not extend to all the features of that to which the kingdom is compared, but only to those features which are required by the argument in hand. And here, accordingly, the kingdom of heaven is "like unto a net that was cast into the sea," not (as supposed by some,[2] who represent that by this word the different natures of those who have come into the net, to-wit, the evil and the righteous, are treated of), as if it is to be thought that, because of the phrase "which gathered of every kind," there are many different natures of the righteous and likewise also of the evil; for to such an interpretation all the Scriptures are opposed, which emphasise the freedom of the will, and censure those who sin and approve those who do right; or otherwise blame could not rightly attach to those of the kinds that were such by nature, nor praise to those of a better kind. For the reason why fishes are good or bad lies not in the souls of the fishes, but is based on that which the Word said with knowledge, "Let the waters bring forth creeping things with living souls,"[3] when, also, "God made great sea-monsters and every soul of creeping creatures which the waters brought forth according to their kinds."[1] There, accordingly, "The waters brought forth every soul of creeping animals according to their kinds," the cause not being in it; but here we are responsible for our being good kinds and worthy of what are called "vessels," or bad and worthy of being cast outside. For it is not the nature in us which is the cause of the evil, but it is the voluntary choice which worketh evil; and so our nature is not the cause of righteousness, as if it were incapable of admitting unrighteousness, but it is the principle which we have admitted that makes men righteous; for also you never see the kinds of things in the water changing from the bad kinds of fishes into the good, or from the better kind to the worse; but you can always behold the righteous or evil among men either coming from wickedness to virtue, or returning from progress towards virtue to the flood of wickedness. Wherefore also in Ezekiel, concerning the man who turns away from unrighteousness to the keeping of the divine commandments, it is thus written: "But if the wicked man turn away from all his wickednesses which he hath done," etc., down to the words, "that he turn from his wicked way and live;"[2] but concerning the man who returns from the advance towards virtue unto the flood of wickedness it is said, "But in the case of the righteous man turning away from his righteousness and committing iniquity," etc., down to the words, "in his sins which he hath sinned in them shall he die."[3] Let those who, from the parable of the drag-net, introduce the doctrine of different natures, tell us in regard to the wicked man who afterwards turned aside from all the wickednesses which he committed and keeps all the commandments of God, and does that which is righteous and merciful, of what nature was he when he was wicked? Clearly not of a nature to be praised. If verily of a nature to be censured, of what kind of nature can he reasonably be described, when he turns away from all his sins which he did? For if he were of the bad class of natures, because of his former deeds, how did he change to that which was better? Or if because of his subsequent deeds you would say that he was of the good class, how being good by nature did he become wicked? And you will also meet with a like dilemma in regard to the righteous man turning away from his righteousness and committing unrighteousness in all

[1] Matt. xiii. 47 [2] Valentinus and his followers. [3] Gen. i. 20.

[1] Gen. i. 21. [2] Ezek. xviii. 20–23. [3] Ezek. xviii. 24.

manner of sins. For before he turned away from righteousness, being occupied with righteous deeds he was not of a bad nature, for a bad nature could not be in righteousness, since a bad tree—that is wickedness—cannot produce good fruits,—the fruits that spring from virtue. Again, on the other hand, if he had been of a good and unchangeable nature he would not have turned away from the good after being called righteous, so as to commit unrighteousness in all his sins which he committed.

12. THE DIVINE SCRIPTURES COMPARED TO A NET.

Now, these things being said, we must hold that "the kingdom of heaven is likened to a net that was cast into the sea and gathered of every kind,[1]" in order to set forth the varied character of the principles of action among men, which are as different as possible from each other, so that the expression "gathered from every kind" embraces both those worthy of praise and those worthy of blame in respect of their proclivities towards the forms of virtues or of vices. And the kingdom of heaven is likened unto the variegated texture of a net, with reference to the Old and the New Scripture which is woven of thoughts of all kinds and greatly varied. As in the case of the fishes that fall into the net, some are found in one part of the net and some in another part, and each at the part at which it was caught, so in the case of those who have come into the net of the Scriptures you would find some caught in the prophetic net; for example, of Isaiah, according to this expression, or of Jeremiah or of Daniel; and others in the net of the law, and others in the Gospel net, and some in the apostolic net; for when one is first captured by the Word or seems to be captured, he is taken from some part of the whole net. And it is nothing strange if some of the fishes caught are encompassed by the whole texture of the net in the Scriptures, and are pressed in on every side and caught, so that they are unable to escape but are, as it were, absolutely enslaved, and not permitted to escape from the net. And this net has been cast into the sea—the wave-tossed life of men in every part of the world, and which swims in the bitter affairs of life. And before our Saviour Jesus Christ this net was not wholly filled; for the net of the law and the prophets had to be completed by Him who says, "Think not that I came to destroy the law and the prophets, I came not to destroy but to fulfil."[1] And the texture of the net has been completed in the Gospels, and in the words of Christ through the Apostles. On this account, therefore, "the kingdom of heaven is like unto a net that was cast into the sea and gathered of every kind." And, apart from what has been said, the expression, "gathered from every kind," may show forth the calling of the Gentiles from every race. And those who attended to the net which was cast into the sea are Jesus Christ, the master of the net, and "the angels who came and ministered unto Him,"[2] who do not draw up the net from the sea, nor carry it to the shore beyond the sea,—namely, to things beyond this life, unless the net be filled full, that is, unless the "fulness of the Gentiles" has come into it. But when it has come, then they draw it up from things here below, and carry it to what is figuratively called the shore, where it will be the work of those who have drawn it up, both to sit by the shore, and there to settle themselves, in order that they may place each of the good in the net into its own order, according to what are here called "vessels," but cast without and away those that are of an opposite character and are called bad. By "without" is meant the furnace of fire as the Saviour interpreted, saying, "So shall it be at the consummation of the age. The angels shall come forth and sever the wicked from among the righteous and shall cast them into the furnace of fire."[3] Only it must be observed, that we are already taught by the parable of the tares and the similitude set forth, that the angels are to be entrusted with the power to distinguish and separate the evil from the righteous; for it is said above, "The Son of man shall send forth His angels, and they shall gather out of His kingdom all things that cause stumbling, and them that do iniquity, and shall cast them into the furnace of fire: there shall be the weeping and gnashing of teeth."[4] But here it is said, "The angels shall come forth and sever the wicked from among the righteous and shall cast them into the furnace of fire."

13. RELATION OF MEN TO ANGELS.

From this it does not follow, as some suppose, that the men who are saved in Christ are superior even to the holy angels; for how can those who are cast by the holy angels into vessels be compared with those

[1] Matt. xiii. 47.

[1] Matt. v. 17.
[2] Matt. iv. 11.
[3] Matt. xiii. 49, 50.
[4] Matt. xiii. 42.

who cast them into vessels, seeing that they have been put under the authority of the angels? While we say this, we are not ignorant that the men who will be saved in Christ surpass some angels—namely, those who have not been entrusted with this office—but not all of them. For we read, "Which things angels desire to look into,"[1] where it is not said "all" angels. And we know also this—"We shall judge angels"[2]—where it is not said "all" angels. Now since these things are written about the net and about those in the net, we say that he who desires that, before the consummation of the age, and before the coming of the angels to sever the wicked from among the righteous, there should be no evil persons "of every kind" in the net, seems not to have understood the Scripture, and to desire the impossible. Wherefore let us not be surprised if, before the severing of the wicked from among the righteous by the angels who are sent forth for this purpose, we see our gatherings also filled with wicked persons. And would that those who will be cast into the furnace of fire may not be greater in number than the righteous! But since we said in the beginning, that the parables and similitudes are not to be accepted in respect of all the things to which they are likened or compared, but only in respect of some things, we must further establish from the things to be said, that in the case of the fishes, so far as their life is concerned, an evil thing happens to them when they are found in the net. For they are deprived of the life which is theirs by nature, and whether they are cast into vessels or cast away, they suffer nothing more than the loss of the life as it is in fishes; but, in the case of those to whom the parable refers, the evil thing is to be in the sea and not to come into the net, in order to be cast along with the good into vessels. And in like manner the bad fishes are cast without and thrown away; but the bad in the similitude before us are cast into "the furnace of fire," that what is said in Ezekiel about the furnace of fire may also overtake them—"And the Word of the Lord came unto me saying, Son of man behold the house of Israel is become to me all mixed with brass and iron," etc., down to the words, "And ye shall know that I the Lord have poured My fury upon you."[3]

14. THE DISCIPLES AS SCRIBES.

"*Have ye understood all these things? They say, Yea.*"[1] Christ Jesus, who knows the things in the hearts of men,[2] as John also taught concerning Him in the Gospel, puts the question not as one ignorant, but having once for all taken upon Him the nature of man, He uses also all the characteristics of a man of which "asking" is one. And there is nothing to be wondered at in the Saviour doing this, since indeed the God of the universe, bearing with the manners of men as a man beareth with the manners of his son, makes inquiry, as—"Adam, where art thou?"[3] and, "Where is Abel thy brother?"[4] But some one with a forced interpretation will say here that the words "have understood" are not to be taken interrogatively but affirmatively; and he will say that the disciples bearing testimony to His affirmation, say, "Yea." Only, whether he is putting a question or making an affirmation, it is necessarily said not "these things" only,—which is demonstrative,—not "all things" only, but "all these things." And here He seems to represent the disciples as having been scribes before the kingdom of heaven;[5] but to this is opposed what is said in the Acts of the Apostles thus, "Now when they beheld the boldness of Peter and John, and perceived that they were unlearned and ignorant men, they marvelled, and they took knowledge of them that they had been with Jesus."[6] Some one may inquire in regard to these things—if they were scribes, how are they spoken of in the Acts as unlearned and ignorant men? Or if they were unlearned and ignorant men, how are they very plainly called scribes by the Saviour? And it might be answered to these inquiries that, as a matter of fact, not all the disciples but only Peter and John are described in the Acts as unlearned and ignorant, but that there were more disciples in regard to whom, because they understood all things, it is said, "Every scribe," etc. Or it might be said that every one who has been instructed in the teaching according to the letter of the law is called a scribe, so that those who were unlearned and ignorant and led captive by the letter of the law are spoken of as scribes in a particular sense. And it is very specially the characteristic of ignorant men, who are unskilled in figurative interpretation and do not understand what is concerned with the mystical[7] exposition of the Scriptures, but believe the bare letter, and, vindicate it, that they call themselves scribes.

[1] 1 Pet. i. 12. [2] 1 Cor. vi. 3. [3] Ezek. xviii. 17-22.

[1] Matt. xiii. 51. [2] John ii. 25, [3] Gen. iii. 9. [4] Gen. iv. 9. [5] Matt. xiii. 52. [6] Acts iv. 13. [7] *Or*, anagogical.

And so one will interpret the words, "Woe unto you Scribes and Pharisees, hypocrites,"[1] as having been said to every one that knows nothing but the letter. Here you will inquire if the scribe of the Gospel be as the scribe of the law, and if the former deals with the Gospel, as the latter with the law, reading and hearing and telling "those things which contain an allegory,"[2] so as, while preserving the historic truth of the events, to understand the unerring principle of mystic interpretation applied to things spiritual, so that the things learned may not be "spiritual things whose characteristic is wickedness,"[3] but may be entirely opposite to such, namely, spiritual things whose characteristic is goodness. And one is a scribe "made a disciple to the kingdom of heaven" in the simpler sense, when he comes from Judaism and receives the teaching of Jesus Christ as defined by the Church; but he is a scribe in a deeper sense, when having received elementary knowledge through the letter of the Scriptures he ascends to things spiritual, which are called the kingdom of the heavens. And according as each thought is attained, and grasped abstractly[4] and proved by example and absolute demonstration, can one understand the kingom of heaven, so that he who abounds in knowledge free from error is in the kingdom of the multitude of what are here represented as "heavens." So, too, you will allegorise the word, "Repent, for the kingdom of the heavens is at hand,"[5] as meaning that the scribes—that is, those who rest satisfied in the bare letter—may repent of this method of interpretation and be instructed in the spiritual teaching which is called the kingdom of the heavens through Jesus Christ the living Word. Wherefore, also, so far as Jesus Christ, "who was in the beginning with God, God the word,"[6] has not His home in a soul, the kingdom of heaven is not in it, but when any one becomes nigh to admission of the Word, to him the kingdom of heaven is nigh. But if the kingdom of heaven and the kingdom of God are the same thing in reality,[7] if not in idea, manifestly to those to whom it is said, "The kingdom of God is within you,"[8] to them also it might be said, "The kingdom of heaven is within you;" and most of all because of the repentance from the letter unto the spirit; since "When one turn to the Lord, the veil over the letter is taken away. But the Lord is the Spirit."[1] And he who is truly a householder is both free and rich; rich because from the office of the scribe he has been made a disciple to the kingdom of heaven, in every word of the Old Testament, and in all knowledge concerning the new teaching of Christ Jesus, and has this riches laid up in his own treasure-house,—in heaven, in which he stores his treasure as one who has been made a disciple to the kingdom of heaven,—where neither moth doth consume, nor thieves break through.[2] And in regard to him, who, as we have said, lays up treasure in heaven, we may truly lay down that not one moth of the passions can touch his spiritual and heavenly possessions. "A moth of the passions," I said, taking the suggestion from the "Proverbs" in which it is written, "As a worm in wood, so pain woundeth the heart of man."[3] For pain is a worm and a moth, which wounds the heart which has not its treasures in heaven and spiritual things, for if a man has his treasure in these—"for where the treasure is, there will the heart be also,"[4]—he has his heart in heaven, and on account of it he says, "Though an host should encamp against me, my heart shall not fear."[5] And so neither can thieves in regard to whom the Saviour said, "All that came before Me are thieves and robbers,"[6] break through those things which are treasured up in heaven, and through the heart which is in heaven and therefore says, "He raised us up with Him, and made us to sit with Him in the heavenly places in Christ,"[7] and, "Our citizenship is in heaven."[8]

15 THE HOUSEHOLDER AND HIS TREASURY.

Now since "every scribe who has been made a disciple to the kingdom of heaven is like unto a man that is a householder who bringeth forth out of his treasury things new and old,"[9] it clearly follows, by "conversion of the proposition," as it is called, that every one who does not bring forth out of his treasury things new and old, is not a scribe who has been made a disciple unto the kingdom of heaven. We must endeavour, therefore, in every way to gather in our heart, "by giving heed to reading, to exhortation, to teaching,"[10] and by "meditating in the law of the Lord day and night,"[11] not only the new oracles of the Gospels and of the Apostles and their Revelation, but

[1] Matt. xxiii. 13.
[2] Gal. iv. 24.
[3] Eph. vi. 12.
[4] *Or*, in an exalted sense.
[5] Matt. iii. 2.
[6] John i. 1, 2.
[7] *Or*, substance.
[8] Luke xvii. 21.

[1] 2 Cor. iii. 16, 17.
[2] Matt. vi. 20.
[3] Prov. xxv. 20.
[4] Matt. vi. 21.
[5] Ps. xxvii. 3.
[6] John. x. 8.
[7] Eph. ii. 6.
[8] Phil. iii. 20.
[9] Matt. xiii. 52.
[10] 1 Tim. iv. 13.
[11] Ps. i, 2.

also the old things in the law "which has the shadow of the good things to come,"[1] and in the prophets who prophesied in accordance with them. And these things will be gathered together, when we also read and know, and remembering them, compare at a fitting time things spiritual with spiritual, not comparing things that cannot be compared with one another, but things which admit of comparison, and which have a certain likeness of diction signifying the same thing, and of thoughts and of opinions, so that by the mouth of two or three or more witnesses[2] from the Scripture, we may establish and confirm every word of God. By means of them also we must refute those who, as far as in them lies, cleave in twain the God head and cut off the New from the Old,[3] so that they are far removed from likeness to the householder who brings forth out of his treasury things new and old. And since he who is likened to any one is different from the one to whom he is likened, the scribe "who is made a disciple unto the kingdom of heaven" will be the one who is likened, but different from him is the householder "who brings out of his treasury things new and old." But he who is likened to him, as in imitation of him, wishes to do that which is like. Perhaps, then, the man who is a householder is Jesus Himself, who brings forth out of His treasury, according to the time of the teaching, things new, things spiritual, which also are always being renewed by Him in the "inner man" of the righteous, who are themselves always being renewed day by day,[4] and old things, things "written and engraven on stones,"[5] and in the stony hearts of the old man, so that by comparison of the letter and by exhibition of the spirit He may enrich the scribe who is made a disciple unto the kingdom of heaven, and make him like unto Himself; until the disciple shall be as the Master, imitating first the imitator of Christ, and after him Christ Himself, according to that which is said by Paul, "Be ye imitators of me even as I also of Christ."[6] And likewise, Jesus the householder may in the simpler sense bring forth out of His treasury things new,—that is, the evangelic teaching—and things old,—that is, the comparison of the sayings which are taken from the law and the prophets, of which we may find examples in the Gospels. And with regard to these things new and old, we must attend also to the spiritual law which says in Leviticus, "And ye shall eat old things, and the old things of the old, and ye shall bring forth the old from before the new; and I will set my tabernacle among you."[1] For we eat with blessing the old things,—the prophetic words,—and the old things of the old things,—the words of the law; and, when the new and evangelical words came, living according to the Gospel we bring forth the old things of the letter from before the new, and He sets His tabernacle in us, fulfilling the promise which He spoke, "I will dwell among them and walk in them."[2]

16. PARABLES IN RELATION TO SIMILITUDES. JESUS IN HIS OWN COUNTRY.

"*And it came to pass, when Jesus had finished these parables, He departed thence. And coming into His own country.*"[3] Since we inquired above whether the things spoken to the multitude were parables, and those spoken to the disciples were similitudes, and set forth observations bearing on this in my judgment not contemptible, you must know that the sentence which is subjoined, "And it came to pass when Jesus had finished these parables, He departed thence," will appear to be in opposition to all these arguments, as applying not only to the parables, but also to the similitudes as we have expounded. We inquire therefore whether all these things are to be rejected, or whether we must speak of two kinds of parables, those spoken to the multitudes, and those announced to the disciples; or whether we are to think of the name of parable as equivocal; or whether the saying, "And it came to pass when Jesus had finished these parables," is to be referred only to the parables above, which come before the similitudes. For, because of the saying, "To you it is given to know the mysteries of the kingdom of heaven, but to the rest in parables,"[4] it was not possible to say to the disciples, inasmuch as they were not of those without, that the Saviour spoke to them in parables. And it follows from this, that the saying, "And it came to pass when Jesus had finished these parables, He departed thence," is to be referred to the parables spoken above, or that the name parable is equivocal, or that there are two kinds of parables, or that these which we have named similitudes were not parables at all. And observe that it was outside of His own country He speaks the parables "which, when He had

[1] Heb. x. 1. [2] Matt. xviii. 16. [3] Marcion and his school. [4] 2 Cor. iv. 16. [5] 2 Cor. iii. 7. [6] 1 Cor. xi. 1.

[1] Lev. xxvi. 10, 11. [2] Lev. xxvi. 12; 2 Cor. vi. 16. [3] Matt. xiii 53, 54. [4] Matt. xiii. 11.

finished, He departed thence; and coming into His own country He taught them in their synagogue." And Mark says, "And He came into His own country and His disciples follow Him."[1] We must therefore inquire whether, by the expression, "His own country," is meant Nazareth or Bethlehem,—Nazareth, because of the saying, "He shall be called a Nazarene,"[2] or Bethlehem, since in it He was born. And further I reflect whether the Evangelists could have said, "coming to Bethlehem," or, "coming to Nazareth." They have not done so, but have named it "His country," because of something being declared in a mystic sense in the passage about His country,—namely, the whole of Judæa,—in which He was dishonoured according to the saying, "A prophet is not without honour, save in his own country."[3] And if any one thinks of Jesus Christ, "a stumbling-block to the Jews,"[4] among whom He is persecuted even until now, but proclaimed among the Gentiles and believed in,—for His word has run over the whole world,—he will see that in His own country Jesus had no honour, but that among those who were "strangers from the covenants,"[5] the Gentiles, He is held in honour. But what things He taught and spake in their synagogue the Evangelists have not recorded, but only that they were so great and of such a nature that all were astonished. And probably the things spoken were too high to be written down. Only be it noted, He taught in their synagogue, not separating from it, nor disregarding it.

17. THE BRETHREN OF JESUS.

And the saying, "*Whence hath this man this wisdom*,"[6] indicates clearly that there was a great and surpassing wisdom in the words of Jesus worthy of the saying, "And lo, a greater than Solomon is here."[7] And He was wont to do greater miracles than those wrought through Elijah and Elisha, and at a still earlier date through Moses and Joshua the son of Nun. And they spoke, wondering, (not knowing that He was the son of a virgin, or not believing it even if it was told to them, but supposing that He was the son of Joseph the carpenter,) "is not this the carpenter's son?"[8] And depreciating the whole of what appeared to be His nearest kindred, they said, "Is not His mother called Mary? And His brethren, James and Joseph and Simon and Judas? And His sisters, are they not all with us?"[9] They thought, then, that He was the son of Joseph and Mary. But some say, basing it on a tradition in the Gospel according to Peter,[1] as it is entitled, or "The Book of James,"[2] that the brethren of Jesus were sons of Joseph by a former wife, whom he married before Mary. Now those who say so wish to preserve the honour of Mary in virginity to the end, so that that body of hers which was appointed to minister to the Word which said, "The Holy Ghost shall come upon thee, and the power of the Most High shall overshadow thee,"[3] might not know intercourse with a man after that the Holy Ghost came into her and the power from on high overshadowed her. And I think it in harmony with reason that Jesus was the first-fruit among men of the purity which consists in chastity, and Mary among women; for it were not pious to ascribe to any other than to her the first-fruit of virginity. And James is he whom Paul says in the Epistle to the Galatians that he saw, "But other of the Apostles saw I none, save James the Lord's brother."[4] And to so great a reputation among the people for righteousness did this James rise, that Flavius Josephus, who wrote the "Antiquities of the Jews" in twenty books, when wishing to exhibit the cause why the people suffered so great misfortunes that even the temple was razed to the ground, said, that these things happened to them in accordance with the wrath of God in consequence of the things which they had dared to do against James the brother of Jesus who is called Christ.[5] And the wonderful thing is, that, though he did not accept Jesus as Christ, he yet gave testimony that the righteousness of James was so great; and he says that the people thought that they had suffered these things because of James. And Jude, who wrote a letter of few lines, it is true, but filled with the healthful words of heavenly grace, said in the preface, "Jude, the servant of Jesus Christ and the brother of James."[6] With regard to Joseph and Simon we have nothing to tell; but the saying, "And His sisters are they not all with us,"[7] seems to me to signify something of this nature—they mind our things, not those of Jesus, and have no unusual portion of surpassing wisdom as Jesus has. And perhaps by these things is indicated a new doubt concerning Him, that Jesus was not a man but something diviner, inasmuch as

[1] Mark vi. 1. See pp. 1–31 of this volume. [2] Matt. ii. 23. [3] Matt. xiii. 57. [4] 1 Cor. i. 23. [5] Eph. ii. 12. [6] Matt. xiii. 54. [7] Matt. xii. 42. [8] Matt. xiii. 55. [9] Matt. xiii. 55, 56.

[1] The Gospel of Peter, of which a fragment was recovered in 1886 and published in 1892. [2] Protevangelium Jacobi, c. 9. [3] Luke i. 35. [4] Gal. i. 19. [5] Jos. *Ant.* xviii. 4. [6] Jude 1. [7] Matt. xiii. 56.

He was, as they supposed, the son of Joseph and Mary, and the brother of four, and of the others—the women—as well, and yet had nothing like to any one of His kindred, and had not from education and teaching come to such a height of wisdom and power. For they also say elsewhere, "How knoweth this man letters having never learned?"[1] which is similar to what is here said. Only, though they say these things and are so perplexed and astonished, they did not believe, but were offended in Him; as if they had been mastered in the eyes of their mind by the powers which, in the time of the passion, He was about to lead in triumph on the cross.

18. PROPHETS IN THEIR OWN COUNTRY.

"*But Jesus said unto them, A prophet is not without honour, save in his own country.*"[2] We must inquire whether the expression has the same force when applied universally to every prophet (as if each one of the prophets was dishonoured in his own country only, but not as if every one who was dishonoured was dishonoured in his country); or, because of the expression being singular, these things were said about one. If, then, these words are spoken about one, these things which have been said suffice, if we refer that which is written to the Saviour. But if it is general, it is not historically true; for Elijah did not suffer dishonour in Tishbeth of Gilead, nor Elisha in Abelmeholah, nor Samuel in Ramathaim, nor Jeremiah in Anathoth. But, figuratively interpreted, it is absolutely true; for we must think of Judæa as their country, and that famous Israel as their kindred, and perhaps of the body as the house. For all suffered dishonour in Judæa from the Israel which is according to the flesh, while they were yet in the body, as it is written in the Acts of the Apostles, as having been spoken in censure to the people, "Which of the prophets did not your fathers persecute, who showed before of the coming of the Righteous one?"[3] And by Paul in the First Epistle to the Thessalonians like things are said: "For ye brethren became imitators of the churches of God which are in Judæa in Christ Jesus, for ye also suffered the same things of your own countrymen even as they did of the Jews, who both killed the Lord Jesus and the prophets, and drave out us, and please not God, and are contrary to all men."[4] A prophet, then, is not without honour among the Gentiles; for either they do not know him at all, or, having learned and received him as a prophet, they honour him. And such are those who are of the Church. Prophets suffer dishonour, first, when they are persecuted, according to historical fact, by the people, and, secondly, when their prophecy is not believed by the people. For if they had believed Moses and the prophets they would have believed Christ, who showed that when men believed Moses and the prophets, belief in Christ logically followed, and that when men did not believe Christ they did not believe Moses.[1] Moreover, as by the transgression of the law he who sins is said to dishonour God, so by not believing in that which is prophesied the prophet is dishonoured by the man who disbelieves the prophecies. And so far as the literal truth is concerned, it is useful to recount what things Jeremiah suffered among the people in relation to which he said, "And I said, I will not speak, nor will I call upon the name of the Lord."[2] And again, elsewhere, "I was continually being mocked."[3] And how great sufferings he endured from the then king of Israel are written in his prophecy. And it is also written that some of the people often came to stone Moses to death; for his fatherland was not the stones of any place, but the people who followed him, among whom also he was dishonoured. And Isaiah is reported to have been sawn asunder by the people; and if any one does not accept the statement because of its being found in the Apocryphal Isaiah,[4] let him believe what is written thus in the Epistle to the Hebrews, "They were stoned, they were sawn asunder, they were tempted;"[5] for the expression, "They were sawn asunder," refers to Isaiah, just as the words, "They were slain with the sword," refer to Zacharias, who was slain "between the sanctuary and the altar,"[6] as the Saviour taught, bearing testimony, as I think, to a Scripture, though not extant in the common and widely circulated books, but perhaps in apocryphal books. And they, too, were dishonoured in their own country among the Jews who went about "in sheep-skins, in goat-skins, being destitute, afflicted," and so on;[7] "For all that will to live godly in Christ Jesus shall suffer persecution."[8] And probably because Paul knew this,

[1] John vii. 15.
[2] Matt. xiii. 57.
[3] Acts vii. 52.
[4] 1 Thess. ii. 14, 15.

[1] John v. 46.
[2] Jer. xx. 9.
[3] Jer. xx. 7.
[4] Probably the *Ascensio Isaiæ*. Cf. Orig. *Ep. ad Afric.* c. 9.
[5] Heb. xi. 37.
[6] Matt. xxiii. 35. Cf. Orig. *Ep. ad Afric.* c. 9.
[7] Heb. xi. 37.
[8] 2 Tim. iii. 12.

"That a prophet has no honour in his own country," though he preached the Word in many places he did not preach it in Tarsus. And the Apostles on this account left Israel and did that which had been enjoined on them by the Saviour, "Make disciples of all the nations,"[1] and, "Ye shall be My witnesses both in Jerusalem and in all Judæa and Samaria, and unto the uttermost part of the earth."[2] For they did that which had been commanded them in Judæa and Jerusalem; but, since a prophet has no honour in his own country, when the Jews did not receive the Word, they went away to the Gentiles. Consider, too, if, because of the fact that the saying, "I will pour forth of My Spirit upon all flesh, and they shall prophesy,"[3] has been fulfilled in the churches from the Gentiles, you can say that those formerly of the world and who by believing became no longer of the world, having received the Holy Spirit in their own country—that is, the world—and prophesying, have not honour, but are dishonoured. Wherefore blessed are they who suffer the same things as the prophets, according to what was said by the Saviour, "For in the same manner did their fathers unto the prophets."[4] Now if any one who attends carefully to these things be hated and attacked, because of his living with rigorous austerity, and his reproof of sinners, as a man who is persecuted and reproached for the sake of righteousness, he will not only not be grieved, but will rejoice and be exceeding glad, being assured that, because of these things, he has great reward in heaven from Him who likened him to the prophets on the ground of his having suffered the same things. Therefore, he who zealously imitates the prophetic life, and attains to the spirit which was in them, must be dishonoured in the world, and in the eyes of sinners, to whom the life of the righteous man is a burden.

19. RELATION OF FAITH AND UNBELIEF TO THE SUPERNATURAL POWERS OF JESUS.

Following this you may see, "*He did not there many mighty works because of their unbelief.*"[5] We are taught by these things that powers were found in those who believed, since "to every one that hath shall be given and he shall have abundance,"[6] but among unbelievers not only did the powers not work, but as Mark wrote, "They could not work."[7] For attend to the words, "He could not there do any mighty works," for it is not said, "He would not," but "He could not;" as if there came to the power when working co-operation from the faith of him on whom the power was working, but this co-operation was hindered in its exercise by unbelief. See, then, that to those who said, "Why could we not cast it out?" He said, "Because of your little faith."[1] And to Peter, when he began to sink, it was said, "O thou of little faith, wherefore didst thou doubt?"[2] But, moreover, she who had the issue of blood, who did not ask for the cure, but only reasoned that if she were to touch the hem of His garment she would be healed, was healed on the spot. And the Saviour, acknowledging the method of healing, says, "Who touched Me? For I perceived that power went forth from Me."[3] And perhaps, as in the case of material things there exists in some things a natural attraction towards some other thing, as in the magnet for iron, and in what is called naphtha for fire, so there is an attraction in such faith towards the divine power, according to what is said, "If ye have faith as a grain of mustard seed, ye shall say unto this mountain, Remove hence to yonder place, and it shall remove."[4] And Matthew and Mark, wishing to set forth the excellency of the divine power, that it has power even in unbelief, but not so great power as it has in the faith of those who are being benefited, seem to me to have said with accuracy, not that He did not "any" mighty works because of their unbelief, but that He did not "many" there.[5] And Mark also does not say, that He could not do any mighty work there, and stop at that point, but added, "Save that He laid His hands upon a few sick folk and healed them,"[6] the power in Him thus overcoming the unbelief. Now it seems to me that, as in the case of material things, tillage is not sufficient in itself for the gathering in of the fruits, unless the air cooperates to this end, nay, rather, He who forms the air with whatever quality He wills and makes it whatever He wills; nor the air apart from tillage, but rather He who by His providence has enacted that the things which spring up from the earth could not spring up apart from tillage; for this He has done once for all in the law, "Let the earth put forth grass sowing seed after its

[1] Matt. xxviii. 19. [2] Acts i. 8. [3] Joel ii. 28
[4] Luke vi. 23. [5] Matt. xiii. 58. [6] Matt. xiii. 12.
[7] Matt. xvii. 19, 20.

[1] Matt. xiv. 31. [2] Luke viii. 45, 46.
[3] Matt. xvii. 20. [4] Matt. xiii. 58.
[5] Mark vi. 5. [6] Mark vi. 5.

kind and after its likeness;"[1] so also neither do the operations of the powers, apart from the faith of those who are being healed, exhibit the absolute work of healing, nor faith, however great it may be, apart from the divine power. And that which is written about wisdom, you may apply also to faith, and to the virtues specifically, so as to make a precept of this kind, "If any one be perfect in wisdom among the sons of men, and the power that comes from Thee be wanting, he will be reckoned as nothing;"[2] or, "If any one be perfect in self-control, so far as is possible for the sons of men, and the control that is from Thee be wanting, he will be reckoned as nothing;" or, "If any one be perfect in righteousness, and in the rest of virtues, and the righteousness and the rest of the virtues that are from Thee be wanting to him, he will be reckoned as nothing." Wherefore, "Let not the wise man glory in his wisdom, nor the strong man in his strength,"[3] for that which is fit matter for glorying is not ours, but is the gift of God; the wisdom is from Him, and the strength is from Him; and so with the rest.

20. DIFFERENT CONCEPTIONS OF JOHN THE BAPTIST.

"*At that season Herod the tetrarch heard the report concerning Jesus and said unto his own servants, This is John the Baptist.*"[4] In Mark[5] it is the same, and also in Luke.[6] The Jews had different opinions, some false, such as the Sadducees held about the resurrection of the dead, that they do not rise, and in regard to angels that they do not exist, but that those things which were written about them were only to be interpreted figuratively, but had no reality in point of fact; and some true opinions, such as were taught by the Pharisees about the resurrection of the dead that they rise. We must therefore here inquire, whether the opinion regarding the soul, mistakenly held by Herod and some from among the people, was somewhat like this—that John, who a little before had been slain by him, had risen from the dead after he had been beheaded, and was the same person under a different name, and being now called Jesus was possessed of the same powers which formerly wrought in John. For what credibility is there in the idea that One, who was so widely known to the whole people, and whose name was noised abroad in the whole of Judæa, whom they declared to be the son of the carpenter and Mary, and to have such and such for brothers and sisters, was thought to be not different from[1] John whose father was Zacharias, and whose mother was Elisabeth, who were themselves not undistinguished among the people? But it is probable that the fact of his being the Son of Zacharias was not unknown to the people, who thought with regard to John that he was truly a prophet, and were so numerous that the Pharisees, in order to avoid the appearance of saying that which was displeasing to the people, were afraid to answer the question, "Was his baptism from heaven or from men?"[2] And perhaps, also, to some of them had come the knowledge of the incident of the vision which was seen in the temple, when Gabriel appeared to Zacharias. What credibility, forsooth, has the erroneous opinion, whether of Herod or of some of the people, that John and Jesus were not two persons, but that it was one and the same person John who rose from the dead after that he had been beheaded and was called Jesus? Some one might say, however, that Herod and some of those of the people held the false dogma of the transmigration of souls into bodies, in consequence of which they thought that the former John had appeared again by a fresh birth, and had come from the dead into life as Jesus. But the time between the birth of John and the birth of Jesus, which was not more than six months, does not permit this false opinion to be considered credible. And perhaps rather some such idea as this was in the mind of Herod, that the powers which wrought in John had passed over to Jesus, in consequence of which He was thought by the people to be John the Baptist. And one might use the following line of argument. Just as because of the spirit and the power of Elijah, and not because of his soul, it is said about John, "This is Elijah which is to come,"[3] the spirit in Elijah and the power in him having gone over to John—so Herod thought that the powers in John wrought in his case works of baptism and teaching,—for John did not one miracle,[4] but in Jesus miraculous portents. It may be said that something of this kind was the thought of those who said that Elijah had appeared in Jesus, or that one of the old prophets had risen.[5] But the opinion of those who said that Jesus was "a prophet even as one of the prophets,"[6] has no bearing on the question. False,

[1] Gen. i. 11.
[2] Wisdom of Solomon ix. 6.
[3] Jer. ix. 23.
[4] Matt. xiv. 1.
[5] Mark vi. 14.
[6] Luke ix. 7.

[1] *Or*, none other than.
[2] Matt. xxi. 25.
[3] Matt. xi. 14.
[4] John x. 41.
[5] Luke ix. 8.
[6] Mark vi. 15.

then, is the saying concerning Jesus, whether that recorded to have been the view of Herod, or that spoken by others. Only, the saying, "That John went before in the spirit and power of Elijah,"[1] which corresponds to the thoughts which they were now cherishing concerning John and Jesus, seems to me more credible. But since we learned, in the first place, that when the Saviour after the temptation heard that John was given up, He retreated into Galilee, and in the second place, that when John was in prison and heard the things about Jesus he sent two of his disciples and said to Him, "Art thou He that cometh, or look we for another?"[2] and in the third place, generally that Herod said about Jesus, "It is John the Baptist, he is risen from the dead,"[3] but we have not previously learned from any quarter the manner in which the Baptist was killed, therefore Matthew has now recorded it, and Mark almost like unto him; but Luke passed over in silence the greater part of the narrative as it is found in them."[4]

21. HEROD AND THE BAPTIST.

The narrative of Matthew is as follows,—"*for Herod had laid hold on John and bound him in the prison.*"[5] In reference to these things, it seems to me, that as the law and the prophets were until John,[6] after whom the grace of prophecy ceased from among the Jews; so the authority of those who had rule among the people, which included the power to kill those whom they thought worthy of death, existed until John; and when the last of the prophets was unlawfully killed by Herod, the king of the Jews was deprived of the power of putting to death; for, if Herod had not been deprived of it, Pilate would not have condemned Jesus to death; but for this Herod would have sufficed along with the council of the chief priests and elders of the people, met for the purpose. And then I think was fulfilled that which was spoken as follows by Jacob to Judah: "A ruler shall not depart from Judah, nor a leader from Israel, until that come which is laid up in store, and he is the expectation of the Gentiles."[7] And perhaps also the Jews were deprived of this power, the Providence of God arranging for the spread of the teaching of Christ among the people, so that even if this were hindered by the Jews, the opposition might not go so far as the slaying of believers, which seemed to be according to law. "But Herod laid hold on John and bound him in prison and put him away,"[1] by this act signifying that, so far as it depended on his power and on the wickedness of the people, he bound and imprisoned the prophetic word, and prevented him from continuing to abide a herald of the truth in freedom as formerly. But this Herod did for the sake of Herodias, the wife of his brother Philip. For John said unto him, "It is not lawful for thee to have her."[2] Now this Philip was tetrarch of the region of Ituræa and of Trachonitis. Some, then, suppose that, when Philip died leaving a daughter, Herodias, Herod married his brother's wife, though the law permitted marriage only when there were no children. But, as we find nowhere clear evidence that Philip was dead, we conclude that a yet greater transgression was done by Herod, namely, that he had induced his brother's wife to revolt from her husband while he was still living.

22. THE DANCING OF HERODIAS. THE KEEPING OF OATHS.

Wherefore John, endued with prophetic boldness and not terrified at the royal dignity of Herod, nor through fear of death keeping silence in regard to so flagrant a sin, filled with a divine spirit said to Herod, "It is not lawful for thee to have her; for it is not lawful for thee to have the wife of thy brother." For Herod having laid hold on John bound him and put him in prison, not daring to slay him outright and to take away the prophetic word from the people; but the wife of the king of Trachonitis—which is a kind of evil opinion and wicked teaching—gave birth to a daughter of the same name, whose movements, seemingly harmonious, pleasing Herod, who was fond of matters connected with birthdays, became the cause of there being no longer a prophetic head among the people. And up to this point I think that the movements of the people of the Jews, which seem to be according to the law, were nothing else than the movements of the daughter of Herodias; but the dancing of Herodias was opposed to that holy dancing with which those who have not danced will be reproached when they hear the words, "We piped unto you, and ye did not dance."[3] And on birthdays, when the lawless word reigns over them, they dance so that their movements please that word. Some one of those before us has observed what is written in Genesis about the birthday of Pharaoh, and has told

[1] Luke i. 17. [2] Matt. xi. 2, 3. [3] Matt. xiv. 2.
[4] The question of John's relation to Jesus and of the supposed transcorporation, is more fully discussed by Origen in his Commentary on John, book vi. 7, p. 353, sqq.
[5] Matt. xiv. 3. [6] Luke xvi. 16. [7] Gen. xlix. 10.

[1] Matt. xiv. 3. [2] Matt. xiv. 3, 4. [3] Matt. xi. 17; Luke vii. 32.

that the worthless man who loves things connected with birth keeps birthday festivals; and we, taking this suggestion from him, find in no Scripture that a birthday was kept by a righteous man. For Herod was more unjust than that famous Pharaoh; for by the latter on his birthday feast a chief baker is killed;[1] but by the former, John, "than whom no one greater hath risen among those born of women,"[2] in regard to whom the Saviour says, "But for what purpose did ye go out? To see a prophet? Yea, I say unto you, and more than a prophet."[3] But thanks be unto God, that, even if the grace of prophecy was taken from the people, a grace greater than all that was poured forth among the Gentiles by our Saviour Jesus Christ, who became "free among the dead;"[4] for "though He were crucified through weakness, yet He liveth through the power of God."[5] Consider also the word in which pure and impure meats are inquired into; but prophecy is despised when it is brought forward in a charger instead of meat. But the Jews have not the head of prophecy, inasmuch as they disown the crown of all prophecy, Christ Jesus; and the prophet is beheaded, because of an oath in a case where the duty was rather to break the oath than to keep the oath; for the charge of rashness in taking an oath and of breaking it because of the rashness is not the same in guilt as the death of a prophet. And not on this account alone is he beheaded, but because "of those who sat at meat with him," who preferred that the prophet should be killed rather than live. And they recline at the same table and also feast along with the evil word which reigns over the Jews, who make merry over his birth. At times you may make a graceful application of the passage to those who swear rashly and wish to hold fast oaths which are taken with a view to unlawful deeds, by saying that not every keeping of oaths is seemly, just as the keeping of the oath of Herod was not. And mark, further, that not openly but secretly and in prison does Herod put John to death. For even the present word of the Jews does not openly deny the prophecies, but virtually and in secret denies them, and is convicted of disbelieving them. For as "if they believed Moses they would have believed Jesus,"[6] so if they had believed the prophets they would have received Him who had been the subject of prophecy. But disbelieving Him they also disbelieve them, and cut off and confine in prison the prophetic word, and hold it dead and divided, and in no way wholesome, since they do not understand it. But we have the whole Jesus, the prophecy concerning Him being fulfilled which said, "A bone shall not be broken."[1]

23. THE WITHDRAWAL OF JESUS.

And the disciples of John having come bury his remains, and "*they went and told Jesus.*"[2] And He withdrew to a desert place,—that is, the Gentiles—and after the killing of the prophet multitudes followed Him from the cities everywhere; seeing which to be great He had compassion on them, and healed their sick; and afterwards with the loaves which were blessed and multiplied from a few loaves He feeds those who followed Him. "*Now when Jesus heard it He withdrew thence in a boat to a desert place apart.*"[3] The letter teaches us to withdraw as far as it is in our power from those who persecute us, and from expected conspiracies through words; for this would be to act according to prudence; and, when one can keep outside of critical positions, to go to meet them is rash and headstrong. For who would still hesitate about avoiding such things, when not only did Jesus retreat in view of what happened to John, but also taught and said, "If they persecute you in this city, flee ye into the other"?[4] When a temptation comes which is not in our power to avoid, we must endure it with exceeding nobleness and courage; but, when it is in our power to avoid it, not to do so is rash. But since after the letter we must also investigate the place according to the mystical meaning, we must say that, when prophecy was plotted against among the Jews and destroyed, because of their giving honour to matters of birthdays, and in respect of their reception of vain movements which, though conceived by the ruler of the wicked and those who feast along with him to be regular and pleasing to them, were irregular and out of tune, if truth be umpire, then Jesus withdraws from the place in which prophecy was attacked and condemned; and He withdraws to the place which had been barren of God among the Gentiles, in order that the Word of God, when the kingdom was taken from the Jews and "given to a nation bringing forth the fruits thereof,"[5] might be among the Gentiles; and, on

[1] Gen. xl. 20. [2] Matt. xi. 11. [3] Luke vii. 26. [4] Ps. lxxxviii. 6. [5] 2 Cor. xiii. 4. [6] John v. 46.

[1] Ex. xii. 46; John xix. 36. [2] Matt. xiv. 12. [3] Matt. xiv. 13. [4] Matt. x. 23. [5] Matt. xxi. 43.

account of it, "the children of the desolate one," who had not been instructed either in the law or the prophets, "might be more than of her who has the husband,"[1] that is, the law. When, then, the word was of old among the Jews, it was not so among them as it is among the Gentiles; wherefore it is said that, "in a boat,"—that is, in the body—He went to the desert place apart, when He heard about the killing of the prophet. And, having come into the desert place apart, He was in it, because that the Word dwelt apart, and His teaching was contrary to the customs and usages which obtained among the Gentiles. And the crowds among the Gentiles, when they heard that Jesus had come to stay in their desert, and that He was apart, as we have already reported, followed Him from their own cities, because each had left the superstitious customs of his fathers and come to the law of Christ. And by land they followed Him, and not in a boat, inasmuch as not with the body but with the soul only, and with the resolution to which they had been persuaded by the Word, they followed the Image of God. And to them Jesus comes out, as they were not able to go to Him, in order that, having gone to those who were without, He might lead within those who were without. And great is the crowd without to whom the Word of God goes out, and, having poured out upon it the light of His "visitation," beholds it; and, seeing that they were rather deserving of being pitied, because they were in such circumstances, as a lover of men He who was impassible suffered the emotion of pity, and not only had pity but healed their sick, who had sicknesses diverse and of every kind arising from their wickedness.

24. THE DIVERSE FORMS OF SPIRITUAL SICKNESS.

And, if you wish to see of what nature are the sicknesses of the soul, contemplate with me the lovers of money, and the lovers of ambition, and the lovers of boys, and if any be fond of women; for these also beholding among the crowds and taking compassion upon them, He healed. For not every sin is to be considered a sickness, but that which has settled down in the whole soul. For so you may see the lovers of money wholly intent on money and upon preserving and gathering it, the lovers of ambition wholly intent on a little glory, for they gape for praise from the masses and the vulgar; and analogously you will understand in the case of the rest which we have named, and if there be any other like to them. Since, then, when expounding the words, "He healed their sick,"[1] we said that not every sin is a sickness, it is fitting to discuss from the Scripture the difference of these. The Apostle indeed says, writing to the Corinthians who had diverse sicknesses, "For this cause many among you are weak and sickly, and not a few sleep."[2] Hear Him in these words, knitting a band and making it plaited of different sins, according as some are weak, and others sickly more than weak, and others, in comparison with both, are asleep. For some, because of impotence of soul, having a tendency to slip into any sin whatever, although they may not be wholly in the grasp of any form of sin, as the sickly are, are only weak; but others who, instead of loving God "with all their soul and all their heart and all their mind," love money, or a little glory, or wife, or children, are suffering from something worse than weakness, and are sickly. And those who sleep are those who, when they ought to be taking heed and watching with the soul, are not doing this, but by reason of great want of attention are nodding in resolution and are drowsy in their reflections, such as "in their dreamings defile the flesh, and set at naught that which is highest in authority, and rail at dignities."[3] And these, because they are asleep, live in an atmosphere of vain and dream-like fancies concerning realities, not admitting the things which are actually true, but deceived by what appears in their vain imaginations, in regard to whom it is said in Isaiah, "Like as when a thirsty man dreams that he is drinking, but when he has risen up is still thirsty, and his soul has cherished a vain hope, so shall be the wealth of all the nations as many as have warred in Jerusalem."[4] If, then, we have seemed to make a digression in recounting the difference between the weak and the sickly and those that sleep, because of that which the Apostle said in the letter to the Corinthians which we have expounded, we have made the digression in our desire to represent what is meant to be understood by the saying, "And He healed their sick."[5]

25. HEALING PRECEDES PATICIPATION IN THE LOAVES OF JESUS.

After this the word says, "*And when*

[1] Isa. liv. 1; Gal. iv. 27.

[1] Matt. xiv. 14. [2] 1 Cor. xi. 30. [3] Jude 8.
[4] Isa. xxix. 8 (LXX., which has "against mount Zion," where Origen has "in Jerusalem").
[5] Matt. xiv. 14.

even was come, His disciples came to Him, saying, The place is desert and the time is already past; send, therefore, the multitudes away, that they may go into the villages and buy themselves food."[1] And first observe that when about to give to the disciples the loaves of blessing, that they might set them before the multitudes, He healed the sick, in order that, having been restored to health, they might participate in the loaves of blessing; for while they are yet sickly, they are not able to receive the loaves of the blessing of Jesus. But if any one, when he ought to listen to the precept, "But let each prove himself, and so let him eat of the bread," etc.,[1] does not obey these words, but in haphazard fashion participates in the bread of the Lord and His cup, he becomes weak or sickly, or even—if I may use the expression—on account of being stupefied by the power of the bread, asleep.

BOOK XI.

INTRODUCTION TO THE FEEDING OF THE FIVE THOUSAND.

And when even was come His disciples came to Him,"[2] that is, at the consummation of the age in regard to which we may fitly say what is found in the Epistle of John, "It is the last hour."[3] They, not yet understanding what the Word was about to do, say to Him, "The place is desert,"[4] seeing the desert condition of the masses in respect of God and the Law and the Word; but they say to Him, "The time is past,"[5] as if the fitting season of the law and prophets had passed. Perhaps they spoke this saying, in reference to the word of Jesus, that because of the beheading of John both the law and the prophets who were until John had ceased.[6] "The time is past," therefore they say, and no food is at hand, because the season of it is no longer present, that those who have followed Thee in the desert may serve the law and the prophets. And, further, the disciples say, "Send them away,"[7] that each one may buy food, if he cannot from the cities, at least from the villages,—places more ignoble. Such things the disciples said, because, after the letter of the law had been abrogated and prophecies had ceased, they despaired of unexpected and new food being found for the multitudes. But see what Jesus answers to the disciples though He does not cry out and plainly say it: "You suppose that, if the great multitude go away from Me in need of food, they will find it in villages rather than with Me, and among bodies of men, not of citizens but of villagers, rather than by abiding with Me. But I declare unto you, that in regard to that of which you suppose they are in need they are not in need, for they have no need to go away; but in regard to that of which you think they have no need—that is, of Me—as if I could not feed them, of this contrary to your expectation they have need. Since, then, I have trained you, and made you fit to give rational food to them who are in need of it, give ye to the crowds who have followed Me to eat; for ye have the power, which ye have received from Me, of giving the multitudes to eat; and if ye had attended to this, ye would have understood that I am far more able to feed them, and ye would not have said, 'Send the multitudes away that they may go and buy food for themselves.'"[2]

2. EXPOSITION OF THE DETAILS OF THE MIRACLE.

Jesus, then, because of the power which He gave to the disciples, even the power of nourishing others, said, Give ye them to eat.[3] But (not denying that they can give loaves, but thinking that there were much too few and not sufficient to feed those who followed Jesus, and not considering that when Jesus takes each loaf—the Word—He extends it as far as He wills, and makes it suffice for all whomsoever He desires to nourish), the disciples say, We have here but five loaves and two fishes.[4] Perhaps by the five loaves they meant to make a veiled reference to the sensible words of the Scriptures, corresponding in number on this account to the five senses, but by the two fishes either to the word expressed[5] and the word conceived,[6] which are a relish, so to speak, to the sensible things contained in the Scriptures;

---

[1] Matt. xiv. 15. [2] Matt. xiv. 15. [3] 1 John ii. 18. [4] Matt. xiv. 15. [5] Matt. xiv. 15. [6] Luke xvi. 16. [7] Matt. xiv. 15.

[1] 1 Cor. xi. 28. [2] Matt. xiv. 15. [3] Matt. xiv. 16. [4] Matt. xiv. 17. [5] λόγος προφορικός. [6] λόγος ἐνδιάθετος.

or, perhaps, to the word which had come to them about the Father and the Son. Wherefore also after His resurrection He ate of a broiled fish,[1] having taken a part from the disciples, and having received that theology about the Father which they were in part able to declare to Him. Such is the contribution we have been able to give to the exposition of the word about the five loaves and the two fishes; and probably those, who are better able than we to gather together the five loaves and the two fishes among themselves, would be able to give a fuller and better interpretation of their meaning. It must be observed, however, that while in Matthew, Mark, and Luke,[2] the disciples say that they have the five loaves and the two fishes, without indicating whether they were wheaten or of barley, John alone says, that the loaves were barley loaves.[3] Wherefore, perhaps, in the Gospel of John the disciples do not acknowledge that the loaves are with them, but say in John, "There is a lad here who has five barley loaves and two fishes."[4] And so long as these five loaves and two fishes were not carried by the disciples of Jesus, they did not increase or multiply, nor were they able to nourish more; but, when the Saviour took them, and in the first placed looked up to heaven, with the rays of His eyes, as it were, drawing down from it power which was to be mingled with the loaves and the fishes which were about to feed the five thousand; and after this blessed the five loaves and the two fishes, increasing and multiplying them by the word and the blessing; and in the third place dividing and breaking He gave to the disciples that they might set them before the multitudes, then the loaves and the fishes were sufficient, so that all ate and were satisfied, and some portions of the loaves which had been blessed they were unable to eat. For so much remained over to the multitudes, which was not according to the capacity of the multitudes but of the disciples who were able to take up that which remained over of the broken pieces, and to place it in baskets filled with that which remained over, which were in number so many as the tribes of Israel. Concerning Joseph, then, it is written in the Psalms, "His hands served in the basket,"[5] but about the disciples of Jesus that they took up that which remained over of the broken pieces twelve baskets, twelve baskets, I take it, not half-full but filled. And there are, I think, up to the present time, and will be until the consummation of the age with the disciples of Jesus, who are superior to the multiudes, the twelve baskets, filled with the broken pieces of living bread which the multitudes cannot eat. Now those who ate of the five loaves which existed before the twelve baskets that remained over, were kindred in nature to the number five; for those who ate had reached the stage of sensible things, since also they were nourished by Him who looked up to heaven and blessed and brake them, and were not boys nor women, but men. For there are, I think, even in sensible foods differences, so that some of them belong to those who "have put away childish things,"[1] and some to those who are still babes and carnal in Christ.

3. THE EXPOSITION OF DETAILS CONTINUED. THE SITTING DOWN ON THE GRASS. THE DIVISION INTO COMPANIES.

We have spoken these things because of the words, "*They that did eat were five thousand men, beside children and women,*"[2] which is an ambiguous expression; for either those who ate were five thousand men, and among those who ate there was no child or woman; or the men only were five thousand, the children and the women not being reckoned. Some, then, as we have said by anticipation, have so understood the passage that neither children nor women were present, when the increase and multiplication of the five loaves and the two fishes took place. Bnt some one might say that, while many ate and according to their desert and capacity participated in the loaves of blessing, some worthy to be numbered, corresponding to the men of twenty years old who are numbered in the Book of Numbers,[3] were Israelitish men, but others who were not worthy of such account and numbering were children and women. Moreover, interpret with me allegorically the children in accordance with the passage, "I could not speak unto you as unto spiritual, but as unto carnal, as unto babes in Christ;"[4] and the women in accordance with the saying, "I wish to present you all as a pure virgin to Christ;"[5] and the men according to the saying, "When I am become a man I have put away childish things."[6] Let us not pass by without exposition the words, "*He commanded the multitudes to sit down on the grass, and He took the five loaves and the two*

[1] Luke xxiv. 42, 43. [2] Matt. xiv. 17; Mark vi. 38; Luke ix. 13. [3] John vi. 9. [4] John vi. 9. [5] Ps. lxxxi. 7.

[1] 1 Cor. xiii. 11. [2] Matt. xiv. 21. [3] Num. i. 3. [4] 1 Cor. iii. 1. [5] 2 Cor. xi. 2. [6] 1 Cor. xiii. 11.

fishes, and looking up to heaven, He blessed, and brake, and gave the loaves to the disciples, and the disciples to the multitudes. And they did all eat."[1] For what is meant by the words, "And He commanded all the multitudes to sit down on the grass?" And what are we to understand in the passage worthy of the command of Jesus? Now, I think that He commanded the multitudes to sit down on the grass because of what is said in Isaiah, "All flesh is grass;"[2] that is to say, He commanded them to put the flesh under, and to keep in subjection "the mind of the flesh,"[3] that so any one might be able to partake of the loaves which Jesus blesses. Then since there are different orders of those who need the food which Jesus supplies and all are not nourished by equal words, on this account I think that Mark has written, "And He commanded them that they should all sit down by companies upon the green grass; and they sat down in ranks by hundreds and by fifties;"[4] but Luke, "And He said unto His disciples, Make them sit down in companies about fifty each."[5] For it was necessary that those who were to find rest in the food of Jesus should either be in the order of the hundred—the sacred number—which is consecrated to God, because of the unit, (in it) or in the order of the fifty—the number which embraces the remission of sins, in accordance with the mystery of the Jubilee which took place every fifty years, and of the feast at Pentecost. And I think that the twelve baskets were in the possession of the disciples to whom it was said "Ye shall sit upon twelve thrones judging the twelve tribes of Israel."[6] And as the throne of him who judges the tribe of Reuben might be said to be a mystery, and the throne of him who judges the tribe of Simeon, and another of him who judges the tribe of Judah, and so on with the others; so there might be a basket of the food of Reuben, and another of Simeon, and another of Levi. But it is not in accordance with our present discourse now to digress so far from the subject in hand as to collect what is said about the twelve tribes, and separately what is said about each of them, and to say what each tribe of Israel may signify.

4. THE MULTITUDES AND THE DISCIPLES CONTRASTED.

"*And straightway He constrained the disciples to enter into the boat, and to go before Him unto the other side, till He should send the multitudes away."*[1] It should be observed how often in the same passages is mentioned the word, "the multitudes," and another word, "the disciples," so that by observing and bringing together the passages about this matter it may be seen that the aim of the Evangelists was to represent by means of the Gospel history the differences of those who come to Jesus; of whom some are the multitudes and are not called disciples, and others are the disciples who are better than the multitudes. It is sufficient, however, for the present, for us to set forth a few sayings, so that any one who is moved by them may do the like with the whole of the Gospels. It is written then—as if the multitudes were below, but the disciples were able to come to Jesus when He went up into the mountain, where the multitudes were not able to be—as follows: "And seeing the multitudes He went up into the mountain, and when He had sat down His disciples came unto Him; and He opened His mouth and taught them saying, Blessed are the poor in spirit," etc.[2] And again in another place, as the multitudes stood in need of healing, it is said, "Many multitudes followed Him and He healed them."[3] We do not find any healing recorded of the disciples; since if any one is already a disciple of Jesus he is whole, and being well he needs Jesus not as a physician but in respect of His other powers. Again in another place, when He was speaking to the multitudes, His mother and His brethren stood without, seeking to speak to Him; this was made known to Him by some one to whom He answered, stretching forth His hand not towards the multitudes but towards the disciples, and said, "Behold My mother and My brethren."[4] And bearing testimony to the disciples as doing the will of the Father which is in heaven, He added, "He is My brother and sister and mother."[5] And again in another place it is written, "All the multitude stood on the beach and He spake to them many things in parables."[6] Then after the parable of the Sowing, it was no longer the multitudes but the disciples who came and said to Him, not "Why speakest thou to us in parables," but, "Why speakest thou to them in parables."[7] Then also He answered and said, not to the multitudes but to the disciples, "To you it is given to know the mysteries of the kingdom of heaven, but to the rest in parables."[8]

---

[1] Matt xiv. 19, 20. [2] Isa. xl. 6. [3] Rom. viii. 6.
[4] Mark vi. 39, 40. [5] Luke ix. 14. [6] Matt. xix. 28.

[1] Matt. xiv. 22. [2] Matt. v. 1–3. [3] Matt. xii. 15.
[4] Matt. xiv. 46–49. [5] Matt. xiv. 50. [6] Matt. xiii. 2, 3.
[7] Matt. xiii. 10. [8] Matt. xiii. 11.

Accordingly, of those who come to the name of Jesus some, who know the mysteries of the kingdom of heaven, would be called disciples; but those to whom such a privilege is not given would be called multitudes, who would be spoken of as inferior to the disciples. For observe carefully that He said to the disciples, "To you it is given to know the mysteries of the kingdom of heaven," but about the multitudes, "To them it is not given."[1] And in another place He dismisses the multitudes indeed, and goes into the house,[2] but He does not dismiss the disciples; and there came to Him into His house, not the multitudes but His disciples, saying, "Declare to us the parable of the tares of the field."[3] Moreover, also, in another place when Jesus heard the things concerning John and withdrew in a boat to a desert place apart, the multitudes followed Him; when He came forth and saw a great multitude He had compassion on them and healed their sick—the sick of the multitudes, not of the disciples.[4] "And when even was come there came to Him," not the multitudes, but the disciples, as being different from the multitudes, saying, "Send the multitudes away that they may go into the villages and buy themselves food."[5] And, further, when Jesus took the five loaves and the two fishes, and looking up to heaven He blessed and brake the loaves, He gave not to the multitudes but to the disciples,[6] that the disciples might give to the multitudes who were not able to take from Him, but received with difficulty at the hands of the disciples the loaves of the blessing of Jesus, and did not eat even all these; for the multitudes were filled and left that which remained over in twelve baskets which were full.

5. THE DISCIPLES IN CONFLICT. JESUS WALKS UPON THE WATERS.

The reason why we have taken up this subject is the passage under discussion which tells that Jesus separated the disciples from the multitudes, and constrained them to enter into the boat and to go before Him unto the other side until He Himself should send the multitudes away;[7] for the multitudes were not able to go away to the other side, as they were not in the mystic sense Hebrews, which are by interpretation, "dwelling on the other side." But this was the work of the disciples of Jesus—I mean to go away to the other side, and to pass beyond things seen and material, as temporal, and to go on to things unseen and eternal. To be dismissed by Jesus was a sufficient act of kindness bestowed on the multitudes by Jesus; for just because they were multitudes they were not able to go away to the other side; and this kind of dismissal no one has the power to effect save Jesus only, and it is not possible for any one to be dismissed unless he has first eaten of the loaves which Jesus blesses. Nor is it possible for any one to eat of the loaves of blessing of Jesus unless he has done as Jesus commanded and sat down upon the grass as we have told. Nor again was it possible for the multitudes to do this unless they had followed Jesus from their own cities, when He withdrew into a desert place apart. And at first, when He was asked by the disciples to send away the multitudes, He did not send them away until He had fed them with the loaves of blessing; but now He sends them away, having first constrained the disciples to enter into the boat; and He sends them away, while they were somewhere below,—for the desert was below,—but He Himself went up into the mountain to pray.[1] And you must observe this, that immediately after the five thousand had been fed, Jesus constrained the disciples to embark into the boat, and to go before Him unto the other side. Only, the disciples were not able to go before Jesus to the other side; but, when they had got as far as the middle of the sea, and the boat was distressed "because the wind was contrary to them,"[2] they were afraid when about the fourth watch of the night Jesus came to them. And if Jesus had not gone up into the boat neither would the wind which was contrary to the disciples who were sailing have ceased, nor would those who were sailing have gone across and come to the other side. And, perhaps, wishing to teach them by experience that it was not possible apart from Him to go to the other side He constrained them to enter into the boat and go before Him to the other side; but, when they were not able to advance farther than the middle of the sea, He appeared to them, and did what is written,[3] and showed that he who arrives at the other side reaches it because Jesus sails along with him. But what is the boat into which Jesus constrained the disciples to enter? Is it perhaps the conflict of temptations and difficulties into which any

[1] Matt. xiii. 11. [2] Matt. xiii. 36. [3] Matt. xiii. 36.
[4] Matt. xiv. 13, 14. [5] Matt. xiv. 15. [6] Matt. xiv. 19.
[7] Matt. xiv. 22.

[1] Matt. xiv. 23. [2] Matt. xiv. 24. [3] Matt. xiv. 25.

one is constrained by the Word, and goes unwillingly, as it were, when the Saviour wishes to train by exercise the disciples in this boat which is distressed by the waves and the contrary wind? But since Mark has made a slight change in the reading, and for "Straightway He constrained the disciples to enter into the boat and to go before Him to the other side," has written, "And straightway He constrained His disciples to enter into the boat and to go before Him unto the other side unto Bethsaida,"[1] we must attend to the word, "He constrained," when first we have seen to the slight variation in Mark who indicates something more definite by the addition of the pronoun; for the same thing is not expressed by the words, straightway "He constrained the disciples." Something more than "the" disciples simply is written in Mark, namely, "His" disciples. Perhaps, therefore, to attend to the expression, the disciples who found it hard to tear themselves away from Jesus, and could not be separated from Him by any ordinary cause, wished to be present with Him; but He having judged that they should make trial of the waves and of the contrary wind, which would not have been contrary if they had been with Jesus, put on them the necessity of being separated from Him and entering into the boat. The Saviour then compels the disciples to enter into the boat of temptations and to go before Him to the other side, and through victory over them to go beyond critical difficulties; but when they had come into the midst of the sea, and of the waves in the temptations, and of the contrary winds which prevented them from going away to the other side, they were not able, struggling as they were without Jesus, to overcome the waves and the contrary wind and reach the other side. Wherefore the Word, taking compassion upon them who had done all that was in their power to reach the other side, came to them walking upon the sea, which for Him had no waves or wind that was able to oppose if He so willed; for it is not written, "He came to them walking upon the waves," but, "upon the waters;"[2] Just as Peter, who at first when Jesus said to him, "Come," went down from the boat and walked not upon "the waves," but upon "the waters"[3] to come to Jesus; but when he doubted he saw that the wind was strong, which was not strong to him who laid aside his little faith and his doubting. But, when Jesus went up with Peter into the boat, the wind ceased, as it had no power to energise against the boat when Jesus had gone up into it.

1 Mark vi. 45. 2 Matt. xiv. 25. 3 Matt. xiv. 29.

6. INTERPRETATION OF THE DETAILS IN THE NARRATIVE. APPLICATION THEREOF TO ALL DISCIPLES.

And then the disciples "*having crossed over came to the land Gennesaret,*"[1] of which word, if we knew the interpretation, we might gain some assistance in the exposition of the present passage. And observe, since God is faithful, and will not suffer the multitudes to be tempted above that they are able,[2] in what way the Son of God constrained the disciples to enter into the boat, as being stronger and able to get as far as the middle of the sea, and to endure the trials by the waves, until they became worthy of divine assistance, and saw Jesus and heard Him when He had gone up, and to cross over and come to the land Gennesaret; but as for the multitudes who, because they were weaker, did not make trial of the boat and the waves and the contrary wind, them He sent away, and went up into the mountain apart to pray.[3] To pray for whom? Was it perhaps to pray for the multitudes that, when they were dismissed after the loaves of blessing, they might do nothing opposed to their dismissal by Jesus? And for the disciples that, when they were constrained by Him to enter into the boat and to go before Him unto the other side, they might suffer nothing in the sea nor from the contrary wind? And I would say with confidence, that, because of the prayer of Jesus to the Father for the disciples, they suffered nothing when sea and wave and contrary wind were striving against them. The simpler disciple, then, may be satisfied with the bare narrative; but let us remember, if ever we fall into distressful temptations, that Jesus has constrained us to enter into their boat, wishing us to go before Him unto the other side; for it is not possible for us to reach the other side, unless we have endured the temptations of waves and contrary wind. Then when we see many difficulties besetting us, and with moderate struggle we have swum through them to some extent, let us consider that our boat is in the midst of the sea, distressed at that time by the waves which wish us to make shipwreck concerning faith or some one of the virtues; but when we see the spirit of the evil one striving against us, let us conceive that then

1 Matt. xiv. 34. 2 Cf. 1 Cor. x. 13. 3 Matt. xiv. 22, 23.

the wind is contrary to us. When then in such suffering we have spent three watches of the night—that is, of the darkness which is in the temptations—striving nobly with all our might and watching ourselves so as not to make shipwreck concerning the faith or some one of the virtues,—the first watch against the father of darkness and wickedness, the second watch against his son "who opposeth and exalteth himself against all that is called God or thing that is worshipped,"[1] and the third watch against the spirit[2] that is opposed to the Holy Spirit, then we believe that when the fourth watch impendeth, when "the night is far spent, and the day is at hand,"[3] the Son of God will come to us, that He may prepare the sea for us, walking upon it. And when we see the Word appearing unto us we shall indeed be troubled before we clearly understand that it is the Saviour who has come to us, supposing that we are still beholding an apparition, and for fear shall cry out; but He Himself straightway will speak to us saying, "Be of good cheer; it is I; be not afraid."[4] And if, warmly moved by His "Be of good cheer," any Peter be found among us, who is on his way to perfection but has not yet become perfect, having gone down from the boat, as if coming out of that temptation in which he was distressed, he will indeed walk at first, wishing to come to Jesus upon the waters; but being as yet of little faith, and as yet doubting, will see that the wind is strong and will be afraid and begin to sink; but he will not sink because he will call upon Jesus with loud voice, and will say to Him, "Lord, save me;"[5] then immediately while such a Peter is yet speaking and saying, "Lord save me," the Word will stretch forth His hand, holding out assistance to such an one, and will take hold of him when he is beginning to sink, and will reproach him for his little faith and doubting.[6] Only, observe that He did not say, "O thou without faith," but, "O thou of little faith,"and that it was said, "Wherefore didst thou doubt," as he had still a measure of faith, but also had a tendency towards that which was opposed to faith.

7. THE HEALING OF THE SICK ON THE OTHER SIDE. THE METHOD OF HEALING.

But after this both Jesus and Peter will go up into the boat, and the wind will cease; and those in the boat, perceiving the great dangers from which they have been saved, will worship Him, saying, not simply, "Thou art the Son of God," as also the two demoniacs said, but, "Of a truth, Thou art the Son of God."[1] This the disciples in the boat say, for I do not think that others than the disciples said so. And when we have undergone all these experiences, having crossed over, we shall come to the land where Jesus commanded us to go before Him. And perhaps, also, some secret and occult mystery with reference to some who were saved by Jesus is indicated by the words, "And when the men of that place knew Him,"—plainly of the place on the other side,—"they sent into all that region round about,"—round about the other side, not on the other side itself, but round about it,—"and they brought unto Him all that were sick."[2] And here observe that they brought unto Him not only many that were sick, but all in that region round about; and the sick who were brought to Him besought Him that they might touch if it were only the border of His garment,[3] beseeching this grace from Him, since they were not like "the woman who had an issue of blood twelve years, and who came behind Him and touched the border of His garment, saying within herself, If I do but touch His garment, I shall be made whole."[4] For observe in what is said about the border of His garment, on account of what the flowing of her blood ceased at once. But those from the country round the land of Gennesaret, to which Jesus and His disciples crossed over and came, did not come of themselves to Jesus, but were brought by those who had sent the tidings, inasmuch as they were not able because of their extreme weakness to come of themselves. Nor did they merely touch the garment, like the woman who had an issue of blood, but they touched after that they had besought Him. Only, of these, "as many as touched were made whole."[5] And whether there be any difference between the "They were made whole,"[6] which is said in their case, and the "being saved,"[7]—for it was said to the woman with the issue of blood, "Thy faith hath saved thee,"[8] you may yourself consider.

8. CONCERNING THE PHARISEES AND SCRIBES WHO CAME AND INQUIRED, WHY DO THY DISCIPLES TRANSGRESS THE TRADITION OF THE ELDERS?

"*Then there came to Him from Jerusalem*

[1] 2 Thess. ii. 4.
[2] The conception of Origen seems to be that opposed to the Divine Trinity there is an evil trinity. Cf. book xii. 20.
[3] Rom. xiii. 12.
[4] Matt. xiv. 27.
[5] Matt. xiv. 30.
[6] Matt. xiv. 31.

[1] Matt. xiv. 33.
[2] Matt. xiv. 35.
[3] Matt. xiv. 36.
[4] Matt. ix. 20, 21.
[5] Matt. xiv. 36.
[6] διεσώθησαν.
[7] σωθῆναι.
[8] Matt. ix. 22.

Pharisees and scribes, saying, Why do Thy disciples transgress the tradition of the elders? For they wash not their hands when they eat bread."[1] He who observes at what time the Pharisees and scribes came from Jerusalem to Jesus, saying, "Why do Thy disciples transgress the tradition of the elders," etc., will perceive that Matthew of necessity wrote not simply that Pharisees and scribes from Jerusalem came to the Saviour to inquire of Him the matters before us, but put it thus, "Then come to Him from Jerusalem." What time, therefore, are we to understand by "then"? At the time when Jesus and His disciples crossed over and came in the boat to the land of Gennesaret, when the wind ceased from the time that Jesus entered into the boat, and when "the men of that place knowing Him sent into all that region round about, and brought unto Him all that were sick, and besought Him that they might touch if it were only the border of His garment, and as many as touched were made whole."[2] At that time came to Him from Jerusalem Pharisees and scribes, not struck with admiration at the power which was in Jesus, which healed those who only touched even the border of His garment, but in a censorious spirit, accusing the disciples before their Teacher, not concerning the transgression of a commandment of God, but of a single tradition of the Jewish elders. And it is probable that this very charge of these censorious persons is a proof of the piety of the disciples of Jesus, who gave to the Pharisees and scribes no opportunity of censure with reference to the transgression of the commandments of God, as they would not have brought the charge of transgression against the disciples, as transgressing the commandment of the elders, if they had had it in their power to censure those whom they accused, and to show that they were transgressing a commandment of God. But do not suppose that these things go to establish the necessity of keeping the law of Moses according to the letter, because the disciples of Jesus up to that time kept it; for not before He suffered did He "redeem us from the curse of the law,"[3] who in suffering for men "became a curse for us." But just as fittingly Paul became a Jew to the Jews that he might gain Jews,[4] what strange thing is it that the Apostles, whose way of life was passed among the Jews, even though they understood the spiritual things in the law, should have used a spirit of accommodation, as Paul also did when he circumcised Timothy,[1] and offered sacrifice in accordance with a certain legal vow, as is written in the Acts of the Apostles?[2] Only, again, they appear fond of bringing accusations, as they have no charge to bring against the disciples of Jesus with reference to a commandment of God, but only with reference to one tradition of the elders. And especially does this love of accusation become manifest in this, that they bring the charge in presence of those very persons who had been healed from their sickness; in appearance against the disciples, but in reality purposing to slander their Teacher, as it was a tradition of the elders that the washing of hands was a thing essential to piety. For they thought that the hands of those who did not wash before eating bread were defiled and unclean, but that the hands of those who had washed them with water became pure and holy, not in a figurative sense, in due relation to the law of Moses according to the letter. But let us, not according to the tradition of the elders among the Jews, but according to sound reason, endeavour to purify our own actions and so to wash the hands of our souls, when we are about to eat the three loaves which we ask from Jesus, who wishes to be our friend;[3] for with hands that are defiled and unwashed and impure, we ought not to partake of the loaves.

9. EXPLANATION OF "CORBAN."

Jesus, however, does not accuse them with reference to a tradition of the Jewish elders, but with regard to two most imperative commandments of God, the one of which was the fifth in the decalogue, being as follows: "Honour thy father and thy mother, that it may be well with thee, and that thy days may be long on the land which the Lord thy God giveth thee;"[4] and the other was written thus in Leviticus, "If a man speak evil of his father or his mother, let him die the death; he has spoken evil of his father or mother, he shall be guilty."[5] But when we wish to examine the very letter of the words as given by Matthew, "He that speaketh evil of father or mother, let him die the death,"[6] consider whether it was taken from the place where it was written, "Whoso striketh his father or mother, let him die the death; and he that speaketh evil of father or mother let him die

[1] Matt. xv. 1, 2.
[2] Matt. xiv. 35, 36.
[3] Gal. iii. 13.
[4] 1 Cor. ix. 20.

[1] Gal. ii. 3.
[2] Acts xxi. 26; xviii. 18.
[3] Cf. Luke xi. 5.
[4] Ex. xx. 12.
[5] Lev. xx. 9.
[6] Matt. xv. 4.

the death."[1] For such are the exact words taken from the Law with regard to the two commandments; but Matthew has quoted them in part and in an abridged form, and not in the very words. But what the nature of the charge is which the Saviour brings against the Pharisees and scribes from Jerusalem, when He says that they transgress the commandment of God because of their tradition we must consider. And God said, "Honour thy father and thy mother,"[2] teaching that the child should pay the honour which is due to his parents. Of this honour to parents one part was to share with them the necessaries of life, such as food and clothing, and if there was any other thing in which it was possible for them to show favour towards their own parents. But the Pharisees and scribes promulgated in opposition to the law a tradition which is found rather obscurely in the Gospel, and which we ourselves would not have thought of, unless one of the Hebrews had given to us the following facts relating to the passage. Sometimes, he says, when money-lenders fell in with stubborn debtors who were able but not willing to pay their debts, they consecrated what was due to the account of the poor, for whom money was cast into the treasury by each of those who wished to give a portion of their goods to the poor according to their ability. They, therefore, said sometimes to their debtors in their own tongue, "That which you owe to me is Corban,"—that is, a gift—"for I have consecrated it to the poor, to the account of piety towards God." Then the debtor, as no longer in debt to men but to God and to piety towards God, was shut up, as it were, even though unwilling, to payment of the debt, no longer to the money-lender, but now to God for the account of the poor, in name of the money-lender. What then the money-lender did to the debtor, that sometimes some sons did to their parents and said to them, "That wherewith thou mightest have been profited by me, father or mother, know that you will receive this from Corban,"[3] from the account of the poor who are consecrated to God. Then the parents, hearing that that which should have been given to them was Corban,—consecrated to God,—no longer wished to take it from their sons, even though they were in extreme need of the necessaries of life. The elders, then, declared to the people a tradition of this kind, "Whosoever said to his father or mother, that which should be given to any of them is Corban and a gift, that man was no longer a debtor to his father or mother in respect of giving to them the necessaries of life." The Saviour censures this tradition, as not being sound but opposed to the commandment of God. For if God says, "Honour thy father and thy mother," but the tradition said, he is not bound to honour his father or mother by a gift, who has consecrated to God, as Corban, that which would have been given to his parents, manifestly the commandment of God concerning the honour due to parents was made void by the tradition of the Pharisees and scribes which said, that he was no longer bound to honour his father or mother, who had, once for all, consecrated to God that which the parents would have received. And the Pharisees, as lovers of money, in order that under pretext of the poor they might receive even that which would have been given to the parents of any one, gave such teaching. And the Gospel testifies to their love of money, saying, "But the Pharisees who were lovers of money heard these things and they scoffed at Him."[1] If, then, any one of those who are called elders among us, or of those who are in any way rulers of the people, profess to give to the poor under the name of the commonweal, rather than to be of those who give to their kindred if they should chance to be in need of the necessaries of life, and those who give cannot do both, this man might with justice be called a brother of those Pharisees who made void the word of God through their own tradition, and were accused by the Saviour as hypocrites. And as a very powerful deterrent to any one from being anxious to take from the account of the poor, and from thinking that "the piety of others is a way of gain,"[2] we have not only these things, but also that which is recorded about the traitor Judas, who in appearance championed the cause of the poor, and said with indignation, "This ointment might have been sold for three hundred pence and given to the poor,"[3] but in reality "was a thief, and having the bag took away what was put therein."[4] If, then, any one in our time who has the bag of the Church speaks likes Judas on behalf of the poor, but takes away what is put therein, let there be assigned to him the portion along with Judas who did these things; on account of which things eating like a gangrene into his soul, the devil cast it into his

[1] Exod. xxi. 15; Lev. xx. 9.
[2] Exod. xx. 12.
[3] Matt. xv. 4.

[1] Luke xvi. 14.
[2] 1 Tim. vi. 5.
[3] Mark xiv. 5; John xii. 5.
[4] John xii. 6.

heart to betray the Saviour; and, when he had received the "fiery dart,"[1] with reference to this end, the devil afterwards himself entered into his soul and took full possession of him. And perhaps, when the Apostle says, "The love of money is a root of all evils,"[2] he says it because of Judas' love of money, which was a root of all the evils that were committed against Jesus.

10. THE TRADITIONS OF THE ELDERS IN COLLISION WITH DIVINE LAW.

But let us return to the subject before us, in which the Saviour abridged and expounded two commandments from the law, the one from the decalogue from Exodus, and the other from Leviticus, or the other from some one of the books of the Pentateuch. Then since we have explained in what way they made void the word of God which said, "Honour thy father and thy mother," by saying, "Thou shalt not honour thy father or thy mother," whosoever shall say to his father or mother, "It is a gift that wherewith thou mightest have been profited by me," some one may inquire whether the words, "He that speaketh evil of father or mother, let him die the death,"[3] are not extraneous. For, granted that he does not honour his father and mother, who consecrates to what is called Corban that which would have been given in honour of father and mother, in what way, therefore, does the tradition of the Pharisees make void the word which said, "He that speaketh evil of father or mother, let him die the death.? But, perhaps, when any one said to his father or his mother, "It is a gift, that wherewith thou mightest have been profited by me,"[4] he, as it were, casts abuse on his father or mother as if he were calling his parents sacrilegious, in taking that which was consecrated to Corban from him who had consecrated it to Corban. The Jews then punish their sons[5] according to the law, as speaking evil of father or mother, when they say to their father or mother, "It is a gift, that wherewith thou mightest have been profited by me," but you by one of your traditions make void two commandments of God. And then you are not ashamed to accuse My disciples who transgress no commandment; for they walk "in all His commandments and ordinances blamelessly,"[6] but transgress a tradition of the elders, so as not to transgress a commandment of God. And if you had held this aim before you, you would have kept the commandment about the honour due to father and mother, and that which said, "He that speaketh evil of father and mother, let him die the death;" but the tradition of the elders which is opposed to these commandments you would not have kept.

11. EXPOSITION OF THE PROPHECY OF ISAIAH QUOTED BY JESUS.

And, after this, wishing to refute completely from the words of the prophets all these traditions of the elders among the Jews, He brought before them a saying, from Isaiah, which in the exact words is as follows: "And the Lord said, This people draws nigh to Me with their mouth," etc.;[1] and, as we said before, Matthew has not written out the prophetical saying in the very words. And, if it be necessary because of its use in the Gospel to interpret it according to our ability, we will take in addition the preceding passage which is, in my judgment, noted with advantage by us for the exposition of that passage in the Gospel which was taken from the prophet. The passage in Isaiah from the beginning is thus, "Be ye faint, and be maddened: be ye drunken, but not with strong drink nor with wine: for the Lord hath given you to drink of the spirit of stupor, and He will close their eyes, both of their prophets, and of their rulers who see things secret. And all these sayings shall be to you as the words of the book, which has been sealed, which if they give to a man who knows letters, saying, Read this, he shall answer, I cannot read, for it is sealed. And this book will be given into the hands of a man who does not know letters, and one will say to him, Read this, and he will say, I know not letters. And the Lord said, This people is nigh to Me," etc., down to the words, "Woe unto them that form counsel in secret, and their works shall be in darkness."[2] Taking up then the passage before us in the Gospel, I have put some of the verses which come before it, and some which follow it, in order to show in what way the Word threatens to close the eyes of those of the people who are astonished and drunken, and have been made to drink of the spirit of deep sleep. And it threatens also to close the eyes of their prophets and their rulers who profess to see things secret,—which things, I think, took place after the advent of the Saviour among that people; for all the words of the whole of the Scriptures,

[1] Eph. vi. 16. [2] 1 Tim. vi. 10. [3] Matt. xv. 4. [4] Matt. xv. 5. [5] *Or*, you, if we read ὑμᾶς. [6] Cf. Luke i. 6.

[1] Isa. xxix. 13. [2] Isa. xxix. 9–15.

and of Isaiah also, have become to them as the words of a sealed book. Now the expression "sealed" is used of a book closed in virtue of its obscurity and not open in virtue of its lucidity, which is equally obscure to those who are not able to read it at all because they do not know letters, and to those who profess to know letters but do not understand the meaning in the things which have been written. Well, then, does he add to this, that when the people, fainting because of their sins and being in a state of madness rage against Him through those sins wherewith they shall be drunken against Him with the spirit of stupor, which shall be given to them to drink by the Lord when He closes their eyes, as unworthy to see, and the eyes of their prophets and of their rulers who profess to see the hidden things of the mysteries in the Divine Scriptures; and, when their eyes are closed, then shall the prophetic words be sealed to them and hidden, as has been the case with those who do not believe in Jesus as the Christ. And when the prophetic sayings have become as the words of a sealed book, not only to those who do not know letters but to those who profess to know, then the Lord said, that the people of the Jews draw nigh to God with their mouth only, and He says that they honour Him with their lips, because their heart by reason of their unbelief in Jesus is far from the Lord. And now, especially, from the time at which they denied our Saviour, it might be said about them by God, "But in vain do they worship Me;"[1] for they no longer teach the precepts of God but of men, and doctrines which are human and no longer of the Spirit of wisdom. Wherefore, when these things happen to them, God has removed the people of the Jews, and has caused to perish the wisdom of the wise men among them; for there is no longer wisdom among them, just as there is no prophecy; but God has utterly destroyed the prudence of the prudent and concealed it,[2] and no longer is it splendid and conspicuous. Wherefore, although they may seem to form some counsel in a deep fashion, because they do it not through the Lord they are called miserable; and even though they profess to tell some secrets of the Divine counsel they lie, since their works are not works of light, but of darkness and night.[3] I have thought it right briefly to set forth the prophecy, and to a certain extent elucidate its meaning, seeing that Matthew made mention of it.

[1] Matt. xv. 9. [2] Isa. xxix. 14. [3] Isa. xxix. 15.

And Mark also made mention of it, from whom we may usefully set down the following words in the place, with reference to the transgression of the elders who held that it was necessary to wash hands when the Jews ate bread, "For the Pharisees and all the Jews, except they wash their hands diligently, eat not, holding the tradition of the elders; and when they come from the market-place except they wash themselves they eat not. And there are some other things which they have received to hold, washings of cups and pots and brazen vessels and couches."[1]

12. THINGS CLEAN AND UNCLEAN ACCORDING TO THE LAW AND THE GOSPEL.

"*And He called to Him the multitude and said unto them, Hear and understand,*" etc.[2] We are clearly taught in these words by the Saviour that, when we read in Leviticus and Deuteronomy the precepts about meat clean and unclean, for the transgression of which we are accused by the material Jews and by the Ebionites who differ little from them, we are not to think that the scope of the Scripture is found in any superficial understanding of them. For if "not that which entereth into the mouth defileth the man, but that which proceedeth out of the mouth,"[3] and especially when, according to Mark, the Saviour said these things "making all meats clean,"[4] manifestly we are not defiled when we eat those things which the Jews who desire to be in bondage to the letter of the law declare to be unclean, but we are then defiled when, whereas our lips ought to be bound with perception and we ought "to make for them what we call a balance and weight,"[5] we speak offhand and discuss matters we ought not, from which there comes to us the spring of sins. And it is indeed becoming to the law of God to forbid those things which arise from wickedness, and to enjoin those things which tend to virtue, but as for things which are in their own nature indifferent to leave them in their own place, as they may, according to our choice and the reason which is in us, be done ill if we sin in them, but if rightly directed by us be done well. And any one who has carefully thought on these matters will see that, even in those things which are thought to be good, it is possible for a man to sin who has taken them up in an evil way and under the impulse of passion, and that these things called impure

[1] Mark vii. 3, 4. [2] Matt. xv. 10. [3] Matt. xv. 11. [4] Mark vii. 19. [5] Ecclus. xxviii. 25.

may be considered pure, if used by us in accordance with reason. As, then, when the Jew sins his circumcision shall be reckoned for uncircumcision, but when one of the Gentiles acts uprightly his uncircumcision shall be reckoned for circumcision,[1] so those things which are thought to be pure shall be reckoned for impure in the case of him who does not use them fittingly, nor when one ought, nor as far as he ought, nor for what reason he ought. But as for the things which are called impure, "All things become pure to the pure," for, "To them that are defiled and unbelieving nothing is pure, since both their minds and their conscience are defiled."[2] And when these are defiled, they make all things whatsoever they touch defiled; as again on the contrary the pure mind and the pure conscience make all things pure, even though they may seem to be impure; for not from intemperance, nor from love of pleasure, nor with doubting which draws a man both ways, do the righteous use meats or drinks, mindful of the precept, "Whether ye eat or drink or whatsoever other thing ye do, do all to the glory of God."[3] And if it be necessary to delineate the foods which are unclean according to the Gospel, we will say that they are such as are supplied by covetousness, and are the result of base love of gain, and are taken up from love of pleasure, and from deifying the belly which is treated with honour, when it, with its appetites, and not reason, rules our souls. But as for us who know that some things are used by demons, or if we do not know, but suspect, and are in doubt about it, if we use such things, we have used them not to the glory of God, nor in the name of Christ; for not only does the suspicion that things have been sacrificed to idols condemn him who eats, but even the doubt concerning this; for "he that doubteth," according to the Apostle, "is condemned if he eat, because he eateth not of faith; and whatsoever is not of faith is sin."[4] He then eats in faith who believes that that which is eaten has not been sacrificed in the temples of idols, and that it is not strangled nor blood;[5] but he eats not of faith who is in doubt about any of these things. And the man who knowing that they have been sacrificed to demons nevertheless uses them, becomes a communicant with demons, while at the same time, his imagination is polluted with reference to demons participating in the sacrifice. And the Apostle, however, knowing that it is not the nature of meats which is the cause of injury to him who uses them or of advantage to him who refrains from their use, but opinions and the reason which is in them, said, "But meat commendeth us not to God, for neither if we eat are we the better, nor if we eat not are we the worse."[1] And since he knew that those who have a loftier conception of what things are pure and what impure according to the law, turning aside from the distinction about the use of things pure and impure, and superstition, I think, in respect of things being different, become indifferent to the use of meats,[2] and on this account are condemned by the Jews as transgressors of law, he said therefore, somewhere, "Let no man therefore judge you in meat or in drink," etc.,[3] teaching us that the things according to the letter are a shadow, but that the true thoughts of the law which are stored up in them are the good things to come, in which one may find what are the pure spiritual meats of the soul, and what are the impure foods in false and contradictory words which injure the man who is nourished in them, "For the law had a shadow of the good things to come."[4]

13. THE OFFENCE OF THE PHARISEES.

And as in many cases we have to consider the astonishment of the Jews at the words of the Saviour, because they were spoken with authority, so also in regard to the words in this place. Having called the multitudes therefore, He said unto them, "Hear and understand,"[5] etc. And He said this, the Pharisees being offended at this saying, as, because of their evil opinions and their worthless interpretation of the law, they were not the plant of his own Father in heaven, and on this account were being rooted up;[6] for they were rooted up as they did not receive the true vine, which was cultivated by the Father, even Jesus Christ.[7] For how could they be a plant of His Father who were offended at the words of Jesus, words which turn men away from the precept, "Handle not, nor taste, nor touch,—all which things were to perish in the using—after the precepts and doctrines of men,"[8] but induce the intelligent hearer of them to seek in regard to them the things which are above and not the things upon the earth as the Jews do?[9] And since, because of their evil opinions, the Pharisees were not the plant of His Father in heaven,

[1] Rom. ii. 25, 26. [2] Tit. i. 15. [3] 1 Cor. x. 31. [4] Rom. xiv. 23. [5] Cf. Acts xv. 20.

[1] 1 Cor. viii. 8. [2] The text is uncertain. [3] Col. ii. 16. [4] Heb. x. 1. [5] Matt. xv. 10. [6] Matt. xv. 13. [7] John xv. 1. [8] Col. ii. 21, 22. [9] Col. iii. 2.

on this account, as about such as were incorrigible, He says to the disciple, "Let them alone;"[1] "Let them alone," He said for this reason, that as they were blind they ought to become conscious of their blindness and seek guides; but they, being unconscious of their own blindness, profess to guide the blind, not reckoning that they would fall into a pit, about which it is written in the Psalms, "He hath made a pit, and digged it, and will fall into the ditch which he hath made."[2] Again, elsewhere it is written, "And seeing the multitudes, He went up into the mountain, and when He had sat down His disciples came unto Him;"[3] but here He stretches forth His hand to the multitude, calling them unto Him, and turning their thoughts away from the literal interpretation of the questions in the law, when He in the first place said to them, who did not yet understand what they heard, "Hear and understand," and thereafter as in parables said to them, "Not that which entereth into the mouth defileth the man, but that which proceedeth out of the mouth."[4]

14. WHY THE PHARISEES WERE NOT A PLANT OF GOD. TEACHING OF ORIGEN ON THE "BREAD OF THE LORD."

After this, it is worth while to look at the phrase which has been assailed in a sophistical way by those who say[5] that the God of the law and the God of the Gospel of Jesus Christ is not the same; for they say that the heavenly Father of Jesus Christ is not the husbandman of those who think that they worship God according to the law of Moses. Jesus Himself said that the Pharisees, who were worshipping the God who created the world and the law, were not a plant which His heavenly Father had planted, and that for this reason it was being rooted up.[6] But you might also say this, that even if it were the Father of Jesus who "brought in and planted the people," when it came out of Egypt, "to the mountain of His own inheritance, to the place which He had prepared for Himself to dwell in,"[7] yet Jesus would have said, in regard to the Pharisees, "Every plant which My heavenly Father planted not, shall be rooted up." Now, to this we will say, that as many as on account of their perverse interpretation of the things in the law were not a plant of His Father in heaven, were blinded in their minds, as not believing the truth, but taking pleasure in unrighteousness,[1] by him who is deified by the sons of this world, and on this account is called by Paul the god of this world.[2] And do not suppose that Paul said that he was truly God; for just as the belly, though it is not the god of those who prize pleasure too highly, being lovers of pleasure rather than lovers of God, is said by Paul to be their god,[3] so the prince of this world, in regard to whom the Saviour says, "Now has the prince of this world been judged,"[4] though he is not God, is said to be the god of those who do not wish to receive the spirit of adoption, in order that they may become sons of that world, and sons of the resurrection from the dead,[5] and who, on this account, abide in the sonship of this world. I have deemed it necessary to introduce these matters, even though they may have been spoken by way of digression, because of the saying, "They are blind guides of the blind."[6] Who are such? The Pharisees, whose minds the god of this world hath blinded as they are unbelieving, because they have not believed in Jesus Christ; and he hath blinded them so that the "light of the Gospel of the glory of God in the face of Christ should not dawn upon them."[7] But not only must we avoid being guided by those blind ones who are conscious that they are in need of guides, because they have not yet received the power of vision of themselves; but even in the case of all who profess to guide us in sound doctrine, we must hear with care, and apply a sound judgment to what is said, lest being guided according to the ignorance of those who are blind, and do not see the things that concern sound doctrine, we ourselves may appear to be blind because we do not see the sense of the Scriptures, so that both he who guides and he who is guided will fall into the ditch of which we have spoken before. Next to this, it is written in what way Peter answered and said to the Saviour, as if he had not understood the saying, "Not that which cometh into the mouth defileth the man, but that which goeth out of the mouth," "Declare unto us the parable."[8] To which the Saviour says, "Are ye also, even yet, without understanding?"[9] As if He had said, "Having been so long time with Me, do ye not yet understand the meaning of what is said, and do ye not perceive that for this reason that which goeth into his mouth does not defile the man, because it passeth into the belly,

[1] Matt. xv. 14. [2] Ps. vii. 15. [3] Matt. v. 1.
[4] Matt. xv. 10, 11. [5] Marcion and his followers.
[6] Matt. xv. 13. [7] Exod. xv. 17.

[1] 2 Thess. ii. 12. [2] 2 Cor. iv. 4. [3] Phil. iii. 19.
[4] John xvi. 11. [5] Cf. Luke xx. 36. [6] Matt. xv. 14.
[7] 2 Cor. iv. 4. [8] Matt. xv. 11. [9] Matt. xv. 16.

and going out from it is cast into the draught?"[1] It was not in respect of the law in which they appeared to believe, that the Pharisees were not a plant of the Father of Jesus, but in respect of their perverse interpretation of the law and the things written in it. For since there are two things to be understood in regard to the law, the ministration of death which was engraven in letters[2] and which had no kinship with the spirit, and the ministration of life which is understood in the spiritual law, those who were able with a sincere heart to say, "We know that the law is spiritual,"[3] and therefore "the law is holy, and the commandment holy and righteous and good,"[4] were the plant which the heavenly Father planted; but those who were not such, but guarded with care the letter which killeth only, were not a plant of God but of him who hardened their heart, and put a veil over it, which veil had power over them so long as they did not turn to the Lord; "for if any one should turn to the Lord, the veil is taken away, and the Lord is the Spirit."[5] Now some one when dealing with the passage might say, that just as "not that which entereth into the mouth defileth the man,"[6] of even though it may be thought by the Jews to be defiled, so not that which entereth into the mouth sanctifieth the man, even though what is called the bread of the Lord may be thought by the simpler disciples to sanctify. And the saying is I think, not to be despised, and on this account, demands clear exposition, which seems to me to be thus; as it is not the meat but the conscience of him who eats with doubt which defiles him that eateth, for "he that doubteth is condemned if he eat, because he eateth not of faith,"[7] and as nothing is pure to him who is defiled and unbelieving, not in itself, but because of his defilement and unbelief, so that which is sanctified through the word of God and prayer[8] does not, in its own nature, sanctify him who uses it, for, if this were so, it would sanctify even him who eats unworthily of the bread of the Lord, and no one on account of this food would become weak or sickly or asleep for something of this kind Paul represented in saying, "For this cause many among you are weak and sickly and not a few sleep."[9] And in the case of the bread of the Lord, accordingly, there is advantage to him who uses it, when with undefiled mind and pure conscience he partakes of the bread. And so neither by not eating, I mean by the very fact that we do not eat of the bread which has been sanctified by the word of God and prayer, are we deprived of any good thing, nor by eating are we the better by any good thing; for the cause of our lacking is wickedness and sins, and the cause of our abounding is righteousness and right actions; so that such is the meaning of what is said by Paul, "For neither if we eat are we the better, nor if we eat not are we the worse."[1] Now, if "everything that entereth into the mouth goes into the belly and is cast out into the draught,"[2] even the meat which has been sanctified through the word of God and prayer, in accordance with the fact that it is material, goes into the belly and is cast out into the draught, but in respect of the prayer which comes upon it, according to the proportion of the faith, becomes a benefit and is a means of clear vision to the mind which looks to that which is beneficial, and it is not the material of the bread but the word which is said over it which is of advantage to him who eats it not unworthily of the Lord. And these things indeed are said of the typical and symbolical body. But many things might be said about the Word Himself who became flesh,[3] and true meat of which he that eateth shall assuredly live for ever, no worthless person being able to eat it; for if it were possible for one who continues worthless to eat of Him who became flesh, who was the Word and the living bread, it would not have been written, that "every one who eats of this bread shall live for ever."[4]

15. EATING WITH UNWASHED HEART DEFILES THE MAN.

Next to this let us see how the things which proceed out and defile the man do not defile the man because of their proceeding out of the mouth, but have the cause of their defilement in the heart, when there come forth out of it, before those things which proceed through the mouth, evil thoughts, of which the species are—murders, adulteries, fornications, thefts, false witness, railings.[5] For these are the things which defile the man, when they come forth out of the heart, and going out from it proceed through the mouth; so that, if they did not come out of the heart, but were retained there somewhere about the heart, and were not allowed to be spoken through the mouth,

[1] Matt. xv. 17. [2] Cf. 2 Cor. iii. 7. [3] Rom. vii. 14. [4] Rom vii. 12. [5] 2 Cor. iii. 16, 17. [6] Matt. xv. 11. [7] Rom. xiv. 23. [8] Cf. 1 Tim. iv. 5. [9] 1 Cor. xi. 30.

[1] 1 Cor. viii. 8. [2] Matt. xv. 17. [3] John i. 14. [4] John vi. 51. [5] Matt. xv. 18, 19.

they would very quickly disappear, and a man would be no more defiled. The spring and source, then, of every sin are evil thoughts; for, unless these gained the mastery, neither murders nor adulteries nor any other such thing would exist. Therefore, each man must keep his own heart with all watchfulness;[1] for when the Lord comes in the day of judgment, "He will bring to light the hidden things of darkness and will make manifest the counsels of the hearts,"[2] "all the thoughts of men meanwhile accusing or else excusing them,"[3] "when their own devices have beset them about."[4] But of such a nature are the evil thoughts that sometimes they make worthy of censure even those things which seem good, and which, so far as the judgment of the masses is concerned, are worthy of praise. Accordingly, if we do alms before men, having in our thoughts the design of appearing to men philanthropic, and of being honoured because of philanthropy, we receive the reward from men;[5] and, universally, everything that is done with the consciousness in the doer that he will be glorified by men, has no reward from Him who beholds in secret, and renders the reward to those who are pure, in secret. So, too, therefore, is it with apparent purity if it is influenced by considerations of vain glory or love of gain; and the teaching which is thought to be the teaching of the Church, if it becomes servile through the word of flattery, either when it is made the excuse for covetousness, or when any one seeks glory from men because of his teaching, is not reckoned to be the teaching of those "who have been set by God in the Church: first, apostles; secondly, prophets; and thirdly, teachers."[6] And you will say the like in the case of him who seeks the office of a bishop for the sake of glory with men, or of flattery from men, or for the sake of the gain received from those who, coming over to the word, give in the name of piety; for a bishop of this kind at any rate does not "desire a good work,"[7] nor can he be without reproach, nor temperate, nor sober-minded, as he is intoxicated with glory and intemperately satiated with it. And the same also you will say about the elders and deacons. And if we seem to some to have made a digression in speaking of these things, consider if it were not necessary that they should be said, because that evil thoughts are the spring of all sins, and can pollute even those actions which, if they were done apart from evil thoughts, would have justified the man who did them. We have thus investigated according to our ability what are the things which defile; but to eat with unwashed hands does not defile the man; but if we must say it with boldness, with unwashed heart to eat anything whatsoever which is the natural food of our reason, defileth the man.

[1] Prov. iv. 23. [2] 1 Cor. iv. 5. [3] Rom. ii. 15. [4] Hos. vii. 2. [5] Matt. vi. 1, 2. [6] 1 Cor. xii. 28. [7] 1 Tim. iii. 1.

16. CONCERNING THE CANAANITISH WOMAN. MEANING OF THE "BORDERS OF TYRE AND SIDON."

"*And Jesus went out thence and withdrew into the parts of Tyre and Sidon. And behold a Canaanitish woman.*"[1] Whence the "thence"? Was it from the land of Gennesaret, concerning which it was said before, "And when they had crossed over they came into the land of Gennesaret?"[2] But He withdrew, perhaps because the Pharisees were offended when they heard that "not that which entereth in, but that which proceedeth out, defileth the man;"[3] and that, because of their being suspected of plotting against Him, it is said, "He withdrew," is manifest from the passage, "And when He heard that John was delivered up He withdrew into Galilee."[4] Perhaps also on this account, when describing the things in this place, Mark says that "He rose up and went into the borders of Tyre, and having entered into the house wished no man to know it."[5] It is probable that He sought to avoid the Pharisees who were offended at His teaching, waiting for the time for His suffering, which was more fitting and rightly appointed. But some one might say that Tyre and Sidon are used for the Gentiles; accordingly when He withdrew from Israel He came into the parts of the Gentiles. Among the Hebrews, then, Tyre is called Sor, and it is interpreted "anguish." Sidon, which is also the Hebrew name, is rendered "hunters." And among the Gentiles likewise the hunters are the evil powers, and among them is great distress, the distress, namely, which exists in wickedness and passions. When Jesus, then, went out from Gennesaret He withdrew indeed from Israel and came, not to Tyre and Sidon, but into "the parts" of Tyre and Sidon, with the result that those of the Gentiles now believe in part; so that if He had visited the whole of Tyre and Sidon, no unbeliever would have been left in it.

[1] Matt. xv. 21, 22. [2] Matt. xiv. 34. [3] Matt. xv. 11. [4] Matt. iv. 12. [5] Mark vii. 24.

Now, according to Mark, "Jesus rose up and went into the borders of Tyre,"[1]—that is, the distress of the Gentiles,—in order that they also from these borders who believe can be saved, when they come out of them; for attend to this: "And behold a Canaanitish woman came out from these borders and cried saying, Have mercy on me, O Lord, Thou Son of David, my daughter is terribly vexed with a demon."[2] And I think that if she had not come out from those borders she would not have been able to cry to Jesus with the great faith to which testimony was borne; and according to the proportion of faith one comes out from the borders among the Gentiles, which "when the Most High divided the nations He set up according to the number of the sons of Israel,"[3] and prevented their further advance. Here, then, certain borders are spoken of as the borders of Tyre and Sidon, but in Exodus the borders of Pharaoh,[4] in which, they say, were formed the plagues against the Egyptians. And we must suppose that each of us when he sins is in the borders of Tyre or Sidon or of Pharaoh and Egypt, or some one of those which are outside the allotted inheritance of God; but when he changes from wickedness to virtue he goes out from the borders of evil, and comes to the borders of the portion of God, there being among these also a difference which will be manifest to those who are able to understand the things that concern the division and the inheritance of Israel, in harmony with the spiritual law. And attend also to the meeting, so to speak, which took place between Jesus and the Canaanitish woman; for He comes as to the parts of Tyre and Sidon, and she comes out of those parts, and cried, saying, "Have mercy on me, O Lord, Thou Son of David."[5] Now the woman was Canaanitish, which is rendered, prepared for humiliation. The righteous, indeed, are prepared for the kingdom of heaven and for the exaltation in the kingdom of God;[6] but sinners are prepared for the humiliation of the wickedness which is in them, and of the deeds which flow from it and prepare them for it, and of the sin which reigns in their mortal body. Only, the Canaanitish woman came out of those borders and went forth from the state of being prepared for humiliation, crying and saying, "Have mercy on me, O Lord, Thou Son of David."

[1] Mark vii. 24.
[2] Matt. xv. 22.
[3] Deut xxxii. 8.
[4] Exod. viii. 2.
[5] Matt. xv. 22.
[6] Cf. Matt. xxv. 34.

17. EXPOSITION OF THE DETAILS IN THE NARRATIVE.

Now bring together from the Gospels those who call Him Son of David, as she, and the blind men in Jericho;[1] and who call Him Son of God, and that without the addition "truly" like the demoniacs who say, "What have we to do with Thee, Thou Son of God;"[2] and who call Him so with the addition "truly," like those in the boat who worshipped Him saying, "Truly Thou art the Son of God."[3] For the bringing together of these passages will, I think, be useful to you with a view to seeing the difference of those who come (to Jesus); some indeed come as to Him "who was born of the seed of David according to the flesh;"[4] but others come to Him who "was declared to be the Son of God with power, according to the spirit of holiness;"[5] and of these some with the "truly," and some without it. Further, observe, that the Canaanitish woman besought Him not about a son, whom she does not seem to have brought forth at all, but about a daughter who was terribly vexed with a demon; but another mother receives back alive her son who was being carried forth dead.[6] And again the ruler of the synagogue makes supplication for a daughter twelve years old, as being dead,[7] but the nobleman about a son as being still sick, and at the point of death.[8] The daughter, accordingly, who was distressed by a demon, and the dead son sprang from two mothers; and the dead daughter, and the son who was sick unto death, sprang from two fathers, of whom the one was a ruler of the synagogue, and the other was a nobleman. And I am persuaded these things contain reasons concerning the diverse kinds of souls which Jesus vivifies and heals. And all the cures that He works among the people, especially those recorded by the Evangelists, took place at that time, that those who would not otherwise have believed unless they saw signs and wonders might believe;[9] for the things aforetime were symbols of the things that are ever being accomplished by the power of Jesus; for there is no time when each of the things which are written is not done by the power of Jesus according to the desert of each. The Canaanitish woman, therefore, because of her race was not worthy even to receive an answer from Jesus, who acknowledged that He had not been sent by the Father

[1] Matt. xx. 30.
[2] Matt. viii. 29.
[3] Matt. xiv. 33.
[4] Rom. i. 3.
[5] Rom. i. 4.
[6] Luke vii. 12.
[7] Matt. ix. 18.
[8] John iv. 46.
[9] John iv. 48.

for any other thing than to the lost sheep of the house of Israel,[1]—a lost race of souls possessed of clear vision; but, because of her resolution and of having worshipped Jesus as Son of God, she obtains an answer, which reproaches her with baseness of birth and exhibits the measure of her worthiness, namely, that she was worthy of crumbs as the little dogs, but not of the loaves. But when she with intensified resolution, accepting the saying of Jesus, puts forth the claim to obtain crumbs even as a little dog, and acknowledges that the masters are of a nobler race, then she gets a second answer, which bears testimony to her faith as great, and a promise that it shall be done unto her as she wills.[2] And corresponding, I think, "to the Jerusalem above, which is free, the mother"[3] of Paul and those like to him, must we conceive of the Canaanitish woman, the mother of her who was terribly distressed with a demon, who was the symbol of the mother of such a soul. And consider whether it is not according to sound reason that there are also many fathers and many mothers corresponding to the fathers of Abraham to whom the patriarch went away,[4] and to Jerusalem the "mother," as Paul says, concerning himself and those like to him. And it is probable that she of whom the Canaanitish woman was a symbol came out of the borders of Tyre and Sidon, of which the places on earth were types, and came to the Saviour and besought Him and even now beseeches Him saying, "Have mercy on me, O Lord, Thou Son of David, my daughter is terribly vexed with a demon."[5] Then also to those without and to the disciples when necessary He answers and says, "I was not sent;"[6] teaching us that there are some lost souls pre-eminently intellectual and clear of vision, figuratively called sheep of the house of Israel; which things, I think, the simpler who are of opinion that they are spoken in regard to the Israel which is after the flesh will of necessity admit, namely, that our Saviour was sent by the Father to no others than to those lost Jews. But we, who can truthfully boast that "if we have once known Christ after the flesh, but now no longer do we know Him so,"[7] are assured that it is pre-eminently the work of the Word to save the more intelligent, for these are more akin to Him than those who are duller. But since the lost sheep of the house of Israel, with the exception of "the remnant according to the election of grace,"[8] disbelieved the Word, on this account "God chose the foolish things of the world,"[1] namely, that which was not Israel, nor clear of vision, that He might put to shame the wise ones of Israel; and He called "the things which are not,"[2] handing over to them an intelligent nation who were able to admit "the foolishness of the preaching,"[3] and of His good pleasure saved those who believe in this, that He might refute "the things which are," having perfected praise for Himself, "out of the mouths of babes and sucklings,"[4] when they became hostile to truth. Now, the Canaanitish woman, having come, worshipped Jesus as God, saying, "Lord, help me," but He answered and said, "It is not possible to take the children's bread and cast it to the little dogs."[5] But some one might inquire also into the meaning of this saying, since,—inasmuch as there was a measure of loaves such that both the children and the dogs of the household could not eat loaves, unless the dogs ate other loaves than those which were well made,—it was not possible according to right reason for the well-made loaf of the children to be given as food to the little dogs. But no such thing appears in the case of the power of Jesus, for of this it was possible both for the children and those called little dogs to partake. Consider, then, whether perhaps with reference to the saying, "It is not possible to take the bread of children," we ought to say that, "He who emptied Himself and took upon Him the form of a servant,"[6] brought a measure of power such as the world was capable of receiving, of which power also He was conscious that a certain quantity went forth from Him as is plain from the words, "Some one did touch Me, for I perceived that power had gone forth from Me."[7] From this measure of power, then, He dispensed, giving a larger portion to those who were pre-eminent and who were called sons, but a smaller portion to those who were not such, as to the little dogs. But though these things were so, nevertheless where there was great faith, to her, who because of her base birth in Canaanitish land was a little dog, He gave as to a child the bread of the children. And perhaps, also, of the words of Jesus there are some loaves which it is possible to give to the more rational, as to children only; and other words, as it were, crumbs from the great house and table of the well-

[1] Matt. xv. 24. [2] Matt. xv. 28. [3] Gal. iv. 26. [4] Gen. xv. 15. [5] Matt. xv. 22. [6] Matt. xv. 24. [7] 2 Cor. v. 16. [8] Rom. xi. 5.

[1] 1 Cor. i. 27. [2] 1 Cor. i. 28. [3] 1 Cor. i. 21. [4] Ps. viii. 2. [5] Matt. xv. 25, 26. [6] Phil. ii. 7. [7] Luke viii. 46.

born and the masters, which may be used by some souls, like the dogs. And according to the law of Moses it is written about certain things, "Ye shall cast them to the dogs,"[1] and it was a matter of care to the Holy Spirit to give instruction about certain foods that they should be left to the dogs. Let others, then, who are strangers to the doctrine of the Church, assume that souls pass from the bodies of men into the bodies of dogs, according to their varying degree of wickedness; but we, who do not find this at all in the divine Scripture, say that the more rational condition changes into one more irrational, undergoing this affection in consequence of great slothfulness and negligence. But, also, in the same way, a will which was more irrational, because of its neglect of reason, sometimes turns and becomes rational, so that that which at one time was a dog, loving to eat of the crumbs that fell from the table of its masters, comes into the condition of a son. For virtue contributes greatly to the making of one a son of God, but wickedness, and mad fury in wanton discourses and shamelessness, contribute to the giving of a man the name of dog according to the word of the Scripture.[2] And the like you will also understand in the case of the other names which are applied to animals without reason. Only, he who is reproached as a dog and yet is not indignant at being called unworthy of the bread of children and with all forbearance repeats the saying of that Canaanitish woman, "Yea, Lord, for even the little dogs eat of the crumbs which fall from their masters'[3] table," will obtain the very gentle answer of Jesus saying to him, "Great is thy faith,"—when he has received so great faith—and saying, "Be it done unto thee even as thou wilt,"[4] so that he himself may be healed, and if he has produced any fruit which stands in need of healing, that this, too, may be cured.

18. CONCERNING THE MULTITUDES WHO WERE HEALED. COMPARISON OF THE MOUNTAIN WHERE JESUS SAT TO THE CHURCH.

"*And Jesus departed thence,*"—manifestly, from what has been said before, from the parts of Tyre and Sidon,—"*and came nigh unto the sea of Galilee,*"[5] which is commonly called the Lake of Gennesaret, and again went up into the mountain where He went up and sat. We may say, then, that into this mountain where Jesus sits, not only the sound in health go up, but along with the sound, those also who were suffering from various disorders. And, perhaps, this mountain to which Jesus went up and sat is that which is more commonly called the Church, which has been set up through the word of God over the rest of the world and the men upon it; whither go not the disciples only, leaving the multitudes as in the case of the beatitudes, but great multitudes who were not accused themselves of being deaf or suffering from any affection, but who had such along with themselves. For you may see, along with the multitudes who come to this mountain where the Son of God sits, some who have become deaf to the things promised, and others blind in soul and not looking at the true light, and others who are lame and not able to walk according to reason, and others who are maimed and not able to work according to reason. Those, accordingly, who are suffering in soul from such things, though they go up along with the multitudes into the mountain where Jesus was, so long as they are outside of the feet of Jesus, are not healed by Him; but when, as men suffering from such disorders, they are cast by the multitude at His feet,[1] and at the extremities of the body of Christ, not being worthy to obtain such things so far as they themselves are concerned, they are then healed by Him. And when you see in the congregation of what is more commonly called the church the catechumens cast behind those who are at the extreme end of it, and as it were at the feet of the body of Jesus—the church—coming to it with their own deafness and blindness and lameness and crookedness, and in time cured according to the Word, you would not err in saying that such having gone up with the multitudes of the church to the mountain where Jesus was, are cast at His feet and are healed; so that the multitude of the church is astonished at beholding transformations which have taken place from so great evils to that which is better, so that it might say, those who were formerly dumb afterwards speak the word of God, and the lame walk, the prophecy of Isaiah being fulfilled, not only in things bodily but in things spiritual, which said, "Then shall the lame man leap as an hart, and the tongue of him that hath an impediment in his speech be plain."[2] And there, unless the expression, "the lame man shall leap as an hart," is to be taken as accidental, we will say that those formerly lame,

[1] Exod. xxii. 31. [2] 2 Sam. xvi. 9. [3] Matt. xv. 27. [4] Matt. xv. 28. [5] Matt. xv. 29.

[1] Matt. xv. 30. [2] Isa. xxxv. 6.

and who now through the power of Jesus leap as an hart are not without design compared to a hart, which is a clean animal, and hostile to serpents and cannot at all be injured by their poison. But also, in respect of the fact that the dumb are seen speaking is the prophecy fulfilled which said, "And the tongue of him that hath an impediment shall be plain," or rather that which said, "Hear ye deaf;" but the blind see according to the prophecy following, "Hear ye deaf, and ye blind look up that ye may see."[1] Now the blind see, when they see the world and from the exceeding great beauty of the things created they contemplate the Creator corresponding in greatness and beauty to them; and when they see clearly "the invisible things of God Himself from the creation of the world, which are perceived through the things that are made;"[2] that is, they see and understand with care and clearness. Now the multitudes seeing these things, glorified the God of Israel,[3] and glorify Him in the persuasion that it is the same God, who is the Father of Him who healed those previously mentioned, and the God of Israel. For He is not the God of the Jews only, but also of the Gentiles.[4] Let us then cause to go up along with ourselves to the mountain where Jesus sits—His church—those who wish to go up to it along with us, the deaf, the blind, the lame, the maimed and many others, and let us cast them at the feet of Jesus that He may heal them, so that the multitudes are astonished at their healing; for it is not the disciples who are described as wondering at such things, although at that time they were present with Jesus, as is manifest from the words, "And Jesus called unto Him His disciples and said, I have compassion on the multitudes,"[5] etc.; and perhaps if you attend carefully to the words, "There came unto Him great multitudes,"[6] you would find that the disciples at that time did not come to Him, but had begun long ago to follow Him and followed Him into the mountain. But there came unto Him those who were inferior to the disciples, and were then for the first time approaching Him, who had not the same experience as those who had gone up with them. Observe, moreover, in the Gospel who are described as having followed Jesus, and who as having come to Him, and who as having been brought to Him, and the division between those who go before and of those who follow; and of those who came, who came to Him in the house, and who when He was elsewhere. For by observation, and by comparing things spiritual with spiritual, you would find many things worthy of the accurate wisdom in the Gospels.

[1] Isa. xlii. 18. [2] Rom. i. 20. [3] Matt. xv. 31. [4] Rom. iii. 29. [5] Matt. xv. 3.2 [6] Matt. xv. 30.

19. CONCERNING THE SEVEN LOAVES. THE NARRATIVE OF THE FEEDING OF THE FOUR THOUSAND COMPARED WITH THAT OF THE FIVE THOUSAND.

"*And Jesus called unto Him His disciples and said.*"[1] Above in the similar history to this about the loaves, before the loaves are spoken of, "Jesus came forth and saw a great multitude and had compassion upon them and healed their sick. And when even was come the disciples came to Him saying, The place is desert and the time is already past, send them away,"[2] etc. But now after the healing of the deaf and the rest, He takes compassion on the multitude which had continued with Him now three days and had nothing to eat. And there the disciples make request concerning the five thousand;[3] but here He speaks of His own accord about the four thousand.[4] Those, too, are fed when it was evening after they had spent a day with Him; but these, who are testified to have continued with Him three days, partake of the loaves lest they might faint by the way. And there the disciples say to Him when He was not inquiring, that they had only five loaves and two fishes; but here to Him making inquiry, they give answer about the seven loaves and the few small fishes. And there He commands the multitudes to sit down or lie upon the grass; for Luke also wrote, "Make them sit down,"[5] and Mark says, "He commanded them all to sit down;"[6] but here He does not command but proclaims[7] to the multitude to sit down. Again, there, the three Evangelists say in the very same words that "He took the five loaves and the two fishes and looking up to heaven He blessed;"[8] but here, as Matthew and Mark have written, "Jesus gave thanks and brake;"[9] there, they recline upon the grass, but here they sit down upon the ground. You will moreover investigate in the accounts in the different places the variation found in John, who wrote in regard to that transaction that Jesus said, "Make the

[1] Matt. xv. 32. [2] Matt. xiv. 15. [3] Matt. xiv. 15. [4] Matt. xv. 32. [5] Luke ix. 14. [6] Mark vi. 39.
[7] ου κελεύει ἀλλὰ παραγγέλλει
[8] Matt. xiv. 19; Mark vi. 41; Luke ix. 16.
[9] Matt. xv 36; Mark viii. 6.

men sit down,"[1] and that, having given thanks, He gave of the loaves to them that were set down, but he did not mention this miracle at all.[2] Attending, then, to the difference of those things which are written in the various places in regard to the loaves, I think that these belong to a different order from those; wherefore these are fed in a mountain, and those in a desert place; and these after they had continued three days with Jesus, but those one day, on the evening of which they were fed. And further, unless it be the same thing for Jesus to do a thing of Himself and to act after having heard from the disciples, consider if those to whom Jesus shows kindness are not superior when He fed them on the spot with a view to showing them kindness. And, if according to John,[3] they were barley loaves of which the twelve baskets remained over, but nothing of this kind is said about these, how are not these superior to the former? And the sick of those He healed,[4] but here He heals these, along with the multitudes, who were not sick but blind, and lame, and deaf, and maimed; wherefore also in regard to these the four thousand marvel,[5] but in regard to the sick no such thing is said. And these I think who ate of the seven loaves for which thanks were given, are superior to those who ate of the five which were blessed; and these who ate the few little fishes to those who ate of the two, and perhaps also these who sat down upon the ground to those who sat down on the grass. And those from fewer loaves leave twelve baskets, but these from a greater number leave seven baskets, inasmuch, as they were able to receive more. And perhaps these tread upon all earthly things and sit down upon them, but those upon the grass—upon their flesh only—for "all flesh is grass."[1] Consider also after this, that Jesus does not wish to send them away fasting lest they faint on the way, as being without the loaves of Jesus, and while they were still on the way—the way to their own concerns—might suffer injury. Take note also of the cases where Jesus is recorded to have sent any one away, that you may see the difference of those who were sent away by Him after being fed, and those who had been sent away otherwise; and, as a pattern of one who was sent away otherwise, take "Woman, thou art loosed from thine infirmity."[2] But further the disciples who are always with Jesus are not sent away by Him; but the multitudes after they have eaten are sent away. Likewise, again, the disciples who conceive nothing great about the Canaanitish woman say, "Send her away, for she crieth after us;"[3] but the Saviour does not at all appear to send her away; for saying unto her, "O woman, great is thy faith, be it done to thee even as thou wilt,"[4] He healed her daughter from that hour: it is not however written that He sent her away. So far at the present time have we been able to investigate and see into the passage before us.

BOOK XII.

1. CONCERNING THOSE WHO ASKED HIM TO SHOW THEM A SIGN FROM HEAVEN.

"*And the Sadducees and Pharisees came, and tempting Him kept asking Him to shew them a sign from heaven.*"[6] The Sadducees and Pharisees who disagreed with each other in regard to the most essential truths,—for the Pharisees champion the doctrine of the resurrection of the dead, hoping that there will be a world to come, while the Sadducees know nothing after this life in store for a man whether he has been advancing towards virtue, or has made no effort at all to come out from the mountains of wickedness,—these, I say, agree that they may tempt Jesus. Now, a similar thing, as Luke has narrated,[5] happened in the case of Herod and Pilate, who became friends with one another that they might kill Jesus; for, perhaps, their hostility with one another would have prevented Herod from asking that He should be put to death, in order to please the people, who said, "Crucify Him, Crucify Him,"[6] and would have influenced Pilate, who was somewhat inclined against His condemnation, his hostility with Herod giving fresh impulse to the inclination which he previously cherished to release Jesus. But their apparent friendship made Herod stronger in

[1] John vi. 10. [2] *Or*, did not mention the occasion of this.
[3] John vi. 13. [4] Matt. xiv. 14. [5] Matt. xv. 31. [6] Matt. xvi. 1.

[1] Isa. xl. 6. [2] Luke xiii. 12, *Literally* 'thou art sent away.'
[3] Matt. xv. 23. [4] Matt. xv. 28. [5] Luke xxiii. 12. [6] Luke xxiii. 21.

his demand against Jesus with Pilate, who wished, perhaps, also because of the newly-formed friendship to do something to gratify Herod and all the nation of the Jews. And often even now you may see in daily life those who hold the most divergent opinions, whether in the philosophy of the Greeks or in other systems of thought, appearing to be of one mind that they may scoff at and attack Jesus Christ in the person of His disciples. And from these things I think you may go on by rational argument to consider, whether when forces join in opposition which are in disagreement with one another, as of Pharaoh with Nebuchadnezzar,[1] and of Tirhakah, king of the Ethiopians, with Sennacherib,[2] a combination then takes place against Jesus and His people. So perhaps, also, "The kings of the earth set themselves and the rulers were gathered together,"[3] though not at all before at harmony with one another, that having taken counsel against the Lord and His Christ. they might slay the Lord of glory.

2. WHY THE PHARISEES ASKED A SIGN FROM HEAVEN.

Now, to this point we have come in our discourse, because of the Pharisees and Sadducees coming together unto Jesus, who disagreed in matters relating to the resurrection, but came, as it were, to an agreement for the sake of tempting our Saviour, and asking Him to show them a sign from heaven. For, not satisfied with the wonderful signs shown among the people in the healing of all forms of disease and sickness, and with the rest of the miracles which our Saviour had done in the knowledge of many, they wished Him to show to them also a sign from heaven. And I conjecture that they suspected that the signs upon earth might possibly not be of God; for they did not hesitate indeed to say, "Jesus casts out demons by Beelzebub the prince of the demons;"[4] and it seemed to them that a sign from heaven could not spring from Beelzebub or any other wicked power. But they erred in regard to both, in regard to signs upon earth as well as to signs from heaven, not being "approved money-changers,"[5] nor knowing how to distinguish between the spirits that are working, which kind are from God, and which have revolted from Him. And they ought to have known that even many of the portents wrought against Egypt in the time of Moses, though they were not from heaven, were clearly from God, and that the fire which fell from heaven upon the sheep of Job was not from God;[1] for that fire belonged to the same one as he to whom belonged those who carried off, and made three bands of horsemen against, the cattle of Job. I think, moreover, that in Isaiah—as if signs could be shown both from the earth and from heaven, the true being from God, but "with all power and signs and lying wonders"[2] those from the evil one—it was said to Ahaz, "Ask for thyself a sign from the Lord thy God in the depth or in the height."[3] For, unless there had been some signs in the depth or in the height which were not from the Lord God, this would not have been said, "Ask for thyself a sign from the Lord thy God in the depth or in the height." But I know well that such an interpretation of the passage, "Ask for thyself a sign from the Lord thy God," will seem to some one rather forced; but give heed to that which is said by the Apostle about the man of sin, the son of perdition, that, "with all power and signs and lying wonders and with all deceit of unrighteousness,"[4] he shall be manifested to them that are perishing, imitating all kinds of wonders, to-wit, those of truth. And as the enchanters and magicians of the Egyptians, as being inferior to the man of sin and the son of perdition, imitated certain powers, both the signs and wonders of truth, doing lying wonders so that the true might not be believed; so I think the man of sin will imitate signs and powers. And perhaps, also, the Pharisees suspected these things because of the prophecies concerning Him; but I inquire whether also the Sadducees tempting Him asked Jesus to show them a sign from heaven. For unless we say that they suspected this, how shall we describe their relation to the portents which Jesus wrought, who continued hard-hearted and were not put to shame by the miraculous things that were done? But if any one supposes that we have given an occasion of defence to the Pharisees and Sadducees, both when they say that the demons were cast out by Jesus through Beelzebub, and when tempting Him, they ask Jesus about a heavenly sign, let him know that we plausibly say that they were drawn away to the end that they might not believe in the miracles of Jesus; but not as to deserve

[1] 2 Kings xxiv. 7.
[2] 2 Kings xix. 9.
[3] Ps. ii. 2.
[4] Matt. ix. 24; xii. 24.
[5] The familiar saying so frequently quoted as Scripture in the Fathers, sometimes ascribed to Jesus by them, sometimes to Paul. See Suicer.

[1] Job i. 16.
[2] 2 Thess. ii. 9.
[3] Isa. vii. 11.
[4] 2 Thess. ii. 9, 10.

forgiveness; for they did not look to the words of the prophets which were being fulfilled in the acts of Jesus, which an evil power was not at all capable of imitating. But to bring back a soul which had gone out, so that it came out of the grave when already stinking and passing the fourth day,[1] was the work of no other than Him who heard the word of the Father, "Let us make man after our image and likeness."[2] But also to command the winds and to make the violence of the sea cease at a word, was the work of no other than Him through whom all things, both the sea itself and the winds, have come into being. Moreover also as to the teaching which stimulates men to the love of the Creator, in harmony with the law and the prophets, and which checks passions and moulds morals according to piety, what else did it indicate to such as were able to see, than that He was truly the Son of God who wrought works so mighty? In respect of which things He said also to the disciples of John, "Go your way and tell John what great things ye see and hear; the blind receive their sight," etc.[3]

3. THE ANSWER OF JESUS TO THEIR REQUEST.

Next let us remark in what way, when asked in regard to one sign, that He might show it from heaven, to the Pharisees and Sadducees who put the question, He answers and says, "*An evil and adulterous generation seeketh after a sign, and there shall be no sign given to it, but the sign of Jonah the prophet*," when also, "*He left them and departed.*"[4] But the sign of Jonah, in truth, according to their question, was not merely a sign but also a sign from heaven; so that even to those who tempted Him and sought a sign from heaven He, nevertheless, out of His own great goodness gave the sign. For if, as Jonah passed three days and three nights in the whale's belly, so the Son of man did in the heart of the earth, and after this rose up from it,—whence but from heaven shall we say that the sign of the resurrection of Christ came? And especially when, at the time of the passion, He became a sign to the robber who obtained favour from Him to enter into the paradise of God; after this, I think, descending into Hades to the dead, "as free among the dead."[5] And the Saviour seems to me to conjoin the sign which was to come from Himself with the reason of the sign in regard to Jonah when He says, not merely that a sign like to that is granted by Him but that very sign; for attend to the words, "And there shall no sign be given to it but the sign of Jonah the prophet."[1] Accordingly that sign was this sign, because that became indicative of this, so that the elucidation of that sign, which was obscure on the face of it, might be found in the fact that the Saviour suffered, and passed three days and three nights in the heart of the earth. At the same time also we learn the general principle that, if the sign signifies something, each of the signs which are recorded, whether as in actual history, or by way of precept, is indicative of something afterwards fulfilled; as for example, the sign of Jonah going out after three days from the whale's belly was indicative of the resurrection of our Saviour, rising after three days and three nights from the dead; and that which is called circumcision is the sign of that which is indicated by Paul in the words: "We are the circumcision."[2] Seek you also every sign in the Old Scriptures as indicative of some passage in the New Scripture, and that which is named a sign in the New Covenant as indicative of something either in the age about to be, or even in the subsequent generations after that the sign has taken place.

4. WHY JESUS CALLED THEM AN ADULTEROUS GENERATION. THE LAW AS HUSBAND.

And He called them, indeed, "an evil generation," because of the quality arising from evil which had been produced in them, for wickedness is voluntary evil-doing, but "adulterous" because that when the Pharisees and Sadducees left that which is figuratively called man, the word of truth or the law, they were debauched by falsehood and the law of sin. For if there are two laws, the law in our members warring against the law of the mind, and the law of the mind,[3] we must say that the law of the mind—that is, the spiritual—is man, to whom the soul was given by God as wife, that is, to the man who is law, according to what is written, "A wife is married to a man by God;"[4] but the other is a paramour of the soul which is subject to it, which also on account of it is called an adulteress. Now that the law is husband of the soul Paul clearly exhibits in the Epistle to the Romans, saying, "The law hath dominion over a man for so long time as he liveth; for the woman that hath a husband is bound to the husband

[1] John xi. 39. [2] Gen. i. 26. [3] Matt. xi. 4, 5. [4] Matt. xvi. 4. [5] Ps. lxxxviii. 6.

[1] Matt. xvi. 4. [2] Phil. iii. 3. [3] Rom. vii. 23. [4] Prov. xix. 14.

while he liveth, to the husband who is law,"[1] etc. For consider in these things that the law hath dominion over the man so long time as the law liveth,—as a husband over a wife. "For the woman that hath a husband," that is, the soul under the law, "is bound to the husband while he liveth," to the husband who is the law; but if the husband —that is, the law die—she is discharged from the law, which is her husband. Now the law dies to him who has gone up to the condition of blessedness, and no longer lives under the law, but acts like to Christ, who, though He became under law for the sake of those under law, that He might gain those under law,[2] did not continue under law, nor did He leave subject to law those who had been freed by Him; for He led them up along with Himself to the divine citizenship which is above the law, which contains, as for the imperfect and such as are still sinners, sacrifices for the remission of sins. He then who is without sin, and stands no longer in need of legal sacrifices, perhaps when he has become perfect has passed beyond even the spiritual law, and comes to the Word beyond it, who became flesh to those who live in the flesh, but to those who no longer at all war after the flesh, He is perceived as being the Word, as [3] He was God in the beginning with God, and reveals the Father. Three things therefore are to be thought of in connection with this place—the woman that hath a husband, who is under a husband—the law; and the woman who is an adulteress, to-wit, the soul, which, while her husband, the law, liveth, has become joined to another husband, namely, the law of the flesh; and the woman who is married to the brother of the dead husband, to the Word who is alive and dies not, who "being raised from the dead dieth no more, for death hath no more dominion over Him."[4] So far then because of the saying, "But if the husband die she is discharged from the law, the husband," and because of this, "so then, while her husband liveth, she shall be called an adulteress, if she be joined to another man," and because of this, "but if the husband die, she is free from the law, so that she is no adulteress though she be joined to another man."[5] But this very saying, "So then while her husband liveth, she shall be called an adulteress," we have brought forward, wishing clearly to show why in answer to the Pharisees and Sadducees who were tempting Him and asking Him to show them a sign from heaven, He said not only "a wicked generation," but an "adulterous" generation.[1] In a general way, then, the law in the members which wars against the law of the mind,[2] as a man who is an adulterer, is an adulterer of the soul. But now also every power that is hostile, which gains the mastery over the human soul, and has intercourse with it, commits adultery with her who had a bridegroom given to her by God, namely, the Word. After these things it is written that "He left them and departed." For how was the bridegroom—the Word—not going to leave the adulterous generation and depart from it? But you might say that the Word of God, leaving the synagogue of the Jews as adulterous, departed from it, and took a wife of fornication,[3] namely, those from the Gentiles; since those who were "Sion, a faithful city,"[4] have become harlots; but these have become like the harlot Rahab, who received the spies of Joshua, and was saved with all her house;[5] after this no longer playing the harlot, but coming to the feet of Jesus, and wetting them with the tears of repentance, and anointing them with the fragrance of the ointment of holy conversation, on account of whom, reproaching Simon the leper,—the former people,—He spoke those things which are written.[6]

5. CONCERNING THE LEAVEN OF THE PHARISEES.

"*And His disciples came to the other side and forgot to take loaves.*"[7] Since the loaves which they had before they came to the other side were no longer useful to the disciples when they came to the other side,—for they needed one kind of loaves before they crossed and a different kind when they crossed,—on this account, being careless of taking loaves when going to the other side, they forgot to take loaves with them. To the other side then came the disciples of Jesus who had passed over from things material to things spiritual, and from things sensible to those which are intellectual. And perhaps that He might turn back those who, by crossing to the other side, "had begun in spirit,"[8] from running back to carnal things, Jesus said to them when on the other side, "Take heed and beware."[9] For there was a certain lump of teaching

[1] Rom. vii. 1, 2. Ἡ γὰρ ὕπανδρος γυνὴ τῷ ζῶντι ἀνδρὶ δέδεται νόμῳ. The reader must note that Origen takes νόμῳ in apposition to ἀνδρὶ.
[2] 1 Cor. ix. 10.
[3] *Or*, who was God.
[4] Rom. vi. 9.
[5] Rom. vii. 2, 3.

[1] Matt. xvi. 4. [2] Rom. vii. 23. [3] Hos. i. 2. [4] Isa. i. 21.
[5] Josh. vi. 25. [6] Luke vii. 37–50. Cf. Matt. xxvi. 6.
[7] Matt. xvi. 5. [8] Cf. Gal. iii. 3. [9] Matt. xvi. 6.

and of truly ancient leaven,—that according to the bare letter, and on this account not freed from those things which arise from wickedness,—which the Pharisees and Sadducees offered, of which Jesus does not wish His own disciples any longer to eat, having made for them a new and spiritual lump, offering Himself to those who gave up the leaven of the Pharisees and Sadducees and had come to Him—"the living bread which came down from heaven and gives life to the world."[1] But since, to him who is no longer going to use the leaven and the lump and the teaching of the Pharisees and the Sadducees, the first thing is to "see" and then to "beware," so that no one, by reason of not seeing and from want of taking heed, may ever partake of their forbidden leaven,—on this account He says to the disciples, first, "see," and then, "beware." It is the mark of the clear-sighted and careful to separate the leaven of the Pharisees and Sadducees and every food that is not of "the unleavened-bread of sincerity and truth"[2] from the living bread, even that which came down from heaven, so that no one who eats may adopt the things of the Pharisees and the Sadducees, but by eating the living and true bread may strengthen his soul. And we might seasonably apply the saying to those who, along with the Christian way of life, prefer to live as the Jews, materially, for these do not see nor beware of the leaven of the Pharisees and Sadducees, but, contrary to the will of Jesus who forbade it, eat the bread of the Pharisees. Yea and also all, who do not wish to understand that the law is spiritual, and has a shadow of the good things to come,[3] and is a shadow of the things to come,[4] neither inquire of what good thing about to be each of the laws is a shadow, nor do they see nor beware of the leaven of the Pharisees; and they also who reject the doctrine of the resurrection of the dead are not on their guard against the leaven of the Sadducees. And there are many among the heterodox who, because of their unbelief in regard to the resurrection of the dead, are imbued with the leaven of the Sadducees. Now, while Jesus said these things, the disciples reasoned, saying not aloud, but in their own hearts, "We took no loaves."[5] And something like this was what they said, "If we had loaves we would not have had to take of the leaven of the Pharisees and the Sadducees; but since, from want of loaves, we run the risk of taking from their leaven, while the Saviour does not wish us to run back to their teaching, therefore He said to us, "Take heed and beware of the leaven of the Pharisees and the Sadducees."[1] And these things then they reasoned; Jesus, while looking to that which was in their hearts, and hearing the reasons in them, as the true overseer of hearts, reproves them because they did not see nor remember the loaves which they received from Him; on account of which, even when they appeared to be in want of loaves, they did not need the leaven of the Pharisees and the Sadducees.

6. THE MEANING OF LEAVEN. JESUS' KNOWLEDGE OF THE HEART.

Then expounding clearly and representing to them, who were being distracted because of the equivocal meaning of loaf and leaven, in an undisguised fashion, that He was not speaking to them about sensible bread but about the leaven in the teaching, He subjoins, "*How is it that ye do not perceive that I spake not to you concerning bread? But beware of the leaven of the Pharisees and the Sadducees.*"[2] And though He had not laid bare the interpretation, but still continued to use metaphorical language, the disciples would have understood that the discourse of the Saviour was about the teaching, figuratively called leaven, which the Pharisees and Sadducees were teaching. So long, then, as we have Jesus with us fulfilling the promise which runs, "Lo, I am with you always unto the consummation of the age,"[3] we cannot fast nor be in want of food, so that, because of want of it we should desire to take and eat the forbidden leaven, even from the Pharisees and Sadducees. Now there may sometimes be a time, when He is with us, that we are without food, as is spoken of in the passage above, "They continue with me now three days and have nothing to eat;"[4] but, even though this should happen, being unwilling to send us away fasting lest we faint on the way, He gives thanks over the loaves which were with the disciples, and causes us to have the seven baskets over from the seven loaves, as we have recorded. And moreover this also is to be observed, in view of those who think that the divinity of the Saviour is not at all demonstrable from the Gospel of Matthew, that the fact that, when the disciples were reasoning among themselves

[1] John vi. 33, 51. [2] 1 Cor. v. 8. [3] Heb. x. 1. [4] Col. ii. 17. [5] Matt. xvi. 7.

[1] Matt. xvi. 6. [2] Matt. xvi. 11. [3] Matt. xxviii. 20. [4] Matt. xv. 32.

and saying, "We have no loaves," Jesus knew their reasonings and said, "Why reason ye among yourselves, O ye of little faith, because ye took no loaves,"[1] was beyond the power of man; for the Lord alone, as Solomon says in the third Book of Kings, knows the hearts of men.[2] But since the disciples understood, when Jesus said, "Beware of the leaven,"[3] that He did not tell them to beware of the loaves but of the teaching of the Pharisees and Sadducees, you will understand that whenever leaven is named it is put figuratively for teaching, whether in the law, or in the Scriptures which come after the law; and so perhaps leaven is not offered upon the altar; for it is not right that prayers should take the form of teaching, but should only be supplications of good things from God. But one might inquire, on account of what has been said about disciples who came to the other side, if any one who has reached the other side can be reproached as one of little faith, and as not yet understanding nor remembering what was done by Jesus. But it is not difficult, I think, to say to this, that in relation to that which is perfect, on the coming of which "that which is in part shall be done away,"[4] all our faith here is little faith, and in regard to that, we who know in part do not yet know nor remember; for we are not able to obtain a memory which is sufficient and able to attain to the magnitude of the nature of the speculations.

7. RELATIVE MAGNITUDE OF SINS OF THE HEART AND ACTUAL SINS.

But we may also learn from this, that in respect of the reasonings only which we reason within ourselves, we are sometimes convicted and reproached as being of little faith. And I think that just as a man commits adultery in his heart only, though not proceeding altogether to the overt act, so he commits in his heart the rest of the things which are forbidden. As then he who has committed adultery in his heart will be punished proportionately to adultery of this kind, so also he who has done in his heart any one of the things forbidden, for example, who has stolen in his heart only, or borne false witness in his heart only, will not be punished as he who has stolen in fact, or who has completed the very act of false testimony, but only as he who has done such things in his heart. There is also the case of the man who while he did not arrive at the evil action,

[1] Matt. xvi. 8.
[2] 1 Kings viii. 39.
[3] Matt. xvi. 6.
[4] 1 Cor. xiii. 10.

came short of it in spite of his own will. For if, in addition to willing it, he has attempted it, but not carried it out, he will be punished not as one who has sinned in his heart alone but in deed. To questions of this sort one might ask, whether any one commits adultery in his heart, even if he does not do the deed of adultery, but lacks self-control in heart only. And the like also you will say concerning the rest of things which are deserving of praise. But the passage possibly contains a plausible fallacy which must be cleared away, I think, in this manner: adultery which takes place in the heart is a less sin, than if one were also to add to it the act. But it is impossible that there can be chastity in the heart, hindering the chaste action—unless indeed one brings forward for an illustration of this the case of the virgin who according to the law was violated in solitude;[1] for it may be granted that the heart of any one may be most pure, [2] but that force in a matter of licentiousness has caused the corruption of the body of her who was chaste. In truth she seems to me to be altogether chaste in secret heart, but no longer to be pure in body such as she was before the act of violence; but though she is not pure outwardly, is she therefore now also unchaste? I have said these things because of the words, "They reasoned among themselves saying, We took no loaves," to which is added, "And Jesus perceiving it, said, O ye of little faith, why reason ye among yourselves,"[3] etc.; for it was necessary that investigation should be made in regard to the censure of things in secret and correlatively to the praise of things in secret.

8. THE LEAVEN FIGURATIVE LIKE THE WATER SPOKEN OF BY JESUS TO THE WOMAN OF SAMARIA.

But I wonder if the disciples thought, before the saying was explained to them by Jesus, that their Teacher and Lord was forbidding them to beware of the sensible leaven of the Pharisees or the Sadducees as impure, and on this account forbidden, lest they might use that leaven because they had not taken loaves. And we might make a like inquiry in regard to other things; but by way of illustration the narrative about the woman of Samaria sufficeth, "Every one that drinketh of this water shall thirst again; but whosoever drinketh of the water that I shall give him shall never thirst."[4] For there, also, so far as the mere form of ex-

[1] Deut. xxii. 25.
[2] *Or*, violence in the licentious person.
[3] Matt. xvi. 7, 8.
[4] John xiv. 13,14.

pression is concerned, the Samaritan woman would seem to have thought that the Saviour was giving a promise about sensible water, when He said, "Whosoever drinketh of the water that I shall give him shall never thirst." And those things then must be figuratively interpreted, and we must examine and compare the water of the spring of Jacob from which the woman of Samaria drew water with the water of Jesus; and here the like must be done; for perhaps the loaves were not baked, but a kind of raw leaven solely, the teaching, namely, of the Pharisees and Sadducees.

9. CONCERNING THE QUESTION OF JESUS IN CÆSAREA, WHO DO MEN SAY THAT I AM? DIFFERENT CONCEPTIONS OF JESUS.

"*Now when Jesus came into the parts of Cæsarea Philippi, He asked His disciples.*"[1] Jesus inquires of the disciples, "Who do men say that I am," that we may learn from the answer of the Apostles the different conceptions then held among the Jews in regard to our Saviour; and perhaps also that the disciples of Jesus might learn to be interested in knowing what is said by men about them;[2] because that will be an advantage to them who do it, by cutting off in every way occasions of evil if anything evil is spoken of, and by increasing the incitements to good, if anything good is spoken of. Only, observe how, on account of the different movements of opinion among the Jews about Jesus, some, under the influence of unsound theories, said that He was John the Baptist, like Herod the tetrarch who said to his servants, "This is John the Baptist, he is risen from the dead, and therefore do the powers work in him;"[3] but others that He who was now called Jesus was Elijah, either having been born a second time, or living from that time in the flesh, and appearing at the present time. But those who said that Jesus was Jeremiah, and not that Jeremiah was a type of the Christ, were perhaps influenced by what is said in the beginning of Jeremiah about Christ, which was not fulfilled in the prophet at that time, but was beginning to be fulfilled in Jesus, whom "God set up over nations and kingdoms to root up, and to break down, and to destroy, and to build up, and to transplant,"[4] having made Him to be a prophet to the Gentiles to whom He proclaimed the word. Moreover also those who said, "that he was a certain one of the prophets,"[1] conceived this opinion concerning Him because of those things which had been said in the prophets as unto them, but which had not been fulfilled in their case. But also the Jews, as worthy of the veil which was upon their heart, held false opinions concerning Jesus; while Peter as not a disciple "of flesh and blood,"[2] but as one fit to receive the revelation of the Father in heaven, confessed that He was the Christ. The saying of Peter to the Saviour, "Thou art the Christ," when the Jews did not know that He was Christ, was indeed a great thing, but greater that he knew Him not only to be Christ, but also "the Son of the living God,"[3] who had also said through the prophets, "I live,"[4] and "They have forsaken Me the spring of living water;"[5]—and He is life also, as from the Father the spring of life, who said, "I am the Life;"[6] And consider carefully, whether, as the spring of the river is not the same thing as the river, the spring of life is not the same as life. And these things we have added because to the saying, "Thou art the Christ, the Son of God," was subjoined the word "living;"[7] for it was necessary to set forth something noteworthy in regard to that which is said about God and the Father of all things as living, both in relation to His absolute life, and in relation to those things which participate in it. But since we said that they were under the influence of unsound opinions who declared that Jesus was John the Baptist, or any one of those named, in saying this let us prove that if they had fallen in with Jesus as He was going away to John for baptism, or with John when he was baptizing Jesus, or if they had heard it from any one, they would not have said that Jesus was John. But also if they had understood the opinions under the influence of which Jesus said, "If ye are willing to receive it, this is Elijah which is to come,"[8] and had heard what was said, as men having ears, some would not have said that He was Elijah. And if those who said that He was Jeremiah had perceived that the most of the prophets took upon themselves certain features that were symbolical of Him, they would not have said that He was Jeremiah; and in like manner the others would not have said that He was one of the prophets.

10. THE ANSWER OF PETER.

And perhaps that which Simon Peter an-

[1] Matt. xvi. 13.
[2] *Or*, Him.
[3] Matt. xiv. 2.
[4] Jer. i. 10.

[1] Matt. xvi. 14.
[2] Matt. xvi. 17.
[3] Matt. xvi. 16.
[4] Jer. xxii. 24.
[5] Jer. ii. 13.
[6] John xiv. 6.
[7] Matt. xvi. 16.
[8] Matt xi. 14.

swered and said, "*Thou art the Christ, the Son of the living God*,"[1] if we say it as Peter, not by flesh and blood revealing it unto us, but by the light from the Father in heaven shining in our heart, we too become as Peter, being pronounced blessed as he was, because that the grounds on which he was pronounced blessed apply also to us, by reason of the fact that flesh and blood have not revealed to us with regard to Jesus that He is Christ, the Son of the living God, but the Father in heaven, from the very heavens, that our citizenship may be in heaven,[2] revealing to us the revelation which carries up to heaven those who take away every veil from the heart, and receive "the spirit of the wisdom and revelation" of God.[3] And if we too have said like Peter, "Thou art the Christ, the Son of the living God," not as if flesh and blood had revealed it unto us, but by light from the Father in heaven having shone in our heart, we become a Peter, and to us there might be said by the Word, "Thou art Peter," etc.[4] For a rock[5] is every disciple of Christ of whom those drank who drank of the spiritual rock which followed them,[6] and upon every such rock is built every word of the church, and the polity in accordance with it; for in each of the perfect, who have the combination of words and deeds and thoughts which fill up the blessedness, is the church built by God.

11. THE PROMISE GIVEN TO PETER NOT RESTRICTED TO HIM, BUT APPLICABLE TO ALL DISCIPLES LIKE HIM.

But if you suppose that upon that one Peter only the whole church is built by God, what would you say about John the son of thunder or each one of the Apostles? Shall we otherwise dare to say, that against Peter in particnlar the gates of Hades shall not prevail, but that they shall prevail against the other Apostles and the perfect? Does not the saying previously made, "The gates of Hades shall not prevail against it,"[7] hold in regard to all and in the case of each of them? And also the saying, "Upon this rock I will build My church"?[8] Are the keys of the kingdom of heaven given by the Lord to Peter only, and will no other of the blessed receive them? But if this promise, "I will give unto thee the keys of the kingdom of heaven,"[9] be common to the others, how shall not all the things previously spoken of, and the things which are subjoined as having been addressed to Peter, be common to them? For in this place these words seem to be addressed as to Peter only, "Whatsoever thou shalt bind on earth shall be bound in heaven,"[1] etc; but in the Gospel of John the Saviour having given the Holy Spirit unto the disciples by breathing upon them said, "Receive ye the Holy Spirit,"[2] etc. Many then will say to the Saviour, "Thou art the Christ, the Son of the living God;" but not all who say this will say it to Him, as not at all having learned it by the revelation of flesh and blood but by the Father in heaven Himself taking away the veil that lay upon their heart, in order that after this "with unveiled face reflecting as a mirror the glory of the Lord"[3] they may speak through the Spirit of God saying concerning Him, "Lord Jesus," and to Him, "Thou art the Christ, the Son of the living God."[4] And if any one says this to Him, not by flesh and blood revealing it unto Him but through the Father in heaven, he will obtain the things that were spoken according to the letter of the Gospel to that Peter, but, as the spirit of the Gospel teaches, to every one who becomes such as that Peter was. For all bear the surname of "rock" who are the imitators of Christ, that is, of the spiritual rock which followed those who are being saved,[5] that they may drink from it the spiritual draught. But these bear the surname of the rock just as Christ does. But also as members of Christ deriving their surname from Him they are called Christians, and from the rock, Peters. And taking occasion from these things you will say that the righteous bear the surname of Christ who is Righteousness, and the wise of Christ who is Wisdom.[6] And so in regard to all His other names, you will apply them by way of surname to the saints; and to all such the saying of the Saviour might be spoken, "Thou art Peter," etc., down to the words, "prevail against it." But what is the "it"? Is it the rock upon which Christ builds the church, or is it the church? For the phrase is ambiguous. Or is it as if the rock and the church were one and the same? This I think to be true; for neither against the rock on which Christ builds the church, nor against the church will the gates of Hades prevail; just as the way of a serpent upon a rock, according to what is written in the Proverbs,[7] cannot be found. Now, if the gates of Hades prevail against any one, such an one cannot be a rock upon which Christ builds the church, nor the church built by

1 Matt. xvi. 16. 2 Phil. iii. 20. 3 Eph. i. 17. 4 Matt. xvi. 18. 5 *Or*, a Peter. 6 1 Cor. x. 4. 7 Matt. xvi. 18. 8 Matt. xvi. 18. 9 Matt. xvi. 19.

1 Matt. xvi. 19. 2 John. xx. 22. 3 2 Cor. iii. 18. 4 Matt. xvi 16 5 1 Cor. x. 4. 6 1 Cor. i. 30. 7 Prov. xxx. 19.

Jesus upon the rock; for the rock is inaccessible to the serpent, and it is stronger than the gates of Hades which are opposing it, so that because of its strength the gates of Hades do not prevail against it; but the church, as a building of Christ who built His own house wisely upon the rock,[1] is incapable of admitting the gates of Hades which prevail against every man who is outside the rock and the church, but have no power against it.

12. EVERY SIN—EVERY FALSE DOCTRINE IS A "GATE OF HADES."

But when we have understood how each of the sins through which there is a way to Hades[2] is a gate of Hades, we shall apprehend that the soul, which has "spot or wrinkle or any such thing,"[3] and because of wickedness is neither holy nor blameless, is neither a rock upon which Christ builds, nor a church, nor part of a church which Christ builds upon the rock. But if any one wishes to put us[4] to shame in regard to these things because of the great majority of those of the church who are thought to believe, it must be said to him not only "Many are called, but few chosen;"[5] but also that which was said by the Saviour to those who come to Him, as it is recorded in Luke in these words, "Strive to enter in by the narrow door, for many, I say unto you, shall seek to enter in through the narrow door and shall not be able;"[6] and also that which is written in the Gospel of Matthew thus, "For narrow is the gate, and strait is the way that leadeth unto life, and few be they that find it."[7] Now, if you attend to the saying, "Many, I say unto you, shall seek to enter in and shall not be able,"[6] you will understand that this refers to those who boast that they are of the church, but live weakly and contrary to the word. Of those, then, who seek to enter in, those who are not able to enter will not be able to do so, because the gates of Hades prevail against them; but in the case of those against whom the gates of Hades will not prevail, those seeking to enter in will be strong, being able to do all things, in Christ Jesus, who strengtheneth them.[8] And in like manner each one of those who are the authors of any evil opinion has become the architect of a certain gate of Hades; but those who co-operate with the teaching of the architect of such things are servants and stewards, who are the bond-servants of the evil doctrine which goes to build up impiety. And though the gates of Hades are many and almost innumerable, no gate of Hades will prevail against the rock or against the church which Christ builds upon it. Notwithstanding, these gates have a certain power by which they gain the mastery over some who do not resist and strive against them; but they are overcome by others who, because they do not turn aside from Him who said, "I am the door,"[1] have rased from their soul all the gates of Hades. And this also we must know that as the gates of cities have each their own names, in the same way the gates of Hades might be named after the species of sins; so that one gate of Hades is called "fornication," through which fornicators go, and another "denial," through which the deniers of God go down into Hades. And likewise already each of the heterodox and of those who have begotten any "knowledge which is falsely so called,"[2] has built a gate of Hades—Marcion one gate, and Basilides another, and Valentinus another.

13. THE "GATES OF HADES" AND THE "GATES OF ZION" CONTRASTED.

In this place, then, the gates of Hades are spoken of; but in the Psalms the prophet gives thanks saying, "He who lifteth me up from the gates of death that I may declare all thy praises in the gates of the daughter of Zion."[3] And from this we learn that it is never possible for any one to be fit to declare the praises of God, unless he has been lifted up from the gates of death, and has come to the gates of Zion. Now the gates of Zion may be conceived as opposed to the gates of death, so that there is one gate of death, dissoluteness, but a gate of Zion, self-control; and so a gate of death, unrighteousness, but a gate of Zion, righteousness, which the prophet shows forth saying, "This is the gate of the Lord, the righteous shall enter into it."[4] And again there is cowardice, a gate of death, but manly courage, a gate of Zion; and want of prudence, a gate of death, but its opposite, prudence, a gate of Zion. But to all the gates of the "knowledge which is falsely so called"[2] one gate is opposed, the gate of knowledge which is free from falsehood. But consider if, because of the say-

[1] Matt. vii. 24.
[2] Or, each of the sins on account of which Christ was about to go to Hades. (Erasmus.)
[3] Eph. v. 27. [4] *Or*, you. [5] Matt. xxii. 14. [6] Luke xiii. 24.
[7] Matt. vii. 14. [8] Phil. iv. 13.

[1] John x. 9. [2] 1 Tim. vi. 20.
[3] Ps. ix. 13, 14. [4] Ps. cxviii. 20.

ing, "our wrestling is not against flesh and blood,"[1] etc., you can say that each power and world-ruler of this darkness, and each one of the "spiritual hosts of wickedness in the heavenly places"[2] is a gate of Hades and a gate of death. Let, then, the principalities and powers with which our wrestling is, be called gates of Hades, but the "ministering spirits"[3] gates of righteousness. But as in the case of the better things many gates are first spoken of, and after the gates, one, in the passage, "Open to me the gates of righteousness, I will enter into them, and will make full confession to the Lord," and "this is the gate of the Lord, by it the righteous shall enter;"[4] so also in the case of those gates which are opposed, many are the gates of Hades and death, each a power; but over all these the wicked one himself. And let us take heed in regard to each sin, as if we were descending into some gate of death if we sin; but when we are lifted up from the gates of death let us declare all the praises of the Lord in the gates of the daughter of Zion; as, for example, in one gate of the daughter of Zion—that which is called self-control—we will declare by our self-control the praises of God; and in another which is called righteousness, by righteousness we will declare the praises of God; and, generally, in all things whatsoever of a praiseworthy character with which we are occupied, in these we are at some gate of the daughter of Zion, declaring at each gate some praise of God. But we must make inquiry whether in one of the Twelve[5] it is said, "They hated him that reproveth in the gates, and they loathed the holy word."[6] Perhaps, then, he who reproves in the gates is of the gates of the daughter of Zion, reproving those who are in sins which are opposed to this gate, even of the gates of Hades or death. But if ye do not so understand the words, "They hated him that reproveth in the gates," either the expression "in the gates" will be held to be superfluous, or investigate how that which is said can be worthy of the prophetic spirit.

14. IN WHAT SENSE THE "KEYS" ARE GIVEN TO PETER, AND EVERY PETER. LIMITATIONS OF THIS POWER.

And after this let us see in what sense it is said to Peter, and to every Peter, "*I will give unto thee the keys of the kingdom of heaven.*"[7] And, in the first place, I think that the saying, "I will give unto thee the keys of the kingdom of heaven," is spoken in consistency with the words, "The gates of Hades shall not prevail against it."[1] For he is worthy to receive from the same Word the keys of the kingdom of heaven, who is fortified against the gates of Hades so that they do not prevail against him, receiving, as it were, for a prize, the keys of the kingdom of heaven, because the gates of Hades had no power against him, that he might open for himself the gates that were closed to those who had been conquered by the gates of Hades. And he enters in, as a temperate man, through an opened gate—the gate of temperance—by the key which opens temperance; and, as a righteous man, by another gate—the gate of righteousness—which is opened by the key of righteousness; and so with the rest of the virtues. For I think that for every virtue of knowledge certain mysteries of wisdom corresponding to the species of the virtue are opened up to him who has lived according to virtue; the Saviour giving to those who are not mastered by the gates of Hades as many keys as there are virtues, which open gates equal in number, which correspond to each virtue according to the revelation of the mysteries. And perhaps, also, each virtue is a kingdom of heaven, and all together are a kingdom of the heavens; so that according to this he is already in the kingdom of the heavens who lives according to the virtues, so that according to this the saying, "Repent, for the kingdom of heaven is at hand,"[2] is to be referred, not to the time, but to deeds and dispositions; for Christ, who is all virtue, has come, and speaks, and on account of this the kingdom of God is within His disciples, and not here or there.[3] But consider how great power the rock has upon which the church is built by Christ, and how great power every one has who says, "Thou art the Christ, the Son of the living God," so that the judgments of this man abide sure, as if God were judging in him, that in the very act of judging the gates of Hades shall not prevail against him. But when one judges unrighteously, and does not bind upon earth according to the Word of God, nor loose upon earth according to His will, the gates of Hades prevail against him; but, in the case of any one against whom the gates of Hades do not prevail, this man judges righteously. Wherefore he has the keys of the kingdom of heaven, opening to those who have been loosed on earth that they may be also loosed in

[1] Eph. vi. 12. [2] Eph. vi. 12. [3] Heb. i. 14.
[4] Ps. cxviii. 19, 20. [5] That is, the Minor Prophets. [6] Amos v. 10.
[7] Matt. xvi. 19.

[1] Matt. xvi. 18. [2] Matt. iii. 2; iv. 17. [3] Luke xvii. 21

heaven, and free; and shutting to those who by his just judgment have been bound on earth that they also may be bound in heaven, and condemned. But when those who maintain the function of the episcopate make use of this word as Peter, and, having received the keys of the kingdom of heaven from the Saviour, teach that things bound by them, that is to say, condemned, are also bound in heaven, and that those which have obtained remission by them are also loosed in heaven, we must say that they speak wholesomely if they have the way of life on account of which it was said to that Peter, "Thou art Peter;"[1] and if they are such that upon them the church is built by Christ, and to them with good reason this could be referred; and the gates of Hades ought not to prevail against him when he wishes to bind and loose. But if he is tightly bound with the cords of his sins,[2] to no purpose does he bind and loose. And perhaps you can say that in the heavens which are in the wise man—that, is the virtues,—the bad man is bound; and again in these the virtuous man is loosed, and has received an indemnity for the sins which he committed before his virtue. But, as the man, who has not the cords of sins nor iniquities compared to a "long rope or to the strap of the yoke of a heifer,"[3] not even God could bind, in like manner, no Peter, whoever he may be; and if any one who is not a Peter, and does not possess the things here spoken of, imagines as a Peter that he will so bind on earth that the things bound are bound in heaven, and will so loose on earth that the things loosed are loosed in heaven, he is puffed up, not understanding the meaning of the Scriptures, and, being puffed up, has fallen into the ruin of the devil.[4]

15. RELATION OF THE FORMER COMMISSION GIVEN BY JESUS TO THE DISCIPLES, TO HIS PRESENT INJUNCTION OF SILENCE. BELIEF AND KNOWLEDGE CONTRASTED.

"*Then enjoined He His disciples that they should tell no man that He was the Christ.*"[5] It is written above that Jesus sent forth these twelve saying unto them, "Go not into any way of the Gentiles,"[6] and the other words which are recorded to have been said to them when He sent them to the apostleship. Did He then wish them when they were already discharging the function of Apostles to proclaim that He was the Christ? For, if He wished it, it is fitting to inquire why He now at all commands the disciples that they should not say that He was the Christ? Or if He did not wish it, how can the things concerning the apostleship be safely maintained? And these things also one may inquire at this place,—whether, when He sent away the Twelve, He did not send them away with the understanding that He was the Christ? But if the Twelve had such understanding, manifestly Peter had it also; how, then, is he now pronounced blessed? For the expression here plainly indicates that now for the first time Peter confessed that Christ was the Son of the living God, Matthew then, according to some of the manuscripts, has written, "Then He commanded His disciples that they should tell no man that He was the Christ," but[1] Mark says, "He charged them that they should tell no man of Him;"[2] and Luke, "He charged them and commanded them to tell this to no man."[3] But what is the "this"? Was it that also according to him, Peter answered and said to the question, "Who say ye that I am,"—"The Christ, the Son of the living God?"[4] You must know, however, that some manuscripts of the Gospel according to Matthew have, "He charged."[5] The difficulty thus started seems to me a very real difficulty; but let a solution which cannot be impugned be sought out, and let the finder of it bring it forward before all, if it be more credible than that which shall be advanced by us as a fairly temperate view.[6] Consider, then, if you can say, that the belief that Jesus is the Christ is inferior to the knowledge of that which is believed. And perhaps also there is a difference in the knowledge of Jesus as the Christ, as every one who knows does not know Him alike. From the words in John, "If ye abide in My word, ye shall know the truth, and the truth shall make you free,"[7] it is plain that belief without knowledge is inferior to knowing; but that there is a difference in the knowledge of Jesus as the Christ, as all who know Him do not know Him equally, is a fact self-evident to any one who gives even a very little consideration to the matter. For who would not acknowledge, for example, that Timothy, though he knew that Jesus was the Christ, had not been enlightened to such an extent in the knowledge of Him as the Apostle had been enlightened? And who would not also admit this—that though many, speaking the

[1] Matt. xvi. 18. [2] Prov. v. 22. [3] Isa. v. 18. [4] 1 Tim. iii. 10. [5] Matt. xvi. 20. [6] Matt. x. 5.

[1] Matt. xvi. 20. [2] Mark viii. 30. [3] Luke ix. 21. [4] Matt. xvi. 15, 16. [5] Matt. xvi. 20. [6] *Or*, which he may regard as mediocre. [7] John viii. 31, 32.

truth, say about God, "He has given to me a true knowledge of things that are," yet they will not say this with equal insight and apprehension of the things known, nor as knowing the same number of things? But it is not only in respect of the difference of knowing that those who know do not know alike, but also according to that which is the source of the knowledge; so that according to this he who knows the Son by the revelation of the Father,[1] as Peter is testified to have known, has the highest beatitude. Now, if these views of ours are sound, you will consider whether the Twelve formerly believed but did not know; but, after believing, they gained also the rudiments of knowledge and knew a few things about Him; and afterwards they continued to advance in knowledge so that they were able to receive the knowledge from the Father who reveals the Son; in which position Peter was, when he was pronounced blessed; for also he is pronounced blessed not merely because he said, "Thou art the Christ," but with the addition, "the Son of the living God." Accordingly Mark and Luke who have recorded that Peter answered and said, "Thou art the Christ," but have not given the addition found in Matthew, have not recorded that he was declared blessed for what had been said, nor the blessing which followed the declaration of blessedness, "Thou art Peter,"[2] etc.

16. GRADUAL GROWTH IN KNOWLEDGE OF THE DISCIPLES.

But now we must first investigate the fact that they were declaring other things about Him as being great and wonderful, but did not yet proclaim that He was the Christ, lest the Saviour may not appear to take away from them the authority to announce that He was the Christ, which He had formerly bestowed upon them. And perhaps some one will support an argument of this kind, saying that on their introduction into the school of Christ the Jews were taught by the disciples glorious things about Jesus, so that in due season there might be built upon these as a foundation the things about Jesus being the Christ; and perhaps many of the things which were said to them were said to all who virtually believed; for not to the Apostles alone did the saying apply, "Before governors and kings also shall ye be brought for My sake for a testimony to them and to the Gentiles;"[3] and perhaps also not to the Apostles absolutely, but to all who were about to believe the word, "And brother shall deliver up brother to death,"[1] etc.; but, "Whosoever shall confess Me,"[2] etc., is said not specially to the Apostles, but also to all believers. According to this, then, through that which was said to the Apostles an outline was given beforehand of the teaching which would afterwards come to be of service both to them and to every teacher.

17. REASONS FOR THAT GRADUAL KNOWLEDGE.

And likewise he who holds that the fact that He was Christ had been formerly proclaimed by the Apostles when they heard the saying, "What I tell you in the darkness, speak ye in the light, and what ye hear in the ear proclaim on the housetops,"[3] will say, that He wished first to give catechetical instruction as it were to those of the Apostles who were to hear the name of Christ, then to permit this, so to speak, to be digested in the minds of the hearers, that, after there had been a period of silence in the proclamation of something of this kind about Him, at a more seasonable time there might be built up upon the former rudiments "Christ Jesus crucified and raised from the dead," which at the beginning not even the Apostles knew; for it is written in the passage now under consideration, "From that time began Jesus to show unto His disciples that He must go unto Jerusalem"[4] and suffer this and that. But if now, for the first time, the Apostles learn from Jesus the things that were about to happen unto Him, namely, that the elders will plot against Him, and that He will be killed, and that after these things, on the third day, He will rise from the dead,—what necessity is there for supposing that those who had been taught by the Apostles concerning Jesus knew them before, or that although Christ was announced to them He was announced to them by way of an introduction which did not clearly elucidate the things concerning Him? For our Saviour wished, when He enjoined the disciples to tell no man that He was the Christ, to reserve the more perfect teaching about Him to a more fitting time, when to those who had seen Him crucified, the disciples who had seen Him crucified and risen could testify the things relating to His resurrection. For if the Apostles, who were always with Him and had seen all the wonderful things which He did, and who bore testimony to His words that they

[1] Matt. xvi. 16. [2] Matt. xvi. 18. [3] Matt. x. 18.

[1] Matt. x. 21. [2] Matt. x. 32. [3] Matt. x. 27. [4] Matt. xvi. 21.

were words of eternal life,[1] were offended on the night on which He was betrayed,—what do you suppose would have been the feelings of those who had formerly learned that He was the Christ? To spare them, I think, He gave this command.

18. JESUS WAS AT FIRST PROCLAIMED BY THE TWELVE AS A WORKER AND A TEACHER ONLY.

But he who holds that the things spoken to the Twelve refer to the times subsequent to this, and that the Apostles had not as yet announced to their hearers that He was the Christ, will say that He wished the conception of the Christ which was involved in the name of Jesus to be reserved for that preaching which was more perfect, and which brought salvation, such as Paul knew of when he said to the Corinthians, "I determined not to know anything among you save Jesus Christ and Him crucified."[2] Wherefore, formerly they proclaimed Jesus as the doer of certain things, and the teacher of certain things; but now when Peter confesses that He was the Christ, the Son of the living God, as He did not wish it to be proclaimed already that He was the Christ, in order that He might be proclaimed at a more suitable time, and that as crucified, He commands His disciples that they should tell no man that He was the Christ. And that this was His meaning, when He forbade proclamation to be made that He was the Christ, is in a measure established by the words, "From that time began Jesus to show unto His disciples how that He must go unto Jerusalem, and suffer many things of the elders," and what is annexed;[3] for then, at the fitting time, He proclaims, so to speak, to the disciples who knew that Jesus was Christ, the Son of the living God, the Father having revealed it to them, that instead of believing in Jesus Christ who had been crucified, they were to believe in Jesus Christ who was about to be crucified. But also, instead of believing in Christ Jesus and Him risen from the dead, He teaches them to believe in Christ Jesus and Him about to be risen from the dead. But since "having put off from Himself the principalities and the powers, He made a show of them openly, triumphing over in the cross,"[4] if any one is ashamed of the cross of Christ, he is ashamed of the dispensation on account of which these powers were triumphed over; and it is fitting that he, who both believes and knows these things, should glory in the cross of our Lord Jesus Christ, through which, when Christ was crucified, the principalities—among which, I think, was also the prince of this world—were made a show of and triumphed over before the believing world. Wherefore, when His suffering was at hand he said, "Now the prince of this world has been judged,"[1] and, "Now shall the prince of this world be cast out," and, "I, if I be lifted from the earth, will draw all men unto Myself;"[2] as he no longer had sufficient power to prevent those going to Jesus who were being drawn by Him.

[1] John vi. 68. [2] 1 Cor. ii. 2. [3] Matt. xvi. 21. [4] Col. ii. 15. [5] Gal. vi. 14.

19. IMPORTANCE OF THE PROCLAMATION OF JESUS AS THE CRUCIFIED.

It is necessary, therefore, to the proclamation of Jesus as Christ, that He should be proclaimed as crucified; and the proclamation that Jesus was the Christ does not seem to me so defective when any of His other miracles is passed over in silence, as when the fact of His crucifixion is passed over. Wherefore, reserving the more perfect proclamation of the things concerning Him by the Apostles, He commanded His disciples that they should tell no man that He was the Christ; and He prepared them to say that He was the Christ crucified and risen from the dead, "when He began" not only to say, nor even to advance to the point of teaching merely, but "to show"[3] to His disciples that He must go to Jerusalem, etc.; for attend to the expression "show"; because just as sensible things are said to be shown so the things spoken by Him to His disciples are said to be shown by Jesus. And I do not think that each of the things seen was shown to those who saw Him suffering many things in body from the elders of the people, with such clearness as was the rational demonstration about Him to the disciples.

20. WHY JESUS HAD TO GO TO JERUSALEM.

"*Then began He to show;*"[4] and probably afterwards when they were able to receive it He shewed more clearly, no longer beginning to show as to those who were learning the introduction, but already also advancing in the showing; and if it is reasonable to conceive that Jesus altogether completed what He began, then, some time, He altogether completed that which He began to show to His disciples about the necessity of His suffering the things which

[1] John xvi. 11. [2] John xii. 31, 32. [3] Matt. xvi. 21. [4] Matt. xvi. 21.

are written. For, when any one apprehends from the Word the perfect knowledge of these things, then it must be said that, from a rational exhibition (the mind seeing the things which are shown,) the exhibition becomes complete for him who has the will and the power to contemplate these things, and does contemplate them. But since "it cannot be that a prophet perish out of Jerusalem,"[1]—a perishing which corresponds to the words, "He that loseth his life for My sake shall find it,"[2]—on this account it was necessary for Him to go to Jerusalem, that having suffered many things in that Jerusalem, He might make "the first-fruits"[3] of the resurrection from the dead in the Jerusalem above, doing away with and breaking up the city upon the earth with all the worship which was maintained in it. For so long as Christ "had not been raised from the dead, the first-fruits of them that are asleep,"[3] and those who become conformed to His death and resurrection had not yet been raised along with Him, the city of God was sought for below, and the temple, and the purifications, and the rest; but when this took place, no longer were the things below sought for, but the things above; and, in order that these might be set up, it was necessary that He should go unto the Jerusalem below, and there suffer many things from the elders in it, and the chief priests and scribes of the people, in order that He might be glorified by the heavenly elders who could receive his bounties, and by diviner high-priests who are ordained under the one High-Priest, and that He might be glorified by the scribes of the people who are occupied with letters "not written with ink"[4] but made clear by the Spirit of the living God, and might be killed in the Jerusalem below, and having risen from the dead might reign in Mount Zion, and the city of the living God—the heavenly Jerusalem.[5] But on the third day He rose from the dead,[6] in order that having delivered them from the wicked one, and his son,[7] in whom was falsehood and unrighteousness and war and everything opposed to that which Christ is, and also from the profane spirit who transforms himself into the Holy Spirit, He might gain for those who had been delivered the right to be baptized in spirit and soul and body, into the name of the Father and the Son and the Holy Spirit, which represent the three days eternally present at the same time to those who by means of them are sons of light.

[1] Luke xiii. 33. [2] Matt. x. 39. [3] 1 Cor. xv. 20.
[4] 2 Cor. iii. 3. [5] Heb. xii. 22.
[6] *Or* (putting a comma after Jerusalem), but that on the third day He might rise.
[7] See xi. c. 6, p. 434, note 2.

21. THE REBUKE OF PETER AND THE ANSWER OF JESUS.

"*And Peter took Him and began to rebuke Him, saying, God be propitious to Thee, Lord, this shall never be unto thee.*"[1] To whom He said, "*Get thee behind Me, Satan; thou art a stumbling-block unto Me; for thou mindest not the things of God but the things of men.*"[2] Since Jesus had begun to show unto His disciples that He must go unto Jerusalem, and suffer many things, Peter up to this point learned the beginnings of those things which were shown.[3] But since he thought that the sufferings were unworthy of Christ the Son of the living God, and below the dignity of the Father who had revealed to him so great things about Christ,—for the things that concerned His coming suffering had not been revealed to him,—on this account he took Him, and as one forgetful of the honour due to the Christ, and that the Son of the living God neither does nor says anything worthy of rebuke, he began to rebuke Him; and as to one who needed propitiation,—for he did not yet know that "God had set Him forth to be a propitiation through faith in His blood,"[4] he said, "God be propitious to thee, O Lord."[5] Approving his purpose, indeed, but rebuking his ignorance, because of the purpose being right, He says to him, "Get thee behind Me,"[6] as to one who, by reason of the things of which he was ignorant and spake not rightly, had abandoned the following of Jesus; but because of his ignorance, as to one who had something antagonistic to the things of God, He said, "Satan," which in the Hebrew means "adversary." But, if Peter had not spoken from ignorance, nor rebuked the Son of the living God, saying unto Him, "God be propitious to thee, Lord, this shall never be unto Thee," Christ would not have said to him, "Get thee behind Me," as to one who had given up being behind Him and following Him; nor would He have said as to one who had spoken things adverse to what He had said, "Satan." But now Satan prevailed over him who had followed Jesus and was going behind Him, to turn aside from following Him and from being behind the Son of God, and to make him, by reason of the words which he spoke in ignorance, worthy

[1] Matt. xvi. 22. [2] Matt. xvi. 23.
[3] These three sentences are supplied from the old Latin version, as at this point there is a hiatus in the MSS.
[4] Rom. iii. 25. [5] Matt. xvi. 22. [6] Matt. xvi. 23.

of being called "Satan" and a stumbling-block to the Son of God, and "as not minding the things of God but the things of men." But that Peter was formerly behind the Son of God, before he committed this sin, is manifest from the words, "Come ye behind Me, and I will make you fishers of men."[1]

22. IMPORTANCE OF THE EXPRESSIONS "BEHIND" AND "TURNED."

But you will compare together His saying to Peter, "Get thee behind me, Satan,"[2] with that said to the devil (who said to Him, "All these things will I give Thee if Thou wilt fall down and worship me"),[3] "get thee hence,"[4] without the addition, "behind Me;" for to be behind Jesus is a good thing. Wherefore it was said, "Come ye behind Me and I will make you fishers of men."[1] And to the same effect is the saying, "He that doth not take his cross and follow behind Me is not worthy of Me."[5] And as a general principle observe the expression "behind"; because it is a good thing when any one goes behind the Lord God and is behind the Christ; but it is the opposite when any one casts the words of God behind him, or when he transgresses the commandment which says, "Do not walk behind thy lusts."[6] And Elijah also, in the third Book of Kings, says to the people, "How long halt ye on both your knees? If God is the Lord, go behind Him, but if Baal is the Lord, go behind him."[7] And Jesus says this to Peter when He "turned," and He does so by way of conferring a favour. And if therefore you will collect more illustrations of the "having turned," and especially those which are ascribed to Jesus, and compare them with one another, you would find that the expression is not superfluous. But it is sufficient at present to bring forward this from the Gospel according to John, "Jesus turned and beheld them—" clearly, Peter and Andrew—"following, and saith unto them, What seek ye?"[8] For observe that, when He "turned," it is for the advantage of those to whom He turned.

23. PETER AS A STUMBLING-BLOCK TO JESUS.

Next we must inquire how He said to Peter, "Thou art a stumbling-block unto Me,"[9] especially when David says, "Great peace have they that love Thy law, and there is no stumbling-block to them."[10] For some one will say, if this is said in the prophet, because of the steadfastness of those who have love, and are incapable of being offended, for "love beareth all things, believeth all things, hopeth all things, endureth all things, love never faileth,"[1] how did the Lord Himself, "who upholdeth all that fall, and raiseth up all that be bowed down,"[2] say to Peter, "Thou art a stumbling-block unto Me"? But it must be said that not only the Saviour, but also he who is perfected in love, cannot be offended. But, so far as it depends on himself, he who says or does such things is a stumbling-block even to him who will not be offended; unless perhaps Jesus calls the disciple who sinned a stumbling-block even to Himself, as much more than Paul He would have said from love, "Who is weak, and I am not weak? Who is made to stumble, and I burn not?"[3] In harmony with which we may put, "Who is made to stumble, and I am not made to stumble?" But if Peter, at that time because of the saying, "God be propitious to Thee, Lord, this shall not be unto Thee,"[4] was called a stumbling-block by Jesus, as not minding the things of God in what he said but the things of men, what is to be said about all those who profess to be made disciples of Jesus, but do not mind the things of God, and do not look to things unseen and eternal, but mind the things of man, and look to things seen and temporal,[5] but that such still more would be stigmatized by Jesus as a stumbling-block to Him, and because stumbling-blocks to Him, as stumbling-blocks to His brethren also? As in regard to them He says, "I was thirsty and ye gave Me no drink,"[6] etc., so also He might say, "When I was running ye caused Me to stumble." Let us not therefore suppose that it is a trivial sin to mind the things of men, since we ought in everything to mind the things of God. And it will be appropriate also to say this to every one that has fallen away from the doctrines of God and the words of the church and a true mind; as, for example, to him who minds as true the teaching of Basilides, or Valentinus, or Marcion, or any one of those who teach the things of men as the things of God.

24. SELF-DENIAL AND CROSS-BEARING.

"*Then Jesus said to His disciples, If any man wills to follow after Me,*" etc.[7] He shows by these words that, to will to come after Jesus and to follow Him, springs from no

[1] Matt. iv. 19. [2] Matt. xvi. 23. [3] Matt. iv. 9. [4] Matt. iv. 10. [5] Matt. x. 38. [6] Ecclus. xviii. 30. [7] 1 Kings xviii. 21. [8] John i. 38. [9] Matt. xvi. 23. [10] Ps. cxix. 165.

[1] 1 Cor. xiii. 7, 8. [2] Ps. cxlv. 14. [3] 2 Cor. xi. 29. [4] Matt. xvi. 22. [5] 2 Cor. iv. 18. [6] Matt. xxv. 42. [7] Matt. xvi. 24.

ordinary manly courage, and that no one who has not denied himself can come after Jesus. And the man denies himself who wipes out by a striking revolution his own former life which had been spent in wickedness; as by way of illustration he who was once licentious denies his licentious self, having become self-controlled even abidingly. But it is probable that some one may put the objection, whether as he denied himself so he also confesses himself, when he denied himself, the unjust, and confesses himself, the righteous one. But, if Christ is righteousness, he who has received righteousness confesses not himself but Christ; so also he who has found wisdom, by the very possession of wisdom, confesses Christ. And such a one indeed as, "with the heart believes unto righteousness, and with the mouth maketh confession unto salvation,"[1] and bears testimony to the works of Christ, as making confession by all these things of Christ before men, will be confessed by Him before His Father in heaven.[2] So also he who has not denied himself but denied the Christ will experience the saying, "I also will deny him."[3] On this account let every thought and every purpose and every word and every action become a denial of ourselves, but a testimony about Christ and in Christ; for I am persuaded that every action of the perfect man is a testimony to Christ Jesus, and that abstinence from every sin is a denial of self, leading him after Christ. And such an one is crucified with Christ, and taking up his own cross follows Him who for our sakes bears His own cross, according to that which is said in John: "They took Jesus therefore and put it on Him," etc., down to the words, "Where they crucified Him."[4] But the Jesus according to John, so to speak, bears the cross for Himself, and bearing it went out; but the Jesus according to Matthew and Mark and Luke, does not bear it for Himself, for Simon of Cyrene bears it.[5] And perhaps this man refers to us, who because of Jesus take up the cross of Jesus, but Jesus Himself takes it upon Himself; for there are, as it were, two conceptions of the cross, the one which Simon of Cyrene bears, and the other which Jesus Himself bears for Himself.

25. REFERENCE TO THE SAYING OF PAUL ABOUT CRUCIFIXION WITH CHRIST.

Moreover in regard to the saying, "Let him deny himself,"[1] the following saying of Paul who denied himself seems appropriate, "Yet I live, and yet no longer I but Christ liveth in me;"[2] for the expression, "I live, yet no longer I," was the voice of one denying himself, as of one who had laid aside his own life and taken on himself the Christ, in order that He might live in him as Righteousness, and as Wisdom, and as Sanctification, and as our Peace,[3] and as the Power of God, who worketh all things in him. But further also, attend to this, that while there are many forms of dying, the Son of God was crucified, being hanged on a tree, in order that all who die unto sin may die to it, in no other way than by the way of the cross. Wherefore they will say, "I have been crucified with Christ," and, "Far be it from me to glory save in the cross of the Lord, through which the world has been crucified unto me and I unto the world."[4] For perhaps also each of those who have been crucified with Christ puts off from himself the principalities and the powers, and makes a show of them and triumphs over them in the cross;[5] or rather, Christ does these things in them.

26. THE LOSS OF LIFE; AND THE SAVING OF IT.

"*For whosoever would save his own life shall lose it.*"[6] The first expression is ambiguous; for it may be understood. in one way thus. If any one as being a lover of life, and thinking that the present life is good, tends carefully his own life with a view to living in the flesh, being afraid to die, as through death going to lose it, this man, by the very willing to save in this way his own life will lose it, placing it outside of the borders of blessedness. But if any one despising the present life because of my word, which has persuaded him to strive in regard to eternal life even unto death for truth, loses his own life, surrendering it for the sake of piety to that which is commonly called death, this man, as for my sake he has lost his life, will save it rather, and keep it in possession. And according to a second way we might interpret the saying as follows. If any one, who has grasped what salvation really is, wishes to procure the salvation of his own life, let this man having taken farewell of this life, and denied himself and taken up his own cross, and following me, lose his own life to the world; for having lost it for my sake and for the sake of all my teaching, he will gain the end of loss of this kind—salvation.

[1] Rom. x. 10. [2] Matt. x. 32. [3] Matt. x. 33. [4] John xix. 17, 18. [5] Matt. xxvii. 32; Mark xv. 21; Luke xxiii. 26.

[1] Matt. xvi. 24. [2] Gal. ii. 20. [3] 1 Cor. i. 30; Eph. ii. 14 [4] Gal. ii 20; vi. 14. [5] Col. ii. 15. [6] Matt. xvi. 25.

27. LIFE LOST TO THE WORLD IS SAVED.

But at the same time also observe that at the beginning it is said, "Whosoever wills," but afterwards, "Whoso shall lose."[1] If we then wish it to be saved let us lose it to the world, as those who have been crucified with Christ and have for our glorying that which is in the cross of our Lord Jesus Christ, through which the world is to be crucified unto us and we unto the world,[2] that we may gain our end, even the salvation of our lives, which begins from the time when we lose it for the sake of the word. But if we think that the salvation of our life is a blessed thing, with reference to the salvation which is in God and the blessednesses with Him, then any loss of life ought to be a good thing, and, for the sake of Christ must prove to be the prelude to the blessed salvation. It seems to me, therefore, following the analogy of self-denial, according to what has been said, that each ought to lose his own life. Let each one therefore lose his own sinning life, that having lost that which is sinful, he may receive that which is saved by right actions; but a man will in no way be profited if he shall gain the whole world. Now he gains the world, I think, to whom the world is not crucified; and to whom the world is not crucified, to that man shall be the loss of his own life. But when two things are put before us, either by gaining one s life to forfeit the world, or by gaining the world to forfeit one's life, much more desirable is the choice, that we should forfeit the world and gain our life by losing it on account of Christ.

28. THE EXCHANGE FOR ONE'S LIFE.

But the saying, "*What shall a man give in exchange for his own life,*"[3] if spoken by way of interrogation, will seem to be able to indicate that an exchange for his own life is given by the man who after his sins has given up his whole substance, that his property may feed the poor, as if he were going by that to obtain salvation; but, if spoken affirmatively, I think, to indicate that there is not anything in man by the giving of which in exchange for his own life which has been overcome by death, he will ransom it out of its hand. A man, therefore, could not give anything as an exchange for his own life, but God gave an exchange for the life of us all, "the precious blood of Christ Jesus,"[4] according as "we

[1] Matt. xvi. 25.
[2] Gal. vi. 14.
[3] Matt. xvi. 26.
[4] 1 Pet. i. 19.

were bought with a price,"[1] "having been redeemed, not with corruptible things as silver or gold, but with precious blood, as of a lamb without blemish and without spot," even of Christ.[2] And in Isaiah it is said to Israel, "I gave Ethiopia in exchange for thee, and Egypt and Syene for thee; from what time thou hast become honourable before Me thou wast glorified."[3] For the exchange, for example, of the first-born of Israel was the first-born of the Egyptians, and the exchange for Israel was the Egyptians who died in the last plagues that came upon Egypt, and in the drowning which took place after the plagues. But, from these things, let him who is able inquire whether the exchange of the true Israel given by God, "who redeems Israel from all his transgressions,"[4] is the true Ethiopia, and, so to speak, spiritual Egypt, and Syene of Egypt; and to inquire with more boldness, perhaps Syene is the exchange for Jerusalem, and Egypt for Judæa, and Ethiopia for those who fear, who are different from Israel, and the house of Levi, and the house of Aaron.

29. THE COMING OF THE SON OF MAN IN GLORY.

"*For the Son of man shall come in the glory of His own Father with His angels.*"[5] Now, indeed, the Son of man has not come in His glory; "for we saw Him, and He had no form nor beauty; but His form was dishonoured and defective compared with the sons of men; He was a man in affliction and toil, and acquainted with the enduring of sickness, because His face was turned away, He was dishonoured and not esteemed."[6] And it was necessary that He should come in such form that He might bear our sins[7] and suffer pain for us; for it did not become Him in glory to bear our sins and suffer pain for us. But He also comes in glory, having prepared[8] the disciples through that epiphany of His which has no form nor beauty; and, having become as they that they might become as He, "conformed to the image of His glory,"[9] since He formerly became conformed to "the body of our humiliation,"[10] when He "emptied Himself and took upon Him the form of a servant,"[11] He is restored to the image of God and also makes them conformed unto it.

[1] 1 Cor. vi. 20.
[2] 1 Pet. i. 18, 19.
[3] Isa. xliii. 3, 4.
[4] Ps. cxxx. 8.
[5] Matt. xvi. 27.
[6] Isa. liii. 2, 3
[7] Isa. liii. 4.
[8] Reading προευτρεπισάς, as the Vetus Inter.
[9] Rom. viii. 29.
[10] Phil. iii. 21.
[11] Phil. ii. 7.

30. THE WORD APPEARS IN DIFFERENT FORMS. THE TIME OF HIS COMING IN GLORY.

But if you will understand the differences of the Word which by "the foolishness of preaching"[1] is proclaimed to those who believe, and spoken in wisdom to them that are perfect, you will see in what way the Word has the form of a slave to those who are learning the rudiments, so that they say, "We saw Him and He had no form or beauty."[2] But to the perfect He comes "in the glory of His own Father,"[3] who might say, "and we beheld His glory, the glory as of the only-begotten from the Father, full of grace and truth."[4] For indeed to the perfect appears the glory of the Word, and the only-begotten of God His Father, and the fulness of grace and likewise of truth, which that man cannot perceive who requires the "foolishness of the preaching," in order to believe. But "the Son of man shall come in the glory of His own Father" not alone, but "with His own angels." And if you can conceive of all those who are fellow-helpers in the glory of the Word, and in the revelation of the Wisdom which is Christ, coming along with Him, you will see in what way the Son of man comes in the glory of His own Father with His own angels. And consider whether you can in this connection say that the prophets who formerly suffered in virtue of their word having "no form or beauty" had an analogous position to the Word who had "no form or beauty." And, as the Son of man comes in the glory of His own Father, so the angels, who are the words in the prophets, are present with Him preserving the measure of their own glory. But when the Word comes in such form with His own angels, He will give to each a part of His own glory and of the brightness of His own angels, according to the action of each. But we say these things not rejecting even the second coming of the Son of God understood in its simpler form. But when shall these things happen? Shall it be when that apostolic oracle is fulfilled which says, "For we must all stand before the judgment-seat of Christ, that each one may receive the things done in the body, according to what he has done, whether it be good or bad?"[5] But if He will render to each according to his deed, not the good deed only, nor the evil apart from the good, it is manifest that He will render to each according to every evil, and according to every good, deed. But I suppose—in this also following the Apostle, but comparing also the sayings of Ezekiel, in which the sins of him who is a perfect convert are wiped out, and the former uprightness of him who has utterly fallen away is not held of account—that in the case of him who is perfected, and has altogether laid aside wickedness, the sins are wiped out, but that, in the case of him who has altogether revolted from piety, if anything good was formerly done by him, it is not taken into account.[1] But to us, who occupy a middle position between the perfect man and the apostate, when we stand before the judgment-seat of Christ,[2] there is rendered what we have done, whether good or bad; for we have not been so pure that our evil deeds are not at all imputed unto us, nor have we fallen away to such an extent that our better actions are forgotten.

31. THE SIMPLER INTERPRETATION OF THE PROMISE ABOUT NOT TASTING OF DEATH.

"*Verily I say unto you there be some of them that stand here that shall not taste of death.*"[3] Some refer these things to the going up—six days after, or, as Luke says,[4] eight days—of the three disciples into the high mountain with Jesus apart; and those who adopt this interpretation say that Peter and the remaining two did not taste of death before they saw the Son of man coming in His own kingdom and in His own glory. For when they saw Jesus transfigured before them so that "His face shone," etc., "they saw the kingdom of God coming with power."[5] For even as some spear-bearers stand around a king, so Moses and Elijah appeared to those who had gone up into the mountains, talking with Jesus. But it is worth while considering whether the sitting on the right hand and on the left hand of the Saviour in His kingdom refers to them, so that the words, "But for whom it is prepared," were[6] spoken because of them. Now this interpretation about the three Apostles not tasting of death until they have seen Jesus transfigured, is adapted to those who are designated by Peter as "new-born babes longing for the reasonable milk which is without guile,"[7] to whom Paul says, "I have fed you with milk, not with meat,"[8] etc. Now, too, every interpretation of a text which is able to build up those who cannot receive greater truths might reasonably be called milk, flowing from the holy ground of the Scriptures, which flows with

[1] 1 Cor. i. 21. [2] Isa. liii. 2. [3] Matt. xvi. 27. [4] John i. 14. [5] 2 Cor. v. 10.

[1] Ezek. xviii. 21–24. [2] 2 Cor. v. 10. [3] Matt. xvi. 28. [4] Luke ix. 28. [5] Mark ix. 1. [6] Matt. xx. 23. [7] 1 Pet. ii. 2. [8] 1 Cor. iii. 2.

milk and honey. But he who has been weaned, like Isaac,[1] worthy of the good cheer and reception which Abraham gave at the weaning of his son, would seek here and in every Scripture food which is different, I think, from that which is meat, indeed, but is not solid food, and from what are figuratively called herbs, which are food to one who has been weaned and is not yet strong but weak, according to the saying, "He that is weak eateth herbs."[2] In like manner also he who has been weaned, like Samuel, and dedicated by his mother to God,[3]—she was Hannah, which is, by interpretation, grace,—would be also a son of grace, seeking, like one nurtured in the temple, flesh of God, the holy food of those who are at once perfect and priests.

32. STANDING BY THE SAVIOUR.

The reflections in regard to the passage before us that occur to us at the present time are these: Some were standing where Jesus was, having the footsteps of the soul firmly planted with Jesus, and the standing of their feet was akin to the standing of which Moses said in the passage, "And I stood on the mountain forty days and forty nights,"[4] who was deemed worthy to have it said to him by God who asked him to stand by Him, "But stand thou here with Me."[5] Those who really stand by Jesus—that is, by the Word of God—do not all stand equally; for among those who stand by Jesus are differences from each other. Wherefore, not all who stand by the Saviour, but some of them as standing better, do not taste of death until they shall have seen the Word who dwelt with men, and on that account called Son of man, coming in His own kingdom; for Jesus does not always come in His own kingdom when He comes, since to the newly initiated He is such that they might say, beholding the Word Himself not glorious nor great, but inferior to many among them, "We saw Him, and He had no form or beauty, but His form was dishonoured, defective compared with all the sons of men."[6] And these things will be said by those who beheld His glory in connection with their own former times, when at first the Word as understood in the synagogue had no form nor beauty to them. To the Word, therefore, who has assumed most manifestly the power above all words, there belongs a royal dignity which is visible to some of those who stand by Jesus, when

[1] Gen. xxi. 8. [2] Rom. xiv. 2. [3] 1 Sam. i. 23, 24. [4] Deut. x. 10. [5] Deut. v. 31. [6] Isa. liii. 2, 3.

they have been able to follow Him as He goes before them and ascends to the lofty mountain of His own manifestation. And of this honour some of those who stand by Jesus are deemed worthy if they be either a Peter against whom the gates of Hades do not prevail, or the sons of thunder,[1] and are begotten of the mighty voice of God who thunders and cries aloud from heaven great things to those who have ears and are wise. Such at least do not taste death.

33. INTERPRETATION OF "TASTING OF DEATH."

But we must seek to understand what is meant by "tasting of death." And He is life who says, "I am the life,"[2] and this life assuredly has been hidden with Christ in God; and, "when Christ our life shall be manifested, then along with Him"[3] shall be manifested those who are worthy of being manifested with Him in glory. But the enemy of this life, who is also the last enemy of all His enemies that shall be destroyed, is death,[4] of which the soul that sinneth dies, having the opposite disposition to that which takes place in the soul that lives uprightly, and in consequence of living uprightly lives. And when it is said in the law, "I have placed life before thy face,"[5] the Scripture says this about Him who said, "I am the Life," and about His enemy, death; the one or other of which each of us by his deeds is always choosing. And when we sin with life before our face, the curse is fulfilled against us which says, "And thy life shall be hanging up before thee," etc., down to the words, "and for the sights of thine eyes which thou shalt see."[6] As, therefore, the Life is also the living bread which came down from heaven and gave life to the world,[7] so His enemy death is dead bread. Now every rational soul is fed either on living bread or dead bread, by the opinions good or bad which it receives. As then in the case of more common foods it is the practice at one time only to taste them, and at another to eat of them more largely; so also, in the case of these loaves, one eats insufficiently only tasting them, but another is satiated,—he that is good or is on the way to being good with the living bread which came down from heaven, but he that is wicked with the dead bread, which is death; and some perhaps sparingly, and sinning a little, only taste of death; but those who have attained to virtue do not even taste of it, but are

[1] Mark iii. 17. [2] John xiv. 6. [3] Col. iii. 3, 4. [4] 1 Cor. xv. 26. [5] Deut. xxx. 15. [6] Deut. xxviii. 66, 67. [7] John vi. 33, 51.

always fed on the living bread. It naturally followed then in the case of Peter, against whom the gates of Hades will not prevail, that he did not taste of death, since any one tastes of death and eats death at the time when the gates of Hades prevail against him; and one eats or tastes of death in proportion as the gates of Hades to a greater or less extent, more or fewer in number, prevail against him. But also for the sons of thunder who were begotten of thunder, which is a heavenly thing, it was impossible to taste of death, which is extremely far removed from thunder, their mother. But these things the Word prophesies to those who shall be perfected, and who by standing with the Word advanced so far that they did not taste of death, until they saw the manifestation and the glory and the kingdom and the excellency of the Word of God in virtue of which He excels every word, which by an appearance of truth draws away and drags about those who are not able to break through the bonds of distraction, and go up to the height of the excellency of the Word of truth.

34. MEANING OF "UNTIL." NO LIMITATION OF PROMISE.

But since some one may think that the promise of the Saviour prescribes a limit of time to their not tasting of death, namely, that they will not taste of death "until"[1] they see the Son of man coming in His own kingdom, but after this will taste of it, let us show that according to the scriptural usage the word "until" signifies that the time concerning the thing signified is pressing, but is not so defined that after the "until," that which is contrary to the thing signified should at all take place. Now, the Saviour says to the eleven disciples when He rose from the dead, this among other things, "Lo, I am with you all the days, even until the consummation of the age."[2] When He said this, did He promise that He was going to be with them until the consummation of the age, but that after the consummation of the age, when another age was at hand, which is "called the age to come," He would be no longer with them?—so that according to this, the condition of the disciples would be better before the consummation of the age than after the consummation of the age? But I do not think that any one will dare to say, that after the consummation of the age the Son of God will be no longer with the disciples, because the expression declares that He will be with them for so long, until the consummation of the age is at hand; for it is clear that the matter under inquiry was, whether the Son of God was forthwith going to be with His disciples before the age to come and the hoped for promises of God which were given as a recompense. But there might have been a question—it being granted that He would be with them—whether sometimes He was present with them, and sometimes not present. Wherefore setting us free from the suspicion that might have arisen from doubt, He declared that now and even all the days He would be with the disciples, and that He would not leave those who had become His disciples until the consummation of the age; (because He said "all the days" He did not deny that by night, when the sun set, He would be present with them.) But if such is the force of the words, "until the consummation of the age," plainly we shall not be compelled to admit that those who see the Son of man coming in His own kingdom shall taste of death, after being deemed worthy of beholding Him in such guise. But as in the case of the passage we brought forward, the urgent necessity was to teach us that "until the consummation of the age" He would not leave us but be with us all the days; so also in this case I think that it is clear to those who know how to look at the logical coherence of things that He who has seen once for all "the Son of man coming in His own kingdom," and seen Him "in His own glory," and seen "the kingdom of God come with power," could not possibly taste of death after the contemplation of things so good and great. But apart from the word of the promise of Jesus, we have conjectured not without reason that we would taste of death, so long as we were not yet held worthy to see "the kingdom of God come with power," and "the Son of man coming in His own glory and in His own kingdom."

35. SCRIPTURAL REFERENCES TO DEATH.

But since here it is written in the three Evangelists, "They shall not taste of death,"[1] but in other writers different things are written concerning death, it may not be out of place to bring forward and examine these passages along with the "taste." In the Psalms, then, it is said, "What man is

[1] Matt. xvi. 28.

[2] Matt. xxviii. 20.

[1] Matt. xvi. 28; Mark ix. 1; Luke ix. 27.

he that shall live and not see death?"[1] And again, in another place, "Let death come upon them and let them go down into Hades alive;"[2] but in one of the prophets, "Death becoming mighty has swallowed them up;"[3] and in the Apocalypse, "Death and Hades follow some."[4] Now in these passages it appears to me that it is one thing to taste of death, but another thing to see death, and another thing for it to come upon some, and that a fourth thing, different from the aforesaid, is signified by the words, "Death becoming mighty has swallowed them up," and a fifth thing, different from these, by the words, "Death and Hades follow them." And if you were to collect them, you would perhaps find also other differences than those which we have mentioned, by a comparison of which with one another and right investigation, you would find the things signified in each place. But here I inquire whether it is a less evil to see death, but a greater evil than seeing to taste of it, but still worse than this that death should follow any one, and not only follow him, but also now come upon him and seize him whom it formerly followed; but to be swallowed up seems to be more grievous than all the things spoken of. But giving heed to what is said, and to the differences of sins committed, you will not, I think, be slow to admit that things of this kind were intended by the Spirit who caused these things to be written in the oracles of God. But, if it be necessary to give an exposition clearer than what has been said of what is signified by seeing the Son of man coming in His own kingdom, or in His own glory, and what is signified by seeing the kingdom of God come with power, these things—whether those that are made to shine in our hearts, or that are found by those who seek, or that enter gradually into our thoughts,—let each one judge as he wills—we will set forth. He who beholds and apprehends the excellency of the Word, as He breaks down and refutes all the plausible forms of things which are truly lies but profess to be truths, sees the Son of man, (according to the word of John, "the Word of God,") coming in His own kingdom; but if such an one were to behold the Word, not only breaking down plausible oppositions, but also representing His own truths with perfect clearness, he would behold His glory in addition to His kingdom. And such an one indeed would see in Him the kingdom of God come with power; and he would see this, as one who is no longer now under the reign of "sin which reigns in the mortal body of those who sin,"[1] but is ever under the orders of the king, who is God of all, whose kingdom is indeed potentially "within us,"[2] but actually, and, as Mark has called it, "with power," and not at all in weakness within the perfect alone. These things, then, Jesus promised to the disciples who were standing, prophesying not about all of them, but about some.

36. CONCERNING THE TRANSFIGURATION OF THE SAVIOUR.

"*Now after six days*," according to Matthew and Mark,[3] "*He taketh with him Peter and James and John his brother, and leads them up into a high mountain apart, and was transfigured before them.*" Now, also, let it be granted, before the exposition that occurs to us in relation to these things, that this took place long ago, and according to the letter. But it seems to me, that those who are led up by Jesus into the high mountain, and are deemed worthy of beholding His transfiguration apart, are not without purpose led up six days after the discourses previously spoken. For since in six days—the perfect number—the whole world,—this perfect work of art,—was made, on this account I think that he who transcends all the things of the world by beholding no longer the things which are seen, for they are temporal, but already the things which are not seen, and only the things which are not seen, because that they are eternal, is represented in the words, "After six days days Jesus took up with Him" certain persons. If therefore any one of us wishes to be taken by Jesus, and led up by Him into the high mountain, and be deemed worthy of beholding His transfiguration apart, let him pass beyond the six days, because he no longer beholds the things which are seen, nor longer loves the world, nor the things in the world,[4] nor lusts after any worldly lust, which is the lust of bodies, and of the riches of the body, and of the glory which is after the flesh, and whatever things whose nature it is to distract and drag away the soul from the things which are better and diviner, and bring it down and fix it fast to the deceit of this age, in wealth and glory, and the rest of the lusts which are the foes of truth. For when he has passed through the six days, as we have

[1] Ps. lxxxix. 48.
[2] Ps. lv. 18.
[3] Isa. xxv. 8.
[4] Rev. vi. 10.

[1] Rom. vi. 12.
[2] Luke xvii. 21.
[3] Matt. xvii. 1; Mark ix. 2.
[4] 1 John ii. 15.

said, he will keep a new Sabbath, rejoicing in the lofty mountain, because he sees Jesus transfigured before him; for the Word has different forms, as He appears to each as is expedient for the beholder, and is manifested to no one beyond the capacity of the beholder.

37. FORCE OF THE WORDS "BEFORE THEM."

But you will ask if, when He was transfigured before those who were led up by Him into the lofty mountain, He appeared to them in the form of God, in which He formerly was, so that He had to those below the form of a servant, but to those who had followed Him after the six days to the lofty mountain, He had not that form, but the form of God. But hear these things, if you can, at the same time giving heed spiritually, that it is not said simply, "He was transfigured," but with a certain necessary addition, which Matthew and Mark have recorded; for, according to both, "He was transfigured before them."[1] And according to this, indeed, you will say that it is possible for Jesus to be transfigured before some with this transfiguration, but before others at the same time not to be transfigured. But if you wish to see the transfiguration of Jesus before those who went up into the lofty mountain apart long with Him, behold with me the Jesus in the Gospels, as more simply apprehended, and as one might say, known "according to the flesh," by those who do not go up, through works and words which are uplifting, to the lofty mountain of wisdom, but known no longer after the flesh, but known in His divinity by means of all the Gospels, and beholden in the form of God according to their knowledge; for before them is Jesus transfigured, and not to any one of those below. But when He is transfigured, His face also shines as the sun, that He may be manifested to the children of light, who have put off the works of darkness, and put on the armour of light,[2] and are no longer the children of darkness or night, but have become the sons of day, and walk honestly as in the day;[3] and being manifested, He will shine unto them not simply as the sun, but as demonstrated to be the sun of righteousness.

38. THE GARMENTS WHITE AS THE LIGHT.

And not only is He transfigured before such disciples, nor does He only add to the transfiguration the shining of His face as the sun; but further also to those who were led up by Him into the high mountain apart, His garments appear white as the light.[1] But the garments of Jesus are the expressions and letters of the Gospels with which He invested Himself. But I think that even the words in the Apostles which indicate the truths concerning Him are garments of Jesus, which become white to those who go up into the high mountain along with Jesus. But since there are differences also of things white, His garments become white as the brightest and purest of all white things; and that is light. When therefore you see any one not only with a thorough understanding of the theology concerning Jesus, but also making clear every expression of the Gospels, do not hesitate to say that to Him the garments of Jesus have become white as the light. But when the Son of God in His transfiguration is so understood and beheld, that His face is a sun, and His garments white as the light, straightway there will appear to him who beholds Jesus in such form Moses,—the law—and Elijah,—in the way of synecdoche, not one prophet only, but all the prophets—holding converse with Jesus; for such is the force of the words "talking with Him;"[2] but, according to Luke, "Moses and Elijah appeared in glory," down to the words, "in Jerusalem."[3] But if any one sees the glory of Moses, having understood the spiritual law as a discourse in harmony with Jesus, and the wisdom in the prophets which is hidden in a mystery,[4] he sees Moses and Elijah in glory when he sees them with Jesus.

39. JESUS WAS TRANSFIGURED—"AS HE WAS PRAYING."

Then, since it will be necessary to expound the passage as given in Mark, "*And as He was praying He was transfigured before them,*"[5] we must say that perhaps it is possible especially to see the Word transfigured before us if we have done the things aforesaid, and gone up into the mountain, and seen the absolute Word holding converse with the Father, and praying to Him for such things as the true High-Priest might pray for to the only true God. But in order that He may thus hold fellowship with God and pray to the Father, He goes up into the mountain; and then, according to Mark, "His garments become white and glistening as the light, so as no fuller on earth can whiten them."[6] And perhaps the fullers

[1] Matt. xvii. 2; Mark ix. 2.
[2] Rom. xiii. 12.
[3] Rom. xiii. 13; 1 Thess. v. 5.

[1] Matt. xvii. 2.
[2] Matt. xvii. 3.
[3] Luke ix. 30, 31.
[4] 1 Cor. ii. 7.
[5] Luke (ix. 28, 29) alone mentions the praying.
[6] Mark ix. 3.

upon the earth are the wise men of this world who are careful about the diction which they consider to be bright and pure, so that even their base thoughts and false dogmas seem to be beautified by their fulling, so to speak; but He who shows His own garments glistering to those who have ascended and brighter than their fulling can make them, is the Word, who exhibits in the expressions of the Scriptures which are despised by many the glistering of the thoughts, when the raiment of Jesus, according to Luke, becomes white and dazzling.[1]

40. DISCUSSION OF THE SAYING OF PETER.

But let us next see what was the thought of Peter when he answered and said to Jesus, "*Lord, it is good for us to be here; let us make three tabernacles,*"[2] etc. And on this account these words call for very special examination, because Mark, in his own person, has added, "For he wist not what to answer,"[3] but Luke, "not knowing," he says, "what he spake."[4] You will consider, therefore, if he spake these things as in a trance, being filled with the spirit which moved him to say these things, which could not be a Holy Spirit; for John taught in the Gospel that, before the resurrection of the Saviour, no one had the Holy Spirit, saying, "For the Spirit was not yet, because Jesus was not yet glorified."[5] But if the Spirit was not yet, and he, not knowing what he said, spoke under the influence of some spirit, the spirit which caused these things to be said was some one of the spirits which had not yet been triumphed over in the cross, nor made a show of along with them, about whom it is written, "Having put off from Himself the principalities and the powers, He made a show of them openly, triumphing over them in the cross.[6]" But this spirit was perhaps that which is called a stumbling-block by Jesus, and which is spoken of as Satan in the passage, "Get thee behind Me, Satan; thou art a stumbling-block unto me."[7] But I know well that such things will offend many who meet with them, because they think that it is opposed to sound reason that he should be spoken ill of who a little before had been pronounced blessed by Jesus, on the ground that the Father in heaven had revealed to him the things concerning the Saviour, to-wit, that He was verily Jesus, and the Christ, and the Son of the living God. But let such an one attend more exactly to the statements about Peter and the rest of the Apostles, how even they made requests as if they were yet alien from Him who was to redeem them from the enemy and purchase them with His own precious blood; or let them also, who will have it that even before the passion of Jesus the Apostles were perfect, tell us whence it came about that "Peter and they that were with him were heavy with sleep."[1] But to anticipate something else of what follows and apply it to the subject in hand, I would raise in turn these questions,—whether it is possible for any one to find occasion of stumbling in Jesus apart from the working of the devil who caused him to stumble; and whether it is possible for any one to deny Jesus, and that in presence of a little maid and a doorkeeper and men most worthless, unless a spirit had been with him in his denial hostile to the Spirit which is given and the wisdom, (which is given) to those who are assisted by God to make confession, according to a certain desert of theirs. But he who has learned to refer the roots of sin to the father of sin, the devil, will not say that apart from him either the Apostles were caused to stumble, or that Peter denied Christ thrice before that well-known cock-crowing. But if this be so, consider whether perhaps with a view to make Jesus stumble, so far as was in his power, and to turn Him aside from the dispensation whose characteristic was suffering that brought salvation to men, which He undertook with great willingness, seeking to effect these things which seemed to contribute to this end, he himself also here wishes as it were, by deceit, to draw away Jesus, as if calling upon Him no longer to condescend to men, and come to them, and undergo death for them, but to abide on the high mountain with Moses and Elijah. But he promised also to build three tabernacles, one apart for Jesus, and one for Moses, and one for Elijah, as if one tabernacle would not have sufficed for the three, if it had been necessary for them to be in tabernacles and in the high mountain. And perhaps also in this he acted with evil intent, when he incited him "who did not know what he said," not desiring that Jesus and Moses and Elijah should be together, but desiring to separate them from one another, under pretext of the three tabernacles. And likewise it was a lie, "It is good for us to be here;"[2] for if it had been a good thing they would also have re-

[1] Luke ix. 29.
[2] Matt. xvii. 4; Mark ix. 5; Luke ix. 33.
[3] Mark ix. 6.
[4] Luke ix. 33.
[5] John vii. 39.
[6] Col. ii. 15.
[7] Matt. xvi. 23.

[1] Luke ix. 32.
[2] Matt. xvii. 4.

mained there. But if it were a lie, you will seek to know who caused the lie to be spoken; and especially since according to John, "When he speaketh a lie he speaketh of his own; for he is a liar and the father thereof;"[1] and as there is no truth apart from the working of Him who says, "I am the Truth,"[2] so there is no lie apart from him who is the enemy of truth. These contrary qualities, accordingly, were still in Peter truth and falsehood; and from truth he said, "Thou art the Christ, the son of the living God,"[3] but from falsehood he said, "May God be propitious to Thee, Lord, this shall not be unto Thee,"[4] and also, "It is good for us to be here."[5] But if any one will not admit that Peter spoke these things from any evil inspiration, but that his words were of his own mere choice, and it is demanded of him how he will interpret, "not knowing what he said," and,[6] "for he did not know what to answer,"[7] he will say, that in the former case Peter held it to be a shameful thing and unworthy of Jesus to admit that the Son of the living God, the Christ, whom already the Father had revealed to him, should be killed; and in the present case that, as having seen the two forms of Jesus and the one at the transfiguration which was much more excellent, being well pleased with that, he said that it was good to make their sojourning in that mountain, in order that he himself and those with him might rejoice as they beheld the transfiguration of Jesus and His face shining as the sun, and His garments white as the light, and, in addition to these things, might always behold in glory those whom they had once seen in glory, Moses and Elijah; and that they might rejoice at the things which they might hear, as they talked and held intercourse with each other, Moses and Elijah with Jesus, and Jesus with them.

41. FIGURATIVE INTERPRETATION OF THE SAME.

But since we have not yet spent our energy in interpreting the things in the place figuratively, but have said these things by way of searching into the mere letter, let us in conformity with these things, consider whether the aforesaid Peter and the sons of thunder who were taken up into the mountain of the dogmas of the truth, and who saw the transfiguration of Jesus and of Moses and Elijah, who appeared in glory with Him, might wish to make tabernacles in themselves for the Word of God who was going to dwell in them, and for His law which had been beholden in glory, and for the prophecy which spake of the decease of Jesus, which He was about to accomplish;[1] and Peter, as one loving the contemplative life, and having preferred that which was delightsome in it to the life among the crowd with its turmoil, said, with the design of benefiting those who desired it, "It is good for us to be here."[2] But since "love seeketh not its own,"[3] Jesus did not do that which Peter thought good; wherefore He descended from the mountain to those who were not able to ascend to it and behold His transfiguration, that they might behold Him in such form as they were able to see Him. It is, therefore, the part of a righteous man who possesses "the love which seeketh not its own"[4] to be free from all, but to bring himself under bondage to all those below that He might gain the more of them.[5] But some one, with reference to what we have alleged about the trance and the working of an evil spirit in Peter, concerning the words, "not knowing what he said,"[6] not accepting that interpretation of ours, may say that there were certain mentioned by Paul "desiring to be teachers of the law,"[7] who do not know about what they speak, but who, though they do not clearly expound the nature of what is said, nor understand their meaning, make confident affirmations of things which they do not know. Of such a nature was the affection of Peter also, for not apprehending what was good with reference to the dispensation of Jesus and of those who appeared in the mountain,—Moses and Elijah,—he says, "It is good for us to be here," etc., "not knowing what he said," "for he wist not what to say," for if "a wise man will understand the things from his own mouth, and carries prudence in his lips,"[8] he who is not so does not understand the things from his own mouth, nor comprehend the nature of the things spoken by him.

42. THE MEANING OF THE "BRIGHT CLOUD."

Next to these come the words, "*While He was yet speaking, behold*, also, *a bright cloud overshadowed them*,"[9] etc. Now, I think that God, wishing to dissuade Peter from making three tabernacles, under which so far as it depended on his choice he was going to dwell, shows a tabernacle better, so to speak, and much more excellent, the cloud. For since it is the function of a tabernacle

[1] John viii. 44. [2] John xiv. 6. [3] Matt. xvi. 16. [4] Matt. xvi. 20. [5] Matt. xvii. 4. [6] Luke ix. 33. [7] Mark ix. 6.

[1] Luke ix. 31. [2] Matt. xvii. 4. [3] 1 Cor. xiii. 5. [4] 1 Cor. xiii. 5. [5] 1 Cor. ix. 19. [6] Luke ix. 33. [7] 1 Tim. i. 7. [8] Prov. xvi. 23. [9] Matt. xvii. 5.

to overshadow him who is in it, and to shelter him, and the bright cloud overshadowed them, God made, as it were, a diviner tabernacle, inasmuch as it was bright, that it might be to them a pattern of the resurrection to come; for a bright cloud overshadows the just, who are at once protected and illuminated and shone upon by it. But what might the bright cloud, which overshadows the just, be? Is it, perhaps, the fatherly power, from which comes the voice of the Father bearing testimony to the Son as beloved and well-pleasing, and exhorting those who were under its shadow to hear Him and no other one? But as He speaks of old, so also always does He speak through what He wills. And perhaps, too, the Holy Spirit is the bright cloud which overshadows the just, and prophesies of the things of God, who works in it, and says, "This is My beloved Son in whom I am well-pleased;" but I would venture also to say that our Saviour is a bright cloud. When, therefore, Peter said, "Let us make here three tabernacles,"[1] . . . one from the Father Himself, and from the Son, and one from the Holy Spirit. For a bright cloud of the Father, Son and Holy Spirit overshadows the genuine disciples of Jesus; or a cloud overshadows the Gospel and the law and the prophets, which is bright to him who is able to see the light of it in the Gospel, and the law, and the prophets. But perhaps the voice from the cloud says to Moses and Elijah, "This is My beloved Son in whom I am well-pleased, hear Him," as they were desirous to see the Son of man, and to hear Him, and to behold Him as He was in glory. And perhaps it teaches the disciples that He who was, in a literal sense, the Son of God, and His beloved in whom He was well-pleased, whom it behoved them especially to hear, was He who was then beheld, and transfigured, and whose face shone as the sun, and who was clothed with garments white as the light.

43. RELATION OF MOSES AND ELIJAH TO JESUS. THE INJUNCTION OF SILENCE.

But after these things it is written that, when they heard the voice from the cloud bearing testimony to the Son, the three Apostles, not being able to bear the glory of the voice and power resting upon it, "fell on their face,"[2] and besought God; for they were sore afraid at the supernatural sight, and the things which were spoken from the sight. But consider if you can also say this with reference to the details in the passage, that the disciples, having understood that the Son of God had been holding conference with Moses, and that it was He who said, "A man shall not see My face and live,"[1] and taking further the testimony of God about Him, as not being able to endure the radiance of the Word, humbled themselves under the mighty hand of God;[2] but, after the touch of the Word, lifting up their eyes they saw Jesus only and no other.[3] Moses, the law, and Elijah, the prophet, became one only with the Gospel of Jesus; and not, as they were formerly three, did they so abide, but the three became one. But consider these things with me in relation to mystical matters; for in regard to the bare meaning of the letter, Moses and Elijah, having appeared in glory and talked with Jesus, went away to the place from which they had come, perhaps to communicate the words which Jesus spake with them, to those who were to be benefited by Him, almost immediately, namely, at the time of the passion, when many bodies of the saints that had fallen asleep, their tombs being opened, were to go to the city which is truly holy—not the Jerusalem which Jesus wept over—and there appear unto many.[4] But after the dispensation in the mountain, when the disciples were coming down from the mountain in order that, when they had come to the multitude, they might serve the Son of God concerning the salvation of the people, Jesus commanded the disciples saying, "Tell the vision to no man until the Son of man rise from the dead."[5] But that saying, "Tell the vision to no man," is like that which was investigated in the passage above, when "He enjoined the disciples to tell no man that He was the Christ."[6] Wherefore the things that were said at that passage may be useful to us also for the passage before us; since Jesus wishes also, in accordance with these, that the things of His glory should not be spoken of, before His glory after the passion; for those who heard, and in particular the multitudes, would have been injured when they saw Him crucified, who had been so glorified. Wherefore since His being glorified in the resurrection was akin to His transfiguration, and to the vision of His face as the sun, on this account He wishes that these things should then be spoken of by the Apostles, when He rose from the dead.

[1] The text is mutilated.
[2] Matt. xvii. 6.

[1] Exod. xxx. 20.
[2] 1 Pet. v. 6.
[3] Matt. xvii. 8.
[4] Matt. xxvii. 52, 53.
[5] Matt. xvii. 9.
[6] Matt. xvi. 20.

BOOK XIII.

I. RELATION OF THE BAPTIST TO ELIJAH. THE THEORY OF TRANSMIGRATION CONSIDERED.

"*The disciples asked Him, saying, Why then say the scribes that Elijah must first come?*"[1] The disciples indeed who went up with Jesus remembered the traditions of the scribes concerning Elijah, that before the advent of Christ, Elijah would come and prepare for Him the souls of those who were going to receive Him. But the vision in the mountain, at which Elijah appeared, did not seem to be in harmony with the things which were said, since to them it seemed that Elijah had not come before Jesus but after Him; wherefore, they say these things, thinking that the scribes lied. But to this the Saviour answers, not setting aside the traditions concerning Elijah, but saying that there was another advent of Elijah before that of Christ of which the scribes were ignorant; and, in regard to this, being ignorant of him, they "had done unto him whatsoever they listed,"[2] as if they had been accomplices in his having been cast into prison by Herod and slain by him; then He says that according as they had done towards Elijah so would He suffer at their hands.[3] And these things indeed as about Elijah the disciples asked and the Saviour answered, but when they heard they understood that the words, "Elijah has already come," and that following which was spoken by the Saviour, had reference to John the Baptist.[4] And let these things be said by way of illustration of the passage before us. But now according to our ability let us make investigation also into the things that are stored up in it. In this place it does not appear to me that by Elijah the soul is spoken of, lest I should fall into the dogma of transmigration, which is foreign to the church of God, and not handed down by the Apostles, nor anywhere set forth in the Scriptures; for it is also in opposition to the saying that "things seen are temporal,"[5] and that "this age shall have a consummation," and also to the fulfilment of the saying, "Heaven and earth shall pass away,"[6] and "the fashion of this world

[1] Matt. xvii. 10.
[2] Matt. xvii. 12.
[3] Matt. xvii. 12.
[4] Matt. xvii. 13.
[5] 2 Cor iv. 18.
[6] Matt. xxiv. 35.

passeth away,"[1] and "the heavens shall perish,"[2] and what follows. For if, by hypothesis, in the constitution of things which has existed from the beginning unto the end of the world, the same soul can be twice in the body, for what cause should it be in it? For if because of sin it should be twice in the body, why should it not be thrice, and repeatedly in it, since punishments, in respect of this life, and of the sins committed in it, shall be rendered to it only by the method of transmigration? But if this be granted as a consequence, perhaps there will never be a time when a soul shall not undergo transmigration; for always because of its former sins will it dwell in the body; and so there will be no place for the corruption of the world, at which "the heaven and the earth shall pass away."[3] And if it be granted, on this hypothesis, that one who is absolutely sinless shall not come into the body by birth, after what length of time do you suppose that a soul shall be found absolutely pure and needing no transmigration? But nevertheless, also, if any one soul is always thus being removed from the definite number of souls and returns no longer to the body, sometime after infinite ages, as it were, birth shall cease; the world being reduced to some one or two or a few more, after the perfecting of whom the world shall perish, the supply of souls coming into the body having failed. But this is not agreeable to the Scripture; for it knows of a multitude of sinners at the time of the destruction of the world. This is manifest from consideration of the saying, "Howbeit when the Son of man cometh shall He find faith on the earth?"[4] So we find it thus said in Matthew, "As were the days of Noah so shall also be the coming of the Son of man; for as they were in the days of the flood," etc.[5] But to those who are then in existence there shall be the exaction of a penalty for their sins, but not by way of transmigration; for, if they are caught while still sinning, either they will be punished after this by a different form of punishment, —and according to this either there will be two general forms of punishment, the one by way of transmigration, and the other

[1] 1 Cor. vii. 31.
[2] Ps. cii. 26.
[3] Matt. xxiv. 35.
[4] Luke xviii. 8.
[5] Matt. xxiv. 37–39.

outside of a body of this kind, and let them declare the causes and differences of these,—or they will not be punished, as if those who were left at the consummation of things had forthwith cast away their sins; or, which is better, there is one form of punishment for those who have sinned in the body, namely, that they should suffer, outside of it, that is, outside the constitution of this life, what is according to the desert of their sins. But to one who has insight into the nature of things it is clear that each of these things is fitted to overturn the doctrine of transmigration. But if, of necessity, the Greeks who introduce the doctrine of transmigration, laying down things in harmony with it, do not acknowledge that the world is coming to corruption, it is fitting that when they have looked the Scriptures straight in the face which plainly declare that the world will perish, they should either disbelieve them, or invent a series of arguments in regard to the interpretation of the things concerning the consummation; which even if they wish they will not be able to do. And this besides we will say to those who may have had the hardihood to aver that the world will not perish, that, if the world does not perish but is to exist for infinite periods of time, there will be no God knowing all things before they come into being. But if, perhaps, He knows in part, either He will know each thing before it comes into being, or certain things, and after these again other things; for things infinite in nature cannot possibly be grasped by that knowledge whose nature it is to limit things known. From this it follows that there cannot be prophecies about all things whatsoever, since all things are infinite.

2. "THE SPIRIT AND POWER OF ELIJAH"—NOT THE SOUL—WERE IN THE BAPTIST.

I have thought it necessary to dwell some time on the examination of the doctrine of transmigration, because of the suspicion of some who suppose that the soul under consideration was the same in Elijah and in John, being called in the former case Elijah, and in the second case John; and that, not apart from God, had he been called John, as is plain from the saying of the angel who appeared to Zacharias, "Fear not, Zacharias, for thy supplication is heard, and thy wife Elisabeth shall bear thee a son, and thou shalt call his name John;"[1] and from the fact that Zacharias regained his speech after he had written in the tablet, that he who had been born should be called John.[1] But if it were the soul of Elijah, then, when he was begotten a second time, he should have been called Elijah; or for the change of name some reason should have been assigned, as in the case of Abram and Abraham, Sarah and Sarrah, Jacob and Israel, Simon and Peter. And yet not even thus would their argument in the case be tenable; for, in the case of the aforesaid, the changes of name took place in one and the same life. But some one might ask, if the soul of Elijah was not first in the Tishbite and secondly in John, what might that be in both which the Saviour called Elijah? And I say that Gabriel in his words to Zacharias suggested what the substance was in Elijah and John that was the same; for he says, "Many of the children of Israel shall he turn to the Lord their God; and he shall go before his face in the spirit and power of Elijah."[2] For, observe, he did not say in the "soul" of Elijah, in which case the doctrine of transmigration might have some ground, but "in the spirit and power of Elijah." For the Scripture well knows the distinction between spirit and soul, as, "May God sanctify you wholly, and may your spirit and soul and body be preserved entire, without blame at the coming of our Lord Jesus Christ;"[3] and the passage, "Bless the Lord, ye spirits and souls of the righteous"[4] as it stands in the book of Daniel, according to the Septuagint, represents the difference between spirit and soul. Elijah, therefore, was not called John because of the soul, but because of the spirit and the power, which in no way conflicts with the teaching of the church, though they were formerly in Elijah, and afterwards in John; and "the spirits of the prophets are subject to the prophets,"[5] but the souls of the prophets are not subject to the prophets, and "the spirit of Elijah rested on Elisha."[6] But we ought to inquire whether the spirit of Elijah is the same as the spirit of God in Elijah, or whether they are different from each other, and whether the spirit of Elijah which was in him was something supernatural, different from the spirit of each man which is in him; for the Apostle clearly indicates that the Spirit of God, though it be in us, is different from the spirit of each man which is in Him, when he says somewhere, "The Spirit itself beareth witness with our spirit that we are the children of God;"[7] and elsewhere,

[1] Luke i. 13.

[1] Luke i. 63. [2] Luke i. 16, 17. [3] 1 Thess. v. 23.
[4] Dan. iii. 86. (Song of the Three Children v. 64.)
[5] 1 Cor. xiv. 32. [6] 2 Kings ii. 15. [7] Rom. viii. 16.

"No one of men knoweth the things of a man save the spirit of the man which is in him; even so the things of God none knoweth save the Spirit of God."[1] But do not marvel in regard to what is said about Elijah, if, just as something strange happened to him different from all the saints who are recorded, in respect of his having been caught up by a whirlwind into heaven,[2] so his spirit had something of choice excellence, so that not only did it rest on Elisha, but also descended along with John at his birth; and that John, separately, "was filled with the Holy Ghost even from his mother's womb," and separately, "came before Christ in the spirit and power of Elijah."[3] For it is possible for several spirits not only worse, but also better, to be in the same man. David accordingly asks to be established by a free spirit,[4] and that a right spirit be renewed in his inward parts.[5] But if, in order that the Saviour may impart to us of "the spirit of wisdom and understanding, the spirit of counsel and might, the spirit of knowledge and reverence,"[6] he was filled also with the spirit of the fear of the Lord; it is possible also that these several good spirits may be conceived as being in the same person. And this also we have brought forward, because of John having come before Christ "in the spirit and power of Elijah,"[7] in order that the saying, "Elijah has already come,"[8] may be referred to the spirit of Elijah that was in John; as also the three disciples who had gone up with Him understood that He spake to them about John the Baptist.[9] Upon Elisha, then, only the spirit of Elijah rested, but John came before,[10] not only in the spirit, but also in the power of Elijah. Wherefore, also, Elisha could not have been called Elijah, but John was Elijah himself. But if it be necessary to adduce the Scripture from which the scribes said that Elijah must first come, listen to Malachi who says, "And behold I will send to you Elijah the Tishbite," etc., down to the words, "Lest I come and smite the earth utterly."[11] And it seems to be indicated by these words, that Elijah was to prepare for the glorious coming of Christ by certain holy words and dispositions in their souls, those who had been made fittest for this, which those upon earth could not have endured, because of the excellency of the glory, unless they had been prepared before hand by Elijah. And likewise, by Elijah,

[1] 1 Cor. ii. 11. [2] 2 Kings ii. 11. [3] Luke i. 15, 17. [4] Ps. li. 12. [5] Ps. li. 10. [6] Isa. xi. 2. [7] Luke i. 17. [8] Matt. xvii. 12. [9] Matt. xvii. 13. [10] Cf. Luke i. 17. [11] Mal. iv. 5, 6.

in this place, I do not understand the soul of that prophet but his spirit and his power; for these it is by which all things shall be restored,[1] so that when they have been restored, and, as a result of that restoration, become capable of receiving the glory of Christ, the Son of God who shall appear in glory may sojourn with them. But if also Elijah be in some sort a word inferior to "the Word who was in the beginning with God, God the Word,"[2] this word also might come as a preparatory discipline to the people prepared by it, that they might be trained for the reception of the perfect Word. But some one may raise the question whether the spirit and power of Elijah, suffered what was suffered in John, according to the words, "They did in him whatsoever they listed."[3] And to this it will be said on the one hand, in simpler fashion that there is nothing strange in the thought, that the things which assist do, because of love, suffer along with those that are assisted; and Jesus indeed says, "Because of the weak I was weak, and I hungered because of the hungry, and I thirsted because of the thirsty,"[4] and, on the other hand, in a deeper sense that the words are not, "But they did unto him whatsoever they listed in him," for the things which suffered leaned upon the spirit and the power of Elijah, the soul of John being in no wise Elijah; and probably also the body (leaned upon them). For in one fashion is the soul in the body, and the spirit, and the power; and in another fashion is the body of the righteous man in these better parts, as leaning upon them, and clinging to them; but "they who are in the flesh cannot please God; but ye are not in the flesh, but in the spirit, if the Spirit of God dwell in you;"[5] for the soul of the sinner is in the flesh, but of the righteous man in spirit. And likewise, further, this might be inquired into, to whom refer the words, "But they did in him whatsoever they listed."[6] Was it to the scribes in regard to whom the disciples inquired and said, "Why then do the scribes say that Elijah must first come?"[7] But it is not at all evident that John suffered anything at the hands of the scribes, except, indeed, that they did not believe him; or, as we said also before, that they were accomplices in the wrongs which Herod dared to inflict on him. But another might say that the words, "But they did in him whatsoever

[1] Matt. xvii. 11. [2] John i. 1. [3] Matt. xvii. 12. [4] Cf. Matt. xxv. 35. [5] Rom. viii. 8, 9. [6] Matt. xvii. 12. [7] Matt. xvii. 10.

they listed," refer not to the scribes but to Herodias and her daughter, and Herod, who did in him whatsoever they listed. And that which follows, "So shall the Son of man suffer from them,"[1] might be referred to the scribes, if the former were referred to them; but, if the former refers to Herod and Herodias and her daughter, the second passage will also refer to them;[2] for Herod also seems to have joined in the vote that Jesus should die, perhaps his wife also taking part with him in the plot against Him.

3. CONCERNING THE EPILEPTIC.

"*And when they were come to the multitude, there came to Him a man kneeling to Him and saying, Lord, have mercy upon my son.*"[3] Those who are suffering, or the kinsfolk of the sufferers, are along with the multitudes; wherefore, when He has dispensed the things that were beyond the multitudes, He descends to them, so that those, who were not able to ascend because of the sicknesses that repressed their soul, might be benefited when the Word descended to them from the loftier regions. But we ought to make inquiry, in respect of what diseases the sufferers believe and pray for their own healing, and in respect of what diseases others do this for them, as, for example, the centurion for his servant, and the nobleman for his son, and the ruler of the synagogue for a daughter, and the Canaanitish woman for her female child who was vexed with a demon, and now the man who kneels to Him on behalf of his epileptic son. And along with these you will investigate when the Saviour heals of Himself and unasked by any one, as for example, the paralytic; for these cures, when compared with one another for this very purpose, and examined together, will exhibit to him who is able to hear "the wisdom of God hidden in a mystery,"[4] many dogmas concerning the different diseases of souls, as well as the method of their healing.

4. SPIRITUAL EPILEPTICS.

But since our present object is not to make inquiry about every case, but about the passage before us, let us, adopting a figurative interpretation, consider who we may say the lunatic was, and who was his father who prayed for him, and what is meant by the sufferer falling not constantly but ofttimes, sometimes into the fire, and sometimes into the water, and what is meant by the fact that he could not be healed by the disciples but by Jesus Himself. For if every sickness and every infirmity, which our Saviour then healed among the people, refers to different disorders in souls, it is also in accordance with reason that by the paralytics are symbolised the palsied in soul, who keep it lying paralysed in the body; but by those who are blind are symbolised those who are blind in respect of things seen by the soul alone, and these are really blind; and by the deaf are symbolised those who are deaf in regard to the reception of the word of salvation. On the same principle it will be necessary that the matters regarding the epileptic should be investigated. Now this affection attacks the sufferers at considerable intervals, during which he who suffers from it seems in no way to differ from the man in good health, at the season when the epilepsy is not working on him. Similar disorders you may find in certain souls, which are often supposed to be healthy in point of temperance and the other virtues; then, sometimes, as if they were seized with a kind of epilepsy arising from their passions, they fall down from the position in which they seemed to stand, and are drawn away by the deceit of this world and other lusts. Perhaps, therefore, you would not err if you said, that such persons, so to speak, are epileptic spiritually, having been cast down by "the spiritual hosts of wickedness in the heavenly places,"[1] and are often ill, at the time when the passions attack their soul; at one time falling into the fire of burnings, when, according to what is said in Hosea, they become adulterers, like a pan heated for the cooking from the burning flame;[2] and, at another time, into the water, when the king of all the dragons in the waters casts them down from the sphere where they appeared to breath freely, so that they come into the depths of the waves of the sea of human life. This interpretation of ours in regard to the lunatic will be supported by him who says in the Book of Wisdom with reference to the even temperament of the just man, "The discourse of a pious man is always wisdom," but, in regard to what we have said, "The fool changes as the moon."[3] And sometimes even in the case of such you may see impulses which might carry away in praise of them those who do not attend to their want of ballast, so that they would say that it was as full moon in their case, or almost full moon. And you might see again the light that seemed to be in them dim-

[1] Matt. xvii. 12. [2] The text is uncertain.
[3] Matt. xvii. 14, 15. [4] 1 Cor. ii. 7.

[1] Eph. vi. 12. [2] Hos. vii. 4. [3] Ecclus. xxvii. 11.

inishing,—as it was not the light of day but the light of night,—fading to so great an extent, that the light which appeared to be seen in them no longer existed. But whether or not those who first gave their names to things, on account of this gave the name of lunacy to the disease epilepsy, you will judge for yourself.

5. THE DEAF AND DUMB SPIRIT.

Now the father of the epileptic—perhaps the angel to whom he had been allotted, if we are to say that every human soul is put in subjection to some angel—prays the Physician of souls for his son that He may heal him who could not be healed from his disorder by the inferior word which was in the disciples. But the dumb and deaf spirit, who was cast out by the Word, must be figuratively understood as the irrational impulses, even towards that which seems to be good, so that, what things any man once did by irrational impulse which seemed to onlookers to be good, he may do no longer irrationally but according to the reason of the teaching of Jesus. Under the inspiration of this Paul also said, "If I have all faith so as to remove mountains;"[1] for he, who has all faith, which is as a grain of mustard seed,[2] removes not one mountain only, but also several analogous to it; for although faith is despised by men and appears to be something very little and contemptible; yet when it meets with good ground, that is the soul, which is able fittingly to receive such seed, it becomes a great tree, so that no one of those things which have no wings, but the birds of heaven which are winged spiritually, are able to lodge in the branches of faith so great.[3]

6. INFLUENCE OF THE MOON AND STARS ON MEN.

Let us now, then, give heed to the very letter of the passage, and first let us inquire, how he who has been cast into darkness and repressed by an impure and deaf and dumb spirit is said to be a "lunatic," and for what reason the expression to be a "lunatic" derives its name from the great light in heaven which is next to the sun, which God appointed "to rule over the night."[4] Let physicians then, discuss the physiology of the matter, inasmuch as they think that there is no impure spirit in the case, but a bodily disorder, and inquiring into the nature of things let them say, that the moist humours which are in the head are moved by a certain sympathy which they have with the light of the moon, which has a moist nature; but as for us, who also believe the Gospel that this sickness is viewed as having been effected by an impure dumb and deaf spirit in those who suffer from it, and who see that those, who are accustomed like the magicians of the Egyptians to promise a cure in regard to such, seem sometimes to be successful in their case, we will say that, perhaps, with the view of slandering the creation of God, in order that "unrighteousness may be spoken loftily, and that they may set their mouth against the heaven,"[1] this impure spirit watches certain configurations of the moon, and so makes it appear from observation of men suffering at such and such a phase of the moon, that the cause of so great an evil is not the dumb and deaf demon, but the great light in heaven which was appointed "to rule by night," and which has no power to originate such a disorder among men. But they all "speak unrighteousness loftily," as many as say, that the cause of all the disorders which exist on the earth, whether of such generally or of each in detail, arises from the disposition of the stars; and such have truly "set their mouth against the heaven," when they say that some of the stars have a malevolent, and others a benevolent influence; since no star was formed by the God of the universe to work evil, according to Jeremiah as it is written in the Lamentations, "Out of the mouth of the Lord shall come things noble and that which is good."[2] And it is probable that as this impure spirit, producing what is called lunacy, observes the phases of the moon, that it may work on him who for certain causes has been committed to it, and who has not made himself worthy of the guardianship of angels, so also there are other spirits and demons who work at certain phases of the rest of the stars; so that not the moon only, but the rest of the stars also may be calumniated by those "who speak unrighteousness loftily." It is worth while, then, to listen to the casters of nativities, who refer the origin of every form of madness and every demoniacal possession to the phases of the moon. That those, then, who suffer from what is called lunacy sometimes fall into the water is evident, and that they also fall into the fire, less frequently indeed, yet it does happen; and it is evident that this disorder is very difficult to cure, so that those who have the power to cure demoniacs sometimes fail in respect of

[1] 1 Cor. xiii. 2.
[2] Matt. xvii. 20.
[3] Cf. Matt. xiii. 31, 32.
[4] Gen. i. 16.

[1] Ps. lxxiii. 8, 9.
[2] Lam. iii. 38. Origen reads τὰ καλὰ instead of τὰ κακὰ.

this, and sometimes with fastings and supplications and more toils, succeed. But you will inquire whether there are such disorders in spirits as well as in men; so that some of them speak, but some of them are speechless, and some of them hear, but some are deaf; for as in them will be found the cause of their being impure, so also, because of their freedom of will, are they condemned to be speechless and deaf; for some men will suffer such condemnation if the prayer of the prophet, as spoken by the Holy Spirit, shall be given heed to, in which it is said of certain sinners, "Let the lying lips be put to silence."[1] And so, perhaps, those who make a bad use of their hearing, and admit the hearing of vanities, will be rendered deaf by Him who said, "Who hath made the stone-deaf and the deaf,"[2] so that they may no longer lend an ear to vain things.

7. THE POWER OF FAITH.

But when the Saviour said, "*O faithless and perverse generation,*"[3] He signifies that wickedness, which is contrary to nature, stealthily enters in from perversity, and makes us perverted. But of the whole race of men on earth, I think, being oppressed by reason of their wickedness and His tarrying with them, the Saviour said, "How long shall I be with you?" We have already, then, spoken in part of the words, "If ye have faith as a grain of mustard seed, ye shall say unto this mountain,"[4] etc.; but nevertheless also we shall speak in this place the things that appear to us fitted to increase perspicuity. The mountains here spoken of, in my opinion, are the hostile powers that have their being in a flood of great wickedness, such as are settled down, so to speak, in some souls of men. Whenever, then, any one has all faith so that he no longer disbelieves in any things which are contained in the Holy Scriptures, and has faith such as was that of Abraham, who believed in God to such a degree that his faith was counted for righteousness, he has all faith as a grain of mustard seed; then will such an one say to this mountain—I mean, the dumb and deaf spirit in him who is called lunatic,—"Remove hence," clearly, from the man who is suffering, perhaps to the abyss, and it shall remove. And the Apostle, taking, I think, his starting-point from this place, says with apostolical authority, "If I have all faith

[1] Ps. xxxi. 18.
[2] Exod. iv. 11.
[3] Matt. xvii. 17.
[4] Matt. xvii. 20.

so as to remove mountains,"[1] for not one mountain merely, but also several analogous to it, he removes who has all faith which is as a grain of mustard-seed; and nothing shall be impossible to him who has so great faith.[2] But let us also attend to this, "This kind goeth not out save by prayer and fasting,"[3] in order that if at any time it is necessary that we should be engaged in the healing of one suffering from such a disorder, we may not adjure, nor put questions, nor speak to the impure spirit as if it heard, but devoting ourselves to prayer and fasting, may be successful as we pray for the sufferer, and by our own fasting may thrust out the unclean spirit from him.

8. JESUS' PREDICTION OF HIS "DELIVERY" INTO THE HANDS OF MEN.

"*And while they abode in Galilee, Jesus said unto them, The Son of man shall be delivered into the hands of men.*"[4] And these things will appear to be of the same effect as those, "that Jesus began to show unto His disciples that He must go unto Jerusalem, and suffer many things of the elders and chief priests and scribes."[5] But it is not so; for it is not the same thing "to show unto the disciples that He must go unto Jerusalem, and suffer many things of the elders and chief priests and scribes," and, after suffering, "be killed," and, after being killed, "be raised up on the third day," as that which was said to them, when they were in Galilee,—which we did not learn before,—that the Son of man "would be delivered up;" for the being delivered up was not mentioned above, but now also it is said that "He is to be delivered up into the hands of men."[6] As for these matters let us inquire by what person or persons He will be delivered up into the hands of men; for there we are taught of whom He will suffer, and in what place He will suffer; but here, in addition, we learn that while His suffering many things takes place at the hands of the aforesaid, they are not the prime causes of His suffering many things, but the one or ones who delivered Him up into the hands of men. For some one will say that the Apostle, interpreting this, says with reference to God, "He that spared not His own Son, but delivered Him up for us all;"[7] but the Son also gave Himself to death for us, so that He was delivered up, not only by the Father but also by Himself. But another will say not merely that, but also collecting

[1] 1 Cor. xiii. 2.
[2] Matt. xvii. 20.
[3] Matt. xvii. 21.
[4] Matt. xvii. 22.
[5] Matt. xvi. 21.
[6] Matt. xvii. 22.
[7] Rom. viii. 32.

the passages together, will say that the Son is first delivered up by God,—then about to be tempted, then to be in conflict, then to suffer for men, or even for the whole world that He might take away its sin,[1]—to the prince of this age, and to the rest of its princes, and then by them delivered into the hands of men who would slay Him. The case of Job will be taken as an illustration. "Lo, all that is his I give into thy hands, but do not touch him;"[2] thereafter, he was, as it were, delivered up by the devil to his princes, namely, to those who took prisoners of war, to the horsemen, to the fire that came down from heaven, to the great wind that came from the desert and broke up his house.[3] But you will consider if, as he delivered up the property of Job to those who took them captive, and to the horsemen, so also he delivered them up to a certain power, subordinate to "the prince of the power of the air, of the spirit that now worketh in the sons of disobedience,"[4] in order that the fire which descended thence on the sheep of Job might seem to fall from heaven, to the man who announced to Job that "fire fell from heaven, and burned up his sheep, and consumed the shepherds likewise."[5] And in the same way you will inquire whether also the sudden mighty wind, that came down from the desert and assailed the four corners of the dwelling, was one of those which are under the devils to whom the devil delivered up the banquet of the sons and daughters of Job, that the house might fall on the children of the just man, and they might die. Let it be granted, then, that, as in the case of Job, the Father first delivered up the Son to the opposing powers, and that then they delivered Him up into the hands of men, among which men Judas also was, into whom after the sop[6] Satan entered, who delivered Him up in a more authoritative manner than Judas. But take care lest on comparing together the delivering up of the Son by the Father to the opposing powers, with the delivering up of the Saviour by them into the hands of men, you should think that what is called the delivering up is the same in the case of both. For understand that the Father in His love of men delivered Him up for us all; but the opposing powers, when they delivered up the Saviour into the hands of men, did not intend to deliver Him up for the salvation of some, but, as far as in them lay, since none of them knew "the wisdom of God which was hidden in a mystery,"[1] they gave Him up to be put to death, that His enemy death might receive Him under its subjection, like those who die in Adam;[2] and also the men who slew Him did so, as they were moulded after the will of those who wished indeed that Jesus should become subject to death. I have deemed it necessary also to examine into these things, because that when Jesus was delivered up into the hands of men, He was not delivered up by men into the hands of men, but by powers to whom the Father delivered up His Son for us all, and in the very act of His being delivered up, and coming under the power of those to whom He was delivered up, destroying him that has the power of death; for "through death He brought to nought him that hath the power of death, that is, the devil, and delivered all them who through fear of death were all their lifetime subject to bondage."[3]

9. SATAN AND THE "DELIVERY" OF JESUS.

Now we must think that the devil has the power of death,—not of that which is common and indifferent, in accordance with which those who are compacted of soul and body die, when their soul is separated from the body,—but of that death which is contrary to and the enemy of Him who said, "I am the Life,"[4] in accordance with which "the soul that sinneth, it shall die."[5] But that it was not God who gave Him up into the hands of men, the Saviour manifestly declares when He says, "If My kingdom were of this world, then would My servants fight that I should not be delivered to the Jews."[6] For, when He was delivered up to the Jews, He was delivered into the hands of men, not by His own servants, but by the prince of this age who says, concerning the powers which are in the sphere of the invisible, the kingdoms which are set up against men, "All these things will I give Thee, if Thou wilt fall down and worship Me."[7] Wherefore also we should think that in regard to them it was said, "The kings of the earth stood side by side, and the rulers were gathered together against the Lord and against His Christ."[8] And those kings, indeed, and those rulers stood side by side and were gathered against the Lord and against His Christ; but we, because we have been benefited by His being delivered by them into the hands of men and slain, say, "Let us break their

[1] John i. 29. [2] Job i. 12. [3] Job i. 15–19. [4] Eph. ii. 2. [5] Job i. 16. [6] John xiii. 27.

[1] 1 Cor. ii. 7, 8. [2] 1 Cor. xv. 22. [3] Heb. ii. 14, 15. [4] John xiv. 6. [5] Ezek. xviii. 4. [6] John xviii. 36. [7] Matt. iv. 9. [8] Ps. ii. 2.

bonds asunder and cast away their yoke from us."[1] For, when we become conformed to the death of Christ, we are no longer under the bonds of the kings of the earth, as we have said, nor under the yoke of the princes of this age, who were gathered together against the Lord. And, on this account, "the Father spared not His own Son, but delivered Him up for us all,"[2] that those, who took Him and delivered Him up into the hands of men, might be laughed at by Him who dwells in the heavens, and might be derided by the Lord, inasmuch as, contrary to their expectation, it was to the destruction of their own kingdom and power, that they received from the Father the Son, who was raised on the third day, by having abolished His enemy death, and made us conformed, not only to the image of His death but also of His resurrection; through whom we walk in newness of life,[3] no longer sitting "in the region and shadow of death,"[4] through the light of God which has sprung up upon us. But when the Saviour said, "The Son of man shall be delivered up into the hands of men, and they shall kill Him, and the third day He shall rise again," they were "exceeding sorry,"[5] giving heed to the fact that He was about to be delivered up into the hands of men, and that He would be killed, as matters gloomy and calling for sorrow, but not attending to the fact that He would rise on the third day, as He needed no longer time "to bring to nought through death him that had the power of death."[6]

10. CONCERNING THOSE WHO DEMANDED THE HALF-SHEKEL.

"*And when they were come to Capernaum, they that received the half-shekel came to Peter.*"[7] There are certain kings of the earth, and the sons of these do not pay toll or tribute; and there are others, different from their sons, who are strangers to the kings of the earth, from whom the kings of the earth receive toll or tribute. And among the kings of the earth, their sons are free as among fathers; but those who are strangers to them, while they are free in relation to things beyond the earth, are as slaves in respect of those who lord it over them and keep them in bondage; as the Egyptians lorded it over the children of Israel, and greatly afflicted their life and violently held them in bondage.[8] It was for the sake of those who were in a bondage, corresponding to the bondage of the Hebrews, that the Son of God took upon Him only the form of a slave,[1] doing no work that was foul or servile. As then, having the form of that slave, He pays toll and tribute not different from that which was paid by His disciple; for the same stater sufficed, even the one coin which was paid for Jesus and His disciple. But this coin was not in the house of Jesus, but it was in the sea, and in the mouth of a fish of the sea which, in my judgment, was benefited when it came up and was caught in the net of Peter, who became a fisher of men, in which net was that which is figuratively called a fish, in order also that the coin with the image of Cæsar might be taken from it, and that it might take its place among those which were caught by them who have learned to become fishers of men. Let him, then, who has the things of Cæsar render them to Cæsar,[2] that afterwards he may be able to render to God the things of God. But since Jesus, who was "the image of the invisible God,"[3] had not the image of Cæsar, for "the prince of this age had nothing in Him,"[4] on this account He takes from its own place, the sea, the image of Cæsar, that He may give it to the kings of the earth for Himself and His disciple, so that those who receive the half-shekel might not imagine that Jesus was the debtor of them and of the kings of the earth; for He paid the debt, not having taken it up, nor having possessed it, nor having acquired it, nor at any time having made it His own possession, so that the image of Cæsar might never be along with the image of the invisible God.

11. THE FREEDOM OF SONS.

And this may be put in another way. There are some who are kings' sons on the earth, and yet they are not sons of those kings, but sons, and sons absolutely; but others, because of their being strangers to the sons of the kings of the earth, and sons of no one of those upon the earth, but on this very account are sons, whether of God or of His Son, or of some one of those who are God's. If, then, the Saviour inquires of Peter, saying, "The kings of the earth from whom do they receive toll or tribute—from their own sons or from strangers?"[5] and Peter replies not from their own sons, but "from strangers," then Jesus says about such as are strangers to the kings of the

[1] Ps. ii. 3. [2] Rm. viii. 32. [3] Rom. vi. 4. [4] Matt. iv. 16. [5] Matt. xvii. 22, 23. [6] Heb. ii. 14. [7] Matt. xvii. 24. [8] Exod. i. 13, 14.

[1] Phil. ii. 7. [2] Mark xii. 17; Luke xx. 25. [3] Col. i. 15. [4] John xiv. 31. [5] Matt. xvii. 25.

earth, and on account of being free are sons, "Therefore the sons are free;" [1] for the sons of the kings of the earth are not free, since "every one that committeth sin is the bond-servant of sin," [2] but they are free who abide in the truth of the word of God, and on this account, know the truth, that they also may become free from sin. If, any one then, is a son simply, and not in this matter wholly a son of the kings of the earth, he is free. And nevertheless, though he is free, he takes care not to offend even the kings of the earth, and their sons, and those who receive the half-shekel; wherefore He says, "Let us not cause them to stumble, but go thou and cast thy net, and take up the fish that first cometh up," [3] etc. But I would inquire of those who are pleased to make myths about different natures, of what sort of nature they were, whether the kings of the earth, or their sons, or those who receive the half-shekel, whom the Saviour does not wish to offend; it appears of a verity, *ex hypothesi*, that they are not of a nature worthy of praise, and yet He took heed not to cause them to stumble, and He prevents any stumbling-block being put in their way, that they may not sin more grievously, and that with a view to their being saved—if they will—even by receiving Him who has spared them from being caused to stumble. And as in a place verily of consolation,—for such is, by interpretation, Capernaum,—comforting the disciple as being both free and a son, He gives to him the power of catching the fish first, that when it came up Peter might be comforted by its coming up and being caught, and by the stater being taken from its mouth, in order to be paid to those whose the stater was, and who demanded as their own such a piece of money.

12. THE STATER ALLEGORIZED.

But you might sometimes gracefully apply the passage to the lover of money, who has nothing in his mouth but things about silver, when you behold him healed by some Peter, who takes the stater, which is the symbol of all his avarice, not only from his mouth and words, but from his whole character. For you will say that such an one was in the sea, and in the bitter affairs of life, and in the waves of the cares and anxieties of avarice, having the stater in his mouth when he was unbelieving and avaricious, but that he came up from the sea and was caught in the rational net, and being benefited by some Peter who has taught him the truth, no longer has the stater in his mouth, but in place of it those things which contain His image, the oracles of God.

[1] Matt. xvii. 26. [2] John viii. 34. [3] Matt. xvii. 27.

13. THE SACRED HALF-SHEKEL.

Moreover to the saying, "They that received the half-shekel came to Peter," [1] you will adduce from Numbers that, for the saints according to the law of God, is paid not a half-shekel simply, but a sacred half-shekel. For it is written, "And thou shalt take five shekels per head, according to the sacred half-shekel." [2] But also on behalf of all the sons of Israel is given a sacred half-shekel per head. Since then it was not possible for the saint of God to possess along with the sacred half-shekels the profane shekels, so to speak, on this account, to them who do not receive the sacred half-shekels, and who asked Peter and said, "Doth not your master pay the half-shekel?" the Saviour commands the stater to be paid, in which was the half-shekel which was found in the mouth of the first fish that came up, in order that it might be given for the Teacher and the disciple.

14. CONCERNING THOSE WHO SAID, WHO IS THE GREATEST? AND CONCERNING THE CHILD THAT WAS CALLED BY JESUS.

"*In that day came the disciples unto Jesus saying, Who then is greatest in the kingdom of heaven?*" [3] In order that we might be taught what it was that the disciples came to Jesus and asked to learn of Him, and how He answered to their inquiry, Matthew, though he might have given an account of this very thing only, has added, according to some manuscripts, "In that hour the disciples came unto Jesus," but, according to others, "In that day;" and it is necessary that we should not leave the meaning of the evangelist without examination. Wherefore giving attention to the words preceding "in that day," or "hour," let us see if it is possible from them to find a way to understand, as being necessary, the addition, "in that day," or "hour." Jesus then had come to Capernaum along with His disciples, where "they that received the half-shekel came to Peter," and asked and said, "Doth not your Master pay the half-shekel?" Then, when Peter answered and said to them, Yea, Jesus giving further a defence with reference to the giving of the half-shekel, sends Peter to drag up the fish into the net, in the mouth of which He said that

[1] Matt. xvii. 24 [2] Num. iii. 47. [3] Matt. xviii. 1.

a stater would be found which was to be given for Himself and Peter. It seems to me, then, that thinking that this was a very great honour which had been bestowed on Peter by Jesus, who judged that he was greater than the rest of His friends, they wished to learn accurately the truth of their suspicion, by making inquiry of Jesus and hearing from Him, whether, as they supposed, He had judged that Peter was greater than they; and at the same time also they hoped to learn the ground on which Peter had been preferred to the rest of the disciples. Matthew then, I think, wishing to make this plain, has subjoined to the words "that take"—the stater, to-wit—"and give unto them for thee and me," the words, "In that day came the disciples unto Jesus, saying, Who then is the greatest in the kingdom of heaven?"[1] And, perhaps, they were also in doubt because of the preference which had been given to the three at the transfiguration, and they were in doubt about this—which of the three was judged by the Lord to be greatest. For John reclined on His breast through love, and we may conclude that before the Supper they had seen many tokens of special honour given by Jesus to John; but Peter on his confession was called blessed in their hearing, because of his saying, "Thou art the Christ, the Son of the living God;"[2] but again because of the saying, "Get thee behind Me, Satan; thou art a stumbling-block unto Me, for thou mindest not the things of God but the things of men,"[3] they were distracted in mind as to whether it was not he but one of the sons of Zebedee, that was the greatest. So much for the words "in that day" or "hour," on which took place the matters relating to the stater.

15. GREATNESS VARIES IN DEGREE.

But next we must seek to understand this: the disciples came to Him, as disciples to a teacher proposing difficult questions, and making inquiry, Who then is greatest in the kingdom of heaven?[4] And, in this respect, we must imitate the disciples of Jesus; for if, at any time, any subject of investigation among us should not be found out let us go with all unanimity in regard to the question in dispute to Jesus, who is present where two or three are gathered together in His name,[5] and is ready by His presence with power to illumine the hearts of those who truly desire to become His disciples, with a view to their apprehension of the matters under inquiry. And likewise it would be nothing strange for us to go to any of those who have been appointed by God as teachers in the church, and propose any question of a like order to this, "Who, then, is greatest in the kingdom of heaven?" What, then, was already known to the disciples of the matters relating to this question? And what was the point under inquiry? That there is not equality in regard to those who are deemed worthy of the kingdom of heaven they had apprehended, and that, as there was not equality, some one was greatest, and so in succession down to the least; but of what nature was the greatest, and what was the way of life of him who was the least, and who occupied the middle position, they further desired to know; unless, indeed, it is more accurate to say that they knew who was least from the words, "Whosoever shall break one of these least commandments, and shall teach men so, shall be called least in the kingdom of heaven;" but who was the greatest of all they did not know, even if they had grasped the meaning of the words, "Whosoever shall do and teach them, the same shall be called great in the kingdom of heaven;"[1] for as there were many great, it was not clear to them who was the greatest of the great, to use a human standard. And that many are great, but the great not equally great, will be manifest from the ascription of the epithet "great" to Isaac, "who waxed great, and became exceedingly great,"[2] and from what is said in the case of Moses, and John the Baptist, and the Saviour. And every one will acknowledge that even though all these were great according to the Scripture, yet the Saviour was greater than they. But whether John also (than whom there was no greater among those born of women),[3] was greater than Isaac and Moses, or whether he was not greater, but equal to both, or to one of them, it would be hazardous to declare. And from the saying, "But Isaac, waxing great, became greater,"[2] until he became not simply great, but with the twice repeated addition, "exceedingly," we may learn that there is a difference among the great, as one is great, and another exceedingly great, and another exceedingly exceedingly great. The disciples, therefore, came to Jesus and sought to learn, who was the greatest in the kingdom of heaven; and perhaps they wished to learn, hearing from

[1] Matt. xvii. 27; xviii. 1. [2] Matt. xvi. 16, 17. [3] Matt. xvi. 23. [4] Matt. xviii. 1. [5] Matt. xviii. 20.

[1] Matt. v. 19. [2] Gen. xxvi. 13. [3] Matt. xi. 11.

Him sometimes like this, "A certain one is greatest in the kingdom of heaven;" but He gives a universal turn to the discourse, showing what was the quality of him who was greatest in the kingdom of heaven. Let us seek to understand, from what is written, to the best of our ability, who this is. "For Jesus called a little child," [1] etc.

16. WHY THE GREAT ARE COMPARED TO LITTLE CHILDREN.

But first we may expound it in simple fashion. One, expounding the word of the Saviour here after the simple method, might say that, if any one who is a man mortifies the lusts of manhood, putting to death by the spirit the deeds of the body, and "always bearing about in the body the putting to death of Jesus," [2] to such a degree that he has the condition of the little child who has not tasted sensual pleasures, and has had no conception of the impulses of manhood, then such an one is converted, and has become as the little children. And the greater the advance he has made towards the condition of the little children in regard to such emotions, by so much the more as compared with those who are in training and have not advanced to so great a height of self-control, is he the greatest in the kingdom of heaven. But that which has been said about little children in respect of lustful pleasures, the same might also be said in regard to the rest of the affections and infirmities and sicknesses of the soul, into which it is not the nature of little children to fall, who have not yet fully attained to the possession of reason; as, for example, that, if any one be converted, and, though a man, such an one becomes as a child in respect of anger; and, as is the child in relation to grief, so that sometimes he laughs and plays at the very time that his father or mother or brother is dead, he who is converted would become such an one as little children; and, having received from the Word a disposition incapable of grief, so that he becomes like the little child in regard to grief. And the like you will say about what is called pleasure, in regard to which the wicked are irrationally lifted up, from which little children do not suffer, nor such as have been converted and become as little children. As, then, it has been accurately demonstrated also by others, that no passion is incident to the little children who have not yet attained to full possession of reason; and if no passion, clearly fear also; but, if there be anything corresponding to the passions, these are faint, and very quickly suppressed, and healed in the case of little children, so that he is worthy of love, who, being converted as the little children, has reached such a point as to have, as it were, his passions in subjection like the little children. And with regard to fear, therefore, similar things to those spoken might be conceived, that the little children do not experience the fear of the wicked, but a different thing, to which those who have an accurate knowledge of questions in regard to the passions and their names give the name of fear; as, for example, in the case of children there is a forgetfulness of their evils at the very time of their tears, for they change in a moment, and laugh and play along with those who were thought to grieve and terrify them, but in truth had wrought in them no such emotion. So too, moreover, one will humble himself like the little child which Jesus called; for neither haughtiness, nor conceit in respect of noble birth, or wealth, or any of those things which are thought to be good, but are not, comes to a little child. Wherefore you may see those who are not altogether infants, up to three or four years of age, like to those who are of mean birth, though they may seem to be of noble birth, and not appearing at all to love rich children rather than the poor. If, therefore, in the same way as according to their age children are affected towards those passions which exalt the senseless, the disciple of Jesus under the influence of reason [1] has humbled himself like the little child which Jesus showed, not being exalted because of vainglory, nor puffed up on the ground of wealth, or raiment, nor elated because of noble birth, in particular are they to be received and imitated in the name of Jesus, who have been converted as the Word showed, like the little child which Jesus took to Him; since especially in such the Christ is, and therefore He says, "Whosoever shall receive one such little child in My name receiveth Me." [2]

17. THE LITTLE ONES AND THEIR STUMBLING-BLOCKS.

But it is a hard task to expound what follows in logical harmony with what has already been said; for one might say, how is it that he who is converted and has become as the little children, is a little one among such as believe in Jesus, and is capable

[1] Matt. xviii. 2.

[2] 2 Cor. iv. 10.

[1] *Or*, the Word.

[2] Matt. xviii. 5.

of being caused to stumble? And likewise let us attempt to explain this coherently. Every one that gives his adherence to Jesus as the Son of God according to the true history concerning Him, and by deeds done according to the Gospel, is on the way to living the life which is according to virtue, is converted and is on the way towards becoming as the little children; and it is impossible for him not to enter into the kingdom of heaven. There are, indeed, many such; but not all, who are converted with a view to becoming like the little children, have reached the point of being made like unto little children; but each wants so much of the likeness to the little children, as he falls short of the disposition of little children towards the passions, of which we have spoken. In the whole multitude, then, of believers, are also those who, having been, as it were, just converted in regard to their becoming as the little children, at the very point of their conversion that they may become as the little children, are called little; and those of them, who are converted that they may become as the little children, but fall far short of having truly become as the little children, are capable of being caused to stumble; each of whom falls so far short of the likeness to them, as he falls short of the disposition of children towards the passions, of which we have spoken, to whom we ought not to give occasions of stumbling-block; but, if it be otherwise, he who has caused him to stumble will require, as contributing towards his cure, to have "an ass's millstone hanged about his neck, and be sunk into the depths of the sea."[1] For, in this way, when he has paid the due penalty in the sea, where is "the dragon which God formed to play in it,"[2] and, so far as is expedient for the end in view, has been punished and undergone suffering, he shall then[3] have his part in those troubles which belong to the depths of the sea, which he endured when he was dragged down by the ass's millstone. For there are also differences of millstones, so that one of them may be, so to call it, the millstone of a man, and another that of an ass; and that is human, about which it is written, "Two women shall be grinding at the mill; one is taken and one is left;"[4] but the millstone of the ass is that which shall be put round him who has given occasion of stumbling-block. But some one might say—I know not whether he would speak soundly or erroneously—that the ass's millstone is the heavy body of the wicked man, which is sunken downwards, and which he will receive at the resurrection that he may be sunk in the abyss which is called the depth of the sea, where "is the dragon which God formed to play therein."[1] But another will refer the creating of a stumbling-block to one of the little ones to the powers that are unseen by men; for from these arise many stumbling-blocks to the little ones pointed out by Jesus. But when they cause to stumble one of the little ones pointed out by Jesus, who are believers in Him, he shall assume an ass's millstone, the corruptible body which presses heavily on the soul, which is itself hung from the neck, which is dragged down to the affairs in this life, that by means of these their conceit may be taken away, and having paid the penalty, they shall come, through means of the ass's millstone, to the condition expedient for them.

[1] Matt. xviii. 6.
[2] Ps. civ. 26.
[3] *Or*, be free from. The *Vetus Inter.* has "*extra dolores.*" It has had ἔξω instead of ἑξῆς.
[4] Matt. xxiv. 41.

18. WHO WAS THE LITTLE CHILD CALLED BY JESUS.

Now another interpretation different from what is called the simpler may be uttered; whether as dogma, or for the sake of exercise, so to speak, let us also inquire what was the little child who was called by Jesus and set in the midst of the disciples. Now consider if you can say that the little child, whom Jesus called, was the Holy Spirit who humbled Himself, when He was called by the Saviour, and set in the midst of the reason of the disciples of Jesus; if, indeed, He wishes us, being turned away from everything else, to be turned towards the examples suggested by the Holy Spirit, so that we may so become as the little children, who are themselves also turned and likened to the Holy Spirit; which little children God gave to the Saviour, according to what is said in Isaiah, "Behold, I and the little children which God has given to me."[2] And it is not possible for any one to enter into the kingdom of heaven, who has not been turned away from the affairs of this world, and made like unto the little children who possess the Holy Spirit; which Holy Spirit was called by Jesus, and, descending from His own perfection to men as a little child, was set by Jesus in the midst of the disciples. It is necessary, then, for him who has turned away from the desires of this world to humble himself not simply as the little child, but, according to what is written,

[1] Ps. civ. 26.
[2] Psa. viii. 18.

"as this little child."[1] But to humble oneself as that little child is to imitate the Holy Spirit, who humbled Himself for the salvation of men. Now, that the Saviour and the Holy Spirit were sent by the Father for the salvation of men has been declared in Isaiah, in the person of the Saviour, saying, "And now the Lord hath sent me and His Spirit."[2] You must know, however, that this expression is ambiguous; for either God sent, but also the Holy Spirit sent, the Saviour; or, as we have taken it, the Father sent both—the Saviour and the Holy Spirit. He, therefore, who has humbled himself more than all those who have humbled themselves in imitation of that little child, is the greatest in the kingdom of heaven. For there are many who are willing to humble themselves as that little child; but the man, who in every respect has become like to the little child who humbled himself, in the name of Jesus—especially in Jesus Himself,—in reality, would be found to be he who is named greater than all in the kingdom of heaven. But as he receives Jesus, whosoever receives one such of the little children in His name, so he rejects Jesus and casts Him out, who does not wish to receive one such little child in the name of Jesus. But if, also, there is a difference in those who are deemed worthy of the Holy Spirit, as believers receive more or less of the Holy Spirit, there would be some little ones among those who believe in God who can be made to stumble: to avenge whose being made to stumble the Word says, with reference to those who had caused them to stumble, "It is profitable for him that an ass's millstone should be hanged about his neck, and that he should be sunk in the depth of the sea."[3] Let these things be said in regard to the passage of Matthew before us.

19. THE PARALLEL PASSAGES IN MARK AND LUKE.

But let us consider also the like account in the other Evangelists. Mark,[4] then, says, that the Twelve reasoned in the way as to which of them was the greatest. Wherefore He sat down, and called them, and teaches who is the greatest, saying, that he who became last of all by means of his moderation and gentleness, would as the greatest obtain the first place, so that he did not receive the place of one who was being ministered unto, but the place of one who ministered, and that not to some but not to others, but to all absolutely; for attend to the words, "If any man would be first he shall be last of all, and minister of all."[1] And next to that He says, that "He,"—Jesus to-wit—"took a little child, and set him in the midst of His own disciples, and taking him in His arms, He said unto them, Whosoever shall receive one of the little children in My name receiveth Me."[2] But what was the little child which Jesus took and placed in His arms, according to the deeper meaning in the passage? Was it the Holy Spirit? And to this little child, indeed, some were likened, of whom He said, "Whosoever shall receive one of such little children in My name receiveth Me." According to Luke, however, the reasoning did not arise spontaneously in the disciples, but was suggested to them by the question, "which of them should be greatest."[3] And Jesus, seeing the reasoning of their heart, as He had eyes that see the reasonings of hearts,—seeing the reasoning of their heart,—without being questioned, according to Luke, "took the little child and set him," not in the midst alone, as Matthew and Mark have said, but now, also, "by His side," and said to the disciples, not only, "Whosoever shall receive one such little child," or, "Whosoever shall receive one of such little ones in My name receiveth Me," but, now going even a step higher, "Whosoever shall receive this little child in My name receiveth Me."[4] It is necessary, therefore, according to Luke, to receive in the name of Jesus that very little child which Jesus took and placed by His side. And I know not if there be any one who can interpret figuratively the word, "Whosoever shall receive this little child in My name." For it is necessary that each of us should receive in the name of Jesus that little child which Jesus then took and set by His side; for he lives as immortal, and we must receive him from Jesus Himself in the name of Jesus; and without being separated from him, Jesus is with him who receives the little child, so that according to this it is said, "Whosoever shall receive this little child in My name receiveth Me." Then, since the Father is inseparable from the Son, He is with him who receives the Son. Wherefore it is said, "And whosoever shall receive Me receives Him that sent Me."[5] But he who has received the little child, and the Saviour, and Him that sent Him, is least of all the disciples of Jesus, making himself little. But, so far as

[1] Matt. xviii. 4. [2] Isa. xlviii. 16. [3] Matt. xviii. 6. [4] Mark ix. 33, 34.

[1] Mark ix. 35. [2] Mark ix. 36, 37. [3] Luke ix. 46. [4] Luke ix. 47, 48. [5] Luke ix. 48.

he belittles himself, to that extent does he become great; as that very thing, which caused him the more to make himself little, contributes to his advance in greatness; for attend to what is said, "He that is least among you all the same is great;" but in other manuscripts we read, "The same shall be great." Now, according to Luke, "If any one shall not receive the kingdom of God as the little child, he shall in no wise enter therein."[1] And this expression is ambiguous; for either it means that he who receives the kingdom of God may become as a little child, or, that he may receive the kingdom of God, which has become to him as a little child. And perhaps here those who receive the kingdom of God receive it, when it is as a little child, but in the world to come no longer as a little child; and they receive the greatness of the perfection in the spiritual manhood, so to speak, which perfection is manifested to all who in the present time receive it, when it is here as a little child.

20. THE WORLD AND OFFENCES. VARIOUS MEANINGS OF WORLD.

"*Woe unto the world because of occasions of stumbling.*"[2] The expression "cosmos," is used in itself and absolutely in the passage, "He was in the cosmos and the cosmos knew Him not,"[3] but it is used relatively and in respect of its connection with that of which it is the cosmos, in the words, "Lest you look up to the heaven, and seeing the sun, and the moon, and all the cosmos of the heavens, you should stray and bow down to them and worship them."[4] And the like you will find in the Book of Esther, spoken about her, when it is written, stripping off all her "cosmos."[5] For the word "cosmos," simply, is not the same as the "cosmos" of heaven, or the "cosmos" of Esther; and this which we are now investigating is another. I think, then, that the world is not this compacted whole of heaven and earth according to the Divine Scriptures, but only the place which is round about the earth, and this is not to be conceived in respect of the whole earth, but only in respect of ours which is inhabited; for the true light "was in the world," that is, in the place which is around, conceived in relation to our part of the earth; "and the world knew Him not,"[6] that is, the men in the region round about, and perhaps also the powers that have an affinity to this place. For it is monstrous to understand by the world here the compacted whole formed of heaven and earth, and those in it; so that it could be said, that the sun and moon and the choir of the stars and the angels in all this world, did not know the true light, and, though ignorant of it, preserved the order which God had appointed for them. But when it is said by the Saviour in the prayer to the Father, "And, now, glorify me, O Father, with Thine own self, with the glory which I had with Thee before the world was,"[1] you must understand by the "world," that which is inhabited by us on the earth; for it was from this world that the Father gave men to the Son, in regard to whom alone the Saviour beseeches His Father, and not for the whole world of men. Moreover, also, when the Saviour says, "And I come to thee and am no longer in the world,"[2] He speaks of the terrestrial world; for it is not to be supposed that He spoke things contradictory when He said, "And I come to thee, and I am no longer in the world," and "I am in the world." But also in this, "And these things I speak in the world,"[3] we must think of the place round about the earth. And this is clearly indicated also by the words, "And the world hated them, because they are not of the world."[4] For it hated us from the time when we no longer "look at the things which are seen, but at the things which are not seen,"[5] because of the teaching of Jesus; not the world of heaven and earth and them that are therein, all compacted together but the men on the earth along with us. And the saying, "They are not of the world,"[6] is equivalent to, They are not of the place round about the earth. And so also the disciples of Jesus are not of this world, as He was not of the world. And further also the saying, "That the world may believe that Thou hast sent Me,"[7] twice spoken in the Gospel according to John, does not refer to the things that are superior to men, but to men who need to believe that the Father sent the Son into the world here. Yea, and also in the Apostle, "Your faith is proclaimed in the whole world."[8]

21. THE "WOE" DOES NOT APPLY TO THE DISCIPLES OF JESUS.

But if there is woe unto men everywhere on the earth, because of occasions of stum-

[1] Luke xviii. 17.
[2] Matt. xviii. 7.
[3] John i. 10.
[4] Deut. iv. 19.
[5] Lomm., following Huet. refers to Esther (The addition to Esther, xiv. 2). But the word κόσμος does not occur in this passage. See Judith x. 4; 1 Macc. ii. 11.
[6] John i. 10.

[1] John xvii. 5.
[2] John xvii. 11.
[3] John xvii. 13.
[4] John xvii. 14.
[5] 2 Cor. iv. 18.
[6] John xvii. 21.
[7] John xvii. 21, 23.
[8] Rom. i. 8.

bling to those who are laid hold of by them; but the disciples are not of the world, as they do not look at things seen, like as the Master is not of this world; to no one of the disciples of Jesus does the "woe because of occasions of stumbling" apply, since "great peace have they who love the law of God, and there is to them no occasion of stumbling."[1] But if any one seems to be called a disciple, but yet is of the world, because of his loving the world, and the things therein,—I mean, the life in the place round about the earth, and the property in it, or the possessions, or any form of wealth whatsoever,—so that the saying, "they are not of the world,"[2] does not fit him; to him, as being really of the world, shall come that which happens to the world, the "woe, because of occasions of stumbling." But let him who wishes to avoid this woe not be a lover of life, but let him say with Paul," "The world is crucified unto me, and I unto the world."[3] For the saints while "in the tabernacle, do groan being burdened"[4] with "the body of humiliation," and do all things that they may become worthy to be found in the mystery of the resurrection, when God shall fashion anew the body of humiliation not of all, but of those who have been truly made disciples to Christ, so that it may be conformed to the body of the glory of Christ.[5] For as none of the "woes" happen to any of the disciples of Christ, so does not this "woe, because of occasions of stumbling;" for, supposing that thousands of occasions should arise, they shall not touch those who are no longer of the world. But if any one, because of his faith wanting ballast, and the instability of his submission in regard to the Word of God, is capable of being caused to stumble, let him know that he is not called by Jesus His disciple. Now we must suppose that so many stumbling-blocks come, that, as a result, the woes extend not to some parts of the earth, but to the whole "world" which is in it.

22. WHAT THE "OCCASIONS OF STUMBLING" ARE.

"*And it must needs be that occasions of stumbling come,*"[6] which I take to be different from the men by whom they come. The occasions then which come are an army of the devil, his angels, and a wicked band of impure spirits, which, seeking out instruments through whom they will work, often find men altogether strangers to piety, and sometimes even some of those who are thought to believe the Word of God, for whom exists a worse woe than that which comes to him who is caused to stumble, just as also it shall be more tolerable for Tyre and Sidon in the day of judgment,[1] than for the places where Jesus did signs and wonders, and yet was not believed. But as one might undertake to make a collection from the Scriptures of those who are pronounced blessed, and of the things in respect of which they are so called, so also he might undertake to do with the woes which are written, and those in whose case the woes are spoken. But that the woe is worse in the case of him who causes to stumble, than in him who is made to stumble, you may prove by the passage, "Whoso shall cause to stumble one of these little ones which believe in Me, it is profitable for him,"[2] etc.; for, while the little one who is made to stumble receives retribution from him who caused him to stumble, it is expedient that the severe and intolerable punishment which is written should befall the man who has caused the stumbling. But if we were to give more careful consideration to these things, we should be on our guard against sinning against the brethren, and wounding their conscience when it is weak, lest we sin against Christ;[3] as often our brethren about us, "for whom Christ died," perish, not only through our knowledge, but also through some other causes connected with us; in the case of whom, we, sinning against Christ, shall pay the penalty, the soul of them who perish through us being required of us.

23. IN WHAT SENSE "NECESSARY."

Next we must test accurately the meaning of the word "necessity" in the passage, "*For there is a necessity that the occasions come,*"[4] and to the like effect in Luke, "It is 'inadmissible' but that occasions of stumbling should come,"[5] instead of "impossible." And as it is necessary that that which is mortal should die, and it is impossible but that it should die, and as it must needs be that he who is in the body should be fed, for it is impossible for one who is not fed to live, so it is necessary and impossible but that occasions of stumbling should arise, since there is a necessity also that wickedness should exist before virtue in men, from which wickedness stumbling-blocks arise; for it is impossible that a man should be found altogether sinless, and who,

[1] Ps. cxix. 165. [2] John xvii. 16. [3] Gal. vi. 14. [4] 2 Cor. v. 4. [5] Phil. iii. 21. [6] Matt. xviii. 7.

[1] Matt. xi. 22. [2] Matt. xviii. 6. [3] 1 Cor. viii. 11, 12. [4] Matt. xviii. 7. [5] Luke xvii 1.

without sin, has attained to virtue. For the wickedness in the evil powers, which is the primal source of the wickedness among men, is altogether eager to work through certain instruments against the men in the world. And perhaps also the wicked powers are more exasperated when they are cast out by the word of Jesus, and their worship is lessened, their customary sacrifices not being offered unto them; and there is a necessity that these offences come; but there is no necessity that they should come through any particular one; wherefore the "woe" falls on the man through whom the stumbling-block comes, as he has given a place to the wicked power whose purpose it is to create a stumbling-block. But do not suppose that by nature, and from constitution, there are certain stumbling-blocks which seek out men through whom they come; for as God did not make death, so neither did He create stumbling-blocks; but free-will begot the stumbling-blocks in some who did not wish to endure toils for virtue.

24. THE OFFENDING HAND, OR FOOT, OR EYE.

And it is well, then, if the eye and the hand are deserving of praise, that the eye cannot with reason say to the hand, "I have no need of thee."[1] But if any one in the whole body of the congregations of the church, who because of his practical gifts has the name of hand, should change and become a hand causing to stumble, let the eye say to such a hand, "I have no need of thee," and, saying it, let him cut it off and cast it from him.[2] And so it is well, if any head be blessed, and the feet worthy of the blessed head, so that the head observing the things which are becoming to itself, may not be able to say to the feet, "I have no need of you." If, however, any foot be found to become a stumbling-block to the whole body, let the head say to such a foot, "I have no need of thee," and having cut it off, let him cast it from himself; for even it is much better that the rest of the body should enter into life, wanting the foot or the hand which caused the stumbling-block, rather than, when the stumbling-block has spread over the whole body, it should be cast into the hell of fire with the two feet or the two hands. And so it is well, that he who can become the eye of the whole body should be worthy of Christ and of the whole body; but if such an eye should ever change, and become a stumbling-block to the whole body, it is well to take it out and cast it outside the whole body, and that the rest of the body without that eye should be saved, rather than that along with it, when the whole body has been corrupted, the whole body should be cast into the hell of fire.[1] For the practical faculty of the soul, if prone to sin, and the walking faculty of the soul, so to speak, if prone to sin, and the faculty of clear vision, if prone to sin, may be the hand that causes to stumble, and the foot that causes to stumble, and the eye that causes to stumble, which things it is better to cast away, and having put them aside to enter into life without them, like as one halt, or maimed, or one-eyed, rather than along with them to lose the whole soul. And likewise in the case of the soul it is a good and blessed thing to use its power for the noblest ends; but if we are going to lose one for any cause, it is better to lose the use of it, that along with the other powers we may be saved.

25. THE EYE OR HAND ALLEGORIZED.

And it is possible to apply these words also to our nearest kinsfolk, who are our members, as it were; being considered to be our members, because of the close relationship; whether by birth, or from any habitual friendship, so to speak; whom we must not spare if they are injuring our soul. For let us cut off from ourselves as a hand or a foot or an eye, a father or mother who wishes us to do that which is contrary to piety, and a son or daughter who, as far as in them lies, would have us revolt from the church of Christ and the love of Him. But even if the wife of our bosom, or a friend who is kindred in soul, become stumbling-blocks to us, let us not spare them, but let us cut them out from ourselves, and cast them outside of our soul, as not being truly our kindred but enemies of our salvation; for "whosoever hates not his father, and mother,"[2] and the others subjoined, when it is the fitting season to hate them as enemies and assailants, that he may be able to win Christ, this man is not worthy of the Son of God. And in respect of these we may say, that from a critical position any lame one, so to speak, is saved, when he has lost a foot—say a brother—and alone obtains the inheritance of the kingdom of God; and a maimed one is saved, when his father is not saved, but they perish, while he is separated from them, that he alone may obtain the benedictions. And so also any one is saved with one eye, who

[1] Cor. xii. 21. [2] Matt. xviii. 8

[1] Cf. Matt. xviii. 9. [2] Luke xiv. 26.

has cut out the eye of his own house, his wife, if she commit fornication, lest having two eyes he may go away into the hell of fire.

26. THE LITTLE ONES AND THEIR ANGELS.

"*See that ye despise not one of these little ones.*"[1] It seems to me that as among the bodies of men there are differences in point of size,—so that some are little, and others great, and others of middle height, and, again, there are differences among the little, as they are more or less little, and the same holds of the great, and of those of middle height,—so also among the souls of men, there are some things which give them the stamp of littleness, and other things the stamp of greatness, so to speak, and generally, after the analogy of things bodily, other things the stamp of mediocrity. But in the case of bodies, it is not due to the action of men but to the spermatic principles, that one is short and little, another great, and another of middle height; but in the case of souls, it is our free-will, and actions of such a kind, and habits of such a kind, that furnish the reason why one is great, or little, or of middle height; and it is of our free-will either by advancing in stature to increase our size, or not advancing to be short. And so indeed I understand the words about Jesus having assumed a human soul, "Jesus advanced;"[2] for as from the free-will there was an advance of His soul in wisdom and grace, so also in stature. And the Apostle says, "Until we all attain unto a full-grown man, unto the measure of the stature of the fulness of Christ;"[3] for we must think that he attains unto a man, and that full-grown, according to the inner man, who has gone through the things of the child, and has reached the stage of the man, and has put away the things of the child, and generally, has perfected the things of the man.[4] And so we must suppose that there is a certain measure of spiritual stature unto which the most perfect soul can attain by magnifying the Lord, and become great. Thus, then, these became great, of whom this is written, Isaac, and Moses, and John, and the Saviour Himself above all; for also about Him Gabriel said, "He shall be great;"[5] but the little ones are "the new-born babes which long for the reasonable milk which is without guile,"[6] such as stand in need of nursing-fathers and nursing-mothers, spoken of in Isaiah when he

[1] Matt. xviii. 10. [2] Luke ii. 52. [3] Eph. iv. 13. [4] Cf. 1 Cor. xiii. 11. [5] Luke i. 32. [6] 1 Pet. ii. 2.

says, about the calling from the Gentiles, "And they shall bring the sons in the bosom, and take their daughters on the shoulders, and kings shall be thy nursing-fathers and their princesses thy nursing-mothers."[1] For these reasons you will, then, attend to the word, "Do not despise one of these little ones,"[2] and consider whether it is their angels who bring them in their bosom, since they have become sons, and also take on their shoulders what are called daughters, and whether from them are the nursing-fathers who are called kings, and the nursing-mothers who are called princesses. And since the little ones, pointed out by our Saviour, are under the stewardship as of nursing-fathers and nursing-mothers, on this account I think that Moses, who believed that he had been already assigned a place among the ranks of the great, said, with regard to the promise, "My angel shall go before you,"[3] "If thou thyself do not go along with me, carry me not up hence."[4] For though the little one even be an heir, yet as being a child he differs nothing from a servant when he is a child,[5] and to the extent to which he is little "has the spirit of bondage to fear;"[6] but he who is not at all any longer such has no longer the spirit of bondage, but already the spirit of adoption, when "perfect love casteth out fear;"[7] it will be plain to thee, how that according to these things "the angel of the Lord" is said "to encamp round about them that fear Him, and to save them."[8] But you will consider, according to these things also, whether these are indeed angels of the little ones "who are led by the spirit of bondage to fear," "when the angel of the Lord encamps round about them that fear Him and delivereth them;" but of the great, whether it is the Lord who is greater than the angels, who might say about each of them, "I am with him in affliction;"[9] and, so long as we are imperfect, and need one to assist us that we may be delivered from evils, we stand in need of an angel of whom Jacob said, "The angel who delivered me from all the evils;"[10] but, when we have become perfected, and have passed through the stage of being subject to nursing-fathers and nursing-mothers and guardians and stewards,[11] we are meet to be governed by the Lord Himself.

[1] Isa. xlix. 22, 23. [2] Matt. xviii. 10. [3] Exod. xxxii. 34. [4] Exod. xxxiii. 15. [5] Gal. iv. 1. [6] Rom. viii. 15. [7] 1 John iv. 18. [8] Ps. xxxiv. 7. [9] Ps. xci. 15. [10] Gen. xlviii. 16. [11] Gal. iv. 4.

27. WHEN THE LITTLE ONES ARE ASSIGNED TO ANGELS.

Then again one might inquire at what time those who are called their angels assume guardianship of the little ones pointed out by Christ; whether they received this commission to discharge concerning them, from what time "by the laver of regeneration,"[1] through which they were born "as new-born babes, they long for the reasonable milk which is without guile,"[2] and no longer are in subjection to any wicked power; or, whether from birth they had been appointed, according to the foreknowledge and predestination of God, over those whom God also foreknew, and foreordained to be conformed to the glory of the Christ.[3] And with reference to the view that they have angels from birth, one might quote, "He who separated me from my mother's womb,"[4] and, "From the womb of my mother thou hast been my protector,"[5] and, "He has assisted me from my mother's womb,"[6] and, "Upon thee I was cast from my mother,"[7] and in the Epistle of Jude, "To them that are beloved in God the Father and are kept for Jesus Christ, being called,"[8] —kept completely by the angels who keep them.

28. CLOSE RELATIONSHIP OF ANGELS TO THEIR "LITTLE ONES."

With reference to the words, "*When through the laver I became a child in Christ,*"[9] it may be said, that there is no holy angel present with those who are still in wickedness, but that during the period of unbelief they are under the angels of Satan;[10] but, after the regeneration, He who has redeemed us with His own blood consigns us to a holy angel, who also, because of his purity, beholds the face of God. And a third exposition of this passage might be something like the following, which would say, that as it is possible for a man to change from unbelief to faith, and from intemperance to temperance, and generally from wickedness to virtue, so also it is possible that the angel, to whom any soul has been entrusted at birth, may be wicked at the first, but afterwards may at some time believe in proportion as the man believes, and may make such advance that he may become one of the angels who always behold the face of the Father in heaven,[1] beginning from the time that he is yoked along with the man who was foreknown and foreordained to believe at that time, the judgments of God, which are unspeakable and unsearchable and like to the depths, fitly bringing together all this harmonious relationship—angels with men. And it may be that as when a man and his wife are both unbelievers, sometimes it is the man who first believes and in time saves his wife, and sometimes the wife who begins and afterwards in time persuades her husband, so it happens with angels and with men. If, however, anything of this kind takes place in the case of other angels or not, you may seek out for yourself. But consider whether it may not be appropriate to say something of this kind in regard to each angel who is so honoured according to the word of the Saviour, that he is said to behold always the face of the Father who is in heaven. But since in what we said above, that the little ones have angels, but that the great have passed beyond such a position, some one will quote in opposition to us from the Acts of the Apostles, where it is written, that a certain maid Rhoda, when Peter knocked at the door, came to answer, and recognizing the voice of Peter, ran in and announced that Peter stood before the gate; but when they who were gathered together in the house wondered, and thought that it was quite impossible that Peter verily stood before the gate, they said, It is his angel.[2] For the objector will say that, as they had learned once for all that each of the believers had some definite angel, they knew that Peter also had one. But he, who adheres to what we have previously said, will say that the word of Rhoda was not necessarily a dogma, and perhaps also the word of those who did not accurately know, when one as being little and God-fearing is governed by angels, and when now by the Lord Himself. After this, in order to establish our conception of the little one which we have brought forward, it will be said that we need no command about "not despising" in the case of the great, but we do need it in the case of the little; wherefore it is not merely said, "Do not despise one of these," pointing to all the disciples, but "one of these little ones,"[3] pointed out by Him, who sees the littleness and the greatness of the soul.

[1] Tit. iii. 5. [2] 1 Pet. ii. 2. [3] Rom. viii. 29. [4] Gal. i. 15. [5] Ps. lxxi. 6. [6] Ps. cxxxix. 13. [7] Ps. xxii. 10. [8] Jude 1. [9] Cf. Tit. iii. 5 1 Pet. ii. 2. [10] The text is perhaps corrupt.

[1] Matt. xviii. 10. [2] Acts xii. 13–15. [3] Matt. xviii. 10.

29. THE LITTLE ONES AND THE PERFECT.

But another might say that the perfect man is here called little, applying the word, "For he that is least among you all, the same is great,"[1] and will affirm that he who humbles himself and becomes a child in the midst of all that believe, though he be an apostle or a bishop, and becomes such "as when a nurse cherisheth her own children,"[2] is the little one pointed out by Jesus, and that the angel of such an one is worthy to behold the face of God. For to say that the little are here called perfect, according to the passage, "He that is least among you all, the same is great,"[3] and as Paul said, "Unto me who am less than the least of all saints was this grace given,"[4] will seem to be in harmony with the saying, "Whoso shall cause one of these little ones to stumble,"[5] and "So it is not the will of My Father in heaven, that one of these little ones should perish."[6] For he, as has been stated, who is now little, could not be made to stumble nor perish, for "great peace have they who love the law of God, and there is no stumbling-block to them;"[7] and he could not perish, who is least of all among all the disciples of Christ, and on this account becomes great; and, since he could not perish, he could say, "Who shall separate us from the love,"[8] etc. But he who wishes to maintain this last exposition will say that the soul even of the just man is changeable, as Ezekiel also testifies, saying, that the righteous man may abandon the commandments of God, so that his former righteousness is not reckoned unto him;[9] wherefore it is said, "Whoso shall cause to stumble one of these little ones,"[5] and, "It is not the will of My Father which is in heaven that one of these little ones should perish."[6]

[As for the exposition of the matters relating to "the hundred sheep," you may consult the homilies on Luke.[10]]

30. THE SINNING BROTHER.

"*If thy brother sin against thee, go, shew him his fault between thee and him alone.*"[11] He, then, who attends closely to the expression, in proof of the surpassing philanthropy of Jesus, will say, that as the words do not suggest a difference of sins, they will act in a singular manner and contrary to the goodness of Jesus, who supply the thought, that these words are to be understood as being limited in their application to lesser sins. But another, also attending closely to the expression, and not wishing to introduce these extraneous thoughts, nor admitting that it is spoken about every sin, will say, that he who commits those great sins is not a brother, even if he be called a brother, as the Apostle says, "If any one that is named a brother be a fornicator, or covetous, or an idolater, etc., with such an one not to eat;"[1] for no one who is an idolater, or a fornicator, or covetous, is a brother; for if he, who seems to bear the name of Christ, though he is named a brother, has something of the features of these, he would not rightly be called a brother. As then he, who says that such words are spoken about every sin, whether the sin be murder, or poisoning, or pæderasty, or anything of that sort, would give occasion of injury to the exceeding goodness of Christ, so, on the contrary, he who distinguishes between the brother and him who is called the brother, might teach that, in the case of the least of the sins of men, he who has not repented after the telling of the fault is to be reckoned as a Gentile and a publican, for sins which are "not unto death,"[2] or, as the law has described them in the Book of Numbers, not "death-bringing."[3] This would seem to be very harsh; for I do not think that any one will readily be found who has not been censured thrice for the same form of sin, say, reviling, with which revilers abuse their neighbours, or those who are carried away by passion, or for over-drinking, or lying and idle words, or any of those things which exist in the masses. You will inquire, therefore, whether any observation of the passage has escaped the notice of those, who are influenced by their conception of the goodness of the Word, and grant pardon to those who have committed the greatest sins, as well as of those who teach that, in the case of the very least sins, he is to be reckoned as a Gentile and a publican, making him a stranger to the church, after he has committed three very trivial transgressions. But the following seems to me to have been overlooked by both of them, namely, the words, "Thou hast gained thy brother."[4] It is assigned by the Word to him only who heard, and He no longer applies it in the case of him who has stumbled twice or thrice and been censured; but that which was to be said about him who was censured twice or thrice, corresponding to

[1] Luke ix. 48. [2] 1 Thess. ii. 7. [3] Luke ix. 48.
[4] Eph. iii. 8. [5] Matt. xviii. 6. [6] Matt. xviii. 14.
[7] Ps. cxix. 165. [8] Rom. viii. 35. [9] Ezek. xxxiii. 12.
[10] Matt. xviii. 12–14. [11] Matt. xviii. 15.

[1] 1 Cor. v. 11. [2] 1 John v. 16.
[3] Num. xviii. 22. [4] Matt. xviii. 15.

the saying, "Thou hast gained thy brother," He has left in the air, so to speak. He is not, therefore, altogether gained, nor will he altogether perish, or he will receive stripes. And attend carefully to the first passage, "If he hear thee, thou hast gained thy brother," and to the second passage, which is literally, "If he hear thee not, take with thyself one or two more, that at the mouth of two or three witnesses every word may be established."[1] What, then, will happen to him who has been censured for the second time, after every word has been established by two or three witnesses, He has left us to conceive. And, again, "If he refuse to hear them"—manifestly, the witnesses who have been taken—"tell it," he says, "to the church;"[2] and He does not say what he will suffer if he does not hear the church, but He taught that if he refused to hear the church, then he who had thrice admonished, and had not been heard, was to regard him for the future as the Gentile and the publican.[3] Therefore he is not altogether gained, nor will he altogether perish. But what at all he will suffer, who at first did not hear, but required witnesses, or even refused to hear these, but was brought to the church, God knows; for we do not declare it, according to the precept, "Judge not that ye be not judged,"[4] "until the Lord come, who will both bring to light the hidden things of darkness and make manifest the counsels of the hearts."[5] But, with reference to the seeming harshness in the case of those who have committed less sins, one might say that it is not possible for him who has not heard twice in succession to hear the third time, so as, on this account, no longer to be as a Gentile or a publican, or no longer to stand in need of the censure in presence of all the church. For we must bear in mind this, "So it is not the will of My Father in heaven that one of these little ones should perish."[6] For if "we must all stand before the judgment-seat of Christ, that each one may receive the things done in the body, according to what he hath done, whether it be good or bad,"[7] let each one with all his power do what he can so that he may not receive punishment for more evil things done in the body, even if he is going to receive back for all the wrongs which he has done; but it should be our ambition to procure the reward for a greater number of good deeds, since "with what measure we mete, it shall be measured to us,"[1] and, "according to the works of our own hands shall it happen unto us,"[2] and not in infinite wise, but either double or sevenfold shall sinners receive for their sins from the hand of the Lord; since He does not render unto any one according to the works of his hands, but more than that which he has done, for "Jerusalem," as Isaiah taught, "received from the hand of the Lord double for her sins;"[3] but the neighbours of Israel, whoever they may be, will receive sevenfold, according to the following expression in the Psalms, "Render unto our neighbours sevenfold into their bosom the reproach with which they have reproached Thee, O Lord."[4] And other forms of payment in return could be found, which, if we apprehend, we shall know that to repent after any sin, whatever its greatness, is advantageous, in order that, in addition to our not being punished for more offences, there may be some hope left to us concerning good deeds done afterwards at some time, even though, before them, thousands of errors have been committed by any one of us. For it would be strange that evil deeds should be reckoned to any one, but the better which are done after the bad should profit nothing; which may also be learned from Ezekiel,[5] by those who pay careful consideration to the things said about such cases.

31. THE POWER TO BIND ON EARTH AND IN HEAVEN.

But to me it seems that, to the case of him who after being thrice admonished was adjudged to be as the Gentile and the publican, it is fitly subjoined, "*Verily, I say unto you,*" —namely, to those who have judged any one to be as the Gentile and the publican,—"*and what things soever ye shall bind on the earth,*"[6] etc.; for with justice has he, who has thrice admonished and not been heard, bound him who is judged to be as a Gentile and a publican; wherefore, when such an one is bound and condemned by one of this character, he remains bound, as no one of those in heaven overturns the judgment of the man who bound him. And, in like manner, he who was admonished once for all, and did things worthy of being gained, having been set free by the admonition of the man who gained him, and no longer bound by the cords of his own sins,[7] for which he was admonished, shall be adjudged to have been set free by those in heaven. Only, it seems to be indicated that the things, which above

[1] Matt. xviii. 15, 16. [2] Matt. xviii. 17. [3] Matt. xviii. 17. [4] Matt. vii. 1. [5] 1 Cor. iv. 5. [6] Matt. xviii. 14. [7] 2 Cor. v. 10.

[1] Matt. vii. 2. [2] Isa. iii. 11. [3] Isa. xl. 2. [4] Ps. lxxix. 12 [5] Ezek. xxxiii. [6] Matt. xviii. 18 [7] Prov. v. 22

were granted to Peter alone, are here given to all who give the three admonitions to all that have sinned; so that, if they be not heard, they will bind on earth him who is judged to be as a Gentile and a publican, as such an one has been bound in heaven. But since it was necessary, even if something in common had been said in the case of Peter and those who had thrice admonished the brethren, that Peter should have some element superior to those who thrice admonished, in the case of Peter, this saying "I will give to thee the keys of the kingdom of the heavens,"[1] has been specially set before the words, "And what things soever ye shall bind on earth," etc. And, indeed, if we were to attend carefully to the evangelical writings, we would also find here, and in relation to those things which seem to be common to Peter and those who have thrice admonished the brethren, a great difference and a pre-eminence in the things said to Peter, compared with the second class. For it is no small difference that Peter received the keys not of one heaven but of more, and in order that whatsoever things he binds on the earth may be bound not in one heaven but in them all, as compared with the many who bind on earth and loose on earth, so that these things are bound and loosed not in the heavens, as in the case of Peter, but in one only; for they do not reach so high a stage, with power as Peter to bind and loose in all the heavens.[1] The better, therefore, is the binder, so much more blessed is he who has been loosed, so that in every part of the heavens his loosing has been accomplished.

BOOK XIV.

1. THE POWER OF HARMONY IN RELATION TO PRAYER.

"*Again I say unto you that if two of you shall agree*[2] *on earth as touching anything that they shall ask, it shall be done for them.*"[3] The word symphony is strictly applied to the harmonies of sounds in music. And there are indeed among musical sounds some accordant and others discordant. But the Evangelic Scripture is familiar with the name as applied to musical matters in the passage, "He heard a symphony and dancing."[4] For it was fitting that when the son who had been lost and found came by penitence into concord with his father a symphony should be heard on the occasion of the joyous mirth of the house. But the wicked Laban was not acquainted with the word symphony in his saying to Jacob, "And if thou hadst told me I would have sent thee away with mirth and with music and with drums and a harp."[5] But akin to the symphony of this nature is that which is written in the second Book of Kings when "the brethren of Aminadab went before the ark, and David and his son played before the Lord on instruments artistically fitted with might and with songs;"[6] for the instruments thus fitted with might and with songs, had in themselves the musical symphony which is so powerful that when two only, bring along with the symphony which has relation to the music that is divine and spiritual, a request to the Father in heaven about anything whatsoever, the Father grants the request to those who ask along with the symphony on earth,—which is most miraculous,—those things which those who have made the symphony spoken of may have asked. So also I understand the apostolic saying "Defraud ye not one the other except it be by agreement for a season that ye may give yourselves unto prayer."[2] For since the word harmony is applied to those who marry according to God in the passage from Proverbs which is as follows: "Fathers will divide their house and substance to their sons, but from God the woman is married to the man,"[3] it is a logical consequence of the harmony being from God, that the name and the deed should enjoy the agreement with a view to prayer, as is indicated in the word, "unless it be by agreement."[4] Then the Word repeating that the agreeing of two on the earth is the same thing as the agreeing with Christ, adds, "For where two or three are gathered together in My name."[5] Therefore the two or three who are gathered together in the name of Christ are those who are in agreement on earth, not two only

---

[1] Matt. xvi. 19. [2] συμφωνήσωσιν. [3] Matt. xviii. 19. [4] Luke xv. 25. [5] Gen. xxxi. 27. [6] 2 Sam. vi. 4, 5.

[1] Matt. xvi. 19. [2] 1 Cor. vii. 5. [3] Prov. xix. 14, ἁρμόζεται. [4] 1 Cor. vii. 5. [5] Matt. xviii. 20.

but sometimes also three. But he who has the power will consider whether this agreement and a congregation of this sort in the midst of which Christ is, can be found in more, since "narrow and straightened is the way that leadeth unto life, and few be they that find it."[1] But perhaps also not even few but two or three make a symphony as Peter and James and John, to whom as making a symphony the Word of God showed His own glory. But two made a symphony, Paul and Sosthenes, when writing the first Epistle to the Corinthians;[2] and after this Paul and Timothy when sending the second Epistle to the same.[3] And even three made a symphony when Paul and Silvanus and Timothy gave instruction by letter to the Thessalonians.[4] But if it be necessary also from the ancient Scriptures to bring forward the three who made a symphony on earth, so that the Word was in the midst of them making them one, attend to the superscription of the Psalms, as for example to that of the forty-first, which is as follows: "Unto the end, unto understanding, for the sons of Korah."[5] For though there were three sons of Korah whose names we find in the Book of Exodus,[6] Aser, which is, by interpretation, "instruction," and the second Elkana, which is translated, "possession of God," and the third Abiasaph, which in the Greek tongue might be rendered, "congregation of the father," yet the prophecies were not divided but were both spoken and written by one spirit, and one voice, and one soul, which wrought with true harmony, and the three speak as one, "As the heart panteth after the springs of the water, so panteth my soul after thee, O God."[7] But also they say in the plural in the forty-fourth Psalm, "O God, we have heard with our ears." But if you wish still further to see those who are making symphony on earth look to those who heard the exhortation, "that ye may be perfected together in the same mind and in the same judgment,"[9] and who strove after the goal, "the soul and the heart of all the believers were one,"[10] who have become such, if it be possible for such a condition to be found in more than two or three, that there is no discord between them, just as there is no discord between the strings of the ten-stringed psaltery with each other. But they were not in symphony in earth who said, "I am of Paul, and I of Apollos, and I of Cephas, and I of Christ,"[1] but there were schisms among them, upon the dissolution of which they were gathered together in company with the spirit in Paul, with the power of the Lord Jesus Christ,[2] that they might no longer "bite and devour one another so that they were consumed by one another;"[3] for discord consumes, as concord brings together, and admits[4] the Son of God who comes in the midst of those who have become at concord. And strictly, indeed, concord takes place in two things generic, through the perfecting together, as the Apostle has called it, of the same mind by an intellectual grasp of the same opinions, and through the perfecting together of the same judgment, by a like way of living. But if whenever two of us agree on earth as touching anything that they shall ask, it shall be done for them of the Father of Jesus who is in heaven,[5] plainly when this is not done for them of the Father in heaven as touching anything that they shall ask, there the two have not been in agreement on earth; and this is the cause why we are not heard when we pray, that we do not agree with one another on earth, neither in opinions nor in life. But further also if we are the body of Christ and God hath set the members each one of them in the body that the members may have the same care one for another, and may agree with one another, and when one member suffers, all the members suffer with it, and if one be glorified, they rejoice with it,[6] we ought to practise the symphony which springs from the divine music, that when we are gathered together in the name of Christ, He may be in the midst of us, the Word of God, and the Wisdom of God, and His Power.[7]

2. THE HARMONY OF HUSBAND AND WIFE.

So much then for the more common understanding of the two or three whom the Word exhorts to be in agreement. But now let us also touch upon another interpretation which was uttered by some one of our predecessors, exhorting those who were married to sanctity and purity; for by the two, he says, whom the Word desires to agree on earth, we must understand the husband and wife, who by agreement defraud each other of bodily intercourse that they may give themselves unto prayer;[8] when if they pray for anything whatever

[1] Matt. vii. 14. [2] 1 Cor. i. 1. [3] 2 Cor. i. 1. [4] 1 Thess. i. 1. [5] Ps. xlii. [6] Exod. vi. 24. [7] Ps. xlii. 1. [8] Ps. xliv. 1. [9] 1 Cor. i. 10. [10] Acts iv. 32.

[1] 1 Cor. i. 12. [2] 1 Cor. v. 4. [3] Gal. v. 15. [4] *Or* reading χωρίζει, following the Vetus Inter, keeps apart. [5] Matt. xviii. 19. [6] 1 Cor. xii. 25, 18, 25, 26. [7] 1 Cor.i. 24. [8] 1 Cor. vii. 5.

that they shall ask, they shall receive it, the request being granted to them by the Father in heaven of Jesus Christ on the ground of such agreement. And this interpretation does not appear to me to cause dissolution of marriage, but to be an incitement to agreement, so that if the one wished to be pure, but the other did not desire it, and on this account he who willed and was able to fulfil the better part, condescended to the one who had not the power or the will, they would not both have the accomplishment from the Father in heaven of Jesus Christ, of anything whatever that they might ask.

3. THE HARMONY OF BODY, SOUL, AND SPIRIT.

And next to this about the married, I am familiar also with another interpretation of the agreement between the two which is as follows. In the wicked, sin reigns over the soul, being settled as on its own throne in this mortal body, so that the soul obeys the lusts thereof;[1] but in the case of those, who have stirred up the sin which formerly reigned over the body as from a throne and who are in conflict with it, "the flesh lusteth against the spirit, and the spirit against the flesh;"[2] but in the case of those who have now become perfected, the spirit has gained the mastery and put to death the deeds of the body, and imparts to the body of its own life, so that already this is fulfilled, "He shall quicken also your mortal bodies because of His Spirit that dwelleth in you;"[3] and there arises a concord of the two, body and spirit, on the earth, on the successful accomplishment of which there is sent up a harmonious prayer also of him who "with the heart believes unto righteousness, but with the mouth maketh confession unto salvation,"[4] so that the heart is no longer far from God, and along with this the righteous man draws nigh to God with his own lips and mouth. But still more blessed is it if the three be gathered together in the name of Jesus that this may be fulfilled, "May God sanctify you wholly, and may your spirit and soul and body be preserved entire without blame at the coming of our Lord Jesus Christ."[5] But some one may inquire with regard to the concord of spirit and body spoken of, if it is possible for these to be at concord without the third being so,—I mean the soul,—and whether it does not follow from the concord of these on the earth after the two have been gathered together in the name of Christ, that the three also are already gathered together in His name, in the midst of whom comes the Son of God as all are dedicated to Him,—I mean the three,—and no one is opposed to Him, there being no antagonism not only on the part of the spirit, but not even of the soul, nor further of the body.

[1] Rom. vi. 12. [2] Gal. v. 17. [3] Rom. viii. 11. [4] Rom. x. 10. [5] 1 Thess. v. 23.

4. HARMONY OF THE OLD AND NEW COVENANTS.

And likewise it is a pleasant thing to endeavour to understand and exhibit the fact of the concord of the two covenants,—of the one before the bodily advent of the Saviour and of the new covenant; for among those things in which the two covenants are at concord so that there is no discord between them would be found prayers, to the effect that about anything whatever they shall ask it shall be done to them from the Father in heaven. And if also you desire the third that unites the two, do not hesitate to say that it is the Holy Spirit, since "the words of the wise," whether they be of those before the advent, or at the time of the advent, or after it, "are as goads, and as nails firmly fixed, which were given by agreement from one shepherd."[1] And do not let this also pass unobserved, that He did not say, where two or three are gathered together in My name, there "shall I be" in the midst of them, but "there am I,"[2] not going to be, not delaying, but at the very moment of the concord being Himself found, and being in the midst of them.

5. THE LIMIT OF FORGIVENESS.

"*Then came Peter and said unto Him, Lord, how often shall my brother sin against me and I forgive him?*"[3] The conception that these things were said in a simple sense by Peter, as if he were inquiring whether he was to forgive his brother when he sinned against him seven times, but no longer if he sinned an eighth time, and by the Saviour, as if He thought that one should sit still and reckon up the sins of his neighbours against him in order that he might forgive seventy times and seven, but that from the seventy-eighth he should not forgive the man who wronged him, seems to me altogether silly and unworthy alike of the progress which Peter had made in the company of Jesus and of the divine magnanimity of Jesus. Perhaps, then, these things also border on an obscurity akin to the words, "Hear My voice, ye

[1] Eccl. xii. 11. [2] Matt. xviii. 20. [3] Matt. xviii. 21.

wives of Lamech,"[1] etc. If any one has already become a friend of Jesus so as to be taught by His spirit which illumines the reason of him who has advanced so far according to his desert, he might know the true meaning, therefore, in regard to these things, and such as Jesus Himself would have clearly expounded it; but we who fall short of the greatness of the friendship of Jesus must be content if we can babble a little about the passage. The number six, then, appears to be working and toilsome, but the number seven to contain the idea of repose. And consider if you can say that he, who loves the world and works the things of the world, and does those things which are material, sins six times, and that the number seven is the end of sin in his case, so that Peter with some such thought in his mind wished to pardon seven sins of those which his brother had committed against him. But since as units the tens and the hundreds have a certain common measure of proportion to the number which is in units, and Jesus knew that the number might be exceeded, on this account, I think, that He added to the number seven also the seventy,[2] and said that there ought to be forgiveness to brethren here, and to them who have sinned in respect to things here. But if any one going beyond the things about the world and this age were to commit sin, even if it were trifling, he could not longer reasonably have forgiveness of sins; for forgiveness extends to the things here, and in relation to the sins committed here, whether the forgiveness comes late or soon; but there is no forgiveness, not even to a brother, who has sinned beyond the seven and seventy times. But you might say that he who has sinned in such wise, whether as against Peter his brother, or as against Peter, against whom the gates of Hades do not prevail, is by sins of this kind in the smaller number of the sin, but according to sins still worse is in the number which has no forgiveness of sins.

6. CONCERNING THE KING WHO MADE A RECKONING WITH HIS OWN SERVANTS, TO WHOM WAS BROUGHT A MAN WHO OWED TEN THOUSAND TALENTS.

"*Therefore I say unto you the kingdom of heaven is likened unto a certain king, who wished to make a reckoning with his own servants.*"[3] The general conception of the parable is to teach us that we should be inclined to forgive the sins committed against us by those who have wronged us, and especially if after the wrongdoing he who has done it supplicates him who has been wronged, asking forgiveness for the sins which he has committed against him. And this the parable wishes to teach us by representing that even when forgiveness has been granted by God to us of the sins in respect of which we have received remission, exaction will be demanded even after the remission, unless we forgive the sins of those who have wronged us, so that there is no longer left in us the least remembrance of the wrong that was done, but the whole heart, assisted by the spirit of forgetfulness of wrongs, which is no common virtue, forgives him who has wronged us those things whieh have been wickedly done against any of us by him, even treacherously. But next to the general conception of the parable, it is right to examine the whole of it more simply according to the letter, so that he who advances with care to the right investigation of each detail of the things previously written may derive profit from the examination of what is said. Now there is, as is probable, an interpretation, transcendental and hard to trace, as it is somewhat mystical, according to which, after the analogy of the parables which are interpreted by the Evangelists, one would investigate each of the details in this; as, for example, who the king was, and who the servants were, and what was the beginning of his making a reckoning, and who was the one debtor who owed many talents, and who was his wife and who his children, and what were the "all things" spoken of besides those which the king ordered to be sold in order that the debt might be paid out of his belongings, and what was meant by the going out of the man who had been forgiven the many talents, and who was the one of the servants who was found and was a debtor not to the householder, but to the man who had been forgiven, and what is meant by the number of the hundred pence, and what by the word, "He took him by the throat saying, Pay what thou owest," and what is the prison into which he who had been forgiven all the talents went out and cast his fellow-servant, and who were the fellow-servants who were grieved and told the lord all that had been done, and who were the tormentors to whom he who had cast his fellow-servant into prison was delivered, and how he who was delivered to the tormentors paid all that was due, so

[1] Gen. iv. 23. [2] Matt. xviii. 22. [3] Matt. xviii. 23.

that he no longer owed anything.[1] But it is probable also that some other things could be added to the number by a more competent investigator, the exposition and interpretation of which I think to be beyond the power of man, and requiring the Spirit of Christ who spoke them in order that Christ may be understood as He spoke; for as "no one among men knows the things of the man, save the spirit which is in him," and "no one knows the things of God, save the Spirit of God,"[2] so no one knows after God the things spoken by Christ in proverbs and parables save the Spirit of Christ, in which he who participates in Christ not only so far as He is Spirit, but in Christ as He is Wisdom, as He is Word, would behold the things which were revealed to him in this passage. But with regard to the interpretation of the loftiest type, we make no profession; nor on the other hand with the assistance of Christ who is the Wisdom of God do we despair of apprehending the things signified in the parable; but whether it shall be the case that such things shall be dictated to us in connection with this Scripture or not, may God in Christ suggest the doing of that which is pleasing to Him, if only there be granted to us also concerning these things, the word of wisdom which is given from God through the Spirit, and the word of knowledge which is supplied according to the Spirit.[3]

7. EXPOSITION CONTINUED: THE KING AND THE SERVANTS.

"*The kingdom of heaven,*" He says, "*is likened,*"[4] etc. But if it be likened to such a king, and one who has done such things, who must we say that it is but the Son of God? For He is the King of the heavens, and as He is absolute Wisdom and absolute Righteousness and absolute Truth, is He not so also absolute Kingdom? But it is not a kingdom of any of those below, nor of a part of those above, but of all the things above, which were called heavens. But if you enquire into the meaning of the words, "Theirs is the kingdom of heaven,"[5] you may say that Christ is theirs in so far as He is absolute Kingdom, reigning in every thought of the man who is no longer under the reign of sin which reigns in the mortal body of those who have subjected themselves to it.[6] And if I say, reigning in every thought, I mean something like this, reigning as Righteousness and Wisdom and Truth and the rest of the virtues in him who has become a heaven, because of bearing the image of the heavenly, and in every power, whether angelic, or the rest that are named saints, not only in this age, but also in that which is to come, and who are worthy of a kingdom of such a kind. Accordingly this kingdom of heaven (when it was made "in the likeness of sinful flesh,"[1] that for sin it might condemn sin, when God made "Him who knew no sin to be sin on behalf of us,"[2] who bear the body of our sin), is likened to a certain king who is understood in relation to Jesus being united to Him, if we may dare so to speak, having more capacity towards being united and becoming entirely one with the "First-born of all creation,"[3] than he, who, being joined to the Lord, becomes one spirit with Him.[4] Now of this kingdom of the heavens which is likened unto a certain king, according to the conception of Jesus, and is united to Him, it is said by anticipation that he wished to make a reckoning with his servants. But he is about to make a reckoning with them in order that it may be manifested how each has employed the tried money of the householder and his rational coins. And the image in the parables was indeed taken from masters who made a reckoning with their own servants; but we shall understand more accurately what is signified by this part of the parable, if we fix our thought on the things done by the slaves who had administered their master's goods, and who were asked to give a reckoning concerning them. For each of them, receiving in different measure from his master's goods, has used them either for that which was right so as to increase the goods of his master, or consumed it riotously on things which he ought not, and spent profusely without judgment and without discretion that which had been put into his hands. But there are those who have wisely administered these goods and goods so great, but have lost others, and whenever they give the reckoning when the master makes a reckoning with them, there is gathered together how much loss each has incurred, and there is reckoned up how much gain each has brought, and according to the worthiness of the way in which he has administered it, he is either honoured or punished, or in some cases the debt is forgiven, but in others the talents are taken away. Well, then, from what has been said, let us

[1] Matt. xviii. 23, 34. [2] 1 Cor. ii. 11. [3] 1 Cor. xii. 8. [4] Matt. xviii. 23. [5] Matt. v. 3. [6] Rom. vi. 12.

[1] Rom. viii. 3. [2] 2 Cor. v. 21. [3] Col. i. 15. [4] 1 Cor. vi. 17.

first look at the rational coins and the tried money of the householder, of which one receives more and another less, for according to the ability of each, to one are given five talents as he has the ability to administer so many, but to another two as not being able to receive the amount of the man before him, and to another one as being also inferior to the second.[1] Are these, then, the only differences, or are we to recognize these differences in the case of certain persons of whom the Gospel goes on to speak while there are also others besides these: In other parables also are found certain persons, as the two debtors, the one who owed five hundred pence, and the other fifty;[2] but whether these had been entrusted with them and had administered them badly as being inferior in ability to him who had been entrusted with a talent, or had received them, we have not learned; but that they owed so much, we seem to be taught from the parable. And there are found other ten servants who were each entrusted with a pound separately.[3] And if any one understood the varied character of the human soul and the wide differences from each other in respect of natural aptitude, or want of aptitude for more or fewer of the virtues, and for these virtues or for those, perhaps he would comprehend how each soul has come with certain coins of the householder which come to light with the full attainment of reason, and with the attention which follows the full attainment of reason, and with exercise in things that are right, or with diligence and exercise in other things, whether they be useful as pursuits, or in part useful and in part not useful, such as the opinions which are not wholly true nor wholly false.

8. THE PRINCIPLE OF THE RECKONING.

But you will here inquire whether all men can be called servants of the king, or some are servants whom he foreknew and foreordained, while there are others who transact business with the servants, and are called bankers.[4] And in like manner you will inquire if there are those outside the number of the slaves from whom the householder declares that he will exact his own with usury, not only men alien from piety, but also some of the believers. Now the servants alone are the stewards of the Word, but the king, making a reckoning with the servants, demands from those who have borrowed from the servants, whether a hundred measures of wheat or a hundred measures of oil,[1] or whatever in point of fact those who are outside of the household of the king have received; for he who owed the hundred measures of wheat or the hundred measures of oil is not found to be, according to the parable, a fellow-servant of the unjust steward, as is evident from the question—how much owest thou to my lord?[2] But mark with me that each deed which is good or seemly is like a gain and an increment, but a wicked deed is like a loss; and as there is a certain gain when the money is greater and another when it is less, and as there are differences of more or less, so according to the good deeds, there is as it were a valuing of gains more or less. To reckon what work is a great gain, and what a less gain, and what a least, is the prerogative of him who alone knows to investigate such things, looking at them in the light of the disposition, and the word, and the deed, and from consideration of the things which are not in our power cooperating with those that are; and so also in the case of things opposite, it is his to say what sin, when a reckoning is made with the servants, is found to be a great loss, and what is less, and what, if we may so call it, is the loss of the very last mite,[3] or the last farthing.[4] The account, therefore, of the entire and whole life is exacted by that which is called the kingdom of heaven which is likened to a king, when "we must all stand before the judgment-seat of Christ that each one may receive the things done in the body according to what he hath done, whether good or bad;"[5] and then when the reckoning is being made, shall there be brought into the reckoning that is made also every idle word that men shall speak,[6] and any cup of cold water only which one has given to drink in the name of a disciple.[7]

9. THE TIME OCCUPIED BY THE RECKONING.

And these things will take place whenever that happens which is written in Daniel, "The books were opened and the judgment was set;"[8] for a record, as it were, is made of all things that have been spoken and done and thought, and by divine power every hidden thing of ours shall be manifested, and everything that is covered shall be revealed,[9] in order that when any one is found who has not "given diligence to be freed from the adversary," he may go in succession through the hands

[1] Matt. xxv. 15.
[2] Luke vii. 41.
[3] Luke xix. 13.
[4] Matt. xxv. 27.

[1] Luke xvi. 6, 7.
[2] Luke xvi. 5.
[3] Luke xii. 59.
[4] Matt. v. 26.
[5] 2 Cor. v. 10.
[6] Matt. xii. 36.
[7] Matt. x. 42.
[8] Dan. vii. 10.
[9] Matt. x. 26; Luke xii. 2.

of the magistrate, and the judge, and the attendant into the prison, until he pays the very last mite;[1] but when one has given diligence to be freed from him and owes nothing to any one, and already has made the pound ten pounds or five pounds, or doubled the five talents, or made the two four, he may obtain the due recompense, entering into the joy of his Lord, either being set over all His possessions,[2] or hearing the word, "Have thou authority over ten cities,"[3] or "Have thou authority over five cities."[4] But we think that these things are spoken of as if they required a long period of time, in order that an account may be made by us of the whole times of the earthly life, so that we might suppose that when the king makes a reckoning with each one of his many servants the matter would require so vast a period of time, until these things come to an end which have existed from the beginning of the world down to the consummation of the age, not of one age, but of many ages. But the truth is not so; for when God wished all at once to rekindle in the memories of all everything that had been done by each one throughout the whole time, in order that each might become conscious of his own doings whether good or bad, He would do it by His ineffable power. For it is not with God as with us; for if we wish to call some things to remembrance, we require sufficient time for the detailed account of what has been said by us, and to bring to our remembrance the things which we wish to remember; but if He wished to call to our memory the things which have been done in this life, in order that becoming conscious of what we have done we may apprehend for what we are punished or honoured, He could do so. But if any one disbelieves the swiftness of the power of God in regard to these matters, he has not yet had a true conception of the God who made the universe, who did not require times to make the vast creation of heaven and earth and the things in them; for, though He may seem to have made these things in six days, there is need of understanding to comprehend in what sense the words "in six days" are said, on account of this, "This is the book of the generation of heaven and earth,"[5] etc. Therefore it may be boldly affirmed that the season of the expected judgment does not require times, but as the resurrection is said to take place "in a moment, in the twinkling of an eye,"[1] so I think will the judgment also be.

[1] Luke xii. 58, 59. [2] Matt. xxiv. 47. [3] Luke xix. 17.
[4] Luke xix. 19. In chap. 12 Origen reads: Be thou also over five cities—as W. & H., and comments on the difference of the reward. The MSS. are therefore in error here.
[5] Gal. ii. 4.

10. THE MAN WHO OWED MANY TALENTS.

Next we must speak in regard to this, "*And when he had begun to reckon, there was brought unto him one which owed many talents.*"[2] The sense of this appears to me to be as follows: The season of beginning the judgment is with the house of God, who says, as also it is written in Ezekiel, to those who are appointed to attend to punishments, "Begin ye with My saints;"[3] and it is like "the twinkling of an eye;" but, the time of making a reckoning includes the same "twinkling," ideally apprehended, for we are not forgetful of what has been previously said of those who owe more. Wherefore it is not written, when he was making reckoning, but it is said, "When he began to reckon," there was brought, at the beginning of his making a reckoning, one who owed many talents; he had lost tens of thousands of talents, having been entrusted with great things, and having had many things committed to his care, but he had brought no gain to his master, but had lost tens of thousands so that he owed many talents; and, perhaps on this account, he owed many talents, seeing that he followed often the woman, who was sitting upon the talent of lead, whose name is wickedness.[4] But observe here that every great sin is a loss of the talents of the master of the house, and such sins are committed by fornicators, adulterers, abusers of themselves with men, effeminate, idolaters, murderers. Perhaps then the one who is brought to the king owing many talents has committed no small sin but all that are great and heinous; and if you were to seek for him among men, perhaps you would find him to be "the man of sin, the son of perdition, he that opposeth and exalteth himself against every God or object of worship;"[5] but if you seek him outside the number of men, who can this be but the devil who has ruined so many who received him, who wrought sin in them. For "man is a great thing, and a pitiful man is precious,"[6] precious so as to be worthy of a talent, whether of gold like as the lamp which was equal to

[1] 1 Cor. xv. 52. [2] Matt. xviii. 24. [3] Ezek. ix. 6.
[4] Zech. v. 7, 8. [5] 2 Thess. ii. 3, 4. [6] Prov. xx. 6.

a talent of gold,[1] or of silver or of any kind of material whatsoever understood intellectually, the symbols of which are recorded in the Words of the Days,[2] when David became enriched with many talents of which the number is mentioned, so many talents of gold, and so many of silver, and of the rest of the material there named, from which the temple of God was built.

11. THE SERVANT WHO OWED A HUNDRED PENCE.

Only, though he cannot pay the talents, for he has lost them, he has a wife and children and other things, of which it is written, "All that he has." [3] And it was possible that when he had been sold along with his own, he would have prospered if some one had bought him, and, by his worth and the things that were his, have paid the whole debt in full; and it was possible that he might no longer be the servant of the king, but become that of his purchaser. And he makes a request that he be not sold along with his own, but may continue to abide in the house of the king; wherefore he fell down and worshipped him, knowing that the king was God, and said, "Have patience with me, and I will pay thee all;" [4] for he was, as is probable, an active man, who knew that he could by a second course of action fill up the whole deficiency of the former loss of many talents. And this truly good king was moved with compassion for the man who owed him many talents and then released him, having bestowed upon him a favour greater than the request which had been made; for the debtor promised to the long-suffering master to pay all his debts, but the Lord moved with compassion for him did not merely forgive him with the idea of receiving his own back as a result of his patience, but even entirely released him and forgave him the whole debt. But this wicked servant, who had besought his master to have patience for his many talents, acted without mercy, for, having found one of his fellow-servants which owed him a hundred pence, he laid hold on him and took him by the throat, saying, "Pay if thou owest." [5] And did he not exhibit the very excess of wickedness who laid hold of his fellow-servant for a hundred pence, and took him by the throat and deprived him of freedom to breathe, when he himself, for the many talents, had neither been laid hold of, nor seized by the throat, but at first was ordered to be sold along with his wife and children and all that was his own; but afterwards, when he had worshipped him, the master was moved with compassion for him, and he was released and forgiven in regard to the whole of the debt. But it were indeed a hard task to tell according to the conception of Jesus who is the one fellow-servant who was found to be owing a hundred pence, not to his own lord, but to him who owed many talents, and who are the fellow-servants who saw the one taking by the throat, and the other taken, and were exceedingly sorry, and represented clearly unto their own lord all that had been done. But what the truth in these matters is, I declare that no one can interpret unless Jesus, who explained all things to His own disciples privately, takes up His abode in his reason, and opens up all the treasures in the parable which are dark, hidden, unseen, and confirms by clear demonstrations the man whom He desires to illumine with the light of the knowledge of the things that are in this parable, that he may at once represent who is brought to the king as the debtor of many talents, and who is the other one who owes to him a hundred pence, etc.; whether he can be the man of sin previously mentioned,[1] or the devil, or neither of these, but some other, whether a man, or some one of those under the sway of the devil; for it is a work of the wisdom of God to exhibit the things have have been prophesied concerning those who are in themselves of a certain nature, or have been made according to such and such qualities, whether among visible powers or also among some men, in whatever way they may have been written by the Holy Spirit. But as we have not yet received the competent mind which is able to be blended with the mind of Christ, and which is capable of attaining to things so great, and which is able with the Spirit to "search all things, even the deep things of God," [2] we, forming an impression still indefinitely with regard to the matters in this passage, are of opinion that the wicked servant indicated by the parable who is here represented in regard to the debt of many talents, refers to some definite one.

12. THE TIME OF THE RECKONING.

But it is fitting to examine at what time the man—the king—in the parable wished

[1] Exod. xxv. 39. [2] Chron. xxii. 14. [3] Matt. xviii. 25. [4] Matt. xviii. 26. [5] Matt. xviii. 28.

[1] 2 Thess. ii. 3. [2] 1 Cor. ii. 10.

to make a reckoning with his own servants, and to what period we ought to refer the things that are said. For if it be after the consummation, or at it at the time of the expected judgment, how are we to maintain the things about him who owed a hundred pence, and was taken by the throat by the man who had been forgiven the many talents? But if, before the judgment, how can we explain the reckoning that was made before this by the king, with his own servants? But we ought to think in a general way about every parable, the interpretation of which has not been recorded by the evangelists, even though Jesus explained all things to His own disciples privately;[1] and for this reason the writers of the Gospels have concealed the clear exposition of the parables, because the things signified by them were beyond the power of the nature of words to express, and every solution and exposition of such parables was of such a kind that not even the whole world itself could contain the books that should be written[2] in relation to such parables. But it may happen that a fitting heart be found, and, because of its purity, able to receive the letters of the exposition of the parable, so that they could be written in it by the Spirit of the living God. But some one will say that, perhaps, we act with impiety, who, because of the secret and mystical import of some of the Scriptures which are of heavenly origin, wish them to be symbolic, and endeavour to expound them, even though it might seem *ex hypothesi* that we had an accurate knowledge of their meaning. But to this we must say that, if there be those who have obtained the gift of accurate apprehension of these things, they know what they ought to do; but as for us, who acknowledge that we fall short of the ability to see into the depth of the things here signified, even though we obtain a somewhat crass perception of the things in the passage, we will say, that some of the things which we seem to find after much examination and inquiry, whether by the grace of God, or by the power of our own mind, we do not venture to commit to writing; but some things, for the sake of our own intellectual discipline, and that of those who may chance to read them, we will to some extent set forth. But let these things, then, be said by way of apology, because of the depth of the parable; but,

[1] Mark iv. 34.

[2] John xxi. 25.

with regard to the question at what time the man—the king—in the parable wished to make a reckoning with his own servants, we will say that it seems that this takes place about the time of the judgment which had been proclaimed. And this is confirmed by two parables, one at the close of the Gospel before us,[1] and one from the Gospel according to Luke.[2] And not to prolong the discussion by quoting the very letter, as any one who wishes can take it from the Scripture himself, we will say that the parable according to Matthew declares, "For it is as when a man going into another country called his own servants, and delivered unto them his own goods, and to one he gave five talents, and to another two, and to another one talent;"[3] then they took action with regard to that which had been entrusted to them, and, after a long time, the lord of those servants cometh, and it is written in the very words, that he also makes a reckoning with them.[4] And compare the words, "And when he began to make a reckoning,"[5] and consider that he called the going of the householder into another country the time at which "we are at home in the body but absent from the Lord;"[6] but his advent, when, "after a long time the lord of those servants cometh,"[7] the time at the consummation in the judgment; for after a long time the lord of those servants cometh and makes a reckoning with them, and those things which follow take place. But the parable in Luke represents with more clearness, that "a certain nobleman went into a far country to receive for himself a kingdom, and to return," and when going, "he called ten servants, and gave to them ten pounds, and said unto them, Trade ye till I come."[8] But the nobleman, being hated by his own citizens, who sent an ambassage after him, as they did not wish him to reign over them, came back again, having received the kingdom, and told the servants to whom he had given the money to be called to himself that he might know what they had gained by trading. And, seeing what they had done, to him who had made the one pound ten pounds, rendering praise in the words, "Well done, thou good servant, because thou wast found faithful in a very little,"[9] he gives to him authority over ten cities, to-wit, those which were under his kingdom. And to another, who had multiplied the pound fivefold, he did not

[1] Matt. xxv. 14-30. [2] Luke xix. 12-27. [3] Matt. xxv. 14, 15. [4] Matt. xxv. 19. [5] Matt. xviii. 24. [6] 2 Cor. v. 6. [7] Matt. xxv. 19. [8] Luke xix. 12, 13. [9] Luke xix. 17.

render the praise which he assigned to the first, nor did he specify the word "authority," as in the case of the first, but said to him, "Be thou also over five cities."[1] But to him who had tied up the pound in a napkin, he said, "Out of thine own mouth will I judge thee, thou wicked servant;"[2] and he said to them that stood by, Take from him the pound, and give it unto him that hath the ten pounds[3] Who, then, in regard to this parable, will not say that the nobleman, who goes into a far country to receive for himself a kingdom and to return, is Christ, going, as it were, into another country to receive the kingdoms of this world, and the things in it? And those who have received the ten talents are those who have been entrusted with the dispensation of the Word which has been committed unto them. And His citizens who did not wish Him to reign over them when He was a citizen in the world in respect of His incarnation,[4] are perhaps Israel who disbelieved Him, and perhaps also the Gentiles who disbelieved Him.

13. NO FORGIVENESS TO THE UNFORGIVING.

Only, I have said these things with the view of referring his return when he comes with his kingdom to the consummation, when he commanded the servants to whom he had given the money to be called to him that he might know what they had gained by trading, and from a desire to demonstrate from this, and from the parable of the Talents, that the passage "he who wished to make a reckoning with his own servants"[5] is to be referred to the consummation when now he is king, receiving the kingdom, on account of which, according to another parable,[6] he went into a far country, to receive for himself a kingdom and to return. Therefore, when he returned after receiving the kingdom, he wished to make a reckoning with his own servants. And "when he had begun to reckon, there was brought unto him one who owed many talents,"[7] and he was brought as to a king by those who had been appointed his ministers—I think, the angels. And perhaps he was one of those under the kingdom who had been entrusted with a great administration and had not dispensed it well, but had wasted what had been entrusted to him, so that he came to owe the many talents which he had lost. This very man, perhaps not having the means to pay, is ordered by the king to be sold along with his wife, by intercourse with whom he became the father of certain children. But it is no easy task to see what is intellectually meant by father and mother and children. What this means in point of truth God may know, and whether He Himself has given insight to us or not, he who can may judge. Only this is our conception of the passage; that, as "the Jerusalem which is above" is "the mother"[1] of Paul and of those like unto him, so there may be a mother of others after the analogy of Jerusalem, the mother, for example, of Syene in Egypt, or Sidon, or as many cities as are named in the Scriptures. Then, as Jerusalem is "a bride adorned for her husband,"[2] Christ, so there may be those mothers of certain powers who have been allotted to them as wives or brides. And as there are certain children of Jerusalem, as mother, and of Christ, as father, so there would be certain children of Syene, or Memphis, or Tyre, or Sidon, and the rulers set over them. Perhaps then, too, this one, the debtor of many talents who was brought to the king, has, as we have said, a wife and children, whom at first the king ordered to be sold, and also all that he had to be sold; but afterwards, being moved with compassion, he released him and forgave him all the debt; not, as if he were ignorant of the future, but, in order that we might understand what happened, it was written that he did so. Each one then of those who have, as we have said, a wife and children will render an account whenever the king comes to make a reckoning, having received the kingdom and having returned; and each of them as a ruler of any Syene or Memphis, or Tyre or Sidon, or any like unto them, has also debtors. This one, then, having been released, and having been forgiven all the debt, "went out from the king and found one of his fellow-servants,"[3] etc.; and, on this account, I suppose that he took him by the throat, when he had gone out from the king, for unless he had gone out he would not have taken his own fellow-servant by the throat. Then observe the accuracy of the Scripture, how that the one fell down and "worshipped," but the other fell down and did not worship but "besought;"[4] and the king being moved with compassion released him and forgave him all the debt, but the servant did not wish even to pity his own fellow-servant; and the king before his release ordered him to be sold and what was his, while he who had been forgiven

[1] Luke xix. 19. See note 4, p. 500. [2] Luke xix. 22.
[3] Luke xix. 24. [4] Luke xix. 14. [5] Matt. xviii. 23.
[6] Luke xix. 12. [7] Matt. xviii. 24.

[1] Gal. iv. 26. [2] Rev. xxi. 2.
[3] Matt. xviii. 28. [4] Matt. xvii. 26, 29.

cast him into prison. And observe that his fellow-servants did not bring any accusation or "said," but "told,"[1] and that he did not use the epithet "wicked" at the beginning in regard to the money lost, but reserved it afterwards for his action towards the fellow-servant. But mark also the moderation of the king; he does not say, You worshipped me, but You besought me; and no longer did he order him and his to be sold, but, what was worse, he delivered him to the tormentors, because of his wickedness.[2] But who may these be but those who have been appointed in the matter of punishments? But at the same time observe, because of the use made of this parable by adherents of heresies, that if they accuse the Creator[3] of being passionate, because of words that declare the wrath of God, they ought also to accuse this king, because that "being wroth," he delivered the debtor to the tormentors. But it must further be said to those whose view it is that no one is delivered by Jesus to the tormentors,—pray, explain to us, good sirs, who is the king who delivered the wicked servant to the tormentors? And let them also attend to this, "So therefore also shall My heavenly Father do unto you;"[4] and to the same persons also might rather be said the things in the parable of the Ten Pounds that the Son of the good God said, "Howbeit these mine enemies which would not that I should reign over them,"[5] etc. The conclusion of the parable, however, is adapted also to the simpler; for all of us who have obtained the forgiveness of our own sins, and have not forgiven our brethren, are taught at once that we shall suffer the lot of him who was forgiven but did not forgive his fellow-servant.

14. HOW JESUS FINISHED HIS WORDS.

"*And it came to pass when Jesus had finished these words.*"[6] He who gives a detailed and complete account of each of the questions before him so that nothing is left out, finishes his own words. But he will give a declaration on this point with more confidence who devotes himself with great diligence to the entire reading of the Old and New Testament; for if the expression, "he finished these words," may be applied to no other, neither to Moses, nor to any of the prophets, but only to Jesus, then one would dare to say that Jesus alone finished His words, He who came to put an end to things, and to fulfil what was defective in the law, by saying, "It was said to them of old time,"[1] etc., and, again, "That the things spoken through the prophets might be fulfilled."[2] But if it is written somewhere also in them, then you may compare and contrast the discourses finished by them with those finished by the Saviour, that you may find the difference between them. And yet at this point, also, investigation might be made whether in the case of the things spoken by way of oracle the expression, "he finished," is applied either to the things spoken by Moses, or any of the prophets, or of both together; for careful observation would suggest very weighty thoughts to those who know how "to compare spiritual things with spiritual," and on this account "speak not in words which man's wisdom teacheth, but which the Spirit teacheth."[3] But perhaps some other one, attending with over-curious spirit to the word "finished," which is assigned to things of a more mystical order, just as we say that some one delivered to those who were under his control mysteries and rites of "perfecting"[4] not in a praiseworthy fashion, and another delivered the mysteries of God to those who are worthy, and rites of "perfecting" proportionate to such mysteries, might say that having initiated them, he made a rite of "perfecting," by which "perfecting" the words were shown to be powerful, so that the gospel of Jesus was preached in the whole world, and by virtue of the divine "perfecting" gained the mastery of every soul which the Father draws to the Son, according to what is said by the Saviour, "No one comes to Me except the Father which has sent Me draw him."[5] Wherefore also "the word" of those who by the grace of God are ambassadors of the gospel, "and their preaching, is not in persuasive words of wisdom, but in demonstration of the spirit of power,"[6] to those for whom the words of the doctrine of Jesus were finished. You will therefore observe how often it is said, "He finished," and of what things it is said, and you will take as an illustration that which is said in regard to the beatitudes, and the whole of

[1] Matt. xviii. 31. [2] Matt. xviii. 34.
[3] That is, the God of the Old Testament—according to Marcion.
[4] Matt. xviii. 35. [5] Luke xix. 27. [6] Matt. xix. 1.

[1] Matt. v. 33. [2] Mark xiv. 49; Matt. xxvi. 56.
[3] 1 Cor. ii. 13.
[4] τελετὰς. Origen's play on the words ἐτέλεσεν and τελετή cannot be fully reproduced in English. The word τελετή, in reference to the mysteries, meant the rite, or participation in the rite, by which one became perfect; and in later Christian usage it was applied to the Sacraments of Baptism and the Lord's Supper. See Suicer.
[5] John vi. 44.
[6] 1 Cor. ii. 4. πνεύματος δυνάμεως. The omission of the καὶ is strange; for in the *Contra Celsum* (i. 2) Origen characterises the argument from prophecy as "the demonstration of the Spirit" and the argument from miracles as "the demonstration of power."

the discourse to which is subjoined, "And it came to pass when Jesus had finished these words, all the multitudes were astonished at His teaching."[1] But now the saying, "Jesus finished these words," is referred also immediately to the very mystical parable according to which the kingdom of heaven is likened unto a king, but also beyond this parable to the sections which were written before it.

15. HOW MEN FOLLOWED JESUS.

Only, when Jesus had finished these words, having spoken them in Galilee about Capernaum, then "He departed thence, and came into the borders of Judæa,"[2] which were different from Galilee. But He came to the borders of Judæa, and not to the middle of it, but, as it were, to the outermost parts, where great multitudes followed Him,[3] whom He healed at "the borders of Judæa beyond Jordan,"—where baptism had been given.[4] But you will observe the difference between the crowds who simply followed, and Peter and the others who gave up everything and followed, and Matthew, who arose and followed him;[5] he did not simply follow, but "having arisen;" for "having arisen" is an important addition. There are always those, then, who follow like the great multitudes, who have not arisen that they may follow, nor have given up all that was theirs formerly, but few are they who have arisen and followed, who also, in the regeneration, shall sit on twelve thrones.[6] Only, if one wishes to be healed, let him follow Jesus.

16. CONCERNING THE PHARISEES AND SCRIBES TEMPTING JESUS (BY ASKING) WHETHER IT WAS LAWFUL FOR A MAN TO PUT AWAY HIS WIFE FOR EVERY CAUSE.

After this it is written that "*there came unto Him the Pharisees tempting Him and saying, Is it lawful for a man to put away his wife for every cause?*"[7] Mark, also, has written to the like effect.[8] Accordingly, of those who came to Jesus and inquired of Him, there were some who put questions to tempt Him; and if our Saviour so transcendent was tempted, which of His disciples who is ordained to teach need be vexed, when he is tempted by some who inquire, not from the love of learning, but from the wish to tempt? And you might find many passages, if you brought them together, in which the Pharisees tempted our Jesus, and others, different from them, as a certain lawyer,[1] and perhaps also a scribe,[2] that by bringing together what is said about those who tempted Him, you might find by investigation what is useful for this kind of inquiries. Only, the Saviour, in response to those who tempted Him, laid down dogmas; for they said, "Is it lawful for a man to put away his own wife for every cause?" and He answered and said, "Have ye not read that He who created them from the beginning made them male and female?"[3] etc. And I think that the Pharisees put forward this word for this reason, that they might attack Him whatever He might say; as, for example, if He had said, "It is lawful," they would have accused Him of dissolving marriages for trifles; but, if He had said, "It is not lawful," they would have accused Him of permitting a man to dwell with a woman, even with sins; so, likewise, in the case of the tribute-money,[4] if He had told them to give, they would have accused Him of making the people subject to the Romans, and not to the law of God, but if He had told them not to give, they would have accused Him of creating war and sedition, and of stirring up those who were not able to stand against so powerful an army. But they did not perceive in what way He answered blamelessly and wisely, in the first place, rejecting the opinion that a wife was to be put away for every cause, and, in the second place, giving answer to the question about the bill of divorcement; for He saw that not every cause is a reasonable ground for the dissolution of marriage, and that the husband must dwell with the wife as the weaker vessel, giving honour,[5] and bearing her burdens in sins;[6] and by what is written in Genesis, He puts to shame the Pharisees who boasted in the Scriptures of Moses, by saying, "Have ye not read that He who created them from the beginning made them male and female," etc., and, subjoining to these words, because of the saying, "And the twain shall become one flesh," teaching in harmony with one flesh, namely, "So that they are no more twain, but one flesh."[7] And, as tending to convince them that they should not put away their wife for every cause, is it said, "What God hath joined together, let not man put asunder."[8] It is to be observed, however, in the exposition of the words quoted from Genesis in the Gospel, that they

---

[1] Matt. vii. 28. [2] Matt. xix. 1. [3] Matt. xix. 2. [4] John i. 28. [5] Matt. ix. 9. [6] Matt. xix. 28. [7] Matt. xix. 3. [8] Mark x. 2.

[1] Matt. xxii. 35. [2] Mark xii. 28. [3] Matt. xix. 4. [4] Matt. xxii. 17. [5] 1 Pet. iii. 7. [6] Gal. vi. 2. [7] Matt. xix. 4–6. [8] Matt. xix. 6.

were not spoken consecutively as they are written in the Gospel; and I think that it is not even said about the same persons, namely, of those who were formed after the image of God, and of those who were formed from the dust of the ground and from one of the ribs of Adam. For where it is said, "Male and female made He them,"[1] the reference is to those formed "after the image," but where He also said, "For this cause shall a man leave his own father and mother,"[2] etc., the reference is not to those formed after the image; for some time after the Lord God formed the man, taking dust from the ground, and from his side the helpmate. And mark, at the same time, that in the case of those who are formed "after the image," the words were not "husband and wife" but "male and female." But we have also observed this in the Hebrew, for man is indicated by the word "is," but male by the word "zachar," and again woman by the word "essa," but female by the word "agkeba." For at no time is it "woman" or "man" "after the image," but the superior class, the male, and the second, the female. But also if a man leave his mother and his father, he cleaves not to the female, but to his own wife, and "they become," since man and woman are one in flesh, "one flesh." Then, describing what ought to be in the case of those who are joined together by God, so that they may be joined together in a manner worthy of God, the Saviour adds, "So that they are no more twain;"[3] and, wherever there is indeed concord, and unison, and harmony, between husband and wife, when he is as ruler and she is obedient to the word, "He shall rule over thee,"[4] then of such persons we may truly say, "They are no more twain." Then since it was necessary that for "him who was joined to the Lord," it should be reserved "that he should become one spirit with Him,"[5] in the case of those who are joined together by God, after the words, "So that they are no more twain," it is said, "but one flesh." And it is God who has joined together the two in one so that they are no more twain, from the time that[6] the woman is married to the man. And, since God has joined them together, on this account in the case of those who are joined together by God, there is a "gift"; and Paul knowing this, that marriage according to the Word of God was a "gift," like as holy celibacy was a gift, says, "But I would that all men were like myself; howbeit, each man hath his own gift from God, one after this manner, and another after that."[1] And those who are joined together by God both mind and keep the precept, "Husbands love your wives, as Christ also the church."[2] The Saviour then commanded, "What God hath joined together, let not man put asunder,"[3] but man wishes to put asunder what God hath joined together, when, "falling away from the sound faith, giving heed to seducing spirits and doctrines of demons, through the hypocrisy of men that speak lies, branded in their own conscience as with a hot iron, forbidding," not only to commit fornication, but "to marry,"[4] he dissolves even those who had been before joined together by the providence of God. Let these things then be said, keeping in view what is expressly said concerning the male and the female, and the man and the woman, as the Saviour taught in the answer to the Pharisees.

17. UNION OF CHRIST AND THE CHURCH.

But since the Apostle understands the words, "*And they twain shall be one flesh*,"[5] of Christ and the church,[6] we must say that Christ keeping the saying, "What God hath joined together let not man put asunder,"[7] did not put away His former wife, so to speak—that is, the former synagogue—for any other cause than that that wife committed fornication, being made an adulteress by the evil one, and along with him plotted against her husband and slew Him, saying, "Away with such a fellow from the earth, crucify Him, crucify Him."[8] It was she therefore who herself revolted, rather than her husband who put her away and dismissed her; wherefore, reproaching her for falling away from him, it says in Isaiah, "Of what kind is the bill of your mother's divorcement, with which I sent her away?"[9] And He who at the beginning created Him "who is in the form of God" after the image, made Him male, and the church female, granting to both oneness after the image. And, for the sake of the church, the Lord—the husband—left the Father whom He saw when He was "in the form of God,"[10] left also His mother, as He was the very son of the Jerusalem which is above, and was joined to His wife who had fallen down here, and these two here became one

[1] Gen. i. 27. [2] Gen. ii. 24. [3] Matt. xix. 6. [4] Gen. iii. 16. [5] 1 Cor. vi. 17. [6] *Or*, by God the woman is married to the man.

[1] 1 Cor. vii. 7. [2] Eph. v. 25. [3] Matt. xix. 6. [4] 1 Tim. iv. 1–3. [5] Matt. xix. 5. [6] Eph. v. 31, 32. [7] Matt. xix. 6. [8] John xix. 6, 15; Luke xxiii. 18. [9] Isa. l. 1. [10] Phil. ii. 6.

flesh. For because of her, He Himself also became flesh, when "the Word became flesh and dwelt among us,"[1] and they are no more two, but now they are one flesh, since it is said to the wife, "Now ye are the body of Christ, and members each in his part;"[2] for the body of Christ is not something apart different from the church, which is His body, and from the members each in his part. And God has joined together these who are not two, but have become one flesh, commanding that men should not separate the church from the Lord. And he who takes heed for himself so as not to be separated, is confident as one who will not possibly be separated and says, "Who shall separate us from the love of Christ?"[3] Here, therefore, the saying, "What God hath joined together, let not man put asunder,"[4] was written with relation to the Pharisees, but to those who are superior to the Pharisees, it could be said, "What then God hath joined together, let nothing put asunder," neither principality nor power; for God, who has joined together is stronger than all those which any one could conceive and name.

18. THE BILL OF DIVORCEMENT.

After this we will discuss the saying of the Pharisees which they said to Jesus, "*Why then did Moses command to give a bill of divorcement and put her away?*"[5] And with good reason we will bring forward for this purpose the passage from Deuteronomy concerning the bill of divorcement, which is as follows: "But if a man taketh a wife and cohabit with her, and it shall be, if she do not find favour in his sight because he hath found in her a thing unseemly," etc., down to the words, "and ye shall not pollute the land which the Lord your God giveth you for an inheritance."[6] Now I inquire whether in these things according to this law, we are to seek nothing in it beyond the letter seeing that God has not given it, or whether to the Pharisees who quoted the saying, "Moses commanded to give a bill of divorcement and put her away," it was of necessity said, "Moses, for your hardness of heart, suffered you to put away your wives; but from the beginning it hath not been so."[7] But if any one ascends to the Gospel of Christ Jesus which teaches that the law is spiritual, he will seek also the spiritual understanding of this law. And he who wishes to interpret these things figuratively will say that, just as it was said by Paul confident in the grace which he had, "A wife is bound for so long time as her husband liveth, but if the husband be dead she is free to be married to whom she will, only in the Lord; but she is happier if she abide as she is, after my judgment, and I think that I also have the Spirit of God"[1] (for here to the words, "after my judgment," lest it should be despised as being without the Spirit of God, he well added, "and I think that I also have the Spirit of God)," so also it would be possible for Moses, by reason of the power given to him to make laws, to the effect that he suffered for the hardness of heart of the people certain things, among which was the putting away of wives, to be persuaded in regard to the laws which he promulgated according to his own judgment, that in these also the legislation took place with the Spirit of God. And he will say that, unless one law is spiritual and another is not such, this is a law, and this is spiritual, and its spiritual significance ought to be investigated.

19. THE DIVORCE OF ISRAEL.

Now, keeping in mind what we said above in regard to the passage from Isaiah about the bill of divorcement, we will say that the mother of the people separated herself from Christ, her husband, without having received the bill of divorcement, but afterwards when there was found in her an unseemly thing, and she did not find favour in his sight, the bill of divorcement was written out for her; for when the new covenant called those of the Gentiles to the house of Him who had cast away his former wife, it virtually gave the bill of divorcement to her who formerly separated from her husband—the law, and the Word. Therefore he, also, having separated from her, married, so to speak, another, having given into the hands of the former the bill of divorcement; wherefore they can no longer do the things enjoined on them by the law, because of the bill of divorcement. And a sign that she has received the bill of divorcement is this, that Jerusalem was destroyed along with what they called the sanctuary of the things in it which were believed to be holy, and with the altar of burnt offerings, and all the worship associated with it. And a further sign of the bill of divorcement is this, that they cannot keep their feasts, even though according to the

---

[1] John i. 14. [2] 1 Cor. xii. 27. [3] Rom. viii. 35. [4] Matt. xix. 6. [5] Matt. xix. 7. [6] Deut. xxiv. 1–4. [7] Matt. xix. 8.

[1] 1 Cor. vii. 39, 40.

letter of the law designedly commanded them, in the place which the Lord God appointed to them for keeping feasts; but there is this also, that the whole synagogue has become unable to stone those who have committed this or that sin; and thousands of things commanded are a sign of the bill of divorcement; and the fact that "there is no more a prophet," and that they say, "We no longer see signs;"[1] for the Lord says, "He hath taken away from Judæa and from Jerusalem," according to the word of Isaiah, "Him that is mighty, and her that is mighty, a powerful giant," etc., down to the words, "a prudent hearer."[2] Now, He who is the Christ may have taken the synagogue to wife and cohabited with her, but it may be that afterwards she found not favour in His sight; and the reason of her not having found favour in His sight was, that there was found in her an unseemly thing; for what was more unseemly than the circumstance that, when it was proposed to them to release one at the feast, they asked for the release of Barabbas the robber, and the condemnation of Jesus?[3] And what was more unseemly than the fact, that they all said in His case, "Crucify Him, crucify Him," and "Away with such a fellow from the earth"?[4] And can this be freed from the charge of unseemliness, "His blood be upon us, and upon our children"?[5] Wherefore, when He was avenged, Jerusalem was compassed with armies, and its desolation was near,[6] and their house was taken away from it, and "the daughter of Zion was left as a booth in a vineyard, and as a lodge in a garden of cucumbers, and as a besieged city."[7] And, about the same time, I think, the husband wrote out a bill of divorcement to his former wife, and gave it into her hands, and sent her away from his own house, and the bond of her who came from the Gentiles has been cancelled about which the Apostle says, "Having blotted out the bond written in ordinances, which was contrary to us, and He hath taken it out of the way, nailing it to the cross;"[8] for Paul also and others became proselytes of Israel for her who came from the Gentiles.[9] The first wife, accordingly, not having found favour before her husband, because in her had been found an unseemly thing, went out from the dwelling of her husband, and, going away, has become joined to another man, to whom she has subjected herself, whether we should call the husband Barabbas the robber, who is figuratively the devil, or some evil power. And in the case of some of that synagogue there has happened the former thing which was written in the law, but in the case of others, that which was second. For the last husband[1] hated his wife and will write out for her some day at the consummation of things a bill of divorcement, when God so orders it, and will give it into her hands and will send her away from his dwelling; for as the good God will put enmity between the serpent and the woman, and between his seed and her seed,[2] so will He order it that the last husband shall hate her.

20. CHRIST AND THE GENTILES.

Now there are those in whose case it has happened that the man dwells with them without having hated them, because they abide in the house of the last husband, who took to himself their synagogue as wife. But also in their case the latter husband dies,[1] perhaps whenever the last enemy of Christ, death, is destroyed. But whichever of these things may happen, whether the former or the latter to the wife, the former husband, it says, who sent her away, will not be able to turn back and take her to be a wife to himself after she has been defiled, since "it is abomination," it says, "before the Lord thy God."[3] But these things will not seem to be consistent with this, "If the fulness of the Gentiles be come in, all Israel shall be saved."[4] But consider if it can be said to this, that, if she shall be saved by her former husband returning and taking her to himself as wife, she will in any case be saved after she has been polluted. A priest, then, will not take to himself as a wife one who has been a harlot and an outcast,[5] but no other, as being inferior to the priest, is hindered from doing so. But if you seek for the harlot in regard to the calling of the Gentiles, you may use the passage, "Take to yourself a wife of fornication, and children of fornication,"[6] etc.; for, as "the priests in the temple profane the sabbath, and are guiltless,"[7] so he who, casting out his former wife, takes in due season "a wife of fornication," having done it according to the command of Him who says, when it is necessary, and so long as it was necessary, "He shall not take a harlot to wife," and, when it was reasonable, He says, "Take to

[1] Ps. lxxiv. 9. [2] Isa. iii. 1–3. [3] Matt. xxvii. 21. [4] John xix. 15. [5] Matt. xxvi. 25. [6] Luke xxi. 20. [7] Isa. i. 8. [8] Col. ii. 14. [9] The text is corrupt.

[1] Deut. xxiv. 3. [2] Gen. iii. 15. [3] Deut. xxiv. 4. [4] Rom. xi. 25, 26. [5] Lev. xxi. 14. [6] Hos. i. 2. [7] Matt. xii. 5.

yourself a wife of fornication." For as the Son of man is Lord of the sabbath,[1] and not the slave of the sabbath as the people are, so He who gives the law has power to give it "until a time of reformation,"[2] and to change the law, and, when the time of the reformation is at hand, also to give after the former way and after the former heart another way and another heart, "in an acceptable time, and in a day of salvation."[3] And let these things be said according to our interpretation of the law in regard to the bill of divorcement.

21. UNION OF ANGELS AND THE SOULS OF MEN.

But some one may inquire whether the human soul can be figuratively called a wife, and the angel who is set over her and is her ruler, with whom as her sovereign she holds conversation, can be called her husband; so that according to this each lawfully dwells along with the soul which is worthy of the guardianship of a divine angel; but sometimes after long sojourning and intercourse a cause may arise in the soul why she does not find favour in the eyes of the angel who is her lord and ruler, because that in it there is found an unseemly thing; and bonds may be written out, as such are written, and a bill of divorcement be written and put into the hands of her who is cast out, so that she may no longer be familiar with her former guardian, when she is cast out from his dwelling. And even she who has gone away from her former dwelling may be joined to another husband, and be unfortunate with him, not only, as in the case of the former, not finding favour in his sight because an unseemly thing was found in her, but even being hated by him.[4] Yea, and even there might be written out from the second husband a bill of divorcement and it might be put into her hands from the last husband who sends her away from his dwelling. But whether there can be such a change of the life of angels with men, as to amount, so far as concerns their relation to us, to their death, one may put the question rash though it be; but be that as it may, she also who has once fallen away from the former husband will not return again to him, for the former husband who sent her away will not be able to turn back and take her as wife to himself, after she was defiled.[5] And if one should dare, using a Scripture which is in circulation in the church, but not acknowledged by all to be divine, to soften down a precept of this kind, the passage might be taken from The Shepherd, concerning some who as soon as they believe are put in subjection to Michael,[1] but falling away from him from love of pleasure, are put in subjection to the angel of luxury,[2] then to the angel of punishment,[3] and after this to the angel of repentance; for you observe that the wife or soul who has once been given to luxury no longer returns to the first ruler, but also besides suffering punishment, is put in subjection to one inferior to Michael; for the angel of penitence is inferior to him. We must therefore take heed lest there be found in us any unseemly thing, and we should not find favour in the eyes of our husband Christ, or of the angel who has been set over us. For if we do not take heed, perhaps we also shall receive the bill of divorcement, and either be bereft of our guardian, or go to another man. But I consider that it is not of good omen to receive, as it were, the marriage of an angel with our own soul.[4]

22. THE MARRIAGE OF CHURCH DIGNITARIES.

But, while dealing with the passage, I would say that we will be able perhaps now to understand and clearly set forth a question which is hard to grasp and see into, with regard to the legislation of the Apostle concerning ecclesiastical matters; for Paul wishes no one of those of the church, who has attained to any eminence beyond the many, as is attained in the administration of the sacraments, to make trial of a second marriage. For laying down the law in regard to bishops in the first Epistle to Timothy, he says, "If a man seeketh the office of a bishop, he desireth a good work. The bishop, therefore, must be without reproach, the husbands of one wife, temperate, sober-minded,"[5] etc.; and, in regard to deacons, "Let the deacons," he says, "be the husbands of one wife, ruling their children and their own houses well,"[6] etc. Yea, and also when appointing widows, he says, "Let there be no one as a widow under threescore years old, having been the wife of one man;"[7] and after this he says the things superadded, as being second or third in importance to this. And, in the Epistle to Titus, "For this cause," he says, "I left thee in Crete that thou shouldest set in order the things that were wanting, and appoint elders

[1] Matt. xii. 8. [2] Heb. ix. 10. [3] 2 Cor. vi. 2.
[4] Cf. Deut. xxiv. 1-3. [5] Deut. xxiv. 4.

[1] Cf. Her. Sim. viii. 3. [2] Cf. Her. Sim. vi. 2. [3] Cf. Her. Sim. vi. 3.
[4] The text is probably corrupt. Perhaps it means the marriage of a *second* angel with our soul.
[5] 1 Tim. iii. 1, 2. [6] 1 Tim. iii. 12. [7] 1 Tim. v. 9.

in every city as I gave thee charge. If any one is blameless, the husband of one wife, having children, that believe "[1]—of course—and so on. Now, when we saw that some who have been married twice may be much better than those who have been married once, we were perplexed why Paul does not at all permit those who have been twice married to be appointed to ecclesiastical dignities; for also it seemed to me that such a thing was worthy of examination, as it was possible that a man, who had been unfortunate in two marriages, and had lost his second wife while he was yet young, might have lived for the rest of his years up to old age in the greatest self-control and chastity. Who, then, would not naturally be perplexed why at all, when a ruler of the church is being sought for, we do not appoint such a man, though he has been twice married, because of the expressions about marriage, but lay hold of the man who has been once married as our ruler, even if he chance to have lived to old age with his wife, and sometimes may not have been disciplined in chastity and temperance? But, from what is said in the law about the bill of divorcement, I reflect whether, seeing that the bishop and the presbyter and the deacon are a symbol of things that truly exist in accordance with these names, he wished to appoint those who were figuratively once married, in order that he who is able to give attention to the matter, may find out from the spiritual law the one who was unworthy of ecclesiastical rule, whose soul did not find favour in the eyes of her husband because there had been found in her an unseemly thing, and she had become worthy of the bill of divorcement; for such a soul, having dwelt along with a second husband, and having been hated by such an one, can no longer, after the second bill of divorcement, return to her former husband.[2] It is likely, therefore, also, that other arguments will be found by those who are wiser than we, and have more ability to see into such things, whether in the law about the bill of divorcement, or in the apostolic writings which prohibit those who have been twice married from ruling over the church or being preferred to preside over it. But, until something shall be found that is better and able by the excessive brilliancy of the light of knowledge to cast into the shade what we have uttered, we have said the things which have occurred to us in regard to the passages.

[1] Tit. i. 5, 6.
[2] Cf. Deut. xxiv. 4.

23. SOME LAWS GIVEN BY CONCESSION TO HUMAN WEAKNESS.

But, even if we have seemed to touch on things too deep for our capacity in the passages, nevertheless, because of the literal expression these things must further be said, that some of the laws were written not as excellent, but as by way of accommodation to the weakness of those to whom the law was given; for something of this kind is indicated in the words, "Moses for your hardness of heart suffered you to put away your wives;"[1] but that which is pre-eminent and superior to the law, which was written for their hardness of heart, is indicated in this, "But from the beginning it hath not been so." But in the new covenant also there are some legal injunctions of the same order as, "Moses for your hardness of heart suffered you to put away your wives;" for example, because of our hardness of heart, it has been written on account of our weakness, "But because of fornications, let each man have his own wife and let each woman have her own husband;"[2] and this, "Let the husband render unto the wife her due, and likewise also the wife unto the husband."[3] To these sayings it is accordingly subjoined, "But this I say by way of permission, not of commandment."[4] But this also, "A wife is bound for so long time as her husband liveth, but if her husband be dead, she is free to be married to whom she will, only in the Lord,"[5] was said by Paul in view of our hardness of heart and weakness, to those who do not wish to desire earnestly the greater gifts[6] and become more blessed. But now contrary to what was written, some even of the rulers of the church have permitted a woman to marry, even when her husband was living, doing contrary to what was written, where it is said, "A wife is bound for so long time as her husband liveth," and "So then if while her husband liveth, she shall be joined to another man she shall be called an adulteress,"[7] not indeed altogether without reason, for it is probable this concession was permitted in comparison with worse things, contrary to what was from the beginning ordained by law, and written.

24. JEWISH CRITICISM OF THE LAW OF CHRIST.

But perhaps some Jewish man of those who dare to oppose the teaching of our Saviour will say, that when Jesus said,

[1] Matt. xix. 8.
[2] 1 Cor. vii. 2.
[3] 1 Cor. viii. 3.
[4] 1 Cor. vii. 6.
[5] 1 Cor. vii. 39.
[6] 1 Cor. xii. 31.
[7] Rom. vii. 3.

"Whosoever shall put away his own wife, saving for the cause of fornication, maketh her an adulteress,"[1] He also gave permission to put away a wife like as well as Moses did, who was said by Him to have given laws for the hardness of heart of the people, and will hold that the saying, "Because he found in her an unseemly thing,"[2] is to be reckoned as the same as fornification on account of which with good cause a wife could be cast away from her husband. But to him it must be said that, if she who committed adultery was according to the law to be stoned, clearly it is not in this sense that the unseemly thing is to be understood. For it is not necessary for adultery or any such great indecency to write a bill of divorcement and give it into the hands of the wife; but indeed perhaps Moses called every sin an unseemly thing, on the discovery of which by the husband in the wife, as not finding favour in the eyes of her husband, the bill of divorcement is written, and the wife is sent away from the house of her husband; "but from the beginning it hath not been so."[3] After this our Saviour says, not at all permitting the dissolution of marriages for any other sin than fornication alone, when detected in the wife, "Whosoever shall but away his own wife, saving for the cause of fornication, maketh her an adulteress."[4] But it might be a subject for inquiry if on this account He hinders any one putting away a wife, unless she be caught in fornication, for any other reason, as for example for poisoning, or for the destruction during the absence of her husband from home of an infant born to them, or for any form of murder whatsoever. And further, if she were found despoiling and pillaging the house of her husband, though she was not guilty of fornication, one might ask if he would with reason cast away such an one, seeing that the Saviour forbids any one to put away his own wife saving for the cause of fornication. In either case there appears to be something monstrous, whether it be really monstrous, I do not know; for to endure sins of such heinousness which seem to be worse than adultery or fornication, will appear to be irrational; but again on the other hand to act contrary to the design of the teaching of the Saviour, every one would acknowledge to be impious. I wonder therefore why He did not say, Let no one put away his own wife saving for the cause of fornication, but says,

[1] Matt. v. 32.
[2] Deut. xxiv. 1.
[3] Matt. xix. 8.
[4] Matt. v. 32.

"Whosoever shall put away his own wife, saving for the cause of fornication, maketh her an adulteress."[1] For confessedly he who puts away his wife when she is not a fornicator, makes her an adulteress, so far as it lies with him, for if, "when the husband is living she shall be called an adulteress if she be joined to another man;"[2] and when by putting her away, he gives to her the excuse of a second marriage, very plainly in this way he makes her an adulteress. But as to whether her being caught in the act of poisoning or committing murder, furnishes any defence of his dismissal of her, you can inquire yourselves; for the husband can also in other ways than by putting her away cause his own wife to commit adultery; as, for example, allowing her to do what she wishes beyond what is fitting, and stooping to friendship with what men she wishes, for often from the simplicity of husbands such false steps happen to wives; but whether there is a ground of defence or not for such husbands in the case of such false steps, you will inquire carefully, and deliver your opinion also in regard to the difficult questions raised by us on the passage. And even he who withholds himself from his wife makes her oftentimes to be an adulteress when he does not satisfy her desires, even though he does so under the appearance of greater gravity and self-control. And perhaps this man is more culpable who, so far as it rests with him, makes her an adulteress when he does not satisfy her desires than he who, for other reason than fornication, has sent her away,—for poisoning or murder or any of the most grievous sins. But as a woman is an adulteress, even though she seem to be married to a man, while the former husband is still living, so also the man who seems to marry her who has been put away, does not so much marry her as commit adultery with her according to the declaration of our Saviour.

25. CHASTITY AND PRAYER.

Now after these things, having considered how many possible accidents may arise in marriages, which it was necessary for the man to endure and in this way suffer very great hardships, or if he did not endure, to transgress the word of Christ, the disciples say to him, taking refuge in celibacy as easier, and more expedient than marriage, though the latter appears to be expedient, "*If the case of the man is so with his*

[1] Matt. v. 32.
[2] Rom. vii. 3.

wife, it is not expedient to marry."[1] And to this the Saviour said, teaching us that absolute chastity is a gift given by God, and not merely the fruit of training, but given by God with prayer, "All men cannot receive the saying, but they to whom it is given."[2] Then seeing that some make a sophistical attack on the saying, "To whom it is given," as if those who wished to remain pure in celibacy, but were mastered by their desires, had an excuse, we must say that, if we believe the Scriptures, why at all do we lay hold of the saying, "But they to whom it is given," but no longer attend to this, "Ask and it shall be given you,"[3] and to that which is added to it, "For every one that asketh receiveth"?[4] For if they "to whom it is given" can receive this saying about absolute purity, let him who wills ask, obeying and believing Him who said, "Ask and it shall be given you,"[3] and not doubting about the saying, "Every one that asketh receiveth."[4] But when there you will inquire who it is that asketh, for no one of those who do not receive has asked, even though he seems to have done so, since it is not lawful to say that the saying, "Every one that asketh receiveth," is a lie. Who then is he that asketh, but he who has

[1] Matt. xix. 10.
[2] Matt. xix. 11.
[3] Matt. vii. 7.
[4] Matt. vii 8.

obeyed Jesus when He says, "If ye stand praying, believe that ye receive, and ye shall receive"?[1] But he that asketh must do everything in his power that he may pray "with the spirit" and pray also "with the understanding,"[2] and pray "without ceasing,"[3] keeping in mind also the saying, "And He spake a parable unto them to the end that they ought always to pray, and not to faint, saying, There was in a city a judge,"[4] etc. And it is useful to know what it is to ask, and what it is to receive, and what is meant by "Every one that asketh, receiveth,"[5] and by "I say unto you though he will not rise and give him, because he is his friend, yet because of his importunity, he will arise and give him as many as he needeth."[6] It is therefore added, "And I say unto you, Ask, and it shall be given you," and so on. Further, let the saying, "All men cannot receive the saying but they to whom it is given,"[7] be a stimulus to us to ask worthily of receiving; and this, "What son is there of you who shall ask his father for a fish, will he for a fish give him a serpent,"[8] etc. God therefore will give the good gift, perfect purity in celibacy and chastity, to those who ask Him with the whole soul, and with faith, and in prayers without ceasing.

[1] Mark xi. 24, 25.
[2] 1 Cor. xiv. 15.
[3] 1 Thess. v. 17.
[4] Luke xviii. 1, 2.
[5] Matt. vii. 8.
[6] Luke xi. 8.
[7] Matt. xix. 11.
[8] Luke xi. 11.

INDICES

THE APOCALYPSES OF PETER, VISIO PAULI, OF MARIA VIRGO, AND OF SEDRACH

INDEX OF SUBJECTS

INDEX OF TEXTS

TESTAMENT OF ABRAHAM, ACTS OF XANTHIPPE AND POLYXENA, AND NARRATIVE OF ZOSIMUS

INDEX OF SUBJECTS

THE EPISTLES OF CLEMENT

INDEX OF SUBJECTS

INDEX OF TEXTS

THE APOLOGY OF ARISTIDES, AND THE PASSION OF THE SCILLITAN MARTYRS

INDEX OF SUBJECTS

ORIGEN'S COMMENTARIES ON THE GOSPELS OF JOHN AND MATTHEW

INDEX OF SUBJECTS

INDEX OF TEXTS